# State Rankings 2014

## *Other titles in the State Fact Finder series*

*Crime State Rankings* (now part of **State Stats**)
*Education State Rankings* (now part of **State Stats**)
*Health Care State Rankings* (now part of **State Stats**)
*City Crime Rankings*

## **State Stats** online database

What is **State Stats**? Drawing together the statistics from the *State Rankings* series of books by CQ Press and Morgan Quitno Press, **State Stats** is a regularly updated database from CQ Press that delivers a dynamic and engaging user experience that is unmatched in other resources. Featuring data from more than 80 different government and nongovernment sources and backed by a rich collection of more than 2,000 current and historical data series on popular topics of research interest, **State Stats** uniquely allows users to discover, view, and export key information measures for the 50 states and the District of Columbia.

Check it out online at http://library.cqpress.com/statestats.

**State Stats** makes research easy by providing in one place annual measures dating back more than 15 years. Data series are displayed in a clear and consistent format with detailed source information. Numerous topics are covered in categories including Agriculture; Crime and Law Enforcement; Defense; Demographics; Economics; Education; Employment and Labor; Geography, Energy, and the Environment; Health and Medicine; Social Welfare; Taxes and Government Finance; Transportation.

The benefit of **State Stats** is in its ease of use and clean and concise presentation of data and trends. An intuitive interface lets users easily browse by state or by topic, and then compare across states or across time. Users can then share, save, and export data. **State Stats** also features CQ Press's CiteNow!® function for generating source citations in APA, MLA, Chicago, or Bluebook styles.

Users can:

- Analyze data patterns by comparing across states, data series, and time

- Create and export custom visuals including line charts, scatter plots, and maps

- Generate tables and download data for statistical research

- Toggle user display between interactive visual and tabular data view

- Engage a moveable timeline to discover trends

- Explore interactive maps featuring zoom and hover functions

**State Stats** is cross-searchable with other CQ Press online products including *CQ Researcher* and the *CQ Press U.S. Political Stats.* Ongoing updates to **State Stats** throughout the year ensure that users have the most current data available.

Working on an advanced data research project? The optional advanced State Stats Data Cart allows for bulk data export across single-click download of complete data series and multiple series.

# State Rankings 2014

## A Statistical View of America

*Editors*

## Kathleen O'Leary Morgan
## and
## Scott Morgan

Los Angeles | London | New Delhi
Singapore | Washington DC

Los Angeles | London | New Delhi
Singapore | Washington DC

FOR INFORMATION:

CQ Press
An Imprint of SAGE Publications, Inc.
2455 Teller Road
Thousand Oaks, California 91320
E-mail: order@sagepub.com

SAGE Publications Ltd.
1 Oliver's Yard
55 City Road
London, EC1Y 1SP
United Kingdom

SAGE Publications India Pvt. Ltd.
B 1/I 1 Mohan Cooperative Industrial Area
Mathura Road, New Delhi 110 044
India

SAGE Publications Asia-Pacific Pte. Ltd.
3 Church Street
#10-04 Samsung Hub
Singapore 049483

Developmental Editor: John Martino
Production Editor: Tracy Buyan
Cover Designer: Michael Dubowe
Marketing Manager: Carmel Schrire

Printed in the United States of America

ISBN 978-1-4833-4784-4 (cloth)
ISBN 978-1-4833-4783-7 (paper)
ISSN 1057-3623

14 15 16 17 18 10 9 8 7 6 5 4 3 2 1

# Contents

# Detailed Table of Contents

## IV. ECONOMY

## V. EDUCATION

## XI. HEALTH

## XII. HOUSEHOLDS AND HOUSING

## XIII. POPULATION

## XIV. SOCIAL WELFARE

## XV. TRANSPORTATION

# Introduction and Methodology

*State Rankings 2014* provides an easily accessible collection of data in a broad range of quality of life factors in the United States. In this latest 2014 edition, *State Ranking* compares data from the 50 states and the District of Columbia in 567 tables in the following 15 different livability categories: agriculture, crime and law enforcement, defense, economy, education, employment and labor, energy and environment, geography, federal government finances, state and local government finances, health, households and housing, population, social welfare, and transportation.

## Purpose of This Book

*State Rankings 2014* translates complicated and often convoluted statistics into meaningful, easy-to-understand information. Too often there is an abundance of data but far too little information putting that data into context. This book allows researchers, legislators, policy analysts, journalists, and the general public to access information in a manner that not only provides basic facts about a state's quality of life, but also gives a meaningful framework by comparing individual states against the rest of the country.

These data and rankings can be used in a variety of ways, by a variety of audiences, including the following examples:

- Policy makers can use the data to help identify areas warranting further study.
- Journalists can easily find impartial state information that puts stories into context.
- The general public can see how a particular state is faring compared to other states.
- Librarians can use the data as a quick reference to assist patrons in research and offer the sources and Web sites included as a starting point for finding other related data.

The comparison rankings in *State Rankings 2014* provide an annual snapshot of how the states are doing in the 15 livability categories mentioned above. There are two principle approaches to using these rankings. The first is to examine how a state is doing compared to all other states via the comparison rankings in this book. The second approach is to compare a state to itself over a given period of time. Both approaches are important to

achieving a good understanding of how and whether a state is making progress. It is important to keep in mind that the rankings are not a definitive determination of which state is the "best." However, since so many issues are surrounded by emotions, tracking them by the numbers can help bring the discussion back to a more balanced, unbiased review that in the end leads to better decisions.

## Data and Limitations

The data featured in *State Rankings 2014* were chosen specifically by the editors from a variety of government and private sector sources. The statistics presented are intended to cover a broad array of quality-of-life subject areas, giving users of the book a solid collection of state information. Nonetheless, the statistics are not inclusive of all the possible data that might be available. The statistics in the book are the latest available from the sources. In a few cases, we have retained tables that have not been updated for several years because we believe our readers will find the data relevant, even if updates are not available. In other cases, we replaced obsolete data with new tables. Long-time users should note in particular that we have updated Government Finances: Federal with new government spending data from the OMB's USASpending.gov, but differences in methodology make that data difficult to compare with past editions.

Previous editions of the book have used the term "most livable" when describing states with the highest livability ranking. This term is no longer being used, because it is purely descriptive—at no time do we attempt to explain *why* a particular state is ranking higher or lower in livability factors than others or against the national average. This explanation—currently sought by social science researchers—is beyond the scope of this book. While our selection of factors clearly affects the rankings, we believe the rankings provide a solid measurement of how the fifty states and Washington, DC are faring with regard to quality of life in the United States. Researchers, practitioners, and others can confidently use the data to understand livability issues and guide policy decisions.

## Methodology

The comparison rankings for *State Rankings 2014* are determined using the same methodology as we have used for the past twenty-plus years. The editors used the previously mentioned 15 livability categories to select 44 quality of life factors from a broad range of economic, educational, health-oriented, public safety, and environmental statistics. Overall comparison rankings were determined by averaging each state's ranking for each category. The scale is one to fifty, the higher the number, the higher the state is in the rankings (i.e., 50 is the best score to receive). Data used are for the most recent year for which comparable numbers are available from most states. All factors are given equal weight.

The 567 tables provided in *State Rankings 2014* then are ranked highest to lowest without any subjective determination as to whether a subject is "positive" or "negative." For the state comparison rankings, the editors do make a subjective determination as to whether something is "positive" or "negative." Twenty-five of the 44 factors were determined to be negative and the remaining nineteen were viewed as positive.

The reason for this division between positive and negative is that if a state ranks first in crime rate (i.e., it has the highest crime rate), its comparison ranking is reduced. Whereas if a state ranks first in per capita personal income (i.e., it has the highest income), its comparison ranking is increased. To account for this, we subtract the rankings for the positive factors from 51 so that a state with the highest ranking in a positive factor ends up with a 50 for that factor (remember, high numbers are best.)

Once we have chosen the factors and divided them into positive and negative groupings, we simply average the ranking for each state in all 44 factors. If a state is missing data for a given factor, its standing is based on the average ranking for the remaining factors. The book uses the latest available data for each livability factor.

As an example, Maine ranks 37th in crime rate (negative factor), 41st in personal bankruptcy rate (negative factor), and ranks 8th in percent of eligible population reported voting in 2010 (positive factor). The 37th and 41st rankings go straight into the comparison formula whereas the number eight ranking in percent of eligible population reported voting is first subtracted from 51 with the resulting 43 going into the ranking. For these three factors for Maine, we would average 37, 41, and 43 with the result being 40.33. If these three factors were the only ones we used, then the resulting average of 40.33 would be the figure we would use to compare Maine to the other 49 states. However, for the *State Rankings* comparison rankings, an additional 41 factors are added into the calculations before the final results are determined.

Designed with the researcher in mind, the numbers shown in *State Rankings* require no additional calculations to convert them from millions, thousands, etc. All states are ranked on a high-to-low basis, with any ties among the states listed alphabetically for a given ranking. Negative numbers are shown in parentheses. For tables displaying national totals (as opposed to rates, per capita, etc.), a separate column is included that shows what percent of the national total each individual state's total represents. This column is headed by "% of USA." This percentage figure is particularly interesting when compared with a state's population in a given year. Rates may be per 10,000 persons, per 100,000 persons, or per some other denominator; these are clearly explained by the text following the national rate and, if necessary, the footnotes.

To further assist readers, source information and footnotes clearly are shown at the bottom of each page, while national totals, rates, and percentages are prominently displayed at the top of each table. Every other line is shaded in gray for easier reading. Numerous information-finding tools are provided: a thorough table of contents, table listings at the beginning of each chapter and a detailed index. In addition, a roster of sources, with addresses, phone numbers and Web sites is found in the back of the book.

# About the Editors

**Kathleen O'Leary Morgan** holds a master's degree in public administration and has served in a number of media and legislative liaison positions within the U.S. Department of Transportation, where she also served as deputy director of congressional affairs.

**Scott Morgan** is an attorney who served as chief counsel to Robert Dole's 1988 presidential campaign.

# The 2014 State Rankings

| RANK | STATE | AVG | 13 RANK | CHANGE |
|---|---|---|---|---|
| 48 | Alabama | 18.95 | 48 | 0 |
| 24 | Alaska | 25.36 | 13 | -11 |
| 43 | Arizona | 20.18 | 39 | -4 |
| 47 | Arkansas | 18.98 | 46 | -1 |
| 36 | California | 22.55 | 31 | -5 |
| 13 | Colorado | 28.43 | 11 | -2 |
| 14 | Connecticut | 28.11 | 15 | 1 |
| 30 | Delaware | 24.43 | 28 | -2 |
| 37 | Florida | 22.39 | 42 | 5 |
| 39 | Georgia | 21.07 | 40 | 1 |
| 22 | Hawaii | 25.73 | 23 | 1 |
| 17 | Idaho | 27.61 | 22 | 5 |
| 27 | Illinois | 24.88 | 27 | 0 |
| 29 | Indiana | 24.48 | 35 | 6 |
| 5 | Iowa | 32.55 | 6 | 1 |
| 18 | Kansas | 27.18 | 16 | -2 |
| 49 | Kentucky | 18.61 | 47 | -2 |
| 40 | Louisiana | 20.61 | 38 | -2 |
| 10 | Maine | 30.25 | 12 | 2 |
| 15 | Maryland | 28.07 | 19 | 4 |
| 8 | Massachusetts | 31.20 | 10 | 2 |
| 32 | Michigan | 23.61 | 34 | 2 |
| 2 | Minnesota | 34.16 | 1 | -1 |
| 50 | Mississippi | 18.48 | 50 | 0 |
| 31 | Missouri | 23.98 | 30 | -1 |
| 20 | Montana | 26.66 | 16 | -4 |
| 4 | Nebraska | 32.70 | 5 | 1 |
| 42 | Nevada | 20.30 | 37 | -5 |
| 1 | New Hampshire | 34.70 | 7 | 6 |
| 16 | New Jersey | 27.66 | 18 | 2 |
| 46 | New Mexico | 19.09 | 45 | -1 |
| 26 | New York | 24.95 | 26 | 0 |
| 34 | North Carolina | 22.82 | 41 | 7 |
| 3 | North Dakota | 33.16 | 2 | -1 |
| 35 | Ohio | 22.61 | 36 | 1 |
| 38 | Oklahoma | 21.68 | 32 | -6 |
| 23 | Oregon | 25.48 | 24 | 1 |
| 33 | Pennsylvania | 23.07 | 33 | 0 |
| 28 | Rhode Island | 24.61 | 29 | 1 |
| 45 | South Carolina | 19.34 | 48 | 3 |
| 11 | South Dakota | 29.36 | 9 | -2 |
| 41 | Tennessee | 20.32 | 44 | 3 |
| 25 | Texas | 24.98 | 25 | 0 |
| 7 | Utah | 31.77 | 7 | 0 |
| 6 | Vermont | 32.05 | 3 | -3 |
| 12 | Virginia | 29.30 | 14 | 2 |
| 19 | Washington | 26.70 | 20 | 1 |
| 44 | West Virginia | 20.00 | 43 | -1 |
| 21 | Wisconsin | 26.48 | 21 | 0 |
| 9 | Wyoming | 31.18 | 4 | -5 |

| RANK | STATE | AVG | 13 RANK | CHANGE |
|---|---|---|---|---|
| 1 | New Hampshire | 34.70 | 7 | 6 |
| 2 | Minnesota | 34.16 | 1 | -1 |
| 3 | North Dakota | 33.16 | 2 | -1 |
| 4 | Nebraska | 32.70 | 5 | 1 |
| 5 | Iowa | 32.55 | 6 | 1 |
| 6 | Vermont | 32.05 | 3 | -3 |
| 7 | Utah | 31.77 | 7 | 0 |
| 8 | Massachusetts | 31.20 | 10 | 2 |
| 9 | Wyoming | 31.18 | 4 | -5 |
| 10 | Maine | 30.25 | 12 | 2 |
| 11 | South Dakota | 29.36 | 9 | -2 |
| 12 | Virginia | 29.30 | 14 | 2 |
| 13 | Colorado | 28.43 | 11 | -2 |
| 14 | Connecticut | 28.11 | 15 | 1 |
| 15 | Maryland | 28.07 | 19 | 4 |
| 16 | New Jersey | 27.66 | 18 | 2 |
| 17 | Idaho | 27.61 | 22 | 5 |
| 18 | Kansas | 27.18 | 16 | -2 |
| 19 | Washington | 26.70 | 20 | 1 |
| 20 | Montana | 26.66 | 16 | -4 |
| 21 | Wisconsin | 26.48 | 21 | 0 |
| 22 | Hawaii | 25.73 | 23 | 1 |
| 23 | Oregon | 25.48 | 24 | 1 |
| 24 | Alaska | 25.36 | 13 | -11 |
| 25 | Texas | 24.98 | 25 | 0 |
| 26 | New York | 24.95 | 26 | 0 |
| 27 | Illinois | 24.88 | 27 | 0 |
| 28 | Rhode Island | 24.61 | 29 | 1 |
| 29 | Indiana | 24.48 | 35 | 6 |
| 30 | Delaware | 24.43 | 28 | -2 |
| 31 | Missouri | 23.98 | 30 | -1 |
| 32 | Michigan | 23.61 | 34 | 2 |
| 33 | Pennsylvania | 23.07 | 33 | 0 |
| 34 | North Carolina | 22.82 | 41 | 7 |
| 35 | Ohio | 22.61 | 36 | 1 |
| 36 | California | 22.55 | 31 | -5 |
| 37 | Florida | 22.39 | 42 | 5 |
| 38 | Oklahoma | 21.68 | 32 | -6 |
| 39 | Georgia | 21.07 | 40 | 1 |
| 40 | Louisiana | 20.61 | 38 | -2 |
| 41 | Tennessee | 20.32 | 44 | 3 |
| 42 | Nevada | 20.30 | 37 | -5 |
| 43 | Arizona | 20.18 | 39 | -4 |
| 44 | West Virginia | 20.00 | 43 | -1 |
| 45 | South Carolina | 19.34 | 48 | 3 |
| 46 | New Mexico | 19.09 | 45 | -1 |
| 47 | Arkansas | 18.98 | 46 | -1 |
| 48 | Alabama | 18.95 | 48 | 0 |
| 49 | Kentucky | 18.61 | 47 | -2 |
| 50 | Mississippi | 18.48 | 50 | 0 |

# Date Each State Admitted to Statehood*

ALPHA ORDER

| RANK | STATE | DATE OF ADMISSION |
|---|---|---|
| 22 | Alabama | December 14, 1819 |
| 49 | Alaska | January 3, 1959 |
| 48 | Arizona | February 14, 1912 |
| 25 | Arkansas | June 15, 1836 |
| 31 | California | September 9, 1850 |
| 38 | Colorado | August 1, 1876 |
| 5 | Connecticut | January 9, 1788 |
| 1 | Delaware | December 7, 1787 |
| 27 | Florida | March 3, 1845 |
| 4 | Georgia | January 2, 1788 |
| 50 | Hawaii | August 21, 1959 |
| 43 | Idaho | July 3, 1890 |
| 21 | Illinois | December 3, 1818 |
| 19 | Indiana | December 11, 1816 |
| 29 | Iowa | December 28, 1846 |
| 34 | Kansas | January 29, 1861 |
| 15 | Kentucky | June 1, 1792 |
| 18 | Louisiana | April 30, 1812 |
| 23 | Maine | March 15, 1820 |
| 7 | Maryland | April 28, 1788 |
| 6 | Massachusetts | February 6, 1788 |
| 26 | Michigan | January 26, 1837 |
| 32 | Minnesota | May 11, 1858 |
| 20 | Mississippi | December 10, 1817 |
| 24 | Missouri | August 10, 1821 |
| 41 | Montana | November 8, 1889 |
| 37 | Nebraska | March 1, 1867 |
| 36 | Nevada | October 31, 1864 |
| 9 | New Hampshire | June 21, 1788 |
| 3 | New Jersey | December 18, 1787 |
| 47 | New Mexico | January 6, 1912 |
| 11 | New York | July 26, 1788 |
| 12 | North Carolina | November 21, 1789 |
| 39 | North Dakota | November 2, 1889 |
| 17 | Ohio | March 1, 1803 |
| 46 | Oklahoma | November 16, 1907 |
| 33 | Oregon | February 14, 1859 |
| 2 | Pennsylvania | December 12, 1787 |
| 13 | Rhode Island | May 29, 1790 |
| 8 | South Carolina | May 23, 1788 |
| 39 | South Dakota | November 2, 1889 |
| 16 | Tennessee | June 1, 1796 |
| 28 | Texas | December 29, 1845 |
| 45 | Utah | January 4, 1896 |
| 14 | Vermont | March 4, 1791 |
| 10 | Virginia | June 26, 1788 |
| 42 | Washington | November 11, 1889 |
| 35 | West Virginia | June 20, 1863 |
| 30 | Wisconsin | May 29, 1848 |
| 44 | Wyoming | July 10, 1890 |

RANK ORDER

| RANK | STATE | DATE OF ADMISSION |
|---|---|---|
| 1 | Delaware | December 7, 1787 |
| 2 | Pennsylvania | December 12, 1787 |
| 3 | New Jersey | December 18, 1787 |
| 4 | Georgia | January 2, 1788 |
| 5 | Connecticut | January 9, 1788 |
| 6 | Massachusetts | February 6, 1788 |
| 7 | Maryland | April 28, 1788 |
| 8 | South Carolina | May 23, 1788 |
| 9 | New Hampshire | June 21, 1788 |
| 10 | Virginia | June 26, 1788 |
| 11 | New York | July 26, 1788 |
| 12 | North Carolina | November 21, 1789 |
| 13 | Rhode Island | May 29, 1790 |
| 14 | Vermont | March 4, 1791 |
| 15 | Kentucky | June 1, 1792 |
| 16 | Tennessee | June 1, 1796 |
| 17 | Ohio | March 1, 1803 |
| 18 | Louisiana | April 30, 1812 |
| 19 | Indiana | December 11, 1816 |
| 20 | Mississippi | December 10, 1817 |
| 21 | Illinois | December 3, 1818 |
| 22 | Alabama | December 14, 1819 |
| 23 | Maine | March 15, 1820 |
| 24 | Missouri | August 10, 1821 |
| 25 | Arkansas | June 15, 1836 |
| 26 | Michigan | January 26, 1837 |
| 27 | Florida | March 3, 1845 |
| 28 | Texas | December 29, 1845 |
| 29 | Iowa | December 28, 1846 |
| 30 | Wisconsin | May 29, 1848 |
| 31 | California | September 9, 1850 |
| 32 | Minnesota | May 11, 1858 |
| 33 | Oregon | February 14, 1859 |
| 34 | Kansas | January 29, 1861 |
| 35 | West Virginia | June 20, 1863 |
| 36 | Nevada | October 31, 1864 |
| 37 | Nebraska | March 1, 1867 |
| 38 | Colorado | August 1, 1876 |
| 39 | North Dakota | November 2, 1889 |
| 39 | South Dakota | November 2, 1889 |
| 41 | Montana | November 8, 1889 |
| 42 | Washington | November 11, 1889 |
| 43 | Idaho | July 3, 1890 |
| 44 | Wyoming | July 10, 1890 |
| 45 | Utah | January 4, 1896 |
| 46 | Oklahoma | November 16, 1907 |
| 47 | New Mexico | January 6, 1912 |
| 48 | Arizona | February 14, 1912 |
| 49 | Alaska | January 3, 1959 |
| 50 | Hawaii | August 21, 1959 |

Source: U.S. Bureau of the Census
"1980 Census of Population" (vol. 1, part A, PC80-1-A)
*First thirteen states show date of ratification of Constitution.

# STATE FAST FACTS

| STATE | NICKNAME | CAPITAL | POPULATION* | AREA** |
|---|---|---|---|---|
| Alabama | Heart of Dixie | Montgomery | 4,833,722 | 52,420 |
| Alaska | The Last Frontier | Juneau | 735,132 | 665,384 |
| Arizona | Grand Canyon State | Phoenix | 6,626,624 | 113,990 |
| Arkansas | The Natural State | Little Rock | 2,959,373 | 53,179 |
| California | Golden State | Sacramento | 38,332,521 | 163,695 |
| Colorado | Centennial State | Denver | 5,268,367 | 104,094 |
| Connecticut | Constitution State | Hartford | 3,596,080 | 5,543 |
| Delaware | First State | Dover | 925,749 | 2,489 |
| Florida | Sunshine State | Tallahassee | 19,552,860 | 65,758 |
| Georgia | Peach State | Atlanta | 9,992,167 | 59,425 |
| Hawaii | Aloha State | Honolulu | 1,404,054 | 10,932 |
| Idaho | Gem State | Boise | 1,612,136 | 83,569 |
| Illinois | Land of Lincoln | Springfield | 12,882,135 | 57,914 |
| Indiana | Hoosier State | Indianapolis | 6,570,902 | 36,420 |
| Iowa | Hawkeye State | Des Moines | 3,090,416 | 56,273 |
| Kansas | Sunflower State | Topeka | 2,893,957 | 82,278 |
| Kentucky | Bluegrass State | Frankfort | 4,395,295 | 40,408 |
| Louisiana | Pelican State | Baton Rouge | 4,625,470 | 52,378 |
| Maine | Pine Tree State | Augusta | 1,328,302 | 35,380 |
| Maryland | Free State | Annapolis | 5,928,814 | 12,406 |
| Massachusetts | Bay State | Boston | 6,692,824 | 10,554 |
| Michigan | Great Lake State | Lansing | 9,895,622 | 96,714 |
| Minnesota | North Star State | St. Paul | 5,420,380 | 86,936 |
| Mississippi | Magnolia State | Jackson | 2,991,207 | 48,432 |
| Missouri | Show Me State | Jefferson City | 6,044,171 | 69,707 |
| Montana | Treasure State | Helena | 1,015,165 | 147,040 |
| Nebraska | Cornhusker State | Lincoln | 1,868,516 | 77,348 |
| Nevada | Silver State | Carson City | 2,790,136 | 110,572 |
| New Hampshire | Granite State | Concord | 1,323,459 | 9,349 |
| New Jersey | Garden State | Trenton | 8,899,339 | 8,723 |
| New Mexico | Land of Enchantment | Santa Fe | 2,085,287 | 121,590 |
| New York | Empire State | Albany | 19,651,127 | 54,555 |
| North Carolina | Tar Heel State | Raleigh | 9,848,060 | 53,819 |
| North Dakota | Peace Garden State | Bismarck | 723,393 | 70,698 |
| Ohio | Buckeye State | Columbus | 11,570,808 | 44,826 |
| Oklahoma | Sooner State | Oklahoma City | 3,850,568 | 69,899 |
| Oregon | Beaver State | Salem | 3,930,065 | 98,379 |
| Pennsylvania | Keystone State | Harrisburg | 12,773,801 | 46,054 |
| Rhode Island | Ocean State | Providence | 1,051,511 | 1,545 |
| South Carolina | Palmetto State | Columbia | 4,774,839 | 32,020 |
| South Dakota | Mount Rushmore State | Pierre | 844,877 | 77,116 |
| Tennessee | Volunteer State | Nashville | 6,495,978 | 42,144 |
| Texas | Lone Star State | Austin | 26,448,193 | 268,596 |
| Utah | Beehive State | Salt Lake City | 2,900,872 | 84,897 |
| Vermont | Green Mountain State | Montpelier | 626,630 | 9,616 |
| Virginia | Old Dominion | Richmond | 8,260,405 | 42,775 |
| Washington | Evergreen State | Olympia | 6,971,406 | 71,298 |
| West Virginia | Mountain State | Charleston | 1,854,304 | 24,230 |
| Wisconsin | Badger State | Madison | 5,742,713 | 65,496 |
| Wyoming | Equality State | Cheyenne | 582,658 | 97,813 |

U.S. Bureau of the Census, "Population Estimates" (December 2013, http://www.census.gov/popest/data/index.html)

**Total of land and water area in square miles.

| STATE SONG | STATE FLOWER | STATE TREE | STATE BIRD |
|---|---|---|---|
| Alabama | Camellia | Southern Pine | Yellowhammer |
| Alaska's Flag | Forget-Me-Not | Sitka Spruce | Willow Ptarmigan |
| Arizona | Saguaro Cactus Blossom | Palo Verde | Cactus Wren |
| Arkansas | Apple Blossom | Pine | Mockingbird |
| I Love You, California | Golden Poppy | California Redwood | California Valley Quail |
| Where the Columbines Grow | Rocky Mountain Columbine | Colorado Blue Spruce | Lark Bunting |
| Yankee Doodle Dandy | Mountain Laurel | White Oak | American Robin |
| Our Delaware | Peach Blossom | American Holly | Blue Hen Chicken |
| Swanee River | Orange Blossom | Sabal Palmetto Palm | Mockingbird |
| Georgia On My Mind | Cherokee Rose | Live Oak | Brown Thrasher |
| Hawaii Ponoi | Yellow Hibiscus | Candlenut | Nene |
| Here We Have Idaho | Syringa | White Pine | Mountain Bluebird |
| Illinois | Purple Violet | White Oak | Cardinal |
| On the Banks of the Wabash, Far Away | Peony | Tulip Poplar | Cardinal |
| The Song of Iowa | Wild Rose | Oak | Eastern Goldfinch |
| Home on the Range | Sunflower | Cottonwood | Western Meadowlark |
| My Old Kentucky Home | Goldenrod | Tulip Tree | Cardinal |
| Give Me Louisiana | Magnolia | Cypress | Eastern Brown Pelican |
| State of Maine Song | White Pine Cone and Tassel | Eastern White Pine | Chickadee |
| Maryland, My Maryland | Black-eyed Susan | White Oak | Baltimore Oriole |
| All Hail to Massachusetts | Mayflower | American Elm | Chickadee |
| Michigan, My Michigan | Apple Blossom | White Pine | Robin |
| Hail! Minnesota | Pink and White Lady's Slipper | Red Pine | Common Loon |
| Go, Mississippi! | Magnolia | Magnolia | Mockingbird |
| Missouri Waltz | Hawthorn | Dogwood | Bluebird |
| Montana | Bitterroot | Ponderosa Pine | Western Meadowlark |
| Beautiful Nebraska | Goldenrod | Cottonwood | Western Meadowlark |
| Home Means Nevada | Sagebrush | Single-Leaf Pinon | Mountain Bluebird |
| Old New Hampshire | Purple Lilac | White Birch | Purple Finch |
| Ode to New Jersey | Purple Violet | Red Oak | Eastern Goldfinch |
| O Fair New Mexico | Yucca | Pinon | Roadrunner |
| I Love New York | Rose | Sugar Maple | Bluebird |
| The Old North State | Dogwood | Pine | Cardinal |
| North Dakota Hymn | Wild Prairie Rose | American Elm | Western Meadowlark |
| Beautiful Ohio | Scarlet Carnation | Buckeye | Cardinal |
| Oklahoma! | Mistletoe | Redbud | Scissortailed Flycatcher |
| Oregon, My Oregon | Oregon Grape | Douglas Fir | Western Meadowlark |
| Hail! Pennsylvania | Mountain Laurel | Hemlock | Ruffed Grouse |
| Rhode Island | Violet | Red Maple | Rhode Island Red |
| Carolina | Yellow Jessamine | Palmetto | Carolina Wren |
| Hail, South Dakota | Pasque Flower | Black Hills Spruce | Ringnecked Pheasant |
| The Tennessee Waltz | Iris | Tulip Poplar | Mockingbird |
| Texas, Our Texas | Bluebonnet | Pecan | Mockingbird |
| Utah, We Love Thee | Sego Lily | Blue Spruce | Seagull |
| Hail, Vermont | Red Clover | Sugar Maple | Hermit Thrush |
| Carry Me Back to Old Virginia | Dogwood | Dogwood | Cardinal |
| Washington, My Home | Western Rhododendron | Western Hemlock | Willow Goldfinch |
| The West Virginia Hills; This Is My West Virginia; and West Virginia, My Home, Sweet Home | Big Rhododendron | Sugar Maple | Cardinal |
| On Wisconsin! | Wood Violet | Sugar Maple | Robin |
| Wyoming | Indian Paintbrush | Cottonwood | Meadowlark |

# I. Agriculture

# Number of Farms in 2012

## National Total = 2,170,000 Farms*

| RANK | STATE | FARMS | % of USA |
|---|---|---|---|
| 21 | Alabama | 46,500 | 2.1% |
| 50 | Alaska | 680 | 0.0% |
| 37 | Arizona | 15,500 | 0.7% |
| 17 | Arkansas | 47,800 | 2.2% |
| 6 | California | 80,500 | 3.7% |
| 26 | Colorado | 36,300 | 1.7% |
| 45 | Connecticut | 4,900 | 0.2% |
| 48 | Delaware | 2,500 | 0.1% |
| 18 | Florida | 47,500 | 2.2% |
| 19 | Georgia | 47,000 | 2.2% |
| 43 | Hawaii | 7,500 | 0.3% |
| 33 | Idaho | 24,500 | 1.1% |
| 10 | Illinois | 74,300 | 3.4% |
| 14 | Indiana | 60,000 | 2.8% |
| 3 | Iowa | 92,200 | 4.2% |
| 12 | Kansas | 65,500 | 3.0% |
| 4 | Kentucky | 85,500 | 3.9% |
| 30 | Louisiana | 29,000 | 1.3% |
| 41 | Maine | 8,100 | 0.4% |
| 38 | Maryland | 12,800 | 0.6% |
| 42 | Massachusetts | 7,700 | 0.4% |
| 15 | Michigan | 54,700 | 2.5% |
| 7 | Minnesota | 79,400 | 3.7% |
| 23 | Mississippi | 42,300 | 1.9% |
| 2 | Missouri | 106,000 | 4.9% |
| 31 | Montana | 28,600 | 1.3% |
| 20 | Nebraska | 46,700 | 2.2% |
| 47 | Nevada | 2,950 | 0.1% |
| 46 | New Hampshire | 4,150 | 0.2% |
| 40 | New Jersey | 10,200 | 0.5% |
| 34 | New Mexico | 23,800 | 1.1% |
| 27 | New York | 36,000 | 1.7% |
| 16 | North Carolina | 50,000 | 2.3% |
| 28 | North Dakota | 31,600 | 1.5% |
| 11 | Ohio | 73,400 | 3.4% |
| 4 | Oklahoma | 85,500 | 3.9% |
| 25 | Oregon | 38,100 | 1.8% |
| 13 | Pennsylvania | 62,100 | 2.9% |
| 49 | Rhode Island | 1,220 | 0.1% |
| 32 | South Carolina | 26,700 | 1.2% |
| 29 | South Dakota | 31,000 | 1.4% |
| 9 | Tennessee | 76,000 | 3.5% |
| 1 | Texas | 244,700 | 11.3% |
| 36 | Utah | 16,400 | 0.8% |
| 44 | Vermont | 7,000 | 0.3% |
| 22 | Virginia | 46,200 | 2.1% |
| 24 | Washington | 39,300 | 1.8% |
| 35 | West Virginia | 22,100 | 1.0% |
| 8 | Wisconsin | 76,800 | 3.5% |
| 39 | Wyoming | 10,800 | 0.5% |

| RANK | STATE | FARMS | % of USA |
|---|---|---|---|
| 1 | Texas | 244,700 | 11.3% |
| 2 | Missouri | 106,000 | 4.9% |
| 3 | Iowa | 92,200 | 4.2% |
| 4 | Kentucky | 85,500 | 3.9% |
| 4 | Oklahoma | 85,500 | 3.9% |
| 6 | California | 80,500 | 3.7% |
| 7 | Minnesota | 79,400 | 3.7% |
| 8 | Wisconsin | 76,800 | 3.5% |
| 9 | Tennessee | 76,000 | 3.5% |
| 10 | Illinois | 74,300 | 3.4% |
| 11 | Ohio | 73,400 | 3.4% |
| 12 | Kansas | 65,500 | 3.0% |
| 13 | Pennsylvania | 62,100 | 2.9% |
| 14 | Indiana | 60,000 | 2.8% |
| 15 | Michigan | 54,700 | 2.5% |
| 16 | North Carolina | 50,000 | 2.3% |
| 17 | Arkansas | 47,800 | 2.2% |
| 18 | Florida | 47,500 | 2.2% |
| 19 | Georgia | 47,000 | 2.2% |
| 20 | Nebraska | 46,700 | 2.2% |
| 21 | Alabama | 46,500 | 2.1% |
| 22 | Virginia | 46,200 | 2.1% |
| 23 | Mississippi | 42,300 | 1.9% |
| 24 | Washington | 39,300 | 1.8% |
| 25 | Oregon | 38,100 | 1.8% |
| 26 | Colorado | 36,300 | 1.7% |
| 27 | New York | 36,000 | 1.7% |
| 28 | North Dakota | 31,600 | 1.5% |
| 29 | South Dakota | 31,000 | 1.4% |
| 30 | Louisiana | 29,000 | 1.3% |
| 31 | Montana | 28,600 | 1.3% |
| 32 | South Carolina | 26,700 | 1.2% |
| 33 | Idaho | 24,500 | 1.1% |
| 34 | New Mexico | 23,800 | 1.1% |
| 35 | West Virginia | 22,100 | 1.0% |
| 36 | Utah | 16,400 | 0.8% |
| 37 | Arizona | 15,500 | 0.7% |
| 38 | Maryland | 12,800 | 0.6% |
| 39 | Wyoming | 10,800 | 0.5% |
| 40 | New Jersey | 10,200 | 0.5% |
| 41 | Maine | 8,100 | 0.4% |
| 42 | Massachusetts | 7,700 | 0.4% |
| 43 | Hawaii | 7,500 | 0.3% |
| 44 | Vermont | 7,000 | 0.3% |
| 45 | Connecticut | 4,900 | 0.2% |
| 46 | New Hampshire | 4,150 | 0.2% |
| 47 | Nevada | 2,950 | 0.1% |
| 48 | Delaware | 2,500 | 0.1% |
| 49 | Rhode Island | 1,220 | 0.1% |
| 50 | Alaska | 680 | 0.0% |
| | District of Columbia | 0 | 0.0% |

Source: U.S. Department of Agriculture, National Agricultural Statistics Service
    "Farms and Land in Farms" (http://usda.mannlib.cornell.edu/MannUsda/viewDocumentInfo.do?documentID=1259)
*A farm is any establishment from which $1,000 or more of agricultural products were sold or would normally be sold during the year.  This includes places with five or more horses, except horses in boarding stables or racetracks.

# Land in Farms in 2012

## National Total = 914,000,000 Acres*

| RANK | STATE | ACRES | % of USA |
|---|---|---|---|
| 31 | Alabama | 8,850,000 | 1.0% |
| 44 | Alaska | 880,000 | 0.1% |
| 15 | Arizona | 26,100,000 | 2.9% |
| 23 | Arkansas | 13,500,000 | 1.5% |
| 16 | California | 25,400,000 | 2.8% |
| 9 | Colorado | 31,300,000 | 3.4% |
| 49 | Connecticut | 400,000 | 0.0% |
| 47 | Delaware | 490,000 | 0.1% |
| 30 | Florida | 9,250,000 | 1.0% |
| 28 | Georgia | 10,400,000 | 1.1% |
| 43 | Hawaii | 1,110,000 | 0.1% |
| 24 | Idaho | 11,400,000 | 1.2% |
| 14 | Illinois | 26,600,000 | 2.9% |
| 20 | Indiana | 14,700,000 | 1.6% |
| 10 | Iowa | 30,700,000 | 3.4% |
| 3 | Kansas | 46,000,000 | 5.0% |
| 21 | Kentucky | 14,000,000 | 1.5% |
| 34 | Louisiana | 7,950,000 | 0.9% |
| 41 | Maine | 1,350,000 | 0.1% |
| 40 | Maryland | 2,050,000 | 0.2% |
| 46 | Massachusetts | 520,000 | 0.1% |
| 29 | Michigan | 9,900,000 | 1.1% |
| 13 | Minnesota | 26,800,000 | 2.9% |
| 25 | Mississippi | 11,150,000 | 1.2% |
| 12 | Missouri | 29,000,000 | 3.2% |
| 2 | Montana | 58,800,000 | 6.4% |
| 4 | Nebraska | 45,500,000 | 5.0% |
| 37 | Nevada | 5,840,000 | 0.6% |
| 48 | New Hampshire | 470,000 | 0.1% |
| 45 | New Jersey | 730,000 | 0.1% |
| 5 | New Mexico | 43,900,000 | 4.8% |
| 36 | New York | 7,000,000 | 0.8% |
| 32 | North Carolina | 8,500,000 | 0.9% |
| 7 | North Dakota | 39,600,000 | 4.3% |
| 22 | Ohio | 13,550,000 | 1.5% |
| 8 | Oklahoma | 34,800,000 | 3.8% |
| 17 | Oregon | 16,500,000 | 1.8% |
| 35 | Pennsylvania | 7,700,000 | 0.8% |
| 50 | Rhode Island | 70,000 | 0.0% |
| 38 | South Carolina | 4,800,000 | 0.5% |
| 6 | South Dakota | 43,650,000 | 4.8% |
| 27 | Tennessee | 10,800,000 | 1.2% |
| 1 | Texas | 128,000,000 | 14.0% |
| 26 | Utah | 11,100,000 | 1.2% |
| 42 | Vermont | 1,220,000 | 0.1% |
| 33 | Virginia | 8,050,000 | 0.9% |
| 19 | Washington | 14,800,000 | 1.6% |
| 39 | West Virginia | 3,620,000 | 0.4% |
| 18 | Wisconsin | 15,000,000 | 1.6% |
| 11 | Wyoming | 30,200,000 | 3.3% |

| RANK | STATE | ACRES | % of USA |
|---|---|---|---|
| 1 | Texas | 128,000,000 | 14.0% |
| 2 | Montana | 58,800,000 | 6.4% |
| 3 | Kansas | 46,000,000 | 5.0% |
| 4 | Nebraska | 45,500,000 | 5.0% |
| 5 | New Mexico | 43,900,000 | 4.8% |
| 6 | South Dakota | 43,650,000 | 4.8% |
| 7 | North Dakota | 39,600,000 | 4.3% |
| 8 | Oklahoma | 34,800,000 | 3.8% |
| 9 | Colorado | 31,300,000 | 3.4% |
| 10 | Iowa | 30,700,000 | 3.4% |
| 11 | Wyoming | 30,200,000 | 3.3% |
| 12 | Missouri | 29,000,000 | 3.2% |
| 13 | Minnesota | 26,800,000 | 2.9% |
| 14 | Illinois | 26,600,000 | 2.9% |
| 15 | Arizona | 26,100,000 | 2.9% |
| 16 | California | 25,400,000 | 2.8% |
| 17 | Oregon | 16,500,000 | 1.8% |
| 18 | Wisconsin | 15,000,000 | 1.6% |
| 19 | Washington | 14,800,000 | 1.6% |
| 20 | Indiana | 14,700,000 | 1.6% |
| 21 | Kentucky | 14,000,000 | 1.5% |
| 22 | Ohio | 13,550,000 | 1.5% |
| 23 | Arkansas | 13,500,000 | 1.5% |
| 24 | Idaho | 11,400,000 | 1.2% |
| 25 | Mississippi | 11,150,000 | 1.2% |
| 26 | Utah | 11,100,000 | 1.2% |
| 27 | Tennessee | 10,800,000 | 1.2% |
| 28 | Georgia | 10,400,000 | 1.1% |
| 29 | Michigan | 9,900,000 | 1.1% |
| 30 | Florida | 9,250,000 | 1.0% |
| 31 | Alabama | 8,850,000 | 1.0% |
| 32 | North Carolina | 8,500,000 | 0.9% |
| 33 | Virginia | 8,050,000 | 0.9% |
| 34 | Louisiana | 7,950,000 | 0.9% |
| 35 | Pennsylvania | 7,700,000 | 0.8% |
| 36 | New York | 7,000,000 | 0.8% |
| 37 | Nevada | 5,840,000 | 0.6% |
| 38 | South Carolina | 4,800,000 | 0.5% |
| 39 | West Virginia | 3,620,000 | 0.4% |
| 40 | Maryland | 2,050,000 | 0.2% |
| 41 | Maine | 1,350,000 | 0.1% |
| 42 | Vermont | 1,220,000 | 0.1% |
| 43 | Hawaii | 1,110,000 | 0.1% |
| 44 | Alaska | 880,000 | 0.1% |
| 45 | New Jersey | 730,000 | 0.1% |
| 46 | Massachusetts | 520,000 | 0.1% |
| 47 | Delaware | 490,000 | 0.1% |
| 48 | New Hampshire | 470,000 | 0.1% |
| 49 | Connecticut | 400,000 | 0.0% |
| 50 | Rhode Island | 70,000 | 0.0% |
| | District of Columbia | 0 | 0.0% |

Source: U.S. Department of Agriculture, National Agricultural Statistics Service
"Farms and Land in Farms" (http://usda.mannlib.cornell.edu/MannUsda/viewDocumentInfo.do?documentID=1259)
*A farm is any establishment from which $1,000 or more of agricultural products were sold or would normally be sold during the year. This includes places with five or more horses, except horses in boarding stables or racetracks.

# Average Number of Acres per Farm in 2012

## National Average = 421 Acres*

ALPHA ORDER

| RANK | STATE | ACRES |
|------|-------|-------|
| 32 | Alabama | 190 |
| 7 | Alaska | 1,294 |
| 5 | Arizona | 1,684 |
| 22 | Arkansas | 282 |
| 21 | California | 316 |
| 10 | Colorado | 862 |
| 47 | Connecticut | 82 |
| 28 | Delaware | 196 |
| 29 | Florida | 195 |
| 27 | Georgia | 221 |
| 43 | Hawaii | 148 |
| 14 | Idaho | 465 |
| 18 | Illinois | 358 |
| 26 | Indiana | 245 |
| 20 | Iowa | 333 |
| 11 | Kansas | 702 |
| 40 | Kentucky | 164 |
| 23 | Louisiana | 274 |
| 39 | Maine | 167 |
| 42 | Maryland | 160 |
| 49 | Massachusetts | 68 |
| 34 | Michigan | 181 |
| 19 | Minnesota | 338 |
| 25 | Mississippi | 264 |
| 23 | Missouri | 274 |
| 2 | Montana | 2,056 |
| 9 | Nebraska | 974 |
| 3 | Nevada | 1,980 |
| 46 | New Hampshire | 113 |
| 48 | New Jersey | 72 |
| 4 | New Mexico | 1,845 |
| 31 | New York | 194 |
| 38 | North Carolina | 170 |
| 8 | North Dakota | 1,253 |
| 33 | Ohio | 185 |
| 16 | Oklahoma | 407 |
| 15 | Oregon | 433 |
| 45 | Pennsylvania | 124 |
| 50 | Rhode Island | 57 |
| 35 | South Carolina | 180 |
| 6 | South Dakota | 1,408 |
| 44 | Tennessee | 142 |
| 13 | Texas | 523 |
| 12 | Utah | 677 |
| 36 | Vermont | 174 |
| 36 | Virginia | 174 |
| 17 | Washington | 377 |
| 40 | West Virginia | 164 |
| 29 | Wisconsin | 195 |
| 1 | Wyoming | 2,796 |

RANK ORDER

| RANK | STATE | ACRES |
|------|-------|-------|
| 1 | Wyoming | 2,796 |
| 2 | Montana | 2,056 |
| 3 | Nevada | 1,980 |
| 4 | New Mexico | 1,845 |
| 5 | Arizona | 1,684 |
| 6 | South Dakota | 1,408 |
| 7 | Alaska | 1,294 |
| 8 | North Dakota | 1,253 |
| 9 | Nebraska | 974 |
| 10 | Colorado | 862 |
| 11 | Kansas | 702 |
| 12 | Utah | 677 |
| 13 | Texas | 523 |
| 14 | Idaho | 465 |
| 15 | Oregon | 433 |
| 16 | Oklahoma | 407 |
| 17 | Washington | 377 |
| 18 | Illinois | 358 |
| 19 | Minnesota | 338 |
| 20 | Iowa | 333 |
| 21 | California | 316 |
| 22 | Arkansas | 282 |
| 23 | Louisiana | 274 |
| 23 | Missouri | 274 |
| 25 | Mississippi | 264 |
| 26 | Indiana | 245 |
| 27 | Georgia | 221 |
| 28 | Delaware | 196 |
| 29 | Florida | 195 |
| 29 | Wisconsin | 195 |
| 31 | New York | 194 |
| 32 | Alabama | 190 |
| 33 | Ohio | 185 |
| 34 | Michigan | 181 |
| 35 | South Carolina | 180 |
| 36 | Vermont | 174 |
| 36 | Virginia | 174 |
| 38 | North Carolina | 170 |
| 39 | Maine | 167 |
| 40 | Kentucky | 164 |
| 40 | West Virginia | 164 |
| 42 | Maryland | 160 |
| 43 | Hawaii | 148 |
| 44 | Tennessee | 142 |
| 45 | Pennsylvania | 124 |
| 46 | New Hampshire | 113 |
| 47 | Connecticut | 82 |
| 48 | New Jersey | 72 |
| 49 | Massachusetts | 68 |
| 50 | Rhode Island | 57 |
| | District of Columbia** | NA |

Source: U.S. Department of Agriculture, National Agricultural Statistics Service
"Farms and Land in Farms" (http://usda.mannlib.cornell.edu/MannUsda/viewDocumentInfo.do?documentID=1259)
*A farm is any establishment from which $1,000 or more of agricultural products were sold or would normally be sold during the year. This includes places with five or more horses, except horses in boarding stables or racetracks.
**Not applicable.

# Average per-Acre Value of Farmland in 2013

## National Average = $2,900 per Acre*

| ALPHA ORDER | | | | RANK ORDER | | |
|---|---|---|---|---|---|---|
| RANK | STATE | PER-ACRE VALUE | | RANK | STATE | PER-ACRE VALUE |
| 36 | Alabama | $2,000 | | 1 | New Jersey | $12,700 |
| NA | Alaska** | NA | | 2 | Rhode Island | 11,800 |
| 20 | Arizona | 3,800 | | 3 | Connecticut | 11,000 |
| 26 | Arkansas | 3,000 | | 4 | Massachusetts | 10,600 |
| 9 | California | 7,300 | | 5 | Iowa | 8,400 |
| 44 | Colorado | 1,280 | | 6 | Delaware | 8,100 |
| 3 | Connecticut | 11,000 | | 7 | Illinois | 7,800 |
| 6 | Delaware | 8,100 | | 8 | Maryland | 7,500 |
| 17 | Florida | 4,500 | | 9 | California | 7,300 |
| 22 | Georgia | 3,600 | | 10 | Indiana | 6,900 |
| NA | Hawaii** | NA | | 11 | Ohio | 5,600 |
| 33 | Idaho | 2,200 | | 12 | Pennsylvania | 5,300 |
| 7 | Illinois | 7,800 | | 13 | Michigan | 4,800 |
| 10 | Indiana | 6,900 | | 14 | Minnesota | 4,750 |
| 5 | Iowa | 8,400 | | 15 | North Carolina | 4,550 |
| 38 | Kansas | 1,900 | | 15 | Virginia | 4,550 |
| 23 | Kentucky | 3,300 | | 17 | Florida | 4,500 |
| 31 | Louisiana | 2,550 | | 18 | New Hampshire | 4,450 |
| 37 | Maine | 1,970 | | 19 | Wisconsin | 4,400 |
| 8 | Maryland | 7,500 | | 20 | Arizona | 3,800 |
| 4 | Massachusetts | 10,600 | | 20 | Tennessee | 3,800 |
| 13 | Michigan | 4,800 | | 22 | Georgia | 3,600 |
| 14 | Minnesota | 4,750 | | 23 | Kentucky | 3,300 |
| 35 | Mississippi | 2,140 | | 24 | Missouri | 3,100 |
| 24 | Missouri | 3,100 | | 25 | Nebraska | 3,050 |
| 46 | Montana | 790 | | 26 | Arkansas | 3,000 |
| 25 | Nebraska | 3,050 | | 27 | South Carolina | 2,850 |
| 45 | Nevada | 1,050 | | 28 | Vermont | 2,800 |
| 18 | New Hampshire | 4,450 | | 29 | West Virginia | 2,750 |
| 1 | New Jersey | 12,700 | | 30 | New York | 2,600 |
| 48 | New Mexico | 550 | | 31 | Louisiana | 2,550 |
| 30 | New York | 2,600 | | 32 | Washington | 2,350 |
| 15 | North Carolina | 4,550 | | 33 | Idaho | 2,200 |
| 42 | North Dakota | 1,690 | | 34 | Oregon | 2,150 |
| 11 | Ohio | 5,600 | | 35 | Mississippi | 2,140 |
| 43 | Oklahoma | 1,590 | | 36 | Alabama | 2,000 |
| 34 | Oregon | 2,150 | | 37 | Maine | 1,970 |
| 12 | Pennsylvania | 5,300 | | 38 | Kansas | 1,900 |
| 2 | Rhode Island | 11,800 | | 38 | Utah | 1,900 |
| 27 | South Carolina | 2,850 | | 40 | Texas | 1,810 |
| 41 | South Dakota | 1,800 | | 41 | South Dakota | 1,800 |
| 20 | Tennessee | 3,800 | | 42 | North Dakota | 1,690 |
| 40 | Texas | 1,810 | | 43 | Oklahoma | 1,590 |
| 38 | Utah | 1,900 | | 44 | Colorado | 1,280 |
| 28 | Vermont | 2,800 | | 45 | Nevada | 1,050 |
| 15 | Virginia | 4,550 | | 46 | Montana | 790 |
| 32 | Washington | 2,350 | | 47 | Wyoming | 560 |
| 29 | West Virginia | 2,750 | | 48 | New Mexico | 550 |
| 19 | Wisconsin | 4,400 | | NA | Alaska** | NA |
| 47 | Wyoming | 560 | | NA | Hawaii** | NA |
| | | | | | District of Columbia** | NA |

Source: U.S. Department of Agriculture, National Agricultural Statistics Service
  "Land Values and Cash Rents" (http://usda.mannlib.cornell.edu/MannUsda/viewDocumentInfo.do?documentID=1446)
*Value of farmland and buildings in nominal dollars.
**Not applicable or available.

# Percent Change in Average per-Acre Value of Farmland: 2012 to 2013

## National Percent Change = 9.4% Increase*

| ALPHA ORDER | | | | RANK ORDER | | |
|---|---|---|---|---|---|---|
| RANK | STATE | PERCENT CHANGE | | RANK | STATE | PERCENT CHANGE |
| 36 | Alabama | 0.0 | | 1 | North Dakota | 36.3 |
| NA | Alaska** | NA | | 2 | South Dakota | 28.6 |
| 16 | Arizona | 5.6 | | 3 | Iowa | 20.0 |
| 18 | Arkansas | 5.3 | | 4 | Kansas | 18.0 |
| 31 | California | 1.4 | | 5 | Nebraska | 17.8 |
| 11 | Colorado | 9.4 | | 6 | Minnesota | 17.3 |
| 42 | Connecticut | (0.9) | | 7 | Illinois | 16.4 |
| 36 | Delaware | 0.0 | | 8 | Michigan | 12.9 |
| 47 | Florida | (2.2) | | 9 | Ohio | 12.0 |
| 23 | Georgia | 2.9 | | 10 | Indiana | 11.3 |
| NA | Hawaii** | NA | | 11 | Colorado | 9.4 |
| 22 | Idaho | 3.8 | | 12 | Kentucky | 8.2 |
| 7 | Illinois | 16.4 | | 13 | Oklahoma | 7.4 |
| 10 | Indiana | 11.3 | | 14 | Missouri | 6.9 |
| 3 | Iowa | 20.0 | | 15 | Louisiana | 6.3 |
| 4 | Kansas | 18.0 | | 16 | Arizona | 5.6 |
| 12 | Kentucky | 8.2 | | 16 | Utah | 5.6 |
| 15 | Louisiana | 6.3 | | 18 | Arkansas | 5.3 |
| 36 | Maine | 0.0 | | 19 | Maryland | 4.2 |
| 19 | Maryland | 4.2 | | 20 | New Jersey | 4.1 |
| 34 | Massachusetts | 1.0 | | 21 | Montana | 3.9 |
| 8 | Michigan | 12.9 | | 22 | Idaho | 3.8 |
| 6 | Minnesota | 17.3 | | 23 | Georgia | 2.9 |
| 36 | Mississippi | 0.0 | | 24 | Tennessee | 2.7 |
| 14 | Missouri | 6.9 | | 25 | Oregon | 2.4 |
| 21 | Montana | 3.9 | | 26 | Virginia | 2.2 |
| 5 | Nebraska | 17.8 | | 26 | Washington | 2.2 |
| 36 | Nevada | 0.0 | | 28 | Pennsylvania | 1.9 |
| 47 | New Hampshire | (2.2) | | 28 | West Virginia | 1.9 |
| 20 | New Jersey | 4.1 | | 30 | Vermont | 1.8 |
| 45 | New Mexico | (1.8) | | 31 | California | 1.4 |
| 46 | New York | (1.9) | | 32 | North Carolina | 1.1 |
| 32 | North Carolina | 1.1 | | 32 | Wisconsin | 1.1 |
| 1 | North Dakota | 36.3 | | 34 | Massachusetts | 1.0 |
| 9 | Ohio | 12.0 | | 35 | Texas | 0.6 |
| 13 | Oklahoma | 7.4 | | 36 | Alabama | 0.0 |
| 25 | Oregon | 2.4 | | 36 | Delaware | 0.0 |
| 28 | Pennsylvania | 1.9 | | 36 | Maine | 0.0 |
| 43 | Rhode Island | (1.7) | | 36 | Mississippi | 0.0 |
| 43 | South Carolina | (1.7) | | 36 | Nevada | 0.0 |
| 2 | South Dakota | 28.6 | | 36 | Wyoming | 0.0 |
| 24 | Tennessee | 2.7 | | 42 | Connecticut | (0.9) |
| 35 | Texas | 0.6 | | 43 | Rhode Island | (1.7) |
| 16 | Utah | 5.6 | | 43 | South Carolina | (1.7) |
| 30 | Vermont | 1.8 | | 45 | New Mexico | (1.8) |
| 26 | Virginia | 2.2 | | 46 | New York | (1.9) |
| 26 | Washington | 2.2 | | 47 | Florida | (2.2) |
| 28 | West Virginia | 1.9 | | 47 | New Hampshire | (2.2) |
| 32 | Wisconsin | 1.1 | | NA | Alaska** | NA |
| 36 | Wyoming | 0.0 | | NA | Hawaii** | NA |
| | | | | District of Columbia** | | NA |

Source: U.S. Department of Agriculture, National Agricultural Statistics Service
   "Land Values and Cash Rents" (http://usda.mannlib.cornell.edu/MannUsda/viewDocumentInfo.do?documentID=1446)
*Value of farmland and buildings in nominal dollars.
**Not applicable or available.

# Net Farm Income in 2012

## National Total = $113,813,381,512*

ALPHA ORDER

| RANK | STATE | FARM INCOME | % of USA |
|---|---|---|---|
| 27 | Alabama | $1,384,611,636 | 1.2% |
| 48 | Alaska | 11,107,512 | 0.0% |
| 33 | Arizona | 902,974,790 | 0.8% |
| 19 | Arkansas | 1,979,479,416 | 1.7% |
| 1 | California | 16,001,126,129 | 14.1% |
| 24 | Colorado | 1,753,342,146 | 1.5% |
| 46 | Connecticut | 75,477,032 | 0.1% |
| 41 | Delaware | 272,204,070 | 0.2% |
| 16 | Florida | 2,522,210,614 | 2.2% |
| 8 | Georgia | 4,214,043,478 | 3.7% |
| 40 | Hawaii | 329,963,992 | 0.3% |
| 14 | Idaho | 2,745,404,023 | 2.4% |
| 9 | Illinois | 4,173,945,737 | 3.7% |
| 11 | Indiana | 3,290,744,166 | 2.9% |
| 2 | Iowa | 9,254,749,955 | 8.1% |
| 13 | Kansas | 3,014,912,796 | 2.6% |
| 25 | Kentucky | 1,540,664,355 | 1.4% |
| 23 | Louisiana | 1,779,420,277 | 1.6% |
| 43 | Maine | 191,601,387 | 0.2% |
| 36 | Maryland | 727,340,301 | 0.6% |
| 45 | Massachusetts | 99,134,587 | 0.1% |
| 17 | Michigan | 2,236,865,568 | 2.0% |
| 3 | Minnesota | 8,172,164,294 | 7.2% |
| 20 | Mississippi | 1,939,511,946 | 1.7% |
| 22 | Missouri | 1,794,697,793 | 1.6% |
| 30 | Montana | 1,294,909,562 | 1.1% |
| 4 | Nebraska | 5,952,229,500 | 5.2% |
| 42 | Nevada | 222,574,672 | 0.2% |
| 50 | New Hampshire | 568,420 | 0.0% |
| 39 | New Jersey | 339,611,038 | 0.3% |
| 28 | New Mexico | 1,358,390,736 | 1.2% |
| 29 | New York | 1,296,263,793 | 1.1% |
| 6 | North Carolina | 4,319,945,655 | 3.8% |
| 7 | North Dakota | 4,279,095,530 | 3.8% |
| 15 | Ohio | 2,567,694,845 | 2.3% |
| 26 | Oklahoma | 1,403,608,323 | 1.2% |
| 31 | Oregon | 959,935,956 | 0.8% |
| 21 | Pennsylvania | 1,833,490,493 | 1.6% |
| 49 | Rhode Island | 4,547,995 | 0.0% |
| 35 | South Carolina | 734,915,397 | 0.6% |
| 10 | South Dakota | 3,643,004,647 | 3.2% |
| 34 | Tennessee | 812,614,316 | 0.7% |
| 5 | Texas | 5,145,163,729 | 4.5% |
| 37 | Utah | 363,640,694 | 0.3% |
| 44 | Vermont | 159,652,106 | 0.1% |
| 32 | Virginia | 932,203,409 | 0.8% |
| 18 | Washington | 2,160,404,109 | 1.9% |
| 47 | West Virginia | 64,224,486 | 0.1% |
| 12 | Wisconsin | 3,200,564,410 | 2.8% |
| 38 | Wyoming | 356,381,692 | 0.3% |

RANK ORDER

| RANK | STATE | FARM INCOME | % of USA |
|---|---|---|---|
| 1 | California | $16,001,126,129 | 14.1% |
| 2 | Iowa | 9,254,749,955 | 8.1% |
| 3 | Minnesota | 8,172,164,294 | 7.2% |
| 4 | Nebraska | 5,952,229,500 | 5.2% |
| 5 | Texas | 5,145,163,729 | 4.5% |
| 6 | North Carolina | 4,319,945,655 | 3.8% |
| 7 | North Dakota | 4,279,095,530 | 3.8% |
| 8 | Georgia | 4,214,043,478 | 3.7% |
| 9 | Illinois | 4,173,945,737 | 3.7% |
| 10 | South Dakota | 3,643,004,647 | 3.2% |
| 11 | Indiana | 3,290,744,166 | 2.9% |
| 12 | Wisconsin | 3,200,564,410 | 2.8% |
| 13 | Kansas | 3,014,912,796 | 2.6% |
| 14 | Idaho | 2,745,404,023 | 2.4% |
| 15 | Ohio | 2,567,694,845 | 2.3% |
| 16 | Florida | 2,522,210,614 | 2.2% |
| 17 | Michigan | 2,236,865,568 | 2.0% |
| 18 | Washington | 2,160,404,109 | 1.9% |
| 19 | Arkansas | 1,979,479,416 | 1.7% |
| 20 | Mississippi | 1,939,511,946 | 1.7% |
| 21 | Pennsylvania | 1,833,490,493 | 1.6% |
| 22 | Missouri | 1,794,697,793 | 1.6% |
| 23 | Louisiana | 1,779,420,277 | 1.6% |
| 24 | Colorado | 1,753,342,146 | 1.5% |
| 25 | Kentucky | 1,540,664,355 | 1.4% |
| 26 | Oklahoma | 1,403,608,323 | 1.2% |
| 27 | Alabama | 1,384,611,636 | 1.2% |
| 28 | New Mexico | 1,358,390,736 | 1.2% |
| 29 | New York | 1,296,263,793 | 1.1% |
| 30 | Montana | 1,294,909,562 | 1.1% |
| 31 | Oregon | 959,935,956 | 0.8% |
| 32 | Virginia | 932,203,409 | 0.8% |
| 33 | Arizona | 902,974,790 | 0.8% |
| 34 | Tennessee | 812,614,316 | 0.7% |
| 35 | South Carolina | 734,915,397 | 0.6% |
| 36 | Maryland | 727,340,301 | 0.6% |
| 37 | Utah | 363,640,694 | 0.3% |
| 38 | Wyoming | 356,381,692 | 0.3% |
| 39 | New Jersey | 339,611,038 | 0.3% |
| 40 | Hawaii | 329,963,992 | 0.3% |
| 41 | Delaware | 272,204,070 | 0.2% |
| 42 | Nevada | 222,574,672 | 0.2% |
| 43 | Maine | 191,601,387 | 0.2% |
| 44 | Vermont | 159,652,106 | 0.1% |
| 45 | Massachusetts | 99,134,587 | 0.1% |
| 46 | Connecticut | 75,477,032 | 0.1% |
| 47 | West Virginia | 64,224,486 | 0.1% |
| 48 | Alaska | 11,107,512 | 0.0% |
| 49 | Rhode Island | 4,547,995 | 0.0% |
| 50 | New Hampshire | 568,420 | 0.0% |
| | District of Columbia | 0 | 0.0% |

Source: U.S. Department of Agriculture, Economic Research Service
"Net Farm Income and Value of Production per Acre for States, 2012
(http://www.ers.usda.gov/data/FarmIncome/FinfidmuXls.htm)
*Net farm income is a measure of the net value of production in a given year. It is determined by subtracting total production expenses from gross farm income.

# Net Farm Income per Operation in 2012

## National Average = $52,625 per Operation*

| ALPHA ORDER | | | | RANK ORDER | | |
|---|---|---|---|---|---|---|
| RANK | STATE | PER OPERATION | | RANK | STATE | PER OPERATION |
| 32 | Alabama | $29,640 | | 1 | California | $199,080 |
| 43 | Alaska | 16,822 | | 2 | North Dakota | 135,324 |
| 13 | Arizona | 58,940 | | 3 | Nebraska | 127,594 |
| 26 | Arkansas | 41,454 | | 4 | South Dakota | 116,864 |
| 1 | California | 199,080 | | 5 | Idaho | 112,065 |
| 20 | Colorado | 48,272 | | 6 | Delaware | 108,976 |
| 45 | Connecticut | 15,498 | | 7 | Minnesota | 103,090 |
| 6 | Delaware | 108,976 | | 8 | Iowa | 100,233 |
| 19 | Florida | 53,235 | | 9 | Georgia | 89,505 |
| 9 | Georgia | 89,505 | | 10 | North Carolina | 86,360 |
| 24 | Hawaii | 43,956 | | 11 | Nevada | 75,240 |
| 5 | Idaho | 112,065 | | 12 | Louisiana | 61,376 |
| 16 | Illinois | 56,206 | | 13 | Arizona | 58,940 |
| 18 | Indiana | 54,880 | | 14 | New Mexico | 57,195 |
| 8 | Iowa | 100,233 | | 15 | Maryland | 56,800 |
| 21 | Kansas | 46,332 | | 16 | Illinois | 56,206 |
| 41 | Kentucky | 18,040 | | 17 | Washington | 55,042 |
| 12 | Louisiana | 61,376 | | 18 | Indiana | 54,880 |
| 36 | Maine | 23,714 | | 19 | Florida | 53,235 |
| 15 | Maryland | 56,800 | | 20 | Colorado | 48,272 |
| 46 | Massachusetts | 12,988 | | 21 | Kansas | 46,332 |
| 27 | Michigan | 40,906 | | 22 | Mississippi | 45,936 |
| 7 | Minnesota | 103,090 | | 23 | Montana | 45,232 |
| 22 | Mississippi | 45,936 | | 24 | Hawaii | 43,956 |
| 42 | Missouri | 16,988 | | 25 | Wisconsin | 41,535 |
| 23 | Montana | 45,232 | | 26 | Arkansas | 41,454 |
| 3 | Nebraska | 127,594 | | 27 | Michigan | 40,906 |
| 11 | Nevada | 75,240 | | 28 | New York | 35,890 |
| 50 | New Hampshire | 113 | | 29 | Ohio | 34,965 |
| 31 | New Jersey | 33,480 | | 30 | Wyoming | 33,552 |
| 14 | New Mexico | 57,195 | | 31 | New Jersey | 33,480 |
| 28 | New York | 35,890 | | 32 | Alabama | 29,640 |
| 10 | North Carolina | 86,360 | | 33 | Pennsylvania | 29,512 |
| 2 | North Dakota | 135,324 | | 34 | South Carolina | 27,540 |
| 29 | Ohio | 34,965 | | 35 | Oregon | 25,114 |
| 44 | Oklahoma | 16,280 | | 36 | Maine | 23,714 |
| 35 | Oregon | 25,114 | | 37 | Vermont | 22,794 |
| 33 | Pennsylvania | 29,512 | | 38 | Utah | 22,341 |
| 48 | Rhode Island | 3,705 | | 39 | Texas | 20,920 |
| 34 | South Carolina | 27,540 | | 40 | Virginia | 20,184 |
| 4 | South Dakota | 116,864 | | 41 | Kentucky | 18,040 |
| 47 | Tennessee | 10,650 | | 42 | Missouri | 16,988 |
| 39 | Texas | 20,920 | | 43 | Alaska | 16,822 |
| 38 | Utah | 22,341 | | 44 | Oklahoma | 16,280 |
| 37 | Vermont | 22,794 | | 45 | Connecticut | 15,498 |
| 40 | Virginia | 20,184 | | 46 | Massachusetts | 12,988 |
| 17 | Washington | 55,042 | | 47 | Tennessee | 10,650 |
| 49 | West Virginia | 2,952 | | 48 | Rhode Island | 3,705 |
| 25 | Wisconsin | 41,535 | | 49 | West Virginia | 2,952 |
| 30 | Wyoming | 33,552 | | 50 | New Hampshire | 113 |
| | | | | | District of Columbia** | NA |

Source: CQ Press using data from U.S. Department of Agriculture, Economic Research Service
   "Net Farm Income and Value of Production per Acre for States, 2012
   (http://www.ers.usda.gov/data-products/farm-income-and-wealth-statistics.aspx)
*Calculated by multiplying average acres per farm by average net farm income per acre.
**Not applicable.

# Net Farm Income per Acre in 2012

## National Average = $125 per Acre*

ALPHA ORDER

| RANK | STATE | PER ACRE |
|---|---|---|
| 23 | Alabama | $156 |
| 48 | Alaska | 13 |
| 43 | Arizona | 35 |
| 25 | Arkansas | 147 |
| 1 | California | 630 |
| 39 | Colorado | 56 |
| 18 | Connecticut | 189 |
| 2 | Delaware | 556 |
| 10 | Florida | 273 |
| 5 | Georgia | 405 |
| 9 | Hawaii | 297 |
| 11 | Idaho | 241 |
| 22 | Illinois | 157 |
| 14 | Indiana | 224 |
| 8 | Iowa | 301 |
| 35 | Kansas | 66 |
| 31 | Kentucky | 110 |
| 14 | Louisiana | 224 |
| 27 | Maine | 142 |
| 6 | Maryland | 355 |
| 17 | Massachusetts | 191 |
| 13 | Michigan | 226 |
| 7 | Minnesota | 305 |
| 21 | Mississippi | 174 |
| 37 | Missouri | 62 |
| 46 | Montana | 22 |
| 28 | Nebraska | 131 |
| 42 | Nevada | 38 |
| 50 | New Hampshire | 1 |
| 4 | New Jersey | 465 |
| 45 | New Mexico | 31 |
| 20 | New York | 185 |
| 3 | North Carolina | 508 |
| 32 | North Dakota | 108 |
| 18 | Ohio | 189 |
| 40 | Oklahoma | 40 |
| 38 | Oregon | 58 |
| 12 | Pennsylvania | 238 |
| 36 | Rhode Island | 65 |
| 24 | South Carolina | 153 |
| 33 | South Dakota | 83 |
| 34 | Tennessee | 75 |
| 40 | Texas | 40 |
| 44 | Utah | 33 |
| 28 | Vermont | 131 |
| 30 | Virginia | 116 |
| 26 | Washington | 146 |
| 47 | West Virginia | 18 |
| 16 | Wisconsin | 213 |
| 49 | Wyoming | 12 |

RANK ORDER

| RANK | STATE | PER ACRE |
|---|---|---|
| 1 | California | $630 |
| 2 | Delaware | 556 |
| 3 | North Carolina | 508 |
| 4 | New Jersey | 465 |
| 5 | Georgia | 405 |
| 6 | Maryland | 355 |
| 7 | Minnesota | 305 |
| 8 | Iowa | 301 |
| 9 | Hawaii | 297 |
| 10 | Florida | 273 |
| 11 | Idaho | 241 |
| 12 | Pennsylvania | 238 |
| 13 | Michigan | 226 |
| 14 | Indiana | 224 |
| 14 | Louisiana | 224 |
| 16 | Wisconsin | 213 |
| 17 | Massachusetts | 191 |
| 18 | Connecticut | 189 |
| 18 | Ohio | 189 |
| 20 | New York | 185 |
| 21 | Mississippi | 174 |
| 22 | Illinois | 157 |
| 23 | Alabama | 156 |
| 24 | South Carolina | 153 |
| 25 | Arkansas | 147 |
| 26 | Washington | 146 |
| 27 | Maine | 142 |
| 28 | Nebraska | 131 |
| 28 | Vermont | 131 |
| 30 | Virginia | 116 |
| 31 | Kentucky | 110 |
| 32 | North Dakota | 108 |
| 33 | South Dakota | 83 |
| 34 | Tennessee | 75 |
| 35 | Kansas | 66 |
| 36 | Rhode Island | 65 |
| 37 | Missouri | 62 |
| 38 | Oregon | 58 |
| 39 | Colorado | 56 |
| 40 | Oklahoma | 40 |
| 40 | Texas | 40 |
| 42 | Nevada | 38 |
| 43 | Arizona | 35 |
| 44 | Utah | 33 |
| 45 | New Mexico | 31 |
| 46 | Montana | 22 |
| 47 | West Virginia | 18 |
| 48 | Alaska | 13 |
| 49 | Wyoming | 12 |
| 50 | New Hampshire | 1 |

| District of Columbia** | NA |
|---|---|

Source: CQ Press using data from U.S. Department of Agriculture, Economic Research Service
"Net Farm Income and Value of Production per Acre for States, 2012
(http://www.ers.usda.gov/data-products/farm-income-and-wealth-statistics.aspx)
*Net farm income is a measure of the net value of production in a given year. It is determined by subtracting total production expenses from gross farm income.
**Not applicable.

# Farm Income: Cash Receipts from Commodities in 2012

## National Total = $395,068,677,000*

<table>
<tr><td colspan="4">ALPHA ORDER</td><td colspan="4">RANK ORDER</td></tr>
<tr><td>RANK</td><td>STATE</td><td>FARM INCOME</td><td>% of USA</td><td>RANK</td><td>STATE</td><td>FARM INCOME</td><td>% of USA</td></tr>
<tr><td>25</td><td>Alabama</td><td>$5,349,114,000</td><td>1.4%</td><td>1</td><td>California</td><td>$44,738,132,000</td><td>11.3%</td></tr>
<tr><td>50</td><td>Alaska</td><td>30,954,000</td><td>0.0%</td><td>2</td><td>Iowa</td><td>31,985,370,000</td><td>8.1%</td></tr>
<tr><td>31</td><td>Arizona</td><td>3,909,695,000</td><td>1.0%</td><td>3</td><td>Nebraska</td><td>24,465,882,000</td><td>6.2%</td></tr>
<tr><td>15</td><td>Arkansas</td><td>9,421,594,000</td><td>2.4%</td><td>4</td><td>Texas</td><td>22,726,067,000</td><td>5.8%</td></tr>
<tr><td>1</td><td>California</td><td>44,738,132,000</td><td>11.3%</td><td>5</td><td>Minnesota</td><td>20,580,696,000</td><td>5.2%</td></tr>
<tr><td>20</td><td>Colorado</td><td>7,638,232,000</td><td>1.9%</td><td>6</td><td>Illinois</td><td>19,649,939,000</td><td>5.0%</td></tr>
<tr><td>46</td><td>Connecticut</td><td>543,829,000</td><td>0.1%</td><td>7</td><td>Kansas</td><td>16,223,254,000</td><td>4.1%</td></tr>
<tr><td>39</td><td>Delaware</td><td>1,180,546,000</td><td>0.3%</td><td>8</td><td>Wisconsin</td><td>12,110,055,000</td><td>3.1%</td></tr>
<tr><td>19</td><td>Florida</td><td>8,252,525,000</td><td>2.1%</td><td>9</td><td>Indiana</td><td>12,052,964,000</td><td>3.1%</td></tr>
<tr><td>14</td><td>Georgia</td><td>9,779,096,000</td><td>2.5%</td><td>10</td><td>North Carolina</td><td>11,706,602,000</td><td>3.0%</td></tr>
<tr><td>41</td><td>Hawaii</td><td>729,321,000</td><td>0.2%</td><td>11</td><td>Ohio</td><td>10,066,756,000</td><td>2.5%</td></tr>
<tr><td>21</td><td>Idaho</td><td>7,586,979,000</td><td>1.9%</td><td>12</td><td>South Dakota</td><td>10,013,470,000</td><td>2.5%</td></tr>
<tr><td>6</td><td>Illinois</td><td>19,649,939,000</td><td>5.0%</td><td>13</td><td>Missouri</td><td>9,940,400,000</td><td>2.5%</td></tr>
<tr><td>9</td><td>Indiana</td><td>12,052,964,000</td><td>3.1%</td><td>14</td><td>Georgia</td><td>9,779,096,000</td><td>2.5%</td></tr>
<tr><td>2</td><td>Iowa</td><td>31,985,370,000</td><td>8.1%</td><td>15</td><td>Arkansas</td><td>9,421,594,000</td><td>2.4%</td></tr>
<tr><td>7</td><td>Kansas</td><td>16,223,254,000</td><td>4.1%</td><td>16</td><td>Washington</td><td>9,293,914,000</td><td>2.4%</td></tr>
<tr><td>27</td><td>Kentucky</td><td>5,284,095,000</td><td>1.3%</td><td>17</td><td>North Dakota</td><td>8,684,221,000</td><td>2.2%</td></tr>
<tr><td>29</td><td>Louisiana</td><td>4,127,882,000</td><td>1.0%</td><td>18</td><td>Michigan</td><td>8,293,622,000</td><td>2.1%</td></tr>
<tr><td>43</td><td>Maine</td><td>702,945,000</td><td>0.2%</td><td>19</td><td>Florida</td><td>8,252,525,000</td><td>2.1%</td></tr>
<tr><td>36</td><td>Maryland</td><td>2,329,861,000</td><td>0.6%</td><td>20</td><td>Colorado</td><td>7,638,232,000</td><td>1.9%</td></tr>
<tr><td>47</td><td>Massachusetts</td><td>510,006,000</td><td>0.1%</td><td>21</td><td>Idaho</td><td>7,586,979,000</td><td>1.9%</td></tr>
<tr><td>18</td><td>Michigan</td><td>8,293,622,000</td><td>2.1%</td><td>22</td><td>Oklahoma</td><td>7,038,174,000</td><td>1.8%</td></tr>
<tr><td>5</td><td>Minnesota</td><td>20,580,696,000</td><td>5.2%</td><td>23</td><td>Pennsylvania</td><td>6,868,357,000</td><td>1.7%</td></tr>
<tr><td>24</td><td>Mississippi</td><td>6,235,891,000</td><td>1.6%</td><td>24</td><td>Mississippi</td><td>6,235,891,000</td><td>1.6%</td></tr>
<tr><td>13</td><td>Missouri</td><td>9,940,400,000</td><td>2.5%</td><td>25</td><td>Alabama</td><td>5,349,114,000</td><td>1.4%</td></tr>
<tr><td>33</td><td>Montana</td><td>3,745,101,000</td><td>0.9%</td><td>26</td><td>New York</td><td>5,287,766,000</td><td>1.3%</td></tr>
<tr><td>3</td><td>Nebraska</td><td>24,465,882,000</td><td>6.2%</td><td>27</td><td>Kentucky</td><td>5,284,095,000</td><td>1.3%</td></tr>
<tr><td>42</td><td>Nevada</td><td>717,590,000</td><td>0.2%</td><td>28</td><td>Oregon</td><td>4,817,294,000</td><td>1.2%</td></tr>
<tr><td>48</td><td>New Hampshire</td><td>183,921,000</td><td>0.0%</td><td>29</td><td>Louisiana</td><td>4,127,882,000</td><td>1.0%</td></tr>
<tr><td>40</td><td>New Jersey</td><td>1,139,186,000</td><td>0.3%</td><td>30</td><td>New Mexico</td><td>4,019,802,000</td><td>1.0%</td></tr>
<tr><td>30</td><td>New Mexico</td><td>4,019,802,000</td><td>1.0%</td><td>31</td><td>Arizona</td><td>3,909,695,000</td><td>1.0%</td></tr>
<tr><td>26</td><td>New York</td><td>5,287,766,000</td><td>1.3%</td><td>32</td><td>Tennessee</td><td>3,849,846,000</td><td>1.0%</td></tr>
<tr><td>10</td><td>North Carolina</td><td>11,706,602,000</td><td>3.0%</td><td>33</td><td>Montana</td><td>3,745,101,000</td><td>0.9%</td></tr>
<tr><td>17</td><td>North Dakota</td><td>8,684,221,000</td><td>2.2%</td><td>34</td><td>Virginia</td><td>3,576,417,000</td><td>0.9%</td></tr>
<tr><td>11</td><td>Ohio</td><td>10,066,756,000</td><td>2.5%</td><td>35</td><td>South Carolina</td><td>2,928,327,000</td><td>0.7%</td></tr>
<tr><td>22</td><td>Oklahoma</td><td>7,038,174,000</td><td>1.8%</td><td>36</td><td>Maryland</td><td>2,329,861,000</td><td>0.6%</td></tr>
<tr><td>28</td><td>Oregon</td><td>4,817,294,000</td><td>1.2%</td><td>37</td><td>Utah</td><td>1,688,836,000</td><td>0.4%</td></tr>
<tr><td>23</td><td>Pennsylvania</td><td>6,868,357,000</td><td>1.7%</td><td>38</td><td>Wyoming</td><td>1,650,684,000</td><td>0.4%</td></tr>
<tr><td>49</td><td>Rhode Island</td><td>62,082,000</td><td>0.0%</td><td>39</td><td>Delaware</td><td>1,180,546,000</td><td>0.3%</td></tr>
<tr><td>35</td><td>South Carolina</td><td>2,928,327,000</td><td>0.7%</td><td>40</td><td>New Jersey</td><td>1,139,186,000</td><td>0.3%</td></tr>
<tr><td>12</td><td>South Dakota</td><td>10,013,470,000</td><td>2.5%</td><td>41</td><td>Hawaii</td><td>729,321,000</td><td>0.2%</td></tr>
<tr><td>32</td><td>Tennessee</td><td>3,849,846,000</td><td>1.0%</td><td>42</td><td>Nevada</td><td>717,590,000</td><td>0.2%</td></tr>
<tr><td>4</td><td>Texas</td><td>22,726,067,000</td><td>5.8%</td><td>43</td><td>Maine</td><td>702,945,000</td><td>0.2%</td></tr>
<tr><td>37</td><td>Utah</td><td>1,688,836,000</td><td>0.4%</td><td>44</td><td>Vermont</td><td>699,313,000</td><td>0.2%</td></tr>
<tr><td>44</td><td>Vermont</td><td>699,313,000</td><td>0.2%</td><td>45</td><td>West Virginia</td><td>652,069,000</td><td>0.2%</td></tr>
<tr><td>34</td><td>Virginia</td><td>3,576,417,000</td><td>0.9%</td><td>46</td><td>Connecticut</td><td>543,829,000</td><td>0.1%</td></tr>
<tr><td>16</td><td>Washington</td><td>9,293,914,000</td><td>2.4%</td><td>47</td><td>Massachusetts</td><td>510,006,000</td><td>0.1%</td></tr>
<tr><td>45</td><td>West Virginia</td><td>652,069,000</td><td>0.2%</td><td>48</td><td>New Hampshire</td><td>183,921,000</td><td>0.0%</td></tr>
<tr><td>8</td><td>Wisconsin</td><td>12,110,055,000</td><td>3.1%</td><td>49</td><td>Rhode Island</td><td>62,082,000</td><td>0.0%</td></tr>
<tr><td>38</td><td>Wyoming</td><td>1,650,684,000</td><td>0.4%</td><td>50</td><td>Alaska</td><td>30,954,000</td><td>0.0%</td></tr>
<tr><td></td><td></td><td></td><td></td><td></td><td>District of Columbia</td><td>0</td><td>0.0%</td></tr>
</table>

Source: U.S. Department of Agriculture, Economic Research Service
"Farm Marketings" (http://www.ers.usda.gov/data-products/farm-income-and-wealth-statistics.aspx)
*Commodities include crops and livestock.

# Farm Income: Crops in 2012

## National Total = $223,484,520,000

| RANK | STATE | FARM INCOME | % of USA |
|---|---|---|---|
| 33 | Alabama | $1,419,722,000 | 0.6% |
| 50 | Alaska | 24,945,000 | 0.0% |
| 30 | Arizona | 2,137,479,000 | 1.0% |
| 16 | Arkansas | 4,774,403,000 | 2.1% |
| 1 | California | 32,583,470,000 | 14.6% |
| 24 | Colorado | 2,898,399,000 | 1.3% |
| 44 | Connecticut | 362,403,000 | 0.2% |
| 42 | Delaware | 377,429,000 | 0.2% |
| 12 | Florida | 6,591,512,000 | 2.9% |
| 18 | Georgia | 4,473,959,000 | 2.0% |
| 38 | Hawaii | 631,244,000 | 0.3% |
| 20 | Idaho | 3,590,281,000 | 1.6% |
| 3 | Illinois | 17,033,617,000 | 7.6% |
| 6 | Indiana | 8,574,545,000 | 3.8% |
| 2 | Iowa | 18,861,660,000 | 8.4% |
| 9 | Kansas | 7,097,141,000 | 3.2% |
| 26 | Kentucky | 2,421,984,000 | 1.1% |
| 23 | Louisiana | 2,962,500,000 | 1.3% |
| 43 | Maine | 363,193,000 | 0.2% |
| 35 | Maryland | 1,142,914,000 | 0.5% |
| 41 | Massachusetts | 398,388,000 | 0.2% |
| 15 | Michigan | 5,329,559,000 | 2.4% |
| 4 | Minnesota | 13,161,060,000 | 5.9% |
| 22 | Mississippi | 3,176,356,000 | 1.4% |
| 14 | Missouri | 5,517,318,000 | 2.5% |
| 28 | Montana | 2,260,720,000 | 1.0% |
| 5 | Nebraska | 12,694,629,000 | 5.7% |
| 45 | Nevada | 287,042,000 | 0.1% |
| 48 | New Hampshire | 89,808,000 | 0.0% |
| 36 | New Jersey | 1,036,048,000 | 0.5% |
| 37 | New Mexico | 828,276,000 | 0.4% |
| 29 | New York | 2,195,210,000 | 1.0% |
| 19 | North Carolina | 4,356,417,000 | 1.9% |
| 8 | North Dakota | 7,555,628,000 | 3.4% |
| 11 | Ohio | 6,794,025,000 | 3.0% |
| 31 | Oklahoma | 1,528,490,000 | 0.7% |
| 21 | Oregon | 3,397,585,000 | 1.5% |
| 25 | Pennsylvania | 2,558,522,000 | 1.1% |
| 49 | Rhode Island | 51,502,000 | 0.0% |
| 34 | South Carolina | 1,370,073,000 | 0.6% |
| 13 | South Dakota | 6,438,535,000 | 2.9% |
| 27 | Tennessee | 2,300,095,000 | 1.0% |
| 7 | Texas | 7,659,939,000 | 3.4% |
| 39 | Utah | 525,456,000 | 0.2% |
| 47 | Vermont | 106,865,000 | 0.0% |
| 32 | Virginia | 1,447,782,000 | 0.6% |
| 10 | Washington | 6,981,651,000 | 3.1% |
| 46 | West Virginia | 126,451,000 | 0.1% |
| 17 | Wisconsin | 4,559,974,000 | 2.0% |
| 40 | Wyoming | 428,313,000 | 0.2% |

| RANK | STATE | FARM INCOME | % of USA |
|---|---|---|---|
| 1 | California | $32,583,470,000 | 14.6% |
| 2 | Iowa | 18,861,660,000 | 8.4% |
| 3 | Illinois | 17,033,617,000 | 7.6% |
| 4 | Minnesota | 13,161,060,000 | 5.9% |
| 5 | Nebraska | 12,694,629,000 | 5.7% |
| 6 | Indiana | 8,574,545,000 | 3.8% |
| 7 | Texas | 7,659,939,000 | 3.4% |
| 8 | North Dakota | 7,555,628,000 | 3.4% |
| 9 | Kansas | 7,097,141,000 | 3.2% |
| 10 | Washington | 6,981,651,000 | 3.1% |
| 11 | Ohio | 6,794,025,000 | 3.0% |
| 12 | Florida | 6,591,512,000 | 2.9% |
| 13 | South Dakota | 6,438,535,000 | 2.9% |
| 14 | Missouri | 5,517,318,000 | 2.5% |
| 15 | Michigan | 5,329,559,000 | 2.4% |
| 16 | Arkansas | 4,774,403,000 | 2.1% |
| 17 | Wisconsin | 4,559,974,000 | 2.0% |
| 18 | Georgia | 4,473,959,000 | 2.0% |
| 19 | North Carolina | 4,356,417,000 | 1.9% |
| 20 | Idaho | 3,590,281,000 | 1.6% |
| 21 | Oregon | 3,397,585,000 | 1.5% |
| 22 | Mississippi | 3,176,356,000 | 1.4% |
| 23 | Louisiana | 2,962,500,000 | 1.3% |
| 24 | Colorado | 2,898,399,000 | 1.3% |
| 25 | Pennsylvania | 2,558,522,000 | 1.1% |
| 26 | Kentucky | 2,421,984,000 | 1.1% |
| 27 | Tennessee | 2,300,095,000 | 1.0% |
| 28 | Montana | 2,260,720,000 | 1.0% |
| 29 | New York | 2,195,210,000 | 1.0% |
| 30 | Arizona | 2,137,479,000 | 1.0% |
| 31 | Oklahoma | 1,528,490,000 | 0.7% |
| 32 | Virginia | 1,447,782,000 | 0.6% |
| 33 | Alabama | 1,419,722,000 | 0.6% |
| 34 | South Carolina | 1,370,073,000 | 0.6% |
| 35 | Maryland | 1,142,914,000 | 0.5% |
| 36 | New Jersey | 1,036,048,000 | 0.5% |
| 37 | New Mexico | 828,276,000 | 0.4% |
| 38 | Hawaii | 631,244,000 | 0.3% |
| 39 | Utah | 525,456,000 | 0.2% |
| 40 | Wyoming | 428,313,000 | 0.2% |
| 41 | Massachusetts | 398,388,000 | 0.2% |
| 42 | Delaware | 377,429,000 | 0.2% |
| 43 | Maine | 363,193,000 | 0.2% |
| 44 | Connecticut | 362,403,000 | 0.2% |
| 45 | Nevada | 287,042,000 | 0.1% |
| 46 | West Virginia | 126,451,000 | 0.1% |
| 47 | Vermont | 106,865,000 | 0.0% |
| 48 | New Hampshire | 89,808,000 | 0.0% |
| 49 | Rhode Island | 51,502,000 | 0.0% |
| 50 | Alaska | 24,945,000 | 0.0% |
| | District of Columbia | 0 | 0.0% |

Source: U.S. Department of Agriculture, Economic Research Service
"Farm Marketings" (http://www.ers.usda.gov/data-products/farm-income-and-wealth-statistics.aspx)

# Farm Income: Livestock in 2012

## National Total = $171,584,157,000*

ALPHA ORDER

| RANK | STATE | FARM INCOME | % of USA |
|------|-------|-------------|----------|
| 16 | Alabama | $3,929,392,000 | 2.3% |
| 50 | Alaska | 6,009,000 | 0.0% |
| 28 | Arizona | 1,772,216,000 | 1.0% |
| 12 | Arkansas | 4,647,191,000 | 2.7% |
| 3 | California | 12,154,662,000 | 7.1% |
| 11 | Colorado | 4,739,833,000 | 2.8% |
| 44 | Connecticut | 181,426,000 | 0.1% |
| 39 | Delaware | 803,117,000 | 0.5% |
| 29 | Florida | 1,661,013,000 | 1.0% |
| 10 | Georgia | 5,305,137,000 | 3.1% |
| 47 | Hawaii | 98,077,000 | 0.1% |
| 15 | Idaho | 3,996,698,000 | 2.3% |
| 25 | Illinois | 2,616,322,000 | 1.5% |
| 18 | Indiana | 3,478,419,000 | 2.0% |
| 2 | Iowa | 13,123,710,000 | 7.6% |
| 5 | Kansas | 9,126,113,000 | 5.3% |
| 24 | Kentucky | 2,862,111,000 | 1.7% |
| 36 | Louisiana | 1,165,382,000 | 0.7% |
| 43 | Maine | 339,752,000 | 0.2% |
| 35 | Maryland | 1,186,947,000 | 0.7% |
| 45 | Massachusetts | 111,618,000 | 0.1% |
| 23 | Michigan | 2,964,063,000 | 1.7% |
| 7 | Minnesota | 7,419,636,000 | 4.3% |
| 22 | Mississippi | 3,059,535,000 | 1.8% |
| 13 | Missouri | 4,423,082,000 | 2.6% |
| 32 | Montana | 1,484,381,000 | 0.9% |
| 4 | Nebraska | 11,771,253,000 | 6.9% |
| 42 | Nevada | 430,548,000 | 0.3% |
| 48 | New Hampshire | 94,113,000 | 0.1% |
| 46 | New Jersey | 103,138,000 | 0.1% |
| 20 | New Mexico | 3,191,526,000 | 1.9% |
| 21 | New York | 3,092,556,000 | 1.8% |
| 8 | North Carolina | 7,350,185,000 | 4.3% |
| 38 | North Dakota | 1,128,593,000 | 0.7% |
| 19 | Ohio | 3,272,731,000 | 1.9% |
| 9 | Oklahoma | 5,509,684,000 | 3.2% |
| 33 | Oregon | 1,419,709,000 | 0.8% |
| 14 | Pennsylvania | 4,309,835,000 | 2.5% |
| 49 | Rhode Island | 10,580,000 | 0.0% |
| 30 | South Carolina | 1,558,254,000 | 0.9% |
| 17 | South Dakota | 3,574,935,000 | 2.1% |
| 31 | Tennessee | 1,549,751,000 | 0.9% |
| 1 | Texas | 15,066,128,000 | 8.8% |
| 37 | Utah | 1,163,380,000 | 0.7% |
| 40 | Vermont | 592,448,000 | 0.3% |
| 27 | Virginia | 2,128,635,000 | 1.2% |
| 26 | Washington | 2,312,263,000 | 1.3% |
| 41 | West Virginia | 525,618,000 | 0.3% |
| 6 | Wisconsin | 7,550,081,000 | 4.4% |
| 34 | Wyoming | 1,222,371,000 | 0.7% |

RANK ORDER

| RANK | STATE | FARM INCOME | % of USA |
|------|-------|-------------|----------|
| 1 | Texas | $15,066,128,000 | 8.8% |
| 2 | Iowa | 13,123,710,000 | 7.6% |
| 3 | California | 12,154,662,000 | 7.1% |
| 4 | Nebraska | 11,771,253,000 | 6.9% |
| 5 | Kansas | 9,126,113,000 | 5.3% |
| 6 | Wisconsin | 7,550,081,000 | 4.4% |
| 7 | Minnesota | 7,419,636,000 | 4.3% |
| 8 | North Carolina | 7,350,185,000 | 4.3% |
| 9 | Oklahoma | 5,509,684,000 | 3.2% |
| 10 | Georgia | 5,305,137,000 | 3.1% |
| 11 | Colorado | 4,739,833,000 | 2.8% |
| 12 | Arkansas | 4,647,191,000 | 2.7% |
| 13 | Missouri | 4,423,082,000 | 2.6% |
| 14 | Pennsylvania | 4,309,835,000 | 2.5% |
| 15 | Idaho | 3,996,698,000 | 2.3% |
| 16 | Alabama | 3,929,392,000 | 2.3% |
| 17 | South Dakota | 3,574,935,000 | 2.1% |
| 18 | Indiana | 3,478,419,000 | 2.0% |
| 19 | Ohio | 3,272,731,000 | 1.9% |
| 20 | New Mexico | 3,191,526,000 | 1.9% |
| 21 | New York | 3,092,556,000 | 1.8% |
| 22 | Mississippi | 3,059,535,000 | 1.8% |
| 23 | Michigan | 2,964,063,000 | 1.7% |
| 24 | Kentucky | 2,862,111,000 | 1.7% |
| 25 | Illinois | 2,616,322,000 | 1.5% |
| 26 | Washington | 2,312,263,000 | 1.3% |
| 27 | Virginia | 2,128,635,000 | 1.2% |
| 28 | Arizona | 1,772,216,000 | 1.0% |
| 29 | Florida | 1,661,013,000 | 1.0% |
| 30 | South Carolina | 1,558,254,000 | 0.9% |
| 31 | Tennessee | 1,549,751,000 | 0.9% |
| 32 | Montana | 1,484,381,000 | 0.9% |
| 33 | Oregon | 1,419,709,000 | 0.8% |
| 34 | Wyoming | 1,222,371,000 | 0.7% |
| 35 | Maryland | 1,186,947,000 | 0.7% |
| 36 | Louisiana | 1,165,382,000 | 0.7% |
| 37 | Utah | 1,163,380,000 | 0.7% |
| 38 | North Dakota | 1,128,593,000 | 0.7% |
| 39 | Delaware | 803,117,000 | 0.5% |
| 40 | Vermont | 592,448,000 | 0.3% |
| 41 | West Virginia | 525,618,000 | 0.3% |
| 42 | Nevada | 430,548,000 | 0.3% |
| 43 | Maine | 339,752,000 | 0.2% |
| 44 | Connecticut | 181,426,000 | 0.1% |
| 45 | Massachusetts | 111,618,000 | 0.1% |
| 46 | New Jersey | 103,138,000 | 0.1% |
| 47 | Hawaii | 98,077,000 | 0.1% |
| 48 | New Hampshire | 94,113,000 | 0.1% |
| 49 | Rhode Island | 10,580,000 | 0.0% |
| 50 | Alaska | 6,009,000 | 0.0% |
| | District of Columbia | 0 | 0.0% |

Source: U.S. Department of Agriculture, Economic Research Service
   "Farm Marketings" (http://www.ers.usda.gov/data-products/farm-income-and-wealth-statistics.aspx)
*Includes livestock products.

# Farm Income: Government Payments in 2012

## National Total = $10,635,118,000*

ALPHA ORDER

| RANK | STATE | FARM INCOME | % of USA |
|------|-------|-------------|----------|
| 30 | Alabama | $117,995,000 | 1.1% |
| 46 | Alaska | 12,358,000 | 0.1% |
| 36 | Arizona | 50,218,000 | 0.5% |
| 10 | Arkansas | 365,119,000 | 3.4% |
| 15 | California | 287,532,000 | 2.7% |
| 22 | Colorado | 215,677,000 | 2.0% |
| 49 | Connecticut | 8,892,000 | 0.1% |
| 43 | Delaware | 15,404,000 | 0.1% |
| 34 | Florida | 69,139,000 | 0.7% |
| 18 | Georgia | 256,716,000 | 2.4% |
| 48 | Hawaii | 11,448,000 | 0.1% |
| 27 | Idaho | 126,650,000 | 1.2% |
| 3 | Illinois | 630,770,000 | 5.9% |
| 12 | Indiana | 322,962,000 | 3.0% |
| 1 | Iowa | 855,352,000 | 8.0% |
| 5 | Kansas | 518,589,000 | 4.9% |
| 13 | Kentucky | 303,414,000 | 2.9% |
| 21 | Louisiana | 219,135,000 | 2.1% |
| 41 | Maine | 21,876,000 | 0.2% |
| 35 | Maryland | 56,199,000 | 0.5% |
| 42 | Massachusetts | 16,975,000 | 0.2% |
| 25 | Michigan | 175,384,000 | 1.6% |
| 4 | Minnesota | 534,668,000 | 5.0% |
| 20 | Mississippi | 219,148,000 | 2.1% |
| 9 | Missouri | 395,991,000 | 3.7% |
| 19 | Montana | 239,263,000 | 2.2% |
| 6 | Nebraska | 480,334,000 | 4.5% |
| 45 | Nevada | 12,877,000 | 0.1% |
| 44 | New Hampshire | 14,874,000 | 0.1% |
| 47 | New Jersey | 11,927,000 | 0.1% |
| 33 | New Mexico | 97,672,000 | 0.9% |
| 32 | New York | 104,277,000 | 1.0% |
| 7 | North Carolina | 430,403,000 | 4.0% |
| 8 | North Dakota | 409,094,000 | 3.8% |
| 17 | Ohio | 279,818,000 | 2.6% |
| 14 | Oklahoma | 295,627,000 | 2.8% |
| 29 | Oregon | 118,040,000 | 1.1% |
| 28 | Pennsylvania | 119,283,000 | 1.1% |
| 50 | Rhode Island | 3,858,000 | 0.0% |
| 31 | South Carolina | 110,159,000 | 1.0% |
| 11 | South Dakota | 330,831,000 | 3.1% |
| 24 | Tennessee | 176,238,000 | 1.7% |
| 2 | Texas | 838,063,000 | 7.9% |
| 38 | Utah | 39,467,000 | 0.4% |
| 40 | Vermont | 22,231,000 | 0.2% |
| 26 | Virginia | 139,942,000 | 1.3% |
| 23 | Washington | 203,661,000 | 1.9% |
| 39 | West Virginia | 25,165,000 | 0.2% |
| 16 | Wisconsin | 281,827,000 | 2.6% |
| 37 | Wyoming | 42,573,000 | 0.4% |

RANK ORDER

| RANK | STATE | FARM INCOME | % of USA |
|------|-------|-------------|----------|
| 1 | Iowa | $855,352,000 | 8.0% |
| 2 | Texas | 838,063,000 | 7.9% |
| 3 | Illinois | 630,770,000 | 5.9% |
| 4 | Minnesota | 534,668,000 | 5.0% |
| 5 | Kansas | 518,589,000 | 4.9% |
| 6 | Nebraska | 480,334,000 | 4.5% |
| 7 | North Carolina | 430,403,000 | 4.0% |
| 8 | North Dakota | 409,094,000 | 3.8% |
| 9 | Missouri | 395,991,000 | 3.7% |
| 10 | Arkansas | 365,119,000 | 3.4% |
| 11 | South Dakota | 330,831,000 | 3.1% |
| 12 | Indiana | 322,962,000 | 3.0% |
| 13 | Kentucky | 303,414,000 | 2.9% |
| 14 | Oklahoma | 295,627,000 | 2.8% |
| 15 | California | 287,532,000 | 2.7% |
| 16 | Wisconsin | 281,827,000 | 2.6% |
| 17 | Ohio | 279,818,000 | 2.6% |
| 18 | Georgia | 256,716,000 | 2.4% |
| 19 | Montana | 239,263,000 | 2.2% |
| 20 | Mississippi | 219,148,000 | 2.1% |
| 21 | Louisiana | 219,135,000 | 2.1% |
| 22 | Colorado | 215,677,000 | 2.0% |
| 23 | Washington | 203,661,000 | 1.9% |
| 24 | Tennessee | 176,238,000 | 1.7% |
| 25 | Michigan | 175,384,000 | 1.6% |
| 26 | Virginia | 139,942,000 | 1.3% |
| 27 | Idaho | 126,650,000 | 1.2% |
| 28 | Pennsylvania | 119,283,000 | 1.1% |
| 29 | Oregon | 118,040,000 | 1.1% |
| 30 | Alabama | 117,995,000 | 1.1% |
| 31 | South Carolina | 110,159,000 | 1.0% |
| 32 | New York | 104,277,000 | 1.0% |
| 33 | New Mexico | 97,672,000 | 0.9% |
| 34 | Florida | 69,139,000 | 0.7% |
| 35 | Maryland | 56,199,000 | 0.5% |
| 36 | Arizona | 50,218,000 | 0.5% |
| 37 | Wyoming | 42,573,000 | 0.4% |
| 38 | Utah | 39,467,000 | 0.4% |
| 39 | West Virginia | 25,165,000 | 0.2% |
| 40 | Vermont | 22,231,000 | 0.2% |
| 41 | Maine | 21,876,000 | 0.2% |
| 42 | Massachusetts | 16,975,000 | 0.2% |
| 43 | Delaware | 15,404,000 | 0.1% |
| 44 | New Hampshire | 14,874,000 | 0.1% |
| 45 | Nevada | 12,877,000 | 0.1% |
| 46 | Alaska | 12,358,000 | 0.1% |
| 47 | New Jersey | 11,927,000 | 0.1% |
| 48 | Hawaii | 11,448,000 | 0.1% |
| 49 | Connecticut | 8,892,000 | 0.1% |
| 50 | Rhode Island | 3,858,000 | 0.0% |
| | District of Columbia | 0 | 0.0% |

Source: U.S. Department of Agriculture, Economic Research Service
    "Farm Income" (http://www.ers.usda.gov/Data/FarmIncome/FinfidmuXls.htm)
*Government payments made directly to farmers in cash.

# Acres Planted in 2013

## National Total = 324,795,000 Acres*

ALPHA ORDER

| RANK | STATE | ACRES | % of USA |
|------|-------|-------|----------|
| 30 | Alabama | 2,410,000 | 0.7% |
| NA | Alaska** | NA | NA |
| 38 | Arizona | 745,000 | 0.2% |
| 15 | Arkansas | 7,682,000 | 2.4% |
| 23 | California | 4,009,000 | 1.2% |
| 18 | Colorado | 5,916,000 | 1.8% |
| 46 | Connecticut | 74,000 | 0.0% |
| 40 | Delaware | 492,000 | 0.2% |
| 35 | Florida | 1,187,000 | 0.4% |
| 24 | Georgia | 3,848,000 | 1.2% |
| 48 | Hawaii | 18,000 | 0.0% |
| 22 | Idaho | 4,502,000 | 1.4% |
| 4 | Illinois | 23,055,000 | 7.1% |
| 10 | Indiana | 12,330,000 | 3.8% |
| 1 | Iowa | 24,320,000 | 7.5% |
| 3 | Kansas | 23,474,000 | 7.2% |
| 16 | Kentucky | 6,567,000 | 2.0% |
| 27 | Louisiana | 3,563,000 | 1.1% |
| 44 | Maine | 269,000 | 0.1% |
| 32 | Maryland | 1,607,000 | 0.5% |
| 45 | Massachusetts | 104,000 | 0.0% |
| 17 | Michigan | 6,504,000 | 2.0% |
| 7 | Minnesota | 19,454,000 | 6.0% |
| 21 | Mississippi | 4,504,000 | 1.4% |
| 9 | Missouri | 14,624,000 | 4.5% |
| 13 | Montana | 9,566,000 | 2.9% |
| 6 | Nebraska | 19,553,000 | 6.0% |
| 41 | Nevada | 380,000 | 0.1% |
| 47 | New Hampshire | 64,000 | 0.0% |
| 42 | New Jersey | 312,000 | 0.1% |
| 37 | New Mexico | 975,000 | 0.3% |
| 28 | New York | 3,148,000 | 1.0% |
| 20 | North Carolina | 5,035,000 | 1.6% |
| 5 | North Dakota | 20,387,000 | 6.3% |
| 12 | Ohio | 10,164,000 | 3.1% |
| 11 | Oklahoma | 10,497,000 | 3.2% |
| 31 | Oregon | 2,144,000 | 0.7% |
| 26 | Pennsylvania | 3,651,000 | 1.1% |
| 49 | Rhode Island | 11,000 | 0.0% |
| 33 | South Carolina | 1,604,000 | 0.5% |
| 8 | South Dakota | 17,855,000 | 5.5% |
| 19 | Tennessee | 5,246,000 | 1.6% |
| 2 | Texas | 24,019,000 | 7.4% |
| 36 | Utah | 1,026,000 | 0.3% |
| 43 | Vermont | 272,000 | 0.1% |
| 29 | Virginia | 2,869,000 | 0.9% |
| 25 | Washington | 3,667,000 | 1.1% |
| 39 | West Virginia | 674,000 | 0.2% |
| 14 | Wisconsin | 7,951,000 | 2.4% |
| 34 | Wyoming | 1,420,000 | 0.4% |

RANK ORDER

| RANK | STATE | ACRES | % of USA |
|------|-------|-------|----------|
| 1 | Iowa | 24,320,000 | 7.5% |
| 2 | Texas | 24,019,000 | 7.4% |
| 3 | Kansas | 23,474,000 | 7.2% |
| 4 | Illinois | 23,055,000 | 7.1% |
| 5 | North Dakota | 20,387,000 | 6.3% |
| 6 | Nebraska | 19,553,000 | 6.0% |
| 7 | Minnesota | 19,454,000 | 6.0% |
| 8 | South Dakota | 17,855,000 | 5.5% |
| 9 | Missouri | 14,624,000 | 4.5% |
| 10 | Indiana | 12,330,000 | 3.8% |
| 11 | Oklahoma | 10,497,000 | 3.2% |
| 12 | Ohio | 10,164,000 | 3.1% |
| 13 | Montana | 9,566,000 | 2.9% |
| 14 | Wisconsin | 7,951,000 | 2.4% |
| 15 | Arkansas | 7,682,000 | 2.4% |
| 16 | Kentucky | 6,567,000 | 2.0% |
| 17 | Michigan | 6,504,000 | 2.0% |
| 18 | Colorado | 5,916,000 | 1.8% |
| 19 | Tennessee | 5,246,000 | 1.6% |
| 20 | North Carolina | 5,035,000 | 1.6% |
| 21 | Mississippi | 4,504,000 | 1.4% |
| 22 | Idaho | 4,502,000 | 1.4% |
| 23 | California | 4,009,000 | 1.2% |
| 24 | Georgia | 3,848,000 | 1.2% |
| 25 | Washington | 3,667,000 | 1.1% |
| 26 | Pennsylvania | 3,651,000 | 1.1% |
| 27 | Louisiana | 3,563,000 | 1.1% |
| 28 | New York | 3,148,000 | 1.0% |
| 29 | Virginia | 2,869,000 | 0.9% |
| 30 | Alabama | 2,410,000 | 0.7% |
| 31 | Oregon | 2,144,000 | 0.7% |
| 32 | Maryland | 1,607,000 | 0.5% |
| 33 | South Carolina | 1,604,000 | 0.5% |
| 34 | Wyoming | 1,420,000 | 0.4% |
| 35 | Florida | 1,187,000 | 0.4% |
| 36 | Utah | 1,026,000 | 0.3% |
| 37 | New Mexico | 975,000 | 0.3% |
| 38 | Arizona | 745,000 | 0.2% |
| 39 | West Virginia | 674,000 | 0.2% |
| 40 | Delaware | 492,000 | 0.2% |
| 41 | Nevada | 380,000 | 0.1% |
| 42 | New Jersey | 312,000 | 0.1% |
| 43 | Vermont | 272,000 | 0.1% |
| 44 | Maine | 269,000 | 0.1% |
| 45 | Massachusetts | 104,000 | 0.0% |
| 46 | Connecticut | 74,000 | 0.0% |
| 47 | New Hampshire | 64,000 | 0.0% |
| 48 | Hawaii | 18,000 | 0.0% |
| 49 | Rhode Island | 11,000 | 0.0% |
| NA | Alaska** | NA | NA |
| | District of Columbia** | NA | NA |

Source: U.S. Department of Agriculture, National Agricultural Statistics Service
"Crop Production: 2013 Summary" (January 2014)
(http://usda.mannlib.cornell.edu/MannUsda/viewDocumentInfo.do?documentID=1047)
*Estimated totals.
**No acreage or not available.

# Acres Harvested in 2013

## National Total = 303,755,000 Acres*

ALPHA ORDER

| RANK | STATE | ACRES | % of USA |
|------|-------|-------|----------|
| 30 | Alabama | 2,309,000 | 0.8% |
| NA | Alaska** | NA | NA |
| 37 | Arizona | 733,000 | 0.2% |
| 15 | Arkansas | 7,560,000 | 2.5% |
| 27 | California | 3,508,000 | 1.2% |
| 19 | Colorado | 4,890,000 | 1.6% |
| 46 | Connecticut | 70,000 | 0.0% |
| 40 | Delaware | 472,000 | 0.2% |
| 35 | Florida | 1,163,000 | 0.4% |
| 24 | Georgia | 3,557,000 | 1.2% |
| 48 | Hawaii | 18,000 | 0.0% |
| 22 | Idaho | 4,338,000 | 1.4% |
| 2 | Illinois | 22,854,000 | 7.5% |
| 10 | Indiana | 12,270,000 | 4.0% |
| 1 | Iowa | 23,981,000 | 7.9% |
| 3 | Kansas | 21,881,000 | 7.2% |
| 16 | Kentucky | 6,447,000 | 2.1% |
| 26 | Louisiana | 3,525,000 | 1.2% |
| 44 | Maine | 260,000 | 0.1% |
| 33 | Maryland | 1,489,000 | 0.5% |
| 45 | Massachusetts | 101,000 | 0.0% |
| 17 | Michigan | 6,433,000 | 2.1% |
| 5 | Minnesota | 19,066,000 | 6.3% |
| 21 | Mississippi | 4,441,000 | 1.5% |
| 9 | Missouri | 14,373,000 | 4.7% |
| 12 | Montana | 9,135,000 | 3.0% |
| 6 | Nebraska | 18,756,000 | 6.2% |
| 41 | Nevada | 365,000 | 0.1% |
| 47 | New Hampshire | 63,000 | 0.0% |
| 42 | New Jersey | 304,000 | 0.1% |
| 39 | New Mexico | 555,000 | 0.2% |
| 28 | New York | 3,093,000 | 1.0% |
| 20 | North Carolina | 4,876,000 | 1.6% |
| 4 | North Dakota | 19,995,000 | 6.6% |
| 11 | Ohio | 10,083,000 | 3.3% |
| 13 | Oklahoma | 7,874,000 | 2.6% |
| 31 | Oregon | 2,099,000 | 0.7% |
| 25 | Pennsylvania | 3,551,000 | 1.2% |
| 49 | Rhode Island | 11,000 | 0.0% |
| 32 | South Carolina | 1,556,000 | 0.5% |
| 7 | South Dakota | 16,874,000 | 5.6% |
| 18 | Tennessee | 5,099,000 | 1.7% |
| 8 | Texas | 16,292,000 | 5.4% |
| 36 | Utah | 964,000 | 0.3% |
| 43 | Vermont | 265,000 | 0.1% |
| 29 | Virginia | 2,754,000 | 0.9% |
| 23 | Washington | 3,605,000 | 1.2% |
| 38 | West Virginia | 670,000 | 0.2% |
| 14 | Wisconsin | 7,633,000 | 2.5% |
| 34 | Wyoming | 1,350,000 | 0.4% |

RANK ORDER

| RANK | STATE | ACRES | % of USA |
|------|-------|-------|----------|
| 1 | Iowa | 23,981,000 | 7.9% |
| 2 | Illinois | 22,854,000 | 7.5% |
| 3 | Kansas | 21,881,000 | 7.2% |
| 4 | North Dakota | 19,995,000 | 6.6% |
| 5 | Minnesota | 19,066,000 | 6.3% |
| 6 | Nebraska | 18,756,000 | 6.2% |
| 7 | South Dakota | 16,874,000 | 5.6% |
| 8 | Texas | 16,292,000 | 5.4% |
| 9 | Missouri | 14,373,000 | 4.7% |
| 10 | Indiana | 12,270,000 | 4.0% |
| 11 | Ohio | 10,083,000 | 3.3% |
| 12 | Montana | 9,135,000 | 3.0% |
| 13 | Oklahoma | 7,874,000 | 2.6% |
| 14 | Wisconsin | 7,633,000 | 2.5% |
| 15 | Arkansas | 7,560,000 | 2.5% |
| 16 | Kentucky | 6,447,000 | 2.1% |
| 17 | Michigan | 6,433,000 | 2.1% |
| 18 | Tennessee | 5,099,000 | 1.7% |
| 19 | Colorado | 4,890,000 | 1.6% |
| 20 | North Carolina | 4,876,000 | 1.6% |
| 21 | Mississippi | 4,441,000 | 1.5% |
| 22 | Idaho | 4,338,000 | 1.4% |
| 23 | Washington | 3,605,000 | 1.2% |
| 24 | Georgia | 3,557,000 | 1.2% |
| 25 | Pennsylvania | 3,551,000 | 1.2% |
| 26 | Louisiana | 3,525,000 | 1.2% |
| 27 | California | 3,508,000 | 1.2% |
| 28 | New York | 3,093,000 | 1.0% |
| 29 | Virginia | 2,754,000 | 0.9% |
| 30 | Alabama | 2,309,000 | 0.8% |
| 31 | Oregon | 2,099,000 | 0.7% |
| 32 | South Carolina | 1,556,000 | 0.5% |
| 33 | Maryland | 1,489,000 | 0.5% |
| 34 | Wyoming | 1,350,000 | 0.4% |
| 35 | Florida | 1,163,000 | 0.4% |
| 36 | Utah | 964,000 | 0.3% |
| 37 | Arizona | 733,000 | 0.2% |
| 38 | West Virginia | 670,000 | 0.2% |
| 39 | New Mexico | 555,000 | 0.2% |
| 40 | Delaware | 472,000 | 0.2% |
| 41 | Nevada | 365,000 | 0.1% |
| 42 | New Jersey | 304,000 | 0.1% |
| 43 | Vermont | 265,000 | 0.1% |
| 44 | Maine | 260,000 | 0.1% |
| 45 | Massachusetts | 101,000 | 0.0% |
| 46 | Connecticut | 70,000 | 0.0% |
| 47 | New Hampshire | 63,000 | 0.0% |
| 48 | Hawaii | 18,000 | 0.0% |
| 49 | Rhode Island | 11,000 | 0.0% |
| NA | Alaska** | NA | NA |
| | District of Columbia** | NA | NA |

Source: U.S. Department of Agriculture, National Agricultural Statistics Service
"Crop Production: 2013 Summary" (January 2014)
(http://usda.mannlib.cornell.edu/MannUsda/viewDocumentInfo.do?documentID=1047)
*Estimated totals.
**No acreage or not available.

# Acres Harvested: Corn in 2013

## National Total = 87,668,000 Acres*

ALPHA ORDER

| RANK | STATE | ACRES | % of USA |
|---|---|---|---|
| 28 | Alabama | 295,000 | 0.3% |
| NA | Alaska** | NA | NA |
| 37 | Arizona | 51,000 | 0.1% |
| 17 | Arkansas | 870,000 | 1.0% |
| 29 | California | 180,000 | 0.2% |
| 16 | Colorado | 990,000 | 1.1% |
| NA | Connecticut** | NA | NA |
| 30 | Delaware | 174,000 | 0.2% |
| 34 | Florida | 78,000 | 0.1% |
| 23 | Georgia | 465,000 | 0.5% |
| NA | Hawaii** | NA | NA |
| 31 | Idaho | 120,000 | 0.1% |
| 2 | Illinois | 11,800,000 | 13.5% |
| 6 | Indiana | 5,850,000 | 6.7% |
| 1 | Iowa | 13,100,000 | 14.9% |
| 7 | Kansas | 4,000,000 | 4.6% |
| 14 | Kentucky | 1,430,000 | 1.6% |
| 22 | Louisiana | 670,000 | 0.8% |
| NA | Maine** | NA | NA |
| 24 | Maryland | 420,000 | 0.5% |
| NA | Massachusetts** | NA | NA |
| 12 | Michigan | 2,250,000 | 2.6% |
| 4 | Minnesota | 8,150,000 | 9.3% |
| 19 | Mississippi | 830,000 | 0.9% |
| 10 | Missouri | 3,200,000 | 3.7% |
| 35 | Montana | 75,000 | 0.1% |
| 3 | Nebraska | 9,550,000 | 10.9% |
| NA | Nevada** | NA | NA |
| NA | New Hampshire** | NA | NA |
| 33 | New Jersey | 80,000 | 0.1% |
| 38 | New Mexico | 39,000 | 0.0% |
| 21 | New York | 690,000 | 0.8% |
| 17 | North Carolina | 870,000 | 1.0% |
| 9 | North Dakota | 3,600,000 | 4.1% |
| 8 | Ohio | 3,740,000 | 4.3% |
| 27 | Oklahoma | 310,000 | 0.4% |
| 39 | Oregon | 36,000 | 0.0% |
| 15 | Pennsylvania | 1,090,000 | 1.2% |
| NA | Rhode Island** | NA | NA |
| 26 | South Carolina | 335,000 | 0.4% |
| 5 | South Dakota | 5,860,000 | 6.7% |
| 20 | Tennessee | 820,000 | 0.9% |
| 13 | Texas | 2,000,000 | 2.3% |
| 41 | Utah | 31,000 | 0.0% |
| NA | Vermont** | NA | NA |
| 25 | Virginia | 360,000 | 0.4% |
| 32 | Washington | 105,000 | 0.1% |
| 39 | West Virginia | 36,000 | 0.0% |
| 11 | Wisconsin | 3,050,000 | 3.5% |
| 36 | Wyoming | 68,000 | 0.1% |

RANK ORDER

| RANK | STATE | ACRES | % of USA |
|---|---|---|---|
| 1 | Iowa | 13,100,000 | 14.9% |
| 2 | Illinois | 11,800,000 | 13.5% |
| 3 | Nebraska | 9,550,000 | 10.9% |
| 4 | Minnesota | 8,150,000 | 9.3% |
| 5 | South Dakota | 5,860,000 | 6.7% |
| 6 | Indiana | 5,850,000 | 6.7% |
| 7 | Kansas | 4,000,000 | 4.6% |
| 8 | Ohio | 3,740,000 | 4.3% |
| 9 | North Dakota | 3,600,000 | 4.1% |
| 10 | Missouri | 3,200,000 | 3.7% |
| 11 | Wisconsin | 3,050,000 | 3.5% |
| 12 | Michigan | 2,250,000 | 2.6% |
| 13 | Texas | 2,000,000 | 2.3% |
| 14 | Kentucky | 1,430,000 | 1.6% |
| 15 | Pennsylvania | 1,090,000 | 1.2% |
| 16 | Colorado | 990,000 | 1.1% |
| 17 | Arkansas | 870,000 | 1.0% |
| 17 | North Carolina | 870,000 | 1.0% |
| 19 | Mississippi | 830,000 | 0.9% |
| 20 | Tennessee | 820,000 | 0.9% |
| 21 | New York | 690,000 | 0.8% |
| 22 | Louisiana | 670,000 | 0.8% |
| 23 | Georgia | 465,000 | 0.5% |
| 24 | Maryland | 420,000 | 0.5% |
| 25 | Virginia | 360,000 | 0.4% |
| 26 | South Carolina | 335,000 | 0.4% |
| 27 | Oklahoma | 310,000 | 0.4% |
| 28 | Alabama | 295,000 | 0.3% |
| 29 | California | 180,000 | 0.2% |
| 30 | Delaware | 174,000 | 0.2% |
| 31 | Idaho | 120,000 | 0.1% |
| 32 | Washington | 105,000 | 0.1% |
| 33 | New Jersey | 80,000 | 0.1% |
| 34 | Florida | 78,000 | 0.1% |
| 35 | Montana | 75,000 | 0.1% |
| 36 | Wyoming | 68,000 | 0.1% |
| 37 | Arizona | 51,000 | 0.1% |
| 38 | New Mexico | 39,000 | 0.0% |
| 39 | Oregon | 36,000 | 0.0% |
| 39 | West Virginia | 36,000 | 0.0% |
| 41 | Utah | 31,000 | 0.0% |
| NA | Alaska** | NA | NA |
| NA | Connecticut** | NA | NA |
| NA | Hawaii** | NA | NA |
| NA | Maine** | NA | NA |
| NA | Massachusetts** | NA | NA |
| NA | Nevada** | NA | NA |
| NA | New Hampshire** | NA | NA |
| NA | Rhode Island** | NA | NA |
| NA | Vermont** | NA | NA |
| | District of Columbia** | NA | NA |

Source: U.S. Department of Agriculture, National Agricultural Statistics Service
"Crop Production: 2013 Summary" (January 2014)
(http://usda.mannlib.cornell.edu/MannUsda/viewDocumentInfo.do?documentID=1047)
*Estimated totals. Acres harvested for grain.
**No acreage or not available.

# Acres Harvested: Soybeans in 2013

## National Total = 75,869,000 Acres*

ALPHA ORDER

RANK ORDER

| RANK | STATE | ACRES | % of USA | | RANK | STATE | ACRES | % of USA |
|---|---|---|---|---|---|---|---|---|
| 22 | Alabama | 425,000 | 0.6% | | 1 | Illinois | 9,420,000 | 12.4% |
| NA | Alaska** | NA | NA | | 2 | Iowa | 9,240,000 | 12.2% |
| NA | Arizona** | NA | NA | | 3 | Minnesota | 6,620,000 | 8.7% |
| 11 | Arkansas | 3,230,000 | 4.3% | | 4 | Missouri | 5,550,000 | 7.3% |
| NA | California** | NA | NA | | 5 | Indiana | 5,190,000 | 6.8% |
| NA | Colorado** | NA | NA | | 6 | Nebraska | 4,760,000 | 6.3% |
| NA | Connecticut** | NA | NA | | 7 | North Dakota | 4,620,000 | 6.1% |
| 27 | Delaware | 163,000 | 0.2% | | 8 | South Dakota | 4,580,000 | 6.0% |
| 30 | Florida | 30,000 | 0.0% | | 9 | Ohio | 4,430,000 | 5.8% |
| 26 | Georgia | 225,000 | 0.3% | | 10 | Kansas | 3,540,000 | 4.7% |
| NA | Hawaii** | NA | NA | | 11 | Arkansas | 3,230,000 | 4.3% |
| NA | Idaho** | NA | NA | | 12 | Mississippi | 1,990,000 | 2.6% |
| 1 | Illinois | 9,420,000 | 12.4% | | 13 | Michigan | 1,890,000 | 2.5% |
| 5 | Indiana | 5,190,000 | 6.8% | | 14 | Kentucky | 1,640,000 | 2.2% |
| 2 | Iowa | 9,240,000 | 12.2% | | 15 | Wisconsin | 1,550,000 | 2.0% |
| 10 | Kansas | 3,540,000 | 4.7% | | 16 | Tennessee | 1,520,000 | 2.0% |
| 14 | Kentucky | 1,640,000 | 2.2% | | 17 | North Carolina | 1,420,000 | 1.9% |
| 18 | Louisiana | 1,110,000 | 1.5% | | 18 | Louisiana | 1,110,000 | 1.5% |
| NA | Maine** | NA | NA | | 19 | Virginia | 590,000 | 0.8% |
| 21 | Maryland | 475,000 | 0.6% | | 20 | Pennsylvania | 535,000 | 0.7% |
| NA | Massachusetts** | NA | NA | | 21 | Maryland | 475,000 | 0.6% |
| 13 | Michigan | 1,890,000 | 2.5% | | 22 | Alabama | 425,000 | 0.6% |
| 3 | Minnesota | 6,620,000 | 8.7% | | 23 | Oklahoma | 335,000 | 0.4% |
| 12 | Mississippi | 1,990,000 | 2.6% | | 24 | South Carolina | 310,000 | 0.4% |
| 4 | Missouri | 5,550,000 | 7.3% | | 25 | New York | 278,000 | 0.4% |
| NA | Montana** | NA | NA | | 26 | Georgia | 225,000 | 0.3% |
| 6 | Nebraska | 4,760,000 | 6.3% | | 27 | Delaware | 163,000 | 0.2% |
| NA | Nevada** | NA | NA | | 28 | Texas | 95,000 | 0.1% |
| NA | New Hampshire** | NA | NA | | 29 | New Jersey | 87,000 | 0.1% |
| 29 | New Jersey | 87,000 | 0.1% | | 30 | Florida | 30,000 | 0.0% |
| NA | New Mexico** | NA | NA | | 31 | West Virginia | 21,000 | 0.0% |
| 25 | New York | 278,000 | 0.4% | | NA | Alaska** | NA | NA |
| 17 | North Carolina | 1,420,000 | 1.9% | | NA | Arizona** | NA | NA |
| 7 | North Dakota | 4,620,000 | 6.1% | | NA | California** | NA | NA |
| 9 | Ohio | 4,430,000 | 5.8% | | NA | Colorado** | NA | NA |
| 23 | Oklahoma | 335,000 | 0.4% | | NA | Connecticut** | NA | NA |
| NA | Oregon** | NA | NA | | NA | Hawaii** | NA | NA |
| 20 | Pennsylvania | 535,000 | 0.7% | | NA | Idaho** | NA | NA |
| NA | Rhode Island** | NA | NA | | NA | Maine** | NA | NA |
| 24 | South Carolina | 310,000 | 0.4% | | NA | Massachusetts** | NA | NA |
| 8 | South Dakota | 4,580,000 | 6.0% | | NA | Montana** | NA | NA |
| 16 | Tennessee | 1,520,000 | 2.0% | | NA | Nevada** | NA | NA |
| 28 | Texas | 95,000 | 0.1% | | NA | New Hampshire** | NA | NA |
| NA | Utah** | NA | NA | | NA | New Mexico** | NA | NA |
| NA | Vermont** | NA | NA | | NA | Oregon** | NA | NA |
| 19 | Virginia | 590,000 | 0.8% | | NA | Rhode Island** | NA | NA |
| NA | Washington** | NA | NA | | NA | Utah** | NA | NA |
| 31 | West Virginia | 21,000 | 0.0% | | NA | Vermont** | NA | NA |
| 15 | Wisconsin | 1,550,000 | 2.0% | | NA | Washington** | NA | NA |
| NA | Wyoming** | NA | NA | | NA | Wyoming** | NA | NA |
| | | | | | District of Columbia** | | NA | NA |

Source: U.S. Department of Agriculture, National Agricultural Statistics Service
    "Crop Production: 2013 Summary" (January 2014)
        (http://usda.mannlib.cornell.edu/MannUsda/viewDocumentInfo.do?documentID=1047)
*Estimated totals.
**No acreage or not available.

# Acres Harvested: Wheat in 2013

## National Total = 45,157,000 Acres*

ALPHA ORDER

| RANK | STATE | ACRES | % of USA |
|---|---|---|---|
| 26 | Alabama | 270,000 | 0.6% |
| NA | Alaska** | NA | NA |
| 35 | Arizona | 89,000 | 0.2% |
| 17 | Arkansas | 615,000 | 1.4% |
| 22 | California | 407,000 | 0.9% |
| 8 | Colorado | 1,649,000 | 3.7% |
| NA | Connecticut** | NA | NA |
| 36 | Delaware | 78,000 | 0.2% |
| 40 | Florida | 19,000 | 0.0% |
| 24 | Georgia | 350,000 | 0.8% |
| NA | Hawaii** | NA | NA |
| 9 | Idaho | 1,241,000 | 2.7% |
| 15 | Illinois | 830,000 | 1.8% |
| 21 | Indiana | 440,000 | 1.0% |
| 39 | Iowa | 21,000 | 0.0% |
| 1 | Kansas | 8,400,000 | 18.6% |
| 18 | Kentucky | 610,000 | 1.4% |
| 30 | Louisiana | 250,000 | 0.6% |
| NA | Maine** | NA | NA |
| 28 | Maryland | 260,000 | 0.6% |
| NA | Massachusetts** | NA | NA |
| 19 | Michigan | 600,000 | 1.3% |
| 10 | Minnesota | 1,187,000 | 2.6% |
| 23 | Mississippi | 385,000 | 0.9% |
| 12 | Missouri | 1,000,000 | 2.2% |
| 3 | Montana | 5,220,000 | 11.6% |
| 11 | Nebraska | 1,130,000 | 2.5% |
| 41 | Nevada | 14,000 | 0.0% |
| NA | New Hampshire** | NA | NA |
| 38 | New Jersey | 29,000 | 0.1% |
| 37 | New Mexico | 70,000 | 0.2% |
| 34 | New York | 115,000 | 0.3% |
| 13 | North Carolina | 920,000 | 2.0% |
| 2 | North Dakota | 6,035,000 | 13.4% |
| 16 | Ohio | 665,000 | 1.5% |
| 4 | Oklahoma | 3,400,000 | 7.5% |
| 14 | Oregon | 868,000 | 1.9% |
| 31 | Pennsylvania | 160,000 | 0.4% |
| NA | Rhode Island** | NA | NA |
| 29 | South Carolina | 255,000 | 0.6% |
| 7 | South Dakota | 1,839,000 | 4.1% |
| 20 | Tennessee | 540,000 | 1.2% |
| 5 | Texas | 2,250,000 | 5.0% |
| 32 | Utah | 124,000 | 0.3% |
| NA | Vermont** | NA | NA |
| 25 | Virginia | 275,000 | 0.6% |
| 6 | Washington | 2,155,000 | 4.8% |
| 42 | West Virginia | 7,000 | 0.0% |
| 27 | Wisconsin | 265,000 | 0.6% |
| 33 | Wyoming | 120,000 | 0.3% |

RANK ORDER

| RANK | STATE | ACRES | % of USA |
|---|---|---|---|
| 1 | Kansas | 8,400,000 | 18.6% |
| 2 | North Dakota | 6,035,000 | 13.4% |
| 3 | Montana | 5,220,000 | 11.6% |
| 4 | Oklahoma | 3,400,000 | 7.5% |
| 5 | Texas | 2,250,000 | 5.0% |
| 6 | Washington | 2,155,000 | 4.8% |
| 7 | South Dakota | 1,839,000 | 4.1% |
| 8 | Colorado | 1,649,000 | 3.7% |
| 9 | Idaho | 1,241,000 | 2.7% |
| 10 | Minnesota | 1,187,000 | 2.6% |
| 11 | Nebraska | 1,130,000 | 2.5% |
| 12 | Missouri | 1,000,000 | 2.2% |
| 13 | North Carolina | 920,000 | 2.0% |
| 14 | Oregon | 868,000 | 1.9% |
| 15 | Illinois | 830,000 | 1.8% |
| 16 | Ohio | 665,000 | 1.5% |
| 17 | Arkansas | 615,000 | 1.4% |
| 18 | Kentucky | 610,000 | 1.4% |
| 19 | Michigan | 600,000 | 1.3% |
| 20 | Tennessee | 540,000 | 1.2% |
| 21 | Indiana | 440,000 | 1.0% |
| 22 | California | 407,000 | 0.9% |
| 23 | Mississippi | 385,000 | 0.9% |
| 24 | Georgia | 350,000 | 0.8% |
| 25 | Virginia | 275,000 | 0.6% |
| 26 | Alabama | 270,000 | 0.6% |
| 27 | Wisconsin | 265,000 | 0.6% |
| 28 | Maryland | 260,000 | 0.6% |
| 29 | South Carolina | 255,000 | 0.6% |
| 30 | Louisiana | 250,000 | 0.6% |
| 31 | Pennsylvania | 160,000 | 0.4% |
| 32 | Utah | 124,000 | 0.3% |
| 33 | Wyoming | 120,000 | 0.3% |
| 34 | New York | 115,000 | 0.3% |
| 35 | Arizona | 89,000 | 0.2% |
| 36 | Delaware | 78,000 | 0.2% |
| 37 | New Mexico | 70,000 | 0.2% |
| 38 | New Jersey | 29,000 | 0.1% |
| 39 | Iowa | 21,000 | 0.0% |
| 40 | Florida | 19,000 | 0.0% |
| 41 | Nevada | 14,000 | 0.0% |
| 42 | West Virginia | 7,000 | 0.0% |
| NA | Alaska** | NA | NA |
| NA | Connecticut** | NA | NA |
| NA | Hawaii** | NA | NA |
| NA | Maine** | NA | NA |
| NA | Massachusetts** | NA | NA |
| NA | New Hampshire** | NA | NA |
| NA | Rhode Island** | NA | NA |
| NA | Vermont** | NA | NA |
| | District of Columbia** | NA | NA |

Source: U.S. Department of Agriculture, National Agricultural Statistics Service
   "Crop Production: 2013 Summary" (January 2014)
      (http://usda.mannlib.cornell.edu/MannUsda/viewDocumentInfo.do?documentID=1047)
*Estimated totals.
**No acreage or not available.

# Cattle on Farms in 2014

## National Total = 87,730,000 Cattle*

ALPHA ORDER

| RANK | STATE | CATTLE | % of USA |
|---|---|---|---|
| 26 | Alabama | 1,240,000 | 1.4% |
| 49 | Alaska | 10,000 | 0.0% |
| 32 | Arizona | 920,000 | 1.0% |
| 17 | Arkansas | 1,660,000 | 1.9% |
| 4 | California | 5,250,000 | 6.0% |
| 11 | Colorado | 2,480,000 | 2.8% |
| 44 | Connecticut | 47,000 | 0.1% |
| 48 | Delaware | 16,000 | 0.0% |
| 18 | Florida | 1,620,000 | 1.8% |
| 30 | Georgia | 1,000,000 | 1.1% |
| 42 | Hawaii | 130,000 | 0.1% |
| 13 | Idaho | 2,190,000 | 2.5% |
| 27 | Illinois | 1,130,000 | 1.3% |
| 33 | Indiana | 870,000 | 1.0% |
| 7 | Iowa | 3,700,000 | 4.2% |
| 3 | Kansas | 5,800,000 | 6.6% |
| 14 | Kentucky | 2,090,000 | 2.4% |
| 36 | Louisiana | 790,000 | 0.9% |
| 43 | Maine | 85,000 | 0.1% |
| 41 | Maryland | 182,000 | 0.2% |
| 45 | Massachusetts | 39,000 | 0.0% |
| 28 | Michigan | 1,120,000 | 1.3% |
| 12 | Minnesota | 2,280,000 | 2.6% |
| 31 | Mississippi | 930,000 | 1.1% |
| 6 | Missouri | 3,800,000 | 4.3% |
| 10 | Montana | 2,550,000 | 2.9% |
| 2 | Nebraska | 6,150,000 | 7.0% |
| 37 | Nevada | 455,000 | 0.5% |
| 46 | New Hampshire | 32,000 | 0.0% |
| 47 | New Jersey | 29,000 | 0.0% |
| 22 | New Mexico | 1,290,000 | 1.5% |
| 21 | New York | 1,450,000 | 1.7% |
| 34 | North Carolina | 810,000 | 0.9% |
| 15 | North Dakota | 1,770,000 | 2.0% |
| 25 | Ohio | 1,250,000 | 1.4% |
| 5 | Oklahoma | 4,300,000 | 4.9% |
| 23 | Oregon | 1,280,000 | 1.5% |
| 18 | Pennsylvania | 1,620,000 | 1.8% |
| 50 | Rhode Island | 5,000 | 0.0% |
| 39 | South Carolina | 360,000 | 0.4% |
| 8 | South Dakota | 3,650,000 | 4.2% |
| 16 | Tennessee | 1,760,000 | 2.0% |
| 1 | Texas | 10,900,000 | 12.4% |
| 35 | Utah | 800,000 | 0.9% |
| 40 | Vermont | 260,000 | 0.3% |
| 20 | Virginia | 1,530,000 | 1.7% |
| 29 | Washington | 1,100,000 | 1.3% |
| 38 | West Virginia | 380,000 | 0.4% |
| 9 | Wisconsin | 3,350,000 | 3.8% |
| 24 | Wyoming | 1,270,000 | 1.4% |

RANK ORDER

| RANK | STATE | CATTLE | % of USA |
|---|---|---|---|
| 1 | Texas | 10,900,000 | 12.4% |
| 2 | Nebraska | 6,150,000 | 7.0% |
| 3 | Kansas | 5,800,000 | 6.6% |
| 4 | California | 5,250,000 | 6.0% |
| 5 | Oklahoma | 4,300,000 | 4.9% |
| 6 | Missouri | 3,800,000 | 4.3% |
| 7 | Iowa | 3,700,000 | 4.2% |
| 8 | South Dakota | 3,650,000 | 4.2% |
| 9 | Wisconsin | 3,350,000 | 3.8% |
| 10 | Montana | 2,550,000 | 2.9% |
| 11 | Colorado | 2,480,000 | 2.8% |
| 12 | Minnesota | 2,280,000 | 2.6% |
| 13 | Idaho | 2,190,000 | 2.5% |
| 14 | Kentucky | 2,090,000 | 2.4% |
| 15 | North Dakota | 1,770,000 | 2.0% |
| 16 | Tennessee | 1,760,000 | 2.0% |
| 17 | Arkansas | 1,660,000 | 1.9% |
| 18 | Florida | 1,620,000 | 1.8% |
| 18 | Pennsylvania | 1,620,000 | 1.8% |
| 20 | Virginia | 1,530,000 | 1.7% |
| 21 | New York | 1,450,000 | 1.7% |
| 22 | New Mexico | 1,290,000 | 1.5% |
| 23 | Oregon | 1,280,000 | 1.5% |
| 24 | Wyoming | 1,270,000 | 1.4% |
| 25 | Ohio | 1,250,000 | 1.4% |
| 26 | Alabama | 1,240,000 | 1.4% |
| 27 | Illinois | 1,130,000 | 1.3% |
| 28 | Michigan | 1,120,000 | 1.3% |
| 29 | Washington | 1,100,000 | 1.3% |
| 30 | Georgia | 1,000,000 | 1.1% |
| 31 | Mississippi | 930,000 | 1.1% |
| 32 | Arizona | 920,000 | 1.0% |
| 33 | Indiana | 870,000 | 1.0% |
| 34 | North Carolina | 810,000 | 0.9% |
| 35 | Utah | 800,000 | 0.9% |
| 36 | Louisiana | 790,000 | 0.9% |
| 37 | Nevada | 455,000 | 0.5% |
| 38 | West Virginia | 380,000 | 0.4% |
| 39 | South Carolina | 360,000 | 0.4% |
| 40 | Vermont | 260,000 | 0.3% |
| 41 | Maryland | 182,000 | 0.2% |
| 42 | Hawaii | 130,000 | 0.1% |
| 43 | Maine | 85,000 | 0.1% |
| 44 | Connecticut | 47,000 | 0.1% |
| 45 | Massachusetts | 39,000 | 0.0% |
| 46 | New Hampshire | 32,000 | 0.0% |
| 47 | New Jersey | 29,000 | 0.0% |
| 48 | Delaware | 16,000 | 0.0% |
| 49 | Alaska | 10,000 | 0.0% |
| 50 | Rhode Island | 5,000 | 0.0% |
| | District of Columbia | 0 | 0.0% |

Source: U.S. Department of Agriculture, National Agricultural Statistics Service
"Cattle" (http://usda.mannlib.cornell.edu/MannUsda/viewDocumentInfo.do?documentID=1017)
*As of January 1, 2014.

# Milk Cows on Farms in 2012

## National Total = 9,233,000 Milk Cows*

| ALPHA ORDER | | | | RANK ORDER | | | |
|---|---|---|---|---|---|---|---|
| RANK | STATE | MILK COWS | % of USA | RANK | STATE | MILK COWS | % of USA |
| 42 | Alabama | 10,000 | 0.1% | 1 | California | 1,782,000 | 19.3% |
| 50 | Alaska | 400 | 0.0% | 2 | Wisconsin | 1,270,000 | 13.8% |
| 13 | Arizona | 188,000 | 2.0% | 3 | New York | 610,000 | 6.6% |
| 42 | Arkansas | 10,000 | 0.1% | 4 | Idaho | 580,000 | 6.3% |
| 1 | California | 1,782,000 | 19.3% | 5 | Pennsylvania | 536,000 | 5.8% |
| 15 | Colorado | 134,000 | 1.5% | 6 | Minnesota | 465,000 | 5.0% |
| 34 | Connecticut | 18,000 | 0.2% | 7 | Texas | 436,000 | 4.7% |
| 47 | Delaware | 4,900 | 0.1% | 8 | Michigan | 375,000 | 4.1% |
| 18 | Florida | 123,000 | 1.3% | 9 | New Mexico | 330,000 | 3.6% |
| 25 | Georgia | 80,000 | 0.9% | 10 | Ohio | 270,000 | 2.9% |
| 48 | Hawaii | 2,000 | 0.0% | 11 | Washington | 262,000 | 2.8% |
| 4 | Idaho | 580,000 | 6.3% | 12 | Iowa | 204,000 | 2.2% |
| 20 | Illinois | 100,000 | 1.1% | 13 | Arizona | 188,000 | 2.0% |
| 14 | Indiana | 175,000 | 1.9% | 14 | Indiana | 175,000 | 1.9% |
| 12 | Iowa | 204,000 | 2.2% | 15 | Colorado | 134,000 | 1.5% |
| 17 | Kansas | 126,000 | 1.4% | 16 | Vermont | 133,000 | 1.4% |
| 26 | Kentucky | 74,000 | 0.8% | 17 | Kansas | 126,000 | 1.4% |
| 36 | Louisiana | 17,000 | 0.2% | 18 | Florida | 123,000 | 1.3% |
| 32 | Maine | 33,000 | 0.4% | 18 | Oregon | 123,000 | 1.3% |
| 28 | Maryland | 51,000 | 0.6% | 20 | Illinois | 100,000 | 1.1% |
| 41 | Massachusetts | 12,000 | 0.1% | 21 | Virginia | 96,000 | 1.0% |
| 8 | Michigan | 375,000 | 4.1% | 22 | Missouri | 94,000 | 1.0% |
| 6 | Minnesota | 465,000 | 5.0% | 23 | South Dakota | 92,000 | 1.0% |
| 38 | Mississippi | 14,000 | 0.2% | 24 | Utah | 90,000 | 1.0% |
| 22 | Missouri | 94,000 | 1.0% | 25 | Georgia | 80,000 | 0.9% |
| 38 | Montana | 14,000 | 0.2% | 26 | Kentucky | 74,000 | 0.8% |
| 27 | Nebraska | 56,000 | 0.6% | 27 | Nebraska | 56,000 | 0.6% |
| 33 | Nevada | 29,000 | 0.3% | 28 | Maryland | 51,000 | 0.6% |
| 38 | New Hampshire | 14,000 | 0.2% | 29 | Tennessee | 50,000 | 0.5% |
| 45 | New Jersey | 7,000 | 0.1% | 30 | Oklahoma | 48,000 | 0.5% |
| 9 | New Mexico | 330,000 | 3.6% | 31 | North Carolina | 46,000 | 0.5% |
| 3 | New York | 610,000 | 6.6% | 32 | Maine | 33,000 | 0.4% |
| 31 | North Carolina | 46,000 | 0.5% | 33 | Nevada | 29,000 | 0.3% |
| 34 | North Dakota | 18,000 | 0.2% | 34 | Connecticut | 18,000 | 0.2% |
| 10 | Ohio | 270,000 | 2.9% | 34 | North Dakota | 18,000 | 0.2% |
| 30 | Oklahoma | 48,000 | 0.5% | 36 | Louisiana | 17,000 | 0.2% |
| 18 | Oregon | 123,000 | 1.3% | 37 | South Carolina | 16,000 | 0.2% |
| 5 | Pennsylvania | 536,000 | 5.8% | 38 | Mississippi | 14,000 | 0.2% |
| 49 | Rhode Island | 1,000 | 0.0% | 38 | Montana | 14,000 | 0.2% |
| 37 | South Carolina | 16,000 | 0.2% | 38 | New Hampshire | 14,000 | 0.2% |
| 23 | South Dakota | 92,000 | 1.0% | 41 | Massachusetts | 12,000 | 0.1% |
| 29 | Tennessee | 50,000 | 0.5% | 42 | Alabama | 10,000 | 0.1% |
| 7 | Texas | 436,000 | 4.7% | 42 | Arkansas | 10,000 | 0.1% |
| 24 | Utah | 90,000 | 1.0% | 42 | West Virginia | 10,000 | 0.1% |
| 16 | Vermont | 133,000 | 1.4% | 45 | New Jersey | 7,000 | 0.1% |
| 21 | Virginia | 96,000 | 1.0% | 46 | Wyoming | 6,000 | 0.1% |
| 11 | Washington | 262,000 | 2.8% | 47 | Delaware | 4,900 | 0.1% |
| 42 | West Virginia | 10,000 | 0.1% | 48 | Hawaii | 2,000 | 0.0% |
| 2 | Wisconsin | 1,270,000 | 13.8% | 49 | Rhode Island | 1,000 | 0.0% |
| 46 | Wyoming | 6,000 | 0.1% | 50 | Alaska | 400 | 0.0% |
| | | | | | District of Columbia | 0 | 0.0% |

Source: U.S. Department of Agriculture, National Agricultural Statistics Service
   "Milk Production, Disposition and Income: 2012 Summary" (April 2013)
   (http://usda.mannlib.cornell.edu/MannUsda/viewDocumentInfo.do?documentID=1105)
*Average number during year.  Excludes heifers not yet fresh.

# Milk Production in 2012

## National Total = 200,324,000,000 Pounds of Milk*

ALPHA ORDER

| RANK | STATE | POUNDS | % of USA |
|---|---|---|---|
| 44 | Alabama | 132,000,000 | 0.1% |
| 50 | Alaska | 5,700,000 | 0.0% |
| 12 | Arizona | 4,508,000,000 | 2.3% |
| 43 | Arkansas | 133,000,000 | 0.1% |
| 1 | California | 41,801,000,000 | 20.9% |
| 15 | Colorado | 3,213,000,000 | 1.6% |
| 34 | Connecticut | 358,000,000 | 0.2% |
| 47 | Delaware | 93,800,000 | 0.0% |
| 19 | Florida | 2,338,000,000 | 1.2% |
| 24 | Georgia | 1,530,000,000 | 0.8% |
| 48 | Hawaii | 28,400,000 | 0.0% |
| 3 | Idaho | 13,558,000,000 | 6.8% |
| 21 | Illinois | 1,951,000,000 | 1.0% |
| 14 | Indiana | 3,739,000,000 | 1.9% |
| 13 | Iowa | 4,433,000,000 | 2.2% |
| 16 | Kansas | 2,731,000,000 | 1.4% |
| 27 | Kentucky | 1,120,000,000 | 0.6% |
| 39 | Louisiana | 224,000,000 | 0.1% |
| 33 | Maine | 613,000,000 | 0.3% |
| 28 | Maryland | 979,000,000 | 0.5% |
| 40 | Massachusetts | 219,000,000 | 0.1% |
| 8 | Michigan | 8,889,000,000 | 4.4% |
| 7 | Minnesota | 9,071,000,000 | 4.5% |
| 41 | Mississippi | 201,000,000 | 0.1% |
| 25 | Missouri | 1,404,000,000 | 0.7% |
| 36 | Montana | 299,000,000 | 0.1% |
| 26 | Nebraska | 1,186,000,000 | 0.6% |
| 32 | Nevada | 666,000,000 | 0.3% |
| 38 | New Hampshire | 275,000,000 | 0.1% |
| 45 | New Jersey | 130,000,000 | 0.1% |
| 9 | New Mexico | 8,149,000,000 | 4.1% |
| 4 | New York | 13,196,000,000 | 6.6% |
| 29 | North Carolina | 940,000,000 | 0.5% |
| 35 | North Dakota | 347,000,000 | 0.2% |
| 11 | Ohio | 5,355,000,000 | 2.7% |
| 30 | Oklahoma | 849,000,000 | 0.4% |
| 18 | Oregon | 2,513,000,000 | 1.3% |
| 5 | Pennsylvania | 10,493,000,000 | 5.2% |
| 49 | Rhode Island | 18,300,000 | 0.0% |
| 37 | South Carolina | 277,000,000 | 0.1% |
| 20 | South Dakota | 1,968,000,000 | 1.0% |
| 31 | Tennessee | 805,000,000 | 0.4% |
| 6 | Texas | 9,596,000,000 | 4.8% |
| 21 | Utah | 1,951,000,000 | 1.0% |
| 17 | Vermont | 2,569,000,000 | 1.3% |
| 23 | Virginia | 1,727,000,000 | 0.9% |
| 10 | Washington | 6,234,000,000 | 3.1% |
| 42 | West Virginia | 158,000,000 | 0.1% |
| 2 | Wisconsin | 27,224,000,000 | 13.6% |
| 46 | Wyoming | 124,900,000 | 0.1% |

RANK ORDER

| RANK | STATE | POUNDS | % of USA |
|---|---|---|---|
| 1 | California | 41,801,000,000 | 20.9% |
| 2 | Wisconsin | 27,224,000,000 | 13.6% |
| 3 | Idaho | 13,558,000,000 | 6.8% |
| 4 | New York | 13,196,000,000 | 6.6% |
| 5 | Pennsylvania | 10,493,000,000 | 5.2% |
| 6 | Texas | 9,596,000,000 | 4.8% |
| 7 | Minnesota | 9,071,000,000 | 4.5% |
| 8 | Michigan | 8,889,000,000 | 4.4% |
| 9 | New Mexico | 8,149,000,000 | 4.1% |
| 10 | Washington | 6,234,000,000 | 3.1% |
| 11 | Ohio | 5,355,000,000 | 2.7% |
| 12 | Arizona | 4,508,000,000 | 2.3% |
| 13 | Iowa | 4,433,000,000 | 2.2% |
| 14 | Indiana | 3,739,000,000 | 1.9% |
| 15 | Colorado | 3,213,000,000 | 1.6% |
| 16 | Kansas | 2,731,000,000 | 1.4% |
| 17 | Vermont | 2,569,000,000 | 1.3% |
| 18 | Oregon | 2,513,000,000 | 1.3% |
| 19 | Florida | 2,338,000,000 | 1.2% |
| 20 | South Dakota | 1,968,000,000 | 1.0% |
| 21 | Illinois | 1,951,000,000 | 1.0% |
| 21 | Utah | 1,951,000,000 | 1.0% |
| 23 | Virginia | 1,727,000,000 | 0.9% |
| 24 | Georgia | 1,530,000,000 | 0.8% |
| 25 | Missouri | 1,404,000,000 | 0.7% |
| 26 | Nebraska | 1,186,000,000 | 0.6% |
| 27 | Kentucky | 1,120,000,000 | 0.6% |
| 28 | Maryland | 979,000,000 | 0.5% |
| 29 | North Carolina | 940,000,000 | 0.5% |
| 30 | Oklahoma | 849,000,000 | 0.4% |
| 31 | Tennessee | 805,000,000 | 0.4% |
| 32 | Nevada | 666,000,000 | 0.3% |
| 33 | Maine | 613,000,000 | 0.3% |
| 34 | Connecticut | 358,000,000 | 0.2% |
| 35 | North Dakota | 347,000,000 | 0.2% |
| 36 | Montana | 299,000,000 | 0.1% |
| 37 | South Carolina | 277,000,000 | 0.1% |
| 38 | New Hampshire | 275,000,000 | 0.1% |
| 39 | Louisiana | 224,000,000 | 0.1% |
| 40 | Massachusetts | 219,000,000 | 0.1% |
| 41 | Mississippi | 201,000,000 | 0.1% |
| 42 | West Virginia | 158,000,000 | 0.1% |
| 43 | Arkansas | 133,000,000 | 0.1% |
| 44 | Alabama | 132,000,000 | 0.1% |
| 45 | New Jersey | 130,000,000 | 0.1% |
| 46 | Wyoming | 124,900,000 | 0.1% |
| 47 | Delaware | 93,800,000 | 0.0% |
| 48 | Hawaii | 28,400,000 | 0.0% |
| 49 | Rhode Island | 18,300,000 | 0.0% |
| 50 | Alaska | 5,700,000 | 0.0% |
| | District of Columbia | 0 | 0.0% |

Source: U.S. Department of Agriculture, National Agricultural Statistics Service
"Milk Production, Disposition and Income: 2012 Summary" (April 2013)
(http://usda.mannlib.cornell.edu/MannUsda/viewDocumentInfo.do?documentID=1105)
*Excludes milk suckled by calves.

# Milk Production per Milk Cow in 2012

## National Average = 21,697 Pounds of Milk per Cow*

ALPHA ORDER

| RANK | STATE | POUNDS |
|------|-------|--------|
| 49 | Alabama | 13,200 |
| 46 | Alaska | 14,250 |
| 2 | Arizona | 23,979 |
| 48 | Arkansas | 13,300 |
| 6 | California | 23,457 |
| 3 | Colorado | 23,978 |
| 22 | Connecticut | 19,889 |
| 31 | Delaware | 19,143 |
| 33 | Florida | 19,008 |
| 32 | Georgia | 19,125 |
| 47 | Hawaii | 14,200 |
| 7 | Idaho | 23,376 |
| 26 | Illinois | 19,510 |
| 16 | Indiana | 21,366 |
| 10 | Iowa | 21,730 |
| 12 | Kansas | 21,675 |
| 43 | Kentucky | 15,135 |
| 50 | Louisiana | 13,176 |
| 34 | Maine | 18,576 |
| 30 | Maryland | 19,196 |
| 37 | Massachusetts | 18,250 |
| 5 | Michigan | 23,704 |
| 27 | Minnesota | 19,508 |
| 45 | Mississippi | 14,357 |
| 44 | Missouri | 14,936 |
| 17 | Montana | 21,357 |
| 18 | Nebraska | 21,179 |
| 8 | Nevada | 22,966 |
| 24 | New Hampshire | 19,643 |
| 35 | New Jersey | 18,571 |
| 1 | New Mexico | 24,694 |
| 13 | New York | 21,633 |
| 20 | North Carolina | 20,435 |
| 29 | North Dakota | 19,278 |
| 23 | Ohio | 19,833 |
| 39 | Oklahoma | 17,688 |
| 21 | Oregon | 20,431 |
| 25 | Pennsylvania | 19,576 |
| 36 | Rhode Island | 18,300 |
| 40 | South Carolina | 17,313 |
| 15 | South Dakota | 21,391 |
| 41 | Tennessee | 16,100 |
| 9 | Texas | 22,009 |
| 11 | Utah | 21,678 |
| 28 | Vermont | 19,316 |
| 38 | Virginia | 17,990 |
| 4 | Washington | 23,794 |
| 42 | West Virginia | 15,800 |
| 14 | Wisconsin | 21,436 |
| 19 | Wyoming | 20,817 |

RANK ORDER

| RANK | STATE | POUNDS |
|------|-------|--------|
| 1 | New Mexico | 24,694 |
| 2 | Arizona | 23,979 |
| 3 | Colorado | 23,978 |
| 4 | Washington | 23,794 |
| 5 | Michigan | 23,704 |
| 6 | California | 23,457 |
| 7 | Idaho | 23,376 |
| 8 | Nevada | 22,966 |
| 9 | Texas | 22,009 |
| 10 | Iowa | 21,730 |
| 11 | Utah | 21,678 |
| 12 | Kansas | 21,675 |
| 13 | New York | 21,633 |
| 14 | Wisconsin | 21,436 |
| 15 | South Dakota | 21,391 |
| 16 | Indiana | 21,366 |
| 17 | Montana | 21,357 |
| 18 | Nebraska | 21,179 |
| 19 | Wyoming | 20,817 |
| 20 | North Carolina | 20,435 |
| 21 | Oregon | 20,431 |
| 22 | Connecticut | 19,889 |
| 23 | Ohio | 19,833 |
| 24 | New Hampshire | 19,643 |
| 25 | Pennsylvania | 19,576 |
| 26 | Illinois | 19,510 |
| 27 | Minnesota | 19,508 |
| 28 | Vermont | 19,316 |
| 29 | North Dakota | 19,278 |
| 30 | Maryland | 19,196 |
| 31 | Delaware | 19,143 |
| 32 | Georgia | 19,125 |
| 33 | Florida | 19,008 |
| 34 | Maine | 18,576 |
| 35 | New Jersey | 18,571 |
| 36 | Rhode Island | 18,300 |
| 37 | Massachusetts | 18,250 |
| 38 | Virginia | 17,990 |
| 39 | Oklahoma | 17,688 |
| 40 | South Carolina | 17,313 |
| 41 | Tennessee | 16,100 |
| 42 | West Virginia | 15,800 |
| 43 | Kentucky | 15,135 |
| 44 | Missouri | 14,936 |
| 45 | Mississippi | 14,357 |
| 46 | Alaska | 14,250 |
| 47 | Hawaii | 14,200 |
| 48 | Arkansas | 13,300 |
| 49 | Alabama | 13,200 |
| 50 | Louisiana | 13,176 |

District of Columbia**                NA

Source: U.S. Department of Agriculture, National Agricultural Statistics Service
  "Milk Production, Disposition and Income: 2012 Summary" (April 2013)
    (http://usda.mannlib.cornell.edu/MannUsda/viewDocumentInfo.do?documentID=1105)
*Excludes milk suckled by calves.
**Not applicable.

# Hogs and Pigs on Farms in 2013

## National Total = 65,940,000 Hogs and Pigs*

| RANK | STATE | HOGS AND PIGS | % of USA | RANK | STATE | HOGS AND PIGS | % of USA |
|------|-------|--------------:|----------|------|-------|--------------:|----------|
| 30 | Alabama | 85,000 | 0.1% | 1 | Iowa | 20,500,000 | 31.1% |
| 48 | Alaska | 1,000 | 0.0% | 2 | North Carolina | 8,700,000 | 13.2% |
| 22 | Arizona | 175,000 | 0.3% | 3 | Minnesota | 8,000,000 | 12.1% |
| 27 | Arkansas | 115,000 | 0.2% | 4 | Illinois | 4,650,000 | 7.1% |
| 28 | California | 95,000 | 0.1% | 5 | Indiana | 3,750,000 | 5.7% |
| 15 | Colorado | 690,000 | 1.0% | 6 | Nebraska | 3,100,000 | 4.7% |
| 43 | Connecticut | 3,500 | 0.0% | 7 | Missouri | 2,850,000 | 4.3% |
| 39 | Delaware | 6,000 | 0.0% | 8 | Ohio | 2,220,000 | 3.4% |
| 33 | Florida | 15,000 | 0.0% | 9 | Oklahoma | 1,990,000 | 3.0% |
| 25 | Georgia | 141,000 | 0.2% | 10 | Kansas | 1,760,000 | 2.7% |
| 34 | Hawaii | 11,500 | 0.0% | 11 | South Dakota | 1,210,000 | 1.8% |
| NA | Idaho** | NA | NA | 12 | Pennsylvania | 1,110,000 | 1.7% |
| 4 | Illinois | 4,650,000 | 7.1% | 13 | Michigan | 1,060,000 | 1.6% |
| 5 | Indiana | 3,750,000 | 5.7% | 14 | Utah | 710,000 | 1.1% |
| 1 | Iowa | 20,500,000 | 31.1% | 15 | Colorado | 690,000 | 1.0% |
| 10 | Kansas | 1,760,000 | 2.7% | 16 | Texas | 600,000 | 0.9% |
| 18 | Kentucky | 315,000 | 0.5% | 17 | Mississippi | 500,000 | 0.8% |
| 38 | Louisiana | 8,000 | 0.0% | 18 | Kentucky | 315,000 | 0.5% |
| 41 | Maine | 4,500 | 0.0% | 19 | Wisconsin | 305,000 | 0.5% |
| 32 | Maryland | 22,000 | 0.0% | 20 | Virginia | 255,000 | 0.4% |
| 36 | Massachusetts | 8,500 | 0.0% | 21 | South Carolina | 245,000 | 0.4% |
| 13 | Michigan | 1,060,000 | 1.6% | 22 | Arizona | 175,000 | 0.3% |
| 3 | Minnesota | 8,000,000 | 12.1% | 22 | Tennessee | 175,000 | 0.3% |
| 17 | Mississippi | 500,000 | 0.8% | 24 | Montana | 166,000 | 0.3% |
| 7 | Missouri | 2,850,000 | 4.3% | 25 | Georgia | 141,000 | 0.2% |
| 24 | Montana | 166,000 | 0.3% | 26 | North Dakota | 135,000 | 0.2% |
| 6 | Nebraska | 3,100,000 | 4.7% | 27 | Arkansas | 115,000 | 0.2% |
| 45 | Nevada | 2,000 | 0.0% | 28 | California | 95,000 | 0.1% |
| 42 | New Hampshire | 3,800 | 0.0% | 29 | Wyoming | 90,000 | 0.1% |
| 35 | New Jersey | 9,000 | 0.0% | 30 | Alabama | 85,000 | 0.1% |
| 47 | New Mexico | 1,200 | 0.0% | 31 | New York | 66,000 | 0.1% |
| 31 | New York | 66,000 | 0.1% | 32 | Maryland | 22,000 | 0.0% |
| 2 | North Carolina | 8,700,000 | 13.2% | 33 | Florida | 15,000 | 0.0% |
| 26 | North Dakota | 135,000 | 0.2% | 34 | Hawaii | 11,500 | 0.0% |
| 8 | Ohio | 2,220,000 | 3.4% | 35 | New Jersey | 9,000 | 0.0% |
| 9 | Oklahoma | 1,990,000 | 3.0% | 36 | Massachusetts | 8,500 | 0.0% |
| 36 | Oregon | 8,500 | 0.0% | 36 | Oregon | 8,500 | 0.0% |
| 12 | Pennsylvania | 1,110,000 | 1.7% | 38 | Louisiana | 8,000 | 0.0% |
| 46 | Rhode Island | 1,900 | 0.0% | 39 | Delaware | 6,000 | 0.0% |
| 21 | South Carolina | 245,000 | 0.4% | 40 | West Virginia | 5,000 | 0.0% |
| 11 | South Dakota | 1,210,000 | 1.8% | 41 | Maine | 4,500 | 0.0% |
| 22 | Tennessee | 175,000 | 0.3% | 42 | New Hampshire | 3,800 | 0.0% |
| 16 | Texas | 600,000 | 0.9% | 43 | Connecticut | 3,500 | 0.0% |
| 14 | Utah | 710,000 | 1.1% | 44 | Vermont | 3,200 | 0.0% |
| 44 | Vermont | 3,200 | 0.0% | 45 | Nevada | 2,000 | 0.0% |
| 20 | Virginia | 255,000 | 0.4% | 46 | Rhode Island | 1,900 | 0.0% |
| NA | Washington** | NA | NA | 47 | New Mexico | 1,200 | 0.0% |
| 40 | West Virginia | 5,000 | 0.0% | 48 | Alaska | 1,000 | 0.0% |
| 19 | Wisconsin | 305,000 | 0.5% | NA | Idaho** | NA | NA |
| 29 | Wyoming | 90,000 | 0.1% | NA | Washington** | NA | NA |
|  |  |  |  |  | District of Columbia | 0 | 0.0% |

ALPHA ORDER

RANK ORDER

Source: U.S. Department of Agriculture, National Agricultural Statistics Service
  "Quarterly Hogs and Pigs" (http://usda.mannlib.cornell.edu/MannUsda/viewDocumentInfo.do?documentID=1086)
*As of December 1, 2013.
**Not available. Figures for Idaho and Washington withheld to avoid disclosing data for individual operations. The two states combined had 62,000 hogs and pigs.

# Chickens in 2012

## National Total = 8,437,900,000 Chickens*

ALPHA ORDER

| RANK | STATE | CHICKENS | % of USA |
|------|-------|----------|----------|
| 2 | Alabama | 1,003,600,000 | 11.9% |
| NA | Alaska*** | NA | NA |
| NA | Arizona*** | NA | NA |
| 3 | Arkansas | 977,100,000 | 11.6% |
| NA | California** | NA | NA |
| NA | Colorado*** | NA | NA |
| NA | Connecticut*** | NA | NA |
| 12 | Delaware | 212,000,000 | 2.5% |
| 18 | Florida | 59,500,000 | 0.7% |
| 1 | Georgia | 1,361,700,000 | 16.1% |
| NA | Hawaii*** | NA | NA |
| NA | Idaho*** | NA | NA |
| NA | Illinois** | NA | NA |
| NA | Indiana** | NA | NA |
| NA | Iowa** | NA | NA |
| NA | Kansas*** | NA | NA |
| 7 | Kentucky | 309,500,000 | 3.7% |
| NA | Louisiana** | NA | NA |
| NA | Maine*** | NA | NA |
| 8 | Maryland | 304,000,000 | 3.6% |
| NA | Massachusetts*** | NA | NA |
| NA | Michigan** | NA | NA |
| 20 | Minnesota | 45,500,000 | 0.5% |
| 5 | Mississippi | 751,300,000 | 8.9% |
| 9 | Missouri | 271,600,000 | 3.2% |
| NA | Montana*** | NA | NA |
| NA | Nebraska** | NA | NA |
| NA | Nevada*** | NA | NA |
| NA | New Hampshire*** | NA | NA |
| NA | New Jersey*** | NA | NA |
| NA | New Mexico*** | NA | NA |
| NA | New York** | NA | NA |
| 4 | North Carolina | 799,700,000 | 9.5% |
| NA | North Dakota*** | NA | NA |
| 17 | Ohio | 63,200,000 | 0.7% |
| 13 | Oklahoma | 211,800,000 | 2.5% |
| NA | Oregon** | NA | NA |
| 15 | Pennsylvania | 154,500,000 | 1.8% |
| NA | Rhode Island*** | NA | NA |
| 11 | South Carolina | 222,800,000 | 2.6% |
| NA | South Dakota*** | NA | NA |
| 14 | Tennessee | 167,600,000 | 2.0% |
| 6 | Texas | 602,500,000 | 7.1% |
| NA | Utah*** | NA | NA |
| NA | Vermont*** | NA | NA |
| 10 | Virginia | 240,500,000 | 2.9% |
| NA | Washington** | NA | NA |
| 16 | West Virginia | 94,000,000 | 1.1% |
| 19 | Wisconsin | 51,700,000 | 0.6% |
| NA | Wyoming*** | NA | NA |

RANK ORDER

| RANK | STATE | CHICKENS | % of USA |
|------|-------|----------|----------|
| 1 | Georgia | 1,361,700,000 | 16.1% |
| 2 | Alabama | 1,003,600,000 | 11.9% |
| 3 | Arkansas | 977,100,000 | 11.6% |
| 4 | North Carolina | 799,700,000 | 9.5% |
| 5 | Mississippi | 751,300,000 | 8.9% |
| 6 | Texas | 602,500,000 | 7.1% |
| 7 | Kentucky | 309,500,000 | 3.7% |
| 8 | Maryland | 304,000,000 | 3.6% |
| 9 | Missouri | 271,600,000 | 3.2% |
| 10 | Virginia | 240,500,000 | 2.9% |
| 11 | South Carolina | 222,800,000 | 2.6% |
| 12 | Delaware | 212,000,000 | 2.5% |
| 13 | Oklahoma | 211,800,000 | 2.5% |
| 14 | Tennessee | 167,600,000 | 2.0% |
| 15 | Pennsylvania | 154,500,000 | 1.8% |
| 16 | West Virginia | 94,000,000 | 1.1% |
| 17 | Ohio | 63,200,000 | 0.7% |
| 18 | Florida | 59,500,000 | 0.7% |
| 19 | Wisconsin | 51,700,000 | 0.6% |
| 20 | Minnesota | 45,500,000 | 0.5% |
| NA | Alaska*** | NA | NA |
| NA | Arizona*** | NA | NA |
| NA | California** | NA | NA |
| NA | Colorado*** | NA | NA |
| NA | Connecticut*** | NA | NA |
| NA | Hawaii*** | NA | NA |
| NA | Idaho*** | NA | NA |
| NA | Illinois** | NA | NA |
| NA | Indiana** | NA | NA |
| NA | Iowa** | NA | NA |
| NA | Kansas*** | NA | NA |
| NA | Louisiana** | NA | NA |
| NA | Maine*** | NA | NA |
| NA | Massachusetts*** | NA | NA |
| NA | Michigan** | NA | NA |
| NA | Montana*** | NA | NA |
| NA | Nebraska** | NA | NA |
| NA | Nevada*** | NA | NA |
| NA | New Hampshire*** | NA | NA |
| NA | New Jersey*** | NA | NA |
| NA | New Mexico*** | NA | NA |
| NA | New York** | NA | NA |
| NA | North Dakota*** | NA | NA |
| NA | Oregon** | NA | NA |
| NA | Rhode Island*** | NA | NA |
| NA | South Dakota*** | NA | NA |
| NA | Utah*** | NA | NA |
| NA | Vermont*** | NA | NA |
| NA | Washington** | NA | NA |
| NA | Wyoming*** | NA | NA |
| | District of Columbia*** | NA | NA |

Source: U.S. Department of Agriculture, National Agricultural Statistics Service
"Poultry - Production and Value: 2012 Summary" (April 2013)
(http://usda.mannlib.cornell.edu/MannUsda/viewDocumentInfo.do?documentID=1130)
*Broilers.  Total includes numbers for states not shown separately but excludes states producing less than 500,000 birds. **These states produced a combined total of 535,800,000 chickens.  They are combined to avoid disclosing individual operations.
National total does not include chickens used for egg production. ***Produces fewer than 500,000 chickens or are not available.

# Eggs Produced in 2012

## National Total = 92,894,000,000 Eggs*

ALPHA ORDER

| RANK | STATE | EGGS | % of USA |
|---|---|---|---|
| 14 | Alabama | 2,139,000,000 | 2.3% |
| NA | Alaska** | NA | NA |
| NA | Arizona** | NA | NA |
| 10 | Arkansas | 3,011,000,000 | 3.2% |
| 5 | California | 5,451,000,000 | 5.9% |
| 20 | Colorado | 1,297,000,000 | 1.4% |
| 30 | Connecticut | 651,000,000 | 0.7% |
| NA | Delaware** | NA | NA |
| 13 | Florida | 2,514,000,000 | 2.7% |
| 7 | Georgia | 4,303,000,000 | 4.6% |
| NA | Hawaii** | NA | NA |
| NA | Idaho** | NA | NA |
| 21 | Illinois | 1,217,000,000 | 1.3% |
| 4 | Indiana | 6,804,000,000 | 7.3% |
| 1 | Iowa | 14,499,000,000 | 15.6% |
| NA | Kansas** | NA | NA |
| 23 | Kentucky | 1,037,000,000 | 1.1% |
| 32 | Louisiana | 533,000,000 | 0.6% |
| 25 | Maine | 998,000,000 | 1.1% |
| 31 | Maryland | 647,000,000 | 0.7% |
| 37 | Massachusetts | 36,000,000 | 0.0% |
| 8 | Michigan | 3,460,000,000 | 3.7% |
| 11 | Minnesota | 2,830,000,000 | 3.0% |
| 17 | Mississippi | 1,381,000,000 | 1.5% |
| 15 | Missouri | 1,968,000,000 | 2.1% |
| 35 | Montana | 119,000,000 | 0.1% |
| 12 | Nebraska | 2,723,000,000 | 2.9% |
| NA | Nevada** | NA | NA |
| NA | New Hampshire** | NA | NA |
| NA | New Jersey** | NA | NA |
| NA | New Mexico** | NA | NA |
| 19 | New York | 1,312,000,000 | 1.4% |
| 9 | North Carolina | 3,086,000,000 | 3.3% |
| NA | North Dakota** | NA | NA |
| 2 | Ohio | 7,685,000,000 | 8.3% |
| 26 | Oklahoma | 741,000,000 | 0.8% |
| 28 | Oregon | 694,000,000 | 0.7% |
| 3 | Pennsylvania | 7,139,000,000 | 7.7% |
| NA | Rhode Island** | NA | NA |
| 22 | South Carolina | 1,129,000,000 | 1.2% |
| 29 | South Dakota | 666,000,000 | 0.7% |
| 33 | Tennessee | 311,000,000 | 0.3% |
| 6 | Texas | 5,098,000,000 | 5.5% |
| 24 | Utah | 1,005,000,000 | 1.1% |
| 36 | Vermont | 60,000,000 | 0.1% |
| 27 | Virginia | 696,000,000 | 0.7% |
| 16 | Washington | 1,905,000,000 | 2.1% |
| 34 | West Virginia | 224,000,000 | 0.2% |
| 18 | Wisconsin | 1,372,000,000 | 1.5% |
| 38 | Wyoming | 2,400,000 | 0.0% |

RANK ORDER

| RANK | STATE | EGGS | % of USA |
|---|---|---|---|
| 1 | Iowa | 14,499,000,000 | 15.6% |
| 2 | Ohio | 7,685,000,000 | 8.3% |
| 3 | Pennsylvania | 7,139,000,000 | 7.7% |
| 4 | Indiana | 6,804,000,000 | 7.3% |
| 5 | California | 5,451,000,000 | 5.9% |
| 6 | Texas | 5,098,000,000 | 5.5% |
| 7 | Georgia | 4,303,000,000 | 4.6% |
| 8 | Michigan | 3,460,000,000 | 3.7% |
| 9 | North Carolina | 3,086,000,000 | 3.3% |
| 10 | Arkansas | 3,011,000,000 | 3.2% |
| 11 | Minnesota | 2,830,000,000 | 3.0% |
| 12 | Nebraska | 2,723,000,000 | 2.9% |
| 13 | Florida | 2,514,000,000 | 2.7% |
| 14 | Alabama | 2,139,000,000 | 2.3% |
| 15 | Missouri | 1,968,000,000 | 2.1% |
| 16 | Washington | 1,905,000,000 | 2.1% |
| 17 | Mississippi | 1,381,000,000 | 1.5% |
| 18 | Wisconsin | 1,372,000,000 | 1.5% |
| 19 | New York | 1,312,000,000 | 1.4% |
| 20 | Colorado | 1,297,000,000 | 1.4% |
| 21 | Illinois | 1,217,000,000 | 1.3% |
| 22 | South Carolina | 1,129,000,000 | 1.2% |
| 23 | Kentucky | 1,037,000,000 | 1.1% |
| 24 | Utah | 1,005,000,000 | 1.1% |
| 25 | Maine | 998,000,000 | 1.1% |
| 26 | Oklahoma | 741,000,000 | 0.8% |
| 27 | Virginia | 696,000,000 | 0.7% |
| 28 | Oregon | 694,000,000 | 0.7% |
| 29 | South Dakota | 666,000,000 | 0.7% |
| 30 | Connecticut | 651,000,000 | 0.7% |
| 31 | Maryland | 647,000,000 | 0.7% |
| 32 | Louisiana | 533,000,000 | 0.6% |
| 33 | Tennessee | 311,000,000 | 0.3% |
| 34 | West Virginia | 224,000,000 | 0.2% |
| 35 | Montana | 119,000,000 | 0.1% |
| 36 | Vermont | 60,000,000 | 0.1% |
| 37 | Massachusetts | 36,000,000 | 0.0% |
| 38 | Wyoming | 2,400,000 | 0.0% |
| NA | Alaska** | NA | NA |
| NA | Arizona** | NA | NA |
| NA | Delaware** | NA | NA |
| NA | Hawaii** | NA | NA |
| NA | Idaho** | NA | NA |
| NA | Kansas** | NA | NA |
| NA | Nevada** | NA | NA |
| NA | New Hampshire** | NA | NA |
| NA | New Jersey** | NA | NA |
| NA | New Mexico** | NA | NA |
| NA | North Dakota** | NA | NA |
| NA | Rhode Island** | NA | NA |
| | District of Columbia | 0 | 0.0% |

Source: U.S. Department of Agriculture, National Agricultural Statistics Service
"Poultry - Production and Value: 2012 Summary" (April 2013)
(http://usda.mannlib.cornell.edu/MannUsda/viewDocumentInfo.do?documentID=1130)
*Includes hatching and market (table) eggs.  **These states produced a combined 2,153,000,000 eggs.  They are combined to avoid disclosing individual operations.

# II. Crime and Law Enforcement

## I. Arrests:

### Important Note Regarding Arrest Numbers

The state arrest numbers reported by the FBI and shown on page 55 are only from those law enforcement agencies that submitted complete arrests reports for 12 months in 2012. The arrest rates were calculated by the editors using population totals provided by the FBI for those jurisdictions reporting. Reports from law enforcement agencies in Alabama, Hawaii, and the District of Columbia were insufficient to calculate rates. Reports from Illinois, Louisiana, Mississippi, New York, Utah, and Washington represented less than 60 percent of their state population. Rates for these states should be interpreted with caution.

## V. Juveniles:

### Important Note Regarding Juvenile Arrest Rates

The juvenile arrest rates shown on page 56 were calculated by the editors as follows:

The state arrest numbers reported by the FBI are only from those law enforcement agencies that submitted complete arrests reports for 12 months in 2012. Included in the FBI report are population totals of these reporting jurisdictions by state. Using these FBI population figures, we first determined what percentage the FBI numbers represented of each state's total resident population. Next, using 2012 Census state estimates for 10- to 17-year-olds, we multiplied the percentages derived from the FBI population figures into the Census Bureau's total juvenile population counts. The resulting juvenile population is the base that was used to determine juvenile arrests per 100,000 juvenile population. The national rate was calculated in the same manner.

Reports from law enforcement agencies in Alabama, Hawaii, and the District of Columbia were insufficient to calculate rates. Reports from Illinois, Louisiana, Mississippi, New York, Utah, and Washington represented less than 60 percent of their state population. Rates for these states should be interpreted with caution.

# Crimes in 2012

## National Total = 10,189,902 Crimes*

ALPHA ORDER

| RANK | STATE | CRIMES | % of USA |
|------|-------|--------|----------|
| 19 | Alabama | 190,571 | 1.9% |
| 46 | Alaska | 24,449 | 0.2% |
| 12 | Arizona | 260,038 | 2.6% |
| 28 | Arkansas | 121,776 | 1.2% |
| 1 | California | 1,210,409 | 11.9% |
| 24 | Colorado | 155,293 | 1.5% |
| 34 | Connecticut | 86,994 | 0.9% |
| 40 | Delaware | 35,659 | 0.3% |
| 3 | Florida | 727,075 | 7.1% |
| 7 | Georgia | 375,920 | 3.7% |
| 39 | Hawaii | 46,147 | 0.5% |
| 42 | Idaho | 34,969 | 0.3% |
| 6 | Illinois | 385,416 | 3.8% |
| 15 | Indiana | 220,634 | 2.2% |
| 36 | Iowa | 77,951 | 0.8% |
| 30 | Kansas | 100,942 | 1.0% |
| 29 | Kentucky | 121,578 | 1.2% |
| 21 | Louisiana | 185,804 | 1.8% |
| 41 | Maine | 34,992 | 0.3% |
| 20 | Maryland | 190,086 | 1.9% |
| 22 | Massachusetts | 170,042 | 1.7% |
| 10 | Michigan | 295,023 | 2.9% |
| 25 | Minnesota | 150,571 | 1.5% |
| 32 | Mississippi | 91,692 | 0.9% |
| 14 | Missouri | 226,745 | 2.2% |
| 45 | Montana | 28,706 | 0.3% |
| 37 | Nebraska | 55,932 | 0.5% |
| 31 | Nevada | 94,273 | 0.9% |
| 43 | New Hampshire | 33,174 | 0.3% |
| 16 | New Jersey | 207,208 | 2.0% |
| 35 | New Mexico | 86,754 | 0.9% |
| 4 | New York | 455,750 | 4.5% |
| 8 | North Carolina | 363,058 | 3.6% |
| 49 | North Dakota | 15,775 | 0.2% |
| 5 | Ohio | 394,478 | 3.9% |
| 26 | Oklahoma | 147,645 | 1.4% |
| 27 | Oregon | 135,376 | 1.3% |
| 9 | Pennsylvania | 320,999 | 3.2% |
| 44 | Rhode Island | 29,668 | 0.3% |
| 17 | South Carolina | 206,947 | 2.0% |
| 47 | South Dakota | 19,850 | 0.2% |
| 13 | Tennessee | 259,214 | 2.5% |
| 2 | Texas | 982,535 | 9.6% |
| 33 | Utah | 91,300 | 0.9% |
| 48 | Vermont | 15,909 | 0.2% |
| 18 | Virginia | 192,549 | 1.9% |
| 11 | Washington | 272,719 | 2.7% |
| 38 | West Virginia | 49,747 | 0.5% |
| 23 | Wisconsin | 156,577 | 1.5% |
| 50 | Wyoming | 14,383 | 0.1% |

RANK ORDER

| RANK | STATE | CRIMES | % of USA |
|------|-------|--------|----------|
| 1 | California | 1,210,409 | 11.9% |
| 2 | Texas | 982,535 | 9.6% |
| 3 | Florida | 727,075 | 7.1% |
| 4 | New York | 455,750 | 4.5% |
| 5 | Ohio | 394,478 | 3.9% |
| 6 | Illinois | 385,416 | 3.8% |
| 7 | Georgia | 375,920 | 3.7% |
| 8 | North Carolina | 363,058 | 3.6% |
| 9 | Pennsylvania | 320,999 | 3.2% |
| 10 | Michigan | 295,023 | 2.9% |
| 11 | Washington | 272,719 | 2.7% |
| 12 | Arizona | 260,038 | 2.6% |
| 13 | Tennessee | 259,214 | 2.5% |
| 14 | Missouri | 226,745 | 2.2% |
| 15 | Indiana | 220,634 | 2.2% |
| 16 | New Jersey | 207,208 | 2.0% |
| 17 | South Carolina | 206,947 | 2.0% |
| 18 | Virginia | 192,549 | 1.9% |
| 19 | Alabama | 190,571 | 1.9% |
| 20 | Maryland | 190,086 | 1.9% |
| 21 | Louisiana | 185,804 | 1.8% |
| 22 | Massachusetts | 170,042 | 1.7% |
| 23 | Wisconsin | 156,577 | 1.5% |
| 24 | Colorado | 155,293 | 1.5% |
| 25 | Minnesota | 150,571 | 1.5% |
| 26 | Oklahoma | 147,645 | 1.4% |
| 27 | Oregon | 135,376 | 1.3% |
| 28 | Arkansas | 121,776 | 1.2% |
| 29 | Kentucky | 121,578 | 1.2% |
| 30 | Kansas | 100,942 | 1.0% |
| 31 | Nevada | 94,273 | 0.9% |
| 32 | Mississippi | 91,692 | 0.9% |
| 33 | Utah | 91,300 | 0.9% |
| 34 | Connecticut | 86,994 | 0.9% |
| 35 | New Mexico | 86,754 | 0.9% |
| 36 | Iowa | 77,951 | 0.8% |
| 37 | Nebraska | 55,932 | 0.5% |
| 38 | West Virginia | 49,747 | 0.5% |
| 39 | Hawaii | 46,147 | 0.5% |
| 40 | Delaware | 35,659 | 0.3% |
| 41 | Maine | 34,992 | 0.3% |
| 42 | Idaho | 34,969 | 0.3% |
| 43 | New Hampshire | 33,174 | 0.3% |
| 44 | Rhode Island | 29,668 | 0.3% |
| 45 | Montana | 28,706 | 0.3% |
| 46 | Alaska | 24,449 | 0.2% |
| 47 | South Dakota | 19,850 | 0.2% |
| 48 | Vermont | 15,909 | 0.2% |
| 49 | North Dakota | 15,775 | 0.2% |
| 50 | Wyoming | 14,383 | 0.1% |
| | District of Columbia | 38,600 | 0.4% |

Source: CQ Press using reported data from the Federal Bureau of Investigation
"Crime in the United States 2012" (Uniform Crime Reports, September 16, 2013, http://www.fbi.gov/about-us/cjis/ucr/)
*Includes murder, rape, robbery, aggravated assault, burglary, larceny-theft, and motor vehicle theft.

# Crime Rate in 2012

## National Rate = 3,246.1 Crimes per 100,000 Population*

| ALPHA ORDER | | | | RANK ORDER | | |
|---|---|---|---|---|---|---|
| RANK | STATE | RATE | | RANK | STATE | RATE |
| 8 | Alabama | 3,952.1 | | 1 | South Carolina | 4,381.0 |
| 21 | Alaska | 3,342.6 | | 2 | New Mexico | 4,159.8 |
| 6 | Arizona | 3,968.1 | | 3 | Arkansas | 4,129.2 |
| 3 | Arkansas | 4,129.2 | | 4 | Louisiana | 4,037.5 |
| 25 | California | 3,181.8 | | 5 | Tennessee | 4,015.0 |
| 28 | Colorado | 2,993.6 | | 6 | Arizona | 3,968.1 |
| 44 | Connecticut | 2,423.0 | | 7 | Washington | 3,954.2 |
| 9 | Delaware | 3,888.3 | | 8 | Alabama | 3,952.1 |
| 14 | Florida | 3,763.8 | | 9 | Delaware | 3,888.3 |
| 11 | Georgia | 3,789.5 | | 10 | Oklahoma | 3,870.3 |
| 22 | Hawaii | 3,314.4 | | 11 | Georgia | 3,789.5 |
| 50 | Idaho | 2,191.4 | | 12 | Texas | 3,770.4 |
| 29 | Illinois | 2,993.5 | | 13 | Missouri | 3,765.3 |
| 20 | Indiana | 3,374.9 | | 14 | Florida | 3,763.8 |
| 40 | Iowa | 2,535.7 | | 15 | North Carolina | 3,722.9 |
| 16 | Kansas | 3,497.8 | | 16 | Kansas | 3,497.8 |
| 34 | Kentucky | 2,775.5 | | 17 | Oregon | 3,471.8 |
| 4 | Louisiana | 4,037.5 | | 18 | Ohio | 3,417.1 |
| 37 | Maine | 2,632.6 | | 19 | Nevada | 3,417.0 |
| 23 | Maryland | 3,230.3 | | 20 | Indiana | 3,374.9 |
| 38 | Massachusetts | 2,558.5 | | 21 | Alaska | 3,342.6 |
| 30 | Michigan | 2,985.0 | | 22 | Hawaii | 3,314.4 |
| 33 | Minnesota | 2,799.2 | | 23 | Maryland | 3,230.3 |
| 26 | Mississippi | 3,071.8 | | 24 | Utah | 3,197.6 |
| 13 | Missouri | 3,765.3 | | 25 | California | 3,181.8 |
| 31 | Montana | 2,855.9 | | 26 | Mississippi | 3,071.8 |
| 27 | Nebraska | 3,014.3 | | 27 | Nebraska | 3,014.3 |
| 19 | Nevada | 3,417.0 | | 28 | Colorado | 2,993.6 |
| 42 | New Hampshire | 2,511.9 | | 29 | Illinois | 2,993.5 |
| 47 | New Jersey | 2,337.5 | | 30 | Michigan | 2,985.0 |
| 2 | New Mexico | 4,159.8 | | 31 | Montana | 2,855.9 |
| 48 | New York | 2,328.8 | | 32 | Rhode Island | 2,824.7 |
| 15 | North Carolina | 3,722.9 | | 33 | Minnesota | 2,799.2 |
| 49 | North Dakota | 2,254.8 | | 34 | Kentucky | 2,775.5 |
| 18 | Ohio | 3,417.1 | | 35 | Wisconsin | 2,734.3 |
| 10 | Oklahoma | 3,870.3 | | 36 | West Virginia | 2,681.2 |
| 17 | Oregon | 3,471.8 | | 37 | Maine | 2,632.6 |
| 41 | Pennsylvania | 2,515.0 | | 38 | Massachusetts | 2,558.5 |
| 32 | Rhode Island | 2,824.7 | | 39 | Vermont | 2,541.3 |
| 1 | South Carolina | 4,381.0 | | 40 | Iowa | 2,535.7 |
| 45 | South Dakota | 2,381.9 | | 41 | Pennsylvania | 2,515.0 |
| 5 | Tennessee | 4,015.0 | | 42 | New Hampshire | 2,511.9 |
| 12 | Texas | 3,770.4 | | 43 | Wyoming | 2,495.2 |
| 24 | Utah | 3,197.6 | | 44 | Connecticut | 2,423.0 |
| 39 | Vermont | 2,541.3 | | 45 | South Dakota | 2,381.9 |
| 46 | Virginia | 2,352.2 | | 46 | Virginia | 2,352.2 |
| 7 | Washington | 3,954.2 | | 47 | New Jersey | 2,337.5 |
| 36 | West Virginia | 2,681.2 | | 48 | New York | 2,328.8 |
| 35 | Wisconsin | 2,734.3 | | 49 | North Dakota | 2,254.8 |
| 43 | Wyoming | 2,495.2 | | 50 | Idaho | 2,191.4 |
| | | | | | District of Columbia | 6,104.5 |

Source: CQ Press using reported data from the Federal Bureau of Investigation
   "Crime in the United States 2012" (Uniform Crime Reports, September 16, 2013, http://www.fbi.gov/about-us/cjis/ucr/)
*Includes murder, rape, robbery, aggravated assault, burglary, larceny-theft, and motor vehicle theft.

# Percent Change in Crime Rate: 2011 to 2012

## National Percent Change = 1.4% Decrease*

| ALPHA ORDER | | | | RANK ORDER | | |
|---|---|---|---|---|---|---|
| RANK | STATE | PERCENT CHANGE | | RANK | STATE | PERCENT CHANGE |
| 26 | Alabama | (1.8) | | 1 | South Dakota | 12.7 |
| 6 | Alaska | 2.9 | | 2 | West Virginia | 11.7 |
| 20 | Arizona | 0.0 | | 3 | Nevada | 8.7 |
| 27 | Arkansas | (2.6) | | 4 | Montana | 7.0 |
| 5 | California | 6.2 | | 5 | California | 6.2 |
| 6 | Colorado | 2.9 | | 6 | Alaska | 2.9 |
| 23 | Connecticut | (0.2) | | 6 | Colorado | 2.9 |
| 28 | Delaware | (2.7) | | 8 | North Dakota | 2.7 |
| 49 | Florida | (6.7) | | 9 | Oregon | 2.1 |
| 46 | Georgia | (5.6) | | 9 | Washington | 2.1 |
| 36 | Hawaii | (3.5) | | 11 | Kansas | 1.6 |
| 39 | Idaho | (3.8) | | 12 | Wisconsin | 1.3 |
| 36 | Illinois | (3.5) | | 13 | New Mexico | 1.2 |
| 35 | Indiana | (3.4) | | 14 | New York | 1.1 |
| 29 | Iowa | (2.8) | | 14 | Oklahoma | 1.1 |
| 11 | Kansas | 1.6 | | 16 | Minnesota | 0.8 |
| 47 | Kentucky | (6.4) | | 17 | Utah | 0.4 |
| 42 | Louisiana | (4.7) | | 18 | Wyoming | 0.2 |
| 25 | Maine | (1.4) | | 19 | Missouri | 0.1 |
| 38 | Maryland | (3.6) | | 20 | Arizona | 0.0 |
| 41 | Massachusetts | (4.5) | | 21 | Michigan | (0.1) |
| 21 | Michigan | (0.1) | | 21 | Nebraska | (0.1) |
| 16 | Minnesota | 0.8 | | 23 | Connecticut | (0.2) |
| 48 | Mississippi | (6.5) | | 24 | Vermont | (0.5) |
| 19 | Missouri | 0.1 | | 25 | Maine | (1.4) |
| 4 | Montana | 7.0 | | 26 | Alabama | (1.8) |
| 21 | Nebraska | (0.1) | | 27 | Arkansas | (2.6) |
| 3 | Nevada | 8.7 | | 28 | Delaware | (2.7) |
| 50 | New Hampshire | (7.1) | | 29 | Iowa | (2.8) |
| 43 | New Jersey | (4.8) | | 29 | Pennsylvania | (2.8) |
| 13 | New Mexico | 1.2 | | 31 | Rhode Island | (2.9) |
| 14 | New York | 1.1 | | 32 | South Carolina | (3.0) |
| 34 | North Carolina | (3.2) | | 33 | Texas | (3.1) |
| 8 | North Dakota | 2.7 | | 34 | North Carolina | (3.2) |
| 45 | Ohio | (5.2) | | 35 | Indiana | (3.4) |
| 14 | Oklahoma | 1.1 | | 36 | Hawaii | (3.5) |
| 9 | Oregon | 2.1 | | 36 | Illinois | (3.5) |
| 29 | Pennsylvania | (2.8) | | 38 | Maryland | (3.6) |
| 31 | Rhode Island | (2.9) | | 39 | Idaho | (3.8) |
| 32 | South Carolina | (3.0) | | 40 | Virginia | (4.2) |
| 1 | South Dakota | 12.7 | | 41 | Massachusetts | (4.5) |
| 43 | Tennessee | (4.8) | | 42 | Louisiana | (4.7) |
| 33 | Texas | (3.1) | | 43 | New Jersey | (4.8) |
| 17 | Utah | 0.4 | | 43 | Tennessee | (4.8) |
| 24 | Vermont | (0.5) | | 45 | Ohio | (5.2) |
| 40 | Virginia | (4.2) | | 46 | Georgia | (5.6) |
| 9 | Washington | 2.1 | | 47 | Kentucky | (6.4) |
| 2 | West Virginia | 11.7 | | 48 | Mississippi | (6.5) |
| 12 | Wisconsin | 1.3 | | 49 | Florida | (6.7) |
| 18 | Wyoming | 0.2 | | 50 | New Hampshire | (7.1) |

District of Columbia                 1.9

Source: CQ Press using reported data from the Federal Bureau of Investigation
   "Crime in the United States 2012" (Uniform Crime Reports, September 16, 2013, http://www.fbi.gov/about-us/cjis/ucr/)
*Includes murder, rape, robbery, aggravated assault, burglary, larceny-theft, and motor vehicle theft.

# Violent Crimes in 2012

## National Total = 1,214,464 Violent Crimes*

ALPHA ORDER

| RANK | STATE | CRIMES | % of USA |
|---|---|---|---|
| 20 | Alabama | 21,693 | 1.8% |
| 40 | Alaska | 4,412 | 0.4% |
| 12 | Arizona | 28,108 | 2.3% |
| 27 | Arkansas | 13,835 | 1.1% |
| 1 | California | 160,944 | 13.3% |
| 25 | Colorado | 16,023 | 1.3% |
| 31 | Connecticut | 10,160 | 0.8% |
| 38 | Delaware | 5,020 | 0.4% |
| 3 | Florida | 94,087 | 7.7% |
| 9 | Georgia | 37,591 | 3.1% |
| 41 | Hawaii | 3,330 | 0.3% |
| 42 | Idaho | 3,318 | 0.3% |
| 5 | Illinois | 53,403 | 4.4% |
| 19 | Indiana | 22,602 | 1.9% |
| 34 | Iowa | 8,112 | 0.7% |
| 30 | Kansas | 10,232 | 0.8% |
| 32 | Kentucky | 9,752 | 0.8% |
| 18 | Louisiana | 22,868 | 1.9% |
| 48 | Maine | 1,631 | 0.1% |
| 13 | Maryland | 28,055 | 2.3% |
| 15 | Massachusetts | 26,953 | 2.2% |
| 6 | Michigan | 44,922 | 3.7% |
| 28 | Minnesota | 12,419 | 1.0% |
| 35 | Mississippi | 7,786 | 0.6% |
| 14 | Missouri | 27,155 | 2.2% |
| 43 | Montana | 2,736 | 0.2% |
| 39 | Nebraska | 4,814 | 0.4% |
| 23 | Nevada | 16,763 | 1.4% |
| 46 | New Hampshire | 2,481 | 0.2% |
| 17 | New Jersey | 25,727 | 2.1% |
| 29 | New Mexico | 11,660 | 1.0% |
| 4 | New York | 79,610 | 6.6% |
| 11 | North Carolina | 34,464 | 2.8% |
| 47 | North Dakota | 1,712 | 0.1% |
| 10 | Ohio | 34,595 | 2.8% |
| 22 | Oklahoma | 17,902 | 1.5% |
| 33 | Oregon | 9,653 | 0.8% |
| 7 | Pennsylvania | 44,503 | 3.7% |
| 45 | Rhode Island | 2,651 | 0.2% |
| 16 | South Carolina | 26,397 | 2.2% |
| 44 | South Dakota | 2,682 | 0.2% |
| 8 | Tennessee | 41,550 | 3.4% |
| 2 | Texas | 106,476 | 8.8% |
| 36 | Utah | 5,876 | 0.5% |
| 50 | Vermont | 893 | 0.1% |
| 26 | Virginia | 15,564 | 1.3% |
| 21 | Washington | 20,386 | 1.7% |
| 37 | West Virginia | 5,869 | 0.5% |
| 24 | Wisconsin | 16,064 | 1.3% |
| 49 | Wyoming | 1,161 | 0.1% |

RANK ORDER

| RANK | STATE | CRIMES | % of USA |
|---|---|---|---|
| 1 | California | 160,944 | 13.3% |
| 2 | Texas | 106,476 | 8.8% |
| 3 | Florida | 94,087 | 7.7% |
| 4 | New York | 79,610 | 6.6% |
| 5 | Illinois | 53,403 | 4.4% |
| 6 | Michigan | 44,922 | 3.7% |
| 7 | Pennsylvania | 44,503 | 3.7% |
| 8 | Tennessee | 41,550 | 3.4% |
| 9 | Georgia | 37,591 | 3.1% |
| 10 | Ohio | 34,595 | 2.8% |
| 11 | North Carolina | 34,464 | 2.8% |
| 12 | Arizona | 28,108 | 2.3% |
| 13 | Maryland | 28,055 | 2.3% |
| 14 | Missouri | 27,155 | 2.2% |
| 15 | Massachusetts | 26,953 | 2.2% |
| 16 | South Carolina | 26,397 | 2.2% |
| 17 | New Jersey | 25,727 | 2.1% |
| 18 | Louisiana | 22,868 | 1.9% |
| 19 | Indiana | 22,602 | 1.9% |
| 20 | Alabama | 21,693 | 1.8% |
| 21 | Washington | 20,386 | 1.7% |
| 22 | Oklahoma | 17,902 | 1.5% |
| 23 | Nevada | 16,763 | 1.4% |
| 24 | Wisconsin | 16,064 | 1.3% |
| 25 | Colorado | 16,023 | 1.3% |
| 26 | Virginia | 15,564 | 1.3% |
| 27 | Arkansas | 13,835 | 1.1% |
| 28 | Minnesota | 12,419 | 1.0% |
| 29 | New Mexico | 11,660 | 1.0% |
| 30 | Kansas | 10,232 | 0.8% |
| 31 | Connecticut | 10,160 | 0.8% |
| 32 | Kentucky | 9,752 | 0.8% |
| 33 | Oregon | 9,653 | 0.8% |
| 34 | Iowa | 8,112 | 0.7% |
| 35 | Mississippi | 7,786 | 0.6% |
| 36 | Utah | 5,876 | 0.5% |
| 37 | West Virginia | 5,869 | 0.5% |
| 38 | Delaware | 5,020 | 0.4% |
| 39 | Nebraska | 4,814 | 0.4% |
| 40 | Alaska | 4,412 | 0.4% |
| 41 | Hawaii | 3,330 | 0.3% |
| 42 | Idaho | 3,318 | 0.3% |
| 43 | Montana | 2,736 | 0.2% |
| 44 | South Dakota | 2,682 | 0.2% |
| 45 | Rhode Island | 2,651 | 0.2% |
| 46 | New Hampshire | 2,481 | 0.2% |
| 47 | North Dakota | 1,712 | 0.1% |
| 48 | Maine | 1,631 | 0.1% |
| 49 | Wyoming | 1,161 | 0.1% |
| 50 | Vermont | 893 | 0.1% |
| | District of Columbia | 7,864 | 0.6% |

Source: Reported data from the Federal Bureau of Investigation
"Crime in the United States 2012" (Uniform Crime Reports, September 16, 2013, http://www.fbi.gov/about-us/cjis/ucr/)
*Violent crimes are offenses of murder, forcible rape, robbery, and aggravated assault.

# Violent Crime Rate in 2012

## National Rate = 386.9 Violent Crimes per 100,000 Population*

ALPHA ORDER

| RANK | STATE | RATE |
|------|-------|------|
| 14 | Alabama | 449.9 |
| 3 | Alaska | 603.2 |
| 15 | Arizona | 428.9 |
| 11 | Arkansas | 469.1 |
| 16 | California | 423.1 |
| 28 | Colorado | 308.9 |
| 32 | Connecticut | 283.0 |
| 6 | Delaware | 547.4 |
| 8 | Florida | 487.1 |
| 21 | Georgia | 378.9 |
| 41 | Hawaii | 239.2 |
| 44 | Idaho | 207.9 |
| 17 | Illinois | 414.8 |
| 25 | Indiana | 345.7 |
| 35 | Iowa | 263.9 |
| 22 | Kansas | 354.6 |
| 43 | Kentucky | 222.6 |
| 7 | Louisiana | 496.9 |
| 50 | Maine | 122.7 |
| 9 | Maryland | 476.8 |
| 20 | Massachusetts | 405.5 |
| 12 | Michigan | 454.5 |
| 42 | Minnesota | 230.9 |
| 36 | Mississippi | 260.8 |
| 13 | Missouri | 450.9 |
| 34 | Montana | 272.2 |
| 37 | Nebraska | 259.4 |
| 2 | Nevada | 607.6 |
| 48 | New Hampshire | 187.9 |
| 31 | New Jersey | 290.2 |
| 4 | New Mexico | 559.1 |
| 19 | New York | 406.8 |
| 23 | North Carolina | 353.4 |
| 40 | North Dakota | 244.7 |
| 29 | Ohio | 299.7 |
| 10 | Oklahoma | 469.3 |
| 39 | Oregon | 247.6 |
| 24 | Pennsylvania | 348.7 |
| 38 | Rhode Island | 252.4 |
| 5 | South Carolina | 558.8 |
| 26 | South Dakota | 321.8 |
| 1 | Tennessee | 643.6 |
| 18 | Texas | 408.6 |
| 45 | Utah | 205.8 |
| 49 | Vermont | 142.6 |
| 47 | Virginia | 190.1 |
| 30 | Washington | 295.6 |
| 27 | West Virginia | 316.3 |
| 33 | Wisconsin | 280.5 |
| 46 | Wyoming | 201.4 |

RANK ORDER

| RANK | STATE | RATE |
|------|-------|------|
| 1 | Tennessee | 643.6 |
| 2 | Nevada | 607.6 |
| 3 | Alaska | 603.2 |
| 4 | New Mexico | 559.1 |
| 5 | South Carolina | 558.8 |
| 6 | Delaware | 547.4 |
| 7 | Louisiana | 496.9 |
| 8 | Florida | 487.1 |
| 9 | Maryland | 476.8 |
| 10 | Oklahoma | 469.3 |
| 11 | Arkansas | 469.1 |
| 12 | Michigan | 454.5 |
| 13 | Missouri | 450.9 |
| 14 | Alabama | 449.9 |
| 15 | Arizona | 428.9 |
| 16 | California | 423.1 |
| 17 | Illinois | 414.8 |
| 18 | Texas | 408.6 |
| 19 | New York | 406.8 |
| 20 | Massachusetts | 405.5 |
| 21 | Georgia | 378.9 |
| 22 | Kansas | 354.6 |
| 23 | North Carolina | 353.4 |
| 24 | Pennsylvania | 348.7 |
| 25 | Indiana | 345.7 |
| 26 | South Dakota | 321.8 |
| 27 | West Virginia | 316.3 |
| 28 | Colorado | 308.9 |
| 29 | Ohio | 299.7 |
| 30 | Washington | 295.6 |
| 31 | New Jersey | 290.2 |
| 32 | Connecticut | 283.0 |
| 33 | Wisconsin | 280.5 |
| 34 | Montana | 272.2 |
| 35 | Iowa | 263.9 |
| 36 | Mississippi | 260.8 |
| 37 | Nebraska | 259.4 |
| 38 | Rhode Island | 252.4 |
| 39 | Oregon | 247.6 |
| 40 | North Dakota | 244.7 |
| 41 | Hawaii | 239.2 |
| 42 | Minnesota | 230.9 |
| 43 | Kentucky | 222.6 |
| 44 | Idaho | 207.9 |
| 45 | Utah | 205.8 |
| 46 | Wyoming | 201.4 |
| 47 | Virginia | 190.1 |
| 48 | New Hampshire | 187.9 |
| 49 | Vermont | 142.6 |
| 50 | Maine | 122.7 |

District of Columbia                1,243.7

Source: Reported data from the Federal Bureau of Investigation
"Crime in the United States 2012" (Uniform Crime Reports, September 16, 2013, http://www.fbi.gov/about-us/cjis/ucr/)
*Violent crimes are offenses of murder, forcible rape, robbery, and aggravated assault.

# Percent Change in Violent Crime Rate: 2011 to 2012

## National Percent Change = 0.0% Change*

| ALPHA ORDER | | | RANK ORDER | | |
|---|---|---|---|---|---|
| RANK | STATE | PERCENT CHANGE | RANK | STATE | PERCENT CHANGE |
| 3 | Alabama | 7.2 | 1 | South Dakota | 25.9 |
| 28 | Alaska | (1.1) | 2 | Wisconsin | 12.3 |
| 9 | Arizona | 3.5 | 3 | Alabama | 7.2 |
| 35 | Arkansas | (2.7) | 4 | Nevada | 7.0 |
| 10 | California | 2.9 | 5 | West Virginia | 6.7 |
| 31 | Colorado | (1.8) | 6 | Tennessee | 5.9 |
| 13 | Connecticut | 2.6 | 7 | Utah | 4.4 |
| 37 | Delaware | (3.4) | 8 | Indiana | 4.2 |
| 44 | Florida | (5.4) | 9 | Arizona | 3.5 |
| 20 | Georgia | 1.1 | 10 | California | 2.9 |
| 42 | Hawaii | (4.9) | 11 | Idaho | 2.8 |
| 11 | Idaho | 2.8 | 12 | Michigan | 2.7 |
| 33 | Illinois | (2.2) | 13 | Connecticut | 2.6 |
| 8 | Indiana | 4.2 | 13 | Iowa | 2.6 |
| 13 | Iowa | 2.6 | 13 | Oklahoma | 2.6 |
| 25 | Kansas | (0.3) | 16 | Rhode Island | 2.5 |
| 47 | Kentucky | (7.1) | 17 | New York | 2.4 |
| 49 | Louisiana | (10.4) | 18 | Nebraska | 2.3 |
| 26 | Maine | (0.5) | 19 | North Carolina | 2.1 |
| 37 | Maryland | (3.4) | 20 | Georgia | 1.1 |
| 43 | Massachusetts | (5.1) | 21 | Missouri | 0.8 |
| 12 | Michigan | 2.7 | 22 | Minnesota | 0.2 |
| 22 | Minnesota | 0.2 | 23 | Washington | 0.1 |
| 36 | Mississippi | (3.0) | 24 | Texas | 0.0 |
| 21 | Missouri | 0.8 | 25 | Kansas | (0.3) |
| 29 | Montana | (1.4) | 26 | Maine | (0.5) |
| 18 | Nebraska | 2.3 | 27 | Oregon | (0.7) |
| 4 | Nevada | 7.0 | 28 | Alaska | (1.1) |
| 50 | New Hampshire | (13.6) | 29 | Montana | (1.4) |
| 45 | New Jersey | (5.7) | 29 | North Dakota | (1.4) |
| 34 | New Mexico | (2.4) | 31 | Colorado | (1.8) |
| 17 | New York | 2.4 | 31 | Ohio | (1.8) |
| 19 | North Carolina | 2.1 | 33 | Illinois | (2.2) |
| 29 | North Dakota | (1.4) | 34 | New Mexico | (2.4) |
| 31 | Ohio | (1.8) | 35 | Arkansas | (2.7) |
| 13 | Oklahoma | 2.6 | 36 | Mississippi | (3.0) |
| 27 | Oregon | (0.7) | 37 | Delaware | (3.4) |
| 40 | Pennsylvania | (3.8) | 37 | Maryland | (3.4) |
| 16 | Rhode Island | 2.5 | 37 | Vermont | (3.4) |
| 46 | South Carolina | (6.4) | 40 | Pennsylvania | (3.8) |
| 1 | South Dakota | 25.9 | 40 | Virginia | (3.8) |
| 6 | Tennessee | 5.9 | 42 | Hawaii | (4.9) |
| 24 | Texas | 0.0 | 43 | Massachusetts | (5.1) |
| 7 | Utah | 4.4 | 44 | Florida | (5.4) |
| 37 | Vermont | (3.4) | 45 | New Jersey | (5.7) |
| 40 | Virginia | (3.8) | 46 | South Carolina | (6.4) |
| 23 | Washington | 0.1 | 47 | Kentucky | (7.1) |
| 5 | West Virginia | 6.7 | 48 | Wyoming | (8.2) |
| 2 | Wisconsin | 12.3 | 49 | Louisiana | (10.4) |
| 48 | Wyoming | (8.2) | 50 | New Hampshire | (13.6) |
| | | | | District of Columbia | 3.6 |

Source: Reported data from the Federal Bureau of Investigation
   "Crime in the United States 2012" (Uniform Crime Reports, September 16, 2013, http://www.fbi.gov/about-us/cjis/ucr/)
*Violent crimes are offenses of murder, forcible rape, robbery, and aggravated assault.

# Murders in 2012

## National Total = 14,827 Murders*

ALPHA ORDER

| RANK | STATE | MURDERS | % of USA |
|------|-------|---------|----------|
| 17 | Alabama | 342 | 2.3% |
| 41 | Alaska | 30 | 0.2% |
| 16 | Arizona | 358 | 2.4% |
| 25 | Arkansas | 173 | 1.2% |
| 1 | California | 1,884 | 12.7% |
| 27 | Colorado | 162 | 1.1% |
| 28 | Connecticut | 146 | 1.0% |
| 36 | Delaware | 57 | 0.4% |
| 3 | Florida | 1,009 | 6.8% |
| 8 | Georgia | 581 | 3.9% |
| 42 | Hawaii | 29 | 0.2% |
| 42 | Idaho | 29 | 0.2% |
| 4 | Illinois | 744 | 5.0% |
| 20 | Indiana | 310 | 2.1% |
| 39 | Iowa | 45 | 0.3% |
| 34 | Kansas | 84 | 0.6% |
| 24 | Kentucky | 195 | 1.3% |
| 9 | Louisiana | 495 | 3.3% |
| 46 | Maine | 25 | 0.2% |
| 15 | Maryland | 369 | 2.5% |
| 30 | Massachusetts | 121 | 0.8% |
| 5 | Michigan | 689 | 4.6% |
| 32 | Minnesota | 99 | 0.7% |
| 21 | Mississippi | 220 | 1.5% |
| 12 | Missouri | 389 | 2.6% |
| 45 | Montana | 27 | 0.2% |
| 37 | Nebraska | 53 | 0.4% |
| 29 | Nevada | 124 | 0.8% |
| 48 | New Hampshire | 15 | 0.1% |
| 13 | New Jersey | 388 | 2.6% |
| 31 | New Mexico | 116 | 0.8% |
| 7 | New York | 684 | 4.6% |
| 11 | North Carolina | 479 | 3.2% |
| 44 | North Dakota | 28 | 0.2% |
| 9 | Ohio | 495 | 3.3% |
| 22 | Oklahoma | 216 | 1.5% |
| 33 | Oregon | 92 | 0.6% |
| 6 | Pennsylvania | 685 | 4.6% |
| 40 | Rhode Island | 34 | 0.2% |
| 18 | South Carolina | 324 | 2.2% |
| 46 | South Dakota | 25 | 0.2% |
| 13 | Tennessee | 388 | 2.6% |
| 2 | Texas | 1,144 | 7.7% |
| 38 | Utah | 50 | 0.3% |
| 50 | Vermont | 8 | 0.1% |
| 19 | Virginia | 314 | 2.1% |
| 23 | Washington | 206 | 1.4% |
| 35 | West Virginia | 72 | 0.5% |
| 25 | Wisconsin | 173 | 1.2% |
| 49 | Wyoming | 14 | 0.1% |

RANK ORDER

| RANK | STATE | MURDERS | % of USA |
|------|-------|---------|----------|
| 1 | California | 1,884 | 12.7% |
| 2 | Texas | 1,144 | 7.7% |
| 3 | Florida | 1,009 | 6.8% |
| 4 | Illinois | 744 | 5.0% |
| 5 | Michigan | 689 | 4.6% |
| 6 | Pennsylvania | 685 | 4.6% |
| 7 | New York | 684 | 4.6% |
| 8 | Georgia | 581 | 3.9% |
| 9 | Louisiana | 495 | 3.3% |
| 9 | Ohio | 495 | 3.3% |
| 11 | North Carolina | 479 | 3.2% |
| 12 | Missouri | 389 | 2.6% |
| 13 | New Jersey | 388 | 2.6% |
| 13 | Tennessee | 388 | 2.6% |
| 15 | Maryland | 369 | 2.5% |
| 16 | Arizona | 358 | 2.4% |
| 17 | Alabama | 342 | 2.3% |
| 18 | South Carolina | 324 | 2.2% |
| 19 | Virginia | 314 | 2.1% |
| 20 | Indiana | 310 | 2.1% |
| 21 | Mississippi | 220 | 1.5% |
| 22 | Oklahoma | 216 | 1.5% |
| 23 | Washington | 206 | 1.4% |
| 24 | Kentucky | 195 | 1.3% |
| 25 | Arkansas | 173 | 1.2% |
| 25 | Wisconsin | 173 | 1.2% |
| 27 | Colorado | 162 | 1.1% |
| 28 | Connecticut | 146 | 1.0% |
| 29 | Nevada | 124 | 0.8% |
| 30 | Massachusetts | 121 | 0.8% |
| 31 | New Mexico | 116 | 0.8% |
| 32 | Minnesota | 99 | 0.7% |
| 33 | Oregon | 92 | 0.6% |
| 34 | Kansas | 84 | 0.6% |
| 35 | West Virginia | 72 | 0.5% |
| 36 | Delaware | 57 | 0.4% |
| 37 | Nebraska | 53 | 0.4% |
| 38 | Utah | 50 | 0.3% |
| 39 | Iowa | 45 | 0.3% |
| 40 | Rhode Island | 34 | 0.2% |
| 41 | Alaska | 30 | 0.2% |
| 42 | Hawaii | 29 | 0.2% |
| 42 | Idaho | 29 | 0.2% |
| 44 | North Dakota | 28 | 0.2% |
| 45 | Montana | 27 | 0.2% |
| 46 | Maine | 25 | 0.2% |
| 46 | South Dakota | 25 | 0.2% |
| 48 | New Hampshire | 15 | 0.1% |
| 49 | Wyoming | 14 | 0.1% |
| 50 | Vermont | 8 | 0.1% |
| | District of Columbia | 88 | 0.6% |

Source: Reported data from the Federal Bureau of Investigation
   "Crime in the United States 2012" (Uniform Crime Reports, September 16, 2013, http://www.fbi.gov/about-us/cjis/ucr/)
*Includes nonnegligent manslaughter.

# Murder Rate in 2012

## National Rate = 4.7 Murders per 100,000 Population*

| ALPHA ORDER | | | RANK ORDER | | |
|---|---|---|---|---|---|
| RANK | STATE | RATE | RANK | STATE | RATE |
| 3 | Alabama | 7.1 | 1 | Louisiana | 10.8 |
| 26 | Alaska | 4.1 | 2 | Mississippi | 7.4 |
| 15 | Arizona | 5.5 | 3 | Alabama | 7.1 |
| 10 | Arkansas | 5.9 | 4 | Michigan | 7.0 |
| 18 | California | 5.0 | 5 | South Carolina | 6.9 |
| 33 | Colorado | 3.1 | 6 | Missouri | 6.5 |
| 26 | Connecticut | 4.1 | 7 | Maryland | 6.3 |
| 8 | Delaware | 6.2 | 8 | Delaware | 6.2 |
| 17 | Florida | 5.2 | 9 | Tennessee | 6.0 |
| 10 | Georgia | 5.9 | 10 | Arkansas | 5.9 |
| 42 | Hawaii | 2.1 | 10 | Georgia | 5.9 |
| 44 | Idaho | 1.8 | 12 | Illinois | 5.8 |
| 12 | Illinois | 5.8 | 13 | Oklahoma | 5.7 |
| 20 | Indiana | 4.7 | 14 | New Mexico | 5.6 |
| 48 | Iowa | 1.5 | 15 | Arizona | 5.5 |
| 37 | Kansas | 2.9 | 16 | Pennsylvania | 5.4 |
| 21 | Kentucky | 4.5 | 17 | Florida | 5.2 |
| 1 | Louisiana | 10.8 | 18 | California | 5.0 |
| 43 | Maine | 1.9 | 19 | North Carolina | 4.9 |
| 7 | Maryland | 6.3 | 20 | Indiana | 4.7 |
| 44 | Massachusetts | 1.8 | 21 | Kentucky | 4.5 |
| 4 | Michigan | 7.0 | 21 | Nevada | 4.5 |
| 44 | Minnesota | 1.8 | 23 | New Jersey | 4.4 |
| 2 | Mississippi | 7.4 | 23 | Texas | 4.4 |
| 6 | Missouri | 6.5 | 25 | Ohio | 4.3 |
| 39 | Montana | 2.7 | 26 | Alaska | 4.1 |
| 37 | Nebraska | 2.9 | 26 | Connecticut | 4.1 |
| 21 | Nevada | 4.5 | 28 | North Dakota | 4.0 |
| 50 | New Hampshire | 1.1 | 29 | West Virginia | 3.9 |
| 23 | New Jersey | 4.4 | 30 | Virginia | 3.8 |
| 14 | New Mexico | 5.6 | 31 | New York | 3.5 |
| 31 | New York | 3.5 | 32 | Rhode Island | 3.2 |
| 19 | North Carolina | 4.9 | 33 | Colorado | 3.1 |
| 28 | North Dakota | 4.0 | 34 | South Dakota | 3.0 |
| 25 | Ohio | 4.3 | 34 | Washington | 3.0 |
| 13 | Oklahoma | 5.7 | 34 | Wisconsin | 3.0 |
| 40 | Oregon | 2.4 | 37 | Kansas | 2.9 |
| 16 | Pennsylvania | 5.4 | 37 | Nebraska | 2.9 |
| 32 | Rhode Island | 3.2 | 39 | Montana | 2.7 |
| 5 | South Carolina | 6.9 | 40 | Oregon | 2.4 |
| 34 | South Dakota | 3.0 | 40 | Wyoming | 2.4 |
| 9 | Tennessee | 6.0 | 42 | Hawaii | 2.1 |
| 23 | Texas | 4.4 | 43 | Maine | 1.9 |
| 44 | Utah | 1.8 | 44 | Idaho | 1.8 |
| 49 | Vermont | 1.3 | 44 | Massachusetts | 1.8 |
| 30 | Virginia | 3.8 | 44 | Minnesota | 1.8 |
| 34 | Washington | 3.0 | 44 | Utah | 1.8 |
| 29 | West Virginia | 3.9 | 48 | Iowa | 1.5 |
| 34 | Wisconsin | 3.0 | 49 | Vermont | 1.3 |
| 40 | Wyoming | 2.4 | 50 | New Hampshire | 1.1 |
| | | | | District of Columbia | 13.9 |

Source: Reported data from the Federal Bureau of Investigation
"Crime in the United States 2012" (Uniform Crime Reports, September 16, 2013, http://www.fbi.gov/about-us/cjis/ucr/)
*Includes nonnegligent manslaughter.

# Percent of Murders Involving Firearms in 2012

## National Percent = 69.3% of Murders*

| RANK | STATE | PERCENT |
| --- | --- | --- |
| NA | Alabama** | NA |
| 43 | Alaska | 37.9 |
| 20 | Arizona | 65.7 |
| 25 | Arkansas | 65.1 |
| 18 | California | 69.4 |
| 35 | Colorado | 57.5 |
| 5 | Connecticut | 76.7 |
| 13 | Delaware | 71.9 |
| NA | Florida** | NA |
| 12 | Georgia | 72.1 |
| NA | Hawaii** | NA |
| 23 | Idaho | 65.4 |
| 1 | Illinois* | 86.2 |
| 9 | Indiana | 74.5 |
| 36 | Iowa | 56.8 |
| 32 | Kansas | 59.5 |
| 28 | Kentucky | 63.5 |
| 2 | Louisiana | 81.3 |
| 37 | Maine | 56.0 |
| 7 | Maryland | 75.9 |
| 34 | Massachusetts | 57.9 |
| 4 | Michigan | 78.6 |
| 42 | Minnesota | 46.1 |
| 7 | Mississippi | 75.9 |
| 11 | Missouri | 72.8 |
| 41 | Montana | 50.0 |
| 3 | Nebraska | 80.8 |
| 30 | Nevada | 60.3 |
| 26 | New Hampshire | 64.3 |
| 15 | New Jersey | 70.9 |
| 29 | New Mexico | 61.5 |
| 31 | New York | 59.7 |
| 20 | North Carolina | 65.7 |
| 46 | North Dakota | 25.0 |
| 19 | Ohio | 67.8 |
| 16 | Oklahoma | 70.3 |
| 40 | Oregon | 51.9 |
| 6 | Pennsylvania | 76.3 |
| 38 | Rhode Island | 55.9 |
| 10 | South Carolina | 73.1 |
| 45 | South Dakota | 28.6 |
| 22 | Tennessee | 65.6 |
| 24 | Texas | 65.3 |
| 33 | Utah | 59.2 |
| 46 | Vermont | 25.0 |
| 17 | Virginia | 70.1 |
| 39 | Washington | 54.6 |
| 14 | West Virginia | 71.2 |
| 27 | Wisconsin | 63.9 |
| 44 | Wyoming | 35.7 |

| RANK | STATE | PERCENT |
| --- | --- | --- |
| 1 | Illinois* | 86.2 |
| 2 | Louisiana | 81.3 |
| 3 | Nebraska | 80.8 |
| 4 | Michigan | 78.6 |
| 5 | Connecticut | 76.7 |
| 6 | Pennsylvania | 76.3 |
| 7 | Maryland | 75.9 |
| 7 | Mississippi | 75.9 |
| 9 | Indiana | 74.5 |
| 10 | South Carolina | 73.1 |
| 11 | Missouri | 72.8 |
| 12 | Georgia | 72.1 |
| 13 | Delaware | 71.9 |
| 14 | West Virginia | 71.2 |
| 15 | New Jersey | 70.9 |
| 16 | Oklahoma | 70.3 |
| 17 | Virginia | 70.1 |
| 18 | California | 69.4 |
| 19 | Ohio | 67.8 |
| 20 | Arizona | 65.7 |
| 20 | North Carolina | 65.7 |
| 22 | Tennessee | 65.6 |
| 23 | Idaho | 65.4 |
| 24 | Texas | 65.3 |
| 25 | Arkansas | 65.1 |
| 26 | New Hampshire | 64.3 |
| 27 | Wisconsin | 63.9 |
| 28 | Kentucky | 63.5 |
| 29 | New Mexico | 61.5 |
| 30 | Nevada | 60.3 |
| 31 | New York | 59.7 |
| 32 | Kansas | 59.5 |
| 33 | Utah | 59.2 |
| 34 | Massachusetts | 57.9 |
| 35 | Colorado | 57.5 |
| 36 | Iowa | 56.8 |
| 37 | Maine | 56.0 |
| 38 | Rhode Island | 55.9 |
| 39 | Washington | 54.6 |
| 40 | Oregon | 51.9 |
| 41 | Montana | 50.0 |
| 42 | Minnesota | 46.1 |
| 43 | Alaska | 37.9 |
| 44 | Wyoming | 35.7 |
| 45 | South Dakota | 28.6 |
| 46 | North Dakota | 25.0 |
| 46 | Vermont | 25.0 |
| NA | Alabama** | NA |
| NA | Florida** | NA |
| NA | Hawaii** | NA |
| | District of Columbia** | NA |

Source: CQ Press using reported data from the Federal Bureau of Investigation
  "Crime in the United States 2012" (Uniform Crime Reports, September 16, 2013, http://www.fbi.gov/about-us/cjis/ucr/)
*Of the 12,711 murders in 2012 for which supplemental data were received by the F.B.I.  There were an additional 2,116 murders
for which the type of murder weapon was not reported to the F.B.I.  Includes nonnegligent manslaughter.  National and state
percents based on reporting jurisdictions only.  Illinois's percent is for Chicago and Rockford only.
**Not available.

# Rapes in 2012

## National Total = 84,376 Rapes*

| ALPHA ORDER | | | | | RANK ORDER | | | |
|---|---|---|---|---|---|---|---|---|
| RANK | STATE | RAPES | % of USA | | RANK | STATE | RAPES | % of USA |
| 22 | Alabama | 1,296 | 1.5% | | 1 | California | 7,837 | 9.3% |
| 39 | Alaska | 583 | 0.7% | | 2 | Texas | 7,711 | 9.1% |
| 9 | Arizona | 2,277 | 2.7% | | 3 | Florida | 5,260 | 6.2% |
| 24 | Arkansas | 1,247 | 1.5% | | 4 | Michigan | 4,589 | 5.4% |
| 1 | California | 7,837 | 9.3% | | 5 | Ohio | 3,658 | 4.3% |
| 12 | Colorado | 2,113 | 2.5% | | 6 | Illinois | 3,570 | 4.2% |
| 34 | Connecticut | 919 | 1.1% | | 7 | Pennsylvania | 3,327 | 3.9% |
| 48 | Delaware | 243 | 0.3% | | 8 | New York | 2,848 | 3.4% |
| 3 | Florida | 5,260 | 6.2% | | 9 | Arizona | 2,277 | 2.7% |
| 11 | Georgia | 2,124 | 2.5% | | 10 | Washington | 2,193 | 2.6% |
| 46 | Hawaii | 285 | 0.3% | | 11 | Georgia | 2,124 | 2.5% |
| 40 | Idaho | 479 | 0.6% | | 12 | Colorado | 2,113 | 2.5% |
| 6 | Illinois | 3,570 | 4.2% | | 13 | Tennessee | 2,032 | 2.4% |
| 16 | Indiana | 1,667 | 2.0% | | 14 | North Carolina | 1,984 | 2.4% |
| 35 | Iowa | 871 | 1.0% | | 15 | South Carolina | 1,679 | 2.0% |
| 29 | Kansas | 1,053 | 1.2% | | 16 | Indiana | 1,667 | 2.0% |
| 23 | Kentucky | 1,272 | 1.5% | | 17 | Massachusetts | 1,642 | 1.9% |
| 27 | Louisiana | 1,158 | 1.4% | | 18 | Minnesota | 1,638 | 1.9% |
| 44 | Maine | 372 | 0.4% | | 19 | Oklahoma | 1,588 | 1.9% |
| 25 | Maryland | 1,235 | 1.5% | | 20 | Missouri | 1,511 | 1.8% |
| 17 | Massachusetts | 1,642 | 1.9% | | 21 | Virginia | 1,452 | 1.7% |
| 4 | Michigan | 4,589 | 5.4% | | 22 | Alabama | 1,296 | 1.5% |
| 18 | Minnesota | 1,638 | 1.9% | | 23 | Kentucky | 1,272 | 1.5% |
| 36 | Mississippi | 822 | 1.0% | | 24 | Arkansas | 1,247 | 1.5% |
| 20 | Missouri | 1,511 | 1.8% | | 25 | Maryland | 1,235 | 1.5% |
| 43 | Montana | 379 | 0.4% | | 26 | Wisconsin | 1,219 | 1.4% |
| 37 | Nebraska | 711 | 0.8% | | 27 | Louisiana | 1,158 | 1.4% |
| 33 | Nevada | 931 | 1.1% | | 28 | Oregon | 1,140 | 1.4% |
| 41 | New Hampshire | 449 | 0.5% | | 29 | Kansas | 1,053 | 1.2% |
| 30 | New Jersey | 1,035 | 1.2% | | 30 | New Jersey | 1,035 | 1.2% |
| 31 | New Mexico | 957 | 1.1% | | 31 | New Mexico | 957 | 1.1% |
| 8 | New York | 2,848 | 3.4% | | 32 | Utah | 943 | 1.1% |
| 14 | North Carolina | 1,984 | 2.4% | | 33 | Nevada | 931 | 1.1% |
| 47 | North Dakota | 272 | 0.3% | | 34 | Connecticut | 919 | 1.1% |
| 5 | Ohio | 3,658 | 4.3% | | 35 | Iowa | 871 | 1.0% |
| 19 | Oklahoma | 1,588 | 1.9% | | 36 | Mississippi | 822 | 1.0% |
| 28 | Oregon | 1,140 | 1.4% | | 37 | Nebraska | 711 | 0.8% |
| 7 | Pennsylvania | 3,327 | 3.9% | | 38 | South Dakota | 585 | 0.7% |
| 45 | Rhode Island | 288 | 0.3% | | 39 | Alaska | 583 | 0.7% |
| 15 | South Carolina | 1,679 | 2.0% | | 40 | Idaho | 479 | 0.6% |
| 38 | South Dakota | 585 | 0.7% | | 41 | New Hampshire | 449 | 0.5% |
| 13 | Tennessee | 2,032 | 2.4% | | 42 | West Virginia | 421 | 0.5% |
| 2 | Texas | 7,711 | 9.1% | | 43 | Montana | 379 | 0.4% |
| 32 | Utah | 943 | 1.1% | | 44 | Maine | 372 | 0.4% |
| 50 | Vermont | 121 | 0.1% | | 45 | Rhode Island | 288 | 0.3% |
| 21 | Virginia | 1,452 | 1.7% | | 46 | Hawaii | 285 | 0.3% |
| 10 | Washington | 2,193 | 2.6% | | 47 | North Dakota | 272 | 0.3% |
| 42 | West Virginia | 421 | 0.5% | | 48 | Delaware | 243 | 0.3% |
| 26 | Wisconsin | 1,219 | 1.4% | | 49 | Wyoming | 154 | 0.2% |
| 49 | Wyoming | 154 | 0.2% | | 50 | Vermont | 121 | 0.1% |
| | | | | | | District of Columbia | 236 | 0.3% |

Source: Reported data from the Federal Bureau of Investigation
    "Crime in the United States 2012" (Uniform Crime Reports, September 16, 2013, http://www.fbi.gov/about-us/cjis/ucr/)
*Forcible rape is the carnal knowledge of a female forcibly and against her will.  Assaults or attempts to commit rape by force or threat of force are included.  However, statutory rape without force and other sex offenses are excluded.

# Rape Rate in 2012

## National Rate = 26.9 Rapes per 100,000 Population*

ALPHA ORDER

| RANK | STATE | RATE |
|---|---|---|
| 31 | Alabama | 26.9 |
| 1 | Alaska | 79.7 |
| 13 | Arizona | 34.7 |
| 5 | Arkansas | 42.3 |
| 44 | California | 20.6 |
| 7 | Colorado | 40.7 |
| 35 | Connecticut | 25.6 |
| 33 | Delaware | 26.5 |
| 30 | Florida | 27.2 |
| 41 | Georgia | 21.4 |
| 45 | Hawaii | 20.5 |
| 21 | Idaho | 30.0 |
| 27 | Illinois | 27.7 |
| 36 | Indiana | 25.5 |
| 25 | Iowa | 28.3 |
| 11 | Kansas | 36.5 |
| 24 | Kentucky | 29.0 |
| 37 | Louisiana | 25.2 |
| 26 | Maine | 28.0 |
| 43 | Maryland | 21.0 |
| 39 | Massachusetts | 24.7 |
| 3 | Michigan | 46.4 |
| 20 | Minnesota | 30.5 |
| 28 | Mississippi | 27.5 |
| 38 | Missouri | 25.1 |
| 10 | Montana | 37.7 |
| 9 | Nebraska | 38.3 |
| 15 | Nevada | 33.7 |
| 14 | New Hampshire | 34.0 |
| 50 | New Jersey | 11.7 |
| 4 | New Mexico | 45.9 |
| 49 | New York | 14.6 |
| 46 | North Carolina | 20.3 |
| 8 | North Dakota | 38.9 |
| 18 | Ohio | 31.7 |
| 6 | Oklahoma | 41.6 |
| 23 | Oregon | 29.2 |
| 34 | Pennsylvania | 26.1 |
| 29 | Rhode Island | 27.4 |
| 12 | South Carolina | 35.5 |
| 2 | South Dakota | 70.2 |
| 19 | Tennessee | 31.5 |
| 22 | Texas | 29.6 |
| 16 | Utah | 33.0 |
| 47 | Vermont | 19.3 |
| 48 | Virginia | 17.7 |
| 17 | Washington | 31.8 |
| 40 | West Virginia | 22.7 |
| 42 | Wisconsin | 21.3 |
| 32 | Wyoming | 26.7 |

RANK ORDER

| RANK | STATE | RATE |
|---|---|---|
| 1 | Alaska | 79.7 |
| 2 | South Dakota | 70.2 |
| 3 | Michigan | 46.4 |
| 4 | New Mexico | 45.9 |
| 5 | Arkansas | 42.3 |
| 6 | Oklahoma | 41.6 |
| 7 | Colorado | 40.7 |
| 8 | North Dakota | 38.9 |
| 9 | Nebraska | 38.3 |
| 10 | Montana | 37.7 |
| 11 | Kansas | 36.5 |
| 12 | South Carolina | 35.5 |
| 13 | Arizona | 34.7 |
| 14 | New Hampshire | 34.0 |
| 15 | Nevada | 33.7 |
| 16 | Utah | 33.0 |
| 17 | Washington | 31.8 |
| 18 | Ohio | 31.7 |
| 19 | Tennessee | 31.5 |
| 20 | Minnesota | 30.5 |
| 21 | Idaho | 30.0 |
| 22 | Texas | 29.6 |
| 23 | Oregon | 29.2 |
| 24 | Kentucky | 29.0 |
| 25 | Iowa | 28.3 |
| 26 | Maine | 28.0 |
| 27 | Illinois | 27.7 |
| 28 | Mississippi | 27.5 |
| 29 | Rhode Island | 27.4 |
| 30 | Florida | 27.2 |
| 31 | Alabama | 26.9 |
| 32 | Wyoming | 26.7 |
| 33 | Delaware | 26.5 |
| 34 | Pennsylvania | 26.1 |
| 35 | Connecticut | 25.6 |
| 36 | Indiana | 25.5 |
| 37 | Louisiana | 25.2 |
| 38 | Missouri | 25.1 |
| 39 | Massachusetts | 24.7 |
| 40 | West Virginia | 22.7 |
| 41 | Georgia | 21.4 |
| 42 | Wisconsin | 21.3 |
| 43 | Maryland | 21.0 |
| 44 | California | 20.6 |
| 45 | Hawaii | 20.5 |
| 46 | North Carolina | 20.3 |
| 47 | Vermont | 19.3 |
| 48 | Virginia | 17.7 |
| 49 | New York | 14.6 |
| 50 | New Jersey | 11.7 |

| District of Columbia | 37.3 |
|---|---|

Source: Reported data from the Federal Bureau of Investigation
"Crime in the United States 2012" (Uniform Crime Reports, September 16, 2013, http://www.fbi.gov/about-us/cjis/ucr/)
*Forcible rape is the carnal knowledge of a female forcibly and against her will. Assaults or attempts to commit rape by force or threat of force are included. However, statutory rape without force and other sex offenses are excluded.

# Robberies in 2012

## National Total = 354,522 Robberies*

ALPHA ORDER

| RANK | STATE | ROBBERIES | % of USA |
|---|---|---|---|
| 20 | Alabama | 5,020 | 1.4% |
| 42 | Alaska | 630 | 0.2% |
| 14 | Arizona | 7,386 | 2.1% |
| 31 | Arkansas | 2,320 | 0.7% |
| 1 | California | 56,521 | 15.9% |
| 28 | Colorado | 3,395 | 1.0% |
| 25 | Connecticut | 3,687 | 1.0% |
| 35 | Delaware | 1,492 | 0.4% |
| 4 | Florida | 23,889 | 6.7% |
| 8 | Georgia | 12,463 | 3.5% |
| 38 | Hawaii | 1,040 | 0.3% |
| 45 | Idaho | 243 | 0.1% |
| 5 | Illinois | 19,471 | 5.5% |
| 15 | Indiana | 6,598 | 1.9% |
| 39 | Iowa | 962 | 0.3% |
| 34 | Kansas | 1,500 | 0.4% |
| 26 | Kentucky | 3,535 | 1.0% |
| 19 | Louisiana | 5,475 | 1.5% |
| 44 | Maine | 423 | 0.1% |
| 11 | Maryland | 10,141 | 2.9% |
| 16 | Massachusetts | 6,552 | 1.8% |
| 10 | Michigan | 10,434 | 2.9% |
| 27 | Minnesota | 3,475 | 1.0% |
| 32 | Mississippi | 2,284 | 0.6% |
| 17 | Missouri | 5,782 | 1.6% |
| 46 | Montana | 191 | 0.1% |
| 36 | Nebraska | 1,130 | 0.3% |
| 21 | Nevada | 4,918 | 1.4% |
| 43 | New Hampshire | 472 | 0.1% |
| 9 | New Jersey | 11,385 | 3.2% |
| 33 | New Mexico | 1,847 | 0.5% |
| 3 | New York | 28,655 | 8.1% |
| 12 | North Carolina | 9,392 | 2.6% |
| 48 | North Dakota | 131 | 0.0% |
| 7 | Ohio | 15,235 | 4.3% |
| 29 | Oklahoma | 3,231 | 0.9% |
| 30 | Oregon | 2,413 | 0.7% |
| 6 | Pennsylvania | 15,673 | 4.4% |
| 41 | Rhode Island | 713 | 0.2% |
| 24 | South Carolina | 4,489 | 1.3% |
| 47 | South Dakota | 158 | 0.0% |
| 13 | Tennessee | 8,169 | 2.3% |
| 2 | Texas | 30,382 | 8.6% |
| 37 | Utah | 1,100 | 0.3% |
| 49 | Vermont | 112 | 0.0% |
| 22 | Virginia | 4,706 | 1.3% |
| 18 | Washington | 5,745 | 1.6% |
| 40 | West Virginia | 838 | 0.2% |
| 23 | Wisconsin | 4,622 | 1.3% |
| 50 | Wyoming | 61 | 0.0% |

RANK ORDER

| RANK | STATE | ROBBERIES | % of USA |
|---|---|---|---|
| 1 | California | 56,521 | 15.9% |
| 2 | Texas | 30,382 | 8.6% |
| 3 | New York | 28,655 | 8.1% |
| 4 | Florida | 23,889 | 6.7% |
| 5 | Illinois | 19,471 | 5.5% |
| 6 | Pennsylvania | 15,673 | 4.4% |
| 7 | Ohio | 15,235 | 4.3% |
| 8 | Georgia | 12,463 | 3.5% |
| 9 | New Jersey | 11,385 | 3.2% |
| 10 | Michigan | 10,434 | 2.9% |
| 11 | Maryland | 10,141 | 2.9% |
| 12 | North Carolina | 9,392 | 2.6% |
| 13 | Tennessee | 8,169 | 2.3% |
| 14 | Arizona | 7,386 | 2.1% |
| 15 | Indiana | 6,598 | 1.9% |
| 16 | Massachusetts | 6,552 | 1.8% |
| 17 | Missouri | 5,782 | 1.6% |
| 18 | Washington | 5,745 | 1.6% |
| 19 | Louisiana | 5,475 | 1.5% |
| 20 | Alabama | 5,020 | 1.4% |
| 21 | Nevada | 4,918 | 1.4% |
| 22 | Virginia | 4,706 | 1.3% |
| 23 | Wisconsin | 4,622 | 1.3% |
| 24 | South Carolina | 4,489 | 1.3% |
| 25 | Connecticut | 3,687 | 1.0% |
| 26 | Kentucky | 3,535 | 1.0% |
| 27 | Minnesota | 3,475 | 1.0% |
| 28 | Colorado | 3,395 | 1.0% |
| 29 | Oklahoma | 3,231 | 0.9% |
| 30 | Oregon | 2,413 | 0.7% |
| 31 | Arkansas | 2,320 | 0.7% |
| 32 | Mississippi | 2,284 | 0.6% |
| 33 | New Mexico | 1,847 | 0.5% |
| 34 | Kansas | 1,500 | 0.4% |
| 35 | Delaware | 1,492 | 0.4% |
| 36 | Nebraska | 1,130 | 0.3% |
| 37 | Utah | 1,100 | 0.3% |
| 38 | Hawaii | 1,040 | 0.3% |
| 39 | Iowa | 962 | 0.3% |
| 40 | West Virginia | 838 | 0.2% |
| 41 | Rhode Island | 713 | 0.2% |
| 42 | Alaska | 630 | 0.2% |
| 43 | New Hampshire | 472 | 0.1% |
| 44 | Maine | 423 | 0.1% |
| 45 | Idaho | 243 | 0.1% |
| 46 | Montana | 191 | 0.1% |
| 47 | South Dakota | 158 | 0.0% |
| 48 | North Dakota | 131 | 0.0% |
| 49 | Vermont | 112 | 0.0% |
| 50 | Wyoming | 61 | 0.0% |
|  | District of Columbia | 4,036 | 1.1% |

Source: Reported data from the Federal Bureau of Investigation
"Crime in the United States 2012" (Uniform Crime Reports, September 16, 2013, http://www.fbi.gov/about-us/cjis/ucr/)
*Robbery is the taking or attempting to take anything of value by force or threat of force.

# Robbery Rate in 2012

## National Rate = 112.9 Robberies per 100,000 Population*

| ALPHA ORDER | | | RANK ORDER | | |
|---|---|---|---|---|---|
| RANK | STATE | RATE | RANK | STATE | RATE |
| 17 | Alabama | 104.1 | 1 | Nevada | 178.3 |
| 25 | Alaska | 86.1 | 2 | Maryland | 172.3 |
| 15 | Arizona | 112.7 | 3 | Delaware | 162.7 |
| 30 | Arkansas | 78.7 | 4 | Illinois | 151.2 |
| 5 | California | 148.6 | 5 | California | 148.6 |
| 34 | Colorado | 65.4 | 6 | New York | 146.4 |
| 18 | Connecticut | 102.7 | 7 | Ohio | 132.0 |
| 3 | Delaware | 162.7 | 8 | New Jersey | 128.4 |
| 11 | Florida | 123.7 | 9 | Tennessee | 126.5 |
| 10 | Georgia | 125.6 | 10 | Georgia | 125.6 |
| 32 | Hawaii | 74.7 | 11 | Florida | 123.7 |
| 49 | Idaho | 15.2 | 12 | Pennsylvania | 122.8 |
| 4 | Illinois | 151.2 | 13 | Louisiana | 119.0 |
| 19 | Indiana | 100.9 | 14 | Texas | 116.6 |
| 44 | Iowa | 31.3 | 15 | Arizona | 112.7 |
| 39 | Kansas | 52.0 | 16 | Michigan | 105.6 |
| 28 | Kentucky | 80.7 | 17 | Alabama | 104.1 |
| 13 | Louisiana | 119.0 | 18 | Connecticut | 102.7 |
| 43 | Maine | 31.8 | 19 | Indiana | 100.9 |
| 2 | Maryland | 172.3 | 20 | Massachusetts | 98.6 |
| 20 | Massachusetts | 98.6 | 21 | North Carolina | 96.3 |
| 16 | Michigan | 105.6 | 22 | Missouri | 96.0 |
| 35 | Minnesota | 64.6 | 23 | South Carolina | 95.0 |
| 31 | Mississippi | 76.5 | 24 | New Mexico | 88.6 |
| 22 | Missouri | 96.0 | 25 | Alaska | 86.1 |
| 45 | Montana | 19.0 | 26 | Oklahoma | 84.7 |
| 37 | Nebraska | 60.9 | 27 | Washington | 83.3 |
| 1 | Nevada | 178.3 | 28 | Kentucky | 80.7 |
| 42 | New Hampshire | 35.7 | 28 | Wisconsin | 80.7 |
| 8 | New Jersey | 128.4 | 30 | Arkansas | 78.7 |
| 24 | New Mexico | 88.6 | 31 | Mississippi | 76.5 |
| 6 | New York | 146.4 | 32 | Hawaii | 74.7 |
| 21 | North Carolina | 96.3 | 33 | Rhode Island | 67.9 |
| 47 | North Dakota | 18.7 | 34 | Colorado | 65.4 |
| 7 | Ohio | 132.0 | 35 | Minnesota | 64.6 |
| 26 | Oklahoma | 84.7 | 36 | Oregon | 61.9 |
| 36 | Oregon | 61.9 | 37 | Nebraska | 60.9 |
| 12 | Pennsylvania | 122.8 | 38 | Virginia | 57.5 |
| 33 | Rhode Island | 67.9 | 39 | Kansas | 52.0 |
| 23 | South Carolina | 95.0 | 40 | West Virginia | 45.2 |
| 45 | South Dakota | 19.0 | 41 | Utah | 38.5 |
| 9 | Tennessee | 126.5 | 42 | New Hampshire | 35.7 |
| 14 | Texas | 116.6 | 43 | Maine | 31.8 |
| 41 | Utah | 38.5 | 44 | Iowa | 31.3 |
| 48 | Vermont | 17.9 | 45 | Montana | 19.0 |
| 38 | Virginia | 57.5 | 45 | South Dakota | 19.0 |
| 27 | Washington | 83.3 | 47 | North Dakota | 18.7 |
| 40 | West Virginia | 45.2 | 48 | Vermont | 17.9 |
| 28 | Wisconsin | 80.7 | 49 | Idaho | 15.2 |
| 50 | Wyoming | 10.6 | 50 | Wyoming | 10.6 |
| | | | | District of Columbia | 638.3 |

Source: Reported data from the Federal Bureau of Investigation
   "Crime in the United States 2012" (Uniform Crime Reports, September 16, 2013, http://www.fbi.gov/about-us/cjis/ucr/)
*Robbery is the taking or attempting to take anything of value by force or threat of force.

# Aggravated Assaults in 2012

## National Total = 760,739 Aggravated Assaults*

ALPHA ORDER

| RANK | STATE | ASSAULTS | % of USA |
|---|---|---|---|
| 18 | Alabama | 15,035 | 2.0% |
| 39 | Alaska | 3,169 | 0.4% |
| 14 | Arizona | 18,087 | 2.4% |
| 25 | Arkansas | 10,095 | 1.3% |
| 1 | California | 94,702 | 12.4% |
| 24 | Colorado | 10,353 | 1.4% |
| 33 | Connecticut | 5,408 | 0.7% |
| 38 | Delaware | 3,228 | 0.4% |
| 3 | Florida | 63,929 | 8.4% |
| 10 | Georgia | 22,423 | 2.9% |
| 43 | Hawaii | 1,976 | 0.3% |
| 41 | Idaho | 2,567 | 0.3% |
| 6 | Illinois | 29,618 | 3.9% |
| 19 | Indiana | 14,027 | 1.8% |
| 31 | Iowa | 6,234 | 0.8% |
| 29 | Kansas | 7,595 | 1.0% |
| 34 | Kentucky | 4,750 | 0.6% |
| 16 | Louisiana | 15,740 | 2.1% |
| 49 | Maine | 811 | 0.1% |
| 15 | Maryland | 16,310 | 2.1% |
| 13 | Massachusetts | 18,638 | 2.4% |
| 7 | Michigan | 29,210 | 3.8% |
| 30 | Minnesota | 7,207 | 0.9% |
| 36 | Mississippi | 4,460 | 0.6% |
| 12 | Missouri | 19,473 | 2.6% |
| 42 | Montana | 2,139 | 0.3% |
| 40 | Nebraska | 2,920 | 0.4% |
| 23 | Nevada | 10,790 | 1.4% |
| 46 | New Hampshire | 1,545 | 0.2% |
| 20 | New Jersey | 12,919 | 1.7% |
| 28 | New Mexico | 8,740 | 1.1% |
| 4 | New York | 47,423 | 6.2% |
| 9 | North Carolina | 22,609 | 3.0% |
| 47 | North Dakota | 1,281 | 0.2% |
| 17 | Ohio | 15,207 | 2.0% |
| 21 | Oklahoma | 12,867 | 1.7% |
| 32 | Oregon | 6,008 | 0.8% |
| 8 | Pennsylvania | 24,818 | 3.3% |
| 45 | Rhode Island | 1,616 | 0.2% |
| 11 | South Carolina | 19,905 | 2.6% |
| 44 | South Dakota | 1,914 | 0.3% |
| 5 | Tennessee | 30,961 | 4.1% |
| 2 | Texas | 67,239 | 8.8% |
| 37 | Utah | 3,783 | 0.5% |
| 50 | Vermont | 652 | 0.1% |
| 27 | Virginia | 9,092 | 1.2% |
| 22 | Washington | 12,242 | 1.6% |
| 35 | West Virginia | 4,538 | 0.6% |
| 26 | Wisconsin | 10,050 | 1.3% |
| 48 | Wyoming | 932 | 0.1% |

RANK ORDER

| RANK | STATE | ASSAULTS | % of USA |
|---|---|---|---|
| 1 | California | 94,702 | 12.4% |
| 2 | Texas | 67,239 | 8.8% |
| 3 | Florida | 63,929 | 8.4% |
| 4 | New York | 47,423 | 6.2% |
| 5 | Tennessee | 30,961 | 4.1% |
| 6 | Illinois | 29,618 | 3.9% |
| 7 | Michigan | 29,210 | 3.8% |
| 8 | Pennsylvania | 24,818 | 3.3% |
| 9 | North Carolina | 22,609 | 3.0% |
| 10 | Georgia | 22,423 | 2.9% |
| 11 | South Carolina | 19,905 | 2.6% |
| 12 | Missouri | 19,473 | 2.6% |
| 13 | Massachusetts | 18,638 | 2.4% |
| 14 | Arizona | 18,087 | 2.4% |
| 15 | Maryland | 16,310 | 2.1% |
| 16 | Louisiana | 15,740 | 2.1% |
| 17 | Ohio | 15,207 | 2.0% |
| 18 | Alabama | 15,035 | 2.0% |
| 19 | Indiana | 14,027 | 1.8% |
| 20 | New Jersey | 12,919 | 1.7% |
| 21 | Oklahoma | 12,867 | 1.7% |
| 22 | Washington | 12,242 | 1.6% |
| 23 | Nevada | 10,790 | 1.4% |
| 24 | Colorado | 10,353 | 1.4% |
| 25 | Arkansas | 10,095 | 1.3% |
| 26 | Wisconsin | 10,050 | 1.3% |
| 27 | Virginia | 9,092 | 1.2% |
| 28 | New Mexico | 8,740 | 1.1% |
| 29 | Kansas | 7,595 | 1.0% |
| 30 | Minnesota | 7,207 | 0.9% |
| 31 | Iowa | 6,234 | 0.8% |
| 32 | Oregon | 6,008 | 0.8% |
| 33 | Connecticut | 5,408 | 0.7% |
| 34 | Kentucky | 4,750 | 0.6% |
| 35 | West Virginia | 4,538 | 0.6% |
| 36 | Mississippi | 4,460 | 0.6% |
| 37 | Utah | 3,783 | 0.5% |
| 38 | Delaware | 3,228 | 0.4% |
| 39 | Alaska | 3,169 | 0.4% |
| 40 | Nebraska | 2,920 | 0.4% |
| 41 | Idaho | 2,567 | 0.3% |
| 42 | Montana | 2,139 | 0.3% |
| 43 | Hawaii | 1,976 | 0.3% |
| 44 | South Dakota | 1,914 | 0.3% |
| 45 | Rhode Island | 1,616 | 0.2% |
| 46 | New Hampshire | 1,545 | 0.2% |
| 47 | North Dakota | 1,281 | 0.2% |
| 48 | Wyoming | 932 | 0.1% |
| 49 | Maine | 811 | 0.1% |
| 50 | Vermont | 652 | 0.1% |
| | District of Columbia | 3,504 | 0.5% |

Source: Reported data from the Federal Bureau of Investigation
"Crime in the United States 2012" (Uniform Crime Reports, September 16, 2013, http://www.fbi.gov/about-us/cjis/ucr/)
*Aggravated assault is an attack for the purpose of inflicting severe bodily injury.

# Aggravated Assault Rate in 2012

## National Rate = 242.3 Aggravated Assaults per 100,000 Population*

| ALPHA ORDER | | | | RANK ORDER | | |
|---|---|---|---|---|---|---|
| RANK | STATE | RATE | | RANK | STATE | RATE |
| 12 | Alabama | 311.8 | | 1 | Tennessee | 479.6 |
| 2 | Alaska | 433.2 | | 2 | Alaska | 433.2 |
| 16 | Arizona | 276.0 | | 3 | South Carolina | 421.4 |
| 7 | Arkansas | 342.3 | | 4 | New Mexico | 419.1 |
| 19 | California | 248.9 | | 5 | Nevada | 391.1 |
| 29 | Colorado | 199.6 | | 6 | Delaware | 352.0 |
| 39 | Connecticut | 150.6 | | 7 | Arkansas | 342.3 |
| 6 | Delaware | 352.0 | | 8 | Louisiana | 342.0 |
| 10 | Florida | 330.9 | | 9 | Oklahoma | 337.3 |
| 25 | Georgia | 226.0 | | 10 | Florida | 330.9 |
| 42 | Hawaii | 141.9 | | 11 | Missouri | 323.4 |
| 35 | Idaho | 160.9 | | 12 | Alabama | 311.8 |
| 23 | Illinois | 230.0 | | 13 | Michigan | 295.5 |
| 26 | Indiana | 214.6 | | 14 | Massachusetts | 280.4 |
| 28 | Iowa | 202.8 | | 15 | Maryland | 277.2 |
| 17 | Kansas | 263.2 | | 16 | Arizona | 276.0 |
| 48 | Kentucky | 108.4 | | 17 | Kansas | 263.2 |
| 8 | Louisiana | 342.0 | | 18 | Texas | 258.0 |
| 50 | Maine | 61.0 | | 19 | California | 248.9 |
| 15 | Maryland | 277.2 | | 20 | West Virginia | 244.6 |
| 14 | Massachusetts | 280.4 | | 21 | New York | 242.3 |
| 13 | Michigan | 295.5 | | 22 | North Carolina | 231.8 |
| 43 | Minnesota | 134.0 | | 23 | Illinois | 230.0 |
| 40 | Mississippi | 149.4 | | 24 | South Dakota | 229.7 |
| 11 | Missouri | 323.4 | | 25 | Georgia | 226.0 |
| 27 | Montana | 212.8 | | 26 | Indiana | 214.6 |
| 36 | Nebraska | 157.4 | | 27 | Montana | 212.8 |
| 5 | Nevada | 391.1 | | 28 | Iowa | 202.8 |
| 46 | New Hampshire | 117.0 | | 29 | Colorado | 199.6 |
| 41 | New Jersey | 145.7 | | 30 | Pennsylvania | 194.4 |
| 4 | New Mexico | 419.1 | | 31 | North Dakota | 183.1 |
| 21 | New York | 242.3 | | 32 | Washington | 177.5 |
| 22 | North Carolina | 231.8 | | 33 | Wisconsin | 175.5 |
| 31 | North Dakota | 183.1 | | 34 | Wyoming | 161.7 |
| 45 | Ohio | 131.7 | | 35 | Idaho | 160.9 |
| 9 | Oklahoma | 337.3 | | 36 | Nebraska | 157.4 |
| 37 | Oregon | 154.1 | | 37 | Oregon | 154.1 |
| 30 | Pennsylvania | 194.4 | | 38 | Rhode Island | 153.9 |
| 38 | Rhode Island | 153.9 | | 39 | Connecticut | 150.6 |
| 3 | South Carolina | 421.4 | | 40 | Mississippi | 149.4 |
| 24 | South Dakota | 229.7 | | 41 | New Jersey | 145.7 |
| 1 | Tennessee | 479.6 | | 42 | Hawaii | 141.9 |
| 18 | Texas | 258.0 | | 43 | Minnesota | 134.0 |
| 44 | Utah | 132.5 | | 44 | Utah | 132.5 |
| 49 | Vermont | 104.2 | | 45 | Ohio | 131.7 |
| 47 | Virginia | 111.1 | | 46 | New Hampshire | 117.0 |
| 32 | Washington | 177.5 | | 47 | Virginia | 111.1 |
| 20 | West Virginia | 244.6 | | 48 | Kentucky | 108.4 |
| 33 | Wisconsin | 175.5 | | 49 | Vermont | 104.2 |
| 34 | Wyoming | 161.7 | | 50 | Maine | 61.0 |
| | | | | District of Columbia | | 554.1 |

Source: Reported data from the Federal Bureau of Investigation
"Crime in the United States 2012" (Uniform Crime Reports, September 16, 2013, http://www.fbi.gov/about-us/cjis/ucr/)
*Aggravated assault is an attack for the purpose of inflicting severe bodily injury.

# Property Crimes in 2012

## National Total = 8,975,438 Property Crimes*

| ALPHA ORDER | | | | | RANK ORDER | | | |
|---|---|---|---|---|---|---|---|---|
| RANK | STATE | CRIMES | % of USA | | RANK | STATE | CRIMES | % of USA |
| 19 | Alabama | 168,878 | 1.9% | | 1 | California | 1,049,465 | 11.7% |
| 46 | Alaska | 20,037 | 0.2% | | 2 | Texas | 876,059 | 9.8% |
| 12 | Arizona | 231,930 | 2.6% | | 3 | Florida | 632,988 | 7.1% |
| 29 | Arkansas | 107,941 | 1.2% | | 4 | New York | 376,140 | 4.2% |
| 1 | California | 1,049,465 | 11.7% | | 5 | Ohio | 359,883 | 4.0% |
| 24 | Colorado | 139,270 | 1.6% | | 6 | Georgia | 338,329 | 3.8% |
| 34 | Connecticut | 76,834 | 0.9% | | 7 | Illinois | 332,013 | 3.7% |
| 43 | Delaware | 30,639 | 0.3% | | 8 | North Carolina | 328,594 | 3.7% |
| 3 | Florida | 632,988 | 7.1% | | 9 | Pennsylvania | 276,496 | 3.1% |
| 6 | Georgia | 338,329 | 3.8% | | 10 | Washington | 252,333 | 2.8% |
| 39 | Hawaii | 42,817 | 0.5% | | 11 | Michigan | 250,101 | 2.8% |
| 41 | Idaho | 31,651 | 0.4% | | 12 | Arizona | 231,930 | 2.6% |
| 7 | Illinois | 332,013 | 3.7% | | 13 | Tennessee | 217,664 | 2.4% |
| 15 | Indiana | 198,032 | 2.2% | | 14 | Missouri | 199,590 | 2.2% |
| 36 | Iowa | 69,839 | 0.8% | | 15 | Indiana | 198,032 | 2.2% |
| 30 | Kansas | 90,710 | 1.0% | | 16 | New Jersey | 181,481 | 2.0% |
| 28 | Kentucky | 111,826 | 1.2% | | 17 | South Carolina | 180,550 | 2.0% |
| 20 | Louisiana | 162,936 | 1.8% | | 18 | Virginia | 176,985 | 2.0% |
| 40 | Maine | 33,361 | 0.4% | | 19 | Alabama | 168,878 | 1.9% |
| 21 | Maryland | 162,031 | 1.8% | | 20 | Louisiana | 162,936 | 1.8% |
| 22 | Massachusetts | 143,089 | 1.6% | | 21 | Maryland | 162,031 | 1.8% |
| 11 | Michigan | 250,101 | 2.8% | | 22 | Massachusetts | 143,089 | 1.6% |
| 25 | Minnesota | 138,152 | 1.5% | | 23 | Wisconsin | 140,513 | 1.6% |
| 32 | Mississippi | 83,906 | 0.9% | | 24 | Colorado | 139,270 | 1.6% |
| 14 | Missouri | 199,590 | 2.2% | | 25 | Minnesota | 138,152 | 1.5% |
| 45 | Montana | 25,970 | 0.3% | | 26 | Oklahoma | 129,743 | 1.4% |
| 37 | Nebraska | 51,118 | 0.6% | | 27 | Oregon | 125,723 | 1.4% |
| 33 | Nevada | 77,510 | 0.9% | | 28 | Kentucky | 111,826 | 1.2% |
| 42 | New Hampshire | 30,693 | 0.3% | | 29 | Arkansas | 107,941 | 1.2% |
| 16 | New Jersey | 181,481 | 2.0% | | 30 | Kansas | 90,710 | 1.0% |
| 35 | New Mexico | 75,094 | 0.8% | | 31 | Utah | 85,424 | 1.0% |
| 4 | New York | 376,140 | 4.2% | | 32 | Mississippi | 83,906 | 0.9% |
| 8 | North Carolina | 328,594 | 3.7% | | 33 | Nevada | 77,510 | 0.9% |
| 49 | North Dakota | 14,063 | 0.2% | | 34 | Connecticut | 76,834 | 0.9% |
| 5 | Ohio | 359,883 | 4.0% | | 35 | New Mexico | 75,094 | 0.8% |
| 26 | Oklahoma | 129,743 | 1.4% | | 36 | Iowa | 69,839 | 0.8% |
| 27 | Oregon | 125,723 | 1.4% | | 37 | Nebraska | 51,118 | 0.6% |
| 9 | Pennsylvania | 276,496 | 3.1% | | 38 | West Virginia | 43,878 | 0.5% |
| 44 | Rhode Island | 27,017 | 0.3% | | 39 | Hawaii | 42,817 | 0.5% |
| 17 | South Carolina | 180,550 | 2.0% | | 40 | Maine | 33,361 | 0.4% |
| 47 | South Dakota | 17,168 | 0.2% | | 41 | Idaho | 31,651 | 0.4% |
| 13 | Tennessee | 217,664 | 2.4% | | 42 | New Hampshire | 30,693 | 0.3% |
| 2 | Texas | 876,059 | 9.8% | | 43 | Delaware | 30,639 | 0.3% |
| 31 | Utah | 85,424 | 1.0% | | 44 | Rhode Island | 27,017 | 0.3% |
| 48 | Vermont | 15,016 | 0.2% | | 45 | Montana | 25,970 | 0.3% |
| 18 | Virginia | 176,985 | 2.0% | | 46 | Alaska | 20,037 | 0.2% |
| 10 | Washington | 252,333 | 2.8% | | 47 | South Dakota | 17,168 | 0.2% |
| 38 | West Virginia | 43,878 | 0.5% | | 48 | Vermont | 15,016 | 0.2% |
| 23 | Wisconsin | 140,513 | 1.6% | | 49 | North Dakota | 14,063 | 0.2% |
| 50 | Wyoming | 13,222 | 0.1% | | 50 | Wyoming | 13,222 | 0.1% |
| | | | | | | District of Columbia | 30,736 | 0.3% |

Source: Reported data from the Federal Bureau of Investigation
"Crime in the United States 2012" (Uniform Crime Reports, September 16, 2013, http://www.fbi.gov/about-us/cjis/ucr/)
*Property crimes are offenses of burglary, larceny-theft, and motor vehicle theft.

# Property Crime Rate in 2012

## National Rate = 2,859.2 Property Crimes per 100,000 Population*

| RANK | STATE (ALPHA ORDER) | RATE | | RANK | STATE (RANK ORDER) | RATE |
|---|---|---|---|---|---|---|
| 7 | Alabama | 3,502.2 | | 1 | South Carolina | 3,822.2 |
| 27 | Alaska | 2,739.4 | | 2 | Arkansas | 3,660.1 |
| 6 | Arizona | 3,539.2 | | 3 | Washington | 3,658.6 |
| 2 | Arkansas | 3,660.1 | | 4 | New Mexico | 3,600.7 |
| 24 | California | 2,758.7 | | 5 | Louisiana | 3,540.6 |
| 28 | Colorado | 2,684.7 | | 6 | Arizona | 3,539.2 |
| 45 | Connecticut | 2,140.0 | | 7 | Alabama | 3,502.2 |
| 13 | Delaware | 3,340.9 | | 8 | Georgia | 3,410.6 |
| 15 | Florida | 3,276.7 | | 9 | Oklahoma | 3,401.0 |
| 8 | Georgia | 3,410.6 | | 10 | Tennessee | 3,371.4 |
| 19 | Hawaii | 3,075.2 | | 11 | North Carolina | 3,369.5 |
| 49 | Idaho | 1,983.5 | | 12 | Texas | 3,361.8 |
| 30 | Illinois | 2,578.7 | | 13 | Delaware | 3,340.9 |
| 20 | Indiana | 3,029.2 | | 14 | Missouri | 3,314.4 |
| 41 | Iowa | 2,271.8 | | 15 | Florida | 3,276.7 |
| 17 | Kansas | 3,143.2 | | 16 | Oregon | 3,224.2 |
| 33 | Kentucky | 2,552.9 | | 17 | Kansas | 3,143.2 |
| 5 | Louisiana | 3,540.6 | | 18 | Ohio | 3,117.4 |
| 35 | Maine | 2,509.9 | | 19 | Hawaii | 3,075.2 |
| 26 | Maryland | 2,753.5 | | 20 | Indiana | 3,029.2 |
| 44 | Massachusetts | 2,153.0 | | 21 | Utah | 2,991.8 |
| 34 | Michigan | 2,530.5 | | 22 | Mississippi | 2,811.0 |
| 32 | Minnesota | 2,568.3 | | 23 | Nevada | 2,809.4 |
| 22 | Mississippi | 2,811.0 | | 24 | California | 2,758.7 |
| 14 | Missouri | 3,314.4 | | 25 | Nebraska | 2,754.9 |
| 29 | Montana | 2,583.7 | | 26 | Maryland | 2,753.5 |
| 25 | Nebraska | 2,754.9 | | 27 | Alaska | 2,739.4 |
| 23 | Nevada | 2,809.4 | | 28 | Colorado | 2,684.7 |
| 39 | New Hampshire | 2,324.0 | | 29 | Montana | 2,583.7 |
| 47 | New Jersey | 2,047.3 | | 30 | Illinois | 2,578.7 |
| 4 | New Mexico | 3,600.7 | | 31 | Rhode Island | 2,572.3 |
| 50 | New York | 1,922.0 | | 32 | Minnesota | 2,568.3 |
| 11 | North Carolina | 3,369.5 | | 33 | Kentucky | 2,552.9 |
| 48 | North Dakota | 2,010.1 | | 34 | Michigan | 2,530.5 |
| 18 | Ohio | 3,117.4 | | 35 | Maine | 2,509.9 |
| 9 | Oklahoma | 3,401.0 | | 36 | Wisconsin | 2,453.8 |
| 16 | Oregon | 3,224.2 | | 37 | Vermont | 2,398.7 |
| 42 | Pennsylvania | 2,166.3 | | 38 | West Virginia | 2,364.9 |
| 31 | Rhode Island | 2,572.3 | | 39 | New Hampshire | 2,324.0 |
| 1 | South Carolina | 3,822.2 | | 40 | Wyoming | 2,293.8 |
| 46 | South Dakota | 2,060.1 | | 41 | Iowa | 2,271.8 |
| 10 | Tennessee | 3,371.4 | | 42 | Pennsylvania | 2,166.3 |
| 12 | Texas | 3,361.8 | | 43 | Virginia | 2,162.1 |
| 21 | Utah | 2,991.8 | | 44 | Massachusetts | 2,153.0 |
| 37 | Vermont | 2,398.7 | | 45 | Connecticut | 2,140.0 |
| 43 | Virginia | 2,162.1 | | 46 | South Dakota | 2,060.1 |
| 3 | Washington | 3,658.6 | | 47 | New Jersey | 2,047.3 |
| 38 | West Virginia | 2,364.9 | | 48 | North Dakota | 2,010.1 |
| 36 | Wisconsin | 2,453.8 | | 49 | Idaho | 1,983.5 |
| 40 | Wyoming | 2,293.8 | | 50 | New York | 1,922.0 |
| | | | | | District of Columbia | 4,860.8 |

Source: Reported data from the Federal Bureau of Investigation
"Crime in the United States 2012" (Uniform Crime Reports, September 16, 2013, http://www.fbi.gov/about-us/cjis/ucr/)
*Property crimes are offenses of burglary, larceny-theft, and motor vehicle theft.

# Percent Change in Property Crime Rate: 2011 to 2012

## National Percent Change = 1.6% Decrease*

ALPHA ORDER

| RANK | STATE | PERCENT CHANGE |
|---|---|---|
| 30 | Alabama | (2.9) |
| 6 | Alaska | 3.8 |
| 21 | Arizona | (0.4) |
| 27 | Arkansas | (2.6) |
| 5 | California | 6.8 |
| 7 | Colorado | 3.4 |
| 23 | Connecticut | (0.6) |
| 27 | Delaware | (2.6) |
| 49 | Florida | (6.8) |
| 45 | Georgia | (6.3) |
| 31 | Hawaii | (3.4) |
| 41 | Idaho | (4.4) |
| 36 | Illinois | (3.7) |
| 39 | Indiana | (4.2) |
| 31 | Iowa | (3.4) |
| 11 | Kansas | 1.8 |
| 45 | Kentucky | (6.3) |
| 38 | Louisiana | (3.9) |
| 25 | Maine | (1.4) |
| 35 | Maryland | (3.6) |
| 41 | Massachusetts | (4.4) |
| 23 | Michigan | (0.6) |
| 14 | Minnesota | 0.8 |
| 49 | Mississippi | (6.8) |
| 19 | Missouri | 0.0 |
| 4 | Montana | 7.9 |
| 20 | Nebraska | (0.3) |
| 3 | Nevada | 9.1 |
| 47 | New Hampshire | (6.5) |
| 43 | New Jersey | (4.7) |
| 11 | New Mexico | 1.8 |
| 14 | New York | 0.8 |
| 36 | North Carolina | (3.7) |
| 8 | North Dakota | 3.2 |
| 44 | Ohio | (5.5) |
| 14 | Oklahoma | 0.8 |
| 9 | Oregon | 2.3 |
| 27 | Pennsylvania | (2.6) |
| 31 | Rhode Island | (3.4) |
| 26 | South Carolina | (2.5) |
| 2 | South Dakota | 10.9 |
| 48 | Tennessee | (6.6) |
| 34 | Texas | (3.5) |
| 17 | Utah | 0.1 |
| 21 | Vermont | (0.4) |
| 39 | Virginia | (4.2) |
| 10 | Washington | 2.2 |
| 1 | West Virginia | 12.5 |
| 17 | Wisconsin | 0.1 |
| 13 | Wyoming | 1.1 |

RANK ORDER

| RANK | STATE | PERCENT CHANGE |
|---|---|---|
| 1 | West Virginia | 12.5 |
| 2 | South Dakota | 10.9 |
| 3 | Nevada | 9.1 |
| 4 | Montana | 7.9 |
| 5 | California | 6.8 |
| 6 | Alaska | 3.8 |
| 7 | Colorado | 3.4 |
| 8 | North Dakota | 3.2 |
| 9 | Oregon | 2.3 |
| 10 | Washington | 2.2 |
| 11 | Kansas | 1.8 |
| 11 | New Mexico | 1.8 |
| 13 | Wyoming | 1.1 |
| 14 | Minnesota | 0.8 |
| 14 | New York | 0.8 |
| 14 | Oklahoma | 0.8 |
| 17 | Utah | 0.1 |
| 17 | Wisconsin | 0.1 |
| 19 | Missouri | 0.0 |
| 20 | Nebraska | (0.3) |
| 21 | Arizona | (0.4) |
| 21 | Vermont | (0.4) |
| 23 | Connecticut | (0.6) |
| 23 | Michigan | (0.6) |
| 25 | Maine | (1.4) |
| 26 | South Carolina | (2.5) |
| 27 | Arkansas | (2.6) |
| 27 | Delaware | (2.6) |
| 27 | Pennsylvania | (2.6) |
| 30 | Alabama | (2.9) |
| 31 | Hawaii | (3.4) |
| 31 | Iowa | (3.4) |
| 31 | Rhode Island | (3.4) |
| 34 | Texas | (3.5) |
| 35 | Maryland | (3.6) |
| 36 | Illinois | (3.7) |
| 36 | North Carolina | (3.7) |
| 38 | Louisiana | (3.9) |
| 39 | Indiana | (4.2) |
| 39 | Virginia | (4.2) |
| 41 | Idaho | (4.4) |
| 41 | Massachusetts | (4.4) |
| 43 | New Jersey | (4.7) |
| 44 | Ohio | (5.5) |
| 45 | Georgia | (6.3) |
| 45 | Kentucky | (6.3) |
| 47 | New Hampshire | (6.5) |
| 48 | Tennessee | (6.6) |
| 49 | Florida | (6.8) |
| 49 | Mississippi | (6.8) |

| | District of Columbia | 1.5 |
|---|---|---|

Source: Reported data from the Federal Bureau of Investigation
  "Crime in the United States 2012" (Uniform Crime Reports, September 16, 2013, http://www.fbi.gov/about-us/cjis/ucr/)
*Property crimes are offenses of burglary, larceny-theft, and motor vehicle theft.

# Burglaries in 2012

## National Total = 2,103,787 Burglaries*

ALPHA ORDER

| RANK | STATE | BURGLARIES | % of USA |
|------|-------|-----------|----------|
| 15 | Alabama | 47,481 | 2.3% |
| 48 | Alaska | 2,950 | 0.1% |
| 13 | Arizona | 52,934 | 2.5% |
| 23 | Arkansas | 31,890 | 1.5% |
| 1 | California | 245,767 | 11.7% |
| 28 | Colorado | 26,157 | 1.2% |
| 35 | Connecticut | 14,711 | 0.7% |
| 41 | Delaware | 7,371 | 0.4% |
| 3 | Florida | 153,563 | 7.3% |
| 6 | Georgia | 86,789 | 4.1% |
| 39 | Hawaii | 7,979 | 0.4% |
| 42 | Idaho | 7,186 | 0.3% |
| 7 | Illinois | 71,101 | 3.4% |
| 14 | Indiana | 47,612 | 2.3% |
| 34 | Iowa | 17,096 | 0.8% |
| 33 | Kansas | 18,767 | 0.9% |
| 24 | Kentucky | 29,587 | 1.4% |
| 19 | Louisiana | 42,140 | 2.0% |
| 40 | Maine | 7,461 | 0.4% |
| 22 | Maryland | 33,732 | 1.6% |
| 21 | Massachusetts | 34,540 | 1.6% |
| 8 | Michigan | 65,665 | 3.1% |
| 29 | Minnesota | 25,378 | 1.2% |
| 26 | Mississippi | 28,076 | 1.3% |
| 17 | Missouri | 42,466 | 2.0% |
| 46 | Montana | 3,894 | 0.2% |
| 38 | Nebraska | 8,735 | 0.4% |
| 30 | Nevada | 22,120 | 1.1% |
| 44 | New Hampshire | 5,444 | 0.3% |
| 18 | New Jersey | 42,338 | 2.0% |
| 32 | New Mexico | 21,384 | 1.0% |
| 9 | New York | 64,553 | 3.1% |
| 5 | North Carolina | 99,323 | 4.7% |
| 49 | North Dakota | 2,377 | 0.1% |
| 4 | Ohio | 103,421 | 4.9% |
| 20 | Oklahoma | 35,731 | 1.7% |
| 31 | Oregon | 21,901 | 1.0% |
| 11 | Pennsylvania | 56,859 | 2.7% |
| 43 | Rhode Island | 5,949 | 0.3% |
| 16 | South Carolina | 45,086 | 2.1% |
| 47 | South Dakota | 3,258 | 0.2% |
| 12 | Tennessee | 56,181 | 2.7% |
| 2 | Texas | 204,810 | 9.7% |
| 36 | Utah | 12,943 | 0.6% |
| 45 | Vermont | 3,965 | 0.2% |
| 25 | Virginia | 29,511 | 1.4% |
| 10 | Washington | 60,725 | 2.9% |
| 37 | West Virginia | 11,291 | 0.5% |
| 27 | Wisconsin | 27,945 | 1.3% |
| 50 | Wyoming | 2,125 | 0.1% |

RANK ORDER

| RANK | STATE | BURGLARIES | % of USA |
|------|-------|-----------|----------|
| 1 | California | 245,767 | 11.7% |
| 2 | Texas | 204,810 | 9.7% |
| 3 | Florida | 153,563 | 7.3% |
| 4 | Ohio | 103,421 | 4.9% |
| 5 | North Carolina | 99,323 | 4.7% |
| 6 | Georgia | 86,789 | 4.1% |
| 7 | Illinois | 71,101 | 3.4% |
| 8 | Michigan | 65,665 | 3.1% |
| 9 | New York | 64,553 | 3.1% |
| 10 | Washington | 60,725 | 2.9% |
| 11 | Pennsylvania | 56,859 | 2.7% |
| 12 | Tennessee | 56,181 | 2.7% |
| 13 | Arizona | 52,934 | 2.5% |
| 14 | Indiana | 47,612 | 2.3% |
| 15 | Alabama | 47,481 | 2.3% |
| 16 | South Carolina | 45,086 | 2.1% |
| 17 | Missouri | 42,466 | 2.0% |
| 18 | New Jersey | 42,338 | 2.0% |
| 19 | Louisiana | 42,140 | 2.0% |
| 20 | Oklahoma | 35,731 | 1.7% |
| 21 | Massachusetts | 34,540 | 1.6% |
| 22 | Maryland | 33,732 | 1.6% |
| 23 | Arkansas | 31,890 | 1.5% |
| 24 | Kentucky | 29,587 | 1.4% |
| 25 | Virginia | 29,511 | 1.4% |
| 26 | Mississippi | 28,076 | 1.3% |
| 27 | Wisconsin | 27,945 | 1.3% |
| 28 | Colorado | 26,157 | 1.2% |
| 29 | Minnesota | 25,378 | 1.2% |
| 30 | Nevada | 22,120 | 1.1% |
| 31 | Oregon | 21,901 | 1.0% |
| 32 | New Mexico | 21,384 | 1.0% |
| 33 | Kansas | 18,767 | 0.9% |
| 34 | Iowa | 17,096 | 0.8% |
| 35 | Connecticut | 14,711 | 0.7% |
| 36 | Utah | 12,943 | 0.6% |
| 37 | West Virginia | 11,291 | 0.5% |
| 38 | Nebraska | 8,735 | 0.4% |
| 39 | Hawaii | 7,979 | 0.4% |
| 40 | Maine | 7,461 | 0.4% |
| 41 | Delaware | 7,371 | 0.4% |
| 42 | Idaho | 7,186 | 0.3% |
| 43 | Rhode Island | 5,949 | 0.3% |
| 44 | New Hampshire | 5,444 | 0.3% |
| 45 | Vermont | 3,965 | 0.2% |
| 46 | Montana | 3,894 | 0.2% |
| 47 | South Dakota | 3,258 | 0.2% |
| 48 | Alaska | 2,950 | 0.1% |
| 49 | North Dakota | 2,377 | 0.1% |
| 50 | Wyoming | 2,125 | 0.1% |
| | District of Columbia | 3,519 | 0.2% |

Source: Reported data from the Federal Bureau of Investigation
   "Crime in the United States 2012" (Uniform Crime Reports, September 16, 2013, http://www.fbi.gov/about-us/cjis/ucr/)
*Burglary is the unlawful entry of a structure to commit a felony or theft.  Attempts are included.

# Burglary Rate in 2012

## National Rate = 670.2 Burglaries per 100,000 Population*

| ALPHA ORDER | | | RANK ORDER | | |
|---|---|---|---|---|---|
| RANK | STATE | RATE | RANK | STATE | RATE |
| 4 | Alabama | 984.7 | 1 | Arkansas | 1,081.3 |
| 44 | Alaska | 403.3 | 2 | New Mexico | 1,025.3 |
| 13 | Arizona | 807.8 | 3 | North Carolina | 1,018.5 |
| 1 | Arkansas | 1,081.3 | 4 | Alabama | 984.7 |
| 23 | California | 646.1 | 5 | South Carolina | 954.5 |
| 34 | Colorado | 504.2 | 6 | Mississippi | 940.6 |
| 43 | Connecticut | 409.7 | 7 | Oklahoma | 936.6 |
| 14 | Delaware | 803.7 | 8 | Louisiana | 915.7 |
| 16 | Florida | 794.9 | 9 | Ohio | 895.9 |
| 11 | Georgia | 874.9 | 10 | Washington | 880.5 |
| 27 | Hawaii | 573.1 | 11 | Georgia | 874.9 |
| 40 | Idaho | 450.3 | 12 | Tennessee | 870.2 |
| 32 | Illinois | 552.2 | 13 | Arizona | 807.8 |
| 18 | Indiana | 728.3 | 14 | Delaware | 803.7 |
| 31 | Iowa | 556.1 | 15 | Nevada | 801.8 |
| 22 | Kansas | 650.3 | 16 | Florida | 794.9 |
| 20 | Kentucky | 675.4 | 17 | Texas | 785.9 |
| 8 | Louisiana | 915.7 | 18 | Indiana | 728.3 |
| 30 | Maine | 561.3 | 19 | Missouri | 705.2 |
| 26 | Maryland | 573.2 | 20 | Kentucky | 675.4 |
| 33 | Massachusetts | 519.7 | 21 | Michigan | 664.4 |
| 21 | Michigan | 664.4 | 22 | Kansas | 650.3 |
| 37 | Minnesota | 471.8 | 23 | California | 646.1 |
| 6 | Mississippi | 940.6 | 24 | Vermont | 633.4 |
| 19 | Missouri | 705.2 | 25 | West Virginia | 608.5 |
| 46 | Montana | 387.4 | 26 | Maryland | 573.2 |
| 38 | Nebraska | 470.8 | 27 | Hawaii | 573.1 |
| 15 | Nevada | 801.8 | 28 | Rhode Island | 566.4 |
| 42 | New Hampshire | 412.2 | 29 | Oregon | 561.7 |
| 36 | New Jersey | 477.6 | 30 | Maine | 561.3 |
| 2 | New Mexico | 1,025.3 | 31 | Iowa | 556.1 |
| 50 | New York | 329.9 | 32 | Illinois | 552.2 |
| 3 | North Carolina | 1,018.5 | 33 | Massachusetts | 519.7 |
| 49 | North Dakota | 339.8 | 34 | Colorado | 504.2 |
| 9 | Ohio | 895.9 | 35 | Wisconsin | 488.0 |
| 7 | Oklahoma | 936.6 | 36 | New Jersey | 477.6 |
| 29 | Oregon | 561.7 | 37 | Minnesota | 471.8 |
| 41 | Pennsylvania | 445.5 | 38 | Nebraska | 470.8 |
| 28 | Rhode Island | 566.4 | 39 | Utah | 453.3 |
| 5 | South Carolina | 954.5 | 40 | Idaho | 450.3 |
| 45 | South Dakota | 391.0 | 41 | Pennsylvania | 445.5 |
| 12 | Tennessee | 870.2 | 42 | New Hampshire | 412.2 |
| 17 | Texas | 785.9 | 43 | Connecticut | 409.7 |
| 39 | Utah | 453.3 | 44 | Alaska | 403.3 |
| 24 | Vermont | 633.4 | 45 | South Dakota | 391.0 |
| 48 | Virginia | 360.5 | 46 | Montana | 387.4 |
| 10 | Washington | 880.5 | 47 | Wyoming | 368.7 |
| 25 | West Virginia | 608.5 | 48 | Virginia | 360.5 |
| 35 | Wisconsin | 488.0 | 49 | North Dakota | 339.8 |
| 47 | Wyoming | 368.7 | 50 | New York | 329.9 |
| | | | | District of Columbia | 556.5 |

Source: Reported data from the Federal Bureau of Investigation
"Crime in the United States 2012" (Uniform Crime Reports, September 16, 2013, http://www.fbi.gov/about-us/cjis/ucr/)
*Burglary is the unlawful entry of a structure to commit a felony or theft. Attempts are included.

# Larceny-Thefts in 2012

## National Total = 6,150,598 Larceny-Thefts*

| ALPHA ORDER | | | | | RANK ORDER | | | |
|---|---|---|---|---|---|---|---|---|
| RANK | STATE | THEFTS | % of USA | | RANK | STATE | THEFTS | % of USA |
| 21 | Alabama | 111,523 | 1.8% | | 1 | California | 635,090 | 10.3% |
| 46 | Alaska | 15,565 | 0.3% | | 2 | Texas | 606,253 | 9.9% |
| 11 | Arizona | 159,838 | 2.6% | | 3 | Florida | 442,095 | 7.2% |
| 29 | Arkansas | 70,327 | 1.1% | | 4 | New York | 294,239 | 4.8% |
| 1 | California | 635,090 | 10.3% | | 5 | Ohio | 236,950 | 3.9% |
| 24 | Colorado | 101,021 | 1.6% | | 6 | Illinois | 235,222 | 3.8% |
| 32 | Connecticut | 55,674 | 0.9% | | 7 | Georgia | 223,004 | 3.6% |
| 43 | Delaware | 21,832 | 0.4% | | 8 | North Carolina | 213,151 | 3.5% |
| 3 | Florida | 442,095 | 7.2% | | 9 | Pennsylvania | 204,609 | 3.3% |
| 7 | Georgia | 223,004 | 3.6% | | 10 | Washington | 165,206 | 2.7% |
| 38 | Hawaii | 31,233 | 0.5% | | 11 | Arizona | 159,838 | 2.6% |
| 42 | Idaho | 23,101 | 0.4% | | 12 | Michigan | 159,321 | 2.6% |
| 6 | Illinois | 235,222 | 3.8% | | 13 | Tennessee | 148,503 | 2.4% |
| 16 | Indiana | 136,759 | 2.2% | | 14 | Missouri | 140,816 | 2.3% |
| 34 | Iowa | 48,720 | 0.8% | | 15 | Virginia | 138,398 | 2.3% |
| 31 | Kansas | 65,165 | 1.1% | | 16 | Indiana | 136,759 | 2.2% |
| 28 | Kentucky | 75,571 | 1.2% | | 17 | New Jersey | 122,662 | 2.0% |
| 20 | Louisiana | 112,915 | 1.8% | | 18 | South Carolina | 122,263 | 2.0% |
| 40 | Maine | 24,905 | 0.4% | | 19 | Maryland | 113,274 | 1.8% |
| 19 | Maryland | 113,274 | 1.8% | | 20 | Louisiana | 112,915 | 1.8% |
| 25 | Massachusetts | 99,317 | 1.6% | | 21 | Alabama | 111,523 | 1.8% |
| 12 | Michigan | 159,321 | 2.6% | | 22 | Wisconsin | 104,352 | 1.7% |
| 23 | Minnesota | 104,316 | 1.7% | | 23 | Minnesota | 104,316 | 1.7% |
| 33 | Mississippi | 51,508 | 0.8% | | 24 | Colorado | 101,021 | 1.6% |
| 14 | Missouri | 140,816 | 2.3% | | 25 | Massachusetts | 99,317 | 1.6% |
| 44 | Montana | 20,387 | 0.3% | | 26 | Oregon | 93,619 | 1.5% |
| 37 | Nebraska | 38,236 | 0.6% | | 27 | Oklahoma | 82,448 | 1.3% |
| 36 | Nevada | 45,372 | 0.7% | | 28 | Kentucky | 75,571 | 1.2% |
| 41 | New Hampshire | 24,226 | 0.4% | | 29 | Arkansas | 70,327 | 1.1% |
| 17 | New Jersey | 122,662 | 2.0% | | 30 | Utah | 66,482 | 1.1% |
| 35 | New Mexico | 48,247 | 0.8% | | 31 | Kansas | 65,165 | 1.1% |
| 4 | New York | 294,239 | 4.8% | | 32 | Connecticut | 55,674 | 0.9% |
| 8 | North Carolina | 213,151 | 3.5% | | 33 | Mississippi | 51,508 | 0.8% |
| 49 | North Dakota | 10,535 | 0.2% | | 34 | Iowa | 48,720 | 0.8% |
| 5 | Ohio | 236,950 | 3.9% | | 35 | New Mexico | 48,247 | 0.8% |
| 27 | Oklahoma | 82,448 | 1.3% | | 36 | Nevada | 45,372 | 0.7% |
| 26 | Oregon | 93,619 | 1.5% | | 37 | Nebraska | 38,236 | 0.6% |
| 9 | Pennsylvania | 204,609 | 3.3% | | 38 | Hawaii | 31,233 | 0.5% |
| 45 | Rhode Island | 18,440 | 0.3% | | 39 | West Virginia | 30,378 | 0.5% |
| 18 | South Carolina | 122,263 | 2.0% | | 40 | Maine | 24,905 | 0.4% |
| 47 | South Dakota | 12,845 | 0.2% | | 41 | New Hampshire | 24,226 | 0.4% |
| 13 | Tennessee | 148,503 | 2.4% | | 42 | Idaho | 23,101 | 0.4% |
| 2 | Texas | 606,253 | 9.9% | | 43 | Delaware | 21,832 | 0.4% |
| 30 | Utah | 66,482 | 1.1% | | 44 | Montana | 20,387 | 0.3% |
| 48 | Vermont | 10,616 | 0.2% | | 45 | Rhode Island | 18,440 | 0.3% |
| 15 | Virginia | 138,398 | 2.3% | | 46 | Alaska | 15,565 | 0.3% |
| 10 | Washington | 165,206 | 2.7% | | 47 | South Dakota | 12,845 | 0.2% |
| 39 | West Virginia | 30,378 | 0.5% | | 48 | Vermont | 10,616 | 0.2% |
| 22 | Wisconsin | 104,352 | 1.7% | | 49 | North Dakota | 10,535 | 0.2% |
| 50 | Wyoming | 10,513 | 0.2% | | 50 | Wyoming | 10,513 | 0.2% |
| | | | | | | District of Columbia | 23,556 | 0.4% |

Source: Reported data from the Federal Bureau of Investigation
    "Crime in the United States 2012" (Uniform Crime Reports, September 16, 2013, http://www.fbi.gov/about-us/cjis/ucr/)
*Larceny-theft is the unlawful taking of property without use of force, violence, or fraud. Attempts are included. Motor vehicle thefts are excluded.

# Larceny-Theft Rate in 2012

## National Rate = 1,959.3 Larceny-Thefts per 100,000 Population*

| ALPHA ORDER | | | RANK ORDER | | |
|---|---|---|---|---|---|
| RANK | STATE | RATE | RANK | STATE | RATE |
| 12 | Alabama | 2,312.8 | 1 | South Carolina | 2,588.3 |
| 20 | Alaska | 2,128.0 | 2 | Louisiana | 2,453.7 |
| 3 | Arizona | 2,439.1 | 3 | Arizona | 2,439.1 |
| 6 | Arkansas | 2,384.7 | 4 | Oregon | 2,400.9 |
| 38 | California | 1,669.5 | 5 | Washington | 2,395.3 |
| 25 | Colorado | 1,947.4 | 6 | Arkansas | 2,384.7 |
| 44 | Connecticut | 1,550.7 | 7 | Delaware | 2,380.6 |
| 7 | Delaware | 2,380.6 | 8 | Missouri | 2,338.4 |
| 14 | Florida | 2,288.6 | 9 | Utah | 2,328.4 |
| 16 | Georgia | 2,248.0 | 10 | Texas | 2,326.4 |
| 17 | Hawaii | 2,243.2 | 11 | New Mexico | 2,313.4 |
| 49 | Idaho | 1,447.7 | 12 | Alabama | 2,312.8 |
| 30 | Illinois | 1,826.9 | 13 | Tennessee | 2,300.1 |
| 21 | Indiana | 2,092.0 | 14 | Florida | 2,288.6 |
| 43 | Iowa | 1,584.8 | 15 | Kansas | 2,258.0 |
| 15 | Kansas | 2,258.0 | 16 | Georgia | 2,248.0 |
| 35 | Kentucky | 1,725.2 | 17 | Hawaii | 2,243.2 |
| 2 | Louisiana | 2,453.7 | 18 | North Carolina | 2,185.7 |
| 28 | Maine | 1,873.7 | 19 | Oklahoma | 2,161.3 |
| 27 | Maryland | 1,924.9 | 20 | Alaska | 2,128.0 |
| 48 | Massachusetts | 1,494.4 | 21 | Indiana | 2,092.0 |
| 41 | Michigan | 1,612.0 | 22 | Nebraska | 2,060.7 |
| 26 | Minnesota | 1,939.3 | 23 | Ohio | 2,052.5 |
| 34 | Mississippi | 1,725.6 | 24 | Montana | 2,028.3 |
| 8 | Missouri | 2,338.4 | 25 | Colorado | 1,947.4 |
| 24 | Montana | 2,028.3 | 26 | Minnesota | 1,939.3 |
| 22 | Nebraska | 2,060.7 | 27 | Maryland | 1,924.9 |
| 39 | Nevada | 1,644.6 | 28 | Maine | 1,873.7 |
| 29 | New Hampshire | 1,834.3 | 29 | New Hampshire | 1,834.3 |
| 50 | New Jersey | 1,383.7 | 30 | Illinois | 1,826.9 |
| 11 | New Mexico | 2,313.4 | 31 | Wyoming | 1,823.9 |
| 47 | New York | 1,503.5 | 32 | Wisconsin | 1,822.3 |
| 18 | North Carolina | 2,185.7 | 33 | Rhode Island | 1,755.7 |
| 46 | North Dakota | 1,505.8 | 34 | Mississippi | 1,725.6 |
| 23 | Ohio | 2,052.5 | 35 | Kentucky | 1,725.2 |
| 19 | Oklahoma | 2,161.3 | 36 | Vermont | 1,695.8 |
| 4 | Oregon | 2,400.9 | 37 | Virginia | 1,690.7 |
| 42 | Pennsylvania | 1,603.1 | 38 | California | 1,669.5 |
| 33 | Rhode Island | 1,755.7 | 39 | Nevada | 1,644.6 |
| 1 | South Carolina | 2,588.3 | 40 | West Virginia | 1,637.3 |
| 45 | South Dakota | 1,541.4 | 41 | Michigan | 1,612.0 |
| 13 | Tennessee | 2,300.1 | 42 | Pennsylvania | 1,603.1 |
| 10 | Texas | 2,326.4 | 43 | Iowa | 1,584.8 |
| 9 | Utah | 2,328.4 | 44 | Connecticut | 1,550.7 |
| 36 | Vermont | 1,695.8 | 45 | South Dakota | 1,541.4 |
| 37 | Virginia | 1,690.7 | 46 | North Dakota | 1,505.8 |
| 5 | Washington | 2,395.3 | 47 | New York | 1,503.5 |
| 40 | West Virginia | 1,637.3 | 48 | Massachusetts | 1,494.4 |
| 32 | Wisconsin | 1,822.3 | 49 | Idaho | 1,447.7 |
| 31 | Wyoming | 1,823.9 | 50 | New Jersey | 1,383.7 |
| | | | | District of Columbia | 3,725.3 |

Source: Reported data from the Federal Bureau of Investigation
"Crime in the United States 2012" (Uniform Crime Reports, September 16, 2013, http://www.fbi.gov/about-us/cjis/ucr/)
*Larceny-theft is the unlawful taking of property without use of force, violence, or fraud. Attempts are included. Motor vehicle thefts are excluded.

# Motor Vehicle Thefts in 2012

## National Total = 721,053 Motor Vehicle Thefts*

| ALPHA ORDER | | | | | RANK ORDER | | | |
|---|---|---|---|---|---|---|---|---|
| RANK | STATE | | THEFTS | % of USA | RANK | STATE | THEFTS | % of USA |
| 23 | Alabama | | 9,874 | 1.4% | 1 | California | 168,608 | 23.4% |
| 42 | Alaska | | 1,522 | 0.2% | 2 | Texas | 64,996 | 9.0% |
| 9 | Arizona | | 19,158 | 2.7% | 3 | Florida | 37,330 | 5.2% |
| 33 | Arkansas | | 5,724 | 0.8% | 4 | Georgia | 28,536 | 4.0% |
| 1 | California | | 168,608 | 23.4% | 5 | Washington | 26,402 | 3.7% |
| 19 | Colorado | | 12,092 | 1.7% | 6 | Illinois | 25,690 | 3.6% |
| 31 | Connecticut | | 6,449 | 0.9% | 7 | Michigan | 25,115 | 3.5% |
| 43 | Delaware | | 1,436 | 0.2% | 8 | Ohio | 19,512 | 2.7% |
| 3 | Florida | | 37,330 | 5.2% | 9 | Arizona | 19,158 | 2.7% |
| 4 | Georgia | | 28,536 | 4.0% | 10 | New York | 17,348 | 2.4% |
| 38 | Hawaii | | 3,605 | 0.5% | 11 | New Jersey | 16,481 | 2.3% |
| 44 | Idaho | | 1,364 | 0.2% | 12 | Missouri | 16,308 | 2.3% |
| 6 | Illinois | | 25,690 | 3.6% | 13 | North Carolina | 16,120 | 2.2% |
| 16 | Indiana | | 13,661 | 1.9% | 14 | Pennsylvania | 15,028 | 2.1% |
| 37 | Iowa | | 4,023 | 0.6% | 15 | Maryland | 15,025 | 2.1% |
| 29 | Kansas | | 6,778 | 0.9% | 16 | Indiana | 13,661 | 1.9% |
| 30 | Kentucky | | 6,668 | 0.9% | 17 | South Carolina | 13,201 | 1.8% |
| 28 | Louisiana | | 7,881 | 1.1% | 18 | Tennessee | 12,980 | 1.8% |
| 48 | Maine | | 995 | 0.1% | 19 | Colorado | 12,092 | 1.7% |
| 15 | Maryland | | 15,025 | 2.1% | 20 | Oklahoma | 11,564 | 1.6% |
| 24 | Massachusetts | | 9,232 | 1.3% | 21 | Oregon | 10,203 | 1.4% |
| 7 | Michigan | | 25,115 | 3.5% | 22 | Nevada | 10,018 | 1.4% |
| 26 | Minnesota | | 8,458 | 1.2% | 23 | Alabama | 9,874 | 1.4% |
| 35 | Mississippi | | 4,322 | 0.6% | 24 | Massachusetts | 9,232 | 1.3% |
| 12 | Missouri | | 16,308 | 2.3% | 25 | Virginia | 9,076 | 1.3% |
| 41 | Montana | | 1,689 | 0.2% | 26 | Minnesota | 8,458 | 1.2% |
| 36 | Nebraska | | 4,147 | 0.6% | 27 | Wisconsin | 8,216 | 1.1% |
| 22 | Nevada | | 10,018 | 1.4% | 28 | Louisiana | 7,881 | 1.1% |
| 47 | New Hampshire | | 1,023 | 0.1% | 29 | Kansas | 6,778 | 0.9% |
| 11 | New Jersey | | 16,481 | 2.3% | 30 | Kentucky | 6,668 | 0.9% |
| 34 | New Mexico | | 5,463 | 0.8% | 31 | Connecticut | 6,449 | 0.9% |
| 10 | New York | | 17,348 | 2.4% | 32 | Utah | 5,999 | 0.8% |
| 13 | North Carolina | | 16,120 | 2.2% | 33 | Arkansas | 5,724 | 0.8% |
| 45 | North Dakota | | 1,151 | 0.2% | 34 | New Mexico | 5,463 | 0.8% |
| 8 | Ohio | | 19,512 | 2.7% | 35 | Mississippi | 4,322 | 0.6% |
| 20 | Oklahoma | | 11,564 | 1.6% | 36 | Nebraska | 4,147 | 0.6% |
| 21 | Oregon | | 10,203 | 1.4% | 37 | Iowa | 4,023 | 0.6% |
| 14 | Pennsylvania | | 15,028 | 2.1% | 38 | Hawaii | 3,605 | 0.5% |
| 39 | Rhode Island | | 2,628 | 0.4% | 39 | Rhode Island | 2,628 | 0.4% |
| 17 | South Carolina | | 13,201 | 1.8% | 40 | West Virginia | 2,209 | 0.3% |
| 46 | South Dakota | | 1,065 | 0.1% | 41 | Montana | 1,689 | 0.2% |
| 18 | Tennessee | | 12,980 | 1.8% | 42 | Alaska | 1,522 | 0.2% |
| 2 | Texas | | 64,996 | 9.0% | 43 | Delaware | 1,436 | 0.2% |
| 32 | Utah | | 5,999 | 0.8% | 44 | Idaho | 1,364 | 0.2% |
| 50 | Vermont | | 435 | 0.1% | 45 | North Dakota | 1,151 | 0.2% |
| 25 | Virginia | | 9,076 | 1.3% | 46 | South Dakota | 1,065 | 0.1% |
| 5 | Washington | | 26,402 | 3.7% | 47 | New Hampshire | 1,023 | 0.1% |
| 40 | West Virginia | | 2,209 | 0.3% | 48 | Maine | 995 | 0.1% |
| 27 | Wisconsin | | 8,216 | 1.1% | 49 | Wyoming | 584 | 0.1% |
| 49 | Wyoming | | 584 | 0.1% | 50 | Vermont | 435 | 0.1% |
| | | | | | | District of Columbia | 3,661 | 0.5% |

Source: Reported data from the Federal Bureau of Investigation
"Crime in the United States 2012" (Uniform Crime Reports, September 16, 2013, http://www.fbi.gov/about-us/cjis/ucr/)
*Includes the theft or attempted theft of a self-propelled vehicle. Excludes motorboats, construction equipment, airplanes, and farming equipment.

# Motor Vehicle Theft Rate in 2012

## National Rate = 229.7 Motor Vehicle Thefts per 100,000 Population*

ALPHA ORDER

| RANK | STATE | RATE |
|---|---|---|
| 22 | Alabama | 204.8 |
| 21 | Alaska | 208.1 |
| 5 | Arizona | 292.3 |
| 25 | Arkansas | 194.1 |
| 1 | California | 443.2 |
| 17 | Colorado | 233.1 |
| 28 | Connecticut | 179.6 |
| 35 | Delaware | 156.6 |
| 26 | Florida | 193.2 |
| 6 | Georgia | 287.7 |
| 11 | Hawaii | 258.9 |
| 47 | Idaho | 85.5 |
| 24 | Illinois | 199.5 |
| 20 | Indiana | 209.0 |
| 40 | Iowa | 130.9 |
| 16 | Kansas | 234.9 |
| 36 | Kentucky | 152.2 |
| 29 | Louisiana | 171.3 |
| 49 | Maine | 74.9 |
| 12 | Maryland | 255.3 |
| 39 | Massachusetts | 138.9 |
| 13 | Michigan | 254.1 |
| 34 | Minnesota | 157.2 |
| 37 | Mississippi | 144.8 |
| 8 | Missouri | 270.8 |
| 31 | Montana | 168.0 |
| 18 | Nebraska | 223.5 |
| 3 | Nevada | 363.1 |
| 48 | New Hampshire | 77.5 |
| 27 | New Jersey | 185.9 |
| 9 | New Mexico | 261.9 |
| 46 | New York | 88.6 |
| 32 | North Carolina | 165.3 |
| 33 | North Dakota | 164.5 |
| 30 | Ohio | 169.0 |
| 4 | Oklahoma | 303.1 |
| 10 | Oregon | 261.7 |
| 43 | Pennsylvania | 117.7 |
| 14 | Rhode Island | 250.2 |
| 7 | South Carolina | 279.5 |
| 41 | South Dakota | 127.8 |
| 23 | Tennessee | 201.0 |
| 15 | Texas | 249.4 |
| 19 | Utah | 210.1 |
| 50 | Vermont | 69.5 |
| 44 | Virginia | 110.9 |
| 2 | Washington | 382.8 |
| 42 | West Virginia | 119.1 |
| 38 | Wisconsin | 143.5 |
| 45 | Wyoming | 101.3 |

RANK ORDER

| RANK | STATE | RATE |
|---|---|---|
| 1 | California | 443.2 |
| 2 | Washington | 382.8 |
| 3 | Nevada | 363.1 |
| 4 | Oklahoma | 303.1 |
| 5 | Arizona | 292.3 |
| 6 | Georgia | 287.7 |
| 7 | South Carolina | 279.5 |
| 8 | Missouri | 270.8 |
| 9 | New Mexico | 261.9 |
| 10 | Oregon | 261.7 |
| 11 | Hawaii | 258.9 |
| 12 | Maryland | 255.3 |
| 13 | Michigan | 254.1 |
| 14 | Rhode Island | 250.2 |
| 15 | Texas | 249.4 |
| 16 | Kansas | 234.9 |
| 17 | Colorado | 233.1 |
| 18 | Nebraska | 223.5 |
| 19 | Utah | 210.1 |
| 20 | Indiana | 209.0 |
| 21 | Alaska | 208.1 |
| 22 | Alabama | 204.8 |
| 23 | Tennessee | 201.0 |
| 24 | Illinois | 199.5 |
| 25 | Arkansas | 194.1 |
| 26 | Florida | 193.2 |
| 27 | New Jersey | 185.9 |
| 28 | Connecticut | 179.6 |
| 29 | Louisiana | 171.3 |
| 30 | Ohio | 169.0 |
| 31 | Montana | 168.0 |
| 32 | North Carolina | 165.3 |
| 33 | North Dakota | 164.5 |
| 34 | Minnesota | 157.2 |
| 35 | Delaware | 156.6 |
| 36 | Kentucky | 152.2 |
| 37 | Mississippi | 144.8 |
| 38 | Wisconsin | 143.5 |
| 39 | Massachusetts | 138.9 |
| 40 | Iowa | 130.9 |
| 41 | South Dakota | 127.8 |
| 42 | West Virginia | 119.1 |
| 43 | Pennsylvania | 117.7 |
| 44 | Virginia | 110.9 |
| 45 | Wyoming | 101.3 |
| 46 | New York | 88.6 |
| 47 | Idaho | 85.5 |
| 48 | New Hampshire | 77.5 |
| 49 | Maine | 74.9 |
| 50 | Vermont | 69.5 |
| | District of Columbia | 579.0 |

Source: Reported data from the Federal Bureau of Investigation
"Crime in the United States 2012" (Uniform Crime Reports, September 16, 2013, http://www.fbi.gov/about-us/cjis/ucr/)
*Includes the theft or attempted theft of a self-propelled vehicle. Excludes motorboats, construction equipment, airplanes, and farming equipment.

# Rate of Consumer Fraud Complaints in 2012

## National Rate = 539.1 Complaints per 100,000 Population*

| ALPHA ORDER | | | | RANK ORDER | | |
|---|---|---|---|---|---|---|
| RANK | STATE | RATE | | RANK | STATE | RATE |
| 30 | Alabama | 403.8 | | 1 | Florida | 693.5 |
| 33 | Alaska | 393.5 | | 2 | Georgia | 590.2 |
| 8 | Arizona | 510.2 | | 3 | Maryland | 564.2 |
| 46 | Arkansas | 344.1 | | 4 | Delaware | 563.2 |
| 11 | California | 492.3 | | 5 | Nevada | 559.9 |
| 6 | Colorado | 545.2 | | 6 | Colorado | 545.2 |
| 17 | Connecticut | 443.0 | | 7 | Virginia | 517.4 |
| 4 | Delaware | 563.2 | | 8 | Arizona | 510.2 |
| 1 | Florida | 693.5 | | 9 | Michigan | 500.9 |
| 2 | Georgia | 590.2 | | 10 | New Hampshire | 499.7 |
| 22 | Hawaii | 429.0 | | 11 | California | 492.3 |
| 27 | Idaho | 419.4 | | 12 | Washington | 488.9 |
| 32 | Illinois | 397.7 | | 13 | New Jersey | 480.2 |
| 38 | Indiana | 374.6 | | 14 | Oregon | 471.8 |
| 49 | Iowa | 296.3 | | 15 | Texas | 458.6 |
| 40 | Kansas | 368.8 | | 16 | Massachusetts | 443.4 |
| 43 | Kentucky | 360.0 | | 17 | Connecticut | 443.0 |
| 31 | Louisiana | 399.9 | | 18 | Pennsylvania | 441.9 |
| 34 | Maine | 393.0 | | 19 | Tennessee | 435.1 |
| 3 | Maryland | 564.2 | | 20 | Ohio | 434.2 |
| 16 | Massachusetts | 443.4 | | 21 | Rhode Island | 433.1 |
| 9 | Michigan | 500.9 | | 22 | Hawaii | 429.0 |
| 35 | Minnesota | 391.3 | | 23 | Missouri | 427.2 |
| 48 | Mississippi | 319.1 | | 24 | North Carolina | 422.6 |
| 23 | Missouri | 427.2 | | 25 | New York | 420.5 |
| 39 | Montana | 371.0 | | 26 | South Carolina | 420.2 |
| 36 | Nebraska | 380.9 | | 27 | Idaho | 419.4 |
| 5 | Nevada | 559.9 | | 28 | New Mexico | 416.0 |
| 10 | New Hampshire | 499.7 | | 29 | North Dakota | 403.9 |
| 13 | New Jersey | 480.2 | | 30 | Alabama | 403.8 |
| 28 | New Mexico | 416.0 | | 31 | Louisiana | 399.9 |
| 25 | New York | 420.5 | | 32 | Illinois | 397.7 |
| 24 | North Carolina | 422.6 | | 33 | Alaska | 393.5 |
| 29 | North Dakota | 403.9 | | 34 | Maine | 393.0 |
| 20 | Ohio | 434.2 | | 35 | Minnesota | 391.3 |
| 45 | Oklahoma | 345.3 | | 36 | Nebraska | 380.9 |
| 14 | Oregon | 471.8 | | 37 | Wisconsin | 378.6 |
| 18 | Pennsylvania | 441.9 | | 38 | Indiana | 374.6 |
| 21 | Rhode Island | 433.1 | | 39 | Montana | 371.0 |
| 26 | South Carolina | 420.2 | | 40 | Kansas | 368.8 |
| 50 | South Dakota | 291.2 | | 41 | Wyoming | 365.5 |
| 19 | Tennessee | 435.1 | | 42 | Vermont | 363.1 |
| 15 | Texas | 458.6 | | 43 | Kentucky | 360.0 |
| 44 | Utah | 347.0 | | 44 | Utah | 347.0 |
| 42 | Vermont | 363.1 | | 45 | Oklahoma | 345.3 |
| 7 | Virginia | 517.4 | | 46 | Arkansas | 344.1 |
| 12 | Washington | 488.9 | | 47 | West Virginia | 334.4 |
| 47 | West Virginia | 334.4 | | 48 | Mississippi | 319.1 |
| 37 | Wisconsin | 378.6 | | 49 | Iowa | 296.3 |
| 41 | Wyoming | 365.5 | | 50 | South Dakota | 291.2 |
| | | | | | District of Columbia | 752.1 |

Source: Federal Trade Commission, Consumer Sentinel
"Consumer Sentinel Network Data Book for January - December 2012" (February 2013, http://www.ftc.gov/sentinel/)
*National rate includes complaints not shown by state.  Rates do not include identity theft or "Do Not Call" registry complaints.

# Rate of Identity Theft Complaints in 2012

## National Rate = 117.6 Complaints per 100,000 Population*

| ALPHA ORDER | | | | RANK ORDER | | |
|---|---|---|---|---|---|---|
| RANK | STATE | RATE | | RANK | STATE | RATE |
| 10 | Alabama | 104.9 | | 1 | Florida | 361.3 |
| 45 | Alaska | 51.7 | | 2 | Georgia | 193.9 |
| 8 | Arizona | 107.3 | | 3 | California | 122.7 |
| 28 | Arkansas | 74.4 | | 4 | Michigan | 122.2 |
| 3 | California | 122.7 | | 5 | New York | 110.1 |
| 15 | Colorado | 93.8 | | 6 | Nevada | 109.9 |
| 22 | Connecticut | 81.2 | | 7 | Texas | 108.6 |
| 13 | Delaware | 98.4 | | 8 | Arizona | 107.3 |
| 1 | Florida | 361.3 | | 9 | Maryland | 105.0 |
| 2 | Georgia | 193.9 | | 10 | Alabama | 104.9 |
| 48 | Hawaii | 47.3 | | 11 | Illinois | 100.9 |
| 38 | Idaho | 56.7 | | 12 | Mississippi | 100.2 |
| 11 | Illinois | 100.9 | | 13 | Delaware | 98.4 |
| 33 | Indiana | 67.5 | | 14 | New Jersey | 95.1 |
| 43 | Iowa | 52.3 | | 15 | Colorado | 93.8 |
| 30 | Kansas | 72.0 | | 16 | Rhode Island | 91.7 |
| 39 | Kentucky | 56.2 | | 17 | South Carolina | 90.6 |
| 21 | Louisiana | 87.6 | | 18 | New Mexico | 89.1 |
| 46 | Maine | 50.1 | | 19 | Pennsylvania | 88.7 |
| 9 | Maryland | 105.0 | | 20 | Tennessee | 88.1 |
| 29 | Massachusetts | 73.4 | | 21 | Louisiana | 87.6 |
| 4 | Michigan | 122.2 | | 22 | Connecticut | 81.2 |
| 34 | Minnesota | 63.9 | | 23 | North Carolina | 81.1 |
| 12 | Mississippi | 100.2 | | 24 | Virginia | 80.8 |
| 27 | Missouri | 74.8 | | 25 | Washington | 77.9 |
| 47 | Montana | 49.8 | | 26 | Ohio | 77.0 |
| 37 | Nebraska | 57.6 | | 27 | Missouri | 74.8 |
| 6 | Nevada | 109.9 | | 28 | Arkansas | 74.4 |
| 36 | New Hampshire | 59.2 | | 29 | Massachusetts | 73.4 |
| 14 | New Jersey | 95.1 | | 30 | Kansas | 72.0 |
| 18 | New Mexico | 89.1 | | 31 | Wisconsin | 70.8 |
| 5 | New York | 110.1 | | 32 | Oklahoma | 67.8 |
| 23 | North Carolina | 81.1 | | 33 | Indiana | 67.5 |
| 49 | North Dakota | 41.2 | | 34 | Minnesota | 63.9 |
| 26 | Ohio | 77.0 | | 35 | Oregon | 63.3 |
| 32 | Oklahoma | 67.8 | | 36 | New Hampshire | 59.2 |
| 35 | Oregon | 63.3 | | 37 | Nebraska | 57.6 |
| 19 | Pennsylvania | 88.7 | | 38 | Idaho | 56.7 |
| 16 | Rhode Island | 91.7 | | 39 | Kentucky | 56.2 |
| 17 | South Carolina | 90.6 | | 40 | Utah | 55.5 |
| 50 | South Dakota | 39.6 | | 41 | Wyoming | 55.2 |
| 20 | Tennessee | 88.1 | | 42 | West Virginia | 54.0 |
| 7 | Texas | 108.6 | | 43 | Iowa | 52.3 |
| 40 | Utah | 55.5 | | 44 | Vermont | 52.1 |
| 44 | Vermont | 52.1 | | 45 | Alaska | 51.7 |
| 24 | Virginia | 80.8 | | 46 | Maine | 50.1 |
| 25 | Washington | 77.9 | | 47 | Montana | 49.8 |
| 42 | West Virginia | 54.0 | | 48 | Hawaii | 47.3 |
| 31 | Wisconsin | 70.8 | | 49 | North Dakota | 41.2 |
| 41 | Wyoming | 55.2 | | 50 | South Dakota | 39.6 |
| | | | | | District of Columbia | 169.1 |

Source: Federal Trade Commission, Consumer Sentinel
"Consumer Sentinel Network Data Book for January - December 2012" (February 2013, http://www.ftc.gov/sentinel/)
*National rate includes complaints not shown by state. Rates do not include consumer fraud or "Do Not Call" registry complaints.

# Reported Arrest Rate in 2012

## National Rate = 3,929.6 Reported Arrests per 100,000 Population*

ALPHA ORDER

| RANK | STATE | RATE |
|---|---|---|
| NA | Alabama** | NA |
| 1 | Alaska | 6,385.8 |
| 17 | Arizona | 4,322.2 |
| 7 | Arkansas | 5,496.4 |
| 39 | California | 3,282.4 |
| 15 | Colorado | 4,547.3 |
| 40 | Connecticut | 3,252.0 |
| 16 | Delaware | 4,328.0 |
| 11 | Florida | 4,976.9 |
| 31 | Georgia | 3,741.4 |
| NA | Hawaii** | NA |
| 23 | Idaho | 4,053.7 |
| NA | Illinois** | NA |
| 32 | Indiana | 3,638.2 |
| 29 | Iowa | 3,788.7 |
| 30 | Kansas | 3,782.6 |
| 18 | Kentucky | 4,279.9 |
| 8 | Louisiana | 5,335.4 |
| 27 | Maine | 3,852.4 |
| 24 | Maryland | 4,014.4 |
| 46 | Massachusetts | 2,245.9 |
| 44 | Michigan | 2,757.8 |
| NA | Minnesota** | NA |
| 2 | Mississippi | 6,147.5 |
| 10 | Missouri | 5,164.7 |
| 37 | Montana | 3,409.8 |
| 14 | Nebraska | 4,592.4 |
| 9 | Nevada | 5,182.0 |
| 26 | New Hampshire | 3,894.9 |
| 28 | New Jersey | 3,802.2 |
| 6 | New Mexico | 5,568.5 |
| 43 | New York** | 3,134.4 |
| 12 | North Carolina | 4,964.9 |
| 19 | North Dakota | 4,244.9 |
| 42 | Ohio | 3,159.5 |
| 33 | Oklahoma | 3,561.3 |
| 35 | Oregon | 3,538.6 |
| 34 | Pennsylvania | 3,541.3 |
| 41 | Rhode Island | 3,178.6 |
| 22 | South Carolina | 4,118.5 |
| 13 | South Dakota | 4,728.8 |
| 3 | Tennessee | 6,077.1 |
| 25 | Texas | 4,000.7 |
| 20 | Utah | 4,193.9 |
| 45 | Vermont | 2,342.9 |
| 21 | Virginia | 4,149.2 |
| 38 | Washington | 3,331.9 |
| 36 | West Virginia | 3,415.1 |
| 4 | Wisconsin | 6,033.1 |
| 5 | Wyoming | 5,843.0 |

RANK ORDER

| RANK | STATE | RATE |
|---|---|---|
| 1 | Alaska | 6,385.8 |
| 2 | Mississippi | 6,147.5 |
| 3 | Tennessee | 6,077.1 |
| 4 | Wisconsin | 6,033.1 |
| 5 | Wyoming | 5,843.0 |
| 6 | New Mexico | 5,568.5 |
| 7 | Arkansas | 5,496.4 |
| 8 | Louisiana | 5,335.4 |
| 9 | Nevada | 5,182.0 |
| 10 | Missouri | 5,164.7 |
| 11 | Florida | 4,976.9 |
| 12 | North Carolina | 4,964.9 |
| 13 | South Dakota | 4,728.8 |
| 14 | Nebraska | 4,592.4 |
| 15 | Colorado | 4,547.3 |
| 16 | Delaware | 4,328.0 |
| 17 | Arizona | 4,322.2 |
| 18 | Kentucky | 4,279.9 |
| 19 | North Dakota | 4,244.9 |
| 20 | Utah | 4,193.9 |
| 21 | Virginia | 4,149.2 |
| 22 | South Carolina | 4,118.5 |
| 23 | Idaho | 4,053.7 |
| 24 | Maryland | 4,014.4 |
| 25 | Texas | 4,000.7 |
| 26 | New Hampshire | 3,894.9 |
| 27 | Maine | 3,852.4 |
| 28 | New Jersey | 3,802.2 |
| 29 | Iowa | 3,788.7 |
| 30 | Kansas | 3,782.6 |
| 31 | Georgia | 3,741.4 |
| 32 | Indiana | 3,638.2 |
| 33 | Oklahoma | 3,561.3 |
| 34 | Pennsylvania | 3,541.3 |
| 35 | Oregon | 3,538.6 |
| 36 | West Virginia | 3,415.1 |
| 37 | Montana | 3,409.8 |
| 38 | Washington | 3,331.9 |
| 39 | California | 3,282.4 |
| 40 | Connecticut | 3,252.0 |
| 41 | Rhode Island | 3,178.6 |
| 42 | Ohio | 3,159.5 |
| 43 | New York** | 3,134.4 |
| 44 | Michigan | 2,757.8 |
| 45 | Vermont | 2,342.9 |
| 46 | Massachusetts | 2,245.9 |
| NA | Alabama** | NA |
| NA | Hawaii** | NA |
| NA | Illinois** | NA |
| NA | Minnesota** | NA |
| | District of Columbia** | NA |

Source: CQ Press using reported data from the Federal Bureau of Investigation
   "Crime in the United States 2012" (Uniform Crime Reports, September 16, 2013, http://www.fbi.gov/about-us/cjis/ucr/)
*By law enforcement agencies submitting complete reports to the F.B.I. for 12 months in 2012.  These rates based on population estimates for areas under the jurisdiction of those agencies reporting.  Arrest rate based on the F.B.I. estimate of total arrests is 3,885.4 reported and unreported arrests per 100,000 population.
**Not available.  New York's figure does not include New York City.

# Reported Juvenile Arrest Rate in 2012

## National Rate = 3,939.8 Reported Arrests per 100,000 Juvenile Population*

ALPHA ORDER

| RANK | STATE | RATE |
|---|---|---|
| NA | Alabama** | NA |
| 13 | Alaska | 5,003.6 |
| 15 | Arizona | 4,958.6 |
| 28 | Arkansas | 3,700.6 |
| 41 | California | 2,836.4 |
| 9 | Colorado | 5,386.2 |
| 39 | Connecticut | 3,021.9 |
| 14 | Delaware | 4,975.8 |
| 23 | Florida | 4,266.8 |
| 32 | Georgia | 3,483.7 |
| NA | Hawaii** | NA |
| 10 | Idaho | 5,287.6 |
| NA | Illinois** | NA |
| 26 | Indiana | 4,099.9 |
| 12 | Iowa | 5,090.8 |
| 37 | Kansas | 3,126.2 |
| 45 | Kentucky | 1,605.6 |
| 7 | Louisiana | 5,472.7 |
| 24 | Maine | 4,250.4 |
| 25 | Maryland | 4,232.4 |
| 44 | Massachusetts | 1,835.9 |
| 42 | Michigan | 2,443.0 |
| NA | Minnesota** | NA |
| 22 | Mississippi | 4,282.4 |
| 16 | Missouri | 4,862.9 |
| 5 | Montana | 7,214.8 |
| 6 | Nebraska | 6,405.9 |
| 21 | Nevada | 4,515.7 |
| 20 | New Hampshire | 4,521.8 |
| 40 | New Jersey | 2,914.8 |
| 17 | New Mexico | 4,855.9 |
| 29 | New York** | 3,690.5 |
| 31 | North Carolina | 3,565.1 |
| 3 | North Dakota | 7,423.2 |
| 35 | Ohio | 3,255.2 |
| 36 | Oklahoma | 3,254.0 |
| 18 | Oregon | 4,602.4 |
| 8 | Pennsylvania | 5,455.1 |
| 30 | Rhode Island | 3,658.0 |
| 33 | South Carolina | 3,429.1 |
| 4 | South Dakota | 7,305.4 |
| 19 | Tennessee | 4,592.2 |
| 27 | Texas | 3,720.5 |
| 11 | Utah | 5,245.2 |
| 43 | Vermont | 1,954.4 |
| 38 | Virginia | 3,066.3 |
| 34 | Washington | 3,412.5 |
| 46 | West Virginia | 1,314.9 |
| 1 | Wisconsin | 11,215.2 |
| 2 | Wyoming | 7,559.6 |

RANK ORDER

| RANK | STATE | RATE |
|---|---|---|
| 1 | Wisconsin | 11,215.2 |
| 2 | Wyoming | 7,559.6 |
| 3 | North Dakota | 7,423.2 |
| 4 | South Dakota | 7,305.4 |
| 5 | Montana | 7,214.8 |
| 6 | Nebraska | 6,405.9 |
| 7 | Louisiana | 5,472.7 |
| 8 | Pennsylvania | 5,455.1 |
| 9 | Colorado | 5,386.2 |
| 10 | Idaho | 5,287.6 |
| 11 | Utah | 5,245.2 |
| 12 | Iowa | 5,090.8 |
| 13 | Alaska | 5,003.6 |
| 14 | Delaware | 4,975.8 |
| 15 | Arizona | 4,958.6 |
| 16 | Missouri | 4,862.9 |
| 17 | New Mexico | 4,855.9 |
| 18 | Oregon | 4,602.4 |
| 19 | Tennessee | 4,592.2 |
| 20 | New Hampshire | 4,521.8 |
| 21 | Nevada | 4,515.7 |
| 22 | Mississippi | 4,282.4 |
| 23 | Florida | 4,266.8 |
| 24 | Maine | 4,250.4 |
| 25 | Maryland | 4,232.4 |
| 26 | Indiana | 4,099.9 |
| 27 | Texas | 3,720.5 |
| 28 | Arkansas | 3,700.6 |
| 29 | New York** | 3,690.5 |
| 30 | Rhode Island | 3,658.0 |
| 31 | North Carolina | 3,565.1 |
| 32 | Georgia | 3,483.7 |
| 33 | South Carolina | 3,429.1 |
| 34 | Washington | 3,412.5 |
| 35 | Ohio | 3,255.2 |
| 36 | Oklahoma | 3,254.0 |
| 37 | Kansas | 3,126.2 |
| 38 | Virginia | 3,066.3 |
| 39 | Connecticut | 3,021.9 |
| 40 | New Jersey | 2,914.8 |
| 41 | California | 2,836.4 |
| 42 | Michigan | 2,443.0 |
| 43 | Vermont | 1,954.4 |
| 44 | Massachusetts | 1,835.9 |
| 45 | Kentucky | 1,605.6 |
| 46 | West Virginia | 1,314.9 |
| NA | Alabama** | NA |
| NA | Hawaii** | NA |
| NA | Illinois** | NA |
| NA | Minnesota** | NA |
| | District of Columbia** | NA |

Source: CQ Press using reported data from the Federal Bureau of Investigation
   "Crime in the United States 2012" (Uniform Crime Reports, September 16, 2013, http://www.fbi.gov/about-us/cjis/ucr/)
*By law enforcement agencies submitting complete reports to the F.B.I. for 12 months in 2012.  Arrests of youths 17 years and younger divided into population of 10 to 17 year olds.
**Not available.  New York's figure does not include New York City.

# Prisoners in State Correctional Institutions: Year End 2012

## National Total = 1,352,582 State Prisoners*

ALPHA ORDER

| RANK | STATE | PRISONERS | % of USA |
|------|-------|-----------|----------|
| 14 | Alabama | 32,431 | 2.4% |
| 41 | Alaska | 5,633 | 0.4% |
| 11 | Arizona | 40,080 | 3.0% |
| 29 | Arkansas | 14,654 | 1.1% |
| 2 | California | 134,534 | 9.9% |
| 25 | Colorado | 20,462 | 1.5% |
| 26 | Connecticut | 17,530 | 1.3% |
| 38 | Delaware | 6,914 | 0.5% |
| 3 | Florida | 101,930 | 7.5% |
| 4 | Georgia | 55,457 | 4.1% |
| 40 | Hawaii | 5,831 | 0.4% |
| 35 | Idaho | 7,985 | 0.6% |
| 8 | Illinois | 49,348 | 3.6% |
| 16 | Indiana | 28,831 | 2.1% |
| 34 | Iowa | 8,733 | 0.6% |
| 33 | Kansas | 9,682 | 0.7% |
| 23 | Kentucky | 22,110 | 1.6% |
| 10 | Louisiana | 40,172 | 3.0% |
| 48 | Maine | 2,108 | 0.2% |
| 24 | Maryland | 21,522 | 1.6% |
| 31 | Massachusetts | 11,308 | 0.8% |
| 9 | Michigan | 43,636 | 3.2% |
| 32 | Minnesota | 9,938 | 0.7% |
| 22 | Mississippi | 22,319 | 1.7% |
| 15 | Missouri | 31,247 | 2.3% |
| 44 | Montana | 3,609 | 0.3% |
| 42 | Nebraska | 4,705 | 0.3% |
| 30 | Nevada | 12,883 | 1.0% |
| 46 | New Hampshire | 2,790 | 0.2% |
| 19 | New Jersey | 23,225 | 1.7% |
| 39 | New Mexico | 6,727 | 0.5% |
| 5 | New York | 54,210 | 4.0% |
| 12 | North Carolina | 37,136 | 2.7% |
| 50 | North Dakota | 1,512 | 0.1% |
| 7 | Ohio | 50,876 | 3.8% |
| 18 | Oklahoma | 25,225 | 1.9% |
| 28 | Oregon | 14,840 | 1.1% |
| 6 | Pennsylvania | 51,125 | 3.8% |
| 45 | Rhode Island | 3,318 | 0.2% |
| 21 | South Carolina | 22,388 | 1.7% |
| 43 | South Dakota | 3,650 | 0.3% |
| 17 | Tennessee | 28,411 | 2.1% |
| 1 | Texas | 166,372 | 12.3% |
| 37 | Utah | 6,962 | 0.5% |
| 49 | Vermont | 2,034 | 0.2% |
| 13 | Virginia | 37,044 | 2.7% |
| 27 | Washington | 17,271 | 1.3% |
| 36 | West Virginia | 7,070 | 0.5% |
| 20 | Wisconsin | 22,600 | 1.7% |
| 47 | Wyoming | 2,204 | 0.2% |

RANK ORDER

| RANK | STATE | PRISONERS | % of USA |
|------|-------|-----------|----------|
| 1 | Texas | 166,372 | 12.3% |
| 2 | California | 134,534 | 9.9% |
| 3 | Florida | 101,930 | 7.5% |
| 4 | Georgia | 55,457 | 4.1% |
| 5 | New York | 54,210 | 4.0% |
| 6 | Pennsylvania | 51,125 | 3.8% |
| 7 | Ohio | 50,876 | 3.8% |
| 8 | Illinois | 49,348 | 3.6% |
| 9 | Michigan | 43,636 | 3.2% |
| 10 | Louisiana | 40,172 | 3.0% |
| 11 | Arizona | 40,080 | 3.0% |
| 12 | North Carolina | 37,136 | 2.7% |
| 13 | Virginia | 37,044 | 2.7% |
| 14 | Alabama | 32,431 | 2.4% |
| 15 | Missouri | 31,247 | 2.3% |
| 16 | Indiana | 28,831 | 2.1% |
| 17 | Tennessee | 28,411 | 2.1% |
| 18 | Oklahoma | 25,225 | 1.9% |
| 19 | New Jersey | 23,225 | 1.7% |
| 20 | Wisconsin | 22,600 | 1.7% |
| 21 | South Carolina | 22,388 | 1.7% |
| 22 | Mississippi | 22,319 | 1.7% |
| 23 | Kentucky | 22,110 | 1.6% |
| 24 | Maryland | 21,522 | 1.6% |
| 25 | Colorado | 20,462 | 1.5% |
| 26 | Connecticut | 17,530 | 1.3% |
| 27 | Washington | 17,271 | 1.3% |
| 28 | Oregon | 14,840 | 1.1% |
| 29 | Arkansas | 14,654 | 1.1% |
| 30 | Nevada | 12,883 | 1.0% |
| 31 | Massachusetts | 11,308 | 0.8% |
| 32 | Minnesota | 9,938 | 0.7% |
| 33 | Kansas | 9,682 | 0.7% |
| 34 | Iowa | 8,733 | 0.6% |
| 35 | Idaho | 7,985 | 0.6% |
| 36 | West Virginia | 7,070 | 0.5% |
| 37 | Utah | 6,962 | 0.5% |
| 38 | Delaware | 6,914 | 0.5% |
| 39 | New Mexico | 6,727 | 0.5% |
| 40 | Hawaii | 5,831 | 0.4% |
| 41 | Alaska | 5,633 | 0.4% |
| 42 | Nebraska | 4,705 | 0.3% |
| 43 | South Dakota | 3,650 | 0.3% |
| 44 | Montana | 3,609 | 0.3% |
| 45 | Rhode Island | 3,318 | 0.2% |
| 46 | New Hampshire | 2,790 | 0.2% |
| 47 | Wyoming | 2,204 | 0.2% |
| 48 | Maine | 2,108 | 0.2% |
| 49 | Vermont | 2,034 | 0.2% |
| 50 | North Dakota | 1,512 | 0.1% |
| | District of Columbia** | NA | NA |

Source: U.S. Department of Justice, Bureau of Justice Statistics
  "Prisoners in 2012" (December 2013, NCJ 243920, http://bjs.ojp.usdoj.gov/)
*As of December 31, 2012. Totals reflect all prisoners, including those sentenced to a year or less and those unsentenced.
National total does not include 217,815 prisoners under federal jurisdiction. State and federal prisoners combined total 1,570,397.
**Responsibility for sentenced felons in D.C. was transferred to the Federal Bureau of Prisons in 2001.

# State Prisoner Imprisonment Rate in 2012

## National Rate = 418 State Prisoners per 100,000 Population*

ALPHA ORDER

| RANK | STATE | RATE |
|---|---|---|
| 3 | Alabama | 650 |
| 21 | Alaska | 401 |
| 6 | Arizona | 583 |
| 11 | Arkansas | 494 |
| 31 | California | 351 |
| 23 | Colorado | 392 |
| 32 | Connecticut | 333 |
| 15 | Delaware | 448 |
| 8 | Florida | 524 |
| 7 | Georgia | 542 |
| 37 | Hawaii | 273 |
| 10 | Idaho | 499 |
| NA | Illinois** | NA |
| 17 | Indiana | 440 |
| 35 | Iowa | 282 |
| 33 | Kansas | 325 |
| 12 | Kentucky | 489 |
| 1 | Louisiana | 893 |
| 47 | Maine | 145 |
| 27 | Maryland | 360 |
| 44 | Massachusetts | 199 |
| 16 | Michigan | 441 |
| 46 | Minnesota | 184 |
| 2 | Mississippi | 717 |
| 9 | Missouri | 518 |
| 28 | Montana | 358 |
| 39 | Nebraska | 247 |
| NA | Nevada** | NA |
| 43 | New Hampshire | 211 |
| 38 | New Jersey | 261 |
| 34 | New Mexico | 315 |
| 36 | New York | 276 |
| 29 | North Carolina | 357 |
| 42 | North Dakota | 213 |
| 17 | Ohio | 440 |
| 4 | Oklahoma | 648 |
| 25 | Oregon | 378 |
| 22 | Pennsylvania | 398 |
| 45 | Rhode Island | 190 |
| 13 | South Carolina | 458 |
| 20 | South Dakota | 434 |
| 19 | Tennessee | 438 |
| 5 | Texas | 601 |
| 40 | Utah | 242 |
| 40 | Vermont | 242 |
| 14 | Virginia | 451 |
| NA | Washington** | NA |
| 25 | West Virginia | 378 |
| 29 | Wisconsin | 357 |
| 24 | Wyoming | 379 |

RANK ORDER

| RANK | STATE | RATE |
|---|---|---|
| 1 | Louisiana | 893 |
| 2 | Mississippi | 717 |
| 3 | Alabama | 650 |
| 4 | Oklahoma | 648 |
| 5 | Texas | 601 |
| 6 | Arizona | 583 |
| 7 | Georgia | 542 |
| 8 | Florida | 524 |
| 9 | Missouri | 518 |
| 10 | Idaho | 499 |
| 11 | Arkansas | 494 |
| 12 | Kentucky | 489 |
| 13 | South Carolina | 458 |
| 14 | Virginia | 451 |
| 15 | Delaware | 448 |
| 16 | Michigan | 441 |
| 17 | Indiana | 440 |
| 17 | Ohio | 440 |
| 19 | Tennessee | 438 |
| 20 | South Dakota | 434 |
| 21 | Alaska | 401 |
| 22 | Pennsylvania | 398 |
| 23 | Colorado | 392 |
| 24 | Wyoming | 379 |
| 25 | Oregon | 378 |
| 25 | West Virginia | 378 |
| 27 | Maryland | 360 |
| 28 | Montana | 358 |
| 29 | North Carolina | 357 |
| 29 | Wisconsin | 357 |
| 31 | California | 351 |
| 32 | Connecticut | 333 |
| 33 | Kansas | 325 |
| 34 | New Mexico | 315 |
| 35 | Iowa | 282 |
| 36 | New York | 276 |
| 37 | Hawaii | 273 |
| 38 | New Jersey | 261 |
| 39 | Nebraska | 247 |
| 40 | Utah | 242 |
| 40 | Vermont | 242 |
| 42 | North Dakota | 213 |
| 43 | New Hampshire | 211 |
| 44 | Massachusetts | 199 |
| 45 | Rhode Island | 190 |
| 46 | Minnesota | 184 |
| 47 | Maine | 145 |
| NA | Illinois** | NA |
| NA | Nevada** | NA |
| NA | Washington** | NA |
| | District of Columbia*** | NA |

Source: U.S. Department of Justice, Bureau of Justice Statistics
    "Prisoners in 2012 - Advance Counts" (July 2013, NCJ 242467, http://bjs.ojp.usdoj.gov/)
*Advance figures as of December 31, 2012.  Includes only inmates sentenced to more than one year.  Does not include federal imprisonment rate of 62 prisoners per 100,000 population.  State and federal combined imprisonment rate is 480 prisoners per 100,000 population.  **Not available.
***Responsibility for sentenced felons in D.C. was transferred to the Federal Bureau of Prisons in 2001.

# Percent Change in Number of State Prisoners: 2011 to 2012

## National Percent Change = 2.2% Decrease*

| ALPHA ORDER | | | | RANK ORDER | | |
|---|---|---|---|---|---|---|
| RANK | STATE | PERCENT CHANGE | | RANK | STATE | PERCENT CHANGE |
| 21 | Alabama | 0.5 | | 1 | New Hampshire | 6.7 |
| 20 | Alaska | 0.6 | | 2 | North Dakota | 6.3 |
| 22 | Arizona | 0.1 | | 3 | Mississippi | 4.4 |
| 49 | Arkansas | (9.0) | | 4 | Kansas | 3.8 |
| 50 | California | (10.1) | | 5 | West Virginia | 3.6 |
| 48 | Colorado | (6.9) | | 6 | South Dakota | 3.3 |
| 45 | Connecticut | (4.3) | | 7 | Idaho | 3.2 |
| 8 | Delaware | 2.6 | | 8 | Delaware | 2.6 |
| 31 | Florida | (1.1) | | 8 | Kentucky | 2.6 |
| 28 | Georgia | (0.9) | | 10 | Oregon | 2.3 |
| 41 | Hawaii | (3.4) | | 11 | Illinois | 1.9 |
| 7 | Idaho | 3.2 | | 11 | Nebraska | 1.9 |
| 11 | Illinois | 1.9 | | 13 | Michigan | 1.6 |
| 25 | Indiana | (0.3) | | 14 | Minnesota | 1.4 |
| 44 | Iowa | (4.2) | | 15 | Missouri | 1.3 |
| 4 | Kansas | 3.8 | | 16 | Louisiana | 1.2 |
| 8 | Kentucky | 2.6 | | 16 | Utah | 1.2 |
| 16 | Louisiana | 1.2 | | 18 | Wyoming | 1.0 |
| 32 | Maine | (1.7) | | 19 | Nevada | 0.8 |
| 46 | Maryland | (4.6) | | 20 | Alaska | 0.6 |
| 37 | Massachusetts | (2.7) | | 21 | Alabama | 0.5 |
| 13 | Michigan | 1.6 | | 22 | Arizona | 0.1 |
| 14 | Minnesota | 1.4 | | 23 | Ohio | (0.2) |
| 3 | Mississippi | 4.4 | | 23 | Tennessee | (0.2) |
| 15 | Missouri | 1.3 | | 25 | Indiana | (0.3) |
| 33 | Montana | (1.9) | | 25 | Wisconsin | (0.3) |
| 11 | Nebraska | 1.9 | | 27 | Rhode Island | (0.6) |
| 19 | Nevada | 0.8 | | 28 | Georgia | (0.9) |
| 1 | New Hampshire | 6.7 | | 28 | Pennsylvania | (0.9) |
| 36 | New Jersey | (2.6) | | 28 | Vermont | (0.9) |
| 43 | New Mexico | (3.9) | | 31 | Florida | (1.1) |
| 34 | New York | (2.2) | | 32 | Maine | (1.7) |
| 47 | North Carolina | (5.8) | | 33 | Montana | (1.9) |
| 2 | North Dakota | 6.3 | | 34 | New York | (2.2) |
| 23 | Ohio | (0.2) | | 35 | South Carolina | (2.3) |
| 39 | Oklahoma | (2.9) | | 36 | New Jersey | (2.6) |
| 10 | Oregon | 2.3 | | 37 | Massachusetts | (2.7) |
| 28 | Pennsylvania | (0.9) | | 38 | Virginia | (2.8) |
| 27 | Rhode Island | (0.6) | | 39 | Oklahoma | (2.9) |
| 35 | South Carolina | (2.3) | | 40 | Washington | (3.2) |
| 6 | South Dakota | 3.3 | | 41 | Hawaii | (3.4) |
| 23 | Tennessee | (0.2) | | 41 | Texas | (3.4) |
| 41 | Texas | (3.4) | | 43 | New Mexico | (3.9) |
| 16 | Utah | 1.2 | | 44 | Iowa | (4.2) |
| 28 | Vermont | (0.9) | | 45 | Connecticut | (4.3) |
| 38 | Virginia | (2.8) | | 46 | Maryland | (4.6) |
| 40 | Washington | (3.2) | | 47 | North Carolina | (5.8) |
| 5 | West Virginia | 3.6 | | 48 | Colorado | (6.9) |
| 25 | Wisconsin | (0.3) | | 49 | Arkansas | (9.0) |
| 18 | Wyoming | 1.0 | | 50 | California | (10.1) |
| | | | | | District of Columbia** | NA |

Source: U.S. Department of Justice, Bureau of Justice Statistics
   "Prisoners in 2012" (December 2013, NCJ 243920, http://bjs.ojp.usdoj.gov/)
*From December 31, 2011 to December 31, 2012. Includes inmates sentenced to more than one year and those sentenced to a year or less or with no sentence. The percent change in number of prisoners under federal jurisdiction during the same period was an 0.7% increase. The combined state and federal decrease was 1.8%.
**Responsibility for sentenced felons in D.C. was transferred to the Federal Bureau of Prisons in 2001.

# Prisoners under Sentence of Death in 2011

## National Total = 3,026 State Prisoners*

<table>
<tr><td colspan="4">ALPHA ORDER</td><td colspan="4">RANK ORDER</td></tr>
<tr><th>RANK</th><th>STATE</th><th>PRISONERS</th><th>% of USA</th><th>RANK</th><th>STATE</th><th>PRISONERS</th><th>% of USA</th></tr>
<tr><td>5</td><td>Alabama</td><td>196</td><td>6.5%</td><td>1</td><td>California</td><td>705</td><td>23.3%</td></tr>
<tr><td>NA</td><td>Alaska**</td><td>NA</td><td>NA</td><td>2</td><td>Florida</td><td>393</td><td>13.0%</td></tr>
<tr><td>8</td><td>Arizona</td><td>130</td><td>4.3%</td><td>3</td><td>Texas</td><td>301</td><td>9.9%</td></tr>
<tr><td>17</td><td>Arkansas</td><td>39</td><td>1.3%</td><td>4</td><td>Pennsylvania</td><td>207</td><td>6.8%</td></tr>
<tr><td>1</td><td>California</td><td>705</td><td>23.3%</td><td>5</td><td>Alabama</td><td>196</td><td>6.5%</td></tr>
<tr><td>31</td><td>Colorado</td><td>3</td><td>0.1%</td><td>6</td><td>North Carolina</td><td>158</td><td>5.2%</td></tr>
<tr><td>24</td><td>Connecticut</td><td>10</td><td>0.3%</td><td>7</td><td>Ohio</td><td>142</td><td>4.7%</td></tr>
<tr><td>20</td><td>Delaware</td><td>18</td><td>0.6%</td><td>8</td><td>Arizona</td><td>130</td><td>4.3%</td></tr>
<tr><td>2</td><td>Florida</td><td>393</td><td>13.0%</td><td>9</td><td>Georgia</td><td>96</td><td>3.2%</td></tr>
<tr><td>9</td><td>Georgia</td><td>96</td><td>3.2%</td><td>10</td><td>Louisiana</td><td>87</td><td>2.9%</td></tr>
<tr><td>NA</td><td>Hawaii**</td><td>NA</td><td>NA</td><td>10</td><td>Tennessee</td><td>87</td><td>2.9%</td></tr>
<tr><td>21</td><td>Idaho</td><td>13</td><td>0.4%</td><td>12</td><td>Nevada</td><td>81</td><td>2.7%</td></tr>
<tr><td>NA</td><td>Illinois**</td><td>NA</td><td>NA</td><td>13</td><td>Oklahoma</td><td>63</td><td>2.1%</td></tr>
<tr><td>22</td><td>Indiana</td><td>12</td><td>0.4%</td><td>14</td><td>Mississippi</td><td>57</td><td>1.9%</td></tr>
<tr><td>NA</td><td>Iowa**</td><td>NA</td><td>NA</td><td>15</td><td>South Carolina</td><td>52</td><td>1.7%</td></tr>
<tr><td>25</td><td>Kansas</td><td>9</td><td>0.3%</td><td>16</td><td>Missouri</td><td>46</td><td>1.5%</td></tr>
<tr><td>19</td><td>Kentucky</td><td>34</td><td>1.1%</td><td>17</td><td>Arkansas</td><td>39</td><td>1.3%</td></tr>
<tr><td>10</td><td>Louisiana</td><td>87</td><td>2.9%</td><td>18</td><td>Oregon</td><td>36</td><td>1.2%</td></tr>
<tr><td>NA</td><td>Maine**</td><td>NA</td><td>NA</td><td>19</td><td>Kentucky</td><td>34</td><td>1.1%</td></tr>
<tr><td>29</td><td>Maryland</td><td>5</td><td>0.2%</td><td>20</td><td>Delaware</td><td>18</td><td>0.6%</td></tr>
<tr><td>NA</td><td>Massachusetts**</td><td>NA</td><td>NA</td><td>21</td><td>Idaho</td><td>13</td><td>0.4%</td></tr>
<tr><td>NA</td><td>Michigan**</td><td>NA</td><td>NA</td><td>22</td><td>Indiana</td><td>12</td><td>0.4%</td></tr>
<tr><td>NA</td><td>Minnesota**</td><td>NA</td><td>NA</td><td>23</td><td>Nebraska</td><td>11</td><td>0.4%</td></tr>
<tr><td>14</td><td>Mississippi</td><td>57</td><td>1.9%</td><td>24</td><td>Connecticut</td><td>10</td><td>0.3%</td></tr>
<tr><td>16</td><td>Missouri</td><td>46</td><td>1.5%</td><td>25</td><td>Kansas</td><td>9</td><td>0.3%</td></tr>
<tr><td>32</td><td>Montana</td><td>2</td><td>0.1%</td><td>25</td><td>Virginia</td><td>9</td><td>0.3%</td></tr>
<tr><td>23</td><td>Nebraska</td><td>11</td><td>0.4%</td><td>27</td><td>Utah</td><td>8</td><td>0.3%</td></tr>
<tr><td>12</td><td>Nevada</td><td>81</td><td>2.7%</td><td>27</td><td>Washington</td><td>8</td><td>0.3%</td></tr>
<tr><td>34</td><td>New Hampshire</td><td>1</td><td>0.0%</td><td>29</td><td>Maryland</td><td>5</td><td>0.2%</td></tr>
<tr><td>NA</td><td>New Jersey**</td><td>NA</td><td>NA</td><td>30</td><td>South Dakota</td><td>4</td><td>0.1%</td></tr>
<tr><td>32</td><td>New Mexico</td><td>2</td><td>0.1%</td><td>31</td><td>Colorado</td><td>3</td><td>0.1%</td></tr>
<tr><td>36</td><td>New York</td><td>0</td><td>0.0%</td><td>32</td><td>Montana</td><td>2</td><td>0.1%</td></tr>
<tr><td>6</td><td>North Carolina</td><td>158</td><td>5.2%</td><td>32</td><td>New Mexico</td><td>2</td><td>0.1%</td></tr>
<tr><td>NA</td><td>North Dakota**</td><td>NA</td><td>NA</td><td>34</td><td>New Hampshire</td><td>1</td><td>0.0%</td></tr>
<tr><td>7</td><td>Ohio</td><td>142</td><td>4.7%</td><td>34</td><td>Wyoming</td><td>1</td><td>0.0%</td></tr>
<tr><td>13</td><td>Oklahoma</td><td>63</td><td>2.1%</td><td>36</td><td>New York</td><td>0</td><td>0.0%</td></tr>
<tr><td>18</td><td>Oregon</td><td>36</td><td>1.2%</td><td>NA</td><td>Alaska**</td><td>NA</td><td>NA</td></tr>
<tr><td>4</td><td>Pennsylvania</td><td>207</td><td>6.8%</td><td>NA</td><td>Hawaii**</td><td>NA</td><td>NA</td></tr>
<tr><td>NA</td><td>Rhode Island**</td><td>NA</td><td>NA</td><td>NA</td><td>Illinois**</td><td>NA</td><td>NA</td></tr>
<tr><td>15</td><td>South Carolina</td><td>52</td><td>1.7%</td><td>NA</td><td>Iowa**</td><td>NA</td><td>NA</td></tr>
<tr><td>30</td><td>South Dakota</td><td>4</td><td>0.1%</td><td>NA</td><td>Maine**</td><td>NA</td><td>NA</td></tr>
<tr><td>10</td><td>Tennessee</td><td>87</td><td>2.9%</td><td>NA</td><td>Massachusetts**</td><td>NA</td><td>NA</td></tr>
<tr><td>3</td><td>Texas</td><td>301</td><td>9.9%</td><td>NA</td><td>Michigan**</td><td>NA</td><td>NA</td></tr>
<tr><td>27</td><td>Utah</td><td>8</td><td>0.3%</td><td>NA</td><td>Minnesota**</td><td>NA</td><td>NA</td></tr>
<tr><td>NA</td><td>Vermont**</td><td>NA</td><td>NA</td><td>NA</td><td>New Jersey**</td><td>NA</td><td>NA</td></tr>
<tr><td>25</td><td>Virginia</td><td>9</td><td>0.3%</td><td>NA</td><td>North Dakota**</td><td>NA</td><td>NA</td></tr>
<tr><td>27</td><td>Washington</td><td>8</td><td>0.3%</td><td>NA</td><td>Rhode Island**</td><td>NA</td><td>NA</td></tr>
<tr><td>NA</td><td>West Virginia**</td><td>NA</td><td>NA</td><td>NA</td><td>Vermont**</td><td>NA</td><td>NA</td></tr>
<tr><td>NA</td><td>Wisconsin**</td><td>NA</td><td>NA</td><td>NA</td><td>West Virginia**</td><td>NA</td><td>NA</td></tr>
<tr><td>34</td><td>Wyoming</td><td>1</td><td>0.0%</td><td>NA</td><td>Wisconsin**</td><td>NA</td><td>NA</td></tr>
<tr><td></td><td></td><td></td><td></td><td></td><td>District of Columbia**</td><td>NA</td><td>NA</td></tr>
</table>

Source: U.S. Department of Justice, Bureau of Justice Statistics
"Capital Punishment 2011" (Bulletin, July 2013, NCJ 242185, http://bjs.ojp.usdoj.gov/)
*As of December 31, 2011.  Does not include 57 federal prisoners under sentence of death.  There were 43 executions in 2011.
**No death penalty as of December 31, 2011.

# Rate of State and Local Police Officers in 2011

## National Rate = 22.1 Officers per 10,000 Population*

ALPHA ORDER

| RANK | STATE | RATE |
|------|-------|------|
| 19 | Alabama | 22.0 |
| 48 | Alaska | 15.7 |
| 13 | Arizona | 22.4 |
| 9 | Arkansas | 24.1 |
| 36 | California | 18.1 |
| 28 | Colorado | 20.3 |
| 15 | Connecticut | 22.2 |
| 32 | Delaware | 19.2 |
| 22 | Florida | 21.6 |
| 20 | Georgia | 21.8 |
| 21 | Hawaii | 21.7 |
| 37 | Idaho | 17.9 |
| 5 | Illinois | 27.5 |
| 38 | Indiana | 17.8 |
| 40 | Iowa | 17.2 |
| 15 | Kansas | 22.2 |
| 41 | Kentucky | 17.1 |
| 3 | Louisiana | 29.5 |
| 46 | Maine | 15.9 |
| 8 | Maryland | 24.2 |
| 3 | Massachusetts | 29.5 |
| 42 | Michigan | 16.6 |
| 45 | Minnesota | 16.0 |
| 11 | Mississippi | 22.7 |
| 13 | Missouri | 22.4 |
| 39 | Montana | 17.7 |
| 28 | Nebraska | 20.3 |
| 33 | Nevada | 19.0 |
| 17 | New Hampshire | 22.1 |
| 2 | New Jersey | 30.3 |
| 24 | New Mexico | 20.8 |
| 1 | New York | 37.4 |
| 12 | North Carolina | 22.5 |
| 34 | North Dakota | 18.3 |
| 31 | Ohio | 20.1 |
| 30 | Oklahoma | 20.2 |
| 44 | Oregon | 16.1 |
| 25 | Pennsylvania | 20.7 |
| 7 | Rhode Island | 24.5 |
| 10 | South Carolina | 23.4 |
| 34 | South Dakota | 18.3 |
| 17 | Tennessee | 22.1 |
| 23 | Texas | 20.9 |
| 49 | Utah | 15.6 |
| 46 | Vermont | 15.9 |
| 27 | Virginia | 20.4 |
| 50 | Washington | 15.5 |
| 43 | West Virginia | 16.4 |
| 25 | Wisconsin | 20.7 |
| 6 | Wyoming | 27.3 |

RANK ORDER

| RANK | STATE | RATE |
|------|-------|------|
| 1 | New York | 37.4 |
| 2 | New Jersey | 30.3 |
| 3 | Louisiana | 29.5 |
| 3 | Massachusetts | 29.5 |
| 5 | Illinois | 27.5 |
| 6 | Wyoming | 27.3 |
| 7 | Rhode Island | 24.5 |
| 8 | Maryland | 24.2 |
| 9 | Arkansas | 24.1 |
| 10 | South Carolina | 23.4 |
| 11 | Mississippi | 22.7 |
| 12 | North Carolina | 22.5 |
| 13 | Arizona | 22.4 |
| 13 | Missouri | 22.4 |
| 15 | Connecticut | 22.2 |
| 15 | Kansas | 22.2 |
| 17 | New Hampshire | 22.1 |
| 17 | Tennessee | 22.1 |
| 19 | Alabama | 22.0 |
| 20 | Georgia | 21.8 |
| 21 | Hawaii | 21.7 |
| 22 | Florida | 21.6 |
| 23 | Texas | 20.9 |
| 24 | New Mexico | 20.8 |
| 25 | Pennsylvania | 20.7 |
| 25 | Wisconsin | 20.7 |
| 27 | Virginia | 20.4 |
| 28 | Colorado | 20.3 |
| 28 | Nebraska | 20.3 |
| 30 | Oklahoma | 20.2 |
| 31 | Ohio | 20.1 |
| 32 | Delaware | 19.2 |
| 33 | Nevada | 19.0 |
| 34 | North Dakota | 18.3 |
| 34 | South Dakota | 18.3 |
| 36 | California | 18.1 |
| 37 | Idaho | 17.9 |
| 38 | Indiana | 17.8 |
| 39 | Montana | 17.7 |
| 40 | Iowa | 17.2 |
| 41 | Kentucky | 17.1 |
| 42 | Michigan | 16.6 |
| 43 | West Virginia | 16.4 |
| 44 | Oregon | 16.1 |
| 45 | Minnesota | 16.0 |
| 46 | Maine | 15.9 |
| 46 | Vermont | 15.9 |
| 48 | Alaska | 15.7 |
| 49 | Utah | 15.6 |
| 50 | Washington | 15.5 |

District of Columbia                62.6

Source: CQ Press using data from U.S. Bureau of the Census, Governments Division
   "Government Employment and Payroll" (http://www.census.gov/govs/apes/index.html)
*Full-time equivalent as of March 2011.  Does not include employees of police departments who are not officers.

# Per Capita State and Local Government Expenditures for Police Protection in 2011
## National Per Capita = $309*

ALPHA ORDER

| RANK | STATE | PER CAPITA |
|------|-------|-----------|
| 35 | Alabama | $237 |
| 2 | Alaska | 452 |
| 12 | Arizona | 325 |
| 49 | Arkansas | 185 |
| 4 | California | 400 |
| 13 | Colorado | 323 |
| 19 | Connecticut | 299 |
| 14 | Delaware | 320 |
| 5 | Florida | 385 |
| 38 | Georgia | 232 |
| 20 | Hawaii | 280 |
| 33 | Idaho | 241 |
| 9 | Illinois | 360 |
| 45 | Indiana | 199 |
| 44 | Iowa | 210 |
| 29 | Kansas | 255 |
| 50 | Kentucky | 161 |
| 11 | Louisiana | 329 |
| 45 | Maine | 199 |
| 8 | Maryland | 370 |
| 14 | Massachusetts | 320 |
| 33 | Michigan | 241 |
| 17 | Minnesota | 309 |
| 43 | Mississippi | 222 |
| 22 | Missouri | 278 |
| 27 | Montana | 258 |
| 41 | Nebraska | 223 |
| 3 | Nevada | 421 |
| 26 | New Hampshire | 267 |
| 6 | New Jersey | 378 |
| 18 | New Mexico | 306 |
| 1 | New York | 462 |
| 30 | North Carolina | 254 |
| 41 | North Dakota | 223 |
| 23 | Ohio | 277 |
| 35 | Oklahoma | 237 |
| 21 | Oregon | 279 |
| 32 | Pennsylvania | 246 |
| 10 | Rhode Island | 339 |
| 40 | South Carolina | 227 |
| 47 | South Dakota | 197 |
| 25 | Tennessee | 268 |
| 28 | Texas | 257 |
| 37 | Utah | 234 |
| 24 | Vermont | 276 |
| 31 | Virginia | 252 |
| 39 | Washington | 230 |
| 48 | West Virginia | 192 |
| 16 | Wisconsin | 310 |
| 7 | Wyoming | 377 |

RANK ORDER

| RANK | STATE | PER CAPITA |
|------|-------|-----------|
| 1 | New York | $462 |
| 2 | Alaska | 452 |
| 3 | Nevada | 421 |
| 4 | California | 400 |
| 5 | Florida | 385 |
| 6 | New Jersey | 378 |
| 7 | Wyoming | 377 |
| 8 | Maryland | 370 |
| 9 | Illinois | 360 |
| 10 | Rhode Island | 339 |
| 11 | Louisiana | 329 |
| 12 | Arizona | 325 |
| 13 | Colorado | 323 |
| 14 | Delaware | 320 |
| 14 | Massachusetts | 320 |
| 16 | Wisconsin | 310 |
| 17 | Minnesota | 309 |
| 18 | New Mexico | 306 |
| 19 | Connecticut | 299 |
| 20 | Hawaii | 280 |
| 21 | Oregon | 279 |
| 22 | Missouri | 278 |
| 23 | Ohio | 277 |
| 24 | Vermont | 276 |
| 25 | Tennessee | 268 |
| 26 | New Hampshire | 267 |
| 27 | Montana | 258 |
| 28 | Texas | 257 |
| 29 | Kansas | 255 |
| 30 | North Carolina | 254 |
| 31 | Virginia | 252 |
| 32 | Pennsylvania | 246 |
| 33 | Idaho | 241 |
| 33 | Michigan | 241 |
| 35 | Alabama | 237 |
| 35 | Oklahoma | 237 |
| 37 | Utah | 234 |
| 38 | Georgia | 232 |
| 39 | Washington | 230 |
| 40 | South Carolina | 227 |
| 41 | Nebraska | 223 |
| 41 | North Dakota | 223 |
| 43 | Mississippi | 222 |
| 44 | Iowa | 210 |
| 45 | Indiana | 199 |
| 45 | Maine | 199 |
| 47 | South Dakota | 197 |
| 48 | West Virginia | 192 |
| 49 | Arkansas | 185 |
| 50 | Kentucky | 161 |

| District of Columbia | 955 |
|---|---|

Source: CQ Press using data from U.S. Bureau of the Census, Governments Division
   "2011 State and Local Government Finances" (http://www.census.gov/govs/local/)
*Direct general expenditures.

# Per Capita State and Local Government Expenditures for Corrections in 2011

## National Per Capita = $235*

ALPHA ORDER

| RANK | STATE | PER CAPITA |
|---|---|---|
| 43 | Alabama | $155 |
| 1 | Alaska | 397 |
| 21 | Arizona | 226 |
| 30 | Arkansas | 184 |
| 2 | California | 361 |
| 15 | Colorado | 237 |
| 27 | Connecticut | 192 |
| 7 | Delaware | 294 |
| 22 | Florida | 225 |
| 17 | Georgia | 230 |
| 50 | Hawaii | 139 |
| 30 | Idaho | 184 |
| 37 | Illinois | 172 |
| 44 | Indiana | 154 |
| 45 | Iowa | 153 |
| 33 | Kansas | 176 |
| 38 | Kentucky | 168 |
| 8 | Louisiana | 286 |
| 46 | Maine | 148 |
| 6 | Maryland | 295 |
| 41 | Massachusetts | 159 |
| 20 | Michigan | 227 |
| 40 | Minnesota | 163 |
| 29 | Mississippi | 186 |
| 47 | Missouri | 143 |
| 14 | Montana | 241 |
| 25 | Nebraska | 198 |
| 12 | Nevada | 255 |
| 48 | New Hampshire | 140 |
| 16 | New Jersey | 234 |
| 5 | New Mexico | 300 |
| 4 | New York | 302 |
| 24 | North Carolina | 199 |
| 32 | North Dakota | 177 |
| 39 | Ohio | 167 |
| 36 | Oklahoma | 173 |
| 10 | Oregon | 271 |
| 13 | Pennsylvania | 254 |
| 28 | Rhode Island | 188 |
| 48 | South Carolina | 140 |
| 26 | South Dakota | 194 |
| 41 | Tennessee | 159 |
| 19 | Texas | 228 |
| 34 | Utah | 175 |
| 23 | Vermont | 202 |
| 9 | Virginia | 273 |
| 17 | Washington | 230 |
| 34 | West Virginia | 175 |
| 11 | Wisconsin | 270 |
| 3 | Wyoming | 356 |

RANK ORDER

| RANK | STATE | PER CAPITA |
|---|---|---|
| 1 | Alaska | $397 |
| 2 | California | 361 |
| 3 | Wyoming | 356 |
| 4 | New York | 302 |
| 5 | New Mexico | 300 |
| 6 | Maryland | 295 |
| 7 | Delaware | 294 |
| 8 | Louisiana | 286 |
| 9 | Virginia | 273 |
| 10 | Oregon | 271 |
| 11 | Wisconsin | 270 |
| 12 | Nevada | 255 |
| 13 | Pennsylvania | 254 |
| 14 | Montana | 241 |
| 15 | Colorado | 237 |
| 16 | New Jersey | 234 |
| 17 | Georgia | 230 |
| 17 | Washington | 230 |
| 19 | Texas | 228 |
| 20 | Michigan | 227 |
| 21 | Arizona | 226 |
| 22 | Florida | 225 |
| 23 | Vermont | 202 |
| 24 | North Carolina | 199 |
| 25 | Nebraska | 198 |
| 26 | South Dakota | 194 |
| 27 | Connecticut | 192 |
| 28 | Rhode Island | 188 |
| 29 | Mississippi | 186 |
| 30 | Arkansas | 184 |
| 30 | Idaho | 184 |
| 32 | North Dakota | 177 |
| 33 | Kansas | 176 |
| 34 | Utah | 175 |
| 34 | West Virginia | 175 |
| 36 | Oklahoma | 173 |
| 37 | Illinois | 172 |
| 38 | Kentucky | 168 |
| 39 | Ohio | 167 |
| 40 | Minnesota | 163 |
| 41 | Massachusetts | 159 |
| 41 | Tennessee | 159 |
| 43 | Alabama | 155 |
| 44 | Indiana | 154 |
| 45 | Iowa | 153 |
| 46 | Maine | 148 |
| 47 | Missouri | 143 |
| 48 | New Hampshire | 140 |
| 48 | South Carolina | 140 |
| 50 | Hawaii | 139 |

| District of Columbia | 415 |
|---|---|

Source: CQ Press using data from U.S. Bureau of the Census, Governments Division
"2011 State and Local Government Finances" (http://www.census.gov/govs/local/)
*Direct general expenditures.

# Per Capita State and Local Government Expenditures for Judicial and Legal Services in 2011
## National Per Capita = $138*

ALPHA ORDER

| RANK | STATE | PER CAPITA |
|------|-------|------------|
| 43 | Alabama | $86 |
| 1 | Alaska | 313 |
| 15 | Arizona | 144 |
| 50 | Arkansas | 70 |
| 2 | California | 236 |
| 17 | Colorado | 132 |
| 5 | Connecticut | 192 |
| 7 | Delaware | 170 |
| 26 | Florida | 115 |
| 36 | Georgia | 103 |
| 6 | Hawaii | 173 |
| 22 | Idaho | 120 |
| 27 | Illinois | 114 |
| 48 | Indiana | 74 |
| 31 | Iowa | 111 |
| 34 | Kansas | 105 |
| 24 | Kentucky | 116 |
| 10 | Louisiana | 159 |
| 49 | Maine | 73 |
| 16 | Maryland | 136 |
| 14 | Massachusetts | 145 |
| 28 | Michigan | 113 |
| 18 | Minnesota | 131 |
| 46 | Mississippi | 76 |
| 44 | Missouri | 79 |
| 11 | Montana | 154 |
| 38 | Nebraska | 97 |
| 9 | Nevada | 165 |
| 41 | New Hampshire | 87 |
| 8 | New Jersey | 167 |
| 12 | New Mexico | 153 |
| 3 | New York | 217 |
| 45 | North Carolina | 78 |
| 31 | North Dakota | 111 |
| 13 | Ohio | 152 |
| 41 | Oklahoma | 87 |
| 28 | Oregon | 113 |
| 18 | Pennsylvania | 131 |
| 24 | Rhode Island | 116 |
| 47 | South Carolina | 75 |
| 39 | South Dakota | 95 |
| 39 | Tennessee | 95 |
| 33 | Texas | 106 |
| 20 | Utah | 122 |
| 30 | Vermont | 112 |
| 37 | Virginia | 102 |
| 20 | Washington | 122 |
| 23 | West Virginia | 117 |
| 35 | Wisconsin | 104 |
| 4 | Wyoming | 204 |

RANK ORDER

| RANK | STATE | PER CAPITA |
|------|-------|------------|
| 1 | Alaska | $313 |
| 2 | California | 236 |
| 3 | New York | 217 |
| 4 | Wyoming | 204 |
| 5 | Connecticut | 192 |
| 6 | Hawaii | 173 |
| 7 | Delaware | 170 |
| 8 | New Jersey | 167 |
| 9 | Nevada | 165 |
| 10 | Louisiana | 159 |
| 11 | Montana | 154 |
| 12 | New Mexico | 153 |
| 13 | Ohio | 152 |
| 14 | Massachusetts | 145 |
| 15 | Arizona | 144 |
| 16 | Maryland | 136 |
| 17 | Colorado | 132 |
| 18 | Minnesota | 131 |
| 18 | Pennsylvania | 131 |
| 20 | Utah | 122 |
| 20 | Washington | 122 |
| 22 | Idaho | 120 |
| 23 | West Virginia | 117 |
| 24 | Kentucky | 116 |
| 24 | Rhode Island | 116 |
| 26 | Florida | 115 |
| 27 | Illinois | 114 |
| 28 | Michigan | 113 |
| 28 | Oregon | 113 |
| 30 | Vermont | 112 |
| 31 | Iowa | 111 |
| 31 | North Dakota | 111 |
| 33 | Texas | 106 |
| 34 | Kansas | 105 |
| 35 | Wisconsin | 104 |
| 36 | Georgia | 103 |
| 37 | Virginia | 102 |
| 38 | Nebraska | 97 |
| 39 | South Dakota | 95 |
| 39 | Tennessee | 95 |
| 41 | New Hampshire | 87 |
| 41 | Oklahoma | 87 |
| 43 | Alabama | 86 |
| 44 | Missouri | 79 |
| 45 | North Carolina | 78 |
| 46 | Mississippi | 76 |
| 47 | South Carolina | 75 |
| 48 | Indiana | 74 |
| 49 | Maine | 73 |
| 50 | Arkansas | 70 |

District of Columbia — 184

Source: CQ Press using data from U.S. Bureau of the Census, Governments Division
"2011 State and Local Government Finances" (http://www.census.gov/govs/local/)
*Direct general expenditures. Includes courts, prosecution and legal services, and public defense.

# III. Defense

# Homeland Security Grants in 2013

## National Total = $913,389,689*

| ALPHA ORDER | | | | | RANK ORDER | | | |
|---|---|---|---|---|---|---|---|---|
| RANK | STATE | GRANTS | % of USA | | RANK | STATE | GRANTS | % of USA |
| 20 | Alabama | $3,459,364 | 0.4% | | 1 | New York | $241,023,122 | 26.4% |
| 20 | Alaska | 3,459,364 | 0.4% | | 2 | California | 168,238,685 | 18.4% |
| 13 | Arizona | 9,472,417 | 1.0% | | 3 | Illinois | 81,950,798 | 9.0% |
| 20 | Arkansas | 3,459,364 | 0.4% | | 4 | Texas | 57,209,688 | 6.3% |
| 2 | California | 168,238,685 | 18.4% | | 5 | Pennsylvania | 29,285,656 | 3.2% |
| 17 | Colorado | 6,459,364 | 0.7% | | 6 | New Jersey | 28,927,276 | 3.2% |
| 20 | Connecticut | 3,459,364 | 0.4% | | 7 | Massachusetts | 22,453,349 | 2.5% |
| 20 | Delaware | 3,459,364 | 0.4% | | 8 | Florida | 18,074,272 | 2.0% |
| 8 | Florida | 18,074,272 | 2.0% | | 9 | Georgia | 11,418,784 | 1.3% |
| 9 | Georgia | 11,418,784 | 1.3% | | 10 | Michigan | 11,289,215 | 1.2% |
| 20 | Hawaii | 3,459,364 | 0.4% | | 11 | Washington | 11,146,176 | 1.2% |
| 20 | Idaho | 3,459,364 | 0.4% | | 12 | Maryland | 10,825,727 | 1.2% |
| 3 | Illinois | 81,950,798 | 9.0% | | 13 | Arizona | 9,472,417 | 1.0% |
| 20 | Indiana | 3,459,364 | 0.4% | | 14 | Minnesota | 8,959,364 | 1.0% |
| 20 | Iowa | 3,459,364 | 0.4% | | 15 | North Carolina | 7,773,429 | 0.9% |
| 20 | Kansas | 3,459,364 | 0.4% | | 16 | Ohio | 6,693,676 | 0.7% |
| 20 | Kentucky | 3,459,364 | 0.4% | | 17 | Colorado | 6,459,364 | 0.7% |
| 20 | Louisiana | 3,459,364 | 0.4% | | 17 | Missouri | 6,459,364 | 0.7% |
| 20 | Maine | 3,459,364 | 0.4% | | 19 | Virginia | 6,446,710 | 0.7% |
| 12 | Maryland | 10,825,727 | 1.2% | | 20 | Alabama | 3,459,364 | 0.4% |
| 7 | Massachusetts | 22,453,349 | 2.5% | | 20 | Alaska | 3,459,364 | 0.4% |
| 10 | Michigan | 11,289,215 | 1.2% | | 20 | Arkansas | 3,459,364 | 0.4% |
| 14 | Minnesota | 8,959,364 | 1.0% | | 20 | Connecticut | 3,459,364 | 0.4% |
| 20 | Mississippi | 3,459,364 | 0.4% | | 20 | Delaware | 3,459,364 | 0.4% |
| 17 | Missouri | 6,459,364 | 0.7% | | 20 | Hawaii | 3,459,364 | 0.4% |
| 20 | Montana | 3,459,364 | 0.4% | | 20 | Idaho | 3,459,364 | 0.4% |
| 20 | Nebraska | 3,459,364 | 0.4% | | 20 | Indiana | 3,459,364 | 0.4% |
| 20 | Nevada | 3,459,364 | 0.4% | | 20 | Iowa | 3,459,364 | 0.4% |
| 20 | New Hampshire | 3,459,364 | 0.4% | | 20 | Kansas | 3,459,364 | 0.4% |
| 6 | New Jersey | 28,927,276 | 3.2% | | 20 | Kentucky | 3,459,364 | 0.4% |
| 20 | New Mexico | 3,459,364 | 0.4% | | 20 | Louisiana | 3,459,364 | 0.4% |
| 1 | New York | 241,023,122 | 26.4% | | 20 | Maine | 3,459,364 | 0.4% |
| 15 | North Carolina | 7,773,429 | 0.9% | | 20 | Mississippi | 3,459,364 | 0.4% |
| 20 | North Dakota | 3,459,364 | 0.4% | | 20 | Montana | 3,459,364 | 0.4% |
| 16 | Ohio | 6,693,676 | 0.7% | | 20 | Nebraska | 3,459,364 | 0.4% |
| 20 | Oklahoma | 3,459,364 | 0.4% | | 20 | Nevada | 3,459,364 | 0.4% |
| 20 | Oregon | 3,459,364 | 0.4% | | 20 | New Hampshire | 3,459,364 | 0.4% |
| 5 | Pennsylvania | 29,285,656 | 3.2% | | 20 | New Mexico | 3,459,364 | 0.4% |
| 20 | Rhode Island | 3,459,364 | 0.4% | | 20 | North Dakota | 3,459,364 | 0.4% |
| 20 | South Carolina | 3,459,364 | 0.4% | | 20 | Oklahoma | 3,459,364 | 0.4% |
| 20 | South Dakota | 3,459,364 | 0.4% | | 20 | Oregon | 3,459,364 | 0.4% |
| 20 | Tennessee | 3,459,364 | 0.4% | | 20 | Rhode Island | 3,459,364 | 0.4% |
| 4 | Texas | 57,209,688 | 6.3% | | 20 | South Carolina | 3,459,364 | 0.4% |
| 20 | Utah | 3,459,364 | 0.4% | | 20 | South Dakota | 3,459,364 | 0.4% |
| 20 | Vermont | 3,459,364 | 0.4% | | 20 | Tennessee | 3,459,364 | 0.4% |
| 19 | Virginia | 6,446,710 | 0.7% | | 20 | Utah | 3,459,364 | 0.4% |
| 11 | Washington | 11,146,176 | 1.2% | | 20 | Vermont | 3,459,364 | 0.4% |
| 20 | West Virginia | 3,459,364 | 0.4% | | 20 | West Virginia | 3,459,364 | 0.4% |
| 20 | Wisconsin | 3,459,364 | 0.4% | | 20 | Wisconsin | 3,459,364 | 0.4% |
| 20 | Wyoming | 3,459,364 | 0.4% | | 20 | Wyoming | 3,459,364 | 0.4% |
| | | | | | | District of Columbia | 55,420,121 | 6.1% |

Source: CQ Press using data from U.S. Department of Homeland Security
"FY 2013 Homeland Security Grant Program (HSGP)" (http://www.fema.gov/media-library/assets/documents/32611?id=7513)
*For fiscal year 2013. National total includes $6,622,212 in grants to U.S. territories. The Homeland Security Grant Program (HSGP) includes three sub-grant programs: State Homeland Security Program (SHSP), Urban Area Security Initiative (UASI), and Operation Stonegarden (OPSG). Law Enforcement Terrorism Prevention Activities (LETPA) allocations are a 25 percent subset of the SHSP and UASI allocations.

# Per Capita Homeland Security Grants in 2013

## National Per Capita = $2.87*

| ALPHA ORDER | | | | RANK ORDER | | |
|---|---|---|---|---|---|---|
| RANK | STATE | PER CAPITA | | RANK | STATE | PER CAPITA |
| 45 | Alabama | $0.72 | | 1 | New York | $12.27 |
| 6 | Alaska | 4.71 | | 2 | Illinois | 6.36 |
| 26 | Arizona | 1.43 | | 3 | Wyoming | 5.94 |
| 31 | Arkansas | 1.17 | | 4 | Vermont | 5.52 |
| 7 | California | 4.39 | | 5 | North Dakota | 4.78 |
| 28 | Colorado | 1.23 | | 6 | Alaska | 4.71 |
| 37 | Connecticut | 0.96 | | 7 | California | 4.39 |
| 9 | Delaware | 3.74 | | 8 | South Dakota | 4.09 |
| 38 | Florida | 0.92 | | 9 | Delaware | 3.74 |
| 33 | Georgia | 1.14 | | 10 | Montana | 3.41 |
| 16 | Hawaii | 2.46 | | 11 | Massachusetts | 3.35 |
| 19 | Idaho | 2.15 | | 12 | Rhode Island | 3.29 |
| 2 | Illinois | 6.36 | | 13 | New Jersey | 3.25 |
| 49 | Indiana | 0.53 | | 14 | New Hampshire | 2.61 |
| 35 | Iowa | 1.12 | | 15 | Maine | 2.60 |
| 29 | Kansas | 1.20 | | 16 | Hawaii | 2.46 |
| 41 | Kentucky | 0.79 | | 17 | Pennsylvania | 2.29 |
| 44 | Louisiana | 0.75 | | 18 | Texas | 2.16 |
| 15 | Maine | 2.60 | | 19 | Idaho | 2.15 |
| 22 | Maryland | 1.83 | | 20 | West Virginia | 1.87 |
| 11 | Massachusetts | 3.35 | | 21 | Nebraska | 1.85 |
| 33 | Michigan | 1.14 | | 22 | Maryland | 1.83 |
| 24 | Minnesota | 1.65 | | 23 | New Mexico | 1.66 |
| 32 | Mississippi | 1.16 | | 24 | Minnesota | 1.65 |
| 36 | Missouri | 1.07 | | 25 | Washington | 1.60 |
| 10 | Montana | 3.41 | | 26 | Arizona | 1.43 |
| 21 | Nebraska | 1.85 | | 27 | Nevada | 1.24 |
| 27 | Nevada | 1.24 | | 28 | Colorado | 1.23 |
| 14 | New Hampshire | 2.61 | | 29 | Kansas | 1.20 |
| 13 | New Jersey | 3.25 | | 30 | Utah | 1.19 |
| 23 | New Mexico | 1.66 | | 31 | Arkansas | 1.17 |
| 1 | New York | 12.27 | | 32 | Mississippi | 1.16 |
| 41 | North Carolina | 0.79 | | 33 | Georgia | 1.14 |
| 5 | North Dakota | 4.78 | | 33 | Michigan | 1.14 |
| 48 | Ohio | 0.58 | | 35 | Iowa | 1.12 |
| 39 | Oklahoma | 0.90 | | 36 | Missouri | 1.07 |
| 40 | Oregon | 0.88 | | 37 | Connecticut | 0.96 |
| 17 | Pennsylvania | 2.29 | | 38 | Florida | 0.92 |
| 12 | Rhode Island | 3.29 | | 39 | Oklahoma | 0.90 |
| 45 | South Carolina | 0.72 | | 40 | Oregon | 0.88 |
| 8 | South Dakota | 4.09 | | 41 | Kentucky | 0.79 |
| 49 | Tennessee | 0.53 | | 41 | North Carolina | 0.79 |
| 18 | Texas | 2.16 | | 43 | Virginia | 0.78 |
| 30 | Utah | 1.19 | | 44 | Louisiana | 0.75 |
| 4 | Vermont | 5.52 | | 45 | Alabama | 0.72 |
| 43 | Virginia | 0.78 | | 45 | South Carolina | 0.72 |
| 25 | Washington | 1.60 | | 47 | Wisconsin | 0.60 |
| 20 | West Virginia | 1.87 | | 48 | Ohio | 0.58 |
| 47 | Wisconsin | 0.60 | | 49 | Indiana | 0.53 |
| 3 | Wyoming | 5.94 | | 49 | Tennessee | 0.53 |
| | | | | | District of Columbia | 85.73 |

Source: CQ Press using data from U.S. Department of Homeland Security
 "FY 2013 Homeland Security Grant Program (HSGP)" (http://www.fema.gov/media-library/assets/documents/32611?id=7513)
*For fiscal year 2013.  National total includes $6,622,212 in grants to U.S. territories.  The Homeland Security Grant Program (HSGP) includes three sub-grant programs: State Homeland Security Program (SHSP), Urban Area Security Initiative (UASI), and Operation Stonegarden (OPSG). Law Enforcement Terrorism Prevention Activities (LETPA) allocations are a 25 percent subset of the SHSP and UASI allocations.

# U.S. Department of Defense Domestic Expenditures in 2009

## National Total = $527,824,146,000*

ALPHA ORDER

| RANK | STATE | EXPENDITURES | % of USA |
|------|-------|--------------|----------|
| 11 | Alabama | $14,291,629,000 | 2.7% |
| 31 | Alaska | 4,888,348,000 | 0.9% |
| 8 | Arizona | 15,308,486,000 | 2.9% |
| 37 | Arkansas | 2,673,622,000 | 0.5% |
| 2 | California | 56,742,620,000 | 10.8% |
| 18 | Colorado | 10,725,693,000 | 2.0% |
| 15 | Connecticut | 12,638,248,000 | 2.4% |
| 47 | Delaware | 876,158,000 | 0.2% |
| 4 | Florida | 22,802,179,000 | 4.3% |
| 6 | Georgia | 18,607,996,000 | 3.5% |
| 25 | Hawaii | 8,800,669,000 | 1.7% |
| 46 | Idaho | 934,634,000 | 0.2% |
| 20 | Illinois | 9,237,211,000 | 1.8% |
| 21 | Indiana | 9,188,013,000 | 1.7% |
| 40 | Iowa | 2,089,452,000 | 0.4% |
| 28 | Kansas | 6,867,835,000 | 1.3% |
| 16 | Kentucky | 12,285,425,000 | 2.3% |
| 22 | Louisiana | 9,149,589,000 | 1.7% |
| 38 | Maine | 2,382,017,000 | 0.5% |
| 5 | Maryland | 19,926,029,000 | 3.8% |
| 9 | Massachusetts | 15,081,759,000 | 2.9% |
| 26 | Michigan | 7,288,503,000 | 1.4% |
| 35 | Minnesota | 2,806,926,000 | 0.5% |
| 29 | Mississippi | 5,689,655,000 | 1.1% |
| 12 | Missouri | 14,281,251,000 | 2.7% |
| 48 | Montana | 853,639,000 | 0.2% |
| 39 | Nebraska | 2,142,336,000 | 0.4% |
| 34 | Nevada | 3,268,456,000 | 0.6% |
| 41 | New Hampshire | 2,014,350,000 | 0.4% |
| 17 | New Jersey | 11,019,807,000 | 2.1% |
| 33 | New Mexico | 3,270,536,000 | 0.6% |
| 13 | New York | 13,562,174,000 | 2.6% |
| 10 | North Carolina | 14,677,953,000 | 2.8% |
| 43 | North Dakota | 1,100,340,000 | 0.2% |
| 19 | Ohio | 10,256,353,000 | 1.9% |
| 27 | Oklahoma | 7,103,675,000 | 1.3% |
| 36 | Oregon | 2,695,604,000 | 0.5% |
| 7 | Pennsylvania | 16,789,144,000 | 3.2% |
| 42 | Rhode Island | 1,431,162,000 | 0.3% |
| 23 | South Carolina | 9,020,997,000 | 1.7% |
| 45 | South Dakota | 1,026,194,000 | 0.2% |
| 30 | Tennessee | 5,362,492,000 | 1.0% |
| 3 | Texas | 42,082,905,000 | 8.0% |
| 32 | Utah | 4,361,476,000 | 0.8% |
| 49 | Vermont | 828,433,000 | 0.2% |
| 1 | Virginia | 56,933,799,000 | 10.8% |
| 14 | Washington | 13,524,233,000 | 2.6% |
| 44 | West Virginia | 1,063,251,000 | 0.2% |
| 24 | Wisconsin | 8,898,053,000 | 1.7% |
| 50 | Wyoming | 566,662,000 | 0.1% |

RANK ORDER

| RANK | STATE | EXPENDITURES | % of USA |
|------|-------|--------------|----------|
| 1 | Virginia | $56,933,799,000 | 10.8% |
| 2 | California | 56,742,620,000 | 10.8% |
| 3 | Texas | 42,082,905,000 | 8.0% |
| 4 | Florida | 22,802,179,000 | 4.3% |
| 5 | Maryland | 19,926,029,000 | 3.8% |
| 6 | Georgia | 18,607,996,000 | 3.5% |
| 7 | Pennsylvania | 16,789,144,000 | 3.2% |
| 8 | Arizona | 15,308,486,000 | 2.9% |
| 9 | Massachusetts | 15,081,759,000 | 2.9% |
| 10 | North Carolina | 14,677,953,000 | 2.8% |
| 11 | Alabama | 14,291,629,000 | 2.7% |
| 12 | Missouri | 14,281,251,000 | 2.7% |
| 13 | New York | 13,562,174,000 | 2.6% |
| 14 | Washington | 13,524,233,000 | 2.6% |
| 15 | Connecticut | 12,638,248,000 | 2.4% |
| 16 | Kentucky | 12,285,425,000 | 2.3% |
| 17 | New Jersey | 11,019,807,000 | 2.1% |
| 18 | Colorado | 10,725,693,000 | 2.0% |
| 19 | Ohio | 10,256,353,000 | 1.9% |
| 20 | Illinois | 9,237,211,000 | 1.8% |
| 21 | Indiana | 9,188,013,000 | 1.7% |
| 22 | Louisiana | 9,149,589,000 | 1.7% |
| 23 | South Carolina | 9,020,997,000 | 1.7% |
| 24 | Wisconsin | 8,898,053,000 | 1.7% |
| 25 | Hawaii | 8,800,669,000 | 1.7% |
| 26 | Michigan | 7,288,503,000 | 1.4% |
| 27 | Oklahoma | 7,103,675,000 | 1.3% |
| 28 | Kansas | 6,867,835,000 | 1.3% |
| 29 | Mississippi | 5,689,655,000 | 1.1% |
| 30 | Tennessee | 5,362,492,000 | 1.0% |
| 31 | Alaska | 4,888,348,000 | 0.9% |
| 32 | Utah | 4,361,476,000 | 0.8% |
| 33 | New Mexico | 3,270,536,000 | 0.6% |
| 34 | Nevada | 3,268,456,000 | 0.6% |
| 35 | Minnesota | 2,806,926,000 | 0.5% |
| 36 | Oregon | 2,695,604,000 | 0.5% |
| 37 | Arkansas | 2,673,622,000 | 0.5% |
| 38 | Maine | 2,382,017,000 | 0.5% |
| 39 | Nebraska | 2,142,336,000 | 0.4% |
| 40 | Iowa | 2,089,452,000 | 0.4% |
| 41 | New Hampshire | 2,014,350,000 | 0.4% |
| 42 | Rhode Island | 1,431,162,000 | 0.3% |
| 43 | North Dakota | 1,100,340,000 | 0.2% |
| 44 | West Virginia | 1,063,251,000 | 0.2% |
| 45 | South Dakota | 1,026,194,000 | 0.2% |
| 46 | Idaho | 934,634,000 | 0.2% |
| 47 | Delaware | 876,158,000 | 0.2% |
| 48 | Montana | 853,639,000 | 0.2% |
| 49 | Vermont | 828,433,000 | 0.2% |
| 50 | Wyoming | 566,662,000 | 0.1% |
| | District of Columbia | 8,406,175,000 | 1.6% |

Source: U.S. Department of Defense
"Atlas/Data Abstract for the United States" (http://siadapp.dmdc.osd.mil/personnel/L03/fy09/09top.htm)
*Expenditures for payroll, grants, and prime contracts ($25,000 or more) for civil and military functions. Does not include payroll, contracts, or grants to U.S. territories and other countries.

# Per Capita U.S. Department of Defense Domestic Expenditures in 2009

## National Per Capita = $1,719*

| ALPHA ORDER | | | RANK ORDER | | |
|---|---|---|---|---|---|
| RANK | STATE | PER CAPITA | RANK | STATE | PER CAPITA |
| 6 | Alabama | $3,035 | 1 | Virginia | $7,223 |
| 2 | Alaska | 6,999 | 2 | Alaska | 6,999 |
| 10 | Arizona | 2,321 | 3 | Hawaii | 6,795 |
| 39 | Arkansas | 925 | 4 | Connecticut | 3,592 |
| 26 | California | 1,535 | 5 | Maryland | 3,496 |
| 12 | Colorado | 2,135 | 6 | Alabama | 3,035 |
| 4 | Connecticut | 3,592 | 7 | Kentucky | 2,848 |
| 38 | Delaware | 990 | 8 | Kansas | 2,436 |
| 35 | Florida | 1,230 | 9 | Missouri | 2,385 |
| 18 | Georgia | 1,893 | 10 | Arizona | 2,321 |
| 3 | Hawaii | 6,795 | 11 | Massachusetts | 2,287 |
| 48 | Idaho | 605 | 12 | Colorado | 2,135 |
| 44 | Illinois | 715 | 13 | Louisiana | 2,037 |
| 28 | Indiana | 1,430 | 14 | Washington | 2,029 |
| 46 | Iowa | 695 | 15 | South Carolina | 1,978 |
| 8 | Kansas | 2,436 | 16 | Mississippi | 1,927 |
| 7 | Kentucky | 2,848 | 16 | Oklahoma | 1,927 |
| 13 | Louisiana | 2,037 | 18 | Georgia | 1,893 |
| 19 | Maine | 1,807 | 19 | Maine | 1,807 |
| 5 | Maryland | 3,496 | 20 | North Dakota | 1,701 |
| 11 | Massachusetts | 2,287 | 21 | Texas | 1,698 |
| 43 | Michigan | 731 | 22 | New Mexico | 1,627 |
| 50 | Minnesota | 533 | 23 | Wisconsin | 1,574 |
| 16 | Mississippi | 1,927 | 24 | Utah | 1,566 |
| 9 | Missouri | 2,385 | 25 | North Carolina | 1,565 |
| 41 | Montana | 876 | 26 | California | 1,535 |
| 36 | Nebraska | 1,192 | 27 | New Hampshire | 1,521 |
| 34 | Nevada | 1,237 | 28 | Indiana | 1,430 |
| 27 | New Hampshire | 1,521 | 29 | Rhode Island | 1,359 |
| 32 | New Jersey | 1,266 | 30 | Pennsylvania | 1,332 |
| 22 | New Mexico | 1,627 | 30 | Vermont | 1,332 |
| 47 | New York | 694 | 32 | New Jersey | 1,266 |
| 25 | North Carolina | 1,565 | 33 | South Dakota | 1,263 |
| 20 | North Dakota | 1,701 | 34 | Nevada | 1,237 |
| 40 | Ohio | 889 | 35 | Florida | 1,230 |
| 16 | Oklahoma | 1,927 | 36 | Nebraska | 1,192 |
| 45 | Oregon | 705 | 37 | Wyoming | 1,041 |
| 30 | Pennsylvania | 1,332 | 38 | Delaware | 990 |
| 29 | Rhode Island | 1,359 | 39 | Arkansas | 925 |
| 15 | South Carolina | 1,978 | 40 | Ohio | 889 |
| 33 | South Dakota | 1,263 | 41 | Montana | 876 |
| 42 | Tennessee | 852 | 42 | Tennessee | 852 |
| 21 | Texas | 1,698 | 43 | Michigan | 731 |
| 24 | Utah | 1,566 | 44 | Illinois | 715 |
| 30 | Vermont | 1,332 | 45 | Oregon | 705 |
| 1 | Virginia | 7,223 | 46 | Iowa | 695 |
| 14 | Washington | 2,029 | 47 | New York | 694 |
| 49 | West Virginia | 584 | 48 | Idaho | 605 |
| 23 | Wisconsin | 1,574 | 49 | West Virginia | 584 |
| 37 | Wyoming | 1,041 | 50 | Minnesota | 533 |
| | | | | District of Columbia | 14,018 |

Source: CQ Press using data from U.S. Department of Defense
  "Atlas/Data Abstract for the United States" (http://siadapp.dmdc.osd.mil/personnel/L03/fy09/09top.htm)
*Expenditures for payroll, grants, and prime contracts ($25,000 or more) for civil and military functions.  Does not include payroll, contracts, or grants to U.S. territories and other countries.

# U.S. Department of Defense Total Contracts in 2009

## National Total = $327,461,911,000*

| RANK | STATE | CONTRACTS | % of USA |
|---|---|---|---|
| 11 | Alabama | $9,501,617,000 | 2.9% |
| 32 | Alaska | 2,180,004,000 | 0.7% |
| 8 | Arizona | 12,064,904,000 | 3.7% |
| 40 | Arkansas | 985,545,000 | 0.3% |
| 1 | California | 41,697,621,000 | 12.7% |
| 21 | Colorado | 5,544,160,000 | 1.7% |
| 9 | Connecticut | 11,817,700,000 | 3.6% |
| 47 | Delaware | 315,358,000 | 0.1% |
| 5 | Florida | 13,188,889,000 | 4.0% |
| 15 | Georgia | 7,039,405,000 | 2.1% |
| 30 | Hawaii | 2,377,271,000 | 0.7% |
| 49 | Idaho | 166,118,000 | 0.1% |
| 20 | Illinois | 5,936,547,000 | 1.8% |
| 16 | Indiana | 6,795,168,000 | 2.1% |
| 39 | Iowa | 1,285,344,000 | 0.4% |
| 27 | Kansas | 3,158,303,000 | 1.0% |
| 17 | Kentucky | 6,534,291,000 | 2.0% |
| 18 | Louisiana | 6,407,579,000 | 2.0% |
| 38 | Maine | 1,407,038,000 | 0.4% |
| 6 | Maryland | 12,911,613,000 | 3.9% |
| 4 | Massachusetts | 13,347,134,000 | 4.1% |
| 22 | Michigan | 5,331,864,000 | 1.6% |
| 37 | Minnesota | 1,529,964,000 | 0.5% |
| 26 | Mississippi | 3,447,072,000 | 1.1% |
| 10 | Missouri | 10,453,949,000 | 3.2% |
| 48 | Montana | 288,759,000 | 0.1% |
| 41 | Nebraska | 931,306,000 | 0.3% |
| 33 | Nevada | 1,818,505,000 | 0.6% |
| 35 | New Hampshire | 1,567,821,000 | 0.5% |
| 13 | New Jersey | 8,226,697,000 | 2.5% |
| 34 | New Mexico | 1,604,488,000 | 0.5% |
| 12 | New York | 8,544,864,000 | 2.6% |
| 25 | North Carolina | 3,994,861,000 | 1.2% |
| 45 | North Dakota | 437,227,000 | 0.1% |
| 19 | Ohio | 6,249,462,000 | 1.9% |
| 29 | Oklahoma | 2,880,203,000 | 0.9% |
| 36 | Oregon | 1,545,991,000 | 0.5% |
| 7 | Pennsylvania | 12,362,728,000 | 3.8% |
| 42 | Rhode Island | 661,794,000 | 0.2% |
| 23 | South Carolina | 5,298,645,000 | 1.6% |
| 44 | South Dakota | 444,618,000 | 0.1% |
| 28 | Tennessee | 3,083,056,000 | 0.9% |
| 3 | Texas | 22,483,566,000 | 6.9% |
| 31 | Utah | 2,206,025,000 | 0.7% |
| 43 | Vermont | 549,931,000 | 0.2% |
| 2 | Virginia | 38,731,568,000 | 11.8% |
| 24 | Washington | 5,173,959,000 | 1.6% |
| 46 | West Virginia | 396,440,000 | 0.1% |
| 14 | Wisconsin | 7,673,970,000 | 2.3% |
| 50 | Wyoming | 140,406,000 | 0.0% |

| RANK | STATE | CONTRACTS | % of USA |
|---|---|---|---|
| 1 | California | $41,697,621,000 | 12.7% |
| 2 | Virginia | 38,731,568,000 | 11.8% |
| 3 | Texas | 22,483,566,000 | 6.9% |
| 4 | Massachusetts | 13,347,134,000 | 4.1% |
| 5 | Florida | 13,188,889,000 | 4.0% |
| 6 | Maryland | 12,911,613,000 | 3.9% |
| 7 | Pennsylvania | 12,362,728,000 | 3.8% |
| 8 | Arizona | 12,064,904,000 | 3.7% |
| 9 | Connecticut | 11,817,700,000 | 3.6% |
| 10 | Missouri | 10,453,949,000 | 3.2% |
| 11 | Alabama | 9,501,617,000 | 2.9% |
| 12 | New York | 8,544,864,000 | 2.6% |
| 13 | New Jersey | 8,226,697,000 | 2.5% |
| 14 | Wisconsin | 7,673,970,000 | 2.3% |
| 15 | Georgia | 7,039,405,000 | 2.1% |
| 16 | Indiana | 6,795,168,000 | 2.1% |
| 17 | Kentucky | 6,534,291,000 | 2.0% |
| 18 | Louisiana | 6,407,579,000 | 2.0% |
| 19 | Ohio | 6,249,462,000 | 1.9% |
| 20 | Illinois | 5,936,547,000 | 1.8% |
| 21 | Colorado | 5,544,160,000 | 1.7% |
| 22 | Michigan | 5,331,864,000 | 1.6% |
| 23 | South Carolina | 5,298,645,000 | 1.6% |
| 24 | Washington | 5,173,959,000 | 1.6% |
| 25 | North Carolina | 3,994,861,000 | 1.2% |
| 26 | Mississippi | 3,447,072,000 | 1.1% |
| 27 | Kansas | 3,158,303,000 | 1.0% |
| 28 | Tennessee | 3,083,056,000 | 0.9% |
| 29 | Oklahoma | 2,880,203,000 | 0.9% |
| 30 | Hawaii | 2,377,271,000 | 0.7% |
| 31 | Utah | 2,206,025,000 | 0.7% |
| 32 | Alaska | 2,180,004,000 | 0.7% |
| 33 | Nevada | 1,818,505,000 | 0.6% |
| 34 | New Mexico | 1,604,488,000 | 0.5% |
| 35 | New Hampshire | 1,567,821,000 | 0.5% |
| 36 | Oregon | 1,545,991,000 | 0.5% |
| 37 | Minnesota | 1,529,964,000 | 0.5% |
| 38 | Maine | 1,407,038,000 | 0.4% |
| 39 | Iowa | 1,285,344,000 | 0.4% |
| 40 | Arkansas | 985,545,000 | 0.3% |
| 41 | Nebraska | 931,306,000 | 0.3% |
| 42 | Rhode Island | 661,794,000 | 0.2% |
| 43 | Vermont | 549,931,000 | 0.2% |
| 44 | South Dakota | 444,618,000 | 0.1% |
| 45 | North Dakota | 437,227,000 | 0.1% |
| 46 | West Virginia | 396,440,000 | 0.1% |
| 47 | Delaware | 315,358,000 | 0.1% |
| 48 | Montana | 288,759,000 | 0.1% |
| 49 | Idaho | 166,118,000 | 0.1% |
| 50 | Wyoming | 140,406,000 | 0.0% |
| | District of Columbia | 4,740,563,000 | 1.4% |

Source: U.S. Department of Defense
"Atlas/Data Abstract for the United States" (http://siadapp.dmdc.osd.mil/personnel/L03/fy09/09top.htm)
*Includes prime contracts ($25,000 or more) for civil and military functions.  Does not include contracts to U.S. territories and other countries.

# Per Capita U.S. Department of Defense Total Contracts in 2009

## National Per Capita = $1,067*

ALPHA ORDER

| RANK | STATE | PER CAPITA |
|---|---|---|
| 6 | Alabama | $2,018 |
| 3 | Alaska | 3,121 |
| 8 | Arizona | 1,829 |
| 45 | Arkansas | 341 |
| 16 | California | 1,128 |
| 18 | Colorado | 1,103 |
| 2 | Connecticut | 3,359 |
| 44 | Delaware | 356 |
| 30 | Florida | 711 |
| 29 | Georgia | 716 |
| 7 | Hawaii | 1,835 |
| 50 | Idaho | 107 |
| 39 | Illinois | 460 |
| 20 | Indiana | 1,058 |
| 41 | Iowa | 427 |
| 17 | Kansas | 1,120 |
| 10 | Kentucky | 1,515 |
| 11 | Louisiana | 1,426 |
| 19 | Maine | 1,067 |
| 4 | Maryland | 2,265 |
| 5 | Massachusetts | 2,024 |
| 36 | Michigan | 535 |
| 47 | Minnesota | 291 |
| 14 | Mississippi | 1,168 |
| 9 | Missouri | 1,746 |
| 46 | Montana | 296 |
| 37 | Nebraska | 518 |
| 31 | Nevada | 688 |
| 13 | New Hampshire | 1,184 |
| 22 | New Jersey | 945 |
| 25 | New Mexico | 798 |
| 40 | New York | 437 |
| 42 | North Carolina | 426 |
| 32 | North Dakota | 676 |
| 35 | Ohio | 541 |
| 27 | Oklahoma | 781 |
| 43 | Oregon | 404 |
| 21 | Pennsylvania | 981 |
| 33 | Rhode Island | 628 |
| 15 | South Carolina | 1,162 |
| 34 | South Dakota | 547 |
| 38 | Tennessee | 490 |
| 23 | Texas | 907 |
| 26 | Utah | 792 |
| 24 | Vermont | 884 |
| 1 | Virginia | 4,914 |
| 28 | Washington | 776 |
| 49 | West Virginia | 218 |
| 12 | Wisconsin | 1,357 |
| 48 | Wyoming | 258 |

RANK ORDER

| RANK | STATE | PER CAPITA |
|---|---|---|
| 1 | Virginia | $4,914 |
| 2 | Connecticut | 3,359 |
| 3 | Alaska | 3,121 |
| 4 | Maryland | 2,265 |
| 5 | Massachusetts | 2,024 |
| 6 | Alabama | 2,018 |
| 7 | Hawaii | 1,835 |
| 8 | Arizona | 1,829 |
| 9 | Missouri | 1,746 |
| 10 | Kentucky | 1,515 |
| 11 | Louisiana | 1,426 |
| 12 | Wisconsin | 1,357 |
| 13 | New Hampshire | 1,184 |
| 14 | Mississippi | 1,168 |
| 15 | South Carolina | 1,162 |
| 16 | California | 1,128 |
| 17 | Kansas | 1,120 |
| 18 | Colorado | 1,103 |
| 19 | Maine | 1,067 |
| 20 | Indiana | 1,058 |
| 21 | Pennsylvania | 981 |
| 22 | New Jersey | 945 |
| 23 | Texas | 907 |
| 24 | Vermont | 884 |
| 25 | New Mexico | 798 |
| 26 | Utah | 792 |
| 27 | Oklahoma | 781 |
| 28 | Washington | 776 |
| 29 | Georgia | 716 |
| 30 | Florida | 711 |
| 31 | Nevada | 688 |
| 32 | North Dakota | 676 |
| 33 | Rhode Island | 628 |
| 34 | South Dakota | 547 |
| 35 | Ohio | 541 |
| 36 | Michigan | 535 |
| 37 | Nebraska | 518 |
| 38 | Tennessee | 490 |
| 39 | Illinois | 460 |
| 40 | New York | 437 |
| 41 | Iowa | 427 |
| 42 | North Carolina | 426 |
| 43 | Oregon | 404 |
| 44 | Delaware | 356 |
| 45 | Arkansas | 341 |
| 46 | Montana | 296 |
| 47 | Minnesota | 291 |
| 48 | Wyoming | 258 |
| 49 | West Virginia | 218 |
| 50 | Idaho | 107 |
| | District of Columbia | 7,905 |

Source: CQ Press using data from U.S. Department of Defense
"Atlas/Data Abstract for the United States" (http://siadapp.dmdc.osd.mil/personnel/L03/fy09/09top.htm)
*Includes prime contracts ($25,000 or more) for civil and military functions. Does not include contracts to U.S. territories and other countries.

# U.S. Department of Defense Grants in 2009

## National Total = $5,192,057,000*

ALPHA ORDER

| RANK | STATE | GRANTS | % of USA |
|---|---|---|---|
| 27 | Alabama | $66,056,000 | 1.3% |
| 35 | Alaska | 48,783,000 | 0.9% |
| 17 | Arizona | 105,948,000 | 2.0% |
| 26 | Arkansas | 66,370,000 | 1.3% |
| 2 | California | 476,541,000 | 9.2% |
| 31 | Colorado | 56,411,000 | 1.1% |
| 18 | Connecticut | 100,249,000 | 1.9% |
| 47 | Delaware | 24,042,000 | 0.5% |
| 7 | Florida | 195,371,000 | 3.8% |
| 21 | Georgia | 73,944,000 | 1.4% |
| 20 | Hawaii | 78,931,000 | 1.5% |
| 28 | Idaho | 59,296,000 | 1.1% |
| 9 | Illinois | 172,126,000 | 3.3% |
| 32 | Indiana | 54,724,000 | 1.1% |
| 30 | Iowa | 56,852,000 | 1.1% |
| 37 | Kansas | 41,857,000 | 0.8% |
| 23 | Kentucky | 70,382,000 | 1.4% |
| 33 | Louisiana | 53,861,000 | 1.0% |
| 12 | Maine | 128,298,000 | 2.5% |
| 1 | Maryland | 476,575,000 | 9.2% |
| 4 | Massachusetts | 243,995,000 | 4.7% |
| 11 | Michigan | 129,652,000 | 2.5% |
| 24 | Minnesota | 68,900,000 | 1.3% |
| 49 | Mississippi | 18,237,000 | 0.4% |
| 38 | Missouri | 40,466,000 | 0.8% |
| 46 | Montana | 24,236,000 | 0.5% |
| 29 | Nebraska | 59,049,000 | 1.1% |
| 43 | Nevada | 35,345,000 | 0.7% |
| 42 | New Hampshire | 35,647,000 | 0.7% |
| 16 | New Jersey | 121,890,000 | 2.3% |
| 39 | New Mexico | 39,587,000 | 0.8% |
| 6 | New York | 198,631,000 | 3.8% |
| 14 | North Carolina | 124,942,000 | 2.4% |
| 44 | North Dakota | 32,174,000 | 0.6% |
| 8 | Ohio | 172,421,000 | 3.3% |
| 15 | Oklahoma | 123,839,000 | 2.4% |
| 19 | Oregon | 98,566,000 | 1.9% |
| 5 | Pennsylvania | 216,030,000 | 4.2% |
| 45 | Rhode Island | 26,333,000 | 0.5% |
| 41 | South Carolina | 39,365,000 | 0.8% |
| 25 | South Dakota | 67,933,000 | 1.3% |
| 36 | Tennessee | 44,134,000 | 0.9% |
| 3 | Texas | 300,450,000 | 5.8% |
| 40 | Utah | 39,483,000 | 0.8% |
| 50 | Vermont | 16,997,000 | 0.3% |
| 10 | Virginia | 130,816,000 | 2.5% |
| 13 | Washington | 126,539,000 | 2.4% |
| 34 | West Virginia | 49,988,000 | 1.0% |
| 22 | Wisconsin | 72,192,000 | 1.4% |
| 48 | Wyoming | 21,236,000 | 0.4% |

RANK ORDER

| RANK | STATE | GRANTS | % of USA |
|---|---|---|---|
| 1 | Maryland | $476,575,000 | 9.2% |
| 2 | California | 476,541,000 | 9.2% |
| 3 | Texas | 300,450,000 | 5.8% |
| 4 | Massachusetts | 243,995,000 | 4.7% |
| 5 | Pennsylvania | 216,030,000 | 4.2% |
| 6 | New York | 198,631,000 | 3.8% |
| 7 | Florida | 195,371,000 | 3.8% |
| 8 | Ohio | 172,421,000 | 3.3% |
| 9 | Illinois | 172,126,000 | 3.3% |
| 10 | Virginia | 130,816,000 | 2.5% |
| 11 | Michigan | 129,652,000 | 2.5% |
| 12 | Maine | 128,298,000 | 2.5% |
| 13 | Washington | 126,539,000 | 2.4% |
| 14 | North Carolina | 124,942,000 | 2.4% |
| 15 | Oklahoma | 123,839,000 | 2.4% |
| 16 | New Jersey | 121,890,000 | 2.3% |
| 17 | Arizona | 105,948,000 | 2.0% |
| 18 | Connecticut | 100,249,000 | 1.9% |
| 19 | Oregon | 98,566,000 | 1.9% |
| 20 | Hawaii | 78,931,000 | 1.5% |
| 21 | Georgia | 73,944,000 | 1.4% |
| 22 | Wisconsin | 72,192,000 | 1.4% |
| 23 | Kentucky | 70,382,000 | 1.4% |
| 24 | Minnesota | 68,900,000 | 1.3% |
| 25 | South Dakota | 67,933,000 | 1.3% |
| 26 | Arkansas | 66,370,000 | 1.3% |
| 27 | Alabama | 66,056,000 | 1.3% |
| 28 | Idaho | 59,296,000 | 1.1% |
| 29 | Nebraska | 59,049,000 | 1.1% |
| 30 | Iowa | 56,852,000 | 1.1% |
| 31 | Colorado | 56,411,000 | 1.1% |
| 32 | Indiana | 54,724,000 | 1.1% |
| 33 | Louisiana | 53,861,000 | 1.0% |
| 34 | West Virginia | 49,988,000 | 1.0% |
| 35 | Alaska | 48,783,000 | 0.9% |
| 36 | Tennessee | 44,134,000 | 0.9% |
| 37 | Kansas | 41,857,000 | 0.8% |
| 38 | Missouri | 40,466,000 | 0.8% |
| 39 | New Mexico | 39,587,000 | 0.8% |
| 40 | Utah | 39,483,000 | 0.8% |
| 41 | South Carolina | 39,365,000 | 0.8% |
| 42 | New Hampshire | 35,647,000 | 0.7% |
| 43 | Nevada | 35,345,000 | 0.7% |
| 44 | North Dakota | 32,174,000 | 0.6% |
| 45 | Rhode Island | 26,333,000 | 0.5% |
| 46 | Montana | 24,236,000 | 0.5% |
| 47 | Delaware | 24,042,000 | 0.5% |
| 48 | Wyoming | 21,236,000 | 0.4% |
| 49 | Mississippi | 18,237,000 | 0.4% |
| 50 | Vermont | 16,997,000 | 0.3% |
| | District of Columbia | 66,367,000 | 1.3% |

Source: U.S. Department of Defense
   "Atlas/Data Abstract for the United States" (http://siadapp.dmdc.osd.mil/personnel/L03/fy09/09top.htm)
*Includes grants for civil and military functions.  Does not include contracts to U.S. territories and other countries.

# Per Capita U.S. Department of Defense Grants in 2009

## National Per Capita = $16.91*

ALPHA ORDER

| RANK | STATE | PER CAPITA |
|---|---|---|
| 31 | Alabama | $14.03 |
| 4 | Alaska | 69.84 |
| 27 | Arizona | 16.06 |
| 20 | Arkansas | 22.97 |
| 38 | California | 12.89 |
| 42 | Colorado | 11.23 |
| 12 | Connecticut | 28.49 |
| 15 | Delaware | 27.16 |
| 43 | Florida | 10.54 |
| 47 | Georgia | 7.52 |
| 5 | Hawaii | 60.94 |
| 8 | Idaho | 38.36 |
| 34 | Illinois | 13.33 |
| 46 | Indiana | 8.52 |
| 23 | Iowa | 18.90 |
| 29 | Kansas | 14.85 |
| 26 | Kentucky | 16.31 |
| 41 | Louisiana | 11.99 |
| 1 | Maine | 97.32 |
| 2 | Maryland | 83.62 |
| 9 | Massachusetts | 37.00 |
| 37 | Michigan | 13.00 |
| 36 | Minnesota | 13.08 |
| 50 | Mississippi | 6.18 |
| 49 | Missouri | 6.76 |
| 19 | Montana | 24.86 |
| 11 | Nebraska | 32.87 |
| 33 | Nevada | 13.37 |
| 16 | New Hampshire | 26.91 |
| 32 | New Jersey | 14.00 |
| 21 | New Mexico | 19.70 |
| 44 | New York | 10.16 |
| 35 | North Carolina | 13.32 |
| 6 | North Dakota | 49.74 |
| 28 | Ohio | 14.94 |
| 10 | Oklahoma | 33.59 |
| 17 | Oregon | 25.76 |
| 24 | Pennsylvania | 17.14 |
| 18 | Rhode Island | 25.00 |
| 45 | South Carolina | 8.63 |
| 2 | South Dakota | 83.62 |
| 48 | Tennessee | 7.01 |
| 40 | Texas | 12.12 |
| 30 | Utah | 14.18 |
| 14 | Vermont | 27.34 |
| 25 | Virginia | 16.60 |
| 22 | Washington | 18.99 |
| 13 | West Virginia | 27.47 |
| 39 | Wisconsin | 12.77 |
| 7 | Wyoming | 39.02 |

RANK ORDER

| RANK | STATE | PER CAPITA |
|---|---|---|
| 1 | Maine | $97.32 |
| 2 | Maryland | 83.62 |
| 2 | South Dakota | 83.62 |
| 4 | Alaska | 69.84 |
| 5 | Hawaii | 60.94 |
| 6 | North Dakota | 49.74 |
| 7 | Wyoming | 39.02 |
| 8 | Idaho | 38.36 |
| 9 | Massachusetts | 37.00 |
| 10 | Oklahoma | 33.59 |
| 11 | Nebraska | 32.87 |
| 12 | Connecticut | 28.49 |
| 13 | West Virginia | 27.47 |
| 14 | Vermont | 27.34 |
| 15 | Delaware | 27.16 |
| 16 | New Hampshire | 26.91 |
| 17 | Oregon | 25.76 |
| 18 | Rhode Island | 25.00 |
| 19 | Montana | 24.86 |
| 20 | Arkansas | 22.97 |
| 21 | New Mexico | 19.70 |
| 22 | Washington | 18.99 |
| 23 | Iowa | 18.90 |
| 24 | Pennsylvania | 17.14 |
| 25 | Virginia | 16.60 |
| 26 | Kentucky | 16.31 |
| 27 | Arizona | 16.06 |
| 28 | Ohio | 14.94 |
| 29 | Kansas | 14.85 |
| 30 | Utah | 14.18 |
| 31 | Alabama | 14.03 |
| 32 | New Jersey | 14.00 |
| 33 | Nevada | 13.37 |
| 34 | Illinois | 13.33 |
| 35 | North Carolina | 13.32 |
| 36 | Minnesota | 13.08 |
| 37 | Michigan | 13.00 |
| 38 | California | 12.89 |
| 39 | Wisconsin | 12.77 |
| 40 | Texas | 12.12 |
| 41 | Louisiana | 11.99 |
| 42 | Colorado | 11.23 |
| 43 | Florida | 10.54 |
| 44 | New York | 10.16 |
| 45 | South Carolina | 8.63 |
| 46 | Indiana | 8.52 |
| 47 | Georgia | 7.52 |
| 48 | Tennessee | 7.01 |
| 49 | Missouri | 6.76 |
| 50 | Mississippi | 6.18 |
| | District of Columbia | 110.67 |

Source: CQ Press using data from U.S. Department of Defense
"Atlas/Data Abstract for the United States" (http://siadapp.dmdc.osd.mil/personnel/L03/fy09/09top.htm)
*Includes grants for civil and military functions. Does not include contracts to U.S. territories and other countries.

# U.S. Department of Defense Domestic Personnel in 2009

## National Total = 2,617,048 Personnel*

ALPHA ORDER

| RANK | STATE | PERSONNEL | % of USA |
|------|-------|-----------|----------|
| 17 | Alabama | 58,789 | 2.2% |
| 26 | Alaska | 33,281 | 1.3% |
| 21 | Arizona | 44,662 | 1.7% |
| 31 | Arkansas | 23,936 | 0.9% |
| 1 | California | 236,963 | 9.1% |
| 15 | Colorado | 59,480 | 2.3% |
| 43 | Connecticut | 10,908 | 0.4% |
| 44 | Delaware | 10,373 | 0.4% |
| 6 | Florida | 105,724 | 4.0% |
| 5 | Georgia | 140,358 | 5.4% |
| 10 | Hawaii | 68,550 | 2.6% |
| 41 | Idaho | 12,575 | 0.5% |
| 19 | Illinois | 50,965 | 1.9% |
| 25 | Indiana | 35,113 | 1.3% |
| 38 | Iowa | 15,419 | 0.6% |
| 20 | Kansas | 44,761 | 1.7% |
| 11 | Kentucky | 65,226 | 2.5% |
| 22 | Louisiana | 42,056 | 1.6% |
| 42 | Maine | 11,829 | 0.5% |
| 8 | Maryland | 80,126 | 3.1% |
| 30 | Massachusetts | 25,458 | 1.0% |
| 29 | Michigan | 29,448 | 1.1% |
| 32 | Minnesota | 23,905 | 0.9% |
| 24 | Mississippi | 36,351 | 1.4% |
| 18 | Missouri | 51,676 | 2.0% |
| 47 | Montana | 9,967 | 0.4% |
| 36 | Nebraska | 18,128 | 0.7% |
| 35 | Nevada | 18,440 | 0.7% |
| 49 | New Hampshire | 5,973 | 0.2% |
| 23 | New Jersey | 39,202 | 1.5% |
| 33 | New Mexico | 23,266 | 0.9% |
| 9 | New York | 72,233 | 2.8% |
| 4 | North Carolina | 159,041 | 6.1% |
| 39 | North Dakota | 13,788 | 0.5% |
| 14 | Ohio | 61,785 | 2.4% |
| 16 | Oklahoma | 59,428 | 2.3% |
| 37 | Oregon | 15,646 | 0.6% |
| 12 | Pennsylvania | 64,619 | 2.5% |
| 45 | Rhode Island | 10,300 | 0.4% |
| 13 | South Carolina | 62,026 | 2.4% |
| 46 | South Dakota | 10,280 | 0.4% |
| 28 | Tennessee | 32,084 | 1.2% |
| 2 | Texas | 235,972 | 9.0% |
| 27 | Utah | 33,054 | 1.3% |
| 50 | Vermont | 5,246 | 0.2% |
| 3 | Virginia | 177,982 | 6.8% |
| 7 | Washington | 93,611 | 3.6% |
| 40 | West Virginia | 12,648 | 0.5% |
| 34 | Wisconsin | 20,689 | 0.8% |
| 48 | Wyoming | 7,818 | 0.3% |

RANK ORDER

| RANK | STATE | PERSONNEL | % of USA |
|------|-------|-----------|----------|
| 1 | California | 236,963 | 9.1% |
| 2 | Texas | 235,972 | 9.0% |
| 3 | Virginia | 177,982 | 6.8% |
| 4 | North Carolina | 159,041 | 6.1% |
| 5 | Georgia | 140,358 | 5.4% |
| 6 | Florida | 105,724 | 4.0% |
| 7 | Washington | 93,611 | 3.6% |
| 8 | Maryland | 80,126 | 3.1% |
| 9 | New York | 72,233 | 2.8% |
| 10 | Hawaii | 68,550 | 2.6% |
| 11 | Kentucky | 65,226 | 2.5% |
| 12 | Pennsylvania | 64,619 | 2.5% |
| 13 | South Carolina | 62,026 | 2.4% |
| 14 | Ohio | 61,785 | 2.4% |
| 15 | Colorado | 59,480 | 2.3% |
| 16 | Oklahoma | 59,428 | 2.3% |
| 17 | Alabama | 58,789 | 2.2% |
| 18 | Missouri | 51,676 | 2.0% |
| 19 | Illinois | 50,965 | 1.9% |
| 20 | Kansas | 44,761 | 1.7% |
| 21 | Arizona | 44,662 | 1.7% |
| 22 | Louisiana | 42,056 | 1.6% |
| 23 | New Jersey | 39,202 | 1.5% |
| 24 | Mississippi | 36,351 | 1.4% |
| 25 | Indiana | 35,113 | 1.3% |
| 26 | Alaska | 33,281 | 1.3% |
| 27 | Utah | 33,054 | 1.3% |
| 28 | Tennessee | 32,084 | 1.2% |
| 29 | Michigan | 29,448 | 1.1% |
| 30 | Massachusetts | 25,458 | 1.0% |
| 31 | Arkansas | 23,936 | 0.9% |
| 32 | Minnesota | 23,905 | 0.9% |
| 33 | New Mexico | 23,266 | 0.9% |
| 34 | Wisconsin | 20,689 | 0.8% |
| 35 | Nevada | 18,440 | 0.7% |
| 36 | Nebraska | 18,128 | 0.7% |
| 37 | Oregon | 15,646 | 0.6% |
| 38 | Iowa | 15,419 | 0.6% |
| 39 | North Dakota | 13,788 | 0.5% |
| 40 | West Virginia | 12,648 | 0.5% |
| 41 | Idaho | 12,575 | 0.5% |
| 42 | Maine | 11,829 | 0.5% |
| 43 | Connecticut | 10,908 | 0.4% |
| 44 | Delaware | 10,373 | 0.4% |
| 45 | Rhode Island | 10,300 | 0.4% |
| 46 | South Dakota | 10,280 | 0.4% |
| 47 | Montana | 9,967 | 0.4% |
| 48 | Wyoming | 7,818 | 0.3% |
| 49 | New Hampshire | 5,973 | 0.2% |
| 50 | Vermont | 5,246 | 0.2% |
| | District of Columbia | 35,890 | 1.4% |

Source: U.S. Department of Defense
   "Atlas/Data Abstract for the United States" (http://siadapp.dmdc.osd.mil/personnel/L03/fy09/09top.htm)
*Includes Active Duty Military, Civilian, Reserve, and National Guard personnel. Does not include personnel in U.S. territories or in other countries.

# U.S. Department of Defense Active Duty Military Personnel in 2009

## National Total = 1,088,465 Personnel*

ALPHA ORDER

| RANK | STATE | PERSONNEL | % of USA |
|------|-------|-----------|----------|
| 20 | Alabama | 11,896 | 1.1% |
| 15 | Alaska | 23,178 | 2.1% |
| 17 | Arizona | 21,343 | 2.0% |
| 28 | Arkansas | 6,717 | 0.6% |
| 2 | California | 117,806 | 10.8% |
| 10 | Colorado | 35,404 | 3.3% |
| 42 | Connecticut | 1,914 | 0.2% |
| 34 | Delaware | 3,870 | 0.4% |
| 8 | Florida | 42,642 | 3.9% |
| 4 | Georgia | 73,988 | 6.8% |
| 9 | Hawaii | 40,874 | 3.8% |
| 32 | Idaho | 4,967 | 0.5% |
| 22 | Illinois | 10,111 | 0.9% |
| 39 | Indiana | 3,108 | 0.3% |
| 46 | Iowa | 1,296 | 0.1% |
| 14 | Kansas | 25,482 | 2.3% |
| 7 | Kentucky | 43,138 | 4.0% |
| 19 | Louisiana | 17,398 | 1.6% |
| 48 | Maine | 730 | 0.1% |
| 13 | Maryland | 29,160 | 2.7% |
| 38 | Massachusetts | 3,205 | 0.3% |
| 40 | Michigan | 2,858 | 0.3% |
| 43 | Minnesota | 1,897 | 0.2% |
| 24 | Mississippi | 9,895 | 0.9% |
| 18 | Missouri | 17,925 | 1.6% |
| 35 | Montana | 3,623 | 0.3% |
| 27 | Nebraska | 6,845 | 0.6% |
| 23 | Nevada | 10,034 | 0.9% |
| 49 | New Hampshire | 675 | 0.1% |
| 29 | New Jersey | 6,673 | 0.6% |
| 21 | New Mexico | 11,038 | 1.0% |
| 12 | New York | 29,553 | 2.7% |
| 3 | North Carolina | 116,073 | 10.7% |
| 26 | North Dakota | 7,209 | 0.7% |
| 25 | Ohio | 8,261 | 0.8% |
| 16 | Oklahoma | 21,673 | 2.0% |
| 44 | Oregon | 1,615 | 0.1% |
| 31 | Pennsylvania | 5,215 | 0.5% |
| 45 | Rhode Island | 1,490 | 0.1% |
| 11 | South Carolina | 32,518 | 3.0% |
| 33 | South Dakota | 3,910 | 0.4% |
| 36 | Tennessee | 3,511 | 0.3% |
| 1 | Texas | 131,548 | 12.1% |
| 30 | Utah | 6,237 | 0.6% |
| 50 | Vermont | 565 | 0.1% |
| 5 | Virginia | 63,160 | 5.8% |
| 6 | Washington | 46,161 | 4.2% |
| 47 | West Virginia | 1,199 | 0.1% |
| 41 | Wisconsin | 2,046 | 0.2% |
| 37 | Wyoming | 3,407 | 0.3% |

RANK ORDER

| RANK | STATE | PERSONNEL | % of USA |
|------|-------|-----------|----------|
| 1 | Texas | 131,548 | 12.1% |
| 2 | California | 117,806 | 10.8% |
| 3 | North Carolina | 116,073 | 10.7% |
| 4 | Georgia | 73,988 | 6.8% |
| 5 | Virginia | 63,160 | 5.8% |
| 6 | Washington | 46,161 | 4.2% |
| 7 | Kentucky | 43,138 | 4.0% |
| 8 | Florida | 42,642 | 3.9% |
| 9 | Hawaii | 40,874 | 3.8% |
| 10 | Colorado | 35,404 | 3.3% |
| 11 | South Carolina | 32,518 | 3.0% |
| 12 | New York | 29,553 | 2.7% |
| 13 | Maryland | 29,160 | 2.7% |
| 14 | Kansas | 25,482 | 2.3% |
| 15 | Alaska | 23,178 | 2.1% |
| 16 | Oklahoma | 21,673 | 2.0% |
| 17 | Arizona | 21,343 | 2.0% |
| 18 | Missouri | 17,925 | 1.6% |
| 19 | Louisiana | 17,398 | 1.6% |
| 20 | Alabama | 11,896 | 1.1% |
| 21 | New Mexico | 11,038 | 1.0% |
| 22 | Illinois | 10,111 | 0.9% |
| 23 | Nevada | 10,034 | 0.9% |
| 24 | Mississippi | 9,895 | 0.9% |
| 25 | Ohio | 8,261 | 0.8% |
| 26 | North Dakota | 7,209 | 0.7% |
| 27 | Nebraska | 6,845 | 0.6% |
| 28 | Arkansas | 6,717 | 0.6% |
| 29 | New Jersey | 6,673 | 0.6% |
| 30 | Utah | 6,237 | 0.6% |
| 31 | Pennsylvania | 5,215 | 0.5% |
| 32 | Idaho | 4,967 | 0.5% |
| 33 | South Dakota | 3,910 | 0.4% |
| 34 | Delaware | 3,870 | 0.4% |
| 35 | Montana | 3,623 | 0.3% |
| 36 | Tennessee | 3,511 | 0.3% |
| 37 | Wyoming | 3,407 | 0.3% |
| 38 | Massachusetts | 3,205 | 0.3% |
| 39 | Indiana | 3,108 | 0.3% |
| 40 | Michigan | 2,858 | 0.3% |
| 41 | Wisconsin | 2,046 | 0.2% |
| 42 | Connecticut | 1,914 | 0.2% |
| 43 | Minnesota | 1,897 | 0.2% |
| 44 | Oregon | 1,615 | 0.1% |
| 45 | Rhode Island | 1,490 | 0.1% |
| 46 | Iowa | 1,296 | 0.1% |
| 47 | West Virginia | 1,199 | 0.1% |
| 48 | Maine | 730 | 0.1% |
| 49 | New Hampshire | 675 | 0.1% |
| 50 | Vermont | 565 | 0.1% |
| | District of Columbia | 13,424 | 1.2% |

Source: U.S. Department of Defense
   "Atlas/Data Abstract for the United States" (http://siadapp.dmdc.osd.mil/personnel/L03/fy09/09top.htm)
*Does not include active duty personnel in U.S. territories, in other countries or others undistributed.

# U.S. Department of Defense Domestic Civilian Personnel in 2009

## National Total = 709,265 Personnel*

ALPHA ORDER

| RANK | STATE | PERSONNEL | % of USA |
|------|-------|-----------|----------|
| 10 | Alabama | 24,794 | 3.5% |
| 32 | Alaska | 5,356 | 0.8% |
| 22 | Arizona | 9,591 | 1.4% |
| 34 | Arkansas | 4,168 | 0.6% |
| 2 | California | 61,365 | 8.7% |
| 18 | Colorado | 11,585 | 1.6% |
| 39 | Connecticut | 2,625 | 0.4% |
| 45 | Delaware | 1,622 | 0.2% |
| 6 | Florida | 28,429 | 4.0% |
| 4 | Georgia | 37,012 | 5.2% |
| 13 | Hawaii | 18,400 | 2.6% |
| 44 | Idaho | 1,716 | 0.2% |
| 14 | Illinois | 15,770 | 2.2% |
| 19 | Indiana | 10,932 | 1.5% |
| 43 | Iowa | 1,733 | 0.2% |
| 27 | Kansas | 7,800 | 1.1% |
| 25 | Kentucky | 8,962 | 1.3% |
| 31 | Louisiana | 6,647 | 0.9% |
| 29 | Maine | 6,946 | 1.0% |
| 5 | Maryland | 34,966 | 4.9% |
| 30 | Massachusetts | 6,918 | 1.0% |
| 24 | Michigan | 8,972 | 1.3% |
| 38 | Minnesota | 2,752 | 0.4% |
| 23 | Mississippi | 9,124 | 1.3% |
| 21 | Missouri | 9,982 | 1.4% |
| 46 | Montana | 1,596 | 0.2% |
| 35 | Nebraska | 3,785 | 0.5% |
| 40 | Nevada | 2,319 | 0.3% |
| 49 | New Hampshire | 1,047 | 0.1% |
| 15 | New Jersey | 15,217 | 2.1% |
| 28 | New Mexico | 7,029 | 1.0% |
| 17 | New York | 12,318 | 1.7% |
| 12 | North Carolina | 20,426 | 2.9% |
| 42 | North Dakota | 1,910 | 0.3% |
| 9 | Ohio | 25,001 | 3.5% |
| 11 | Oklahoma | 22,115 | 3.1% |
| 36 | Oregon | 3,561 | 0.5% |
| 8 | Pennsylvania | 27,107 | 3.8% |
| 33 | Rhode Island | 4,372 | 0.6% |
| 20 | South Carolina | 10,406 | 1.5% |
| 47 | South Dakota | 1,388 | 0.2% |
| 26 | Tennessee | 7,967 | 1.1% |
| 3 | Texas | 48,057 | 6.8% |
| 16 | Utah | 14,818 | 2.1% |
| 50 | Vermont | 729 | 0.1% |
| 1 | Virginia | 89,713 | 12.6% |
| 7 | Washington | 27,980 | 3.9% |
| 41 | West Virginia | 2,146 | 0.3% |
| 37 | Wisconsin | 2,810 | 0.4% |
| 48 | Wyoming | 1,193 | 0.2% |

RANK ORDER

| RANK | STATE | PERSONNEL | % of USA |
|------|-------|-----------|----------|
| 1 | Virginia | 89,713 | 12.6% |
| 2 | California | 61,365 | 8.7% |
| 3 | Texas | 48,057 | 6.8% |
| 4 | Georgia | 37,012 | 5.2% |
| 5 | Maryland | 34,966 | 4.9% |
| 6 | Florida | 28,429 | 4.0% |
| 7 | Washington | 27,980 | 3.9% |
| 8 | Pennsylvania | 27,107 | 3.8% |
| 9 | Ohio | 25,001 | 3.5% |
| 10 | Alabama | 24,794 | 3.5% |
| 11 | Oklahoma | 22,115 | 3.1% |
| 12 | North Carolina | 20,426 | 2.9% |
| 13 | Hawaii | 18,400 | 2.6% |
| 14 | Illinois | 15,770 | 2.2% |
| 15 | New Jersey | 15,217 | 2.1% |
| 16 | Utah | 14,818 | 2.1% |
| 17 | New York | 12,318 | 1.7% |
| 18 | Colorado | 11,585 | 1.6% |
| 19 | Indiana | 10,932 | 1.5% |
| 20 | South Carolina | 10,406 | 1.5% |
| 21 | Missouri | 9,982 | 1.4% |
| 22 | Arizona | 9,591 | 1.4% |
| 23 | Mississippi | 9,124 | 1.3% |
| 24 | Michigan | 8,972 | 1.3% |
| 25 | Kentucky | 8,962 | 1.3% |
| 26 | Tennessee | 7,967 | 1.1% |
| 27 | Kansas | 7,800 | 1.1% |
| 28 | New Mexico | 7,029 | 1.0% |
| 29 | Maine | 6,946 | 1.0% |
| 30 | Massachusetts | 6,918 | 1.0% |
| 31 | Louisiana | 6,647 | 0.9% |
| 32 | Alaska | 5,356 | 0.8% |
| 33 | Rhode Island | 4,372 | 0.6% |
| 34 | Arkansas | 4,168 | 0.6% |
| 35 | Nebraska | 3,785 | 0.5% |
| 36 | Oregon | 3,561 | 0.5% |
| 37 | Wisconsin | 2,810 | 0.4% |
| 38 | Minnesota | 2,752 | 0.4% |
| 39 | Connecticut | 2,625 | 0.4% |
| 40 | Nevada | 2,319 | 0.3% |
| 41 | West Virginia | 2,146 | 0.3% |
| 42 | North Dakota | 1,910 | 0.3% |
| 43 | Iowa | 1,733 | 0.2% |
| 44 | Idaho | 1,716 | 0.2% |
| 45 | Delaware | 1,622 | 0.2% |
| 46 | Montana | 1,596 | 0.2% |
| 47 | South Dakota | 1,388 | 0.2% |
| 48 | Wyoming | 1,193 | 0.2% |
| 49 | New Hampshire | 1,047 | 0.1% |
| 50 | Vermont | 729 | 0.1% |
|  | District of Columbia | 16,088 | 2.3% |

Source: U.S. Department of Defense
   "Atlas/Data Abstract for the United States" (http://siadapp.dmdc.osd.mil/personnel/L03/fy09/09top.htm)
*Does not include civilian personnel in U.S. territories or civilian personnel in other countries.  Includes military and civil functions.

# U.S. Department of Defense Reserve and National Guard Personnel in 2009

## National Total = 819,318 Personnel*

ALPHA ORDER

RANK ORDER

| RANK | STATE | PERSONNEL | % of USA | | RANK | STATE | PERSONNEL | % of USA |
|---|---|---|---|---|---|---|---|---|
| 12 | Alabama | 22,099 | 2.7% | | 1 | California | 57,792 | 7.1% |
| 44 | Alaska | 4,747 | 0.6% | | 2 | Texas | 56,367 | 6.9% |
| 26 | Arizona | 13,728 | 1.7% | | 3 | Florida | 34,653 | 4.2% |
| 28 | Arkansas | 13,051 | 1.6% | | 4 | Pennsylvania | 32,297 | 3.9% |
| 1 | California | 57,792 | 7.1% | | 5 | New York | 30,362 | 3.7% |
| 29 | Colorado | 12,491 | 1.5% | | 6 | Georgia | 29,358 | 3.6% |
| 37 | Connecticut | 6,369 | 0.8% | | 7 | Ohio | 28,523 | 3.5% |
| 42 | Delaware | 4,881 | 0.6% | | 8 | Virginia | 25,109 | 3.1% |
| 3 | Florida | 34,653 | 4.2% | | 9 | Illinois | 25,084 | 3.1% |
| 6 | Georgia | 29,358 | 3.6% | | 10 | Missouri | 23,769 | 2.9% |
| 35 | Hawaii | 9,276 | 1.1% | | 11 | North Carolina | 22,542 | 2.8% |
| 39 | Idaho | 5,892 | 0.7% | | 12 | Alabama | 22,099 | 2.7% |
| 9 | Illinois | 25,084 | 3.1% | | 13 | Indiana | 21,073 | 2.6% |
| 13 | Indiana | 21,073 | 2.6% | | 14 | Tennessee | 20,606 | 2.5% |
| 30 | Iowa | 12,390 | 1.5% | | 15 | Washington | 19,470 | 2.4% |
| 32 | Kansas | 11,479 | 1.4% | | 16 | Minnesota | 19,256 | 2.4% |
| 27 | Kentucky | 13,126 | 1.6% | | 17 | South Carolina | 19,102 | 2.3% |
| 18 | Louisiana | 18,011 | 2.2% | | 18 | Louisiana | 18,011 | 2.2% |
| 48 | Maine | 4,153 | 0.5% | | 19 | Michigan | 17,618 | 2.2% |
| 22 | Maryland | 16,000 | 2.0% | | 20 | Mississippi | 17,332 | 2.1% |
| 25 | Massachusetts | 15,335 | 1.9% | | 21 | New Jersey | 17,312 | 2.1% |
| 19 | Michigan | 17,618 | 2.2% | | 22 | Maryland | 16,000 | 2.0% |
| 16 | Minnesota | 19,256 | 2.4% | | 23 | Wisconsin | 15,833 | 1.9% |
| 20 | Mississippi | 17,332 | 2.1% | | 24 | Oklahoma | 15,640 | 1.9% |
| 10 | Missouri | 23,769 | 2.9% | | 25 | Massachusetts | 15,335 | 1.9% |
| 43 | Montana | 4,748 | 0.6% | | 26 | Arizona | 13,728 | 1.7% |
| 36 | Nebraska | 7,498 | 0.9% | | 27 | Kentucky | 13,126 | 1.6% |
| 38 | Nevada | 6,087 | 0.7% | | 28 | Arkansas | 13,051 | 1.6% |
| 47 | New Hampshire | 4,251 | 0.5% | | 29 | Colorado | 12,491 | 1.5% |
| 21 | New Jersey | 17,312 | 2.1% | | 30 | Iowa | 12,390 | 1.5% |
| 40 | New Mexico | 5,199 | 0.6% | | 31 | Utah | 11,999 | 1.5% |
| 5 | New York | 30,362 | 3.7% | | 32 | Kansas | 11,479 | 1.4% |
| 11 | North Carolina | 22,542 | 2.8% | | 33 | Oregon | 10,470 | 1.3% |
| 45 | North Dakota | 4,669 | 0.6% | | 34 | West Virginia | 9,303 | 1.1% |
| 7 | Ohio | 28,523 | 3.5% | | 35 | Hawaii | 9,276 | 1.1% |
| 24 | Oklahoma | 15,640 | 1.9% | | 36 | Nebraska | 7,498 | 0.9% |
| 33 | Oregon | 10,470 | 1.3% | | 37 | Connecticut | 6,369 | 0.8% |
| 4 | Pennsylvania | 32,297 | 3.9% | | 38 | Nevada | 6,087 | 0.7% |
| 46 | Rhode Island | 4,438 | 0.5% | | 39 | Idaho | 5,892 | 0.7% |
| 17 | South Carolina | 19,102 | 2.3% | | 40 | New Mexico | 5,199 | 0.6% |
| 41 | South Dakota | 4,982 | 0.6% | | 41 | South Dakota | 4,982 | 0.6% |
| 14 | Tennessee | 20,606 | 2.5% | | 42 | Delaware | 4,881 | 0.6% |
| 2 | Texas | 56,367 | 6.9% | | 43 | Montana | 4,748 | 0.6% |
| 31 | Utah | 11,999 | 1.5% | | 44 | Alaska | 4,747 | 0.6% |
| 49 | Vermont | 3,952 | 0.5% | | 45 | North Dakota | 4,669 | 0.6% |
| 8 | Virginia | 25,109 | 3.1% | | 46 | Rhode Island | 4,438 | 0.5% |
| 15 | Washington | 19,470 | 2.4% | | 47 | New Hampshire | 4,251 | 0.5% |
| 34 | West Virginia | 9,303 | 1.1% | | 48 | Maine | 4,153 | 0.5% |
| 23 | Wisconsin | 15,833 | 1.9% | | 49 | Vermont | 3,952 | 0.5% |
| 50 | Wyoming | 3,218 | 0.4% | | 50 | Wyoming | 3,218 | 0.4% |
| | | | | | | District of Columbia | 6,378 | 0.8% |

Source: U.S. Department of Defense
"Atlas/Data Abstract for the United States" (http://siadapp.dmdc.osd.mil/personnel/L03/fy09/09top.htm)
*Does not include reserve and national guard personnel in U.S. territories.

# U.S. Department of Defense Total Compensation in 2009

## National Total = $195,170,178,000*

ALPHA ORDER

| RANK | STATE | COMPENSATION | % of USA |
|---|---|---|---|
| 13 | Alabama | $4,723,956,000 | 2.4% |
| 24 | Alaska | 2,659,561,000 | 1.4% |
| 20 | Arizona | 3,137,634,000 | 1.6% |
| 31 | Arkansas | 1,621,707,000 | 0.8% |
| 3 | California | 14,568,458,000 | 7.5% |
| 11 | Colorado | 5,125,122,000 | 2.6% |
| 41 | Connecticut | 720,299,000 | 0.4% |
| 46 | Delaware | 536,758,000 | 0.3% |
| 6 | Florida | 9,417,919,000 | 4.8% |
| 4 | Georgia | 11,494,647,000 | 5.9% |
| 9 | Hawaii | 6,344,467,000 | 3.3% |
| 42 | Idaho | 709,220,000 | 0.4% |
| 21 | Illinois | 3,128,538,000 | 1.6% |
| 25 | Indiana | 2,338,121,000 | 1.2% |
| 39 | Iowa | 747,256,000 | 0.4% |
| 19 | Kansas | 3,667,675,000 | 1.9% |
| 10 | Kentucky | 5,680,752,000 | 2.9% |
| 22 | Louisiana | 2,688,149,000 | 1.4% |
| 38 | Maine | 846,681,000 | 0.4% |
| 8 | Maryland | 6,537,841,000 | 3.3% |
| 32 | Massachusetts | 1,490,630,000 | 0.8% |
| 29 | Michigan | 1,826,987,000 | 0.9% |
| 34 | Minnesota | 1,208,062,000 | 0.6% |
| 27 | Mississippi | 2,224,346,000 | 1.1% |
| 17 | Missouri | 3,786,836,000 | 1.9% |
| 45 | Montana | 540,644,000 | 0.3% |
| 35 | Nebraska | 1,151,981,000 | 0.6% |
| 33 | Nevada | 1,414,606,000 | 0.7% |
| 48 | New Hampshire | 410,882,000 | 0.2% |
| 23 | New Jersey | 2,671,220,000 | 1.4% |
| 30 | New Mexico | 1,626,461,000 | 0.8% |
| 12 | New York | 4,818,679,000 | 2.5% |
| 5 | North Carolina | 10,558,150,000 | 5.4% |
| 43 | North Dakota | 630,939,000 | 0.3% |
| 16 | Ohio | 3,834,470,000 | 2.0% |
| 15 | Oklahoma | 4,099,633,000 | 2.1% |
| 37 | Oregon | 1,051,047,000 | 0.5% |
| 14 | Pennsylvania | 4,210,386,000 | 2.2% |
| 40 | Rhode Island | 743,035,000 | 0.4% |
| 18 | South Carolina | 3,682,987,000 | 1.9% |
| 47 | South Dakota | 513,643,000 | 0.3% |
| 26 | Tennessee | 2,235,302,000 | 1.1% |
| 1 | Texas | 19,298,889,000 | 9.9% |
| 28 | Utah | 2,115,968,000 | 1.1% |
| 50 | Vermont | 261,505,000 | 0.1% |
| 2 | Virginia | 18,071,415,000 | 9.3% |
| 7 | Washington | 8,223,735,000 | 4.2% |
| 44 | West Virginia | 616,823,000 | 0.3% |
| 36 | Wisconsin | 1,151,891,000 | 0.6% |
| 49 | Wyoming | 405,020,000 | 0.2% |

RANK ORDER

| RANK | STATE | COMPENSATION | % of USA |
|---|---|---|---|
| 1 | Texas | $19,298,889,000 | 9.9% |
| 2 | Virginia | 18,071,415,000 | 9.3% |
| 3 | California | 14,568,458,000 | 7.5% |
| 4 | Georgia | 11,494,647,000 | 5.9% |
| 5 | North Carolina | 10,558,150,000 | 5.4% |
| 6 | Florida | 9,417,919,000 | 4.8% |
| 7 | Washington | 8,223,735,000 | 4.2% |
| 8 | Maryland | 6,537,841,000 | 3.3% |
| 9 | Hawaii | 6,344,467,000 | 3.3% |
| 10 | Kentucky | 5,680,752,000 | 2.9% |
| 11 | Colorado | 5,125,122,000 | 2.6% |
| 12 | New York | 4,818,679,000 | 2.5% |
| 13 | Alabama | 4,723,956,000 | 2.4% |
| 14 | Pennsylvania | 4,210,386,000 | 2.2% |
| 15 | Oklahoma | 4,099,633,000 | 2.1% |
| 16 | Ohio | 3,834,470,000 | 2.0% |
| 17 | Missouri | 3,786,836,000 | 1.9% |
| 18 | South Carolina | 3,682,987,000 | 1.9% |
| 19 | Kansas | 3,667,675,000 | 1.9% |
| 20 | Arizona | 3,137,634,000 | 1.6% |
| 21 | Illinois | 3,128,538,000 | 1.6% |
| 22 | Louisiana | 2,688,149,000 | 1.4% |
| 23 | New Jersey | 2,671,220,000 | 1.4% |
| 24 | Alaska | 2,659,561,000 | 1.4% |
| 25 | Indiana | 2,338,121,000 | 1.2% |
| 26 | Tennessee | 2,235,302,000 | 1.1% |
| 27 | Mississippi | 2,224,346,000 | 1.1% |
| 28 | Utah | 2,115,968,000 | 1.1% |
| 29 | Michigan | 1,826,987,000 | 0.9% |
| 30 | New Mexico | 1,626,461,000 | 0.8% |
| 31 | Arkansas | 1,621,707,000 | 0.8% |
| 32 | Massachusetts | 1,490,630,000 | 0.8% |
| 33 | Nevada | 1,414,606,000 | 0.7% |
| 34 | Minnesota | 1,208,062,000 | 0.6% |
| 35 | Nebraska | 1,151,981,000 | 0.6% |
| 36 | Wisconsin | 1,151,891,000 | 0.6% |
| 37 | Oregon | 1,051,047,000 | 0.5% |
| 38 | Maine | 846,681,000 | 0.4% |
| 39 | Iowa | 747,256,000 | 0.4% |
| 40 | Rhode Island | 743,035,000 | 0.4% |
| 41 | Connecticut | 720,299,000 | 0.4% |
| 42 | Idaho | 709,220,000 | 0.4% |
| 43 | North Dakota | 630,939,000 | 0.3% |
| 44 | West Virginia | 616,823,000 | 0.3% |
| 45 | Montana | 540,644,000 | 0.3% |
| 46 | Delaware | 536,758,000 | 0.3% |
| 47 | South Dakota | 513,643,000 | 0.3% |
| 48 | New Hampshire | 410,882,000 | 0.2% |
| 49 | Wyoming | 405,020,000 | 0.2% |
| 50 | Vermont | 261,505,000 | 0.1% |
| | District of Columbia | 3,599,245,000 | 1.8% |

Source: U.S. Department of Defense
"Atlas/Data Abstract for the United States" (http://siadapp.dmdc.osd.mil/personnel/L03/fy09/09top.htm)
*Includes Civilian Pay, Military Active Duty Pay, Reserve, National Guard Pay, and Retired Military Pay.  Based on location of recipient.  Does not include recipients in U.S. territories and other countries.

# U.S. Department of Defense Military Active Duty Pay in 2009

## National Total = $84,459,939,000*

ALPHA ORDER

| RANK | STATE | PAYROLL | % of USA |
|------|-------|---------|----------|
| 20 | Alabama | $1,254,790,000 | 1.5% |
| 13 | Alaska | 2,077,719,000 | 2.5% |
| 19 | Arizona | 1,262,572,000 | 1.5% |
| 28 | Arkansas | 435,036,000 | 0.5% |
| 5 | California | 5,182,809,000 | 6.1% |
| 9 | Colorado | 2,965,503,000 | 3.5% |
| 41 | Connecticut | 198,163,000 | 0.2% |
| 38 | Delaware | 216,219,000 | 0.3% |
| 10 | Florida | 2,816,465,000 | 3.3% |
| 3 | Georgia | 6,668,434,000 | 7.9% |
| 6 | Hawaii | 4,529,364,000 | 5.4% |
| 36 | Idaho | 261,607,000 | 0.3% |
| 21 | Illinois | 738,269,000 | 0.9% |
| 31 | Indiana | 350,647,000 | 0.4% |
| 45 | Iowa | 140,071,000 | 0.2% |
| 12 | Kansas | 2,465,253,000 | 2.9% |
| 8 | Kentucky | 4,339,243,000 | 5.1% |
| 17 | Louisiana | 1,417,143,000 | 1.7% |
| 47 | Maine | 113,348,000 | 0.1% |
| 14 | Maryland | 2,012,820,000 | 2.4% |
| 33 | Massachusetts | 319,863,000 | 0.4% |
| 35 | Michigan | 263,638,000 | 0.3% |
| 39 | Minnesota | 206,036,000 | 0.2% |
| 23 | Mississippi | 629,352,000 | 0.7% |
| 18 | Missouri | 1,310,799,000 | 1.6% |
| 42 | Montana | 187,506,000 | 0.2% |
| 29 | Nebraska | 434,949,000 | 0.5% |
| 24 | Nevada | 600,019,000 | 0.7% |
| 49 | New Hampshire | 73,429,000 | 0.1% |
| 27 | New Jersey | 543,053,000 | 0.6% |
| 26 | New Mexico | 571,288,000 | 0.7% |
| 11 | New York | 2,701,191,000 | 3.2% |
| 2 | North Carolina | 7,012,462,000 | 8.3% |
| 32 | North Dakota | 335,954,000 | 0.4% |
| 22 | Ohio | 640,496,000 | 0.8% |
| 15 | Oklahoma | 1,678,570,000 | 2.0% |
| 44 | Oregon | 140,868,000 | 0.2% |
| 25 | Pennsylvania | 574,034,000 | 0.7% |
| 46 | Rhode Island | 120,400,000 | 0.1% |
| 16 | South Carolina | 1,530,304,000 | 1.8% |
| 40 | South Dakota | 198,438,000 | 0.2% |
| 34 | Tennessee | 282,250,000 | 0.3% |
| 1 | Texas | 11,128,462,000 | 13.2% |
| 30 | Utah | 431,738,000 | 0.5% |
| 50 | Vermont | 64,177,000 | 0.1% |
| 4 | Virginia | 6,214,491,000 | 7.4% |
| 7 | Washington | 4,407,343,000 | 5.2% |
| 48 | West Virginia | 106,870,000 | 0.1% |
| 37 | Wisconsin | 222,262,000 | 0.3% |
| 43 | Wyoming | 177,223,000 | 0.2% |

RANK ORDER

| RANK | STATE | PAYROLL | % of USA |
|------|-------|---------|----------|
| 1 | Texas | $11,128,462,000 | 13.2% |
| 2 | North Carolina | 7,012,462,000 | 8.3% |
| 3 | Georgia | 6,668,434,000 | 7.9% |
| 4 | Virginia | 6,214,491,000 | 7.4% |
| 5 | California | 5,182,809,000 | 6.1% |
| 6 | Hawaii | 4,529,364,000 | 5.4% |
| 7 | Washington | 4,407,343,000 | 5.2% |
| 8 | Kentucky | 4,339,243,000 | 5.1% |
| 9 | Colorado | 2,965,503,000 | 3.5% |
| 10 | Florida | 2,816,465,000 | 3.3% |
| 11 | New York | 2,701,191,000 | 3.2% |
| 12 | Kansas | 2,465,253,000 | 2.9% |
| 13 | Alaska | 2,077,719,000 | 2.5% |
| 14 | Maryland | 2,012,820,000 | 2.4% |
| 15 | Oklahoma | 1,678,570,000 | 2.0% |
| 16 | South Carolina | 1,530,304,000 | 1.8% |
| 17 | Louisiana | 1,417,143,000 | 1.7% |
| 18 | Missouri | 1,310,799,000 | 1.6% |
| 19 | Arizona | 1,262,572,000 | 1.5% |
| 20 | Alabama | 1,254,790,000 | 1.5% |
| 21 | Illinois | 738,269,000 | 0.9% |
| 22 | Ohio | 640,496,000 | 0.8% |
| 23 | Mississippi | 629,352,000 | 0.7% |
| 24 | Nevada | 600,019,000 | 0.7% |
| 25 | Pennsylvania | 574,034,000 | 0.7% |
| 26 | New Mexico | 571,288,000 | 0.7% |
| 27 | New Jersey | 543,053,000 | 0.6% |
| 28 | Arkansas | 435,036,000 | 0.5% |
| 29 | Nebraska | 434,949,000 | 0.5% |
| 30 | Utah | 431,738,000 | 0.5% |
| 31 | Indiana | 350,647,000 | 0.4% |
| 32 | North Dakota | 335,954,000 | 0.4% |
| 33 | Massachusetts | 319,863,000 | 0.4% |
| 34 | Tennessee | 282,250,000 | 0.3% |
| 35 | Michigan | 263,638,000 | 0.3% |
| 36 | Idaho | 261,607,000 | 0.3% |
| 37 | Wisconsin | 222,262,000 | 0.3% |
| 38 | Delaware | 216,219,000 | 0.3% |
| 39 | Minnesota | 206,036,000 | 0.2% |
| 40 | South Dakota | 198,438,000 | 0.2% |
| 41 | Connecticut | 198,163,000 | 0.2% |
| 42 | Montana | 187,506,000 | 0.2% |
| 43 | Wyoming | 177,223,000 | 0.2% |
| 44 | Oregon | 140,868,000 | 0.2% |
| 45 | Iowa | 140,071,000 | 0.2% |
| 46 | Rhode Island | 120,400,000 | 0.1% |
| 47 | Maine | 113,348,000 | 0.1% |
| 48 | West Virginia | 106,870,000 | 0.1% |
| 49 | New Hampshire | 73,429,000 | 0.1% |
| 50 | Vermont | 64,177,000 | 0.1% |
| | District of Columbia | 1,906,999,000 | 2.3% |

Source: U.S. Department of Defense
"Atlas/Data Abstract for the United States" (http://siadapp.dmdc.osd.mil/personnel/L03/fy09/09top.htm)
*Based on location of recipient. Does not include recipients in U.S. territories and other countries.

# U.S. Department of Defense Civilian Pay in 2009

## National Total = $49,735,662,000*

ALPHA ORDER

| RANK | STATE | PAYROLL | % of USA |
|---|---|---|---|
| 9 | Alabama | $1,808,239,000 | 3.6% |
| 33 | Alaska | 321,206,000 | 0.6% |
| 22 | Arizona | 626,966,000 | 1.3% |
| 35 | Arkansas | 235,881,000 | 0.5% |
| 2 | California | 4,570,024,000 | 9.2% |
| 17 | Colorado | 786,177,000 | 1.6% |
| 37 | Connecticut | 184,190,000 | 0.4% |
| 45 | Delaware | 98,410,000 | 0.2% |
| 6 | Florida | 1,942,655,000 | 3.9% |
| 5 | Georgia | 2,288,362,000 | 4.6% |
| 14 | Hawaii | 1,163,627,000 | 2.3% |
| 44 | Idaho | 100,861,000 | 0.2% |
| 15 | Illinois | 1,069,790,000 | 2.2% |
| 20 | Indiana | 705,646,000 | 1.4% |
| 43 | Iowa | 102,185,000 | 0.2% |
| 29 | Kansas | 471,455,000 | 0.9% |
| 26 | Kentucky | 508,305,000 | 1.0% |
| 31 | Louisiana | 414,120,000 | 0.8% |
| 30 | Maine | 440,345,000 | 0.9% |
| 3 | Maryland | 2,995,038,000 | 6.0% |
| 25 | Massachusetts | 539,474,000 | 1.1% |
| 19 | Michigan | 705,769,000 | 1.4% |
| 38 | Minnesota | 177,452,000 | 0.4% |
| 24 | Mississippi | 585,976,000 | 1.2% |
| 23 | Missouri | 586,610,000 | 1.2% |
| 46 | Montana | 91,395,000 | 0.2% |
| 34 | Nebraska | 250,642,000 | 0.5% |
| 40 | Nevada | 143,070,000 | 0.3% |
| 48 | New Hampshire | 74,277,000 | 0.1% |
| 12 | New Jersey | 1,290,072,000 | 2.6% |
| 27 | New Mexico | 483,878,000 | 1.0% |
| 18 | New York | 784,658,000 | 1.6% |
| 13 | North Carolina | 1,210,521,000 | 2.4% |
| 42 | North Dakota | 108,116,000 | 0.2% |
| 8 | Ohio | 1,824,865,000 | 3.7% |
| 11 | Oklahoma | 1,339,260,000 | 2.7% |
| 36 | Oregon | 231,630,000 | 0.5% |
| 10 | Pennsylvania | 1,788,532,000 | 3.6% |
| 32 | Rhode Island | 391,187,000 | 0.8% |
| 21 | South Carolina | 638,047,000 | 1.3% |
| 47 | South Dakota | 76,881,000 | 0.2% |
| 28 | Tennessee | 476,959,000 | 1.0% |
| 4 | Texas | 2,917,913,000 | 5.9% |
| 16 | Utah | 954,215,000 | 1.9% |
| 50 | Vermont | 44,921,000 | 0.1% |
| 1 | Virginia | 7,447,686,000 | 15.0% |
| 7 | Washington | 1,873,338,000 | 3.8% |
| 41 | West Virginia | 126,119,000 | 0.3% |
| 39 | Wisconsin | 160,743,000 | 0.3% |
| 49 | Wyoming | 69,027,000 | 0.1% |

RANK ORDER

| RANK | STATE | PAYROLL | % of USA |
|---|---|---|---|
| 1 | Virginia | $7,447,686,000 | 15.0% |
| 2 | California | 4,570,024,000 | 9.2% |
| 3 | Maryland | 2,995,038,000 | 6.0% |
| 4 | Texas | 2,917,913,000 | 5.9% |
| 5 | Georgia | 2,288,362,000 | 4.6% |
| 6 | Florida | 1,942,655,000 | 3.9% |
| 7 | Washington | 1,873,338,000 | 3.8% |
| 8 | Ohio | 1,824,865,000 | 3.7% |
| 9 | Alabama | 1,808,239,000 | 3.6% |
| 10 | Pennsylvania | 1,788,532,000 | 3.6% |
| 11 | Oklahoma | 1,339,260,000 | 2.7% |
| 12 | New Jersey | 1,290,072,000 | 2.6% |
| 13 | North Carolina | 1,210,521,000 | 2.4% |
| 14 | Hawaii | 1,163,627,000 | 2.3% |
| 15 | Illinois | 1,069,790,000 | 2.2% |
| 16 | Utah | 954,215,000 | 1.9% |
| 17 | Colorado | 786,177,000 | 1.6% |
| 18 | New York | 784,658,000 | 1.6% |
| 19 | Michigan | 705,769,000 | 1.4% |
| 20 | Indiana | 705,646,000 | 1.4% |
| 21 | South Carolina | 638,047,000 | 1.3% |
| 22 | Arizona | 626,966,000 | 1.3% |
| 23 | Missouri | 586,610,000 | 1.2% |
| 24 | Mississippi | 585,976,000 | 1.2% |
| 25 | Massachusetts | 539,474,000 | 1.1% |
| 26 | Kentucky | 508,305,000 | 1.0% |
| 27 | New Mexico | 483,878,000 | 1.0% |
| 28 | Tennessee | 476,959,000 | 1.0% |
| 29 | Kansas | 471,455,000 | 0.9% |
| 30 | Maine | 440,345,000 | 0.9% |
| 31 | Louisiana | 414,120,000 | 0.8% |
| 32 | Rhode Island | 391,187,000 | 0.8% |
| 33 | Alaska | 321,206,000 | 0.6% |
| 34 | Nebraska | 250,642,000 | 0.5% |
| 35 | Arkansas | 235,881,000 | 0.5% |
| 36 | Oregon | 231,630,000 | 0.5% |
| 37 | Connecticut | 184,190,000 | 0.4% |
| 38 | Minnesota | 177,452,000 | 0.4% |
| 39 | Wisconsin | 160,743,000 | 0.3% |
| 40 | Nevada | 143,070,000 | 0.3% |
| 41 | West Virginia | 126,119,000 | 0.3% |
| 42 | North Dakota | 108,116,000 | 0.2% |
| 43 | Iowa | 102,185,000 | 0.2% |
| 44 | Idaho | 100,861,000 | 0.2% |
| 45 | Delaware | 98,410,000 | 0.2% |
| 46 | Montana | 91,395,000 | 0.2% |
| 47 | South Dakota | 76,881,000 | 0.2% |
| 48 | New Hampshire | 74,277,000 | 0.1% |
| 49 | Wyoming | 69,027,000 | 0.1% |
| 50 | Vermont | 44,921,000 | 0.1% |
|  | District of Columbia | 1,508,947,000 | 3.0% |

Source: U.S. Department of Defense
   "Atlas/Data Abstract for the United States" (http://siadapp.dmdc.osd.mil/personnel/L03/fy09/09top.htm)
*Based on location of recipient.  Does not include recipients in U.S. territories and other countries.

# U.S. Department of Defense Reserve and National Guard Pay in 2009

## National Total = $22,758,996,000*

| RANK | STATE | PAYROLL | % of USA |
|---|---|---|---|
| 11 | Alabama | $617,055,000 | 2.7% |
| 46 | Alaska | 90,592,000 | 0.4% |
| 36 | Arizona | 180,724,000 | 0.8% |
| 18 | Arkansas | 518,376,000 | 2.3% |
| 2 | California | 1,391,094,000 | 6.1% |
| 33 | Colorado | 285,229,000 | 1.3% |
| 38 | Connecticut | 149,873,000 | 0.7% |
| 49 | Delaware | 74,623,000 | 0.3% |
| 7 | Florida | 826,134,000 | 3.6% |
| 6 | Georgia | 868,244,000 | 3.8% |
| 30 | Hawaii | 315,642,000 | 1.4% |
| 41 | Idaho | 116,236,000 | 0.5% |
| 10 | Illinois | 680,329,000 | 3.0% |
| 5 | Indiana | 905,556,000 | 4.0% |
| 29 | Iowa | 321,928,000 | 1.4% |
| 28 | Kansas | 334,444,000 | 1.5% |
| 27 | Kentucky | 391,231,000 | 1.7% |
| 26 | Louisiana | 410,608,000 | 1.8% |
| 47 | Maine | 87,175,000 | 0.4% |
| 25 | Maryland | 421,636,000 | 1.9% |
| 31 | Massachusetts | 312,302,000 | 1.4% |
| 24 | Michigan | 437,538,000 | 1.9% |
| 17 | Minnesota | 557,666,000 | 2.5% |
| 16 | Mississippi | 558,821,000 | 2.5% |
| 3 | Missouri | 1,268,807,000 | 5.6% |
| 43 | Montana | 110,398,000 | 0.5% |
| 35 | Nebraska | 198,307,000 | 0.9% |
| 37 | Nevada | 151,343,000 | 0.7% |
| 48 | New Hampshire | 78,753,000 | 0.3% |
| 19 | New Jersey | 507,311,000 | 2.2% |
| 39 | New Mexico | 148,491,000 | 0.7% |
| 8 | New York | 782,279,000 | 3.4% |
| 9 | North Carolina | 729,587,000 | 3.2% |
| 44 | North Dakota | 110,138,000 | 0.5% |
| 12 | Ohio | 609,867,000 | 2.7% |
| 20 | Oklahoma | 496,151,000 | 2.2% |
| 32 | Oregon | 300,719,000 | 1.3% |
| 4 | Pennsylvania | 1,011,822,000 | 4.4% |
| 40 | Rhode Island | 117,397,000 | 0.5% |
| 21 | South Carolina | 485,464,000 | 2.1% |
| 42 | South Dakota | 115,571,000 | 0.5% |
| 14 | Tennessee | 572,830,000 | 2.5% |
| 1 | Texas | 1,520,699,000 | 6.7% |
| 23 | Utah | 448,935,000 | 2.0% |
| 45 | Vermont | 92,561,000 | 0.4% |
| 13 | Virginia | 603,453,000 | 2.7% |
| 15 | Washington | 563,322,000 | 2.5% |
| 34 | West Virginia | 216,627,000 | 1.0% |
| 22 | Wisconsin | 470,144,000 | 2.1% |
| 50 | Wyoming | 70,775,000 | 0.3% |

| RANK | STATE | PAYROLL | % of USA |
|---|---|---|---|
| 1 | Texas | $1,520,699,000 | 6.7% |
| 2 | California | 1,391,094,000 | 6.1% |
| 3 | Missouri | 1,268,807,000 | 5.6% |
| 4 | Pennsylvania | 1,011,822,000 | 4.4% |
| 5 | Indiana | 905,556,000 | 4.0% |
| 6 | Georgia | 868,244,000 | 3.8% |
| 7 | Florida | 826,134,000 | 3.6% |
| 8 | New York | 782,279,000 | 3.4% |
| 9 | North Carolina | 729,587,000 | 3.2% |
| 10 | Illinois | 680,329,000 | 3.0% |
| 11 | Alabama | 617,055,000 | 2.7% |
| 12 | Ohio | 609,867,000 | 2.7% |
| 13 | Virginia | 603,453,000 | 2.7% |
| 14 | Tennessee | 572,830,000 | 2.5% |
| 15 | Washington | 563,322,000 | 2.5% |
| 16 | Mississippi | 558,821,000 | 2.5% |
| 17 | Minnesota | 557,666,000 | 2.5% |
| 18 | Arkansas | 518,376,000 | 2.3% |
| 19 | New Jersey | 507,311,000 | 2.2% |
| 20 | Oklahoma | 496,151,000 | 2.2% |
| 21 | South Carolina | 485,464,000 | 2.1% |
| 22 | Wisconsin | 470,144,000 | 2.1% |
| 23 | Utah | 448,935,000 | 2.0% |
| 24 | Michigan | 437,538,000 | 1.9% |
| 25 | Maryland | 421,636,000 | 1.9% |
| 26 | Louisiana | 410,608,000 | 1.8% |
| 27 | Kentucky | 391,231,000 | 1.7% |
| 28 | Kansas | 334,444,000 | 1.5% |
| 29 | Iowa | 321,928,000 | 1.4% |
| 30 | Hawaii | 315,642,000 | 1.4% |
| 31 | Massachusetts | 312,302,000 | 1.4% |
| 32 | Oregon | 300,719,000 | 1.3% |
| 33 | Colorado | 285,229,000 | 1.3% |
| 34 | West Virginia | 216,627,000 | 1.0% |
| 35 | Nebraska | 198,307,000 | 0.9% |
| 36 | Arizona | 180,724,000 | 0.8% |
| 37 | Nevada | 151,343,000 | 0.7% |
| 38 | Connecticut | 149,873,000 | 0.7% |
| 39 | New Mexico | 148,491,000 | 0.7% |
| 40 | Rhode Island | 117,397,000 | 0.5% |
| 41 | Idaho | 116,236,000 | 0.5% |
| 42 | South Dakota | 115,571,000 | 0.5% |
| 43 | Montana | 110,398,000 | 0.5% |
| 44 | North Dakota | 110,138,000 | 0.5% |
| 45 | Vermont | 92,561,000 | 0.4% |
| 46 | Alaska | 90,592,000 | 0.4% |
| 47 | Maine | 87,175,000 | 0.4% |
| 48 | New Hampshire | 78,753,000 | 0.3% |
| 49 | Delaware | 74,623,000 | 0.3% |
| 50 | Wyoming | 70,775,000 | 0.3% |
| | District of Columbia | 124,189,000 | 0.5% |

Source: U.S. Department of Defense
    "Atlas/Data Abstract for the United States" (http://siadapp.dmdc.osd.mil/personnel/L03/fy09/09top.htm)
*Based on location of recipient. Does not include recipients in U.S. territories and other countries.

# U.S. Department of Defense Retired Military Pay in 2009

## National Total = $38,215,581,000*

ALPHA ORDER

| RANK | STATE | PAYROLL | % of USA |
|---|---|---|---|
| 11 | Alabama | $1,043,872,000 | 2.7% |
| 42 | Alaska | 170,044,000 | 0.4% |
| 10 | Arizona | 1,067,372,000 | 2.8% |
| 24 | Arkansas | 432,414,000 | 1.1% |
| 4 | California | 3,424,531,000 | 9.0% |
| 9 | Colorado | 1,088,213,000 | 2.8% |
| 39 | Connecticut | 188,073,000 | 0.5% |
| 45 | Delaware | 147,506,000 | 0.4% |
| 1 | Florida | 3,832,665,000 | 10.0% |
| 5 | Georgia | 1,669,607,000 | 4.4% |
| 30 | Hawaii | 335,834,000 | 0.9% |
| 37 | Idaho | 230,516,000 | 0.6% |
| 16 | Illinois | 640,150,000 | 1.7% |
| 29 | Indiana | 376,272,000 | 1.0% |
| 41 | Iowa | 183,072,000 | 0.5% |
| 27 | Kansas | 396,523,000 | 1.0% |
| 23 | Kentucky | 441,973,000 | 1.2% |
| 22 | Louisiana | 446,278,000 | 1.2% |
| 38 | Maine | 205,813,000 | 0.5% |
| 8 | Maryland | 1,108,347,000 | 2.9% |
| 32 | Massachusetts | 318,991,000 | 0.8% |
| 26 | Michigan | 420,042,000 | 1.1% |
| 36 | Minnesota | 266,908,000 | 0.7% |
| 21 | Mississippi | 450,197,000 | 1.2% |
| 17 | Missouri | 620,620,000 | 1.6% |
| 44 | Montana | 151,345,000 | 0.4% |
| 35 | Nebraska | 268,083,000 | 0.7% |
| 20 | Nevada | 520,174,000 | 1.4% |
| 40 | New Hampshire | 184,423,000 | 0.5% |
| 31 | New Jersey | 330,784,000 | 0.9% |
| 25 | New Mexico | 422,804,000 | 1.1% |
| 19 | New York | 550,551,000 | 1.4% |
| 6 | North Carolina | 1,605,580,000 | 4.2% |
| 49 | North Dakota | 76,731,000 | 0.2% |
| 15 | Ohio | 759,242,000 | 2.0% |
| 18 | Oklahoma | 585,652,000 | 1.5% |
| 28 | Oregon | 377,830,000 | 1.0% |
| 14 | Pennsylvania | 835,998,000 | 2.2% |
| 47 | Rhode Island | 114,051,000 | 0.3% |
| 12 | South Carolina | 1,029,172,000 | 2.7% |
| 46 | South Dakota | 122,753,000 | 0.3% |
| 13 | Tennessee | 903,263,000 | 2.4% |
| 3 | Texas | 3,731,815,000 | 9.8% |
| 34 | Utah | 281,080,000 | 0.7% |
| 50 | Vermont | 59,846,000 | 0.2% |
| 2 | Virginia | 3,805,785,000 | 10.0% |
| 7 | Washington | 1,379,732,000 | 3.6% |
| 43 | West Virginia | 167,207,000 | 0.4% |
| 33 | Wisconsin | 298,742,000 | 0.8% |
| 48 | Wyoming | 87,995,000 | 0.2% |

RANK ORDER

| RANK | STATE | PAYROLL | % of USA |
|---|---|---|---|
| 1 | Florida | $3,832,665,000 | 10.0% |
| 2 | Virginia | 3,805,785,000 | 10.0% |
| 3 | Texas | 3,731,815,000 | 9.8% |
| 4 | California | 3,424,531,000 | 9.0% |
| 5 | Georgia | 1,669,607,000 | 4.4% |
| 6 | North Carolina | 1,605,580,000 | 4.2% |
| 7 | Washington | 1,379,732,000 | 3.6% |
| 8 | Maryland | 1,108,347,000 | 2.9% |
| 9 | Colorado | 1,088,213,000 | 2.8% |
| 10 | Arizona | 1,067,372,000 | 2.8% |
| 11 | Alabama | 1,043,872,000 | 2.7% |
| 12 | South Carolina | 1,029,172,000 | 2.7% |
| 13 | Tennessee | 903,263,000 | 2.4% |
| 14 | Pennsylvania | 835,998,000 | 2.2% |
| 15 | Ohio | 759,242,000 | 2.0% |
| 16 | Illinois | 640,150,000 | 1.7% |
| 17 | Missouri | 620,620,000 | 1.6% |
| 18 | Oklahoma | 585,652,000 | 1.5% |
| 19 | New York | 550,551,000 | 1.4% |
| 20 | Nevada | 520,174,000 | 1.4% |
| 21 | Mississippi | 450,197,000 | 1.2% |
| 22 | Louisiana | 446,278,000 | 1.2% |
| 23 | Kentucky | 441,973,000 | 1.2% |
| 24 | Arkansas | 432,414,000 | 1.1% |
| 25 | New Mexico | 422,804,000 | 1.1% |
| 26 | Michigan | 420,042,000 | 1.1% |
| 27 | Kansas | 396,523,000 | 1.0% |
| 28 | Oregon | 377,830,000 | 1.0% |
| 29 | Indiana | 376,272,000 | 1.0% |
| 30 | Hawaii | 335,834,000 | 0.9% |
| 31 | New Jersey | 330,784,000 | 0.9% |
| 32 | Massachusetts | 318,991,000 | 0.8% |
| 33 | Wisconsin | 298,742,000 | 0.8% |
| 34 | Utah | 281,080,000 | 0.7% |
| 35 | Nebraska | 268,083,000 | 0.7% |
| 36 | Minnesota | 266,908,000 | 0.7% |
| 37 | Idaho | 230,516,000 | 0.6% |
| 38 | Maine | 205,813,000 | 0.5% |
| 39 | Connecticut | 188,073,000 | 0.5% |
| 40 | New Hampshire | 184,423,000 | 0.5% |
| 41 | Iowa | 183,072,000 | 0.5% |
| 42 | Alaska | 170,044,000 | 0.4% |
| 43 | West Virginia | 167,207,000 | 0.4% |
| 44 | Montana | 151,345,000 | 0.4% |
| 45 | Delaware | 147,506,000 | 0.4% |
| 46 | South Dakota | 122,753,000 | 0.3% |
| 47 | Rhode Island | 114,051,000 | 0.3% |
| 48 | Wyoming | 87,995,000 | 0.2% |
| 49 | North Dakota | 76,731,000 | 0.2% |
| 50 | Vermont | 59,846,000 | 0.2% |
| | District of Columbia | 59,110,000 | 0.2% |

Source: U.S. Department of Defense
  "Atlas/Data Abstract for the United States" (http://siadapp.dmdc.osd.mil/personnel/L03/fy09/09top.htm)
*Based on location of recipient.  Does not include recipients in U.S. territories and other countries.

# Veterans in 2013

## National Total = 21,972,964 Veterans*

ALPHA ORDER

| RANK | STATE | VETERANS | % of USA |
|------|-------|----------|----------|
| 20 | Alabama | 414,963 | 1.9% |
| 46 | Alaska | 74,671 | 0.3% |
| 13 | Arizona | 527,400 | 2.4% |
| 29 | Arkansas | 250,095 | 1.1% |
| 1 | California | 1,795,455 | 8.2% |
| 22 | Colorado | 390,824 | 1.8% |
| 34 | Connecticut | 207,759 | 0.9% |
| 44 | Delaware | 78,016 | 0.4% |
| 3 | Florida | 1,520,563 | 6.9% |
| 8 | Georgia | 774,464 | 3.5% |
| 41 | Hawaii | 116,947 | 0.5% |
| 39 | Idaho | 138,108 | 0.6% |
| 10 | Illinois | 744,710 | 3.4% |
| 16 | Indiana | 490,380 | 2.2% |
| 30 | Iowa | 233,815 | 1.1% |
| 33 | Kansas | 223,708 | 1.0% |
| 26 | Kentucky | 339,334 | 1.5% |
| 28 | Louisiana | 315,342 | 1.4% |
| 40 | Maine | 127,694 | 0.6% |
| 17 | Maryland | 443,076 | 2.0% |
| 23 | Massachusetts | 374,809 | 1.7% |
| 11 | Michigan | 660,773 | 3.0% |
| 24 | Minnesota | 360,754 | 1.6% |
| 32 | Mississippi | 225,469 | 1.0% |
| 15 | Missouri | 497,874 | 2.3% |
| 43 | Montana | 101,597 | 0.5% |
| 38 | Nebraska | 138,773 | 0.6% |
| 31 | Nevada | 225,933 | 1.0% |
| 42 | New Hampshire | 110,778 | 0.5% |
| 18 | New Jersey | 425,094 | 1.9% |
| 36 | New Mexico | 170,699 | 0.8% |
| 5 | New York | 885,796 | 4.0% |
| 9 | North Carolina | 769,384 | 3.5% |
| 49 | North Dakota | 56,213 | 0.3% |
| 6 | Ohio | 877,894 | 4.0% |
| 25 | Oklahoma | 340,395 | 1.5% |
| 27 | Oregon | 322,355 | 1.5% |
| 4 | Pennsylvania | 953,644 | 4.3% |
| 47 | Rhode Island | 69,206 | 0.3% |
| 19 | South Carolina | 420,968 | 1.9% |
| 45 | South Dakota | 75,687 | 0.3% |
| 14 | Tennessee | 521,267 | 2.4% |
| 2 | Texas | 1,667,740 | 7.6% |
| 37 | Utah | 150,771 | 0.7% |
| 50 | Vermont | 48,812 | 0.2% |
| 7 | Virginia | 840,398 | 3.8% |
| 12 | Washington | 602,272 | 2.7% |
| 35 | West Virginia | 173,389 | 0.8% |
| 21 | Wisconsin | 409,419 | 1.9% |
| 48 | Wyoming | 56,518 | 0.3% |

RANK ORDER

| RANK | STATE | VETERANS | % of USA |
|------|-------|----------|----------|
| 1 | California | 1,795,455 | 8.2% |
| 2 | Texas | 1,667,740 | 7.6% |
| 3 | Florida | 1,520,563 | 6.9% |
| 4 | Pennsylvania | 953,644 | 4.3% |
| 5 | New York | 885,796 | 4.0% |
| 6 | Ohio | 877,894 | 4.0% |
| 7 | Virginia | 840,398 | 3.8% |
| 8 | Georgia | 774,464 | 3.5% |
| 9 | North Carolina | 769,384 | 3.5% |
| 10 | Illinois | 744,710 | 3.4% |
| 11 | Michigan | 660,773 | 3.0% |
| 12 | Washington | 602,272 | 2.7% |
| 13 | Arizona | 527,400 | 2.4% |
| 14 | Tennessee | 521,267 | 2.4% |
| 15 | Missouri | 497,874 | 2.3% |
| 16 | Indiana | 490,380 | 2.2% |
| 17 | Maryland | 443,076 | 2.0% |
| 18 | New Jersey | 425,094 | 1.9% |
| 19 | South Carolina | 420,968 | 1.9% |
| 20 | Alabama | 414,963 | 1.9% |
| 21 | Wisconsin | 409,419 | 1.9% |
| 22 | Colorado | 390,824 | 1.8% |
| 23 | Massachusetts | 374,809 | 1.7% |
| 24 | Minnesota | 360,754 | 1.6% |
| 25 | Oklahoma | 340,395 | 1.5% |
| 26 | Kentucky | 339,334 | 1.5% |
| 27 | Oregon | 322,355 | 1.5% |
| 28 | Louisiana | 315,342 | 1.4% |
| 29 | Arkansas | 250,095 | 1.1% |
| 30 | Iowa | 233,815 | 1.1% |
| 31 | Nevada | 225,933 | 1.0% |
| 32 | Mississippi | 225,469 | 1.0% |
| 33 | Kansas | 223,708 | 1.0% |
| 34 | Connecticut | 207,759 | 0.9% |
| 35 | West Virginia | 173,389 | 0.8% |
| 36 | New Mexico | 170,699 | 0.8% |
| 37 | Utah | 150,771 | 0.7% |
| 38 | Nebraska | 138,773 | 0.6% |
| 39 | Idaho | 138,108 | 0.6% |
| 40 | Maine | 127,694 | 0.6% |
| 41 | Hawaii | 116,947 | 0.5% |
| 42 | New Hampshire | 110,778 | 0.5% |
| 43 | Montana | 101,597 | 0.5% |
| 44 | Delaware | 78,016 | 0.4% |
| 45 | South Dakota | 75,687 | 0.3% |
| 46 | Alaska | 74,671 | 0.3% |
| 47 | Rhode Island | 69,206 | 0.3% |
| 48 | Wyoming | 56,518 | 0.3% |
| 49 | North Dakota | 56,213 | 0.3% |
| 50 | Vermont | 48,812 | 0.2% |
| | District of Columbia | 31,166 | 0.1% |

Source: U.S. Department of Veteran Affairs
"Veteran Data and Information" (http://www.va.gov/vetdata/Veteran_Population.asp)
*Estimates based on 2010 data.  Includes 199,794 veterans in U.S. territories or other countries.

# Percent of Adult Population Who Are Veterans in 2013

## National Percent = 9.1%*

ALPHA ORDER

| RANK | STATE | PERCENT |
|------|-------|---------|
| 12 | Alabama | 11.2 |
| 1 | Alaska | 13.7 |
| 18 | Arizona | 10.7 |
| 12 | Arkansas | 11.2 |
| 48 | California | 6.2 |
| 30 | Colorado | 9.9 |
| 46 | Connecticut | 7.4 |
| 14 | Delaware | 11.0 |
| 30 | Florida | 9.9 |
| 23 | Georgia | 10.4 |
| 18 | Hawaii | 10.7 |
| 7 | Idaho | 11.8 |
| 45 | Illinois | 7.6 |
| 30 | Indiana | 9.9 |
| 30 | Iowa | 9.9 |
| 24 | Kansas | 10.3 |
| 27 | Kentucky | 10.1 |
| 39 | Louisiana | 9.1 |
| 5 | Maine | 12.0 |
| 35 | Maryland | 9.8 |
| 47 | Massachusetts | 7.1 |
| 41 | Michigan | 8.7 |
| 40 | Minnesota | 8.8 |
| 27 | Mississippi | 10.1 |
| 16 | Missouri | 10.8 |
| 3 | Montana | 13.0 |
| 29 | Nebraska | 10.0 |
| 16 | Nevada | 10.8 |
| 20 | New Hampshire | 10.6 |
| 48 | New Jersey | 6.2 |
| 15 | New Mexico | 10.9 |
| 50 | New York | 5.8 |
| 24 | North Carolina | 10.3 |
| 24 | North Dakota | 10.3 |
| 30 | Ohio | 9.9 |
| 7 | Oklahoma | 11.8 |
| 20 | Oregon | 10.6 |
| 37 | Pennsylvania | 9.5 |
| 43 | Rhode Island | 8.3 |
| 10 | South Carolina | 11.6 |
| 5 | South Dakota | 12.0 |
| 22 | Tennessee | 10.5 |
| 41 | Texas | 8.7 |
| 44 | Utah | 7.7 |
| 36 | Vermont | 9.7 |
| 2 | Virginia | 13.3 |
| 11 | Washington | 11.3 |
| 7 | West Virginia | 11.8 |
| 38 | Wisconsin | 9.3 |
| 4 | Wyoming | 12.8 |

RANK ORDER

| RANK | STATE | PERCENT |
|------|-------|---------|
| 1 | Alaska | 13.7 |
| 2 | Virginia | 13.3 |
| 3 | Montana | 13.0 |
| 4 | Wyoming | 12.8 |
| 5 | Maine | 12.0 |
| 5 | South Dakota | 12.0 |
| 7 | Idaho | 11.8 |
| 7 | Oklahoma | 11.8 |
| 7 | West Virginia | 11.8 |
| 10 | South Carolina | 11.6 |
| 11 | Washington | 11.3 |
| 12 | Alabama | 11.2 |
| 12 | Arkansas | 11.2 |
| 14 | Delaware | 11.0 |
| 15 | New Mexico | 10.9 |
| 16 | Missouri | 10.8 |
| 16 | Nevada | 10.8 |
| 18 | Arizona | 10.7 |
| 18 | Hawaii | 10.7 |
| 20 | New Hampshire | 10.6 |
| 20 | Oregon | 10.6 |
| 22 | Tennessee | 10.5 |
| 23 | Georgia | 10.4 |
| 24 | Kansas | 10.3 |
| 24 | North Carolina | 10.3 |
| 24 | North Dakota | 10.3 |
| 27 | Kentucky | 10.1 |
| 27 | Mississippi | 10.1 |
| 29 | Nebraska | 10.0 |
| 30 | Colorado | 9.9 |
| 30 | Florida | 9.9 |
| 30 | Indiana | 9.9 |
| 30 | Iowa | 9.9 |
| 30 | Ohio | 9.9 |
| 35 | Maryland | 9.8 |
| 36 | Vermont | 9.7 |
| 37 | Pennsylvania | 9.5 |
| 38 | Wisconsin | 9.3 |
| 39 | Louisiana | 9.1 |
| 40 | Minnesota | 8.8 |
| 41 | Michigan | 8.7 |
| 41 | Texas | 8.7 |
| 43 | Rhode Island | 8.3 |
| 44 | Utah | 7.7 |
| 45 | Illinois | 7.6 |
| 46 | Connecticut | 7.4 |
| 47 | Massachusetts | 7.1 |
| 48 | California | 6.2 |
| 48 | New Jersey | 6.2 |
| 50 | New York | 5.8 |

District of Columbia 6.0

Source: CQ Press using data from U.S. Department of Veteran Affairs
 "Veteran Data and Information" (http://www.va.gov/vetdata/Veteran_Population.asp)
*Estimates based on 2010 data. National figures does not include veterans in U.S. territories or other countries. Percent calculated with population 18 years old and older in 2012.

# U.S. Military Fatalities in Iraq and Afghanistan as of January 28, 2014

## National Total = 6,779 Fatalities*

ALPHA ORDER

| RANK | STATE | FATALITIES | % of USA |
|---|---|---|---|
| 25 | Alabama | 105 | 1.5% |
| 46 | Alaska | 23 | 0.3% |
| 13 | Arizona | 151 | 2.2% |
| 29 | Arkansas | 89 | 1.3% |
| 1 | California | 725 | 10.7% |
| 26 | Colorado | 100 | 1.5% |
| 38 | Connecticut | 47 | 0.7% |
| 49 | Delaware | 19 | 0.3% |
| 3 | Florida | 342 | 5.0% |
| 9 | Georgia | 214 | 3.2% |
| 43 | Hawaii | 36 | 0.5% |
| 36 | Idaho | 50 | 0.7% |
| 7 | Illinois | 249 | 3.7% |
| 12 | Indiana | 154 | 2.3% |
| 32 | Iowa | 72 | 1.1% |
| 31 | Kansas | 73 | 1.1% |
| 23 | Kentucky | 109 | 1.6% |
| 20 | Louisiana | 123 | 1.8% |
| 36 | Maine | 50 | 0.7% |
| 22 | Maryland | 117 | 1.7% |
| 18 | Massachusetts | 124 | 1.8% |
| 8 | Michigan | 224 | 3.3% |
| 27 | Minnesota | 96 | 1.4% |
| 30 | Mississippi | 80 | 1.2% |
| 15 | Missouri | 143 | 2.1% |
| 40 | Montana | 40 | 0.6% |
| 33 | Nebraska | 60 | 0.9% |
| 35 | Nevada | 54 | 0.8% |
| 42 | New Hampshire | 38 | 0.6% |
| 20 | New Jersey | 123 | 1.8% |
| 34 | New Mexico | 55 | 0.8% |
| 4 | New York | 292 | 4.3% |
| 11 | North Carolina | 186 | 2.7% |
| 48 | North Dakota | 20 | 0.3% |
| 6 | Ohio | 275 | 4.1% |
| 17 | Oklahoma | 125 | 1.8% |
| 24 | Oregon | 108 | 1.6% |
| 5 | Pennsylvania | 290 | 4.3% |
| 50 | Rhode Island | 16 | 0.2% |
| 28 | South Carolina | 94 | 1.4% |
| 45 | South Dakota | 24 | 0.4% |
| 16 | Tennessee | 140 | 2.1% |
| 2 | Texas | 600 | 8.9% |
| 38 | Utah | 47 | 0.7% |
| 44 | Vermont | 26 | 0.4% |
| 10 | Virginia | 196 | 2.9% |
| 14 | Washington | 147 | 2.2% |
| 41 | West Virginia | 39 | 0.6% |
| 18 | Wisconsin | 124 | 1.8% |
| 47 | Wyoming | 22 | 0.3% |

RANK ORDER

| RANK | STATE | FATALITIES | % of USA |
|---|---|---|---|
| 1 | California | 725 | 10.7% |
| 2 | Texas | 600 | 8.9% |
| 3 | Florida | 342 | 5.0% |
| 4 | New York | 292 | 4.3% |
| 5 | Pennsylvania | 290 | 4.3% |
| 6 | Ohio | 275 | 4.1% |
| 7 | Illinois | 249 | 3.7% |
| 8 | Michigan | 224 | 3.3% |
| 9 | Georgia | 214 | 3.2% |
| 10 | Virginia | 196 | 2.9% |
| 11 | North Carolina | 186 | 2.7% |
| 12 | Indiana | 154 | 2.3% |
| 13 | Arizona | 151 | 2.2% |
| 14 | Washington | 147 | 2.2% |
| 15 | Missouri | 143 | 2.1% |
| 16 | Tennessee | 140 | 2.1% |
| 17 | Oklahoma | 125 | 1.8% |
| 18 | Massachusetts | 124 | 1.8% |
| 18 | Wisconsin | 124 | 1.8% |
| 20 | Louisiana | 123 | 1.8% |
| 20 | New Jersey | 123 | 1.8% |
| 22 | Maryland | 117 | 1.7% |
| 23 | Kentucky | 109 | 1.6% |
| 24 | Oregon | 108 | 1.6% |
| 25 | Alabama | 105 | 1.5% |
| 26 | Colorado | 100 | 1.5% |
| 27 | Minnesota | 96 | 1.4% |
| 28 | South Carolina | 94 | 1.4% |
| 29 | Arkansas | 89 | 1.3% |
| 30 | Mississippi | 80 | 1.2% |
| 31 | Kansas | 73 | 1.1% |
| 32 | Iowa | 72 | 1.1% |
| 33 | Nebraska | 60 | 0.9% |
| 34 | New Mexico | 55 | 0.8% |
| 35 | Nevada | 54 | 0.8% |
| 36 | Idaho | 50 | 0.7% |
| 36 | Maine | 50 | 0.7% |
| 38 | Connecticut | 47 | 0.7% |
| 38 | Utah | 47 | 0.7% |
| 40 | Montana | 40 | 0.6% |
| 41 | West Virginia | 39 | 0.6% |
| 42 | New Hampshire | 38 | 0.6% |
| 43 | Hawaii | 36 | 0.5% |
| 44 | Vermont | 26 | 0.4% |
| 45 | South Dakota | 24 | 0.4% |
| 46 | Alaska | 23 | 0.3% |
| 47 | Wyoming | 22 | 0.3% |
| 48 | North Dakota | 20 | 0.3% |
| 49 | Delaware | 19 | 0.3% |
| 50 | Rhode Island | 16 | 0.2% |
| | District of Columbia | 10 | 0.1% |

Source: U.S. Department of Defense, Defense Casualty Analysis System
   "U.S. Military Casualties" (https://www.dmdc.osd.mil/dcas/pages/report_sum_all.xhtml)
*Total includes 113 deaths of soldiers from U.S. territories. Total does not include deaths of United Kingdom soldiers or other coalition nations. Includes 5,322 combat and 1,457 noncombat deaths. Includes 4,476 deaths in Iraq and 2,303 deaths in Afghanistan.

# Rate of U.S. Military Fatalities in Iraq and Afghanistan as of January 28, 2014

## National Rate = 2.1 Fatalities per 100,000 Population*

ALPHA ORDER

| RANK | STATE | RATE |
|------|-------|------|
| 29 | Alabama | 2.2 |
| 7 | Alaska | 3.1 |
| 23 | Arizona | 2.3 |
| 9 | Arkansas | 3.0 |
| 38 | California | 1.9 |
| 38 | Colorado | 1.9 |
| 50 | Connecticut | 1.3 |
| 32 | Delaware | 2.1 |
| 45 | Florida | 1.7 |
| 32 | Georgia | 2.1 |
| 16 | Hawaii | 2.6 |
| 7 | Idaho | 3.1 |
| 38 | Illinois | 1.9 |
| 23 | Indiana | 2.3 |
| 23 | Iowa | 2.3 |
| 18 | Kansas | 2.5 |
| 18 | Kentucky | 2.5 |
| 13 | Louisiana | 2.7 |
| 3 | Maine | 3.8 |
| 36 | Maryland | 2.0 |
| 38 | Massachusetts | 1.9 |
| 23 | Michigan | 2.3 |
| 44 | Minnesota | 1.8 |
| 13 | Mississippi | 2.7 |
| 20 | Missouri | 2.4 |
| 2 | Montana | 3.9 |
| 5 | Nebraska | 3.2 |
| 38 | Nevada | 1.9 |
| 10 | New Hampshire | 2.9 |
| 49 | New Jersey | 1.4 |
| 16 | New Mexico | 2.6 |
| 47 | New York | 1.5 |
| 38 | North Carolina | 1.9 |
| 11 | North Dakota | 2.8 |
| 20 | Ohio | 2.4 |
| 5 | Oklahoma | 3.2 |
| 13 | Oregon | 2.7 |
| 23 | Pennsylvania | 2.3 |
| 47 | Rhode Island | 1.5 |
| 36 | South Carolina | 2.0 |
| 11 | South Dakota | 2.8 |
| 29 | Tennessee | 2.2 |
| 23 | Texas | 2.3 |
| 46 | Utah | 1.6 |
| 1 | Vermont | 4.1 |
| 20 | Virginia | 2.4 |
| 32 | Washington | 2.1 |
| 32 | West Virginia | 2.1 |
| 29 | Wisconsin | 2.2 |
| 3 | Wyoming | 3.8 |

RANK ORDER

| RANK | STATE | RATE |
|------|-------|------|
| 1 | Vermont | 4.1 |
| 2 | Montana | 3.9 |
| 3 | Maine | 3.8 |
| 3 | Wyoming | 3.8 |
| 5 | Nebraska | 3.2 |
| 5 | Oklahoma | 3.2 |
| 7 | Alaska | 3.1 |
| 7 | Idaho | 3.1 |
| 9 | Arkansas | 3.0 |
| 10 | New Hampshire | 2.9 |
| 11 | North Dakota | 2.8 |
| 11 | South Dakota | 2.8 |
| 13 | Louisiana | 2.7 |
| 13 | Mississippi | 2.7 |
| 13 | Oregon | 2.7 |
| 16 | Hawaii | 2.6 |
| 16 | New Mexico | 2.6 |
| 18 | Kansas | 2.5 |
| 18 | Kentucky | 2.5 |
| 20 | Missouri | 2.4 |
| 20 | Ohio | 2.4 |
| 20 | Virginia | 2.4 |
| 23 | Arizona | 2.3 |
| 23 | Indiana | 2.3 |
| 23 | Iowa | 2.3 |
| 23 | Michigan | 2.3 |
| 23 | Pennsylvania | 2.3 |
| 23 | Texas | 2.3 |
| 29 | Alabama | 2.2 |
| 29 | Tennessee | 2.2 |
| 29 | Wisconsin | 2.2 |
| 32 | Delaware | 2.1 |
| 32 | Georgia | 2.1 |
| 32 | Washington | 2.1 |
| 32 | West Virginia | 2.1 |
| 36 | Maryland | 2.0 |
| 36 | South Carolina | 2.0 |
| 38 | California | 1.9 |
| 38 | Colorado | 1.9 |
| 38 | Illinois | 1.9 |
| 38 | Massachusetts | 1.9 |
| 38 | Nevada | 1.9 |
| 38 | North Carolina | 1.9 |
| 44 | Minnesota | 1.8 |
| 45 | Florida | 1.7 |
| 46 | Utah | 1.6 |
| 47 | New York | 1.5 |
| 47 | Rhode Island | 1.5 |
| 49 | New Jersey | 1.4 |
| 50 | Connecticut | 1.3 |
| | District of Columbia | 1.5 |

Source: CQ Press using data from U.S. Department of Defense, Defense Casualty Analysis System
   "U.S. Military Casualties" (https://www.dmdc.osd.mil/dcas/pages/report_sum_all.xhtml)
*National rate does not include deaths of soldiers from U.S. territories. Includes combat and noncombat deaths. Calculated with 2013 population estimates.

# U.S. Military Wounded in Iraq and Afghanistan as of January 28, 2014

## National Total = 51,874 Wounded*

| RANK | STATE | WOUNDED | % of USA |
|------|-------|---------|----------|
| 18 | Alabama | 851 | 1.6% |
| 46 | Alaska | 156 | 0.3% |
| 14 | Arizona | 1,138 | 2.2% |
| 29 | Arkansas | 643 | 1.2% |
| 1 | California | 4,790 | 9.2% |
| 22 | Colorado | 805 | 1.6% |
| 35 | Connecticut | 418 | 0.8% |
| 50 | Delaware | 81 | 0.2% |
| 3 | Florida | 2,451 | 4.7% |
| 9 | Georgia | 1,463 | 2.8% |
| 43 | Hawaii | 207 | 0.4% |
| 36 | Idaho | 387 | 0.7% |
| 7 | Illinois | 1,732 | 3.3% |
| 15 | Indiana | 1,088 | 2.1% |
| 31 | Iowa | 617 | 1.2% |
| 30 | Kansas | 622 | 1.2% |
| 27 | Kentucky | 742 | 1.4% |
| 21 | Louisiana | 826 | 1.6% |
| 41 | Maine | 316 | 0.6% |
| 28 | Maryland | 667 | 1.3% |
| 20 | Massachusetts | 831 | 1.6% |
| 8 | Michigan | 1,619 | 3.1% |
| 26 | Minnesota | 745 | 1.4% |
| 33 | Mississippi | 437 | 0.8% |
| 13 | Missouri | 1,175 | 2.3% |
| 40 | Montana | 323 | 0.6% |
| 39 | Nebraska | 334 | 0.6% |
| 37 | Nevada | 369 | 0.7% |
| 42 | New Hampshire | 293 | 0.6% |
| 24 | New Jersey | 753 | 1.5% |
| 34 | New Mexico | 420 | 0.8% |
| 4 | New York | 2,291 | 4.4% |
| 10 | North Carolina | 1,420 | 2.7% |
| 49 | North Dakota | 116 | 0.2% |
| 5 | Ohio | 2,021 | 3.9% |
| 19 | Oklahoma | 847 | 1.6% |
| 23 | Oregon | 780 | 1.5% |
| 6 | Pennsylvania | 1,976 | 3.8% |
| 45 | Rhode Island | 163 | 0.3% |
| 25 | South Carolina | 747 | 1.4% |
| 44 | South Dakota | 194 | 0.4% |
| 16 | Tennessee | 1,000 | 1.9% |
| 2 | Texas | 4,296 | 8.3% |
| 32 | Utah | 449 | 0.9% |
| 47 | Vermont | 151 | 0.3% |
| 12 | Virginia | 1,181 | 2.3% |
| 11 | Washington | 1,278 | 2.5% |
| 38 | West Virginia | 357 | 0.7% |
| 17 | Wisconsin | 908 | 1.8% |
| 48 | Wyoming | 149 | 0.3% |

| RANK | STATE | WOUNDED | % of USA |
|------|-------|---------|----------|
| 1 | California | 4,790 | 9.2% |
| 2 | Texas | 4,296 | 8.3% |
| 3 | Florida | 2,451 | 4.7% |
| 4 | New York | 2,291 | 4.4% |
| 5 | Ohio | 2,021 | 3.9% |
| 6 | Pennsylvania | 1,976 | 3.8% |
| 7 | Illinois | 1,732 | 3.3% |
| 8 | Michigan | 1,619 | 3.1% |
| 9 | Georgia | 1,463 | 2.8% |
| 10 | North Carolina | 1,420 | 2.7% |
| 11 | Washington | 1,278 | 2.5% |
| 12 | Virginia | 1,181 | 2.3% |
| 13 | Missouri | 1,175 | 2.3% |
| 14 | Arizona | 1,138 | 2.2% |
| 15 | Indiana | 1,088 | 2.1% |
| 16 | Tennessee | 1,000 | 1.9% |
| 17 | Wisconsin | 908 | 1.8% |
| 18 | Alabama | 851 | 1.6% |
| 19 | Oklahoma | 847 | 1.6% |
| 20 | Massachusetts | 831 | 1.6% |
| 21 | Louisiana | 826 | 1.6% |
| 22 | Colorado | 805 | 1.6% |
| 23 | Oregon | 780 | 1.5% |
| 24 | New Jersey | 753 | 1.5% |
| 25 | South Carolina | 747 | 1.4% |
| 26 | Minnesota | 745 | 1.4% |
| 27 | Kentucky | 742 | 1.4% |
| 28 | Maryland | 667 | 1.3% |
| 29 | Arkansas | 643 | 1.2% |
| 30 | Kansas | 622 | 1.2% |
| 31 | Iowa | 617 | 1.2% |
| 32 | Utah | 449 | 0.9% |
| 33 | Mississippi | 437 | 0.8% |
| 34 | New Mexico | 420 | 0.8% |
| 35 | Connecticut | 418 | 0.8% |
| 36 | Idaho | 387 | 0.7% |
| 37 | Nevada | 369 | 0.7% |
| 38 | West Virginia | 357 | 0.7% |
| 39 | Nebraska | 334 | 0.6% |
| 40 | Montana | 323 | 0.6% |
| 41 | Maine | 316 | 0.6% |
| 42 | New Hampshire | 293 | 0.6% |
| 43 | Hawaii | 207 | 0.4% |
| 44 | South Dakota | 194 | 0.4% |
| 45 | Rhode Island | 163 | 0.3% |
| 46 | Alaska | 156 | 0.3% |
| 47 | Vermont | 151 | 0.3% |
| 48 | Wyoming | 149 | 0.3% |
| 49 | North Dakota | 116 | 0.2% |
| 50 | Delaware | 81 | 0.2% |
| | District of Columbia | 29 | 0.1% |

Source: U.S. Department of Defense, Defense Casualty Analysis System
"U.S. Military Casualties" (https://www.dmdc.osd.mil/dcas/pages/report_sum_all.xhtml)
*Total includes 4,222 wounded soldiers from U.S. territories. Total does not include wounded soldiers of United Kingdom or other coalition nations. Only includes wounded in action. Includes 32,236 wounded in Iraq and 19,638 wounded in Afghanistan.

# IV. Economy

# Gross Domestic Product in 2012

## National Total = $15,566,077,000,000*

ALPHA ORDER

| RANK | STATE | G.D.P. | % of USA |
|------|-------|--------|----------|
| 26 | Alabama | $183,547,000,000 | 1.2% |
| 44 | Alaska | 51,859,000,000 | 0.3% |
| 20 | Arizona | 266,891,000,000 | 1.7% |
| 34 | Arkansas | 109,557,000,000 | 0.7% |
| 1 | California | 2,003,479,000,000 | 12.9% |
| 19 | Colorado | 274,048,000,000 | 1.8% |
| 24 | Connecticut | 229,317,000,000 | 1.5% |
| 40 | Delaware | 65,984,000,000 | 0.4% |
| 4 | Florida | 777,164,000,000 | 5.0% |
| 11 | Georgia | 433,569,000,000 | 2.8% |
| 38 | Hawaii | 72,424,000,000 | 0.5% |
| 42 | Idaho | 58,243,000,000 | 0.4% |
| 5 | Illinois | 695,238,000,000 | 4.5% |
| 16 | Indiana | 298,625,000,000 | 1.9% |
| 30 | Iowa | 152,436,000,000 | 1.0% |
| 31 | Kansas | 138,953,000,000 | 0.9% |
| 28 | Kentucky | 173,466,000,000 | 1.1% |
| 23 | Louisiana | 243,264,000,000 | 1.6% |
| 43 | Maine | 53,656,000,000 | 0.3% |
| 15 | Maryland | 317,678,000,000 | 2.0% |
| 12 | Massachusetts | 403,823,000,000 | 2.6% |
| 13 | Michigan | 400,504,000,000 | 2.6% |
| 17 | Minnesota | 294,729,000,000 | 1.9% |
| 35 | Mississippi | 101,490,000,000 | 0.7% |
| 22 | Missouri | 258,832,000,000 | 1.7% |
| 48 | Montana | 40,422,000,000 | 0.3% |
| 36 | Nebraska | 99,557,000,000 | 0.6% |
| 32 | Nevada | 133,584,000,000 | 0.9% |
| 41 | New Hampshire | 64,697,000,000 | 0.4% |
| 8 | New Jersey | 508,003,000,000 | 3.3% |
| 37 | New Mexico | 80,600,000,000 | 0.5% |
| 3 | New York | 1,205,930,000,000 | 7.7% |
| 9 | North Carolina | 455,973,000,000 | 2.9% |
| 46 | North Dakota | 46,016,000,000 | 0.3% |
| 7 | Ohio | 509,393,000,000 | 3.3% |
| 29 | Oklahoma | 160,953,000,000 | 1.0% |
| 25 | Oregon | 198,702,000,000 | 1.3% |
| 6 | Pennsylvania | 600,897,000,000 | 3.9% |
| 45 | Rhode Island | 50,956,000,000 | 0.3% |
| 27 | South Carolina | 176,217,000,000 | 1.1% |
| 47 | South Dakota | 42,464,000,000 | 0.3% |
| 18 | Tennessee | 277,036,000,000 | 1.8% |
| 2 | Texas | 1,397,369,000,000 | 9.0% |
| 33 | Utah | 130,486,000,000 | 0.8% |
| 50 | Vermont | 27,296,000,000 | 0.2% |
| 10 | Virginia | 445,876,000,000 | 2.9% |
| 14 | Washington | 375,730,000,000 | 2.4% |
| 39 | West Virginia | 69,380,000,000 | 0.4% |
| 21 | Wisconsin | 261,548,000,000 | 1.7% |
| 49 | Wyoming | 38,422,000,000 | 0.2% |

RANK ORDER

| RANK | STATE | G.D.P. | % of USA |
|------|-------|--------|----------|
| 1 | California | $2,003,479,000,000 | 12.9% |
| 2 | Texas | 1,397,369,000,000 | 9.0% |
| 3 | New York | 1,205,930,000,000 | 7.7% |
| 4 | Florida | 777,164,000,000 | 5.0% |
| 5 | Illinois | 695,238,000,000 | 4.5% |
| 6 | Pennsylvania | 600,897,000,000 | 3.9% |
| 7 | Ohio | 509,393,000,000 | 3.3% |
| 8 | New Jersey | 508,003,000,000 | 3.3% |
| 9 | North Carolina | 455,973,000,000 | 2.9% |
| 10 | Virginia | 445,876,000,000 | 2.9% |
| 11 | Georgia | 433,569,000,000 | 2.8% |
| 12 | Massachusetts | 403,823,000,000 | 2.6% |
| 13 | Michigan | 400,504,000,000 | 2.6% |
| 14 | Washington | 375,730,000,000 | 2.4% |
| 15 | Maryland | 317,678,000,000 | 2.0% |
| 16 | Indiana | 298,625,000,000 | 1.9% |
| 17 | Minnesota | 294,729,000,000 | 1.9% |
| 18 | Tennessee | 277,036,000,000 | 1.8% |
| 19 | Colorado | 274,048,000,000 | 1.8% |
| 20 | Arizona | 266,891,000,000 | 1.7% |
| 21 | Wisconsin | 261,548,000,000 | 1.7% |
| 22 | Missouri | 258,832,000,000 | 1.7% |
| 23 | Louisiana | 243,264,000,000 | 1.6% |
| 24 | Connecticut | 229,317,000,000 | 1.5% |
| 25 | Oregon | 198,702,000,000 | 1.3% |
| 26 | Alabama | 183,547,000,000 | 1.2% |
| 27 | South Carolina | 176,217,000,000 | 1.1% |
| 28 | Kentucky | 173,466,000,000 | 1.1% |
| 29 | Oklahoma | 160,953,000,000 | 1.0% |
| 30 | Iowa | 152,436,000,000 | 1.0% |
| 31 | Kansas | 138,953,000,000 | 0.9% |
| 32 | Nevada | 133,584,000,000 | 0.9% |
| 33 | Utah | 130,486,000,000 | 0.8% |
| 34 | Arkansas | 109,557,000,000 | 0.7% |
| 35 | Mississippi | 101,490,000,000 | 0.7% |
| 36 | Nebraska | 99,557,000,000 | 0.6% |
| 37 | New Mexico | 80,600,000,000 | 0.5% |
| 38 | Hawaii | 72,424,000,000 | 0.5% |
| 39 | West Virginia | 69,380,000,000 | 0.4% |
| 40 | Delaware | 65,984,000,000 | 0.4% |
| 41 | New Hampshire | 64,697,000,000 | 0.4% |
| 42 | Idaho | 58,243,000,000 | 0.4% |
| 43 | Maine | 53,656,000,000 | 0.3% |
| 44 | Alaska | 51,859,000,000 | 0.3% |
| 45 | Rhode Island | 50,956,000,000 | 0.3% |
| 46 | North Dakota | 46,016,000,000 | 0.3% |
| 47 | South Dakota | 42,464,000,000 | 0.3% |
| 48 | Montana | 40,422,000,000 | 0.3% |
| 49 | Wyoming | 38,422,000,000 | 0.2% |
| 50 | Vermont | 27,296,000,000 | 0.2% |
| | District of Columbia | 109,793,000,000 | 0.7% |

Source: U.S. Department of Commerce, Bureau of Economic Analysis
    "Gross Domestic Product Data" (http://www.bea.gov/iTable/index_regional.cfm)
*G.D.P. is the market value of goods and services produced by the labor and property located in a state.  It is the state
counterpart to the nation's Gross Domestic Product.  This was formerly known as Gross State Product (G.S.P.).

# Percent Change in Gross Domestic Product: 2008 to 2012
## (Adjusted to Constant 2005 Dollars)
## National Percent Change = 3.2% Increase*

ALPHA ORDER

| RANK | STATE | PERCENT CHANGE |
|---|---|---|
| 36 | Alabama | 0.9 |
| 5 | Alaska | 9.0 |
| 49 | Arizona | (4.4) |
| 32 | Arkansas | 2.5 |
| 43 | California | (0.3) |
| 25 | Colorado | 3.9 |
| 48 | Connecticut | (2.6) |
| 18 | Delaware | 4.5 |
| 47 | Florida | (2.5) |
| 40 | Georgia | 0.0 |
| 27 | Hawaii | 3.0 |
| 44 | Idaho | (0.8) |
| 34 | Illinois | 2.3 |
| 10 | Indiana | 5.6 |
| 16 | Iowa | 4.9 |
| 25 | Kansas | 3.9 |
| 21 | Kentucky | 4.4 |
| 6 | Louisiana | 7.9 |
| 36 | Maine | 0.9 |
| 9 | Maryland | 6.3 |
| 12 | Massachusetts | 5.3 |
| 36 | Michigan | 0.9 |
| 18 | Minnesota | 4.5 |
| 44 | Mississippi | (0.8) |
| 41 | Missouri | (0.2) |
| 18 | Montana | 4.5 |
| 8 | Nebraska | 7.3 |
| 50 | Nevada | (5.5) |
| 22 | New Hampshire | 4.2 |
| 46 | New Jersey | (1.3) |
| 33 | New Mexico | 2.4 |
| 14 | New York | 5.2 |
| 24 | North Carolina | 4.0 |
| 1 | North Dakota | 35.0 |
| 35 | Ohio | 1.2 |
| 29 | Oklahoma | 2.9 |
| 3 | Oregon | 10.1 |
| 31 | Pennsylvania | 2.6 |
| 39 | Rhode Island | 0.8 |
| 27 | South Carolina | 3.0 |
| 16 | South Dakota | 4.9 |
| 22 | Tennessee | 4.2 |
| 2 | Texas | 12.5 |
| 7 | Utah | 7.7 |
| 15 | Vermont | 5.0 |
| 12 | Virginia | 5.3 |
| 11 | Washington | 5.5 |
| 4 | West Virginia | 9.3 |
| 29 | Wisconsin | 2.9 |
| 41 | Wyoming | (0.2) |

RANK ORDER

| RANK | STATE | PERCENT CHANGE |
|---|---|---|
| 1 | North Dakota | 35.0 |
| 2 | Texas | 12.5 |
| 3 | Oregon | 10.1 |
| 4 | West Virginia | 9.3 |
| 5 | Alaska | 9.0 |
| 6 | Louisiana | 7.9 |
| 7 | Utah | 7.7 |
| 8 | Nebraska | 7.3 |
| 9 | Maryland | 6.3 |
| 10 | Indiana | 5.6 |
| 11 | Washington | 5.5 |
| 12 | Massachusetts | 5.3 |
| 12 | Virginia | 5.3 |
| 14 | New York | 5.2 |
| 15 | Vermont | 5.0 |
| 16 | Iowa | 4.9 |
| 16 | South Dakota | 4.9 |
| 18 | Delaware | 4.5 |
| 18 | Minnesota | 4.5 |
| 18 | Montana | 4.5 |
| 21 | Kentucky | 4.4 |
| 22 | New Hampshire | 4.2 |
| 22 | Tennessee | 4.2 |
| 24 | North Carolina | 4.0 |
| 25 | Colorado | 3.9 |
| 25 | Kansas | 3.9 |
| 27 | Hawaii | 3.0 |
| 27 | South Carolina | 3.0 |
| 29 | Oklahoma | 2.9 |
| 29 | Wisconsin | 2.9 |
| 31 | Pennsylvania | 2.6 |
| 32 | Arkansas | 2.5 |
| 33 | New Mexico | 2.4 |
| 34 | Illinois | 2.3 |
| 35 | Ohio | 1.2 |
| 36 | Alabama | 0.9 |
| 36 | Maine | 0.9 |
| 36 | Michigan | 0.9 |
| 39 | Rhode Island | 0.8 |
| 40 | Georgia | 0.0 |
| 41 | Missouri | (0.2) |
| 41 | Wyoming | (0.2) |
| 43 | California | (0.3) |
| 44 | Idaho | (0.8) |
| 44 | Mississippi | (0.8) |
| 46 | New Jersey | (1.3) |
| 47 | Florida | (2.5) |
| 48 | Connecticut | (2.6) |
| 49 | Arizona | (4.4) |
| 50 | Nevada | (5.5) |
|  | District of Columbia | 4.9 |

Source: CQ Press using data from U.S. Department of Commerce, Bureau of Economic Analysis
"Gross Domestic Product Data" (http://www.bea.gov/iTable/index_regional.cfm)
*G.D.P. is the market value of goods and services produced by the labor and property located in a state. It is the state counterpart to the nation's Gross Domestic Product. This was formerly known as Gross State Product (G.S.P.). Adjusted for inflation using chained 2005 dollars.

# Average Annual Change in Gross Domestic Product: 2008 to 2012
## (Adjusted to Constant 2005 Dollars)
## National Annual Percent Change = 0.6% Increase*

ALPHA ORDER

| RANK | STATE | PERCENT CHANGE |
|------|-------|----------------|
| 35 | Alabama | 0.2 |
| 5 | Alaska | 1.7 |
| 49 | Arizona | (0.9) |
| 31 | Arkansas | 0.5 |
| 43 | California | (0.1) |
| 22 | Colorado | 0.8 |
| 47 | Connecticut | (0.5) |
| 18 | Delaware | 0.9 |
| 47 | Florida | (0.5) |
| 40 | Georgia | 0.0 |
| 27 | Hawaii | 0.6 |
| 44 | Idaho | (0.2) |
| 31 | Illinois | 0.5 |
| 10 | Indiana | 1.1 |
| 12 | Iowa | 1.0 |
| 22 | Kansas | 0.8 |
| 18 | Kentucky | 0.9 |
| 6 | Louisiana | 1.5 |
| 35 | Maine | 0.2 |
| 9 | Maryland | 1.2 |
| 12 | Massachusetts | 1.0 |
| 35 | Michigan | 0.2 |
| 18 | Minnesota | 0.9 |
| 44 | Mississippi | (0.2) |
| 40 | Missouri | 0.0 |
| 18 | Montana | 0.9 |
| 8 | Nebraska | 1.4 |
| 50 | Nevada | (1.1) |
| 22 | New Hampshire | 0.8 |
| 46 | New Jersey | (0.3) |
| 31 | New Mexico | 0.5 |
| 12 | New York | 1.0 |
| 22 | North Carolina | 0.8 |
| 1 | North Dakota | 6.2 |
| 35 | Ohio | 0.2 |
| 27 | Oklahoma | 0.6 |
| 3 | Oregon | 2.0 |
| 31 | Pennsylvania | 0.5 |
| 35 | Rhode Island | 0.2 |
| 27 | South Carolina | 0.6 |
| 12 | South Dakota | 1.0 |
| 22 | Tennessee | 0.8 |
| 2 | Texas | 2.4 |
| 6 | Utah | 1.5 |
| 12 | Vermont | 1.0 |
| 12 | Virginia | 1.0 |
| 10 | Washington | 1.1 |
| 4 | West Virginia | 1.8 |
| 27 | Wisconsin | 0.6 |
| 40 | Wyoming | 0.0 |

RANK ORDER

| RANK | STATE | PERCENT CHANGE |
|------|-------|----------------|
| 1 | North Dakota | 6.2 |
| 2 | Texas | 2.4 |
| 3 | Oregon | 2.0 |
| 4 | West Virginia | 1.8 |
| 5 | Alaska | 1.7 |
| 6 | Louisiana | 1.5 |
| 6 | Utah | 1.5 |
| 8 | Nebraska | 1.4 |
| 9 | Maryland | 1.2 |
| 10 | Indiana | 1.1 |
| 10 | Washington | 1.1 |
| 12 | Iowa | 1.0 |
| 12 | Massachusetts | 1.0 |
| 12 | New York | 1.0 |
| 12 | South Dakota | 1.0 |
| 12 | Vermont | 1.0 |
| 12 | Virginia | 1.0 |
| 18 | Delaware | 0.9 |
| 18 | Kentucky | 0.9 |
| 18 | Minnesota | 0.9 |
| 18 | Montana | 0.9 |
| 22 | Colorado | 0.8 |
| 22 | Kansas | 0.8 |
| 22 | New Hampshire | 0.8 |
| 22 | North Carolina | 0.8 |
| 22 | Tennessee | 0.8 |
| 27 | Hawaii | 0.6 |
| 27 | Oklahoma | 0.6 |
| 27 | South Carolina | 0.6 |
| 27 | Wisconsin | 0.6 |
| 31 | Arkansas | 0.5 |
| 31 | Illinois | 0.5 |
| 31 | New Mexico | 0.5 |
| 31 | Pennsylvania | 0.5 |
| 35 | Alabama | 0.2 |
| 35 | Maine | 0.2 |
| 35 | Michigan | 0.2 |
| 35 | Ohio | 0.2 |
| 35 | Rhode Island | 0.2 |
| 40 | Georgia | 0.0 |
| 40 | Missouri | 0.0 |
| 40 | Wyoming | 0.0 |
| 43 | California | (0.1) |
| 44 | Idaho | (0.2) |
| 44 | Mississippi | (0.2) |
| 46 | New Jersey | (0.3) |
| 47 | Connecticut | (0.5) |
| 47 | Florida | (0.5) |
| 49 | Arizona | (0.9) |
| 50 | Nevada | (1.1) |
| | District of Columbia | 1.0 |

Source: CQ Press using data from U.S. Department of Commerce, Bureau of Economic Analysis
"Gross Domestic Product Data" (http://www.bea.gov/iTable/index_regional.cfm)

*G.D.P. is the market value of goods and services produced by the labor and property located in a state. It is the state counterpart to the nation's Gross Domestic Product. This was formerly known as Gross State Product (G.S.P.). Adjusted for inflation using chained 2005 dollars.

# Per Capita Gross Domestic Product in 2012

## National Per Capita = $49,587*

| ALPHA ORDER | | | | RANK ORDER | | |
|---|---|---|---|---|---|---|
| RANK | STATE | PER CAPITA | | RANK | STATE | PER CAPITA |
| 45 | Alabama | $38,064 | | 1 | Delaware | $71,949 |
| 2 | Alaska | 70,899 | | 2 | Alaska | 70,899 |
| 38 | Arizona | 40,726 | | 3 | Wyoming | 66,657 |
| 48 | Arkansas | 37,149 | | 4 | North Dakota | 65,772 |
| 18 | California | 52,666 | | 5 | Connecticut | 63,870 |
| 17 | Colorado | 52,828 | | 6 | New York | 61,621 |
| 5 | Connecticut | 63,870 | | 7 | Massachusetts | 60,760 |
| 1 | Delaware | 71,949 | | 8 | New Jersey | 57,307 |
| 41 | Florida | 40,231 | | 9 | Minnesota | 54,791 |
| 33 | Georgia | 43,707 | | 10 | Washington | 54,477 |
| 19 | Hawaii | 52,017 | | 11 | Virginia | 54,469 |
| 49 | Idaho | 36,499 | | 12 | Illinois | 53,998 |
| 12 | Illinois | 53,998 | | 13 | Maryland | 53,985 |
| 30 | Indiana | 45,680 | | 14 | Nebraska | 53,654 |
| 22 | Iowa | 49,586 | | 15 | Texas | 53,623 |
| 26 | Kansas | 48,149 | | 16 | Louisiana | 52,862 |
| 43 | Kentucky | 39,600 | | 17 | Colorado | 52,828 |
| 16 | Louisiana | 52,862 | | 18 | California | 52,666 |
| 40 | Maine | 40,367 | | 19 | Hawaii | 52,017 |
| 13 | Maryland | 53,985 | | 20 | Oregon | 50,958 |
| 7 | Massachusetts | 60,760 | | 21 | South Dakota | 50,956 |
| 39 | Michigan | 40,523 | | 22 | Iowa | 49,586 |
| 9 | Minnesota | 54,791 | | 23 | New Hampshire | 48,986 |
| 50 | Mississippi | 34,001 | | 24 | Rhode Island | 48,516 |
| 35 | Missouri | 42,981 | | 25 | Nevada | 48,419 |
| 42 | Montana | 40,215 | | 26 | Kansas | 48,149 |
| 14 | Nebraska | 53,654 | | 27 | Pennsylvania | 47,079 |
| 25 | Nevada | 48,419 | | 28 | North Carolina | 46,757 |
| 23 | New Hampshire | 48,986 | | 29 | Utah | 45,700 |
| 8 | New Jersey | 57,307 | | 30 | Indiana | 45,680 |
| 44 | New Mexico | 38,647 | | 31 | Wisconsin | 45,674 |
| 6 | New York | 61,621 | | 32 | Ohio | 44,125 |
| 28 | North Carolina | 46,757 | | 33 | Georgia | 43,707 |
| 4 | North Dakota | 65,772 | | 34 | Vermont | 43,603 |
| 32 | Ohio | 44,125 | | 35 | Missouri | 42,981 |
| 37 | Oklahoma | 42,192 | | 36 | Tennessee | 42,910 |
| 20 | Oregon | 50,958 | | 37 | Oklahoma | 42,192 |
| 27 | Pennsylvania | 47,079 | | 38 | Arizona | 40,726 |
| 24 | Rhode Island | 48,516 | | 39 | Michigan | 40,523 |
| 47 | South Carolina | 37,305 | | 40 | Maine | 40,367 |
| 21 | South Dakota | 50,956 | | 41 | Florida | 40,231 |
| 36 | Tennessee | 42,910 | | 42 | Montana | 40,215 |
| 15 | Texas | 53,623 | | 43 | Kentucky | 39,600 |
| 29 | Utah | 45,700 | | 44 | New Mexico | 38,647 |
| 34 | Vermont | 43,603 | | 45 | Alabama | 38,064 |
| 11 | Virginia | 54,469 | | 46 | West Virginia | 37,393 |
| 10 | Washington | 54,477 | | 47 | South Carolina | 37,305 |
| 46 | West Virginia | 37,393 | | 48 | Arkansas | 37,149 |
| 31 | Wisconsin | 45,674 | | 49 | Idaho | 36,499 |
| 3 | Wyoming | 66,657 | | 50 | Mississippi | 34,001 |

| | | |
|---|---|---|
| | District of Columbia | 173,634 |

Source: CQ Press using data from U.S. Department of Commerce, Bureau of Economic Analysis
"Gross Domestic Product Data" (http://www.bea.gov/iTable/index_regional.cfm)
*G.D.P. is the market value of goods and services produced by the labor and property located in a state. It is the state counterpart to the nation's Gross Domestic Product. This was formerly known as Gross State Product (G.S.P.).

# Percent Change in Per Capita Gross Domestic Product: 2008 to 2012
## (Adjusted to Constant 2005 Dollars)
## National Percent Change = 0.0% Change*

ALPHA ORDER

| RANK | STATE | PERCENT CHANGE |
|------|-------|----------------|
| 36 | Alabama | (1.3) |
| 14 | Alaska | 2.4 |
| 49 | Arizona | (8.3) |
| 32 | Arkansas | (0.1) |
| 44 | California | (4.1) |
| 40 | Colorado | (2.1) |
| 43 | Connecticut | (3.8) |
| 27 | Delaware | 0.7 |
| 48 | Florida | (6.5) |
| 44 | Georgia | (4.1) |
| 38 | Hawaii | (1.5) |
| 46 | Idaho | (4.6) |
| 20 | Illinois | 1.3 |
| 8 | Indiana | 3.8 |
| 11 | Iowa | 3.0 |
| 23 | Kansas | 1.1 |
| 15 | Kentucky | 2.2 |
| 6 | Louisiana | 4.0 |
| 24 | Maine | 1.0 |
| 12 | Maryland | 2.7 |
| 13 | Massachusetts | 2.5 |
| 17 | Michigan | 1.6 |
| 16 | Minnesota | 1.9 |
| 40 | Mississippi | (2.1) |
| 39 | Missouri | (1.8) |
| 18 | Montana | 1.5 |
| 7 | Nebraska | 3.9 |
| 50 | Nevada | (9.1) |
| 8 | New Hampshire | 3.8 |
| 42 | New Jersey | (3.0) |
| 36 | New Mexico | (1.3) |
| 10 | New York | 3.3 |
| 33 | North Carolina | (0.7) |
| 1 | North Dakota | 26.9 |
| 25 | Ohio | 0.9 |
| 34 | Oklahoma | (1.0) |
| 3 | Oregon | 6.5 |
| 19 | Pennsylvania | 1.4 |
| 20 | Rhode Island | 1.3 |
| 35 | South Carolina | (1.2) |
| 29 | South Dakota | 0.6 |
| 26 | Tennessee | 0.8 |
| 4 | Texas | 4.9 |
| 30 | Utah | 0.4 |
| 5 | Vermont | 4.7 |
| 27 | Virginia | 0.7 |
| 30 | Washington | 0.4 |
| 2 | West Virginia | 8.4 |
| 20 | Wisconsin | 1.3 |
| 47 | Wyoming | (5.5) |

RANK ORDER

| RANK | STATE | PERCENT CHANGE |
|------|-------|----------------|
| 1 | North Dakota | 26.9 |
| 2 | West Virginia | 8.4 |
| 3 | Oregon | 6.5 |
| 4 | Texas | 4.9 |
| 5 | Vermont | 4.7 |
| 6 | Louisiana | 4.0 |
| 7 | Nebraska | 3.9 |
| 8 | Indiana | 3.8 |
| 8 | New Hampshire | 3.8 |
| 10 | New York | 3.3 |
| 11 | Iowa | 3.0 |
| 12 | Maryland | 2.7 |
| 13 | Massachusetts | 2.5 |
| 14 | Alaska | 2.4 |
| 15 | Kentucky | 2.2 |
| 16 | Minnesota | 1.9 |
| 17 | Michigan | 1.6 |
| 18 | Montana | 1.5 |
| 19 | Pennsylvania | 1.4 |
| 20 | Illinois | 1.3 |
| 20 | Rhode Island | 1.3 |
| 20 | Wisconsin | 1.3 |
| 23 | Kansas | 1.1 |
| 24 | Maine | 1.0 |
| 25 | Ohio | 0.9 |
| 26 | Tennessee | 0.8 |
| 27 | Delaware | 0.7 |
| 27 | Virginia | 0.7 |
| 29 | South Dakota | 0.6 |
| 30 | Utah | 0.4 |
| 30 | Washington | 0.4 |
| 32 | Arkansas | (0.1) |
| 33 | North Carolina | (0.7) |
| 34 | Oklahoma | (1.0) |
| 35 | South Carolina | (1.2) |
| 36 | Alabama | (1.3) |
| 36 | New Mexico | (1.3) |
| 38 | Hawaii | (1.5) |
| 39 | Missouri | (1.8) |
| 40 | Colorado | (2.1) |
| 40 | Mississippi | (2.1) |
| 42 | New Jersey | (3.0) |
| 43 | Connecticut | (3.8) |
| 44 | California | (4.1) |
| 44 | Georgia | (4.1) |
| 46 | Idaho | (4.6) |
| 47 | Wyoming | (5.5) |
| 48 | Florida | (6.5) |
| 49 | Arizona | (8.3) |
| 50 | Nevada | (9.1) |

| | | |
|--|--|--|
| | District of Columbia | (3.7) |

Source: CQ Press using data from U.S. Department of Commerce, Bureau of Economic Analysis
  "Gross Domestic Product Data" (http://www.bea.gov/iTable/index_regional.cfm)
*G.D.P. is the market value of goods and services produced by the labor and property located in a state. It is the state counterpart to the nation's Gross Domestic Product. This was formerly known as Gross State Product (G.S.P.). Adjusted for inflation using chained 2005 dollars.

# Personal Income in 2012

## National Total = $13,401,868,693,000*

ALPHA ORDER

ALPHA ORDER | | | | | RANK ORDER | | | |

| RANK | STATE | INCOME | % of USA | | RANK | STATE | INCOME | % of USA |
|------|-------|--------|----------|---|------|-------|--------|----------|
| 25 | Alabama | $171,782,909,000 | 1.3% | | 1 | California | $1,711,110,319,000 | 12.8% |
| 48 | Alaska | 34,215,563,000 | 0.3% | | 2 | Texas | 1,080,709,649,000 | 8.1% |
| 19 | Arizona | 235,780,739,000 | 1.8% | | 3 | New York | 1,019,514,062,000 | 7.6% |
| 33 | Arkansas | 102,402,574,000 | 0.8% | | 4 | Florida | 779,338,815,000 | 5.8% |
| 1 | California | 1,711,110,319,000 | 12.8% | | 5 | Illinois | 577,008,488,000 | 4.3% |
| 21 | Colorado | 234,142,330,000 | 1.7% | | 6 | Pennsylvania | 556,692,387,000 | 4.2% |
| 23 | Connecticut | 211,499,831,000 | 1.6% | | 7 | New Jersey | 475,393,092,000 | 3.5% |
| 44 | Delaware | 38,462,662,000 | 0.3% | | 8 | Ohio | 453,556,274,000 | 3.4% |
| 4 | Florida | 779,338,815,000 | 5.8% | | 9 | Virginia | 385,403,843,000 | 2.9% |
| 11 | Georgia | 365,740,189,000 | 2.7% | | 10 | Michigan | 370,598,555,000 | 2.8% |
| 40 | Hawaii | 61,294,803,000 | 0.5% | | 11 | Georgia | 365,740,189,000 | 2.7% |
| 41 | Idaho | 53,853,716,000 | 0.4% | | 12 | Massachusetts | 363,459,345,000 | 2.7% |
| 5 | Illinois | 577,008,488,000 | 4.3% | | 13 | North Carolina | 361,301,305,000 | 2.7% |
| 18 | Indiana | 241,242,521,000 | 1.8% | | 14 | Washington | 313,212,035,000 | 2.3% |
| 30 | Iowa | 129,503,257,000 | 1.0% | | 15 | Maryland | 305,826,774,000 | 2.3% |
| 31 | Kansas | 120,732,283,000 | 0.9% | | 16 | Minnesota | 248,663,407,000 | 1.9% |
| 27 | Kentucky | 153,494,780,000 | 1.1% | | 17 | Tennessee | 243,256,486,000 | 1.8% |
| 24 | Louisiana | 181,372,591,000 | 1.4% | | 18 | Indiana | 241,242,521,000 | 1.8% |
| 42 | Maine | 52,477,565,000 | 0.4% | | 19 | Arizona | 235,780,739,000 | 1.8% |
| 15 | Maryland | 305,826,774,000 | 2.3% | | 20 | Missouri | 235,153,679,000 | 1.8% |
| 12 | Massachusetts | 363,459,345,000 | 2.7% | | 21 | Colorado | 234,142,330,000 | 1.7% |
| 10 | Michigan | 370,598,555,000 | 2.8% | | 22 | Wisconsin | 232,129,105,000 | 1.7% |
| 16 | Minnesota | 248,663,407,000 | 1.9% | | 23 | Connecticut | 211,499,831,000 | 1.6% |
| 35 | Mississippi | 98,721,708,000 | 0.7% | | 24 | Louisiana | 181,372,591,000 | 1.4% |
| 20 | Missouri | 235,153,679,000 | 1.8% | | 25 | Alabama | 171,782,909,000 | 1.3% |
| 45 | Montana | 37,561,941,000 | 0.3% | | 26 | South Carolina | 161,863,730,000 | 1.2% |
| 36 | Nebraska | 80,052,414,000 | 0.6% | | 27 | Kentucky | 153,494,780,000 | 1.1% |
| 32 | Nevada | 103,076,310,000 | 0.8% | | 28 | Oregon | 151,241,129,000 | 1.1% |
| 39 | New Hampshire | 62,150,236,000 | 0.5% | | 29 | Oklahoma | 148,798,993,000 | 1.1% |
| 7 | New Jersey | 475,393,092,000 | 3.5% | | 30 | Iowa | 129,503,257,000 | 1.0% |
| 37 | New Mexico | 73,159,160,000 | 0.5% | | 31 | Kansas | 120,732,283,000 | 0.9% |
| 3 | New York | 1,019,514,062,000 | 7.6% | | 32 | Nevada | 103,076,310,000 | 0.8% |
| 13 | North Carolina | 361,301,305,000 | 2.7% | | 33 | Arkansas | 102,402,574,000 | 0.8% |
| 47 | North Dakota | 36,305,820,000 | 0.3% | | 34 | Utah | 98,797,168,000 | 0.7% |
| 8 | Ohio | 453,556,274,000 | 3.4% | | 35 | Mississippi | 98,721,708,000 | 0.7% |
| 29 | Oklahoma | 148,798,993,000 | 1.1% | | 36 | Nebraska | 80,052,414,000 | 0.6% |
| 28 | Oregon | 151,241,129,000 | 1.1% | | 37 | New Mexico | 73,159,160,000 | 0.5% |
| 6 | Pennsylvania | 556,692,387,000 | 4.2% | | 38 | West Virginia | 63,968,460,000 | 0.5% |
| 43 | Rhode Island | 47,253,091,000 | 0.4% | | 39 | New Hampshire | 62,150,236,000 | 0.5% |
| 26 | South Carolina | 161,863,730,000 | 1.2% | | 40 | Hawaii | 61,294,803,000 | 0.5% |
| 46 | South Dakota | 36,383,703,000 | 0.3% | | 41 | Idaho | 53,853,716,000 | 0.4% |
| 17 | Tennessee | 243,256,486,000 | 1.8% | | 42 | Maine | 52,477,565,000 | 0.4% |
| 2 | Texas | 1,080,709,649,000 | 8.1% | | 43 | Rhode Island | 47,253,091,000 | 0.4% |
| 34 | Utah | 98,797,168,000 | 0.7% | | 44 | Delaware | 38,462,662,000 | 0.3% |
| 50 | Vermont | 26,914,633,000 | 0.2% | | 45 | Montana | 37,561,941,000 | 0.3% |
| 9 | Virginia | 385,403,843,000 | 2.9% | | 46 | South Dakota | 36,383,703,000 | 0.3% |
| 14 | Washington | 313,212,035,000 | 2.3% | | 47 | North Dakota | 36,305,820,000 | 0.3% |
| 38 | West Virginia | 63,968,460,000 | 0.5% | | 48 | Alaska | 34,215,563,000 | 0.3% |
| 22 | Wisconsin | 232,129,105,000 | 1.7% | | 49 | Wyoming | 28,053,707,000 | 0.2% |
| 49 | Wyoming | 28,053,707,000 | 0.2% | | 50 | Vermont | 26,914,633,000 | 0.2% |
| | | | | | | District of Columbia | 47,240,557,000 | 0.4% |

Source: U.S. Department of Commerce, Bureau of Economic Analysis
"Annual State Personal Income" (http://www.bea.gov/iTable/iTable.cfm?ReqID=70&step=1)
*The national total shown here is the sum of the state estimates.  It differs from the national income and product accounts (NIPA) estimate of personal income because it omits the earnings of federal civilian and military personnel stationed abroad and of U.S. residents employed abroad temporarily by private U.S. firms.

# Change in Personal Income: 2011 to 2012

## National Percent Change = 3.5% Increase*

ALPHA ORDER

| RANK | STATE | PERCENT CHANGE |
|---|---|---|
| 42 | Alabama | 2.6 |
| 15 | Alaska | 3.7 |
| 15 | Arizona | 3.7 |
| 25 | Arkansas | 3.3 |
| 9 | California | 4.0 |
| 10 | Colorado | 3.9 |
| 49 | Connecticut | 2.0 |
| 47 | Delaware | 2.3 |
| 28 | Florida | 3.2 |
| 18 | Georgia | 3.6 |
| 10 | Hawaii | 3.9 |
| 25 | Idaho | 3.3 |
| 42 | Illinois | 2.6 |
| 15 | Indiana | 3.7 |
| 37 | Iowa | 2.8 |
| 35 | Kansas | 2.9 |
| 23 | Kentucky | 3.4 |
| 37 | Louisiana | 2.8 |
| 28 | Maine | 3.2 |
| 18 | Maryland | 3.6 |
| 28 | Massachusetts | 3.2 |
| 22 | Michigan | 3.5 |
| 6 | Minnesota | 4.4 |
| 18 | Mississippi | 3.6 |
| 34 | Missouri | 3.0 |
| 4 | Montana | 4.5 |
| 47 | Nebraska | 2.3 |
| 44 | Nevada | 2.4 |
| 37 | New Hampshire | 2.8 |
| 37 | New Jersey | 2.8 |
| 35 | New Mexico | 2.9 |
| 44 | New York | 2.4 |
| 10 | North Carolina | 3.9 |
| 1 | North Dakota | 12.4 |
| 14 | Ohio | 3.8 |
| 7 | Oklahoma | 4.2 |
| 8 | Oregon | 4.1 |
| 25 | Pennsylvania | 3.3 |
| 44 | Rhode Island | 2.4 |
| 18 | South Carolina | 3.6 |
| 50 | South Dakota | (0.2) |
| 10 | Tennessee | 3.9 |
| 2 | Texas | 4.9 |
| 3 | Utah | 4.7 |
| 23 | Vermont | 3.4 |
| 28 | Virginia | 3.2 |
| 4 | Washington | 4.5 |
| 28 | West Virginia | 3.2 |
| 41 | Wisconsin | 2.7 |
| 33 | Wyoming | 3.1 |

RANK ORDER

| RANK | STATE | PERCENT CHANGE |
|---|---|---|
| 1 | North Dakota | 12.4 |
| 2 | Texas | 4.9 |
| 3 | Utah | 4.7 |
| 4 | Montana | 4.5 |
| 4 | Washington | 4.5 |
| 6 | Minnesota | 4.4 |
| 7 | Oklahoma | 4.2 |
| 8 | Oregon | 4.1 |
| 9 | California | 4.0 |
| 10 | Colorado | 3.9 |
| 10 | Hawaii | 3.9 |
| 10 | North Carolina | 3.9 |
| 10 | Tennessee | 3.9 |
| 14 | Ohio | 3.8 |
| 15 | Alaska | 3.7 |
| 15 | Arizona | 3.7 |
| 15 | Indiana | 3.7 |
| 18 | Georgia | 3.6 |
| 18 | Maryland | 3.6 |
| 18 | Mississippi | 3.6 |
| 18 | South Carolina | 3.6 |
| 22 | Michigan | 3.5 |
| 23 | Kentucky | 3.4 |
| 23 | Vermont | 3.4 |
| 25 | Arkansas | 3.3 |
| 25 | Idaho | 3.3 |
| 25 | Pennsylvania | 3.3 |
| 28 | Florida | 3.2 |
| 28 | Maine | 3.2 |
| 28 | Massachusetts | 3.2 |
| 28 | Virginia | 3.2 |
| 28 | West Virginia | 3.2 |
| 33 | Wyoming | 3.1 |
| 34 | Missouri | 3.0 |
| 35 | Kansas | 2.9 |
| 35 | New Mexico | 2.9 |
| 37 | Iowa | 2.8 |
| 37 | Louisiana | 2.8 |
| 37 | New Hampshire | 2.8 |
| 37 | New Jersey | 2.8 |
| 41 | Wisconsin | 2.7 |
| 42 | Alabama | 2.6 |
| 42 | Illinois | 2.6 |
| 44 | Nevada | 2.4 |
| 44 | New York | 2.4 |
| 44 | Rhode Island | 2.4 |
| 47 | Delaware | 2.3 |
| 47 | Nebraska | 2.3 |
| 49 | Connecticut | 2.0 |
| 50 | South Dakota | (0.2) |
| | District of Columbia | 3.6 |

Source: U.S. Department of Commerce, Bureau of Economic Analysis
   "Annual State Personal Income" (http://www.bea.gov/iTable/iTable.cfm?ReqID=70&step=1)
*Based on revised 2011 figures.

# Per Capita Personal Income in 2012

## National Per Capita = $42,693*

ALPHA ORDER

| RANK | STATE | PER CAPITA |
|---|---|---|
| 42 | Alabama | $35,625 |
| 10 | Alaska | 46,778 |
| 41 | Arizona | 35,979 |
| 45 | Arkansas | 34,723 |
| 15 | California | 44,980 |
| 13 | Colorado | 45,135 |
| 1 | Connecticut | 58,908 |
| 23 | Delaware | 41,940 |
| 27 | Florida | 40,344 |
| 40 | Georgia | 36,869 |
| 17 | Hawaii | 44,024 |
| 49 | Idaho | 33,749 |
| 16 | Illinois | 44,815 |
| 39 | Indiana | 36,902 |
| 22 | Iowa | 42,126 |
| 24 | Kansas | 41,835 |
| 44 | Kentucky | 35,041 |
| 29 | Louisiana | 39,413 |
| 28 | Maine | 39,481 |
| 5 | Maryland | 51,971 |
| 2 | Massachusetts | 54,687 |
| 35 | Michigan | 37,497 |
| 11 | Minnesota | 46,227 |
| 50 | Mississippi | 33,073 |
| 31 | Missouri | 39,049 |
| 36 | Montana | 37,370 |
| 20 | Nebraska | 43,143 |
| 37 | Nevada | 37,361 |
| 9 | New Hampshire | 47,058 |
| 3 | New Jersey | 53,628 |
| 43 | New Mexico | 35,079 |
| 4 | New York | 52,095 |
| 38 | North Carolina | 37,049 |
| 6 | North Dakota | 51,893 |
| 30 | Ohio | 39,289 |
| 32 | Oklahoma | 39,006 |
| 33 | Oregon | 38,786 |
| 19 | Pennsylvania | 43,616 |
| 14 | Rhode Island | 44,990 |
| 48 | South Carolina | 34,266 |
| 18 | South Dakota | 43,659 |
| 34 | Tennessee | 37,678 |
| 25 | Texas | 41,471 |
| 46 | Utah | 34,601 |
| 21 | Vermont | 42,994 |
| 8 | Virginia | 47,082 |
| 12 | Washington | 45,413 |
| 47 | West Virginia | 34,477 |
| 26 | Wisconsin | 40,537 |
| 7 | Wyoming | 48,670 |

RANK ORDER

| RANK | STATE | PER CAPITA |
|---|---|---|
| 1 | Connecticut | $58,908 |
| 2 | Massachusetts | 54,687 |
| 3 | New Jersey | 53,628 |
| 4 | New York | 52,095 |
| 5 | Maryland | 51,971 |
| 6 | North Dakota | 51,893 |
| 7 | Wyoming | 48,670 |
| 8 | Virginia | 47,082 |
| 9 | New Hampshire | 47,058 |
| 10 | Alaska | 46,778 |
| 11 | Minnesota | 46,227 |
| 12 | Washington | 45,413 |
| 13 | Colorado | 45,135 |
| 14 | Rhode Island | 44,990 |
| 15 | California | 44,980 |
| 16 | Illinois | 44,815 |
| 17 | Hawaii | 44,024 |
| 18 | South Dakota | 43,659 |
| 19 | Pennsylvania | 43,616 |
| 20 | Nebraska | 43,143 |
| 21 | Vermont | 42,994 |
| 22 | Iowa | 42,126 |
| 23 | Delaware | 41,940 |
| 24 | Kansas | 41,835 |
| 25 | Texas | 41,471 |
| 26 | Wisconsin | 40,537 |
| 27 | Florida | 40,344 |
| 28 | Maine | 39,481 |
| 29 | Louisiana | 39,413 |
| 30 | Ohio | 39,289 |
| 31 | Missouri | 39,049 |
| 32 | Oklahoma | 39,006 |
| 33 | Oregon | 38,786 |
| 34 | Tennessee | 37,678 |
| 35 | Michigan | 37,497 |
| 36 | Montana | 37,370 |
| 37 | Nevada | 37,361 |
| 38 | North Carolina | 37,049 |
| 39 | Indiana | 36,902 |
| 40 | Georgia | 36,869 |
| 41 | Arizona | 35,979 |
| 42 | Alabama | 35,625 |
| 43 | New Mexico | 35,079 |
| 44 | Kentucky | 35,041 |
| 45 | Arkansas | 34,723 |
| 46 | Utah | 34,601 |
| 47 | West Virginia | 34,477 |
| 48 | South Carolina | 34,266 |
| 49 | Idaho | 33,749 |
| 50 | Mississippi | 33,073 |
| | District of Columbia | 74,710 |

Source: U.S. Department of Commerce, Bureau of Economic Analysis
   "Annual State Personal Income" (http://www.bea.gov/iTable/iTable.cfm?ReqID=70&step=1)
*The national figure is based on the sum of the state estimates.  It differs from the national income and product accounts
(NIPA) estimate of personal income because it omits the earnings of federal civilian and military personnel stationed abroad and
of U.S. residents employed abroad temporarily by private U.S. firms.

# Change in Per Capita Personal Income: 2011 to 2012

## National Percent Change = 2.7% Increase*

ALPHA ORDER

| RANK | STATE | PERCENT CHANGE |
|------|-------|----------------|
| 41 | Alabama | 2.1 |
| 34 | Alaska | 2.4 |
| 24 | Arizona | 2.6 |
| 20 | Arkansas | 2.9 |
| 15 | California | 3.1 |
| 30 | Colorado | 2.5 |
| 45 | Connecticut | 1.7 |
| 48 | Delaware | 1.2 |
| 44 | Florida | 1.8 |
| 30 | Georgia | 2.5 |
| 24 | Hawaii | 2.6 |
| 24 | Idaho | 2.6 |
| 30 | Illinois | 2.5 |
| 7 | Indiana | 3.4 |
| 34 | Iowa | 2.4 |
| 37 | Kansas | 2.3 |
| 15 | Kentucky | 3.1 |
| 40 | Louisiana | 2.2 |
| 15 | Maine | 3.1 |
| 24 | Maryland | 2.6 |
| 37 | Massachusetts | 2.3 |
| 7 | Michigan | 3.4 |
| 4 | Minnesota | 3.7 |
| 7 | Mississippi | 3.4 |
| 21 | Missouri | 2.8 |
| 2 | Montana | 3.8 |
| 46 | Nebraska | 1.6 |
| 49 | Nevada | 1.1 |
| 24 | New Hampshire | 2.6 |
| 37 | New Jersey | 2.3 |
| 21 | New Mexico | 2.8 |
| 43 | New York | 1.9 |
| 21 | North Carolina | 2.8 |
| 1 | North Dakota | 9.9 |
| 2 | Ohio | 3.8 |
| 5 | Oklahoma | 3.5 |
| 7 | Oregon | 3.4 |
| 15 | Pennsylvania | 3.1 |
| 30 | Rhode Island | 2.5 |
| 24 | South Carolina | 2.6 |
| 50 | South Dakota | (1.3) |
| 19 | Tennessee | 3.0 |
| 12 | Texas | 3.3 |
| 12 | Utah | 3.3 |
| 7 | Vermont | 3.4 |
| 41 | Virginia | 2.1 |
| 5 | Washington | 3.5 |
| 14 | West Virginia | 3.2 |
| 34 | Wisconsin | 2.4 |
| 46 | Wyoming | 1.6 |

RANK ORDER

| RANK | STATE | PERCENT CHANGE |
|------|-------|----------------|
| 1 | North Dakota | 9.9 |
| 2 | Montana | 3.8 |
| 2 | Ohio | 3.8 |
| 4 | Minnesota | 3.7 |
| 5 | Oklahoma | 3.5 |
| 5 | Washington | 3.5 |
| 7 | Indiana | 3.4 |
| 7 | Michigan | 3.4 |
| 7 | Mississippi | 3.4 |
| 7 | Oregon | 3.4 |
| 7 | Vermont | 3.4 |
| 12 | Texas | 3.3 |
| 12 | Utah | 3.3 |
| 14 | West Virginia | 3.2 |
| 15 | California | 3.1 |
| 15 | Kentucky | 3.1 |
| 15 | Maine | 3.1 |
| 15 | Pennsylvania | 3.1 |
| 19 | Tennessee | 3.0 |
| 20 | Arkansas | 2.9 |
| 21 | Missouri | 2.8 |
| 21 | New Mexico | 2.8 |
| 21 | North Carolina | 2.8 |
| 24 | Arizona | 2.6 |
| 24 | Hawaii | 2.6 |
| 24 | Idaho | 2.6 |
| 24 | Maryland | 2.6 |
| 24 | New Hampshire | 2.6 |
| 24 | South Carolina | 2.6 |
| 30 | Colorado | 2.5 |
| 30 | Georgia | 2.5 |
| 30 | Illinois | 2.5 |
| 30 | Rhode Island | 2.5 |
| 34 | Alaska | 2.4 |
| 34 | Iowa | 2.4 |
| 34 | Wisconsin | 2.4 |
| 37 | Kansas | 2.3 |
| 37 | Massachusetts | 2.3 |
| 37 | New Jersey | 2.3 |
| 40 | Louisiana | 2.2 |
| 41 | Alabama | 2.1 |
| 41 | Virginia | 2.1 |
| 43 | New York | 1.9 |
| 44 | Florida | 1.8 |
| 45 | Connecticut | 1.7 |
| 46 | Nebraska | 1.6 |
| 46 | Wyoming | 1.6 |
| 48 | Delaware | 1.2 |
| 49 | Nevada | 1.1 |
| 50 | South Dakota | (1.3) |
| | District of Columbia | 1.3 |

Source: U.S. Department of Commerce, Bureau of Economic Analysis
    "Annual State Personal Income" (http://www.bea.gov/iTable/iTable.cfm?ReqID=70&step=1)
*Based on revised 2011 figures.

# Per Capita Disposable Personal Income in 2012

## National Per Capita = $38,000*

ALPHA ORDER

ALPHA ORDER

| RANK | STATE | PER CAPITA |
|---|---|---|
| 42 | Alabama | $32,467 |
| 9 | Alaska | 42,306 |
| 41 | Arizona | 32,797 |
| 45 | Arkansas | 31,675 |
| 17 | California | 39,416 |
| 15 | Colorado | 40,069 |
| 1 | Connecticut | 49,562 |
| 25 | Delaware | 36,983 |
| 26 | Florida | 36,760 |
| 40 | Georgia | 33,168 |
| 16 | Hawaii | 39,956 |
| 49 | Idaho | 30,913 |
| 18 | Illinois | 39,242 |
| 39 | Indiana | 33,217 |
| 22 | Iowa | 38,257 |
| 24 | Kansas | 37,539 |
| 44 | Kentucky | 31,676 |
| 28 | Louisiana | 36,042 |
| 29 | Maine | 35,834 |
| 5 | Maryland | 45,324 |
| 2 | Massachusetts | 46,947 |
| 37 | Michigan | 33,672 |
| 12 | Minnesota | 40,670 |
| 50 | Mississippi | 30,449 |
| 31 | Missouri | 35,229 |
| 36 | Montana | 33,734 |
| 20 | Nebraska | 38,883 |
| 35 | Nevada | 33,866 |
| 8 | New Hampshire | 42,502 |
| 3 | New Jersey | 46,856 |
| 43 | New Mexico | 32,314 |
| 6 | New York | 44,355 |
| 38 | North Carolina | 33,333 |
| 4 | North Dakota | 46,460 |
| 32 | Ohio | 35,153 |
| 30 | Oklahoma | 35,461 |
| 34 | Oregon | 34,466 |
| 21 | Pennsylvania | 38,739 |
| 14 | Rhode Island | 40,361 |
| 46 | South Carolina | 31,346 |
| 13 | South Dakota | 40,427 |
| 33 | Tennessee | 34,898 |
| 23 | Texas | 37,723 |
| 47 | Utah | 31,329 |
| 19 | Vermont | 38,981 |
| 10 | Virginia | 41,369 |
| 11 | Washington | 41,259 |
| 48 | West Virginia | 31,270 |
| 27 | Wisconsin | 36,230 |
| 7 | Wyoming | 43,788 |

RANK ORDER

| RANK | STATE | PER CAPITA |
|---|---|---|
| 1 | Connecticut | $49,562 |
| 2 | Massachusetts | 46,947 |
| 3 | New Jersey | 46,856 |
| 4 | North Dakota | 46,460 |
| 5 | Maryland | 45,324 |
| 6 | New York | 44,355 |
| 7 | Wyoming | 43,788 |
| 8 | New Hampshire | 42,502 |
| 9 | Alaska | 42,306 |
| 10 | Virginia | 41,369 |
| 11 | Washington | 41,259 |
| 12 | Minnesota | 40,670 |
| 13 | South Dakota | 40,427 |
| 14 | Rhode Island | 40,361 |
| 15 | Colorado | 40,069 |
| 16 | Hawaii | 39,956 |
| 17 | California | 39,416 |
| 18 | Illinois | 39,242 |
| 19 | Vermont | 38,981 |
| 20 | Nebraska | 38,883 |
| 21 | Pennsylvania | 38,739 |
| 22 | Iowa | 38,257 |
| 23 | Texas | 37,723 |
| 24 | Kansas | 37,539 |
| 25 | Delaware | 36,983 |
| 26 | Florida | 36,760 |
| 27 | Wisconsin | 36,230 |
| 28 | Louisiana | 36,042 |
| 29 | Maine | 35,834 |
| 30 | Oklahoma | 35,461 |
| 31 | Missouri | 35,229 |
| 32 | Ohio | 35,153 |
| 33 | Tennessee | 34,898 |
| 34 | Oregon | 34,466 |
| 35 | Nevada | 33,866 |
| 36 | Montana | 33,734 |
| 37 | Michigan | 33,672 |
| 38 | North Carolina | 33,333 |
| 39 | Indiana | 33,217 |
| 40 | Georgia | 33,168 |
| 41 | Arizona | 32,797 |
| 42 | Alabama | 32,467 |
| 43 | New Mexico | 32,314 |
| 44 | Kentucky | 31,676 |
| 45 | Arkansas | 31,675 |
| 46 | South Carolina | 31,346 |
| 47 | Utah | 31,329 |
| 48 | West Virginia | 31,270 |
| 49 | Idaho | 30,913 |
| 50 | Mississippi | 30,449 |

| District of Columbia | 65,677 |
|---|---|

Source: U.S. Department of Commerce, Bureau of Economic Analysis
   "Annual State Personal Income" (http://www.bea.gov/iTable/iTable.cfm?ReqID=70&step=1)
*Disposable personal income is personal income less personal tax and nontax payments. It is the income available to persons for spending or saving.

# Median Household Income in 2012

## National Median = $51,336*

ALPHA ORDER

| RANK | STATE | INCOME |
|---|---|---|
| 43 | Alabama | $43,350 |
| 7 | Alaska | 61,066 |
| 30 | Arizona | 48,689 |
| 49 | Arkansas | 40,606 |
| 13 | California | 56,222 |
| 8 | Colorado | 60,180 |
| 3 | Connecticut | 66,844 |
| 18 | Delaware | 54,307 |
| 38 | Florida | 46,175 |
| 36 | Georgia | 47,171 |
| 10 | Hawaii | 59,748 |
| 31 | Idaho | 48,640 |
| 22 | Illinois | 52,284 |
| 37 | Indiana | 46,707 |
| 23 | Iowa | 52,110 |
| 32 | Kansas | 48,538 |
| 47 | Kentucky | 41,687 |
| 48 | Louisiana | 40,660 |
| 27 | Maine | 50,121 |
| 1 | Maryland | 69,920 |
| 5 | Massachusetts | 64,153 |
| 29 | Michigan | 49,549 |
| 11 | Minnesota | 58,641 |
| 50 | Mississippi | 39,592 |
| 34 | Missouri | 48,248 |
| 44 | Montana | 43,226 |
| 17 | Nebraska | 54,755 |
| 28 | Nevada | 49,759 |
| 2 | New Hampshire | 68,415 |
| 4 | New Jersey | 65,548 |
| 41 | New Mexico | 44,605 |
| 25 | New York | 50,600 |
| 40 | North Carolina | 44,620 |
| 16 | North Dakota | 55,673 |
| 39 | Ohio | 46,093 |
| 35 | Oklahoma | 47,755 |
| 21 | Oregon | 52,555 |
| 24 | Pennsylvania | 51,245 |
| 19 | Rhode Island | 53,495 |
| 45 | South Carolina | 43,078 |
| 33 | South Dakota | 48,461 |
| 46 | Tennessee | 42,266 |
| 26 | Texas | 50,591 |
| 12 | Utah | 58,235 |
| 15 | Vermont | 55,808 |
| 6 | Virginia | 64,043 |
| 9 | Washington | 59,790 |
| 42 | West Virginia | 43,765 |
| 20 | Wisconsin | 53,083 |
| 14 | Wyoming | 56,044 |

RANK ORDER

| RANK | STATE | INCOME |
|---|---|---|
| 1 | Maryland | $69,920 |
| 2 | New Hampshire | 68,415 |
| 3 | Connecticut | 66,844 |
| 4 | New Jersey | 65,548 |
| 5 | Massachusetts | 64,153 |
| 6 | Virginia | 64,043 |
| 7 | Alaska | 61,066 |
| 8 | Colorado | 60,180 |
| 9 | Washington | 59,790 |
| 10 | Hawaii | 59,748 |
| 11 | Minnesota | 58,641 |
| 12 | Utah | 58,235 |
| 13 | California | 56,222 |
| 14 | Wyoming | 56,044 |
| 15 | Vermont | 55,808 |
| 16 | North Dakota | 55,673 |
| 17 | Nebraska | 54,755 |
| 18 | Delaware | 54,307 |
| 19 | Rhode Island | 53,495 |
| 20 | Wisconsin | 53,083 |
| 21 | Oregon | 52,555 |
| 22 | Illinois | 52,284 |
| 23 | Iowa | 52,110 |
| 24 | Pennsylvania | 51,245 |
| 25 | New York | 50,600 |
| 26 | Texas | 50,591 |
| 27 | Maine | 50,121 |
| 28 | Nevada | 49,759 |
| 29 | Michigan | 49,549 |
| 30 | Arizona | 48,689 |
| 31 | Idaho | 48,640 |
| 32 | Kansas | 48,538 |
| 33 | South Dakota | 48,461 |
| 34 | Missouri | 48,248 |
| 35 | Oklahoma | 47,755 |
| 36 | Georgia | 47,171 |
| 37 | Indiana | 46,707 |
| 38 | Florida | 46,175 |
| 39 | Ohio | 46,093 |
| 40 | North Carolina | 44,620 |
| 41 | New Mexico | 44,605 |
| 42 | West Virginia | 43,765 |
| 43 | Alabama | 43,350 |
| 44 | Montana | 43,226 |
| 45 | South Carolina | 43,078 |
| 46 | Tennessee | 42,266 |
| 47 | Kentucky | 41,687 |
| 48 | Louisiana | 40,660 |
| 49 | Arkansas | 40,606 |
| 50 | Mississippi | 39,592 |
| | District of Columbia | 60,534 |

Source: U.S. Bureau of the Census

"Median Household Income by State" (http://www.census.gov/hhes/www/income/data/historical/household/index.html)

*This is a 3-year-average of inflation-adjusted single-year medians for the years 2010 through 2012.

# Bankruptcy Filings in 2013

## National Total = 1,072,807 Bankruptcies*

ALPHA ORDER

ALPHA ORDER

| RANK | STATE | BANKRUPTCIES | % of USA |
|---|---|---|---|
| 12 | Alabama | 27,678 | 2.5% |
| 50 | Alaska | 638 | 0.1% |
| 17 | Arizona | 24,046 | 2.2% |
| 30 | Arkansas | 12,580 | 1.1% |
| 1 | California | 149,203 | 13.5% |
| 18 | Colorado | 23,976 | 2.2% |
| 34 | Connecticut | 7,321 | 0.7% |
| 40 | Delaware | 3,581 | 0.3% |
| 2 | Florida | 77,923 | 7.0% |
| 4 | Georgia | 60,305 | 5.4% |
| 44 | Hawaii | 2,313 | 0.2% |
| 36 | Idaho | 5,643 | 0.5% |
| 3 | Illinois | 68,125 | 6.2% |
| 10 | Indiana | 34,495 | 3.1% |
| 35 | Iowa | 5,892 | 0.5% |
| 32 | Kansas | 8,604 | 0.8% |
| 22 | Kentucky | 18,672 | 1.7% |
| 23 | Louisiana | 15,972 | 1.4% |
| 43 | Maine | 2,575 | 0.2% |
| 20 | Maryland | 23,193 | 2.1% |
| 28 | Massachusetts | 13,201 | 1.2% |
| 6 | Michigan | 44,032 | 4.0% |
| 24 | Minnesota | 15,003 | 1.4% |
| 29 | Mississippi | 12,938 | 1.2% |
| 15 | Missouri | 25,951 | 2.3% |
| 45 | Montana | 1,851 | 0.2% |
| 37 | Nebraska | 5,362 | 0.5% |
| 26 | Nevada | 14,483 | 1.3% |
| 42 | New Hampshire | 3,376 | 0.3% |
| 11 | New Jersey | 28,882 | 2.6% |
| 38 | New Mexico | 4,502 | 0.4% |
| 9 | New York | 37,192 | 3.4% |
| 21 | North Carolina | 19,438 | 1.8% |
| 49 | North Dakota | 872 | 0.1% |
| 5 | Ohio | 48,695 | 4.4% |
| 31 | Oklahoma | 10,981 | 1.0% |
| 27 | Oregon | 13,677 | 1.2% |
| 13 | Pennsylvania | 27,563 | 2.5% |
| 41 | Rhode Island | 3,547 | 0.3% |
| 33 | South Carolina | 7,618 | 0.7% |
| 46 | South Dakota | 1,366 | 0.1% |
| 7 | Tennessee | 42,910 | 3.9% |
| 8 | Texas | 42,780 | 3.9% |
| 25 | Utah | 14,939 | 1.3% |
| 48 | Vermont | 933 | 0.1% |
| 14 | Virginia | 26,578 | 2.4% |
| 16 | Washington | 25,730 | 2.3% |
| 39 | West Virginia | 3,765 | 0.3% |
| 19 | Wisconsin | 23,473 | 2.1% |
| 47 | Wyoming | 1,241 | 0.1% |

RANK ORDER

| RANK | STATE | BANKRUPTCIES | % of USA |
|---|---|---|---|
| 1 | California | 149,203 | 13.5% |
| 2 | Florida | 77,923 | 7.0% |
| 3 | Illinois | 68,125 | 6.2% |
| 4 | Georgia | 60,305 | 5.4% |
| 5 | Ohio | 48,695 | 4.4% |
| 6 | Michigan | 44,032 | 4.0% |
| 7 | Tennessee | 42,910 | 3.9% |
| 8 | Texas | 42,780 | 3.9% |
| 9 | New York | 37,192 | 3.4% |
| 10 | Indiana | 34,495 | 3.1% |
| 11 | New Jersey | 28,882 | 2.6% |
| 12 | Alabama | 27,678 | 2.5% |
| 13 | Pennsylvania | 27,563 | 2.5% |
| 14 | Virginia | 26,578 | 2.4% |
| 15 | Missouri | 25,951 | 2.3% |
| 16 | Washington | 25,730 | 2.3% |
| 17 | Arizona | 24,046 | 2.2% |
| 18 | Colorado | 23,976 | 2.2% |
| 19 | Wisconsin | 23,473 | 2.1% |
| 20 | Maryland | 23,193 | 2.1% |
| 21 | North Carolina | 19,438 | 1.8% |
| 22 | Kentucky | 18,672 | 1.7% |
| 23 | Louisiana | 15,972 | 1.4% |
| 24 | Minnesota | 15,003 | 1.4% |
| 25 | Utah | 14,939 | 1.3% |
| 26 | Nevada | 14,483 | 1.3% |
| 27 | Oregon | 13,677 | 1.2% |
| 28 | Massachusetts | 13,201 | 1.2% |
| 29 | Mississippi | 12,938 | 1.2% |
| 30 | Arkansas | 12,580 | 1.1% |
| 31 | Oklahoma | 10,981 | 1.0% |
| 32 | Kansas | 8,604 | 0.8% |
| 33 | South Carolina | 7,618 | 0.7% |
| 34 | Connecticut | 7,321 | 0.7% |
| 35 | Iowa | 5,892 | 0.5% |
| 36 | Idaho | 5,643 | 0.5% |
| 37 | Nebraska | 5,362 | 0.5% |
| 38 | New Mexico | 4,502 | 0.4% |
| 39 | West Virginia | 3,765 | 0.3% |
| 40 | Delaware | 3,581 | 0.3% |
| 41 | Rhode Island | 3,547 | 0.3% |
| 42 | New Hampshire | 3,376 | 0.3% |
| 43 | Maine | 2,575 | 0.2% |
| 44 | Hawaii | 2,313 | 0.2% |
| 45 | Montana | 1,851 | 0.2% |
| 46 | South Dakota | 1,366 | 0.1% |
| 47 | Wyoming | 1,241 | 0.1% |
| 48 | Vermont | 933 | 0.1% |
| 49 | North Dakota | 872 | 0.1% |
| 50 | Alaska | 638 | 0.1% |
| | District of Columbia | 855 | 0.1% |

Source: CQ Press using data from Administrative Office of the U.S. Courts
   "Table F-2, U.S. Bankruptcy Courts" (http://www.uscourts.gov/Statistics/BankruptcyStatistics.aspx)
*For 12 months through September 2013. Includes business (34,892) and non-business (1,072,807) filings. Includes all chapters of bankruptcy. National total includes 10,794 bankruptcies in U.S. territories.

# Personal Bankruptcy Rate in 2013

## National Rate = 336 Personal Bankruptcies per 100,000 Population*

ALPHA ORDER

| RANK | STATE | RATE |
|---|---|---|
| 3 | Alabama | 563 |
| 50 | Alaska | 78 |
| 20 | Arizona | 349 |
| 13 | Arkansas | 415 |
| 18 | California | 376 |
| 8 | Colorado | 440 |
| 37 | Connecticut | 195 |
| 30 | Delaware | 270 |
| 16 | Florida | 383 |
| 2 | Georgia | 587 |
| 44 | Hawaii | 158 |
| 21 | Idaho | 339 |
| 4 | Illinois | 516 |
| 5 | Indiana | 515 |
| 40 | Iowa | 183 |
| 27 | Kansas | 291 |
| 12 | Kentucky | 416 |
| 23 | Louisiana | 337 |
| 41 | Maine | 182 |
| 17 | Maryland | 382 |
| 38 | Massachusetts | 191 |
| 9 | Michigan | 434 |
| 31 | Minnesota | 268 |
| 10 | Mississippi | 423 |
| 11 | Missouri | 419 |
| 43 | Montana | 175 |
| 28 | Nebraska | 278 |
| 7 | Nevada | 499 |
| 32 | New Hampshire | 235 |
| 25 | New Jersey | 314 |
| 33 | New Mexico | 208 |
| 42 | New York | 181 |
| 39 | North Carolina | 190 |
| 49 | North Dakota | 116 |
| 14 | Ohio | 413 |
| 29 | Oklahoma | 277 |
| 22 | Oregon | 338 |
| 33 | Pennsylvania | 208 |
| 24 | Rhode Island | 325 |
| 46 | South Carolina | 154 |
| 45 | South Dakota | 155 |
| 1 | Tennessee | 650 |
| 47 | Texas | 152 |
| 6 | Utah | 504 |
| 48 | Vermont | 143 |
| 25 | Virginia | 314 |
| 19 | Washington | 358 |
| 36 | West Virginia | 196 |
| 15 | Wisconsin | 399 |
| 35 | Wyoming | 200 |

RANK ORDER

| RANK | STATE | RATE |
|---|---|---|
| 1 | Tennessee | 650 |
| 2 | Georgia | 587 |
| 3 | Alabama | 563 |
| 4 | Illinois | 516 |
| 5 | Indiana | 515 |
| 6 | Utah | 504 |
| 7 | Nevada | 499 |
| 8 | Colorado | 440 |
| 9 | Michigan | 434 |
| 10 | Mississippi | 423 |
| 11 | Missouri | 419 |
| 12 | Kentucky | 416 |
| 13 | Arkansas | 415 |
| 14 | Ohio | 413 |
| 15 | Wisconsin | 399 |
| 16 | Florida | 383 |
| 17 | Maryland | 382 |
| 18 | California | 376 |
| 19 | Washington | 358 |
| 20 | Arizona | 349 |
| 21 | Idaho | 339 |
| 22 | Oregon | 338 |
| 23 | Louisiana | 337 |
| 24 | Rhode Island | 325 |
| 25 | New Jersey | 314 |
| 25 | Virginia | 314 |
| 27 | Kansas | 291 |
| 28 | Nebraska | 278 |
| 29 | Oklahoma | 277 |
| 30 | Delaware | 270 |
| 31 | Minnesota | 268 |
| 32 | New Hampshire | 235 |
| 33 | New Mexico | 208 |
| 33 | Pennsylvania | 208 |
| 35 | Wyoming | 200 |
| 36 | West Virginia | 196 |
| 37 | Connecticut | 195 |
| 38 | Massachusetts | 191 |
| 39 | North Carolina | 190 |
| 40 | Iowa | 183 |
| 41 | Maine | 182 |
| 42 | New York | 181 |
| 43 | Montana | 175 |
| 44 | Hawaii | 158 |
| 45 | South Dakota | 155 |
| 46 | South Carolina | 154 |
| 47 | Texas | 152 |
| 48 | Vermont | 143 |
| 49 | North Dakota | 116 |
| 50 | Alaska | 78 |
| | District of Columbia | 122 |

Source: CQ Press using data from Administrative Office of the U.S. Courts
"Table F-2, U.S. Bankruptcy Courts" (http://www.uscourts.gov/Statistics/BankruptcyStatistics.aspx)
*For 12 months through September 2013. National rate does not include bankruptcies or population in U.S. territories. Includes all nonbusiness bankruptcies.

# Percent Change in Personal Bankruptcy Rate: 2012 to 2013

## National Percent Change = 12.7% Decrease*

| ALPHA ORDER | | | RANK ORDER | | |
|---|---|---|---|---|---|
| RANK | STATE | PERCENT CHANGE | RANK | STATE | PERCENT CHANGE |
| 4 | Alabama | (3.4) | 1 | Mississippi | 1.4 |
| 50 | Alaska | (27.8) | 2 | Louisiana | (1.7) |
| 44 | Arizona | (20.9) | 3 | Illinois | (2.1) |
| 5 | Arkansas | (3.5) | 4 | Alabama | (3.4) |
| 47 | California | (25.5) | 5 | Arkansas | (3.5) |
| 30 | Colorado | (14.2) | 6 | Maryland | (4.0) |
| 31 | Connecticut | (14.5) | 7 | Tennessee | (4.3) |
| 45 | Delaware | (21.1) | 8 | Missouri | (5.0) |
| 15 | Florida | (8.4) | 9 | Indiana | (6.0) |
| 22 | Georgia | (10.5) | 10 | South Carolina | (6.1) |
| 32 | Hawaii | (14.6) | 10 | Wyoming | (6.1) |
| 39 | Idaho | (15.7) | 12 | Ohio | (6.6) |
| 3 | Illinois | (2.1) | 13 | Kansas | (7.3) |
| 9 | Indiana | (6.0) | 14 | West Virginia | (8.0) |
| 27 | Iowa | (12.4) | 15 | Florida | (8.4) |
| 13 | Kansas | (7.3) | 16 | New Mexico | (8.8) |
| 18 | Kentucky | (9.0) | 16 | Pennsylvania | (8.8) |
| 2 | Louisiana | (1.7) | 18 | Kentucky | (9.0) |
| 42 | Maine | (17.3) | 19 | Nebraska | (9.4) |
| 6 | Maryland | (4.0) | 20 | Vermont | (9.5) |
| 49 | Massachusetts | (26.8) | 20 | Wisconsin | (9.5) |
| 32 | Michigan | (14.6) | 22 | Georgia | (10.5) |
| 37 | Minnesota | (15.5) | 23 | Utah | (10.6) |
| 1 | Mississippi | 1.4 | 24 | Washington | (10.9) |
| 8 | Missouri | (5.0) | 25 | Oklahoma | (11.5) |
| 32 | Montana | (14.6) | 26 | North Carolina | (12.0) |
| 19 | Nebraska | (9.4) | 27 | Iowa | (12.4) |
| 48 | Nevada | (26.5) | 28 | New Jersey | (13.7) |
| 43 | New Hampshire | (20.1) | 29 | Virginia | (14.0) |
| 28 | New Jersey | (13.7) | 30 | Colorado | (14.2) |
| 16 | New Mexico | (8.8) | 31 | Connecticut | (14.5) |
| 32 | New York | (14.6) | 32 | Hawaii | (14.6) |
| 26 | North Carolina | (12.0) | 32 | Michigan | (14.6) |
| 45 | North Dakota | (21.1) | 32 | Montana | (14.6) |
| 12 | Ohio | (6.6) | 32 | New York | (14.6) |
| 25 | Oklahoma | (11.5) | 32 | Texas | (14.6) |
| 37 | Oregon | (15.5) | 37 | Minnesota | (15.5) |
| 16 | Pennsylvania | (8.8) | 37 | Oregon | (15.5) |
| 40 | Rhode Island | (16.2) | 39 | Idaho | (15.7) |
| 10 | South Carolina | (6.1) | 40 | Rhode Island | (16.2) |
| 41 | South Dakota | (16.7) | 41 | South Dakota | (16.7) |
| 7 | Tennessee | (4.3) | 42 | Maine | (17.3) |
| 32 | Texas | (14.6) | 43 | New Hampshire | (20.1) |
| 23 | Utah | (10.6) | 44 | Arizona | (20.9) |
| 20 | Vermont | (9.5) | 45 | Delaware | (21.1) |
| 29 | Virginia | (14.0) | 45 | North Dakota | (21.1) |
| 24 | Washington | (10.9) | 47 | California | (25.5) |
| 14 | West Virginia | (8.0) | 48 | Nevada | (26.5) |
| 20 | Wisconsin | (9.5) | 49 | Massachusetts | (26.8) |
| 10 | Wyoming | (6.1) | 50 | Alaska | (27.8) |
| | | | | District of Columbia | (9.0) |

Source: CQ Press using data from Administrative Office of the U.S. Courts
   "Table F-2, U.S. Bankruptcy Courts" (http://www.uscourts.gov/Statistics/BankruptcyStatistics.aspx)
*Twelve months ending in September 2012 to 12 months ending in September 2013.  National rate does not include bankruptcies or population in U.S. territories.  Includes all nonbusiness bankruptcies.

# Business Bankruptcy Rate in 2011

## National Rate = 0.8% of Existing Firms*

| ALPHA ORDER | | | RANK ORDER | | |
|---|---|---|---|---|---|
| RANK | STATE | RATE | RANK | STATE | RATE |
| 14 | Alabama | 0.8 | 1 | Delaware | 3.3 |
| 46 | Alaska | 0.4 | 2 | Nevada | 2.1 |
| 4 | Arizona | 1.3 | 3 | New Hampshire | 1.5 |
| 14 | Arkansas | 0.8 | 4 | Arizona | 1.3 |
| 6 | California | 1.1 | 4 | Georgia | 1.3 |
| 10 | Colorado | 0.9 | 6 | California | 1.1 |
| 37 | Connecticut | 0.5 | 7 | Florida | 1.0 |
| 1 | Delaware | 3.3 | 7 | Tennessee | 1.0 |
| 7 | Florida | 1.0 | 7 | Utah | 1.0 |
| 4 | Georgia | 1.3 | 10 | Colorado | 0.9 |
| 20 | Hawaii | 0.7 | 10 | Michigan | 0.9 |
| 14 | Idaho | 0.8 | 10 | Mississippi | 0.9 |
| 14 | Illinois | 0.8 | 10 | Texas | 0.9 |
| 20 | Indiana | 0.7 | 14 | Alabama | 0.8 |
| 28 | Iowa | 0.6 | 14 | Arkansas | 0.8 |
| 37 | Kansas | 0.5 | 14 | Idaho | 0.8 |
| 20 | Kentucky | 0.7 | 14 | Illinois | 0.8 |
| 14 | Louisiana | 0.8 | 14 | Louisiana | 0.8 |
| 20 | Maine | 0.7 | 14 | Washington | 0.8 |
| 28 | Maryland | 0.6 | 20 | Hawaii | 0.7 |
| 46 | Massachusetts | 0.4 | 20 | Indiana | 0.7 |
| 10 | Michigan | 0.9 | 20 | Kentucky | 0.7 |
| 28 | Minnesota | 0.6 | 20 | Maine | 0.7 |
| 10 | Mississippi | 0.9 | 20 | North Carolina | 0.7 |
| 37 | Missouri | 0.5 | 20 | Ohio | 0.7 |
| 46 | Montana | 0.4 | 20 | West Virginia | 0.7 |
| 37 | Nebraska | 0.5 | 20 | Wisconsin | 0.7 |
| 2 | Nevada | 2.1 | 28 | Iowa | 0.6 |
| 3 | New Hampshire | 1.5 | 28 | Maryland | 0.6 |
| 28 | New Jersey | 0.6 | 28 | Minnesota | 0.6 |
| 28 | New Mexico | 0.6 | 28 | New Jersey | 0.6 |
| 37 | New York | 0.5 | 28 | New Mexico | 0.6 |
| 20 | North Carolina | 0.7 | 28 | Oklahoma | 0.6 |
| 49 | North Dakota | 0.3 | 28 | Oregon | 0.6 |
| 20 | Ohio | 0.7 | 28 | Rhode Island | 0.6 |
| 28 | Oklahoma | 0.6 | 28 | Virginia | 0.6 |
| 28 | Oregon | 0.6 | 37 | Connecticut | 0.5 |
| 37 | Pennsylvania | 0.5 | 37 | Kansas | 0.5 |
| 28 | Rhode Island | 0.6 | 37 | Missouri | 0.5 |
| 37 | South Carolina | 0.5 | 37 | Nebraska | 0.5 |
| 37 | South Dakota | 0.5 | 37 | New York | 0.5 |
| 7 | Tennessee | 1.0 | 37 | Pennsylvania | 0.5 |
| 10 | Texas | 0.9 | 37 | South Carolina | 0.5 |
| 7 | Utah | 1.0 | 37 | South Dakota | 0.5 |
| 50 | Vermont | 0.2 | 37 | Wyoming | 0.5 |
| 28 | Virginia | 0.6 | 46 | Alaska | 0.4 |
| 14 | Washington | 0.8 | 46 | Massachusetts | 0.4 |
| 20 | West Virginia | 0.7 | 46 | Montana | 0.4 |
| 20 | Wisconsin | 0.7 | 49 | North Dakota | 0.3 |
| 37 | Wyoming | 0.5 | 50 | Vermont | 0.2 |
| | | | | District of Columbia | 0.4 |

Source: CQ Press using data from U.S. Small Business Administration
   "The Small Business Economy 2012" (http://www.sba.gov/advocacy/849/6282)
*Firms can be in more than one state. Firms filing for bankruptcy in 2011 as a percent of employer firms existing at the beginning of 2011 based on 2010 counts.

# 2014 State Business Tax Climate Index

## National Average Score = 5.24*

| ALPHA ORDER | | | | RANK ORDER | | |
|---|---|---|---|---|---|---|
| RANK | STATE | SCORE | | RANK | STATE | SCORE |
| 21 | Alabama | 5.21 | | 1 | Wyoming | 7.58 |
| 4 | Alaska | 7.24 | | 2 | South Dakota | 7.52 |
| 22 | Arizona | 5.20 | | 3 | Nevada | 7.46 |
| 34 | Arkansas | 4.89 | | 4 | Alaska | 7.24 |
| 48 | California | 3.76 | | 5 | Florida | 6.91 |
| 19 | Colorado | 5.27 | | 6 | Washington | 6.32 |
| 42 | Connecticut | 4.47 | | 7 | Montana | 6.24 |
| 13 | Delaware | 5.75 | | 8 | New Hampshire | 6.08 |
| 5 | Florida | 6.91 | | 9 | Utah | 6.01 |
| 32 | Georgia | 4.92 | | 10 | Indiana | 5.99 |
| 30 | Hawaii | 5.02 | | 11 | Texas | 5.91 |
| 18 | Idaho | 5.31 | | 12 | Oregon | 5.75 |
| 31 | Illinois | 5.00 | | 13 | Delaware | 5.75 |
| 10 | Indiana | 5.99 | | 14 | Michigan | 5.73 |
| 40 | Iowa | 4.55 | | 15 | Tennessee | 5.59 |
| 20 | Kansas | 5.22 | | 16 | Missouri | 5.47 |
| 27 | Kentucky | 5.08 | | 17 | Mississippi | 5.36 |
| 33 | Louisiana | 4.90 | | 18 | Idaho | 5.31 |
| 29 | Maine | 5.04 | | 19 | Colorado | 5.27 |
| 41 | Maryland | 4.49 | | 20 | Kansas | 5.22 |
| 25 | Massachusetts | 5.09 | | 21 | Alabama | 5.21 |
| 14 | Michigan | 5.73 | | 22 | Arizona | 5.20 |
| 47 | Minnesota | 4.06 | | 23 | West Virginia | 5.19 |
| 17 | Mississippi | 5.36 | | 24 | Pennsylvania | 5.11 |
| 16 | Missouri | 5.47 | | 25 | Massachusetts | 5.09 |
| 7 | Montana | 6.24 | | 26 | Virginia | 5.09 |
| 34 | Nebraska | 4.89 | | 27 | Kentucky | 5.08 |
| 3 | Nevada | 7.46 | | 28 | North Dakota | 5.05 |
| 8 | New Hampshire | 6.08 | | 29 | Maine | 5.04 |
| 49 | New Jersey | 3.45 | | 30 | Hawaii | 5.02 |
| 38 | New Mexico | 4.72 | | 31 | Illinois | 5.00 |
| 50 | New York | 3.45 | | 32 | Georgia | 4.92 |
| 44 | North Carolina | 4.35 | | 33 | Louisiana | 4.90 |
| 28 | North Dakota | 5.05 | | 34 | Arkansas | 4.89 |
| 39 | Ohio | 4.58 | | 34 | Nebraska | 4.89 |
| 36 | Oklahoma | 4.88 | | 36 | Oklahoma | 4.88 |
| 12 | Oregon | 5.75 | | 37 | South Carolina | 4.86 |
| 24 | Pennsylvania | 5.11 | | 38 | New Mexico | 4.72 |
| 46 | Rhode Island | 4.14 | | 39 | Ohio | 4.58 |
| 37 | South Carolina | 4.86 | | 40 | Iowa | 4.55 |
| 2 | South Dakota | 7.52 | | 41 | Maryland | 4.49 |
| 15 | Tennessee | 5.59 | | 42 | Connecticut | 4.47 |
| 11 | Texas | 5.91 | | 43 | Wisconsin | 4.43 |
| 9 | Utah | 6.01 | | 44 | North Carolina | 4.35 |
| 45 | Vermont | 4.14 | | 45 | Vermont | 4.14 |
| 26 | Virginia | 5.09 | | 46 | Rhode Island | 4.14 |
| 6 | Washington | 6.32 | | 47 | Minnesota | 4.06 |
| 23 | West Virginia | 5.19 | | 48 | California | 3.76 |
| 43 | Wisconsin | 4.43 | | 49 | New Jersey | 3.45 |
| 1 | Wyoming | 7.58 | | 50 | New York | 3.45 |
| | | | | | District of Columbia | 4.37 |

Source: The Tax Foundation
   "State Business Tax Climate Index" (October 2013, http://taxfoundation.org/article/2014-state-business-tax-climate-index)
*This index looks at levels of taxation and complexity of compliance to compare the states on how "business friendly" each state is compared to the others.  The scale for each factor considered is one to ten, with ten being the "best."  Rankings are based on unrounded scores and reflect those of The Tax Foundation.

# Fortune 500 Companies in 2013

## National Total = 500 Companies*

ALPHA ORDER

| RANK | STATE | COMPANIES | % of USA |
|------|-------|-----------|----------|
| 35 | Alabama | 1 | 0.2% |
| 39 | Alaska | 0 | 0.0% |
| 21 | Arizona | 6 | 1.2% |
| 21 | Arkansas | 6 | 1.2% |
| 1 | California | 54 | 10.8% |
| 16 | Colorado | 10 | 2.0% |
| 11 | Connecticut | 16 | 3.2% |
| 32 | Delaware | 2 | 0.4% |
| 13 | Florida | 15 | 3.0% |
| 11 | Georgia | 16 | 3.2% |
| 39 | Hawaii | 0 | 0.0% |
| 35 | Idaho | 1 | 0.2% |
| 4 | Illinois | 32 | 6.4% |
| 21 | Indiana | 6 | 1.2% |
| 32 | Iowa | 2 | 0.4% |
| 29 | Kansas | 3 | 0.6% |
| 24 | Kentucky | 5 | 1.0% |
| 29 | Louisiana | 3 | 0.6% |
| 39 | Maine | 0 | 0.0% |
| 26 | Maryland | 4 | 0.8% |
| 14 | Massachusetts | 12 | 2.4% |
| 9 | Michigan | 19 | 3.8% |
| 9 | Minnesota | 19 | 3.8% |
| 39 | Mississippi | 0 | 0.0% |
| 16 | Missouri | 10 | 2.0% |
| 39 | Montana | 0 | 0.0% |
| 24 | Nebraska | 5 | 1.0% |
| 26 | Nevada | 4 | 0.8% |
| 39 | New Hampshire | 0 | 0.0% |
| 7 | New Jersey | 21 | 4.2% |
| 39 | New Mexico | 0 | 0.0% |
| 2 | New York | 52 | 10.4% |
| 14 | North Carolina | 12 | 2.4% |
| 39 | North Dakota | 0 | 0.0% |
| 5 | Ohio | 27 | 5.4% |
| 26 | Oklahoma | 4 | 0.8% |
| 32 | Oregon | 2 | 0.4% |
| 7 | Pennsylvania | 21 | 4.2% |
| 29 | Rhode Island | 3 | 0.6% |
| 35 | South Carolina | 1 | 0.2% |
| 39 | South Dakota | 0 | 0.0% |
| 19 | Tennessee | 9 | 1.8% |
| 2 | Texas | 52 | 10.4% |
| 35 | Utah | 1 | 0.2% |
| 39 | Vermont | 0 | 0.0% |
| 6 | Virginia | 23 | 4.6% |
| 20 | Washington | 8 | 1.6% |
| 39 | West Virginia | 0 | 0.0% |
| 16 | Wisconsin | 10 | 2.0% |
| 39 | Wyoming | 0 | 0.0% |

RANK ORDER

| RANK | STATE | COMPANIES | % of USA |
|------|-------|-----------|----------|
| 1 | California | 54 | 10.8% |
| 2 | New York | 52 | 10.4% |
| 2 | Texas | 52 | 10.4% |
| 4 | Illinois | 32 | 6.4% |
| 5 | Ohio | 27 | 5.4% |
| 6 | Virginia | 23 | 4.6% |
| 7 | New Jersey | 21 | 4.2% |
| 7 | Pennsylvania | 21 | 4.2% |
| 9 | Michigan | 19 | 3.8% |
| 9 | Minnesota | 19 | 3.8% |
| 11 | Connecticut | 16 | 3.2% |
| 11 | Georgia | 16 | 3.2% |
| 13 | Florida | 15 | 3.0% |
| 14 | Massachusetts | 12 | 2.4% |
| 14 | North Carolina | 12 | 2.4% |
| 16 | Colorado | 10 | 2.0% |
| 16 | Missouri | 10 | 2.0% |
| 16 | Wisconsin | 10 | 2.0% |
| 19 | Tennessee | 9 | 1.8% |
| 20 | Washington | 8 | 1.6% |
| 21 | Arizona | 6 | 1.2% |
| 21 | Arkansas | 6 | 1.2% |
| 21 | Indiana | 6 | 1.2% |
| 24 | Kentucky | 5 | 1.0% |
| 24 | Nebraska | 5 | 1.0% |
| 26 | Maryland | 4 | 0.8% |
| 26 | Nevada | 4 | 0.8% |
| 26 | Oklahoma | 4 | 0.8% |
| 29 | Kansas | 3 | 0.6% |
| 29 | Louisiana | 3 | 0.6% |
| 29 | Rhode Island | 3 | 0.6% |
| 32 | Delaware | 2 | 0.4% |
| 32 | Iowa | 2 | 0.4% |
| 32 | Oregon | 2 | 0.4% |
| 35 | Alabama | 1 | 0.2% |
| 35 | Idaho | 1 | 0.2% |
| 35 | South Carolina | 1 | 0.2% |
| 35 | Utah | 1 | 0.2% |
| 39 | Alaska | 0 | 0.0% |
| 39 | Hawaii | 0 | 0.0% |
| 39 | Maine | 0 | 0.0% |
| 39 | Mississippi | 0 | 0.0% |
| 39 | Montana | 0 | 0.0% |
| 39 | New Hampshire | 0 | 0.0% |
| 39 | New Mexico | 0 | 0.0% |
| 39 | North Dakota | 0 | 0.0% |
| 39 | South Dakota | 0 | 0.0% |
| 39 | Vermont | 0 | 0.0% |
| 39 | West Virginia | 0 | 0.0% |
| 39 | Wyoming | 0 | 0.0% |
| | District of Columbia | 3 | 0.6% |

Source: Fortune magazine
   "Fortune 500" (April 8, 2013, Vol. 167, No. 5)
*By state where each company's headquarters is located.

# Employer Firms in 2010

## National Total = 5,734,538 Firms*

| ALPHA ORDER | | | | | RANK ORDER | | | |
|---|---|---|---|---|---|---|---|---|
| RANK | STATE | FIRMS | % of USA | | RANK | STATE | FIRMS | % of USA |
| 26 | Alabama | 75,518 | 1.3% | | 1 | California | 690,454 | 12.0% |
| 50 | Alaska | 16,462 | 0.3% | | 2 | New York | 444,895 | 7.8% |
| 21 | Arizona | 102,175 | 1.8% | | 3 | Florida | 400,840 | 7.0% |
| 33 | Arkansas | 51,072 | 0.9% | | 4 | Texas | 394,392 | 6.9% |
| 1 | California | 690,454 | 12.0% | | 5 | Illinois | 253,612 | 4.4% |
| 15 | Colorado | 125,820 | 2.2% | | 6 | Pennsylvania | 231,192 | 4.0% |
| 27 | Connecticut | 72,747 | 1.3% | | 7 | New Jersey | 193,722 | 3.4% |
| 46 | Delaware | 19,679 | 0.3% | | 8 | Ohio | 190,184 | 3.3% |
| 3 | Florida | 400,840 | 7.0% | | 9 | Michigan | 174,345 | 3.0% |
| 10 | Georgia | 170,245 | 3.0% | | 10 | Georgia | 170,245 | 3.0% |
| 43 | Hawaii | 25,383 | 0.4% | | 11 | North Carolina | 168,938 | 2.9% |
| 37 | Idaho | 36,660 | 0.6% | | 12 | Virginia | 149,271 | 2.6% |
| 5 | Illinois | 253,612 | 4.4% | | 13 | Washington | 144,377 | 2.5% |
| 18 | Indiana | 110,961 | 1.9% | | 14 | Massachusetts | 137,406 | 2.4% |
| 30 | Iowa | 63,402 | 1.1% | | 15 | Colorado | 125,820 | 2.2% |
| 31 | Kansas | 59,170 | 1.0% | | 16 | Missouri | 117,832 | 2.1% |
| 29 | Kentucky | 69,572 | 1.2% | | 17 | Minnesota | 117,687 | 2.1% |
| 24 | Louisiana | 81,299 | 1.4% | | 18 | Indiana | 110,961 | 1.9% |
| 39 | Maine | 33,773 | 0.6% | | 19 | Wisconsin | 110,435 | 1.9% |
| 20 | Maryland | 108,246 | 1.9% | | 20 | Maryland | 108,246 | 1.9% |
| 14 | Massachusetts | 137,406 | 2.4% | | 21 | Arizona | 102,175 | 1.8% |
| 9 | Michigan | 174,345 | 3.0% | | 22 | Tennessee | 97,976 | 1.7% |
| 17 | Minnesota | 117,687 | 2.1% | | 23 | Oregon | 87,996 | 1.5% |
| 35 | Mississippi | 45,813 | 0.8% | | 24 | Louisiana | 81,299 | 1.4% |
| 16 | Missouri | 117,832 | 2.1% | | 25 | South Carolina | 78,883 | 1.4% |
| 40 | Montana | 31,358 | 0.5% | | 26 | Alabama | 75,518 | 1.3% |
| 36 | Nebraska | 41,974 | 0.7% | | 27 | Connecticut | 72,747 | 1.3% |
| 34 | Nevada | 47,352 | 0.8% | | 28 | Oklahoma | 71,972 | 1.3% |
| 41 | New Hampshire | 31,025 | 0.5% | | 29 | Kentucky | 69,572 | 1.2% |
| 7 | New Jersey | 193,722 | 3.4% | | 30 | Iowa | 63,402 | 1.1% |
| 38 | New Mexico | 35,655 | 0.6% | | 31 | Kansas | 59,170 | 1.0% |
| 2 | New York | 444,895 | 7.8% | | 32 | Utah | 57,664 | 1.0% |
| 11 | North Carolina | 168,938 | 2.9% | | 33 | Arkansas | 51,072 | 0.9% |
| 48 | North Dakota | 18,169 | 0.3% | | 34 | Nevada | 47,352 | 0.8% |
| 8 | Ohio | 190,184 | 3.3% | | 35 | Mississippi | 45,813 | 0.8% |
| 28 | Oklahoma | 71,972 | 1.3% | | 36 | Nebraska | 41,974 | 0.7% |
| 23 | Oregon | 87,996 | 1.5% | | 37 | Idaho | 36,660 | 0.6% |
| 6 | Pennsylvania | 231,192 | 4.0% | | 38 | New Mexico | 35,655 | 0.6% |
| 44 | Rhode Island | 24,556 | 0.4% | | 39 | Maine | 33,773 | 0.6% |
| 25 | South Carolina | 78,883 | 1.4% | | 40 | Montana | 31,358 | 0.5% |
| 45 | South Dakota | 21,637 | 0.4% | | 41 | New Hampshire | 31,025 | 0.5% |
| 22 | Tennessee | 97,976 | 1.7% | | 42 | West Virginia | 29,609 | 0.5% |
| 4 | Texas | 394,392 | 6.9% | | 43 | Hawaii | 25,383 | 0.4% |
| 32 | Utah | 57,664 | 1.0% | | 44 | Rhode Island | 24,556 | 0.4% |
| 47 | Vermont | 18,596 | 0.3% | | 45 | South Dakota | 21,637 | 0.4% |
| 12 | Virginia | 149,271 | 2.6% | | 46 | Delaware | 19,679 | 0.3% |
| 13 | Washington | 144,377 | 2.5% | | 47 | Vermont | 18,596 | 0.3% |
| 42 | West Virginia | 29,609 | 0.5% | | 48 | North Dakota | 18,169 | 0.3% |
| 19 | Wisconsin | 110,435 | 1.9% | | 49 | Wyoming | 17,585 | 0.3% |
| 49 | Wyoming | 17,585 | 0.3% | | 50 | Alaska | 16,462 | 0.3% |
| | | | | | | District of Columbia | 16,913 | 0.3% |

Source: U.S. Small Business Administration
"The Small Business Economy 2012" (http://www.sba.gov/advocacy/849/6282)
*Updated figures.  State totals do not add to the U.S. figure as firms can be in more than one state.

# New Employer Firms in 2011

## National Total = 1,433,703 New Firms*

ALPHA ORDER

| RANK | STATE | FIRMS | % of USA |
|------|-------|-------|----------|
| 29 | Alabama | 14,335 | 1.0% |
| 49 | Alaska | 4,466 | 0.3% |
| 16 | Arizona | 30,030 | 2.1% |
| 25 | Arkansas | 17,175 | 1.2% |
| 1 | California | 165,536 | 11.5% |
| 13 | Colorado | 36,375 | 2.5% |
| 34 | Connecticut | 10,999 | 0.8% |
| 46 | Delaware | 5,081 | 0.4% |
| 2 | Florida | 129,059 | 9.0% |
| 7 | Georgia | 52,788 | 3.7% |
| 45 | Hawaii | 5,117 | 0.4% |
| 35 | Idaho | 10,797 | 0.8% |
| 5 | Illinois | 60,208 | 4.2% |
| 19 | Indiana | 23,681 | 1.7% |
| 33 | Iowa | 12,719 | 0.9% |
| 32 | Kansas | 12,893 | 0.9% |
| 27 | Kentucky | 16,230 | 1.1% |
| 24 | Louisiana | 17,398 | 1.2% |
| 36 | Maine | 9,228 | 0.6% |
| 17 | Maryland | 28,586 | 2.0% |
| 14 | Massachusetts | 33,323 | 2.3% |
| 10 | Michigan | 40,946 | 2.9% |
| 18 | Minnesota | 27,700 | 1.9% |
| 37 | Mississippi | 8,987 | 0.6% |
| 20 | Missouri | 22,058 | 1.5% |
| 40 | Montana | 8,522 | 0.6% |
| 38 | Nebraska | 8,732 | 0.6% |
| 31 | Nevada | 13,597 | 0.9% |
| 41 | New Hampshire | 8,287 | 0.6% |
| 11 | New Jersey | 39,494 | 2.8% |
| 39 | New Mexico | 8,675 | 0.6% |
| 3 | New York | 108,231 | 7.5% |
| 8 | North Carolina | 42,758 | 3.0% |
| 44 | North Dakota | 5,289 | 0.4% |
| 12 | Ohio | 38,296 | 2.7% |
| 30 | Oklahoma | 14,244 | 1.0% |
| 22 | Oregon | 21,487 | 1.5% |
| 6 | Pennsylvania | 54,929 | 3.8% |
| 42 | Rhode Island | 6,786 | 0.5% |
| 26 | South Carolina | 17,168 | 1.2% |
| 47 | South Dakota | 4,829 | 0.3% |
| 28 | Tennessee | 15,954 | 1.1% |
| 4 | Texas | 87,955 | 6.1% |
| 23 | Utah | 18,411 | 1.3% |
| 48 | Vermont | 4,604 | 0.3% |
| 9 | Virginia | 41,879 | 2.9% |
| 15 | Washington | 30,416 | 2.1% |
| 43 | West Virginia | 6,463 | 0.5% |
| 21 | Wisconsin | 21,713 | 1.5% |
| 50 | Wyoming | 4,151 | 0.3% |

RANK ORDER

| RANK | STATE | FIRMS | % of USA |
|------|-------|-------|----------|
| 1 | California | 165,536 | 11.5% |
| 2 | Florida | 129,059 | 9.0% |
| 3 | New York | 108,231 | 7.5% |
| 4 | Texas | 87,955 | 6.1% |
| 5 | Illinois | 60,208 | 4.2% |
| 6 | Pennsylvania | 54,929 | 3.8% |
| 7 | Georgia | 52,788 | 3.7% |
| 8 | North Carolina | 42,758 | 3.0% |
| 9 | Virginia | 41,879 | 2.9% |
| 10 | Michigan | 40,946 | 2.9% |
| 11 | New Jersey | 39,494 | 2.8% |
| 12 | Ohio | 38,296 | 2.7% |
| 13 | Colorado | 36,375 | 2.5% |
| 14 | Massachusetts | 33,323 | 2.3% |
| 15 | Washington | 30,416 | 2.1% |
| 16 | Arizona | 30,030 | 2.1% |
| 17 | Maryland | 28,586 | 2.0% |
| 18 | Minnesota | 27,700 | 1.9% |
| 19 | Indiana | 23,681 | 1.7% |
| 20 | Missouri | 22,058 | 1.5% |
| 21 | Wisconsin | 21,713 | 1.5% |
| 22 | Oregon | 21,487 | 1.5% |
| 23 | Utah | 18,411 | 1.3% |
| 24 | Louisiana | 17,398 | 1.2% |
| 25 | Arkansas | 17,175 | 1.2% |
| 26 | South Carolina | 17,168 | 1.2% |
| 27 | Kentucky | 16,230 | 1.1% |
| 28 | Tennessee | 15,954 | 1.1% |
| 29 | Alabama | 14,335 | 1.0% |
| 30 | Oklahoma | 14,244 | 1.0% |
| 31 | Nevada | 13,597 | 0.9% |
| 32 | Kansas | 12,893 | 0.9% |
| 33 | Iowa | 12,719 | 0.9% |
| 34 | Connecticut | 10,999 | 0.8% |
| 35 | Idaho | 10,797 | 0.8% |
| 36 | Maine | 9,228 | 0.6% |
| 37 | Mississippi | 8,987 | 0.6% |
| 38 | Nebraska | 8,732 | 0.6% |
| 39 | New Mexico | 8,675 | 0.6% |
| 40 | Montana | 8,522 | 0.6% |
| 41 | New Hampshire | 8,287 | 0.6% |
| 42 | Rhode Island | 6,786 | 0.5% |
| 43 | West Virginia | 6,463 | 0.5% |
| 44 | North Dakota | 5,289 | 0.4% |
| 45 | Hawaii | 5,117 | 0.4% |
| 46 | Delaware | 5,081 | 0.4% |
| 47 | South Dakota | 4,829 | 0.3% |
| 48 | Vermont | 4,604 | 0.3% |
| 49 | Alaska | 4,466 | 0.3% |
| 50 | Wyoming | 4,151 | 0.3% |
| | District of Columbia | 5,118 | 0.4% |

Source: U.S. Small Business Administration
   "The Small Business Economy 2012" (http://www.sba.gov/advocacy/849/6282)
*Establishment openings and closings represent quarterly business turnover for new and existing establishments, which can belong to small or large firms (seasonally adjusted).

# Rate of New Employer Firms in 2011

## National Rate = 25.0% of Existing Firms*

<table>
<tr><td colspan="3">ALPHA ORDER</td><td colspan="3">RANK ORDER</td></tr>
<tr><th>RANK</th><th>STATE</th><th>RATE</th><th>RANK</th><th>STATE</th><th>RATE</th></tr>
<tr><td>47</td><td>Alabama</td><td>19.0</td><td>1</td><td>Arkansas</td><td>33.6</td></tr>
<tr><td>14</td><td>Alaska</td><td>27.1</td><td>2</td><td>Florida</td><td>32.2</td></tr>
<tr><td>6</td><td>Arizona</td><td>29.4</td><td>3</td><td>Utah</td><td>31.9</td></tr>
<tr><td>1</td><td>Arkansas</td><td>33.6</td><td>4</td><td>Georgia</td><td>31.0</td></tr>
<tr><td>24</td><td>California</td><td>24.0</td><td>5</td><td>Idaho</td><td>29.5</td></tr>
<tr><td>8</td><td>Colorado</td><td>28.9</td><td>6</td><td>Arizona</td><td>29.4</td></tr>
<tr><td>50</td><td>Connecticut</td><td>15.1</td><td>7</td><td>North Dakota</td><td>29.1</td></tr>
<tr><td>17</td><td>Delaware</td><td>25.8</td><td>8</td><td>Colorado</td><td>28.9</td></tr>
<tr><td>2</td><td>Florida</td><td>32.2</td><td>9</td><td>Nevada</td><td>28.7</td></tr>
<tr><td>4</td><td>Georgia</td><td>31.0</td><td>10</td><td>Virginia</td><td>28.1</td></tr>
<tr><td>41</td><td>Hawaii</td><td>20.2</td><td>11</td><td>Rhode Island</td><td>27.6</td></tr>
<tr><td>5</td><td>Idaho</td><td>29.5</td><td>12</td><td>Maine</td><td>27.3</td></tr>
<tr><td>26</td><td>Illinois</td><td>23.7</td><td>13</td><td>Montana</td><td>27.2</td></tr>
<tr><td>37</td><td>Indiana</td><td>21.3</td><td>14</td><td>Alaska</td><td>27.1</td></tr>
<tr><td>42</td><td>Iowa</td><td>20.1</td><td>15</td><td>New Hampshire</td><td>26.7</td></tr>
<tr><td>33</td><td>Kansas</td><td>21.8</td><td>16</td><td>Maryland</td><td>26.4</td></tr>
<tr><td>30</td><td>Kentucky</td><td>23.3</td><td>17</td><td>Delaware</td><td>25.8</td></tr>
<tr><td>36</td><td>Louisiana</td><td>21.4</td><td>18</td><td>North Carolina</td><td>25.3</td></tr>
<tr><td>12</td><td>Maine</td><td>27.3</td><td>19</td><td>Vermont</td><td>24.8</td></tr>
<tr><td>16</td><td>Maryland</td><td>26.4</td><td>20</td><td>Oregon</td><td>24.4</td></tr>
<tr><td>21</td><td>Massachusetts</td><td>24.3</td><td>21</td><td>Massachusetts</td><td>24.3</td></tr>
<tr><td>28</td><td>Michigan</td><td>23.5</td><td>21</td><td>New Mexico</td><td>24.3</td></tr>
<tr><td>28</td><td>Minnesota</td><td>23.5</td><td>21</td><td>New York</td><td>24.3</td></tr>
<tr><td>46</td><td>Mississippi</td><td>19.6</td><td>24</td><td>California</td><td>24.0</td></tr>
<tr><td>48</td><td>Missouri</td><td>18.7</td><td>25</td><td>Pennsylvania</td><td>23.8</td></tr>
<tr><td>13</td><td>Montana</td><td>27.2</td><td>26</td><td>Illinois</td><td>23.7</td></tr>
<tr><td>39</td><td>Nebraska</td><td>20.8</td><td>27</td><td>Wyoming</td><td>23.6</td></tr>
<tr><td>9</td><td>Nevada</td><td>28.7</td><td>28</td><td>Michigan</td><td>23.5</td></tr>
<tr><td>15</td><td>New Hampshire</td><td>26.7</td><td>28</td><td>Minnesota</td><td>23.5</td></tr>
<tr><td>40</td><td>New Jersey</td><td>20.4</td><td>30</td><td>Kentucky</td><td>23.3</td></tr>
<tr><td>21</td><td>New Mexico</td><td>24.3</td><td>31</td><td>South Dakota</td><td>22.3</td></tr>
<tr><td>21</td><td>New York</td><td>24.3</td><td>31</td><td>Texas</td><td>22.3</td></tr>
<tr><td>18</td><td>North Carolina</td><td>25.3</td><td>33</td><td>Kansas</td><td>21.8</td></tr>
<tr><td>7</td><td>North Dakota</td><td>29.1</td><td>33</td><td>South Carolina</td><td>21.8</td></tr>
<tr><td>42</td><td>Ohio</td><td>20.1</td><td>33</td><td>West Virginia</td><td>21.8</td></tr>
<tr><td>44</td><td>Oklahoma</td><td>19.8</td><td>36</td><td>Louisiana</td><td>21.4</td></tr>
<tr><td>20</td><td>Oregon</td><td>24.4</td><td>37</td><td>Indiana</td><td>21.3</td></tr>
<tr><td>25</td><td>Pennsylvania</td><td>23.8</td><td>38</td><td>Washington</td><td>21.1</td></tr>
<tr><td>11</td><td>Rhode Island</td><td>27.6</td><td>39</td><td>Nebraska</td><td>20.8</td></tr>
<tr><td>33</td><td>South Carolina</td><td>21.8</td><td>40</td><td>New Jersey</td><td>20.4</td></tr>
<tr><td>31</td><td>South Dakota</td><td>22.3</td><td>41</td><td>Hawaii</td><td>20.2</td></tr>
<tr><td>49</td><td>Tennessee</td><td>16.3</td><td>42</td><td>Iowa</td><td>20.1</td></tr>
<tr><td>31</td><td>Texas</td><td>22.3</td><td>42</td><td>Ohio</td><td>20.1</td></tr>
<tr><td>3</td><td>Utah</td><td>31.9</td><td>44</td><td>Oklahoma</td><td>19.8</td></tr>
<tr><td>19</td><td>Vermont</td><td>24.8</td><td>45</td><td>Wisconsin</td><td>19.7</td></tr>
<tr><td>10</td><td>Virginia</td><td>28.1</td><td>46</td><td>Mississippi</td><td>19.6</td></tr>
<tr><td>38</td><td>Washington</td><td>21.1</td><td>47</td><td>Alabama</td><td>19.0</td></tr>
<tr><td>33</td><td>West Virginia</td><td>21.8</td><td>48</td><td>Missouri</td><td>18.7</td></tr>
<tr><td>45</td><td>Wisconsin</td><td>19.7</td><td>49</td><td>Tennessee</td><td>16.3</td></tr>
<tr><td>27</td><td>Wyoming</td><td>23.6</td><td>50</td><td>Connecticut</td><td>15.1</td></tr>
<tr><td></td><td></td><td></td><td></td><td>District of Columbia</td><td>30.3</td></tr>
</table>

Source: CQ Press using data from U.S. Small Business Administration
"The Small Business Economy 2012" (http://www.sba.gov/advocacy/849/6282)
*Establishment openings and closings represent quarterly business turnover for new and existing establishments, which can belong to small or large firms (seasonally adjusted). Firms can be in more than one state. Rate represents the number of employer firms started in 2011 as a percent of existing firms at the beginning of 2011 based on 2010 counts.

# Employer Firm Terminations in 2011

## National Total = 1,434,390 Terminations*

ALPHA ORDER

| RANK | STATE | FIRMS | % of USA |
|---|---|---|---|
| 30 | Alabama | 14,770 | 1.0% |
| 48 | Alaska | 4,237 | 0.3% |
| 16 | Arizona | 29,889 | 2.1% |
| 24 | Arkansas | 17,085 | 1.2% |
| 1 | California | 172,682 | 12.1% |
| 13 | Colorado | 35,152 | 2.5% |
| 35 | Connecticut | 11,196 | 0.8% |
| 45 | Delaware | 5,392 | 0.4% |
| 2 | Florida | 124,471 | 8.7% |
| 7 | Georgia | 53,005 | 3.7% |
| 44 | Hawaii | 6,384 | 0.4% |
| 34 | Idaho | 11,674 | 0.8% |
| 5 | Illinois | 59,944 | 4.2% |
| 19 | Indiana | 24,147 | 1.7% |
| 32 | Iowa | 12,842 | 0.9% |
| 33 | Kansas | 12,706 | 0.9% |
| 27 | Kentucky | 16,340 | 1.1% |
| 25 | Louisiana | 16,659 | 1.2% |
| 37 | Maine | 9,003 | 0.6% |
| 17 | Maryland | 28,988 | 2.0% |
| 14 | Massachusetts | 32,654 | 2.3% |
| 8 | Michigan | 40,531 | 2.8% |
| 18 | Minnesota | 25,370 | 1.8% |
| 36 | Mississippi | 9,415 | 0.7% |
| 21 | Missouri | 22,493 | 1.6% |
| 41 | Montana | 8,136 | 0.6% |
| 40 | Nebraska | 8,179 | 0.6% |
| 31 | Nevada | 12,928 | 0.9% |
| 39 | New Hampshire | 8,219 | 0.6% |
| 12 | New Jersey | 38,268 | 2.7% |
| 38 | New Mexico | 8,806 | 0.6% |
| 3 | New York | 106,278 | 7.5% |
| 10 | North Carolina | 39,453 | 2.8% |
| 49 | North Dakota | 4,027 | 0.3% |
| 9 | Ohio | 40,221 | 2.8% |
| 28 | Oklahoma | 16,069 | 1.1% |
| 22 | Oregon | 21,889 | 1.5% |
| 6 | Pennsylvania | 57,766 | 4.1% |
| 42 | Rhode Island | 6,740 | 0.5% |
| 23 | South Carolina | 17,106 | 1.2% |
| 47 | South Dakota | 4,684 | 0.3% |
| 29 | Tennessee | 15,856 | 1.1% |
| 4 | Texas | 83,154 | 5.8% |
| 26 | Utah | 16,493 | 1.2% |
| 46 | Vermont | 4,686 | 0.3% |
| 11 | Virginia | 39,279 | 2.8% |
| 15 | Washington | 31,557 | 2.2% |
| 43 | West Virginia | 6,466 | 0.5% |
| 20 | Wisconsin | 22,707 | 1.6% |
| 50 | Wyoming | 4,010 | 0.3% |

RANK ORDER

| RANK | STATE | FIRMS | % of USA |
|---|---|---|---|
| 1 | California | 172,682 | 12.1% |
| 2 | Florida | 124,471 | 8.7% |
| 3 | New York | 106,278 | 7.5% |
| 4 | Texas | 83,154 | 5.8% |
| 5 | Illinois | 59,944 | 4.2% |
| 6 | Pennsylvania | 57,766 | 4.1% |
| 7 | Georgia | 53,005 | 3.7% |
| 8 | Michigan | 40,531 | 2.8% |
| 9 | Ohio | 40,221 | 2.8% |
| 10 | North Carolina | 39,453 | 2.8% |
| 11 | Virginia | 39,279 | 2.8% |
| 12 | New Jersey | 38,268 | 2.7% |
| 13 | Colorado | 35,152 | 2.5% |
| 14 | Massachusetts | 32,654 | 2.3% |
| 15 | Washington | 31,557 | 2.2% |
| 16 | Arizona | 29,889 | 2.1% |
| 17 | Maryland | 28,988 | 2.0% |
| 18 | Minnesota | 25,370 | 1.8% |
| 19 | Indiana | 24,147 | 1.7% |
| 20 | Wisconsin | 22,707 | 1.6% |
| 21 | Missouri | 22,493 | 1.6% |
| 22 | Oregon | 21,889 | 1.5% |
| 23 | South Carolina | 17,106 | 1.2% |
| 24 | Arkansas | 17,085 | 1.2% |
| 25 | Louisiana | 16,659 | 1.2% |
| 26 | Utah | 16,493 | 1.2% |
| 27 | Kentucky | 16,340 | 1.1% |
| 28 | Oklahoma | 16,069 | 1.1% |
| 29 | Tennessee | 15,856 | 1.1% |
| 30 | Alabama | 14,770 | 1.0% |
| 31 | Nevada | 12,928 | 0.9% |
| 32 | Iowa | 12,842 | 0.9% |
| 33 | Kansas | 12,706 | 0.9% |
| 34 | Idaho | 11,674 | 0.8% |
| 35 | Connecticut | 11,196 | 0.8% |
| 36 | Mississippi | 9,415 | 0.7% |
| 37 | Maine | 9,003 | 0.6% |
| 38 | New Mexico | 8,806 | 0.6% |
| 39 | New Hampshire | 8,219 | 0.6% |
| 40 | Nebraska | 8,179 | 0.6% |
| 41 | Montana | 8,136 | 0.6% |
| 42 | Rhode Island | 6,740 | 0.5% |
| 43 | West Virginia | 6,466 | 0.5% |
| 44 | Hawaii | 6,384 | 0.4% |
| 45 | Delaware | 5,392 | 0.4% |
| 46 | Vermont | 4,686 | 0.3% |
| 47 | South Dakota | 4,684 | 0.3% |
| 48 | Alaska | 4,237 | 0.3% |
| 49 | North Dakota | 4,027 | 0.3% |
| 50 | Wyoming | 4,010 | 0.3% |
| | District of Columbia | 4,384 | 0.3% |

Source: U.S. Small Business Administration
    "The Small Business Economy 2012" (http://www.sba.gov/advocacy/849/6282)
*Establishment openings and closings represent quarterly business turnover for new and existing establishments, which can belong to small or large firms (seasonally adjusted).

# Rate of Employer Firm Terminations in 2011

## National Rate = 24.8% of Existing Firms*

ALPHA ORDER

RANK ORDER

| RANK | STATE | RATE |
|------|-------|------|
| 46 | Alabama | 19.6 |
| 16 | Alaska | 25.7 |
| 5 | Arizona | 29.3 |
| 1 | Arkansas | 33.5 |
| 19 | California | 25.0 |
| 7 | Colorado | 27.9 |
| 50 | Connecticut | 15.4 |
| 8 | Delaware | 27.4 |
| 3 | Florida | 31.1 |
| 3 | Georgia | 31.1 |
| 17 | Hawaii | 25.2 |
| 2 | Idaho | 31.8 |
| 25 | Illinois | 23.6 |
| 33 | Indiana | 21.8 |
| 44 | Iowa | 20.3 |
| 38 | Kansas | 21.5 |
| 26 | Kentucky | 23.5 |
| 43 | Louisiana | 20.5 |
| 12 | Maine | 26.7 |
| 11 | Maryland | 26.8 |
| 24 | Massachusetts | 23.8 |
| 28 | Michigan | 23.2 |
| 36 | Minnesota | 21.6 |
| 41 | Mississippi | 20.6 |
| 48 | Missouri | 19.1 |
| 15 | Montana | 25.9 |
| 47 | Nebraska | 19.5 |
| 10 | Nevada | 27.3 |
| 13 | New Hampshire | 26.5 |
| 45 | New Jersey | 19.8 |
| 22 | New Mexico | 24.7 |
| 23 | New York | 23.9 |
| 27 | North Carolina | 23.4 |
| 31 | North Dakota | 22.2 |
| 39 | Ohio | 21.1 |
| 30 | Oklahoma | 22.3 |
| 21 | Oregon | 24.9 |
| 19 | Pennsylvania | 25.0 |
| 8 | Rhode Island | 27.4 |
| 35 | South Carolina | 21.7 |
| 36 | South Dakota | 21.6 |
| 49 | Tennessee | 16.2 |
| 39 | Texas | 21.1 |
| 6 | Utah | 28.6 |
| 17 | Vermont | 25.2 |
| 14 | Virginia | 26.3 |
| 32 | Washington | 21.9 |
| 33 | West Virginia | 21.8 |
| 41 | Wisconsin | 20.6 |
| 29 | Wyoming | 22.8 |

| RANK | STATE | RATE |
|------|-------|------|
| 1 | Arkansas | 33.5 |
| 2 | Idaho | 31.8 |
| 3 | Florida | 31.1 |
| 3 | Georgia | 31.1 |
| 5 | Arizona | 29.3 |
| 6 | Utah | 28.6 |
| 7 | Colorado | 27.9 |
| 8 | Delaware | 27.4 |
| 8 | Rhode Island | 27.4 |
| 10 | Nevada | 27.3 |
| 11 | Maryland | 26.8 |
| 12 | Maine | 26.7 |
| 13 | New Hampshire | 26.5 |
| 14 | Virginia | 26.3 |
| 15 | Montana | 25.9 |
| 16 | Alaska | 25.7 |
| 17 | Hawaii | 25.2 |
| 17 | Vermont | 25.2 |
| 19 | California | 25.0 |
| 19 | Pennsylvania | 25.0 |
| 21 | Oregon | 24.9 |
| 22 | New Mexico | 24.7 |
| 23 | New York | 23.9 |
| 24 | Massachusetts | 23.8 |
| 25 | Illinois | 23.6 |
| 26 | Kentucky | 23.5 |
| 27 | North Carolina | 23.4 |
| 28 | Michigan | 23.2 |
| 29 | Wyoming | 22.8 |
| 30 | Oklahoma | 22.3 |
| 31 | North Dakota | 22.2 |
| 32 | Washington | 21.9 |
| 33 | Indiana | 21.8 |
| 33 | West Virginia | 21.8 |
| 35 | South Carolina | 21.7 |
| 36 | Minnesota | 21.6 |
| 36 | South Dakota | 21.6 |
| 38 | Kansas | 21.5 |
| 39 | Ohio | 21.1 |
| 39 | Texas | 21.1 |
| 41 | Mississippi | 20.6 |
| 41 | Wisconsin | 20.6 |
| 43 | Louisiana | 20.5 |
| 44 | Iowa | 20.3 |
| 45 | New Jersey | 19.8 |
| 46 | Alabama | 19.6 |
| 47 | Nebraska | 19.5 |
| 48 | Missouri | 19.1 |
| 49 | Tennessee | 16.2 |
| 50 | Connecticut | 15.4 |

| | | |
|---|---|---|
| | District of Columbia | 25.9 |

Source: CQ Press using data from U.S. Small Business Administration
"The Small Business Economy 2012" (http://www.sba.gov/advocacy/849/6282)

*Establishment openings and closings represent quarterly business turnover for new and existing establishments, which can belong to small or large firms (seasonally adjusted). Firms can be in more than one state. Rate represents the number of employer firms ceasing operations in 2011 as a percent of existing firms at the beginning of 2011 based on 2010 counts. Some state terminations result in successor firms which are not listed as new firms, thus making terminations higher than formations for most states.

# V. Education

*(Continued)*

*(Continued)*

# Estimated Percent of School-Age Population in Public Schools in 2011

## National Percent = 92.0%*

ALPHA ORDER

| RANK | STATE | PERCENT |
|------|-------|---------|
| 22 | Alabama | 91.8 |
| 3 | Alaska | 98.7 |
| 26 | Arizona | 91.2 |
| 9 | Arkansas | 93.8 |
| 11 | California | 93.4 |
| 6 | Colorado | 95.0 |
| 19 | Connecticut | 92.5 |
| 47 | Delaware | 86.9 |
| 34 | Florida | 90.5 |
| 17 | Georgia | 92.8 |
| 50 | Hawaii | 83.1 |
| 40 | Idaho | 89.3 |
| 20 | Illinois | 92.1 |
| 38 | Indiana | 89.7 |
| 8 | Iowa | 94.4 |
| 16 | Kansas | 93.0 |
| 27 | Kentucky | 91.0 |
| 47 | Louisiana | 86.9 |
| 9 | Maine | 93.8 |
| 47 | Maryland | 86.9 |
| 21 | Massachusetts | 91.9 |
| 18 | Michigan | 92.7 |
| 33 | Minnesota | 90.6 |
| 32 | Mississippi | 90.7 |
| 39 | Missouri | 89.4 |
| 42 | Montana | 88.2 |
| 29 | Nebraska | 90.8 |
| 25 | Nevada | 91.6 |
| 23 | New Hampshire | 91.7 |
| 15 | New Jersey | 93.1 |
| 34 | New Mexico | 90.5 |
| 46 | New York | 87.6 |
| 36 | North Carolina | 89.9 |
| 29 | North Dakota | 90.8 |
| 41 | Ohio | 88.5 |
| 5 | Oklahoma | 98.5 |
| 27 | Oregon | 91.0 |
| 43 | Pennsylvania | 88.0 |
| 43 | Rhode Island | 88.0 |
| 12 | South Carolina | 93.3 |
| 45 | South Dakota | 87.9 |
| 29 | Tennessee | 90.8 |
| 3 | Texas | 98.7 |
| 7 | Utah | 94.7 |
| 1 | Vermont | 102.1 |
| 14 | Virginia | 93.2 |
| 23 | Washington | 91.7 |
| 2 | West Virginia | 100.5 |
| 37 | Wisconsin | 89.8 |
| 12 | Wyoming | 93.3 |

RANK ORDER

| RANK | STATE | PERCENT |
|------|-------|---------|
| 1 | Vermont | 102.1 |
| 2 | West Virginia | 100.5 |
| 3 | Alaska | 98.7 |
| 3 | Texas | 98.7 |
| 5 | Oklahoma | 98.5 |
| 6 | Colorado | 95.0 |
| 7 | Utah | 94.7 |
| 8 | Iowa | 94.4 |
| 9 | Arkansas | 93.8 |
| 9 | Maine | 93.8 |
| 11 | California | 93.4 |
| 12 | South Carolina | 93.3 |
| 12 | Wyoming | 93.3 |
| 14 | Virginia | 93.2 |
| 15 | New Jersey | 93.1 |
| 16 | Kansas | 93.0 |
| 17 | Georgia | 92.8 |
| 18 | Michigan | 92.7 |
| 19 | Connecticut | 92.5 |
| 20 | Illinois | 92.1 |
| 21 | Massachusetts | 91.9 |
| 22 | Alabama | 91.8 |
| 23 | New Hampshire | 91.7 |
| 23 | Washington | 91.7 |
| 25 | Nevada | 91.6 |
| 26 | Arizona | 91.2 |
| 27 | Kentucky | 91.0 |
| 27 | Oregon | 91.0 |
| 29 | Nebraska | 90.8 |
| 29 | North Dakota | 90.8 |
| 29 | Tennessee | 90.8 |
| 32 | Mississippi | 90.7 |
| 33 | Minnesota | 90.6 |
| 34 | Florida | 90.5 |
| 34 | New Mexico | 90.5 |
| 36 | North Carolina | 89.9 |
| 37 | Wisconsin | 89.8 |
| 38 | Indiana | 89.7 |
| 39 | Missouri | 89.4 |
| 40 | Idaho | 89.3 |
| 41 | Ohio | 88.5 |
| 42 | Montana | 88.2 |
| 43 | Pennsylvania | 88.0 |
| 43 | Rhode Island | 88.0 |
| 45 | South Dakota | 87.9 |
| 46 | New York | 87.6 |
| 47 | Delaware | 86.9 |
| 47 | Louisiana | 86.9 |
| 47 | Maryland | 86.9 |
| 50 | Hawaii | 83.1 |

District of Columbia 103.1

Source: CQ Press using data from U.S. Department of Education, National Center for Education Statistics
    "Common Core of Data (CCD) Database" (http://nces.ed.gov/ccd/)
*Estimate based on 2011 Census population estimates for 5- to 17-year-olds compared to estimated 2010-2011 school year
public school student membership.  Student membership figures include counts for pre-kindergarten programs.  Figures higher
than 100 percent reflect using different sources for population and for student membership.

# Regular Public Elementary and Secondary School Districts in 2011

## National Total = 13,592 Districts*

ALPHA ORDER

| RANK | STATE | DISTRICTS | % of USA |
|------|-------|-----------|----------|
| 35 | Alabama | 133 | 1.0% |
| 43 | Alaska | 53 | 0.4% |
| 23 | Arizona | 224 | 1.6% |
| 21 | Arkansas | 239 | 1.8% |
| 2 | California | 955 | 7.0% |
| 27 | Colorado | 178 | 1.3% |
| 30 | Connecticut | 169 | 1.2% |
| 48 | Delaware | 19 | 0.1% |
| 41 | Florida | 67 | 0.5% |
| 26 | Georgia | 180 | 1.3% |
| 50 | Hawaii | 1 | 0.0% |
| 36 | Idaho | 116 | 0.9% |
| 3 | Illinois | 868 | 6.4% |
| 18 | Indiana | 293 | 2.2% |
| 13 | Iowa | 359 | 2.6% |
| 15 | Kansas | 312 | 2.3% |
| 29 | Kentucky | 174 | 1.3% |
| 40 | Louisiana | 70 | 0.5% |
| 22 | Maine | 235 | 1.7% |
| 47 | Maryland | 24 | 0.2% |
| 20 | Massachusetts | 244 | 1.8% |
| 7 | Michigan | 551 | 4.1% |
| 14 | Minnesota | 337 | 2.5% |
| 31 | Mississippi | 152 | 1.1% |
| 9 | Missouri | 522 | 3.8% |
| 12 | Montana | 417 | 3.1% |
| 19 | Nebraska | 251 | 1.8% |
| 49 | Nevada | 17 | 0.1% |
| 27 | New Hampshire | 178 | 1.3% |
| 6 | New Jersey | 613 | 4.5% |
| 38 | New Mexico | 89 | 0.7% |
| 4 | New York | 695 | 5.1% |
| 37 | North Carolina | 115 | 0.8% |
| 25 | North Dakota | 183 | 1.3% |
| 5 | Ohio | 615 | 4.5% |
| 8 | Oklahoma | 526 | 3.9% |
| 24 | Oregon | 186 | 1.4% |
| 10 | Pennsylvania | 500 | 3.7% |
| 46 | Rhode Island | 32 | 0.2% |
| 39 | South Carolina | 86 | 0.6% |
| 31 | South Dakota | 152 | 1.1% |
| 33 | Tennessee | 137 | 1.0% |
| 1 | Texas | 1,031 | 7.6% |
| 45 | Utah | 41 | 0.3% |
| 17 | Vermont | 294 | 2.2% |
| 34 | Virginia | 134 | 1.0% |
| 16 | Washington | 295 | 2.2% |
| 42 | West Virginia | 55 | 0.4% |
| 11 | Wisconsin | 424 | 3.1% |
| 44 | Wyoming | 49 | 0.4% |

RANK ORDER

| RANK | STATE | DISTRICTS | % of USA |
|------|-------|-----------|----------|
| 1 | Texas | 1,031 | 7.6% |
| 2 | California | 955 | 7.0% |
| 3 | Illinois | 868 | 6.4% |
| 4 | New York | 695 | 5.1% |
| 5 | Ohio | 615 | 4.5% |
| 6 | New Jersey | 613 | 4.5% |
| 7 | Michigan | 551 | 4.1% |
| 8 | Oklahoma | 526 | 3.9% |
| 9 | Missouri | 522 | 3.8% |
| 10 | Pennsylvania | 500 | 3.7% |
| 11 | Wisconsin | 424 | 3.1% |
| 12 | Montana | 417 | 3.1% |
| 13 | Iowa | 359 | 2.6% |
| 14 | Minnesota | 337 | 2.5% |
| 15 | Kansas | 312 | 2.3% |
| 16 | Washington | 295 | 2.2% |
| 17 | Vermont | 294 | 2.2% |
| 18 | Indiana | 293 | 2.2% |
| 19 | Nebraska | 251 | 1.8% |
| 20 | Massachusetts | 244 | 1.8% |
| 21 | Arkansas | 239 | 1.8% |
| 22 | Maine | 235 | 1.7% |
| 23 | Arizona | 224 | 1.6% |
| 24 | Oregon | 186 | 1.4% |
| 25 | North Dakota | 183 | 1.3% |
| 26 | Georgia | 180 | 1.3% |
| 27 | Colorado | 178 | 1.3% |
| 27 | New Hampshire | 178 | 1.3% |
| 29 | Kentucky | 174 | 1.3% |
| 30 | Connecticut | 169 | 1.2% |
| 31 | Mississippi | 152 | 1.1% |
| 31 | South Dakota | 152 | 1.1% |
| 33 | Tennessee | 137 | 1.0% |
| 34 | Virginia | 134 | 1.0% |
| 35 | Alabama | 133 | 1.0% |
| 36 | Idaho | 116 | 0.9% |
| 37 | North Carolina | 115 | 0.8% |
| 38 | New Mexico | 89 | 0.7% |
| 39 | South Carolina | 86 | 0.6% |
| 40 | Louisiana | 70 | 0.5% |
| 41 | Florida | 67 | 0.5% |
| 42 | West Virginia | 55 | 0.4% |
| 43 | Alaska | 53 | 0.4% |
| 44 | Wyoming | 49 | 0.4% |
| 45 | Utah | 41 | 0.3% |
| 46 | Rhode Island | 32 | 0.2% |
| 47 | Maryland | 24 | 0.2% |
| 48 | Delaware | 19 | 0.1% |
| 49 | Nevada | 17 | 0.1% |
| 50 | Hawaii | 1 | 0.0% |
| | District of Columbia | 2 | 0.0% |

Source: U.S. Department of Education, National Center for Education Statistics
   "Numbers and Types of Public Elementary and Secondary Education Agencies" (http://nces.ed.gov/pubs2012/2012326.pdf)
*For school year 2010-2011.  Regular school districts are agencies responsible for providing free public education for school-age children residing within their jurisdiction.  Included in these figures are districts that reported having no students.  This can occur when a small district has no pupils or contracts with another district to seducate the students under its jurisdiction.

# Public Elementary and Secondary Schools in 2012

## National Total = 98,328 Schools*

ALPHA ORDER

| RANK | STATE | SCHOOLS | % of USA |
|---|---|---|---|
| 23 | Alabama | 1,618 | 1.6% |
| 44 | Alaska | 511 | 0.5% |
| 15 | Arizona | 2,252 | 2.3% |
| 32 | Arkansas | 1,108 | 1.1% |
| 1 | California | 10,170 | 10.3% |
| 20 | Colorado | 1,813 | 1.8% |
| 31 | Connecticut | 1,150 | 1.2% |
| 50 | Delaware | 221 | 0.2% |
| 5 | Florida | 4,212 | 4.3% |
| 13 | Georgia | 2,388 | 2.4% |
| 49 | Hawaii | 287 | 0.3% |
| 38 | Idaho | 762 | 0.8% |
| 4 | Illinois | 4,336 | 4.4% |
| 18 | Indiana | 1,933 | 2.0% |
| 27 | Iowa | 1,411 | 1.4% |
| 28 | Kansas | 1,359 | 1.4% |
| 24 | Kentucky | 1,565 | 1.6% |
| 26 | Louisiana | 1,437 | 1.5% |
| 42 | Maine | 621 | 0.6% |
| 25 | Maryland | 1,451 | 1.5% |
| 19 | Massachusetts | 1,835 | 1.9% |
| 7 | Michigan | 3,550 | 3.6% |
| 12 | Minnesota | 2,392 | 2.4% |
| 34 | Mississippi | 1,069 | 1.1% |
| 11 | Missouri | 2,408 | 2.4% |
| 37 | Montana | 826 | 0.8% |
| 33 | Nebraska | 1,090 | 1.1% |
| 41 | Nevada | 649 | 0.7% |
| 45 | New Hampshire | 477 | 0.5% |
| 9 | New Jersey | 2,596 | 2.6% |
| 36 | New Mexico | 866 | 0.9% |
| 3 | New York | 4,752 | 4.8% |
| 10 | North Carolina | 2,577 | 2.6% |
| 43 | North Dakota | 513 | 0.5% |
| 6 | Ohio | 3,714 | 3.8% |
| 22 | Oklahoma | 1,774 | 1.8% |
| 29 | Oregon | 1,261 | 1.3% |
| 8 | Pennsylvania | 3,181 | 3.2% |
| 48 | Rhode Island | 308 | 0.3% |
| 30 | South Carolina | 1,223 | 1.2% |
| 40 | South Dakota | 704 | 0.7% |
| 21 | Tennessee | 1,802 | 1.8% |
| 2 | Texas | 8,697 | 8.8% |
| 35 | Utah | 1,020 | 1.0% |
| 47 | Vermont | 320 | 0.3% |
| 17 | Virginia | 2,170 | 2.2% |
| 14 | Washington | 2,365 | 2.4% |
| 39 | West Virginia | 759 | 0.8% |
| 16 | Wisconsin | 2,243 | 2.3% |
| 46 | Wyoming | 354 | 0.4% |

RANK ORDER

| RANK | STATE | SCHOOLS | % of USA |
|---|---|---|---|
| 1 | California | 10,170 | 10.3% |
| 2 | Texas | 8,697 | 8.8% |
| 3 | New York | 4,752 | 4.8% |
| 4 | Illinois | 4,336 | 4.4% |
| 5 | Florida | 4,212 | 4.3% |
| 6 | Ohio | 3,714 | 3.8% |
| 7 | Michigan | 3,550 | 3.6% |
| 8 | Pennsylvania | 3,181 | 3.2% |
| 9 | New Jersey | 2,596 | 2.6% |
| 10 | North Carolina | 2,577 | 2.6% |
| 11 | Missouri | 2,408 | 2.4% |
| 12 | Minnesota | 2,392 | 2.4% |
| 13 | Georgia | 2,388 | 2.4% |
| 14 | Washington | 2,365 | 2.4% |
| 15 | Arizona | 2,252 | 2.3% |
| 16 | Wisconsin | 2,243 | 2.3% |
| 17 | Virginia | 2,170 | 2.2% |
| 18 | Indiana | 1,933 | 2.0% |
| 19 | Massachusetts | 1,835 | 1.9% |
| 20 | Colorado | 1,813 | 1.8% |
| 21 | Tennessee | 1,802 | 1.8% |
| 22 | Oklahoma | 1,774 | 1.8% |
| 23 | Alabama | 1,618 | 1.6% |
| 24 | Kentucky | 1,565 | 1.6% |
| 25 | Maryland | 1,451 | 1.5% |
| 26 | Louisiana | 1,437 | 1.5% |
| 27 | Iowa | 1,411 | 1.4% |
| 28 | Kansas | 1,359 | 1.4% |
| 29 | Oregon | 1,261 | 1.3% |
| 30 | South Carolina | 1,223 | 1.2% |
| 31 | Connecticut | 1,150 | 1.2% |
| 32 | Arkansas | 1,108 | 1.1% |
| 33 | Nebraska | 1,090 | 1.1% |
| 34 | Mississippi | 1,069 | 1.1% |
| 35 | Utah | 1,020 | 1.0% |
| 36 | New Mexico | 866 | 0.9% |
| 37 | Montana | 826 | 0.8% |
| 38 | Idaho | 762 | 0.8% |
| 39 | West Virginia | 759 | 0.8% |
| 40 | South Dakota | 704 | 0.7% |
| 41 | Nevada | 649 | 0.7% |
| 42 | Maine | 621 | 0.6% |
| 43 | North Dakota | 513 | 0.5% |
| 44 | Alaska | 511 | 0.5% |
| 45 | New Hampshire | 477 | 0.5% |
| 46 | Wyoming | 354 | 0.4% |
| 47 | Vermont | 320 | 0.3% |
| 48 | Rhode Island | 308 | 0.3% |
| 49 | Hawaii | 287 | 0.3% |
| 50 | Delaware | 221 | 0.2% |
|  | District of Columbia | 228 | 0.2% |

Source: U.S. Department of Education, National Center for Education Statistics
   "Selected Statistics From the Common Core of Data: School Year 2011-12" (http://nces.ed.gov/pubs2013/2013441.pdf)
*For school year 2011-2012.

# Private Elementary and Secondary Schools in 2012

## National Total = 30,861 Schools*

ALPHA ORDER

| RANK | STATE | SCHOOLS | % of USA |
|---|---|---|---|
| 25 | Alabama | 402 | 1.3% |
| 48 | Alaska | 51 | 0.2% |
| 28 | Arizona | 341 | 1.1% |
| 32 | Arkansas | 234 | 0.8% |
| 1 | California | 3,479 | 11.3% |
| 22 | Colorado | 414 | 1.3% |
| 23 | Connecticut | 406 | 1.3% |
| 42 | Delaware | 124 | 0.4% |
| 4 | Florida | 1,880 | 6.1% |
| 16 | Georgia | 710 | 2.3% |
| 41 | Hawaii | 134 | 0.4% |
| 42 | Idaho | 124 | 0.4% |
| 5 | Illinois | 1,572 | 5.1% |
| 9 | Indiana | 969 | 3.1% |
| 30 | Iowa | 300 | 1.0% |
| 24 | Kansas** | 404 | 1.3% |
| 29 | Kentucky | 329 | 1.1% |
| 26 | Louisiana | 394 | 1.3% |
| 38 | Maine | 157 | 0.5% |
| 15 | Maryland | 736 | 2.4% |
| 12 | Massachusetts | 803 | 2.6% |
| 13 | Michigan | 791 | 2.6% |
| 20 | Minnesota | 504 | 1.6% |
| 34 | Mississippi | 221 | 0.7% |
| 8 | Missouri** | 1,270 | 4.1% |
| 46 | Montana | 111 | 0.4% |
| 33 | Nebraska | 222 | 0.7% |
| 38 | Nevada | 157 | 0.5% |
| 31 | New Hampshire | 278 | 0.9% |
| 7 | New Jersey | 1,289 | 4.2% |
| 36 | New Mexico | 174 | 0.6% |
| 3 | New York | 1,931 | 6.3% |
| 17 | North Carolina | 642 | 2.1% |
| 49 | North Dakota | 46 | 0.1% |
| 10 | Ohio | 968 | 3.1% |
| 35 | Oklahoma | 181 | 0.6% |
| 21 | Oregon | 432 | 1.4% |
| 2 | Pennsylvania | 2,325 | 7.5% |
| 40 | Rhode Island | 144 | 0.5% |
| 27 | South Carolina | 378 | 1.2% |
| 47 | South Dakota | 74 | 0.2% |
| 19 | Tennessee | 512 | 1.7% |
| 6 | Texas | 1,502 | 4.9% |
| 37 | Utah | 160 | 0.5% |
| 45 | Vermont | 114 | 0.4% |
| 14 | Virginia | 755 | 2.4% |
| 18 | Washington | 633 | 2.1% |
| 42 | West Virginia | 124 | 0.4% |
| 11 | Wisconsin | 844 | 2.7% |
| 50 | Wyoming | 38 | 0.1% |

RANK ORDER

| RANK | STATE | SCHOOLS | % of USA |
|---|---|---|---|
| 1 | California | 3,479 | 11.3% |
| 2 | Pennsylvania | 2,325 | 7.5% |
| 3 | New York | 1,931 | 6.3% |
| 4 | Florida | 1,880 | 6.1% |
| 5 | Illinois | 1,572 | 5.1% |
| 6 | Texas | 1,502 | 4.9% |
| 7 | New Jersey | 1,289 | 4.2% |
| 8 | Missouri** | 1,270 | 4.1% |
| 9 | Indiana | 969 | 3.1% |
| 10 | Ohio | 968 | 3.1% |
| 11 | Wisconsin | 844 | 2.7% |
| 12 | Massachusetts | 803 | 2.6% |
| 13 | Michigan | 791 | 2.6% |
| 14 | Virginia | 755 | 2.4% |
| 15 | Maryland | 736 | 2.4% |
| 16 | Georgia | 710 | 2.3% |
| 17 | North Carolina | 642 | 2.1% |
| 18 | Washington | 633 | 2.1% |
| 19 | Tennessee | 512 | 1.7% |
| 20 | Minnesota | 504 | 1.6% |
| 21 | Oregon | 432 | 1.4% |
| 22 | Colorado | 414 | 1.3% |
| 23 | Connecticut | 406 | 1.3% |
| 24 | Kansas** | 404 | 1.3% |
| 25 | Alabama | 402 | 1.3% |
| 26 | Louisiana | 394 | 1.3% |
| 27 | South Carolina | 378 | 1.2% |
| 28 | Arizona | 341 | 1.1% |
| 29 | Kentucky | 329 | 1.1% |
| 30 | Iowa | 300 | 1.0% |
| 31 | New Hampshire | 278 | 0.9% |
| 32 | Arkansas | 234 | 0.8% |
| 33 | Nebraska | 222 | 0.7% |
| 34 | Mississippi | 221 | 0.7% |
| 35 | Oklahoma | 181 | 0.6% |
| 36 | New Mexico | 174 | 0.6% |
| 37 | Utah | 160 | 0.5% |
| 38 | Maine | 157 | 0.5% |
| 38 | Nevada | 157 | 0.5% |
| 40 | Rhode Island | 144 | 0.5% |
| 41 | Hawaii | 134 | 0.4% |
| 42 | Delaware | 124 | 0.4% |
| 42 | Idaho | 124 | 0.4% |
| 42 | West Virginia | 124 | 0.4% |
| 45 | Vermont | 114 | 0.4% |
| 46 | Montana | 111 | 0.4% |
| 47 | South Dakota | 74 | 0.2% |
| 48 | Alaska | 51 | 0.2% |
| 49 | North Dakota | 46 | 0.1% |
| 50 | Wyoming | 38 | 0.1% |
| | District of Columbia | 79 | 0.3% |

Source: U.S. Department of Education, National Center for Education Statistics
    "Characteristics of Private Schools in the United States" (http://nces.ed.gov/pubsearch/pubsinfo.asp?pubid=2013316)
*For school year 2011-2012.  Includes private schools that provide instruction for one or more grades kindergarten through 12 (or comparable ungraded levels).
**Interpret data for these states with caution.

# Private Elementary and Secondary School Enrollment in 2012

## National Total = 4,494,845 Students*

ALPHA ORDER

| RANK | STATE | STUDENTS | % of USA |
|---|---|---|---|
| 22 | Alabama | 67,479 | 1.5% |
| 49 | Alaska | 4,087 | 0.1% |
| 29 | Arizona | 43,134 | 1.0% |
| 35 | Arkansas | 25,164 | 0.6% |
| 1 | California | 523,088 | 11.6% |
| 27 | Colorado | 45,697 | 1.0% |
| 24 | Connecticut | 58,399 | 1.3% |
| 37 | Delaware | 21,667 | 0.5% |
| 3 | Florida | 284,238 | 6.3% |
| 9 | Georgia | 120,488 | 2.7% |
| 33 | Hawaii | 33,994 | 0.8% |
| 44 | Idaho | 11,262 | 0.3% |
| 5 | Illinois | 226,265 | 5.0% |
| 16 | Indiana | 111,872 | 2.5% |
| 25 | Iowa | 58,180 | 1.3% |
| 31 | Kansas | 39,016 | 0.9% |
| 23 | Kentucky | 60,590 | 1.3% |
| 14 | Louisiana | 112,645 | 2.5% |
| 41 | Maine | 17,011 | 0.4% |
| 10 | Maryland | 117,657 | 2.6% |
| 13 | Massachusetts | 112,684 | 2.5% |
| 11 | Michigan | 116,461 | 2.6% |
| 21 | Minnesota | 76,693 | 1.7% |
| 28 | Mississippi | 45,419 | 1.0% |
| 12 | Missouri | 115,553 | 2.6% |
| 46 | Montana | 8,561 | 0.2% |
| 32 | Nebraska | 36,163 | 0.8% |
| 39 | Nevada | 20,396 | 0.5% |
| 38 | New Hampshire | 21,264 | 0.5% |
| 8 | New Jersey | 166,508 | 3.7% |
| 40 | New Mexico | 19,360 | 0.4% |
| 2 | New York | 430,293 | 9.6% |
| 17 | North Carolina | 106,661 | 2.4% |
| 48 | North Dakota | 6,535 | 0.1% |
| 7 | Ohio | 190,810 | 4.2% |
| 34 | Oklahoma | 30,063 | 0.7% |
| 30 | Oregon | 42,694 | 0.9% |
| 4 | Pennsylvania | 240,993 | 5.4% |
| 36 | Rhode Island | 22,539 | 0.5% |
| 26 | South Carolina | 47,259 | 1.1% |
| 45 | South Dakota | 10,266 | 0.2% |
| 19 | Tennessee | 81,499 | 1.8% |
| 6 | Texas | 223,469 | 5.0% |
| 42 | Utah | 15,498 | 0.3% |
| 47 | Vermont | 8,323 | 0.2% |
| 18 | Virginia | 98,439 | 2.2% |
| 20 | Washington | 77,279 | 1.7% |
| 43 | West Virginia | 11,890 | 0.3% |
| 15 | Wisconsin | 112,025 | 2.5% |
| 50 | Wyoming | 1,947 | 0.0% |

RANK ORDER

| RANK | STATE | STUDENTS | % of USA |
|---|---|---|---|
| 1 | California | 523,088 | 11.6% |
| 2 | New York | 430,293 | 9.6% |
| 3 | Florida | 284,238 | 6.3% |
| 4 | Pennsylvania | 240,993 | 5.4% |
| 5 | Illinois | 226,265 | 5.0% |
| 6 | Texas | 223,469 | 5.0% |
| 7 | Ohio | 190,810 | 4.2% |
| 8 | New Jersey | 166,508 | 3.7% |
| 9 | Georgia | 120,488 | 2.7% |
| 10 | Maryland | 117,657 | 2.6% |
| 11 | Michigan | 116,461 | 2.6% |
| 12 | Missouri | 115,553 | 2.6% |
| 13 | Massachusetts | 112,684 | 2.5% |
| 14 | Louisiana | 112,645 | 2.5% |
| 15 | Wisconsin | 112,025 | 2.5% |
| 16 | Indiana | 111,872 | 2.5% |
| 17 | North Carolina | 106,661 | 2.4% |
| 18 | Virginia | 98,439 | 2.2% |
| 19 | Tennessee | 81,499 | 1.8% |
| 20 | Washington | 77,279 | 1.7% |
| 21 | Minnesota | 76,693 | 1.7% |
| 22 | Alabama | 67,479 | 1.5% |
| 23 | Kentucky | 60,590 | 1.3% |
| 24 | Connecticut | 58,399 | 1.3% |
| 25 | Iowa | 58,180 | 1.3% |
| 26 | South Carolina | 47,259 | 1.1% |
| 27 | Colorado | 45,697 | 1.0% |
| 28 | Mississippi | 45,419 | 1.0% |
| 29 | Arizona | 43,134 | 1.0% |
| 30 | Oregon | 42,694 | 0.9% |
| 31 | Kansas | 39,016 | 0.9% |
| 32 | Nebraska | 36,163 | 0.8% |
| 33 | Hawaii | 33,994 | 0.8% |
| 34 | Oklahoma | 30,063 | 0.7% |
| 35 | Arkansas | 25,164 | 0.6% |
| 36 | Rhode Island | 22,539 | 0.5% |
| 37 | Delaware | 21,667 | 0.5% |
| 38 | New Hampshire | 21,264 | 0.5% |
| 39 | Nevada | 20,396 | 0.5% |
| 40 | New Mexico | 19,360 | 0.4% |
| 41 | Maine | 17,011 | 0.4% |
| 42 | Utah | 15,498 | 0.3% |
| 43 | West Virginia | 11,890 | 0.3% |
| 44 | Idaho | 11,262 | 0.3% |
| 45 | South Dakota | 10,266 | 0.2% |
| 46 | Montana | 8,561 | 0.2% |
| 47 | Vermont | 8,323 | 0.2% |
| 48 | North Dakota | 6,535 | 0.1% |
| 49 | Alaska | 4,087 | 0.1% |
| 50 | Wyoming | 1,947 | 0.0% |
| | District of Columbia | 15,368 | 0.3% |

Source: U.S. Department of Education, National Center for Education Statistics
"Characteristics of Private Schools in the United States" (http://nces.ed.gov/pubsearch/pubsinfo.asp?pubid=2013316)
*For school year 2011-2012. Includes private schools that provide instruction for one or more grades kindergarten through 12 (or comparable ungraded levels).

# Enrollment in Public Elementary and Secondary Schools in 2012

## National Total = 49,521,669 Students*

| RANK | STATE | STUDENTS | % of USA |
|------|-------|----------|----------|
| 23 | Alabama | 744,621 | 1.5% |
| 45 | Alaska | 131,167 | 0.3% |
| 13 | Arizona | 1,080,319 | 2.2% |
| 34 | Arkansas | 483,114 | 1.0% |
| 1 | California | 6,287,834 | 12.7% |
| 20 | Colorado | 854,265 | 1.7% |
| 30 | Connecticut | 554,437 | 1.1% |
| 46 | Delaware | 128,946 | 0.3% |
| 4 | Florida | 2,668,156 | 5.4% |
| 8 | Georgia | 1,685,016 | 3.4% |
| 42 | Hawaii | 182,706 | 0.4% |
| 39 | Idaho | 279,873 | 0.6% |
| 5 | Illinois | 2,083,097 | 4.2% |
| 15 | Indiana | 1,040,765 | 2.1% |
| 31 | Iowa | 495,870 | 1.0% |
| 33 | Kansas | 486,108 | 1.0% |
| 26 | Kentucky | 681,987 | 1.4% |
| 25 | Louisiana | 703,390 | 1.4% |
| 41 | Maine | 188,969 | 0.4% |
| 21 | Maryland | 854,086 | 1.7% |
| 17 | Massachusetts | 953,369 | 1.9% |
| 9 | Michigan | 1,573,537 | 3.2% |
| 22 | Minnesota | 839,738 | 1.7% |
| 32 | Mississippi | 490,619 | 1.0% |
| 18 | Missouri | 916,584 | 1.9% |
| 44 | Montana | 142,349 | 0.3% |
| 37 | Nebraska | 301,296 | 0.6% |
| 35 | Nevada | 439,634 | 0.9% |
| 40 | New Hampshire | 191,900 | 0.4% |
| 11 | New Jersey | 1,356,431 | 2.7% |
| 36 | New Mexico | 337,225 | 0.7% |
| 3 | New York | 2,704,718 | 5.5% |
| 10 | North Carolina | 1,507,864 | 3.0% |
| 48 | North Dakota | 97,646 | 0.2% |
| 7 | Ohio | 1,740,030 | 3.5% |
| 27 | Oklahoma | 666,120 | 1.3% |
| 29 | Oregon | 568,208 | 1.1% |
| 6 | Pennsylvania | 1,771,395 | 3.6% |
| 43 | Rhode Island | 142,854 | 0.3% |
| 24 | South Carolina | 727,186 | 1.5% |
| 47 | South Dakota | 128,016 | 0.3% |
| 16 | Tennessee | 999,693 | 2.0% |
| 2 | Texas | 5,000,470 | 10.1% |
| 28 | Utah | 598,832 | 1.2% |
| 50 | Vermont | 89,908 | 0.2% |
| 12 | Virginia | 1,257,883 | 2.5% |
| 14 | Washington | 1,045,453 | 2.1% |
| 38 | West Virginia | 282,870 | 0.6% |
| 19 | Wisconsin | 871,105 | 1.8% |
| 49 | Wyoming | 90,099 | 0.2% |

### RANK ORDER

| RANK | STATE | STUDENTS | % of USA |
|------|-------|----------|----------|
| 1 | California | 6,287,834 | 12.7% |
| 2 | Texas | 5,000,470 | 10.1% |
| 3 | New York | 2,704,718 | 5.5% |
| 4 | Florida | 2,668,156 | 5.4% |
| 5 | Illinois | 2,083,097 | 4.2% |
| 6 | Pennsylvania | 1,771,395 | 3.6% |
| 7 | Ohio | 1,740,030 | 3.5% |
| 8 | Georgia | 1,685,016 | 3.4% |
| 9 | Michigan | 1,573,537 | 3.2% |
| 10 | North Carolina | 1,507,864 | 3.0% |
| 11 | New Jersey | 1,356,431 | 2.7% |
| 12 | Virginia | 1,257,883 | 2.5% |
| 13 | Arizona | 1,080,319 | 2.2% |
| 14 | Washington | 1,045,453 | 2.1% |
| 15 | Indiana | 1,040,765 | 2.1% |
| 16 | Tennessee | 999,693 | 2.0% |
| 17 | Massachusetts | 953,369 | 1.9% |
| 18 | Missouri | 916,584 | 1.9% |
| 19 | Wisconsin | 871,105 | 1.8% |
| 20 | Colorado | 854,265 | 1.7% |
| 21 | Maryland | 854,086 | 1.7% |
| 22 | Minnesota | 839,738 | 1.7% |
| 23 | Alabama | 744,621 | 1.5% |
| 24 | South Carolina | 727,186 | 1.5% |
| 25 | Louisiana | 703,390 | 1.4% |
| 26 | Kentucky | 681,987 | 1.4% |
| 27 | Oklahoma | 666,120 | 1.3% |
| 28 | Utah | 598,832 | 1.2% |
| 29 | Oregon | 568,208 | 1.1% |
| 30 | Connecticut | 554,437 | 1.1% |
| 31 | Iowa | 495,870 | 1.0% |
| 32 | Mississippi | 490,619 | 1.0% |
| 33 | Kansas | 486,108 | 1.0% |
| 34 | Arkansas | 483,114 | 1.0% |
| 35 | Nevada | 439,634 | 0.9% |
| 36 | New Mexico | 337,225 | 0.7% |
| 37 | Nebraska | 301,296 | 0.6% |
| 38 | West Virginia | 282,870 | 0.6% |
| 39 | Idaho | 279,873 | 0.6% |
| 40 | New Hampshire | 191,900 | 0.4% |
| 41 | Maine | 188,969 | 0.4% |
| 42 | Hawaii | 182,706 | 0.4% |
| 43 | Rhode Island | 142,854 | 0.3% |
| 44 | Montana | 142,349 | 0.3% |
| 45 | Alaska | 131,167 | 0.3% |
| 46 | Delaware | 128,946 | 0.3% |
| 47 | South Dakota | 128,016 | 0.3% |
| 48 | North Dakota | 97,646 | 0.2% |
| 49 | Wyoming | 90,099 | 0.2% |
| 50 | Vermont | 89,908 | 0.2% |
| | District of Columbia | 73,911 | 0.1% |

ALPHA ORDER

Source: U.S. Department of Education, National Center for Education Statistics
"Selected Statistics From the Common Core of Data: School Year 2011-12" (http://nces.ed.gov/pubs2013/2013441.pdf)
*For school year 2011-2012.

# Public Elementary and Secondary School Teachers in 2012

## National Total = 3,103,263 Teachers*

ALPHA ORDER

| RANK | STATE | TEACHERS | % of USA |
|---|---|---|---|
| 24 | Alabama | 47,723 | 1.5% |
| 49 | Alaska | 8,088 | 0.3% |
| 21 | Arizona | 50,800 | 1.6% |
| 31 | Arkansas | 33,983 | 1.1% |
| 2 | California | 268,689 | 8.7% |
| 23 | Colorado | 48,078 | 1.5% |
| 26 | Connecticut | 43,805 | 1.4% |
| 46 | Delaware | 8,587 | 0.3% |
| 4 | Florida | 175,006 | 5.6% |
| 7 | Georgia | 111,133 | 3.6% |
| 42 | Hawaii | 11,458 | 0.4% |
| 39 | Idaho | 15,990 | 0.5% |
| 5 | Illinois | 131,777 | 4.2% |
| 16 | Indiana | 62,339 | 2.0% |
| 30 | Iowa | 34,658 | 1.1% |
| 29 | Kansas | 37,407 | 1.2% |
| 27 | Kentucky | 41,860 | 1.3% |
| 22 | Louisiana | 48,657 | 1.6% |
| 41 | Maine | 14,888 | 0.5% |
| 17 | Maryland | 57,589 | 1.9% |
| 13 | Massachusetts | 69,342 | 2.2% |
| 12 | Michigan | 86,997 | 2.8% |
| 20 | Minnesota | 52,832 | 1.7% |
| 32 | Mississippi | 32,007 | 1.0% |
| 15 | Missouri | 66,252 | 2.1% |
| 44 | Montana | 10,153 | 0.3% |
| 35 | Nebraska | 22,182 | 0.7% |
| 37 | Nevada | 21,132 | 0.7% |
| 40 | New Hampshire | 15,049 | 0.5% |
| 8 | New Jersey | 109,719 | 3.5% |
| 36 | New Mexico | 21,957 | 0.7% |
| 3 | New York | 209,527 | 6.8% |
| 10 | North Carolina | 97,308 | 3.1% |
| 47 | North Dakota | 8,525 | 0.3% |
| 9 | Ohio | 107,972 | 3.5% |
| 28 | Oklahoma | 41,349 | 1.3% |
| 33 | Oregon | 26,791 | 0.9% |
| 6 | Pennsylvania | 124,646 | 4.0% |
| 43 | Rhode Island | 11,414 | 0.4% |
| 25 | South Carolina | 46,782 | 1.5% |
| 45 | South Dakota | 9,247 | 0.3% |
| 14 | Tennessee | 66,382 | 2.1% |
| 1 | Texas | 324,282 | 10.4% |
| 34 | Utah | 25,970 | 0.8% |
| 48 | Vermont | 8,364 | 0.3% |
| 11 | Virginia | 90,832 | 2.9% |
| 19 | Washington | 53,119 | 1.7% |
| 38 | West Virginia | 20,247 | 0.7% |
| 18 | Wisconsin | 56,245 | 1.8% |
| 50 | Wyoming | 7,847 | 0.3% |

RANK ORDER

| RANK | STATE | TEACHERS | % of USA |
|---|---|---|---|
| 1 | Texas | 324,282 | 10.4% |
| 2 | California | 268,689 | 8.7% |
| 3 | New York | 209,527 | 6.8% |
| 4 | Florida | 175,006 | 5.6% |
| 5 | Illinois | 131,777 | 4.2% |
| 6 | Pennsylvania | 124,646 | 4.0% |
| 7 | Georgia | 111,133 | 3.6% |
| 8 | New Jersey | 109,719 | 3.5% |
| 9 | Ohio | 107,972 | 3.5% |
| 10 | North Carolina | 97,308 | 3.1% |
| 11 | Virginia | 90,832 | 2.9% |
| 12 | Michigan | 86,997 | 2.8% |
| 13 | Massachusetts | 69,342 | 2.2% |
| 14 | Tennessee | 66,382 | 2.1% |
| 15 | Missouri | 66,252 | 2.1% |
| 16 | Indiana | 62,339 | 2.0% |
| 17 | Maryland | 57,589 | 1.9% |
| 18 | Wisconsin | 56,245 | 1.8% |
| 19 | Washington | 53,119 | 1.7% |
| 20 | Minnesota | 52,832 | 1.7% |
| 21 | Arizona | 50,800 | 1.6% |
| 22 | Louisiana | 48,657 | 1.6% |
| 23 | Colorado | 48,078 | 1.5% |
| 24 | Alabama | 47,723 | 1.5% |
| 25 | South Carolina | 46,782 | 1.5% |
| 26 | Connecticut | 43,805 | 1.4% |
| 27 | Kentucky | 41,860 | 1.3% |
| 28 | Oklahoma | 41,349 | 1.3% |
| 29 | Kansas | 37,407 | 1.2% |
| 30 | Iowa | 34,658 | 1.1% |
| 31 | Arkansas | 33,983 | 1.1% |
| 32 | Mississippi | 32,007 | 1.0% |
| 33 | Oregon | 26,791 | 0.9% |
| 34 | Utah | 25,970 | 0.8% |
| 35 | Nebraska | 22,182 | 0.7% |
| 36 | New Mexico | 21,957 | 0.7% |
| 37 | Nevada | 21,132 | 0.7% |
| 38 | West Virginia | 20,247 | 0.7% |
| 39 | Idaho | 15,990 | 0.5% |
| 40 | New Hampshire | 15,049 | 0.5% |
| 41 | Maine | 14,888 | 0.5% |
| 42 | Hawaii | 11,458 | 0.4% |
| 43 | Rhode Island | 11,414 | 0.4% |
| 44 | Montana | 10,153 | 0.3% |
| 45 | South Dakota | 9,247 | 0.3% |
| 46 | Delaware | 8,587 | 0.3% |
| 47 | North Dakota | 8,525 | 0.3% |
| 48 | Vermont | 8,364 | 0.3% |
| 49 | Alaska | 8,088 | 0.3% |
| 50 | Wyoming | 7,847 | 0.3% |
| | District of Columbia | 6,278 | 0.2% |

Source: U.S. Department of Education, National Center for Education Statistics
"Selected Statistics From the Common Core of Data: School Year 2011-12" (http://nces.ed.gov/pubs2013/2013441.pdf)
*For school year 2011-2012. Counts are full-time equivalent figures.

# Pupil-Teacher Ratio in Public Elementary and Secondary Schools in 2012

## National Ratio = 16.0 Pupils Per Teacher*

| ALPHA ORDER | | | | RANK ORDER | | |
|---|---|---|---|---|---|---|
| RANK | STATE | RATIO | | RANK | STATE | RATIO |
| 18 | Alabama | 15.6 | | 1 | California | 23.4 |
| 12 | Alaska | 16.2 | | 2 | Utah | 23.1 |
| 3 | Arizona | 21.3 | | 3 | Arizona | 21.3 |
| 32 | Arkansas | 14.2 | | 4 | Oregon | 21.2 |
| 1 | California | 23.4 | | 5 | Nevada | 20.8 |
| 8 | Colorado | 17.8 | | 6 | Washington | 19.7 |
| 44 | Connecticut | 12.7 | | 7 | Michigan | 18.1 |
| 28 | Delaware | 15.0 | | 8 | Colorado | 17.8 |
| 25 | Florida | 15.2 | | 9 | Idaho | 17.5 |
| 25 | Georgia | 15.2 | | 10 | Indiana | 16.7 |
| 15 | Hawaii | 15.9 | | 11 | Kentucky | 16.3 |
| 9 | Idaho | 17.5 | | 12 | Alaska | 16.2 |
| 17 | Illinois | 15.8 | | 13 | Ohio | 16.1 |
| 10 | Indiana | 16.7 | | 13 | Oklahoma | 16.1 |
| 31 | Iowa | 14.3 | | 15 | Hawaii | 15.9 |
| 41 | Kansas | 13.0 | | 15 | Minnesota | 15.9 |
| 11 | Kentucky | 16.3 | | 17 | Illinois | 15.8 |
| 30 | Louisiana | 14.5 | | 18 | Alabama | 15.6 |
| 44 | Maine | 12.7 | | 19 | North Carolina | 15.5 |
| 29 | Maryland | 14.8 | | 19 | South Carolina | 15.5 |
| 39 | Massachusetts | 13.7 | | 19 | Wisconsin | 15.5 |
| 7 | Michigan | 18.1 | | 22 | New Mexico | 15.4 |
| 15 | Minnesota | 15.9 | | 22 | Texas | 15.4 |
| 24 | Mississippi | 15.3 | | 24 | Mississippi | 15.3 |
| 36 | Missouri | 13.8 | | 25 | Florida | 15.2 |
| 34 | Montana | 14.0 | | 25 | Georgia | 15.2 |
| 40 | Nebraska | 13.6 | | 27 | Tennessee | 15.1 |
| 5 | Nevada | 20.8 | | 28 | Delaware | 15.0 |
| 43 | New Hampshire | 12.8 | | 29 | Maryland | 14.8 |
| 47 | New Jersey | 12.4 | | 30 | Louisiana | 14.5 |
| 22 | New Mexico | 15.4 | | 31 | Iowa | 14.3 |
| 42 | New York | 12.9 | | 32 | Arkansas | 14.2 |
| 19 | North Carolina | 15.5 | | 32 | Pennsylvania | 14.2 |
| 48 | North Dakota | 11.5 | | 34 | Montana | 14.0 |
| 13 | Ohio | 16.1 | | 34 | West Virginia | 14.0 |
| 13 | Oklahoma | 16.1 | | 36 | Missouri | 13.8 |
| 4 | Oregon | 21.2 | | 36 | South Dakota | 13.8 |
| 32 | Pennsylvania | 14.2 | | 36 | Virginia | 13.8 |
| 46 | Rhode Island | 12.5 | | 39 | Massachusetts | 13.7 |
| 19 | South Carolina | 15.5 | | 40 | Nebraska | 13.6 |
| 36 | South Dakota | 13.8 | | 41 | Kansas | 13.0 |
| 27 | Tennessee | 15.1 | | 42 | New York | 12.9 |
| 22 | Texas | 15.4 | | 43 | New Hampshire | 12.8 |
| 2 | Utah | 23.1 | | 44 | Connecticut | 12.7 |
| 50 | Vermont | 10.7 | | 44 | Maine | 12.7 |
| 36 | Virginia | 13.8 | | 46 | Rhode Island | 12.5 |
| 6 | Washington | 19.7 | | 47 | New Jersey | 12.4 |
| 34 | West Virginia | 14.0 | | 48 | North Dakota | 11.5 |
| 19 | Wisconsin | 15.5 | | 48 | Wyoming | 11.5 |
| 48 | Wyoming | 11.5 | | 50 | Vermont | 10.7 |
| | | | | | District of Columbia | 11.8 |

Source: U.S. Department of Education, National Center for Education Statistics
"Selected Statistics From the Common Core of Data: School Year 2011-12" (http://nces.ed.gov/pubs2013/2013441.pdf)
*For school year 2011-2012. Based on full-time equivalency counts of teachers.

# Estimated Average Salary of Public School Teachers in 2013
## (National Education Association)
## National Average = $56,383*

ALPHA ORDER

| RANK | STATE | SALARY |
|------|-------|--------|
| 38 | Alabama | $47,949 |
| 6 | Alaska | 65,468 |
| 29 | Arizona | 49,885 |
| 44 | Arkansas | 46,632 |
| 4 | California | 69,324 |
| 31 | Colorado | 49,844 |
| 3 | Connecticut | 69,766 |
| 11 | Delaware | 59,679 |
| 43 | Florida | 46,944 |
| 22 | Georgia | 52,880 |
| 20 | Hawaii | 54,300 |
| 32 | Idaho | 49,734 |
| 12 | Illinois | 59,113 |
| 25 | Indiana | 51,456 |
| 24 | Iowa | 51,528 |
| 41 | Kansas | 47,464 |
| 27 | Kentucky | 50,326 |
| 26 | Louisiana | 51,381 |
| 36 | Maine | 48,119 |
| 7 | Maryland | 65,265 |
| 2 | Massachusetts | 73,129 |
| 10 | Michigan | 61,560 |
| 16 | Minnesota | 56,268 |
| 49 | Mississippi | 41,994 |
| 40 | Missouri | 47,517 |
| 28 | Montana | 49,999 |
| 34 | Nebraska | 48,931 |
| 17 | Nevada | 55,957 |
| 18 | New Hampshire | 55,599 |
| 5 | New Jersey | 68,797 |
| 45 | New Mexico | 46,573 |
| 1 | New York | 75,279 |
| 47 | North Carolina | 45,947 |
| 42 | North Dakota | 47,344 |
| 14 | Ohio | 58,092 |
| 48 | Oklahoma | 44,128 |
| 13 | Oregon | 58,758 |
| 8 | Pennsylvania | 63,521 |
| 9 | Rhode Island | 63,474 |
| 39 | South Carolina | 47,924 |
| 50 | South Dakota | 39,580 |
| 35 | Tennessee | 48,289 |
| 37 | Texas | 48,110 |
| 33 | Utah | 49,393 |
| 23 | Vermont | 52,526 |
| 30 | Virginia | 49,869 |
| 21 | Washington | 53,571 |
| 46 | West Virginia | 46,405 |
| 19 | Wisconsin | 55,171 |
| 15 | Wyoming | 57,920 |

RANK ORDER

| RANK | STATE | SALARY |
|------|-------|--------|
| 1 | New York | $75,279 |
| 2 | Massachusetts | 73,129 |
| 3 | Connecticut | 69,766 |
| 4 | California | 69,324 |
| 5 | New Jersey | 68,797 |
| 6 | Alaska | 65,468 |
| 7 | Maryland | 65,265 |
| 8 | Pennsylvania | 63,521 |
| 9 | Rhode Island | 63,474 |
| 10 | Michigan | 61,560 |
| 11 | Delaware | 59,679 |
| 12 | Illinois | 59,113 |
| 13 | Oregon | 58,758 |
| 14 | Ohio | 58,092 |
| 15 | Wyoming | 57,920 |
| 16 | Minnesota | 56,268 |
| 17 | Nevada | 55,957 |
| 18 | New Hampshire | 55,599 |
| 19 | Wisconsin | 55,171 |
| 20 | Hawaii | 54,300 |
| 21 | Washington | 53,571 |
| 22 | Georgia | 52,880 |
| 23 | Vermont | 52,526 |
| 24 | Iowa | 51,528 |
| 25 | Indiana | 51,456 |
| 26 | Louisiana | 51,381 |
| 27 | Kentucky | 50,326 |
| 28 | Montana | 49,999 |
| 29 | Arizona | 49,885 |
| 30 | Virginia | 49,869 |
| 31 | Colorado | 49,844 |
| 32 | Idaho | 49,734 |
| 33 | Utah | 49,393 |
| 34 | Nebraska | 48,931 |
| 35 | Tennessee | 48,289 |
| 36 | Maine | 48,119 |
| 37 | Texas | 48,110 |
| 38 | Alabama | 47,949 |
| 39 | South Carolina | 47,924 |
| 40 | Missouri | 47,517 |
| 41 | Kansas | 47,464 |
| 42 | North Dakota | 47,344 |
| 43 | Florida | 46,944 |
| 44 | Arkansas | 46,632 |
| 45 | New Mexico | 46,573 |
| 46 | West Virginia | 46,405 |
| 47 | North Carolina | 45,947 |
| 48 | Oklahoma | 44,128 |
| 49 | Mississippi | 41,994 |
| 50 | South Dakota | 39,580 |
| | District of Columbia | 70,906 |

Source: National Education Association, Washington, D.C.
   "Rankings and Estimates" (Copyright © 2012, NEA, used with permission, http://www.nea.org/home/54597.htm)
*Estimates for school year 2012-2013 for classroom teachers.

# Average Teacher's Salary as a Percent of Average Annual Pay in 2012

## National Average = 113.4% of Average Annual Pay*

ALPHA ORDER

| RANK | STATE | PERCENT |
|---|---|---|
| 33 | Alabama | 114.3 |
| 12 | Alaska | 126.3 |
| 41 | Arizona | 108.1 |
| 19 | Arkansas | 121.6 |
| 20 | California | 121.4 |
| 48 | Colorado | 97.8 |
| 37 | Connecticut | 112.1 |
| 30 | Delaware | 114.5 |
| 41 | Florida | 108.1 |
| 32 | Georgia | 114.4 |
| 14 | Hawaii | 124.9 |
| 1 | Idaho | 135.9 |
| 38 | Illinois | 111.8 |
| 16 | Indiana | 123.6 |
| 13 | Iowa | 126.1 |
| 30 | Kansas | 114.5 |
| 15 | Kentucky | 123.7 |
| 26 | Louisiana | 117.3 |
| 16 | Maine | 123.6 |
| 22 | Maryland | 119.3 |
| 23 | Massachusetts | 118.9 |
| 4 | Michigan | 131.8 |
| 36 | Minnesota | 112.7 |
| 27 | Mississippi | 116.6 |
| 39 | Missouri | 110.0 |
| 3 | Montana | 132.8 |
| 16 | Nebraska | 123.6 |
| 11 | Nevada | 126.5 |
| 34 | New Hampshire | 113.7 |
| 28 | New Jersey | 115.8 |
| 35 | New Mexico | 113.3 |
| 24 | New York | 118.6 |
| 44 | North Carolina | 106.6 |
| 47 | North Dakota | 101.7 |
| 7 | Ohio | 129.7 |
| 45 | Oklahoma | 106.3 |
| 5 | Oregon | 131.2 |
| 8 | Pennsylvania | 129.6 |
| 2 | Rhode Island | 134.5 |
| 20 | South Carolina | 121.4 |
| 43 | South Dakota | 107.3 |
| 40 | Tennessee | 108.5 |
| 49 | Texas | 95.4 |
| 25 | Utah | 118.1 |
| 10 | Vermont | 126.7 |
| 49 | Virginia | 95.4 |
| 46 | Washington | 101.8 |
| 29 | West Virginia | 115.4 |
| 6 | Wisconsin | 129.8 |
| 9 | Wyoming | 129.1 |

RANK ORDER

| RANK | STATE | PERCENT |
|---|---|---|
| 1 | Idaho | 135.9 |
| 2 | Rhode Island | 134.5 |
| 3 | Montana | 132.8 |
| 4 | Michigan | 131.8 |
| 5 | Oregon | 131.2 |
| 6 | Wisconsin | 129.8 |
| 7 | Ohio | 129.7 |
| 8 | Pennsylvania | 129.6 |
| 9 | Wyoming | 129.1 |
| 10 | Vermont | 126.7 |
| 11 | Nevada | 126.5 |
| 12 | Alaska | 126.3 |
| 13 | Iowa | 126.1 |
| 14 | Hawaii | 124.9 |
| 15 | Kentucky | 123.7 |
| 16 | Indiana | 123.6 |
| 16 | Maine | 123.6 |
| 16 | Nebraska | 123.6 |
| 19 | Arkansas | 121.6 |
| 20 | California | 121.4 |
| 20 | South Carolina | 121.4 |
| 22 | Maryland | 119.3 |
| 23 | Massachusetts | 118.9 |
| 24 | New York | 118.6 |
| 25 | Utah | 118.1 |
| 26 | Louisiana | 117.3 |
| 27 | Mississippi | 116.6 |
| 28 | New Jersey | 115.8 |
| 29 | West Virginia | 115.4 |
| 30 | Delaware | 114.5 |
| 30 | Kansas | 114.5 |
| 32 | Georgia | 114.4 |
| 33 | Alabama | 114.3 |
| 34 | New Hampshire | 113.7 |
| 35 | New Mexico | 113.3 |
| 36 | Minnesota | 112.7 |
| 37 | Connecticut | 112.1 |
| 38 | Illinois | 111.8 |
| 39 | Missouri | 110.0 |
| 40 | Tennessee | 108.5 |
| 41 | Arizona | 108.1 |
| 41 | Florida | 108.1 |
| 43 | South Dakota | 107.3 |
| 44 | North Carolina | 106.6 |
| 45 | Oklahoma | 106.3 |
| 46 | Washington | 101.8 |
| 47 | North Dakota | 101.7 |
| 48 | Colorado | 97.8 |
| 49 | Texas | 95.4 |
| 49 | Virginia | 95.4 |
| | District of Columbia | 84.3 |

Source: CQ Press using data from National Education Association, Washington, D.C.

"Rankings and Estimates" (Copyright © 2012, NEA, used with permission, http://www.nea.org/home/54597.htm)

"Quarterly Census of Employment and Wages" (http://www.bls.gov/cew/home.htm)

*Average of public elementary and secondary teacher salary for school years 2011-2012 and 2012-2013 compared to each state's 2012 average annual pay for all workers covered by federal unemployment.

# Percent of Public School Fourth Graders
# Proficient or Better in Reading in 2013
# National Percent = 34%*

ALPHA ORDER

| RANK | STATE | PERCENT |
|------|-------|---------|
| 37 | Alabama | 31 |
| 44 | Alaska | 27 |
| 41 | Arizona | 28 |
| 35 | Arkansas | 32 |
| 44 | California | 27 |
| 8 | Colorado | 41 |
| 4 | Connecticut | 43 |
| 13 | Delaware | 38 |
| 12 | Florida | 39 |
| 29 | Georgia | 34 |
| 39 | Hawaii | 30 |
| 33 | Idaho | 33 |
| 29 | Illinois | 34 |
| 13 | Indiana | 38 |
| 13 | Iowa | 38 |
| 13 | Kansas | 38 |
| 24 | Kentucky | 36 |
| 48 | Louisiana | 23 |
| 18 | Maine | 37 |
| 2 | Maryland | 45 |
| 1 | Massachusetts | 47 |
| 37 | Michigan | 31 |
| 8 | Minnesota | 41 |
| 49 | Mississippi | 21 |
| 25 | Missouri | 35 |
| 25 | Montana | 35 |
| 18 | Nebraska | 37 |
| 44 | Nevada | 27 |
| 2 | New Hampshire | 45 |
| 6 | New Jersey | 42 |
| 49 | New Mexico | 21 |
| 18 | New York | 37 |
| 25 | North Carolina | 35 |
| 29 | North Dakota | 34 |
| 18 | Ohio | 37 |
| 39 | Oklahoma | 30 |
| 33 | Oregon | 33 |
| 10 | Pennsylvania | 40 |
| 13 | Rhode Island | 38 |
| 41 | South Carolina | 28 |
| 35 | South Dakota | 32 |
| 29 | Tennessee | 34 |
| 41 | Texas | 28 |
| 18 | Utah | 37 |
| 6 | Vermont | 42 |
| 4 | Virginia | 43 |
| 10 | Washington | 40 |
| 44 | West Virginia | 27 |
| 25 | Wisconsin | 35 |
| 18 | Wyoming | 37 |

RANK ORDER

| RANK | STATE | PERCENT |
|------|-------|---------|
| 1 | Massachusetts | 47 |
| 2 | Maryland | 45 |
| 2 | New Hampshire | 45 |
| 4 | Connecticut | 43 |
| 4 | Virginia | 43 |
| 6 | New Jersey | 42 |
| 6 | Vermont | 42 |
| 8 | Colorado | 41 |
| 8 | Minnesota | 41 |
| 10 | Pennsylvania | 40 |
| 10 | Washington | 40 |
| 12 | Florida | 39 |
| 13 | Delaware | 38 |
| 13 | Indiana | 38 |
| 13 | Iowa | 38 |
| 13 | Kansas | 38 |
| 13 | Rhode Island | 38 |
| 18 | Maine | 37 |
| 18 | Nebraska | 37 |
| 18 | New York | 37 |
| 18 | Ohio | 37 |
| 18 | Utah | 37 |
| 18 | Wyoming | 37 |
| 24 | Kentucky | 36 |
| 25 | Missouri | 35 |
| 25 | Montana | 35 |
| 25 | North Carolina | 35 |
| 25 | Wisconsin | 35 |
| 29 | Georgia | 34 |
| 29 | Illinois | 34 |
| 29 | North Dakota | 34 |
| 29 | Tennessee | 34 |
| 33 | Idaho | 33 |
| 33 | Oregon | 33 |
| 35 | Arkansas | 32 |
| 35 | South Dakota | 32 |
| 37 | Alabama | 31 |
| 37 | Michigan | 31 |
| 39 | Hawaii | 30 |
| 39 | Oklahoma | 30 |
| 41 | Arizona | 28 |
| 41 | South Carolina | 28 |
| 41 | Texas | 28 |
| 44 | Alaska | 27 |
| 44 | California | 27 |
| 44 | Nevada | 27 |
| 44 | West Virginia | 27 |
| 48 | Louisiana | 23 |
| 49 | Mississippi | 21 |
| 49 | New Mexico | 21 |
| | District of Columbia | 23 |

Source: U.S. Department of Education, National Center for Education Statistics
   "The Nation's Report Card: Reading 2013" (http://nces.ed.gov/nationsreportcard/)
*There are four achievement levels: Below Basic, Basic, Proficient, and Advanced.  Proficient represents solid academic
mastery for 4th graders.  Students reaching this level have demonstrated competency over challenging subject matter, including
subject matter knowledge, application of such knowledge to real-world situations, and analytical skills appropriate to the subject
matter.

# Percent of Public School Eighth Graders
## Proficient or Better in Reading in 2013
## National Percent = 34%*

ALPHA ORDER

| RANK | STATE | PERCENT |
|---|---|---|
| 46 | Alabama | 25 |
| 37 | Alaska | 31 |
| 44 | Arizona | 28 |
| 39 | Arkansas | 30 |
| 41 | California | 29 |
| 10 | Colorado | 40 |
| 3 | Connecticut | 45 |
| 31 | Delaware | 33 |
| 31 | Florida | 33 |
| 36 | Georgia | 32 |
| 44 | Hawaii | 28 |
| 14 | Idaho | 38 |
| 21 | Illinois | 36 |
| 28 | Indiana | 35 |
| 18 | Iowa | 37 |
| 21 | Kansas | 36 |
| 14 | Kentucky | 38 |
| 48 | Louisiana | 24 |
| 14 | Maine | 38 |
| 6 | Maryland | 42 |
| 1 | Massachusetts | 48 |
| 31 | Michigan | 33 |
| 9 | Minnesota | 41 |
| 50 | Mississippi | 20 |
| 21 | Missouri | 36 |
| 10 | Montana | 40 |
| 18 | Nebraska | 37 |
| 39 | Nevada | 30 |
| 5 | New Hampshire | 44 |
| 2 | New Jersey | 46 |
| 49 | New Mexico | 22 |
| 28 | New York | 35 |
| 31 | North Carolina | 33 |
| 30 | North Dakota | 34 |
| 12 | Ohio | 39 |
| 41 | Oklahoma | 29 |
| 18 | Oregon | 37 |
| 6 | Pennsylvania | 42 |
| 21 | Rhode Island | 36 |
| 41 | South Carolina | 29 |
| 21 | South Dakota | 36 |
| 31 | Tennessee | 33 |
| 37 | Texas | 31 |
| 12 | Utah | 39 |
| 3 | Vermont | 45 |
| 21 | Virginia | 36 |
| 6 | Washington | 42 |
| 46 | West Virginia | 25 |
| 21 | Wisconsin | 36 |
| 14 | Wyoming | 38 |

RANK ORDER

| RANK | STATE | PERCENT |
|---|---|---|
| 1 | Massachusetts | 48 |
| 2 | New Jersey | 46 |
| 3 | Connecticut | 45 |
| 3 | Vermont | 45 |
| 5 | New Hampshire | 44 |
| 6 | Maryland | 42 |
| 6 | Pennsylvania | 42 |
| 6 | Washington | 42 |
| 9 | Minnesota | 41 |
| 10 | Colorado | 40 |
| 10 | Montana | 40 |
| 12 | Ohio | 39 |
| 12 | Utah | 39 |
| 14 | Idaho | 38 |
| 14 | Kentucky | 38 |
| 14 | Maine | 38 |
| 14 | Wyoming | 38 |
| 18 | Iowa | 37 |
| 18 | Nebraska | 37 |
| 18 | Oregon | 37 |
| 21 | Illinois | 36 |
| 21 | Kansas | 36 |
| 21 | Missouri | 36 |
| 21 | Rhode Island | 36 |
| 21 | South Dakota | 36 |
| 21 | Virginia | 36 |
| 21 | Wisconsin | 36 |
| 28 | Indiana | 35 |
| 28 | New York | 35 |
| 30 | North Dakota | 34 |
| 31 | Delaware | 33 |
| 31 | Florida | 33 |
| 31 | Michigan | 33 |
| 31 | North Carolina | 33 |
| 31 | Tennessee | 33 |
| 36 | Georgia | 32 |
| 37 | Alaska | 31 |
| 37 | Texas | 31 |
| 39 | Arkansas | 30 |
| 39 | Nevada | 30 |
| 41 | California | 29 |
| 41 | Oklahoma | 29 |
| 41 | South Carolina | 29 |
| 44 | Arizona | 28 |
| 44 | Hawaii | 28 |
| 46 | Alabama | 25 |
| 46 | West Virginia | 25 |
| 48 | Louisiana | 24 |
| 49 | New Mexico | 22 |
| 50 | Mississippi | 20 |

| District of Columbia | | 17 |
|---|---|---|

Source: U.S. Department of Education, National Center for Education Statistics
   "The Nation's Report Card: Reading 2013" (http://nces.ed.gov/nationsreportcard/)
*There are four achievement levels: Below Basic, Basic, Proficient, and Advanced.  Proficient represents solid academic mastery for 8th graders.  Students reaching this level have demonstrated competency over challenging subject matter, including subject matter knowledge, application of such knowledge to real-world situations, and analytical skills appropriate to the subject matter.

# Percent of Public School Fourth Graders Proficient or Better in Mathematics in 2013
## National Percent = 41%*

| RANK | STATE | PERCENT |
|------|-------|---------|
| 48 | Alabama | 30 |
| 40 | Alaska | 37 |
| 30 | Arizona | 40 |
| 36 | Arkansas | 39 |
| 46 | California | 33 |
| 6 | Colorado | 50 |
| 19 | Connecticut | 45 |
| 25 | Delaware | 42 |
| 27 | Florida | 41 |
| 36 | Georgia | 39 |
| 18 | Hawaii | 46 |
| 30 | Idaho | 40 |
| 36 | Illinois | 39 |
| 4 | Indiana | 52 |
| 8 | Iowa | 48 |
| 8 | Kansas | 48 |
| 27 | Kentucky | 41 |
| 49 | Louisiana | 26 |
| 14 | Maine | 47 |
| 14 | Maryland | 47 |
| 3 | Massachusetts | 58 |
| 40 | Michigan | 37 |
| 1 | Minnesota | 59 |
| 49 | Mississippi | 26 |
| 36 | Missouri | 39 |
| 19 | Montana | 45 |
| 19 | Nebraska | 45 |
| 45 | Nevada | 34 |
| 1 | New Hampshire | 59 |
| 7 | New Jersey | 49 |
| 47 | New Mexico | 31 |
| 30 | New York | 40 |
| 19 | North Carolina | 45 |
| 8 | North Dakota | 48 |
| 8 | Ohio | 48 |
| 42 | Oklahoma | 36 |
| 30 | Oregon | 40 |
| 23 | Pennsylvania | 44 |
| 25 | Rhode Island | 42 |
| 43 | South Carolina | 35 |
| 30 | South Dakota | 40 |
| 30 | Tennessee | 40 |
| 27 | Texas | 41 |
| 23 | Utah | 44 |
| 4 | Vermont | 52 |
| 14 | Virginia | 47 |
| 8 | Washington | 48 |
| 43 | West Virginia | 35 |
| 14 | Wisconsin | 47 |
| 8 | Wyoming | 48 |

| RANK | STATE | PERCENT |
|------|-------|---------|
| 1 | Minnesota | 59 |
| 1 | New Hampshire | 59 |
| 3 | Massachusetts | 58 |
| 4 | Indiana | 52 |
| 4 | Vermont | 52 |
| 6 | Colorado | 50 |
| 7 | New Jersey | 49 |
| 8 | Iowa | 48 |
| 8 | Kansas | 48 |
| 8 | North Dakota | 48 |
| 8 | Ohio | 48 |
| 8 | Washington | 48 |
| 8 | Wyoming | 48 |
| 14 | Maine | 47 |
| 14 | Maryland | 47 |
| 14 | Virginia | 47 |
| 14 | Wisconsin | 47 |
| 18 | Hawaii | 46 |
| 19 | Connecticut | 45 |
| 19 | Montana | 45 |
| 19 | Nebraska | 45 |
| 19 | North Carolina | 45 |
| 23 | Pennsylvania | 44 |
| 23 | Utah | 44 |
| 25 | Delaware | 42 |
| 25 | Rhode Island | 42 |
| 27 | Florida | 41 |
| 27 | Kentucky | 41 |
| 27 | Texas | 41 |
| 30 | Arizona | 40 |
| 30 | Idaho | 40 |
| 30 | New York | 40 |
| 30 | Oregon | 40 |
| 30 | South Dakota | 40 |
| 30 | Tennessee | 40 |
| 36 | Arkansas | 39 |
| 36 | Georgia | 39 |
| 36 | Illinois | 39 |
| 36 | Missouri | 39 |
| 40 | Alaska | 37 |
| 40 | Michigan | 37 |
| 42 | Oklahoma | 36 |
| 43 | South Carolina | 35 |
| 43 | West Virginia | 35 |
| 45 | Nevada | 34 |
| 46 | California | 33 |
| 47 | New Mexico | 31 |
| 48 | Alabama | 30 |
| 49 | Louisiana | 26 |
| 49 | Mississippi | 26 |

| | | |
|---|---|---|
| | District of Columbia | 28 |

Source: U.S. Department of Education, National Center for Education Statistics
"The Nation's Report Card: Mathematics 2013" (http://nces.ed.gov/nationsreportcard/)
*There are four achievement levels: Below Basic, Basic, Proficient, and Advanced. Proficient represents solid academic mastery for 4th graders. Students reaching this level have demonstrated competency over challenging subject matter, including subject matter knowledge, application of such knowledge to real-world situations, and analytical skills appropriate to the subject matter.

# Percent of Public School Eighth Graders Proficient or Better in Mathematics in 2013
## National Percent = 34%*

ALPHA ORDER

| RANK | STATE | PERCENT |
|------|-------|---------|
| 50 | Alabama | 20 |
| 30 | Alaska | 33 |
| 35 | Arizona | 31 |
| 41 | Arkansas | 28 |
| 41 | California | 28 |
| 6 | Colorado | 42 |
| 20 | Connecticut | 37 |
| 30 | Delaware | 33 |
| 35 | Florida | 31 |
| 40 | Georgia | 29 |
| 33 | Hawaii | 32 |
| 22 | Idaho | 36 |
| 22 | Illinois | 36 |
| 15 | Indiana | 38 |
| 22 | Iowa | 36 |
| 10 | Kansas | 40 |
| 38 | Kentucky | 30 |
| 48 | Louisiana | 21 |
| 10 | Maine | 40 |
| 20 | Maryland | 37 |
| 1 | Massachusetts | 55 |
| 38 | Michigan | 30 |
| 3 | Minnesota | 47 |
| 48 | Mississippi | 21 |
| 30 | Missouri | 33 |
| 10 | Montana | 40 |
| 22 | Nebraska | 36 |
| 41 | Nevada | 28 |
| 3 | New Hampshire | 47 |
| 2 | New Jersey | 49 |
| 47 | New Mexico | 23 |
| 33 | New York | 32 |
| 22 | North Carolina | 36 |
| 9 | North Dakota | 41 |
| 10 | Ohio | 40 |
| 45 | Oklahoma | 25 |
| 29 | Oregon | 34 |
| 6 | Pennsylvania | 42 |
| 22 | Rhode Island | 36 |
| 35 | South Carolina | 31 |
| 15 | South Dakota | 38 |
| 41 | Tennessee | 28 |
| 15 | Texas | 38 |
| 22 | Utah | 36 |
| 3 | Vermont | 47 |
| 15 | Virginia | 38 |
| 6 | Washington | 42 |
| 46 | West Virginia | 24 |
| 10 | Wisconsin | 40 |
| 15 | Wyoming | 38 |

RANK ORDER

| RANK | STATE | PERCENT |
|------|-------|---------|
| 1 | Massachusetts | 55 |
| 2 | New Jersey | 49 |
| 3 | Minnesota | 47 |
| 3 | New Hampshire | 47 |
| 3 | Vermont | 47 |
| 6 | Colorado | 42 |
| 6 | Pennsylvania | 42 |
| 6 | Washington | 42 |
| 9 | North Dakota | 41 |
| 10 | Kansas | 40 |
| 10 | Maine | 40 |
| 10 | Montana | 40 |
| 10 | Ohio | 40 |
| 10 | Wisconsin | 40 |
| 15 | Indiana | 38 |
| 15 | South Dakota | 38 |
| 15 | Texas | 38 |
| 15 | Virginia | 38 |
| 15 | Wyoming | 38 |
| 20 | Connecticut | 37 |
| 20 | Maryland | 37 |
| 22 | Idaho | 36 |
| 22 | Illinois | 36 |
| 22 | Iowa | 36 |
| 22 | Nebraska | 36 |
| 22 | North Carolina | 36 |
| 22 | Rhode Island | 36 |
| 22 | Utah | 36 |
| 29 | Oregon | 34 |
| 30 | Alaska | 33 |
| 30 | Delaware | 33 |
| 30 | Missouri | 33 |
| 33 | Hawaii | 32 |
| 33 | New York | 32 |
| 35 | Arizona | 31 |
| 35 | Florida | 31 |
| 35 | South Carolina | 31 |
| 38 | Kentucky | 30 |
| 38 | Michigan | 30 |
| 40 | Georgia | 29 |
| 41 | Arkansas | 28 |
| 41 | California | 28 |
| 41 | Nevada | 28 |
| 41 | Tennessee | 28 |
| 45 | Oklahoma | 25 |
| 46 | West Virginia | 24 |
| 47 | New Mexico | 23 |
| 48 | Louisiana | 21 |
| 48 | Mississippi | 21 |
| 50 | Alabama | 20 |
|  | District of Columbia | 19 |

Source: U.S. Department of Education, National Center for Education Statistics
  "The Nation's Report Card: Mathematics 2013" (http://nces.ed.gov/nationsreportcard/)
*There are four achievement levels: Below Basic, Basic, Proficient, and Advanced. Proficient represents solid academic mastery for 8th graders. Students reaching this level have demonstrated competency over challenging subject matter, including subject matter knowledge, application of such knowledge to real-world situations, and analytical skills appropriate to the subject matter.

# Percent of Population Graduated from High School in 2012

## National Percent = 86.4%*

RANK STATE                          PERCENT

| ALPHA ORDER | | | | RANK ORDER | | |
|---|---|---|---|---|---|---|
| **RANK** | **STATE** | **PERCENT** | | **RANK** | **STATE** | **PERCENT** |
| 45 | Alabama | 84.0 | | 1 | Montana | 92.8 |
| 3 | Alaska | 92.0 | | 2 | Minnesota | 92.5 |
| 35 | Arizona | 85.7 | | 3 | Alaska | 92.0 |
| 42 | Arkansas | 84.8 | | 4 | New Hampshire | 91.8 |
| 49 | California | 81.5 | | 5 | North Dakota | 91.7 |
| 12 | Colorado | 90.6 | | 5 | Vermont | 91.7 |
| 18 | Connecticut | 89.9 | | 5 | Wyoming | 91.7 |
| 26 | Delaware | 88.5 | | 8 | Iowa | 91.6 |
| 33 | Florida | 86.5 | | 8 | Maine | 91.6 |
| 39 | Georgia | 85.0 | | 10 | Utah | 91.0 |
| 15 | Hawaii | 90.4 | | 11 | Wisconsin | 90.7 |
| 20 | Idaho | 89.8 | | 12 | Colorado | 90.6 |
| 30 | Illinois | 87.6 | | 13 | Nebraska | 90.5 |
| 30 | Indiana | 87.6 | | 13 | South Dakota | 90.5 |
| 8 | Iowa | 91.6 | | 15 | Hawaii | 90.4 |
| 17 | Kansas | 90.2 | | 15 | Washington | 90.4 |
| 46 | Kentucky | 83.8 | | 17 | Kansas | 90.2 |
| 47 | Louisiana | 83.0 | | 18 | Connecticut | 89.9 |
| 8 | Maine | 91.6 | | 18 | Oregon | 89.9 |
| 23 | Maryland | 89.1 | | 20 | Idaho | 89.8 |
| 21 | Massachusetts | 89.7 | | 21 | Massachusetts | 89.7 |
| 22 | Michigan | 89.2 | | 22 | Michigan | 89.2 |
| 2 | Minnesota | 92.5 | | 23 | Maryland | 89.1 |
| 48 | Mississippi | 82.3 | | 24 | Pennsylvania | 88.9 |
| 28 | Missouri | 88.0 | | 25 | Ohio | 88.8 |
| 1 | Montana | 92.8 | | 26 | Delaware | 88.5 |
| 13 | Nebraska | 90.5 | | 27 | New Jersey | 88.3 |
| 40 | Nevada | 84.9 | | 28 | Missouri | 88.0 |
| 4 | New Hampshire | 91.8 | | 29 | Virginia | 87.9 |
| 27 | New Jersey | 88.3 | | 30 | Illinois | 87.6 |
| 44 | New Mexico | 84.4 | | 30 | Indiana | 87.6 |
| 36 | New York | 85.3 | | 32 | Oklahoma | 86.7 |
| 37 | North Carolina | 85.2 | | 33 | Florida | 86.5 |
| 5 | North Dakota | 91.7 | | 34 | Rhode Island | 86.1 |
| 25 | Ohio | 88.8 | | 35 | Arizona | 85.7 |
| 32 | Oklahoma | 86.7 | | 36 | New York | 85.3 |
| 18 | Oregon | 89.9 | | 37 | North Carolina | 85.2 |
| 24 | Pennsylvania | 88.9 | | 38 | Tennessee | 85.1 |
| 34 | Rhode Island | 86.1 | | 39 | Georgia | 85.0 |
| 40 | South Carolina | 84.9 | | 40 | Nevada | 84.9 |
| 13 | South Dakota | 90.5 | | 40 | South Carolina | 84.9 |
| 38 | Tennessee | 85.1 | | 42 | Arkansas | 84.8 |
| 50 | Texas | 81.4 | | 43 | West Virginia | 84.5 |
| 10 | Utah | 91.0 | | 44 | New Mexico | 84.4 |
| 5 | Vermont | 91.7 | | 45 | Alabama | 84.0 |
| 29 | Virginia | 87.9 | | 46 | Kentucky | 83.8 |
| 15 | Washington | 90.4 | | 47 | Louisiana | 83.0 |
| 43 | West Virginia | 84.5 | | 48 | Mississippi | 82.3 |
| 11 | Wisconsin | 90.7 | | 49 | California | 81.5 |
| 5 | Wyoming | 91.7 | | 50 | Texas | 81.4 |
| | | | | | District of Columbia | 88.6 |

Source: U.S. Bureau of the Census
    "2012 American Community Survey-Table R1501" (http://www.census.gov/acs/www/index.html)
*Persons age 25 and older.  Includes equivalency status.

# Public High School Graduates in 2010

## National Total = 3,128,022 Graduates*

ALPHA ORDER

RANK ORDER

| RANK | STATE | GRADUATES | % of USA | RANK | STATE | GRADUATES | % of USA |
|---|---|---|---|---|---|---|---|
| 23 | Alabama | 43,166 | 1.4% | 1 | California | 404,987 | 12.9% |
| 45 | Alaska | 8,245 | 0.3% | 2 | Texas | 280,894 | 9.0% |
| 19 | Arizona | 61,145 | 2.0% | 3 | New York | 183,826 | 5.9% |
| 33 | Arkansas | 28,276 | 0.9% | 4 | Florida | 156,130 | 5.0% |
| 1 | California | 404,987 | 12.9% | 5 | Illinois | 139,035 | 4.4% |
| 22 | Colorado | 49,321 | 1.6% | 6 | Pennsylvania | 131,182 | 4.2% |
| 29 | Connecticut | 34,495 | 1.1% | 7 | Ohio | 123,437 | 3.9% |
| 47 | Delaware | 8,133 | 0.3% | 8 | Michigan | 110,682 | 3.5% |
| 4 | Florida | 156,130 | 5.0% | 9 | New Jersey | 96,225 | 3.1% |
| 10 | Georgia | 91,561 | 2.9% | 10 | Georgia | 91,561 | 2.9% |
| 42 | Hawaii | 10,998 | 0.4% | 11 | North Carolina | 88,704 | 2.8% |
| 38 | Idaho | 17,793 | 0.6% | 12 | Virginia | 81,511 | 2.6% |
| 5 | Illinois | 139,035 | 4.4% | 13 | Washington | 66,046 | 2.1% |
| 15 | Indiana | 64,551 | 2.1% | 14 | Wisconsin | 64,687 | 2.1% |
| 30 | Iowa | 34,462 | 1.1% | 15 | Indiana | 64,551 | 2.1% |
| 31 | Kansas | 31,642 | 1.0% | 16 | Massachusetts | 64,462 | 2.1% |
| 24 | Kentucky | 42,664 | 1.4% | 17 | Missouri | 63,994 | 2.0% |
| 27 | Louisiana | 36,573 | 1.2% | 18 | Tennessee | 62,408 | 2.0% |
| 41 | Maine | 14,069 | 0.4% | 19 | Arizona | 61,145 | 2.0% |
| 21 | Maryland | 59,078 | 1.9% | 20 | Minnesota | 59,667 | 1.9% |
| 16 | Massachusetts | 64,462 | 2.1% | 21 | Maryland | 59,078 | 1.9% |
| 8 | Michigan | 110,682 | 3.5% | 22 | Colorado | 49,321 | 1.6% |
| 20 | Minnesota | 59,667 | 1.9% | 23 | Alabama | 43,166 | 1.4% |
| 34 | Mississippi | 25,478 | 0.8% | 24 | Kentucky | 42,664 | 1.4% |
| 17 | Missouri | 63,994 | 2.0% | 25 | South Carolina | 40,438 | 1.3% |
| 43 | Montana | 10,075 | 0.3% | 26 | Oklahoma | 38,503 | 1.2% |
| 36 | Nebraska | 19,370 | 0.6% | 27 | Louisiana | 36,573 | 1.2% |
| 35 | Nevada | 20,956 | 0.7% | 28 | Oregon | 34,671 | 1.1% |
| 40 | New Hampshire | 15,034 | 0.5% | 29 | Connecticut | 34,495 | 1.1% |
| 9 | New Jersey | 96,225 | 3.1% | 30 | Iowa | 34,462 | 1.1% |
| 37 | New Mexico | 18,595 | 0.6% | 31 | Kansas | 31,642 | 1.0% |
| 3 | New York | 183,826 | 5.9% | 32 | Utah | 31,481 | 1.0% |
| 11 | North Carolina | 88,704 | 2.8% | 33 | Arkansas | 28,276 | 0.9% |
| 49 | North Dakota | 7,155 | 0.2% | 34 | Mississippi | 25,478 | 0.8% |
| 7 | Ohio | 123,437 | 3.9% | 35 | Nevada | 20,956 | 0.7% |
| 26 | Oklahoma | 38,503 | 1.2% | 36 | Nebraska | 19,370 | 0.6% |
| 28 | Oregon | 34,671 | 1.1% | 37 | New Mexico | 18,595 | 0.6% |
| 6 | Pennsylvania | 131,182 | 4.2% | 38 | Idaho | 17,793 | 0.6% |
| 44 | Rhode Island | 9,908 | 0.3% | 39 | West Virginia | 17,651 | 0.6% |
| 25 | South Carolina | 40,438 | 1.3% | 40 | New Hampshire | 15,034 | 0.5% |
| 46 | South Dakota | 8,162 | 0.3% | 41 | Maine | 14,069 | 0.4% |
| 18 | Tennessee | 62,408 | 2.0% | 42 | Hawaii | 10,998 | 0.4% |
| 2 | Texas | 280,894 | 9.0% | 43 | Montana | 10,075 | 0.3% |
| 32 | Utah | 31,481 | 1.0% | 44 | Rhode Island | 9,908 | 0.3% |
| 48 | Vermont | 7,199 | 0.2% | 45 | Alaska | 8,245 | 0.3% |
| 12 | Virginia | 81,511 | 2.6% | 46 | South Dakota | 8,162 | 0.3% |
| 13 | Washington | 66,046 | 2.1% | 47 | Delaware | 8,133 | 0.3% |
| 39 | West Virginia | 17,651 | 0.6% | 48 | Vermont | 7,199 | 0.2% |
| 14 | Wisconsin | 64,687 | 2.1% | 49 | North Dakota | 7,155 | 0.2% |
| 50 | Wyoming | 5,695 | 0.2% | 50 | Wyoming | 5,695 | 0.2% |
| | | | | | District of Columbia | 3,602 | 0.1% |

Source: U.S. Department of Education, National Center for Education Statistics
   "Public School Graduates and Dropouts from the Common Core of Data: School Year 2009-10" (NCES 2013309)
   (http://nces.ed.gov/pubsearch/pubsinfo.asp?pubid=2013309)
*Diploma recipients for school year 2009-2010.  Excludes persons receiving high school equivalency certificates.

# Averaged Freshman Graduation Rate for Public High Schools in 2010

## National Average = 78.2%*

| ALPHA ORDER | | | | RANK ORDER | | |
|---|---|---|---|---|---|---|
| RANK | STATE | PERCENT | | RANK | STATE | PERCENT |
| 43 | Alabama | 71.8 | | 1 | Vermont | 91.4 |
| 37 | Alaska | 75.5 | | 2 | Wisconsin | 91.1 |
| 42 | Arizona | 74.7 | | 3 | North Dakota | 88.4 |
| 41 | Arkansas | 75.0 | | 4 | Minnesota | 88.2 |
| 29 | California | 78.2 | | 5 | Iowa | 87.9 |
| 24 | Colorado | 79.8 | | 6 | New Jersey | 87.2 |
| 40 | Connecticut | 75.1 | | 7 | New Hampshire | 86.3 |
| 37 | Delaware | 75.5 | | 8 | Kansas | 84.5 |
| 44 | Florida | 70.8 | | 9 | Pennsylvania | 84.1 |
| 45 | Georgia | 69.9 | | 10 | Idaho | 84.0 |
| 39 | Hawaii | 75.4 | | 11 | Nebraska | 83.8 |
| 10 | Idaho | 84.0 | | 12 | Missouri | 83.7 |
| 16 | Illinois | 81.9 | | 13 | Maine | 82.8 |
| 30 | Indiana | 77.2 | | 14 | Massachusetts | 82.6 |
| 5 | Iowa | 87.9 | | 15 | Maryland | 82.2 |
| 8 | Kansas | 84.5 | | 16 | Illinois | 81.9 |
| 23 | Kentucky | 79.9 | | 16 | Montana | 81.9 |
| 46 | Louisiana | 68.8 | | 18 | South Dakota | 81.8 |
| 13 | Maine | 82.8 | | 19 | Ohio | 81.4 |
| 15 | Maryland | 82.2 | | 20 | Virginia | 81.2 |
| 14 | Massachusetts | 82.6 | | 21 | Tennessee | 80.4 |
| 36 | Michigan | 75.9 | | 22 | Wyoming | 80.3 |
| 4 | Minnesota | 88.2 | | 23 | Kentucky | 79.9 |
| 49 | Mississippi | 63.8 | | 24 | Colorado | 79.8 |
| 12 | Missouri | 83.7 | | 25 | Texas | 78.9 |
| 16 | Montana | 81.9 | | 26 | Utah | 78.6 |
| 11 | Nebraska | 83.8 | | 27 | Oklahoma | 78.5 |
| 50 | Nevada | 57.8 | | 28 | West Virginia | 78.3 |
| 7 | New Hampshire | 86.3 | | 29 | California | 78.2 |
| 6 | New Jersey | 87.2 | | 30 | Indiana | 77.2 |
| 48 | New Mexico | 67.3 | | 30 | Washington | 77.2 |
| 35 | New York | 76.0 | | 32 | North Carolina | 76.9 |
| 32 | North Carolina | 76.9 | | 33 | Rhode Island | 76.4 |
| 3 | North Dakota | 88.4 | | 34 | Oregon | 76.3 |
| 19 | Ohio | 81.4 | | 35 | New York | 76.0 |
| 27 | Oklahoma | 78.5 | | 36 | Michigan | 75.9 |
| 34 | Oregon | 76.3 | | 37 | Alaska | 75.5 |
| 9 | Pennsylvania | 84.1 | | 37 | Delaware | 75.5 |
| 33 | Rhode Island | 76.4 | | 39 | Hawaii | 75.4 |
| 47 | South Carolina | 68.2 | | 40 | Connecticut | 75.1 |
| 18 | South Dakota | 81.8 | | 41 | Arkansas | 75.0 |
| 21 | Tennessee | 80.4 | | 42 | Arizona | 74.7 |
| 25 | Texas | 78.9 | | 43 | Alabama | 71.8 |
| 26 | Utah | 78.6 | | 44 | Florida | 70.8 |
| 1 | Vermont | 91.4 | | 45 | Georgia | 69.9 |
| 20 | Virginia | 81.2 | | 46 | Louisiana | 68.8 |
| 30 | Washington | 77.2 | | 47 | South Carolina | 68.2 |
| 28 | West Virginia | 78.3 | | 48 | New Mexico | 67.3 |
| 2 | Wisconsin | 91.1 | | 49 | Mississippi | 63.8 |
| 22 | Wyoming | 80.3 | | 50 | Nevada | 57.8 |
| | | | | District of Columbia | | 59.9 |

Source: U.S. Department of Education, National Center for Education Statistics
"Public School Graduates and Dropouts from the Common Core of Data: School Year 2009-10" (NCES 2013309)
(http://nces.ed.gov/pubsearch/pubsinfo.asp?pubid=2013309)
*This rate is an estimate of the percentage of an entering freshman class graduating in 4 years. For 2009-10, it equals the total number of diploma recipients in 2009-10 divided by the average membership of the 8th-grade class in 2005-06, the 9th-grade class in 2006-07, and the 10th-grade class in 2007-08.

# Public High School Dropout Rate in 2010

## National Rate = 3.4%*

ALPHA ORDER

| RANK | STATE | RATE |
|---|---|---|
| 45 | Alabama | 1.8 |
| 3 | Alaska | 6.9 |
| 1 | Arizona | 7.8 |
| 21 | Arkansas | 3.6 |
| 10 | California | 4.6 |
| 6 | Colorado | 5.3 |
| 27 | Connecticut | 3.0 |
| 19 | Delaware | 3.9 |
| 38 | Florida | 2.3 |
| 20 | Georgia | 3.8 |
| 7 | Hawaii | 5.2 |
| 49 | Idaho | 1.4 |
| 29 | Illinois | 2.9 |
| 46 | Indiana | 1.6 |
| 24 | Iowa | 3.4 |
| 42 | Kansas | 2.1 |
| 26 | Kentucky | 3.2 |
| 8 | Louisiana | 4.8 |
| 15 | Maine | 4.2 |
| 31 | Maryland | 2.7 |
| 30 | Massachusetts | 2.8 |
| 13 | Michigan | 4.3 |
| 46 | Minnesota | 1.6 |
| 2 | Mississippi | 7.4 |
| 23 | Missouri | 3.5 |
| 13 | Montana | 4.3 |
| 39 | Nebraska | 2.2 |
| 12 | Nevada | 4.5 |
| 50 | New Hampshire | 1.2 |
| 46 | New Jersey | 1.6 |
| 3 | New Mexico | 6.9 |
| 21 | New York | 3.6 |
| 9 | North Carolina | 4.7 |
| 39 | North Dakota | 2.2 |
| 15 | Ohio | 4.2 |
| 36 | Oklahoma | 2.4 |
| 24 | Oregon | 3.4 |
| 42 | Pennsylvania | 2.1 |
| 10 | Rhode Island | 4.6 |
| 27 | South Carolina | 3.0 |
| 34 | South Dakota | 2.6 |
| 31 | Tennessee | 2.7 |
| 31 | Texas | 2.7 |
| 34 | Utah | 2.6 |
| 36 | Vermont | 2.4 |
| 42 | Virginia | 2.1 |
| 15 | Washington | 4.2 |
| 18 | West Virginia | 4.0 |
| 39 | Wisconsin | 2.2 |
| 5 | Wyoming | 6.0 |

RANK ORDER

| RANK | STATE | RATE |
|---|---|---|
| 1 | Arizona | 7.8 |
| 2 | Mississippi | 7.4 |
| 3 | Alaska | 6.9 |
| 3 | New Mexico | 6.9 |
| 5 | Wyoming | 6.0 |
| 6 | Colorado | 5.3 |
| 7 | Hawaii | 5.2 |
| 8 | Louisiana | 4.8 |
| 9 | North Carolina | 4.7 |
| 10 | California | 4.6 |
| 10 | Rhode Island | 4.6 |
| 12 | Nevada | 4.5 |
| 13 | Michigan | 4.3 |
| 13 | Montana | 4.3 |
| 15 | Maine | 4.2 |
| 15 | Ohio | 4.2 |
| 15 | Washington | 4.2 |
| 18 | West Virginia | 4.0 |
| 19 | Delaware | 3.9 |
| 20 | Georgia | 3.8 |
| 21 | Arkansas | 3.6 |
| 21 | New York | 3.6 |
| 23 | Missouri | 3.5 |
| 24 | Iowa | 3.4 |
| 24 | Oregon | 3.4 |
| 26 | Kentucky | 3.2 |
| 27 | Connecticut | 3.0 |
| 27 | South Carolina | 3.0 |
| 29 | Illinois | 2.9 |
| 30 | Massachusetts | 2.8 |
| 31 | Maryland | 2.7 |
| 31 | Tennessee | 2.7 |
| 31 | Texas | 2.7 |
| 34 | South Dakota | 2.6 |
| 34 | Utah | 2.6 |
| 36 | Oklahoma | 2.4 |
| 36 | Vermont | 2.4 |
| 38 | Florida | 2.3 |
| 39 | Nebraska | 2.2 |
| 39 | North Dakota | 2.2 |
| 39 | Wisconsin | 2.2 |
| 42 | Kansas | 2.1 |
| 42 | Pennsylvania | 2.1 |
| 42 | Virginia | 2.1 |
| 45 | Alabama | 1.8 |
| 46 | Indiana | 1.6 |
| 46 | Minnesota | 1.6 |
| 46 | New Jersey | 1.6 |
| 49 | Idaho | 1.4 |
| 50 | New Hampshire | 1.2 |
| | District of Columbia | 7.0 |

Source: U.S. Department of Education, National Center for Education Statistics
"Public School Graduates and Dropouts from the Common Core of Data: School Year 2009-10" (NCES 2013309)
(http://nces.ed.gov/pubsearch/pubsinfo.asp?pubid=2013309)
*"Event" dropout rates showing the number of 9th-12th grade dropouts divided by the number of students enrolled at the beginning of the school year in those grades.

# ACT Average Composite Score in 2013

## National Average = 20.9*

ALPHA ORDER

| RANK | STATE | AVERAGE SCORE |
|------|-------|---------------|
| 36 | Alabama | 20.4 |
| 28 | Alaska | 21.1 |
| 44 | Arizona | 19.6 |
| 39 | Arkansas | 20.2 |
| 15 | California | 22.2 |
| 36 | Colorado | 20.4 |
| 2 | Connecticut | 24.0 |
| 9 | Delaware | 22.9 |
| 44 | Florida | 19.6 |
| 31 | Georgia | 20.7 |
| 40 | Hawaii | 20.1 |
| 16 | Idaho | 22.1 |
| 33 | Illinois | 20.6 |
| 22 | Indiana | 21.7 |
| 16 | Iowa | 22.1 |
| 20 | Kansas | 21.8 |
| 44 | Kentucky | 19.6 |
| 47 | Louisiana | 19.5 |
| 4 | Maine | 23.5 |
| 14 | Maryland | 22.3 |
| 1 | Massachusetts | 24.1 |
| 41 | Michigan | 19.9 |
| 6 | Minnesota | 23.0 |
| 49 | Mississippi | 18.9 |
| 23 | Missouri | 21.6 |
| 26 | Montana | 21.3 |
| 24 | Nebraska | 21.5 |
| 26 | Nevada | 21.3 |
| 3 | New Hampshire | 23.8 |
| 6 | New Jersey | 23.0 |
| 41 | New Mexico | 19.9 |
| 5 | New York | 23.4 |
| 50 | North Carolina | 18.7 |
| 35 | North Dakota | 20.5 |
| 20 | Ohio | 21.8 |
| 30 | Oklahoma | 20.8 |
| 24 | Oregon | 21.5 |
| 11 | Pennsylvania | 22.7 |
| 11 | Rhode Island | 22.7 |
| 36 | South Carolina | 20.4 |
| 19 | South Dakota | 21.9 |
| 47 | Tennessee | 19.5 |
| 29 | Texas | 20.9 |
| 31 | Utah | 20.7 |
| 6 | Vermont | 23.0 |
| 13 | Virginia | 22.6 |
| 10 | Washington | 22.8 |
| 33 | West Virginia | 20.6 |
| 16 | Wisconsin | 22.1 |
| 43 | Wyoming | 19.8 |

RANK ORDER

| RANK | STATE | AVERAGE SCORE |
|------|-------|---------------|
| 1 | Massachusetts | 24.1 |
| 2 | Connecticut | 24.0 |
| 3 | New Hampshire | 23.8 |
| 4 | Maine | 23.5 |
| 5 | New York | 23.4 |
| 6 | Minnesota | 23.0 |
| 6 | New Jersey | 23.0 |
| 6 | Vermont | 23.0 |
| 9 | Delaware | 22.9 |
| 10 | Washington | 22.8 |
| 11 | Pennsylvania | 22.7 |
| 11 | Rhode Island | 22.7 |
| 13 | Virginia | 22.6 |
| 14 | Maryland | 22.3 |
| 15 | California | 22.2 |
| 16 | Idaho | 22.1 |
| 16 | Iowa | 22.1 |
| 16 | Wisconsin | 22.1 |
| 19 | South Dakota | 21.9 |
| 20 | Kansas | 21.8 |
| 20 | Ohio | 21.8 |
| 22 | Indiana | 21.7 |
| 23 | Missouri | 21.6 |
| 24 | Nebraska | 21.5 |
| 24 | Oregon | 21.5 |
| 26 | Montana | 21.3 |
| 26 | Nevada | 21.3 |
| 28 | Alaska | 21.1 |
| 29 | Texas | 20.9 |
| 30 | Oklahoma | 20.8 |
| 31 | Georgia | 20.7 |
| 31 | Utah | 20.7 |
| 33 | Illinois | 20.6 |
| 33 | West Virginia | 20.6 |
| 35 | North Dakota | 20.5 |
| 36 | Alabama | 20.4 |
| 36 | Colorado | 20.4 |
| 36 | South Carolina | 20.4 |
| 39 | Arkansas | 20.2 |
| 40 | Hawaii | 20.1 |
| 41 | Michigan | 19.9 |
| 41 | New Mexico | 19.9 |
| 43 | Wyoming | 19.8 |
| 44 | Arizona | 19.6 |
| 44 | Florida | 19.6 |
| 44 | Kentucky | 19.6 |
| 47 | Louisiana | 19.5 |
| 47 | Tennessee | 19.5 |
| 49 | Mississippi | 18.9 |
| 50 | North Carolina | 18.7 |
| | District of Columbia | 20.4 |

Source: The American College Testing Program (Copyright © 2013)
   "Average ACT Scores by State" (http://www.act.org/newsroom/)
*The ACT score range is 1 to 36.  Approximately 1.8 million 2013 U.S. high school students took the test. Caution should be used in using ACT scores to compare states.  The percentage of high school students taking the test varies greatly from one state to another.  For example, all 11th grade students in Colorado, Illinois, Kentucky, Louisiana, Michigan,  Tennessee, Utah, and Wyoming are required to take the test but, in Maine, only 8 percent of 11th grade students took the test.

# Education Expenditures by State and Local Governments in 2011

## National Total = $861,130,583,000*

ALPHA ORDER

| RANK | STATE | EXPENDITURES | % of USA |
|------|-------|--------------|----------|
| 21 | Alabama | $13,370,655,000 | 1.6% |
| 41 | Alaska | 3,376,705,000 | 0.4% |
| 20 | Arizona | 13,385,017,000 | 1.6% |
| 31 | Arkansas | 8,446,175,000 | 1.0% |
| 1 | California | 102,228,064,000 | 11.9% |
| 22 | Colorado | 13,203,613,000 | 1.5% |
| 26 | Connecticut | 11,789,282,000 | 1.4% |
| 43 | Delaware | 3,134,169,000 | 0.4% |
| 4 | Florida | 38,691,438,000 | 4.5% |
| 10 | Georgia | 24,832,351,000 | 2.9% |
| 42 | Hawaii | 3,345,400,000 | 0.4% |
| 44 | Idaho | 3,131,029,000 | 0.4% |
| 6 | Illinois | 34,669,254,000 | 4.0% |
| 17 | Indiana | 16,270,151,000 | 1.9% |
| 29 | Iowa | 9,636,273,000 | 1.1% |
| 32 | Kansas | 8,366,291,000 | 1.0% |
| 27 | Kentucky | 11,466,117,000 | 1.3% |
| 24 | Louisiana | 12,118,671,000 | 1.4% |
| 40 | Maine | 3,458,596,000 | 0.4% |
| 15 | Maryland | 18,258,312,000 | 2.1% |
| 14 | Massachusetts | 18,761,469,000 | 2.2% |
| 9 | Michigan | 28,697,437,000 | 3.3% |
| 18 | Minnesota | 15,388,894,000 | 1.8% |
| 34 | Mississippi | 7,250,853,000 | 0.8% |
| 19 | Missouri | 13,746,802,000 | 1.6% |
| 46 | Montana | 2,596,472,000 | 0.3% |
| 36 | Nebraska | 5,700,817,000 | 0.7% |
| 38 | Nevada | 5,576,914,000 | 0.6% |
| 39 | New Hampshire | 3,772,584,000 | 0.4% |
| 8 | New Jersey | 30,551,441,000 | 3.5% |
| 35 | New Mexico | 6,778,349,000 | 0.8% |
| 3 | New York | 71,545,006,000 | 8.3% |
| 11 | North Carolina | 23,735,316,000 | 2.8% |
| 49 | North Dakota | 2,231,853,000 | 0.3% |
| 7 | Ohio | 33,310,313,000 | 3.9% |
| 30 | Oklahoma | 9,393,181,000 | 1.1% |
| 28 | Oregon | 10,513,873,000 | 1.2% |
| 5 | Pennsylvania | 35,400,439,000 | 4.1% |
| 45 | Rhode Island | 3,049,159,000 | 0.4% |
| 25 | South Carolina | 12,066,922,000 | 1.4% |
| 50 | South Dakota | 2,086,181,000 | 0.2% |
| 23 | Tennessee | 12,759,853,000 | 1.5% |
| 2 | Texas | 74,047,357,000 | 8.6% |
| 33 | Utah | 7,773,247,000 | 0.9% |
| 48 | Vermont | 2,377,847,000 | 0.3% |
| 12 | Virginia | 22,270,393,000 | 2.6% |
| 13 | Washington | 18,785,682,000 | 2.2% |
| 37 | West Virginia | 5,595,864,000 | 0.6% |
| 16 | Wisconsin | 17,350,331,000 | 2.0% |
| 47 | Wyoming | 2,495,867,000 | 0.3% |

RANK ORDER

| RANK | STATE | EXPENDITURES | % of USA |
|------|-------|--------------|----------|
| 1 | California | $102,228,064,000 | 11.9% |
| 2 | Texas | 74,047,357,000 | 8.6% |
| 3 | New York | 71,545,006,000 | 8.3% |
| 4 | Florida | 38,691,438,000 | 4.5% |
| 5 | Pennsylvania | 35,400,439,000 | 4.1% |
| 6 | Illinois | 34,669,254,000 | 4.0% |
| 7 | Ohio | 33,310,313,000 | 3.9% |
| 8 | New Jersey | 30,551,441,000 | 3.5% |
| 9 | Michigan | 28,697,437,000 | 3.3% |
| 10 | Georgia | 24,832,351,000 | 2.9% |
| 11 | North Carolina | 23,735,316,000 | 2.8% |
| 12 | Virginia | 22,270,393,000 | 2.6% |
| 13 | Washington | 18,785,682,000 | 2.2% |
| 14 | Massachusetts | 18,761,469,000 | 2.2% |
| 15 | Maryland | 18,258,312,000 | 2.1% |
| 16 | Wisconsin | 17,350,331,000 | 2.0% |
| 17 | Indiana | 16,270,151,000 | 1.9% |
| 18 | Minnesota | 15,388,894,000 | 1.8% |
| 19 | Missouri | 13,746,802,000 | 1.6% |
| 20 | Arizona | 13,385,017,000 | 1.6% |
| 21 | Alabama | 13,370,655,000 | 1.6% |
| 22 | Colorado | 13,203,613,000 | 1.5% |
| 23 | Tennessee | 12,759,853,000 | 1.5% |
| 24 | Louisiana | 12,118,671,000 | 1.4% |
| 25 | South Carolina | 12,066,922,000 | 1.4% |
| 26 | Connecticut | 11,789,282,000 | 1.4% |
| 27 | Kentucky | 11,466,117,000 | 1.3% |
| 28 | Oregon | 10,513,873,000 | 1.2% |
| 29 | Iowa | 9,636,273,000 | 1.1% |
| 30 | Oklahoma | 9,393,181,000 | 1.1% |
| 31 | Arkansas | 8,446,175,000 | 1.0% |
| 32 | Kansas | 8,366,291,000 | 1.0% |
| 33 | Utah | 7,773,247,000 | 0.9% |
| 34 | Mississippi | 7,250,853,000 | 0.8% |
| 35 | New Mexico | 6,778,349,000 | 0.8% |
| 36 | Nebraska | 5,700,817,000 | 0.7% |
| 37 | West Virginia | 5,595,864,000 | 0.6% |
| 38 | Nevada | 5,576,914,000 | 0.6% |
| 39 | New Hampshire | 3,772,584,000 | 0.4% |
| 40 | Maine | 3,458,596,000 | 0.4% |
| 41 | Alaska | 3,376,705,000 | 0.4% |
| 42 | Hawaii | 3,345,400,000 | 0.4% |
| 43 | Delaware | 3,134,169,000 | 0.4% |
| 44 | Idaho | 3,131,029,000 | 0.4% |
| 45 | Rhode Island | 3,049,159,000 | 0.4% |
| 46 | Montana | 2,596,472,000 | 0.3% |
| 47 | Wyoming | 2,495,867,000 | 0.3% |
| 48 | Vermont | 2,377,847,000 | 0.3% |
| 49 | North Dakota | 2,231,853,000 | 0.3% |
| 50 | South Dakota | 2,086,181,000 | 0.2% |
| | District of Columbia | 2,342,304,000 | 0.3% |

Source: U.S. Bureau of the Census, Governments Division
"2011 State and Local Government Finances" (http://www.census.gov/govs/local/)
*Direct general expenditures for higher, secondary, elementary, and, "other" education. Includes capital outlays.

# Per Capita State and Local Government Expenditures for Education in 2011

## National Per Capita = $2,764*

ALPHA ORDER

| RANK | STATE | PER CAPITA |
|------|-------|------------|
| 24 | Alabama | $2,783 |
| 1 | Alaska | 4,665 |
| 46 | Arizona | 2,070 |
| 21 | Arkansas | 2,874 |
| 30 | California | 2,713 |
| 37 | Colorado | 2,581 |
| 7 | Connecticut | 3,287 |
| 6 | Delaware | 3,451 |
| 48 | Florida | 2,028 |
| 39 | Georgia | 2,531 |
| 44 | Hawaii | 2,427 |
| 50 | Idaho | 1,977 |
| 31 | Illinois | 2,696 |
| 40 | Indiana | 2,497 |
| 10 | Iowa | 3,145 |
| 15 | Kansas | 2,915 |
| 33 | Kentucky | 2,626 |
| 32 | Louisiana | 2,649 |
| 34 | Maine | 2,603 |
| 11 | Maryland | 3,127 |
| 23 | Massachusetts | 2,840 |
| 16 | Michigan | 2,906 |
| 20 | Minnesota | 2,878 |
| 43 | Mississippi | 2,435 |
| 45 | Missouri | 2,288 |
| 34 | Montana | 2,603 |
| 12 | Nebraska | 3,095 |
| 47 | Nevada | 2,050 |
| 22 | New Hampshire | 2,863 |
| 5 | New Jersey | 3,458 |
| 8 | New Mexico | 3,261 |
| 4 | New York | 3,669 |
| 42 | North Carolina | 2,459 |
| 9 | North Dakota | 3,259 |
| 19 | Ohio | 2,886 |
| 41 | Oklahoma | 2,482 |
| 29 | Oregon | 2,718 |
| 25 | Pennsylvania | 2,778 |
| 17 | Rhode Island | 2,902 |
| 36 | South Carolina | 2,582 |
| 38 | South Dakota | 2,533 |
| 49 | Tennessee | 1,994 |
| 18 | Texas | 2,889 |
| 26 | Utah | 2,762 |
| 3 | Vermont | 3,795 |
| 28 | Virginia | 2,748 |
| 27 | Washington | 2,753 |
| 14 | West Virginia | 3,017 |
| 13 | Wisconsin | 3,039 |
| 2 | Wyoming | 4,399 |

RANK ORDER

| RANK | STATE | PER CAPITA |
|------|-------|------------|
| 1 | Alaska | $4,665 |
| 2 | Wyoming | 4,399 |
| 3 | Vermont | 3,795 |
| 4 | New York | 3,669 |
| 5 | New Jersey | 3,458 |
| 6 | Delaware | 3,451 |
| 7 | Connecticut | 3,287 |
| 8 | New Mexico | 3,261 |
| 9 | North Dakota | 3,259 |
| 10 | Iowa | 3,145 |
| 11 | Maryland | 3,127 |
| 12 | Nebraska | 3,095 |
| 13 | Wisconsin | 3,039 |
| 14 | West Virginia | 3,017 |
| 15 | Kansas | 2,915 |
| 16 | Michigan | 2,906 |
| 17 | Rhode Island | 2,902 |
| 18 | Texas | 2,889 |
| 19 | Ohio | 2,886 |
| 20 | Minnesota | 2,878 |
| 21 | Arkansas | 2,874 |
| 22 | New Hampshire | 2,863 |
| 23 | Massachusetts | 2,840 |
| 24 | Alabama | 2,783 |
| 25 | Pennsylvania | 2,778 |
| 26 | Utah | 2,762 |
| 27 | Washington | 2,753 |
| 28 | Virginia | 2,748 |
| 29 | Oregon | 2,718 |
| 30 | California | 2,713 |
| 31 | Illinois | 2,696 |
| 32 | Louisiana | 2,649 |
| 33 | Kentucky | 2,626 |
| 34 | Maine | 2,603 |
| 34 | Montana | 2,603 |
| 36 | South Carolina | 2,582 |
| 37 | Colorado | 2,581 |
| 38 | South Dakota | 2,533 |
| 39 | Georgia | 2,531 |
| 40 | Indiana | 2,497 |
| 41 | Oklahoma | 2,482 |
| 42 | North Carolina | 2,459 |
| 43 | Mississippi | 2,435 |
| 44 | Hawaii | 2,427 |
| 45 | Missouri | 2,288 |
| 46 | Arizona | 2,070 |
| 47 | Nevada | 2,050 |
| 48 | Florida | 2,028 |
| 49 | Tennessee | 1,994 |
| 50 | Idaho | 1,977 |

| | District of Columbia | 3,784 |

Source: CQ Press using data from U.S. Bureau of the Census, Governments Division
"2011 State and Local Government Finances" (http://www.census.gov/govs/local/)
*Direct general expenditures for higher, secondary, elementary, and, "other" education. Includes capital outlays.

# Expenditures for Education as a Percent of
# All State and Local Government Expenditures in 2011
## National Percent = 33.3%*

| RANK | STATE | PERCENT |
|------|-------|---------|
| 9 | Alabama | 37.8 |
| 50 | Alaska | 26.4 |
| 38 | Arizona | 31.4 |
| 1 | Arkansas | 40.6 |
| 46 | California | 28.9 |
| 36 | Colorado | 32.0 |
| 21 | Connecticut | 35.3 |
| 14 | Delaware | 36.5 |
| 48 | Florida | 28.0 |
| 5 | Georgia | 38.8 |
| 49 | Hawaii | 27.4 |
| 44 | Idaho | 29.9 |
| 28 | Illinois | 33.2 |
| 19 | Indiana | 35.5 |
| 16 | Iowa | 36.4 |
| 16 | Kansas | 36.4 |
| 19 | Kentucky | 35.5 |
| 47 | Louisiana | 28.3 |
| 39 | Maine | 30.5 |
| 12 | Maryland | 36.6 |
| 39 | Massachusetts | 30.5 |
| 4 | Michigan | 38.9 |
| 33 | Minnesota | 32.6 |
| 41 | Mississippi | 30.4 |
| 29 | Missouri | 33.1 |
| 36 | Montana | 32.0 |
| 3 | Nebraska | 39.3 |
| 45 | Nevada | 29.8 |
| 11 | New Hampshire | 36.9 |
| 10 | New Jersey | 37.5 |
| 24 | New Mexico | 34.9 |
| 41 | New York | 30.4 |
| 21 | North Carolina | 35.3 |
| 25 | North Dakota | 34.7 |
| 21 | Ohio | 35.3 |
| 14 | Oklahoma | 36.5 |
| 29 | Oregon | 33.1 |
| 33 | Pennsylvania | 32.6 |
| 31 | Rhode Island | 33.0 |
| 26 | South Carolina | 33.9 |
| 27 | South Dakota | 33.8 |
| 43 | Tennessee | 30.3 |
| 2 | Texas | 39.9 |
| 8 | Utah | 38.2 |
| 7 | Vermont | 38.5 |
| 12 | Virginia | 36.6 |
| 35 | Washington | 32.5 |
| 6 | West Virginia | 38.7 |
| 16 | Wisconsin | 36.4 |
| 31 | Wyoming | 33.0 |

| RANK | STATE | PERCENT |
|------|-------|---------|
| 1 | Arkansas | 40.6 |
| 2 | Texas | 39.9 |
| 3 | Nebraska | 39.3 |
| 4 | Michigan | 38.9 |
| 5 | Georgia | 38.8 |
| 6 | West Virginia | 38.7 |
| 7 | Vermont | 38.5 |
| 8 | Utah | 38.2 |
| 9 | Alabama | 37.8 |
| 10 | New Jersey | 37.5 |
| 11 | New Hampshire | 36.9 |
| 12 | Maryland | 36.6 |
| 12 | Virginia | 36.6 |
| 14 | Delaware | 36.5 |
| 14 | Oklahoma | 36.5 |
| 16 | Iowa | 36.4 |
| 16 | Kansas | 36.4 |
| 16 | Wisconsin | 36.4 |
| 19 | Indiana | 35.5 |
| 19 | Kentucky | 35.5 |
| 21 | Connecticut | 35.3 |
| 21 | North Carolina | 35.3 |
| 21 | Ohio | 35.3 |
| 24 | New Mexico | 34.9 |
| 25 | North Dakota | 34.7 |
| 26 | South Carolina | 33.9 |
| 27 | South Dakota | 33.8 |
| 28 | Illinois | 33.2 |
| 29 | Missouri | 33.1 |
| 29 | Oregon | 33.1 |
| 31 | Rhode Island | 33.0 |
| 31 | Wyoming | 33.0 |
| 33 | Minnesota | 32.6 |
| 33 | Pennsylvania | 32.6 |
| 35 | Washington | 32.5 |
| 36 | Colorado | 32.0 |
| 36 | Montana | 32.0 |
| 38 | Arizona | 31.4 |
| 39 | Maine | 30.5 |
| 39 | Massachusetts | 30.5 |
| 41 | Mississippi | 30.4 |
| 41 | New York | 30.4 |
| 43 | Tennessee | 30.3 |
| 44 | Idaho | 29.9 |
| 45 | Nevada | 29.8 |
| 46 | California | 28.9 |
| 47 | Louisiana | 28.3 |
| 48 | Florida | 28.0 |
| 49 | Hawaii | 27.4 |
| 50 | Alaska | 26.4 |
| | District of Columbia | 22.6 |

Source: CQ Press using data from U.S. Bureau of the Census, Governments Division
"2011 State and Local Government Finances" (http://www.census.gov/govs/local/)
*Direct general expenditures for higher, secondary, elementary, and "other" education as a percent of all direct general expenditures. Includes capital outlays.

# State and Local Government Expenditures for Elementary and Secondary Education in 2011
## National Total = $564,862,357,000*

ALPHA ORDER

| RANK | STATE | EXPENDITURES | % of USA |
|---|---|---|---|
| 25 | Alabama | $7,602,838,000 | 1.3% |
| 40 | Alaska | 2,459,961,000 | 0.4% |
| 24 | Arizona | 8,066,255,000 | 1.4% |
| 31 | Arkansas | 5,361,913,000 | 0.9% |
| 1 | California | 63,482,302,000 | 11.2% |
| 22 | Colorado | 8,185,316,000 | 1.4% |
| 21 | Connecticut | 8,535,528,000 | 1.5% |
| 45 | Delaware | 1,733,515,000 | 0.3% |
| 4 | Florida | 26,304,058,000 | 4.7% |
| 10 | Georgia | 16,880,214,000 | 3.0% |
| 43 | Hawaii | 1,938,691,000 | 0.3% |
| 44 | Idaho | 1,898,594,000 | 0.3% |
| 6 | Illinois | 24,526,656,000 | 4.3% |
| 18 | Indiana | 9,737,968,000 | 1.7% |
| 29 | Iowa | 5,749,910,000 | 1.0% |
| 32 | Kansas | 5,258,252,000 | 0.9% |
| 27 | Kentucky | 6,754,701,000 | 1.2% |
| 23 | Louisiana | 8,173,663,000 | 1.4% |
| 41 | Maine | 2,443,312,000 | 0.4% |
| 14 | Maryland | 12,026,838,000 | 2.1% |
| 13 | Massachusetts | 13,019,880,000 | 2.3% |
| 9 | Michigan | 17,511,552,000 | 3.1% |
| 17 | Minnesota | 9,984,789,000 | 1.8% |
| 33 | Mississippi | 4,275,596,000 | 0.8% |
| 19 | Missouri | 9,425,857,000 | 1.7% |
| 47 | Montana | 1,621,407,000 | 0.3% |
| 37 | Nebraska | 3,580,214,000 | 0.6% |
| 36 | Nevada | 4,012,361,000 | 0.7% |
| 39 | New Hampshire | 2,768,396,000 | 0.5% |
| 7 | New Jersey | 23,429,839,000 | 4.1% |
| 35 | New Mexico | 4,058,681,000 | 0.7% |
| 2 | New York | 55,420,282,000 | 9.8% |
| 12 | North Carolina | 13,133,835,000 | 2.3% |
| 50 | North Dakota | 1,233,523,000 | 0.2% |
| 8 | Ohio | 22,089,312,000 | 3.9% |
| 30 | Oklahoma | 5,506,234,000 | 1.0% |
| 28 | Oregon | 6,019,375,000 | 1.1% |
| 5 | Pennsylvania | 24,682,167,000 | 4.4% |
| 42 | Rhode Island | 2,201,660,000 | 0.4% |
| 26 | South Carolina | 7,590,661,000 | 1.3% |
| 49 | South Dakota | 1,304,302,000 | 0.2% |
| 20 | Tennessee | 8,610,554,000 | 1.5% |
| 3 | Texas | 47,014,113,000 | 8.3% |
| 34 | Utah | 4,084,498,000 | 0.7% |
| 48 | Vermont | 1,471,329,000 | 0.3% |
| 11 | Virginia | 14,277,830,000 | 2.5% |
| 15 | Washington | 11,421,314,000 | 2.0% |
| 38 | West Virginia | 3,314,898,000 | 0.6% |
| 16 | Wisconsin | 10,862,164,000 | 1.9% |
| 46 | Wyoming | 1,640,623,000 | 0.3% |

RANK ORDER

| RANK | STATE | EXPENDITURES | % of USA |
|---|---|---|---|
| 1 | California | $63,482,302,000 | 11.2% |
| 2 | New York | 55,420,282,000 | 9.8% |
| 3 | Texas | 47,014,113,000 | 8.3% |
| 4 | Florida | 26,304,058,000 | 4.7% |
| 5 | Pennsylvania | 24,682,167,000 | 4.4% |
| 6 | Illinois | 24,526,656,000 | 4.3% |
| 7 | New Jersey | 23,429,839,000 | 4.1% |
| 8 | Ohio | 22,089,312,000 | 3.9% |
| 9 | Michigan | 17,511,552,000 | 3.1% |
| 10 | Georgia | 16,880,214,000 | 3.0% |
| 11 | Virginia | 14,277,830,000 | 2.5% |
| 12 | North Carolina | 13,133,835,000 | 2.3% |
| 13 | Massachusetts | 13,019,880,000 | 2.3% |
| 14 | Maryland | 12,026,838,000 | 2.1% |
| 15 | Washington | 11,421,314,000 | 2.0% |
| 16 | Wisconsin | 10,862,164,000 | 1.9% |
| 17 | Minnesota | 9,984,789,000 | 1.8% |
| 18 | Indiana | 9,737,968,000 | 1.7% |
| 19 | Missouri | 9,425,857,000 | 1.7% |
| 20 | Tennessee | 8,610,554,000 | 1.5% |
| 21 | Connecticut | 8,535,528,000 | 1.5% |
| 22 | Colorado | 8,185,316,000 | 1.4% |
| 23 | Louisiana | 8,173,663,000 | 1.4% |
| 24 | Arizona | 8,066,255,000 | 1.4% |
| 25 | Alabama | 7,602,838,000 | 1.3% |
| 26 | South Carolina | 7,590,661,000 | 1.3% |
| 27 | Kentucky | 6,754,701,000 | 1.2% |
| 28 | Oregon | 6,019,375,000 | 1.1% |
| 29 | Iowa | 5,749,910,000 | 1.0% |
| 30 | Oklahoma | 5,506,234,000 | 1.0% |
| 31 | Arkansas | 5,361,913,000 | 0.9% |
| 32 | Kansas | 5,258,252,000 | 0.9% |
| 33 | Mississippi | 4,275,596,000 | 0.8% |
| 34 | Utah | 4,084,498,000 | 0.7% |
| 35 | New Mexico | 4,058,681,000 | 0.7% |
| 36 | Nevada | 4,012,361,000 | 0.7% |
| 37 | Nebraska | 3,580,214,000 | 0.6% |
| 38 | West Virginia | 3,314,898,000 | 0.6% |
| 39 | New Hampshire | 2,768,396,000 | 0.5% |
| 40 | Alaska | 2,459,961,000 | 0.4% |
| 41 | Maine | 2,443,312,000 | 0.4% |
| 42 | Rhode Island | 2,201,660,000 | 0.4% |
| 43 | Hawaii | 1,938,691,000 | 0.3% |
| 44 | Idaho | 1,898,594,000 | 0.3% |
| 45 | Delaware | 1,733,515,000 | 0.3% |
| 46 | Wyoming | 1,640,623,000 | 0.3% |
| 47 | Montana | 1,621,407,000 | 0.3% |
| 48 | Vermont | 1,471,329,000 | 0.3% |
| 49 | South Dakota | 1,304,302,000 | 0.2% |
| 50 | North Dakota | 1,233,523,000 | 0.2% |
| | District of Columbia | 2,174,626,000 | 0.4% |

Source: U.S. Bureau of the Census, Governments Division
   "2011 State and Local Government Finances" (http://www.census.gov/govs/local/)
*Direct general expenditures. Includes capital outlays.

# Per Capita State and Local Government Expenditures for Elementary and Secondary Education in 2011
## National Per Capita = $1,813*

ALPHA ORDER

| RANK | STATE | PER CAPITA |
|------|-------|------------|
| 36 | Alabama | $1,583 |
| 1 | Alaska | 3,398 |
| 49 | Arizona | 1,247 |
| 23 | Arkansas | 1,825 |
| 30 | California | 1,685 |
| 34 | Colorado | 1,600 |
| 5 | Connecticut | 2,380 |
| 15 | Delaware | 1,909 |
| 46 | Florida | 1,378 |
| 29 | Georgia | 1,720 |
| 45 | Hawaii | 1,407 |
| 50 | Idaho | 1,199 |
| 16 | Illinois | 1,907 |
| 40 | Indiana | 1,494 |
| 18 | Iowa | 1,877 |
| 22 | Kansas | 1,832 |
| 39 | Kentucky | 1,547 |
| 25 | Louisiana | 1,787 |
| 20 | Maine | 1,839 |
| 9 | Maryland | 2,060 |
| 10 | Massachusetts | 1,971 |
| 27 | Michigan | 1,773 |
| 19 | Minnesota | 1,867 |
| 44 | Mississippi | 1,436 |
| 37 | Missouri | 1,569 |
| 32 | Montana | 1,625 |
| 12 | Nebraska | 1,943 |
| 41 | Nevada | 1,475 |
| 7 | New Hampshire | 2,101 |
| 4 | New Jersey | 2,652 |
| 11 | New Mexico | 1,953 |
| 3 | New York | 2,842 |
| 47 | North Carolina | 1,361 |
| 24 | North Dakota | 1,801 |
| 14 | Ohio | 1,914 |
| 42 | Oklahoma | 1,455 |
| 38 | Oregon | 1,556 |
| 13 | Pennsylvania | 1,937 |
| 8 | Rhode Island | 2,096 |
| 33 | South Carolina | 1,624 |
| 35 | South Dakota | 1,584 |
| 48 | Tennessee | 1,345 |
| 21 | Texas | 1,834 |
| 43 | Utah | 1,451 |
| 6 | Vermont | 2,348 |
| 28 | Virginia | 1,762 |
| 31 | Washington | 1,674 |
| 25 | West Virginia | 1,787 |
| 17 | Wisconsin | 1,902 |
| 2 | Wyoming | 2,892 |

RANK ORDER

| RANK | STATE | PER CAPITA |
|------|-------|------------|
| 1 | Alaska | $3,398 |
| 2 | Wyoming | 2,892 |
| 3 | New York | 2,842 |
| 4 | New Jersey | 2,652 |
| 5 | Connecticut | 2,380 |
| 6 | Vermont | 2,348 |
| 7 | New Hampshire | 2,101 |
| 8 | Rhode Island | 2,096 |
| 9 | Maryland | 2,060 |
| 10 | Massachusetts | 1,971 |
| 11 | New Mexico | 1,953 |
| 12 | Nebraska | 1,943 |
| 13 | Pennsylvania | 1,937 |
| 14 | Ohio | 1,914 |
| 15 | Delaware | 1,909 |
| 16 | Illinois | 1,907 |
| 17 | Wisconsin | 1,902 |
| 18 | Iowa | 1,877 |
| 19 | Minnesota | 1,867 |
| 20 | Maine | 1,839 |
| 21 | Texas | 1,834 |
| 22 | Kansas | 1,832 |
| 23 | Arkansas | 1,825 |
| 24 | North Dakota | 1,801 |
| 25 | Louisiana | 1,787 |
| 25 | West Virginia | 1,787 |
| 27 | Michigan | 1,773 |
| 28 | Virginia | 1,762 |
| 29 | Georgia | 1,720 |
| 30 | California | 1,685 |
| 31 | Washington | 1,674 |
| 32 | Montana | 1,625 |
| 33 | South Carolina | 1,624 |
| 34 | Colorado | 1,600 |
| 35 | South Dakota | 1,584 |
| 36 | Alabama | 1,583 |
| 37 | Missouri | 1,569 |
| 38 | Oregon | 1,556 |
| 39 | Kentucky | 1,547 |
| 40 | Indiana | 1,494 |
| 41 | Nevada | 1,475 |
| 42 | Oklahoma | 1,455 |
| 43 | Utah | 1,451 |
| 44 | Mississippi | 1,436 |
| 45 | Hawaii | 1,407 |
| 46 | Florida | 1,378 |
| 47 | North Carolina | 1,361 |
| 48 | Tennessee | 1,345 |
| 49 | Arizona | 1,247 |
| 50 | Idaho | 1,199 |
| | District of Columbia | 3,513 |

Source: CQ Press using data from U.S. Bureau of the Census, Governments Division
"2011 State and Local Government Finances" (http://www.census.gov/govs/local/)
*Direct general expenditures. Includes capital outlays.

# Expenditures for Elementary and Secondary Education as a Percent of All State and Local Government Expenditures in 2011
## National Percent = 21.9%*

ALPHA ORDER

| RANK | STATE | PERCENT |
|------|-------|---------|
| 23 | Alabama | 21.5 |
| 41 | Alaska | 19.2 |
| 45 | Arizona | 18.9 |
| 4 | Arkansas | 25.8 |
| 48 | California | 17.9 |
| 38 | Colorado | 19.8 |
| 5 | Connecticut | 25.6 |
| 35 | Delaware | 20.2 |
| 43 | Florida | 19.1 |
| 3 | Georgia | 26.4 |
| 50 | Hawaii | 15.9 |
| 47 | Idaho | 18.1 |
| 13 | Illinois | 23.5 |
| 28 | Indiana | 21.2 |
| 21 | Iowa | 21.7 |
| 16 | Kansas | 22.9 |
| 32 | Kentucky | 20.9 |
| 43 | Louisiana | 19.1 |
| 23 | Maine | 21.5 |
| 8 | Maryland | 24.1 |
| 28 | Massachusetts | 21.2 |
| 10 | Michigan | 23.8 |
| 31 | Minnesota | 21.1 |
| 48 | Mississippi | 17.9 |
| 19 | Missouri | 22.7 |
| 37 | Montana | 20.0 |
| 7 | Nebraska | 24.7 |
| 23 | Nevada | 21.5 |
| 2 | New Hampshire | 27.0 |
| 1 | New Jersey | 28.7 |
| 32 | New Mexico | 20.9 |
| 12 | New York | 23.6 |
| 40 | North Carolina | 19.5 |
| 41 | North Dakota | 19.2 |
| 14 | Ohio | 23.4 |
| 26 | Oklahoma | 21.4 |
| 45 | Oregon | 18.9 |
| 19 | Pennsylvania | 22.7 |
| 9 | Rhode Island | 23.9 |
| 27 | South Carolina | 21.3 |
| 28 | South Dakota | 21.2 |
| 34 | Tennessee | 20.5 |
| 6 | Texas | 25.3 |
| 36 | Utah | 20.1 |
| 10 | Vermont | 23.8 |
| 14 | Virginia | 23.4 |
| 38 | Washington | 19.8 |
| 16 | West Virginia | 22.9 |
| 18 | Wisconsin | 22.8 |
| 21 | Wyoming | 21.7 |

RANK ORDER

| RANK | STATE | PERCENT |
|------|-------|---------|
| 1 | New Jersey | 28.7 |
| 2 | New Hampshire | 27.0 |
| 3 | Georgia | 26.4 |
| 4 | Arkansas | 25.8 |
| 5 | Connecticut | 25.6 |
| 6 | Texas | 25.3 |
| 7 | Nebraska | 24.7 |
| 8 | Maryland | 24.1 |
| 9 | Rhode Island | 23.9 |
| 10 | Michigan | 23.8 |
| 10 | Vermont | 23.8 |
| 12 | New York | 23.6 |
| 13 | Illinois | 23.5 |
| 14 | Ohio | 23.4 |
| 14 | Virginia | 23.4 |
| 16 | Kansas | 22.9 |
| 16 | West Virginia | 22.9 |
| 18 | Wisconsin | 22.8 |
| 19 | Missouri | 22.7 |
| 19 | Pennsylvania | 22.7 |
| 21 | Iowa | 21.7 |
| 21 | Wyoming | 21.7 |
| 23 | Alabama | 21.5 |
| 23 | Maine | 21.5 |
| 23 | Nevada | 21.5 |
| 26 | Oklahoma | 21.4 |
| 27 | South Carolina | 21.3 |
| 28 | Indiana | 21.2 |
| 28 | Massachusetts | 21.2 |
| 28 | South Dakota | 21.2 |
| 31 | Minnesota | 21.1 |
| 32 | Kentucky | 20.9 |
| 32 | New Mexico | 20.9 |
| 34 | Tennessee | 20.5 |
| 35 | Delaware | 20.2 |
| 36 | Utah | 20.1 |
| 37 | Montana | 20.0 |
| 38 | Colorado | 19.8 |
| 38 | Washington | 19.8 |
| 40 | North Carolina | 19.5 |
| 41 | Alaska | 19.2 |
| 41 | North Dakota | 19.2 |
| 43 | Florida | 19.1 |
| 43 | Louisiana | 19.1 |
| 45 | Arizona | 18.9 |
| 45 | Oregon | 18.9 |
| 47 | Idaho | 18.1 |
| 48 | California | 17.9 |
| 48 | Mississippi | 17.9 |
| 50 | Hawaii | 15.9 |

| | District of Columbia | 20.9 |

Source: CQ Press using data from U.S. Bureau of the Census, Governments Division
"2011 State and Local Government Finances" (http://www.census.gov/govs/local/)
*Direct general expenditures as a percent of all direct general expenditures. Includes capital outlays.

# Estimated Per Pupil Public Elementary and Secondary School Current Expenditures in 2013
## National Per Pupil = $11,068*

| ALPHA ORDER | | | | RANK ORDER | | |
|---|---|---|---|---|---|---|
| RANK | STATE | PER PUPIL | | RANK | STATE | PER PUPIL |
| 41 | Alabama | $8,779 | | 1 | Vermont | $19,752 |
| 4 | Alaska | 18,192 | | 2 | New York | 19,523 |
| 50 | Arizona | 6,949 | | 3 | New Jersey | 19,291 |
| 14 | Arkansas | 13,215 | | 4 | Alaska | 18,192 |
| 38 | California | 9,202 | | 5 | Rhode Island | 17,666 |
| 28 | Colorado | 10,199 | | 6 | Wyoming | 16,577 |
| 7 | Connecticut | 16,272 | | 7 | Connecticut | 16,272 |
| 11 | Delaware | 14,890 | | 8 | New Hampshire | 15,394 |
| 43 | Florida | 8,637 | | 9 | Maryland | 15,287 |
| 33 | Georgia | 9,654 | | 10 | Massachusetts | 15,211 |
| 19 | Hawaii | 11,569 | | 11 | Delaware | 14,890 |
| 44 | Idaho | 8,528 | | 12 | Pennsylvania | 14,467 |
| 15 | Illinois | 12,927 | | 13 | Michigan | 13,686 |
| 22 | Indiana | 11,129 | | 14 | Arkansas | 13,215 |
| 36 | Iowa | 9,411 | | 15 | Illinois | 12,927 |
| 32 | Kansas | 9,689 | | 16 | Wisconsin | 12,555 |
| 31 | Kentucky | 9,891 | | 17 | West Virginia | 12,116 |
| 27 | Louisiana | 10,310 | | 18 | Minnesota | 11,632 |
| 24 | Maine | 10,414 | | 19 | Hawaii | 11,569 |
| 9 | Maryland | 15,287 | | 20 | Virginia | 11,457 |
| 10 | Massachusetts | 15,211 | | 21 | Oregon | 11,254 |
| 13 | Michigan | 13,686 | | 22 | Indiana | 11,129 |
| 18 | Minnesota | 11,632 | | 23 | Montana | 10,645 |
| 35 | Mississippi | 9,427 | | 24 | Maine | 10,414 |
| 29 | Missouri | 10,093 | | 25 | New Mexico | 10,397 |
| 23 | Montana | 10,645 | | 26 | Washington | 10,313 |
| 34 | Nebraska | 9,621 | | 27 | Louisiana | 10,310 |
| 45 | Nevada | 8,501 | | 28 | Colorado | 10,199 |
| 8 | New Hampshire | 15,394 | | 29 | Missouri | 10,093 |
| 3 | New Jersey | 19,291 | | 30 | Ohio | 9,941 |
| 25 | New Mexico | 10,397 | | 31 | Kentucky | 9,891 |
| 2 | New York | 19,523 | | 32 | Kansas | 9,689 |
| 47 | North Carolina | 8,433 | | 33 | Georgia | 9,654 |
| 40 | North Dakota | 8,849 | | 34 | Nebraska | 9,621 |
| 30 | Ohio | 9,941 | | 35 | Mississippi | 9,427 |
| 46 | Oklahoma | 8,481 | | 36 | Iowa | 9,411 |
| 21 | Oregon | 11,254 | | 37 | South Dakota | 9,347 |
| 12 | Pennsylvania | 14,467 | | 38 | California | 9,202 |
| 5 | Rhode Island | 17,666 | | 39 | South Carolina | 8,898 |
| 39 | South Carolina | 8,898 | | 40 | North Dakota | 8,849 |
| 37 | South Dakota | 9,347 | | 41 | Alabama | 8,779 |
| 42 | Tennessee | 8,695 | | 42 | Tennessee | 8,695 |
| 48 | Texas | 7,886 | | 43 | Florida | 8,637 |
| 49 | Utah | 7,129 | | 44 | Idaho | 8,528 |
| 1 | Vermont | 19,752 | | 45 | Nevada | 8,501 |
| 20 | Virginia | 11,457 | | 46 | Oklahoma | 8,481 |
| 26 | Washington | 10,313 | | 47 | North Carolina | 8,433 |
| 17 | West Virginia | 12,116 | | 48 | Texas | 7,886 |
| 16 | Wisconsin | 12,555 | | 49 | Utah | 7,129 |
| 6 | Wyoming | 16,577 | | 50 | Arizona | 6,949 |
| | | | | | District of Columbia | 14,406 |

Source: National Education Association, Washington, D.C.

"Rankings and Estimates" (Copyright © 2012, NEA, used with permission, http://www.nea.org/home/54597.htm)

*Estimates for school year 2012-2013. Based on student membership.

# Higher Education Expenditures by State and Local Governments in 2011

## National Total = $252,270,144,000*

ALPHA ORDER

ALPHA ORDER

| RANK | STATE | EXPENDITURES | % of USA |
|---|---|---|---|
| 17 | Alabama | $4,965,533,000 | 2.0% |
| 44 | Alaska | 804,687,000 | 0.3% |
| 19 | Arizona | 4,581,965,000 | 1.8% |
| 34 | Arkansas | 2,415,979,000 | 1.0% |
| 1 | California | 33,924,657,000 | 13.4% |
| 20 | Colorado | 4,524,651,000 | 1.8% |
| 32 | Connecticut | 2,634,179,000 | 1.0% |
| 41 | Delaware | 1,069,356,000 | 0.4% |
| 5 | Florida | 9,561,941,000 | 3.8% |
| 13 | Georgia | 5,760,641,000 | 2.3% |
| 38 | Hawaii | 1,311,756,000 | 0.5% |
| 40 | Idaho | 1,081,700,000 | 0.4% |
| 8 | Illinois | 8,688,799,000 | 3.4% |
| 16 | Indiana | 5,522,656,000 | 2.2% |
| 25 | Iowa | 3,473,156,000 | 1.4% |
| 31 | Kansas | 2,844,866,000 | 1.1% |
| 23 | Kentucky | 3,774,528,000 | 1.5% |
| 30 | Louisiana | 3,138,128,000 | 1.2% |
| 46 | Maine | 794,851,000 | 0.3% |
| 15 | Maryland | 5,554,128,000 | 2.2% |
| 18 | Massachusetts | 4,666,758,000 | 1.8% |
| 4 | Michigan | 10,219,623,000 | 4.1% |
| 21 | Minnesota | 4,405,616,000 | 1.7% |
| 33 | Mississippi | 2,587,705,000 | 1.0% |
| 24 | Missouri | 3,616,927,000 | 1.4% |
| 45 | Montana | 797,111,000 | 0.3% |
| 36 | Nebraska | 1,859,131,000 | 0.7% |
| 39 | Nevada | 1,283,450,000 | 0.5% |
| 43 | New Hampshire | 842,663,000 | 0.3% |
| 14 | New Jersey | 5,702,285,000 | 2.3% |
| 35 | New Mexico | 2,392,724,000 | 0.9% |
| 3 | New York | 14,190,472,000 | 5.6% |
| 6 | North Carolina | 9,289,635,000 | 3.7% |
| 42 | North Dakota | 884,248,000 | 0.4% |
| 9 | Ohio | 8,590,415,000 | 3.4% |
| 26 | Oklahoma | 3,358,720,000 | 1.3% |
| 22 | Oregon | 4,146,073,000 | 1.6% |
| 7 | Pennsylvania | 8,860,132,000 | 3.5% |
| 50 | Rhode Island | 615,842,000 | 0.2% |
| 27 | South Carolina | 3,358,072,000 | 1.3% |
| 49 | South Dakota | 672,371,000 | 0.3% |
| 28 | Tennessee | 3,324,173,000 | 1.3% |
| 2 | Texas | 24,833,195,000 | 9.8% |
| 29 | Utah | 3,308,138,000 | 1.3% |
| 47 | Vermont | 734,522,000 | 0.3% |
| 10 | Virginia | 7,067,344,000 | 2.8% |
| 11 | Washington | 5,926,165,000 | 2.3% |
| 37 | West Virginia | 1,586,126,000 | 0.6% |
| 12 | Wisconsin | 5,869,385,000 | 2.3% |
| 48 | Wyoming | 685,288,000 | 0.3% |

RANK ORDER

| RANK | STATE | EXPENDITURES | % of USA |
|---|---|---|---|
| 1 | California | $33,924,657,000 | 13.4% |
| 2 | Texas | 24,833,195,000 | 9.8% |
| 3 | New York | 14,190,472,000 | 5.6% |
| 4 | Michigan | 10,219,623,000 | 4.1% |
| 5 | Florida | 9,561,941,000 | 3.8% |
| 6 | North Carolina | 9,289,635,000 | 3.7% |
| 7 | Pennsylvania | 8,860,132,000 | 3.5% |
| 8 | Illinois | 8,688,799,000 | 3.4% |
| 9 | Ohio | 8,590,415,000 | 3.4% |
| 10 | Virginia | 7,067,344,000 | 2.8% |
| 11 | Washington | 5,926,165,000 | 2.3% |
| 12 | Wisconsin | 5,869,385,000 | 2.3% |
| 13 | Georgia | 5,760,641,000 | 2.3% |
| 14 | New Jersey | 5,702,285,000 | 2.3% |
| 15 | Maryland | 5,554,128,000 | 2.2% |
| 16 | Indiana | 5,522,656,000 | 2.2% |
| 17 | Alabama | 4,965,533,000 | 2.0% |
| 18 | Massachusetts | 4,666,758,000 | 1.8% |
| 19 | Arizona | 4,581,965,000 | 1.8% |
| 20 | Colorado | 4,524,651,000 | 1.8% |
| 21 | Minnesota | 4,405,616,000 | 1.7% |
| 22 | Oregon | 4,146,073,000 | 1.6% |
| 23 | Kentucky | 3,774,528,000 | 1.5% |
| 24 | Missouri | 3,616,927,000 | 1.4% |
| 25 | Iowa | 3,473,156,000 | 1.4% |
| 26 | Oklahoma | 3,358,720,000 | 1.3% |
| 27 | South Carolina | 3,358,072,000 | 1.3% |
| 28 | Tennessee | 3,324,173,000 | 1.3% |
| 29 | Utah | 3,308,138,000 | 1.3% |
| 30 | Louisiana | 3,138,128,000 | 1.2% |
| 31 | Kansas | 2,844,866,000 | 1.1% |
| 32 | Connecticut | 2,634,179,000 | 1.0% |
| 33 | Mississippi | 2,587,705,000 | 1.0% |
| 34 | Arkansas | 2,415,979,000 | 1.0% |
| 35 | New Mexico | 2,392,724,000 | 0.9% |
| 36 | Nebraska | 1,859,131,000 | 0.7% |
| 37 | West Virginia | 1,586,126,000 | 0.6% |
| 38 | Hawaii | 1,311,756,000 | 0.5% |
| 39 | Nevada | 1,283,450,000 | 0.5% |
| 40 | Idaho | 1,081,700,000 | 0.4% |
| 41 | Delaware | 1,069,356,000 | 0.4% |
| 42 | North Dakota | 884,248,000 | 0.4% |
| 43 | New Hampshire | 842,663,000 | 0.3% |
| 44 | Alaska | 804,687,000 | 0.3% |
| 45 | Montana | 797,111,000 | 0.3% |
| 46 | Maine | 794,851,000 | 0.3% |
| 47 | Vermont | 734,522,000 | 0.3% |
| 48 | Wyoming | 685,288,000 | 0.3% |
| 49 | South Dakota | 672,371,000 | 0.3% |
| 50 | Rhode Island | 615,842,000 | 0.2% |
| | District of Columbia | 167,678,000 | 0.1% |

Source: U.S. Bureau of the Census, Governments Division
   "2011 State and Local Government Finances" (http://www.census.gov/govs/local/)
*Direct general expenditures. Includes capital outlays.

# Per Capita State and Local Government Expenditures for Higher Education in 2011
## National Per Capita = $810*

ALPHA ORDER

| RANK | STATE | PER CAPITA |
|------|-------|------------|
| 11 | Alabama | $1,034 |
| 8 | Alaska | 1,112 |
| 36 | Arizona | 708 |
| 29 | Arkansas | 822 |
| 19 | California | 900 |
| 21 | Colorado | 884 |
| 33 | Connecticut | 734 |
| 3 | Delaware | 1,178 |
| 49 | Florida | 501 |
| 46 | Georgia | 587 |
| 17 | Hawaii | 952 |
| 40 | Idaho | 683 |
| 41 | Illinois | 676 |
| 27 | Indiana | 848 |
| 7 | Iowa | 1,134 |
| 14 | Kansas | 991 |
| 25 | Kentucky | 864 |
| 39 | Louisiana | 686 |
| 45 | Maine | 598 |
| 18 | Maryland | 951 |
| 37 | Massachusetts | 706 |
| 10 | Michigan | 1,035 |
| 28 | Minnesota | 824 |
| 23 | Mississippi | 869 |
| 44 | Missouri | 602 |
| 31 | Montana | 799 |
| 13 | Nebraska | 1,009 |
| 50 | Nevada | 472 |
| 43 | New Hampshire | 639 |
| 42 | New Jersey | 645 |
| 6 | New Mexico | 1,151 |
| 34 | New York | 728 |
| 16 | North Carolina | 963 |
| 1 | North Dakota | 1,291 |
| 32 | Ohio | 744 |
| 20 | Oklahoma | 888 |
| 9 | Oregon | 1,072 |
| 38 | Pennsylvania | 695 |
| 47 | Rhode Island | 586 |
| 35 | South Carolina | 719 |
| 30 | South Dakota | 816 |
| 48 | Tennessee | 519 |
| 15 | Texas | 969 |
| 4 | Utah | 1,175 |
| 5 | Vermont | 1,172 |
| 22 | Virginia | 872 |
| 23 | Washington | 869 |
| 26 | West Virginia | 855 |
| 12 | Wisconsin | 1,028 |
| 2 | Wyoming | 1,208 |

RANK ORDER

| RANK | STATE | PER CAPITA |
|------|-------|------------|
| 1 | North Dakota | $1,291 |
| 2 | Wyoming | 1,208 |
| 3 | Delaware | 1,178 |
| 4 | Utah | 1,175 |
| 5 | Vermont | 1,172 |
| 6 | New Mexico | 1,151 |
| 7 | Iowa | 1,134 |
| 8 | Alaska | 1,112 |
| 9 | Oregon | 1,072 |
| 10 | Michigan | 1,035 |
| 11 | Alabama | 1,034 |
| 12 | Wisconsin | 1,028 |
| 13 | Nebraska | 1,009 |
| 14 | Kansas | 991 |
| 15 | Texas | 969 |
| 16 | North Carolina | 963 |
| 17 | Hawaii | 952 |
| 18 | Maryland | 951 |
| 19 | California | 900 |
| 20 | Oklahoma | 888 |
| 21 | Colorado | 884 |
| 22 | Virginia | 872 |
| 23 | Mississippi | 869 |
| 23 | Washington | 869 |
| 25 | Kentucky | 864 |
| 26 | West Virginia | 855 |
| 27 | Indiana | 848 |
| 28 | Minnesota | 824 |
| 29 | Arkansas | 822 |
| 30 | South Dakota | 816 |
| 31 | Montana | 799 |
| 32 | Ohio | 744 |
| 33 | Connecticut | 734 |
| 34 | New York | 728 |
| 35 | South Carolina | 719 |
| 36 | Arizona | 708 |
| 37 | Massachusetts | 706 |
| 38 | Pennsylvania | 695 |
| 39 | Louisiana | 686 |
| 40 | Idaho | 683 |
| 41 | Illinois | 676 |
| 42 | New Jersey | 645 |
| 43 | New Hampshire | 639 |
| 44 | Missouri | 602 |
| 45 | Maine | 598 |
| 46 | Georgia | 587 |
| 47 | Rhode Island | 586 |
| 48 | Tennessee | 519 |
| 49 | Florida | 501 |
| 50 | Nevada | 472 |

District of Columbia — 271

Source: CQ Press using data from U.S. Bureau of the Census, Governments Division
"2011 State and Local Government Finances" (http://www.census.gov/govs/local/)
*Direct general expenditures. Includes capital outlays.

# Expenditures for Higher Education as a Percent
## of All State and Local Government Expenditures in 2011
## National Percent = 9.8%*

ALPHA ORDER

| RANK | STATE | PERCENT |
|------|-------|---------|
| 2 | Alabama | 14.0 |
| 49 | Alaska | 6.3 |
| 25 | Arizona | 10.7 |
| 18 | Arkansas | 11.6 |
| 30 | California | 9.6 |
| 21 | Colorado | 11.0 |
| 40 | Connecticut | 7.9 |
| 11 | Delaware | 12.5 |
| 46 | Florida | 6.9 |
| 35 | Georgia | 9.0 |
| 25 | Hawaii | 10.7 |
| 27 | Idaho | 10.3 |
| 37 | Illinois | 8.3 |
| 15 | Indiana | 12.0 |
| 7 | Iowa | 13.1 |
| 12 | Kansas | 12.4 |
| 17 | Kentucky | 11.7 |
| 43 | Louisiana | 7.3 |
| 44 | Maine | 7.0 |
| 20 | Maryland | 11.1 |
| 42 | Massachusetts | 7.6 |
| 3 | Michigan | 13.9 |
| 32 | Minnesota | 9.3 |
| 23 | Mississippi | 10.9 |
| 36 | Missouri | 8.7 |
| 29 | Montana | 9.8 |
| 10 | Nebraska | 12.8 |
| 46 | Nevada | 6.9 |
| 38 | New Hampshire | 8.2 |
| 44 | New Jersey | 7.0 |
| 13 | New Mexico | 12.3 |
| 50 | New York | 6.0 |
| 4 | North Carolina | 13.8 |
| 4 | North Dakota | 13.8 |
| 33 | Ohio | 9.1 |
| 8 | Oklahoma | 13.0 |
| 8 | Oregon | 13.0 |
| 38 | Pennsylvania | 8.2 |
| 48 | Rhode Island | 6.7 |
| 31 | South Carolina | 9.4 |
| 23 | South Dakota | 10.9 |
| 40 | Tennessee | 7.9 |
| 6 | Texas | 13.4 |
| 1 | Utah | 16.2 |
| 16 | Vermont | 11.9 |
| 18 | Virginia | 11.6 |
| 27 | Washington | 10.3 |
| 21 | West Virginia | 11.0 |
| 13 | Wisconsin | 12.3 |
| 33 | Wyoming | 9.1 |

RANK ORDER

| RANK | STATE | PERCENT |
|------|-------|---------|
| 1 | Utah | 16.2 |
| 2 | Alabama | 14.0 |
| 3 | Michigan | 13.9 |
| 4 | North Carolina | 13.8 |
| 4 | North Dakota | 13.8 |
| 6 | Texas | 13.4 |
| 7 | Iowa | 13.1 |
| 8 | Oklahoma | 13.0 |
| 8 | Oregon | 13.0 |
| 10 | Nebraska | 12.8 |
| 11 | Delaware | 12.5 |
| 12 | Kansas | 12.4 |
| 13 | New Mexico | 12.3 |
| 13 | Wisconsin | 12.3 |
| 15 | Indiana | 12.0 |
| 16 | Vermont | 11.9 |
| 17 | Kentucky | 11.7 |
| 18 | Arkansas | 11.6 |
| 18 | Virginia | 11.6 |
| 20 | Maryland | 11.1 |
| 21 | Colorado | 11.0 |
| 21 | West Virginia | 11.0 |
| 23 | Mississippi | 10.9 |
| 23 | South Dakota | 10.9 |
| 25 | Arizona | 10.7 |
| 25 | Hawaii | 10.7 |
| 27 | Idaho | 10.3 |
| 27 | Washington | 10.3 |
| 29 | Montana | 9.8 |
| 30 | California | 9.6 |
| 31 | South Carolina | 9.4 |
| 32 | Minnesota | 9.3 |
| 33 | Ohio | 9.1 |
| 33 | Wyoming | 9.1 |
| 35 | Georgia | 9.0 |
| 36 | Missouri | 8.7 |
| 37 | Illinois | 8.3 |
| 38 | New Hampshire | 8.2 |
| 38 | Pennsylvania | 8.2 |
| 40 | Connecticut | 7.9 |
| 40 | Tennessee | 7.9 |
| 42 | Massachusetts | 7.6 |
| 43 | Louisiana | 7.3 |
| 44 | Maine | 7.0 |
| 44 | New Jersey | 7.0 |
| 46 | Florida | 6.9 |
| 46 | Nevada | 6.9 |
| 48 | Rhode Island | 6.7 |
| 49 | Alaska | 6.3 |
| 50 | New York | 6.0 |

| District of Columbia | 1.6 |
|---|---|

Source: CQ Press using data from U.S. Bureau of the Census, Governments Division
   "2011 State and Local Government Finances" (http://www.census.gov/govs/local/)
*Direct general expenditures for higher education as a percent of all direct general expenditures. Includes capital outlays.

# Average Faculty Salary at Institutions of Higher Education in 2012

## National Average = $76,570*

ALPHA ORDER

| RANK | STATE | AVERAGE SALARY |
|------|-------|----------------|
| 36 | Alabama | $65,998 |
| 18 | Alaska | 73,864 |
| 14 | Arizona | 77,222 |
| 50 | Arkansas | 56,191 |
| 4 | California | 92,320 |
| 26 | Colorado | 70,383 |
| 3 | Connecticut | 93,210 |
| 5 | Delaware | 92,312 |
| 22 | Florida | 71,329 |
| 33 | Georgia | 68,530 |
| 13 | Hawaii | 78,370 |
| 46 | Idaho | 58,903 |
| 11 | Illinois | 80,111 |
| 19 | Indiana | 73,459 |
| 29 | Iowa | 69,902 |
| 39 | Kansas | 63,848 |
| 43 | Kentucky | 61,554 |
| 38 | Louisiana | 64,453 |
| 21 | Maine | 71,775 |
| 15 | Maryland | 75,721 |
| 1 | Massachusetts | 96,523 |
| 9 | Michigan | 81,359 |
| 23 | Minnesota | 71,060 |
| 49 | Mississippi | 56,368 |
| 32 | Missouri | 68,547 |
| 47 | Montana | 57,198 |
| 35 | Nebraska | 67,684 |
| 12 | Nevada | 79,496 |
| 10 | New Hampshire | 80,698 |
| 2 | New Jersey | 95,945 |
| 41 | New Mexico | 62,196 |
| 6 | New York | 88,638 |
| 34 | North Carolina | 68,153 |
| 42 | North Dakota | 62,134 |
| 20 | Ohio | 72,355 |
| 40 | Oklahoma | 62,687 |
| 31 | Oregon | 68,890 |
| 8 | Pennsylvania | 81,942 |
| 7 | Rhode Island | 86,931 |
| 44 | South Carolina | 61,027 |
| 48 | South Dakota | 56,633 |
| 37 | Tennessee | 65,592 |
| 25 | Texas | 70,637 |
| 16 | Utah | 74,816 |
| 17 | Vermont | 73,991 |
| 24 | Virginia | 71,030 |
| 30 | Washington | 69,146 |
| 45 | West Virginia | 60,041 |
| 27 | Wisconsin | 70,265 |
| 28 | Wyoming | 70,155 |

RANK ORDER

| RANK | STATE | AVERAGE SALARY |
|------|-------|----------------|
| 1 | Massachusetts | $96,523 |
| 2 | New Jersey | 95,945 |
| 3 | Connecticut | 93,210 |
| 4 | California | 92,320 |
| 5 | Delaware | 92,312 |
| 6 | New York | 88,638 |
| 7 | Rhode Island | 86,931 |
| 8 | Pennsylvania | 81,942 |
| 9 | Michigan | 81,359 |
| 10 | New Hampshire | 80,698 |
| 11 | Illinois | 80,111 |
| 12 | Nevada | 79,496 |
| 13 | Hawaii | 78,370 |
| 14 | Arizona | 77,222 |
| 15 | Maryland | 75,721 |
| 16 | Utah | 74,816 |
| 17 | Vermont | 73,991 |
| 18 | Alaska | 73,864 |
| 19 | Indiana | 73,459 |
| 20 | Ohio | 72,355 |
| 21 | Maine | 71,775 |
| 22 | Florida | 71,329 |
| 23 | Minnesota | 71,060 |
| 24 | Virginia | 71,030 |
| 25 | Texas | 70,637 |
| 26 | Colorado | 70,383 |
| 27 | Wisconsin | 70,265 |
| 28 | Wyoming | 70,155 |
| 29 | Iowa | 69,902 |
| 30 | Washington | 69,146 |
| 31 | Oregon | 68,890 |
| 32 | Missouri | 68,547 |
| 33 | Georgia | 68,530 |
| 34 | North Carolina | 68,153 |
| 35 | Nebraska | 67,684 |
| 36 | Alabama | 65,998 |
| 37 | Tennessee | 65,592 |
| 38 | Louisiana | 64,453 |
| 39 | Kansas | 63,848 |
| 40 | Oklahoma | 62,687 |
| 41 | New Mexico | 62,196 |
| 42 | North Dakota | 62,134 |
| 43 | Kentucky | 61,554 |
| 44 | South Carolina | 61,027 |
| 45 | West Virginia | 60,041 |
| 46 | Idaho | 58,903 |
| 47 | Montana | 57,198 |
| 48 | South Dakota | 56,633 |
| 49 | Mississippi | 56,368 |
| 50 | Arkansas | 56,191 |
| | District of Columbia | 99,141 |

Source: U.S. Department of Education, National Center for Education Statistics
"Digest of Education Statistics 2012" (http://nces.ed.gov/programs/digest/index.asp)
*For 2011-2012 school year. For full-time instructional faculty on 9-month contracts at four-year and two-year public and private degree-granting institutions.

# Average Student Costs at Public Institutions of Higher Education in 2012

## National Average = $16,789*

| ALPHA ORDER | | | | RANK ORDER | | |
|---|---|---|---|---|---|---|
| RANK | STATE | AVERAGE COSTS | | RANK | STATE | AVERAGE COSTS |
| 28 | Alabama | $15,499 | | 1 | New Hampshire | $23,315 |
| 35 | Alaska | 14,528 | | 2 | New Jersey | 23,165 |
| 12 | Arizona | 19,227 | | 3 | Vermont | 22,496 |
| 42 | Arkansas | 13,044 | | 4 | Illinois | 21,142 |
| 7 | California | 20,780 | | 5 | Delaware | 20,980 |
| 22 | Colorado | 17,169 | | 5 | Pennsylvania | 20,980 |
| 10 | Connecticut | 19,815 | | 7 | California | 20,780 |
| 5 | Delaware | 20,980 | | 8 | Rhode Island | 20,634 |
| 37 | Florida | 13,590 | | 9 | Massachusetts | 20,339 |
| 31 | Georgia | 14,799 | | 10 | Connecticut | 19,815 |
| 24 | Hawaii | 16,356 | | 11 | Michigan | 19,230 |
| 48 | Idaho | 12,340 | | 12 | Arizona | 19,227 |
| 4 | Illinois | 21,142 | | 13 | Ohio | 18,668 |
| 23 | Indiana | 17,043 | | 14 | Maine | 18,618 |
| 26 | Iowa | 15,653 | | 15 | South Carolina | 18,076 |
| 38 | Kansas | 13,457 | | 16 | Virginia | 17,967 |
| 25 | Kentucky | 15,913 | | 17 | Oregon | 17,591 |
| 46 | Louisiana | 12,602 | | 18 | Washington | 17,588 |
| 14 | Maine | 18,618 | | 19 | New York | 17,558 |
| 20 | Maryland | 17,446 | | 20 | Maryland | 17,446 |
| 9 | Massachusetts | 20,339 | | 21 | Minnesota | 17,286 |
| 11 | Michigan | 19,230 | | 22 | Colorado | 17,169 |
| 21 | Minnesota | 17,286 | | 23 | Indiana | 17,043 |
| 44 | Mississippi | 12,814 | | 24 | Hawaii | 16,356 |
| 27 | Missouri | 15,634 | | 25 | Kentucky | 15,913 |
| 41 | Montana | 13,103 | | 26 | Iowa | 15,653 |
| 34 | Nebraska | 14,584 | | 27 | Missouri | 15,634 |
| 30 | Nevada | 15,033 | | 28 | Alabama | 15,499 |
| 1 | New Hampshire | 23,315 | | 29 | Texas | 15,355 |
| 2 | New Jersey | 23,165 | | 30 | Nevada | 15,033 |
| 43 | New Mexico | 12,874 | | 31 | Georgia | 14,799 |
| 19 | New York | 17,558 | | 32 | Wisconsin | 14,710 |
| 36 | North Carolina | 13,687 | | 33 | Tennessee | 14,622 |
| 45 | North Dakota | 12,801 | | 34 | Nebraska | 14,584 |
| 13 | Ohio | 18,668 | | 35 | Alaska | 14,528 |
| 47 | Oklahoma | 12,585 | | 36 | North Carolina | 13,687 |
| 17 | Oregon | 17,591 | | 37 | Florida | 13,590 |
| 5 | Pennsylvania | 20,980 | | 38 | Kansas | 13,457 |
| 8 | Rhode Island | 20,634 | | 39 | West Virginia | 13,444 |
| 15 | South Carolina | 18,076 | | 40 | South Dakota | 13,321 |
| 40 | South Dakota | 13,321 | | 41 | Montana | 13,103 |
| 33 | Tennessee | 14,622 | | 42 | Arkansas | 13,044 |
| 29 | Texas | 15,355 | | 43 | New Mexico | 12,874 |
| 50 | Utah | 11,319 | | 44 | Mississippi | 12,814 |
| 3 | Vermont | 22,496 | | 45 | North Dakota | 12,801 |
| 16 | Virginia | 17,967 | | 46 | Louisiana | 12,602 |
| 18 | Washington | 17,588 | | 47 | Oklahoma | 12,585 |
| 39 | West Virginia | 13,444 | | 48 | Idaho | 12,340 |
| 32 | Wisconsin | 14,710 | | 49 | Wyoming | 12,022 |
| 49 | Wyoming | 12,022 | | 50 | Utah | 11,319 |
| | | | | | District of Columbia** | NA |

Source: U.S. Department of Education, National Center for Education Statistics
   "Digest of Education Statistics 2012" (http://nces.ed.gov/programs/digest/index.asp)
*Data for 2011-2012 school year.  Based on average in-state tuition, room and board, and fees for full-time students in public four-year institutions for an entire academic year.
**Not available.

# Average Student Costs at Private Institutions of Higher Education in 2012

## National Average = $33,716*

| ALPHA ORDER | | | | RANK ORDER | | |
|---|---|---|---|---|---|---|
| RANK | STATE | AVERAGE COSTS | | RANK | STATE | AVERAGE COSTS |
| 43 | Alabama | $22,021 | | 1 | Massachusetts | $48,343 |
| 24 | Alaska | 29,695 | | 2 | Connecticut | 46,854 |
| 45 | Arizona | 20,466 | | 3 | Rhode Island | 44,448 |
| 38 | Arkansas | 24,032 | | 4 | Vermont | 43,606 |
| 11 | California | 39,039 | | 5 | New York | 43,559 |
| 28 | Colorado | 29,021 | | 6 | Maryland | 43,109 |
| 2 | Connecticut | 46,854 | | 7 | Pennsylvania | 42,168 |
| 40 | Delaware | 23,800 | | 8 | Maine | 41,201 |
| 25 | Florida | 29,594 | | 9 | New Jersey | 41,053 |
| 22 | Georgia | 31,956 | | 10 | New Hampshire | 40,574 |
| 36 | Hawaii | 24,875 | | 11 | California | 39,039 |
| 49 | Idaho | 14,095 | | 12 | Oregon | 38,723 |
| 15 | Illinois | 35,219 | | 13 | Washington | 38,295 |
| 18 | Indiana | 34,094 | | 14 | Louisiana | 36,354 |
| 41 | Iowa | 23,052 | | 15 | Illinois | 35,219 |
| 31 | Kansas | 27,484 | | 16 | Ohio | 34,771 |
| 33 | Kentucky | 26,326 | | 17 | North Carolina | 34,695 |
| 14 | Louisiana | 36,354 | | 18 | Indiana | 34,094 |
| 8 | Maine | 41,201 | | 19 | Minnesota | 33,461 |
| 6 | Maryland | 43,109 | | 20 | Texas | 33,215 |
| 1 | Massachusetts | 48,343 | | 21 | Wisconsin | 32,599 |
| 37 | Michigan | 24,740 | | 22 | Georgia | 31,956 |
| 19 | Minnesota | 33,461 | | 23 | Tennessee | 30,052 |
| 44 | Mississippi | 20,741 | | 24 | Alaska | 29,695 |
| 32 | Missouri | 26,810 | | 25 | Florida | 29,594 |
| 35 | Montana | 25,388 | | 26 | Nevada | 29,164 |
| 34 | Nebraska | 25,846 | | 27 | Virginia | 29,098 |
| 26 | Nevada | 29,164 | | 28 | Colorado | 29,021 |
| 10 | New Hampshire | 40,574 | | 29 | Oklahoma | 28,285 |
| 9 | New Jersey | 41,053 | | 30 | South Carolina | 27,685 |
| 39 | New Mexico | 23,808 | | 31 | Kansas | 27,484 |
| 5 | New York | 43,559 | | 32 | Missouri | 26,810 |
| 17 | North Carolina | 34,695 | | 33 | Kentucky | 26,326 |
| 47 | North Dakota | 16,386 | | 34 | Nebraska | 25,846 |
| 16 | Ohio | 34,771 | | 35 | Montana | 25,388 |
| 29 | Oklahoma | 28,285 | | 36 | Hawaii | 24,875 |
| 12 | Oregon | 38,723 | | 37 | Michigan | 24,740 |
| 7 | Pennsylvania | 42,168 | | 38 | Arkansas | 24,032 |
| 3 | Rhode Island | 44,448 | | 39 | New Mexico | 23,808 |
| 30 | South Carolina | 27,685 | | 40 | Delaware | 23,800 |
| 42 | South Dakota | 22,802 | | 41 | Iowa | 23,052 |
| 23 | Tennessee | 30,052 | | 42 | South Dakota | 22,802 |
| 20 | Texas | 33,215 | | 43 | Alabama | 22,021 |
| 48 | Utah | 14,859 | | 44 | Mississippi | 20,741 |
| 4 | Vermont | 43,606 | | 45 | Arizona | 20,466 |
| 27 | Virginia | 29,098 | | 46 | West Virginia | 18,828 |
| 13 | Washington | 38,295 | | 47 | North Dakota | 16,386 |
| 46 | West Virginia | 18,828 | | 48 | Utah | 14,859 |
| 21 | Wisconsin | 32,599 | | 49 | Idaho | 14,095 |
| NA | Wyoming** | NA | | NA | Wyoming** | NA |
| | | | | | District of Columbia | 47,122 |

Source: U.S. Department of Education, National Center for Education Statistics
"Digest of Education Statistics 2012" (http://nces.ed.gov/programs/digest/index.asp)
*Data for 2011-2012 school year. Based on average in-state tuition, room and board, and fees for full-time students in private four-year institutions for an entire academic year.
**Not available.

# Institutions of Higher Education in 2012

## National Total = 4,706 Institutions*

ALPHA ORDER

| RANK | STATE | INSTITUTIONS | % of USA |
|------|-------|--------------|----------|
| 23 | Alabama | 76 | 1.6% |
| 50 | Alaska | 9 | 0.2% |
| 20 | Arizona | 87 | 1.8% |
| 31 | Arkansas | 51 | 1.1% |
| 1 | California | 460 | 9.8% |
| 17 | Colorado | 91 | 1.9% |
| 32 | Connecticut | 47 | 1.0% |
| 48 | Delaware | 12 | 0.3% |
| 5 | Florida | 240 | 5.1% |
| 9 | Georgia | 139 | 3.0% |
| 44 | Hawaii | 21 | 0.4% |
| 46 | Idaho | 18 | 0.4% |
| 7 | Illinois | 182 | 3.9% |
| 16 | Indiana | 107 | 2.3% |
| 26 | Iowa | 67 | 1.4% |
| 26 | Kansas | 67 | 1.4% |
| 21 | Kentucky | 79 | 1.7% |
| 24 | Louisiana | 73 | 1.6% |
| 38 | Maine | 32 | 0.7% |
| 29 | Maryland | 62 | 1.3% |
| 12 | Massachusetts | 124 | 2.6% |
| 14 | Michigan | 111 | 2.4% |
| 13 | Minnesota | 116 | 2.5% |
| 35 | Mississippi | 42 | 0.9% |
| 10 | Missouri | 137 | 2.9% |
| 43 | Montana | 22 | 0.5% |
| 35 | Nebraska | 42 | 0.9% |
| 40 | Nevada | 26 | 0.6% |
| 39 | New Hampshire | 29 | 0.6% |
| 25 | New Jersey | 68 | 1.4% |
| 34 | New Mexico | 44 | 0.9% |
| 2 | New York | 303 | 6.4% |
| 8 | North Carolina | 148 | 3.1% |
| 44 | North Dakota | 21 | 0.4% |
| 6 | Ohio | 222 | 4.7% |
| 28 | Oklahoma | 63 | 1.3% |
| 29 | Oregon | 62 | 1.3% |
| 3 | Pennsylvania | 265 | 5.6% |
| 47 | Rhode Island | 13 | 0.3% |
| 22 | South Carolina | 77 | 1.6% |
| 41 | South Dakota | 25 | 0.5% |
| 14 | Tennessee | 111 | 2.4% |
| 4 | Texas | 260 | 5.5% |
| 35 | Utah | 42 | 0.9% |
| 42 | Vermont | 24 | 0.5% |
| 11 | Virginia | 131 | 2.8% |
| 18 | Washington | 88 | 1.9% |
| 33 | West Virginia | 46 | 1.0% |
| 18 | Wisconsin | 88 | 1.9% |
| 49 | Wyoming | 11 | 0.2% |

RANK ORDER

| RANK | STATE | INSTITUTIONS | % of USA |
|------|-------|--------------|----------|
| 1 | California | 460 | 9.8% |
| 2 | New York | 303 | 6.4% |
| 3 | Pennsylvania | 265 | 5.6% |
| 4 | Texas | 260 | 5.5% |
| 5 | Florida | 240 | 5.1% |
| 6 | Ohio | 222 | 4.7% |
| 7 | Illinois | 182 | 3.9% |
| 8 | North Carolina | 148 | 3.1% |
| 9 | Georgia | 139 | 3.0% |
| 10 | Missouri | 137 | 2.9% |
| 11 | Virginia | 131 | 2.8% |
| 12 | Massachusetts | 124 | 2.6% |
| 13 | Minnesota | 116 | 2.5% |
| 14 | Michigan | 111 | 2.4% |
| 14 | Tennessee | 111 | 2.4% |
| 16 | Indiana | 107 | 2.3% |
| 17 | Colorado | 91 | 1.9% |
| 18 | Washington | 88 | 1.9% |
| 18 | Wisconsin | 88 | 1.9% |
| 20 | Arizona | 87 | 1.8% |
| 21 | Kentucky | 79 | 1.7% |
| 22 | South Carolina | 77 | 1.6% |
| 23 | Alabama | 76 | 1.6% |
| 24 | Louisiana | 73 | 1.6% |
| 25 | New Jersey | 68 | 1.4% |
| 26 | Iowa | 67 | 1.4% |
| 26 | Kansas | 67 | 1.4% |
| 28 | Oklahoma | 63 | 1.3% |
| 29 | Maryland | 62 | 1.3% |
| 29 | Oregon | 62 | 1.3% |
| 31 | Arkansas | 51 | 1.1% |
| 32 | Connecticut | 47 | 1.0% |
| 33 | West Virginia | 46 | 1.0% |
| 34 | New Mexico | 44 | 0.9% |
| 35 | Mississippi | 42 | 0.9% |
| 35 | Nebraska | 42 | 0.9% |
| 35 | Utah | 42 | 0.9% |
| 38 | Maine | 32 | 0.7% |
| 39 | New Hampshire | 29 | 0.6% |
| 40 | Nevada | 26 | 0.6% |
| 41 | South Dakota | 25 | 0.5% |
| 42 | Vermont | 24 | 0.5% |
| 43 | Montana | 22 | 0.5% |
| 44 | Hawaii | 21 | 0.4% |
| 44 | North Dakota | 21 | 0.4% |
| 46 | Idaho | 18 | 0.4% |
| 47 | Rhode Island | 13 | 0.3% |
| 48 | Delaware | 12 | 0.3% |
| 49 | Wyoming | 11 | 0.2% |
| 50 | Alaska | 9 | 0.2% |
| | District of Columbia | 20 | 0.4% |

Source: U.S. Department of Education, National Center for Education Statistics
    "Digest of Education Statistics 2012" (http://nces.ed.gov/programs/digest/index.asp)
*For 2011-2012 school year.  Consists of 2,968 four-year and 1,738 two-year public and private (profit and not-for-profit)
degree-granting institutions.  Includes five U.S. Service Schools not shown by state.

# Enrollment in Institutions of Higher Education in 2011

## National Total = 20,994,113 Students*

| RANK | STATE | STUDENTS | % of USA |
|------|-------|----------|----------|
| 24 | Alabama | 318,686 | 1.5% |
| 50 | Alaska | 34,932 | 0.2% |
| 6 | Arizona | 796,986 | 3.8% |
| 33 | Arkansas | 179,281 | 0.9% |
| 1 | California | 2,685,893 | 12.8% |
| 22 | Colorado | 365,820 | 1.7% |
| 32 | Connecticut | 201,638 | 1.0% |
| 44 | Delaware | 56,516 | 0.3% |
| 4 | Florida | 1,143,698 | 5.4% |
| 12 | Georgia | 565,459 | 2.7% |
| 41 | Hawaii | 79,018 | 0.4% |
| 39 | Idaho | 90,142 | 0.4% |
| 5 | Illinois | 892,881 | 4.3% |
| 14 | Indiana | 457,824 | 2.2% |
| 21 | Iowa | 372,146 | 1.8% |
| 31 | Kansas | 216,662 | 1.0% |
| 25 | Kentucky | 293,766 | 1.4% |
| 26 | Louisiana | 265,856 | 1.3% |
| 43 | Maine | 72,297 | 0.3% |
| 18 | Maryland | 380,097 | 1.8% |
| 13 | Massachusetts | 508,554 | 2.4% |
| 9 | Michigan | 685,526 | 3.3% |
| 15 | Minnesota | 457,752 | 2.2% |
| 34 | Mississippi | 179,090 | 0.9% |
| 16 | Missouri | 456,997 | 2.2% |
| 47 | Montana | 54,042 | 0.3% |
| 37 | Nebraska | 142,875 | 0.7% |
| 38 | Nevada | 121,013 | 0.6% |
| 42 | New Hampshire | 77,444 | 0.4% |
| 17 | New Jersey | 443,750 | 2.1% |
| 36 | New Mexico | 157,555 | 0.8% |
| 3 | New York | 1,318,142 | 6.3% |
| 11 | North Carolina | 585,013 | 2.8% |
| 46 | North Dakota | 55,772 | 0.3% |
| 8 | Ohio | 735,026 | 3.5% |
| 30 | Oklahoma | 230,154 | 1.1% |
| 29 | Oregon | 259,061 | 1.2% |
| 7 | Pennsylvania | 787,789 | 3.8% |
| 40 | Rhode Island | 84,644 | 0.4% |
| 28 | South Carolina | 260,002 | 1.2% |
| 45 | South Dakota | 55,899 | 0.3% |
| 23 | Tennessee | 350,275 | 1.7% |
| 2 | Texas | 1,564,387 | 7.5% |
| 27 | Utah | 264,396 | 1.3% |
| 48 | Vermont | 45,143 | 0.2% |
| 10 | Virginia | 588,465 | 2.8% |
| 20 | Washington | 372,841 | 1.8% |
| 35 | West Virginia | 162,308 | 0.8% |
| 19 | Wisconsin | 376,603 | 1.8% |
| 49 | Wyoming | 38,092 | 0.2% |

| RANK | STATE | STUDENTS | % of USA |
|------|-------|----------|----------|
| 1 | California | 2,685,893 | 12.8% |
| 2 | Texas | 1,564,387 | 7.5% |
| 3 | New York | 1,318,142 | 6.3% |
| 4 | Florida | 1,143,698 | 5.4% |
| 5 | Illinois | 892,881 | 4.3% |
| 6 | Arizona | 796,986 | 3.8% |
| 7 | Pennsylvania | 787,789 | 3.8% |
| 8 | Ohio | 735,026 | 3.5% |
| 9 | Michigan | 685,526 | 3.3% |
| 10 | Virginia | 588,465 | 2.8% |
| 11 | North Carolina | 585,013 | 2.8% |
| 12 | Georgia | 565,459 | 2.7% |
| 13 | Massachusetts | 508,554 | 2.4% |
| 14 | Indiana | 457,824 | 2.2% |
| 15 | Minnesota | 457,752 | 2.2% |
| 16 | Missouri | 456,997 | 2.2% |
| 17 | New Jersey | 443,750 | 2.1% |
| 18 | Maryland | 380,097 | 1.8% |
| 19 | Wisconsin | 376,603 | 1.8% |
| 20 | Washington | 372,841 | 1.8% |
| 21 | Iowa | 372,146 | 1.8% |
| 22 | Colorado | 365,820 | 1.7% |
| 23 | Tennessee | 350,275 | 1.7% |
| 24 | Alabama | 318,686 | 1.5% |
| 25 | Kentucky | 293,766 | 1.4% |
| 26 | Louisiana | 265,856 | 1.3% |
| 27 | Utah | 264,396 | 1.3% |
| 28 | South Carolina | 260,002 | 1.2% |
| 29 | Oregon | 259,061 | 1.2% |
| 30 | Oklahoma | 230,154 | 1.1% |
| 31 | Kansas | 216,662 | 1.0% |
| 32 | Connecticut | 201,638 | 1.0% |
| 33 | Arkansas | 179,281 | 0.9% |
| 34 | Mississippi | 179,090 | 0.9% |
| 35 | West Virginia | 162,308 | 0.8% |
| 36 | New Mexico | 157,555 | 0.8% |
| 37 | Nebraska | 142,875 | 0.7% |
| 38 | Nevada | 121,013 | 0.6% |
| 39 | Idaho | 90,142 | 0.4% |
| 40 | Rhode Island | 84,644 | 0.4% |
| 41 | Hawaii | 79,018 | 0.4% |
| 42 | New Hampshire | 77,444 | 0.4% |
| 43 | Maine | 72,297 | 0.3% |
| 44 | Delaware | 56,516 | 0.3% |
| 45 | South Dakota | 55,899 | 0.3% |
| 46 | North Dakota | 55,772 | 0.3% |
| 47 | Montana | 54,042 | 0.3% |
| 48 | Vermont | 45,143 | 0.2% |
| 49 | Wyoming | 38,092 | 0.2% |
| 50 | Alaska | 34,932 | 0.2% |
| | District of Columbia | 90,213 | 0.4% |

Source: U.S. Department of Education, National Center for Education Statistics
    "Digest of Education Statistics 2012" (http://nces.ed.gov/programs/digest/index.asp)
*Fall 2011 enrollment.  Includes full-time and part-time students at Title IV eligible, degree-granting four-year and two-year institutions.  National total includes 15,692 students at U.S. Service Schools not shown by state.

# Enrollment Rate in Institutions of Higher Education in 2011

## National Rate = 676 Students per 1,000 Population 18 to 24 Years Old*

ALPHA ORDER

| RANK | STATE | RATE |
|------|-------|------|
| 28 | Alabama | 657 |
| 50 | Alaska | 455 |
| 1 | Arizona | 1,237 |
| 30 | Arkansas | 628 |
| 22 | California | 676 |
| 11 | Colorado | 731 |
| 36 | Connecticut | 609 |
| 34 | Delaware | 617 |
| 29 | Florida | 646 |
| 44 | Georgia | 568 |
| 37 | Hawaii | 598 |
| 41 | Idaho | 575 |
| 13 | Illinois | 714 |
| 17 | Indiana | 696 |
| 2 | Iowa | 1,198 |
| 10 | Kansas | 739 |
| 15 | Kentucky | 701 |
| 46 | Louisiana | 558 |
| 31 | Maine | 624 |
| 21 | Maryland | 677 |
| 9 | Massachusetts | 748 |
| 18 | Michigan | 690 |
| 4 | Minnesota | 908 |
| 40 | Mississippi | 579 |
| 6 | Missouri | 772 |
| 47 | Montana | 555 |
| 6 | Nebraska | 772 |
| 49 | Nevada | 483 |
| 33 | New Hampshire | 621 |
| 42 | New Jersey | 573 |
| 8 | New Mexico | 761 |
| 26 | New York | 664 |
| 35 | North Carolina | 613 |
| 26 | North Dakota | 664 |
| 24 | Ohio | 666 |
| 39 | Oklahoma | 593 |
| 14 | Oregon | 711 |
| 32 | Pennsylvania | 622 |
| 16 | Rhode Island | 699 |
| 48 | South Carolina | 541 |
| 23 | South Dakota | 673 |
| 43 | Tennessee | 571 |
| 38 | Texas | 595 |
| 5 | Utah | 808 |
| 19 | Vermont | 682 |
| 12 | Virginia | 723 |
| 45 | Washington | 560 |
| 3 | West Virginia | 946 |
| 20 | Wisconsin | 678 |
| 24 | Wyoming | 666 |

RANK ORDER

| RANK | STATE | RATE |
|------|-------|------|
| 1 | Arizona | 1,237 |
| 2 | Iowa | 1,198 |
| 3 | West Virginia | 946 |
| 4 | Minnesota | 908 |
| 5 | Utah | 808 |
| 6 | Missouri | 772 |
| 6 | Nebraska | 772 |
| 8 | New Mexico | 761 |
| 9 | Massachusetts | 748 |
| 10 | Kansas | 739 |
| 11 | Colorado | 731 |
| 12 | Virginia | 723 |
| 13 | Illinois | 714 |
| 14 | Oregon | 711 |
| 15 | Kentucky | 701 |
| 16 | Rhode Island | 699 |
| 17 | Indiana | 696 |
| 18 | Michigan | 690 |
| 19 | Vermont | 682 |
| 20 | Wisconsin | 678 |
| 21 | Maryland | 677 |
| 22 | California | 676 |
| 23 | South Dakota | 673 |
| 24 | Ohio | 666 |
| 24 | Wyoming | 666 |
| 26 | New York | 664 |
| 26 | North Dakota | 664 |
| 28 | Alabama | 657 |
| 29 | Florida | 646 |
| 30 | Arkansas | 628 |
| 31 | Maine | 624 |
| 32 | Pennsylvania | 622 |
| 33 | New Hampshire | 621 |
| 34 | Delaware | 617 |
| 35 | North Carolina | 613 |
| 36 | Connecticut | 609 |
| 37 | Hawaii | 598 |
| 38 | Texas | 595 |
| 39 | Oklahoma | 593 |
| 40 | Mississippi | 579 |
| 41 | Idaho | 575 |
| 42 | New Jersey | 573 |
| 43 | Tennessee | 571 |
| 44 | Georgia | 568 |
| 45 | Washington | 560 |
| 46 | Louisiana | 558 |
| 47 | Montana | 555 |
| 48 | South Carolina | 541 |
| 49 | Nevada | 483 |
| 50 | Alaska | 455 |

| District of Columbia | 1,071 |
|---|---|

Source: CQ Press using data from U.S. Department of Education, National Center for Education Statistics
"Digest of Education Statistics 2012" (http://nces.ed.gov/programs/digest/index.asp)
*Based on fall 2011 enrollment and population. National rate includes U.S. Service Schools. Includes students at four-year and two-year public and private degree-granting institutions. Enrollment based on location of institution. Population based on residence.

# Enrollment in Public Institutions of Higher Education in 2011

## National Total = 15,110,196 Students*

ALPHA ORDER

| RANK | STATE | STUDENTS | % of USA |
|---|---|---|---|
| 21 | Alabama | 260,523 | 1.7% |
| 49 | Alaska | 32,158 | 0.2% |
| 12 | Arizona | 366,116 | 2.4% |
| 33 | Arkansas | 158,760 | 1.1% |
| 1 | California | 2,178,629 | 14.4% |
| 19 | Colorado | 269,298 | 1.8% |
| 35 | Connecticut | 126,487 | 0.8% |
| 47 | Delaware | 40,698 | 0.3% |
| 3 | Florida | 803,200 | 5.3% |
| 9 | Georgia | 428,708 | 2.8% |
| 40 | Hawaii | 60,330 | 0.4% |
| 39 | Idaho | 65,753 | 0.4% |
| 5 | Illinois | 577,043 | 3.8% |
| 14 | Indiana | 340,264 | 2.3% |
| 31 | Iowa | 178,491 | 1.2% |
| 29 | Kansas | 186,475 | 1.2% |
| 23 | Kentucky | 233,427 | 1.5% |
| 25 | Louisiana | 225,210 | 1.5% |
| 41 | Maine | 50,253 | 0.3% |
| 16 | Maryland | 314,383 | 2.1% |
| 24 | Massachusetts | 227,005 | 1.5% |
| 6 | Michigan | 554,741 | 3.7% |
| 18 | Minnesota | 274,192 | 1.8% |
| 32 | Mississippi | 160,611 | 1.1% |
| 20 | Missouri | 260,585 | 1.7% |
| 42 | Montana | 48,912 | 0.3% |
| 36 | Nebraska | 106,794 | 0.7% |
| 37 | Nevada | 105,048 | 0.7% |
| 45 | New Hampshire | 43,333 | 0.3% |
| 13 | New Jersey | 359,458 | 2.4% |
| 34 | New Mexico | 146,515 | 1.0% |
| 4 | New York | 731,914 | 4.8% |
| 8 | North Carolina | 470,989 | 3.1% |
| 43 | North Dakota | 48,868 | 0.3% |
| 7 | Ohio | 542,774 | 3.6% |
| 28 | Oklahoma | 197,373 | 1.3% |
| 26 | Oregon | 215,466 | 1.4% |
| 10 | Pennsylvania | 428,269 | 2.8% |
| 46 | Rhode Island | 43,254 | 0.3% |
| 27 | South Carolina | 208,302 | 1.4% |
| 44 | South Dakota | 43,729 | 0.3% |
| 22 | Tennessee | 241,917 | 1.6% |
| 2 | Texas | 1,367,005 | 9.0% |
| 30 | Utah | 179,208 | 1.2% |
| 50 | Vermont | 27,132 | 0.2% |
| 11 | Virginia | 413,761 | 2.7% |
| 15 | Washington | 317,066 | 2.1% |
| 38 | West Virginia | 95,634 | 0.6% |
| 17 | Wisconsin | 296,795 | 2.0% |
| 48 | Wyoming | 36,368 | 0.2% |

RANK ORDER

| RANK | STATE | STUDENTS | % of USA |
|---|---|---|---|
| 1 | California | 2,178,629 | 14.4% |
| 2 | Texas | 1,367,005 | 9.0% |
| 3 | Florida | 803,200 | 5.3% |
| 4 | New York | 731,914 | 4.8% |
| 5 | Illinois | 577,043 | 3.8% |
| 6 | Michigan | 554,741 | 3.7% |
| 7 | Ohio | 542,774 | 3.6% |
| 8 | North Carolina | 470,989 | 3.1% |
| 9 | Georgia | 428,708 | 2.8% |
| 10 | Pennsylvania | 428,269 | 2.8% |
| 11 | Virginia | 413,761 | 2.7% |
| 12 | Arizona | 366,116 | 2.4% |
| 13 | New Jersey | 359,458 | 2.4% |
| 14 | Indiana | 340,264 | 2.3% |
| 15 | Washington | 317,066 | 2.1% |
| 16 | Maryland | 314,383 | 2.1% |
| 17 | Wisconsin | 296,795 | 2.0% |
| 18 | Minnesota | 274,192 | 1.8% |
| 19 | Colorado | 269,298 | 1.8% |
| 20 | Missouri | 260,585 | 1.7% |
| 21 | Alabama | 260,523 | 1.7% |
| 22 | Tennessee | 241,917 | 1.6% |
| 23 | Kentucky | 233,427 | 1.5% |
| 24 | Massachusetts | 227,005 | 1.5% |
| 25 | Louisiana | 225,210 | 1.5% |
| 26 | Oregon | 215,466 | 1.4% |
| 27 | South Carolina | 208,302 | 1.4% |
| 28 | Oklahoma | 197,373 | 1.3% |
| 29 | Kansas | 186,475 | 1.2% |
| 30 | Utah | 179,208 | 1.2% |
| 31 | Iowa | 178,491 | 1.2% |
| 32 | Mississippi | 160,611 | 1.1% |
| 33 | Arkansas | 158,760 | 1.1% |
| 34 | New Mexico | 146,515 | 1.0% |
| 35 | Connecticut | 126,487 | 0.8% |
| 36 | Nebraska | 106,794 | 0.7% |
| 37 | Nevada | 105,048 | 0.7% |
| 38 | West Virginia | 95,634 | 0.6% |
| 39 | Idaho | 65,753 | 0.4% |
| 40 | Hawaii | 60,330 | 0.4% |
| 41 | Maine | 50,253 | 0.3% |
| 42 | Montana | 48,912 | 0.3% |
| 43 | North Dakota | 48,868 | 0.3% |
| 44 | South Dakota | 43,729 | 0.3% |
| 45 | New Hampshire | 43,333 | 0.3% |
| 46 | Rhode Island | 43,254 | 0.3% |
| 47 | Delaware | 40,698 | 0.3% |
| 48 | Wyoming | 36,368 | 0.2% |
| 49 | Alaska | 32,158 | 0.2% |
| 50 | Vermont | 27,132 | 0.2% |
|  | District of Columbia | 5,280 | 0.0% |

Source: U.S. Department of Education, National Center for Education Statistics
    "Digest of Education Statistics 2012" (http://nces.ed.gov/programs/digest/index.asp)
*Fall 2011 enrollment.  Includes full-time and part-time students at Title IV eligible, degree-granting four-year and two-year
institutions.  National total includes 15,692 students at U.S. Service Schools not shown by state.

# Enrollment in Private Institutions of Higher Education in 2011

## National Total = 5,883,917 Students*

ALPHA ORDER

| RANK | STATE | STUDENTS | % of USA |
|---|---|---|---|
| 27 | Alabama | 58,163 | 1.0% |
| 49 | Alaska | 2,774 | 0.0% |
| 3 | Arizona | 430,870 | 7.3% |
| 39 | Arkansas | 20,521 | 0.3% |
| 2 | California | 507,264 | 8.6% |
| 19 | Colorado | 96,522 | 1.6% |
| 23 | Connecticut | 75,151 | 1.3% |
| 44 | Delaware | 15,818 | 0.3% |
| 5 | Florida | 340,498 | 5.8% |
| 14 | Georgia | 136,751 | 2.3% |
| 40 | Hawaii | 18,688 | 0.3% |
| 37 | Idaho | 24,389 | 0.4% |
| 6 | Illinois | 315,838 | 5.4% |
| 16 | Indiana | 117,560 | 2.0% |
| 10 | Iowa | 193,655 | 3.3% |
| 36 | Kansas | 30,187 | 0.5% |
| 26 | Kentucky | 60,339 | 1.0% |
| 32 | Louisiana | 40,646 | 0.7% |
| 38 | Maine | 22,044 | 0.4% |
| 25 | Maryland | 65,714 | 1.1% |
| 7 | Massachusetts | 281,549 | 4.8% |
| 15 | Michigan | 130,785 | 2.2% |
| 12 | Minnesota | 183,560 | 3.1% |
| 41 | Mississippi | 18,479 | 0.3% |
| 9 | Missouri | 196,412 | 3.3% |
| 48 | Montana | 5,130 | 0.1% |
| 33 | Nebraska | 36,081 | 0.6% |
| 43 | Nevada | 15,965 | 0.3% |
| 34 | New Hampshire | 34,111 | 0.6% |
| 21 | New Jersey | 84,292 | 1.4% |
| 46 | New Mexico | 11,040 | 0.2% |
| 1 | New York | 586,228 | 10.0% |
| 17 | North Carolina | 114,024 | 1.9% |
| 47 | North Dakota | 6,904 | 0.1% |
| 11 | Ohio | 192,252 | 3.3% |
| 35 | Oklahoma | 32,781 | 0.6% |
| 30 | Oregon | 43,595 | 0.7% |
| 4 | Pennsylvania | 359,520 | 6.1% |
| 31 | Rhode Island | 41,390 | 0.7% |
| 29 | South Carolina | 51,700 | 0.9% |
| 45 | South Dakota | 12,170 | 0.2% |
| 18 | Tennessee | 108,358 | 1.8% |
| 8 | Texas | 197,382 | 3.4% |
| 20 | Utah | 85,188 | 1.4% |
| 42 | Vermont | 18,011 | 0.3% |
| 13 | Virginia | 174,704 | 3.0% |
| 28 | Washington | 55,775 | 0.9% |
| 24 | West Virginia | 66,674 | 1.1% |
| 22 | Wisconsin | 79,808 | 1.4% |
| 50 | Wyoming | 1,724 | 0.0% |

RANK ORDER

| RANK | STATE | STUDENTS | % of USA |
|---|---|---|---|
| 1 | New York | 586,228 | 10.0% |
| 2 | California | 507,264 | 8.6% |
| 3 | Arizona | 430,870 | 7.3% |
| 4 | Pennsylvania | 359,520 | 6.1% |
| 5 | Florida | 340,498 | 5.8% |
| 6 | Illinois | 315,838 | 5.4% |
| 7 | Massachusetts | 281,549 | 4.8% |
| 8 | Texas | 197,382 | 3.4% |
| 9 | Missouri | 196,412 | 3.3% |
| 10 | Iowa | 193,655 | 3.3% |
| 11 | Ohio | 192,252 | 3.3% |
| 12 | Minnesota | 183,560 | 3.1% |
| 13 | Virginia | 174,704 | 3.0% |
| 14 | Georgia | 136,751 | 2.3% |
| 15 | Michigan | 130,785 | 2.2% |
| 16 | Indiana | 117,560 | 2.0% |
| 17 | North Carolina | 114,024 | 1.9% |
| 18 | Tennessee | 108,358 | 1.8% |
| 19 | Colorado | 96,522 | 1.6% |
| 20 | Utah | 85,188 | 1.4% |
| 21 | New Jersey | 84,292 | 1.4% |
| 22 | Wisconsin | 79,808 | 1.4% |
| 23 | Connecticut | 75,151 | 1.3% |
| 24 | West Virginia | 66,674 | 1.1% |
| 25 | Maryland | 65,714 | 1.1% |
| 26 | Kentucky | 60,339 | 1.0% |
| 27 | Alabama | 58,163 | 1.0% |
| 28 | Washington | 55,775 | 0.9% |
| 29 | South Carolina | 51,700 | 0.9% |
| 30 | Oregon | 43,595 | 0.7% |
| 31 | Rhode Island | 41,390 | 0.7% |
| 32 | Louisiana | 40,646 | 0.7% |
| 33 | Nebraska | 36,081 | 0.6% |
| 34 | New Hampshire | 34,111 | 0.6% |
| 35 | Oklahoma | 32,781 | 0.6% |
| 36 | Kansas | 30,187 | 0.5% |
| 37 | Idaho | 24,389 | 0.4% |
| 38 | Maine | 22,044 | 0.4% |
| 39 | Arkansas | 20,521 | 0.3% |
| 40 | Hawaii | 18,688 | 0.3% |
| 41 | Mississippi | 18,479 | 0.3% |
| 42 | Vermont | 18,011 | 0.3% |
| 43 | Nevada | 15,965 | 0.3% |
| 44 | Delaware | 15,818 | 0.3% |
| 45 | South Dakota | 12,170 | 0.2% |
| 46 | New Mexico | 11,040 | 0.2% |
| 47 | North Dakota | 6,904 | 0.1% |
| 48 | Montana | 5,130 | 0.1% |
| 49 | Alaska | 2,774 | 0.0% |
| 50 | Wyoming | 1,724 | 0.0% |
| | District of Columbia | 84,933 | 1.4% |

Source: U.S. Department of Education, National Center for Education Statistics
   "Digest of Education Statistics 2012" (http://nces.ed.gov/programs/digest/index.asp)
*Fall 2011 enrollment.  Includes full-time and part-time students at Title IV eligible, degree-granting four-year and two-year institutions.

# Percent of Population with a Bachelor's Degree or More in 2012

## National Percent = 29.1%*

| ALPHA ORDER | | | | RANK ORDER | | |
|---|---|---|---|---|---|---|
| RANK | STATE | PERCENT | | RANK | STATE | PERCENT |
| 44 | Alabama | 23.3 | | 1 | Massachusetts | 39.3 |
| 23 | Alaska | 28.0 | | 2 | Colorado | 37.5 |
| 28 | Arizona | 27.3 | | 3 | Connecticut | 37.1 |
| 48 | Arkansas | 21.0 | | 4 | Maryland | 36.9 |
| 14 | California | 30.9 | | 5 | New Jersey | 36.2 |
| 2 | Colorado | 37.5 | | 6 | Vermont | 35.8 |
| 3 | Connecticut | 37.1 | | 7 | Virginia | 35.5 |
| 19 | Delaware | 29.5 | | 8 | New Hampshire | 34.6 |
| 30 | Florida | 26.8 | | 9 | New York | 33.4 |
| 22 | Georgia | 28.2 | | 10 | Minnesota | 33.2 |
| 17 | Hawaii | 30.1 | | 11 | Washington | 31.7 |
| 37 | Idaho | 25.5 | | 12 | Illinois | 31.6 |
| 12 | Illinois | 31.6 | | 13 | Rhode Island | 31.4 |
| 43 | Indiana | 23.4 | | 14 | California | 30.9 |
| 33 | Iowa | 26.3 | | 15 | Utah | 30.7 |
| 16 | Kansas | 30.4 | | 16 | Kansas | 30.4 |
| 47 | Kentucky | 21.8 | | 17 | Hawaii | 30.1 |
| 46 | Louisiana | 22.0 | | 18 | Oregon | 29.9 |
| 23 | Maine | 28.0 | | 19 | Delaware | 29.5 |
| 4 | Maryland | 36.9 | | 20 | Montana | 29.4 |
| 1 | Massachusetts | 39.3 | | 21 | Nebraska | 29.0 |
| 36 | Michigan | 26.0 | | 22 | Georgia | 28.2 |
| 10 | Minnesota | 33.2 | | 23 | Alaska | 28.0 |
| 49 | Mississippi | 20.7 | | 23 | Maine | 28.0 |
| 32 | Missouri | 26.4 | | 25 | North Dakota | 27.9 |
| 20 | Montana | 29.4 | | 26 | Pennsylvania | 27.8 |
| 21 | Nebraska | 29.0 | | 27 | North Carolina | 27.4 |
| 45 | Nevada | 22.4 | | 28 | Arizona | 27.3 |
| 8 | New Hampshire | 34.6 | | 29 | Wisconsin | 27.1 |
| 5 | New Jersey | 36.2 | | 30 | Florida | 26.8 |
| 35 | New Mexico | 26.1 | | 31 | Texas | 26.7 |
| 9 | New York | 33.4 | | 32 | Missouri | 26.4 |
| 27 | North Carolina | 27.4 | | 33 | Iowa | 26.3 |
| 25 | North Dakota | 27.9 | | 33 | South Dakota | 26.3 |
| 38 | Ohio | 25.2 | | 35 | New Mexico | 26.1 |
| 42 | Oklahoma | 23.8 | | 36 | Michigan | 26.0 |
| 18 | Oregon | 29.9 | | 37 | Idaho | 25.5 |
| 26 | Pennsylvania | 27.8 | | 38 | Ohio | 25.2 |
| 13 | Rhode Island | 31.4 | | 39 | South Carolina | 25.1 |
| 39 | South Carolina | 25.1 | | 40 | Wyoming | 24.7 |
| 33 | South Dakota | 26.3 | | 41 | Tennessee | 24.3 |
| 41 | Tennessee | 24.3 | | 42 | Oklahoma | 23.8 |
| 31 | Texas | 26.7 | | 43 | Indiana | 23.4 |
| 15 | Utah | 30.7 | | 44 | Alabama | 23.3 |
| 6 | Vermont | 35.8 | | 45 | Nevada | 22.4 |
| 7 | Virginia | 35.5 | | 46 | Louisiana | 22.0 |
| 11 | Washington | 31.7 | | 47 | Kentucky | 21.8 |
| 50 | West Virginia | 18.6 | | 48 | Arkansas | 21.0 |
| 29 | Wisconsin | 27.1 | | 49 | Mississippi | 20.7 |
| 40 | Wyoming | 24.7 | | 50 | West Virginia | 18.6 |
| | | | | | District of Columbia | 53.0 |

Source: U.S. Bureau of the Census
"2012 American Community Survey-Table R1502" (http://www.census.gov/acs/www/index.html)
*Persons age 25 and older.

# Percent of Population Who Have Completed an Advanced Degree in 2012

## National Percent = 10.9%*

ALPHA ORDER

| RANK | STATE | PERCENT |
|------|-------|---------|
| 37 | Alabama | 8.6 |
| 17 | Alaska | 10.9 |
| 24 | Arizona | 10.2 |
| 50 | Arkansas | 7.2 |
| 13 | California | 11.3 |
| 8 | Colorado | 13.7 |
| 3 | Connecticut | 16.6 |
| 12 | Delaware | 11.4 |
| 29 | Florida | 9.6 |
| 22 | Georgia | 10.4 |
| 21 | Hawaii | 10.5 |
| 41 | Idaho | 8.2 |
| 11 | Illinois | 12.0 |
| 39 | Indiana | 8.4 |
| 41 | Iowa | 8.2 |
| 17 | Kansas | 10.9 |
| 36 | Kentucky | 8.9 |
| 47 | Louisiana | 7.5 |
| 26 | Maine | 9.8 |
| 2 | Maryland | 16.9 |
| 1 | Massachusetts | 17.1 |
| 25 | Michigan | 10.0 |
| 20 | Minnesota | 10.8 |
| 46 | Mississippi | 7.6 |
| 27 | Missouri | 9.7 |
| 33 | Montana | 9.2 |
| 27 | Nebraska | 9.7 |
| 47 | Nevada | 7.5 |
| 10 | New Hampshire | 12.6 |
| 7 | New Jersey | 13.8 |
| 16 | New Mexico | 11.2 |
| 5 | New York | 14.4 |
| 30 | North Carolina | 9.3 |
| 39 | North Dakota | 8.4 |
| 30 | Ohio | 9.3 |
| 44 | Oklahoma | 7.9 |
| 13 | Oregon | 11.3 |
| 17 | Pennsylvania | 10.9 |
| 9 | Rhode Island | 12.8 |
| 34 | South Carolina | 9.1 |
| 43 | South Dakota | 8.1 |
| 37 | Tennessee | 8.6 |
| 35 | Texas | 9.0 |
| 22 | Utah | 10.4 |
| 6 | Vermont | 13.9 |
| 4 | Virginia | 14.9 |
| 13 | Washington | 11.3 |
| 49 | West Virginia | 7.3 |
| 30 | Wisconsin | 9.3 |
| 45 | Wyoming | 7.8 |

RANK ORDER

| RANK | STATE | PERCENT |
|------|-------|---------|
| 1 | Massachusetts | 17.1 |
| 2 | Maryland | 16.9 |
| 3 | Connecticut | 16.6 |
| 4 | Virginia | 14.9 |
| 5 | New York | 14.4 |
| 6 | Vermont | 13.9 |
| 7 | New Jersey | 13.8 |
| 8 | Colorado | 13.7 |
| 9 | Rhode Island | 12.8 |
| 10 | New Hampshire | 12.6 |
| 11 | Illinois | 12.0 |
| 12 | Delaware | 11.4 |
| 13 | California | 11.3 |
| 13 | Oregon | 11.3 |
| 13 | Washington | 11.3 |
| 16 | New Mexico | 11.2 |
| 17 | Alaska | 10.9 |
| 17 | Kansas | 10.9 |
| 17 | Pennsylvania | 10.9 |
| 20 | Minnesota | 10.8 |
| 21 | Hawaii | 10.5 |
| 22 | Georgia | 10.4 |
| 22 | Utah | 10.4 |
| 24 | Arizona | 10.2 |
| 25 | Michigan | 10.0 |
| 26 | Maine | 9.8 |
| 27 | Missouri | 9.7 |
| 27 | Nebraska | 9.7 |
| 29 | Florida | 9.6 |
| 30 | North Carolina | 9.3 |
| 30 | Ohio | 9.3 |
| 30 | Wisconsin | 9.3 |
| 33 | Montana | 9.2 |
| 34 | South Carolina | 9.1 |
| 35 | Texas | 9.0 |
| 36 | Kentucky | 8.9 |
| 37 | Alabama | 8.6 |
| 37 | Tennessee | 8.6 |
| 39 | Indiana | 8.4 |
| 39 | North Dakota | 8.4 |
| 41 | Idaho | 8.2 |
| 41 | Iowa | 8.2 |
| 43 | South Dakota | 8.1 |
| 44 | Oklahoma | 7.9 |
| 45 | Wyoming | 7.8 |
| 46 | Mississippi | 7.6 |
| 47 | Louisiana | 7.5 |
| 47 | Nevada | 7.5 |
| 49 | West Virginia | 7.3 |
| 50 | Arkansas | 7.2 |

District of Columbia     30.0

Source: U.S. Bureau of the Census

"2012 American Community Survey-Table R1503" (http://www.census.gov/acs/www/index.html)

*Persons age 25 and older who have earned a master's degree or higher.

# Public Libraries and Branches in 2010

## National Total = 16,417 Libraries and Branches*

ALPHA ORDER

| RANK | STATE | LIBRARIES | % of USA |
|---|---|---|---|
| 22 | Alabama | 289 | 1.8% |
| 44 | Alaska | 91 | 0.6% |
| 31 | Arizona | 216 | 1.3% |
| 30 | Arkansas | 219 | 1.3% |
| 1 | California | 1,107 | 6.7% |
| 24 | Colorado | 250 | 1.5% |
| 27 | Connecticut | 230 | 1.4% |
| 50 | Delaware | 32 | 0.2% |
| 9 | Florida | 525 | 3.2% |
| 14 | Georgia | 392 | 2.4% |
| 49 | Hawaii | 51 | 0.3% |
| 39 | Idaho | 139 | 0.8% |
| 4 | Illinois | 783 | 4.8% |
| 12 | Indiana | 434 | 2.6% |
| 8 | Iowa | 553 | 3.4% |
| 16 | Kansas | 358 | 2.2% |
| 34 | Kentucky | 200 | 1.2% |
| 20 | Louisiana | 336 | 2.0% |
| 29 | Maine | 221 | 1.3% |
| 36 | Maryland | 184 | 1.1% |
| 11 | Massachusetts | 455 | 2.8% |
| 6 | Michigan | 653 | 4.0% |
| 18 | Minnesota | 357 | 2.2% |
| 25 | Mississippi | 235 | 1.4% |
| 16 | Missouri | 358 | 2.2% |
| 42 | Montana | 110 | 0.7% |
| 26 | Nebraska | 234 | 1.4% |
| 45 | Nevada | 86 | 0.5% |
| 28 | New Hampshire | 226 | 1.4% |
| 13 | New Jersey | 432 | 2.6% |
| 43 | New Mexico | 108 | 0.7% |
| 2 | New York | 1,066 | 6.5% |
| 15 | North Carolina | 387 | 2.4% |
| 46 | North Dakota | 82 | 0.5% |
| 5 | Ohio | 720 | 4.4% |
| 33 | Oklahoma | 207 | 1.3% |
| 32 | Oregon | 215 | 1.3% |
| 7 | Pennsylvania | 634 | 3.9% |
| 48 | Rhode Island | 73 | 0.4% |
| 35 | South Carolina | 193 | 1.2% |
| 41 | South Dakota | 125 | 0.8% |
| 22 | Tennessee | 289 | 1.8% |
| 3 | Texas | 852 | 5.2% |
| 40 | Utah | 126 | 0.8% |
| 38 | Vermont | 161 | 1.0% |
| 19 | Virginia | 354 | 2.2% |
| 21 | Washington | 334 | 2.0% |
| 37 | West Virginia | 174 | 1.1% |
| 10 | Wisconsin | 460 | 2.8% |
| 47 | Wyoming | 76 | 0.5% |

RANK ORDER

| RANK | STATE | LIBRARIES | % of USA |
|---|---|---|---|
| 1 | California | 1,107 | 6.7% |
| 2 | New York | 1,066 | 6.5% |
| 3 | Texas | 852 | 5.2% |
| 4 | Illinois | 783 | 4.8% |
| 5 | Ohio | 720 | 4.4% |
| 6 | Michigan | 653 | 4.0% |
| 7 | Pennsylvania | 634 | 3.9% |
| 8 | Iowa | 553 | 3.4% |
| 9 | Florida | 525 | 3.2% |
| 10 | Wisconsin | 460 | 2.8% |
| 11 | Massachusetts | 455 | 2.8% |
| 12 | Indiana | 434 | 2.6% |
| 13 | New Jersey | 432 | 2.6% |
| 14 | Georgia | 392 | 2.4% |
| 15 | North Carolina | 387 | 2.4% |
| 16 | Kansas | 358 | 2.2% |
| 16 | Missouri | 358 | 2.2% |
| 18 | Minnesota | 357 | 2.2% |
| 19 | Virginia | 354 | 2.2% |
| 20 | Louisiana | 336 | 2.0% |
| 21 | Washington | 334 | 2.0% |
| 22 | Alabama | 289 | 1.8% |
| 22 | Tennessee | 289 | 1.8% |
| 24 | Colorado | 250 | 1.5% |
| 25 | Mississippi | 235 | 1.4% |
| 26 | Nebraska | 234 | 1.4% |
| 27 | Connecticut | 230 | 1.4% |
| 28 | New Hampshire | 226 | 1.4% |
| 29 | Maine | 221 | 1.3% |
| 30 | Arkansas | 219 | 1.3% |
| 31 | Arizona | 216 | 1.3% |
| 32 | Oregon | 215 | 1.3% |
| 33 | Oklahoma | 207 | 1.3% |
| 34 | Kentucky | 200 | 1.2% |
| 35 | South Carolina | 193 | 1.2% |
| 36 | Maryland | 184 | 1.1% |
| 37 | West Virginia | 174 | 1.1% |
| 38 | Vermont | 161 | 1.0% |
| 39 | Idaho | 139 | 0.8% |
| 40 | Utah | 126 | 0.8% |
| 41 | South Dakota | 125 | 0.8% |
| 42 | Montana | 110 | 0.7% |
| 43 | New Mexico | 108 | 0.7% |
| 44 | Alaska | 91 | 0.6% |
| 45 | Nevada | 86 | 0.5% |
| 46 | North Dakota | 82 | 0.5% |
| 47 | Wyoming | 76 | 0.5% |
| 48 | Rhode Island | 73 | 0.4% |
| 49 | Hawaii | 51 | 0.3% |
| 50 | Delaware | 32 | 0.2% |
|  | District of Columbia | 25 | 0.2% |

Source: Institute of Museum and Library Services
   "Public Library Survey Fiscal Year 2010" (January 2013, http://www.imls.gov/research/default.aspx)
*For fiscal year 2010. Total of central and branch outlets. Does not include bookmobiles. There are 8,951 public libraries.

# Rate of Public Libraries and Branches in 2010

## National Average = 18,842 Population per Library*

ALPHA ORDER

| RANK | STATE | RATE |
|------|-------|------|
| 25 | Alabama | 16,556 |
| 43 | Alaska | 7,847 |
| 5 | Arizona | 29,680 |
| 35 | Arkansas | 13,346 |
| 2 | California | 33,726 |
| 17 | Colorado | 20,194 |
| 28 | Connecticut | 15,551 |
| 7 | Delaware | 28,120 |
| 1 | Florida | 35,897 |
| 9 | Georgia | 24,783 |
| 8 | Hawaii | 26,750 |
| 38 | Idaho | 11,301 |
| 26 | Illinois | 16,399 |
| 30 | Indiana | 14,954 |
| 49 | Iowa | 5,516 |
| 42 | Kansas | 7,986 |
| 15 | Kentucky | 21,733 |
| 34 | Louisiana | 13,524 |
| 47 | Maine | 6,007 |
| 3 | Maryland | 31,457 |
| 32 | Massachusetts | 14,425 |
| 29 | Michigan | 15,127 |
| 31 | Minnesota | 14,876 |
| 36 | Mississippi | 12,635 |
| 24 | Missouri | 16,749 |
| 40 | Montana | 9,007 |
| 44 | Nebraska | 7,819 |
| 4 | Nevada | 31,439 |
| 48 | New Hampshire | 5,827 |
| 16 | New Jersey | 20,378 |
| 20 | New Mexico | 19,118 |
| 21 | New York | 18,198 |
| 10 | North Carolina | 24,700 |
| 41 | North Dakota | 8,224 |
| 27 | Ohio | 16,025 |
| 22 | Oklahoma | 18,162 |
| 23 | Oregon | 17,852 |
| 19 | Pennsylvania | 20,049 |
| 33 | Rhode Island | 14,421 |
| 11 | South Carolina | 24,020 |
| 46 | South Dakota | 6,530 |
| 14 | Tennessee | 21,995 |
| 6 | Texas | 29,628 |
| 13 | Utah | 22,025 |
| 50 | Vermont | 3,888 |
| 12 | Virginia | 22,670 |
| 18 | Washington | 20,191 |
| 39 | West Virginia | 10,655 |
| 37 | Wisconsin | 12,369 |
| 45 | Wyoming | 7,426 |

RANK ORDER

| RANK | STATE | RATE |
|------|-------|------|
| 1 | Florida | 35,897 |
| 2 | California | 33,726 |
| 3 | Maryland | 31,457 |
| 4 | Nevada | 31,439 |
| 5 | Arizona | 29,680 |
| 6 | Texas | 29,628 |
| 7 | Delaware | 28,120 |
| 8 | Hawaii | 26,750 |
| 9 | Georgia | 24,783 |
| 10 | North Carolina | 24,700 |
| 11 | South Carolina | 24,020 |
| 12 | Virginia | 22,670 |
| 13 | Utah | 22,025 |
| 14 | Tennessee | 21,995 |
| 15 | Kentucky | 21,733 |
| 16 | New Jersey | 20,378 |
| 17 | Colorado | 20,194 |
| 18 | Washington | 20,191 |
| 19 | Pennsylvania | 20,049 |
| 20 | New Mexico | 19,118 |
| 21 | New York | 18,198 |
| 22 | Oklahoma | 18,162 |
| 23 | Oregon | 17,852 |
| 24 | Missouri | 16,749 |
| 25 | Alabama | 16,556 |
| 26 | Illinois | 16,399 |
| 27 | Ohio | 16,025 |
| 28 | Connecticut | 15,551 |
| 29 | Michigan | 15,127 |
| 30 | Indiana | 14,954 |
| 31 | Minnesota | 14,876 |
| 32 | Massachusetts | 14,425 |
| 33 | Rhode Island | 14,421 |
| 34 | Louisiana | 13,524 |
| 35 | Arkansas | 13,346 |
| 36 | Mississippi | 12,635 |
| 37 | Wisconsin | 12,369 |
| 38 | Idaho | 11,301 |
| 39 | West Virginia | 10,655 |
| 40 | Montana | 9,007 |
| 41 | North Dakota | 8,224 |
| 42 | Kansas | 7,986 |
| 43 | Alaska | 7,847 |
| 44 | Nebraska | 7,819 |
| 45 | Wyoming | 7,426 |
| 46 | South Dakota | 6,530 |
| 47 | Maine | 6,007 |
| 48 | New Hampshire | 5,827 |
| 49 | Iowa | 5,516 |
| 50 | Vermont | 3,888 |

| District of Columbia | 24,200 |
|---|---|

Source: CQ Press using data from Institute of Museum and Library Services
"Public Library Survey Fiscal Year 2010" (January 2013, http://www.imls.gov/research/default.aspx)
*For fiscal year 2010. Based on total of central and branch outlets. Does not include bookmobiles.

# Rate of Books in Public Libraries in 2010

## National Rate = 2,613 Books per 1,000 Population*

| ALPHA ORDER | | | RANK ORDER | | |
|---|---|---|---|---|---|
| RANK | STATE | RATE | RANK | STATE | RATE |
| 40 | Alabama | 2,017 | 1 | Massachusetts | 4,996 |
| 19 | Alaska | 3,314 | 2 | Vermont | 4,646 |
| 50 | Arizona | 1,395 | 3 | New Hampshire | 4,532 |
| 33 | Arkansas | 2,248 | 4 | Maine | 4,527 |
| 41 | California | 2,002 | 5 | Wyoming | 4,426 |
| 32 | Colorado | 2,328 | 6 | Rhode Island | 4,404 |
| 7 | Connecticut | 4,104 | 7 | Connecticut | 4,104 |
| 38 | Delaware | 2,065 | 8 | Iowa | 3,972 |
| 45 | Florida | 1,754 | 9 | Indiana | 3,949 |
| 47 | Georgia | 1,726 | 10 | Ohio | 3,919 |
| 28 | Hawaii | 2,541 | 11 | New York | 3,767 |
| 25 | Idaho | 2,748 | 12 | South Dakota | 3,585 |
| 14 | Illinois | 3,522 | 13 | Michigan | 3,576 |
| 9 | Indiana | 3,949 | 14 | Illinois | 3,522 |
| 8 | Iowa | 3,972 | 15 | North Dakota | 3,520 |
| 16 | Kansas | 3,519 | 16 | Kansas | 3,519 |
| 37 | Kentucky | 2,077 | 17 | Wisconsin | 3,479 |
| 26 | Louisiana | 2,622 | 18 | New Jersey | 3,366 |
| 4 | Maine | 4,527 | 19 | Alaska | 3,314 |
| 30 | Maryland | 2,411 | 20 | Nebraska | 3,201 |
| 1 | Massachusetts | 4,996 | 21 | Minnesota | 2,936 |
| 13 | Michigan | 3,576 | 22 | Missouri | 2,890 |
| 21 | Minnesota | 2,936 | 23 | West Virginia | 2,839 |
| 43 | Mississippi | 1,876 | 24 | Montana | 2,820 |
| 22 | Missouri | 2,890 | 25 | Idaho | 2,748 |
| 24 | Montana | 2,820 | 26 | Louisiana | 2,622 |
| 20 | Nebraska | 3,201 | 27 | Oregon | 2,618 |
| 48 | Nevada | 1,681 | 28 | Hawaii | 2,541 |
| 3 | New Hampshire | 4,532 | 29 | Utah | 2,477 |
| 18 | New Jersey | 3,366 | 30 | Maryland | 2,411 |
| 36 | New Mexico | 2,144 | 31 | Virginia | 2,358 |
| 11 | New York | 3,767 | 32 | Colorado | 2,328 |
| 46 | North Carolina | 1,753 | 33 | Arkansas | 2,248 |
| 15 | North Dakota | 3,520 | 34 | Washington | 2,206 |
| 10 | Ohio | 3,919 | 35 | Pennsylvania | 2,186 |
| 42 | Oklahoma | 1,956 | 36 | New Mexico | 2,144 |
| 27 | Oregon | 2,618 | 37 | Kentucky | 2,077 |
| 35 | Pennsylvania | 2,186 | 38 | Delaware | 2,065 |
| 6 | Rhode Island | 4,404 | 38 | South Carolina | 2,065 |
| 38 | South Carolina | 2,065 | 40 | Alabama | 2,017 |
| 12 | South Dakota | 3,585 | 41 | California | 2,002 |
| 44 | Tennessee | 1,862 | 42 | Oklahoma | 1,956 |
| 49 | Texas | 1,657 | 43 | Mississippi | 1,876 |
| 29 | Utah | 2,477 | 44 | Tennessee | 1,862 |
| 2 | Vermont | 4,646 | 45 | Florida | 1,754 |
| 31 | Virginia | 2,358 | 46 | North Carolina | 1,753 |
| 34 | Washington | 2,206 | 47 | Georgia | 1,726 |
| 23 | West Virginia | 2,839 | 48 | Nevada | 1,681 |
| 17 | Wisconsin | 3,479 | 49 | Texas | 1,657 |
| 5 | Wyoming | 4,426 | 50 | Arizona | 1,395 |
| | | | | District of Columbia | 3,147 |

Source: CQ Press using data from Institute of Museum and Library Services
"Public Library Survey Fiscal Year 2010" (January 2013, http://www.imls.gov/research/default.aspx)
*For fiscal year 2010. Includes serial back files in print.

# Rate of Electronic Books in Public Libraries in 2010

## National Rate = 60 Electronic Books per 1,000 Population*

ALPHA ORDER

| RANK | STATE | RATE |
|---|---|---|
| 11 | Alabama | 88 |
| 8 | Alaska | 139 |
| 20 | Arizona | 43 |
| 39 | Arkansas | 9 |
| 30 | California | 20 |
| 19 | Colorado | 48 |
| 40 | Connecticut | 8 |
| 46 | Delaware | 4 |
| 16 | Florida | 54 |
| 47 | Georgia | 3 |
| 37 | Hawaii | 10 |
| 35 | Idaho | 13 |
| 17 | Illinois | 51 |
| 31 | Indiana | 18 |
| 41 | Iowa | 7 |
| 47 | Kansas | 3 |
| 23 | Kentucky | 34 |
| 34 | Louisiana | 14 |
| 9 | Maine | 110 |
| 32 | Maryland | 16 |
| 23 | Massachusetts | 34 |
| 21 | Michigan | 35 |
| 2 | Minnesota | 405 |
| 43 | Mississippi | 6 |
| 23 | Missouri | 34 |
| 3 | Montana | 307 |
| 5 | Nebraska | 219 |
| 28 | Nevada | 29 |
| 6 | New Hampshire | 167 |
| 26 | New Jersey | 32 |
| 43 | New Mexico | 6 |
| 15 | New York | 56 |
| 21 | North Carolina | 35 |
| 12 | North Dakota | 82 |
| 4 | Ohio | 249 |
| 47 | Oklahoma | 3 |
| 7 | Oregon | 166 |
| 17 | Pennsylvania | 51 |
| 13 | Rhode Island | 78 |
| 33 | South Carolina | 15 |
| 14 | South Dakota | 70 |
| 45 | Tennessee | 5 |
| 37 | Texas | 10 |
| 27 | Utah | 30 |
| 41 | Vermont | 7 |
| 9 | Virginia | 110 |
| 29 | Washington | 26 |
| 35 | West Virginia | 13 |
| 1 | Wisconsin | 483 |
| 50 | Wyoming | 1 |

RANK ORDER

| RANK | STATE | RATE |
|---|---|---|
| 1 | Wisconsin | 483 |
| 2 | Minnesota | 405 |
| 3 | Montana | 307 |
| 4 | Ohio | 249 |
| 5 | Nebraska | 219 |
| 6 | New Hampshire | 167 |
| 7 | Oregon | 166 |
| 8 | Alaska | 139 |
| 9 | Maine | 110 |
| 9 | Virginia | 110 |
| 11 | Alabama | 88 |
| 12 | North Dakota | 82 |
| 13 | Rhode Island | 78 |
| 14 | South Dakota | 70 |
| 15 | New York | 56 |
| 16 | Florida | 54 |
| 17 | Illinois | 51 |
| 17 | Pennsylvania | 51 |
| 19 | Colorado | 48 |
| 20 | Arizona | 43 |
| 21 | Michigan | 35 |
| 21 | North Carolina | 35 |
| 23 | Kentucky | 34 |
| 23 | Massachusetts | 34 |
| 23 | Missouri | 34 |
| 26 | New Jersey | 32 |
| 27 | Utah | 30 |
| 28 | Nevada | 29 |
| 29 | Washington | 26 |
| 30 | California | 20 |
| 31 | Indiana | 18 |
| 32 | Maryland | 16 |
| 33 | South Carolina | 15 |
| 34 | Louisiana | 14 |
| 35 | Idaho | 13 |
| 35 | West Virginia | 13 |
| 37 | Hawaii | 10 |
| 37 | Texas | 10 |
| 39 | Arkansas | 9 |
| 40 | Connecticut | 8 |
| 41 | Iowa | 7 |
| 41 | Vermont | 7 |
| 43 | Mississippi | 6 |
| 43 | New Mexico | 6 |
| 45 | Tennessee | 5 |
| 46 | Delaware | 4 |
| 47 | Georgia | 3 |
| 47 | Kansas | 3 |
| 47 | Oklahoma | 3 |
| 50 | Wyoming | 1 |
| | District of Columbia | 21 |

Source: CQ Press using data from Institute of Museum and Library Services
"Public Library Survey Fiscal Year 2010" (January 2013, http://www.imls.gov/research/default.aspx)
*For fiscal year 2010.

# Internet Terminals in Public Libraries in 2010

## National Total = 244,842 Terminals*

| ALPHA ORDER | | | | | RANK ORDER | | | |
|---|---|---|---|---|---|---|---|---|
| RANK | STATE | TERMINALS | % of USA | | RANK | STATE | TERMINALS | % of USA |
| 18 | Alabama | 4,773 | 1.9% | | 1 | California | 18,846 | 7.7% |
| 47 | Alaska | 610 | 0.2% | | 2 | New York | 16,681 | 6.8% |
| 22 | Arizona | 4,403 | 1.8% | | 3 | Texas | 16,347 | 6.7% |
| 33 | Arkansas | 2,144 | 0.9% | | 4 | Florida | 15,564 | 6.4% |
| 1 | California | 18,846 | 7.7% | | 5 | Illinois | 11,841 | 4.8% |
| 21 | Colorado | 4,470 | 1.8% | | 6 | Ohio | 11,388 | 4.7% |
| 27 | Connecticut | 3,783 | 1.5% | | 7 | Michigan | 10,484 | 4.3% |
| 49 | Delaware | 543 | 0.2% | | 8 | Indiana | 8,114 | 3.3% |
| 4 | Florida | 15,564 | 6.4% | | 9 | Georgia | 7,599 | 3.1% |
| 9 | Georgia | 7,599 | 3.1% | | 10 | Pennsylvania | 7,440 | 3.0% |
| 50 | Hawaii | 274 | 0.1% | | 11 | New Jersey | 7,110 | 2.9% |
| 37 | Idaho | 1,455 | 0.6% | | 12 | North Carolina | 6,764 | 2.8% |
| 5 | Illinois | 11,841 | 4.8% | | 13 | Virginia | 6,104 | 2.5% |
| 8 | Indiana | 8,114 | 3.3% | | 14 | Massachusetts | 5,597 | 2.3% |
| 25 | Iowa | 4,090 | 1.7% | | 15 | Washington | 5,555 | 2.3% |
| 29 | Kansas | 3,441 | 1.4% | | 16 | Wisconsin | 5,274 | 2.2% |
| 26 | Kentucky | 3,876 | 1.6% | | 17 | Minnesota | 5,201 | 2.1% |
| 19 | Louisiana | 4,557 | 1.9% | | 18 | Alabama | 4,773 | 1.9% |
| 36 | Maine | 1,470 | 0.6% | | 19 | Louisiana | 4,557 | 1.9% |
| 23 | Maryland | 4,239 | 1.7% | | 20 | Missouri | 4,472 | 1.8% |
| 14 | Massachusetts | 5,597 | 2.3% | | 21 | Colorado | 4,470 | 1.8% |
| 7 | Michigan | 10,484 | 4.3% | | 22 | Arizona | 4,403 | 1.8% |
| 17 | Minnesota | 5,201 | 2.1% | | 23 | Maryland | 4,239 | 1.7% |
| 32 | Mississippi | 2,409 | 1.0% | | 24 | Tennessee | 4,234 | 1.7% |
| 20 | Missouri | 4,472 | 1.8% | | 25 | Iowa | 4,090 | 1.7% |
| 43 | Montana | 958 | 0.4% | | 26 | Kentucky | 3,876 | 1.6% |
| 34 | Nebraska | 1,903 | 0.8% | | 27 | Connecticut | 3,783 | 1.5% |
| 41 | Nevada | 1,264 | 0.5% | | 28 | South Carolina | 3,493 | 1.4% |
| 39 | New Hampshire | 1,343 | 0.5% | | 29 | Kansas | 3,441 | 1.4% |
| 11 | New Jersey | 7,110 | 2.9% | | 30 | Oregon | 2,781 | 1.1% |
| 38 | New Mexico | 1,373 | 0.6% | | 31 | Oklahoma | 2,414 | 1.0% |
| 2 | New York | 16,681 | 6.8% | | 32 | Mississippi | 2,409 | 1.0% |
| 12 | North Carolina | 6,764 | 2.8% | | 33 | Arkansas | 2,144 | 0.9% |
| 48 | North Dakota | 567 | 0.2% | | 34 | Nebraska | 1,903 | 0.8% |
| 6 | Ohio | 11,388 | 4.7% | | 35 | Utah | 1,756 | 0.7% |
| 31 | Oklahoma | 2,414 | 1.0% | | 36 | Maine | 1,470 | 0.6% |
| 30 | Oregon | 2,781 | 1.1% | | 37 | Idaho | 1,455 | 0.6% |
| 10 | Pennsylvania | 7,440 | 3.0% | | 38 | New Mexico | 1,373 | 0.6% |
| 42 | Rhode Island | 1,216 | 0.5% | | 39 | New Hampshire | 1,343 | 0.5% |
| 28 | South Carolina | 3,493 | 1.4% | | 40 | West Virginia | 1,324 | 0.5% |
| 45 | South Dakota | 906 | 0.4% | | 41 | Nevada | 1,264 | 0.5% |
| 24 | Tennessee | 4,234 | 1.7% | | 42 | Rhode Island | 1,216 | 0.5% |
| 3 | Texas | 16,347 | 6.7% | | 43 | Montana | 958 | 0.4% |
| 35 | Utah | 1,756 | 0.7% | | 44 | Vermont | 937 | 0.4% |
| 44 | Vermont | 937 | 0.4% | | 45 | South Dakota | 906 | 0.4% |
| 13 | Virginia | 6,104 | 2.5% | | 46 | Wyoming | 776 | 0.3% |
| 15 | Washington | 5,555 | 2.3% | | 47 | Alaska | 610 | 0.2% |
| 40 | West Virginia | 1,324 | 0.5% | | 48 | North Dakota | 567 | 0.2% |
| 16 | Wisconsin | 5,274 | 2.2% | | 49 | Delaware | 543 | 0.2% |
| 46 | Wyoming | 776 | 0.3% | | 50 | Hawaii | 274 | 0.1% |
| | | | | | | District of Columbia | 679 | 0.3% |

Source: Institute of Museum and Library Services
"Public Library Survey Fiscal Year 2010" (January 2013, http://www.imls.gov/research/default.aspx)
*For fiscal year 2010. Total of public-use Internet terminals in central and branch outlets.

# Rate of Internet Terminals in Public Libraries in 2010

## National Rate = 14.9 Terminals per Library*

| RANK | STATE | RATE |
|------|-------|------|
| 16 | Alabama | 16.5 |
| 46 | Alaska | 6.7 |
| 3 | Arizona | 20.4 |
| 38 | Arkansas | 9.8 |
| 12 | California | 17.0 |
| 9 | Colorado | 17.9 |
| 18 | Connecticut | 16.4 |
| 12 | Delaware | 17.0 |
| 1 | Florida | 29.6 |
| 4 | Georgia | 19.4 |
| 50 | Hawaii | 5.4 |
| 35 | Idaho | 10.5 |
| 22 | Illinois | 15.1 |
| 7 | Indiana | 18.7 |
| 43 | Iowa | 7.4 |
| 39 | Kansas | 9.6 |
| 4 | Kentucky | 19.4 |
| 27 | Louisiana | 13.6 |
| 46 | Maine | 6.7 |
| 2 | Maryland | 23.0 |
| 31 | Massachusetts | 12.3 |
| 19 | Michigan | 16.1 |
| 25 | Minnesota | 14.6 |
| 36 | Mississippi | 10.3 |
| 30 | Missouri | 12.5 |
| 40 | Montana | 8.7 |
| 41 | Nebraska | 8.1 |
| 23 | Nevada | 14.7 |
| 48 | New Hampshire | 5.9 |
| 16 | New Jersey | 16.5 |
| 29 | New Mexico | 12.7 |
| 21 | New York | 15.6 |
| 10 | North Carolina | 17.5 |
| 45 | North Dakota | 6.9 |
| 20 | Ohio | 15.8 |
| 32 | Oklahoma | 11.7 |
| 28 | Oregon | 12.9 |
| 32 | Pennsylvania | 11.7 |
| 14 | Rhode Island | 16.7 |
| 8 | South Carolina | 18.1 |
| 44 | South Dakota | 7.2 |
| 23 | Tennessee | 14.7 |
| 6 | Texas | 19.2 |
| 26 | Utah | 13.9 |
| 49 | Vermont | 5.8 |
| 11 | Virginia | 17.2 |
| 15 | Washington | 16.6 |
| 42 | West Virginia | 7.6 |
| 34 | Wisconsin | 11.5 |
| 37 | Wyoming | 10.2 |

| RANK | STATE | RATE |
|------|-------|------|
| 1 | Florida | 29.6 |
| 2 | Maryland | 23.0 |
| 3 | Arizona | 20.4 |
| 4 | Georgia | 19.4 |
| 4 | Kentucky | 19.4 |
| 6 | Texas | 19.2 |
| 7 | Indiana | 18.7 |
| 8 | South Carolina | 18.1 |
| 9 | Colorado | 17.9 |
| 10 | North Carolina | 17.5 |
| 11 | Virginia | 17.2 |
| 12 | California | 17.0 |
| 12 | Delaware | 17.0 |
| 14 | Rhode Island | 16.7 |
| 15 | Washington | 16.6 |
| 16 | Alabama | 16.5 |
| 16 | New Jersey | 16.5 |
| 18 | Connecticut | 16.4 |
| 19 | Michigan | 16.1 |
| 20 | Ohio | 15.8 |
| 21 | New York | 15.6 |
| 22 | Illinois | 15.1 |
| 23 | Nevada | 14.7 |
| 23 | Tennessee | 14.7 |
| 25 | Minnesota | 14.6 |
| 26 | Utah | 13.9 |
| 27 | Louisiana | 13.6 |
| 28 | Oregon | 12.9 |
| 29 | New Mexico | 12.7 |
| 30 | Missouri | 12.5 |
| 31 | Massachusetts | 12.3 |
| 32 | Oklahoma | 11.7 |
| 32 | Pennsylvania | 11.7 |
| 34 | Wisconsin | 11.5 |
| 35 | Idaho | 10.5 |
| 36 | Mississippi | 10.3 |
| 37 | Wyoming | 10.2 |
| 38 | Arkansas | 9.8 |
| 39 | Kansas | 9.6 |
| 40 | Montana | 8.7 |
| 41 | Nebraska | 8.1 |
| 42 | West Virginia | 7.6 |
| 43 | Iowa | 7.4 |
| 44 | South Dakota | 7.2 |
| 45 | North Dakota | 6.9 |
| 46 | Alaska | 6.7 |
| 46 | Maine | 6.7 |
| 48 | New Hampshire | 5.9 |
| 49 | Vermont | 5.8 |
| 50 | Hawaii | 5.4 |

| District of Columbia | 27.2 |
|---|---|

Source: CQ Press using data from Institute of Museum and Library Services
"Public Library Survey Fiscal Year 2010" (January 2013, http://www.imls.gov/research/default.aspx)
*For fiscal year 2010. Total of public-use Internet terminals in central and branch outlets divided by the number of outlets.

# Per Capita State Art Agencies' Legislative Appropriations in 2014

## National Per Capita = $0.89*

ALPHA ORDER

| RANK | STATE | PER CAPITA |
|---|---|---|
| 23 | Alabama | $0.74 |
| 12 | Alaska | 1.09 |
| 47 | Arizona | 0.15 |
| 28 | Arkansas | 0.69 |
| 46 | California | 0.15 |
| 42 | Colorado | 0.38 |
| 11 | Connecticut | 1.54 |
| 3 | Delaware | 3.57 |
| 19 | Florida | 0.82 |
| 50 | Georgia | 0.06 |
| 2 | Hawaii | 3.65 |
| 41 | Idaho | 0.43 |
| 21 | Illinois | 0.78 |
| 39 | Indiana | 0.45 |
| 40 | Iowa | 0.43 |
| 49 | Kansas | 0.07 |
| 29 | Kentucky | 0.64 |
| 36 | Louisiana | 0.50 |
| 34 | Maine | 0.57 |
| 4 | Maryland | 2.57 |
| 9 | Massachusetts | 1.66 |
| 26 | Michigan | 0.71 |
| 1 | Minnesota | 6.31 |
| 31 | Mississippi | 0.60 |
| 20 | Missouri | 0.79 |
| 33 | Montana | 0.57 |
| 22 | Nebraska | 0.78 |
| 38 | Nevada | 0.46 |
| 43 | New Hampshire | 0.29 |
| 8 | New Jersey | 1.84 |
| 27 | New Mexico | 0.69 |
| 5 | New York | 2.03 |
| 24 | North Carolina | 0.72 |
| 15 | North Dakota | 1.04 |
| 17 | Ohio | 0.98 |
| 14 | Oklahoma | 1.04 |
| 32 | Oregon | 0.57 |
| 25 | Pennsylvania | 0.71 |
| 7 | Rhode Island | 1.87 |
| 30 | South Carolina | 0.63 |
| 18 | South Dakota | 0.87 |
| 13 | Tennessee | 1.07 |
| 44 | Texas | 0.21 |
| 10 | Utah | 1.56 |
| 16 | Vermont | 1.02 |
| 37 | Virginia | 0.47 |
| 45 | Washington | 0.16 |
| 35 | West Virginia | 0.55 |
| 48 | Wisconsin | 0.13 |
| 6 | Wyoming | 2.01 |

RANK ORDER

| RANK | STATE | PER CAPITA |
|---|---|---|
| 1 | Minnesota | $6.31 |
| 2 | Hawaii | 3.65 |
| 3 | Delaware | 3.57 |
| 4 | Maryland | 2.57 |
| 5 | New York | 2.03 |
| 6 | Wyoming | 2.01 |
| 7 | Rhode Island | 1.87 |
| 8 | New Jersey | 1.84 |
| 9 | Massachusetts | 1.66 |
| 10 | Utah | 1.56 |
| 11 | Connecticut | 1.54 |
| 12 | Alaska | 1.09 |
| 13 | Tennessee | 1.07 |
| 14 | Oklahoma | 1.04 |
| 15 | North Dakota | 1.04 |
| 16 | Vermont | 1.02 |
| 17 | Ohio | 0.98 |
| 18 | South Dakota | 0.87 |
| 19 | Florida | 0.82 |
| 20 | Missouri | 0.79 |
| 21 | Illinois | 0.78 |
| 22 | Nebraska | 0.78 |
| 23 | Alabama | 0.74 |
| 24 | North Carolina | 0.72 |
| 25 | Pennsylvania | 0.71 |
| 26 | Michigan | 0.71 |
| 27 | New Mexico | 0.69 |
| 28 | Arkansas | 0.69 |
| 29 | Kentucky | 0.64 |
| 30 | South Carolina | 0.63 |
| 31 | Mississippi | 0.60 |
| 32 | Oregon | 0.57 |
| 33 | Montana | 0.57 |
| 34 | Maine | 0.57 |
| 35 | West Virginia | 0.55 |
| 36 | Louisiana | 0.50 |
| 37 | Virginia | 0.47 |
| 38 | Nevada | 0.46 |
| 39 | Indiana | 0.45 |
| 40 | Iowa | $0.43 |
| 41 | Idaho | 0.43 |
| 42 | Colorado | 0.38 |
| 43 | New Hampshire | 0.29 |
| 44 | Texas | 0.21 |
| 45 | Washington | 0.16 |
| 46 | California | 0.15 |
| 47 | Arizona | 0.15 |
| 48 | Wisconsin | 0.13 |
| 49 | Kansas | 0.07 |
| 50 | Georgia | 0.06 |
| | District of Columbia | 18.69 |

Source: CQ Press using data from National Assembly of State Arts Agencies
   "Current State Arts Agency Budgets" (http://www.nasaa-arts.org/Research/Funding/)

*Projected figures for fiscal year 2014. Includes line item appropriations. Line items are legislative appropriations that are not controlled by the state art agencies but are passed through their budgets directly to another entity. Calculated using 2013 census population estimates. National per capita does not include appropriations or population in U.S. territories.

# Federal Allocations for Head Start Program in 2012

## National Total = $7,682,420,000*

ALPHA ORDER

| RANK | STATE | EXPENDITURES | % of USA |
|------|-------|-------------|----------|
| 16 | Alabama | $125,717,736 | 1.6% |
| 49 | Alaska | 14,373,541 | 0.2% |
| 19 | Arizona | 121,746,967 | 1.6% |
| 29 | Arkansas | 75,176,442 | 1.0% |
| 1 | California | 957,971,585 | 12.5% |
| 28 | Colorado | 80,798,717 | 1.1% |
| 34 | Connecticut | 58,755,649 | 0.8% |
| 47 | Delaware | 15,341,871 | 0.2% |
| 5 | Florida | 313,310,850 | 4.1% |
| 9 | Georgia | 198,596,452 | 2.6% |
| 41 | Hawaii | 25,594,284 | 0.3% |
| 40 | Idaho | 27,252,585 | 0.4% |
| 4 | Illinois | 314,325,492 | 4.1% |
| 22 | Indiana | 115,222,711 | 1.5% |
| 33 | Iowa | 59,267,964 | 0.8% |
| 32 | Kansas | 59,800,770 | 0.8% |
| 17 | Kentucky | 125,505,972 | 1.6% |
| 12 | Louisiana | 167,980,835 | 2.2% |
| 38 | Maine | 31,534,389 | 0.4% |
| 26 | Maryland | 89,394,017 | 1.2% |
| 18 | Massachusetts | 122,724,674 | 1.6% |
| 7 | Michigan | 267,668,992 | 3.5% |
| 27 | Minnesota | 83,787,316 | 1.1% |
| 10 | Mississippi | 180,315,944 | 2.3% |
| 14 | Missouri | 138,965,174 | 1.8% |
| 43 | Montana | 23,985,541 | 0.3% |
| 37 | Nebraska | 42,187,836 | 0.5% |
| 39 | Nevada | 29,960,223 | 0.4% |
| 46 | New Hampshire | 15,540,919 | 0.2% |
| 13 | New Jersey | 149,580,131 | 1.9% |
| 31 | New Mexico | 62,550,656 | 0.8% |
| 3 | New York | 493,984,026 | 6.4% |
| 11 | North Carolina | 171,736,149 | 2.2% |
| 45 | North Dakota | 20,059,789 | 0.3% |
| 6 | Ohio | 286,668,880 | 3.7% |
| 25 | Oklahoma | 97,666,553 | 1.3% |
| 30 | Oregon | 70,304,700 | 0.9% |
| 8 | Pennsylvania | 261,801,900 | 3.4% |
| 42 | Rhode Island | 25,043,856 | 0.3% |
| 24 | South Carolina | 99,208,187 | 1.3% |
| 44 | South Dakota | 21,605,345 | 0.3% |
| 15 | Tennessee | 137,123,145 | 1.8% |
| 2 | Texas | 559,620,987 | 7.3% |
| 36 | Utah | 45,113,078 | 0.6% |
| 48 | Vermont | 15,143,423 | 0.2% |
| 21 | Virginia | 115,286,747 | 1.5% |
| 20 | Washington | 117,458,766 | 1.5% |
| 35 | West Virginia | 58,201,030 | 0.8% |
| 23 | Wisconsin | 105,184,250 | 1.4% |
| 50 | Wyoming | 13,438,273 | 0.2% |

RANK ORDER

| RANK | STATE | EXPENDITURES | % of USA |
|------|-------|-------------|----------|
| 1 | California | $957,971,585 | 12.5% |
| 2 | Texas | 559,620,987 | 7.3% |
| 3 | New York | 493,984,026 | 6.4% |
| 4 | Illinois | 314,325,492 | 4.1% |
| 5 | Florida | 313,310,850 | 4.1% |
| 6 | Ohio | 286,668,880 | 3.7% |
| 7 | Michigan | 267,668,992 | 3.5% |
| 8 | Pennsylvania | 261,801,900 | 3.4% |
| 9 | Georgia | 198,596,452 | 2.6% |
| 10 | Mississippi | 180,315,944 | 2.3% |
| 11 | North Carolina | 171,736,149 | 2.2% |
| 12 | Louisiana | 167,980,835 | 2.2% |
| 13 | New Jersey | 149,580,131 | 1.9% |
| 14 | Missouri | 138,965,174 | 1.8% |
| 15 | Tennessee | 137,123,145 | 1.8% |
| 16 | Alabama | 125,717,736 | 1.6% |
| 17 | Kentucky | 125,505,972 | 1.6% |
| 18 | Massachusetts | 122,724,674 | 1.6% |
| 19 | Arizona | 121,746,967 | 1.6% |
| 20 | Washington | 117,458,766 | 1.5% |
| 21 | Virginia | 115,286,747 | 1.5% |
| 22 | Indiana | 115,222,711 | 1.5% |
| 23 | Wisconsin | 105,184,250 | 1.4% |
| 24 | South Carolina | 99,208,187 | 1.3% |
| 25 | Oklahoma | 97,666,553 | 1.3% |
| 26 | Maryland | 89,394,017 | 1.2% |
| 27 | Minnesota | 83,787,316 | 1.1% |
| 28 | Colorado | 80,798,717 | 1.1% |
| 29 | Arkansas | 75,176,442 | 1.0% |
| 30 | Oregon | 70,304,700 | 0.9% |
| 31 | New Mexico | 62,550,656 | 0.8% |
| 32 | Kansas | 59,800,770 | 0.8% |
| 33 | Iowa | 59,267,964 | 0.8% |
| 34 | Connecticut | 58,755,649 | 0.8% |
| 35 | West Virginia | 58,201,030 | 0.8% |
| 36 | Utah | 45,113,078 | 0.6% |
| 37 | Nebraska | 42,187,836 | 0.5% |
| 38 | Maine | 31,534,389 | 0.4% |
| 39 | Nevada | 29,960,223 | 0.4% |
| 40 | Idaho | 27,252,585 | 0.4% |
| 41 | Hawaii | 25,594,284 | 0.3% |
| 42 | Rhode Island | 25,043,856 | 0.3% |
| 43 | Montana | 23,985,541 | 0.3% |
| 44 | South Dakota | 21,605,345 | 0.3% |
| 45 | North Dakota | 20,059,789 | 0.3% |
| 46 | New Hampshire | 15,540,919 | 0.2% |
| 47 | Delaware | 15,341,871 | 0.2% |
| 48 | Vermont | 15,143,423 | 0.2% |
| 49 | Alaska | 14,373,541 | 0.2% |
| 50 | Wyoming | 13,438,273 | 0.2% |
| | District of Columbia | 27,867,030 | 0.4% |

Source: U.S. Department of Health and Human Services, Administration for Children and Families
 "Head Start Fact Sheet Fiscal Year 2012" (http://eclkc.ohs.acf.hhs.gov/hslc/mr/factsheets)
*For fiscal year 2012. National total includes $550,266,135 to Migrant and Native American programs and $295,379,244 to U.S. territories. Does not include $286,124,000 in "support activities" expenditures.

# Head Start Program Enrollment in 2012

## National Total = 956,497 Children*

ALPHA ORDER

| RANK | STATE | ENROLLMENT | % of USA |
|---|---|---|---|
| 15 | Alabama | 17,301 | 1.8% |
| 49 | Alaska | 1,761 | 0.2% |
| 21 | Arizona | 14,137 | 1.5% |
| 29 | Arkansas | 10,814 | 1.1% |
| 1 | California | 104,950 | 10.9% |
| 30 | Colorado | 10,624 | 1.1% |
| 35 | Connecticut | 7,357 | 0.8% |
| 46 | Delaware | 2,209 | 0.2% |
| 6 | Florida | 38,304 | 4.0% |
| 10 | Georgia | 25,112 | 2.6% |
| 39 | Hawaii | 3,187 | 0.3% |
| 40 | Idaho | 3,135 | 0.3% |
| 4 | Illinois | 41,644 | 4.3% |
| 18 | Indiana | 15,515 | 1.6% |
| 32 | Iowa | 8,133 | 0.8% |
| 31 | Kansas | 8,751 | 0.9% |
| 16 | Kentucky | 16,938 | 1.8% |
| 11 | Louisiana | 22,054 | 2.3% |
| 38 | Maine | 3,536 | 0.4% |
| 28 | Maryland | 10,885 | 1.1% |
| 23 | Massachusetts | 13,295 | 1.4% |
| 8 | Michigan | 35,961 | 3.7% |
| 27 | Minnesota | 11,410 | 1.2% |
| 9 | Mississippi | 27,323 | 2.8% |
| 13 | Missouri | 18,186 | 1.9% |
| 42 | Montana | 3,071 | 0.3% |
| 37 | Nebraska | 5,452 | 0.6% |
| 41 | Nevada | 3,100 | 0.3% |
| 48 | New Hampshire | 1,764 | 0.2% |
| 17 | New Jersey | 15,661 | 1.6% |
| 34 | New Mexico | 7,839 | 0.8% |
| 3 | New York | 51,696 | 5.4% |
| 12 | North Carolina | 20,484 | 2.1% |
| 45 | North Dakota | 2,498 | 0.3% |
| 5 | Ohio | 39,106 | 4.1% |
| 22 | Oklahoma | 13,925 | 1.4% |
| 25 | Oregon | 12,502 | 1.3% |
| 7 | Pennsylvania | 36,955 | 3.8% |
| 44 | Rhode Island | 2,966 | 0.3% |
| 24 | South Carolina | 13,225 | 1.4% |
| 43 | South Dakota | 2,987 | 0.3% |
| 14 | Tennessee | 17,323 | 1.8% |
| 2 | Texas | 71,963 | 7.5% |
| 36 | Utah | 6,117 | 0.6% |
| 50 | Vermont | 1,562 | 0.2% |
| 19 | Virginia | 14,462 | 1.5% |
| 26 | Washington | 12,404 | 1.3% |
| 33 | West Virginia | 8,075 | 0.8% |
| 20 | Wisconsin | 14,407 | 1.5% |
| 47 | Wyoming | 1,824 | 0.2% |

RANK ORDER

| RANK | STATE | ENROLLMENT | % of USA |
|---|---|---|---|
| 1 | California | 104,950 | 10.9% |
| 2 | Texas | 71,963 | 7.5% |
| 3 | New York | 51,696 | 5.4% |
| 4 | Illinois | 41,644 | 4.3% |
| 5 | Ohio | 39,106 | 4.1% |
| 6 | Florida | 38,304 | 4.0% |
| 7 | Pennsylvania | 36,955 | 3.8% |
| 8 | Michigan | 35,961 | 3.7% |
| 9 | Mississippi | 27,323 | 2.8% |
| 10 | Georgia | 25,112 | 2.6% |
| 11 | Louisiana | 22,054 | 2.3% |
| 12 | North Carolina | 20,484 | 2.1% |
| 13 | Missouri | 18,186 | 1.9% |
| 14 | Tennessee | 17,323 | 1.8% |
| 15 | Alabama | 17,301 | 1.8% |
| 16 | Kentucky | 16,938 | 1.8% |
| 17 | New Jersey | 15,661 | 1.6% |
| 18 | Indiana | 15,515 | 1.6% |
| 19 | Virginia | 14,462 | 1.5% |
| 20 | Wisconsin | 14,407 | 1.5% |
| 21 | Arizona | 14,137 | 1.5% |
| 22 | Oklahoma | 13,925 | 1.4% |
| 23 | Massachusetts | 13,295 | 1.4% |
| 24 | South Carolina | 13,225 | 1.4% |
| 25 | Oregon | 12,502 | 1.3% |
| 26 | Washington | 12,404 | 1.3% |
| 27 | Minnesota | 11,410 | 1.2% |
| 28 | Maryland | 10,885 | 1.1% |
| 29 | Arkansas | 10,814 | 1.1% |
| 30 | Colorado | 10,624 | 1.1% |
| 31 | Kansas | 8,751 | 0.9% |
| 32 | Iowa | 8,133 | 0.8% |
| 33 | West Virginia | 8,075 | 0.8% |
| 34 | New Mexico | 7,839 | 0.8% |
| 35 | Connecticut | 7,357 | 0.8% |
| 36 | Utah | 6,117 | 0.6% |
| 37 | Nebraska | 5,452 | 0.6% |
| 38 | Maine | 3,536 | 0.4% |
| 39 | Hawaii | 3,187 | 0.3% |
| 40 | Idaho | 3,135 | 0.3% |
| 41 | Nevada | 3,100 | 0.3% |
| 42 | Montana | 3,071 | 0.3% |
| 43 | South Dakota | 2,987 | 0.3% |
| 44 | Rhode Island | 2,966 | 0.3% |
| 45 | North Dakota | 2,498 | 0.3% |
| 46 | Delaware | 2,209 | 0.2% |
| 47 | Wyoming | 1,824 | 0.2% |
| 48 | New Hampshire | 1,764 | 0.2% |
| 49 | Alaska | 1,761 | 0.2% |
| 50 | Vermont | 1,562 | 0.2% |
|  | District of Columbia | 3,328 | 0.3% |

Source: U.S. Department of Health and Human Services, Administration for Children and Families
   "Head Start Fact Sheet Fiscal Year 2012" (http://eclkc.ohs.acf.hhs.gov/hslc/mr/factsheets)
*For fiscal year 2012. National total includes 58,661 enrollees in Migrant and Native American programs and 40,618 enrollees in U.S. territories.

# VI. Employment and Labor

# Average Annual Pay in 2012

## National Average = $49,289*

ALPHA ORDER

| RANK | STATE | ANNUAL PAY |
|------|-------|-----------|
| 32 | Alabama | $41,990 |
| 11 | Alaska | 50,614 |
| 21 | Arizona | 45,593 |
| 46 | Arkansas | 38,226 |
| 5 | California | 56,784 |
| 13 | Colorado | 50,563 |
| 2 | Connecticut | 62,085 |
| 9 | Delaware | 51,734 |
| 29 | Florida | 43,211 |
| 19 | Georgia | 46,267 |
| 27 | Hawaii | 43,385 |
| 49 | Idaho | 36,152 |
| 7 | Illinois | 52,194 |
| 36 | Indiana | 41,240 |
| 41 | Iowa | 40,343 |
| 37 | Kansas | 41,118 |
| 40 | Kentucky | 40,451 |
| 28 | Louisiana | 43,300 |
| 45 | Maine | 38,606 |
| 6 | Maryland | 54,035 |
| 3 | Massachusetts | 60,898 |
| 17 | Michigan | 46,720 |
| 14 | Minnesota | 49,349 |
| 50 | Mississippi | 35,875 |
| 31 | Missouri | 42,695 |
| 47 | Montana | 37,096 |
| 44 | Nebraska | 39,268 |
| 26 | Nevada | 43,667 |
| 16 | New Hampshire | 48,272 |
| 4 | New Jersey | 58,644 |
| 39 | New Mexico | 40,698 |
| 1 | New York | 62,669 |
| 30 | North Carolina | 43,110 |
| 20 | North Dakota | 45,909 |
| 24 | Ohio | 44,244 |
| 34 | Oklahoma | 41,633 |
| 23 | Oregon | 44,258 |
| 15 | Pennsylvania | 48,397 |
| 18 | Rhode Island | 46,716 |
| 43 | South Carolina | 39,286 |
| 48 | South Dakota | 36,534 |
| 25 | Tennessee | 43,961 |
| 12 | Texas | 50,579 |
| 35 | Utah | 41,301 |
| 38 | Vermont | 40,967 |
| 10 | Virginia | 51,646 |
| 8 | Washington | 51,962 |
| 42 | West Virginia | 39,727 |
| 33 | Wisconsin | 41,966 |
| 22 | Wyoming | 44,580 |

RANK ORDER

| RANK | STATE | ANNUAL PAY |
|------|-------|-----------|
| 1 | New York | $62,669 |
| 2 | Connecticut | 62,085 |
| 3 | Massachusetts | 60,898 |
| 4 | New Jersey | 58,644 |
| 5 | California | 56,784 |
| 6 | Maryland | 54,035 |
| 7 | Illinois | 52,194 |
| 8 | Washington | 51,962 |
| 9 | Delaware | 51,734 |
| 10 | Virginia | 51,646 |
| 11 | Alaska | 50,614 |
| 12 | Texas | 50,579 |
| 13 | Colorado | 50,563 |
| 14 | Minnesota | 49,349 |
| 15 | Pennsylvania | 48,397 |
| 16 | New Hampshire | 48,272 |
| 17 | Michigan | 46,720 |
| 18 | Rhode Island | 46,716 |
| 19 | Georgia | 46,267 |
| 20 | North Dakota | 45,909 |
| 21 | Arizona | 45,593 |
| 22 | Wyoming | 44,580 |
| 23 | Oregon | 44,258 |
| 24 | Ohio | 44,244 |
| 25 | Tennessee | 43,961 |
| 26 | Nevada | 43,667 |
| 27 | Hawaii | 43,385 |
| 28 | Louisiana | 43,300 |
| 29 | Florida | 43,211 |
| 30 | North Carolina | 43,110 |
| 31 | Missouri | 42,695 |
| 32 | Alabama | 41,990 |
| 33 | Wisconsin | 41,966 |
| 34 | Oklahoma | 41,633 |
| 35 | Utah | 41,301 |
| 36 | Indiana | 41,240 |
| 37 | Kansas | 41,118 |
| 38 | Vermont | 40,967 |
| 39 | New Mexico | 40,698 |
| 40 | Kentucky | 40,451 |
| 41 | Iowa | 40,343 |
| 42 | West Virginia | 39,727 |
| 43 | South Carolina | 39,286 |
| 44 | Nebraska | 39,268 |
| 45 | Maine | 38,606 |
| 46 | Arkansas | 38,226 |
| 47 | Montana | 37,096 |
| 48 | South Dakota | 36,534 |
| 49 | Idaho | 36,152 |
| 50 | Mississippi | 35,875 |
| | District of Columbia | 82,783 |

Source: U.S. Department of Labor, Bureau of Labor Statistics
   "Quarterly Census of Employment and Wages" (http://www.bls.gov/cew/home.htm)
*Computed by dividing total annual wages of employees covered by unemployment insurance programs by the average monthly number of these employees.  Includes bonuses, cash value of meals and lodging, tips and, in many states, employer contributions to certain deferred compensation plans such as 401(k) plans.

# Percent Change in Average Annual Pay: 2011 to 2012

## National Percent Change = 2.6% Change*

| ALPHA ORDER | | | | RANK ORDER | | |
|---|---|---|---|---|---|---|
| RANK | STATE | PERCENT CHANGE | | RANK | STATE | PERCENT CHANGE |
| 37 | Alabama | 2.0 | | 1 | North Dakota | 9.9 |
| 22 | Alaska | 2.5 | | 2 | Oklahoma | 3.8 |
| 27 | Arizona | 2.3 | | 2 | Texas | 3.8 |
| 22 | Arkansas | 2.5 | | 4 | Montana | 3.6 |
| 7 | California | 3.2 | | 5 | Tennessee | 3.5 |
| 10 | Colorado | 3.0 | | 6 | Washington | 3.4 |
| 46 | Connecticut | 1.5 | | 7 | California | 3.2 |
| 26 | Delaware | 2.4 | | 7 | South Dakota | 3.2 |
| 33 | Florida | 2.1 | | 9 | Minnesota | 3.1 |
| 19 | Georgia | 2.6 | | 10 | Colorado | 3.0 |
| 33 | Hawaii | 2.1 | | 10 | Missouri | 3.0 |
| 46 | Idaho | 1.5 | | 10 | Ohio | 3.0 |
| 16 | Illinois | 2.7 | | 13 | Iowa | 2.9 |
| 22 | Indiana | 2.5 | | 13 | Pennsylvania | 2.9 |
| 13 | Iowa | 2.9 | | 15 | Kansas | 2.8 |
| 15 | Kansas | 2.8 | | 16 | Illinois | 2.7 |
| 37 | Kentucky | 2.0 | | 16 | Oregon | 2.7 |
| 30 | Louisiana | 2.2 | | 16 | Wyoming | 2.7 |
| 46 | Maine | 1.5 | | 19 | Georgia | 2.6 |
| 40 | Maryland | 1.9 | | 19 | Mississippi | 2.6 |
| 33 | Massachusetts | 2.1 | | 19 | Nebraska | 2.6 |
| 40 | Michigan | 1.9 | | 22 | Alaska | 2.5 |
| 9 | Minnesota | 3.1 | | 22 | Arkansas | 2.5 |
| 19 | Mississippi | 2.6 | | 22 | Indiana | 2.5 |
| 10 | Missouri | 3.0 | | 22 | Utah | 2.5 |
| 4 | Montana | 3.6 | | 26 | Delaware | 2.4 |
| 19 | Nebraska | 2.6 | | 27 | Arizona | 2.3 |
| 50 | Nevada | 1.3 | | 27 | North Carolina | 2.3 |
| 33 | New Hampshire | 2.1 | | 27 | Wisconsin | 2.3 |
| 40 | New Jersey | 1.9 | | 30 | Louisiana | 2.2 |
| 43 | New Mexico | 1.7 | | 30 | Rhode Island | 2.2 |
| 49 | New York | 1.4 | | 30 | South Carolina | 2.2 |
| 27 | North Carolina | 2.3 | | 33 | Florida | 2.1 |
| 1 | North Dakota | 9.9 | | 33 | Hawaii | 2.1 |
| 10 | Ohio | 3.0 | | 33 | Massachusetts | 2.1 |
| 2 | Oklahoma | 3.8 | | 33 | New Hampshire | 2.1 |
| 16 | Oregon | 2.7 | | 37 | Alabama | 2.0 |
| 13 | Pennsylvania | 2.9 | | 37 | Kentucky | 2.0 |
| 30 | Rhode Island | 2.2 | | 37 | Virginia | 2.0 |
| 30 | South Carolina | 2.2 | | 40 | Maryland | 1.9 |
| 7 | South Dakota | 3.2 | | 40 | Michigan | 1.9 |
| 5 | Tennessee | 3.5 | | 40 | New Jersey | 1.9 |
| 2 | Texas | 3.8 | | 43 | New Mexico | 1.7 |
| 22 | Utah | 2.5 | | 43 | Vermont | 1.7 |
| 43 | Vermont | 1.7 | | 45 | West Virginia | 1.6 |
| 37 | Virginia | 2.0 | | 46 | Connecticut | 1.5 |
| 6 | Washington | 3.4 | | 46 | Idaho | 1.5 |
| 45 | West Virginia | 1.6 | | 46 | Maine | 1.5 |
| 27 | Wisconsin | 2.3 | | 49 | New York | 1.4 |
| 16 | Wyoming | 2.7 | | 50 | Nevada | 1.3 |
| | | | | | District of Columbia | 1.5 |

Source: CQ Press using data from U.S. Department of Labor, Bureau of Labor Statistics
    "Quarterly Census of Employment and Wages" (http://www.bls.gov/cew/home.htm)
*Includes bonuses, cash value of meals and lodging, tips and, in many states, employer contributions to certain deferred compensation plans such as 401(k) plans.

# Median Earnings of Male Full-Time Workers in 2012

## National Median = $47,473

ALPHA ORDER

| RANK | STATE | EARNINGS |
|---|---|---|
| 31 | Alabama | $44,567 |
| 5 | Alaska | 57,068 |
| 34 | Arizona | 43,618 |
| 49 | Arkansas | 40,153 |
| 16 | California | 50,139 |
| 15 | Colorado | 50,509 |
| 1 | Connecticut | 61,097 |
| 14 | Delaware | 50,689 |
| 47 | Florida | 40,889 |
| 33 | Georgia | 43,707 |
| 25 | Hawaii | 45,748 |
| 43 | Idaho | 41,664 |
| 11 | Illinois | 51,262 |
| 26 | Indiana | 45,620 |
| 27 | Iowa | 45,305 |
| 30 | Kansas | 44,765 |
| 37 | Kentucky | 42,321 |
| 21 | Louisiana | 47,249 |
| 38 | Maine | 42,280 |
| 4 | Maryland | 57,447 |
| 3 | Massachusetts | 60,243 |
| 17 | Michigan | 49,897 |
| 13 | Minnesota | 50,885 |
| 50 | Mississippi | 40,081 |
| 35 | Missouri | 42,974 |
| 44 | Montana | 41,656 |
| 36 | Nebraska | 42,878 |
| 39 | Nevada | 42,137 |
| 6 | New Hampshire | 54,136 |
| 2 | New Jersey | 60,878 |
| 46 | New Mexico | 41,211 |
| 10 | New York | 51,274 |
| 40 | North Carolina | 41,859 |
| 24 | North Dakota | 45,888 |
| 23 | Ohio | 46,789 |
| 45 | Oklahoma | 41,415 |
| 20 | Oregon | 47,402 |
| 18 | Pennsylvania | 49,330 |
| 12 | Rhode Island | 50,975 |
| 42 | South Carolina | 41,740 |
| 48 | South Dakota | 40,721 |
| 41 | Tennessee | 41,828 |
| 28 | Texas | 44,802 |
| 19 | Utah | 48,540 |
| 29 | Vermont | 44,776 |
| 8 | Virginia | 52,125 |
| 7 | Washington | 52,529 |
| 32 | West Virginia | 44,159 |
| 22 | Wisconsin | 46,898 |
| 9 | Wyoming | 51,932 |

RANK ORDER

| RANK | STATE | EARNINGS |
|---|---|---|
| 1 | Connecticut | $61,097 |
| 2 | New Jersey | 60,878 |
| 3 | Massachusetts | 60,243 |
| 4 | Maryland | 57,447 |
| 5 | Alaska | 57,068 |
| 6 | New Hampshire | 54,136 |
| 7 | Washington | 52,529 |
| 8 | Virginia | 52,125 |
| 9 | Wyoming | 51,932 |
| 10 | New York | 51,274 |
| 11 | Illinois | 51,262 |
| 12 | Rhode Island | 50,975 |
| 13 | Minnesota | 50,885 |
| 14 | Delaware | 50,689 |
| 15 | Colorado | 50,509 |
| 16 | California | 50,139 |
| 17 | Michigan | 49,897 |
| 18 | Pennsylvania | 49,330 |
| 19 | Utah | 48,540 |
| 20 | Oregon | 47,402 |
| 21 | Louisiana | 47,249 |
| 22 | Wisconsin | 46,898 |
| 23 | Ohio | 46,789 |
| 24 | North Dakota | 45,888 |
| 25 | Hawaii | 45,748 |
| 26 | Indiana | 45,620 |
| 27 | Iowa | 45,305 |
| 28 | Texas | 44,802 |
| 29 | Vermont | 44,776 |
| 30 | Kansas | 44,765 |
| 31 | Alabama | 44,567 |
| 32 | West Virginia | 44,159 |
| 33 | Georgia | 43,707 |
| 34 | Arizona | 43,618 |
| 35 | Missouri | 42,974 |
| 36 | Nebraska | 42,878 |
| 37 | Kentucky | 42,321 |
| 38 | Maine | 42,280 |
| 39 | Nevada | 42,137 |
| 40 | North Carolina | 41,859 |
| 41 | Tennessee | 41,828 |
| 42 | South Carolina | 41,740 |
| 43 | Idaho | 41,664 |
| 44 | Montana | 41,656 |
| 45 | Oklahoma | 41,415 |
| 46 | New Mexico | 41,211 |
| 47 | Florida | 40,889 |
| 48 | South Dakota | 40,721 |
| 49 | Arkansas | 40,153 |
| 50 | Mississippi | 40,081 |
|  | District of Columbia | 66,754 |

Source: U.S. Bureau of the Census
"2012 American Community Survey-Table R2001" (http://www.census.gov/acs/www/index.html)

# Median Earnings of Female Full-Time Workers in 2012

## National Median = $37,412

ALPHA ORDER

ALPHA ORDER

| RANK | STATE | EARNINGS |
|------|-------|----------|
| 44 | Alabama | $31,674 |
| 6 | Alaska | 42,345 |
| 23 | Arizona | 35,974 |
| 49 | Arkansas | 30,843 |
| 7 | California | 41,956 |
| 14 | Colorado | 40,402 |
| 2 | Connecticut | 47,900 |
| 9 | Delaware | 41,120 |
| 30 | Florida | 34,202 |
| 25 | Georgia | 35,479 |
| 16 | Hawaii | 38,040 |
| 47 | Idaho | 31,296 |
| 15 | Illinois | 40,309 |
| 34 | Indiana | 33,419 |
| 27 | Iowa | 35,106 |
| 31 | Kansas | 34,131 |
| 41 | Kentucky | 32,157 |
| 45 | Louisiana | 31,586 |
| 28 | Maine | 35,057 |
| 1 | Maryland | 49,000 |
| 4 | Massachusetts | 47,651 |
| 20 | Michigan | 36,772 |
| 13 | Minnesota | 40,595 |
| 50 | Mississippi | 30,287 |
| 38 | Missouri | 32,868 |
| 43 | Montana | 31,775 |
| 35 | Nebraska | 33,218 |
| 24 | Nevada | 35,941 |
| 8 | New Hampshire | 41,774 |
| 3 | New Jersey | 47,878 |
| 37 | New Mexico | 33,074 |
| 5 | New York | 43,000 |
| 29 | North Carolina | 34,421 |
| 33 | North Dakota | 33,877 |
| 22 | Ohio | 35,984 |
| 46 | Oklahoma | 31,543 |
| 19 | Oregon | 37,381 |
| 18 | Pennsylvania | 37,414 |
| 11 | Rhode Island | 41,074 |
| 39 | South Carolina | 32,402 |
| 42 | South Dakota | 31,792 |
| 40 | Tennessee | 32,398 |
| 26 | Texas | 35,453 |
| 32 | Utah | 34,062 |
| 17 | Vermont | 38,017 |
| 10 | Virginia | 41,104 |
| 12 | Washington | 41,062 |
| 48 | West Virginia | 30,885 |
| 21 | Wisconsin | 36,535 |
| 36 | Wyoming | 33,152 |

RANK ORDER

| RANK | STATE | EARNINGS |
|------|-------|----------|
| 1 | Maryland | $49,000 |
| 2 | Connecticut | 47,900 |
| 3 | New Jersey | 47,878 |
| 4 | Massachusetts | 47,651 |
| 5 | New York | 43,000 |
| 6 | Alaska | 42,345 |
| 7 | California | 41,956 |
| 8 | New Hampshire | 41,774 |
| 9 | Delaware | 41,120 |
| 10 | Virginia | 41,104 |
| 11 | Rhode Island | 41,074 |
| 12 | Washington | 41,062 |
| 13 | Minnesota | 40,595 |
| 14 | Colorado | 40,402 |
| 15 | Illinois | 40,309 |
| 16 | Hawaii | 38,040 |
| 17 | Vermont | 38,017 |
| 18 | Pennsylvania | 37,414 |
| 19 | Oregon | 37,381 |
| 20 | Michigan | 36,772 |
| 21 | Wisconsin | 36,535 |
| 22 | Ohio | 35,984 |
| 23 | Arizona | 35,974 |
| 24 | Nevada | 35,941 |
| 25 | Georgia | 35,479 |
| 26 | Texas | 35,453 |
| 27 | Iowa | 35,106 |
| 28 | Maine | 35,057 |
| 29 | North Carolina | 34,421 |
| 30 | Florida | 34,202 |
| 31 | Kansas | 34,131 |
| 32 | Utah | 34,062 |
| 33 | North Dakota | 33,877 |
| 34 | Indiana | 33,419 |
| 35 | Nebraska | 33,218 |
| 36 | Wyoming | 33,152 |
| 37 | New Mexico | 33,074 |
| 38 | Missouri | 32,868 |
| 39 | South Carolina | 32,402 |
| 40 | Tennessee | 32,398 |
| 41 | Kentucky | 32,157 |
| 42 | South Dakota | 31,792 |
| 43 | Montana | 31,775 |
| 44 | Alabama | 31,674 |
| 45 | Louisiana | 31,586 |
| 46 | Oklahoma | 31,543 |
| 47 | Idaho | 31,296 |
| 48 | West Virginia | 30,885 |
| 49 | Arkansas | 30,843 |
| 50 | Mississippi | 30,287 |
| | District of Columbia | 60,116 |

Source: U.S. Bureau of the Census
"2012 American Community Survey-Table R2002" (http://www.census.gov/acs/www/index.html)

# State Minimum Wage Rates in 2014

## National Rate = $7.25 per Hour*

<table>
<tr><td colspan="3">ALPHA ORDER</td><td colspan="3">RANK ORDER</td></tr>
<tr><td>RANK</td><td>STATE</td><td>MINIMUM WAGE</td><td>RANK</td><td>STATE</td><td>MINIMUM WAGE</td></tr>
<tr><td>NA</td><td>Alabama**</td><td>NA</td><td>1</td><td>Washington</td><td>$9.32</td></tr>
<tr><td>17</td><td>Alaska</td><td>7.75</td><td>2</td><td>Oregon</td><td>9.10</td></tr>
<tr><td>15</td><td>Arizona</td><td>7.90</td><td>3</td><td>Vermont</td><td>8.73</td></tr>
<tr><td>42</td><td>Arkansas</td><td>6.25</td><td>4</td><td>Connecticut</td><td>8.70</td></tr>
<tr><td>8</td><td>California</td><td>8.00</td><td>5</td><td>Illinois</td><td>8.25</td></tr>
<tr><td>8</td><td>Colorado</td><td>8.00</td><td>5</td><td>Nevada</td><td>8.25</td></tr>
<tr><td>4</td><td>Connecticut</td><td>8.70</td><td>5</td><td>New Jersey</td><td>8.25</td></tr>
<tr><td>22</td><td>Delaware</td><td>7.25</td><td>8</td><td>California</td><td>8.00</td></tr>
<tr><td>14</td><td>Florida</td><td>7.93</td><td>8</td><td>Colorado</td><td>8.00</td></tr>
<tr><td>44</td><td>Georgia</td><td>5.15</td><td>8</td><td>Massachusetts</td><td>8.00</td></tr>
<tr><td>22</td><td>Hawaii</td><td>7.25</td><td>8</td><td>New York</td><td>8.00</td></tr>
<tr><td>22</td><td>Idaho</td><td>7.25</td><td>8</td><td>Rhode Island</td><td>8.00</td></tr>
<tr><td>5</td><td>Illinois</td><td>8.25</td><td>13</td><td>Ohio</td><td>7.95</td></tr>
<tr><td>22</td><td>Indiana</td><td>7.25</td><td>14</td><td>Florida</td><td>7.93</td></tr>
<tr><td>22</td><td>Iowa</td><td>7.25</td><td>15</td><td>Arizona</td><td>7.90</td></tr>
<tr><td>22</td><td>Kansas</td><td>7.25</td><td>15</td><td>Montana</td><td>7.90</td></tr>
<tr><td>22</td><td>Kentucky</td><td>7.25</td><td>17</td><td>Alaska</td><td>7.75</td></tr>
<tr><td>NA</td><td>Louisiana**</td><td>NA</td><td>18</td><td>Maine</td><td>7.50</td></tr>
<tr><td>18</td><td>Maine</td><td>7.50</td><td>18</td><td>Missouri</td><td>7.50</td></tr>
<tr><td>22</td><td>Maryland</td><td>7.25</td><td>18</td><td>New Mexico</td><td>7.50</td></tr>
<tr><td>8</td><td>Massachusetts</td><td>8.00</td><td>21</td><td>Michigan</td><td>7.40</td></tr>
<tr><td>21</td><td>Michigan</td><td>7.40</td><td>22</td><td>Delaware</td><td>7.25</td></tr>
<tr><td>43</td><td>Minnesota</td><td>6.15</td><td>22</td><td>Hawaii</td><td>7.25</td></tr>
<tr><td>NA</td><td>Mississippi**</td><td>NA</td><td>22</td><td>Idaho</td><td>7.25</td></tr>
<tr><td>18</td><td>Missouri</td><td>7.50</td><td>22</td><td>Indiana</td><td>7.25</td></tr>
<tr><td>15</td><td>Montana</td><td>7.90</td><td>22</td><td>Iowa</td><td>7.25</td></tr>
<tr><td>22</td><td>Nebraska</td><td>7.25</td><td>22</td><td>Kansas</td><td>7.25</td></tr>
<tr><td>5</td><td>Nevada</td><td>8.25</td><td>22</td><td>Kentucky</td><td>7.25</td></tr>
<tr><td>22</td><td>New Hampshire</td><td>7.25</td><td>22</td><td>Maryland</td><td>7.25</td></tr>
<tr><td>5</td><td>New Jersey</td><td>8.25</td><td>22</td><td>Nebraska</td><td>7.25</td></tr>
<tr><td>18</td><td>New Mexico</td><td>7.50</td><td>22</td><td>New Hampshire</td><td>7.25</td></tr>
<tr><td>8</td><td>New York</td><td>8.00</td><td>22</td><td>North Carolina</td><td>7.25</td></tr>
<tr><td>22</td><td>North Carolina</td><td>7.25</td><td>22</td><td>North Dakota</td><td>7.25</td></tr>
<tr><td>22</td><td>North Dakota</td><td>7.25</td><td>22</td><td>Oklahoma</td><td>7.25</td></tr>
<tr><td>13</td><td>Ohio</td><td>7.95</td><td>22</td><td>Pennsylvania</td><td>7.25</td></tr>
<tr><td>22</td><td>Oklahoma</td><td>7.25</td><td>22</td><td>South Dakota</td><td>7.25</td></tr>
<tr><td>2</td><td>Oregon</td><td>9.10</td><td>22</td><td>Texas</td><td>7.25</td></tr>
<tr><td>22</td><td>Pennsylvania</td><td>7.25</td><td>22</td><td>Utah</td><td>7.25</td></tr>
<tr><td>8</td><td>Rhode Island</td><td>8.00</td><td>22</td><td>Virginia</td><td>7.25</td></tr>
<tr><td>NA</td><td>South Carolina**</td><td>NA</td><td>22</td><td>West Virginia</td><td>7.25</td></tr>
<tr><td>22</td><td>South Dakota</td><td>7.25</td><td>22</td><td>Wisconsin</td><td>7.25</td></tr>
<tr><td>NA</td><td>Tennessee**</td><td>NA</td><td>42</td><td>Arkansas</td><td>6.25</td></tr>
<tr><td>22</td><td>Texas</td><td>7.25</td><td>43</td><td>Minnesota</td><td>6.15</td></tr>
<tr><td>22</td><td>Utah</td><td>7.25</td><td>44</td><td>Georgia</td><td>5.15</td></tr>
<tr><td>3</td><td>Vermont</td><td>8.73</td><td>44</td><td>Wyoming</td><td>5.15</td></tr>
<tr><td>22</td><td>Virginia</td><td>7.25</td><td>NA</td><td>Alabama**</td><td>NA</td></tr>
<tr><td>1</td><td>Washington</td><td>9.32</td><td>NA</td><td>Louisiana**</td><td>NA</td></tr>
<tr><td>22</td><td>West Virginia</td><td>7.25</td><td>NA</td><td>Mississippi**</td><td>NA</td></tr>
<tr><td>22</td><td>Wisconsin</td><td>7.25</td><td>NA</td><td>South Carolina**</td><td>NA</td></tr>
<tr><td>44</td><td>Wyoming</td><td>5.15</td><td>NA</td><td>Tennessee**</td><td>NA</td></tr>
<tr><td></td><td></td><td></td><td></td><td>District of Columbia</td><td>8.25</td></tr>
</table>

Source: U.S. Department of Labor, Employment Standards Administration
"Minimum Wage Laws in the States" (http://www.dol.gov/esa/minwage/america.htm)
*As of January 1, 2014.  State minimum wage rates are for those employers and jobs not covered by the federal program.
**No separate state program.

# Average Hourly Earnings of Production Workers
## on Manufacturing Payrolls in 2013
## National Average = $24.64*

| RANK | STATE | HOURLY EARNINGS |
|------|-------|-----------------|
| 36 | Alabama | $18.31 |
| 3 | Alaska | 22.27 |
| 27 | Arizona | 18.96 |
| 49 | Arkansas | 15.33 |
| 8 | California | 21.12 |
| 2 | Colorado | 24.60 |
| 7 | Connecticut | 21.53 |
| 47 | Delaware | 16.65 |
| 9 | Florida | 20.78 |
| 39 | Georgia | 18.25 |
| 23 | Hawaii | 19.11 |
| 6 | Idaho | 21.59 |
| 17 | Illinois | 19.42 |
| 31 | Indiana | 18.60 |
| 30 | Iowa | 18.70 |
| 33 | Kansas | 18.55 |
| 19 | Kentucky | 19.38 |
| 3 | Louisiana | 22.27 |
| 10 | Maine | 20.70 |
| 14 | Maryland | 19.91 |
| 5 | Massachusetts | 21.92 |
| 13 | Michigan | 20.09 |
| 12 | Minnesota | 20.15 |
| 38 | Mississippi | 18.29 |
| 25 | Missouri | 19.07 |
| 44 | Montana | 17.12 |
| 46 | Nebraska | 16.92 |
| 48 | Nevada | 16.44 |
| 31 | New Hampshire | 18.60 |
| 21 | New Jersey | 19.19 |
| 42 | New Mexico | 17.35 |
| 16 | New York | 19.45 |
| 45 | North Carolina | 16.97 |
| 28 | North Dakota | 18.89 |
| 15 | Ohio | 19.84 |
| 40 | Oklahoma | 18.07 |
| 23 | Oregon | 19.11 |
| 20 | Pennsylvania | 19.31 |
| 22 | Rhode Island | 19.18 |
| 26 | South Carolina | 19.04 |
| 43 | South Dakota | 17.20 |
| 41 | Tennessee | 17.60 |
| 11 | Texas | 20.50 |
| 36 | Utah | 18.31 |
| 35 | Vermont | 18.44 |
| 18 | Virginia | 19.40 |
| 1 | Washington | 25.48 |
| 34 | West Virginia | 18.45 |
| 29 | Wisconsin | 18.88 |
| NA | Wyoming** | NA |

| RANK | STATE | HOURLY EARNINGS |
|------|-------|-----------------|
| 1 | Washington | $25.48 |
| 2 | Colorado | 24.60 |
| 3 | Alaska | 22.27 |
| 3 | Louisiana | 22.27 |
| 5 | Massachusetts | 21.92 |
| 6 | Idaho | 21.59 |
| 7 | Connecticut | 21.53 |
| 8 | California | 21.12 |
| 9 | Florida | 20.78 |
| 10 | Maine | 20.70 |
| 11 | Texas | 20.50 |
| 12 | Minnesota | 20.15 |
| 13 | Michigan | 20.09 |
| 14 | Maryland | 19.91 |
| 15 | Ohio | 19.84 |
| 16 | New York | 19.45 |
| 17 | Illinois | 19.42 |
| 18 | Virginia | 19.40 |
| 19 | Kentucky | 19.38 |
| 20 | Pennsylvania | 19.31 |
| 21 | New Jersey | 19.19 |
| 22 | Rhode Island | 19.18 |
| 23 | Hawaii | 19.11 |
| 23 | Oregon | 19.11 |
| 25 | Missouri | 19.07 |
| 26 | South Carolina | 19.04 |
| 27 | Arizona | 18.96 |
| 28 | North Dakota | 18.89 |
| 29 | Wisconsin | 18.88 |
| 30 | Iowa | 18.70 |
| 31 | Indiana | 18.60 |
| 31 | New Hampshire | 18.60 |
| 33 | Kansas | 18.55 |
| 34 | West Virginia | 18.45 |
| 35 | Vermont | 18.44 |
| 36 | Alabama | 18.31 |
| 36 | Utah | 18.31 |
| 38 | Mississippi | 18.29 |
| 39 | Georgia | 18.25 |
| 40 | Oklahoma | 18.07 |
| 41 | Tennessee | 17.60 |
| 42 | New Mexico | 17.35 |
| 43 | South Dakota | 17.20 |
| 44 | Montana | 17.12 |
| 45 | North Carolina | 16.97 |
| 46 | Nebraska | 16.92 |
| 47 | Delaware | 16.65 |
| 48 | Nevada | 16.44 |
| 49 | Arkansas | 15.33 |
| NA | Wyoming** | NA |
| | District of Columbia** | NA |

Source: U.S. Department of Labor, Bureau of Labor Statistics
"State and Metro Area Employment, Hours and Earnings" (http://www.bls.gov/sae/home.htm)
*Preliminary data for December 2013.  Not seasonally adjusted except for national figure.
**Not available.

# Average Weekly Earnings of Production Workers on Manufacturing Payrolls in 2013
## National Average = $1,010.24*

| ALPHA ORDER | | | RANK ORDER | | |
|---|---|---|---|---|---|
| RANK | STATE | WEEKLY EARNINGS | RANK | STATE | WEEKLY EARNINGS |
| 25 | Alabama | $783.67 | 1 | Washington | $1,067.61 |
| 38 | Alaska | 730.46 | 2 | Louisiana | 1,019.97 |
| 30 | Arizona | 777.36 | 3 | Colorado | 974.16 |
| 48 | Arkansas | 625.46 | 4 | Massachusetts | 920.64 |
| 10 | California | 884.93 | 5 | Michigan | 906.06 |
| 3 | Colorado | 974.16 | 6 | Texas | 904.05 |
| 7 | Connecticut | 902.11 | 7 | Connecticut | 902.11 |
| 47 | Delaware | 672.66 | 8 | Maine | 892.17 |
| 9 | Florida | 885.23 | 9 | Florida | 885.23 |
| 29 | Georgia | 779.28 | 10 | California | 884.93 |
| 34 | Hawaii | 756.76 | 11 | Idaho | 876.55 |
| 11 | Idaho | 876.55 | 12 | Ohio | 853.12 |
| 15 | Illinois | 833.12 | 13 | Kentucky | 848.84 |
| 32 | Indiana | 775.62 | 14 | Minnesota | 848.32 |
| 26 | Iowa | 783.53 | 15 | Illinois | 833.12 |
| 16 | Kansas | 825.48 | 16 | Kansas | 825.48 |
| 13 | Kentucky | 848.84 | 17 | Virginia | 818.68 |
| 2 | Louisiana | 1,019.97 | 18 | South Carolina | 811.10 |
| 8 | Maine | 892.17 | 19 | New Jersey | 807.90 |
| 20 | Maryland | 802.37 | 20 | Maryland | 802.37 |
| 4 | Massachusetts | 920.64 | 21 | New York | 801.34 |
| 5 | Michigan | 906.06 | 22 | Rhode Island | 795.97 |
| 14 | Minnesota | 848.32 | 23 | Missouri | 795.22 |
| 27 | Mississippi | 780.98 | 24 | New Hampshire | 786.78 |
| 23 | Missouri | 795.22 | 25 | Alabama | 783.67 |
| 49 | Montana | 618.03 | 26 | Iowa | 783.53 |
| 39 | Nebraska | 729.25 | 27 | Mississippi | 780.98 |
| 46 | Nevada | 690.48 | 28 | Pennsylvania | 780.12 |
| 24 | New Hampshire | 786.78 | 29 | Georgia | 779.28 |
| 19 | New Jersey | 807.90 | 30 | Arizona | 777.36 |
| 45 | New Mexico | 699.21 | 31 | Oregon | 775.87 |
| 21 | New York | 801.34 | 32 | Indiana | 775.62 |
| 40 | North Carolina | 726.32 | 33 | Wisconsin | 770.30 |
| 44 | North Dakota | 714.04 | 34 | Hawaii | 756.76 |
| 12 | Ohio | 853.12 | 35 | West Virginia | 741.69 |
| 37 | Oklahoma | 739.06 | 36 | Utah | 741.56 |
| 31 | Oregon | 775.87 | 37 | Oklahoma | 739.06 |
| 28 | Pennsylvania | 780.12 | 38 | Alaska | 730.46 |
| 22 | Rhode Island | 795.97 | 39 | Nebraska | 729.25 |
| 18 | South Carolina | 811.10 | 40 | North Carolina | 726.32 |
| 41 | South Dakota | 725.84 | 41 | South Dakota | 725.84 |
| 42 | Tennessee | 723.36 | 42 | Tennessee | 723.36 |
| 6 | Texas | 904.05 | 43 | Vermont | 719.16 |
| 36 | Utah | 741.56 | 44 | North Dakota | 714.04 |
| 43 | Vermont | 719.16 | 45 | New Mexico | 699.21 |
| 17 | Virginia | 818.68 | 46 | Nevada | 690.48 |
| 1 | Washington | 1,067.61 | 47 | Delaware | 672.66 |
| 35 | West Virginia | 741.69 | 48 | Arkansas | 625.46 |
| 33 | Wisconsin | 770.30 | 49 | Montana | 618.03 |
| NA | Wyoming** | NA | NA | Wyoming** | NA |
| | | | District of Columbia** | | NA |

Source: U.S. Department of Labor, Bureau of Labor Statistics
"State and Metro Area Employment, Hours and Earnings" (http://www.bls.gov/sae/home.htm)
*Preliminary data for December 2013. Not seasonally adjusted except for national figure.
**Not available.

# Average Work Week of Production Workers on Manufacturing Payrolls in 2013
## National Average = 41.0 Hours per Week*

ALPHA ORDER

| RANK | STATE | WEEKLY HOURS |
|------|-------|--------------|
| 10 | Alabama | 42.8 |
| 49 | Alaska | 32.8 |
| 32 | Arizona | 41.0 |
| 34 | Arkansas | 40.8 |
| 23 | California | 41.9 |
| 44 | Colorado | 39.6 |
| 23 | Connecticut | 41.9 |
| 39 | Delaware | 40.4 |
| 14 | Florida | 42.6 |
| 12 | Georgia | 42.7 |
| 44 | Hawaii | 39.6 |
| 36 | Idaho | 40.6 |
| 9 | Illinois | 42.9 |
| 27 | Indiana | 41.7 |
| 23 | Iowa | 41.9 |
| 3 | Kansas | 44.5 |
| 5 | Kentucky | 43.8 |
| 1 | Louisiana | 45.8 |
| 6 | Maine | 43.1 |
| 41 | Maryland | 40.3 |
| 21 | Massachusetts | 42.0 |
| 2 | Michigan | 45.1 |
| 19 | Minnesota | 42.1 |
| 12 | Mississippi | 42.7 |
| 27 | Missouri | 41.7 |
| 48 | Montana | 36.1 |
| 6 | Nebraska | 43.1 |
| 21 | Nevada | 42.0 |
| 16 | New Hampshire | 42.3 |
| 19 | New Jersey | 42.1 |
| 41 | New Mexico | 40.3 |
| 30 | New York | 41.2 |
| 10 | North Carolina | 42.8 |
| 47 | North Dakota | 37.8 |
| 8 | Ohio | 43.0 |
| 33 | Oklahoma | 40.9 |
| 36 | Oregon | 40.6 |
| 39 | Pennsylvania | 40.4 |
| 29 | Rhode Island | 41.5 |
| 14 | South Carolina | 42.6 |
| 17 | South Dakota | 42.2 |
| 31 | Tennessee | 41.1 |
| 4 | Texas | 44.1 |
| 38 | Utah | 40.5 |
| 46 | Vermont | 39.0 |
| 17 | Virginia | 42.2 |
| 23 | Washington | 41.9 |
| 43 | West Virginia | 40.2 |
| 34 | Wisconsin | 40.8 |
| NA | Wyoming** | NA |

RANK ORDER

| RANK | STATE | WEEKLY HOURS |
|------|-------|--------------|
| 1 | Louisiana | 45.8 |
| 2 | Michigan | 45.1 |
| 3 | Kansas | 44.5 |
| 4 | Texas | 44.1 |
| 5 | Kentucky | 43.8 |
| 6 | Maine | 43.1 |
| 6 | Nebraska | 43.1 |
| 8 | Ohio | 43.0 |
| 9 | Illinois | 42.9 |
| 10 | Alabama | 42.8 |
| 10 | North Carolina | 42.8 |
| 12 | Georgia | 42.7 |
| 12 | Mississippi | 42.7 |
| 14 | Florida | 42.6 |
| 14 | South Carolina | 42.6 |
| 16 | New Hampshire | 42.3 |
| 17 | South Dakota | 42.2 |
| 17 | Virginia | 42.2 |
| 19 | Minnesota | 42.1 |
| 19 | New Jersey | 42.1 |
| 21 | Massachusetts | 42.0 |
| 21 | Nevada | 42.0 |
| 23 | California | 41.9 |
| 23 | Connecticut | 41.9 |
| 23 | Iowa | 41.9 |
| 23 | Washington | 41.9 |
| 27 | Indiana | 41.7 |
| 27 | Missouri | 41.7 |
| 29 | Rhode Island | 41.5 |
| 30 | New York | 41.2 |
| 31 | Tennessee | 41.1 |
| 32 | Arizona | 41.0 |
| 33 | Oklahoma | 40.9 |
| 34 | Arkansas | 40.8 |
| 34 | Wisconsin | 40.8 |
| 36 | Idaho | 40.6 |
| 36 | Oregon | 40.6 |
| 38 | Utah | 40.5 |
| 39 | Delaware | 40.4 |
| 39 | Pennsylvania | 40.4 |
| 41 | Maryland | 40.3 |
| 41 | New Mexico | 40.3 |
| 43 | West Virginia | 40.2 |
| 44 | Colorado | 39.6 |
| 44 | Hawaii | 39.6 |
| 46 | Vermont | 39.0 |
| 47 | North Dakota | 37.8 |
| 48 | Montana | 36.1 |
| 49 | Alaska | 32.8 |
| NA | Wyoming** | NA |
| | District of Columbia** | NA |

Source: U.S. Department of Labor, Bureau of Labor Statistics
"State and Metro Area Employment, Hours and Earnings" (http://www.bls.gov/sae/home.htm)
*Preliminary data for December 2013. Not seasonally adjusted except for national figure.
**Not available.

# Average Weekly Unemployment Benefit in 2013

## National Average = $309.21 a Week

ALPHA ORDER

ALPHA ORDER

| RANK | STATE | BENEFIT |
|---|---|---|
| 49 | Alabama | $207.13 |
| 40 | Alaska | 249.56 |
| 47 | Arizona | 220.67 |
| 29 | Arkansas | 289.12 |
| 23 | California | 300.94 |
| 9 | Colorado | 356.94 |
| 12 | Connecticut | 344.80 |
| 42 | Delaware | 245.01 |
| 46 | Florida | 231.84 |
| 38 | Georgia | 266.72 |
| 2 | Hawaii | 423.81 |
| 39 | Idaho | 264.15 |
| 17 | Illinois | 322.87 |
| 43 | Indiana | 242.40 |
| 15 | Iowa | 335.72 |
| 14 | Kansas | 340.50 |
| 28 | Kentucky | 291.78 |
| 48 | Louisiana | 207.46 |
| 33 | Maine | 285.54 |
| 16 | Maryland | 329.35 |
| 1 | Massachusetts | 426.70 |
| 27 | Michigan | 292.51 |
| 6 | Minnesota | 376.70 |
| 50 | Mississippi | 194.27 |
| 44 | Missouri | 241.26 |
| 30 | Montana | 288.83 |
| 34 | Nebraska | 275.91 |
| 22 | Nevada | 302.93 |
| 31 | New Hampshire | 287.55 |
| 3 | New Jersey | 397.83 |
| 25 | New Mexico | 294.78 |
| 21 | New York | 308.32 |
| 32 | North Carolina | 287.51 |
| 4 | North Dakota | 396.80 |
| 18 | Ohio | 317.33 |
| 26 | Oklahoma | 292.93 |
| 19 | Oregon | 316.42 |
| 8 | Pennsylvania | 359.58 |
| 10 | Rhode Island | 350.61 |
| 41 | South Carolina | 248.13 |
| 37 | South Dakota | 272.50 |
| 45 | Tennessee | 236.88 |
| 13 | Texas | 341.35 |
| 11 | Utah | 345.43 |
| 20 | Vermont | 310.87 |
| 24 | Virginia | 295.81 |
| 5 | Washington | 388.58 |
| 36 | West Virginia | 274.52 |
| 35 | Wisconsin | 274.97 |
| 7 | Wyoming | 360.35 |

RANK ORDER

| RANK | STATE | BENEFIT |
|---|---|---|
| 1 | Massachusetts | $426.70 |
| 2 | Hawaii | 423.81 |
| 3 | New Jersey | 397.83 |
| 4 | North Dakota | 396.80 |
| 5 | Washington | 388.58 |
| 6 | Minnesota | 376.70 |
| 7 | Wyoming | 360.35 |
| 8 | Pennsylvania | 359.58 |
| 9 | Colorado | 356.94 |
| 10 | Rhode Island | 350.61 |
| 11 | Utah | 345.43 |
| 12 | Connecticut | 344.80 |
| 13 | Texas | 341.35 |
| 14 | Kansas | 340.50 |
| 15 | Iowa | 335.72 |
| 16 | Maryland | 329.35 |
| 17 | Illinois | 322.87 |
| 18 | Ohio | 317.33 |
| 19 | Oregon | 316.42 |
| 20 | Vermont | 310.87 |
| 21 | New York | 308.32 |
| 22 | Nevada | 302.93 |
| 23 | California | 300.94 |
| 24 | Virginia | 295.81 |
| 25 | New Mexico | 294.78 |
| 26 | Oklahoma | 292.93 |
| 27 | Michigan | 292.51 |
| 28 | Kentucky | 291.78 |
| 29 | Arkansas | 289.12 |
| 30 | Montana | 288.83 |
| 31 | New Hampshire | 287.55 |
| 32 | North Carolina | 287.51 |
| 33 | Maine | 285.54 |
| 34 | Nebraska | 275.91 |
| 35 | Wisconsin | 274.97 |
| 36 | West Virginia | 274.52 |
| 37 | South Dakota | 272.50 |
| 38 | Georgia | 266.72 |
| 39 | Idaho | 264.15 |
| 40 | Alaska | 249.56 |
| 41 | South Carolina | 248.13 |
| 42 | Delaware | 245.01 |
| 43 | Indiana | 242.40 |
| 44 | Missouri | 241.26 |
| 45 | Tennessee | 236.88 |
| 46 | Florida | 231.84 |
| 47 | Arizona | 220.67 |
| 48 | Louisiana | 207.46 |
| 49 | Alabama | 207.13 |
| 50 | Mississippi | 194.27 |
| | District of Columbia | 299.46 |

Source: CQ Press using data from U.S. Department of Labor, Bureau of Labor Statistics
"Unemployment Insurance Data Summary" (http://workforcesecurity.doleta.gov/unemploy/finance.asp)

# Workers' Compensation Benefit Payments in 2011

## National Total = $60,210,113,000*

| ALPHA ORDER | | | |
|---|---|---|---|
| RANK | STATE | PAYMENTS | % of USA |
| 29 | Alabama | $616,022,000 | 1.0% |
| 42 | Alaska | 238,789,000 | 0.4% |
| 25 | Arizona | 711,801,000 | 1.2% |
| 45 | Arkansas | 189,123,000 | 0.3% |
| 1 | California | 10,477,086,000 | 17.4% |
| 24 | Colorado | 760,599,000 | 1.3% |
| 20 | Connecticut | 865,920,000 | 1.4% |
| 44 | Delaware | 219,971,000 | 0.4% |
| 5 | Florida | 2,711,148,000 | 4.5% |
| 11 | Georgia | 1,389,746,000 | 2.3% |
| 40 | Hawaii | 246,780,000 | 0.4% |
| 41 | Idaho | 245,429,000 | 0.4% |
| 3 | Illinois | 3,074,406,000 | 5.1% |
| 28 | Indiana | 625,111,000 | 1.0% |
| 27 | Iowa | 626,720,000 | 1.0% |
| 32 | Kansas | 435,641,000 | 0.7% |
| 26 | Kentucky | 656,441,000 | 1.1% |
| 19 | Louisiana | 869,762,000 | 1.4% |
| 39 | Maine | 252,017,000 | 0.4% |
| 15 | Maryland | 1,006,998,000 | 1.7% |
| 16 | Massachusetts | 962,596,000 | 1.6% |
| 12 | Michigan | 1,301,061,000 | 2.2% |
| 14 | Minnesota | 1,011,017,000 | 1.7% |
| 34 | Mississippi | 334,430,000 | 0.6% |
| 22 | Missouri | 813,686,000 | 1.4% |
| 38 | Montana | 252,550,000 | 0.4% |
| 35 | Nebraska | 321,306,000 | 0.5% |
| 33 | Nevada | 381,176,000 | 0.6% |
| 43 | New Hampshire | 227,488,000 | 0.4% |
| 8 | New Jersey | 2,168,517,000 | 3.6% |
| 36 | New Mexico | 275,783,000 | 0.5% |
| 2 | New York | 5,097,055,000 | 8.5% |
| 10 | North Carolina | 1,420,429,000 | 2.4% |
| 49 | North Dakota | 125,960,000 | 0.2% |
| 7 | Ohio | 2,232,596,000 | 3.7% |
| 21 | Oklahoma | 839,308,000 | 1.4% |
| 30 | Oregon | 568,516,000 | 0.9% |
| 4 | Pennsylvania | 2,894,165,000 | 4.8% |
| 46 | Rhode Island | 168,291,000 | 0.3% |
| 18 | South Carolina | 874,227,000 | 1.5% |
| 50 | South Dakota | 90,844,000 | 0.2% |
| 23 | Tennessee | 783,729,000 | 1.3% |
| 9 | Texas | 1,604,137,000 | 2.7% |
| 37 | Utah | 256,742,000 | 0.4% |
| 48 | Vermont | 136,795,000 | 0.2% |
| 17 | Virginia | 875,090,000 | 1.5% |
| 6 | Washington | 2,316,713,000 | 3.8% |
| 31 | West Virginia | 505,924,000 | 0.8% |
| 13 | Wisconsin | 1,099,950,000 | 1.8% |
| 47 | Wyoming | 162,388,000 | 0.3% |

| RANK ORDER | | | |
|---|---|---|---|
| RANK | STATE | PAYMENTS | % of USA |
| 1 | California | $10,477,086,000 | 17.4% |
| 2 | New York | 5,097,055,000 | 8.5% |
| 3 | Illinois | 3,074,406,000 | 5.1% |
| 4 | Pennsylvania | 2,894,165,000 | 4.8% |
| 5 | Florida | 2,711,148,000 | 4.5% |
| 6 | Washington | 2,316,713,000 | 3.8% |
| 7 | Ohio | 2,232,596,000 | 3.7% |
| 8 | New Jersey | 2,168,517,000 | 3.6% |
| 9 | Texas | 1,604,137,000 | 2.7% |
| 10 | North Carolina | 1,420,429,000 | 2.4% |
| 11 | Georgia | 1,389,746,000 | 2.3% |
| 12 | Michigan | 1,301,061,000 | 2.2% |
| 13 | Wisconsin | 1,099,950,000 | 1.8% |
| 14 | Minnesota | 1,011,017,000 | 1.7% |
| 15 | Maryland | 1,006,998,000 | 1.7% |
| 16 | Massachusetts | 962,596,000 | 1.6% |
| 17 | Virginia | 875,090,000 | 1.5% |
| 18 | South Carolina | 874,227,000 | 1.5% |
| 19 | Louisiana | 869,762,000 | 1.4% |
| 20 | Connecticut | 865,920,000 | 1.4% |
| 21 | Oklahoma | 839,308,000 | 1.4% |
| 22 | Missouri | 813,686,000 | 1.4% |
| 23 | Tennessee | 783,729,000 | 1.3% |
| 24 | Colorado | 760,599,000 | 1.3% |
| 25 | Arizona | 711,801,000 | 1.2% |
| 26 | Kentucky | 656,441,000 | 1.1% |
| 27 | Iowa | 626,720,000 | 1.0% |
| 28 | Indiana | 625,111,000 | 1.0% |
| 29 | Alabama | 616,022,000 | 1.0% |
| 30 | Oregon | 568,516,000 | 0.9% |
| 31 | West Virginia | 505,924,000 | 0.8% |
| 32 | Kansas | 435,641,000 | 0.7% |
| 33 | Nevada | 381,176,000 | 0.6% |
| 34 | Mississippi | 334,430,000 | 0.6% |
| 35 | Nebraska | 321,306,000 | 0.5% |
| 36 | New Mexico | 275,783,000 | 0.5% |
| 37 | Utah | 256,742,000 | 0.4% |
| 38 | Montana | 252,550,000 | 0.4% |
| 39 | Maine | 252,017,000 | 0.4% |
| 40 | Hawaii | 246,780,000 | 0.4% |
| 41 | Idaho | 245,429,000 | 0.4% |
| 42 | Alaska | 238,789,000 | 0.4% |
| 43 | New Hampshire | 227,488,000 | 0.4% |
| 44 | Delaware | 219,971,000 | 0.4% |
| 45 | Arkansas | 189,123,000 | 0.3% |
| 46 | Rhode Island | 168,291,000 | 0.3% |
| 47 | Wyoming | 162,388,000 | 0.3% |
| 48 | Vermont | 136,795,000 | 0.2% |
| 49 | North Dakota | 125,960,000 | 0.2% |
| 50 | South Dakota | 90,844,000 | 0.2% |
| | District of Columbia | 111,141,000 | 0.2% |

Source: National Academy of Social Insurance (Washington, DC)
"Workers' Compensation: Benefits, Coverage, and Costs, 2011" (http://www.nasi.org)
*Estimated payments from private insurance, state and federal funds, and self insurance. National total includes payments for federal civilian employee program, Black Lung Program, and other federal programs.

# Workers' Compensation Benefit Payment per Covered Worker in 2011

## National Average = $478*

ALPHA ORDER

| RANK | STATE | AVERAGE |
|------|-------|---------|
| 33 | Alabama | $367 |
| 2 | Alaska | 783 |
| 44 | Arizona | 306 |
| 50 | Arkansas | 175 |
| 4 | California | 732 |
| 35 | Colorado | 354 |
| 12 | Connecticut | 543 |
| 11 | Delaware | 555 |
| 24 | Florida | 405 |
| 28 | Georgia | 388 |
| 19 | Hawaii | 442 |
| 23 | Idaho | 412 |
| 10 | Illinois | 562 |
| 47 | Indiana | 231 |
| 19 | Iowa | 442 |
| 38 | Kansas | 344 |
| 26 | Kentucky | 389 |
| 15 | Louisiana | 480 |
| 18 | Maine | 448 |
| 21 | Maryland | 432 |
| 43 | Massachusetts | 307 |
| 35 | Michigan | 354 |
| 25 | Minnesota | 396 |
| 41 | Mississippi | 335 |
| 40 | Missouri | 338 |
| 5 | Montana | 622 |
| 32 | Nebraska | 368 |
| 37 | Nevada | 348 |
| 31 | New Hampshire | 380 |
| 9 | New Jersey | 588 |
| 30 | New Mexico | 383 |
| 6 | New York | 614 |
| 26 | North Carolina | 389 |
| 38 | North Dakota | 344 |
| 17 | Ohio | 457 |
| 7 | Oklahoma | 610 |
| 34 | Oregon | 358 |
| 13 | Pennsylvania | 535 |
| 29 | Rhode Island | 385 |
| 14 | South Carolina | 520 |
| 46 | South Dakota | 240 |
| 42 | Tennessee | 319 |
| 49 | Texas | 192 |
| 48 | Utah | 226 |
| 16 | Vermont | 477 |
| 45 | Virginia | 264 |
| 1 | Washington | 856 |
| 3 | West Virginia | 767 |
| 22 | Wisconsin | 430 |
| 8 | Wyoming | 608 |

RANK ORDER

| RANK | STATE | AVERAGE |
|------|-------|---------|
| 1 | Washington | $856 |
| 2 | Alaska | 783 |
| 3 | West Virginia | 767 |
| 4 | California | 732 |
| 5 | Montana | 622 |
| 6 | New York | 614 |
| 7 | Oklahoma | 610 |
| 8 | Wyoming | 608 |
| 9 | New Jersey | 588 |
| 10 | Illinois | 562 |
| 11 | Delaware | 555 |
| 12 | Connecticut | 543 |
| 13 | Pennsylvania | 535 |
| 14 | South Carolina | 520 |
| 15 | Louisiana | 480 |
| 16 | Vermont | 477 |
| 17 | Ohio | 457 |
| 18 | Maine | 448 |
| 19 | Hawaii | 442 |
| 19 | Iowa | 442 |
| 21 | Maryland | 432 |
| 22 | Wisconsin | 430 |
| 23 | Idaho | 412 |
| 24 | Florida | 405 |
| 25 | Minnesota | 396 |
| 26 | Kentucky | 389 |
| 26 | North Carolina | 389 |
| 28 | Georgia | 388 |
| 29 | Rhode Island | 385 |
| 30 | New Mexico | 383 |
| 31 | New Hampshire | 380 |
| 32 | Nebraska | 368 |
| 33 | Alabama | 367 |
| 34 | Oregon | 358 |
| 35 | Colorado | 354 |
| 35 | Michigan | 354 |
| 37 | Nevada | 348 |
| 38 | Kansas | 344 |
| 38 | North Dakota | 344 |
| 40 | Missouri | 338 |
| 41 | Mississippi | 335 |
| 42 | Tennessee | 319 |
| 43 | Massachusetts | 307 |
| 44 | Arizona | 306 |
| 45 | Virginia | 264 |
| 46 | South Dakota | 240 |
| 47 | Indiana | 231 |
| 48 | Utah | 226 |
| 49 | Texas | 192 |
| 50 | Arkansas | 175 |
| | District of Columbia | 225 |

Source: CQ Press using data from National Academy of Social Insurance (Washington, DC)
   "Workers' Compensation: Benefits, Coverage, and Costs, 2011" (http://www.nasi.org)
*Estimated payments from private insurance, state and federal funds, and self insurance.  National rate includes payments for federal civilian employee program, Black Lung Program, and other federal programs. Total divided by number of workers covered by workers' compensation.

# Percent Change in Workers' Compensation Benefit Payments: 2010 to 2011

## National Percent Change = 3.5% Increase*

| ALPHA ORDER | | | RANK ORDER | | |
|---|---|---|---|---|---|
| RANK | STATE | PERCENT CHANGE | RANK | STATE | PERCENT CHANGE |
| 40 | Alabama | (2.1) | 1 | Virginia | 12.5 |
| 7 | Alaska | 7.9 | 2 | Iowa | 12.2 |
| 25 | Arizona | 1.4 | 3 | New York | 10.7 |
| 46 | Arkansas | (6.9) | 4 | North Dakota | 9.5 |
| 6 | California | 8.4 | 5 | Connecticut | 8.9 |
| 44 | Colorado | (5.3) | 6 | California | 8.4 |
| 5 | Connecticut | 8.9 | 7 | Alaska | 7.9 |
| 18 | Delaware | 3.8 | 8 | Kansas | 7.5 |
| 10 | Florida | 6.5 | 9 | Texas | 6.9 |
| 42 | Georgia | (4.3) | 10 | Florida | 6.5 |
| 24 | Hawaii | 1.8 | 11 | Maryland | 5.6 |
| 19 | Idaho | 3.6 | 12 | Utah | 5.5 |
| 20 | Illinois | 2.8 | 13 | New Jersey | 5.4 |
| 17 | Indiana | 4.4 | 14 | Rhode Island | 5.2 |
| 2 | Iowa | 12.2 | 15 | North Carolina | 5.1 |
| 8 | Kansas | 7.5 | 16 | Louisiana | 4.5 |
| 36 | Kentucky | (0.8) | 17 | Indiana | 4.4 |
| 16 | Louisiana | 4.5 | 18 | Delaware | 3.8 |
| 28 | Maine | 0.2 | 19 | Idaho | 3.6 |
| 11 | Maryland | 5.6 | 20 | Illinois | 2.8 |
| 43 | Massachusetts | (5.0) | 21 | Wisconsin | 2.6 |
| 22 | Michigan | 2.3 | 22 | Michigan | 2.3 |
| 41 | Minnesota | (2.3) | 22 | Nebraska | 2.3 |
| 37 | Mississippi | (0.9) | 24 | Hawaii | 1.8 |
| 26 | Missouri | 1.0 | 25 | Arizona | 1.4 |
| 44 | Montana | (5.3) | 26 | Missouri | 1.0 |
| 22 | Nebraska | 2.3 | 27 | Washington | 0.3 |
| 50 | Nevada | (11.3) | 28 | Maine | 0.2 |
| 48 | New Hampshire | (9.6) | 29 | New Mexico | (0.1) |
| 13 | New Jersey | 5.4 | 29 | Tennessee | (0.1) |
| 29 | New Mexico | (0.1) | 31 | Vermont | (0.2) |
| 3 | New York | 10.7 | 32 | Pennsylvania | (0.5) |
| 15 | North Carolina | 5.1 | 32 | West Virginia | (0.5) |
| 4 | North Dakota | 9.5 | 34 | Oklahoma | (0.6) |
| 38 | Ohio | (1.6) | 35 | Wyoming | (0.7) |
| 34 | Oklahoma | (0.6) | 36 | Kentucky | (0.8) |
| 49 | Oregon | (10.1) | 37 | Mississippi | (0.9) |
| 32 | Pennsylvania | (0.5) | 38 | Ohio | (1.6) |
| 14 | Rhode Island | 5.2 | 39 | South Carolina | (1.9) |
| 39 | South Carolina | (1.9) | 40 | Alabama | (2.1) |
| 47 | South Dakota | (9.5) | 41 | Minnesota | (2.3) |
| 29 | Tennessee | (0.1) | 42 | Georgia | (4.3) |
| 9 | Texas | 6.9 | 43 | Massachusetts | (5.0) |
| 12 | Utah | 5.5 | 44 | Colorado | (5.3) |
| 31 | Vermont | (0.2) | 44 | Montana | (5.3) |
| 1 | Virginia | 12.5 | 46 | Arkansas | (6.9) |
| 27 | Washington | 0.3 | 47 | South Dakota | (9.5) |
| 32 | West Virginia | (0.5) | 48 | New Hampshire | (9.6) |
| 21 | Wisconsin | 2.6 | 49 | Oregon | (10.1) |
| 35 | Wyoming | (0.7) | 50 | Nevada | (11.3) |
| | | | | District of Columbia | 5.4 |

Source: National Academy of Social Insurance (Washington, DC)
   "Workers' Compensation: Benefits, Coverage, and Costs, 2011" (http://www.nasi.org)
*Estimated payments from private insurance, state and federal funds, and self insurance. National rate includes payments for federal civilian employee program, Black Lung Program, and other federal programs.

# Civilian Labor Force in 2013

## National Total = 154,937,000 Workers*

ALPHA ORDER

| RANK | STATE | LABOR FORCE | % of USA |
|---|---|---|---|
| 24 | Alabama | 2,117,600 | 1.4% |
| 48 | Alaska | 366,000 | 0.2% |
| 20 | Arizona | 2,988,300 | 1.9% |
| 34 | Arkansas | 1,327,900 | 0.9% |
| 1 | California | 18,568,200 | 12.0% |
| 22 | Colorado | 2,736,100 | 1.8% |
| 28 | Connecticut | 1,848,500 | 1.2% |
| 46 | Delaware | 439,500 | 0.3% |
| 4 | Florida | 9,405,300 | 6.1% |
| 8 | Georgia | 4,728,100 | 3.1% |
| 42 | Hawaii | 655,600 | 0.4% |
| 39 | Idaho | 772,600 | 0.5% |
| 5 | Illinois | 6,538,700 | 4.2% |
| 15 | Indiana | 3,180,000 | 2.1% |
| 30 | Iowa | 1,672,500 | 1.1% |
| 31 | Kansas | 1,487,400 | 1.0% |
| 26 | Kentucky | 2,047,200 | 1.3% |
| 25 | Louisiana | 2,090,500 | 1.3% |
| 41 | Maine | 709,000 | 0.5% |
| 16 | Maryland | 3,109,400 | 2.0% |
| 13 | Massachusetts | 3,481,300 | 2.2% |
| 9 | Michigan | 4,694,300 | 3.0% |
| 21 | Minnesota | 2,971,600 | 1.9% |
| 35 | Mississippi | 1,272,900 | 0.8% |
| 19 | Missouri | 3,016,800 | 1.9% |
| 44 | Montana | 510,400 | 0.3% |
| 36 | Nebraska | 1,021,600 | 0.7% |
| 33 | Nevada | 1,362,400 | 0.9% |
| 40 | New Hampshire | 740,700 | 0.5% |
| 11 | New Jersey | 4,506,000 | 2.9% |
| 37 | New Mexico | 920,100 | 0.6% |
| 3 | New York | 9,631,500 | 6.2% |
| 10 | North Carolina | 4,656,300 | 3.0% |
| 47 | North Dakota | 403,600 | 0.3% |
| 7 | Ohio | 5,737,800 | 3.7% |
| 29 | Oklahoma | 1,821,600 | 1.2% |
| 27 | Oregon | 1,915,300 | 1.2% |
| 6 | Pennsylvania | 6,443,500 | 4.2% |
| 43 | Rhode Island | 550,500 | 0.4% |
| 23 | South Carolina | 2,153,600 | 1.4% |
| 45 | South Dakota | 450,400 | 0.3% |
| 18 | Tennessee | 3,042,600 | 2.0% |
| 2 | Texas | 12,852,600 | 8.3% |
| 32 | Utah | 1,427,900 | 0.9% |
| 49 | Vermont | 349,900 | 0.2% |
| 12 | Virginia | 4,225,200 | 2.7% |
| 14 | Washington | 3,455,700 | 2.2% |
| 38 | West Virginia | 794,600 | 0.5% |
| 17 | Wisconsin | 3,071,700 | 2.0% |
| 50 | Wyoming | 308,500 | 0.2% |

RANK ORDER

| RANK | STATE | LABOR FORCE | % of USA |
|---|---|---|---|
| 1 | California | 18,568,200 | 12.0% |
| 2 | Texas | 12,852,600 | 8.3% |
| 3 | New York | 9,631,500 | 6.2% |
| 4 | Florida | 9,405,300 | 6.1% |
| 5 | Illinois | 6,538,700 | 4.2% |
| 6 | Pennsylvania | 6,443,500 | 4.2% |
| 7 | Ohio | 5,737,800 | 3.7% |
| 8 | Georgia | 4,728,100 | 3.1% |
| 9 | Michigan | 4,694,300 | 3.0% |
| 10 | North Carolina | 4,656,300 | 3.0% |
| 11 | New Jersey | 4,506,000 | 2.9% |
| 12 | Virginia | 4,225,200 | 2.7% |
| 13 | Massachusetts | 3,481,300 | 2.2% |
| 14 | Washington | 3,455,700 | 2.2% |
| 15 | Indiana | 3,180,000 | 2.1% |
| 16 | Maryland | 3,109,400 | 2.0% |
| 17 | Wisconsin | 3,071,700 | 2.0% |
| 18 | Tennessee | 3,042,600 | 2.0% |
| 19 | Missouri | 3,016,800 | 1.9% |
| 20 | Arizona | 2,988,300 | 1.9% |
| 21 | Minnesota | 2,971,600 | 1.9% |
| 22 | Colorado | 2,736,100 | 1.8% |
| 23 | South Carolina | 2,153,600 | 1.4% |
| 24 | Alabama | 2,117,600 | 1.4% |
| 25 | Louisiana | 2,090,500 | 1.3% |
| 26 | Kentucky | 2,047,200 | 1.3% |
| 27 | Oregon | 1,915,300 | 1.2% |
| 28 | Connecticut | 1,848,500 | 1.2% |
| 29 | Oklahoma | 1,821,600 | 1.2% |
| 30 | Iowa | 1,672,500 | 1.1% |
| 31 | Kansas | 1,487,400 | 1.0% |
| 32 | Utah | 1,427,900 | 0.9% |
| 33 | Nevada | 1,362,400 | 0.9% |
| 34 | Arkansas | 1,327,900 | 0.9% |
| 35 | Mississippi | 1,272,900 | 0.8% |
| 36 | Nebraska | 1,021,600 | 0.7% |
| 37 | New Mexico | 920,100 | 0.6% |
| 38 | West Virginia | 794,600 | 0.5% |
| 39 | Idaho | 772,600 | 0.5% |
| 40 | New Hampshire | 740,700 | 0.5% |
| 41 | Maine | 709,000 | 0.5% |
| 42 | Hawaii | 655,600 | 0.4% |
| 43 | Rhode Island | 550,500 | 0.4% |
| 44 | Montana | 510,400 | 0.3% |
| 45 | South Dakota | 450,400 | 0.3% |
| 46 | Delaware | 439,500 | 0.3% |
| 47 | North Dakota | 403,600 | 0.3% |
| 48 | Alaska | 366,000 | 0.2% |
| 49 | Vermont | 349,900 | 0.2% |
| 50 | Wyoming | 308,500 | 0.2% |
| | District of Columbia | 366,300 | 0.2% |

Source: U.S. Department of Labor, Bureau of Labor Statistics

"Regional and State Employment and Unemployment" (press release, January 28, 2014, www.bls.gov/bls/newsrels.htm)

*Seasonally adjusted preliminary data as of December 2013. National total calculated through a different formula.

# Employed Civilian Labor Force in 2013

## National Total = 144,586,000 Employed Workers*

ALPHA ORDER

| RANK | STATE | EMPLOYED | % of USA |
|------|-------|----------|----------|
| 24 | Alabama | 1,987,900 | 1.4% |
| 48 | Alaska | 342,700 | 0.2% |
| 21 | Arizona | 2,761,800 | 1.9% |
| 34 | Arkansas | 1,229,400 | 0.9% |
| 1 | California | 17,036,100 | 11.8% |
| 22 | Colorado | 2,567,100 | 1.8% |
| 29 | Connecticut | 1,712,000 | 1.2% |
| 46 | Delaware | 412,100 | 0.3% |
| 4 | Florida | 8,821,400 | 6.1% |
| 8 | Georgia | 4,378,200 | 3.0% |
| 42 | Hawaii | 625,800 | 0.4% |
| 39 | Idaho | 728,600 | 0.5% |
| 6 | Illinois | 5,973,400 | 4.1% |
| 15 | Indiana | 2,961,900 | 2.0% |
| 30 | Iowa | 1,602,300 | 1.1% |
| 31 | Kansas | 1,414,800 | 1.0% |
| 26 | Kentucky | 1,883,500 | 1.3% |
| 25 | Louisiana | 1,971,300 | 1.4% |
| 41 | Maine | 664,700 | 0.5% |
| 16 | Maryland | 2,919,100 | 2.0% |
| 13 | Massachusetts | 3,237,500 | 2.2% |
| 10 | Michigan | 4,300,100 | 3.0% |
| 19 | Minnesota | 2,834,300 | 2.0% |
| 35 | Mississippi | 1,171,300 | 0.8% |
| 18 | Missouri | 2,840,200 | 2.0% |
| 44 | Montana | 483,800 | 0.3% |
| 36 | Nebraska | 985,200 | 0.7% |
| 33 | Nevada | 1,242,100 | 0.9% |
| 40 | New Hampshire | 703,000 | 0.5% |
| 11 | New Jersey | 4,177,400 | 2.9% |
| 37 | New Mexico | 861,300 | 0.6% |
| 3 | New York | 8,950,400 | 6.2% |
| 9 | North Carolina | 4,333,600 | 3.0% |
| 47 | North Dakota | 393,100 | 0.3% |
| 7 | Ohio | 5,322,300 | 3.7% |
| 28 | Oklahoma | 1,723,800 | 1.2% |
| 27 | Oregon | 1,780,500 | 1.2% |
| 5 | Pennsylvania | 6,000,200 | 4.1% |
| 43 | Rhode Island | 500,600 | 0.3% |
| 23 | South Carolina | 2,011,200 | 1.4% |
| 45 | South Dakota | 434,400 | 0.3% |
| 20 | Tennessee | 2,804,900 | 1.9% |
| 2 | Texas | 12,087,900 | 8.4% |
| 32 | Utah | 1,370,100 | 0.9% |
| 49 | Vermont | 335,200 | 0.2% |
| 12 | Virginia | 4,006,400 | 2.8% |
| 14 | Washington | 3,227,800 | 2.2% |
| 38 | West Virginia | 747,900 | 0.5% |
| 17 | Wisconsin | 2,880,300 | 2.0% |
| 50 | Wyoming | 295,000 | 0.2% |

RANK ORDER

| RANK | STATE | EMPLOYED | % of USA |
|------|-------|----------|----------|
| 1 | California | 17,036,100 | 11.8% |
| 2 | Texas | 12,087,900 | 8.4% |
| 3 | New York | 8,950,400 | 6.2% |
| 4 | Florida | 8,821,400 | 6.1% |
| 5 | Pennsylvania | 6,000,200 | 4.1% |
| 6 | Illinois | 5,973,400 | 4.1% |
| 7 | Ohio | 5,322,300 | 3.7% |
| 8 | Georgia | 4,378,200 | 3.0% |
| 9 | North Carolina | 4,333,600 | 3.0% |
| 10 | Michigan | 4,300,100 | 3.0% |
| 11 | New Jersey | 4,177,400 | 2.9% |
| 12 | Virginia | 4,006,400 | 2.8% |
| 13 | Massachusetts | 3,237,500 | 2.2% |
| 14 | Washington | 3,227,800 | 2.2% |
| 15 | Indiana | 2,961,900 | 2.0% |
| 16 | Maryland | 2,919,100 | 2.0% |
| 17 | Wisconsin | 2,880,300 | 2.0% |
| 18 | Missouri | 2,840,200 | 2.0% |
| 19 | Minnesota | 2,834,300 | 2.0% |
| 20 | Tennessee | 2,804,900 | 1.9% |
| 21 | Arizona | 2,761,800 | 1.9% |
| 22 | Colorado | 2,567,100 | 1.8% |
| 23 | South Carolina | 2,011,200 | 1.4% |
| 24 | Alabama | 1,987,900 | 1.4% |
| 25 | Louisiana | 1,971,300 | 1.4% |
| 26 | Kentucky | 1,883,500 | 1.3% |
| 27 | Oregon | 1,780,500 | 1.2% |
| 28 | Oklahoma | 1,723,800 | 1.2% |
| 29 | Connecticut | 1,712,000 | 1.2% |
| 30 | Iowa | 1,602,300 | 1.1% |
| 31 | Kansas | 1,414,800 | 1.0% |
| 32 | Utah | 1,370,100 | 0.9% |
| 33 | Nevada | 1,242,100 | 0.9% |
| 34 | Arkansas | 1,229,400 | 0.9% |
| 35 | Mississippi | 1,171,300 | 0.8% |
| 36 | Nebraska | 985,200 | 0.7% |
| 37 | New Mexico | 861,300 | 0.6% |
| 38 | West Virginia | 747,900 | 0.5% |
| 39 | Idaho | 728,600 | 0.5% |
| 40 | New Hampshire | 703,000 | 0.5% |
| 41 | Maine | 664,700 | 0.5% |
| 42 | Hawaii | 625,800 | 0.4% |
| 43 | Rhode Island | 500,600 | 0.3% |
| 44 | Montana | 483,800 | 0.3% |
| 45 | South Dakota | 434,400 | 0.3% |
| 46 | Delaware | 412,100 | 0.3% |
| 47 | North Dakota | 393,100 | 0.3% |
| 48 | Alaska | 342,700 | 0.2% |
| 49 | Vermont | 335,200 | 0.2% |
| 50 | Wyoming | 295,000 | 0.2% |
| | District of Columbia | 336,800 | 0.2% |

Source: CQ Press using data from U.S. Department of Labor, Bureau of Labor Statistics
"Regional and State Employment and Unemployment" (press release, January 28, 2014, www.bls.gov/bls/newsrels.htm)
*Seasonally adjusted preliminary data as of December 2013. National total calculated through a different formula.

# Employment to Population Ratio in 2013

## National Percent = 58.2% of Population 16 Years and Older Employed*

ALPHA ORDER

| RANK | STATE | PERCENT |
|---|---|---|
| 48 | Alabama | 52.0 |
| 16 | Alaska | 60.7 |
| 44 | Arizona | 54.0 |
| 46 | Arkansas | 53.1 |
| 32 | California | 57.0 |
| 12 | Colorado | 62.8 |
| 22 | Connecticut | 59.1 |
| 37 | Delaware | 56.0 |
| 38 | Florida | 55.9 |
| 33 | Georgia | 56.8 |
| 39 | Hawaii | 55.8 |
| 18 | Idaho | 60.0 |
| 25 | Illinois | 58.7 |
| 30 | Indiana | 57.8 |
| 6 | Iowa | 65.9 |
| 11 | Kansas | 63.1 |
| 43 | Kentucky | 54.2 |
| 40 | Louisiana | 54.7 |
| 17 | Maine | 60.6 |
| 13 | Maryland | 62.1 |
| 19 | Massachusetts | 59.8 |
| 42 | Michigan | 54.5 |
| 3 | Minnesota | 66.7 |
| 49 | Mississippi | 50.4 |
| 21 | Missouri | 59.4 |
| 19 | Montana | 59.8 |
| 2 | Nebraska | 68.3 |
| 31 | Nevada | 57.2 |
| 7 | New Hampshire | 65.0 |
| 23 | New Jersey | 59.0 |
| 47 | New Mexico | 52.9 |
| 35 | New York | 56.6 |
| 36 | North Carolina | 56.2 |
| 1 | North Dakota | 70.0 |
| 27 | Ohio | 57.9 |
| 27 | Oklahoma | 57.9 |
| 33 | Oregon | 56.8 |
| 27 | Pennsylvania | 57.9 |
| 26 | Rhode Island | 58.2 |
| 45 | South Carolina | 53.4 |
| 3 | South Dakota | 66.7 |
| 40 | Tennessee | 54.7 |
| 15 | Texas | 61.0 |
| 3 | Utah | 66.7 |
| 9 | Vermont | 64.7 |
| 14 | Virginia | 61.3 |
| 24 | Washington | 58.8 |
| 50 | West Virginia | 49.3 |
| 10 | Wisconsin | 63.2 |
| 8 | Wyoming | 64.8 |

RANK ORDER

| RANK | STATE | PERCENT |
|---|---|---|
| 1 | North Dakota | 70.0 |
| 2 | Nebraska | 68.3 |
| 3 | Minnesota | 66.7 |
| 3 | South Dakota | 66.7 |
| 3 | Utah | 66.7 |
| 6 | Iowa | 65.9 |
| 7 | New Hampshire | 65.0 |
| 8 | Wyoming | 64.8 |
| 9 | Vermont | 64.7 |
| 10 | Wisconsin | 63.2 |
| 11 | Kansas | 63.1 |
| 12 | Colorado | 62.8 |
| 13 | Maryland | 62.1 |
| 14 | Virginia | 61.3 |
| 15 | Texas | 61.0 |
| 16 | Alaska | 60.7 |
| 17 | Maine | 60.6 |
| 18 | Idaho | 60.0 |
| 19 | Massachusetts | 59.8 |
| 19 | Montana | 59.8 |
| 21 | Missouri | 59.4 |
| 22 | Connecticut | 59.1 |
| 23 | New Jersey | 59.0 |
| 24 | Washington | 58.8 |
| 25 | Illinois | 58.7 |
| 26 | Rhode Island | 58.2 |
| 27 | Ohio | 57.9 |
| 27 | Oklahoma | 57.9 |
| 27 | Pennsylvania | 57.9 |
| 30 | Indiana | 57.8 |
| 31 | Nevada | 57.2 |
| 32 | California | 57.0 |
| 33 | Georgia | 56.8 |
| 33 | Oregon | 56.8 |
| 35 | New York | 56.6 |
| 36 | North Carolina | 56.2 |
| 37 | Delaware | 56.0 |
| 38 | Florida | 55.9 |
| 39 | Hawaii | 55.8 |
| 40 | Louisiana | 54.7 |
| 40 | Tennessee | 54.7 |
| 42 | Michigan | 54.5 |
| 43 | Kentucky | 54.2 |
| 44 | Arizona | 54.0 |
| 45 | South Carolina | 53.4 |
| 46 | Arkansas | 53.1 |
| 47 | New Mexico | 52.9 |
| 48 | Alabama | 52.0 |
| 49 | Mississippi | 50.4 |
| 50 | West Virginia | 49.3 |
| | District of Columbia | 63.1 |

Source: CQ Press using data from U.S. Department of Labor, Bureau of Labor Statistics
"Regional and State Employment and Unemployment" (press release, January 28, 2014, www.bls.gov/bls/newsrels.htm)
*Seasonally adjusted preliminary data as of December 2013.  Calculated with 2012 population data.

# Unemployed Civilian Labor Force in 2013

## National Total = 10,351,000 Unemployed Workers*

ALPHA ORDER

| RANK | STATE | UNEMPLOYED | % of USA |
|---|---|---|---|
| 27 | Alabama | 129,700 | 1.3% |
| 46 | Alaska | 23,300 | 0.2% |
| 15 | Arizona | 226,500 | 2.2% |
| 31 | Arkansas | 98,500 | 1.0% |
| 1 | California | 1,532,100 | 14.8% |
| 21 | Colorado | 169,000 | 1.6% |
| 25 | Connecticut | 136,500 | 1.3% |
| 44 | Delaware | 27,400 | 0.3% |
| 4 | Florida | 583,900 | 5.6% |
| 9 | Georgia | 349,900 | 3.4% |
| 43 | Hawaii | 29,800 | 0.3% |
| 40 | Idaho | 44,000 | 0.4% |
| 5 | Illinois | 565,300 | 5.5% |
| 17 | Indiana | 218,100 | 2.1% |
| 34 | Iowa | 70,200 | 0.7% |
| 33 | Kansas | 72,600 | 0.7% |
| 22 | Kentucky | 163,700 | 1.6% |
| 29 | Louisiana | 119,200 | 1.2% |
| 39 | Maine | 44,300 | 0.4% |
| 19 | Maryland | 190,300 | 1.8% |
| 12 | Massachusetts | 243,800 | 2.4% |
| 8 | Michigan | 394,200 | 3.8% |
| 24 | Minnesota | 137,300 | 1.3% |
| 30 | Mississippi | 101,600 | 1.0% |
| 20 | Missouri | 176,600 | 1.7% |
| 45 | Montana | 26,600 | 0.3% |
| 42 | Nebraska | 36,400 | 0.4% |
| 28 | Nevada | 120,300 | 1.2% |
| 41 | New Hampshire | 37,700 | 0.4% |
| 10 | New Jersey | 328,600 | 3.2% |
| 35 | New Mexico | 58,800 | 0.6% |
| 3 | New York | 681,100 | 6.6% |
| 11 | North Carolina | 322,700 | 3.1% |
| 50 | North Dakota | 10,500 | 0.1% |
| 7 | Ohio | 415,500 | 4.0% |
| 32 | Oklahoma | 97,800 | 0.9% |
| 26 | Oregon | 134,800 | 1.3% |
| 6 | Pennsylvania | 443,300 | 4.3% |
| 37 | Rhode Island | 49,900 | 0.5% |
| 23 | South Carolina | 142,400 | 1.4% |
| 47 | South Dakota | 16,000 | 0.2% |
| 13 | Tennessee | 237,700 | 2.3% |
| 2 | Texas | 764,700 | 7.4% |
| 36 | Utah | 57,800 | 0.6% |
| 48 | Vermont | 14,700 | 0.1% |
| 16 | Virginia | 218,800 | 2.1% |
| 14 | Washington | 227,900 | 2.2% |
| 38 | West Virginia | 46,700 | 0.5% |
| 18 | Wisconsin | 191,400 | 1.8% |
| 49 | Wyoming | 13,500 | 0.1% |

RANK ORDER

| RANK | STATE | UNEMPLOYED | % of USA |
|---|---|---|---|
| 1 | California | 1,532,100 | 14.8% |
| 2 | Texas | 764,700 | 7.4% |
| 3 | New York | 681,100 | 6.6% |
| 4 | Florida | 583,900 | 5.6% |
| 5 | Illinois | 565,300 | 5.5% |
| 6 | Pennsylvania | 443,300 | 4.3% |
| 7 | Ohio | 415,500 | 4.0% |
| 8 | Michigan | 394,200 | 3.8% |
| 9 | Georgia | 349,900 | 3.4% |
| 10 | New Jersey | 328,600 | 3.2% |
| 11 | North Carolina | 322,700 | 3.1% |
| 12 | Massachusetts | 243,800 | 2.4% |
| 13 | Tennessee | 237,700 | 2.3% |
| 14 | Washington | 227,900 | 2.2% |
| 15 | Arizona | 226,500 | 2.2% |
| 16 | Virginia | 218,800 | 2.1% |
| 17 | Indiana | 218,100 | 2.1% |
| 18 | Wisconsin | 191,400 | 1.8% |
| 19 | Maryland | 190,300 | 1.8% |
| 20 | Missouri | 176,600 | 1.7% |
| 21 | Colorado | 169,000 | 1.6% |
| 22 | Kentucky | 163,700 | 1.6% |
| 23 | South Carolina | 142,400 | 1.4% |
| 24 | Minnesota | 137,300 | 1.3% |
| 25 | Connecticut | 136,500 | 1.3% |
| 26 | Oregon | 134,800 | 1.3% |
| 27 | Alabama | 129,700 | 1.3% |
| 28 | Nevada | 120,300 | 1.2% |
| 29 | Louisiana | 119,200 | 1.2% |
| 30 | Mississippi | 101,600 | 1.0% |
| 31 | Arkansas | 98,500 | 1.0% |
| 32 | Oklahoma | 97,800 | 0.9% |
| 33 | Kansas | 72,600 | 0.7% |
| 34 | Iowa | 70,200 | 0.7% |
| 35 | New Mexico | 58,800 | 0.6% |
| 36 | Utah | 57,800 | 0.6% |
| 37 | Rhode Island | 49,900 | 0.5% |
| 38 | West Virginia | 46,700 | 0.5% |
| 39 | Maine | 44,300 | 0.4% |
| 40 | Idaho | 44,000 | 0.4% |
| 41 | New Hampshire | 37,700 | 0.4% |
| 42 | Nebraska | 36,400 | 0.4% |
| 43 | Hawaii | 29,800 | 0.3% |
| 44 | Delaware | 27,400 | 0.3% |
| 45 | Montana | 26,600 | 0.3% |
| 46 | Alaska | 23,300 | 0.2% |
| 47 | South Dakota | 16,000 | 0.2% |
| 48 | Vermont | 14,700 | 0.1% |
| 49 | Wyoming | 13,500 | 0.1% |
| 50 | North Dakota | 10,500 | 0.1% |
| | District of Columbia | 29,500 | 0.3% |

Source: U.S. Department of Labor, Bureau of Labor Statistics
"Regional and State Employment and Unemployment" (press release, January 28, 2014, www.bls.gov/bls/newsrels.htm)
*Seasonally adjusted preliminary data as of December 2013. National total calculated through a different formula.

# Unemployment Rate in 2013

## National Rate = 6.7% of Labor Force Unemployed*

ALPHA ORDER

| RANK | STATE | PERCENT |
| --- | --- | --- |
| 30 | Alabama | 6.1 |
| 23 | Alaska | 6.4 |
| 9 | Arizona | 7.6 |
| 10 | Arkansas | 7.4 |
| 5 | California | 8.3 |
| 25 | Colorado | 6.2 |
| 10 | Connecticut | 7.4 |
| 25 | Delaware | 6.2 |
| 25 | Florida | 6.2 |
| 10 | Georgia | 7.4 |
| 43 | Hawaii | 4.5 |
| 35 | Idaho | 5.7 |
| 3 | Illinois | 8.6 |
| 18 | Indiana | 6.9 |
| 45 | Iowa | 4.2 |
| 41 | Kansas | 4.9 |
| 6 | Kentucky | 8.0 |
| 35 | Louisiana | 5.7 |
| 25 | Maine | 6.2 |
| 30 | Maryland | 6.1 |
| 16 | Massachusetts | 7.0 |
| 4 | Michigan | 8.4 |
| 42 | Minnesota | 4.6 |
| 6 | Mississippi | 8.0 |
| 33 | Missouri | 5.9 |
| 38 | Montana | 5.2 |
| 48 | Nebraska | 3.6 |
| 2 | Nevada | 8.8 |
| 40 | New Hampshire | 5.1 |
| 13 | New Jersey | 7.3 |
| 23 | New Mexico | 6.4 |
| 15 | New York | 7.1 |
| 18 | North Carolina | 6.9 |
| 50 | North Dakota | 2.6 |
| 14 | Ohio | 7.2 |
| 37 | Oklahoma | 5.4 |
| 16 | Oregon | 7.0 |
| 18 | Pennsylvania | 6.9 |
| 1 | Rhode Island | 9.1 |
| 21 | South Carolina | 6.6 |
| 48 | South Dakota | 3.6 |
| 8 | Tennessee | 7.8 |
| 32 | Texas | 6.0 |
| 47 | Utah | 4.1 |
| 45 | Vermont | 4.2 |
| 38 | Virginia | 5.2 |
| 21 | Washington | 6.6 |
| 33 | West Virginia | 5.9 |
| 25 | Wisconsin | 6.2 |
| 44 | Wyoming | 4.4 |

RANK ORDER

| RANK | STATE | PERCENT |
| --- | --- | --- |
| 1 | Rhode Island | 9.1 |
| 2 | Nevada | 8.8 |
| 3 | Illinois | 8.6 |
| 4 | Michigan | 8.4 |
| 5 | California | 8.3 |
| 6 | Kentucky | 8.0 |
| 6 | Mississippi | 8.0 |
| 8 | Tennessee | 7.8 |
| 9 | Arizona | 7.6 |
| 10 | Arkansas | 7.4 |
| 10 | Connecticut | 7.4 |
| 10 | Georgia | 7.4 |
| 13 | New Jersey | 7.3 |
| 14 | Ohio | 7.2 |
| 15 | New York | 7.1 |
| 16 | Massachusetts | 7.0 |
| 16 | Oregon | 7.0 |
| 18 | Indiana | 6.9 |
| 18 | North Carolina | 6.9 |
| 18 | Pennsylvania | 6.9 |
| 21 | South Carolina | 6.6 |
| 21 | Washington | 6.6 |
| 23 | Alaska | 6.4 |
| 23 | New Mexico | 6.4 |
| 25 | Colorado | 6.2 |
| 25 | Delaware | 6.2 |
| 25 | Florida | 6.2 |
| 25 | Maine | 6.2 |
| 25 | Wisconsin | 6.2 |
| 30 | Alabama | 6.1 |
| 30 | Maryland | 6.1 |
| 32 | Texas | 6.0 |
| 33 | Missouri | 5.9 |
| 33 | West Virginia | 5.9 |
| 35 | Idaho | 5.7 |
| 35 | Louisiana | 5.7 |
| 37 | Oklahoma | 5.4 |
| 38 | Montana | 5.2 |
| 38 | Virginia | 5.2 |
| 40 | New Hampshire | 5.1 |
| 41 | Kansas | 4.9 |
| 42 | Minnesota | 4.6 |
| 43 | Hawaii | 4.5 |
| 44 | Wyoming | 4.4 |
| 45 | Iowa | 4.2 |
| 45 | Vermont | 4.2 |
| 47 | Utah | 4.1 |
| 48 | Nebraska | 3.6 |
| 48 | South Dakota | 3.6 |
| 50 | North Dakota | 2.6 |

District of Columbia    8.1

Source: U.S. Department of Labor, Bureau of Labor Statistics
   "Regional and State Employment and Unemployment" (press release, January 28, 2014, www.bls.gov/bls/newsrels.htm)
*Seasonally adjusted preliminary data as of December 2013.  National figure calculated through a different formula.

# Women in Civilian Labor Force in 2012

## National Total = 72,684,000 Women*

ALPHA ORDER

| RANK | STATE | WOMEN | % of USA |
|---|---|---|---|
| 24 | Alabama | 1,026,000 | 1.4% |
| 49 | Alaska | 168,000 | 0.2% |
| 20 | Arizona | 1,385,000 | 1.9% |
| 33 | Arkansas | 634,000 | 0.9% |
| 1 | California | 8,358,000 | 11.5% |
| 22 | Colorado | 1,256,000 | 1.7% |
| 28 | Connecticut | 898,000 | 1.2% |
| 45 | Delaware | 221,000 | 0.3% |
| 4 | Florida | 4,467,000 | 6.1% |
| 8 | Georgia | 2,291,000 | 3.2% |
| 42 | Hawaii | 303,000 | 0.4% |
| 40 | Idaho | 342,000 | 0.5% |
| 5 | Illinois | 3,117,000 | 4.3% |
| 17 | Indiana | 1,478,000 | 2.0% |
| 30 | Iowa | 784,000 | 1.1% |
| 31 | Kansas | 699,000 | 1.0% |
| 25 | Kentucky | 979,000 | 1.3% |
| 26 | Louisiana | 972,000 | 1.3% |
| 41 | Maine | 338,000 | 0.5% |
| 15 | Maryland | 1,546,000 | 2.1% |
| 13 | Massachusetts | 1,720,000 | 2.4% |
| 10 | Michigan | 2,199,000 | 3.0% |
| 21 | Minnesota | 1,383,000 | 1.9% |
| 32 | Mississippi | 637,000 | 0.9% |
| 19 | Missouri | 1,437,000 | 2.0% |
| 44 | Montana | 241,000 | 0.3% |
| 36 | Nebraska | 487,000 | 0.7% |
| 34 | Nevada | 626,000 | 0.9% |
| 39 | New Hampshire | 353,000 | 0.5% |
| 11 | New Jersey | 2,164,000 | 3.0% |
| 37 | New Mexico | 450,000 | 0.6% |
| 3 | New York | 4,540,000 | 6.2% |
| 9 | North Carolina | 2,221,000 | 3.1% |
| 47 | North Dakota | 184,000 | 0.3% |
| 7 | Ohio | 2,710,000 | 3.7% |
| 29 | Oklahoma | 824,000 | 1.1% |
| 27 | Oregon | 926,000 | 1.3% |
| 6 | Pennsylvania | 3,060,000 | 4.2% |
| 43 | Rhode Island | 273,000 | 0.4% |
| 23 | South Carolina | 1,060,000 | 1.5% |
| 46 | South Dakota | 206,000 | 0.3% |
| 18 | Tennessee | 1,438,000 | 2.0% |
| 2 | Texas | 5,731,000 | 7.9% |
| 35 | Utah | 597,000 | 0.8% |
| 48 | Vermont | 173,000 | 0.2% |
| 12 | Virginia | 1,989,000 | 2.7% |
| 14 | Washington | 1,620,000 | 2.2% |
| 38 | West Virginia | 373,000 | 0.5% |
| 16 | Wisconsin | 1,479,000 | 2.0% |
| 50 | Wyoming | 137,000 | 0.2% |

RANK ORDER

| RANK | STATE | WOMEN | % of USA |
|---|---|---|---|
| 1 | California | 8,358,000 | 11.5% |
| 2 | Texas | 5,731,000 | 7.9% |
| 3 | New York | 4,540,000 | 6.2% |
| 4 | Florida | 4,467,000 | 6.1% |
| 5 | Illinois | 3,117,000 | 4.3% |
| 6 | Pennsylvania | 3,060,000 | 4.2% |
| 7 | Ohio | 2,710,000 | 3.7% |
| 8 | Georgia | 2,291,000 | 3.2% |
| 9 | North Carolina | 2,221,000 | 3.1% |
| 10 | Michigan | 2,199,000 | 3.0% |
| 11 | New Jersey | 2,164,000 | 3.0% |
| 12 | Virginia | 1,989,000 | 2.7% |
| 13 | Massachusetts | 1,720,000 | 2.4% |
| 14 | Washington | 1,620,000 | 2.2% |
| 15 | Maryland | 1,546,000 | 2.1% |
| 16 | Wisconsin | 1,479,000 | 2.0% |
| 17 | Indiana | 1,478,000 | 2.0% |
| 18 | Tennessee | 1,438,000 | 2.0% |
| 19 | Missouri | 1,437,000 | 2.0% |
| 20 | Arizona | 1,385,000 | 1.9% |
| 21 | Minnesota | 1,383,000 | 1.9% |
| 22 | Colorado | 1,256,000 | 1.7% |
| 23 | South Carolina | 1,060,000 | 1.5% |
| 24 | Alabama | 1,026,000 | 1.4% |
| 25 | Kentucky | 979,000 | 1.3% |
| 26 | Louisiana | 972,000 | 1.3% |
| 27 | Oregon | 926,000 | 1.3% |
| 28 | Connecticut | 898,000 | 1.2% |
| 29 | Oklahoma | 824,000 | 1.1% |
| 30 | Iowa | 784,000 | 1.1% |
| 31 | Kansas | 699,000 | 1.0% |
| 32 | Mississippi | 637,000 | 0.9% |
| 33 | Arkansas | 634,000 | 0.9% |
| 34 | Nevada | 626,000 | 0.9% |
| 35 | Utah | 597,000 | 0.8% |
| 36 | Nebraska | 487,000 | 0.7% |
| 37 | New Mexico | 450,000 | 0.6% |
| 38 | West Virginia | 373,000 | 0.5% |
| 39 | New Hampshire | 353,000 | 0.5% |
| 40 | Idaho | 342,000 | 0.5% |
| 41 | Maine | 338,000 | 0.5% |
| 42 | Hawaii | 303,000 | 0.4% |
| 43 | Rhode Island | 273,000 | 0.4% |
| 44 | Montana | 241,000 | 0.3% |
| 45 | Delaware | 221,000 | 0.3% |
| 46 | South Dakota | 206,000 | 0.3% |
| 47 | North Dakota | 184,000 | 0.3% |
| 48 | Vermont | 173,000 | 0.2% |
| 49 | Alaska | 168,000 | 0.2% |
| 50 | Wyoming | 137,000 | 0.2% |
| | District of Columbia | 184,000 | 0.3% |

Source: U.S. Department of Labor, Bureau of Labor Statistics
    "Geographic Profiles of Employment and Unemployment, 2012" (http://www.bls.gov/gps/)
*Annual averages.

# Percent of Women in the Civilian Labor Force in 2012

## National Percent = 57.7% of Women*

ALPHA ORDER

| RANK | STATE | PERCENT |
|------|-------|---------|
| 49 | Alabama | 52.0 |
| 10 | Alaska | 63.6 |
| 46 | Arizona | 54.0 |
| 45 | Arkansas | 54.1 |
| 36 | California | 55.7 |
| 13 | Colorado | 62.0 |
| 16 | Connecticut | 60.7 |
| 26 | Delaware | 58.3 |
| 38 | Florida | 55.5 |
| 26 | Georgia | 58.3 |
| 39 | Hawaii | 55.2 |
| 33 | Idaho | 56.5 |
| 18 | Illinois | 60.3 |
| 32 | Indiana | 57.0 |
| 7 | Iowa | 64.5 |
| 11 | Kansas | 62.5 |
| 35 | Kentucky | 55.8 |
| 48 | Louisiana | 52.9 |
| 17 | Maine | 60.5 |
| 9 | Maryland | 63.7 |
| 14 | Massachusetts | 61.7 |
| 44 | Michigan | 54.5 |
| 4 | Minnesota | 65.0 |
| 47 | Mississippi | 53.3 |
| 22 | Missouri | 59.3 |
| 18 | Montana | 60.3 |
| 1 | Nebraska | 67.7 |
| 25 | Nevada | 58.4 |
| 5 | New Hampshire | 64.7 |
| 21 | New Jersey | 59.7 |
| 41 | New Mexico | 54.9 |
| 36 | New York | 55.7 |
| 34 | North Carolina | 56.1 |
| 2 | North Dakota | 67.6 |
| 30 | Ohio | 57.8 |
| 40 | Oklahoma | 55.1 |
| 24 | Oregon | 58.5 |
| 29 | Pennsylvania | 57.9 |
| 15 | Rhode Island | 61.6 |
| 41 | South Carolina | 54.9 |
| 8 | South Dakota | 64.2 |
| 43 | Tennessee | 54.7 |
| 31 | Texas | 57.7 |
| 26 | Utah | 58.3 |
| 3 | Vermont | 66.1 |
| 20 | Virginia | 60.2 |
| 23 | Washington | 59.1 |
| 50 | West Virginia | 48.9 |
| 5 | Wisconsin | 64.7 |
| 12 | Wyoming | 62.3 |

RANK ORDER

| RANK | STATE | PERCENT |
|------|-------|---------|
| 1 | Nebraska | 67.7 |
| 2 | North Dakota | 67.6 |
| 3 | Vermont | 66.1 |
| 4 | Minnesota | 65.0 |
| 5 | New Hampshire | 64.7 |
| 5 | Wisconsin | 64.7 |
| 7 | Iowa | 64.5 |
| 8 | South Dakota | 64.2 |
| 9 | Maryland | 63.7 |
| 10 | Alaska | 63.6 |
| 11 | Kansas | 62.5 |
| 12 | Wyoming | 62.3 |
| 13 | Colorado | 62.0 |
| 14 | Massachusetts | 61.7 |
| 15 | Rhode Island | 61.6 |
| 16 | Connecticut | 60.7 |
| 17 | Maine | 60.5 |
| 18 | Illinois | 60.3 |
| 18 | Montana | 60.3 |
| 20 | Virginia | 60.2 |
| 21 | New Jersey | 59.7 |
| 22 | Missouri | 59.3 |
| 23 | Washington | 59.1 |
| 24 | Oregon | 58.5 |
| 25 | Nevada | 58.4 |
| 26 | Delaware | 58.3 |
| 26 | Georgia | 58.3 |
| 26 | Utah | 58.3 |
| 29 | Pennsylvania | 57.9 |
| 30 | Ohio | 57.8 |
| 31 | Texas | 57.7 |
| 32 | Indiana | 57.0 |
| 33 | Idaho | 56.5 |
| 34 | North Carolina | 56.1 |
| 35 | Kentucky | 55.8 |
| 36 | California | 55.7 |
| 36 | New York | 55.7 |
| 38 | Florida | 55.5 |
| 39 | Hawaii | 55.2 |
| 40 | Oklahoma | 55.1 |
| 41 | New Mexico | 54.9 |
| 41 | South Carolina | 54.9 |
| 43 | Tennessee | 54.7 |
| 44 | Michigan | 54.5 |
| 45 | Arkansas | 54.1 |
| 46 | Arizona | 54.0 |
| 47 | Mississippi | 53.3 |
| 48 | Louisiana | 52.9 |
| 49 | Alabama | 52.0 |
| 50 | West Virginia | 48.9 |

| | District of Columbia | 65.3 |

Source: U.S. Department of Labor, Bureau of Labor Statistics
"Geographic Profiles of Employment and Unemployment, 2012" (http://www.bls.gov/gps/)
*Annual averages.

# Percent of Civilian Labor Force Comprised of Women in 2012

## National Percent = 46.9% of Civilian Labor Force*

ALPHA ORDER

| RANK | STATE | PERCENT |
|---|---|---|
| 26 | Alabama | 47.2 |
| 41 | Alaska | 45.9 |
| 41 | Arizona | 45.9 |
| 31 | Arkansas | 47.0 |
| 47 | California | 45.2 |
| 41 | Colorado | 45.9 |
| 10 | Connecticut | 47.7 |
| 2 | Delaware | 49.3 |
| 10 | Florida | 47.7 |
| 17 | Georgia | 47.5 |
| 33 | Hawaii | 46.9 |
| 49 | Idaho | 44.3 |
| 26 | Illinois | 47.2 |
| 33 | Indiana | 46.9 |
| 10 | Iowa | 47.7 |
| 23 | Kansas | 47.3 |
| 19 | Kentucky | 47.4 |
| 35 | Louisiana | 46.8 |
| 7 | Maine | 48.1 |
| 1 | Maryland | 49.6 |
| 2 | Massachusetts | 49.3 |
| 28 | Michigan | 47.1 |
| 31 | Minnesota | 47.0 |
| 9 | Mississippi | 48.0 |
| 10 | Missouri | 47.7 |
| 15 | Montana | 47.6 |
| 15 | Nebraska | 47.6 |
| 44 | Nevada | 45.4 |
| 10 | New Hampshire | 47.7 |
| 28 | New Jersey | 47.1 |
| 19 | New Mexico | 47.4 |
| 17 | New York | 47.5 |
| 23 | North Carolina | 47.3 |
| 38 | North Dakota | 46.5 |
| 19 | Ohio | 47.4 |
| 44 | Oklahoma | 45.4 |
| 23 | Oregon | 47.3 |
| 28 | Pennsylvania | 47.1 |
| 4 | Rhode Island | 49.0 |
| 5 | South Carolina | 48.9 |
| 35 | South Dakota | 46.8 |
| 39 | Tennessee | 46.4 |
| 46 | Texas | 45.3 |
| 50 | Utah | 43.7 |
| 6 | Vermont | 48.6 |
| 19 | Virginia | 47.4 |
| 37 | Washington | 46.7 |
| 40 | West Virginia | 46.2 |
| 7 | Wisconsin | 48.1 |
| 48 | Wyoming | 44.5 |

RANK ORDER

| RANK | STATE | PERCENT |
|---|---|---|
| 1 | Maryland | 49.6 |
| 2 | Delaware | 49.3 |
| 2 | Massachusetts | 49.3 |
| 4 | Rhode Island | 49.0 |
| 5 | South Carolina | 48.9 |
| 6 | Vermont | 48.6 |
| 7 | Maine | 48.1 |
| 7 | Wisconsin | 48.1 |
| 9 | Mississippi | 48.0 |
| 10 | Connecticut | 47.7 |
| 10 | Florida | 47.7 |
| 10 | Iowa | 47.7 |
| 10 | Missouri | 47.7 |
| 10 | New Hampshire | 47.7 |
| 15 | Montana | 47.6 |
| 15 | Nebraska | 47.6 |
| 17 | Georgia | 47.5 |
| 17 | New York | 47.5 |
| 19 | Kentucky | 47.4 |
| 19 | New Mexico | 47.4 |
| 19 | Ohio | 47.4 |
| 19 | Virginia | 47.4 |
| 23 | Kansas | 47.3 |
| 23 | North Carolina | 47.3 |
| 23 | Oregon | 47.3 |
| 26 | Alabama | 47.2 |
| 26 | Illinois | 47.2 |
| 28 | Michigan | 47.1 |
| 28 | New Jersey | 47.1 |
| 28 | Pennsylvania | 47.1 |
| 31 | Arkansas | 47.0 |
| 31 | Minnesota | 47.0 |
| 33 | Hawaii | 46.9 |
| 33 | Indiana | 46.9 |
| 35 | Louisiana | 46.8 |
| 35 | South Dakota | 46.8 |
| 37 | Washington | 46.7 |
| 38 | North Dakota | 46.5 |
| 39 | Tennessee | 46.4 |
| 40 | West Virginia | 46.2 |
| 41 | Alaska | 45.9 |
| 41 | Arizona | 45.9 |
| 41 | Colorado | 45.9 |
| 44 | Nevada | 45.4 |
| 44 | Oklahoma | 45.4 |
| 46 | Texas | 45.3 |
| 47 | California | 45.2 |
| 48 | Wyoming | 44.5 |
| 49 | Idaho | 44.3 |
| 50 | Utah | 43.7 |
| | District of Columbia | 50.7 |

Source: CQ Press using data from U.S. Department of Labor, Bureau of Labor Statistics
"Geographic Profiles of Employment and Unemployment, 2012" (http://www.bls.gov/gps/)
*Annual averages.

# Percent of Children under 6 Years Old with All Parents Working in 2012

## National Percent = 64.9%

| ALPHA ORDER | | | | RANK ORDER | | |
|---|---|---|---|---|---|---|
| RANK | STATE | PERCENT | | RANK | STATE | PERCENT |
| 39 | Alabama | 63.2 | | 1 | Minnesota | 74.8 |
| 44 | Alaska | 61.2 | | 2 | Iowa | 74.4 |
| 42 | Arizona | 61.4 | | 3 | South Dakota | 74.0 |
| 32 | Arkansas | 64.6 | | 4 | North Dakota | 73.8 |
| 45 | California | 60.8 | | 5 | Rhode Island | 73.1 |
| 41 | Colorado | 62.5 | | 6 | Nebraska | 72.6 |
| 11 | Connecticut | 70.5 | | 7 | Vermont | 72.4 |
| 14 | Delaware | 68.4 | | 8 | Maryland | 71.7 |
| 20 | Florida | 67.3 | | 9 | Wisconsin | 71.4 |
| 37 | Georgia | 63.7 | | 10 | Louisiana | 70.7 |
| 36 | Hawaii | 64.4 | | 11 | Connecticut | 70.5 |
| 46 | Idaho | 60.2 | | 12 | Massachusetts | 69.9 |
| 16 | Illinois | 68.0 | | 13 | South Carolina | 68.7 |
| 23 | Indiana | 67.0 | | 14 | Delaware | 68.4 |
| 2 | Iowa | 74.4 | | 15 | Ohio | 68.1 |
| 22 | Kansas | 67.1 | | 16 | Illinois | 68.0 |
| 27 | Kentucky | 65.2 | | 17 | Mississippi | 67.9 |
| 10 | Louisiana | 70.7 | | 18 | New Hampshire | 67.8 |
| 29 | Maine | 65.1 | | 19 | Missouri | 67.6 |
| 8 | Maryland | 71.7 | | 20 | Florida | 67.3 |
| 12 | Massachusetts | 69.9 | | 20 | Pennsylvania | 67.3 |
| 24 | Michigan | 66.7 | | 22 | Kansas | 67.1 |
| 1 | Minnesota | 74.8 | | 23 | Indiana | 67.0 |
| 17 | Mississippi | 67.9 | | 24 | Michigan | 66.7 |
| 19 | Missouri | 67.6 | | 25 | New Jersey | 66.4 |
| 31 | Montana | 64.8 | | 26 | Virginia | 66.2 |
| 6 | Nebraska | 72.6 | | 27 | Kentucky | 65.2 |
| 30 | Nevada | 65.0 | | 27 | North Carolina | 65.2 |
| 18 | New Hampshire | 67.8 | | 29 | Maine | 65.1 |
| 25 | New Jersey | 66.4 | | 30 | Nevada | 65.0 |
| 40 | New Mexico | 62.6 | | 31 | Montana | 64.8 |
| 32 | New York | 64.6 | | 32 | Arkansas | 64.6 |
| 27 | North Carolina | 65.2 | | 32 | New York | 64.6 |
| 4 | North Dakota | 73.8 | | 34 | Oklahoma | 64.5 |
| 15 | Ohio | 68.1 | | 34 | Wyoming | 64.5 |
| 34 | Oklahoma | 64.5 | | 36 | Hawaii | 64.4 |
| 43 | Oregon | 61.3 | | 37 | Georgia | 63.7 |
| 20 | Pennsylvania | 67.3 | | 38 | Tennessee | 63.4 |
| 5 | Rhode Island | 73.1 | | 39 | Alabama | 63.2 |
| 13 | South Carolina | 68.7 | | 40 | New Mexico | 62.6 |
| 3 | South Dakota | 74.0 | | 41 | Colorado | 62.5 |
| 38 | Tennessee | 63.4 | | 42 | Arizona | 61.4 |
| 47 | Texas | 59.8 | | 43 | Oregon | 61.3 |
| 50 | Utah | 51.8 | | 44 | Alaska | 61.2 |
| 7 | Vermont | 72.4 | | 45 | California | 60.8 |
| 26 | Virginia | 66.2 | | 46 | Idaho | 60.2 |
| 48 | Washington | 58.2 | | 47 | Texas | 59.8 |
| 49 | West Virginia | 56.3 | | 48 | Washington | 58.2 |
| 9 | Wisconsin | 71.4 | | 49 | West Virginia | 56.3 |
| 34 | Wyoming | 64.5 | | 50 | Utah | 51.8 |
| | | | | District of Columbia | | 75.8 |

Source: U.S. Bureau of the Census
"2012 American Community Survey-Table R2302" (http://www.census.gov/acs/www/index.html)

# Job Growth: 2012 to 2013

## National Percent Change = 1.6% Increase*

<table>
<tr><td colspan="3">ALPHA ORDER</td><td colspan="3">RANK ORDER</td></tr>
<tr><th>RANK</th><th>STATE</th><th>PERCENT CHANGE</th><th>RANK</th><th>STATE</th><th>PERCENT CHANGE</th></tr>
<tr><td>44</td><td>Alabama</td><td>0.6</td><td>1</td><td>North Dakota</td><td>4.0</td></tr>
<tr><td>50</td><td>Alaska</td><td>(0.7)</td><td>2</td><td>Florida</td><td>2.6</td></tr>
<tr><td>7</td><td>Arizona</td><td>2.0</td><td>3</td><td>Oregon</td><td>2.4</td></tr>
<tr><td>28</td><td>Arkansas</td><td>1.1</td><td>4</td><td>Texas</td><td>2.3</td></tr>
<tr><td>17</td><td>California</td><td>1.6</td><td>5</td><td>Delaware</td><td>2.2</td></tr>
<tr><td>9</td><td>Colorado</td><td>1.9</td><td>5</td><td>Georgia</td><td>2.2</td></tr>
<tr><td>41</td><td>Connecticut</td><td>0.7</td><td>7</td><td>Arizona</td><td>2.0</td></tr>
<tr><td>5</td><td>Delaware</td><td>2.2</td><td>7</td><td>South Carolina</td><td>2.0</td></tr>
<tr><td>2</td><td>Florida</td><td>2.6</td><td>9</td><td>Colorado</td><td>1.9</td></tr>
<tr><td>5</td><td>Georgia</td><td>2.2</td><td>9</td><td>Washington</td><td>1.9</td></tr>
<tr><td>17</td><td>Hawaii</td><td>1.6</td><td>11</td><td>Indiana</td><td>1.8</td></tr>
<tr><td>24</td><td>Idaho</td><td>1.3</td><td>11</td><td>Nevada</td><td>1.8</td></tr>
<tr><td>28</td><td>Illinois</td><td>1.1</td><td>13</td><td>Massachusetts</td><td>1.7</td></tr>
<tr><td>11</td><td>Indiana</td><td>1.8</td><td>13</td><td>Minnesota</td><td>1.7</td></tr>
<tr><td>37</td><td>Iowa</td><td>0.8</td><td>13</td><td>Mississippi</td><td>1.7</td></tr>
<tr><td>41</td><td>Kansas</td><td>0.7</td><td>13</td><td>Utah</td><td>1.7</td></tr>
<tr><td>47</td><td>Kentucky</td><td>0.3</td><td>17</td><td>California</td><td>1.6</td></tr>
<tr><td>34</td><td>Louisiana</td><td>1.0</td><td>17</td><td>Hawaii</td><td>1.6</td></tr>
<tr><td>28</td><td>Maine</td><td>1.1</td><td>17</td><td>Michigan</td><td>1.6</td></tr>
<tr><td>22</td><td>Maryland</td><td>1.4</td><td>17</td><td>North Carolina</td><td>1.6</td></tr>
<tr><td>13</td><td>Massachusetts</td><td>1.7</td><td>17</td><td>Wisconsin</td><td>1.6</td></tr>
<tr><td>17</td><td>Michigan</td><td>1.6</td><td>22</td><td>Maryland</td><td>1.4</td></tr>
<tr><td>13</td><td>Minnesota</td><td>1.7</td><td>22</td><td>South Dakota</td><td>1.4</td></tr>
<tr><td>13</td><td>Mississippi</td><td>1.7</td><td>24</td><td>Idaho</td><td>1.3</td></tr>
<tr><td>24</td><td>Missouri</td><td>1.3</td><td>24</td><td>Missouri</td><td>1.3</td></tr>
<tr><td>41</td><td>Montana</td><td>0.7</td><td>24</td><td>Wyoming</td><td>1.3</td></tr>
<tr><td>28</td><td>Nebraska</td><td>1.1</td><td>27</td><td>Oklahoma</td><td>1.2</td></tr>
<tr><td>11</td><td>Nevada</td><td>1.8</td><td>28</td><td>Arkansas</td><td>1.1</td></tr>
<tr><td>37</td><td>New Hampshire</td><td>0.8</td><td>28</td><td>Illinois</td><td>1.1</td></tr>
<tr><td>47</td><td>New Jersey</td><td>0.3</td><td>28</td><td>Maine</td><td>1.1</td></tr>
<tr><td>46</td><td>New Mexico</td><td>0.4</td><td>28</td><td>Nebraska</td><td>1.1</td></tr>
<tr><td>28</td><td>New York</td><td>1.1</td><td>28</td><td>New York</td><td>1.1</td></tr>
<tr><td>17</td><td>North Carolina</td><td>1.6</td><td>28</td><td>Tennessee</td><td>1.1</td></tr>
<tr><td>1</td><td>North Dakota</td><td>4.0</td><td>34</td><td>Louisiana</td><td>1.0</td></tr>
<tr><td>45</td><td>Ohio</td><td>0.5</td><td>34</td><td>Vermont</td><td>1.0</td></tr>
<tr><td>27</td><td>Oklahoma</td><td>1.2</td><td>34</td><td>West Virginia</td><td>1.0</td></tr>
<tr><td>3</td><td>Oregon</td><td>2.4</td><td>37</td><td>Iowa</td><td>0.8</td></tr>
<tr><td>47</td><td>Pennsylvania</td><td>0.3</td><td>37</td><td>New Hampshire</td><td>0.8</td></tr>
<tr><td>37</td><td>Rhode Island</td><td>0.8</td><td>37</td><td>Rhode Island</td><td>0.8</td></tr>
<tr><td>7</td><td>South Carolina</td><td>2.0</td><td>37</td><td>Virginia</td><td>0.8</td></tr>
<tr><td>22</td><td>South Dakota</td><td>1.4</td><td>41</td><td>Connecticut</td><td>0.7</td></tr>
<tr><td>28</td><td>Tennessee</td><td>1.1</td><td>41</td><td>Kansas</td><td>0.7</td></tr>
<tr><td>4</td><td>Texas</td><td>2.3</td><td>41</td><td>Montana</td><td>0.7</td></tr>
<tr><td>13</td><td>Utah</td><td>1.7</td><td>44</td><td>Alabama</td><td>0.6</td></tr>
<tr><td>34</td><td>Vermont</td><td>1.0</td><td>45</td><td>Ohio</td><td>0.5</td></tr>
<tr><td>37</td><td>Virginia</td><td>0.8</td><td>46</td><td>New Mexico</td><td>0.4</td></tr>
<tr><td>9</td><td>Washington</td><td>1.9</td><td>47</td><td>Kentucky</td><td>0.3</td></tr>
<tr><td>34</td><td>West Virginia</td><td>1.0</td><td>47</td><td>New Jersey</td><td>0.3</td></tr>
<tr><td>17</td><td>Wisconsin</td><td>1.6</td><td>47</td><td>Pennsylvania</td><td>0.3</td></tr>
<tr><td>24</td><td>Wyoming</td><td>1.3</td><td>50</td><td>Alaska</td><td>(0.7)</td></tr>
<tr><td></td><td></td><td></td><td></td><td>District of Columbia</td><td>(0.1)</td></tr>
</table>

Source: CQ Press using data from U.S. Department of Labor, Bureau of Labor Statistics
   "Regional and State Employment and Unemployment" (press release, January 28, 2014, www.bls.gov/bls/newsrels.htm)
*Nonfarm jobs.  December 2012 to December 2013, seasonally adjusted.  National figure based on nonfarm employment from a different survey.

# Employees on Nonfarm Payrolls in 2013

## National Total = 136,877,000 Employees*

ALPHA ORDER

| RANK | STATE | EMPLOYEES | % of USA |
|---|---|---|---|
| 25 | Alabama | 1,894,900 | 1.4% |
| 48 | Alaska | 333,100 | 0.2% |
| 21 | Arizona | 2,537,600 | 1.9% |
| 33 | Arkansas | 1,193,500 | 0.9% |
| 1 | California | 14,767,800 | 10.8% |
| 22 | Colorado | 2,379,700 | 1.7% |
| 28 | Connecticut | 1,651,200 | 1.2% |
| 46 | Delaware | 430,600 | 0.3% |
| 4 | Florida | 7,645,000 | 5.6% |
| 10 | Georgia | 4,078,300 | 3.0% |
| 41 | Hawaii | 621,100 | 0.5% |
| 40 | Idaho | 637,400 | 0.5% |
| 5 | Illinois | 5,835,100 | 4.3% |
| 14 | Indiana | 2,975,500 | 2.2% |
| 30 | Iowa | 1,528,500 | 1.1% |
| 31 | Kansas | 1,375,900 | 1.0% |
| 26 | Kentucky | 1,842,800 | 1.3% |
| 23 | Louisiana | 1,964,000 | 1.4% |
| 42 | Maine | 600,500 | 0.4% |
| 20 | Maryland | 2,625,200 | 1.9% |
| 13 | Massachusetts | 3,354,600 | 2.5% |
| 9 | Michigan | 4,092,700 | 3.0% |
| 17 | Minnesota | 2,797,700 | 2.0% |
| 35 | Mississippi | 1,127,100 | 0.8% |
| 19 | Missouri | 2,721,800 | 2.0% |
| 45 | Montana | 448,500 | 0.3% |
| 36 | Nebraska | 971,800 | 0.7% |
| 34 | Nevada | 1,180,100 | 0.9% |
| 39 | New Hampshire | 640,300 | 0.5% |
| 11 | New Jersey | 3,942,300 | 2.9% |
| 37 | New Mexico | 810,400 | 0.6% |
| 3 | New York | 8,943,800 | 6.5% |
| 8 | North Carolina | 4,096,800 | 3.0% |
| 44 | North Dakota | 456,100 | 0.3% |
| 7 | Ohio | 5,200,600 | 3.8% |
| 29 | Oklahoma | 1,636,800 | 1.2% |
| 27 | Oregon | 1,682,700 | 1.2% |
| 6 | Pennsylvania | 5,761,600 | 4.2% |
| 43 | Rhode Island | 469,200 | 0.3% |
| 24 | South Carolina | 1,913,300 | 1.4% |
| 47 | South Dakota | 421,900 | 0.3% |
| 18 | Tennessee | 2,771,100 | 2.0% |
| 2 | Texas | 11,277,100 | 8.2% |
| 32 | Utah | 1,288,000 | 0.9% |
| 49 | Vermont | 309,100 | 0.2% |
| 12 | Virginia | 3,777,300 | 2.8% |
| 15 | Washington | 2,940,200 | 2.1% |
| 38 | West Virginia | 773,900 | 0.6% |
| 16 | Wisconsin | 2,840,500 | 2.1% |
| 50 | Wyoming | 292,600 | 0.2% |

RANK ORDER

| RANK | STATE | EMPLOYEES | % of USA |
|---|---|---|---|
| 1 | California | 14,767,800 | 10.8% |
| 2 | Texas | 11,277,100 | 8.2% |
| 3 | New York | 8,943,800 | 6.5% |
| 4 | Florida | 7,645,000 | 5.6% |
| 5 | Illinois | 5,835,100 | 4.3% |
| 6 | Pennsylvania | 5,761,600 | 4.2% |
| 7 | Ohio | 5,200,600 | 3.8% |
| 8 | North Carolina | 4,096,800 | 3.0% |
| 9 | Michigan | 4,092,700 | 3.0% |
| 10 | Georgia | 4,078,300 | 3.0% |
| 11 | New Jersey | 3,942,300 | 2.9% |
| 12 | Virginia | 3,777,300 | 2.8% |
| 13 | Massachusetts | 3,354,600 | 2.5% |
| 14 | Indiana | 2,975,500 | 2.2% |
| 15 | Washington | 2,940,200 | 2.1% |
| 16 | Wisconsin | 2,840,500 | 2.1% |
| 17 | Minnesota | 2,797,700 | 2.0% |
| 18 | Tennessee | 2,771,100 | 2.0% |
| 19 | Missouri | 2,721,800 | 2.0% |
| 20 | Maryland | 2,625,200 | 1.9% |
| 21 | Arizona | 2,537,600 | 1.9% |
| 22 | Colorado | 2,379,700 | 1.7% |
| 23 | Louisiana | 1,964,000 | 1.4% |
| 24 | South Carolina | 1,913,300 | 1.4% |
| 25 | Alabama | 1,894,900 | 1.4% |
| 26 | Kentucky | 1,842,800 | 1.3% |
| 27 | Oregon | 1,682,700 | 1.2% |
| 28 | Connecticut | 1,651,200 | 1.2% |
| 29 | Oklahoma | 1,636,800 | 1.2% |
| 30 | Iowa | 1,528,500 | 1.1% |
| 31 | Kansas | 1,375,900 | 1.0% |
| 32 | Utah | 1,288,000 | 0.9% |
| 33 | Arkansas | 1,193,500 | 0.9% |
| 34 | Nevada | 1,180,100 | 0.9% |
| 35 | Mississippi | 1,127,100 | 0.8% |
| 36 | Nebraska | 971,800 | 0.7% |
| 37 | New Mexico | 810,400 | 0.6% |
| 38 | West Virginia | 773,900 | 0.6% |
| 39 | New Hampshire | 640,300 | 0.5% |
| 40 | Idaho | 637,400 | 0.5% |
| 41 | Hawaii | 621,100 | 0.5% |
| 42 | Maine | 600,500 | 0.4% |
| 43 | Rhode Island | 469,200 | 0.3% |
| 44 | North Dakota | 456,100 | 0.3% |
| 45 | Montana | 448,500 | 0.3% |
| 46 | Delaware | 430,600 | 0.3% |
| 47 | South Dakota | 421,900 | 0.3% |
| 48 | Alaska | 333,100 | 0.2% |
| 49 | Vermont | 309,100 | 0.2% |
| 50 | Wyoming | 292,600 | 0.2% |
| | District of Columbia | 732,400 | 0.5% |

Source: U.S. Department of Labor, Bureau of Labor Statistics
"Regional and State Employment and Unemployment" (press release, January 28, 2014, www.bls.gov/bls/newsrels.htm)
*Seasonally adjusted preliminary data as of December 2013. National total calculated through a different formula.

# Employees in Construction in 2013

## National Total = 5,833,000 Employees*

<table>
<tr><td colspan="4">ALPHA ORDER</td><td colspan="4">RANK ORDER</td></tr>
<tr><td>RANK</td><td>STATE</td><td>EMPLOYEES</td><td>% of USA</td><td>RANK</td><td>STATE</td><td>EMPLOYEES</td><td>% of USA</td></tr>
<tr><td>25</td><td>Alabama</td><td>78,400</td><td>1.3%</td><td>1</td><td>California</td><td>632,100</td><td>10.8%</td></tr>
<tr><td>47</td><td>Alaska</td><td>18,600</td><td>0.3%</td><td>2</td><td>Texas</td><td>611,100</td><td>10.5%</td></tr>
<tr><td>16</td><td>Arizona</td><td>123,300</td><td>2.1%</td><td>3</td><td>Florida</td><td>373,600</td><td>6.4%</td></tr>
<tr><td>35</td><td>Arkansas</td><td>47,400</td><td>0.8%</td><td>4</td><td>New York</td><td>316,600</td><td>5.4%</td></tr>
<tr><td>1</td><td>California</td><td>632,100</td><td>10.8%</td><td>5</td><td>Pennsylvania</td><td>220,500</td><td>3.8%</td></tr>
<tr><td>17</td><td>Colorado</td><td>122,800</td><td>2.1%</td><td>6</td><td>Illinois</td><td>183,100</td><td>3.1%</td></tr>
<tr><td>32</td><td>Connecticut</td><td>56,000</td><td>1.0%</td><td>7</td><td>Ohio</td><td>176,700</td><td>3.0%</td></tr>
<tr><td>48</td><td>Delaware**</td><td>18,200</td><td>0.3%</td><td>8</td><td>Virginia</td><td>176,200</td><td>3.0%</td></tr>
<tr><td>3</td><td>Florida</td><td>373,600</td><td>6.4%</td><td>9</td><td>North Carolina</td><td>166,400</td><td>2.9%</td></tr>
<tr><td>11</td><td>Georgia</td><td>149,400</td><td>2.6%</td><td>10</td><td>Maryland**</td><td>150,600</td><td>2.6%</td></tr>
<tr><td>39</td><td>Hawaii**</td><td>32,100</td><td>0.6%</td><td>11</td><td>Georgia</td><td>149,400</td><td>2.6%</td></tr>
<tr><td>41</td><td>Idaho</td><td>31,100</td><td>0.5%</td><td>12</td><td>Washington</td><td>142,400</td><td>2.4%</td></tr>
<tr><td>6</td><td>Illinois</td><td>183,100</td><td>3.1%</td><td>13</td><td>Louisiana</td><td>133,700</td><td>2.3%</td></tr>
<tr><td>19</td><td>Indiana</td><td>115,900</td><td>2.0%</td><td>14</td><td>New Jersey</td><td>127,500</td><td>2.2%</td></tr>
<tr><td>29</td><td>Iowa</td><td>66,400</td><td>1.1%</td><td>15</td><td>Michigan</td><td>126,600</td><td>2.2%</td></tr>
<tr><td>33</td><td>Kansas</td><td>55,900</td><td>1.0%</td><td>16</td><td>Arizona</td><td>123,300</td><td>2.1%</td></tr>
<tr><td>30</td><td>Kentucky</td><td>64,700</td><td>1.1%</td><td>17</td><td>Colorado</td><td>122,800</td><td>2.1%</td></tr>
<tr><td>13</td><td>Louisiana</td><td>133,700</td><td>2.3%</td><td>18</td><td>Massachusetts</td><td>119,100</td><td>2.0%</td></tr>
<tr><td>42</td><td>Maine</td><td>25,600</td><td>0.4%</td><td>19</td><td>Indiana</td><td>115,900</td><td>2.0%</td></tr>
<tr><td>10</td><td>Maryland**</td><td>150,600</td><td>2.6%</td><td>20</td><td>Missouri</td><td>108,900</td><td>1.9%</td></tr>
<tr><td>18</td><td>Massachusetts</td><td>119,100</td><td>2.0%</td><td>21</td><td>Tennessee**</td><td>108,000</td><td>1.9%</td></tr>
<tr><td>15</td><td>Michigan</td><td>126,600</td><td>2.2%</td><td>22</td><td>Minnesota</td><td>99,100</td><td>1.7%</td></tr>
<tr><td>22</td><td>Minnesota</td><td>99,100</td><td>1.7%</td><td>23</td><td>Wisconsin</td><td>94,300</td><td>1.6%</td></tr>
<tr><td>31</td><td>Mississippi</td><td>56,400</td><td>1.0%</td><td>24</td><td>South Carolina</td><td>83,100</td><td>1.4%</td></tr>
<tr><td>20</td><td>Missouri</td><td>108,900</td><td>1.9%</td><td>25</td><td>Alabama</td><td>78,400</td><td>1.3%</td></tr>
<tr><td>45</td><td>Montana</td><td>21,400</td><td>0.4%</td><td>26</td><td>Oregon</td><td>72,500</td><td>1.2%</td></tr>
<tr><td>36</td><td>Nebraska**</td><td>43,200</td><td>0.7%</td><td>27</td><td>Utah</td><td>69,600</td><td>1.2%</td></tr>
<tr><td>34</td><td>Nevada</td><td>54,600</td><td>0.9%</td><td>28</td><td>Oklahoma</td><td>68,100</td><td>1.2%</td></tr>
<tr><td>44</td><td>New Hampshire</td><td>22,500</td><td>0.4%</td><td>29</td><td>Iowa</td><td>66,400</td><td>1.1%</td></tr>
<tr><td>14</td><td>New Jersey</td><td>127,500</td><td>2.2%</td><td>30</td><td>Kentucky</td><td>64,700</td><td>1.1%</td></tr>
<tr><td>37</td><td>New Mexico</td><td>40,900</td><td>0.7%</td><td>31</td><td>Mississippi</td><td>56,400</td><td>1.0%</td></tr>
<tr><td>4</td><td>New York</td><td>316,600</td><td>5.4%</td><td>32</td><td>Connecticut</td><td>56,000</td><td>1.0%</td></tr>
<tr><td>9</td><td>North Carolina</td><td>166,400</td><td>2.9%</td><td>33</td><td>Kansas</td><td>55,900</td><td>1.0%</td></tr>
<tr><td>40</td><td>North Dakota</td><td>31,700</td><td>0.5%</td><td>34</td><td>Nevada</td><td>54,600</td><td>0.9%</td></tr>
<tr><td>7</td><td>Ohio</td><td>176,700</td><td>3.0%</td><td>35</td><td>Arkansas</td><td>47,400</td><td>0.8%</td></tr>
<tr><td>28</td><td>Oklahoma</td><td>68,100</td><td>1.2%</td><td>36</td><td>Nebraska**</td><td>43,200</td><td>0.7%</td></tr>
<tr><td>26</td><td>Oregon</td><td>72,500</td><td>1.2%</td><td>37</td><td>New Mexico</td><td>40,900</td><td>0.7%</td></tr>
<tr><td>5</td><td>Pennsylvania</td><td>220,500</td><td>3.8%</td><td>38</td><td>West Virginia</td><td>34,500</td><td>0.6%</td></tr>
<tr><td>49</td><td>Rhode Island</td><td>15,400</td><td>0.3%</td><td>39</td><td>Hawaii**</td><td>32,100</td><td>0.6%</td></tr>
<tr><td>24</td><td>South Carolina</td><td>83,100</td><td>1.4%</td><td>40</td><td>North Dakota</td><td>31,700</td><td>0.5%</td></tr>
<tr><td>45</td><td>South Dakota**</td><td>21,400</td><td>0.4%</td><td>41</td><td>Idaho</td><td>31,100</td><td>0.5%</td></tr>
<tr><td>21</td><td>Tennessee**</td><td>108,000</td><td>1.9%</td><td>42</td><td>Maine</td><td>25,600</td><td>0.4%</td></tr>
<tr><td>2</td><td>Texas</td><td>611,100</td><td>10.5%</td><td>43</td><td>Wyoming</td><td>23,600</td><td>0.4%</td></tr>
<tr><td>27</td><td>Utah</td><td>69,600</td><td>1.2%</td><td>44</td><td>New Hampshire</td><td>22,500</td><td>0.4%</td></tr>
<tr><td>50</td><td>Vermont</td><td>14,700</td><td>0.3%</td><td>45</td><td>Montana</td><td>21,400</td><td>0.4%</td></tr>
<tr><td>8</td><td>Virginia</td><td>176,200</td><td>3.0%</td><td>45</td><td>South Dakota**</td><td>21,400</td><td>0.4%</td></tr>
<tr><td>12</td><td>Washington</td><td>142,400</td><td>2.4%</td><td>47</td><td>Alaska</td><td>18,600</td><td>0.3%</td></tr>
<tr><td>38</td><td>West Virginia</td><td>34,500</td><td>0.6%</td><td>48</td><td>Delaware**</td><td>18,200</td><td>0.3%</td></tr>
<tr><td>23</td><td>Wisconsin</td><td>94,300</td><td>1.6%</td><td>49</td><td>Rhode Island</td><td>15,400</td><td>0.3%</td></tr>
<tr><td>43</td><td>Wyoming</td><td>23,600</td><td>0.4%</td><td>50</td><td>Vermont</td><td>14,700</td><td>0.3%</td></tr>
<tr><td></td><td></td><td></td><td></td><td></td><td>District of Columbia**</td><td>13,000</td><td>0.2%</td></tr>
</table>

Source: U.S. Department of Labor, Bureau of Labor Statistics
  "Regional and State Employment and Unemployment" (press release, January 28, 2014, www.bls.gov/bls/newsrels.htm)
*Seasonally adjusted preliminary data as of December 2013.  National total calculated through a different formula.
**Figures for states include employees in mining and logging.

# Percent of Nonfarm Employees in Construction in 2013

## National Percent = 4.3% of Employees*

| ALPHA ORDER | | | | RANK ORDER | | |
|---|---|---|---|---|---|---|
| **RANK** | **STATE** | **PERCENT** | | **RANK** | **STATE** | **PERCENT** |
| 30 | Alabama | 4.1 | | 1 | Wyoming | 8.1 |
| 5 | Alaska | 5.6 | | 2 | North Dakota | 7.0 |
| 13 | Arizona | 4.9 | | 3 | Louisiana | 6.8 |
| 33 | Arkansas | 4.0 | | 4 | Maryland** | 5.7 |
| 23 | California | 4.3 | | 5 | Alaska | 5.6 |
| 8 | Colorado | 5.2 | | 6 | Texas | 5.4 |
| 44 | Connecticut | 3.4 | | 6 | Utah | 5.4 |
| 28 | Delaware** | 4.2 | | 8 | Colorado | 5.2 |
| 13 | Florida | 4.9 | | 8 | Hawaii** | 5.2 |
| 38 | Georgia | 3.7 | | 10 | South Dakota** | 5.1 |
| 8 | Hawaii** | 5.2 | | 11 | Mississippi | 5.0 |
| 13 | Idaho | 4.9 | | 11 | New Mexico | 5.0 |
| 49 | Illinois | 3.1 | | 13 | Arizona | 4.9 |
| 35 | Indiana | 3.9 | | 13 | Florida | 4.9 |
| 23 | Iowa | 4.3 | | 13 | Idaho | 4.9 |
| 30 | Kansas | 4.1 | | 16 | Montana | 4.8 |
| 40 | Kentucky | 3.5 | | 16 | Vermont | 4.8 |
| 3 | Louisiana | 6.8 | | 16 | Washington | 4.8 |
| 23 | Maine | 4.3 | | 19 | Virginia | 4.7 |
| 4 | Maryland** | 5.7 | | 20 | Nevada | 4.6 |
| 39 | Massachusetts | 3.6 | | 21 | West Virginia | 4.5 |
| 49 | Michigan | 3.1 | | 22 | Nebraska** | 4.4 |
| 40 | Minnesota | 3.5 | | 23 | California | 4.3 |
| 11 | Mississippi | 5.0 | | 23 | Iowa | 4.3 |
| 33 | Missouri | 4.0 | | 23 | Maine | 4.3 |
| 16 | Montana | 4.8 | | 23 | Oregon | 4.3 |
| 22 | Nebraska** | 4.4 | | 23 | South Carolina | 4.3 |
| 20 | Nevada | 4.6 | | 28 | Delaware** | 4.2 |
| 40 | New Hampshire | 3.5 | | 28 | Oklahoma | 4.2 |
| 48 | New Jersey | 3.2 | | 30 | Alabama | 4.1 |
| 11 | New Mexico | 5.0 | | 30 | Kansas | 4.1 |
| 40 | New York | 3.5 | | 30 | North Carolina | 4.1 |
| 30 | North Carolina | 4.1 | | 33 | Arkansas | 4.0 |
| 2 | North Dakota | 7.0 | | 33 | Missouri | 4.0 |
| 44 | Ohio | 3.4 | | 35 | Indiana | 3.9 |
| 28 | Oklahoma | 4.2 | | 35 | Tennessee** | 3.9 |
| 23 | Oregon | 4.3 | | 37 | Pennsylvania | 3.8 |
| 37 | Pennsylvania | 3.8 | | 38 | Georgia | 3.7 |
| 46 | Rhode Island | 3.3 | | 39 | Massachusetts | 3.6 |
| 23 | South Carolina | 4.3 | | 40 | Kentucky | 3.5 |
| 10 | South Dakota** | 5.1 | | 40 | Minnesota | 3.5 |
| 35 | Tennessee** | 3.9 | | 40 | New Hampshire | 3.5 |
| 6 | Texas | 5.4 | | 40 | New York | 3.5 |
| 6 | Utah | 5.4 | | 44 | Connecticut | 3.4 |
| 16 | Vermont | 4.8 | | 44 | Ohio | 3.4 |
| 19 | Virginia | 4.7 | | 46 | Rhode Island | 3.3 |
| 16 | Washington | 4.8 | | 46 | Wisconsin | 3.3 |
| 21 | West Virginia | 4.5 | | 48 | New Jersey | 3.2 |
| 46 | Wisconsin | 3.3 | | 49 | Illinois | 3.1 |
| 1 | Wyoming | 8.1 | | 49 | Michigan | 3.1 |
| | | | | | District of Columbia** | 1.8 |

Source: CQ Press using data from U.S. Department of Labor, Bureau of Labor Statistics
   "Regional and State Employment and Unemployment" (press release, January 28, 2014, www.bls.gov/bls/newsrels.htm)
*Seasonally adjusted preliminary data as of December 2013.  National figure calculated through a different formula.
**Figures for states include employees in mining and logging.

# Employees in Education and Health Services in 2013

## National Total = 20,823,000 Employees*

| RANK | STATE | EMPLOYEES | % of USA |
|------|-------|-----------|----------|
| 29 | Alabama | 219,500 | 1.1% |
| 49 | Alaska | 47,500 | 0.2% |
| 21 | Arizona | 381,300 | 1.8% |
| 32 | Arkansas | 176,500 | 0.8% |
| 1 | California | 1,934,500 | 9.3% |
| 23 | Colorado | 295,300 | 1.4% |
| 22 | Connecticut | 328,300 | 1.6% |
| 44 | Delaware | 70,700 | 0.3% |
| 5 | Florida | 1,136,400 | 5.5% |
| 12 | Georgia | 518,100 | 2.5% |
| 43 | Hawaii | 77,600 | 0.4% |
| 42 | Idaho | 92,800 | 0.4% |
| 6 | Illinois | 880,700 | 4.2% |
| 15 | Indiana | 443,200 | 2.1% |
| 28 | Iowa | 225,600 | 1.1% |
| 31 | Kansas | 188,600 | 0.9% |
| 25 | Kentucky | 259,900 | 1.2% |
| 24 | Louisiana | 284,300 | 1.4% |
| 38 | Maine | 121,100 | 0.6% |
| 16 | Maryland | 428,500 | 2.1% |
| 8 | Massachusetts | 709,900 | 3.4% |
| 10 | Michigan | 639,000 | 3.1% |
| 14 | Minnesota | 497,500 | 2.4% |
| 35 | Mississippi | 134,000 | 0.6% |
| 17 | Missouri | 425,400 | 2.0% |
| 45 | Montana | 69,500 | 0.3% |
| 34 | Nebraska | 142,000 | 0.7% |
| 40 | Nevada | 112,500 | 0.5% |
| 39 | New Hampshire | 117,700 | 0.6% |
| 9 | New Jersey | 645,300 | 3.1% |
| 37 | New Mexico | 121,600 | 0.6% |
| 2 | New York | 1,835,400 | 8.8% |
| 11 | North Carolina | 565,600 | 2.7% |
| 48 | North Dakota | 59,500 | 0.3% |
| 6 | Ohio | 880,700 | 4.2% |
| 27 | Oklahoma | 226,700 | 1.1% |
| 26 | Oregon | 244,300 | 1.2% |
| 4 | Pennsylvania | 1,175,300 | 5.6% |
| 41 | Rhode Island | 103,600 | 0.5% |
| 30 | South Carolina | 213,800 | 1.0% |
| 46 | South Dakota | 68,200 | 0.3% |
| 19 | Tennessee | 404,900 | 1.9% |
| 3 | Texas | 1,512,200 | 7.3% |
| 33 | Utah | 171,500 | 0.8% |
| 47 | Vermont | 62,000 | 0.3% |
| 13 | Virginia | 499,700 | 2.4% |
| 20 | Washington | 397,100 | 1.9% |
| 36 | West Virginia | 128,900 | 0.6% |
| 18 | Wisconsin | 421,200 | 2.0% |
| 50 | Wyoming | 26,800 | 0.1% |

| RANK | STATE | EMPLOYEES | % of USA |
|------|-------|-----------|----------|
| 1 | California | 1,934,500 | 9.3% |
| 2 | New York | 1,835,400 | 8.8% |
| 3 | Texas | 1,512,200 | 7.3% |
| 4 | Pennsylvania | 1,175,300 | 5.6% |
| 5 | Florida | 1,136,400 | 5.5% |
| 6 | Illinois | 880,700 | 4.2% |
| 6 | Ohio | 880,700 | 4.2% |
| 8 | Massachusetts | 709,900 | 3.4% |
| 9 | New Jersey | 645,300 | 3.1% |
| 10 | Michigan | 639,000 | 3.1% |
| 11 | North Carolina | 565,600 | 2.7% |
| 12 | Georgia | 518,100 | 2.5% |
| 13 | Virginia | 499,700 | 2.4% |
| 14 | Minnesota | 497,500 | 2.4% |
| 15 | Indiana | 443,200 | 2.1% |
| 16 | Maryland | 428,500 | 2.1% |
| 17 | Missouri | 425,400 | 2.0% |
| 18 | Wisconsin | 421,200 | 2.0% |
| 19 | Tennessee | 404,900 | 1.9% |
| 20 | Washington | 397,100 | 1.9% |
| 21 | Arizona | 381,300 | 1.8% |
| 22 | Connecticut | 328,300 | 1.6% |
| 23 | Colorado | 295,300 | 1.4% |
| 24 | Louisiana | 284,300 | 1.4% |
| 25 | Kentucky | 259,900 | 1.2% |
| 26 | Oregon | 244,300 | 1.2% |
| 27 | Oklahoma | 226,700 | 1.1% |
| 28 | Iowa | 225,600 | 1.1% |
| 29 | Alabama | 219,500 | 1.1% |
| 30 | South Carolina | 213,800 | 1.0% |
| 31 | Kansas | 188,600 | 0.9% |
| 32 | Arkansas | 176,500 | 0.8% |
| 33 | Utah | 171,500 | 0.8% |
| 34 | Nebraska | 142,000 | 0.7% |
| 35 | Mississippi | 134,000 | 0.6% |
| 36 | West Virginia | 128,900 | 0.6% |
| 37 | New Mexico | 121,600 | 0.6% |
| 38 | Maine | 121,100 | 0.6% |
| 39 | New Hampshire | 117,700 | 0.6% |
| 40 | Nevada | 112,500 | 0.5% |
| 41 | Rhode Island | 103,600 | 0.5% |
| 42 | Idaho | 92,800 | 0.4% |
| 43 | Hawaii | 77,600 | 0.4% |
| 44 | Delaware | 70,700 | 0.3% |
| 45 | Montana | 69,500 | 0.3% |
| 46 | South Dakota | 68,200 | 0.3% |
| 47 | Vermont | 62,000 | 0.3% |
| 48 | North Dakota | 59,500 | 0.3% |
| 49 | Alaska | 47,500 | 0.2% |
| 50 | Wyoming | 26,800 | 0.1% |
| | District of Columbia | 116,900 | 0.6% |

Source: U.S. Department of Labor, Bureau of Labor Statistics
  "Regional and State Employment and Unemployment" (press release, January 28, 2014, www.bls.gov/bls/newsrels.htm)
*Seasonally adjusted preliminary data as of December 2013.  National total calculated through a different formula.

# Percent of Nonfarm Employees in Education and Health Services in 2013

## National Percent = 15.2% of Employees*

ALPHA ORDER

| RANK | STATE | PERCENT |
|------|-------|---------|
| 47 | Alabama | 11.6 |
| 32 | Alaska | 14.3 |
| 20 | Arizona | 15.0 |
| 24 | Arkansas | 14.8 |
| 41 | California | 13.1 |
| 45 | Colorado | 12.4 |
| 7 | Connecticut | 19.9 |
| 12 | Delaware | 16.4 |
| 22 | Florida | 14.9 |
| 43 | Georgia | 12.7 |
| 44 | Hawaii | 12.5 |
| 27 | Idaho | 14.6 |
| 19 | Illinois | 15.1 |
| 22 | Indiana | 14.9 |
| 24 | Iowa | 14.8 |
| 36 | Kansas | 13.7 |
| 33 | Kentucky | 14.1 |
| 30 | Louisiana | 14.5 |
| 5 | Maine | 20.2 |
| 14 | Maryland | 16.3 |
| 2 | Massachusetts | 21.2 |
| 16 | Michigan | 15.6 |
| 9 | Minnesota | 17.8 |
| 46 | Mississippi | 11.9 |
| 16 | Missouri | 15.6 |
| 18 | Montana | 15.5 |
| 27 | Nebraska | 14.6 |
| 49 | Nevada | 9.5 |
| 8 | New Hampshire | 18.4 |
| 12 | New Jersey | 16.4 |
| 20 | New Mexico | 15.0 |
| 3 | New York | 20.5 |
| 35 | North Carolina | 13.8 |
| 42 | North Dakota | 13.0 |
| 10 | Ohio | 16.9 |
| 34 | Oklahoma | 13.9 |
| 30 | Oregon | 14.5 |
| 4 | Pennsylvania | 20.4 |
| 1 | Rhode Island | 22.1 |
| 48 | South Carolina | 11.2 |
| 15 | South Dakota | 16.2 |
| 27 | Tennessee | 14.6 |
| 38 | Texas | 13.4 |
| 39 | Utah | 13.3 |
| 6 | Vermont | 20.1 |
| 40 | Virginia | 13.2 |
| 37 | Washington | 13.5 |
| 11 | West Virginia | 16.7 |
| 24 | Wisconsin | 14.8 |
| 50 | Wyoming | 9.2 |

RANK ORDER

| RANK | STATE | PERCENT |
|------|-------|---------|
| 1 | Rhode Island | 22.1 |
| 2 | Massachusetts | 21.2 |
| 3 | New York | 20.5 |
| 4 | Pennsylvania | 20.4 |
| 5 | Maine | 20.2 |
| 6 | Vermont | 20.1 |
| 7 | Connecticut | 19.9 |
| 8 | New Hampshire | 18.4 |
| 9 | Minnesota | 17.8 |
| 10 | Ohio | 16.9 |
| 11 | West Virginia | 16.7 |
| 12 | Delaware | 16.4 |
| 12 | New Jersey | 16.4 |
| 14 | Maryland | 16.3 |
| 15 | South Dakota | 16.2 |
| 16 | Michigan | 15.6 |
| 16 | Missouri | 15.6 |
| 18 | Montana | 15.5 |
| 19 | Illinois | 15.1 |
| 20 | Arizona | 15.0 |
| 20 | New Mexico | 15.0 |
| 22 | Florida | 14.9 |
| 22 | Indiana | 14.9 |
| 24 | Arkansas | 14.8 |
| 24 | Iowa | 14.8 |
| 24 | Wisconsin | 14.8 |
| 27 | Idaho | 14.6 |
| 27 | Nebraska | 14.6 |
| 27 | Tennessee | 14.6 |
| 30 | Louisiana | 14.5 |
| 30 | Oregon | 14.5 |
| 32 | Alaska | 14.3 |
| 33 | Kentucky | 14.1 |
| 34 | Oklahoma | 13.9 |
| 35 | North Carolina | 13.8 |
| 36 | Kansas | 13.7 |
| 37 | Washington | 13.5 |
| 38 | Texas | 13.4 |
| 39 | Utah | 13.3 |
| 40 | Virginia | 13.2 |
| 41 | California | 13.1 |
| 42 | North Dakota | 13.0 |
| 43 | Georgia | 12.7 |
| 44 | Hawaii | 12.5 |
| 45 | Colorado | 12.4 |
| 46 | Mississippi | 11.9 |
| 47 | Alabama | 11.6 |
| 48 | South Carolina | 11.2 |
| 49 | Nevada | 9.5 |
| 50 | Wyoming | 9.2 |

| District of Columbia | 16.0 |
|---|---|

Source: CQ Press using data from U.S. Department of Labor, Bureau of Labor Statistics
   "Regional and State Employment and Unemployment" (press release, January 28, 2014, www.bls.gov/bls/newsrels.htm)
*Seasonally adjusted preliminary data as of December 2013.  National figure calculated through a different formula.

# Employees in Financial Activities in 2013

## National Total = 7,915,000 Employees*

ALPHA ORDER

| RANK | STATE | EMPLOYEES | % of USA |
|------|-------|-----------|----------|
| 27 | Alabama | 93,300 | 1.2% |
| 48 | Alaska | 13,200 | 0.2% |
| 14 | Arizona | 189,000 | 2.4% |
| 35 | Arkansas | 51,100 | 0.6% |
| 1 | California | 783,200 | 9.9% |
| 19 | Colorado | 143,900 | 1.8% |
| 23 | Connecticut | 129,500 | 1.6% |
| 37 | Delaware | 44,500 | 0.6% |
| 4 | Florida | 509,000 | 6.4% |
| 9 | Georgia | 233,800 | 3.0% |
| 45 | Hawaii | 27,400 | 0.3% |
| 42 | Idaho | 30,900 | 0.4% |
| 5 | Illinois | 370,300 | 4.7% |
| 22 | Indiana | 134,000 | 1.7% |
| 24 | Iowa | 102,900 | 1.3% |
| 31 | Kansas | 77,500 | 1.0% |
| 29 | Kentucky | 88,200 | 1.1% |
| 26 | Louisiana | 94,800 | 1.2% |
| 41 | Maine | 31,600 | 0.4% |
| 18 | Maryland | 144,200 | 1.8% |
| 10 | Massachusetts | 207,400 | 2.6% |
| 13 | Michigan | 195,000 | 2.5% |
| 15 | Minnesota | 179,400 | 2.3% |
| 36 | Mississippi | 44,900 | 0.6% |
| 16 | Missouri | 170,800 | 2.2% |
| 47 | Montana | 21,900 | 0.3% |
| 33 | Nebraska | 71,400 | 0.9% |
| 34 | Nevada | 54,200 | 0.7% |
| 39 | New Hampshire | 35,200 | 0.4% |
| 8 | New Jersey | 248,400 | 3.1% |
| 38 | New Mexico | 37,000 | 0.5% |
| 2 | New York | 680,400 | 8.6% |
| 11 | North Carolina | 206,700 | 2.6% |
| 46 | North Dakota | 23,500 | 0.3% |
| 7 | Ohio | 278,600 | 3.5% |
| 30 | Oklahoma | 80,300 | 1.0% |
| 28 | Oregon | 88,900 | 1.1% |
| 6 | Pennsylvania | 312,300 | 3.9% |
| 40 | Rhode Island | 32,100 | 0.4% |
| 25 | South Carolina | 101,800 | 1.3% |
| 43 | South Dakota | 29,700 | 0.4% |
| 21 | Tennessee | 139,700 | 1.8% |
| 3 | Texas | 672,100 | 8.5% |
| 32 | Utah | 73,000 | 0.9% |
| 49 | Vermont | 12,300 | 0.2% |
| 12 | Virginia | 199,300 | 2.5% |
| 20 | Washington | 143,300 | 1.8% |
| 44 | West Virginia | 28,500 | 0.4% |
| 17 | Wisconsin | 159,600 | 2.0% |
| 50 | Wyoming | 10,500 | 0.1% |

RANK ORDER

| RANK | STATE | EMPLOYEES | % of USA |
|------|-------|-----------|----------|
| 1 | California | 783,200 | 9.9% |
| 2 | New York | 680,400 | 8.6% |
| 3 | Texas | 672,100 | 8.5% |
| 4 | Florida | 509,000 | 6.4% |
| 5 | Illinois | 370,300 | 4.7% |
| 6 | Pennsylvania | 312,300 | 3.9% |
| 7 | Ohio | 278,600 | 3.5% |
| 8 | New Jersey | 248,400 | 3.1% |
| 9 | Georgia | 233,800 | 3.0% |
| 10 | Massachusetts | 207,400 | 2.6% |
| 11 | North Carolina | 206,700 | 2.6% |
| 12 | Virginia | 199,300 | 2.5% |
| 13 | Michigan | 195,000 | 2.5% |
| 14 | Arizona | 189,000 | 2.4% |
| 15 | Minnesota | 179,400 | 2.3% |
| 16 | Missouri | 170,800 | 2.2% |
| 17 | Wisconsin | 159,600 | 2.0% |
| 18 | Maryland | 144,200 | 1.8% |
| 19 | Colorado | 143,900 | 1.8% |
| 20 | Washington | 143,300 | 1.8% |
| 21 | Tennessee | 139,700 | 1.8% |
| 22 | Indiana | 134,000 | 1.7% |
| 23 | Connecticut | 129,500 | 1.6% |
| 24 | Iowa | 102,900 | 1.3% |
| 25 | South Carolina | 101,800 | 1.3% |
| 26 | Louisiana | 94,800 | 1.2% |
| 27 | Alabama | 93,300 | 1.2% |
| 28 | Oregon | 88,900 | 1.1% |
| 29 | Kentucky | 88,200 | 1.1% |
| 30 | Oklahoma | 80,300 | 1.0% |
| 31 | Kansas | 77,500 | 1.0% |
| 32 | Utah | 73,000 | 0.9% |
| 33 | Nebraska | 71,400 | 0.9% |
| 34 | Nevada | 54,200 | 0.7% |
| 35 | Arkansas | 51,100 | 0.6% |
| 36 | Mississippi | 44,900 | 0.6% |
| 37 | Delaware | 44,500 | 0.6% |
| 38 | New Mexico | 37,000 | 0.5% |
| 39 | New Hampshire | 35,200 | 0.4% |
| 40 | Rhode Island | 32,100 | 0.4% |
| 41 | Maine | 31,600 | 0.4% |
| 42 | Idaho | 30,900 | 0.4% |
| 43 | South Dakota | 29,700 | 0.4% |
| 44 | West Virginia | 28,500 | 0.4% |
| 45 | Hawaii | 27,400 | 0.3% |
| 46 | North Dakota | 23,500 | 0.3% |
| 47 | Montana | 21,900 | 0.3% |
| 48 | Alaska | 13,200 | 0.2% |
| 49 | Vermont | 12,300 | 0.2% |
| 50 | Wyoming | 10,500 | 0.1% |
| | District of Columbia | 28,900 | 0.4% |

Source: U.S. Department of Labor, Bureau of Labor Statistics
   "Regional and State Employment and Unemployment" (press release, January 28, 2014, www.bls.gov/bls/newsrels.htm)
*Seasonally adjusted preliminary data as of December 2013. National total calculated through a different formula. Financial activities include insurance and real estate.

# Percent of Nonfarm Employees in Financial Activities in 2013

## National Percent = 5.8% of Employees*

ALPHA ORDER

| RANK | STATE | PERCENT |
|---|---|---|
| 33 | Alabama | 4.9 |
| 46 | Alaska | 4.0 |
| 4 | Arizona | 7.4 |
| 45 | Arkansas | 4.3 |
| 25 | California | 5.3 |
| 15 | Colorado | 6.0 |
| 2 | Connecticut | 7.8 |
| 1 | Delaware | 10.3 |
| 8 | Florida | 6.7 |
| 17 | Georgia | 5.7 |
| 44 | Hawaii | 4.4 |
| 37 | Idaho | 4.8 |
| 11 | Illinois | 6.3 |
| 43 | Indiana | 4.5 |
| 8 | Iowa | 6.7 |
| 19 | Kansas | 5.6 |
| 37 | Kentucky | 4.8 |
| 37 | Louisiana | 4.8 |
| 25 | Maine | 5.3 |
| 21 | Maryland | 5.5 |
| 14 | Massachusetts | 6.2 |
| 37 | Michigan | 4.8 |
| 10 | Minnesota | 6.4 |
| 46 | Mississippi | 4.0 |
| 11 | Missouri | 6.3 |
| 33 | Montana | 4.9 |
| 5 | Nebraska | 7.3 |
| 41 | Nevada | 4.6 |
| 21 | New Hampshire | 5.5 |
| 11 | New Jersey | 6.3 |
| 41 | New Mexico | 4.6 |
| 3 | New York | 7.6 |
| 31 | North Carolina | 5.0 |
| 30 | North Dakota | 5.2 |
| 23 | Ohio | 5.4 |
| 33 | Oklahoma | 4.9 |
| 25 | Oregon | 5.3 |
| 23 | Pennsylvania | 5.4 |
| 7 | Rhode Island | 6.8 |
| 25 | South Carolina | 5.3 |
| 6 | South Dakota | 7.0 |
| 31 | Tennessee | 5.0 |
| 15 | Texas | 6.0 |
| 17 | Utah | 5.7 |
| 46 | Vermont | 4.0 |
| 25 | Virginia | 5.3 |
| 33 | Washington | 4.9 |
| 49 | West Virginia | 3.7 |
| 19 | Wisconsin | 5.6 |
| 50 | Wyoming | 3.6 |

RANK ORDER

| RANK | STATE | PERCENT |
|---|---|---|
| 1 | Delaware | 10.3 |
| 2 | Connecticut | 7.8 |
| 3 | New York | 7.6 |
| 4 | Arizona | 7.4 |
| 5 | Nebraska | 7.3 |
| 6 | South Dakota | 7.0 |
| 7 | Rhode Island | 6.8 |
| 8 | Florida | 6.7 |
| 8 | Iowa | 6.7 |
| 10 | Minnesota | 6.4 |
| 11 | Illinois | 6.3 |
| 11 | Missouri | 6.3 |
| 11 | New Jersey | 6.3 |
| 14 | Massachusetts | 6.2 |
| 15 | Colorado | 6.0 |
| 15 | Texas | 6.0 |
| 17 | Georgia | 5.7 |
| 17 | Utah | 5.7 |
| 19 | Kansas | 5.6 |
| 19 | Wisconsin | 5.6 |
| 21 | Maryland | 5.5 |
| 21 | New Hampshire | 5.5 |
| 23 | Ohio | 5.4 |
| 23 | Pennsylvania | 5.4 |
| 25 | California | 5.3 |
| 25 | Maine | 5.3 |
| 25 | Oregon | 5.3 |
| 25 | South Carolina | 5.3 |
| 25 | Virginia | 5.3 |
| 30 | North Dakota | 5.2 |
| 31 | North Carolina | 5.0 |
| 31 | Tennessee | 5.0 |
| 33 | Alabama | 4.9 |
| 33 | Montana | 4.9 |
| 33 | Oklahoma | 4.9 |
| 33 | Washington | 4.9 |
| 37 | Idaho | 4.8 |
| 37 | Kentucky | 4.8 |
| 37 | Louisiana | 4.8 |
| 37 | Michigan | 4.8 |
| 41 | Nevada | 4.6 |
| 41 | New Mexico | 4.6 |
| 43 | Indiana | 4.5 |
| 44 | Hawaii | 4.4 |
| 45 | Arkansas | 4.3 |
| 46 | Alaska | 4.0 |
| 46 | Mississippi | 4.0 |
| 46 | Vermont | 4.0 |
| 49 | West Virginia | 3.7 |
| 50 | Wyoming | 3.6 |

| | | |
|---|---|---|
| | District of Columbia | 3.9 |

Source: CQ Press using data from U.S. Department of Labor, Bureau of Labor Statistics
   "Regional and State Employment and Unemployment" (press release, January 28, 2014, www.bls.gov/bls/newsrels.htm)
*Seasonally adjusted preliminary data as of December 2013.  National figure calculated through a different formula.  Financial activities include insurance and real estate.

# Employees in Government in 2013

## National Total = 21,849,000 Employees*

| RANK | STATE | EMPLOYEES | % of USA |
|---|---|---|---|
| 23 | Alabama | 369,300 | 1.7% |
| 44 | Alaska | 82,500 | 0.4% |
| 21 | Arizona | 411,300 | 1.9% |
| 34 | Arkansas | 215,100 | 1.0% |
| 1 | California | 2,353,100 | 10.8% |
| 22 | Colorado | 404,600 | 1.9% |
| 32 | Connecticut | 237,200 | 1.1% |
| 48 | Delaware | 63,400 | 0.3% |
| 4 | Florida | 1,071,800 | 4.9% |
| 10 | Georgia | 671,100 | 3.1% |
| 39 | Hawaii | 125,300 | 0.6% |
| 40 | Idaho | 118,600 | 0.5% |
| 5 | Illinois | 827,100 | 3.8% |
| 16 | Indiana | 435,800 | 2.0% |
| 30 | Iowa | 252,100 | 1.2% |
| 29 | Kansas | 258,100 | 1.2% |
| 27 | Kentucky | 334,400 | 1.5% |
| 26 | Louisiana | 343,000 | 1.6% |
| 41 | Maine | 97,800 | 0.4% |
| 14 | Maryland | 506,400 | 2.3% |
| 15 | Massachusetts | 442,000 | 2.0% |
| 12 | Michigan | 603,900 | 2.8% |
| 19 | Minnesota | 417,100 | 1.9% |
| 31 | Mississippi | 244,200 | 1.1% |
| 17 | Missouri | 431,800 | 2.0% |
| 43 | Montana | 89,300 | 0.4% |
| 36 | Nebraska | 168,600 | 0.8% |
| 38 | Nevada | 152,700 | 0.7% |
| 42 | New Hampshire | 89,800 | 0.4% |
| 11 | New Jersey | 628,400 | 2.9% |
| 35 | New Mexico | 191,600 | 0.9% |
| 3 | New York | 1,440,100 | 6.6% |
| 7 | North Carolina | 714,300 | 3.3% |
| 45 | North Dakota | 79,700 | 0.4% |
| 6 | Ohio | 740,000 | 3.4% |
| 25 | Oklahoma | 351,700 | 1.6% |
| 28 | Oregon | 292,100 | 1.3% |
| 9 | Pennsylvania | 711,600 | 3.3% |
| 49 | Rhode Island | 59,500 | 0.3% |
| 24 | South Carolina | 354,200 | 1.6% |
| 46 | South Dakota | 78,200 | 0.4% |
| 18 | Tennessee | 418,100 | 1.9% |
| 2 | Texas | 1,809,200 | 8.3% |
| 33 | Utah | 217,800 | 1.0% |
| 50 | Vermont | 54,300 | 0.2% |
| 8 | Virginia | 713,800 | 3.3% |
| 13 | Washington | 539,400 | 2.5% |
| 37 | West Virginia | 155,500 | 0.7% |
| 20 | Wisconsin | 414,600 | 1.9% |
| 47 | Wyoming | 74,100 | 0.3% |

| RANK | STATE | EMPLOYEES | % of USA |
|---|---|---|---|
| 1 | California | 2,353,100 | 10.8% |
| 2 | Texas | 1,809,200 | 8.3% |
| 3 | New York | 1,440,100 | 6.6% |
| 4 | Florida | 1,071,800 | 4.9% |
| 5 | Illinois | 827,100 | 3.8% |
| 6 | Ohio | 740,000 | 3.4% |
| 7 | North Carolina | 714,300 | 3.3% |
| 8 | Virginia | 713,800 | 3.3% |
| 9 | Pennsylvania | 711,600 | 3.3% |
| 10 | Georgia | 671,100 | 3.1% |
| 11 | New Jersey | 628,400 | 2.9% |
| 12 | Michigan | 603,900 | 2.8% |
| 13 | Washington | 539,400 | 2.5% |
| 14 | Maryland | 506,400 | 2.3% |
| 15 | Massachusetts | 442,000 | 2.0% |
| 16 | Indiana | 435,800 | 2.0% |
| 17 | Missouri | 431,800 | 2.0% |
| 18 | Tennessee | 418,100 | 1.9% |
| 19 | Minnesota | 417,100 | 1.9% |
| 20 | Wisconsin | 414,600 | 1.9% |
| 21 | Arizona | 411,300 | 1.9% |
| 22 | Colorado | 404,600 | 1.9% |
| 23 | Alabama | 369,300 | 1.7% |
| 24 | South Carolina | 354,200 | 1.6% |
| 25 | Oklahoma | 351,700 | 1.6% |
| 26 | Louisiana | 343,000 | 1.6% |
| 27 | Kentucky | 334,400 | 1.5% |
| 28 | Oregon | 292,100 | 1.3% |
| 29 | Kansas | 258,100 | 1.2% |
| 30 | Iowa | 252,100 | 1.2% |
| 31 | Mississippi | 244,200 | 1.1% |
| 32 | Connecticut | 237,200 | 1.1% |
| 33 | Utah | 217,800 | 1.0% |
| 34 | Arkansas | 215,100 | 1.0% |
| 35 | New Mexico | 191,600 | 0.9% |
| 36 | Nebraska | 168,600 | 0.8% |
| 37 | West Virginia | 155,500 | 0.7% |
| 38 | Nevada | 152,700 | 0.7% |
| 39 | Hawaii | 125,300 | 0.6% |
| 40 | Idaho | 118,600 | 0.5% |
| 41 | Maine | 97,800 | 0.4% |
| 42 | New Hampshire | 89,800 | 0.4% |
| 43 | Montana | 89,300 | 0.4% |
| 44 | Alaska | 82,500 | 0.4% |
| 45 | North Dakota | 79,700 | 0.4% |
| 46 | South Dakota | 78,200 | 0.4% |
| 47 | Wyoming | 74,100 | 0.3% |
| 48 | Delaware | 63,400 | 0.3% |
| 49 | Rhode Island | 59,500 | 0.3% |
| 50 | Vermont | 54,300 | 0.2% |
| | District of Columbia | 235,700 | 1.1% |

Source: U.S. Department of Labor, Bureau of Labor Statistics
"Regional and State Employment and Unemployment" (press release, January 28, 2014, www.bls.gov/bls/newsrels.htm)
*Seasonally adjusted preliminary data as of December 2013. National total calculated through a different formula.

# Percent of Nonfarm Employees in Government in 2013

## National Percent = 16.0% of Employees*

| ALPHA ORDER | | | | RANK ORDER | | |
|---|---|---|---|---|---|---|
| RANK | STATE | PERCENT | | RANK | STATE | PERCENT |
| 9 | Alabama | 19.5 | | 1 | Wyoming | 25.3 |
| 2 | Alaska | 24.8 | | 2 | Alaska | 24.8 |
| 30 | Arizona | 16.2 | | 3 | New Mexico | 23.6 |
| 18 | Arkansas | 18.0 | | 4 | Mississippi | 21.7 |
| 33 | California | 15.9 | | 5 | Oklahoma | 21.5 |
| 25 | Colorado | 17.0 | | 6 | Hawaii | 20.2 |
| 42 | Connecticut | 14.4 | | 7 | West Virginia | 20.1 |
| 39 | Delaware | 14.7 | | 8 | Montana | 19.9 |
| 45 | Florida | 14.0 | | 9 | Alabama | 19.5 |
| 27 | Georgia | 16.5 | | 10 | Maryland | 19.3 |
| 6 | Hawaii | 20.2 | | 11 | Virginia | 18.9 |
| 13 | Idaho | 18.6 | | 12 | Kansas | 18.8 |
| 43 | Illinois | 14.2 | | 13 | Idaho | 18.6 |
| 40 | Indiana | 14.6 | | 14 | South Carolina | 18.5 |
| 27 | Iowa | 16.5 | | 14 | South Dakota | 18.5 |
| 12 | Kansas | 18.8 | | 16 | Washington | 18.3 |
| 17 | Kentucky | 18.1 | | 17 | Kentucky | 18.1 |
| 20 | Louisiana | 17.5 | | 18 | Arkansas | 18.0 |
| 29 | Maine | 16.3 | | 19 | Vermont | 17.6 |
| 10 | Maryland | 19.3 | | 20 | Louisiana | 17.5 |
| 47 | Massachusetts | 13.2 | | 20 | North Dakota | 17.5 |
| 38 | Michigan | 14.8 | | 22 | North Carolina | 17.4 |
| 37 | Minnesota | 14.9 | | 22 | Oregon | 17.4 |
| 4 | Mississippi | 21.7 | | 24 | Nebraska | 17.3 |
| 33 | Missouri | 15.9 | | 25 | Colorado | 17.0 |
| 8 | Montana | 19.9 | | 26 | Utah | 16.9 |
| 24 | Nebraska | 17.3 | | 27 | Georgia | 16.5 |
| 48 | Nevada | 12.9 | | 27 | Iowa | 16.5 |
| 45 | New Hampshire | 14.0 | | 29 | Maine | 16.3 |
| 33 | New Jersey | 15.9 | | 30 | Arizona | 16.2 |
| 3 | New Mexico | 23.6 | | 31 | New York | 16.1 |
| 31 | New York | 16.1 | | 32 | Texas | 16.0 |
| 22 | North Carolina | 17.4 | | 33 | California | 15.9 |
| 20 | North Dakota | 17.5 | | 33 | Missouri | 15.9 |
| 43 | Ohio | 14.2 | | 33 | New Jersey | 15.9 |
| 5 | Oklahoma | 21.5 | | 36 | Tennessee | 15.1 |
| 22 | Oregon | 17.4 | | 37 | Minnesota | 14.9 |
| 50 | Pennsylvania | 12.4 | | 38 | Michigan | 14.8 |
| 49 | Rhode Island | 12.7 | | 39 | Delaware | 14.7 |
| 14 | South Carolina | 18.5 | | 40 | Indiana | 14.6 |
| 14 | South Dakota | 18.5 | | 40 | Wisconsin | 14.6 |
| 36 | Tennessee | 15.1 | | 42 | Connecticut | 14.4 |
| 32 | Texas | 16.0 | | 43 | Illinois | 14.2 |
| 26 | Utah | 16.9 | | 43 | Ohio | 14.2 |
| 19 | Vermont | 17.6 | | 45 | Florida | 14.0 |
| 11 | Virginia | 18.9 | | 45 | New Hampshire | 14.0 |
| 16 | Washington | 18.3 | | 47 | Massachusetts | 13.2 |
| 7 | West Virginia | 20.1 | | 48 | Nevada | 12.9 |
| 40 | Wisconsin | 14.6 | | 49 | Rhode Island | 12.7 |
| 1 | Wyoming | 25.3 | | 50 | Pennsylvania | 12.4 |

| | | |
|---|---|---|
| | District of Columbia | 32.2 |

Source: CQ Press using data from U.S. Department of Labor, Bureau of Labor Statistics
   "Regional and State Employment and Unemployment" (press release, January 28, 2014, www.bls.gov/bls/newsrels.htm)
*Seasonally adjusted preliminary data as of December 2013.  National figure calculated through a different formula.

# Employees in Leisure and Hospitality in 2013

## National Total = 14,291,000 Employees*

ALPHA ORDER

| RANK | STATE | EMPLOYEES | % of USA |
|---|---|---|---|
| 26 | Alabama | 181,200 | 1.3% |
| 50 | Alaska | 32,200 | 0.2% |
| 20 | Arizona | 278,500 | 1.9% |
| 36 | Arkansas | 103,400 | 0.7% |
| 1 | California | 1,696,300 | 11.9% |
| 17 | Colorado | 291,800 | 2.0% |
| 30 | Connecticut | 145,600 | 1.0% |
| 46 | Delaware | 45,200 | 0.3% |
| 3 | Florida | 1,039,700 | 7.3% |
| 9 | Georgia | 422,900 | 3.0% |
| 35 | Hawaii | 113,000 | 0.8% |
| 42 | Idaho | 62,000 | 0.4% |
| 5 | Illinois | 545,100 | 3.8% |
| 15 | Indiana | 299,700 | 2.1% |
| 31 | Iowa | 134,600 | 0.9% |
| 34 | Kansas | 120,800 | 0.8% |
| 27 | Kentucky | 180,400 | 1.3% |
| 25 | Louisiana | 219,800 | 1.5% |
| 41 | Maine | 64,800 | 0.5% |
| 23 | Maryland | 252,700 | 1.8% |
| 13 | Massachusetts | 334,400 | 2.3% |
| 10 | Michigan | 394,600 | 2.8% |
| 22 | Minnesota | 253,800 | 1.8% |
| 33 | Mississippi | 124,300 | 0.9% |
| 19 | Missouri | 283,300 | 2.0% |
| 43 | Montana | 59,800 | 0.4% |
| 38 | Nebraska | 83,300 | 0.6% |
| 14 | Nevada | 324,800 | 2.3% |
| 40 | New Hampshire | 65,400 | 0.5% |
| 12 | New Jersey | 352,800 | 2.5% |
| 37 | New Mexico | 89,100 | 0.6% |
| 4 | New York | 827,400 | 5.8% |
| 8 | North Carolina | 435,500 | 3.0% |
| 47 | North Dakota | 38,400 | 0.3% |
| 7 | Ohio | 506,800 | 3.5% |
| 29 | Oklahoma | 156,400 | 1.1% |
| 28 | Oregon | 179,600 | 1.3% |
| 6 | Pennsylvania | 533,900 | 3.7% |
| 44 | Rhode Island | 53,300 | 0.4% |
| 24 | South Carolina | 230,700 | 1.6% |
| 45 | South Dakota | 45,400 | 0.3% |
| 16 | Tennessee | 292,700 | 2.0% |
| 2 | Texas | 1,144,900 | 8.0% |
| 32 | Utah | 126,500 | 0.9% |
| 48 | Vermont | 35,400 | 0.2% |
| 11 | Virginia | 367,900 | 2.6% |
| 18 | Washington | 288,400 | 2.0% |
| 39 | West Virginia | 74,500 | 0.5% |
| 21 | Wisconsin | 276,200 | 1.9% |
| 49 | Wyoming | 34,200 | 0.2% |

RANK ORDER

| RANK | STATE | EMPLOYEES | % of USA |
|---|---|---|---|
| 1 | California | 1,696,300 | 11.9% |
| 2 | Texas | 1,144,900 | 8.0% |
| 3 | Florida | 1,039,700 | 7.3% |
| 4 | New York | 827,400 | 5.8% |
| 5 | Illinois | 545,100 | 3.8% |
| 6 | Pennsylvania | 533,900 | 3.7% |
| 7 | Ohio | 506,800 | 3.5% |
| 8 | North Carolina | 435,500 | 3.0% |
| 9 | Georgia | 422,900 | 3.0% |
| 10 | Michigan | 394,600 | 2.8% |
| 11 | Virginia | 367,900 | 2.6% |
| 12 | New Jersey | 352,800 | 2.5% |
| 13 | Massachusetts | 334,400 | 2.3% |
| 14 | Nevada | 324,800 | 2.3% |
| 15 | Indiana | 299,700 | 2.1% |
| 16 | Tennessee | 292,700 | 2.0% |
| 17 | Colorado | 291,800 | 2.0% |
| 18 | Washington | 288,400 | 2.0% |
| 19 | Missouri | 283,300 | 2.0% |
| 20 | Arizona | 278,500 | 1.9% |
| 21 | Wisconsin | 276,200 | 1.9% |
| 22 | Minnesota | 253,800 | 1.8% |
| 23 | Maryland | 252,700 | 1.8% |
| 24 | South Carolina | 230,700 | 1.6% |
| 25 | Louisiana | 219,800 | 1.5% |
| 26 | Alabama | 181,200 | 1.3% |
| 27 | Kentucky | 180,400 | 1.3% |
| 28 | Oregon | 179,600 | 1.3% |
| 29 | Oklahoma | 156,400 | 1.1% |
| 30 | Connecticut | 145,600 | 1.0% |
| 31 | Iowa | 134,600 | 0.9% |
| 32 | Utah | 126,500 | 0.9% |
| 33 | Mississippi | 124,300 | 0.9% |
| 34 | Kansas | 120,800 | 0.8% |
| 35 | Hawaii | 113,000 | 0.8% |
| 36 | Arkansas | 103,400 | 0.7% |
| 37 | New Mexico | 89,100 | 0.6% |
| 38 | Nebraska | 83,300 | 0.6% |
| 39 | West Virginia | 74,500 | 0.5% |
| 40 | New Hampshire | 65,400 | 0.5% |
| 41 | Maine | 64,800 | 0.5% |
| 42 | Idaho | 62,000 | 0.4% |
| 43 | Montana | 59,800 | 0.4% |
| 44 | Rhode Island | 53,300 | 0.4% |
| 45 | South Dakota | 45,400 | 0.3% |
| 46 | Delaware | 45,200 | 0.3% |
| 47 | North Dakota | 38,400 | 0.3% |
| 48 | Vermont | 35,400 | 0.2% |
| 49 | Wyoming | 34,200 | 0.2% |
| 50 | Alaska | 32,200 | 0.2% |
| | District of Columbia | 68,800 | 0.5% |

Source: U.S. Department of Labor, Bureau of Labor Statistics
   "Regional and State Employment and Unemployment" (press release, January 28, 2014, www.bls.gov/bls/newsrels.htm)
*Seasonally adjusted preliminary data as of December 2013.  National total calculated through a different formula.

# Percent of Nonfarm Employees in Leisure and Hospitality in 2013

## National Percent = 10.4% of Employees*

ALPHA ORDER

| RANK | STATE | PERCENT |
|---|---|---|
| 35 | Alabama | 9.6 |
| 30 | Alaska | 9.7 |
| 12 | Arizona | 11.0 |
| 48 | Arkansas | 8.7 |
| 8 | California | 11.5 |
| 5 | Colorado | 12.3 |
| 45 | Connecticut | 8.8 |
| 20 | Delaware | 10.5 |
| 3 | Florida | 13.6 |
| 21 | Georgia | 10.4 |
| 2 | Hawaii | 18.2 |
| 30 | Idaho | 9.7 |
| 40 | Illinois | 9.3 |
| 25 | Indiana | 10.1 |
| 45 | Iowa | 8.8 |
| 45 | Kansas | 8.8 |
| 27 | Kentucky | 9.8 |
| 11 | Louisiana | 11.2 |
| 15 | Maine | 10.8 |
| 35 | Maryland | 9.6 |
| 26 | Massachusetts | 10.0 |
| 35 | Michigan | 9.6 |
| 43 | Minnesota | 9.1 |
| 12 | Mississippi | 11.0 |
| 21 | Missouri | 10.4 |
| 4 | Montana | 13.3 |
| 49 | Nebraska | 8.6 |
| 1 | Nevada | 27.5 |
| 23 | New Hampshire | 10.2 |
| 44 | New Jersey | 8.9 |
| 12 | New Mexico | 11.0 |
| 40 | New York | 9.3 |
| 18 | North Carolina | 10.6 |
| 50 | North Dakota | 8.4 |
| 30 | Ohio | 9.7 |
| 35 | Oklahoma | 9.6 |
| 17 | Oregon | 10.7 |
| 40 | Pennsylvania | 9.3 |
| 10 | Rhode Island | 11.4 |
| 6 | South Carolina | 12.1 |
| 15 | South Dakota | 10.8 |
| 18 | Tennessee | 10.6 |
| 23 | Texas | 10.2 |
| 27 | Utah | 9.8 |
| 8 | Vermont | 11.5 |
| 30 | Virginia | 9.7 |
| 27 | Washington | 9.8 |
| 35 | West Virginia | 9.6 |
| 30 | Wisconsin | 9.7 |
| 7 | Wyoming | 11.7 |

RANK ORDER

| RANK | STATE | PERCENT |
|---|---|---|
| 1 | Nevada | 27.5 |
| 2 | Hawaii | 18.2 |
| 3 | Florida | 13.6 |
| 4 | Montana | 13.3 |
| 5 | Colorado | 12.3 |
| 6 | South Carolina | 12.1 |
| 7 | Wyoming | 11.7 |
| 8 | California | 11.5 |
| 8 | Vermont | 11.5 |
| 10 | Rhode Island | 11.4 |
| 11 | Louisiana | 11.2 |
| 12 | Arizona | 11.0 |
| 12 | Mississippi | 11.0 |
| 12 | New Mexico | 11.0 |
| 15 | Maine | 10.8 |
| 15 | South Dakota | 10.8 |
| 17 | Oregon | 10.7 |
| 18 | North Carolina | 10.6 |
| 18 | Tennessee | 10.6 |
| 20 | Delaware | 10.5 |
| 21 | Georgia | 10.4 |
| 21 | Missouri | 10.4 |
| 23 | New Hampshire | 10.2 |
| 23 | Texas | 10.2 |
| 25 | Indiana | 10.1 |
| 26 | Massachusetts | 10.0 |
| 27 | Kentucky | 9.8 |
| 27 | Utah | 9.8 |
| 27 | Washington | 9.8 |
| 30 | Alaska | 9.7 |
| 30 | Idaho | 9.7 |
| 30 | Ohio | 9.7 |
| 30 | Virginia | 9.7 |
| 30 | Wisconsin | 9.7 |
| 35 | Alabama | 9.6 |
| 35 | Maryland | 9.6 |
| 35 | Michigan | 9.6 |
| 35 | Oklahoma | 9.6 |
| 35 | West Virginia | 9.6 |
| 40 | Illinois | 9.3 |
| 40 | New York | 9.3 |
| 40 | Pennsylvania | 9.3 |
| 43 | Minnesota | 9.1 |
| 44 | New Jersey | 8.9 |
| 45 | Connecticut | 8.8 |
| 45 | Iowa | 8.8 |
| 45 | Kansas | 8.8 |
| 48 | Arkansas | 8.7 |
| 49 | Nebraska | 8.6 |
| 50 | North Dakota | 8.4 |

| | District of Columbia | 9.4 |
|---|---|---|

Source: CQ Press using data from U.S. Department of Labor, Bureau of Labor Statistics
   "Regional and State Employment and Unemployment" (press release, January 28, 2014, www.bls.gov/bls/newsrels.htm)
*Seasonally adjusted preliminary data as of December 2013.  National figure calculated through a different formula.

# Employees in Manufacturing in 2013

## National Total = 12,028,000 Employees*

ALPHA ORDER

| RANK | STATE | EMPLOYEES | % of USA |
|---|---|---|---|
| NA | Alabama** | NA | NA |
| 47 | Alaska | 10,400 | 0.1% |
| 27 | Arizona | 154,000 | 1.3% |
| 26 | Arkansas | 154,700 | 1.3% |
| 1 | California | 1,251,500 | 10.4% |
| 30 | Colorado | 134,900 | 1.1% |
| 25 | Connecticut | 159,200 | 1.3% |
| 44 | Delaware | 25,500 | 0.2% |
| 13 | Florida | 322,400 | 2.7% |
| 11 | Georgia | 357,600 | 3.0% |
| 46 | Hawaii | 13,900 | 0.1% |
| 35 | Idaho | 58,100 | 0.5% |
| 4 | Illinois | 577,600 | 4.8% |
| 7 | Indiana | 491,200 | 4.1% |
| 22 | Iowa | 215,600 | 1.8% |
| 24 | Kansas | 164,900 | 1.4% |
| 21 | Kentucky | 222,500 | 1.8% |
| 28 | Louisiana | 145,700 | 1.2% |
| 36 | Maine | 50,100 | 0.4% |
| 32 | Maryland | 102,500 | 0.9% |
| 17 | Massachusetts | 248,500 | 2.1% |
| 6 | Michigan | 563,200 | 4.7% |
| 14 | Minnesota | 306,800 | 2.6% |
| 29 | Mississippi | 138,000 | 1.1% |
| 16 | Missouri | 250,300 | 2.1% |
| 45 | Montana | 18,200 | 0.2% |
| 33 | Nebraska | 96,600 | 0.8% |
| 40 | Nevada | 40,000 | 0.3% |
| 34 | New Hampshire | 65,900 | 0.5% |
| 18 | New Jersey | 247,600 | 2.1% |
| 42 | New Mexico | 28,300 | 0.2% |
| 9 | New York | 444,900 | 3.7% |
| 10 | North Carolina | 444,200 | 3.7% |
| 43 | North Dakota | 25,700 | 0.2% |
| 3 | Ohio | 663,000 | 5.5% |
| NA | Oklahoma** | NA | NA |
| 23 | Oregon | 176,200 | 1.5% |
| 5 | Pennsylvania | 564,700 | 4.7% |
| 39 | Rhode Island | 40,500 | 0.3% |
| 20 | South Carolina | 224,700 | 1.9% |
| 38 | South Dakota | 42,600 | 0.4% |
| 12 | Tennessee | 325,300 | 2.7% |
| 2 | Texas | 878,000 | 7.3% |
| 31 | Utah | 121,500 | 1.0% |
| 41 | Vermont | 32,200 | 0.3% |
| 19 | Virginia | 232,900 | 1.9% |
| 15 | Washington | 281,800 | 2.3% |
| 37 | West Virginia | 48,600 | 0.4% |
| 8 | Wisconsin | 468,200 | 3.9% |
| 48 | Wyoming | 9,800 | 0.1% |

RANK ORDER

| RANK | STATE | EMPLOYEES | % of USA |
|---|---|---|---|
| 1 | California | 1,251,500 | 10.4% |
| 2 | Texas | 878,000 | 7.3% |
| 3 | Ohio | 663,000 | 5.5% |
| 4 | Illinois | 577,600 | 4.8% |
| 5 | Pennsylvania | 564,700 | 4.7% |
| 6 | Michigan | 563,200 | 4.7% |
| 7 | Indiana | 491,200 | 4.1% |
| 8 | Wisconsin | 468,200 | 3.9% |
| 9 | New York | 444,900 | 3.7% |
| 10 | North Carolina | 444,200 | 3.7% |
| 11 | Georgia | 357,600 | 3.0% |
| 12 | Tennessee | 325,300 | 2.7% |
| 13 | Florida | 322,400 | 2.7% |
| 14 | Minnesota | 306,800 | 2.6% |
| 15 | Washington | 281,800 | 2.3% |
| 16 | Missouri | 250,300 | 2.1% |
| 17 | Massachusetts | 248,500 | 2.1% |
| 18 | New Jersey | 247,600 | 2.1% |
| 19 | Virginia | 232,900 | 1.9% |
| 20 | South Carolina | 224,700 | 1.9% |
| 21 | Kentucky | 222,500 | 1.8% |
| 22 | Iowa | 215,600 | 1.8% |
| 23 | Oregon | 176,200 | 1.5% |
| 24 | Kansas | 164,900 | 1.4% |
| 25 | Connecticut | 159,200 | 1.3% |
| 26 | Arkansas | 154,700 | 1.3% |
| 27 | Arizona | 154,000 | 1.3% |
| 28 | Louisiana | 145,700 | 1.2% |
| 29 | Mississippi | 138,000 | 1.1% |
| 30 | Colorado | 134,900 | 1.1% |
| 31 | Utah | 121,500 | 1.0% |
| 32 | Maryland | 102,500 | 0.9% |
| 33 | Nebraska | 96,600 | 0.8% |
| 34 | New Hampshire | 65,900 | 0.5% |
| 35 | Idaho | 58,100 | 0.5% |
| 36 | Maine | 50,100 | 0.4% |
| 37 | West Virginia | 48,600 | 0.4% |
| 38 | South Dakota | 42,600 | 0.4% |
| 39 | Rhode Island | 40,500 | 0.3% |
| 40 | Nevada | 40,000 | 0.3% |
| 41 | Vermont | 32,200 | 0.3% |
| 42 | New Mexico | 28,300 | 0.2% |
| 43 | North Dakota | 25,700 | 0.2% |
| 44 | Delaware | 25,500 | 0.2% |
| 45 | Montana | 18,200 | 0.2% |
| 46 | Hawaii | 13,900 | 0.1% |
| 47 | Alaska | 10,400 | 0.1% |
| 48 | Wyoming | 9,800 | 0.1% |
| NA | Alabama** | NA | NA |
| NA | Oklahoma** | NA | NA |
| | District of Columbia** | NA | NA |

Source: U.S. Department of Labor, Bureau of Labor Statistics

"Regional and State Employment and Unemployment" (press release, January 28, 2014, www.bls.gov/bls/newsrels.htm)

*Seasonally adjusted preliminary data as of December 2013. National total calculated through a different formula.

**The Bureau of Labor Statistics does not publish seasonally adjusted figures in this category for these states.

# Percent of Nonfarm Employees in Manufacturing in 2013

## National Percent = 8.8% of Employees*

| ALPHA ORDER | | | | RANK ORDER | | |
|---|---|---|---|---|---|---|
| RANK | STATE | PERCENT | | RANK | STATE | PERCENT |
| NA | Alabama** | NA | | 1 | Indiana | 16.5 |
| 47 | Alaska | 3.1 | | 1 | Wisconsin | 16.5 |
| 36 | Arizona | 6.1 | | 3 | Iowa | 14.1 |
| 5 | Arkansas | 13.0 | | 4 | Michigan | 13.8 |
| 28 | California | 8.5 | | 5 | Arkansas | 13.0 |
| 38 | Colorado | 5.7 | | 6 | Ohio | 12.7 |
| 21 | Connecticut | 9.6 | | 7 | Mississippi | 12.2 |
| 37 | Delaware | 5.9 | | 8 | Kentucky | 12.1 |
| 41 | Florida | 4.2 | | 9 | Kansas | 12.0 |
| 26 | Georgia | 8.8 | | 10 | South Carolina | 11.7 |
| 48 | Hawaii | 2.2 | | 10 | Tennessee | 11.7 |
| 25 | Idaho | 9.1 | | 12 | Minnesota | 11.0 |
| 18 | Illinois | 9.9 | | 13 | North Carolina | 10.8 |
| 1 | Indiana | 16.5 | | 14 | Oregon | 10.5 |
| 3 | Iowa | 14.1 | | 15 | Vermont | 10.4 |
| 9 | Kansas | 12.0 | | 16 | New Hampshire | 10.3 |
| 8 | Kentucky | 12.1 | | 17 | South Dakota | 10.1 |
| 31 | Louisiana | 7.4 | | 18 | Illinois | 9.9 |
| 29 | Maine | 8.3 | | 18 | Nebraska | 9.9 |
| 43 | Maryland | 3.9 | | 20 | Pennsylvania | 9.8 |
| 31 | Massachusetts | 7.4 | | 21 | Connecticut | 9.6 |
| 4 | Michigan | 13.8 | | 21 | Washington | 9.6 |
| 12 | Minnesota | 11.0 | | 23 | Utah | 9.4 |
| 7 | Mississippi | 12.2 | | 24 | Missouri | 9.2 |
| 24 | Missouri | 9.2 | | 25 | Idaho | 9.1 |
| 42 | Montana | 4.1 | | 26 | Georgia | 8.8 |
| 18 | Nebraska | 9.9 | | 27 | Rhode Island | 8.6 |
| 45 | Nevada | 3.4 | | 28 | California | 8.5 |
| 16 | New Hampshire | 10.3 | | 29 | Maine | 8.3 |
| 33 | New Jersey | 6.3 | | 30 | Texas | 7.8 |
| 44 | New Mexico | 3.5 | | 31 | Louisiana | 7.4 |
| 40 | New York | 5.0 | | 31 | Massachusetts | 7.4 |
| 13 | North Carolina | 10.8 | | 33 | New Jersey | 6.3 |
| 39 | North Dakota | 5.6 | | 33 | West Virginia | 6.3 |
| 6 | Ohio | 12.7 | | 35 | Virginia | 6.2 |
| NA | Oklahoma** | NA | | 36 | Arizona | 6.1 |
| 14 | Oregon | 10.5 | | 37 | Delaware | 5.9 |
| 20 | Pennsylvania | 9.8 | | 38 | Colorado | 5.7 |
| 27 | Rhode Island | 8.6 | | 39 | North Dakota | 5.6 |
| 10 | South Carolina | 11.7 | | 40 | New York | 5.0 |
| 17 | South Dakota | 10.1 | | 41 | Florida | 4.2 |
| 10 | Tennessee | 11.7 | | 42 | Montana | 4.1 |
| 30 | Texas | 7.8 | | 43 | Maryland | 3.9 |
| 23 | Utah | 9.4 | | 44 | New Mexico | 3.5 |
| 15 | Vermont | 10.4 | | 45 | Nevada | 3.4 |
| 35 | Virginia | 6.2 | | 46 | Wyoming | 3.3 |
| 21 | Washington | 9.6 | | 47 | Alaska | 3.1 |
| 33 | West Virginia | 6.3 | | 48 | Hawaii | 2.2 |
| 1 | Wisconsin | 16.5 | | NA | Alabama** | NA |
| 46 | Wyoming | 3.3 | | NA | Oklahoma** | NA |
| | | | | | District of Columbia** | NA |

Source: CQ Press using data from U.S. Department of Labor, Bureau of Labor Statistics
   "Regional and State Employment and Unemployment" (press release, January 28, 2014, www.bls.gov/bls/newsrels.htm)
*Seasonally adjusted preliminary data as of December 2013.  National figure calculated through a different formula.
**The Bureau of Labor Statistics does not publish seasonally adjusted figures in this category for these states.

# Employees in Mining and Logging in 2013

## National Total = 886,000 Employees*

ALPHA ORDER

| RANK | STATE | EMPLOYEES | % of USA |
|------|-------|-----------|----------|
| 17 | Alabama | 12,400 | 1.4% |
| 12 | Alaska | 18,200 | 2.1% |
| 15 | Arizona | 12,900 | 1.5% |
| 21 | Arkansas | 10,300 | 1.2% |
| 8 | California | 29,900 | 3.4% |
| 7 | Colorado | 30,400 | 3.4% |
| 43 | Connecticut | 500 | 0.1% |
| NA | Delaware** | NA | NA |
| 30 | Florida | 5,700 | 0.6% |
| 24 | Georgia | 8,600 | 1.0% |
| NA | Hawaii** | NA | NA |
| 33 | Idaho | 4,100 | 0.5% |
| 20 | Illinois | 10,400 | 1.2% |
| 27 | Indiana | 7,200 | 0.8% |
| 38 | Iowa | 2,200 | 0.2% |
| 19 | Kansas | 10,600 | 1.2% |
| 11 | Kentucky | 18,300 | 2.1% |
| 3 | Louisiana | 54,500 | 6.2% |
| 37 | Maine | 2,700 | 0.3% |
| NA | Maryland** | NA | NA |
| 40 | Massachusetts | 900 | 0.1% |
| 25 | Michigan | 7,900 | 0.9% |
| 26 | Minnesota | 7,300 | 0.8% |
| 23 | Mississippi | 9,400 | 1.1% |
| 34 | Missouri | 3,900 | 0.4% |
| 22 | Montana | 9,600 | 1.1% |
| NA | Nebraska** | NA | NA |
| 13 | Nevada | 16,900 | 1.9% |
| 40 | New Hampshire | 900 | 0.1% |
| 39 | New Jersey | 1,200 | 0.1% |
| 10 | New Mexico | 25,200 | 2.8% |
| 32 | New York | 5,000 | 0.6% |
| 31 | North Carolina | 5,400 | 0.6% |
| 6 | North Dakota | 35,300 | 4.0% |
| 16 | Ohio | 12,800 | 1.4% |
| 2 | Oklahoma | 54,600 | 6.2% |
| 28 | Oregon | 6,800 | 0.8% |
| 5 | Pennsylvania | 36,500 | 4.1% |
| 44 | Rhode Island | 200 | 0.0% |
| 35 | South Carolina | 3,700 | 0.4% |
| NA | South Dakota** | NA | NA |
| NA | Tennessee** | NA | NA |
| 1 | Texas | 288,900 | 32.6% |
| 14 | Utah | 13,300 | 1.5% |
| 42 | Vermont | 800 | 0.1% |
| 18 | Virginia | 10,800 | 1.2% |
| 29 | Washington | 5,900 | 0.7% |
| 4 | West Virginia | 36,900 | 4.2% |
| 36 | Wisconsin | 3,500 | 0.4% |
| 9 | Wyoming | 25,900 | 2.9% |

RANK ORDER

| RANK | STATE | EMPLOYEES | % of USA |
|------|-------|-----------|----------|
| 1 | Texas | 288,900 | 32.6% |
| 2 | Oklahoma | 54,600 | 6.2% |
| 3 | Louisiana | 54,500 | 6.2% |
| 4 | West Virginia | 36,900 | 4.2% |
| 5 | Pennsylvania | 36,500 | 4.1% |
| 6 | North Dakota | 35,300 | 4.0% |
| 7 | Colorado | 30,400 | 3.4% |
| 8 | California | 29,900 | 3.4% |
| 9 | Wyoming | 25,900 | 2.9% |
| 10 | New Mexico | 25,200 | 2.8% |
| 11 | Kentucky | 18,300 | 2.1% |
| 12 | Alaska | 18,200 | 2.1% |
| 13 | Nevada | 16,900 | 1.9% |
| 14 | Utah | 13,300 | 1.5% |
| 15 | Arizona | 12,900 | 1.5% |
| 16 | Ohio | 12,800 | 1.4% |
| 17 | Alabama | 12,400 | 1.4% |
| 18 | Virginia | 10,800 | 1.2% |
| 19 | Kansas | 10,600 | 1.2% |
| 20 | Illinois | 10,400 | 1.2% |
| 21 | Arkansas | 10,300 | 1.2% |
| 22 | Montana | 9,600 | 1.1% |
| 23 | Mississippi | 9,400 | 1.1% |
| 24 | Georgia | 8,600 | 1.0% |
| 25 | Michigan | 7,900 | 0.9% |
| 26 | Minnesota | 7,300 | 0.8% |
| 27 | Indiana | 7,200 | 0.8% |
| 28 | Oregon | 6,800 | 0.8% |
| 29 | Washington | 5,900 | 0.7% |
| 30 | Florida | 5,700 | 0.6% |
| 31 | North Carolina | 5,400 | 0.6% |
| 32 | New York | 5,000 | 0.6% |
| 33 | Idaho | 4,100 | 0.5% |
| 34 | Missouri | 3,900 | 0.4% |
| 35 | South Carolina | 3,700 | 0.4% |
| 36 | Wisconsin | 3,500 | 0.4% |
| 37 | Maine | 2,700 | 0.3% |
| 38 | Iowa | 2,200 | 0.2% |
| 39 | New Jersey | 1,200 | 0.1% |
| 40 | Massachusetts | 900 | 0.1% |
| 40 | New Hampshire | 900 | 0.1% |
| 42 | Vermont | 800 | 0.1% |
| 43 | Connecticut | 500 | 0.1% |
| 44 | Rhode Island | 200 | 0.0% |
| NA | Delaware** | NA | NA |
| NA | Hawaii** | NA | NA |
| NA | Maryland** | NA | NA |
| NA | Nebraska** | NA | NA |
| NA | South Dakota** | NA | NA |
| NA | Tennessee** | NA | NA |
| | District of Columbia** | NA | NA |

Source: U.S. Department of Labor, Bureau of Labor Statistics
   "Regional and State Employment and Unemployment" (press release, January 28, 2014, www.bls.gov/bls/newsrels.htm)
*Not seasonally adjusted preliminary data as of December 2013.  National total calculated through a different formula.
**The Bureau of Labor Statistics does not publish figures in this category for these states.

# Percent of Nonfarm Employees in Mining and Logging in 2013

## National Percent = 0.6% of Employees*

ALPHA ORDER

| RANK | STATE | PERCENT |
|------|-------|---------|
| 17 | Alabama | 0.7 |
| 3 | Alaska | 5.7 |
| 20 | Arizona | 0.5 |
| 14 | Arkansas | 0.9 |
| 26 | California | 0.2 |
| 11 | Colorado | 1.3 |
| 41 | Connecticut | 0.0 |
| NA | Delaware** | NA |
| 34 | Florida | 0.1 |
| 26 | Georgia | 0.2 |
| NA | Hawaii** | NA |
| 18 | Idaho | 0.6 |
| 26 | Illinois | 0.2 |
| 26 | Indiana | 0.2 |
| 34 | Iowa | 0.1 |
| 15 | Kansas | 0.8 |
| 12 | Kentucky | 1.0 |
| 7 | Louisiana | 2.8 |
| 21 | Maine | 0.4 |
| NA | Maryland** | NA |
| 41 | Massachusetts | 0.0 |
| 26 | Michigan | 0.2 |
| 23 | Minnesota | 0.3 |
| 15 | Mississippi | 0.8 |
| 34 | Missouri | 0.1 |
| 9 | Montana | 2.2 |
| NA | Nebraska** | NA |
| 10 | Nevada | 1.4 |
| 34 | New Hampshire | 0.1 |
| 41 | New Jersey | 0.0 |
| 6 | New Mexico | 3.1 |
| 34 | New York | 0.1 |
| 34 | North Carolina | 0.1 |
| 2 | North Dakota | 7.7 |
| 26 | Ohio | 0.2 |
| 5 | Oklahoma | 3.3 |
| 21 | Oregon | 0.4 |
| 18 | Pennsylvania | 0.6 |
| 41 | Rhode Island | 0.0 |
| 26 | South Carolina | 0.2 |
| NA | South Dakota** | NA |
| NA | Tennessee** | NA |
| 8 | Texas | 2.5 |
| 12 | Utah | 1.0 |
| 23 | Vermont | 0.3 |
| 23 | Virginia | 0.3 |
| 26 | Washington | 0.2 |
| 4 | West Virginia | 4.7 |
| 34 | Wisconsin | 0.1 |
| 1 | Wyoming | 8.9 |

RANK ORDER

| RANK | STATE | PERCENT |
|------|-------|---------|
| 1 | Wyoming | 8.9 |
| 2 | North Dakota | 7.7 |
| 3 | Alaska | 5.7 |
| 4 | West Virginia | 4.7 |
| 5 | Oklahoma | 3.3 |
| 6 | New Mexico | 3.1 |
| 7 | Louisiana | 2.8 |
| 8 | Texas | 2.5 |
| 9 | Montana | 2.2 |
| 10 | Nevada | 1.4 |
| 11 | Colorado | 1.3 |
| 12 | Kentucky | 1.0 |
| 12 | Utah | 1.0 |
| 14 | Arkansas | 0.9 |
| 15 | Kansas | 0.8 |
| 15 | Mississippi | 0.8 |
| 17 | Alabama | 0.7 |
| 18 | Idaho | 0.6 |
| 18 | Pennsylvania | 0.6 |
| 20 | Arizona | 0.5 |
| 21 | Maine | 0.4 |
| 21 | Oregon | 0.4 |
| 23 | Minnesota | 0.3 |
| 23 | Vermont | 0.3 |
| 23 | Virginia | 0.3 |
| 26 | California | 0.2 |
| 26 | Georgia | 0.2 |
| 26 | Illinois | 0.2 |
| 26 | Indiana | 0.2 |
| 26 | Michigan | 0.2 |
| 26 | Ohio | 0.2 |
| 26 | South Carolina | 0.2 |
| 26 | Washington | 0.2 |
| 34 | Florida | 0.1 |
| 34 | Iowa | 0.1 |
| 34 | Missouri | 0.1 |
| 34 | New Hampshire | 0.1 |
| 34 | New York | 0.1 |
| 34 | North Carolina | 0.1 |
| 34 | Wisconsin | 0.1 |
| 41 | Connecticut | 0.0 |
| 41 | Massachusetts | 0.0 |
| 41 | New Jersey | 0.0 |
| 41 | Rhode Island | 0.0 |
| NA | Delaware** | NA |
| NA | Hawaii** | NA |
| NA | Maryland** | NA |
| NA | Nebraska** | NA |
| NA | South Dakota** | NA |
| NA | Tennessee** | NA |

District of Columbia**          NA

Source: CQ Press using data from U.S. Department of Labor, Bureau of Labor Statistics
   "Regional and State Employment and Unemployment" (press release, January 28, 2014, www.bls.gov/bls/newsrels.htm)
*Not seasonally adjusted preliminary data as of December 2013.  National figure calculated through a different formula.
**The Bureau of Labor Statistics does not publish seasonally adjusted figures in this category for these states.

# Employees in Professional and Business Services in 2013

## National Total = 18,789,000 Employees*

| ALPHA ORDER | | | | | RANK ORDER | | | |
|---|---|---|---|---|---|---|---|---|
| RANK | STATE | EMPLOYEES | % of USA | | RANK | STATE | EMPLOYEES | % of USA |
| 24 | Alabama | 220,500 | 1.2% | | 1 | California | 2,326,600 | 12.4% |
| 48 | Alaska | 28,400 | 0.2% | | 2 | Texas | 1,492,100 | 7.9% |
| 16 | Arizona | 363,800 | 1.9% | | 3 | New York | 1,200,400 | 6.4% |
| 34 | Arkansas | 126,100 | 0.7% | | 4 | Florida | 1,109,300 | 5.9% |
| 1 | California | 2,326,600 | 12.4% | | 5 | Illinois | 898,300 | 4.8% |
| 15 | Colorado | 377,800 | 2.0% | | 6 | Pennsylvania | 745,600 | 4.0% |
| 28 | Connecticut | 202,900 | 1.1% | | 7 | Ohio | 681,100 | 3.6% |
| 42 | Delaware | 61,100 | 0.3% | | 8 | Virginia | 675,600 | 3.6% |
| 4 | Florida | 1,109,300 | 5.9% | | 9 | New Jersey | 618,100 | 3.3% |
| 10 | Georgia | 598,000 | 3.2% | | 10 | Georgia | 598,000 | 3.2% |
| 39 | Hawaii | 77,400 | 0.4% | | 11 | Michigan | 596,900 | 3.2% |
| 38 | Idaho | 78,600 | 0.4% | | 12 | North Carolina | 565,000 | 3.0% |
| 5 | Illinois | 898,300 | 4.8% | | 13 | Massachusetts | 509,700 | 2.7% |
| 21 | Indiana | 311,800 | 1.7% | | 14 | Maryland | 430,800 | 2.3% |
| 33 | Iowa | 134,000 | 0.7% | | 15 | Colorado | 377,800 | 2.0% |
| 31 | Kansas | 161,300 | 0.9% | | 16 | Arizona | 363,800 | 1.9% |
| 25 | Kentucky | 208,100 | 1.1% | | 17 | Washington | 357,600 | 1.9% |
| 26 | Louisiana | 205,500 | 1.1% | | 18 | Missouri | 350,100 | 1.9% |
| 43 | Maine | 59,900 | 0.3% | | 19 | Tennessee | 347,600 | 1.9% |
| 14 | Maryland | 430,800 | 2.3% | | 20 | Minnesota | 341,800 | 1.8% |
| 13 | Massachusetts | 509,700 | 2.7% | | 21 | Indiana | 311,800 | 1.7% |
| 11 | Michigan | 596,900 | 3.2% | | 22 | Wisconsin | 304,200 | 1.6% |
| 20 | Minnesota | 341,800 | 1.8% | | 23 | South Carolina | 240,000 | 1.3% |
| 36 | Mississippi | 106,400 | 0.6% | | 24 | Alabama | 220,500 | 1.2% |
| 18 | Missouri | 350,100 | 1.9% | | 25 | Kentucky | 208,100 | 1.1% |
| 45 | Montana | 42,900 | 0.2% | | 26 | Louisiana | 205,500 | 1.1% |
| 35 | Nebraska | 108,400 | 0.6% | | 27 | Oregon | 204,500 | 1.1% |
| 32 | Nevada | 145,300 | 0.8% | | 28 | Connecticut | 202,900 | 1.1% |
| 40 | New Hampshire | 70,400 | 0.4% | | 29 | Oklahoma | 186,300 | 1.0% |
| 9 | New Jersey | 618,100 | 3.3% | | 30 | Utah | 170,500 | 0.9% |
| 37 | New Mexico | 97,500 | 0.5% | | 31 | Kansas | 161,300 | 0.9% |
| 3 | New York | 1,200,400 | 6.4% | | 32 | Nevada | 145,300 | 0.8% |
| 12 | North Carolina | 565,000 | 3.0% | | 33 | Iowa | 134,000 | 0.7% |
| 46 | North Dakota | 34,400 | 0.2% | | 34 | Arkansas | 126,100 | 0.7% |
| 7 | Ohio | 681,100 | 3.6% | | 35 | Nebraska | 108,400 | 0.6% |
| 29 | Oklahoma | 186,300 | 1.0% | | 36 | Mississippi | 106,400 | 0.6% |
| 27 | Oregon | 204,500 | 1.1% | | 37 | New Mexico | 97,500 | 0.5% |
| 6 | Pennsylvania | 745,600 | 4.0% | | 38 | Idaho | 78,600 | 0.4% |
| 44 | Rhode Island | 59,000 | 0.3% | | 39 | Hawaii | 77,400 | 0.4% |
| 23 | South Carolina | 240,000 | 1.3% | | 40 | New Hampshire | 70,400 | 0.4% |
| 47 | South Dakota | 29,300 | 0.2% | | 41 | West Virginia | 66,800 | 0.4% |
| 19 | Tennessee | 347,600 | 1.9% | | 42 | Delaware | 61,100 | 0.3% |
| 2 | Texas | 1,492,100 | 7.9% | | 43 | Maine | 59,900 | 0.3% |
| 30 | Utah | 170,500 | 0.9% | | 44 | Rhode Island | 59,000 | 0.3% |
| 49 | Vermont | 27,000 | 0.1% | | 45 | Montana | 42,900 | 0.2% |
| 8 | Virginia | 675,600 | 3.6% | | 46 | North Dakota | 34,400 | 0.2% |
| 17 | Washington | 357,600 | 1.9% | | 47 | South Dakota | 29,300 | 0.2% |
| 41 | West Virginia | 66,800 | 0.4% | | 48 | Alaska | 28,400 | 0.2% |
| 22 | Wisconsin | 304,200 | 1.6% | | 49 | Vermont | 27,000 | 0.1% |
| 50 | Wyoming | 18,300 | 0.1% | | 50 | Wyoming | 18,300 | 0.1% |
| | | | | | | District of Columbia | 156,300 | 0.8% |

Source: U.S. Department of Labor, Bureau of Labor Statistics
   "Regional and State Employment and Unemployment" (press release, January 28, 2014, www.bls.gov/bls/newsrels.htm)
*Seasonally adjusted preliminary data as of December 2013. National total calculated through a different formula.

# Percent of Nonfarm Employees in Professional and Business Services in 2013

## National Percent = 13.7% of Employees*

ALPHA ORDER

| RANK | STATE | PERCENT |
|------|-------|---------|
| 32 | Alabama | 11.6 |
| 47 | Alaska | 8.5 |
| 11 | Arizona | 14.3 |
| 38 | Arkansas | 10.6 |
| 4 | California | 15.8 |
| 3 | Colorado | 15.9 |
| 24 | Connecticut | 12.3 |
| 12 | Delaware | 14.2 |
| 10 | Florida | 14.5 |
| 8 | Georgia | 14.7 |
| 21 | Hawaii | 12.5 |
| 24 | Idaho | 12.3 |
| 6 | Illinois | 15.4 |
| 39 | Indiana | 10.5 |
| 44 | Iowa | 8.8 |
| 31 | Kansas | 11.7 |
| 34 | Kentucky | 11.3 |
| 39 | Louisiana | 10.5 |
| 41 | Maine | 10.0 |
| 2 | Maryland | 16.4 |
| 7 | Massachusetts | 15.2 |
| 9 | Michigan | 14.6 |
| 27 | Minnesota | 12.2 |
| 43 | Mississippi | 9.4 |
| 18 | Missouri | 12.9 |
| 42 | Montana | 9.6 |
| 35 | Nebraska | 11.2 |
| 24 | Nevada | 12.3 |
| 36 | New Hampshire | 11.0 |
| 5 | New Jersey | 15.7 |
| 30 | New Mexico | 12.0 |
| 14 | New York | 13.4 |
| 13 | North Carolina | 13.8 |
| 48 | North Dakota | 7.5 |
| 17 | Ohio | 13.1 |
| 33 | Oklahoma | 11.4 |
| 27 | Oregon | 12.2 |
| 18 | Pennsylvania | 12.9 |
| 20 | Rhode Island | 12.6 |
| 21 | South Carolina | 12.5 |
| 49 | South Dakota | 6.9 |
| 21 | Tennessee | 12.5 |
| 15 | Texas | 13.2 |
| 15 | Utah | 13.2 |
| 45 | Vermont | 8.7 |
| 1 | Virginia | 17.9 |
| 27 | Washington | 12.2 |
| 46 | West Virginia | 8.6 |
| 37 | Wisconsin | 10.7 |
| 50 | Wyoming | 6.3 |

RANK ORDER

| RANK | STATE | PERCENT |
|------|-------|---------|
| 1 | Virginia | 17.9 |
| 2 | Maryland | 16.4 |
| 3 | Colorado | 15.9 |
| 4 | California | 15.8 |
| 5 | New Jersey | 15.7 |
| 6 | Illinois | 15.4 |
| 7 | Massachusetts | 15.2 |
| 8 | Georgia | 14.7 |
| 9 | Michigan | 14.6 |
| 10 | Florida | 14.5 |
| 11 | Arizona | 14.3 |
| 12 | Delaware | 14.2 |
| 13 | North Carolina | 13.8 |
| 14 | New York | 13.4 |
| 15 | Texas | 13.2 |
| 15 | Utah | 13.2 |
| 17 | Ohio | 13.1 |
| 18 | Missouri | 12.9 |
| 18 | Pennsylvania | 12.9 |
| 20 | Rhode Island | 12.6 |
| 21 | Hawaii | 12.5 |
| 21 | South Carolina | 12.5 |
| 21 | Tennessee | 12.5 |
| 24 | Connecticut | 12.3 |
| 24 | Idaho | 12.3 |
| 24 | Nevada | 12.3 |
| 27 | Minnesota | 12.2 |
| 27 | Oregon | 12.2 |
| 27 | Washington | 12.2 |
| 30 | New Mexico | 12.0 |
| 31 | Kansas | 11.7 |
| 32 | Alabama | 11.6 |
| 33 | Oklahoma | 11.4 |
| 34 | Kentucky | 11.3 |
| 35 | Nebraska | 11.2 |
| 36 | New Hampshire | 11.0 |
| 37 | Wisconsin | 10.7 |
| 38 | Arkansas | 10.6 |
| 39 | Indiana | 10.5 |
| 39 | Louisiana | 10.5 |
| 41 | Maine | 10.0 |
| 42 | Montana | 9.6 |
| 43 | Mississippi | 9.4 |
| 44 | Iowa | 8.8 |
| 45 | Vermont | 8.7 |
| 46 | West Virginia | 8.6 |
| 47 | Alaska | 8.5 |
| 48 | North Dakota | 7.5 |
| 49 | South Dakota | 6.9 |
| 50 | Wyoming | 6.3 |

| District of Columbia | 21.3 |
|---|---|

Source: CQ Press using data from U.S. Department of Labor, Bureau of Labor Statistics
"Regional and State Employment and Unemployment" (press release, January 28, 2014, www.bls.gov/bls/newsrels.htm)
*Seasonally adjusted preliminary data as of December 2013. National figure calculated through a different formula.

# Employees in Trade, Transportation, and Public Utilities in 2013

## National Total = 26,286,000 Employees*

| ALPHA ORDER | | | | RANK ORDER | | | |
|---|---|---|---|---|---|---|---|
| RANK | STATE | EMPLOYEES | % of USA | RANK | STATE | EMPLOYEES | % of USA |
| 25 | Alabama | 368,200 | 1.4% | 1 | California | 2,805,700 | 10.7% |
| 48 | Alaska | 63,900 | 0.2% | 2 | Texas | 2,274,000 | 8.7% |
| 20 | Arizona | 497,900 | 1.9% | 3 | Florida | 1,620,900 | 6.2% |
| 33 | Arkansas | 253,100 | 1.0% | 4 | New York | 1,550,400 | 5.9% |
| 1 | California | 2,805,700 | 10.7% | 5 | Illinois | 1,185,000 | 4.5% |
| 22 | Colorado | 413,400 | 1.6% | 6 | Pennsylvania | 1,113,500 | 4.2% |
| 29 | Connecticut | 300,700 | 1.1% | 7 | Ohio | 986,300 | 3.8% |
| 46 | Delaware | 76,200 | 0.3% | 8 | Georgia | 864,200 | 3.3% |
| 3 | Florida | 1,620,900 | 6.2% | 9 | New Jersey | 835,300 | 3.2% |
| 8 | Georgia | 864,200 | 3.3% | 10 | North Carolina | 774,400 | 2.9% |
| 42 | Hawaii | 116,900 | 0.4% | 11 | Michigan | 745,600 | 2.8% |
| 40 | Idaho | 130,500 | 0.5% | 12 | Virginia | 640,400 | 2.4% |
| 5 | Illinois | 1,185,000 | 4.5% | 13 | Indiana | 589,800 | 2.2% |
| 13 | Indiana | 589,800 | 2.2% | 14 | Tennessee | 589,100 | 2.2% |
| 28 | Iowa | 312,400 | 1.2% | 15 | Massachusetts | 563,100 | 2.1% |
| 31 | Kansas | 257,200 | 1.0% | 16 | Washington | 562,900 | 2.1% |
| 24 | Kentucky | 376,000 | 1.4% | 17 | Missouri | 524,700 | 2.0% |
| 23 | Louisiana | 394,300 | 1.5% | 18 | Minnesota | 521,800 | 2.0% |
| 41 | Maine | 119,200 | 0.5% | 19 | Wisconsin | 513,300 | 2.0% |
| 21 | Maryland | 459,700 | 1.7% | 20 | Arizona | 497,900 | 1.9% |
| 15 | Massachusetts | 563,100 | 2.1% | 21 | Maryland | 459,700 | 1.7% |
| 11 | Michigan | 745,600 | 2.8% | 22 | Colorado | 413,400 | 1.6% |
| 18 | Minnesota | 521,800 | 2.0% | 23 | Louisiana | 394,300 | 1.5% |
| 35 | Mississippi | 219,800 | 0.8% | 24 | Kentucky | 376,000 | 1.4% |
| 17 | Missouri | 524,700 | 2.0% | 25 | Alabama | 368,200 | 1.4% |
| 44 | Montana | 90,500 | 0.3% | 26 | South Carolina | 366,500 | 1.4% |
| 36 | Nebraska | 204,800 | 0.8% | 27 | Oregon | 323,300 | 1.2% |
| 34 | Nevada | 232,900 | 0.9% | 28 | Iowa | 312,400 | 1.2% |
| 37 | New Hampshire | 138,400 | 0.5% | 29 | Connecticut | 300,700 | 1.1% |
| 9 | New Jersey | 835,300 | 3.2% | 30 | Oklahoma | 295,200 | 1.1% |
| 38 | New Mexico | 137,300 | 0.5% | 31 | Kansas | 257,200 | 1.0% |
| 4 | New York | 1,550,400 | 5.9% | 32 | Utah | 253,600 | 1.0% |
| 10 | North Carolina | 774,400 | 2.9% | 33 | Arkansas | 253,100 | 1.0% |
| 43 | North Dakota | 104,800 | 0.4% | 34 | Nevada | 232,900 | 0.9% |
| 7 | Ohio | 986,300 | 3.8% | 35 | Mississippi | 219,800 | 0.8% |
| 30 | Oklahoma | 295,200 | 1.1% | 36 | Nebraska | 204,800 | 0.8% |
| 27 | Oregon | 323,300 | 1.2% | 37 | New Hampshire | 138,400 | 0.5% |
| 6 | Pennsylvania | 1,113,500 | 4.2% | 38 | New Mexico | 137,300 | 0.5% |
| 47 | Rhode Island | 74,700 | 0.3% | 39 | West Virginia | 136,700 | 0.5% |
| 26 | South Carolina | 366,500 | 1.4% | 40 | Idaho | 130,500 | 0.5% |
| 45 | South Dakota | 84,900 | 0.3% | 41 | Maine | 119,200 | 0.5% |
| 14 | Tennessee | 589,100 | 2.2% | 42 | Hawaii | 116,900 | 0.4% |
| 2 | Texas | 2,274,000 | 8.7% | 43 | North Dakota | 104,800 | 0.4% |
| 32 | Utah | 253,600 | 1.0% | 44 | Montana | 90,500 | 0.3% |
| 49 | Vermont | 55,700 | 0.2% | 45 | South Dakota | 84,900 | 0.3% |
| 12 | Virginia | 640,400 | 2.4% | 46 | Delaware | 76,200 | 0.3% |
| 16 | Washington | 562,900 | 2.1% | 47 | Rhode Island | 74,700 | 0.3% |
| 39 | West Virginia | 136,700 | 0.5% | 48 | Alaska | 63,900 | 0.2% |
| 19 | Wisconsin | 513,300 | 2.0% | 49 | Vermont | 55,700 | 0.2% |
| 50 | Wyoming | 55,100 | 0.2% | 50 | Wyoming | 55,100 | 0.2% |
| | | | | | District of Columbia | 27,600 | 0.1% |

Source: U.S. Department of Labor, Bureau of Labor Statistics
    "Regional and State Employment and Unemployment" (press release, January 28, 2014, www.bls.gov/bls/newsrels.htm)
*Seasonally adjusted preliminary data as of December 2013.  National total calculated through a different formula.

# Percent of Nonfarm Employees in
# Trade, Transportation, and Public Utilities in 2013
# National Percent = 19.2% of Employees*

ALPHA ORDER

| RANK | STATE | PERCENT |
|------|-------|---------|
| 23 | Alabama | 19.4 |
| 26 | Alaska | 19.2 |
| 21 | Arizona | 19.6 |
| 4 | Arkansas | 21.2 |
| 30 | California | 19.0 |
| 45 | Colorado | 17.4 |
| 37 | Connecticut | 18.2 |
| 42 | Delaware | 17.7 |
| 4 | Florida | 21.2 |
| 4 | Georgia | 21.2 |
| 33 | Hawaii | 18.8 |
| 9 | Idaho | 20.5 |
| 12 | Illinois | 20.3 |
| 18 | Indiana | 19.8 |
| 10 | Iowa | 20.4 |
| 35 | Kansas | 18.7 |
| 10 | Kentucky | 20.4 |
| 15 | Louisiana | 20.1 |
| 17 | Maine | 19.9 |
| 44 | Maryland | 17.5 |
| 49 | Massachusetts | 16.8 |
| 37 | Michigan | 18.2 |
| 35 | Minnesota | 18.7 |
| 22 | Mississippi | 19.5 |
| 24 | Missouri | 19.3 |
| 13 | Montana | 20.2 |
| 8 | Nebraska | 21.1 |
| 19 | Nevada | 19.7 |
| 2 | New Hampshire | 21.6 |
| 4 | New Jersey | 21.2 |
| 48 | New Mexico | 16.9 |
| 46 | New York | 17.3 |
| 32 | North Carolina | 18.9 |
| 1 | North Dakota | 23.0 |
| 30 | Ohio | 19.0 |
| 40 | Oklahoma | 18.0 |
| 26 | Oregon | 19.2 |
| 24 | Pennsylvania | 19.3 |
| 50 | Rhode Island | 15.9 |
| 26 | South Carolina | 19.2 |
| 15 | South Dakota | 20.1 |
| 3 | Tennessee | 21.3 |
| 13 | Texas | 20.2 |
| 19 | Utah | 19.7 |
| 40 | Vermont | 18.0 |
| 47 | Virginia | 17.0 |
| 29 | Washington | 19.1 |
| 42 | West Virginia | 17.7 |
| 39 | Wisconsin | 18.1 |
| 33 | Wyoming | 18.8 |

RANK ORDER

| RANK | STATE | PERCENT |
|------|-------|---------|
| 1 | North Dakota | 23.0 |
| 2 | New Hampshire | 21.6 |
| 3 | Tennessee | 21.3 |
| 4 | Arkansas | 21.2 |
| 4 | Florida | 21.2 |
| 4 | Georgia | 21.2 |
| 4 | New Jersey | 21.2 |
| 8 | Nebraska | 21.1 |
| 9 | Idaho | 20.5 |
| 10 | Iowa | 20.4 |
| 10 | Kentucky | 20.4 |
| 12 | Illinois | 20.3 |
| 13 | Montana | 20.2 |
| 13 | Texas | 20.2 |
| 15 | Louisiana | 20.1 |
| 15 | South Dakota | 20.1 |
| 17 | Maine | 19.9 |
| 18 | Indiana | 19.8 |
| 19 | Nevada | 19.7 |
| 19 | Utah | 19.7 |
| 21 | Arizona | 19.6 |
| 22 | Mississippi | 19.5 |
| 23 | Alabama | 19.4 |
| 24 | Missouri | 19.3 |
| 24 | Pennsylvania | 19.3 |
| 26 | Alaska | 19.2 |
| 26 | Oregon | 19.2 |
| 26 | South Carolina | 19.2 |
| 29 | Washington | 19.1 |
| 30 | California | 19.0 |
| 30 | Ohio | 19.0 |
| 32 | North Carolina | 18.9 |
| 33 | Hawaii | 18.8 |
| 33 | Wyoming | 18.8 |
| 35 | Kansas | 18.7 |
| 35 | Minnesota | 18.7 |
| 37 | Connecticut | 18.2 |
| 37 | Michigan | 18.2 |
| 39 | Wisconsin | 18.1 |
| 40 | Oklahoma | 18.0 |
| 40 | Vermont | 18.0 |
| 42 | Delaware | 17.7 |
| 42 | West Virginia | 17.7 |
| 44 | Maryland | 17.5 |
| 45 | Colorado | 17.4 |
| 46 | New York | 17.3 |
| 47 | Virginia | 17.0 |
| 48 | New Mexico | 16.9 |
| 49 | Massachusetts | 16.8 |
| 50 | Rhode Island | 15.9 |
| | District of Columbia | 3.8 |

Source: CQ Press using data from U.S. Department of Labor, Bureau of Labor Statistics
"Regional and State Employment and Unemployment" (press release, January 28, 2014, www.bls.gov/bls/newsrels.htm)
*Seasonally adjusted preliminary data as of December 2013. National figure calculated through a different formula.

# VII. Energy and Environment

# Energy Consumption in 2011

## National Total = 97,387,300,000,000,000 BTUs*

ALPHA ORDER

| RANK | STATE | BTUs | % of USA |
|---|---|---|---|
| 17 | Alabama | 1,931,300,000,000,000 | 2.0% |
| 38 | Alaska | 637,900,000,000,000 | 0.7% |
| 26 | Arizona | 1,431,500,000,000,000 | 1.5% |
| 31 | Arkansas | 1,117,100,000,000,000 | 1.1% |
| 2 | California | 7,858,400,000,000,000 | 8.1% |
| 25 | Colorado | 1,480,800,000,000,000 | 1.5% |
| 35 | Connecticut | 741,600,000,000,000 | 0.8% |
| 48 | Delaware | 271,600,000,000,000 | 0.3% |
| 3 | Florida | 4,217,100,000,000,000 | 4.3% |
| 9 | Georgia | 3,002,100,000,000,000 | 3.1% |
| 47 | Hawaii | 286,000,000,000,000 | 0.3% |
| 42 | Idaho | 525,600,000,000,000 | 0.5% |
| 5 | Illinois | 3,977,800,000,000,000 | 4.1% |
| 10 | Indiana | 2,869,200,000,000,000 | 2.9% |
| 24 | Iowa | 1,512,600,000,000,000 | 1.6% |
| 30 | Kansas | 1,162,500,000,000,000 | 1.2% |
| 18 | Kentucky | 1,911,400,000,000,000 | 2.0% |
| 4 | Louisiana | 4,055,300,000,000,000 | 4.2% |
| 43 | Maine | 412,500,000,000,000 | 0.4% |
| 27 | Maryland | 1,426,400,000,000,000 | 1.5% |
| 28 | Massachusetts | 1,395,100,000,000,000 | 1.4% |
| 11 | Michigan | 2,802,700,000,000,000 | 2.9% |
| 20 | Minnesota | 1,866,600,000,000,000 | 1.9% |
| 29 | Mississippi | 1,163,400,000,000,000 | 1.2% |
| 19 | Missouri | 1,878,100,000,000,000 | 1.9% |
| 44 | Montana | 397,500,000,000,000 | 0.4% |
| 33 | Nebraska | 871,400,000,000,000 | 0.9% |
| 39 | Nevada | 632,500,000,000,000 | 0.6% |
| 46 | New Hampshire | 292,100,000,000,000 | 0.3% |
| 13 | New Jersey | 2,438,500,000,000,000 | 2.5% |
| 37 | New Mexico | 688,000,000,000,000 | 0.7% |
| 8 | New York | 3,614,800,000,000,000 | 3.7% |
| 12 | North Carolina | 2,572,700,000,000,000 | 2.6% |
| 41 | North Dakota | 526,200,000,000,000 | 0.5% |
| 6 | Ohio | 3,827,600,000,000,000 | 3.9% |
| 23 | Oklahoma | 1,594,600,000,000,000 | 1.6% |
| 32 | Oregon | 1,014,200,000,000,000 | 1.0% |
| 7 | Pennsylvania | 3,725,300,000,000,000 | 3.8% |
| 49 | Rhode Island | 183,900,000,000,000 | 0.2% |
| 22 | South Carolina | 1,610,300,000,000,000 | 1.7% |
| 45 | South Dakota | 382,400,000,000,000 | 0.4% |
| 15 | Tennessee | 2,201,100,000,000,000 | 2.3% |
| 1 | Texas | 12,206,600,000,000,000 | 12.5% |
| 34 | Utah | 797,200,000,000,000 | 0.8% |
| 50 | Vermont | 149,300,000,000,000 | 0.2% |
| 14 | Virginia | 2,388,500,000,000,000 | 2.5% |
| 16 | Washington | 2,080,200,000,000,000 | 2.1% |
| 36 | West Virginia | 724,300,000,000,000 | 0.7% |
| 21 | Wisconsin | 1,789,200,000,000,000 | 1.8% |
| 40 | Wyoming | 553,000,000,000,000 | 0.6% |

RANK ORDER

| RANK | STATE | BTUs | % of USA |
|---|---|---|---|
| 1 | Texas | 12,206,600,000,000,000 | 12.5% |
| 2 | California | 7,858,400,000,000,000 | 8.1% |
| 3 | Florida | 4,217,100,000,000,000 | 4.3% |
| 4 | Louisiana | 4,055,300,000,000,000 | 4.2% |
| 5 | Illinois | 3,977,800,000,000,000 | 4.1% |
| 6 | Ohio | 3,827,600,000,000,000 | 3.9% |
| 7 | Pennsylvania | 3,725,300,000,000,000 | 3.8% |
| 8 | New York | 3,614,800,000,000,000 | 3.7% |
| 9 | Georgia | 3,002,100,000,000,000 | 3.1% |
| 10 | Indiana | 2,869,200,000,000,000 | 2.9% |
| 11 | Michigan | 2,802,700,000,000,000 | 2.9% |
| 12 | North Carolina | 2,572,700,000,000,000 | 2.6% |
| 13 | New Jersey | 2,438,500,000,000,000 | 2.5% |
| 14 | Virginia | 2,388,500,000,000,000 | 2.5% |
| 15 | Tennessee | 2,201,100,000,000,000 | 2.3% |
| 16 | Washington | 2,080,200,000,000,000 | 2.1% |
| 17 | Alabama | 1,931,300,000,000,000 | 2.0% |
| 18 | Kentucky | 1,911,400,000,000,000 | 2.0% |
| 19 | Missouri | 1,878,100,000,000,000 | 1.9% |
| 20 | Minnesota | 1,866,600,000,000,000 | 1.9% |
| 21 | Wisconsin | 1,789,200,000,000,000 | 1.8% |
| 22 | South Carolina | 1,610,300,000,000,000 | 1.7% |
| 23 | Oklahoma | 1,594,600,000,000,000 | 1.6% |
| 24 | Iowa | 1,512,600,000,000,000 | 1.6% |
| 25 | Colorado | 1,480,800,000,000,000 | 1.5% |
| 26 | Arizona | 1,431,500,000,000,000 | 1.5% |
| 27 | Maryland | 1,426,400,000,000,000 | 1.5% |
| 28 | Massachusetts | 1,395,100,000,000,000 | 1.4% |
| 29 | Mississippi | 1,163,400,000,000,000 | 1.2% |
| 30 | Kansas | 1,162,500,000,000,000 | 1.2% |
| 31 | Arkansas | 1,117,100,000,000,000 | 1.1% |
| 32 | Oregon | 1,014,200,000,000,000 | 1.0% |
| 33 | Nebraska | 871,400,000,000,000 | 0.9% |
| 34 | Utah | 797,200,000,000,000 | 0.8% |
| 35 | Connecticut | 741,600,000,000,000 | 0.8% |
| 36 | West Virginia | 724,300,000,000,000 | 0.7% |
| 37 | New Mexico | 688,000,000,000,000 | 0.7% |
| 38 | Alaska | 637,900,000,000,000 | 0.7% |
| 39 | Nevada | 632,500,000,000,000 | 0.6% |
| 40 | Wyoming | 553,000,000,000,000 | 0.6% |
| 41 | North Dakota | 526,200,000,000,000 | 0.5% |
| 42 | Idaho | 525,600,000,000,000 | 0.5% |
| 43 | Maine | 412,500,000,000,000 | 0.4% |
| 44 | Montana | 397,500,000,000,000 | 0.4% |
| 45 | South Dakota | 382,400,000,000,000 | 0.4% |
| 46 | New Hampshire | 292,100,000,000,000 | 0.3% |
| 47 | Hawaii | 286,000,000,000,000 | 0.3% |
| 48 | Delaware | 271,600,000,000,000 | 0.3% |
| 49 | Rhode Island | 183,900,000,000,000 | 0.2% |
| 50 | Vermont | 149,300,000,000,000 | 0.2% |
| | District of Columbia | 180,300,000,000,000 | 0.2% |

Source: U.S. Department of Energy, Energy Information Administration
   "State Energy Data 2011: Consumption" (http://www.eia.gov/state/seds/)
*British Thermal Units: The amount of heat required to raise the temperature of one pound of water one degree.  National total
includes 11.1 trillion Btu of net imports of coal coke that are not allocated to the states.

# Per Capita Energy Consumption in 2011

## National Per Capita = 312,551,695 BTUs*

ALPHA ORDER

| RANK | STATE | PER CAPITA |
|------|-------|-----------|
| 13 | Alabama | 402,045,178 |
| 3 | Alaska | 881,247,755 |
| 43 | Arizona | 221,343,788 |
| 17 | Arkansas | 380,149,337 |
| 46 | California | 208,534,497 |
| 33 | Colorado | 289,427,794 |
| 48 | Connecticut | 206,762,898 |
| 30 | Delaware | 299,073,818 |
| 44 | Florida | 220,995,813 |
| 28 | Georgia | 305,947,744 |
| 47 | Hawaii | 207,527,742 |
| 21 | Idaho | 331,871,818 |
| 27 | Illinois | 309,321,673 |
| 9 | Indiana | 440,307,638 |
| 5 | Iowa | 493,652,779 |
| 12 | Kansas | 404,997,795 |
| 10 | Kentucky | 437,710,422 |
| 2 | Louisiana | 886,449,711 |
| 26 | Maine | 310,490,281 |
| 39 | Maryland | 244,264,477 |
| 45 | Massachusetts | 211,154,740 |
| 34 | Michigan | 283,765,968 |
| 18 | Minnesota | 349,073,429 |
| 15 | Mississippi | 390,736,121 |
| 25 | Missouri | 312,548,677 |
| 14 | Montana | 398,429,536 |
| 7 | Nebraska | 473,012,657 |
| 41 | Nevada | 232,534,371 |
| 42 | New Hampshire | 221,656,130 |
| 36 | New Jersey | 276,011,619 |
| 23 | New Mexico | 330,980,231 |
| 49 | New York | 185,358,998 |
| 37 | North Carolina | 266,570,567 |
| 4 | North Dakota | 768,466,863 |
| 22 | Ohio | 331,652,169 |
| 11 | Oklahoma | 421,387,768 |
| 38 | Oregon | 262,187,166 |
| 32 | Pennsylvania | 292,319,146 |
| 50 | Rhode Island | 175,035,169 |
| 19 | South Carolina | 344,570,959 |
| 8 | South Dakota | 464,307,006 |
| 20 | Tennessee | 343,933,322 |
| 6 | Texas | 476,229,156 |
| 35 | Utah | 283,262,867 |
| 40 | Vermont | 238,273,071 |
| 31 | Virginia | 294,717,032 |
| 29 | Washington | 304,868,621 |
| 16 | West Virginia | 390,477,587 |
| 24 | Wisconsin | 313,353,625 |
| 1 | Wyoming | 974,696,663 |

RANK ORDER

| RANK | STATE | PER CAPITA |
|------|-------|-----------|
| 1 | Wyoming | 974,696,663 |
| 2 | Louisiana | 886,449,711 |
| 3 | Alaska | 881,247,755 |
| 4 | North Dakota | 768,466,863 |
| 5 | Iowa | 493,652,779 |
| 6 | Texas | 476,229,156 |
| 7 | Nebraska | 473,012,657 |
| 8 | South Dakota | 464,307,006 |
| 9 | Indiana | 440,307,638 |
| 10 | Kentucky | 437,710,422 |
| 11 | Oklahoma | 421,387,768 |
| 12 | Kansas | 404,997,795 |
| 13 | Alabama | 402,045,178 |
| 14 | Montana | 398,429,536 |
| 15 | Mississippi | 390,736,121 |
| 16 | West Virginia | 390,477,587 |
| 17 | Arkansas | 380,149,337 |
| 18 | Minnesota | 349,073,429 |
| 19 | South Carolina | 344,570,959 |
| 20 | Tennessee | 343,933,322 |
| 21 | Idaho | 331,871,818 |
| 22 | Ohio | 331,652,169 |
| 23 | New Mexico | 330,980,231 |
| 24 | Wisconsin | 313,353,625 |
| 25 | Missouri | 312,548,677 |
| 26 | Maine | 310,490,281 |
| 27 | Illinois | 309,321,673 |
| 28 | Georgia | 305,947,744 |
| 29 | Washington | 304,868,621 |
| 30 | Delaware | 299,073,818 |
| 31 | Virginia | 294,717,032 |
| 32 | Pennsylvania | 292,319,146 |
| 33 | Colorado | 289,427,794 |
| 34 | Michigan | 283,765,968 |
| 35 | Utah | 283,262,867 |
| 36 | New Jersey | 276,011,619 |
| 37 | North Carolina | 266,570,567 |
| 38 | Oregon | 262,187,166 |
| 39 | Maryland | 244,264,477 |
| 40 | Vermont | 238,273,071 |
| 41 | Nevada | 232,534,371 |
| 42 | New Hampshire | 221,656,130 |
| 43 | Arizona | 221,343,788 |
| 44 | Florida | 220,995,813 |
| 45 | Massachusetts | 211,154,740 |
| 46 | California | 208,534,497 |
| 47 | Hawaii | 207,527,742 |
| 48 | Connecticut | 206,762,898 |
| 49 | New York | 185,358,998 |
| 50 | Rhode Island | 175,035,169 |

District of Columbia      291,266,841

Source: CQ Press using data from U.S. Department of Energy, Energy Information Administration
   "State Energy Data 2011: Consumption" (http://www.eia.gov/state/seds/)
*British Thermal Units: The amount of heat required to raise the temperature of one pound of water one degree. National total
includes 11.1 trillion Btu of net imports of coal coke that are not allocated to the states.

# Energy Prices in 2011

## National Rate = $21.71 per Million BTUs*

ALPHA ORDER

| RANK | STATE | RATE |
|---|---|---|
| 38 | Alabama | $19.85 |
| 10 | Alaska | 25.17 |
| 7 | Arizona | 25.23 |
| 41 | Arkansas | 19.63 |
| 13 | California | 24.14 |
| 28 | Colorado | 21.07 |
| 2 | Connecticut | 27.81 |
| 10 | Delaware | 25.17 |
| 9 | Florida | 25.18 |
| 25 | Georgia | 21.30 |
| 1 | Hawaii | 38.41 |
| 44 | Idaho | 19.22 |
| 43 | Illinois | 19.29 |
| 49 | Indiana | 17.52 |
| 47 | Iowa | 17.86 |
| 29 | Kansas | 20.81 |
| 35 | Kentucky | 20.35 |
| 48 | Louisiana | 17.69 |
| 24 | Maine | 21.67 |
| 8 | Maryland | 25.22 |
| 5 | Massachusetts | 25.90 |
| 31 | Michigan | 20.65 |
| 42 | Minnesota | 19.61 |
| 32 | Mississippi | 20.56 |
| 20 | Missouri | 22.26 |
| 23 | Montana | 21.72 |
| 45 | Nebraska | 19.08 |
| 15 | Nevada | 23.16 |
| 4 | New Hampshire | 27.36 |
| 14 | New Jersey | 24.00 |
| 17 | New Mexico | 22.69 |
| 10 | New York | 25.17 |
| 16 | North Carolina | 22.93 |
| 50 | North Dakota | 17.25 |
| 34 | Ohio | 20.43 |
| 40 | Oklahoma | 19.71 |
| 21 | Oregon | 22.02 |
| 18 | Pennsylvania | 22.58 |
| 6 | Rhode Island | 25.88 |
| 27 | South Carolina | 21.24 |
| 37 | South Dakota | 19.91 |
| 22 | Tennessee | 21.92 |
| 33 | Texas | 20.53 |
| 39 | Utah | 19.81 |
| 3 | Vermont | 27.77 |
| 19 | Virginia | 22.50 |
| 26 | Washington | 21.25 |
| 36 | West Virginia | 20.04 |
| 30 | Wisconsin | 20.70 |
| 46 | Wyoming | 17.90 |

RANK ORDER

| RANK | STATE | RATE |
|---|---|---|
| 1 | Hawaii | $38.41 |
| 2 | Connecticut | 27.81 |
| 3 | Vermont | 27.77 |
| 4 | New Hampshire | 27.36 |
| 5 | Massachusetts | 25.90 |
| 6 | Rhode Island | 25.88 |
| 7 | Arizona | 25.23 |
| 8 | Maryland | 25.22 |
| 9 | Florida | 25.18 |
| 10 | Alaska | 25.17 |
| 10 | Delaware | 25.17 |
| 10 | New York | 25.17 |
| 13 | California | 24.14 |
| 14 | New Jersey | 24.00 |
| 15 | Nevada | 23.16 |
| 16 | North Carolina | 22.93 |
| 17 | New Mexico | 22.69 |
| 18 | Pennsylvania | 22.58 |
| 19 | Virginia | 22.50 |
| 20 | Missouri | 22.26 |
| 21 | Oregon | 22.02 |
| 22 | Tennessee | 21.92 |
| 23 | Montana | 21.72 |
| 24 | Maine | 21.67 |
| 25 | Georgia | 21.30 |
| 26 | Washington | 21.25 |
| 27 | South Carolina | 21.24 |
| 28 | Colorado | 21.07 |
| 29 | Kansas | 20.81 |
| 30 | Wisconsin | 20.70 |
| 31 | Michigan | 20.65 |
| 32 | Mississippi | 20.56 |
| 33 | Texas | 20.53 |
| 34 | Ohio | 20.43 |
| 35 | Kentucky | 20.35 |
| 36 | West Virginia | 20.04 |
| 37 | South Dakota | 19.91 |
| 38 | Alabama | 19.85 |
| 39 | Utah | 19.81 |
| 40 | Oklahoma | 19.71 |
| 41 | Arkansas | 19.63 |
| 42 | Minnesota | 19.61 |
| 43 | Illinois | 19.29 |
| 44 | Idaho | 19.22 |
| 45 | Nebraska | 19.08 |
| 46 | Wyoming | 17.90 |
| 47 | Iowa | 17.86 |
| 48 | Louisiana | 17.69 |
| 49 | Indiana | 17.52 |
| 50 | North Dakota | 17.25 |
| | District of Columbia | 27.04 |

Source: U.S. Department of Energy, Energy Information Administration
    "State Energy Data 2011: Prices and Expenditures" (http://www.eia.gov/state/seds/)
*British Thermal Units: The amount of heat required to raise the temperature of one pound of water one degree.

# Energy Expenditures in 2011

## National Total = $1,394,088,400,000*

ALPHA ORDER

| RANK | STATE | EXPENDITURES | % of USA |
|---|---|---|---|
| 19 | Alabama | $24,479,300,000 | 1.8% |
| 39 | Alaska | 7,739,300,000 | 0.6% |
| 24 | Arizona | 22,464,700,000 | 1.6% |
| 33 | Arkansas | 14,046,700,000 | 1.0% |
| 2 | California | 136,096,400,000 | 9.8% |
| 27 | Colorado | 19,332,700,000 | 1.4% |
| 29 | Connecticut | 15,365,100,000 | 1.1% |
| 48 | Delaware | 3,956,500,000 | 0.3% |
| 3 | Florida | 68,013,200,000 | 4.9% |
| 10 | Georgia | 42,404,700,000 | 3.0% |
| 40 | Hawaii | 7,608,300,000 | 0.5% |
| 42 | Idaho | 6,585,600,000 | 0.5% |
| 7 | Illinois | 50,925,200,000 | 3.7% |
| 14 | Indiana | 32,518,500,000 | 2.3% |
| 28 | Iowa | 17,164,100,000 | 1.2% |
| 32 | Kansas | 14,866,800,000 | 1.1% |
| 23 | Kentucky | 23,149,200,000 | 1.7% |
| 8 | Louisiana | 46,833,100,000 | 3.4% |
| 41 | Maine | 7,317,300,000 | 0.5% |
| 22 | Maryland | 23,203,900,000 | 1.7% |
| 16 | Massachusetts | 27,248,300,000 | 2.0% |
| 11 | Michigan | 39,498,900,000 | 2.8% |
| 21 | Minnesota | 24,316,200,000 | 1.7% |
| 30 | Mississippi | 15,169,000,000 | 1.1% |
| 18 | Missouri | 26,750,300,000 | 1.9% |
| 45 | Montana | 5,576,300,000 | 0.4% |
| 35 | Nebraska | 9,971,200,000 | 0.7% |
| 36 | Nevada | 9,670,800,000 | 0.7% |
| 44 | New Hampshire | 5,964,600,000 | 0.4% |
| 9 | New Jersey | 43,214,000,000 | 3.1% |
| 38 | New Mexico | 8,845,800,000 | 0.6% |
| 4 | New York | 65,876,900,000 | 4.7% |
| 12 | North Carolina | 36,102,400,000 | 2.6% |
| 43 | North Dakota | 6,409,300,000 | 0.5% |
| 6 | Ohio | 50,995,500,000 | 3.7% |
| 26 | Oklahoma | 19,765,500,000 | 1.4% |
| 31 | Oregon | 14,941,000,000 | 1.1% |
| 5 | Pennsylvania | 55,163,800,000 | 4.0% |
| 49 | Rhode Island | 3,818,300,000 | 0.3% |
| 25 | South Carolina | 21,174,900,000 | 1.5% |
| 47 | South Dakota | 4,546,700,000 | 0.3% |
| 15 | Tennessee | 29,699,400,000 | 2.1% |
| 1 | Texas | 169,290,000,000 | 12.1% |
| 34 | Utah | 10,430,700,000 | 0.7% |
| 50 | Vermont | 3,151,000,000 | 0.2% |
| 13 | Virginia | 33,914,700,000 | 2.4% |
| 17 | Washington | 27,124,400,000 | 1.9% |
| 37 | West Virginia | 8,887,900,000 | 0.6% |
| 20 | Wisconsin | 24,356,400,000 | 1.7% |
| 46 | Wyoming | 5,406,100,000 | 0.4% |

RANK ORDER

| RANK | STATE | EXPENDITURES | % of USA |
|---|---|---|---|
| 1 | Texas | $169,290,000,000 | 12.1% |
| 2 | California | 136,096,400,000 | 9.8% |
| 3 | Florida | 68,013,200,000 | 4.9% |
| 4 | New York | 65,876,900,000 | 4.7% |
| 5 | Pennsylvania | 55,163,800,000 | 4.0% |
| 6 | Ohio | 50,995,500,000 | 3.7% |
| 7 | Illinois | 50,925,200,000 | 3.7% |
| 8 | Louisiana | 46,833,100,000 | 3.4% |
| 9 | New Jersey | 43,214,000,000 | 3.1% |
| 10 | Georgia | 42,404,700,000 | 3.0% |
| 11 | Michigan | 39,498,900,000 | 2.8% |
| 12 | North Carolina | 36,102,400,000 | 2.6% |
| 13 | Virginia | 33,914,700,000 | 2.4% |
| 14 | Indiana | 32,518,500,000 | 2.3% |
| 15 | Tennessee | 29,699,400,000 | 2.1% |
| 16 | Massachusetts | 27,248,300,000 | 2.0% |
| 17 | Washington | 27,124,400,000 | 1.9% |
| 18 | Missouri | 26,750,300,000 | 1.9% |
| 19 | Alabama | 24,479,300,000 | 1.8% |
| 20 | Wisconsin | 24,356,400,000 | 1.7% |
| 21 | Minnesota | 24,316,200,000 | 1.7% |
| 22 | Maryland | 23,203,900,000 | 1.7% |
| 23 | Kentucky | 23,149,200,000 | 1.7% |
| 24 | Arizona | 22,464,700,000 | 1.6% |
| 25 | South Carolina | 21,174,900,000 | 1.5% |
| 26 | Oklahoma | 19,765,500,000 | 1.4% |
| 27 | Colorado | 19,332,700,000 | 1.4% |
| 28 | Iowa | 17,164,100,000 | 1.2% |
| 29 | Connecticut | 15,365,100,000 | 1.1% |
| 30 | Mississippi | 15,169,000,000 | 1.1% |
| 31 | Oregon | 14,941,000,000 | 1.1% |
| 32 | Kansas | 14,866,800,000 | 1.1% |
| 33 | Arkansas | 14,046,700,000 | 1.0% |
| 34 | Utah | 10,430,700,000 | 0.7% |
| 35 | Nebraska | 9,971,200,000 | 0.7% |
| 36 | Nevada | 9,670,800,000 | 0.7% |
| 37 | West Virginia | 8,887,900,000 | 0.6% |
| 38 | New Mexico | 8,845,800,000 | 0.6% |
| 39 | Alaska | 7,739,300,000 | 0.6% |
| 40 | Hawaii | 7,608,300,000 | 0.5% |
| 41 | Maine | 7,317,300,000 | 0.5% |
| 42 | Idaho | 6,585,600,000 | 0.5% |
| 43 | North Dakota | 6,409,300,000 | 0.5% |
| 44 | New Hampshire | 5,964,600,000 | 0.4% |
| 45 | Montana | 5,576,300,000 | 0.4% |
| 46 | Wyoming | 5,406,100,000 | 0.4% |
| 47 | South Dakota | 4,546,700,000 | 0.3% |
| 48 | Delaware | 3,956,500,000 | 0.3% |
| 49 | Rhode Island | 3,818,300,000 | 0.3% |
| 50 | Vermont | 3,151,000,000 | 0.2% |
| | District of Columbia | 2,396,000,000 | 0.2% |

Source: U.S. Department of Energy, Energy Information Administration
    "State Energy Data 2011: Prices and Expenditures" (http://www.eia.gov/state/seds/)
*The national total includes $342 million for coal coke net imports, which are not allocated to the states.

# Per Capita Energy Expenditures in 2011

## National Per Capita = $4,474

| ALPHA ORDER | | | | RANK ORDER | | |
|---|---|---|---|---|---|---|
| RANK | STATE | PER CAPITA | | RANK | STATE | PER CAPITA |
| 15 | Alabama | $5,096 | | 1 | Alaska | $10,692 |
| 1 | Alaska | 10,692 | | 2 | Louisiana | 10,237 |
| 49 | Arizona | 3,474 | | 3 | Wyoming | 9,529 |
| 21 | Arkansas | 4,780 | | 4 | North Dakota | 9,360 |
| 46 | California | 3,612 | | 5 | Texas | 6,605 |
| 42 | Colorado | 3,779 | | 6 | Iowa | 5,602 |
| 31 | Connecticut | 4,284 | | 7 | Montana | 5,589 |
| 28 | Delaware | 4,357 | | 8 | Hawaii | 5,521 |
| 47 | Florida | 3,564 | | 8 | South Dakota | 5,521 |
| 30 | Georgia | 4,322 | | 10 | Maine | 5,508 |
| 8 | Hawaii | 5,521 | | 11 | Nebraska | 5,413 |
| 35 | Idaho | 4,158 | | 12 | Kentucky | 5,301 |
| 40 | Illinois | 3,960 | | 13 | Oklahoma | 5,223 |
| 18 | Indiana | 4,990 | | 14 | Kansas | 5,179 |
| 6 | Iowa | 5,602 | | 15 | Alabama | 5,096 |
| 14 | Kansas | 5,179 | | 16 | Mississippi | 5,095 |
| 12 | Kentucky | 5,301 | | 17 | Vermont | 5,029 |
| 2 | Louisiana | 10,237 | | 18 | Indiana | 4,990 |
| 10 | Maine | 5,508 | | 19 | New Jersey | 4,891 |
| 39 | Maryland | 3,974 | | 20 | West Virginia | 4,792 |
| 36 | Massachusetts | 4,124 | | 21 | Arkansas | 4,780 |
| 37 | Michigan | 3,999 | | 22 | Tennessee | 4,641 |
| 23 | Minnesota | 4,547 | | 23 | Minnesota | 4,547 |
| 16 | Mississippi | 5,095 | | 24 | South Carolina | 4,531 |
| 26 | Missouri | 4,452 | | 25 | New Hampshire | 4,526 |
| 7 | Montana | 5,589 | | 26 | Missouri | 4,452 |
| 11 | Nebraska | 5,413 | | 27 | Ohio | 4,419 |
| 48 | Nevada | 3,555 | | 28 | Delaware | 4,357 |
| 25 | New Hampshire | 4,526 | | 29 | Pennsylvania | 4,329 |
| 19 | New Jersey | 4,891 | | 30 | Georgia | 4,322 |
| 33 | New Mexico | 4,256 | | 31 | Connecticut | 4,284 |
| 50 | New York | 3,378 | | 32 | Wisconsin | 4,266 |
| 43 | North Carolina | 3,741 | | 33 | New Mexico | 4,256 |
| 4 | North Dakota | 9,360 | | 34 | Virginia | 4,185 |
| 27 | Ohio | 4,419 | | 35 | Idaho | 4,158 |
| 13 | Oklahoma | 5,223 | | 36 | Massachusetts | 4,124 |
| 41 | Oregon | 3,862 | | 37 | Michigan | 3,999 |
| 29 | Pennsylvania | 4,329 | | 38 | Washington | 3,975 |
| 45 | Rhode Island | 3,634 | | 39 | Maryland | 3,974 |
| 24 | South Carolina | 4,531 | | 40 | Illinois | 3,960 |
| 8 | South Dakota | 5,521 | | 41 | Oregon | 3,862 |
| 22 | Tennessee | 4,641 | | 42 | Colorado | 3,779 |
| 5 | Texas | 6,605 | | 43 | North Carolina | 3,741 |
| 44 | Utah | 3,706 | | 44 | Utah | 3,706 |
| 17 | Vermont | 5,029 | | 45 | Rhode Island | 3,634 |
| 34 | Virginia | 4,185 | | 46 | California | 3,612 |
| 38 | Washington | 3,975 | | 47 | Florida | 3,564 |
| 20 | West Virginia | 4,792 | | 48 | Nevada | 3,555 |
| 32 | Wisconsin | 4,266 | | 49 | Arizona | 3,474 |
| 3 | Wyoming | 9,529 | | 50 | New York | 3,378 |
| | | | | | District of Columbia | 3,871 |

Source: CQ Press using data from U.S. Department of Energy, Energy Information Administration
"State Energy Data 2011: Prices and Expenditures" (http://www.eia.gov/state/seds/)

# Average Monthly Electric Bill for Industrial Customers in 2012

## National Average = $7,483 per Month

<table>
<tr><td colspan="3"><u>ALPHA ORDER</u></td><td colspan="3"><u>RANK ORDER</u></td></tr>
<tr><td>RANK</td><td>STATE</td><td>MONTHLY BILL</td><td>RANK</td><td>STATE</td><td>MONTHLY BILL</td></tr>
<tr><td>8</td><td>Alabama</td><td>$24,425</td><td>1</td><td>Hawaii</td><td>$133,212</td></tr>
<tr><td>13</td><td>Alaska</td><td>15,329</td><td>2</td><td>Tennessee</td><td>85,815</td></tr>
<tr><td>24</td><td>Arizona</td><td>8,754</td><td>3</td><td>Vermont</td><td>53,495</td></tr>
<tr><td>48</td><td>Arkansas</td><td>2,386</td><td>4</td><td>Illinois</td><td>36,206</td></tr>
<tr><td>33</td><td>California</td><td>5,561</td><td>5</td><td>South Carolina</td><td>32,173</td></tr>
<tr><td>32</td><td>Colorado</td><td>5,571</td><td>6</td><td>Wisconsin</td><td>31,542</td></tr>
<tr><td>26</td><td>Connecticut</td><td>8,104</td><td>7</td><td>Kentucky</td><td>27,621</td></tr>
<tr><td>10</td><td>Delaware</td><td>22,464</td><td>8</td><td>Alabama</td><td>24,425</td></tr>
<tr><td>29</td><td>Florida</td><td>6,316</td><td>9</td><td>Virginia</td><td>24,389</td></tr>
<tr><td>23</td><td>Georgia</td><td>8,972</td><td>10</td><td>Delaware</td><td>22,464</td></tr>
<tr><td>1</td><td>Hawaii</td><td>133,212</td><td>11</td><td>Nevada</td><td>19,800</td></tr>
<tr><td>49</td><td>Idaho</td><td>1,648</td><td>12</td><td>Michigan</td><td>15,471</td></tr>
<tr><td>4</td><td>Illinois</td><td>36,206</td><td>13</td><td>Alaska</td><td>15,329</td></tr>
<tr><td>16</td><td>Indiana</td><td>13,734</td><td>14</td><td>Ohio</td><td>14,150</td></tr>
<tr><td>18</td><td>Iowa</td><td>11,868</td><td>15</td><td>North Carolina</td><td>13,843</td></tr>
<tr><td>45</td><td>Kansas</td><td>2,607</td><td>16</td><td>Indiana</td><td>13,734</td></tr>
<tr><td>7</td><td>Kentucky</td><td>27,621</td><td>17</td><td>Mississippi</td><td>12,267</td></tr>
<tr><td>28</td><td>Louisiana</td><td>6,655</td><td>18</td><td>Iowa</td><td>11,868</td></tr>
<tr><td>27</td><td>Maine</td><td>7,243</td><td>19</td><td>Pennsylvania</td><td>11,591</td></tr>
<tr><td>44</td><td>Maryland</td><td>3,393</td><td>20</td><td>Minnesota</td><td>11,585</td></tr>
<tr><td>25</td><td>Massachusetts</td><td>8,383</td><td>21</td><td>Missouri</td><td>9,707</td></tr>
<tr><td>12</td><td>Michigan</td><td>15,471</td><td>22</td><td>New York</td><td>9,390</td></tr>
<tr><td>20</td><td>Minnesota</td><td>11,585</td><td>23</td><td>Georgia</td><td>8,972</td></tr>
<tr><td>17</td><td>Mississippi</td><td>12,267</td><td>24</td><td>Arizona</td><td>8,754</td></tr>
<tr><td>21</td><td>Missouri</td><td>9,707</td><td>25</td><td>Massachusetts</td><td>8,383</td></tr>
<tr><td>46</td><td>Montana</td><td>2,439</td><td>26</td><td>Connecticut</td><td>8,104</td></tr>
<tr><td>50</td><td>Nebraska</td><td>1,285</td><td>27</td><td>Maine</td><td>7,243</td></tr>
<tr><td>11</td><td>Nevada</td><td>19,800</td><td>28</td><td>Louisiana</td><td>6,655</td></tr>
<tr><td>31</td><td>New Hampshire</td><td>5,590</td><td>29</td><td>Florida</td><td>6,316</td></tr>
<tr><td>35</td><td>New Jersey</td><td>5,344</td><td>30</td><td>North Dakota</td><td>6,079</td></tr>
<tr><td>40</td><td>New Mexico</td><td>4,276</td><td>31</td><td>New Hampshire</td><td>5,590</td></tr>
<tr><td>22</td><td>New York</td><td>9,390</td><td>32</td><td>Colorado</td><td>5,571</td></tr>
<tr><td>15</td><td>North Carolina</td><td>13,843</td><td>33</td><td>California</td><td>5,561</td></tr>
<tr><td>30</td><td>North Dakota</td><td>6,079</td><td>34</td><td>Wyoming</td><td>5,487</td></tr>
<tr><td>14</td><td>Ohio</td><td>14,150</td><td>35</td><td>New Jersey</td><td>5,344</td></tr>
<tr><td>42</td><td>Oklahoma</td><td>3,850</td><td>36</td><td>South Dakota</td><td>5,159</td></tr>
<tr><td>47</td><td>Oregon</td><td>2,399</td><td>37</td><td>West Virginia</td><td>5,013</td></tr>
<tr><td>19</td><td>Pennsylvania</td><td>11,591</td><td>38</td><td>Utah</td><td>4,822</td></tr>
<tr><td>41</td><td>Rhode Island</td><td>4,264</td><td>39</td><td>Texas</td><td>4,750</td></tr>
<tr><td>5</td><td>South Carolina</td><td>32,173</td><td>40</td><td>New Mexico</td><td>4,276</td></tr>
<tr><td>36</td><td>South Dakota</td><td>5,159</td><td>41</td><td>Rhode Island</td><td>4,264</td></tr>
<tr><td>2</td><td>Tennessee</td><td>85,815</td><td>42</td><td>Oklahoma</td><td>3,850</td></tr>
<tr><td>39</td><td>Texas</td><td>4,750</td><td>43</td><td>Washington</td><td>3,427</td></tr>
<tr><td>38</td><td>Utah</td><td>4,822</td><td>44</td><td>Maryland</td><td>3,393</td></tr>
<tr><td>3</td><td>Vermont</td><td>53,495</td><td>45</td><td>Kansas</td><td>2,607</td></tr>
<tr><td>9</td><td>Virginia</td><td>24,389</td><td>46</td><td>Montana</td><td>2,439</td></tr>
<tr><td>43</td><td>Washington</td><td>3,427</td><td>47</td><td>Oregon</td><td>2,399</td></tr>
<tr><td>37</td><td>West Virginia</td><td>5,013</td><td>48</td><td>Arkansas</td><td>2,386</td></tr>
<tr><td>6</td><td>Wisconsin</td><td>31,542</td><td>49</td><td>Idaho</td><td>1,648</td></tr>
<tr><td>34</td><td>Wyoming</td><td>5,487</td><td>50</td><td>Nebraska</td><td>1,285</td></tr>
<tr><td colspan="3"></td><td colspan="2">District of Columbia</td><td>993,225</td></tr>
</table>

Source: U.S. Department of Energy, Energy Information Administration
"Electric Sales, Revenue and Average Price 2012" (http://www.eia.gov/electricity/sales_revenue_price/index.cfm)

# Average Monthly Electric Bill for Commercial Customers in 2012

## National Average = $629 per Month

ALPHA ORDER

| RANK | STATE | MONTHLY BILL |
|---|---|---|
| 23 | Alabama | $541 |
| 9 | Alaska | 733 |
| 6 | Arizona | 772 |
| 46 | Arkansas | 428 |
| 8 | California | 742 |
| 41 | Colorado | 449 |
| 3 | Connecticut | 1,053 |
| 10 | Delaware | 702 |
| 14 | Florida | 639 |
| 12 | Georgia | 670 |
| 1 | Hawaii | 1,566 |
| 50 | Idaho | 334 |
| 20 | Illinois | 573 |
| 25 | Indiana | 531 |
| 48 | Iowa | 368 |
| 25 | Kansas | 531 |
| 39 | Kentucky | 458 |
| 21 | Louisiana | 560 |
| 44 | Maine | 437 |
| 2 | Maryland | 1,060 |
| 27 | Massachusetts | 525 |
| 11 | Michigan | 673 |
| 18 | Minnesota | 595 |
| 36 | Mississippi | 464 |
| 22 | Missouri | 558 |
| 48 | Montana | 368 |
| 44 | Nebraska | 437 |
| 43 | Nevada | 440 |
| 35 | New Hampshire | 475 |
| 5 | New Jersey | 833 |
| 29 | New Mexico | 518 |
| 4 | New York | 919 |
| 31 | North Carolina | 515 |
| 23 | North Dakota | 541 |
| 17 | Ohio | 602 |
| 40 | Oklahoma | 454 |
| 38 | Oregon | 460 |
| 34 | Pennsylvania | 491 |
| 16 | Rhode Island | 623 |
| 32 | South Carolina | 497 |
| 42 | South Dakota | 446 |
| 29 | Tennessee | 518 |
| 13 | Texas | 668 |
| 15 | Utah | 626 |
| 36 | Vermont | 464 |
| 7 | Virginia | 751 |
| 27 | Washington | 525 |
| 47 | West Virginia | 393 |
| 18 | Wisconsin | 595 |
| 33 | Wyoming | 492 |

RANK ORDER

| RANK | STATE | MONTHLY BILL |
|---|---|---|
| 1 | Hawaii | $1,566 |
| 2 | Maryland | 1,060 |
| 3 | Connecticut | 1,053 |
| 4 | New York | 919 |
| 5 | New Jersey | 833 |
| 6 | Arizona | 772 |
| 7 | Virginia | 751 |
| 8 | California | 742 |
| 9 | Alaska | 733 |
| 10 | Delaware | 702 |
| 11 | Michigan | 673 |
| 12 | Georgia | 670 |
| 13 | Texas | 668 |
| 14 | Florida | 639 |
| 15 | Utah | 626 |
| 16 | Rhode Island | 623 |
| 17 | Ohio | 602 |
| 18 | Minnesota | 595 |
| 18 | Wisconsin | 595 |
| 20 | Illinois | 573 |
| 21 | Louisiana | 560 |
| 22 | Missouri | 558 |
| 23 | Alabama | 541 |
| 23 | North Dakota | 541 |
| 25 | Indiana | 531 |
| 25 | Kansas | 531 |
| 27 | Massachusetts | 525 |
| 27 | Washington | 525 |
| 29 | New Mexico | 518 |
| 29 | Tennessee | 518 |
| 31 | North Carolina | 515 |
| 32 | South Carolina | 497 |
| 33 | Wyoming | 492 |
| 34 | Pennsylvania | 491 |
| 35 | New Hampshire | 475 |
| 36 | Mississippi | 464 |
| 36 | Vermont | 464 |
| 38 | Oregon | 460 |
| 39 | Kentucky | 458 |
| 40 | Oklahoma | 454 |
| 41 | Colorado | 449 |
| 42 | South Dakota | 446 |
| 43 | Nevada | 440 |
| 44 | Maine | 437 |
| 44 | Nebraska | 437 |
| 46 | Arkansas | 428 |
| 47 | West Virginia | 393 |
| 48 | Iowa | 368 |
| 48 | Montana | 368 |
| 50 | Idaho | 334 |
| | District of Columbia | 3,288 |

Source: U.S. Department of Energy, Energy Information Administration
"Electric Sales, Revenue and Average Price 2012" (http://www.eia.gov/electricity/sales_revenue_price/index.cfm)

# Average Monthly Electric Bill for Residential Customers in 2012

## National Average = $107 per Month

ALPHA ORDER

| RANK | STATE | MONTHLY BILL |
|------|-------|--------------|
| 2 | Alabama | $135 |
| 14 | Alaska | 117 |
| 13 | Arizona | 120 |
| 28 | Arkansas | 104 |
| 40 | California | 88 |
| 47 | Colorado | 81 |
| 7 | Connecticut | 127 |
| 5 | Delaware | 128 |
| 9 | Florida | 123 |
| 9 | Georgia | 123 |
| 1 | Hawaii | 203 |
| 40 | Idaho | 88 |
| 43 | Illinois | 87 |
| 25 | Indiana | 105 |
| 35 | Iowa | 94 |
| 22 | Kansas | 106 |
| 20 | Kentucky | 107 |
| 25 | Louisiana | 105 |
| 49 | Maine | 78 |
| 4 | Maryland | 129 |
| 35 | Massachusetts | 94 |
| 34 | Michigan | 95 |
| 39 | Minnesota | 90 |
| 12 | Mississippi | 122 |
| 18 | Missouri | 108 |
| 45 | Montana | 85 |
| 29 | Nebraska | 100 |
| 16 | Nevada | 111 |
| 30 | New Hampshire | 99 |
| 17 | New Jersey | 109 |
| 50 | New Mexico | 75 |
| 22 | New York | 106 |
| 14 | North Carolina | 117 |
| 30 | North Dakota | 99 |
| 25 | Ohio | 105 |
| 18 | Oklahoma | 108 |
| 35 | Oregon | 94 |
| 20 | Pennsylvania | 107 |
| 44 | Rhode Island | 86 |
| 3 | South Carolina | 132 |
| 30 | South Dakota | 99 |
| 9 | Tennessee | 123 |
| 5 | Texas | 128 |
| 48 | Utah | 79 |
| 33 | Vermont | 96 |
| 8 | Virginia | 124 |
| 40 | Washington | 88 |
| 22 | West Virginia | 106 |
| 38 | Wisconsin | 93 |
| 45 | Wyoming | 85 |

RANK ORDER

| RANK | STATE | MONTHLY BILL |
|------|-------|--------------|
| 1 | Hawaii | $203 |
| 2 | Alabama | 135 |
| 3 | South Carolina | 132 |
| 4 | Maryland | 129 |
| 5 | Delaware | 128 |
| 5 | Texas | 128 |
| 7 | Connecticut | 127 |
| 8 | Virginia | 124 |
| 9 | Florida | 123 |
| 9 | Georgia | 123 |
| 9 | Tennessee | 123 |
| 12 | Mississippi | 122 |
| 13 | Arizona | 120 |
| 14 | Alaska | 117 |
| 14 | North Carolina | 117 |
| 16 | Nevada | 111 |
| 17 | New Jersey | 109 |
| 18 | Missouri | 108 |
| 18 | Oklahoma | 108 |
| 20 | Kentucky | 107 |
| 20 | Pennsylvania | 107 |
| 22 | Kansas | 106 |
| 22 | New York | 106 |
| 22 | West Virginia | 106 |
| 25 | Indiana | 105 |
| 25 | Louisiana | 105 |
| 25 | Ohio | 105 |
| 28 | Arkansas | 104 |
| 29 | Nebraska | 100 |
| 30 | New Hampshire | 99 |
| 30 | North Dakota | 99 |
| 30 | South Dakota | 99 |
| 33 | Vermont | 96 |
| 34 | Michigan | 95 |
| 35 | Iowa | 94 |
| 35 | Massachusetts | 94 |
| 35 | Oregon | 94 |
| 38 | Wisconsin | 93 |
| 39 | Minnesota | 90 |
| 40 | California | 88 |
| 40 | Idaho | 88 |
| 40 | Washington | 88 |
| 43 | Illinois | 87 |
| 44 | Rhode Island | 86 |
| 45 | Montana | 85 |
| 45 | Wyoming | 85 |
| 47 | Colorado | 81 |
| 48 | Utah | 79 |
| 49 | Maine | 78 |
| 50 | New Mexico | 75 |
| | District of Columbia | 89 |

Source: U.S. Department of Energy, Energy Information Administration
"Electric Sales, Revenue and Average Price 2012" (http://www.eia.gov/electricity/sales_revenue_price/index.cfm)

# Electricity Generated through Renewable Sources in 2010

## National Total = 427,376,076,000 Kilowatthours*

ALPHA ORDER

| RANK | STATE | KWH | % of USA |
|---|---|---|---|
| 6 | Alabama | 11,081,240,000 | 2.6% |
| 44 | Alaska | 1,452,053,000 | 0.3% |
| 14 | Arizona | 6,941,067,000 | 1.6% |
| 20 | Arkansas | 5,282,905,000 | 1.2% |
| 2 | California | 58,880,591,000 | 13.8% |
| 22 | Colorado | 5,132,796,000 | 1.2% |
| 45 | Connecticut | 1,130,327,000 | 0.3% |
| 50 | Delaware | 138,197,000 | 0.0% |
| 23 | Florida | 4,664,197,000 | 1.1% |
| 18 | Georgia | 6,502,265,000 | 1.5% |
| 48 | Hawaii | 817,391,000 | 0.2% |
| 9 | Idaho | 10,168,254,000 | 2.4% |
| 21 | Illinois | 5,256,702,000 | 1.2% |
| 30 | Indiana | 3,699,378,000 | 0.9% |
| 8 | Iowa | 10,308,651,000 | 2.4% |
| 32 | Kansas | 3,472,565,000 | 0.8% |
| 33 | Kentucky | 3,020,121,000 | 0.7% |
| 31 | Louisiana | 3,576,570,000 | 0.8% |
| 11 | Maine | 7,962,664,000 | 1.9% |
| 38 | Maryland | 2,241,061,000 | 0.5% |
| 37 | Massachusetts | 2,270,073,000 | 0.5% |
| 28 | Michigan | 4,083,005,000 | 1.0% |
| 12 | Minnesota | 7,480,043,000 | 1.8% |
| 42 | Mississippi | 1,504,270,000 | 0.4% |
| 35 | Missouri | 2,526,944,000 | 0.6% |
| 7 | Montana | 10,441,819,000 | 2.4% |
| 41 | Nebraska | 1,807,009,000 | 0.4% |
| 25 | Nevada | 4,443,943,000 | 1.0% |
| 34 | New Hampshire | 2,709,801,000 | 0.6% |
| 47 | New Jersey | 868,173,000 | 0.2% |
| 39 | New Mexico | 2,071,802,000 | 0.5% |
| 4 | New York | 30,286,245,000 | 7.1% |
| 15 | North Carolina | 6,839,691,000 | 1.6% |
| 19 | North Dakota | 6,150,146,000 | 1.4% |
| 46 | Ohio | 1,129,113,000 | 0.3% |
| 13 | Oklahoma | 6,968,744,000 | 1.6% |
| 3 | Oregon | 35,299,140,000 | 8.3% |
| 17 | Pennsylvania | 6,577,376,000 | 1.5% |
| 49 | Rhode Island | 143,779,000 | 0.0% |
| 27 | South Carolina | 4,249,508,000 | 1.0% |
| 16 | South Dakota | 6,610,551,000 | 1.5% |
| 10 | Tennessee | 9,125,345,000 | 2.1% |
| 5 | Texas | 28,966,660,000 | 6.8% |
| 43 | Utah | 1,476,479,000 | 0.3% |
| 40 | Vermont | 1,829,226,000 | 0.4% |
| 29 | Virginia | 3,719,831,000 | 0.9% |
| 1 | Washington | 74,905,346,000 | 17.5% |
| 36 | West Virginia | 2,306,533,000 | 0.5% |
| 24 | Wisconsin | 4,585,808,000 | 1.1% |
| 26 | Wyoming | 4,270,680,000 | 1.0% |

RANK ORDER

| RANK | STATE | KWH | % of USA |
|---|---|---|---|
| 1 | Washington | 74,905,346,000 | 17.5% |
| 2 | California | 58,880,591,000 | 13.8% |
| 3 | Oregon | 35,299,140,000 | 8.3% |
| 4 | New York | 30,286,245,000 | 7.1% |
| 5 | Texas | 28,966,660,000 | 6.8% |
| 6 | Alabama | 11,081,240,000 | 2.6% |
| 7 | Montana | 10,441,819,000 | 2.4% |
| 8 | Iowa | 10,308,651,000 | 2.4% |
| 9 | Idaho | 10,168,254,000 | 2.4% |
| 10 | Tennessee | 9,125,345,000 | 2.1% |
| 11 | Maine | 7,962,664,000 | 1.9% |
| 12 | Minnesota | 7,480,043,000 | 1.8% |
| 13 | Oklahoma | 6,968,744,000 | 1.6% |
| 14 | Arizona | 6,941,067,000 | 1.6% |
| 15 | North Carolina | 6,839,691,000 | 1.6% |
| 16 | South Dakota | 6,610,551,000 | 1.5% |
| 17 | Pennsylvania | 6,577,376,000 | 1.5% |
| 18 | Georgia | 6,502,265,000 | 1.5% |
| 19 | North Dakota | 6,150,146,000 | 1.4% |
| 20 | Arkansas | 5,282,905,000 | 1.2% |
| 21 | Illinois | 5,256,702,000 | 1.2% |
| 22 | Colorado | 5,132,796,000 | 1.2% |
| 23 | Florida | 4,664,197,000 | 1.1% |
| 24 | Wisconsin | 4,585,808,000 | 1.1% |
| 25 | Nevada | 4,443,943,000 | 1.0% |
| 26 | Wyoming | 4,270,680,000 | 1.0% |
| 27 | South Carolina | 4,249,508,000 | 1.0% |
| 28 | Michigan | 4,083,005,000 | 1.0% |
| 29 | Virginia | 3,719,831,000 | 0.9% |
| 30 | Indiana | 3,699,378,000 | 0.9% |
| 31 | Louisiana | 3,576,570,000 | 0.8% |
| 32 | Kansas | 3,472,565,000 | 0.8% |
| 33 | Kentucky | 3,020,121,000 | 0.7% |
| 34 | New Hampshire | 2,709,801,000 | 0.6% |
| 35 | Missouri | 2,526,944,000 | 0.6% |
| 36 | West Virginia | 2,306,533,000 | 0.5% |
| 37 | Massachusetts | 2,270,073,000 | 0.5% |
| 38 | Maryland | 2,241,061,000 | 0.5% |
| 39 | New Mexico | 2,071,802,000 | 0.5% |
| 40 | Vermont | 1,829,226,000 | 0.4% |
| 41 | Nebraska | 1,807,009,000 | 0.4% |
| 42 | Mississippi | 1,504,270,000 | 0.4% |
| 43 | Utah | 1,476,479,000 | 0.3% |
| 44 | Alaska | 1,452,053,000 | 0.3% |
| 45 | Connecticut | 1,130,327,000 | 0.3% |
| 46 | Ohio | 1,129,113,000 | 0.3% |
| 47 | New Jersey | 868,173,000 | 0.2% |
| 48 | Hawaii | 817,391,000 | 0.2% |
| 49 | Rhode Island | 143,779,000 | 0.0% |
| 50 | Delaware | 138,197,000 | 0.0% |
| | District of Columbia** | NA | NA |

Source: U.S. Department of Energy, Energy Information Administration
"Renewable Energy Trends, 2010" (http://www.eia.gov/renewable/annual/trends/)
*Includes hydroelectric, geothermal, solar, wind, MSW/landfill gas, wood/wood waste and other biomass.
**Not reported.

# Percent of Electricity Generated through Renewable Sources in 2010

## National Percent = 10.4%*

ALPHA ORDER

| RANK | STATE | PERCENT |
|------|-------|---------|
| 22 | Alabama | 7.3 |
| 10 | Alaska | 21.5 |
| 26 | Arizona | 6.2 |
| 20 | Arkansas | 8.7 |
| 7 | California | 28.8 |
| 17 | Colorado | 10.1 |
| 38 | Connecticut | 3.4 |
| 46 | Delaware | 2.5 |
| 47 | Florida | 2.0 |
| 33 | Georgia | 4.7 |
| 21 | Hawaii | 7.5 |
| 1 | Idaho | 84.6 |
| 45 | Illinois | 2.6 |
| 40 | Indiana | 3.0 |
| 11 | Iowa | 17.9 |
| 23 | Kansas | 7.2 |
| 39 | Kentucky | 3.1 |
| 36 | Louisiana | 3.5 |
| 5 | Maine | 46.8 |
| 30 | Maryland | 5.1 |
| 28 | Massachusetts | 5.3 |
| 35 | Michigan | 3.7 |
| 13 | Minnesota | 13.9 |
| 43 | Mississippi | 2.8 |
| 44 | Missouri | 2.7 |
| 6 | Montana | 35.1 |
| 32 | Nebraska | 4.9 |
| 14 | Nevada | 12.6 |
| 15 | New Hampshire | 12.2 |
| 49 | New Jersey | 1.3 |
| 27 | New Mexico | 5.7 |
| 9 | New York | 22.1 |
| 28 | North Carolina | 5.3 |
| 12 | North Dakota | 17.7 |
| 50 | Ohio | 0.8 |
| 18 | Oklahoma | 9.6 |
| 4 | Oregon | 64.0 |
| 41 | Pennsylvania | 2.9 |
| 48 | Rhode Island | 1.9 |
| 34 | South Carolina | 4.1 |
| 3 | South Dakota | 65.8 |
| 16 | Tennessee | 11.1 |
| 25 | Texas | 7.0 |
| 36 | Utah | 3.5 |
| 8 | Vermont | 27.6 |
| 30 | Virginia | 5.1 |
| 2 | Washington | 72.4 |
| 41 | West Virginia | 2.9 |
| 24 | Wisconsin | 7.1 |
| 19 | Wyoming | 8.9 |

RANK ORDER

| RANK | STATE | PERCENT |
|------|-------|---------|
| 1 | Idaho | 84.6 |
| 2 | Washington | 72.4 |
| 3 | South Dakota | 65.8 |
| 4 | Oregon | 64.0 |
| 5 | Maine | 46.8 |
| 6 | Montana | 35.1 |
| 7 | California | 28.8 |
| 8 | Vermont | 27.6 |
| 9 | New York | 22.1 |
| 10 | Alaska | 21.5 |
| 11 | Iowa | 17.9 |
| 12 | North Dakota | 17.7 |
| 13 | Minnesota | 13.9 |
| 14 | Nevada | 12.6 |
| 15 | New Hampshire | 12.2 |
| 16 | Tennessee | 11.1 |
| 17 | Colorado | 10.1 |
| 18 | Oklahoma | 9.6 |
| 19 | Wyoming | 8.9 |
| 20 | Arkansas | 8.7 |
| 21 | Hawaii | 7.5 |
| 22 | Alabama | 7.3 |
| 23 | Kansas | 7.2 |
| 24 | Wisconsin | 7.1 |
| 25 | Texas | 7.0 |
| 26 | Arizona | 6.2 |
| 27 | New Mexico | 5.7 |
| 28 | Massachusetts | 5.3 |
| 28 | North Carolina | 5.3 |
| 30 | Maryland | 5.1 |
| 30 | Virginia | 5.1 |
| 32 | Nebraska | 4.9 |
| 33 | Georgia | 4.7 |
| 34 | South Carolina | 4.1 |
| 35 | Michigan | 3.7 |
| 36 | Louisiana | 3.5 |
| 36 | Utah | 3.5 |
| 38 | Connecticut | 3.4 |
| 39 | Kentucky | 3.1 |
| 40 | Indiana | 3.0 |
| 41 | Pennsylvania | 2.9 |
| 41 | West Virginia | 2.9 |
| 43 | Mississippi | 2.8 |
| 44 | Missouri | 2.7 |
| 45 | Illinois | 2.6 |
| 46 | Delaware | 2.5 |
| 47 | Florida | 2.0 |
| 48 | Rhode Island | 1.9 |
| 49 | New Jersey | 1.3 |
| 50 | Ohio | 0.8 |
| | District of Columbia** | NA |

Source: U.S. Department of Energy, Energy Information Administration
   "Renewable Energy Trends, 2010" (http://www.eia.gov/renewable/annual/trends/)
*Includes hydroelectric, geothermal, solar, wind, MSW/landfill gas, wood/wood waste and other biomass.
**Not reported.

# Average Price of Natural Gas Delivered to Industrial Customers in 2012

## National Average = $3.89 per Thousand Cubic Feet

ALPHA ORDER

| RANK | STATE | RATE |
|---|---|---|
| 43 | Alabama | $4.35 |
| 32 | Alaska | 5.11 |
| 25 | Arizona | 5.78 |
| 19 | Arkansas | 6.38 |
| 26 | California | 5.77 |
| 24 | Colorado | 5.79 |
| 8 | Connecticut | 8.83 |
| 2 | Delaware | 11.61 |
| 17 | Florida | 6.96 |
| 40 | Georgia | 4.60 |
| 1 | Hawaii | 30.89 |
| 27 | Idaho | 5.73 |
| 28 | Illinois | 5.64 |
| 21 | Indiana | 6.19 |
| 38 | Iowa | 4.70 |
| 47 | Kansas | 3.95 |
| 46 | Kentucky | 3.96 |
| 50 | Louisiana | 2.96 |
| 4 | Maine | 10.35 |
| 10 | Maryland | 8.01 |
| 5 | Massachusetts | 9.82 |
| 15 | Michigan | 7.38 |
| 41 | Minnesota | 4.48 |
| 37 | Mississippi | 4.86 |
| 11 | Missouri | 7.93 |
| 14 | Montana | 7.54 |
| 44 | Nebraska | 4.34 |
| 16 | Nevada | 7.34 |
| 3 | New Hampshire | 10.48 |
| 12 | New Jersey | 7.87 |
| 35 | New Mexico | 4.87 |
| 18 | New York | 6.92 |
| 20 | North Carolina | 6.37 |
| 41 | North Dakota | 4.48 |
| 29 | Ohio | 5.48 |
| 13 | Oklahoma | 7.65 |
| 22 | Oregon | 5.87 |
| 7 | Pennsylvania | 9.58 |
| 6 | Rhode Island | 9.78 |
| 45 | South Carolina | 4.30 |
| 30 | South Dakota | 5.37 |
| 33 | Tennessee | 4.94 |
| 49 | Texas | 3.02 |
| 39 | Utah | 4.69 |
| 34 | Vermont | 4.89 |
| 31 | Virginia | 5.29 |
| 9 | Washington | 8.77 |
| 48 | West Virginia | 3.56 |
| 23 | Wisconsin | 5.81 |
| 35 | Wyoming | 4.87 |

RANK ORDER

| RANK | STATE | RATE |
|---|---|---|
| 1 | Hawaii | $30.89 |
| 2 | Delaware | 11.61 |
| 3 | New Hampshire | 10.48 |
| 4 | Maine | 10.35 |
| 5 | Massachusetts | 9.82 |
| 6 | Rhode Island | 9.78 |
| 7 | Pennsylvania | 9.58 |
| 8 | Connecticut | 8.83 |
| 9 | Washington | 8.77 |
| 10 | Maryland | 8.01 |
| 11 | Missouri | 7.93 |
| 12 | New Jersey | 7.87 |
| 13 | Oklahoma | 7.65 |
| 14 | Montana | 7.54 |
| 15 | Michigan | 7.38 |
| 16 | Nevada | 7.34 |
| 17 | Florida | 6.96 |
| 18 | New York | 6.92 |
| 19 | Arkansas | 6.38 |
| 20 | North Carolina | 6.37 |
| 21 | Indiana | 6.19 |
| 22 | Oregon | 5.87 |
| 23 | Wisconsin | 5.81 |
| 24 | Colorado | 5.79 |
| 25 | Arizona | 5.78 |
| 26 | California | 5.77 |
| 27 | Idaho | 5.73 |
| 28 | Illinois | 5.64 |
| 29 | Ohio | 5.48 |
| 30 | South Dakota | 5.37 |
| 31 | Virginia | 5.29 |
| 32 | Alaska | 5.11 |
| 33 | Tennessee | 4.94 |
| 34 | Vermont | 4.89 |
| 35 | New Mexico | 4.87 |
| 35 | Wyoming | 4.87 |
| 37 | Mississippi | 4.86 |
| 38 | Iowa | 4.70 |
| 39 | Utah | 4.69 |
| 40 | Georgia | 4.60 |
| 41 | Minnesota | 4.48 |
| 41 | North Dakota | 4.48 |
| 43 | Alabama | 4.35 |
| 44 | Nebraska | 4.34 |
| 45 | South Carolina | 4.30 |
| 46 | Kentucky | 3.96 |
| 47 | Kansas | 3.95 |
| 48 | West Virginia | 3.56 |
| 49 | Texas | 3.02 |
| 50 | Louisiana | 2.96 |

District of Columbia*          NA

Source: U.S. Department of Energy, Energy Information Administration
    "Natural Gas" (http://www.eia.gov/naturalgas/)
*Not available.

# Average Price of Natural Gas Delivered to Commercial Customers in 2012

## National Average = $8.10 per Thousand Cubic Feet

ALPHA ORDER

| RANK | STATE | RATE |
|---|---|---|
| 3 | Alabama | $12.55 |
| 29 | Alaska | 8.09 |
| 16 | Arizona | 9.35 |
| 30 | Arkansas | 7.99 |
| 42 | California | 7.05 |
| 35 | Colorado | 7.58 |
| 25 | Connecticut | 8.40 |
| 2 | Delaware | 13.31 |
| 9 | Florida | 10.41 |
| 13 | Georgia | 9.74 |
| 1 | Hawaii | 47.03 |
| 38 | Idaho | 7.35 |
| 33 | Illinois | 7.77 |
| 34 | Indiana | 7.68 |
| 40 | Iowa | 7.13 |
| 19 | Kansas | 8.82 |
| 28 | Kentucky | 8.28 |
| 24 | Louisiana | 8.44 |
| 5 | Maine | 12.22 |
| 11 | Maryland | 10.00 |
| 8 | Massachusetts | 10.68 |
| 27 | Michigan | 8.35 |
| 47 | Minnesota | 6.38 |
| 37 | Mississippi | 7.38 |
| 14 | Missouri | 9.54 |
| 31 | Montana | 7.98 |
| 49 | Nebraska | 6.19 |
| 36 | Nevada | 7.43 |
| 7 | New Hampshire | 11.95 |
| 23 | New Jersey | 8.50 |
| 48 | New Mexico | 6.31 |
| 32 | New York | 7.84 |
| 22 | North Carolina | 8.62 |
| 50 | North Dakota | 6.04 |
| 41 | Ohio | 7.11 |
| 17 | Oklahoma | 8.95 |
| 18 | Oregon | 8.91 |
| 10 | Pennsylvania | 10.24 |
| 4 | Rhode Island | 12.31 |
| 21 | South Carolina | 8.67 |
| 46 | South Dakota | 6.45 |
| 26 | Tennessee | 8.36 |
| 45 | Texas | 6.63 |
| 43 | Utah | 7.00 |
| 6 | Vermont | 12.09 |
| 20 | Virginia | 8.77 |
| 12 | Washington | 9.82 |
| 15 | West Virginia | 9.39 |
| 39 | Wisconsin | 7.34 |
| 44 | Wyoming | 6.72 |

RANK ORDER

| RANK | STATE | RATE |
|---|---|---|
| 1 | Hawaii | $47.03 |
| 2 | Delaware | 13.31 |
| 3 | Alabama | 12.55 |
| 4 | Rhode Island | 12.31 |
| 5 | Maine | 12.22 |
| 6 | Vermont | 12.09 |
| 7 | New Hampshire | 11.95 |
| 8 | Massachusetts | 10.68 |
| 9 | Florida | 10.41 |
| 10 | Pennsylvania | 10.24 |
| 11 | Maryland | 10.00 |
| 12 | Washington | 9.82 |
| 13 | Georgia | 9.74 |
| 14 | Missouri | 9.54 |
| 15 | West Virginia | 9.39 |
| 16 | Arizona | 9.35 |
| 17 | Oklahoma | 8.95 |
| 18 | Oregon | 8.91 |
| 19 | Kansas | 8.82 |
| 20 | Virginia | 8.77 |
| 21 | South Carolina | 8.67 |
| 22 | North Carolina | 8.62 |
| 23 | New Jersey | 8.50 |
| 24 | Louisiana | 8.44 |
| 25 | Connecticut | 8.40 |
| 26 | Tennessee | 8.36 |
| 27 | Michigan | 8.35 |
| 28 | Kentucky | 8.28 |
| 29 | Alaska | 8.09 |
| 30 | Arkansas | 7.99 |
| 31 | Montana | 7.98 |
| 32 | New York | 7.84 |
| 33 | Illinois | 7.77 |
| 34 | Indiana | 7.68 |
| 35 | Colorado | 7.58 |
| 36 | Nevada | 7.43 |
| 37 | Mississippi | 7.38 |
| 38 | Idaho | 7.35 |
| 39 | Wisconsin | 7.34 |
| 40 | Iowa | 7.13 |
| 41 | Ohio | 7.11 |
| 42 | California | 7.05 |
| 43 | Utah | 7.00 |
| 44 | Wyoming | 6.72 |
| 45 | Texas | 6.63 |
| 46 | South Dakota | 6.45 |
| 47 | Minnesota | 6.38 |
| 48 | New Mexico | 6.31 |
| 49 | Nebraska | 6.19 |
| 50 | North Dakota | 6.04 |
| | District of Columbia | 11.19 |

Source: U.S. Department of Energy, Energy Information Administration
"Natural Gas" (http://www.eia.gov/naturalgas/)

# Average Price of Natural Gas Delivered to Residential Customers in 2012

## National Average = $10.71 per Thousand Cubic Feet

ALPHA ORDER

| RANK | STATE | RATE |
|---|---|---|
| 5 | Alabama | $16.20 |
| 42 | Alaska | 8.47 |
| 7 | Arizona | 15.75 |
| 21 | Arkansas | 11.82 |
| 37 | California | 9.14 |
| 45 | Colorado | 8.31 |
| 10 | Connecticut | 14.17 |
| 8 | Delaware | 15.24 |
| 2 | Florida | 18.31 |
| 4 | Georgia | 16.23 |
| 1 | Hawaii | 52.86 |
| 46 | Idaho | 8.26 |
| 46 | Illinois | 8.26 |
| 38 | Indiana | 8.94 |
| 35 | Iowa | 9.46 |
| 31 | Kansas | 10.13 |
| 29 | Kentucky | 10.19 |
| 22 | Louisiana | 11.54 |
| 6 | Maine | 15.94 |
| 18 | Maryland | 12.17 |
| 13 | Massachusetts | 13.22 |
| 26 | Michigan | 10.86 |
| 49 | Minnesota | 8.00 |
| 34 | Mississippi | 9.59 |
| 16 | Missouri | 12.25 |
| 48 | Montana | 8.06 |
| 41 | Nebraska | 8.68 |
| 30 | Nevada | 10.14 |
| 11 | New Hampshire | 13.74 |
| 25 | New Jersey | 11.09 |
| 40 | New Mexico | 8.69 |
| 14 | New York | 12.97 |
| 17 | North Carolina | 12.19 |
| 50 | North Dakota | 7.43 |
| 33 | Ohio | 9.91 |
| 24 | Oklahoma | 11.10 |
| 23 | Oregon | 11.22 |
| 19 | Pennsylvania | 11.99 |
| 9 | Rhode Island | 14.29 |
| 12 | South Carolina | 13.25 |
| 44 | South Dakota | 8.39 |
| 32 | Tennessee | 9.95 |
| 28 | Texas | 10.55 |
| 39 | Utah | 8.70 |
| 3 | Vermont | 16.73 |
| 15 | Virginia | 12.42 |
| 20 | Washington | 11.87 |
| 27 | West Virginia | 10.83 |
| 36 | Wisconsin | 9.27 |
| 43 | Wyoming | 8.42 |

RANK ORDER

| RANK | STATE | RATE |
|---|---|---|
| 1 | Hawaii | $52.86 |
| 2 | Florida | 18.31 |
| 3 | Vermont | 16.73 |
| 4 | Georgia | 16.23 |
| 5 | Alabama | 16.20 |
| 6 | Maine | 15.94 |
| 7 | Arizona | 15.75 |
| 8 | Delaware | 15.24 |
| 9 | Rhode Island | 14.29 |
| 10 | Connecticut | 14.17 |
| 11 | New Hampshire | 13.74 |
| 12 | South Carolina | 13.25 |
| 13 | Massachusetts | 13.22 |
| 14 | New York | 12.97 |
| 15 | Virginia | 12.42 |
| 16 | Missouri | 12.25 |
| 17 | North Carolina | 12.19 |
| 18 | Maryland | 12.17 |
| 19 | Pennsylvania | 11.99 |
| 20 | Washington | 11.87 |
| 21 | Arkansas | 11.82 |
| 22 | Louisiana | 11.54 |
| 23 | Oregon | 11.22 |
| 24 | Oklahoma | 11.10 |
| 25 | New Jersey | 11.09 |
| 26 | Michigan | 10.86 |
| 27 | West Virginia | 10.83 |
| 28 | Texas | 10.55 |
| 29 | Kentucky | 10.19 |
| 30 | Nevada | 10.14 |
| 31 | Kansas | 10.13 |
| 32 | Tennessee | 9.95 |
| 33 | Ohio | 9.91 |
| 34 | Mississippi | 9.59 |
| 35 | Iowa | 9.46 |
| 36 | Wisconsin | 9.27 |
| 37 | California | 9.14 |
| 38 | Indiana | 8.94 |
| 39 | Utah | 8.70 |
| 40 | New Mexico | 8.69 |
| 41 | Nebraska | 8.68 |
| 42 | Alaska | 8.47 |
| 43 | Wyoming | 8.42 |
| 44 | South Dakota | 8.39 |
| 45 | Colorado | 8.31 |
| 46 | Idaho | 8.26 |
| 46 | Illinois | 8.26 |
| 48 | Montana | 8.06 |
| 49 | Minnesota | 8.00 |
| 50 | North Dakota | 7.43 |

| District of Columbia | 12.10 |
|---|---|

Source: U.S. Department of Energy, Energy Information Administration
"Natural Gas" (http://www.eia.gov/naturalgas/)

# Natural Gas Consumption in 2012

## National Total = 25,533,448,000,000 Cubic Feet*

ALPHA ORDER

| RANK | STATE | CUBIC FEET | % of USA |
|---|---|---|---|
| 11 | Alabama | 666,738,000,000 | 2.6% |
| 22 | Alaska | 343,110,000,000 | 1.3% |
| 23 | Arizona | 332,079,000,000 | 1.3% |
| 24 | Arkansas | 295,811,000,000 | 1.2% |
| 2 | California | 2,403,385,000,000 | 9.4% |
| 16 | Colorado | 443,367,000,000 | 1.7% |
| 33 | Connecticut | 229,159,000,000 | 0.9% |
| 41 | Delaware | 101,676,000,000 | 0.4% |
| 4 | Florida | 1,328,469,000,000 | 5.2% |
| 14 | Georgia | 615,768,000,000 | 2.4% |
| 50 | Hawaii | 2,689,000,000 | 0.0% |
| 43 | Idaho | 89,004,000,000 | 0.3% |
| 7 | Illinois | 938,145,000,000 | 3.7% |
| 13 | Indiana | 650,180,000,000 | 2.5% |
| 25 | Iowa | 295,183,000,000 | 1.2% |
| 29 | Kansas | 262,170,000,000 | 1.0% |
| 34 | Kentucky | 224,591,000,000 | 0.9% |
| 3 | Louisiana | 1,482,299,000,000 | 5.8% |
| 48 | Maine | 68,266,000,000 | 0.3% |
| 37 | Maryland | 208,948,000,000 | 0.8% |
| 18 | Massachusetts | 416,351,000,000 | 1.6% |
| 9 | Michigan | 790,149,000,000 | 3.1% |
| 17 | Minnesota | 419,529,000,000 | 1.6% |
| 15 | Mississippi | 474,189,000,000 | 1.9% |
| 30 | Missouri | 255,875,000,000 | 1.0% |
| 44 | Montana | 73,399,000,000 | 0.3% |
| 38 | Nebraska | 158,758,000,000 | 0.6% |
| 27 | Nevada | 273,505,000,000 | 1.1% |
| 46 | New Hampshire | 72,069,000,000 | 0.3% |
| 12 | New Jersey | 652,060,000,000 | 2.6% |
| 32 | New Mexico | 244,584,000,000 | 1.0% |
| 5 | New York | 1,223,059,000,000 | 4.8% |
| 21 | North Carolina | 363,945,000,000 | 1.4% |
| 45 | North Dakota | 72,740,000,000 | 0.3% |
| 8 | Ohio | 842,959,000,000 | 3.3% |
| 10 | Oklahoma | 691,992,000,000 | 2.7% |
| 36 | Oregon | 215,830,000,000 | 0.8% |
| 6 | Pennsylvania | 1,037,979,000,000 | 4.1% |
| 42 | Rhode Island | 95,477,000,000 | 0.4% |
| 31 | South Carolina | 244,850,000,000 | 1.0% |
| 47 | South Dakota | 70,238,000,000 | 0.3% |
| 26 | Tennessee | 277,289,000,000 | 1.1% |
| 1 | Texas | 3,871,786,000,000 | 15.2% |
| 35 | Utah | 223,040,000,000 | 0.9% |
| 49 | Vermont | 8,191,000,000 | 0.0% |
| 19 | Virginia | 410,108,000,000 | 1.6% |
| 28 | Washington | 264,252,000,000 | 1.0% |
| 40 | West Virginia | 129,612,000,000 | 0.5% |
| 20 | Wisconsin | 402,657,000,000 | 1.6% |
| 39 | Wyoming | 153,383,000,000 | 0.6% |

RANK ORDER

| RANK | STATE | CUBIC FEET | % of USA |
|---|---|---|---|
| 1 | Texas | 3,871,786,000,000 | 15.2% |
| 2 | California | 2,403,385,000,000 | 9.4% |
| 3 | Louisiana | 1,482,299,000,000 | 5.8% |
| 4 | Florida | 1,328,469,000,000 | 5.2% |
| 5 | New York | 1,223,059,000,000 | 4.8% |
| 6 | Pennsylvania | 1,037,979,000,000 | 4.1% |
| 7 | Illinois | 938,145,000,000 | 3.7% |
| 8 | Ohio | 842,959,000,000 | 3.3% |
| 9 | Michigan | 790,149,000,000 | 3.1% |
| 10 | Oklahoma | 691,992,000,000 | 2.7% |
| 11 | Alabama | 666,738,000,000 | 2.6% |
| 12 | New Jersey | 652,060,000,000 | 2.6% |
| 13 | Indiana | 650,180,000,000 | 2.5% |
| 14 | Georgia | 615,768,000,000 | 2.4% |
| 15 | Mississippi | 474,189,000,000 | 1.9% |
| 16 | Colorado | 443,367,000,000 | 1.7% |
| 17 | Minnesota | 419,529,000,000 | 1.6% |
| 18 | Massachusetts | 416,351,000,000 | 1.6% |
| 19 | Virginia | 410,108,000,000 | 1.6% |
| 20 | Wisconsin | 402,657,000,000 | 1.6% |
| 21 | North Carolina | 363,945,000,000 | 1.4% |
| 22 | Alaska | 343,110,000,000 | 1.3% |
| 23 | Arizona | 332,079,000,000 | 1.3% |
| 24 | Arkansas | 295,811,000,000 | 1.2% |
| 25 | Iowa | 295,183,000,000 | 1.2% |
| 26 | Tennessee | 277,289,000,000 | 1.1% |
| 27 | Nevada | 273,505,000,000 | 1.1% |
| 28 | Washington | 264,252,000,000 | 1.0% |
| 29 | Kansas | 262,170,000,000 | 1.0% |
| 30 | Missouri | 255,875,000,000 | 1.0% |
| 31 | South Carolina | 244,850,000,000 | 1.0% |
| 32 | New Mexico | 244,584,000,000 | 1.0% |
| 33 | Connecticut | 229,159,000,000 | 0.9% |
| 34 | Kentucky | 224,591,000,000 | 0.9% |
| 35 | Utah | 223,040,000,000 | 0.9% |
| 36 | Oregon | 215,830,000,000 | 0.8% |
| 37 | Maryland | 208,948,000,000 | 0.8% |
| 38 | Nebraska | 158,758,000,000 | 0.6% |
| 39 | Wyoming | 153,383,000,000 | 0.6% |
| 40 | West Virginia | 129,612,000,000 | 0.5% |
| 41 | Delaware | 101,676,000,000 | 0.4% |
| 42 | Rhode Island | 95,477,000,000 | 0.4% |
| 43 | Idaho | 89,004,000,000 | 0.3% |
| 44 | Montana | 73,399,000,000 | 0.3% |
| 45 | North Dakota | 72,740,000,000 | 0.3% |
| 46 | New Hampshire | 72,069,000,000 | 0.3% |
| 47 | South Dakota | 70,238,000,000 | 0.3% |
| 48 | Maine | 68,266,000,000 | 0.3% |
| 49 | Vermont | 8,191,000,000 | 0.0% |
| 50 | Hawaii | 2,689,000,000 | 0.0% |
| | District of Columbia | 28,572,000,000 | 0.1% |

Source: U.S. Department of Energy, Energy Information Administration
"Natural Gas Annual 2012" (http://www.eia.gov/naturalgas/annual/)
*National total includes 93,985,000,000 cubic feet of consumption in the Gulf of Mexico not shown by state.

# Coal Mines in 2012

## National Total = 1,229 Mines*

ALPHA ORDER

| RANK | STATE | MINES | % of USA |
|---|---|---|---|
| 5 | Alabama | 46 | 3.7% |
| 22 | Alaska | 1 | 0.1% |
| 22 | Arizona | 1 | 0.1% |
| 19 | Arkansas | 2 | 0.2% |
| NA | California** | NA | NA |
| 12 | Colorado | 12 | 1.0% |
| NA | Connecticut** | NA | NA |
| NA | Delaware** | NA | NA |
| NA | Florida** | NA | NA |
| NA | Georgia** | NA | NA |
| NA | Hawaii** | NA | NA |
| NA | Idaho** | NA | NA |
| 8 | Illinois | 24 | 2.0% |
| 7 | Indiana | 29 | 2.4% |
| NA | Iowa** | NA | NA |
| 22 | Kansas | 1 | 0.1% |
| 1 | Kentucky | 357 | 29.0% |
| 19 | Louisiana | 2 | 0.2% |
| NA | Maine** | NA | NA |
| 9 | Maryland | 21 | 1.7% |
| NA | Massachusetts** | NA | NA |
| NA | Michigan** | NA | NA |
| NA | Minnesota** | NA | NA |
| 22 | Mississippi | 1 | 0.1% |
| 19 | Missouri | 2 | 0.2% |
| 16 | Montana | 6 | 0.5% |
| NA | Nebraska** | NA | NA |
| NA | Nevada** | NA | NA |
| NA | New Hampshire** | NA | NA |
| NA | New Jersey** | NA | NA |
| 17 | New Mexico | 4 | 0.3% |
| NA | New York** | NA | NA |
| NA | North Carolina** | NA | NA |
| 17 | North Dakota | 4 | 0.3% |
| 6 | Ohio | 39 | 3.2% |
| 15 | Oklahoma | 7 | 0.6% |
| NA | Oregon** | NA | NA |
| 3 | Pennsylvania | 235 | 19.1% |
| NA | Rhode Island** | NA | NA |
| NA | South Carolina** | NA | NA |
| NA | South Dakota** | NA | NA |
| 11 | Tennessee | 14 | 1.1% |
| 12 | Texas | 12 | 1.0% |
| 14 | Utah | 9 | 0.7% |
| NA | Vermont** | NA | NA |
| 4 | Virginia | 96 | 7.8% |
| NA | Washington** | NA | NA |
| 2 | West Virginia | 264 | 21.5% |
| NA | Wisconsin** | NA | NA |
| 10 | Wyoming | 18 | 1.5% |

RANK ORDER

| RANK | STATE | MINES | % of USA |
|---|---|---|---|
| 1 | Kentucky | 357 | 29.0% |
| 2 | West Virginia | 264 | 21.5% |
| 3 | Pennsylvania | 235 | 19.1% |
| 4 | Virginia | 96 | 7.8% |
| 5 | Alabama | 46 | 3.7% |
| 6 | Ohio | 39 | 3.2% |
| 7 | Indiana | 29 | 2.4% |
| 8 | Illinois | 24 | 2.0% |
| 9 | Maryland | 21 | 1.7% |
| 10 | Wyoming | 18 | 1.5% |
| 11 | Tennessee | 14 | 1.1% |
| 12 | Colorado | 12 | 1.0% |
| 12 | Texas | 12 | 1.0% |
| 14 | Utah | 9 | 0.7% |
| 15 | Oklahoma | 7 | 0.6% |
| 16 | Montana | 6 | 0.5% |
| 17 | New Mexico | 4 | 0.3% |
| 17 | North Dakota | 4 | 0.3% |
| 19 | Arkansas | 2 | 0.2% |
| 19 | Louisiana | 2 | 0.2% |
| 19 | Missouri | 2 | 0.2% |
| 22 | Alaska | 1 | 0.1% |
| 22 | Arizona | 1 | 0.1% |
| 22 | Kansas | 1 | 0.1% |
| 22 | Mississippi | 1 | 0.1% |
| NA | California** | NA | NA |
| NA | Connecticut** | NA | NA |
| NA | Delaware** | NA | NA |
| NA | Florida** | NA | NA |
| NA | Georgia** | NA | NA |
| NA | Hawaii** | NA | NA |
| NA | Idaho** | NA | NA |
| NA | Iowa** | NA | NA |
| NA | Maine** | NA | NA |
| NA | Massachusetts** | NA | NA |
| NA | Michigan** | NA | NA |
| NA | Minnesota** | NA | NA |
| NA | Nebraska** | NA | NA |
| NA | Nevada** | NA | NA |
| NA | New Hampshire** | NA | NA |
| NA | New Jersey** | NA | NA |
| NA | New York** | NA | NA |
| NA | North Carolina** | NA | NA |
| NA | Oregon** | NA | NA |
| NA | Rhode Island** | NA | NA |
| NA | South Carolina** | NA | NA |
| NA | South Dakota** | NA | NA |
| NA | Vermont** | NA | NA |
| NA | Washington** | NA | NA |
| NA | Wisconsin** | NA | NA |
| | District of Columbia** | NA | NA |

Source: U.S. Department of Energy, Energy Information Administration
   "Annual Coal Report" (released December 12, 2013, http://www.eia.gov/coal/annual/)
*National total includes 22 coal mines in refuse recovery not shown by state.
**Not available or no mines.

# Coal Production in 2012

## National Total = 1,016,458,000 Short Tons*

ALPHA ORDER

| RANK | STATE | SHORT TONS | % of USA |
|---|---|---|---|
| 13 | Alabama | 19,321,000 | 1.9% |
| 20 | Alaska | 2,052,000 | 0.2% |
| 16 | Arizona | 7,493,000 | 0.7% |
| 24 | Arkansas | 98,000 | 0.0% |
| NA | California** | NA | NA |
| 9 | Colorado | 28,566,000 | 2.8% |
| NA | Connecticut** | NA | NA |
| NA | Delaware** | NA | NA |
| NA | Florida** | NA | NA |
| NA | Georgia** | NA | NA |
| NA | Hawaii** | NA | NA |
| NA | Idaho** | NA | NA |
| 5 | Illinois | 48,486,000 | 4.8% |
| 7 | Indiana | 36,720,000 | 3.6% |
| NA | Iowa** | NA | NA |
| 25 | Kansas | 16,000 | 0.0% |
| 3 | Kentucky | 90,862,000 | 8.9% |
| 17 | Louisiana | 3,971,000 | 0.4% |
| NA | Maine** | NA | NA |
| 19 | Maryland | 2,283,000 | 0.2% |
| NA | Massachusetts** | NA | NA |
| NA | Michigan** | NA | NA |
| NA | Minnesota** | NA | NA |
| 18 | Mississippi | 2,953,000 | 0.3% |
| 23 | Missouri | 422,000 | 0.0% |
| 8 | Montana | 36,694,000 | 3.6% |
| NA | Nebraska** | NA | NA |
| NA | Nevada** | NA | NA |
| NA | New Hampshire | NA | NA |
| NA | New Jersey** | NA | NA |
| 12 | New Mexico | 22,452,000 | 2.2% |
| NA | New York** | NA | NA |
| NA | North Carolina** | NA | NA |
| 10 | North Dakota | 27,529,000 | 2.7% |
| 11 | Ohio | 26,328,000 | 2.6% |
| 22 | Oklahoma | 1,054,000 | 0.1% |
| NA | Oregon** | NA | NA |
| 4 | Pennsylvania | 54,719,000 | 5.4% |
| NA | Rhode Island** | NA | NA |
| NA | South Carolina** | NA | NA |
| NA | South Dakota** | NA | NA |
| 21 | Tennessee | 1,090,000 | 0.1% |
| 6 | Texas | 44,178,000 | 4.3% |
| 15 | Utah | 17,016,000 | 1.7% |
| NA | Vermont** | NA | NA |
| 14 | Virginia | 18,965,000 | 1.9% |
| NA | Washington** | NA | NA |
| 2 | West Virginia | 120,425,000 | 11.8% |
| NA | Wisconsin** | NA | NA |
| 1 | Wyoming | 401,442,000 | 39.5% |

RANK ORDER

| RANK | STATE | SHORT TONS | % of USA |
|---|---|---|---|
| 1 | Wyoming | 401,442,000 | 39.5% |
| 2 | West Virginia | 120,425,000 | 11.8% |
| 3 | Kentucky | 90,862,000 | 8.9% |
| 4 | Pennsylvania | 54,719,000 | 5.4% |
| 5 | Illinois | 48,486,000 | 4.8% |
| 6 | Texas | 44,178,000 | 4.3% |
| 7 | Indiana | 36,720,000 | 3.6% |
| 8 | Montana | 36,694,000 | 3.6% |
| 9 | Colorado | 28,566,000 | 2.8% |
| 10 | North Dakota | 27,529,000 | 2.7% |
| 11 | Ohio | 26,328,000 | 2.6% |
| 12 | New Mexico | 22,452,000 | 2.2% |
| 13 | Alabama | 19,321,000 | 1.9% |
| 14 | Virginia | 18,965,000 | 1.9% |
| 15 | Utah | 17,016,000 | 1.7% |
| 16 | Arizona | 7,493,000 | 0.7% |
| 17 | Louisiana | 3,971,000 | 0.4% |
| 18 | Mississippi | 2,953,000 | 0.3% |
| 19 | Maryland | 2,283,000 | 0.2% |
| 20 | Alaska | 2,052,000 | 0.2% |
| 21 | Tennessee | 1,090,000 | 0.1% |
| 22 | Oklahoma | 1,054,000 | 0.1% |
| 23 | Missouri | 422,000 | 0.0% |
| 24 | Arkansas | 98,000 | 0.0% |
| 25 | Kansas | 16,000 | 0.0% |
| NA | California** | NA | NA |
| NA | Connecticut** | NA | NA |
| NA | Delaware** | NA | NA |
| NA | Florida** | NA | NA |
| NA | Georgia** | NA | NA |
| NA | Hawaii** | NA | NA |
| NA | Idaho** | NA | NA |
| NA | Iowa** | NA | NA |
| NA | Maine** | NA | NA |
| NA | Massachusetts** | NA | NA |
| NA | Michigan** | NA | NA |
| NA | Minnesota** | NA | NA |
| NA | Nebraska** | NA | NA |
| NA | Nevada** | NA | NA |
| NA | New Hampshire** | NA | NA |
| NA | New Jersey** | NA | NA |
| NA | New York** | NA | NA |
| NA | North Carolina** | NA | NA |
| NA | Oregon** | NA | NA |
| NA | Rhode Island** | NA | NA |
| NA | South Carolina** | NA | NA |
| NA | South Dakota** | NA | NA |
| NA | Vermont** | NA | NA |
| NA | Washington** | NA | NA |
| NA | Wisconsin** | NA | NA |
| | District of Columbia** | NA | NA |

Source: U.S. Department of Energy, Energy Information Administration
"Annual Coal Report" (released December 12, 2013, http://www.eia.gov/coal/annual/)
*National total includes 1,324,000 short tons from refuse recovery not shown by state.
**Not available or no production.

# Gasoline Used in 2012

## National Total = 134,998,800,000 Gallons*

| ALPHA ORDER | | | | | RANK ORDER | | | |
|---|---|---|---|---|---|---|---|---|
| **RANK** | **STATE** | **GALLONS** | **% of USA** | | **RANK** | **STATE** | **GALLONS** | **% of USA** |
| 22 | Alabama | 2,577,035,000 | 1.9% | | 1 | California | 14,525,691,000 | 10.8% |
| 50 | Alaska | 288,738,000 | 0.2% | | 2 | Texas | 12,444,478,000 | 9.2% |
| 20 | Arizona | 2,616,978,000 | 1.9% | | 3 | Florida | 8,150,577,000 | 6.0% |
| 32 | Arkansas | 1,434,181,000 | 1.1% | | 4 | New York | 5,424,144,000 | 4.0% |
| 1 | California | 14,525,691,000 | 10.8% | | 5 | Pennsylvania | 5,036,098,000 | 3.7% |
| 26 | Colorado | 2,137,244,000 | 1.6% | | 6 | Ohio | 4,979,306,000 | 3.7% |
| 31 | Connecticut | 1,449,384,000 | 1.1% | | 7 | Georgia | 4,691,478,000 | 3.5% |
| 46 | Delaware | 436,706,000 | 0.3% | | 8 | Illinois | 4,649,208,000 | 3.4% |
| 3 | Florida | 8,150,577,000 | 6.0% | | 9 | Michigan | 4,460,239,000 | 3.3% |
| 7 | Georgia | 4,691,478,000 | 3.5% | | 10 | North Carolina | 4,311,886,000 | 3.2% |
| 44 | Hawaii | 450,286,000 | 0.3% | | 11 | New Jersey | 4,058,680,000 | 3.0% |
| 39 | Idaho | 704,611,000 | 0.5% | | 12 | Virginia | 3,933,092,000 | 2.9% |
| 8 | Illinois | 4,649,208,000 | 3.4% | | 13 | Tennessee | 3,167,178,000 | 2.3% |
| 15 | Indiana | 3,017,750,000 | 2.2% | | 14 | Missouri | 3,109,356,000 | 2.3% |
| 29 | Iowa | 1,636,231,000 | 1.2% | | 15 | Indiana | 3,017,750,000 | 2.2% |
| 33 | Kansas | 1,260,688,000 | 0.9% | | 16 | Massachusetts | 2,779,752,000 | 2.1% |
| 25 | Kentucky | 2,147,737,000 | 1.6% | | 17 | Maryland | 2,721,780,000 | 2.0% |
| 24 | Louisiana | 2,247,906,000 | 1.7% | | 18 | Washington | 2,685,167,000 | 2.0% |
| 41 | Maine | 658,213,000 | 0.5% | | 19 | South Carolina | 2,639,209,000 | 2.0% |
| 17 | Maryland | 2,721,780,000 | 2.0% | | 20 | Arizona | 2,616,978,000 | 1.9% |
| 16 | Massachusetts | 2,779,752,000 | 2.1% | | 21 | Minnesota | 2,579,198,000 | 1.9% |
| 9 | Michigan | 4,460,239,000 | 3.3% | | 22 | Alabama | 2,577,035,000 | 1.9% |
| 21 | Minnesota | 2,579,198,000 | 1.9% | | 23 | Wisconsin | 2,506,856,000 | 1.9% |
| 28 | Mississippi | 1,657,284,000 | 1.2% | | 24 | Louisiana | 2,247,906,000 | 1.7% |
| 14 | Missouri | 3,109,356,000 | 2.3% | | 25 | Kentucky | 2,147,737,000 | 1.6% |
| 42 | Montana | 506,158,000 | 0.4% | | 26 | Colorado | 2,137,244,000 | 1.6% |
| 37 | Nebraska | 844,237,000 | 0.6% | | 27 | Oklahoma | 1,924,486,000 | 1.4% |
| 34 | Nevada | 1,083,614,000 | 0.8% | | 28 | Mississippi | 1,657,284,000 | 1.2% |
| 40 | New Hampshire | 699,964,000 | 0.5% | | 29 | Iowa | 1,636,231,000 | 1.2% |
| 11 | New Jersey | 4,058,680,000 | 3.0% | | 30 | Oregon | 1,468,762,000 | 1.1% |
| 36 | New Mexico | 961,686,000 | 0.7% | | 31 | Connecticut | 1,449,384,000 | 1.1% |
| 4 | New York | 5,424,144,000 | 4.0% | | 32 | Arkansas | 1,434,181,000 | 1.1% |
| 10 | North Carolina | 4,311,886,000 | 3.2% | | 33 | Kansas | 1,260,688,000 | 0.9% |
| 45 | North Dakota | 438,732,000 | 0.3% | | 34 | Nevada | 1,083,614,000 | 0.8% |
| 6 | Ohio | 4,979,306,000 | 3.7% | | 35 | Utah | 1,072,492,000 | 0.8% |
| 27 | Oklahoma | 1,924,486,000 | 1.4% | | 36 | New Mexico | 961,686,000 | 0.7% |
| 30 | Oregon | 1,468,762,000 | 1.1% | | 37 | Nebraska | 844,237,000 | 0.6% |
| 5 | Pennsylvania | 5,036,098,000 | 3.7% | | 38 | West Virginia | 809,016,000 | 0.6% |
| 48 | Rhode Island | 365,350,000 | 0.3% | | 39 | Idaho | 704,611,000 | 0.5% |
| 19 | South Carolina | 2,639,209,000 | 2.0% | | 40 | New Hampshire | 699,964,000 | 0.5% |
| 43 | South Dakota | 464,982,000 | 0.3% | | 41 | Maine | 658,213,000 | 0.5% |
| 13 | Tennessee | 3,167,178,000 | 2.3% | | 42 | Montana | 506,158,000 | 0.4% |
| 2 | Texas | 12,444,478,000 | 9.2% | | 43 | South Dakota | 464,982,000 | 0.3% |
| 35 | Utah | 1,072,492,000 | 0.8% | | 44 | Hawaii | 450,286,000 | 0.3% |
| 49 | Vermont | 316,725,000 | 0.2% | | 45 | North Dakota | 438,732,000 | 0.3% |
| 12 | Virginia | 3,933,092,000 | 2.9% | | 46 | Delaware | 436,706,000 | 0.3% |
| 18 | Washington | 2,685,167,000 | 2.0% | | 47 | Wyoming | 371,512,000 | 0.3% |
| 38 | West Virginia | 809,016,000 | 0.6% | | 48 | Rhode Island | 365,350,000 | 0.3% |
| 23 | Wisconsin | 2,506,856,000 | 1.9% | | 49 | Vermont | 316,725,000 | 0.2% |
| 47 | Wyoming | 371,512,000 | 0.3% | | 50 | Alaska | 288,738,000 | 0.2% |
| | | | | | | District of Columbia | 96,739,000 | 0.1% |

Source: U.S. Department of Transportation, Federal Highway Administration
"Highway Statistics 2012" (Table MF-21, http://www.fhwa.dot.gov/policyinformation/statistics/2012/)
*Includes gasoline for highway and nonhighway uses as well as for losses allowed for evaporation and handling. "Gasoline" includes gasohol but excludes "special fuels" such as diesel.

# Per Capita Gasoline Used in 2012

## National Per Capita = 431 Gallons*

ALPHA ORDER

| RANK | STATE | PER CAPITA |
|---|---|---|
| 5 | Alabama | 539 |
| 41 | Alaska | 397 |
| 39 | Arizona | 401 |
| 16 | Arkansas | 483 |
| 44 | California | 385 |
| 37 | Colorado | 410 |
| 38 | Connecticut | 409 |
| 17 | Delaware | 478 |
| 35 | Florida | 422 |
| 19 | Georgia | 476 |
| 49 | Hawaii | 340 |
| 34 | Idaho | 426 |
| 47 | Illinois | 367 |
| 23 | Indiana | 465 |
| 3 | Iowa | 559 |
| 28 | Kansas | 450 |
| 13 | Kentucky | 495 |
| 12 | Louisiana | 501 |
| 11 | Maine | 510 |
| 27 | Maryland | 453 |
| 36 | Massachusetts | 420 |
| 26 | Michigan | 454 |
| 24 | Minnesota | 463 |
| 7 | Mississippi | 535 |
| 9 | Missouri | 518 |
| 15 | Montana | 492 |
| 29 | Nebraska | 449 |
| 42 | Nevada | 394 |
| 8 | New Hampshire | 534 |
| 21 | New Jersey | 468 |
| 25 | New Mexico | 457 |
| 50 | New York | 283 |
| 29 | North Carolina | 449 |
| 2 | North Dakota | 587 |
| 33 | Ohio | 431 |
| 17 | Oklahoma | 478 |
| 45 | Oregon | 382 |
| 40 | Pennsylvania | 399 |
| 48 | Rhode Island | 358 |
| 4 | South Carolina | 549 |
| 6 | South Dakota | 538 |
| 13 | Tennessee | 495 |
| 20 | Texas | 470 |
| 46 | Utah | 379 |
| 10 | Vermont | 516 |
| 22 | Virginia | 467 |
| 43 | Washington | 391 |
| 31 | West Virginia | 444 |
| 32 | Wisconsin | 439 |
| 1 | Wyoming | 594 |

RANK ORDER

| RANK | STATE | PER CAPITA |
|---|---|---|
| 1 | Wyoming | 594 |
| 2 | North Dakota | 587 |
| 3 | Iowa | 559 |
| 4 | South Carolina | 549 |
| 5 | Alabama | 539 |
| 6 | South Dakota | 538 |
| 7 | Mississippi | 535 |
| 8 | New Hampshire | 534 |
| 9 | Missouri | 518 |
| 10 | Vermont | 516 |
| 11 | Maine | 510 |
| 12 | Louisiana | 501 |
| 13 | Kentucky | 495 |
| 13 | Tennessee | 495 |
| 15 | Montana | 492 |
| 16 | Arkansas | 483 |
| 17 | Delaware | 478 |
| 17 | Oklahoma | 478 |
| 19 | Georgia | 476 |
| 20 | Texas | 470 |
| 21 | New Jersey | 468 |
| 22 | Virginia | 467 |
| 23 | Indiana | 465 |
| 24 | Minnesota | 463 |
| 25 | New Mexico | 457 |
| 26 | Michigan | 454 |
| 27 | Maryland | 453 |
| 28 | Kansas | 450 |
| 29 | Nebraska | 449 |
| 29 | North Carolina | 449 |
| 31 | West Virginia | 444 |
| 32 | Wisconsin | 439 |
| 33 | Ohio | 431 |
| 34 | Idaho | 426 |
| 35 | Florida | 422 |
| 36 | Massachusetts | 420 |
| 37 | Colorado | 410 |
| 38 | Connecticut | 409 |
| 39 | Arizona | 401 |
| 40 | Pennsylvania | 399 |
| 41 | Alaska | 397 |
| 42 | Nevada | 394 |
| 43 | Washington | 391 |
| 44 | California | 385 |
| 45 | Oregon | 382 |
| 46 | Utah | 379 |
| 47 | Illinois | 367 |
| 48 | Rhode Island | 358 |
| 49 | Hawaii | 340 |
| 50 | New York | 283 |

| District of Columbia | 170 |
|---|---|

Source: CQ Press using data from U.S. Department of Transportation, Federal Highway Administration
"Highway Statistics 2012" (Table MF-21, http://www.fhwa.dot.gov/policyinformation/statistics/2012/)
*Includes gasoline for highway and nonhighway uses as well as for losses allowed for evaporation and handling. "Gasoline" includes gasohol but excludes "special fuels" such as diesel.

# Daily Production of Crude Oil in 2012

## National Total = 6,482,309 Barrels a Day*

ALPHA ORDER

| RANK | STATE | BARRELS | % of USA |
|------|-------|---------|----------|
| 15 | Alabama | 26,025 | 0.4% |
| 4 | Alaska | 525,596 | 8.1% |
| 30 | Arizona | 142 | 0.0% |
| 17 | Arkansas | 17,858 | 0.3% |
| 3 | California | 536,404 | 8.3% |
| 9 | Colorado | 134,888 | 2.1% |
| NA | Connecticut** | NA | NA |
| NA | Delaware** | NA | NA |
| 24 | Florida | 5,833 | 0.1% |
| NA | Georgia** | NA | NA |
| NA | Hawaii** | NA | NA |
| NA | Idaho** | NA | NA |
| 14 | Illinois | 26,765 | 0.4% |
| 23 | Indiana | 6,421 | 0.1% |
| NA | Iowa** | NA | NA |
| 10 | Kansas | 119,347 | 1.8% |
| 20 | Kentucky | 8,738 | 0.1% |
| 7 | Louisiana | 192,954 | 3.0% |
| NA | Maine** | NA | NA |
| NA | Maryland** | NA | NA |
| NA | Massachusetts** | NA | NA |
| 16 | Michigan | 20,194 | 0.3% |
| NA | Minnesota** | NA | NA |
| 13 | Mississippi | 65,995 | 1.0% |
| 29 | Missouri | 473 | 0.0% |
| 12 | Montana | 72,391 | 1.1% |
| 21 | Nebraska | 8,260 | 0.1% |
| 26 | Nevada | 1,005 | 0.0% |
| NA | New Hampshire** | NA | NA |
| NA | New Jersey** | NA | NA |
| 6 | New Mexico | 232,798 | 3.6% |
| 27 | New York | 964 | 0.0% |
| NA | North Carolina** | NA | NA |
| 2 | North Dakota | 662,530 | 10.2% |
| 18 | Ohio | 13,325 | 0.2% |
| 5 | Oklahoma | 238,134 | 3.7% |
| NA | Oregon** | NA | NA |
| 19 | Pennsylvania | 11,880 | 0.2% |
| NA | Rhode Island** | NA | NA |
| NA | South Carolina** | NA | NA |
| 25 | South Dakota | 4,792 | 0.1% |
| 28 | Tennessee | 787 | 0.0% |
| 1 | Texas | 1,986,336 | 30.6% |
| 11 | Utah | 82,686 | 1.3% |
| NA | Vermont** | NA | NA |
| 31 | Virginia | 25 | 0.0% |
| NA | Washington** | NA | NA |
| 22 | West Virginia | 7,030 | 0.1% |
| NA | Wisconsin** | NA | NA |
| 8 | Wyoming | 157,716 | 2.4% |

RANK ORDER

| RANK | STATE | BARRELS | % of USA |
|------|-------|---------|----------|
| 1 | Texas | 1,986,336 | 30.6% |
| 2 | North Dakota | 662,530 | 10.2% |
| 3 | California | 536,404 | 8.3% |
| 4 | Alaska | 525,596 | 8.1% |
| 5 | Oklahoma | 238,134 | 3.7% |
| 6 | New Mexico | 232,798 | 3.6% |
| 7 | Louisiana | 192,954 | 3.0% |
| 8 | Wyoming | 157,716 | 2.4% |
| 9 | Colorado | 134,888 | 2.1% |
| 10 | Kansas | 119,347 | 1.8% |
| 11 | Utah | 82,686 | 1.3% |
| 12 | Montana | 72,391 | 1.1% |
| 13 | Mississippi | 65,995 | 1.0% |
| 14 | Illinois | 26,765 | 0.4% |
| 15 | Alabama | 26,025 | 0.4% |
| 16 | Michigan | 20,194 | 0.3% |
| 17 | Arkansas | 17,858 | 0.3% |
| 18 | Ohio | 13,325 | 0.2% |
| 19 | Pennsylvania | 11,880 | 0.2% |
| 20 | Kentucky | 8,738 | 0.1% |
| 21 | Nebraska | 8,260 | 0.1% |
| 22 | West Virginia | 7,030 | 0.1% |
| 23 | Indiana | 6,421 | 0.1% |
| 24 | Florida | 5,833 | 0.1% |
| 25 | South Dakota | 4,792 | 0.1% |
| 26 | Nevada | 1,005 | 0.0% |
| 27 | New York | 964 | 0.0% |
| 28 | Tennessee | 787 | 0.0% |
| 29 | Missouri | 473 | 0.0% |
| 30 | Arizona | 142 | 0.0% |
| 31 | Virginia | 25 | 0.0% |
| NA | Connecticut** | NA | NA |
| NA | Delaware** | NA | NA |
| NA | Georgia** | NA | NA |
| NA | Hawaii** | NA | NA |
| NA | Idaho** | NA | NA |
| NA | Iowa** | NA | NA |
| NA | Maine** | NA | NA |
| NA | Maryland** | NA | NA |
| NA | Massachusetts** | NA | NA |
| NA | Minnesota** | NA | NA |
| NA | New Hampshire** | NA | NA |
| NA | New Jersey** | NA | NA |
| NA | North Carolina** | NA | NA |
| NA | Oregon** | NA | NA |
| NA | Rhode Island** | NA | NA |
| NA | South Carolina** | NA | NA |
| NA | Vermont** | NA | NA |
| NA | Washington** | NA | NA |
| NA | Wisconsin** | NA | NA |
| | District of Columbia** | NA | NA |

Source: CQ Press using data from U.S. Department of Energy, Energy Information Administration
"Petroleum Supply Annual 2012, Volume 1" (http://tonto.eia.doe.gov/dnav/pet/pet_crd_crpdn_adc_mbbl_m.htm)
*National total includes 1,314,019 barrels a day in federal offshore production. Figures for Alaska, California, Louisiana, and Texas include state offshore production.
**No reported production.

# Fossil Fuel Emissions in 2011

## National Total = 5,407,900,000 Metric Tons of Carbon Dioxide (CO2)*

| ALPHA ORDER | | | | | RANK ORDER | | | |
|---|---|---|---|---|---|---|---|---|
| RANK | STATE | TONS OF CO2 | % of USA | | RANK | STATE | TONS OF CO2 | % of USA |
| 14 | Alabama | 129,620,000 | 2.4% | | 1 | Texas | 679,720,000 | 12.6% |
| 38 | Alaska | 38,160,000 | 0.7% | | 2 | California | 360,000,000 | 6.7% |
| 22 | Arizona | 93,280,000 | 1.7% | | 3 | Pennsylvania | 246,790,000 | 4.6% |
| 30 | Arkansas | 67,560,000 | 1.2% | | 4 | Ohio | 236,630,000 | 4.4% |
| 2 | California | 360,000,000 | 6.7% | | 5 | Florida | 230,980,000 | 4.3% |
| 24 | Colorado | 91,980,000 | 1.7% | | 6 | Illinois | 230,580,000 | 4.3% |
| 40 | Connecticut | 35,300,000 | 0.7% | | 7 | Louisiana | 215,400,000 | 4.0% |
| 48 | Delaware | 13,110,000 | 0.2% | | 8 | Indiana | 208,260,000 | 3.9% |
| 5 | Florida | 230,980,000 | 4.3% | | 9 | New York | 166,320,000 | 3.1% |
| 11 | Georgia | 156,430,000 | 2.9% | | 10 | Michigan | 160,260,000 | 3.0% |
| 43 | Hawaii | 19,310,000 | 0.4% | | 11 | Georgia | 156,430,000 | 2.9% |
| 46 | Idaho | 16,030,000 | 0.3% | | 12 | Kentucky | 148,360,000 | 2.7% |
| 6 | Illinois | 230,580,000 | 4.3% | | 13 | Missouri | 135,540,000 | 2.5% |
| 8 | Indiana | 208,260,000 | 3.9% | | 14 | Alabama | 129,620,000 | 2.4% |
| 25 | Iowa | 87,420,000 | 1.6% | | 15 | North Carolina | 127,920,000 | 2.4% |
| 27 | Kansas | 72,360,000 | 1.3% | | 16 | New Jersey | 117,560,000 | 2.2% |
| 12 | Kentucky | 148,360,000 | 2.7% | | 17 | Oklahoma | 107,920,000 | 2.0% |
| 7 | Louisiana | 215,400,000 | 4.0% | | 18 | Tennessee | 105,730,000 | 2.0% |
| 44 | Maine | 17,630,000 | 0.3% | | 19 | Virginia | 99,860,000 | 1.8% |
| 31 | Maryland | 65,800,000 | 1.2% | | 20 | Wisconsin | 98,050,000 | 1.8% |
| 29 | Massachusetts | 68,890,000 | 1.3% | | 21 | West Virginia | 95,970,000 | 1.8% |
| 10 | Michigan | 160,260,000 | 3.0% | | 22 | Arizona | 93,280,000 | 1.7% |
| 23 | Minnesota | 92,690,000 | 1.7% | | 23 | Minnesota | 92,690,000 | 1.7% |
| 34 | Mississippi | 61,210,000 | 1.1% | | 24 | Colorado | 91,980,000 | 1.7% |
| 13 | Missouri | 135,540,000 | 2.5% | | 25 | Iowa | 87,420,000 | 1.6% |
| 42 | Montana | 31,900,000 | 0.6% | | 26 | South Carolina | 80,210,000 | 1.5% |
| 36 | Nebraska | 52,260,000 | 1.0% | | 27 | Kansas | 72,360,000 | 1.3% |
| 41 | Nevada | 33,850,000 | 0.6% | | 28 | Washington | 70,810,000 | 1.3% |
| 45 | New Hampshire | 16,410,000 | 0.3% | | 29 | Massachusetts | 68,890,000 | 1.3% |
| 16 | New Jersey | 117,560,000 | 2.2% | | 30 | Arkansas | 67,560,000 | 1.2% |
| 35 | New Mexico | 56,600,000 | 1.0% | | 31 | Maryland | 65,800,000 | 1.2% |
| 9 | New York | 166,320,000 | 3.1% | | 32 | Utah | 63,970,000 | 1.2% |
| 15 | North Carolina | 127,920,000 | 2.4% | | 33 | Wyoming | 63,890,000 | 1.2% |
| 37 | North Dakota | 50,340,000 | 0.9% | | 34 | Mississippi | 61,210,000 | 1.1% |
| 4 | Ohio | 236,630,000 | 4.4% | | 35 | New Mexico | 56,600,000 | 1.0% |
| 17 | Oklahoma | 107,920,000 | 2.0% | | 36 | Nebraska | 52,260,000 | 1.0% |
| 39 | Oregon | 37,250,000 | 0.7% | | 37 | North Dakota | 50,340,000 | 0.9% |
| 3 | Pennsylvania | 246,790,000 | 4.6% | | 38 | Alaska | 38,160,000 | 0.7% |
| 49 | Rhode Island | 11,050,000 | 0.2% | | 39 | Oregon | 37,250,000 | 0.7% |
| 26 | South Carolina | 80,210,000 | 1.5% | | 40 | Connecticut | 35,300,000 | 0.7% |
| 47 | South Dakota | 14,760,000 | 0.3% | | 41 | Nevada | 33,850,000 | 0.6% |
| 18 | Tennessee | 105,730,000 | 2.0% | | 42 | Montana | 31,900,000 | 0.6% |
| 1 | Texas | 679,720,000 | 12.6% | | 43 | Hawaii | 19,310,000 | 0.4% |
| 32 | Utah | 63,970,000 | 1.2% | | 44 | Maine | 17,630,000 | 0.3% |
| 50 | Vermont | 5,900,000 | 0.1% | | 45 | New Hampshire | 16,410,000 | 0.3% |
| 19 | Virginia | 99,860,000 | 1.8% | | 46 | Idaho | 16,030,000 | 0.3% |
| 28 | Washington | 70,810,000 | 1.3% | | 47 | South Dakota | 14,760,000 | 0.3% |
| 21 | West Virginia | 95,970,000 | 1.8% | | 48 | Delaware | 13,110,000 | 0.2% |
| 20 | Wisconsin | 98,050,000 | 1.8% | | 49 | Rhode Island | 11,050,000 | 0.2% |
| 33 | Wyoming | 63,890,000 | 1.2% | | 50 | Vermont | 5,900,000 | 0.1% |
| | | | | | | District of Columbia | 3,170,000 | 0.1% |

Source: U.S. Environmental Protection Agency
  "Energy CO2 Emissions by State"  (http://www.epa.gov/statelocalclimate/resources/state_energyco2inv.html)
*Carbon dioxide (CO2) emissions from fossil fuel combustion.  This  represents the largest source (92%) of total CO2 emissions
from all emission sources.  Emissions are based on the location where fossil fuels are used. Fuels can be used in one state to
generate electricity consumed in another.

# Per Capita Fossil Fuel Emissions in 2011

## National Per Capita = 17.4 Metric Tons of Carbon Dioxide (CO2)*

ALPHA ORDER

| RANK | STATE | PER CAPITA |
|---|---|---|
| 13 | Alabama | 27.0 |
| 3 | Alaska | 52.8 |
| 31 | Arizona | 14.4 |
| 16 | Arkansas | 23.0 |
| 47 | California | 9.6 |
| 22 | Colorado | 18.0 |
| 46 | Connecticut | 9.8 |
| 31 | Delaware | 14.4 |
| 40 | Florida | 12.1 |
| 30 | Georgia | 15.9 |
| 33 | Hawaii | 14.0 |
| 45 | Idaho | 10.1 |
| 23 | Illinois | 17.9 |
| 7 | Indiana | 32.0 |
| 9 | Iowa | 28.5 |
| 15 | Kansas | 25.2 |
| 6 | Kentucky | 34.0 |
| 5 | Louisiana | 47.1 |
| 34 | Maine | 13.3 |
| 41 | Maryland | 11.3 |
| 43 | Massachusetts | 10.4 |
| 29 | Michigan | 16.2 |
| 25 | Minnesota | 17.3 |
| 19 | Mississippi | 20.6 |
| 18 | Missouri | 22.6 |
| 7 | Montana | 32.0 |
| 11 | Nebraska | 28.4 |
| 37 | Nevada | 12.5 |
| 38 | New Hampshire | 12.4 |
| 34 | New Jersey | 13.3 |
| 12 | New Mexico | 27.2 |
| 50 | New York | 8.5 |
| 34 | North Carolina | 13.3 |
| 2 | North Dakota | 73.5 |
| 20 | Ohio | 20.5 |
| 9 | Oklahoma | 28.5 |
| 47 | Oregon | 9.6 |
| 21 | Pennsylvania | 19.4 |
| 42 | Rhode Island | 10.5 |
| 26 | South Carolina | 17.2 |
| 23 | South Dakota | 17.9 |
| 28 | Tennessee | 16.5 |
| 14 | Texas | 26.5 |
| 17 | Utah | 22.7 |
| 49 | Vermont | 9.4 |
| 39 | Virginia | 12.3 |
| 43 | Washington | 10.4 |
| 4 | West Virginia | 51.7 |
| 26 | Wisconsin | 17.2 |
| 1 | Wyoming | 112.6 |

RANK ORDER

| RANK | STATE | PER CAPITA |
|---|---|---|
| 1 | Wyoming | 112.6 |
| 2 | North Dakota | 73.5 |
| 3 | Alaska | 52.8 |
| 4 | West Virginia | 51.7 |
| 5 | Louisiana | 47.1 |
| 6 | Kentucky | 34.0 |
| 7 | Indiana | 32.0 |
| 7 | Montana | 32.0 |
| 9 | Iowa | 28.5 |
| 9 | Oklahoma | 28.5 |
| 11 | Nebraska | 28.4 |
| 12 | New Mexico | 27.2 |
| 13 | Alabama | 27.0 |
| 14 | Texas | 26.5 |
| 15 | Kansas | 25.2 |
| 16 | Arkansas | 23.0 |
| 17 | Utah | 22.7 |
| 18 | Missouri | 22.6 |
| 19 | Mississippi | 20.6 |
| 20 | Ohio | 20.5 |
| 21 | Pennsylvania | 19.4 |
| 22 | Colorado | 18.0 |
| 23 | Illinois | 17.9 |
| 23 | South Dakota | 17.9 |
| 25 | Minnesota | 17.3 |
| 26 | South Carolina | 17.2 |
| 26 | Wisconsin | 17.2 |
| 28 | Tennessee | 16.5 |
| 29 | Michigan | 16.2 |
| 30 | Georgia | 15.9 |
| 31 | Arizona | 14.4 |
| 31 | Delaware | 14.4 |
| 33 | Hawaii | 14.0 |
| 34 | Maine | 13.3 |
| 34 | New Jersey | 13.3 |
| 34 | North Carolina | 13.3 |
| 37 | Nevada | 12.5 |
| 38 | New Hampshire | 12.4 |
| 39 | Virginia | 12.3 |
| 40 | Florida | 12.1 |
| 41 | Maryland | 11.3 |
| 42 | Rhode Island | 10.5 |
| 43 | Massachusetts | 10.4 |
| 43 | Washington | 10.4 |
| 45 | Idaho | 10.1 |
| 46 | Connecticut | 9.8 |
| 47 | California | 9.6 |
| 47 | Oregon | 9.6 |
| 49 | Vermont | 9.4 |
| 50 | New York | 8.5 |

| | | |
|---|---|---|
| | District of Columbia | 5.1 |

Source: CQ Press using data from U.S. Environmental Protection Agency
   "Energy CO2 Emissions by State"  (http://www.epa.gov/statelocalclimate/resources/state_energyco2inv.html)
*Carbon dioxide (CO2) emissions from fossil fuel combustion.  This represents the largest source (92%) of total CO2 emissions from all emission sources.  Emissions are based on the location where fossil fuels are used. Fuels can be used in one state to generate electricity consumed in another.

# Percent Change in Fossil Fuel Emissions: 2007 to 2011

## National Percent Change = 8.4% Decrease*

ALPHA ORDER

| RANK | STATE | PERCENT CHANGE |
|------|-------|----------------|
| 28 | Alabama | (10.8) |
| 34 | Alaska | (13.1) |
| 21 | Arizona | (8.5) |
| 2 | Arkansas | 6.7 |
| 30 | California | (11.4) |
| 17 | Colorado | (6.5) |
| 33 | Connecticut | (12.5) |
| 50 | Delaware | (23.2) |
| 23 | Florida | (9.8) |
| 38 | Georgia | (14.9) |
| 48 | Hawaii | (19.7) |
| 10 | Idaho | (2.5) |
| 14 | Illinois | (5.0) |
| 24 | Indiana | (9.9) |
| 6 | Iowa | 0.6 |
| 18 | Kansas | (7.6) |
| 15 | Kentucky | (5.2) |
| 5 | Louisiana | 0.8 |
| 42 | Maine | (16.1) |
| 40 | Maryland | (15.8) |
| 35 | Massachusetts | (14.0) |
| 31 | Michigan | (11.5) |
| 19 | Minnesota | (7.8) |
| 26 | Mississippi | (10.2) |
| 12 | Missouri | (3.6) |
| 41 | Montana | (16.0) |
| 1 | Nebraska | 17.6 |
| 47 | Nevada | (19.1) |
| 36 | New Hampshire | (14.3) |
| 29 | New Jersey | (10.9) |
| 12 | New Mexico | (3.6) |
| 45 | New York | (17.1) |
| 43 | North Carolina | (16.4) |
| 4 | North Dakota | 2.4 |
| 32 | Ohio | (11.8) |
| 9 | Oklahoma | (1.3) |
| 39 | Oregon | (15.2) |
| 26 | Pennsylvania | (10.2) |
| 8 | Rhode Island | (0.8) |
| 22 | South Carolina | (9.7) |
| 3 | South Dakota | 6.3 |
| 46 | Tennessee | (17.9) |
| 7 | Texas | (0.3) |
| 20 | Utah | (8.0) |
| 25 | Vermont | (10.1) |
| 49 | Virginia | (21.7) |
| 37 | Washington | (14.6) |
| 44 | West Virginia | (16.6) |
| 16 | Wisconsin | (6.2) |
| 11 | Wyoming | (3.4) |

RANK ORDER

| RANK | STATE | PERCENT CHANGE |
|------|-------|----------------|
| 1 | Nebraska | 17.6 |
| 2 | Arkansas | 6.7 |
| 3 | South Dakota | 6.3 |
| 4 | North Dakota | 2.4 |
| 5 | Louisiana | 0.8 |
| 6 | Iowa | 0.6 |
| 7 | Texas | (0.3) |
| 8 | Rhode Island | (0.8) |
| 9 | Oklahoma | (1.3) |
| 10 | Idaho | (2.5) |
| 11 | Wyoming | (3.4) |
| 12 | Missouri | (3.6) |
| 12 | New Mexico | (3.6) |
| 14 | Illinois | (5.0) |
| 15 | Kentucky | (5.2) |
| 16 | Wisconsin | (6.2) |
| 17 | Colorado | (6.5) |
| 18 | Kansas | (7.6) |
| 19 | Minnesota | (7.8) |
| 20 | Utah | (8.0) |
| 21 | Arizona | (8.5) |
| 22 | South Carolina | (9.7) |
| 23 | Florida | (9.8) |
| 24 | Indiana | (9.9) |
| 25 | Vermont | (10.1) |
| 26 | Mississippi | (10.2) |
| 26 | Pennsylvania | (10.2) |
| 28 | Alabama | (10.8) |
| 29 | New Jersey | (10.9) |
| 30 | California | (11.4) |
| 31 | Michigan | (11.5) |
| 32 | Ohio | (11.8) |
| 33 | Connecticut | (12.5) |
| 34 | Alaska | (13.1) |
| 35 | Massachusetts | (14.0) |
| 36 | New Hampshire | (14.3) |
| 37 | Washington | (14.6) |
| 38 | Georgia | (14.9) |
| 39 | Oregon | (15.2) |
| 40 | Maryland | (15.8) |
| 41 | Montana | (16.0) |
| 42 | Maine | (16.1) |
| 43 | North Carolina | (16.4) |
| 44 | West Virginia | (16.6) |
| 45 | New York | (17.1) |
| 46 | Tennessee | (17.9) |
| 47 | Nevada | (19.1) |
| 48 | Hawaii | (19.7) |
| 49 | Virginia | (21.7) |
| 50 | Delaware | (23.2) |
| | District of Columbia | (7.0) |

Source: CQ Press using data from U.S. Environmental Protection Agency
"Energy CO2 Emissions by State" (http://www.epa.gov/statelocalclimate/resources/state_energyco2inv.html)
*Based on metric tons of carbon dioxide (CO2).

# Toxic Releases: Total Pollution Released in 2012

## National Total = 3,626,883,669 Pounds of Toxins*

| ALPHA ORDER | | | | RANK ORDER | | | |
|---|---|---|---|---|---|---|---|
| RANK | STATE | POUNDS | % of USA | RANK | STATE | POUNDS | % of USA |
| 11 | Alabama | 81,590,091 | 2.2% | 1 | Alaska | 876,721,634 | 24.2% |
| 1 | Alaska | 876,721,634 | 24.2% | 2 | Nevada | 285,874,773 | 7.9% |
| 10 | Arizona | 85,509,846 | 2.4% | 3 | Texas | 226,457,216 | 6.2% |
| 27 | Arkansas | 35,290,419 | 1.0% | 4 | Utah | 191,961,034 | 5.3% |
| 30 | California | 31,707,203 | 0.9% | 5 | Louisiana | 143,289,289 | 4.0% |
| 31 | Colorado | 28,606,663 | 0.8% | 6 | Indiana | 139,647,681 | 3.9% |
| 47 | Connecticut | 2,141,978 | 0.1% | 7 | Illinois | 120,290,946 | 3.3% |
| 43 | Delaware | 7,568,205 | 0.2% | 8 | Ohio | 116,871,981 | 3.2% |
| 18 | Florida | 62,918,425 | 1.7% | 9 | Pennsylvania | 97,878,672 | 2.7% |
| 16 | Georgia | 65,392,625 | 1.8% | 10 | Arizona | 85,509,846 | 2.4% |
| 46 | Hawaii | 2,693,617 | 0.1% | 11 | Alabama | 81,590,091 | 2.2% |
| 26 | Idaho | 38,675,265 | 1.1% | 12 | Tennessee | 78,787,463 | 2.2% |
| 7 | Illinois | 120,290,946 | 3.3% | 13 | Kentucky | 77,986,319 | 2.2% |
| 6 | Indiana | 139,647,681 | 3.9% | 14 | Michigan | 70,038,763 | 1.9% |
| 25 | Iowa | 39,655,624 | 1.1% | 15 | Missouri | 69,735,412 | 1.9% |
| 36 | Kansas | 19,416,528 | 0.5% | 16 | Georgia | 65,392,625 | 1.8% |
| 13 | Kentucky | 77,986,319 | 2.2% | 17 | Oklahoma | 65,389,776 | 1.8% |
| 5 | Louisiana | 143,289,289 | 4.0% | 18 | Florida | 62,918,425 | 1.7% |
| 41 | Maine | 12,046,792 | 0.3% | 19 | Montana | 59,210,084 | 1.6% |
| 42 | Maryland | 8,262,420 | 0.2% | 20 | Mississippi | 55,622,343 | 1.5% |
| 45 | Massachusetts | 3,567,275 | 0.1% | 21 | North Carolina | 54,214,451 | 1.5% |
| 14 | Michigan | 70,038,763 | 1.9% | 22 | South Carolina | 49,310,415 | 1.4% |
| 32 | Minnesota | 27,350,939 | 0.8% | 23 | Virginia | 42,361,499 | 1.2% |
| 20 | Mississippi | 55,622,343 | 1.5% | 24 | West Virginia | 39,743,554 | 1.1% |
| 15 | Missouri | 69,735,412 | 1.9% | 25 | Iowa | 39,655,624 | 1.1% |
| 19 | Montana | 59,210,084 | 1.6% | 26 | Idaho | 38,675,265 | 1.1% |
| 34 | Nebraska | 23,590,024 | 0.7% | 27 | Arkansas | 35,290,419 | 1.0% |
| 2 | Nevada | 285,874,773 | 7.9% | 28 | North Dakota | 34,480,922 | 1.0% |
| 48 | New Hampshire | 822,371 | 0.0% | 29 | Wisconsin | 34,040,973 | 0.9% |
| 40 | New Jersey | 12,768,089 | 0.4% | 30 | California | 31,707,203 | 0.9% |
| 33 | New Mexico | 24,763,210 | 0.7% | 31 | Colorado | 28,606,663 | 0.8% |
| 38 | New York | 17,257,529 | 0.5% | 32 | Minnesota | 27,350,939 | 0.8% |
| 21 | North Carolina | 54,214,451 | 1.5% | 33 | New Mexico | 24,763,210 | 0.7% |
| 28 | North Dakota | 34,480,922 | 1.0% | 34 | Nebraska | 23,590,024 | 0.7% |
| 8 | Ohio | 116,871,981 | 3.2% | 35 | Oregon | 23,198,111 | 0.6% |
| 17 | Oklahoma | 65,389,776 | 1.8% | 36 | Kansas | 19,416,528 | 0.5% |
| 35 | Oregon | 23,198,111 | 0.6% | 37 | Washington | 19,238,953 | 0.5% |
| 9 | Pennsylvania | 97,878,672 | 2.7% | 38 | New York | 17,257,529 | 0.5% |
| 50 | Rhode Island | 268,558 | 0.0% | 39 | Wyoming | 17,153,005 | 0.5% |
| 22 | South Carolina | 49,310,415 | 1.4% | 40 | New Jersey | 12,768,089 | 0.4% |
| 44 | South Dakota | 5,176,520 | 0.1% | 41 | Maine | 12,046,792 | 0.3% |
| 12 | Tennessee | 78,787,463 | 2.2% | 42 | Maryland | 8,262,420 | 0.2% |
| 3 | Texas | 226,457,216 | 6.2% | 43 | Delaware | 7,568,205 | 0.2% |
| 4 | Utah | 191,961,034 | 5.3% | 44 | South Dakota | 5,176,520 | 0.1% |
| 49 | Vermont | 310,901 | 0.0% | 45 | Massachusetts | 3,567,275 | 0.1% |
| 23 | Virginia | 42,361,499 | 1.2% | 46 | Hawaii | 2,693,617 | 0.1% |
| 37 | Washington | 19,238,953 | 0.5% | 47 | Connecticut | 2,141,978 | 0.1% |
| 24 | West Virginia | 39,743,554 | 1.1% | 48 | New Hampshire | 822,371 | 0.0% |
| 29 | Wisconsin | 34,040,973 | 0.9% | 49 | Vermont | 310,901 | 0.0% |
| 39 | Wyoming | 17,153,005 | 0.5% | 50 | Rhode Island | 268,558 | 0.0% |
| | | | | | District of Columbia | 27,283 | 0.0% |

Source: U.S. Environmental Protection Agency, Office of Pollution Prevention and Toxics Information Management
   "2012 Toxics Release Inventory"  (http://www.epa.gov/triexplorer/)
*National total does not include 5,259,081 pounds of toxins in U.S. territories.  Includes discharges to air, surface water, underground injection, and surface land.  Includes both original (or manufacturing) industries and those added by EPA since it began tracking releases.

# Toxic Releases: Total Air Emissions in 2012

## National Total = 753,223,676 Pounds*

| ALPHA ORDER | | | | RANK ORDER | | | |
|---|---|---|---|---|---|---|---|
| RANK | STATE | POUNDS | % of USA | RANK | STATE | POUNDS | % of USA |
| 7 | Alabama | 33,168,902 | 4.4% | 1 | Texas | 60,486,694 | 8.0% |
| 48 | Alaska | 446,348 | 0.1% | 2 | Louisiana | 51,628,735 | 6.9% |
| 37 | Arizona | 2,194,736 | 0.3% | 3 | Ohio | 44,312,754 | 5.9% |
| 20 | Arkansas | 16,395,622 | 2.2% | 4 | Georgia | 41,361,693 | 5.5% |
| 28 | California | 7,520,124 | 1.0% | 5 | Kentucky | 41,171,493 | 5.5% |
| 35 | Colorado | 2,780,261 | 0.4% | 6 | Indiana | 38,892,127 | 5.2% |
| 46 | Connecticut | 855,661 | 0.1% | 7 | Alabama | 33,168,902 | 4.4% |
| 44 | Delaware | 1,109,209 | 0.1% | 8 | Illinois | 29,029,593 | 3.9% |
| 13 | Florida | 25,072,828 | 3.3% | 9 | Tennessee | 28,327,560 | 3.8% |
| 4 | Georgia | 41,361,693 | 5.5% | 10 | South Carolina | 28,217,707 | 3.7% |
| 39 | Hawaii | 1,876,897 | 0.2% | 11 | Pennsylvania | 27,765,131 | 3.7% |
| 33 | Idaho | 4,572,651 | 0.6% | 12 | North Carolina | 26,641,726 | 3.5% |
| 8 | Illinois | 29,029,593 | 3.9% | 13 | Florida | 25,072,828 | 3.3% |
| 6 | Indiana | 38,892,127 | 5.2% | 14 | Michigan | 24,182,233 | 3.2% |
| 18 | Iowa | 19,570,214 | 2.6% | 15 | Mississippi | 20,965,865 | 2.8% |
| 24 | Kansas | 9,996,714 | 1.3% | 16 | Virginia | 20,763,540 | 2.8% |
| 5 | Kentucky | 41,171,493 | 5.5% | 17 | Oklahoma | 19,726,926 | 2.6% |
| 2 | Louisiana | 51,628,735 | 6.9% | 18 | Iowa | 19,570,214 | 2.6% |
| 34 | Maine | 4,447,162 | 0.6% | 19 | West Virginia | 18,146,053 | 2.4% |
| 31 | Maryland | 5,209,145 | 0.7% | 20 | Arkansas | 16,395,622 | 2.2% |
| 41 | Massachusetts | 1,543,846 | 0.2% | 21 | North Dakota | 14,749,715 | 2.0% |
| 14 | Michigan | 24,182,233 | 3.2% | 22 | Wisconsin | 12,786,089 | 1.7% |
| 26 | Minnesota | 9,177,885 | 1.2% | 23 | Missouri | 11,561,486 | 1.5% |
| 15 | Mississippi | 20,965,865 | 2.8% | 24 | Kansas | 9,996,714 | 1.3% |
| 23 | Missouri | 11,561,486 | 1.5% | 25 | Washington | 9,898,022 | 1.3% |
| 40 | Montana | 1,761,481 | 0.2% | 26 | Minnesota | 9,177,885 | 1.2% |
| 32 | Nebraska | 4,627,598 | 0.6% | 27 | Utah | 8,070,094 | 1.1% |
| 42 | Nevada | 1,265,370 | 0.2% | 28 | California | 7,520,124 | 1.0% |
| 47 | New Hampshire | 616,504 | 0.1% | 29 | New York | 6,758,936 | 0.9% |
| 38 | New Jersey | 2,142,968 | 0.3% | 30 | Oregon | 6,622,188 | 0.9% |
| 45 | New Mexico | 1,043,897 | 0.1% | 31 | Maryland | 5,209,145 | 0.7% |
| 29 | New York | 6,758,936 | 0.9% | 32 | Nebraska | 4,627,598 | 0.6% |
| 12 | North Carolina | 26,641,726 | 3.5% | 33 | Idaho | 4,572,651 | 0.6% |
| 21 | North Dakota | 14,749,715 | 2.0% | 34 | Maine | 4,447,162 | 0.6% |
| 3 | Ohio | 44,312,754 | 5.9% | 35 | Colorado | 2,780,261 | 0.4% |
| 17 | Oklahoma | 19,726,926 | 2.6% | 36 | Wyoming | 2,386,422 | 0.3% |
| 30 | Oregon | 6,622,188 | 0.9% | 37 | Arizona | 2,194,736 | 0.3% |
| 11 | Pennsylvania | 27,765,131 | 3.7% | 38 | New Jersey | 2,142,968 | 0.3% |
| 49 | Rhode Island | 107,255 | 0.0% | 39 | Hawaii | 1,876,897 | 0.2% |
| 10 | South Carolina | 28,217,707 | 3.7% | 40 | Montana | 1,761,481 | 0.2% |
| 43 | South Dakota | 1,219,388 | 0.2% | 41 | Massachusetts | 1,543,846 | 0.2% |
| 9 | Tennessee | 28,327,560 | 3.8% | 42 | Nevada | 1,265,370 | 0.2% |
| 1 | Texas | 60,486,694 | 8.0% | 43 | South Dakota | 1,219,388 | 0.2% |
| 27 | Utah | 8,070,094 | 1.1% | 44 | Delaware | 1,109,209 | 0.1% |
| 50 | Vermont | 37,001 | 0.0% | 45 | New Mexico | 1,043,897 | 0.1% |
| 16 | Virginia | 20,763,540 | 2.8% | 46 | Connecticut | 855,661 | 0.1% |
| 25 | Washington | 9,898,022 | 1.3% | 47 | New Hampshire | 616,504 | 0.1% |
| 19 | West Virginia | 18,146,053 | 2.4% | 48 | Alaska | 446,348 | 0.1% |
| 22 | Wisconsin | 12,786,089 | 1.7% | 49 | Rhode Island | 107,255 | 0.0% |
| 36 | Wyoming | 2,386,422 | 0.3% | 50 | Vermont | 37,001 | 0.0% |
| | | | | | District of Columbia | 11,227 | 0.0% |

Source: U.S. Environmental Protection Agency, Office of Pollution Prevention and Toxics Information Management
   "2012 Toxics Release Inventory" (http://www.epa.gov/triexplorer/)
*Includes fugitive and point source air emissions. National total does not include 4,251,939 pounds of emissions in U.S. territories. Includes both original (or manufacturing) industries and those added by EPA since it began tracking releases.

# Toxic Releases: Total Surface Water Discharges in 2012

## National Total = 206,992,950 Pounds*

| ALPHA ORDER | | | | | RANK ORDER | | | |
|---|---|---|---|---|---|---|---|---|
| RANK | STATE | POUNDS | % of USA | | RANK | STATE | POUNDS | % of USA |
| 4 | Alabama | 12,290,924 | 5.9% | | 1 | Indiana | 18,311,874 | 8.8% |
| 37 | Alaska | 570,475 | 0.3% | | 2 | Texas | 16,572,655 | 8.0% |
| 48 | Arizona | 1,177 | 0.0% | | 3 | Louisiana | 12,644,689 | 6.1% |
| 17 | Arkansas | 4,250,380 | 2.1% | | 4 | Alabama | 12,290,924 | 5.9% |
| 26 | California | 2,358,874 | 1.1% | | 5 | Virginia | 11,822,567 | 5.7% |
| 36 | Colorado | 849,619 | 0.4% | | 6 | Nebraska | 10,522,803 | 5.1% |
| 40 | Connecticut | 223,997 | 0.1% | | 7 | Pennsylvania | 10,475,081 | 5.1% |
| 20 | Delaware | 3,777,904 | 1.8% | | 8 | Georgia | 10,132,249 | 4.9% |
| 32 | Florida | 1,332,673 | 0.6% | | 9 | North Carolina | 8,899,571 | 4.3% |
| 8 | Georgia | 10,132,249 | 4.9% | | 10 | Ohio | 7,569,944 | 3.7% |
| 38 | Hawaii | 435,662 | 0.2% | | 11 | Kentucky | 7,417,795 | 3.6% |
| 25 | Idaho | 2,470,923 | 1.2% | | 12 | Iowa | 6,829,092 | 3.3% |
| 14 | Illinois | 6,130,604 | 3.0% | | 13 | New Jersey | 6,191,385 | 3.0% |
| 1 | Indiana | 18,311,874 | 8.8% | | 14 | Illinois | 6,130,604 | 3.0% |
| 12 | Iowa | 6,829,092 | 3.3% | | 15 | New York | 5,307,015 | 2.6% |
| 39 | Kansas | 302,239 | 0.1% | | 16 | Mississippi | 4,957,679 | 2.4% |
| 11 | Kentucky | 7,417,795 | 3.6% | | 17 | Arkansas | 4,250,380 | 2.1% |
| 3 | Louisiana | 12,644,689 | 6.1% | | 18 | Oklahoma | 4,219,626 | 2.0% |
| 22 | Maine | 3,105,291 | 1.5% | | 19 | Tennessee | 4,114,915 | 2.0% |
| 35 | Maryland | 1,084,344 | 0.5% | | 20 | Delaware | 3,777,904 | 1.8% |
| 47 | Massachusetts | 5,551 | 0.0% | | 21 | South Carolina | 3,347,493 | 1.6% |
| 31 | Michigan | 1,779,947 | 0.9% | | 22 | Maine | 3,105,291 | 1.5% |
| 30 | Minnesota | 1,861,487 | 0.9% | | 23 | Wisconsin | 2,797,260 | 1.4% |
| 16 | Mississippi | 4,957,679 | 2.4% | | 24 | Washington | 2,728,520 | 1.3% |
| 27 | Missouri | 2,176,282 | 1.1% | | 25 | Idaho | 2,470,923 | 1.2% |
| 41 | Montana | 195,669 | 0.1% | | 26 | California | 2,358,874 | 1.1% |
| 6 | Nebraska | 10,522,803 | 5.1% | | 27 | Missouri | 2,176,282 | 1.1% |
| 34 | Nevada | 1,169,685 | 0.6% | | 28 | West Virginia | 2,161,592 | 1.0% |
| 49 | New Hampshire | 797 | 0.0% | | 29 | South Dakota | 1,895,777 | 0.9% |
| 13 | New Jersey | 6,191,385 | 3.0% | | 30 | Minnesota | 1,861,487 | 0.9% |
| 45 | New Mexico | 39,784 | 0.0% | | 31 | Michigan | 1,779,947 | 0.9% |
| 15 | New York | 5,307,015 | 2.6% | | 32 | Florida | 1,332,673 | 0.6% |
| 9 | North Carolina | 8,899,571 | 4.3% | | 33 | Oregon | 1,288,342 | 0.6% |
| 42 | North Dakota | 151,308 | 0.1% | | 34 | Nevada | 1,169,685 | 0.6% |
| 10 | Ohio | 7,569,944 | 3.7% | | 35 | Maryland | 1,084,344 | 0.5% |
| 18 | Oklahoma | 4,219,626 | 2.0% | | 36 | Colorado | 849,619 | 0.4% |
| 33 | Oregon | 1,288,342 | 0.6% | | 37 | Alaska | 570,475 | 0.3% |
| 7 | Pennsylvania | 10,475,081 | 5.1% | | 38 | Hawaii | 435,662 | 0.2% |
| 50 | Rhode Island | 600 | 0.0% | | 39 | Kansas | 302,239 | 0.1% |
| 21 | South Carolina | 3,347,493 | 1.6% | | 40 | Connecticut | 223,997 | 0.1% |
| 29 | South Dakota | 1,895,777 | 0.9% | | 41 | Montana | 195,669 | 0.1% |
| 19 | Tennessee | 4,114,915 | 2.0% | | 42 | North Dakota | 151,308 | 0.1% |
| 2 | Texas | 16,572,655 | 8.0% | | 43 | Utah | 104,515 | 0.1% |
| 43 | Utah | 104,515 | 0.1% | | 44 | Vermont | 98,218 | 0.0% |
| 44 | Vermont | 98,218 | 0.0% | | 45 | New Mexico | 39,784 | 0.0% |
| 5 | Virginia | 11,822,567 | 5.7% | | 46 | Wyoming | 15,149 | 0.0% |
| 24 | Washington | 2,728,520 | 1.3% | | 47 | Massachusetts | 5,551 | 0.0% |
| 28 | West Virginia | 2,161,592 | 1.0% | | 48 | Arizona | 1,177 | 0.0% |
| 23 | Wisconsin | 2,797,260 | 1.4% | | 49 | New Hampshire | 797 | 0.0% |
| 46 | Wyoming | 15,149 | 0.0% | | 50 | Rhode Island | 600 | 0.0% |
| | | | | | | District of Columbia | 948 | 0.0% |

Source: U.S. Environmental Protection Agency, Office of Pollution Prevention and Toxics Information Management
"2012 Toxics Release Inventory" (http://www.epa.gov/triexplorer/)
*National total does not include 276,939 pounds of discharges in U.S. territories. Includes both original (or manufacturing) industries and those added by EPA since it began tracking releases.

# Hazardous Waste Sites on the National Priority List in 2014

## National Total = 1,373 Sites*

| ALPHA ORDER | | | | RANK ORDER | | | |
|---|---|---|---|---|---|---|---|
| RANK | STATE | SITES | % of USA | RANK | STATE | SITES | % of USA |
| 26 | Alabama | 15 | 1.1% | 1 | New Jersey | 116 | 8.4% |
| 45 | Alaska | 6 | 0.4% | 2 | California | 98 | 7.1% |
| 40 | Arizona | 9 | 0.7% | 3 | Pennsylvania | 97 | 7.1% |
| 39 | Arkansas | 10 | 0.7% | 4 | New York | 87 | 6.3% |
| 2 | California | 98 | 7.1% | 5 | Michigan | 67 | 4.9% |
| 21 | Colorado | 20 | 1.5% | 6 | Florida | 56 | 4.1% |
| 26 | Connecticut | 15 | 1.1% | 7 | Texas | 51 | 3.7% |
| 31 | Delaware | 14 | 1.0% | 8 | Washington | 50 | 3.6% |
| 6 | Florida | 56 | 4.1% | 9 | Illinois | 48 | 3.5% |
| 24 | Georgia | 17 | 1.2% | 10 | Ohio | 43 | 3.1% |
| 46 | Hawaii | 3 | 0.2% | 11 | North Carolina | 39 | 2.8% |
| 40 | Idaho | 9 | 0.7% | 11 | Wisconsin | 39 | 2.8% |
| 9 | Illinois | 48 | 3.5% | 13 | Indiana | 37 | 2.7% |
| 13 | Indiana | 37 | 2.7% | 14 | Missouri | 33 | 2.4% |
| 35 | Iowa | 12 | 0.9% | 15 | Massachusetts | 32 | 2.3% |
| 34 | Kansas | 13 | 0.9% | 16 | Virginia | 31 | 2.3% |
| 31 | Kentucky | 14 | 1.0% | 17 | Minnesota | 25 | 1.8% |
| 35 | Louisiana | 12 | 0.9% | 17 | South Carolina | 25 | 1.8% |
| 31 | Maine | 14 | 1.0% | 19 | New Hampshire | 22 | 1.6% |
| 20 | Maryland | 21 | 1.5% | 20 | Maryland | 21 | 1.5% |
| 15 | Massachusetts | 32 | 2.3% | 21 | Colorado | 20 | 1.5% |
| 5 | Michigan | 67 | 4.9% | 22 | Utah | 19 | 1.4% |
| 17 | Minnesota | 25 | 1.8% | 23 | Montana | 18 | 1.3% |
| 40 | Mississippi | 9 | 0.7% | 24 | Georgia | 17 | 1.2% |
| 14 | Missouri | 33 | 2.4% | 24 | Tennessee | 17 | 1.2% |
| 23 | Montana | 18 | 1.3% | 26 | Alabama | 15 | 1.1% |
| 26 | Nebraska | 15 | 1.1% | 26 | Connecticut | 15 | 1.1% |
| 49 | Nevada | 1 | 0.1% | 26 | Nebraska | 15 | 1.1% |
| 19 | New Hampshire | 22 | 1.6% | 26 | New Mexico | 15 | 1.1% |
| 1 | New Jersey | 116 | 8.4% | 26 | Oregon | 15 | 1.1% |
| 26 | New Mexico | 15 | 1.1% | 31 | Delaware | 14 | 1.0% |
| 4 | New York | 87 | 6.3% | 31 | Kentucky | 14 | 1.0% |
| 11 | North Carolina | 39 | 2.8% | 31 | Maine | 14 | 1.0% |
| 50 | North Dakota | 0 | 0.0% | 34 | Kansas | 13 | 0.9% |
| 10 | Ohio | 43 | 3.1% | 35 | Iowa | 12 | 0.9% |
| 44 | Oklahoma | 8 | 0.6% | 35 | Louisiana | 12 | 0.9% |
| 26 | Oregon | 15 | 1.1% | 35 | Rhode Island | 12 | 0.9% |
| 3 | Pennsylvania | 97 | 7.1% | 38 | Vermont | 11 | 0.8% |
| 35 | Rhode Island | 12 | 0.9% | 39 | Arkansas | 10 | 0.7% |
| 17 | South Carolina | 25 | 1.8% | 40 | Arizona | 9 | 0.7% |
| 47 | South Dakota | 2 | 0.1% | 40 | Idaho | 9 | 0.7% |
| 24 | Tennessee | 17 | 1.2% | 40 | Mississippi | 9 | 0.7% |
| 7 | Texas | 51 | 3.7% | 40 | West Virginia | 9 | 0.7% |
| 22 | Utah | 19 | 1.4% | 44 | Oklahoma | 8 | 0.6% |
| 38 | Vermont | 11 | 0.8% | 45 | Alaska | 6 | 0.4% |
| 16 | Virginia | 31 | 2.3% | 46 | Hawaii | 3 | 0.2% |
| 8 | Washington | 50 | 3.6% | 47 | South Dakota | 2 | 0.1% |
| 40 | West Virginia | 9 | 0.7% | 47 | Wyoming | 2 | 0.1% |
| 11 | Wisconsin | 39 | 2.8% | 49 | Nevada | 1 | 0.1% |
| 47 | Wyoming | 2 | 0.1% | 50 | North Dakota | 0 | 0.0% |
| | | | | District of Columbia | | 1 | 0.1% |

Source: U.S. Environmental Protection Agency
   "National Priorities List (NPL) Sites in the United States" (http://www.epa.gov/superfund/sites/npl/)
*As of January 7, 2014.  Includes final and proposed General Superfund and Federal Facilities Sites.  National total includes 16 sites in Puerto Rico, two in Guam, and one in the U.S. Virgin Islands.

# Hazardous Waste Sites on the National Priority List
## per 10,000 Square Miles in 2014
## National Rate = 3.6 Sites per 10,000 Square Miles*

ALPHA ORDER

| RANK | STATE | RATE |
|------|-------|------|
| 27 | Alabama | 2.9 |
| 48 | Alaska | 0.1 |
| 45 | Arizona | 0.8 |
| 34 | Arkansas | 1.9 |
| 20 | California | 6.0 |
| 34 | Colorado | 1.9 |
| 5 | Connecticut | 27.1 |
| 3 | Delaware | 56.3 |
| 13 | Florida | 8.5 |
| 27 | Georgia | 2.9 |
| 30 | Hawaii | 2.7 |
| 43 | Idaho | 1.1 |
| 14 | Illinois | 8.3 |
| 11 | Indiana | 10.2 |
| 33 | Iowa | 2.1 |
| 39 | Kansas | 1.6 |
| 26 | Kentucky | 3.5 |
| 31 | Louisiana | 2.3 |
| 23 | Maine | 4.0 |
| 8 | Maryland | 16.9 |
| 4 | Massachusetts | 30.3 |
| 19 | Michigan | 6.9 |
| 27 | Minnesota | 2.9 |
| 34 | Mississippi | 1.9 |
| 22 | Missouri | 4.7 |
| 41 | Montana | 1.2 |
| 34 | Nebraska | 1.9 |
| 48 | Nevada | 0.1 |
| 6 | New Hampshire | 23.5 |
| 1 | New Jersey | 133.0 |
| 41 | New Mexico | 1.2 |
| 9 | New York | 15.9 |
| 16 | North Carolina | 7.2 |
| 50 | North Dakota | 0.0 |
| 12 | Ohio | 9.6 |
| 43 | Oklahoma | 1.1 |
| 40 | Oregon | 1.5 |
| 7 | Pennsylvania | 21.1 |
| 2 | Rhode Island | 77.7 |
| 15 | South Carolina | 7.8 |
| 46 | South Dakota | 0.3 |
| 23 | Tennessee | 4.0 |
| 34 | Texas | 1.9 |
| 32 | Utah | 2.2 |
| 10 | Vermont | 11.4 |
| 16 | Virginia | 7.2 |
| 18 | Washington | 7.0 |
| 25 | West Virginia | 3.7 |
| 20 | Wisconsin | 6.0 |
| 47 | Wyoming | 0.2 |

RANK ORDER

| RANK | STATE | RATE |
|------|-------|------|
| 1 | New Jersey | 133.0 |
| 2 | Rhode Island | 77.7 |
| 3 | Delaware | 56.3 |
| 4 | Massachusetts | 30.3 |
| 5 | Connecticut | 27.1 |
| 6 | New Hampshire | 23.5 |
| 7 | Pennsylvania | 21.1 |
| 8 | Maryland | 16.9 |
| 9 | New York | 15.9 |
| 10 | Vermont | 11.4 |
| 11 | Indiana | 10.2 |
| 12 | Ohio | 9.6 |
| 13 | Florida | 8.5 |
| 14 | Illinois | 8.3 |
| 15 | South Carolina | 7.8 |
| 16 | North Carolina | 7.2 |
| 16 | Virginia | 7.2 |
| 18 | Washington | 7.0 |
| 19 | Michigan | 6.9 |
| 20 | California | 6.0 |
| 20 | Wisconsin | 6.0 |
| 22 | Missouri | 4.7 |
| 23 | Maine | 4.0 |
| 23 | Tennessee | 4.0 |
| 25 | West Virginia | 3.7 |
| 26 | Kentucky | 3.5 |
| 27 | Alabama | 2.9 |
| 27 | Georgia | 2.9 |
| 27 | Minnesota | 2.9 |
| 30 | Hawaii | 2.7 |
| 31 | Louisiana | 2.3 |
| 32 | Utah | 2.2 |
| 33 | Iowa | 2.1 |
| 34 | Arkansas | 1.9 |
| 34 | Colorado | 1.9 |
| 34 | Mississippi | 1.9 |
| 34 | Nebraska | 1.9 |
| 34 | Texas | 1.9 |
| 39 | Kansas | 1.6 |
| 40 | Oregon | 1.5 |
| 41 | Montana | 1.2 |
| 41 | New Mexico | 1.2 |
| 43 | Idaho | 1.1 |
| 43 | Oklahoma | 1.1 |
| 45 | Arizona | 0.8 |
| 46 | South Dakota | 0.3 |
| 47 | Wyoming | 0.2 |
| 48 | Alaska | 0.1 |
| 48 | Nevada | 0.1 |
| 50 | North Dakota | 0.0 |
| | District of Columbia** | NA |

Source: CQ Press using data from U.S. Environmental Protection Agency
"National Priorities List (NPL) Sites in the United States" (http://www.epa.gov/superfund/sites/npl/)
*As of January 7, 2014. Includes final and proposed General Superfund and Federal Facilities Sites. National rate excludes sites and square miles in Puerto Rico, Guam and the Virgin Islands. Based on land and water area of states.
**The District of Columbia has one site in its 68 square miles.

# Hazardous Waste Sites Deleted from the National Priorities List as of 2014

## National Total = 374 Sites*

| ALPHA ORDER | | | | RANK ORDER | | | |
|---|---|---|---|---|---|---|---|
| RANK | STATE | SITES | % of USA | RANK | STATE | SITES | % of USA |
| 43 | Alabama | 1 | 0.3% | 1 | New Jersey | 33 | 8.8% |
| 31 | Alaska | 3 | 0.8% | 2 | New York | 30 | 8.0% |
| 31 | Arizona | 3 | 0.8% | 3 | Pennsylvania | 29 | 7.8% |
| 13 | Arkansas | 7 | 1.9% | 4 | Florida | 24 | 6.4% |
| 8 | California | 13 | 3.5% | 5 | Minnesota | 21 | 5.6% |
| 31 | Colorado | 3 | 0.8% | 6 | Michigan | 19 | 5.1% |
| 31 | Connecticut | 3 | 0.8% | 7 | Washington | 17 | 4.5% |
| 13 | Delaware | 7 | 1.9% | 8 | California | 13 | 3.5% |
| 4 | Florida | 24 | 6.4% | 9 | Louisiana | 12 | 3.2% |
| 22 | Georgia | 5 | 1.3% | 9 | Texas | 12 | 3.2% |
| 43 | Hawaii | 1 | 0.3% | 11 | Iowa | 10 | 2.7% |
| 31 | Idaho | 3 | 0.8% | 12 | Indiana | 9 | 2.4% |
| 22 | Illinois | 5 | 1.3% | 13 | Arkansas | 7 | 1.9% |
| 12 | Indiana | 9 | 2.4% | 13 | Delaware | 7 | 1.9% |
| 11 | Iowa | 10 | 2.7% | 13 | Ohio | 7 | 1.9% |
| 22 | Kansas | 5 | 1.3% | 13 | Oklahoma | 7 | 1.9% |
| 17 | Kentucky | 6 | 1.6% | 17 | Kentucky | 6 | 1.6% |
| 9 | Louisiana | 12 | 3.2% | 17 | Massachusetts | 6 | 1.6% |
| 38 | Maine | 2 | 0.5% | 17 | South Carolina | 6 | 1.6% |
| 27 | Maryland | 4 | 1.1% | 17 | Tennessee | 6 | 1.6% |
| 17 | Massachusetts | 6 | 1.6% | 17 | Wisconsin | 6 | 1.6% |
| 6 | Michigan | 19 | 5.1% | 22 | Georgia | 5 | 1.3% |
| 5 | Minnesota | 21 | 5.6% | 22 | Illinois | 5 | 1.3% |
| 31 | Mississippi | 3 | 0.8% | 22 | Kansas | 5 | 1.3% |
| 22 | Missouri | 5 | 1.3% | 22 | Missouri | 5 | 1.3% |
| 48 | Montana | 0 | 0.0% | 22 | Utah | 5 | 1.3% |
| 43 | Nebraska | 1 | 0.3% | 27 | Maryland | 4 | 1.1% |
| 48 | Nevada | 0 | 0.0% | 27 | New Mexico | 4 | 1.1% |
| 48 | New Hampshire | 0 | 0.0% | 27 | Oregon | 4 | 1.1% |
| 1 | New Jersey | 33 | 8.8% | 27 | Virginia | 4 | 1.1% |
| 27 | New Mexico | 4 | 1.1% | 31 | Alaska | 3 | 0.8% |
| 2 | New York | 30 | 8.0% | 31 | Arizona | 3 | 0.8% |
| 31 | North Carolina | 3 | 0.8% | 31 | Colorado | 3 | 0.8% |
| 38 | North Dakota | 2 | 0.5% | 31 | Connecticut | 3 | 0.8% |
| 13 | Ohio | 7 | 1.9% | 31 | Idaho | 3 | 0.8% |
| 13 | Oklahoma | 7 | 1.9% | 31 | Mississippi | 3 | 0.8% |
| 27 | Oregon | 4 | 1.1% | 31 | North Carolina | 3 | 0.8% |
| 3 | Pennsylvania | 29 | 7.8% | 38 | Maine | 2 | 0.5% |
| 43 | Rhode Island | 1 | 0.3% | 38 | North Dakota | 2 | 0.5% |
| 17 | South Carolina | 6 | 1.6% | 38 | South Dakota | 2 | 0.5% |
| 38 | South Dakota | 2 | 0.5% | 38 | Vermont | 2 | 0.5% |
| 17 | Tennessee | 6 | 1.6% | 38 | West Virginia | 2 | 0.5% |
| 9 | Texas | 12 | 3.2% | 43 | Alabama | 1 | 0.3% |
| 22 | Utah | 5 | 1.3% | 43 | Hawaii | 1 | 0.3% |
| 38 | Vermont | 2 | 0.5% | 43 | Nebraska | 1 | 0.3% |
| 27 | Virginia | 4 | 1.1% | 43 | Rhode Island | 1 | 0.3% |
| 7 | Washington | 17 | 4.5% | 43 | Wyoming | 1 | 0.3% |
| 38 | West Virginia | 2 | 0.5% | 48 | Montana | 0 | 0.0% |
| 17 | Wisconsin | 6 | 1.6% | 48 | Nevada | 0 | 0.0% |
| 43 | Wyoming | 1 | 0.3% | 48 | New Hampshire | 0 | 0.0% |
| | | | | | District of Columbia | 0 | 0.0% |

Source: U.S. Environmental Protection Agency
   "National Priorities List (NPL) Sites in the United States" (http://www.epa.gov/superfund/sites/npl/)
*Cumulative total as of January 7, 2014.  National total includes six sites in Puerto Rico and four in other U.S. territories.

# VIII. Geography

# Total Area of States in Square Miles in 2010

## National Total = 3,796,742 Square Miles*

ALPHA ORDER

| RANK | STATE | MILES | % of USA |
|------|-------|-------|----------|
| 30 | Alabama | 52,420 | 1.4% |
| 1 | Alaska | 665,384 | 17.5% |
| 6 | Arizona | 113,990 | 3.0% |
| 29 | Arkansas | 53,179 | 1.4% |
| 3 | California | 163,695 | 4.3% |
| 8 | Colorado | 104,094 | 2.7% |
| 48 | Connecticut | 5,543 | 0.1% |
| 49 | Delaware | 2,489 | 0.1% |
| 22 | Florida | 65,758 | 1.7% |
| 24 | Georgia | 59,425 | 1.6% |
| 43 | Hawaii | 10,932 | 0.3% |
| 14 | Idaho | 83,569 | 2.2% |
| 25 | Illinois | 57,914 | 1.5% |
| 38 | Indiana | 36,420 | 1.0% |
| 26 | Iowa | 56,273 | 1.5% |
| 15 | Kansas | 82,278 | 2.2% |
| 37 | Kentucky | 40,408 | 1.1% |
| 31 | Louisiana | 52,378 | 1.4% |
| 39 | Maine | 35,380 | 0.9% |
| 42 | Maryland | 12,406 | 0.3% |
| 44 | Massachusetts | 10,554 | 0.3% |
| 11 | Michigan | 96,714 | 2.5% |
| 12 | Minnesota | 86,936 | 2.3% |
| 32 | Mississippi | 48,432 | 1.3% |
| 21 | Missouri | 69,707 | 1.8% |
| 4 | Montana | 147,040 | 3.9% |
| 16 | Nebraska | 77,348 | 2.0% |
| 7 | Nevada | 110,572 | 2.9% |
| 46 | New Hampshire | 9,349 | 0.2% |
| 47 | New Jersey | 8,723 | 0.2% |
| 5 | New Mexico | 121,590 | 3.2% |
| 27 | New York | 54,555 | 1.4% |
| 28 | North Carolina | 53,819 | 1.4% |
| 19 | North Dakota | 70,698 | 1.9% |
| 34 | Ohio | 44,826 | 1.2% |
| 20 | Oklahoma | 69,899 | 1.8% |
| 9 | Oregon | 98,379 | 2.6% |
| 33 | Pennsylvania | 46,054 | 1.2% |
| 50 | Rhode Island | 1,545 | 0.0% |
| 40 | South Carolina | 32,020 | 0.8% |
| 17 | South Dakota | 77,116 | 2.0% |
| 36 | Tennessee | 42,144 | 1.1% |
| 2 | Texas | 268,596 | 7.1% |
| 13 | Utah | 84,897 | 2.2% |
| 45 | Vermont | 9,616 | 0.3% |
| 35 | Virginia | 42,775 | 1.1% |
| 18 | Washington | 71,298 | 1.9% |
| 41 | West Virginia | 24,230 | 0.6% |
| 23 | Wisconsin | 65,496 | 1.7% |
| 10 | Wyoming | 97,813 | 2.6% |

RANK ORDER

| RANK | STATE | MILES | % of USA |
|------|-------|-------|----------|
| 1 | Alaska | 665,384 | 17.5% |
| 2 | Texas | 268,596 | 7.1% |
| 3 | California | 163,695 | 4.3% |
| 4 | Montana | 147,040 | 3.9% |
| 5 | New Mexico | 121,590 | 3.2% |
| 6 | Arizona | 113,990 | 3.0% |
| 7 | Nevada | 110,572 | 2.9% |
| 8 | Colorado | 104,094 | 2.7% |
| 9 | Oregon | 98,379 | 2.6% |
| 10 | Wyoming | 97,813 | 2.6% |
| 11 | Michigan | 96,714 | 2.5% |
| 12 | Minnesota | 86,936 | 2.3% |
| 13 | Utah | 84,897 | 2.2% |
| 14 | Idaho | 83,569 | 2.2% |
| 15 | Kansas | 82,278 | 2.2% |
| 16 | Nebraska | 77,348 | 2.0% |
| 17 | South Dakota | 77,116 | 2.0% |
| 18 | Washington | 71,298 | 1.9% |
| 19 | North Dakota | 70,698 | 1.9% |
| 20 | Oklahoma | 69,899 | 1.8% |
| 21 | Missouri | 69,707 | 1.8% |
| 22 | Florida | 65,758 | 1.7% |
| 23 | Wisconsin | 65,496 | 1.7% |
| 24 | Georgia | 59,425 | 1.6% |
| 25 | Illinois | 57,914 | 1.5% |
| 26 | Iowa | 56,273 | 1.5% |
| 27 | New York | 54,555 | 1.4% |
| 28 | North Carolina | 53,819 | 1.4% |
| 29 | Arkansas | 53,179 | 1.4% |
| 30 | Alabama | 52,420 | 1.4% |
| 31 | Louisiana | 52,378 | 1.4% |
| 32 | Mississippi | 48,432 | 1.3% |
| 33 | Pennsylvania | 46,054 | 1.2% |
| 34 | Ohio | 44,826 | 1.2% |
| 35 | Virginia | 42,775 | 1.1% |
| 36 | Tennessee | 42,144 | 1.1% |
| 37 | Kentucky | 40,408 | 1.1% |
| 38 | Indiana | 36,420 | 1.0% |
| 39 | Maine | 35,380 | 0.9% |
| 40 | South Carolina | 32,020 | 0.8% |
| 41 | West Virginia | 24,230 | 0.6% |
| 42 | Maryland | 12,406 | 0.3% |
| 43 | Hawaii | 10,932 | 0.3% |
| 44 | Massachusetts | 10,554 | 0.3% |
| 45 | Vermont | 9,616 | 0.3% |
| 46 | New Hampshire | 9,349 | 0.2% |
| 47 | New Jersey | 8,723 | 0.2% |
| 48 | Connecticut | 5,543 | 0.1% |
| 49 | Delaware | 2,489 | 0.1% |
| 50 | Rhode Island | 1,545 | 0.0% |
| | District of Columbia | 68 | 0.0% |

Source: U.S. Bureau of the Census
"State Area Measurements" (http://www.census.gov/geo/reference/state-area.html)
*Total of land and water area.  Revised figures as of January 1, 2010

# Land Area of States in Square Miles in 2010

## National Total = 3,531,905 Square Miles of Land Area*

ALPHA ORDER

| RANK | STATE | MILES | % of USA |
|---|---|---|---|
| 28 | Alabama | 50,645 | 1.4% |
| 1 | Alaska | 570,641 | 16.2% |
| 6 | Arizona | 113,594 | 3.2% |
| 27 | Arkansas | 52,035 | 1.5% |
| 3 | California | 155,779 | 4.4% |
| 8 | Colorado | 103,642 | 2.9% |
| 48 | Connecticut | 4,842 | 0.1% |
| 49 | Delaware | 1,949 | 0.1% |
| 26 | Florida | 53,625 | 1.5% |
| 21 | Georgia | 57,513 | 1.6% |
| 47 | Hawaii | 6,423 | 0.2% |
| 11 | Idaho | 82,643 | 2.3% |
| 24 | Illinois | 55,519 | 1.6% |
| 38 | Indiana | 35,826 | 1.0% |
| 23 | Iowa | 55,857 | 1.6% |
| 13 | Kansas | 81,759 | 2.3% |
| 37 | Kentucky | 39,486 | 1.1% |
| 33 | Louisiana | 43,204 | 1.2% |
| 39 | Maine | 30,843 | 0.9% |
| 42 | Maryland | 9,707 | 0.3% |
| 45 | Massachusetts | 7,800 | 0.2% |
| 22 | Michigan | 56,539 | 1.6% |
| 14 | Minnesota | 79,627 | 2.3% |
| 31 | Mississippi | 46,923 | 1.3% |
| 18 | Missouri | 68,742 | 1.9% |
| 4 | Montana | 145,546 | 4.1% |
| 15 | Nebraska | 76,824 | 2.2% |
| 7 | Nevada | 109,781 | 3.1% |
| 44 | New Hampshire | 8,953 | 0.3% |
| 46 | New Jersey | 7,354 | 0.2% |
| 5 | New Mexico | 121,298 | 3.4% |
| 30 | New York | 47,126 | 1.3% |
| 29 | North Carolina | 48,618 | 1.4% |
| 17 | North Dakota | 69,001 | 2.0% |
| 35 | Ohio | 40,861 | 1.2% |
| 19 | Oklahoma | 68,595 | 1.9% |
| 10 | Oregon | 95,988 | 2.7% |
| 32 | Pennsylvania | 44,743 | 1.3% |
| 50 | Rhode Island | 1,034 | 0.0% |
| 40 | South Carolina | 30,061 | 0.9% |
| 16 | South Dakota | 75,811 | 2.1% |
| 34 | Tennessee | 41,235 | 1.2% |
| 2 | Texas | 261,232 | 7.4% |
| 12 | Utah | 82,170 | 2.3% |
| 43 | Vermont | 9,217 | 0.3% |
| 36 | Virginia | 39,490 | 1.1% |
| 20 | Washington | 66,456 | 1.9% |
| 41 | West Virginia | 24,038 | 0.7% |
| 25 | Wisconsin | 54,158 | 1.5% |
| 9 | Wyoming | 97,093 | 2.7% |

RANK ORDER

| RANK | STATE | MILES | % of USA |
|---|---|---|---|
| 1 | Alaska | 570,641 | 16.2% |
| 2 | Texas | 261,232 | 7.4% |
| 3 | California | 155,779 | 4.4% |
| 4 | Montana | 145,546 | 4.1% |
| 5 | New Mexico | 121,298 | 3.4% |
| 6 | Arizona | 113,594 | 3.2% |
| 7 | Nevada | 109,781 | 3.1% |
| 8 | Colorado | 103,642 | 2.9% |
| 9 | Wyoming | 97,093 | 2.7% |
| 10 | Oregon | 95,988 | 2.7% |
| 11 | Idaho | 82,643 | 2.3% |
| 12 | Utah | 82,170 | 2.3% |
| 13 | Kansas | 81,759 | 2.3% |
| 14 | Minnesota | 79,627 | 2.3% |
| 15 | Nebraska | 76,824 | 2.2% |
| 16 | South Dakota | 75,811 | 2.1% |
| 17 | North Dakota | 69,001 | 2.0% |
| 18 | Missouri | 68,742 | 1.9% |
| 19 | Oklahoma | 68,595 | 1.9% |
| 20 | Washington | 66,456 | 1.9% |
| 21 | Georgia | 57,513 | 1.6% |
| 22 | Michigan | 56,539 | 1.6% |
| 23 | Iowa | 55,857 | 1.6% |
| 24 | Illinois | 55,519 | 1.6% |
| 25 | Wisconsin | 54,158 | 1.5% |
| 26 | Florida | 53,625 | 1.5% |
| 27 | Arkansas | 52,035 | 1.5% |
| 28 | Alabama | 50,645 | 1.4% |
| 29 | North Carolina | 48,618 | 1.4% |
| 30 | New York | 47,126 | 1.3% |
| 31 | Mississippi | 46,923 | 1.3% |
| 32 | Pennsylvania | 44,743 | 1.3% |
| 33 | Louisiana | 43,204 | 1.2% |
| 34 | Tennessee | 41,235 | 1.2% |
| 35 | Ohio | 40,861 | 1.2% |
| 36 | Virginia | 39,490 | 1.1% |
| 37 | Kentucky | 39,486 | 1.1% |
| 38 | Indiana | 35,826 | 1.0% |
| 39 | Maine | 30,843 | 0.9% |
| 40 | South Carolina | 30,061 | 0.9% |
| 41 | West Virginia | 24,038 | 0.7% |
| 42 | Maryland | 9,707 | 0.3% |
| 43 | Vermont | 9,217 | 0.3% |
| 44 | New Hampshire | 8,953 | 0.3% |
| 45 | Massachusetts | 7,800 | 0.2% |
| 46 | New Jersey | 7,354 | 0.2% |
| 47 | Hawaii | 6,423 | 0.2% |
| 48 | Connecticut | 4,842 | 0.1% |
| 49 | Delaware | 1,949 | 0.1% |
| 50 | Rhode Island | 1,034 | 0.0% |
| | District of Columbia | 61 | 0.0% |

Source: U.S. Bureau of the Census
   "State Area Measurements" (http://www.census.gov/geo/reference/state-area.html)
*Includes dry land temporarily or partially covered by water, such as marshland, swamps, etc.; streams and canals under one-eighth mile wide; and lakes, reservoirs, and ponds under 40 acres.  Revised figures as of August 2010.

# Water Area of States in Square Miles in 2010

## National Total = 264,837 Square Miles of Water*

ALPHA ORDER

| RANK | STATE | MILES | % of USA |
|---|---|---|---|
| 23 | Alabama | 1,775 | 0.7% |
| 1 | Alaska | 94,743 | 35.8% |
| 48 | Arizona | 396 | 0.1% |
| 31 | Arkansas | 1,143 | 0.4% |
| 6 | California | 7,916 | 3.0% |
| 44 | Colorado | 452 | 0.2% |
| 38 | Connecticut | 701 | 0.3% |
| 40 | Delaware | 540 | 0.2% |
| 3 | Florida | 12,133 | 4.6% |
| 22 | Georgia | 1,912 | 0.7% |
| 13 | Hawaii | 4,509 | 1.7% |
| 33 | Idaho | 926 | 0.3% |
| 19 | Illinois | 2,395 | 0.9% |
| 39 | Indiana | 593 | 0.2% |
| 45 | Iowa | 416 | 0.2% |
| 42 | Kansas | 520 | 0.2% |
| 34 | Kentucky | 921 | 0.3% |
| 5 | Louisiana | 9,174 | 3.5% |
| 12 | Maine | 4,537 | 1.7% |
| 18 | Maryland | 2,699 | 1.0% |
| 16 | Massachusetts | 2,754 | 1.0% |
| 2 | Michigan | 40,175 | 15.2% |
| 9 | Minnesota | 7,309 | 2.8% |
| 25 | Mississippi | 1,509 | 0.6% |
| 32 | Missouri | 965 | 0.4% |
| 26 | Montana | 1,494 | 0.6% |
| 41 | Nebraska | 524 | 0.2% |
| 36 | Nevada | 791 | 0.3% |
| 47 | New Hampshire | 397 | 0.1% |
| 27 | New Jersey | 1,368 | 0.5% |
| 49 | New Mexico | 292 | 0.1% |
| 7 | New York | 7,429 | 2.8% |
| 10 | North Carolina | 5,201 | 2.0% |
| 24 | North Dakota | 1,698 | 0.6% |
| 14 | Ohio | 3,965 | 1.5% |
| 30 | Oklahoma | 1,304 | 0.5% |
| 20 | Oregon | 2,391 | 0.9% |
| 28 | Pennsylvania | 1,312 | 0.5% |
| 43 | Rhode Island | 511 | 0.2% |
| 21 | South Carolina | 1,960 | 0.7% |
| 29 | South Dakota | 1,305 | 0.5% |
| 35 | Tennessee | 909 | 0.3% |
| 8 | Texas | 7,365 | 2.8% |
| 17 | Utah | 2,727 | 1.0% |
| 46 | Vermont | 400 | 0.2% |
| 15 | Virginia | 3,285 | 1.2% |
| 11 | Washington | 4,842 | 1.8% |
| 50 | West Virginia | 192 | 0.1% |
| 4 | Wisconsin | 11,339 | 4.3% |
| 37 | Wyoming | 720 | 0.3% |

RANK ORDER

| RANK | STATE | MILES | % of USA |
|---|---|---|---|
| 1 | Alaska | 94,743 | 35.8% |
| 2 | Michigan | 40,175 | 15.2% |
| 3 | Florida | 12,133 | 4.6% |
| 4 | Wisconsin | 11,339 | 4.3% |
| 5 | Louisiana | 9,174 | 3.5% |
| 6 | California | 7,916 | 3.0% |
| 7 | New York | 7,429 | 2.8% |
| 8 | Texas | 7,365 | 2.8% |
| 9 | Minnesota | 7,309 | 2.8% |
| 10 | North Carolina | 5,201 | 2.0% |
| 11 | Washington | 4,842 | 1.8% |
| 12 | Maine | 4,537 | 1.7% |
| 13 | Hawaii | 4,509 | 1.7% |
| 14 | Ohio | 3,965 | 1.5% |
| 15 | Virginia | 3,285 | 1.2% |
| 16 | Massachusetts | 2,754 | 1.0% |
| 17 | Utah | 2,727 | 1.0% |
| 18 | Maryland | 2,699 | 1.0% |
| 19 | Illinois | 2,395 | 0.9% |
| 20 | Oregon | 2,391 | 0.9% |
| 21 | South Carolina | 1,960 | 0.7% |
| 22 | Georgia | 1,912 | 0.7% |
| 23 | Alabama | 1,775 | 0.7% |
| 24 | North Dakota | 1,698 | 0.6% |
| 25 | Mississippi | 1,509 | 0.6% |
| 26 | Montana | 1,494 | 0.6% |
| 27 | New Jersey | 1,368 | 0.5% |
| 28 | Pennsylvania | 1,312 | 0.5% |
| 29 | South Dakota | 1,305 | 0.5% |
| 30 | Oklahoma | 1,304 | 0.5% |
| 31 | Arkansas | 1,143 | 0.4% |
| 32 | Missouri | 965 | 0.4% |
| 33 | Idaho | 926 | 0.3% |
| 34 | Kentucky | 921 | 0.3% |
| 35 | Tennessee | 909 | 0.3% |
| 36 | Nevada | 791 | 0.3% |
| 37 | Wyoming | 720 | 0.3% |
| 38 | Connecticut | 701 | 0.3% |
| 39 | Indiana | 593 | 0.2% |
| 40 | Delaware | 540 | 0.2% |
| 41 | Nebraska | 524 | 0.2% |
| 42 | Kansas | 520 | 0.2% |
| 43 | Rhode Island | 511 | 0.2% |
| 44 | Colorado | 452 | 0.2% |
| 45 | Iowa | 416 | 0.2% |
| 46 | Vermont | 400 | 0.2% |
| 47 | New Hampshire | 397 | 0.1% |
| 48 | Arizona | 396 | 0.1% |
| 49 | New Mexico | 292 | 0.1% |
| 50 | West Virginia | 192 | 0.1% |
| | District of Columbia | 7 | 0.0% |

Source: U.S. Bureau of the Census
"State Area Measurements" (http://www.census.gov/geo/reference/state-area.html)
*Includes permanent inland water surface, such as lakes, reservoirs, and ponds having an area of 40 acres or more, canals one-eighth mile or more in width; coastal waters behind or sheltered by headlands or islands separated by less than 1 nautical mile of water, and islands under 40 acres in area. Excludes areas of oceans, bays, etc., lying within U.S. jurisdiction but not defined as inland water. Revised figures as of August 2010.

# Highest Point of Elevation in Feet

## National High Point = 20,320 Feet Above Sea Level (Mt. McKinley, Alaska)

ALPHA ORDER

| RANK | STATE | HIGHEST POINT |
|------|-------|---------------|
| 35 | Alabama | 2,407 |
| 1 | Alaska | 20,320 |
| 12 | Arizona | 12,633 |
| 34 | Arkansas | 2,753 |
| 2 | California | 14,494 |
| 3 | Colorado | 14,433 |
| 36 | Connecticut | 2,380 |
| 49 | Delaware | 448 |
| 50 | Florida | 345 |
| 25 | Georgia | 4,784 |
| 6 | Hawaii | 13,796 |
| 11 | Idaho | 12,662 |
| 45 | Illinois | 1,235 |
| 44 | Indiana | 1,257 |
| 42 | Iowa | 1,670 |
| 28 | Kansas | 4,039 |
| 27 | Kentucky | 4,145 |
| 48 | Louisiana | 535 |
| 22 | Maine | 5,268 |
| 32 | Maryland | 3,360 |
| 31 | Massachusetts | 3,491 |
| 38 | Michigan | 1,979 |
| 37 | Minnesota | 2,301 |
| 47 | Mississippi | 806 |
| 41 | Missouri | 1,772 |
| 10 | Montana | 12,799 |
| 20 | Nebraska | 5,424 |
| 9 | Nevada | 13,140 |
| 18 | New Hampshire | 6,288 |
| 40 | New Jersey | 1,803 |
| 8 | New Mexico | 13,161 |
| 21 | New York | 5,344 |
| 16 | North Carolina | 6,684 |
| 30 | North Dakota | 3,506 |
| 43 | Ohio | 1,550 |
| 23 | Oklahoma | 4,973 |
| 13 | Oregon | 11,239 |
| 33 | Pennsylvania | 3,213 |
| 46 | Rhode Island | 812 |
| 29 | South Carolina | 3,560 |
| 15 | South Dakota | 7,242 |
| 17 | Tennessee | 6,643 |
| 14 | Texas | 8,749 |
| 7 | Utah | 13,528 |
| 26 | Vermont | 4,393 |
| 19 | Virginia | 5,729 |
| 4 | Washington | 14,411 |
| 24 | West Virginia | 4,863 |
| 39 | Wisconsin | 1,951 |
| 5 | Wyoming | 13,804 |

RANK ORDER

| RANK | STATE | HIGHEST POINT |
|------|-------|---------------|
| 1 | Alaska | 20,320 |
| 2 | California | 14,494 |
| 3 | Colorado | 14,433 |
| 4 | Washington | 14,411 |
| 5 | Wyoming | 13,804 |
| 6 | Hawaii | 13,796 |
| 7 | Utah | 13,528 |
| 8 | New Mexico | 13,161 |
| 9 | Nevada | 13,140 |
| 10 | Montana | 12,799 |
| 11 | Idaho | 12,662 |
| 12 | Arizona | 12,633 |
| 13 | Oregon | 11,239 |
| 14 | Texas | 8,749 |
| 15 | South Dakota | 7,242 |
| 16 | North Carolina | 6,684 |
| 17 | Tennessee | 6,643 |
| 18 | New Hampshire | 6,288 |
| 19 | Virginia | 5,729 |
| 20 | Nebraska | 5,424 |
| 21 | New York | 5,344 |
| 22 | Maine | 5,268 |
| 23 | Oklahoma | 4,973 |
| 24 | West Virginia | 4,863 |
| 25 | Georgia | 4,784 |
| 26 | Vermont | 4,393 |
| 27 | Kentucky | 4,145 |
| 28 | Kansas | 4,039 |
| 29 | South Carolina | 3,560 |
| 30 | North Dakota | 3,506 |
| 31 | Massachusetts | 3,491 |
| 32 | Maryland | 3,360 |
| 33 | Pennsylvania | 3,213 |
| 34 | Arkansas | 2,753 |
| 35 | Alabama | 2,407 |
| 36 | Connecticut | 2,380 |
| 37 | Minnesota | 2,301 |
| 38 | Michigan | 1,979 |
| 39 | Wisconsin | 1,951 |
| 40 | New Jersey | 1,803 |
| 41 | Missouri | 1,772 |
| 42 | Iowa | 1,670 |
| 43 | Ohio | 1,550 |
| 44 | Indiana | 1,257 |
| 45 | Illinois | 1,235 |
| 46 | Rhode Island | 812 |
| 47 | Mississippi | 806 |
| 48 | Louisiana | 535 |
| 49 | Delaware | 448 |
| 50 | Florida | 345 |
| | District of Columbia | 410 |

Source: U.S. Department of Interior, U.S. Geological Survey
"Elevations and Distances in the United States" (http://erg.usgs.gov/isb/pubs/booklets/elvadist/elvadist.html)

# Lowest Point of Elevation in Feet

## National Low Point = 282 Feet Below Sea Level (Death Valley, California)*

ALPHA ORDER | | | RANK ORDER

| RANK | STATE | LOWEST POINT | RANK | STATE | LOWEST POINT |
|------|-------|--------------|------|-------|--------------|
| 3 | Alabama | 0 | 1 | California | (282) |
| 3 | Alaska | 0 | 2 | Louisiana | (8) |
| 26 | Arizona | 70 | 3 | Alabama* | 0 |
| 25 | Arkansas | 55 | 3 | Alaska | 0 |
| 1 | California | (282) | 3 | Connecticut | 0 |
| 50 | Colorado | 3,315 | 3 | Delaware | 0 |
| 3 | Connecticut | 0 | 3 | Florida | 0 |
| 3 | Delaware | 0 | 3 | Georgia | 0 |
| 3 | Florida | 0 | 3 | Hawaii | 0 |
| 3 | Georgia | 0 | 3 | Maine | 0 |
| 3 | Hawaii | 0 | 3 | Maryland | 0 |
| 42 | Idaho | 710 | 3 | Massachusetts | 0 |
| 32 | Illinois | 279 | 3 | Mississippi | 0 |
| 34 | Indiana | 320 | 3 | New Hampshire | 0 |
| 37 | Iowa | 480 | 3 | New Jersey | 0 |
| 41 | Kansas | 679 | 3 | New York | 0 |
| 31 | Kentucky | 257 | 3 | North Carolina | 0 |
| 2 | Louisiana | (8) | 3 | Oregon | 0 |
| 3 | Maine | 0 | 3 | Pennsylvania | 0 |
| 3 | Maryland | 0 | 3 | Rhode Island | 0 |
| 3 | Massachusetts | 0 | 3 | South Carolina | 0 |
| 38 | Michigan | 571 | 3 | Texas | 0 |
| 40 | Minnesota | 601 | 3 | Virginia | 0 |
| 3 | Mississippi | 0 | 3 | Washington | 0 |
| 29 | Missouri | 230 | 25 | Arkansas | 55 |
| 46 | Montana | 1,800 | 26 | Arizona | 70 |
| 44 | Nebraska | 840 | 27 | Vermont | 95 |
| 36 | Nevada | 479 | 28 | Tennessee | 178 |
| 3 | New Hampshire | 0 | 29 | Missouri | 230 |
| 3 | New Jersey | 0 | 30 | West Virginia | 240 |
| 48 | New Mexico | 2,842 | 31 | Kentucky | 257 |
| 3 | New York | 0 | 32 | Illinois | 279 |
| 3 | North Carolina | 0 | 33 | Oklahoma | 289 |
| 43 | North Dakota | 750 | 34 | Indiana | 320 |
| 35 | Ohio | 455 | 35 | Ohio | 455 |
| 33 | Oklahoma | 289 | 36 | Nevada | 479 |
| 3 | Oregon | 0 | 37 | Iowa | 480 |
| 3 | Pennsylvania | 0 | 38 | Michigan | 571 |
| 3 | Rhode Island | 0 | 39 | Wisconsin | 579 |
| 3 | South Carolina | 0 | 40 | Minnesota | 601 |
| 45 | South Dakota | 966 | 41 | Kansas | 679 |
| 28 | Tennessee | 178 | 42 | Idaho | 710 |
| 3 | Texas | 0 | 43 | North Dakota | 750 |
| 47 | Utah | 2,000 | 44 | Nebraska | 840 |
| 27 | Vermont | 95 | 45 | South Dakota | 966 |
| 3 | Virginia | 0 | 46 | Montana | 1,800 |
| 3 | Washington | 0 | 47 | Utah | 2,000 |
| 30 | West Virginia | 240 | 48 | New Mexico | 2,842 |
| 39 | Wisconsin | 579 | 49 | Wyoming | 3,099 |
| 49 | Wyoming | 3,099 | 50 | Colorado | 3,315 |
| | | | | District of Columbia | 1 |

Source: U.S. Department of Interior, U.S. Geological Survey
   "Elevations and Distances in the United States" (http://erg.usgs.gov/isb/pubs/booklets/elvadist/elvadist.html)
*States with "0" have sea level as lowest point.

# Approximate Mean Elevation in Feet

## Approximate National Mean Elevation = 2,500 Feet Above Sea Level

ALPHA ORDER

| RANK | STATE | MEAN ELEVATION |
|------|-------|----------------|
| 40 | Alabama | 500 |
| 15 | Alaska | 1,900 |
| 7 | Arizona | 4,100 |
| 36 | Arkansas | 650 |
| 11 | California | 2,900 |
| 1 | Colorado | 6,800 |
| 40 | Connecticut | 500 |
| 50 | Delaware | 60 |
| 48 | Florida | 100 |
| 37 | Georgia | 600 |
| 10 | Hawaii | 3,030 |
| 6 | Idaho | 5,000 |
| 37 | Illinois | 600 |
| 34 | Indiana | 700 |
| 22 | Iowa | 1,100 |
| 14 | Kansas | 2,000 |
| 33 | Kentucky | 750 |
| 48 | Louisiana | 100 |
| 37 | Maine | 600 |
| 43 | Maryland | 350 |
| 40 | Massachusetts | 500 |
| 29 | Michigan | 900 |
| 21 | Minnesota | 1,200 |
| 45 | Mississippi | 300 |
| 32 | Missouri | 800 |
| 8 | Montana | 3,400 |
| 12 | Nebraska | 2,600 |
| 5 | Nevada | 5,500 |
| 25 | New Hampshire | 1,000 |
| 46 | New Jersey | 250 |
| 4 | New Mexico | 5,700 |
| 25 | New York | 1,000 |
| 34 | North Carolina | 700 |
| 15 | North Dakota | 1,900 |
| 31 | Ohio | 850 |
| 20 | Oklahoma | 1,300 |
| 9 | Oregon | 3,300 |
| 22 | Pennsylvania | 1,100 |
| 47 | Rhode Island | 200 |
| 43 | South Carolina | 350 |
| 13 | South Dakota | 2,200 |
| 29 | Tennessee | 900 |
| 17 | Texas | 1,700 |
| 3 | Utah | 6,100 |
| 25 | Vermont | 1,000 |
| 28 | Virginia | 950 |
| 17 | Washington | 1,700 |
| 19 | West Virginia | 1,500 |
| 24 | Wisconsin | 1,050 |
| 2 | Wyoming | 6,700 |

RANK ORDER

| RANK | STATE | MEAN ELEVATION |
|------|-------|----------------|
| 1 | Colorado | 6,800 |
| 2 | Wyoming | 6,700 |
| 3 | Utah | 6,100 |
| 4 | New Mexico | 5,700 |
| 5 | Nevada | 5,500 |
| 6 | Idaho | 5,000 |
| 7 | Arizona | 4,100 |
| 8 | Montana | 3,400 |
| 9 | Oregon | 3,300 |
| 10 | Hawaii | 3,030 |
| 11 | California | 2,900 |
| 12 | Nebraska | 2,600 |
| 13 | South Dakota | 2,200 |
| 14 | Kansas | 2,000 |
| 15 | Alaska | 1,900 |
| 15 | North Dakota | 1,900 |
| 17 | Texas | 1,700 |
| 17 | Washington | 1,700 |
| 19 | West Virginia | 1,500 |
| 20 | Oklahoma | 1,300 |
| 21 | Minnesota | 1,200 |
| 22 | Iowa | 1,100 |
| 22 | Pennsylvania | 1,100 |
| 24 | Wisconsin | 1,050 |
| 25 | New Hampshire | 1,000 |
| 25 | New York | 1,000 |
| 25 | Vermont | 1,000 |
| 28 | Virginia | 950 |
| 29 | Michigan | 900 |
| 29 | Tennessee | 900 |
| 31 | Ohio | 850 |
| 32 | Missouri | 800 |
| 33 | Kentucky | 750 |
| 34 | Indiana | 700 |
| 34 | North Carolina | 700 |
| 36 | Arkansas | 650 |
| 37 | Georgia | 600 |
| 37 | Illinois | 600 |
| 37 | Maine | 600 |
| 40 | Alabama | 500 |
| 40 | Connecticut | 500 |
| 40 | Massachusetts | 500 |
| 43 | Maryland | 350 |
| 43 | South Carolina | 350 |
| 45 | Mississippi | 300 |
| 46 | New Jersey | 250 |
| 47 | Rhode Island | 200 |
| 48 | Florida | 100 |
| 48 | Louisiana | 100 |
| 50 | Delaware | 60 |
|  | District of Columbia | 150 |

Source: U.S. Department of Interior, U.S. Geological Survey
"Elevations and Distances in the United States" (http://erg.usgs.gov/isb/pubs/booklets/elvadist/elvadist.html)

# Normal Daily Mean Temperature*

ALPHA ORDER

| RANK | STATE | MEAN TEMPERATURE |
|---|---|---|
| 7 | Alabama | 63.7 |
| 50 | Alaska | 31.9 |
| 6 | Arizona | 63.9 |
| 10 | Arkansas | 62.0 |
| 12 | California | 60.3 |
| 38 | Colorado | 48.4 |
| 27 | Connecticut | 51.2 |
| 20 | Delaware** | 54.4 |
| 2 | Florida | 72.0 |
| 8 | Georgia | 63.6 |
| 1 | Hawaii | 75.7 |
| 31 | Idaho | 50.3 |
| 33 | Illinois | 50.1 |
| 24 | Indiana | 52.0 |
| 39 | Iowa | 48.1 |
| 22 | Kansas | 54.0 |
| 17 | Kentucky | 55.8 |
| 3 | Louisiana | 67.4 |
| 47 | Maine | 42.5 |
| 19 | Maryland** | 54.6 |
| 37 | Massachusetts | 49.3 |
| 45 | Michigan | 44.7 |
| 48 | Minnesota | 41.4 |
| 9 | Mississippi | 63.4 |
| 18 | Missouri | 55.2 |
| 46 | Montana | 44.0 |
| 36 | Nebraska | 49.4 |
| 24 | Nevada | 52.0 |
| 41 | New Hampshire** | 45.9 |
| 20 | New Jersey | 54.4 |
| 16 | New Mexico | 57.0 |
| 32 | New York | 50.2 |
| 13 | North Carolina | 60.1 |
| 49 | North Dakota | 41.3 |
| 34 | Ohio | 50.0 |
| 11 | Oklahoma | 60.5 |
| 28 | Oregon | 51.1 |
| 26 | Pennsylvania | 51.6 |
| 28 | Rhode Island** | 51.1 |
| 5 | South Carolina | 64.0 |
| 42 | South Dakota | 45.2 |
| 14 | Tennessee | 58.7 |
| 4 | Texas | 66.8 |
| 28 | Utah | 51.1 |
| 42 | Vermont** | 45.2 |
| 15 | Virginia | 57.2 |
| 34 | Washington | 50.0 |
| 23 | West Virginia | 52.7 |
| 40 | Wisconsin | 46.3 |
| 44 | Wyoming | 44.8 |

RANK ORDER

| RANK | STATE | MEAN TEMPERATURE |
|---|---|---|
| 1 | Hawaii | 75.7 |
| 2 | Florida | 72.0 |
| 3 | Louisiana | 67.4 |
| 4 | Texas | 66.8 |
| 5 | South Carolina | 64.0 |
| 6 | Arizona | 63.9 |
| 7 | Alabama | 63.7 |
| 8 | Georgia | 63.6 |
| 9 | Mississippi | 63.4 |
| 10 | Arkansas | 62.0 |
| 11 | Oklahoma | 60.5 |
| 12 | California | 60.3 |
| 13 | North Carolina | 60.1 |
| 14 | Tennessee | 58.7 |
| 15 | Virginia | 57.2 |
| 16 | New Mexico | 57.0 |
| 17 | Kentucky | 55.8 |
| 18 | Missouri | 55.2 |
| 19 | Maryland** | 54.6 |
| 20 | Delaware** | 54.4 |
| 20 | New Jersey | 54.4 |
| 22 | Kansas | 54.0 |
| 23 | West Virginia | 52.7 |
| 24 | Indiana | 52.0 |
| 24 | Nevada | 52.0 |
| 26 | Pennsylvania | 51.6 |
| 27 | Connecticut | 51.2 |
| 28 | Oregon | 51.1 |
| 28 | Rhode Island** | 51.1 |
| 28 | Utah | 51.1 |
| 31 | Idaho | 50.3 |
| 32 | New York | 50.2 |
| 33 | Illinois | 50.1 |
| 34 | Ohio | 50.0 |
| 34 | Washington | 50.0 |
| 36 | Nebraska | 49.4 |
| 37 | Massachusetts | 49.3 |
| 38 | Colorado | 48.4 |
| 39 | Iowa | 48.1 |
| 40 | Wisconsin | 46.3 |
| 41 | New Hampshire** | 45.9 |
| 42 | South Dakota | 45.2 |
| 42 | Vermont** | 45.2 |
| 44 | Wyoming | 44.8 |
| 45 | Michigan | 44.7 |
| 46 | Montana | 44.0 |
| 47 | Maine | 42.5 |
| 48 | Minnesota | 41.4 |
| 49 | North Dakota | 41.3 |
| 50 | Alaska | 31.9 |
|  | District of Columbia | 55.9 |

Source: CQ Press using data from U.S. Department of Commerce, National Oceanic and Atmospheric Administration
"Comparative Climatic Data Through 2012" (ftp://ftp.ncdc.noaa.gov/pub/data/ccd-data/CCD-2012.pdf)

*Based on 30-year averages, 1971-2000.

**Percentages from these states are from a single location. All other states are from two or more reporting cities within each state, which were averaged to determine each state's average.

# Percent of Days That Are Sunny*

ALPHA ORDER

| RANK | STATE | PERCENT OF DAYS SUNNY |
|------|-------|----------------------|
| 26 | Alabama | 58 |
| 50 | Alaska | 38 |
| 1 | Arizona | 85 |
| 8 | Arkansas | 66 |
| 4 | California | 72 |
| 4 | Colorado | 72 |
| 34 | Connecticut** | 56 |
| 36 | Delaware** | 55 |
| 7 | Florida | 67 |
| 16 | Georgia | 63 |
| 8 | Hawaii | 66 |
| 14 | Idaho | 64 |
| 31 | Illinois | 57 |
| 26 | Indiana | 58 |
| 22 | Iowa | 60 |
| 8 | Kansas | 66 |
| 36 | Kentucky | 55 |
| 14 | Louisiana | 64 |
| 31 | Maine** | 57 |
| 31 | Maryland** | 57 |
| 36 | Massachusetts | 55 |
| 44 | Michigan | 49 |
| 36 | Minnesota | 55 |
| 16 | Mississippi | 63 |
| 26 | Missouri | 58 |
| 24 | Montana | 59 |
| 16 | Nebraska | 63 |
| 2 | Nevada | 76 |
| 48 | New Hampshire | 44 |
| 34 | New Jersey** | 56 |
| 3 | New Mexico | 75 |
| 42 | New York | 51 |
| 22 | North Carolina | 60 |
| 24 | North Dakota | 59 |
| 42 | Ohio | 51 |
| 12 | Oklahoma | 65 |
| 46 | Oregon** | 48 |
| 41 | Pennsylvania | 53 |
| 26 | Rhode Island** | 58 |
| 20 | South Carolina | 62 |
| 16 | South Dakota | 63 |
| 26 | Tennessee | 58 |
| 12 | Texas | 65 |
| 6 | Utah | 68 |
| 44 | Vermont** | 49 |
| 21 | Virginia | 61 |
| 47 | Washington | 45 |
| 49 | West Virginia** | 40 |
| 40 | Wisconsin | 54 |
| 8 | Wyoming | 66 |

RANK ORDER

| RANK | STATE | PERCENT OF DAYS SUNNY |
|------|-------|----------------------|
| 1 | Arizona | 85 |
| 2 | Nevada | 76 |
| 3 | New Mexico | 75 |
| 4 | California | 72 |
| 4 | Colorado | 72 |
| 6 | Utah | 68 |
| 7 | Florida | 67 |
| 8 | Arkansas | 66 |
| 8 | Hawaii | 66 |
| 8 | Kansas | 66 |
| 8 | Wyoming | 66 |
| 12 | Oklahoma | 65 |
| 12 | Texas | 65 |
| 14 | Idaho | 64 |
| 14 | Louisiana | 64 |
| 16 | Georgia | 63 |
| 16 | Mississippi | 63 |
| 16 | Nebraska | 63 |
| 16 | South Dakota | 63 |
| 20 | South Carolina | 62 |
| 21 | Virginia | 61 |
| 22 | Iowa | 60 |
| 22 | North Carolina | 60 |
| 24 | Montana | 59 |
| 24 | North Dakota | 59 |
| 26 | Alabama | 58 |
| 26 | Indiana | 58 |
| 26 | Missouri | 58 |
| 26 | Rhode Island** | 58 |
| 26 | Tennessee | 58 |
| 31 | Illinois | 57 |
| 31 | Maine** | 57 |
| 31 | Maryland** | 57 |
| 34 | Connecticut** | 56 |
| 34 | New Jersey** | 56 |
| 36 | Delaware** | 55 |
| 36 | Kentucky | 55 |
| 36 | Massachusetts | 55 |
| 36 | Minnesota | 55 |
| 40 | Wisconsin | 54 |
| 41 | Pennsylvania | 53 |
| 42 | New York | 51 |
| 42 | Ohio | 51 |
| 44 | Michigan | 49 |
| 44 | Vermont** | 49 |
| 46 | Oregon** | 48 |
| 47 | Washington | 45 |
| 48 | New Hampshire | 44 |
| 49 | West Virginia** | 40 |
| 50 | Alaska | 38 |
| | District of Columbia** | 56 |

Source: CQ Press using data from U.S. Department of Commerce, National Oceanic and Atmospheric Administration
    "Comparative Climatic Data Through 2012" (ftp://ftp.ncdc.noaa.gov/pub/data/ccd-data/CCD-2012.pdf)
*As a percent of possible sunshine updated through 2012.
**Percentages from these states are from a single location.  All other states are from two or more reporting cities within each state, which were averaged to determine each state's average.

# Average Wind Speed (MPH)*

ALPHA ORDER

| RANK | STATE | MILES PER HOUR |
|------|-------|----------------|
| 41 | Alabama | 7.6 |
| 24 | Alaska | 9.3 |
| 42 | Arizona | 7.5 |
| 40 | Arkansas | 7.7 |
| 46 | California | 6.9 |
| 32 | Colorado | 8.5 |
| 19 | Connecticut | 9.6 |
| 26 | Delaware** | 9.0 |
| 33 | Florida | 8.3 |
| 45 | Georgia | 7.4 |
| 5 | Hawaii | 10.9 |
| 22 | Idaho | 9.4 |
| 18 | Illinois | 9.8 |
| 22 | Indiana | 9.4 |
| 6 | Iowa | 10.7 |
| 2 | Kansas | 12.0 |
| 39 | Kentucky | 7.8 |
| 36 | Louisiana | 8.1 |
| 27 | Maine | 8.9 |
| 30 | Maryland** | 8.6 |
| 1 | Massachusetts | 12.5 |
| 21 | Michigan | 9.5 |
| 11 | Minnesota | 10.2 |
| 48 | Mississippi | 6.5 |
| 13 | Missouri | 10.1 |
| 25 | Montana | 9.2 |
| 9 | Nebraska | 10.3 |
| 37 | Nevada | 8.0 |
| 47 | New Hampshire** | 6.7 |
| 15 | New Jersey | 10.0 |
| 16 | New Mexico | 9.9 |
| 11 | New York | 10.2 |
| 34 | North Carolina | 8.2 |
| 7 | North Dakota | 10.6 |
| 19 | Ohio | 9.6 |
| 3 | Oklahoma | 11.2 |
| 38 | Oregon | 7.9 |
| 30 | Pennsylvania | 8.6 |
| 8 | Rhode Island | 10.5 |
| 42 | South Carolina | 7.5 |
| 4 | South Dakota | 11.1 |
| 48 | Tennessee | 6.5 |
| 9 | Texas | 10.3 |
| 29 | Utah** | 8.8 |
| 27 | Vermont** | 8.9 |
| 34 | Virginia | 8.2 |
| 42 | Washington | 7.5 |
| 48 | West Virginia | 6.5 |
| 16 | Wisconsin | 9.9 |
| 13 | Wyoming | 10.1 |

RANK ORDER

| RANK | STATE | MILES PER HOUR |
|------|-------|----------------|
| 1 | Massachusetts | 12.5 |
| 2 | Kansas | 12.0 |
| 3 | Oklahoma | 11.2 |
| 4 | South Dakota | 11.1 |
| 5 | Hawaii | 10.9 |
| 6 | Iowa | 10.7 |
| 7 | North Dakota | 10.6 |
| 8 | Rhode Island | 10.5 |
| 9 | Nebraska | 10.3 |
| 9 | Texas | 10.3 |
| 11 | Minnesota | 10.2 |
| 11 | New York | 10.2 |
| 13 | Missouri | 10.1 |
| 13 | Wyoming | 10.1 |
| 15 | New Jersey | 10.0 |
| 16 | New Mexico | 9.9 |
| 16 | Wisconsin | 9.9 |
| 18 | Illinois | 9.8 |
| 19 | Connecticut | 9.6 |
| 19 | Ohio | 9.6 |
| 21 | Michigan | 9.5 |
| 22 | Idaho | 9.4 |
| 22 | Indiana | 9.4 |
| 24 | Alaska | 9.3 |
| 25 | Montana | 9.2 |
| 26 | Delaware** | 9.0 |
| 27 | Maine | 8.9 |
| 27 | Vermont** | 8.9 |
| 29 | Utah** | 8.8 |
| 30 | Maryland** | 8.6 |
| 30 | Pennsylvania | 8.6 |
| 32 | Colorado | 8.5 |
| 33 | Florida | 8.3 |
| 34 | North Carolina | 8.2 |
| 34 | Virginia | 8.2 |
| 36 | Louisiana | 8.1 |
| 37 | Nevada | 8.0 |
| 38 | Oregon | 7.9 |
| 39 | Kentucky | 7.8 |
| 40 | Arkansas | 7.7 |
| 41 | Alabama | 7.6 |
| 42 | Arizona | 7.5 |
| 42 | South Carolina | 7.5 |
| 42 | Washington | 7.5 |
| 45 | Georgia | 7.4 |
| 46 | California | 6.9 |
| 47 | New Hampshire** | 6.7 |
| 48 | Mississippi | 6.5 |
| 48 | Tennessee | 6.5 |
| 48 | West Virginia | 6.5 |
| | District of Columbia | 8.4 |

Source: CQ Press using data from U.S. Department of Commerce, National Oceanic and Atmospheric Administration
"Comparative Climatic Data Through 2012" (ftp://ftp.ncdc.noaa.gov/pub/data/ccd-data/CCD-2012.pdf)

*Updated through 2012.

**Averages from these states are from a single location. All other states are from two or more reporting cities within each state, which were averaged to determine each state's average.

# Tornadoes in 2013

## National Total = 942 Tornadoes*

ALPHA ORDER

| RANK | STATE | TORNADOES | % of USA |
|------|-------|-----------|----------|
| 15 | Alabama | 27 | 2.9% |
| 43 | Alaska | 0 | 0.0% |
| 38 | Arizona | 1 | 0.1% |
| 13 | Arkansas | 30 | 3.2% |
| 31 | California | 6 | 0.6% |
| 15 | Colorado | 27 | 2.9% |
| 33 | Connecticut | 3 | 0.3% |
| 38 | Delaware | 1 | 0.1% |
| 10 | Florida | 37 | 3.9% |
| 15 | Georgia | 27 | 2.9% |
| 43 | Hawaii | 0 | 0.0% |
| 32 | Idaho | 5 | 0.5% |
| 1 | Illinois | 69 | 7.3% |
| 9 | Indiana | 41 | 4.4% |
| 13 | Iowa | 30 | 3.2% |
| 4 | Kansas | 58 | 6.2% |
| 7 | Kentucky | 50 | 5.3% |
| 12 | Louisiana | 34 | 3.6% |
| 38 | Maine | 1 | 0.1% |
| 25 | Maryland | 10 | 1.1% |
| 38 | Massachusetts | 1 | 0.1% |
| 22 | Michigan | 13 | 1.4% |
| 24 | Minnesota | 11 | 1.2% |
| 11 | Mississippi | 36 | 3.8% |
| 6 | Missouri | 54 | 5.7% |
| 25 | Montana | 10 | 1.1% |
| 2 | Nebraska | 65 | 6.9% |
| 43 | Nevada | 0 | 0.0% |
| 43 | New Hampshire | 0 | 0.0% |
| 33 | New Jersey | 3 | 0.3% |
| 43 | New Mexico | 0 | 0.0% |
| 27 | New York | 9 | 1.0% |
| 23 | North Carolina | 12 | 1.3% |
| 19 | North Dakota | 17 | 1.8% |
| 18 | Ohio | 26 | 2.8% |
| 5 | Oklahoma | 56 | 5.9% |
| 33 | Oregon | 3 | 0.3% |
| 27 | Pennsylvania | 9 | 1.0% |
| 43 | Rhode Island | 0 | 0.0% |
| 29 | South Carolina | 8 | 0.8% |
| 20 | South Dakota | 15 | 1.6% |
| 8 | Tennessee | 43 | 4.6% |
| 2 | Texas | 65 | 6.9% |
| 38 | Utah | 1 | 0.1% |
| 43 | Vermont | 0 | 0.0% |
| 33 | Virginia | 3 | 0.3% |
| 37 | Washington | 2 | 0.2% |
| 43 | West Virginia | 0 | 0.0% |
| 20 | Wisconsin | 15 | 1.6% |
| 29 | Wyoming | 8 | 0.8% |

RANK ORDER

| RANK | STATE | TORNADOES | % of USA |
|------|-------|-----------|----------|
| 1 | Illinois | 69 | 7.3% |
| 2 | Nebraska | 65 | 6.9% |
| 2 | Texas | 65 | 6.9% |
| 4 | Kansas | 58 | 6.2% |
| 5 | Oklahoma | 56 | 5.9% |
| 6 | Missouri | 54 | 5.7% |
| 7 | Kentucky | 50 | 5.3% |
| 8 | Tennessee | 43 | 4.6% |
| 9 | Indiana | 41 | 4.4% |
| 10 | Florida | 37 | 3.9% |
| 11 | Mississippi | 36 | 3.8% |
| 12 | Louisiana | 34 | 3.6% |
| 13 | Arkansas | 30 | 3.2% |
| 13 | Iowa | 30 | 3.2% |
| 15 | Alabama | 27 | 2.9% |
| 15 | Colorado | 27 | 2.9% |
| 15 | Georgia | 27 | 2.9% |
| 18 | Ohio | 26 | 2.8% |
| 19 | North Dakota | 17 | 1.8% |
| 20 | South Dakota | 15 | 1.6% |
| 20 | Wisconsin | 15 | 1.6% |
| 22 | Michigan | 13 | 1.4% |
| 23 | North Carolina | 12 | 1.3% |
| 24 | Minnesota | 11 | 1.2% |
| 25 | Maryland | 10 | 1.1% |
| 25 | Montana | 10 | 1.1% |
| 27 | New York | 9 | 1.0% |
| 27 | Pennsylvania | 9 | 1.0% |
| 29 | South Carolina | 8 | 0.8% |
| 29 | Wyoming | 8 | 0.8% |
| 31 | California | 6 | 0.6% |
| 32 | Idaho | 5 | 0.5% |
| 33 | Connecticut | 3 | 0.3% |
| 33 | New Jersey | 3 | 0.3% |
| 33 | Oregon | 3 | 0.3% |
| 33 | Virginia | 3 | 0.3% |
| 37 | Washington | 2 | 0.2% |
| 38 | Arizona | 1 | 0.1% |
| 38 | Delaware | 1 | 0.1% |
| 38 | Maine | 1 | 0.1% |
| 38 | Massachusetts | 1 | 0.1% |
| 38 | Utah | 1 | 0.1% |
| 43 | Alaska | 0 | 0.0% |
| 43 | Hawaii | 0 | 0.0% |
| 43 | Nevada | 0 | 0.0% |
| 43 | New Hampshire | 0 | 0.0% |
| 43 | New Mexico | 0 | 0.0% |
| 43 | Rhode Island | 0 | 0.0% |
| 43 | Vermont | 0 | 0.0% |
| 43 | West Virginia | 0 | 0.0% |
| | District of Columbia | 0 | 0.0% |

Source: National Weather Service, Storm Prediction Center
"Annual Severe Weather Report Summary - 2013" (www.spc.ncep.noaa.gov/climo/online/monthly/2013_annual_summary.html)
*Preliminary figures. Tornadoes striking more than one state are counted in each state.

# Hazardous Weather Fatalities in 2012

## National Total = 519 Fatalities*

ALPHA ORDER

| RANK | STATE | FATALITIES | % of USA |
|------|-------|-----------|----------|
| 11 | Alabama | 17 | 3.3% |
| 37 | Alaska | 1 | 0.2% |
| 19 | Arizona | 9 | 1.7% |
| 21 | Arkansas | 8 | 1.5% |
| 9 | California | 20 | 3.9% |
| 23 | Colorado | 7 | 1.3% |
| 30 | Connecticut | 3 | 0.6% |
| 46 | Delaware | 0 | 0.0% |
| 4 | Florida | 29 | 5.6% |
| 37 | Georgia | 1 | 0.2% |
| 37 | Hawaii | 1 | 0.2% |
| 37 | Idaho | 1 | 0.2% |
| 2 | Illinois | 47 | 9.1% |
| 10 | Indiana | 19 | 3.7% |
| 30 | Iowa | 3 | 0.6% |
| 30 | Kansas | 3 | 0.6% |
| 5 | Kentucky | 27 | 5.2% |
| 15 | Louisiana | 12 | 2.3% |
| 46 | Maine | 0 | 0.0% |
| 27 | Maryland | 5 | 1.0% |
| 46 | Massachusetts | 0 | 0.0% |
| 19 | Michigan | 9 | 1.7% |
| 23 | Minnesota | 7 | 1.3% |
| 28 | Mississippi | 4 | 0.8% |
| 3 | Missouri | 42 | 8.1% |
| 28 | Montana | 4 | 0.8% |
| 37 | Nebraska | 1 | 0.2% |
| 15 | Nevada | 12 | 2.3% |
| 37 | New Hampshire | 1 | 0.2% |
| 6 | New Jersey | 24 | 4.6% |
| 37 | New Mexico | 1 | 0.2% |
| 1 | New York | 57 | 11.0% |
| 15 | North Carolina | 12 | 2.3% |
| 46 | North Dakota | 0 | 0.0% |
| 18 | Ohio | 11 | 2.1% |
| 12 | Oklahoma | 14 | 2.7% |
| 30 | Oregon | 3 | 0.6% |
| 8 | Pennsylvania | 23 | 4.4% |
| 46 | Rhode Island | 0 | 0.0% |
| 36 | South Carolina | 2 | 0.4% |
| 37 | South Dakota | 1 | 0.2% |
| 14 | Tennessee | 13 | 2.5% |
| 6 | Texas | 24 | 4.6% |
| 25 | Utah | 6 | 1.2% |
| 30 | Vermont | 3 | 0.6% |
| 21 | Virginia | 8 | 1.5% |
| 25 | Washington | 6 | 1.2% |
| 37 | West Virginia | 1 | 0.2% |
| 12 | Wisconsin | 14 | 2.7% |
| 30 | Wyoming | 3 | 0.6% |

RANK ORDER

| RANK | STATE | FATALITIES | % of USA |
|------|-------|-----------|----------|
| 1 | New York | 57 | 11.0% |
| 2 | Illinois | 47 | 9.1% |
| 3 | Missouri | 42 | 8.1% |
| 4 | Florida | 29 | 5.6% |
| 5 | Kentucky | 27 | 5.2% |
| 6 | New Jersey | 24 | 4.6% |
| 6 | Texas | 24 | 4.6% |
| 8 | Pennsylvania | 23 | 4.4% |
| 9 | California | 20 | 3.9% |
| 10 | Indiana | 19 | 3.7% |
| 11 | Alabama | 17 | 3.3% |
| 12 | Oklahoma | 14 | 2.7% |
| 12 | Wisconsin | 14 | 2.7% |
| 14 | Tennessee | 13 | 2.5% |
| 15 | Louisiana | 12 | 2.3% |
| 15 | Nevada | 12 | 2.3% |
| 15 | North Carolina | 12 | 2.3% |
| 18 | Ohio | 11 | 2.1% |
| 19 | Arizona | 9 | 1.7% |
| 19 | Michigan | 9 | 1.7% |
| 21 | Arkansas | 8 | 1.5% |
| 21 | Virginia | 8 | 1.5% |
| 23 | Colorado | 7 | 1.3% |
| 23 | Minnesota | 7 | 1.3% |
| 25 | Utah | 6 | 1.2% |
| 25 | Washington | 6 | 1.2% |
| 27 | Maryland | 5 | 1.0% |
| 28 | Mississippi | 4 | 0.8% |
| 28 | Montana | 4 | 0.8% |
| 30 | Connecticut | 3 | 0.6% |
| 30 | Iowa | 3 | 0.6% |
| 30 | Kansas | 3 | 0.6% |
| 30 | Oregon | 3 | 0.6% |
| 30 | Vermont | 3 | 0.6% |
| 30 | Wyoming | 3 | 0.6% |
| 36 | South Carolina | 2 | 0.4% |
| 37 | Alaska | 1 | 0.2% |
| 37 | Georgia | 1 | 0.2% |
| 37 | Hawaii | 1 | 0.2% |
| 37 | Idaho | 1 | 0.2% |
| 37 | Nebraska | 1 | 0.2% |
| 37 | New Hampshire | 1 | 0.2% |
| 37 | New Mexico | 1 | 0.2% |
| 37 | South Dakota | 1 | 0.2% |
| 37 | West Virginia | 1 | 0.2% |
| 46 | Delaware | 0 | 0.0% |
| 46 | Maine | 0 | 0.0% |
| 46 | Massachusetts | 0 | 0.0% |
| 46 | North Dakota | 0 | 0.0% |
| 46 | Rhode Island | 0 | 0.0% |
| | District of Columbia | 0 | 0.0% |

Source: National Weather Service, Water and Weather Services
"2012 Summary of Hazardous Weather Fatalities" (http://www.nws.noaa.gov/om/hazstats/state12.pdf)
*Includes lightning, tornado, thunderstorm, extreme temperature, flood, coastal storm, rip current, hurricane, winter storm, fog, avalanche, and other weather events. National total does not include 12 fatalities in U.S. waters or territories.

# Cost of Damage from Hazardous Weather in 2012

## National Total = $38,677,580,000*

ALPHA ORDER

| RANK | STATE | DAMAGE | % of USA |
|------|-------|--------|----------|
| 42 | Alabama | $7,450,000 | 0.0% |
| 36 | Alaska | 24,150,000 | 0.1% |
| 37 | Arizona | 21,700,000 | 0.1% |
| 12 | Arkansas | 180,590,000 | 0.5% |
| 30 | California | 37,020,000 | 0.1% |
| 5 | Colorado | 1,162,830,000 | 3.0% |
| 45 | Connecticut | 7,020,000 | 0.0% |
| 43 | Delaware | 7,430,000 | 0.0% |
| 15 | Florida | 129,230,000 | 0.3% |
| 21 | Georgia | 61,390,000 | 0.2% |
| 50 | Hawaii | 200,000 | 0.0% |
| 10 | Idaho | 479,600,000 | 1.2% |
| 4 | Illinois | 1,179,750,000 | 3.1% |
| 19 | Indiana | 73,060,000 | 0.2% |
| 3 | Iowa | 2,796,300,000 | 7.2% |
| 9 | Kansas | 540,780,000 | 1.4% |
| 13 | Kentucky | 165,080,000 | 0.4% |
| 6 | Louisiana | 810,650,000 | 2.1% |
| 49 | Maine | 1,100,000 | 0.0% |
| 25 | Maryland | 47,900,000 | 0.1% |
| 35 | Massachusetts | 26,190,000 | 0.1% |
| 11 | Michigan | 197,070,000 | 0.5% |
| 22 | Minnesota | 60,840,000 | 0.2% |
| 29 | Mississippi | 39,130,000 | 0.1% |
| 20 | Missouri | 72,410,000 | 0.2% |
| 41 | Montana | 8,580,000 | 0.0% |
| 8 | Nebraska | 550,880,000 | 1.4% |
| 17 | Nevada | 82,150,000 | 0.2% |
| 47 | New Hampshire | 5,280,000 | 0.0% |
| 1 | New Jersey | 24,996,860,000 | 64.6% |
| 28 | New Mexico | 39,330,000 | 0.1% |
| 27 | New York | 39,940,000 | 0.1% |
| 24 | North Carolina | 57,060,000 | 0.1% |
| 46 | North Dakota | 6,000,000 | 0.0% |
| 14 | Ohio | 135,990,000 | 0.4% |
| 7 | Oklahoma | 656,180,000 | 1.7% |
| 32 | Oregon | 30,760,000 | 0.1% |
| 26 | Pennsylvania | 42,770,000 | 0.1% |
| 39 | Rhode Island | 11,860,000 | 0.0% |
| 40 | South Carolina | 9,380,000 | 0.0% |
| 44 | South Dakota | 7,260,000 | 0.0% |
| 18 | Tennessee | 81,770,000 | 0.2% |
| 2 | Texas | 3,518,070,000 | 9.1% |
| 34 | Utah | 27,230,000 | 0.1% |
| 38 | Vermont | 14,630,000 | 0.0% |
| 23 | Virginia | 57,580,000 | 0.1% |
| 33 | Washington | 28,450,000 | 0.1% |
| 16 | West Virginia | 102,560,000 | 0.3% |
| 31 | Wisconsin | 32,930,000 | 0.1% |
| 48 | Wyoming | 5,110,000 | 0.0% |

RANK ORDER

| RANK | STATE | DAMAGE | % of USA |
|------|-------|--------|----------|
| 1 | New Jersey | $24,996,860,000 | 64.6% |
| 2 | Texas | 3,518,070,000 | 9.1% |
| 3 | Iowa | 2,796,300,000 | 7.2% |
| 4 | Illinois | 1,179,750,000 | 3.1% |
| 5 | Colorado | 1,162,830,000 | 3.0% |
| 6 | Louisiana | 810,650,000 | 2.1% |
| 7 | Oklahoma | 656,180,000 | 1.7% |
| 8 | Nebraska | 550,880,000 | 1.4% |
| 9 | Kansas | 540,780,000 | 1.4% |
| 10 | Idaho | 479,600,000 | 1.2% |
| 11 | Michigan | 197,070,000 | 0.5% |
| 12 | Arkansas | 180,590,000 | 0.5% |
| 13 | Kentucky | 165,080,000 | 0.4% |
| 14 | Ohio | 135,990,000 | 0.4% |
| 15 | Florida | 129,230,000 | 0.3% |
| 16 | West Virginia | 102,560,000 | 0.3% |
| 17 | Nevada | 82,150,000 | 0.2% |
| 18 | Tennessee | 81,770,000 | 0.2% |
| 19 | Indiana | 73,060,000 | 0.2% |
| 20 | Missouri | 72,410,000 | 0.2% |
| 21 | Georgia | 61,390,000 | 0.2% |
| 22 | Minnesota | 60,840,000 | 0.2% |
| 23 | Virginia | 57,580,000 | 0.1% |
| 24 | North Carolina | 57,060,000 | 0.1% |
| 25 | Maryland | 47,900,000 | 0.1% |
| 26 | Pennsylvania | 42,770,000 | 0.1% |
| 27 | New York | 39,940,000 | 0.1% |
| 28 | New Mexico | 39,330,000 | 0.1% |
| 29 | Mississippi | 39,130,000 | 0.1% |
| 30 | California | 37,020,000 | 0.1% |
| 31 | Wisconsin | 32,930,000 | 0.1% |
| 32 | Oregon | 30,760,000 | 0.1% |
| 33 | Washington | 28,450,000 | 0.1% |
| 34 | Utah | 27,230,000 | 0.1% |
| 35 | Massachusetts | 26,190,000 | 0.1% |
| 36 | Alaska | 24,150,000 | 0.1% |
| 37 | Arizona | 21,700,000 | 0.1% |
| 38 | Vermont | 14,630,000 | 0.0% |
| 39 | Rhode Island | 11,860,000 | 0.0% |
| 40 | South Carolina | 9,380,000 | 0.0% |
| 41 | Montana | 8,580,000 | 0.0% |
| 42 | Alabama | 7,450,000 | 0.0% |
| 43 | Delaware | 7,430,000 | 0.0% |
| 44 | South Dakota | 7,260,000 | 0.0% |
| 45 | Connecticut | 7,020,000 | 0.0% |
| 46 | North Dakota | 6,000,000 | 0.0% |
| 47 | New Hampshire | 5,280,000 | 0.0% |
| 48 | Wyoming | 5,110,000 | 0.0% |
| 49 | Maine | 1,100,000 | 0.0% |
| 50 | Hawaii | 200,000 | 0.0% |
| | District of Columbia | 100,000 | 0.0% |

Source: National Weather Service, Water and Weather Services
   "2012 Summary of Hazardous Weather Fatalities" (http://www.nws.noaa.gov/om/hazstats/state12.pdf)
*Includes property and crop damage from lightning, tornado, thunderstorm, extreme temperature, flood, coastal storm, rip current, hurricane, winter storm, fog, avalanche, and other weather events. National total does not include damage costs in U.S. territories.

# National Park Service Land in 2013

## National Total = 84,479,316 Acres*

ALPHA ORDER

| RANK | STATE | ACRES | % of USA |
|---|---|---|---|
| 41 | Alabama | 22,737 | 0.0% |
| 1 | Alaska | 54,654,067 | 64.7% |
| 3 | Arizona | 2,962,815 | 3.5% |
| 25 | Arkansas | 104,977 | 0.1% |
| 2 | California | 8,142,048 | 9.6% |
| 11 | Colorado | 725,198 | 0.9% |
| 46 | Connecticut | 7,782 | 0.0% |
| 48 | Delaware | 900 | 0.0% |
| 4 | Florida | 2,638,210 | 3.1% |
| 34 | Georgia | 63,326 | 0.1% |
| 17 | Hawaii | 369,166 | 0.4% |
| 13 | Idaho | 518,224 | 0.6% |
| 49 | Illinois | 115 | 0.0% |
| 43 | Indiana | 15,540 | 0.0% |
| 47 | Iowa | 2,713 | 0.0% |
| 44 | Kansas | 11,636 | 0.0% |
| 27 | Kentucky | 95,699 | 0.1% |
| 39 | Louisiana | 23,545 | 0.0% |
| 29 | Maine | 91,706 | 0.1% |
| 31 | Maryland | 73,893 | 0.1% |
| 35 | Massachusetts | 57,962 | 0.1% |
| 12 | Michigan | 718,151 | 0.9% |
| 20 | Minnesota | 301,330 | 0.4% |
| 24 | Mississippi | 118,739 | 0.1% |
| 30 | Missouri | 83,477 | 0.1% |
| 8 | Montana | 1,274,364 | 1.5% |
| 36 | Nebraska | 45,675 | 0.1% |
| 10 | Nevada | 778,512 | 0.9% |
| 42 | New Hampshire | 21,932 | 0.0% |
| 26 | New Jersey | 99,243 | 0.1% |
| 15 | New Mexico | 391,078 | 0.5% |
| 32 | New York | 73,000 | 0.1% |
| 14 | North Carolina | 407,045 | 0.5% |
| 33 | North Dakota | 72,568 | 0.1% |
| 37 | Ohio | 34,804 | 0.0% |
| 45 | Oklahoma | 10,241 | 0.0% |
| 21 | Oregon | 199,319 | 0.2% |
| 22 | Pennsylvania | 138,015 | 0.2% |
| 50 | Rhode Island | 5 | 0.0% |
| 38 | South Carolina | 32,348 | 0.0% |
| 19 | South Dakota | 302,998 | 0.4% |
| 16 | Tennessee | 386,458 | 0.5% |
| 9 | Texas | 1,247,913 | 1.5% |
| 6 | Utah | 2,117,683 | 2.5% |
| 40 | Vermont | 23,265 | 0.0% |
| 18 | Virginia | 363,307 | 0.4% |
| 7 | Washington | 1,967,532 | 2.3% |
| 28 | West Virginia | 92,697 | 0.1% |
| 23 | Wisconsin | 133,755 | 0.2% |
| 5 | Wyoming | 2,396,424 | 2.8% |

RANK ORDER

| RANK | STATE | ACRES | % of USA |
|---|---|---|---|
| 1 | Alaska | 54,654,067 | 64.7% |
| 2 | California | 8,142,048 | 9.6% |
| 3 | Arizona | 2,962,815 | 3.5% |
| 4 | Florida | 2,638,210 | 3.1% |
| 5 | Wyoming | 2,396,424 | 2.8% |
| 6 | Utah | 2,117,683 | 2.5% |
| 7 | Washington | 1,967,532 | 2.3% |
| 8 | Montana | 1,274,364 | 1.5% |
| 9 | Texas | 1,247,913 | 1.5% |
| 10 | Nevada | 778,512 | 0.9% |
| 11 | Colorado | 725,198 | 0.9% |
| 12 | Michigan | 718,151 | 0.9% |
| 13 | Idaho | 518,224 | 0.6% |
| 14 | North Carolina | 407,045 | 0.5% |
| 15 | New Mexico | 391,078 | 0.5% |
| 16 | Tennessee | 386,458 | 0.5% |
| 17 | Hawaii | 369,166 | 0.4% |
| 18 | Virginia | 363,307 | 0.4% |
| 19 | South Dakota | 302,998 | 0.4% |
| 20 | Minnesota | 301,330 | 0.4% |
| 21 | Oregon | 199,319 | 0.2% |
| 22 | Pennsylvania | 138,015 | 0.2% |
| 23 | Wisconsin | 133,755 | 0.2% |
| 24 | Mississippi | 118,739 | 0.1% |
| 25 | Arkansas | 104,977 | 0.1% |
| 26 | New Jersey | 99,243 | 0.1% |
| 27 | Kentucky | 95,699 | 0.1% |
| 28 | West Virginia | 92,697 | 0.1% |
| 29 | Maine | 91,706 | 0.1% |
| 30 | Missouri | 83,477 | 0.1% |
| 31 | Maryland | 73,893 | 0.1% |
| 32 | New York | 73,000 | 0.1% |
| 33 | North Dakota | 72,568 | 0.1% |
| 34 | Georgia | 63,326 | 0.1% |
| 35 | Massachusetts | 57,962 | 0.1% |
| 36 | Nebraska | 45,675 | 0.1% |
| 37 | Ohio | 34,804 | 0.0% |
| 38 | South Carolina | 32,348 | 0.0% |
| 39 | Louisiana | 23,545 | 0.0% |
| 40 | Vermont | 23,265 | 0.0% |
| 41 | Alabama | 22,737 | 0.0% |
| 42 | New Hampshire | 21,932 | 0.0% |
| 43 | Indiana | 15,540 | 0.0% |
| 44 | Kansas | 11,636 | 0.0% |
| 45 | Oklahoma | 10,241 | 0.0% |
| 46 | Connecticut | 7,782 | 0.0% |
| 47 | Iowa | 2,713 | 0.0% |
| 48 | Delaware | 900 | 0.0% |
| 49 | Illinois | 115 | 0.0% |
| 50 | Rhode Island | 5 | 0.0% |
| | District of Columbia | 7,131 | 0.0% |

Source: National Park Service
   "Listing of Acreage by State" (unpublished data)
*As of December 31, 2013.  Includes federal and nonfederal land in national parks, monuments, historic sites, recreation areas, preserves, battlefields, grasslands, seashores, parkways, trails, and rivers.  Does not include land in national forest or wildlife areas.  Includes 58,050 acres in U.S. territories.

# Recreation Visits to National Park Service Areas in 2012

## National Total = 282,765,682 Visits*

ALPHA ORDER

| RANK | STATE | VISITS | % of USA |
|---|---|---|---|
| 36 | Alabama | 717,724 | 0.3% |
| 27 | Alaska | 2,412,524 | 0.9% |
| 7 | Arizona | 9,979,972 | 3.5% |
| 24 | Arkansas | 2,727,454 | 1.0% |
| 1 | California | 35,991,200 | 12.7% |
| 16 | Colorado | 5,811,546 | 2.1% |
| 49 | Connecticut | 21,465 | 0.0% |
| 50 | Delaware | 0 | 0.0% |
| 6 | Florida | 10,366,613 | 3.7% |
| 12 | Georgia | 7,350,309 | 2.6% |
| 17 | Hawaii | 5,119,035 | 1.8% |
| 40 | Idaho | 553,554 | 0.2% |
| 42 | Illinois | 295,464 | 0.1% |
| 29 | Indiana | 2,148,903 | 0.8% |
| 44 | Iowa | 207,352 | 0.1% |
| 45 | Kansas | 101,752 | 0.0% |
| 30 | Kentucky | 1,717,853 | 0.6% |
| 38 | Louisiana | 625,913 | 0.2% |
| 26 | Maine | 2,431,052 | 0.9% |
| 13 | Maryland | 6,658,643 | 2.4% |
| 5 | Massachusetts | 10,487,447 | 3.7% |
| 28 | Michigan | 2,192,477 | 0.8% |
| 39 | Minnesota | 601,274 | 0.2% |
| 14 | Mississippi | 6,449,713 | 2.3% |
| 21 | Missouri | 4,171,826 | 1.5% |
| 20 | Montana | 4,451,755 | 1.6% |
| 41 | Nebraska | 304,046 | 0.1% |
| 19 | Nevada | 4,808,929 | 1.7% |
| 47 | New Hampshire | 33,663 | 0.0% |
| 18 | New Jersey | 4,885,202 | 1.7% |
| 33 | New Mexico | 1,502,808 | 0.5% |
| 4 | New York | 12,633,278 | 4.5% |
| 3 | North Carolina | 17,706,032 | 6.3% |
| 37 | North Dakota | 669,242 | 0.2% |
| 25 | Ohio | 2,611,158 | 0.9% |
| 34 | Oklahoma | 1,497,654 | 0.5% |
| 35 | Oregon | 875,271 | 0.3% |
| 9 | Pennsylvania | 8,768,869 | 3.1% |
| 46 | Rhode Island | 51,944 | 0.0% |
| 31 | South Carolina | 1,566,756 | 0.6% |
| 22 | South Dakota | 3,950,666 | 1.4% |
| 10 | Tennessee | 8,414,094 | 3.0% |
| 23 | Texas | 3,939,160 | 1.4% |
| 8 | Utah | 9,503,304 | 3.4% |
| 48 | Vermont | 32,403 | 0.0% |
| 2 | Virginia | 23,398,517 | 8.3% |
| 11 | Washington | 7,529,549 | 2.7% |
| 32 | West Virginia | 1,543,425 | 0.5% |
| 43 | Wisconsin | 273,933 | 0.1% |
| 15 | Wyoming | 6,194,752 | 2.2% |

RANK ORDER

| RANK | STATE | VISITS | % of USA |
|---|---|---|---|
| 1 | California | 35,991,200 | 12.7% |
| 2 | Virginia | 23,398,517 | 8.3% |
| 3 | North Carolina | 17,706,032 | 6.3% |
| 4 | New York | 12,633,278 | 4.5% |
| 5 | Massachusetts | 10,487,447 | 3.7% |
| 6 | Florida | 10,366,613 | 3.7% |
| 7 | Arizona | 9,979,972 | 3.5% |
| 8 | Utah | 9,503,304 | 3.4% |
| 9 | Pennsylvania | 8,768,869 | 3.1% |
| 10 | Tennessee | 8,414,094 | 3.0% |
| 11 | Washington | 7,529,549 | 2.7% |
| 12 | Georgia | 7,350,309 | 2.6% |
| 13 | Maryland | 6,658,643 | 2.4% |
| 14 | Mississippi | 6,449,713 | 2.3% |
| 15 | Wyoming | 6,194,752 | 2.2% |
| 16 | Colorado | 5,811,546 | 2.1% |
| 17 | Hawaii | 5,119,035 | 1.8% |
| 18 | New Jersey | 4,885,202 | 1.7% |
| 19 | Nevada | 4,808,929 | 1.7% |
| 20 | Montana | 4,451,755 | 1.6% |
| 21 | Missouri | 4,171,826 | 1.5% |
| 22 | South Dakota | 3,950,666 | 1.4% |
| 23 | Texas | 3,939,160 | 1.4% |
| 24 | Arkansas | 2,727,454 | 1.0% |
| 25 | Ohio | 2,611,158 | 0.9% |
| 26 | Maine | 2,431,052 | 0.9% |
| 27 | Alaska | 2,412,524 | 0.9% |
| 28 | Michigan | 2,192,477 | 0.8% |
| 29 | Indiana | 2,148,903 | 0.8% |
| 30 | Kentucky | 1,717,853 | 0.6% |
| 31 | South Carolina | 1,566,756 | 0.6% |
| 32 | West Virginia | 1,543,425 | 0.5% |
| 33 | New Mexico | 1,502,808 | 0.5% |
| 34 | Oklahoma | 1,497,654 | 0.5% |
| 35 | Oregon | 875,271 | 0.3% |
| 36 | Alabama | 717,724 | 0.3% |
| 37 | North Dakota | 669,242 | 0.2% |
| 38 | Louisiana | 625,913 | 0.2% |
| 39 | Minnesota | 601,274 | 0.2% |
| 40 | Idaho | 553,554 | 0.2% |
| 41 | Nebraska | 304,046 | 0.1% |
| 42 | Illinois | 295,464 | 0.1% |
| 43 | Wisconsin | 273,933 | 0.1% |
| 44 | Iowa | 207,352 | 0.1% |
| 45 | Kansas | 101,752 | 0.0% |
| 46 | Rhode Island | 51,944 | 0.0% |
| 47 | New Hampshire | 33,663 | 0.0% |
| 48 | Vermont | 32,403 | 0.0% |
| 49 | Connecticut | 21,465 | 0.0% |
| 50 | Delaware | 0 | 0.0% |
| | District of Columbia | 34,286,073 | 12.1% |

Source: National Park Service, Public Use Statistics Office
 "National Park Service Statistical Abstract 2012" (https://irma.nps.gov/Stats/Reports/AbstractsandForecasts)
*National total includes 2,192,133 visits in U.S. territories.

# Percent Change in National Park Service Recreation Visits: 2011 to 2012

## National Percent Change = 1.4% Increase*

ALPHA ORDER

| RANK | STATE | PERCENT CHANGE |
|------|-------|----------------|
| 42 | Alabama | (5.0) |
| 19 | Alaska | 3.4 |
| 37 | Arizona | (1.5) |
| 43 | Arkansas | (5.3) |
| 30 | California | 1.5 |
| 33 | Colorado | (0.1) |
| 40 | Connecticut | (4.2) |
| NA | Delaware** | NA |
| 39 | Florida | (2.0) |
| 25 | Georgia | 2.5 |
| 12 | Hawaii | 7.0 |
| 46 | Idaho | (8.0) |
| 34 | Illinois | (0.3) |
| 24 | Indiana | 2.6 |
| 41 | Iowa | (4.4) |
| 3 | Kansas | 12.6 |
| 20 | Kentucky | 3.1 |
| 9 | Louisiana | 8.3 |
| 27 | Maine | 2.4 |
| 7 | Maryland | 9.8 |
| 25 | Massachusetts | 2.5 |
| 4 | Michigan | 11.8 |
| 14 | Minnesota | 5.0 |
| 45 | Mississippi | (7.7) |
| 13 | Missouri | 6.6 |
| 8 | Montana | 9.6 |
| 6 | Nebraska | 10.1 |
| 38 | Nevada | (1.6) |
| 21 | New Hampshire | 3.0 |
| 47 | New Jersey | (8.8) |
| 32 | New Mexico | 0.8 |
| 49 | New York | (22.0) |
| 21 | North Carolina | 3.0 |
| 2 | North Dakota | 13.1 |
| 11 | Ohio | 8.0 |
| 1 | Oklahoma | 22.4 |
| 16 | Oregon | 4.2 |
| 23 | Pennsylvania | 2.8 |
| 29 | Rhode Island | 2.0 |
| 36 | South Carolina | (1.4) |
| 18 | South Dakota | 3.8 |
| 9 | Tennessee | 8.3 |
| 44 | Texas | (6.5) |
| 27 | Utah | 2.4 |
| 5 | Vermont | 11.5 |
| 34 | Virginia | (0.3) |
| 30 | Washington | 1.5 |
| 15 | West Virginia | 4.4 |
| 48 | Wisconsin | (12.5) |
| 17 | Wyoming | 4.0 |

RANK ORDER

| RANK | STATE | PERCENT CHANGE |
|------|-------|----------------|
| 1 | Oklahoma | 22.4 |
| 2 | North Dakota | 13.1 |
| 3 | Kansas | 12.6 |
| 4 | Michigan | 11.8 |
| 5 | Vermont | 11.5 |
| 6 | Nebraska | 10.1 |
| 7 | Maryland | 9.8 |
| 8 | Montana | 9.6 |
| 9 | Louisiana | 8.3 |
| 9 | Tennessee | 8.3 |
| 11 | Ohio | 8.0 |
| 12 | Hawaii | 7.0 |
| 13 | Missouri | 6.6 |
| 14 | Minnesota | 5.0 |
| 15 | West Virginia | 4.4 |
| 16 | Oregon | 4.2 |
| 17 | Wyoming | 4.0 |
| 18 | South Dakota | 3.8 |
| 19 | Alaska | 3.4 |
| 20 | Kentucky | 3.1 |
| 21 | New Hampshire | 3.0 |
| 21 | North Carolina | 3.0 |
| 23 | Pennsylvania | 2.8 |
| 24 | Indiana | 2.6 |
| 25 | Georgia | 2.5 |
| 25 | Massachusetts | 2.5 |
| 27 | Maine | 2.4 |
| 27 | Utah | 2.4 |
| 29 | Rhode Island | 2.0 |
| 30 | California | 1.5 |
| 30 | Washington | 1.5 |
| 32 | New Mexico | 0.8 |
| 33 | Colorado | (0.1) |
| 34 | Illinois | (0.3) |
| 34 | Virginia | (0.3) |
| 36 | South Carolina | (1.4) |
| 37 | Arizona | (1.5) |
| 38 | Nevada | (1.6) |
| 39 | Florida | (2.0) |
| 40 | Connecticut | (4.2) |
| 41 | Iowa | (4.4) |
| 42 | Alabama | (5.0) |
| 43 | Arkansas | (5.3) |
| 44 | Texas | (6.5) |
| 45 | Mississippi | (7.7) |
| 46 | Idaho | (8.0) |
| 47 | New Jersey | (8.8) |
| 48 | Wisconsin | (12.5) |
| 49 | New York | (22.0) |
| NA | Delaware** | NA |
| | District of Columbia | 12.1 |

Source: National Park Service, Public Use Statistics Office
"National Park Service Statistical Abstract 2012" (https://irma.nps.gov/Stats/Reports/AbstractsandForecasts)
*National percent change includes visits in U.S. territories.
**Not applicable.

# State Parks, Recreation Areas, and Natural Areas in 2010

## National Total = 7,810 Areas*

ALPHA ORDER

| RANK | STATE | AREAS | % of USA |
|------|-------|-------|----------|
| 50 | Alabama | 22 | 0.3% |
| 11 | Alaska | 139 | 1.8% |
| 45 | Arizona | 32 | 0.4% |
| 34 | Arkansas | 52 | 0.7% |
| 5 | California | 278 | 3.6% |
| 9 | Colorado | 168 | 2.2% |
| 12 | Connecticut | 137 | 1.8% |
| 43 | Delaware | 34 | 0.4% |
| 10 | Florida | 160 | 2.0% |
| 26 | Georgia | 73 | 0.9% |
| 28 | Hawaii | 68 | 0.9% |
| 43 | Idaho | 34 | 0.4% |
| 4 | Illinois | 319 | 4.1% |
| 42 | Indiana | 37 | 0.5% |
| 8 | Iowa | 179 | 2.3% |
| 47 | Kansas | 25 | 0.3% |
| 35 | Kentucky | 51 | 0.7% |
| 31 | Louisiana | 60 | 0.8% |
| 13 | Maine | 136 | 1.7% |
| 30 | Maryland | 65 | 0.8% |
| 3 | Massachusetts | 339 | 4.3% |
| 18 | Michigan | 98 | 1.3% |
| 1 | Minnesota | 1,783 | 22.8% |
| 47 | Mississippi | 25 | 0.3% |
| 21 | Missouri | 85 | 1.1% |
| 28 | Montana | 68 | 0.9% |
| 21 | Nebraska | 85 | 1.1% |
| 47 | Nevada | 25 | 0.3% |
| 19 | New Hampshire | 91 | 1.2% |
| 16 | New Jersey | 117 | 1.5% |
| 41 | New Mexico | 38 | 0.5% |
| 2 | New York | 1,418 | 18.2% |
| 27 | North Carolina | 70 | 0.9% |
| 46 | North Dakota | 31 | 0.4% |
| 25 | Ohio | 75 | 1.0% |
| 39 | Oklahoma | 42 | 0.5% |
| 6 | Oregon | 257 | 3.3% |
| 15 | Pennsylvania | 121 | 1.5% |
| 24 | Rhode Island | 77 | 1.0% |
| 32 | South Carolina | 56 | 0.7% |
| 14 | South Dakota | 131 | 1.7% |
| 33 | Tennessee | 53 | 0.7% |
| 20 | Texas | 90 | 1.2% |
| 36 | Utah | 50 | 0.6% |
| 17 | Vermont | 103 | 1.3% |
| 38 | Virginia | 43 | 0.6% |
| 7 | Washington | 201 | 2.6% |
| 37 | West Virginia | 47 | 0.6% |
| 23 | Wisconsin | 82 | 1.0% |
| 40 | Wyoming | 40 | 0.5% |

RANK ORDER

| RANK | STATE | AREAS | % of USA |
|------|-------|-------|----------|
| 1 | Minnesota | 1,783 | 22.8% |
| 2 | New York | 1,418 | 18.2% |
| 3 | Massachusetts | 339 | 4.3% |
| 4 | Illinois | 319 | 4.1% |
| 5 | California | 278 | 3.6% |
| 6 | Oregon | 257 | 3.3% |
| 7 | Washington | 201 | 2.6% |
| 8 | Iowa | 179 | 2.3% |
| 9 | Colorado | 168 | 2.2% |
| 10 | Florida | 160 | 2.0% |
| 11 | Alaska | 139 | 1.8% |
| 12 | Connecticut | 137 | 1.8% |
| 13 | Maine | 136 | 1.7% |
| 14 | South Dakota | 131 | 1.7% |
| 15 | Pennsylvania | 121 | 1.5% |
| 16 | New Jersey | 117 | 1.5% |
| 17 | Vermont | 103 | 1.3% |
| 18 | Michigan | 98 | 1.3% |
| 19 | New Hampshire | 91 | 1.2% |
| 20 | Texas | 90 | 1.2% |
| 21 | Missouri | 85 | 1.1% |
| 21 | Nebraska | 85 | 1.1% |
| 23 | Wisconsin | 82 | 1.0% |
| 24 | Rhode Island | 77 | 1.0% |
| 25 | Ohio | 75 | 1.0% |
| 26 | Georgia | 73 | 0.9% |
| 27 | North Carolina | 70 | 0.9% |
| 28 | Hawaii | 68 | 0.9% |
| 28 | Montana | 68 | 0.9% |
| 30 | Maryland | 65 | 0.8% |
| 31 | Louisiana | 60 | 0.8% |
| 32 | South Carolina | 56 | 0.7% |
| 33 | Tennessee | 53 | 0.7% |
| 34 | Arkansas | 52 | 0.7% |
| 35 | Kentucky | 51 | 0.7% |
| 36 | Utah | 50 | 0.6% |
| 37 | West Virginia | 47 | 0.6% |
| 38 | Virginia | 43 | 0.6% |
| 39 | Oklahoma | 42 | 0.5% |
| 40 | Wyoming | 40 | 0.5% |
| 41 | New Mexico | 38 | 0.5% |
| 42 | Indiana | 37 | 0.5% |
| 43 | Delaware | 34 | 0.4% |
| 43 | Idaho | 34 | 0.4% |
| 45 | Arizona | 32 | 0.4% |
| 46 | North Dakota | 31 | 0.4% |
| 47 | Kansas | 25 | 0.3% |
| 47 | Mississippi | 25 | 0.3% |
| 47 | Nevada | 25 | 0.3% |
| 50 | Alabama | 22 | 0.3% |
| | District of Columbia** | NA | NA |

Source: The National Association of State Parks Directors
"Annual Information Exchange" (http://www.naspd.org/)
*For the period July 1, 2009 through June 30, 2010. Includes operating and nonoperating state parks, recreation areas, natural areas, and other areas.
**Not applicable.

# Visitors to State Parks and Recreation Areas in 2010

## National Total = 740,733,016 Visitors*

| RANK | STATE | VISITORS | % of USA |
|------|-------|----------|----------|
| 40 | Alabama | 3,838,568 | 0.5% |
| 35 | Alaska | 5,405,238 | 0.7% |
| 44 | Arizona | 2,267,407 | 0.3% |
| 25 | Arkansas | 8,830,816 | 1.2% |
| 1 | California | 65,036,234 | 8.8% |
| 18 | Colorado | 12,285,251 | 1.7% |
| 26 | Connecticut | 8,208,751 | 1.1% |
| 36 | Delaware | 4,947,148 | 0.7% |
| 11 | Florida | 20,110,021 | 2.7% |
| 23 | Georgia | 9,722,243 | 1.3% |
| 21 | Hawaii | 10,425,185 | 1.4% |
| 39 | Idaho | 4,649,326 | 0.6% |
| 6 | Illinois | 42,293,523 | 5.7% |
| 14 | Indiana | 15,846,351 | 2.1% |
| 17 | Iowa | 14,373,901 | 1.9% |
| 28 | Kansas | 7,800,100 | 1.1% |
| 33 | Kentucky | 7,013,120 | 0.9% |
| 45 | Louisiana | 2,068,794 | 0.3% |
| 43 | Maine | 2,602,097 | 0.4% |
| 22 | Maryland | 10,131,635 | 1.4% |
| 8 | Massachusetts | 35,270,780 | 4.8% |
| 10 | Michigan | 21,167,130 | 2.9% |
| 24 | Minnesota | 8,922,135 | 1.2% |
| 48 | Mississippi | 1,217,409 | 0.2% |
| 13 | Missouri | 16,214,980 | 2.2% |
| 46 | Montana | 1,896,183 | 0.3% |
| 19 | Nebraska | 11,143,763 | 1.5% |
| 42 | Nevada | 3,045,556 | 0.4% |
| 47 | New Hampshire | 1,585,665 | 0.2% |
| 12 | New Jersey | 17,163,594 | 2.3% |
| 37 | New Mexico | 4,768,710 | 0.6% |
| 2 | New York | 56,322,000 | 7.6% |
| 15 | North Carolina | 14,899,149 | 2.0% |
| 49 | North Dakota | 1,086,058 | 0.1% |
| 3 | Ohio | 53,813,556 | 7.3% |
| 20 | Oklahoma | 11,087,826 | 1.5% |
| 5 | Oregon | 43,755,240 | 5.9% |
| 7 | Pennsylvania | 38,523,251 | 5.2% |
| 34 | Rhode Island | 5,871,944 | 0.8% |
| 27 | South Carolina | 8,197,483 | 1.1% |
| 29 | South Dakota | 7,785,502 | 1.1% |
| 9 | Tennessee | 29,918,632 | 4.0% |
| 30 | Texas | 7,473,693 | 1.0% |
| 38 | Utah | 4,682,959 | 0.6% |
| 50 | Vermont | 758,282 | 0.1% |
| 31 | Virginia | 7,463,460 | 1.0% |
| 4 | Washington | 44,134,793 | 6.0% |
| 32 | West Virginia | 7,171,461 | 1.0% |
| 16 | Wisconsin | 14,469,998 | 2.0% |
| 41 | Wyoming | 3,066,115 | 0.4% |

| RANK | STATE | VISITORS | % of USA |
|------|-------|----------|----------|
| 1 | California | 65,036,234 | 8.8% |
| 2 | New York | 56,322,000 | 7.6% |
| 3 | Ohio | 53,813,556 | 7.3% |
| 4 | Washington | 44,134,793 | 6.0% |
| 5 | Oregon | 43,755,240 | 5.9% |
| 6 | Illinois | 42,293,523 | 5.7% |
| 7 | Pennsylvania | 38,523,251 | 5.2% |
| 8 | Massachusetts | 35,270,780 | 4.8% |
| 9 | Tennessee | 29,918,632 | 4.0% |
| 10 | Michigan | 21,167,130 | 2.9% |
| 11 | Florida | 20,110,021 | 2.7% |
| 12 | New Jersey | 17,163,594 | 2.3% |
| 13 | Missouri | 16,214,980 | 2.2% |
| 14 | Indiana | 15,846,351 | 2.1% |
| 15 | North Carolina | 14,899,149 | 2.0% |
| 16 | Wisconsin | 14,469,998 | 2.0% |
| 17 | Iowa | 14,373,901 | 1.9% |
| 18 | Colorado | 12,285,251 | 1.7% |
| 19 | Nebraska | 11,143,763 | 1.5% |
| 20 | Oklahoma | 11,087,826 | 1.5% |
| 21 | Hawaii | 10,425,185 | 1.4% |
| 22 | Maryland | 10,131,635 | 1.4% |
| 23 | Georgia | 9,722,243 | 1.3% |
| 24 | Minnesota | 8,922,135 | 1.2% |
| 25 | Arkansas | 8,830,816 | 1.2% |
| 26 | Connecticut | 8,208,751 | 1.1% |
| 27 | South Carolina | 8,197,483 | 1.1% |
| 28 | Kansas | 7,800,100 | 1.1% |
| 29 | South Dakota | 7,785,502 | 1.1% |
| 30 | Texas | 7,473,693 | 1.0% |
| 31 | Virginia | 7,463,460 | 1.0% |
| 32 | West Virginia | 7,171,461 | 1.0% |
| 33 | Kentucky | 7,013,120 | 0.9% |
| 34 | Rhode Island | 5,871,944 | 0.8% |
| 35 | Alaska | 5,405,238 | 0.7% |
| 36 | Delaware | 4,947,148 | 0.7% |
| 37 | New Mexico | 4,768,710 | 0.6% |
| 38 | Utah | 4,682,959 | 0.6% |
| 39 | Idaho | 4,649,326 | 0.6% |
| 40 | Alabama | 3,838,568 | 0.5% |
| 41 | Wyoming | 3,066,115 | 0.4% |
| 42 | Nevada | 3,045,556 | 0.4% |
| 43 | Maine | 2,602,097 | 0.4% |
| 44 | Arizona | 2,267,407 | 0.3% |
| 45 | Louisiana | 2,068,794 | 0.3% |
| 46 | Montana | 1,896,183 | 0.3% |
| 47 | New Hampshire | 1,585,665 | 0.2% |
| 48 | Mississippi | 1,217,409 | 0.2% |
| 49 | North Dakota | 1,086,058 | 0.1% |
| 50 | Vermont | 758,282 | 0.1% |
| | District of Columbia** | NA | NA |

Source: The National Association of State Parks Directors
"Annual Information Exchange" (http://www.naspd.org/)
*For the period July 1, 2009 through June 30, 2010. Includes operating and nonoperating state parks, recreation areas, natural areas, and other areas. Includes day and overnight visitors.
**Not applicable.

# IX. Government Finances: Federal

# Internal Revenue Service Gross Collections in 2012

## National Total = $2,524,320,134,000*

| ALPHA ORDER | | | | | | RANK ORDER | | | |
|---|---|---|---|---|---|---|---|---|---|
| RANK | STATE | COLLECTIONS | % of USA | | | RANK | STATE | COLLECTIONS | % of USA |
| 31 | Alabama | $20,882,949,000 | 0.8% | | | 1 | California | $292,563,574,000 | 11.6% |
| 47 | Alaska | 4,898,780,000 | 0.2% | | | 2 | Texas | 219,459,878,000 | 8.7% |
| 23 | Arizona | 34,850,436,000 | 1.4% | | | 3 | New York | 201,167,954,000 | 8.0% |
| 26 | Arkansas | 25,299,832,000 | 1.0% | | | 4 | Illinois | 124,431,227,000 | 4.9% |
| 1 | California | 292,563,574,000 | 11.6% | | | 5 | Florida | 122,249,635,000 | 4.8% |
| 22 | Colorado | 41,252,701,000 | 1.6% | | | 6 | New Jersey | 111,377,490,000 | 4.4% |
| 19 | Connecticut | 47,262,702,000 | 1.9% | | | 7 | Ohio | 111,094,276,000 | 4.4% |
| 30 | Delaware | 21,835,412,000 | 0.9% | | | 8 | Pennsylvania | 108,961,515,000 | 4.3% |
| 5 | Florida | 122,249,635,000 | 4.8% | | | 9 | Massachusetts | 79,826,976,000 | 3.2% |
| 11 | Georgia | 65,498,308,000 | 2.6% | | | 10 | Minnesota | 78,685,402,000 | 3.1% |
| 42 | Hawaii | 6,511,578,000 | 0.3% | | | 11 | Georgia | 65,498,308,000 | 2.6% |
| 41 | Idaho | 7,622,490,000 | 0.3% | | | 12 | Virginia | 64,297,400,000 | 2.5% |
| 4 | Illinois | 124,431,227,000 | 4.9% | | | 13 | North Carolina | 61,600,064,000 | 2.4% |
| 16 | Indiana | 51,238,512,000 | 2.0% | | | 14 | Michigan | 59,210,158,000 | 2.3% |
| 33 | Iowa | 18,753,596,000 | 0.7% | | | 15 | Washington | 52,443,862,000 | 2.1% |
| 29 | Kansas | 21,904,615,000 | 0.9% | | | 16 | Indiana | 51,238,512,000 | 2.0% |
| 27 | Kentucky | 25,085,813,000 | 1.0% | | | 17 | Missouri | 48,413,247,000 | 1.9% |
| 24 | Louisiana | 34,811,072,000 | 1.4% | | | 18 | Maryland | 48,107,002,000 | 1.9% |
| 44 | Maine | 6,229,189,000 | 0.2% | | | 19 | Connecticut | 47,262,702,000 | 1.9% |
| 18 | Maryland | 48,107,002,000 | 1.9% | | | 20 | Tennessee | 47,010,303,000 | 1.9% |
| 9 | Massachusetts | 79,826,976,000 | 3.2% | | | 21 | Wisconsin | 41,498,033,000 | 1.6% |
| 14 | Michigan | 59,210,158,000 | 2.3% | | | 22 | Colorado | 41,252,701,000 | 1.6% |
| 10 | Minnesota | 78,685,402,000 | 3.1% | | | 23 | Arizona | 34,850,436,000 | 1.4% |
| 38 | Mississippi | 10,458,549,000 | 0.4% | | | 24 | Louisiana | 34,811,072,000 | 1.4% |
| 17 | Missouri | 48,413,247,000 | 1.9% | | | 25 | Oklahoma | 27,087,264,000 | 1.1% |
| 48 | Montana | 4,383,727,000 | 0.2% | | | 26 | Arkansas | 25,299,832,000 | 1.0% |
| 32 | Nebraska | 19,795,254,000 | 0.8% | | | 27 | Kentucky | 25,085,813,000 | 1.0% |
| 36 | Nevada | 13,727,425,000 | 0.5% | | | 28 | Oregon | 22,716,602,000 | 0.9% |
| 39 | New Hampshire | 8,807,691,000 | 0.3% | | | 29 | Kansas | 21,904,615,000 | 0.9% |
| 6 | New Jersey | 111,377,490,000 | 4.4% | | | 30 | Delaware | 21,835,412,000 | 0.9% |
| 40 | New Mexico | 7,866,206,000 | 0.3% | | | 31 | Alabama | 20,882,949,000 | 0.8% |
| 3 | New York | 201,167,954,000 | 8.0% | | | 32 | Nebraska | 19,795,254,000 | 0.8% |
| 13 | North Carolina | 61,600,064,000 | 2.4% | | | 33 | Iowa | 18,753,596,000 | 0.7% |
| 45 | North Dakota | 5,664,860,000 | 0.2% | | | 34 | South Carolina | 18,557,166,000 | 0.7% |
| 7 | Ohio | 111,094,276,000 | 4.4% | | | 35 | Utah | 15,642,129,000 | 0.6% |
| 25 | Oklahoma | 27,087,264,000 | 1.1% | | | 36 | Nevada | 13,727,425,000 | 0.5% |
| 28 | Oregon | 22,716,602,000 | 0.9% | | | 37 | Rhode Island | 10,992,338,000 | 0.4% |
| 8 | Pennsylvania | 108,961,515,000 | 4.3% | | | 38 | Mississippi | 10,458,549,000 | 0.4% |
| 37 | Rhode Island | 10,992,338,000 | 0.4% | | | 39 | New Hampshire | 8,807,691,000 | 0.3% |
| 34 | South Carolina | 18,557,166,000 | 0.7% | | | 40 | New Mexico | 7,866,206,000 | 0.3% |
| 46 | South Dakota | 5,136,249,000 | 0.2% | | | 41 | Idaho | 7,622,490,000 | 0.3% |
| 20 | Tennessee | 47,010,303,000 | 1.9% | | | 42 | Hawaii | 6,511,578,000 | 0.3% |
| 2 | Texas | 219,459,878,000 | 8.7% | | | 43 | West Virginia | 6,498,502,000 | 0.3% |
| 35 | Utah | 15,642,129,000 | 0.6% | | | 44 | Maine | 6,229,189,000 | 0.2% |
| 50 | Vermont | 3,524,887,000 | 0.1% | | | 45 | North Dakota | 5,664,860,000 | 0.2% |
| 12 | Virginia | 64,297,400,000 | 2.5% | | | 46 | South Dakota | 5,136,249,000 | 0.2% |
| 15 | Washington | 52,443,862,000 | 2.1% | | | 47 | Alaska | 4,898,780,000 | 0.2% |
| 43 | West Virginia | 6,498,502,000 | 0.3% | | | 48 | Montana | 4,383,727,000 | 0.2% |
| 21 | Wisconsin | 41,498,033,000 | 1.6% | | | 49 | Wyoming | 3,828,379,000 | 0.2% |
| 49 | Wyoming | 3,828,379,000 | 0.2% | | | 50 | Vermont | 3,524,887,000 | 0.1% |
| | | | | | | | District of Columbia | 20,747,652,000 | 0.8% |

Source: U.S. Department of the Treasury, Internal Revenue Service
"Fiscal Year 2012 IRS Data Book" (http://www.irs.gov/uac/SOI-Tax-Stats-IRS-Data-Book)
*Total includes $12,549,273,000 from U.S. citizens abroad and other miscellaneous returns not shown separately.

# Per Capita Internal Revenue Service Gross Collections in 2012

## National Per Capita = $8,001*

<table>
<tr><th colspan="3">ALPHA ORDER</th><th colspan="3">RANK ORDER</th></tr>
<tr><th>RANK</th><th>STATE</th><th>PER CAPITA</th><th>RANK</th><th>STATE</th><th>PER CAPITA</th></tr>
<tr><td>46</td><td>Alabama</td><td>$4,331</td><td>1</td><td>Delaware</td><td>$23,809</td></tr>
<tr><td>27</td><td>Alaska</td><td>6,697</td><td>2</td><td>Minnesota</td><td>14,628</td></tr>
<tr><td>40</td><td>Arizona</td><td>5,318</td><td>3</td><td>Connecticut</td><td>13,164</td></tr>
<tr><td>11</td><td>Arkansas</td><td>8,579</td><td>4</td><td>New Jersey</td><td>12,564</td></tr>
<tr><td>20</td><td>California</td><td>7,691</td><td>5</td><td>Massachusetts</td><td>12,011</td></tr>
<tr><td>17</td><td>Colorado</td><td>7,952</td><td>6</td><td>Nebraska</td><td>10,668</td></tr>
<tr><td>3</td><td>Connecticut</td><td>13,164</td><td>7</td><td>Rhode Island</td><td>10,466</td></tr>
<tr><td>1</td><td>Delaware</td><td>23,809</td><td>8</td><td>New York</td><td>10,279</td></tr>
<tr><td>31</td><td>Florida</td><td>6,328</td><td>9</td><td>Illinois</td><td>9,664</td></tr>
<tr><td>30</td><td>Georgia</td><td>6,603</td><td>10</td><td>Ohio</td><td>9,623</td></tr>
<tr><td>44</td><td>Hawaii</td><td>4,677</td><td>11</td><td>Arkansas</td><td>8,579</td></tr>
<tr><td>42</td><td>Idaho</td><td>4,777</td><td>12</td><td>Pennsylvania</td><td>8,537</td></tr>
<tr><td>9</td><td>Illinois</td><td>9,664</td><td>13</td><td>Texas</td><td>8,422</td></tr>
<tr><td>19</td><td>Indiana</td><td>7,838</td><td>14</td><td>Maryland</td><td>8,175</td></tr>
<tr><td>34</td><td>Iowa</td><td>6,100</td><td>15</td><td>North Dakota</td><td>8,097</td></tr>
<tr><td>22</td><td>Kansas</td><td>7,590</td><td>16</td><td>Missouri</td><td>8,039</td></tr>
<tr><td>37</td><td>Kentucky</td><td>5,727</td><td>17</td><td>Colorado</td><td>7,952</td></tr>
<tr><td>23</td><td>Louisiana</td><td>7,565</td><td>18</td><td>Virginia</td><td>7,855</td></tr>
<tr><td>43</td><td>Maine</td><td>4,686</td><td>19</td><td>Indiana</td><td>7,838</td></tr>
<tr><td>14</td><td>Maryland</td><td>8,175</td><td>20</td><td>California</td><td>7,691</td></tr>
<tr><td>5</td><td>Massachusetts</td><td>12,011</td><td>21</td><td>Washington</td><td>7,604</td></tr>
<tr><td>35</td><td>Michigan</td><td>5,991</td><td>22</td><td>Kansas</td><td>7,590</td></tr>
<tr><td>2</td><td>Minnesota</td><td>14,628</td><td>23</td><td>Louisiana</td><td>7,565</td></tr>
<tr><td>49</td><td>Mississippi</td><td>3,504</td><td>24</td><td>Tennessee</td><td>7,281</td></tr>
<tr><td>16</td><td>Missouri</td><td>8,039</td><td>25</td><td>Wisconsin</td><td>7,247</td></tr>
<tr><td>45</td><td>Montana</td><td>4,361</td><td>26</td><td>Oklahoma</td><td>7,101</td></tr>
<tr><td>6</td><td>Nebraska</td><td>10,668</td><td>27</td><td>Alaska</td><td>6,697</td></tr>
<tr><td>41</td><td>Nevada</td><td>4,976</td><td>28</td><td>New Hampshire</td><td>6,669</td></tr>
<tr><td>28</td><td>New Hampshire</td><td>6,669</td><td>29</td><td>Wyoming</td><td>6,642</td></tr>
<tr><td>4</td><td>New Jersey</td><td>12,564</td><td>30</td><td>Georgia</td><td>6,603</td></tr>
<tr><td>48</td><td>New Mexico</td><td>3,772</td><td>31</td><td>Florida</td><td>6,328</td></tr>
<tr><td>8</td><td>New York</td><td>10,279</td><td>32</td><td>North Carolina</td><td>6,317</td></tr>
<tr><td>32</td><td>North Carolina</td><td>6,317</td><td>33</td><td>South Dakota</td><td>6,163</td></tr>
<tr><td>15</td><td>North Dakota</td><td>8,097</td><td>34</td><td>Iowa</td><td>6,100</td></tr>
<tr><td>10</td><td>Ohio</td><td>9,623</td><td>35</td><td>Michigan</td><td>5,991</td></tr>
<tr><td>26</td><td>Oklahoma</td><td>7,101</td><td>36</td><td>Oregon</td><td>5,826</td></tr>
<tr><td>36</td><td>Oregon</td><td>5,826</td><td>37</td><td>Kentucky</td><td>5,727</td></tr>
<tr><td>12</td><td>Pennsylvania</td><td>8,537</td><td>38</td><td>Vermont</td><td>5,631</td></tr>
<tr><td>7</td><td>Rhode Island</td><td>10,466</td><td>39</td><td>Utah</td><td>5,478</td></tr>
<tr><td>47</td><td>South Carolina</td><td>3,929</td><td>40</td><td>Arizona</td><td>5,318</td></tr>
<tr><td>33</td><td>South Dakota</td><td>6,163</td><td>41</td><td>Nevada</td><td>4,976</td></tr>
<tr><td>24</td><td>Tennessee</td><td>7,281</td><td>42</td><td>Idaho</td><td>4,777</td></tr>
<tr><td>13</td><td>Texas</td><td>8,422</td><td>43</td><td>Maine</td><td>4,686</td></tr>
<tr><td>39</td><td>Utah</td><td>5,478</td><td>44</td><td>Hawaii</td><td>4,677</td></tr>
<tr><td>38</td><td>Vermont</td><td>5,631</td><td>45</td><td>Montana</td><td>4,361</td></tr>
<tr><td>18</td><td>Virginia</td><td>7,855</td><td>46</td><td>Alabama</td><td>4,331</td></tr>
<tr><td>21</td><td>Washington</td><td>7,604</td><td>47</td><td>South Carolina</td><td>3,929</td></tr>
<tr><td>50</td><td>West Virginia</td><td>3,502</td><td>48</td><td>New Mexico</td><td>3,772</td></tr>
<tr><td>25</td><td>Wisconsin</td><td>7,247</td><td>49</td><td>Mississippi</td><td>3,504</td></tr>
<tr><td>29</td><td>Wyoming</td><td>6,642</td><td>50</td><td>West Virginia</td><td>3,502</td></tr>
<tr><td></td><td></td><td></td><td></td><td>District of Columbia</td><td>32,812</td></tr>
</table>

Source: CQ Press using data from U.S. Department of the Treasury, Internal Revenue Service
   "Fiscal Year 2012 IRS Data Book" (http://www.irs.gov/uac/SOI-Tax-Stats-IRS-Data-Book)
*National per capita does not include collections from U.S. citizens abroad and other miscellaneous returns not shown separately.

# Federal Individual Income Tax Collections in 2012

## National Total = $2,172,233,368,000*

ALPHA ORDER

| RANK | STATE | COLLECTIONS | % of USA |
|---|---|---|---|
| 28 | Alabama | $19,500,672,000 | 0.9% |
| 47 | Alaska | 4,640,174,000 | 0.2% |
| 24 | Arizona | 29,968,613,000 | 1.4% |
| 30 | Arkansas | 18,266,603,000 | 0.8% |
| 1 | California | 249,275,399,000 | 11.5% |
| 21 | Colorado | 36,113,422,000 | 1.7% |
| 20 | Connecticut | 40,875,490,000 | 1.9% |
| 33 | Delaware | 14,602,084,000 | 0.7% |
| 4 | Florida | 113,188,889,000 | 5.2% |
| 13 | Georgia | 53,987,301,000 | 2.5% |
| 43 | Hawaii | 5,922,132,000 | 0.3% |
| 41 | Idaho | 7,169,783,000 | 0.3% |
| 5 | Illinois | 103,654,375,000 | 4.8% |
| 16 | Indiana | 47,141,859,000 | 2.2% |
| 31 | Iowa | 17,210,796,000 | 0.8% |
| 29 | Kansas | 18,510,512,000 | 0.9% |
| 25 | Kentucky | 22,986,776,000 | 1.1% |
| 23 | Louisiana | 33,187,181,000 | 1.5% |
| 44 | Maine | 5,542,557,000 | 0.3% |
| 17 | Maryland | 45,186,159,000 | 2.1% |
| 9 | Massachusetts | 73,152,183,000 | 3.4% |
| 11 | Michigan | 54,959,506,000 | 2.5% |
| 10 | Minnesota | 61,712,466,000 | 2.8% |
| 37 | Mississippi | 9,693,914,000 | 0.4% |
| 19 | Missouri | 40,997,767,000 | 1.9% |
| 48 | Montana | 4,147,270,000 | 0.2% |
| 34 | Nebraska | 13,470,845,000 | 0.6% |
| 36 | Nevada | 12,737,643,000 | 0.6% |
| 39 | New Hampshire | 8,370,452,000 | 0.4% |
| 8 | New Jersey | 92,020,482,000 | 4.2% |
| 40 | New Mexico | 7,494,229,000 | 0.3% |
| 2 | New York | 176,938,759,000 | 8.1% |
| 12 | North Carolina | 54,747,979,000 | 2.5% |
| 45 | North Dakota | 5,268,271,000 | 0.2% |
| 6 | Ohio | 95,611,009,000 | 4.4% |
| 27 | Oklahoma | 19,789,170,000 | 0.9% |
| 26 | Oregon | 21,131,294,000 | 1.0% |
| 7 | Pennsylvania | 94,747,441,000 | 4.4% |
| 38 | Rhode Island | 8,607,614,000 | 0.4% |
| 32 | South Carolina | 17,064,717,000 | 0.8% |
| 46 | South Dakota | 4,840,542,000 | 0.2% |
| 18 | Tennessee | 41,867,521,000 | 1.9% |
| 3 | Texas | 171,880,172,000 | 7.9% |
| 35 | Utah | 13,227,408,000 | 0.6% |
| 50 | Vermont | 3,236,379,000 | 0.1% |
| 14 | Virginia | 53,807,056,000 | 2.5% |
| 15 | Washington | 47,600,345,000 | 2.2% |
| 42 | West Virginia | 6,082,100,000 | 0.3% |
| 22 | Wisconsin | 35,757,347,000 | 1.6% |
| 49 | Wyoming | 3,495,933,000 | 0.2% |

RANK ORDER

| RANK | STATE | COLLECTIONS | % of USA |
|---|---|---|---|
| 1 | California | $249,275,399,000 | 11.5% |
| 2 | New York | 176,938,759,000 | 8.1% |
| 3 | Texas | 171,880,172,000 | 7.9% |
| 4 | Florida | 113,188,889,000 | 5.2% |
| 5 | Illinois | 103,654,375,000 | 4.8% |
| 6 | Ohio | 95,611,009,000 | 4.4% |
| 7 | Pennsylvania | 94,747,441,000 | 4.4% |
| 8 | New Jersey | 92,020,482,000 | 4.2% |
| 9 | Massachusetts | 73,152,183,000 | 3.4% |
| 10 | Minnesota | 61,712,466,000 | 2.8% |
| 11 | Michigan | 54,959,506,000 | 2.5% |
| 12 | North Carolina | 54,747,979,000 | 2.5% |
| 13 | Georgia | 53,987,301,000 | 2.5% |
| 14 | Virginia | 53,807,056,000 | 2.5% |
| 15 | Washington | 47,600,345,000 | 2.2% |
| 16 | Indiana | 47,141,859,000 | 2.2% |
| 17 | Maryland | 45,186,159,000 | 2.1% |
| 18 | Tennessee | 41,867,521,000 | 1.9% |
| 19 | Missouri | 40,997,767,000 | 1.9% |
| 20 | Connecticut | 40,875,490,000 | 1.9% |
| 21 | Colorado | 36,113,422,000 | 1.7% |
| 22 | Wisconsin | 35,757,347,000 | 1.6% |
| 23 | Louisiana | 33,187,181,000 | 1.5% |
| 24 | Arizona | 29,968,613,000 | 1.4% |
| 25 | Kentucky | 22,986,776,000 | 1.1% |
| 26 | Oregon | 21,131,294,000 | 1.0% |
| 27 | Oklahoma | 19,789,170,000 | 0.9% |
| 28 | Alabama | 19,500,672,000 | 0.9% |
| 29 | Kansas | 18,510,512,000 | 0.9% |
| 30 | Arkansas | 18,266,603,000 | 0.8% |
| 31 | Iowa | 17,210,796,000 | 0.8% |
| 32 | South Carolina | 17,064,717,000 | 0.8% |
| 33 | Delaware | 14,602,084,000 | 0.7% |
| 34 | Nebraska | 13,470,845,000 | 0.6% |
| 35 | Utah | 13,227,408,000 | 0.6% |
| 36 | Nevada | 12,737,643,000 | 0.6% |
| 37 | Mississippi | 9,693,914,000 | 0.4% |
| 38 | Rhode Island | 8,607,614,000 | 0.4% |
| 39 | New Hampshire | 8,370,452,000 | 0.4% |
| 40 | New Mexico | 7,494,229,000 | 0.3% |
| 41 | Idaho | 7,169,783,000 | 0.3% |
| 42 | West Virginia | 6,082,100,000 | 0.3% |
| 43 | Hawaii | 5,922,132,000 | 0.3% |
| 44 | Maine | 5,542,557,000 | 0.3% |
| 45 | North Dakota | 5,268,271,000 | 0.2% |
| 46 | South Dakota | 4,840,542,000 | 0.2% |
| 47 | Alaska | 4,640,174,000 | 0.2% |
| 48 | Montana | 4,147,270,000 | 0.2% |
| 49 | Wyoming | 3,495,933,000 | 0.2% |
| 50 | Vermont | 3,236,379,000 | 0.1% |
| | District of Columbia | 20,139,227,000 | 0.9% |

Source: U.S. Department of the Treasury, Internal Revenue Service
"Fiscal Year 2012 IRS Data Book" (http://www.irs.gov/uac/SOI-Tax-Stats-IRS-Data-Book)
*Total includes $10,705,550,000 from U.S. citizens abroad and other miscellaneous returns not shown separately.

# Average Revenue Collection per Federal Individual Income Tax Return in 2012

## National Average = $14,853 per Return*

ALPHA ORDER

| RANK | STATE | PER RETURN |
|---|---|---|
| 43 | Alabama | $9,310 |
| 27 | Alaska | 12,555 |
| 39 | Arizona | 10,820 |
| 20 | Arkansas | 14,854 |
| 21 | California | 14,719 |
| 18 | Colorado | 15,061 |
| 3 | Connecticut | 23,474 |
| 1 | Delaware | 33,854 |
| 37 | Florida | 11,625 |
| 34 | Georgia | 11,960 |
| 44 | Hawaii | 8,992 |
| 40 | Idaho | 10,762 |
| 8 | Illinois | 16,983 |
| 12 | Indiana | 15,675 |
| 31 | Iowa | 12,173 |
| 24 | Kansas | 13,988 |
| 30 | Kentucky | 12,291 |
| 10 | Louisiana | 16,476 |
| 45 | Maine | 8,808 |
| 11 | Maryland | 16,015 |
| 4 | Massachusetts | 22,628 |
| 36 | Michigan | 11,794 |
| 2 | Minnesota | 23,846 |
| 50 | Mississippi | 7,538 |
| 17 | Missouri | 15,090 |
| 46 | Montana | 8,682 |
| 13 | Nebraska | 15,533 |
| 42 | Nevada | 9,869 |
| 28 | New Hampshire | 12,401 |
| 5 | New Jersey | 21,306 |
| 48 | New Mexico | 8,216 |
| 6 | New York | 18,915 |
| 26 | North Carolina | 12,844 |
| 14 | North Dakota | 15,500 |
| 7 | Ohio | 17,410 |
| 29 | Oklahoma | 12,326 |
| 32 | Oregon | 12,082 |
| 15 | Pennsylvania | 15,349 |
| 9 | Rhode Island | 16,799 |
| 47 | South Carolina | 8,234 |
| 35 | South Dakota | 11,819 |
| 22 | Tennessee | 14,468 |
| 16 | Texas | 15,221 |
| 38 | Utah | 11,479 |
| 41 | Vermont | 10,152 |
| 23 | Virginia | 14,235 |
| 19 | Washington | 14,908 |
| 49 | West Virginia | 7,708 |
| 25 | Wisconsin | 12,921 |
| 33 | Wyoming | 12,000 |

RANK ORDER

| RANK | STATE | PER RETURN |
|---|---|---|
| 1 | Delaware | $33,854 |
| 2 | Minnesota | 23,846 |
| 3 | Connecticut | 23,474 |
| 4 | Massachusetts | 22,628 |
| 5 | New Jersey | 21,306 |
| 6 | New York | 18,915 |
| 7 | Ohio | 17,410 |
| 8 | Illinois | 16,983 |
| 9 | Rhode Island | 16,799 |
| 10 | Louisiana | 16,476 |
| 11 | Maryland | 16,015 |
| 12 | Indiana | 15,675 |
| 13 | Nebraska | 15,533 |
| 14 | North Dakota | 15,500 |
| 15 | Pennsylvania | 15,349 |
| 16 | Texas | 15,221 |
| 17 | Missouri | 15,090 |
| 18 | Colorado | 15,061 |
| 19 | Washington | 14,908 |
| 20 | Arkansas | 14,854 |
| 21 | California | 14,719 |
| 22 | Tennessee | 14,468 |
| 23 | Virginia | 14,235 |
| 24 | Kansas | 13,988 |
| 25 | Wisconsin | 12,921 |
| 26 | North Carolina | 12,844 |
| 27 | Alaska | 12,555 |
| 28 | New Hampshire | 12,401 |
| 29 | Oklahoma | 12,326 |
| 30 | Kentucky | 12,291 |
| 31 | Iowa | 12,173 |
| 32 | Oregon | 12,082 |
| 33 | Wyoming | 12,000 |
| 34 | Georgia | 11,960 |
| 35 | South Dakota | 11,819 |
| 36 | Michigan | 11,794 |
| 37 | Florida | 11,625 |
| 38 | Utah | 11,479 |
| 39 | Arizona | 10,820 |
| 40 | Idaho | 10,762 |
| 41 | Vermont | 10,152 |
| 42 | Nevada | 9,869 |
| 43 | Alabama | 9,310 |
| 44 | Hawaii | 8,992 |
| 45 | Maine | 8,808 |
| 46 | Montana | 8,682 |
| 47 | South Carolina | 8,234 |
| 48 | New Mexico | 8,216 |
| 49 | West Virginia | 7,708 |
| 50 | Mississippi | 7,538 |
| | District of Columbia | 61,602 |

Source: CQ Press using data from U.S. Department of the Treasury, Internal Revenue Service
"Fiscal Year 2012 IRS Data Book" (http://www.irs.gov/uac/SOI-Tax-Stats-IRS-Data-Book)
*National Rate includes collections and returns from U.S. citizens abroad and other miscellaneous returns not shown separately.

# Adjusted Gross Income in 2011

## National Total = $8,378,794,024,000*

ALPHA ORDER

| RANK | STATE | A.G.I. | % of USA |
|---|---|---|---|
| 24 | Alabama | $100,317,597,000 | 1.2% |
| 46 | Alaska | 21,706,335,000 | 0.3% |
| 21 | Arizona | 141,315,182,000 | 1.7% |
| 34 | Arkansas | 57,281,450,000 | 0.7% |
| 1 | California | 1,066,049,949,000 | 12.7% |
| 17 | Colorado | 150,645,967,000 | 1.8% |
| 20 | Connecticut | 146,101,673,000 | 1.7% |
| 44 | Delaware | 24,590,469,000 | 0.3% |
| 4 | Florida | 485,461,200,000 | 5.8% |
| 12 | Georgia | 223,940,849,000 | 2.7% |
| 40 | Hawaii | 34,372,459,000 | 0.4% |
| 41 | Idaho | 30,728,223,000 | 0.4% |
| 5 | Illinois | 371,414,191,000 | 4.4% |
| 19 | Indiana | 147,573,636,000 | 1.8% |
| 30 | Iowa | 75,359,890,000 | 0.9% |
| 31 | Kansas | 73,272,170,000 | 0.9% |
| 28 | Kentucky | 88,207,428,000 | 1.1% |
| 25 | Louisiana | 99,162,456,000 | 1.2% |
| 42 | Maine | 30,652,089,000 | 0.4% |
| 15 | Maryland | 194,974,934,000 | 2.3% |
| 10 | Massachusetts | 241,984,679,000 | 2.9% |
| 11 | Michigan | 234,472,007,000 | 2.8% |
| 16 | Minnesota | 157,793,380,000 | 1.9% |
| 35 | Mississippi | 52,669,845,000 | 0.6% |
| 23 | Missouri | 138,422,030,000 | 1.7% |
| 45 | Montana | 22,419,479,000 | 0.3% |
| 36 | Nebraska | 46,459,002,000 | 0.6% |
| 32 | Nevada | 67,018,285,000 | 0.8% |
| 37 | New Hampshire | 42,423,770,000 | 0.5% |
| 7 | New Jersey | 316,448,772,000 | 3.8% |
| 38 | New Mexico | 41,850,497,000 | 0.5% |
| 3 | New York | 646,261,837,000 | 7.7% |
| 13 | North Carolina | 215,963,437,000 | 2.6% |
| 48 | North Dakota | 20,833,480,000 | 0.2% |
| 8 | Ohio | 277,608,472,000 | 3.3% |
| 29 | Oklahoma | 84,813,229,000 | 1.0% |
| 27 | Oregon | 91,954,276,000 | 1.1% |
| 6 | Pennsylvania | 348,612,836,000 | 4.2% |
| 43 | Rhode Island | 29,193,327,000 | 0.3% |
| 26 | South Carolina | 96,747,846,000 | 1.2% |
| 47 | South Dakota | 21,289,609,000 | 0.3% |
| 22 | Tennessee | 140,012,114,000 | 1.7% |
| 2 | Texas | 665,901,147,000 | 7.9% |
| 33 | Utah | 61,131,021,000 | 0.7% |
| 50 | Vermont | 16,394,126,000 | 0.2% |
| 9 | Virginia | 252,170,828,000 | 3.0% |
| 14 | Washington | 200,197,882,000 | 2.4% |
| 39 | West Virginia | 37,424,201,000 | 0.4% |
| 18 | Wisconsin | 148,183,780,000 | 1.8% |
| 49 | Wyoming | 18,086,478,000 | 0.2% |

RANK ORDER

| RANK | STATE | A.G.I. | % of USA |
|---|---|---|---|
| 1 | California | $1,066,049,949,000 | 12.7% |
| 2 | Texas | 665,901,147,000 | 7.9% |
| 3 | New York | 646,261,837,000 | 7.7% |
| 4 | Florida | 485,461,200,000 | 5.8% |
| 5 | Illinois | 371,414,191,000 | 4.4% |
| 6 | Pennsylvania | 348,612,836,000 | 4.2% |
| 7 | New Jersey | 316,448,772,000 | 3.8% |
| 8 | Ohio | 277,608,472,000 | 3.3% |
| 9 | Virginia | 252,170,828,000 | 3.0% |
| 10 | Massachusetts | 241,984,679,000 | 2.9% |
| 11 | Michigan | 234,472,007,000 | 2.8% |
| 12 | Georgia | 223,940,849,000 | 2.7% |
| 13 | North Carolina | 215,963,437,000 | 2.6% |
| 14 | Washington | 200,197,882,000 | 2.4% |
| 15 | Maryland | 194,974,934,000 | 2.3% |
| 16 | Minnesota | 157,793,380,000 | 1.9% |
| 17 | Colorado | 150,645,967,000 | 1.8% |
| 18 | Wisconsin | 148,183,780,000 | 1.8% |
| 19 | Indiana | 147,573,636,000 | 1.8% |
| 20 | Connecticut | 146,101,673,000 | 1.7% |
| 21 | Arizona | 141,315,182,000 | 1.7% |
| 22 | Tennessee | 140,012,114,000 | 1.7% |
| 23 | Missouri | 138,422,030,000 | 1.7% |
| 24 | Alabama | 100,317,597,000 | 1.2% |
| 25 | Louisiana | 99,162,456,000 | 1.2% |
| 26 | South Carolina | 96,747,846,000 | 1.2% |
| 27 | Oregon | 91,954,276,000 | 1.1% |
| 28 | Kentucky | 88,207,428,000 | 1.1% |
| 29 | Oklahoma | 84,813,229,000 | 1.0% |
| 30 | Iowa | 75,359,890,000 | 0.9% |
| 31 | Kansas | 73,272,170,000 | 0.9% |
| 32 | Nevada | 67,018,285,000 | 0.8% |
| 33 | Utah | 61,131,021,000 | 0.7% |
| 34 | Arkansas | 57,281,450,000 | 0.7% |
| 35 | Mississippi | 52,669,845,000 | 0.6% |
| 36 | Nebraska | 46,459,002,000 | 0.6% |
| 37 | New Hampshire | 42,423,770,000 | 0.5% |
| 38 | New Mexico | 41,850,497,000 | 0.5% |
| 39 | West Virginia | 37,424,201,000 | 0.4% |
| 40 | Hawaii | 34,372,459,000 | 0.4% |
| 41 | Idaho | 30,728,223,000 | 0.4% |
| 42 | Maine | 30,652,089,000 | 0.4% |
| 43 | Rhode Island | 29,193,327,000 | 0.3% |
| 44 | Delaware | 24,590,469,000 | 0.3% |
| 45 | Montana | 22,419,479,000 | 0.3% |
| 46 | Alaska | 21,706,335,000 | 0.3% |
| 47 | South Dakota | 21,289,609,000 | 0.3% |
| 48 | North Dakota | 20,833,480,000 | 0.2% |
| 49 | Wyoming | 18,086,478,000 | 0.2% |
| 50 | Vermont | 16,394,126,000 | 0.2% |
| | District of Columbia | 25,217,823,000 | 0.3% |

Source: U.S. Department of the Treasury, Internal Revenue Service
"Individual Tax Statistics, State Income" (http://www.irs.gov/taxstats/index.html)
*Total includes $55,706,382,000 from U.S. citizens abroad and other miscellaneous returns not shown separately.

# Per Capita Adjusted Gross Income in 2011

## National Per Capita = $26,712*

ALPHA ORDER

| RANK | STATE | PER CAPITA |
|---|---|---|
| 43 | Alabama | $20,883 |
| 10 | Alaska | 29,987 |
| 40 | Arizona | 21,851 |
| 48 | Arkansas | 19,493 |
| 15 | California | 28,289 |
| 12 | Colorado | 29,444 |
| 1 | Connecticut | 40,734 |
| 18 | Delaware | 27,078 |
| 24 | Florida | 25,440 |
| 34 | Georgia | 22,822 |
| 26 | Hawaii | 24,941 |
| 49 | Idaho | 19,402 |
| 14 | Illinois | 28,882 |
| 35 | Indiana | 22,647 |
| 28 | Iowa | 24,594 |
| 23 | Kansas | 25,527 |
| 45 | Kentucky | 20,199 |
| 42 | Louisiana | 21,676 |
| 32 | Maine | 23,072 |
| 4 | Maryland | 33,389 |
| 2 | Massachusetts | 36,625 |
| 31 | Michigan | 23,740 |
| 11 | Minnesota | 29,509 |
| 50 | Mississippi | 17,690 |
| 33 | Missouri | 23,036 |
| 36 | Montana | 22,472 |
| 25 | Nebraska | 25,219 |
| 27 | Nevada | 24,639 |
| 6 | New Hampshire | 32,193 |
| 3 | New Jersey | 35,819 |
| 47 | New Mexico | 20,133 |
| 5 | New York | 33,139 |
| 38 | North Carolina | 22,377 |
| 9 | North Dakota | 30,425 |
| 29 | Ohio | 24,054 |
| 37 | Oklahoma | 22,413 |
| 30 | Oregon | 23,772 |
| 17 | Pennsylvania | 27,355 |
| 16 | Rhode Island | 27,786 |
| 44 | South Carolina | 20,702 |
| 22 | South Dakota | 25,850 |
| 39 | Tennessee | 21,878 |
| 20 | Texas | 25,980 |
| 41 | Utah | 21,721 |
| 19 | Vermont | 26,164 |
| 8 | Virginia | 31,115 |
| 13 | Washington | 29,340 |
| 46 | West Virginia | 20,176 |
| 21 | Wisconsin | 25,952 |
| 7 | Wyoming | 31,879 |

RANK ORDER

| RANK | STATE | PER CAPITA |
|---|---|---|
| 1 | Connecticut | $40,734 |
| 2 | Massachusetts | 36,625 |
| 3 | New Jersey | 35,819 |
| 4 | Maryland | 33,389 |
| 5 | New York | 33,139 |
| 6 | New Hampshire | 32,193 |
| 7 | Wyoming | 31,879 |
| 8 | Virginia | 31,115 |
| 9 | North Dakota | 30,425 |
| 10 | Alaska | 29,987 |
| 11 | Minnesota | 29,509 |
| 12 | Colorado | 29,444 |
| 13 | Washington | 29,340 |
| 14 | Illinois | 28,882 |
| 15 | California | 28,289 |
| 16 | Rhode Island | 27,786 |
| 17 | Pennsylvania | 27,355 |
| 18 | Delaware | 27,078 |
| 19 | Vermont | 26,164 |
| 20 | Texas | 25,980 |
| 21 | Wisconsin | 25,952 |
| 22 | South Dakota | 25,850 |
| 23 | Kansas | 25,527 |
| 24 | Florida | 25,440 |
| 25 | Nebraska | 25,219 |
| 26 | Hawaii | 24,941 |
| 27 | Nevada | 24,639 |
| 28 | Iowa | 24,594 |
| 29 | Ohio | 24,054 |
| 30 | Oregon | 23,772 |
| 31 | Michigan | 23,740 |
| 32 | Maine | 23,072 |
| 33 | Missouri | 23,036 |
| 34 | Georgia | 22,822 |
| 35 | Indiana | 22,647 |
| 36 | Montana | 22,472 |
| 37 | Oklahoma | 22,413 |
| 38 | North Carolina | 22,377 |
| 39 | Tennessee | 21,878 |
| 40 | Arizona | 21,851 |
| 41 | Utah | 21,721 |
| 42 | Louisiana | 21,676 |
| 43 | Alabama | 20,883 |
| 44 | South Carolina | 20,702 |
| 45 | Kentucky | 20,199 |
| 46 | West Virginia | 20,176 |
| 47 | New Mexico | 20,133 |
| 48 | Arkansas | 19,493 |
| 49 | Idaho | 19,402 |
| 50 | Mississippi | 17,690 |
| | District of Columbia | 40,738 |

Source: CQ Press using data from U.S. Department of the Treasury, Internal Revenue Service
"Individual Tax Statistics, State Income" (http://www.irs.gov/taxstats/index.html)
*National per capita does not include income from U.S. citizens abroad and other miscellaneous returns not shown separately.

# Federal Business Income Tax Collections in 2012

## National Total = $281,461,580,000*

### ALPHA ORDER

| RANK | STATE | COLLECTIONS | % of USA |
|------|-------|-------------|----------|
| 35 | Alabama | $1,102,865,000 | 0.4% |
| 47 | Alaska | 191,060,000 | 0.1% |
| 25 | Arizona | 3,408,925,000 | 1.2% |
| 14 | Arkansas | 6,304,626,000 | 2.2% |
| 1 | California | 37,181,407,000 | 13.2% |
| 21 | Colorado | 3,968,517,000 | 1.4% |
| 17 | Connecticut | 5,431,458,000 | 1.9% |
| 11 | Delaware | 7,087,549,000 | 2.5% |
| 12 | Florida | 6,609,351,000 | 2.3% |
| 10 | Georgia | 8,417,016,000 | 3.0% |
| 40 | Hawaii | 398,720,000 | 0.1% |
| 41 | Idaho | 367,921,000 | 0.1% |
| 5 | Illinois | 17,337,038,000 | 6.2% |
| 26 | Indiana | 3,228,361,000 | 1.1% |
| 32 | Iowa | 1,315,070,000 | 0.5% |
| 29 | Kansas | 1,980,014,000 | 0.7% |
| 31 | Kentucky | 1,764,142,000 | 0.6% |
| 36 | Louisiana | 1,102,737,000 | 0.4% |
| 39 | Maine | 509,393,000 | 0.2% |
| 27 | Maryland | 2,626,431,000 | 0.9% |
| 18 | Massachusetts | 5,278,522,000 | 1.9% |
| 23 | Michigan | 3,841,440,000 | 1.4% |
| 6 | Minnesota | 16,121,685,000 | 5.7% |
| 38 | Mississippi | 609,194,000 | 0.2% |
| 16 | Missouri | 6,082,671,000 | 2.2% |
| 49 | Montana | 156,415,000 | 0.1% |
| 15 | Nebraska | 6,149,516,000 | 2.2% |
| 37 | Nevada | 757,762,000 | 0.3% |
| 46 | New Hampshire | 205,260,000 | 0.1% |
| 4 | New Jersey | 17,459,934,000 | 6.2% |
| 50 | New Mexico | 150,549,000 | 0.1% |
| 3 | New York | 21,269,375,000 | 7.6% |
| 13 | North Carolina | 6,411,802,000 | 2.3% |
| 43 | North Dakota | 301,698,000 | 0.1% |
| 7 | Ohio | 11,604,143,000 | 4.1% |
| 20 | Oklahoma | 3,982,694,000 | 1.4% |
| 33 | Oregon | 1,229,807,000 | 0.4% |
| 8 | Pennsylvania | 11,222,657,000 | 4.0% |
| 28 | Rhode Island | 2,327,315,000 | 0.8% |
| 34 | South Carolina | 1,211,525,000 | 0.4% |
| 45 | South Dakota | 235,097,000 | 0.1% |
| 22 | Tennessee | 3,903,991,000 | 1.4% |
| 2 | Texas | 27,984,282,000 | 9.9% |
| 30 | Utah | 1,809,517,000 | 0.6% |
| 44 | Vermont | 255,605,000 | 0.1% |
| 9 | Virginia | 9,994,059,000 | 3.6% |
| 24 | Washington | 3,793,982,000 | 1.3% |
| 42 | West Virginia | 315,740,000 | 0.1% |
| 19 | Wisconsin | 4,641,696,000 | 1.6% |
| 48 | Wyoming | 175,685,000 | 0.1% |

### RANK ORDER

| RANK | STATE | COLLECTIONS | % of USA |
|------|-------|-------------|----------|
| 1 | California | $37,181,407,000 | 13.2% |
| 2 | Texas | 27,984,282,000 | 9.9% |
| 3 | New York | 21,269,375,000 | 7.6% |
| 4 | New Jersey | 17,459,934,000 | 6.2% |
| 5 | Illinois | 17,337,038,000 | 6.2% |
| 6 | Minnesota | 16,121,685,000 | 5.7% |
| 7 | Ohio | 11,604,143,000 | 4.1% |
| 8 | Pennsylvania | 11,222,657,000 | 4.0% |
| 9 | Virginia | 9,994,059,000 | 3.6% |
| 10 | Georgia | 8,417,016,000 | 3.0% |
| 11 | Delaware | 7,087,549,000 | 2.5% |
| 12 | Florida | 6,609,351,000 | 2.3% |
| 13 | North Carolina | 6,411,802,000 | 2.3% |
| 14 | Arkansas | 6,304,626,000 | 2.2% |
| 15 | Nebraska | 6,149,516,000 | 2.2% |
| 16 | Missouri | 6,082,671,000 | 2.2% |
| 17 | Connecticut | 5,431,458,000 | 1.9% |
| 18 | Massachusetts | 5,278,522,000 | 1.9% |
| 19 | Wisconsin | 4,641,696,000 | 1.6% |
| 20 | Oklahoma | 3,982,694,000 | 1.4% |
| 21 | Colorado | 3,968,517,000 | 1.4% |
| 22 | Tennessee | 3,903,991,000 | 1.4% |
| 23 | Michigan | 3,841,440,000 | 1.4% |
| 24 | Washington | 3,793,982,000 | 1.3% |
| 25 | Arizona | 3,408,925,000 | 1.2% |
| 26 | Indiana | 3,228,361,000 | 1.1% |
| 27 | Maryland | 2,626,431,000 | 0.9% |
| 28 | Rhode Island | 2,327,315,000 | 0.8% |
| 29 | Kansas | 1,980,014,000 | 0.7% |
| 30 | Utah | 1,809,517,000 | 0.6% |
| 31 | Kentucky | 1,764,142,000 | 0.6% |
| 32 | Iowa | 1,315,070,000 | 0.5% |
| 33 | Oregon | 1,229,807,000 | 0.4% |
| 34 | South Carolina | 1,211,525,000 | 0.4% |
| 35 | Alabama | 1,102,865,000 | 0.4% |
| 36 | Louisiana | 1,102,737,000 | 0.4% |
| 37 | Nevada | 757,762,000 | 0.3% |
| 38 | Mississippi | 609,194,000 | 0.2% |
| 39 | Maine | 509,393,000 | 0.2% |
| 40 | Hawaii | 398,720,000 | 0.1% |
| 41 | Idaho | 367,921,000 | 0.1% |
| 42 | West Virginia | 315,740,000 | 0.1% |
| 43 | North Dakota | 301,698,000 | 0.1% |
| 44 | Vermont | 255,605,000 | 0.1% |
| 45 | South Dakota | 235,097,000 | 0.1% |
| 46 | New Hampshire | 205,260,000 | 0.1% |
| 47 | Alaska | 191,060,000 | 0.1% |
| 48 | Wyoming | 175,685,000 | 0.1% |
| 49 | Montana | 156,415,000 | 0.1% |
| 50 | New Mexico | 150,549,000 | 0.1% |
|  | District of Columbia | 392,793,000 | 0.1% |

Source: U.S. Department of the Treasury, Internal Revenue Service
  "Fiscal Year 2012 IRS Data Book" (http://www.irs.gov/uac/SOI-Tax-Stats-IRS-Data-Book)
*Total includes collections and returns from international sources and others not distributed by state. Includes taxes on
corporation income (Form 1120 series) and unrelated business income from tax-exempt organizations.

# Average Revenue Collection per Federal Business Income Tax Return in 2012

## National Average = $41,196 per Return*

| ALPHA ORDER | | | | RANK ORDER | | |
|---|---|---|---|---|---|---|
| RANK | STATE | PER RETURN | | RANK | STATE | PER RETURN |
| 35 | Alabama | $15,743 | | 1 | Delaware | $289,950 |
| 37 | Alaska | 15,483 | | 2 | Nebraska | 140,892 |
| 23 | Arizona | 28,889 | | 3 | Minnesota | 123,788 |
| 4 | Arkansas | 115,465 | | 4 | Arkansas | 115,465 |
| 16 | California | 49,139 | | 5 | Connecticut | 99,883 |
| 27 | Colorado | 25,580 | | 6 | Rhode Island | 93,253 |
| 5 | Connecticut | 99,883 | | 7 | New Jersey | 87,000 |
| 1 | Delaware | 289,950 | | 8 | Ohio | 64,686 |
| 48 | Florida | 8,380 | | 9 | Texas | 63,997 |
| 19 | Georgia | 37,605 | | 10 | Virginia | 60,480 |
| 40 | Hawaii | 14,227 | | 11 | Missouri | 60,106 |
| 45 | Idaho | 10,367 | | 12 | Tennessee | 57,340 |
| 14 | Illinois | 50,966 | | 13 | Oklahoma | 54,495 |
| 24 | Indiana | 28,438 | | 14 | Illinois | 50,966 |
| 29 | Iowa | 21,081 | | 15 | Pennsylvania | 50,182 |
| 18 | Kansas | 38,161 | | 16 | California | 49,139 |
| 26 | Kentucky | 26,104 | | 17 | Wisconsin | 49,087 |
| 42 | Louisiana | 13,276 | | 18 | Kansas | 38,161 |
| 33 | Maine | 16,470 | | 19 | Georgia | 37,605 |
| 30 | Maryland | 20,807 | | 20 | Massachusetts | 36,563 |
| 20 | Massachusetts | 36,563 | | 21 | North Carolina | 33,115 |
| 32 | Michigan | 19,811 | | 22 | New York | 32,461 |
| 3 | Minnesota | 123,788 | | 23 | Arizona | 28,889 |
| 39 | Mississippi | 14,867 | | 24 | Indiana | 28,438 |
| 11 | Missouri | 60,106 | | 25 | Washington | 27,808 |
| 50 | Montana | 4,552 | | 26 | Kentucky | 26,104 |
| 2 | Nebraska | 140,892 | | 27 | Colorado | 25,580 |
| 44 | Nevada | 10,597 | | 28 | Utah | 25,203 |
| 47 | New Hampshire | 9,093 | | 29 | Iowa | 21,081 |
| 7 | New Jersey | 87,000 | | 30 | Maryland | 20,807 |
| 49 | New Mexico | 4,959 | | 31 | North Dakota | 20,113 |
| 22 | New York | 32,461 | | 32 | Michigan | 19,811 |
| 21 | North Carolina | 33,115 | | 33 | Maine | 16,470 |
| 31 | North Dakota | 20,113 | | 34 | Oregon | 16,030 |
| 8 | Ohio | 64,686 | | 35 | Alabama | 15,743 |
| 13 | Oklahoma | 54,495 | | 36 | Vermont | 15,573 |
| 34 | Oregon | 16,030 | | 37 | Alaska | 15,483 |
| 15 | Pennsylvania | 50,182 | | 38 | West Virginia | 15,471 |
| 6 | Rhode Island | 93,253 | | 39 | Mississippi | 14,867 |
| 41 | South Carolina | 14,160 | | 40 | Hawaii | 14,227 |
| 43 | South Dakota | 12,681 | | 41 | South Carolina | 14,160 |
| 12 | Tennessee | 57,340 | | 42 | Louisiana | 13,276 |
| 9 | Texas | 63,997 | | 43 | South Dakota | 12,681 |
| 28 | Utah | 25,203 | | 44 | Nevada | 10,597 |
| 36 | Vermont | 15,573 | | 45 | Idaho | 10,367 |
| 10 | Virginia | 60,480 | | 46 | Wyoming | 9,857 |
| 25 | Washington | 27,808 | | 47 | New Hampshire | 9,093 |
| 38 | West Virginia | 15,471 | | 48 | Florida | 8,380 |
| 17 | Wisconsin | 49,087 | | 49 | New Mexico | 4,959 |
| 46 | Wyoming | 9,857 | | 50 | Montana | 4,552 |
| | | | | | District of Columbia | 23,397 |

Source: CQ Press using data from U.S. Department of the Treasury, Internal Revenue Service
  "Fiscal Year 2012 IRS Data Book" (http://www.irs.gov/uac/SOI-Tax-Stats-IRS-Data-Book)
*National average does not include income from U.S. citizens abroad and other miscellaneous returns not shown separately.
Includes taxes on corporation income (Form 1120 series) and unrelated business income from tax-exempt organizations.

# Federal Tax Returns Filed in 2012

## National Total = 237,345,350 Returns*

ALPHA ORDER

| RANK | STATE | RETURNS | % of USA |
|---|---|---|---|
| 25 | Alabama | 3,147,518 | 1.3% |
| 48 | Alaska | 596,965 | 0.3% |
| 17 | Arizona | 4,427,579 | 1.9% |
| 34 | Arkansas | 1,955,546 | 0.8% |
| 1 | California | 28,198,973 | 11.9% |
| 22 | Colorado | 4,248,818 | 1.8% |
| 27 | Connecticut | 2,937,407 | 1.2% |
| 45 | Delaware | 741,786 | 0.3% |
| 3 | Florida | 16,473,456 | 6.9% |
| 10 | Georgia | 6,998,715 | 2.9% |
| 41 | Hawaii | 1,082,377 | 0.5% |
| 39 | Idaho | 1,140,121 | 0.5% |
| 5 | Illinois | 9,941,483 | 4.2% |
| 15 | Indiana | 4,573,728 | 1.9% |
| 30 | Iowa | 2,373,242 | 1.0% |
| 31 | Kansas | 2,194,379 | 0.9% |
| 28 | Kentucky | 2,848,123 | 1.2% |
| 23 | Louisiana | 3,188,326 | 1.3% |
| 42 | Maine | 1,078,155 | 0.5% |
| 16 | Maryland | 4,568,093 | 1.9% |
| 13 | Massachusetts | 5,435,185 | 2.3% |
| 9 | Michigan | 7,188,168 | 3.0% |
| 20 | Minnesota | 4,319,712 | 1.8% |
| 35 | Mississippi | 1,890,372 | 0.8% |
| 18 | Missouri | 4,400,636 | 1.9% |
| 43 | Montana | 909,370 | 0.4% |
| 36 | Nebraska | 1,465,428 | 0.6% |
| 32 | Nevada | 2,049,796 | 0.9% |
| 40 | New Hampshire | 1,099,721 | 0.5% |
| 8 | New Jersey | 7,373,699 | 3.1% |
| 37 | New Mexico | 1,423,252 | 0.6% |
| 4 | New York | 15,713,652 | 6.6% |
| 11 | North Carolina | 6,662,337 | 2.8% |
| 47 | North Dakota | 626,940 | 0.3% |
| 7 | Ohio | 8,406,967 | 3.5% |
| 29 | Oklahoma | 2,669,079 | 1.1% |
| 26 | Oregon | 3,019,820 | 1.3% |
| 6 | Pennsylvania | 9,735,275 | 4.1% |
| 44 | Rhode Island | 851,844 | 0.4% |
| 24 | South Carolina | 3,176,909 | 1.3% |
| 46 | South Dakota | 732,691 | 0.3% |
| 21 | Tennessee | 4,291,438 | 1.8% |
| 2 | Texas | 17,834,945 | 7.5% |
| 33 | Utah | 1,966,432 | 0.8% |
| 49 | Vermont | 567,858 | 0.2% |
| 12 | Virginia | 6,076,121 | 2.6% |
| 14 | Washington | 5,338,459 | 2.2% |
| 38 | West Virginia | 1,173,944 | 0.5% |
| 19 | Wisconsin | 4,373,339 | 1.8% |
| 50 | Wyoming | 530,793 | 0.2% |

RANK ORDER

| RANK | STATE | RETURNS | % of USA |
|---|---|---|---|
| 1 | California | 28,198,973 | 11.9% |
| 2 | Texas | 17,834,945 | 7.5% |
| 3 | Florida | 16,473,456 | 6.9% |
| 4 | New York | 15,713,652 | 6.6% |
| 5 | Illinois | 9,941,483 | 4.2% |
| 6 | Pennsylvania | 9,735,275 | 4.1% |
| 7 | Ohio | 8,406,967 | 3.5% |
| 8 | New Jersey | 7,373,699 | 3.1% |
| 9 | Michigan | 7,188,168 | 3.0% |
| 10 | Georgia | 6,998,715 | 2.9% |
| 11 | North Carolina | 6,662,337 | 2.8% |
| 12 | Virginia | 6,076,121 | 2.6% |
| 13 | Massachusetts | 5,435,185 | 2.3% |
| 14 | Washington | 5,338,459 | 2.2% |
| 15 | Indiana | 4,573,728 | 1.9% |
| 16 | Maryland | 4,568,093 | 1.9% |
| 17 | Arizona | 4,427,579 | 1.9% |
| 18 | Missouri | 4,400,636 | 1.9% |
| 19 | Wisconsin | 4,373,339 | 1.8% |
| 20 | Minnesota | 4,319,712 | 1.8% |
| 21 | Tennessee | 4,291,438 | 1.8% |
| 22 | Colorado | 4,248,818 | 1.8% |
| 23 | Louisiana | 3,188,326 | 1.3% |
| 24 | South Carolina | 3,176,909 | 1.3% |
| 25 | Alabama | 3,147,518 | 1.3% |
| 26 | Oregon | 3,019,820 | 1.3% |
| 27 | Connecticut | 2,937,407 | 1.2% |
| 28 | Kentucky | 2,848,123 | 1.2% |
| 29 | Oklahoma | 2,669,079 | 1.1% |
| 30 | Iowa | 2,373,242 | 1.0% |
| 31 | Kansas | 2,194,379 | 0.9% |
| 32 | Nevada | 2,049,796 | 0.9% |
| 33 | Utah | 1,966,432 | 0.8% |
| 34 | Arkansas | 1,955,546 | 0.8% |
| 35 | Mississippi | 1,890,372 | 0.8% |
| 36 | Nebraska | 1,465,428 | 0.6% |
| 37 | New Mexico | 1,423,252 | 0.6% |
| 38 | West Virginia | 1,173,944 | 0.5% |
| 39 | Idaho | 1,140,121 | 0.5% |
| 40 | New Hampshire | 1,099,721 | 0.5% |
| 41 | Hawaii | 1,082,377 | 0.5% |
| 42 | Maine | 1,078,155 | 0.5% |
| 43 | Montana | 909,370 | 0.4% |
| 44 | Rhode Island | 851,844 | 0.4% |
| 45 | Delaware | 741,786 | 0.3% |
| 46 | South Dakota | 732,691 | 0.3% |
| 47 | North Dakota | 626,940 | 0.3% |
| 48 | Alaska | 596,965 | 0.3% |
| 49 | Vermont | 567,858 | 0.2% |
| 50 | Wyoming | 530,793 | 0.2% |
| | District of Columbia | 567,560 | 0.2% |

Source: U.S. Department of the Treasury, Internal Revenue Service
"Fiscal Year 2012 IRS Data Book" (http://www.irs.gov/uac/SOI-Tax-Stats-IRS-Data-Book)
*Total includes returns from international sources and other miscellaneous returns not shown separately.

# Percent of Federal Returns Filed Electronically in 2012

## National Percent = 60.9%*

ALPHA ORDER

| RANK | STATE | PERCENT |
|---|---|---|
| 7 | Alabama | 64.2 |
| 33 | Alaska | 59.8 |
| 30 | Arizona | 60.3 |
| 18 | Arkansas | 61.7 |
| 35 | California | 59.7 |
| 45 | Colorado | 57.1 |
| 35 | Connecticut | 59.7 |
| 32 | Delaware | 60.0 |
| 25 | Florida | 60.6 |
| 3 | Georgia | 65.0 |
| 50 | Hawaii | 52.3 |
| 38 | Idaho | 59.5 |
| 33 | Illinois | 59.8 |
| 11 | Indiana | 63.4 |
| 28 | Iowa | 60.4 |
| 16 | Kansas | 62.3 |
| 12 | Kentucky | 63.3 |
| 21 | Louisiana | 61.1 |
| 46 | Maine | 56.7 |
| 44 | Maryland | 57.8 |
| 4 | Massachusetts | 64.6 |
| 5 | Michigan | 64.4 |
| 17 | Minnesota | 62.0 |
| 6 | Mississippi | 64.3 |
| 28 | Missouri | 60.4 |
| 47 | Montana | 55.7 |
| 20 | Nebraska | 61.2 |
| 15 | Nevada | 63.0 |
| 31 | New Hampshire | 60.2 |
| 22 | New Jersey | 61.0 |
| 37 | New Mexico | 59.6 |
| 1 | New York | 66.0 |
| 24 | North Carolina | 60.7 |
| 49 | North Dakota | 54.5 |
| 9 | Ohio | 63.6 |
| 23 | Oklahoma | 60.8 |
| 41 | Oregon | 58.9 |
| 25 | Pennsylvania | 60.6 |
| 2 | Rhode Island | 65.5 |
| 8 | South Carolina | 63.9 |
| 42 | South Dakota | 58.1 |
| 9 | Tennessee | 63.6 |
| 19 | Texas | 61.3 |
| 12 | Utah | 63.3 |
| 48 | Vermont | 54.8 |
| 38 | Virginia | 59.5 |
| 40 | Washington | 59.2 |
| 27 | West Virginia | 60.5 |
| 14 | Wisconsin | 63.2 |
| 43 | Wyoming | 58.0 |

RANK ORDER

| RANK | STATE | PERCENT |
|---|---|---|
| 1 | New York | 66.0 |
| 2 | Rhode Island | 65.5 |
| 3 | Georgia | 65.0 |
| 4 | Massachusetts | 64.6 |
| 5 | Michigan | 64.4 |
| 6 | Mississippi | 64.3 |
| 7 | Alabama | 64.2 |
| 8 | South Carolina | 63.9 |
| 9 | Ohio | 63.6 |
| 9 | Tennessee | 63.6 |
| 11 | Indiana | 63.4 |
| 12 | Kentucky | 63.3 |
| 12 | Utah | 63.3 |
| 14 | Wisconsin | 63.2 |
| 15 | Nevada | 63.0 |
| 16 | Kansas | 62.3 |
| 17 | Minnesota | 62.0 |
| 18 | Arkansas | 61.7 |
| 19 | Texas | 61.3 |
| 20 | Nebraska | 61.2 |
| 21 | Louisiana | 61.1 |
| 22 | New Jersey | 61.0 |
| 23 | Oklahoma | 60.8 |
| 24 | North Carolina | 60.7 |
| 25 | Florida | 60.6 |
| 25 | Pennsylvania | 60.6 |
| 27 | West Virginia | 60.5 |
| 28 | Iowa | 60.4 |
| 28 | Missouri | 60.4 |
| 30 | Arizona | 60.3 |
| 31 | New Hampshire | 60.2 |
| 32 | Delaware | 60.0 |
| 33 | Alaska | 59.8 |
| 33 | Illinois | 59.8 |
| 35 | California | 59.7 |
| 35 | Connecticut | 59.7 |
| 37 | New Mexico | 59.6 |
| 38 | Idaho | 59.5 |
| 38 | Virginia | 59.5 |
| 40 | Washington | 59.2 |
| 41 | Oregon | 58.9 |
| 42 | South Dakota | 58.1 |
| 43 | Wyoming | 58.0 |
| 44 | Maryland | 57.8 |
| 45 | Colorado | 57.1 |
| 46 | Maine | 56.7 |
| 47 | Montana | 55.7 |
| 48 | Vermont | 54.8 |
| 49 | North Dakota | 54.5 |
| 50 | Hawaii | 52.3 |
|  | District of Columbia | 57.5 |

Source: CQ Press using data from U.S. Department of the Treasury, Internal Revenue Service
"Fiscal Year 2012 IRS Data Book" (http://www.irs.gov/uac/SOI-Tax-Stats-IRS-Data-Book)
*Total includes returns from international sources and other miscellaneous returns. Includes corporate, individual, partnership, estate, employment and other returns. Excludes returns that cannot be filed electronically including informational returns. Forty-seven percent of individual income tax returns were filed electronically.

# Federal Individual Income Tax Returns Filed in 2012

## National Total = 146,243,886 Returns*

ALPHA ORDER

| RANK | STATE | RETURNS | % of USA |
|---|---|---|---|
| 23 | Alabama | 2,094,553 | 1.4% |
| 47 | Alaska | 369,581 | 0.3% |
| 18 | Arizona | 2,769,832 | 1.9% |
| 34 | Arkansas | 1,229,757 | 0.8% |
| 1 | California | 16,935,887 | 11.6% |
| 22 | Colorado | 2,397,815 | 1.6% |
| 28 | Connecticut | 1,741,293 | 1.2% |
| 45 | Delaware | 431,325 | 0.3% |
| 3 | Florida | 9,736,734 | 6.7% |
| 9 | Georgia | 4,514,150 | 3.1% |
| 41 | Hawaii | 658,626 | 0.5% |
| 40 | Idaho | 666,204 | 0.5% |
| 6 | Illinois | 6,103,373 | 4.2% |
| 15 | Indiana | 3,007,521 | 2.1% |
| 30 | Iowa | 1,413,882 | 1.0% |
| 31 | Kansas | 1,323,293 | 0.9% |
| 26 | Kentucky | 1,870,180 | 1.3% |
| 25 | Louisiana | 2,014,306 | 1.4% |
| 42 | Maine | 629,281 | 0.4% |
| 17 | Maryland | 2,821,455 | 1.9% |
| 13 | Massachusetts | 3,232,880 | 2.2% |
| 8 | Michigan | 4,660,114 | 3.2% |
| 21 | Minnesota | 2,587,955 | 1.8% |
| 33 | Mississippi | 1,285,923 | 0.9% |
| 20 | Missouri | 2,716,941 | 1.9% |
| 44 | Montana | 477,712 | 0.3% |
| 37 | Nebraska | 867,235 | 0.6% |
| 32 | Nevada | 1,290,641 | 0.9% |
| 39 | New Hampshire | 674,965 | 0.5% |
| 10 | New Jersey | 4,319,000 | 3.0% |
| 36 | New Mexico | 912,132 | 0.6% |
| 4 | New York | 9,354,490 | 6.4% |
| 11 | North Carolina | 4,262,480 | 2.9% |
| 48 | North Dakota | 339,892 | 0.2% |
| 7 | Ohio | 5,491,871 | 3.8% |
| 29 | Oklahoma | 1,605,475 | 1.1% |
| 27 | Oregon | 1,748,979 | 1.2% |
| 5 | Pennsylvania | 6,172,712 | 4.2% |
| 43 | Rhode Island | 512,377 | 0.4% |
| 24 | South Carolina | 2,072,346 | 1.4% |
| 46 | South Dakota | 409,547 | 0.3% |
| 16 | Tennessee | 2,893,799 | 2.0% |
| 2 | Texas | 11,292,464 | 7.7% |
| 35 | Utah | 1,152,313 | 0.8% |
| 49 | Vermont | 318,780 | 0.2% |
| 12 | Virginia | 3,779,854 | 2.6% |
| 14 | Washington | 3,192,891 | 2.2% |
| 38 | West Virginia | 789,106 | 0.5% |
| 19 | Wisconsin | 2,767,383 | 1.9% |
| 50 | Wyoming | 291,332 | 0.2% |

RANK ORDER

| RANK | STATE | RETURNS | % of USA |
|---|---|---|---|
| 1 | California | 16,935,887 | 11.6% |
| 2 | Texas | 11,292,464 | 7.7% |
| 3 | Florida | 9,736,734 | 6.7% |
| 4 | New York | 9,354,490 | 6.4% |
| 5 | Pennsylvania | 6,172,712 | 4.2% |
| 6 | Illinois | 6,103,373 | 4.2% |
| 7 | Ohio | 5,491,871 | 3.8% |
| 8 | Michigan | 4,660,114 | 3.2% |
| 9 | Georgia | 4,514,150 | 3.1% |
| 10 | New Jersey | 4,319,000 | 3.0% |
| 11 | North Carolina | 4,262,480 | 2.9% |
| 12 | Virginia | 3,779,854 | 2.6% |
| 13 | Massachusetts | 3,232,880 | 2.2% |
| 14 | Washington | 3,192,891 | 2.2% |
| 15 | Indiana | 3,007,521 | 2.1% |
| 16 | Tennessee | 2,893,799 | 2.0% |
| 17 | Maryland | 2,821,455 | 1.9% |
| 18 | Arizona | 2,769,832 | 1.9% |
| 19 | Wisconsin | 2,767,383 | 1.9% |
| 20 | Missouri | 2,716,941 | 1.9% |
| 21 | Minnesota | 2,587,955 | 1.8% |
| 22 | Colorado | 2,397,815 | 1.6% |
| 23 | Alabama | 2,094,553 | 1.4% |
| 24 | South Carolina | 2,072,346 | 1.4% |
| 25 | Louisiana | 2,014,306 | 1.4% |
| 26 | Kentucky | 1,870,180 | 1.3% |
| 27 | Oregon | 1,748,979 | 1.2% |
| 28 | Connecticut | 1,741,293 | 1.2% |
| 29 | Oklahoma | 1,605,475 | 1.1% |
| 30 | Iowa | 1,413,882 | 1.0% |
| 31 | Kansas | 1,323,293 | 0.9% |
| 32 | Nevada | 1,290,641 | 0.9% |
| 33 | Mississippi | 1,285,923 | 0.9% |
| 34 | Arkansas | 1,229,757 | 0.8% |
| 35 | Utah | 1,152,313 | 0.8% |
| 36 | New Mexico | 912,132 | 0.6% |
| 37 | Nebraska | 867,235 | 0.6% |
| 38 | West Virginia | 789,106 | 0.5% |
| 39 | New Hampshire | 674,965 | 0.5% |
| 40 | Idaho | 666,204 | 0.5% |
| 41 | Hawaii | 658,626 | 0.5% |
| 42 | Maine | 629,281 | 0.4% |
| 43 | Rhode Island | 512,377 | 0.4% |
| 44 | Montana | 477,712 | 0.3% |
| 45 | Delaware | 431,325 | 0.3% |
| 46 | South Dakota | 409,547 | 0.3% |
| 47 | Alaska | 369,581 | 0.3% |
| 48 | North Dakota | 339,892 | 0.2% |
| 49 | Vermont | 318,780 | 0.2% |
| 50 | Wyoming | 291,332 | 0.2% |
| | District of Columbia | 326,925 | 0.2% |

Source: U.S. Department of the Treasury, Internal Revenue Service
"Fiscal Year 2012 IRS Data Book" (http://www.irs.gov/uac/SOI-Tax-Stats-IRS-Data-Book)
*Total includes returns from international sources and other miscellaneous returns not shown separately.

# Federal Business Income Tax Returns Filed in 2012

## National Total = 6,842,630 Returns*

ALPHA ORDER

| RANK | STATE | RETURNS | % of USA |
|------|-------|---------|----------|
| 28 | Alabama | 70,056 | 1.0% |
| 50 | Alaska | 12,340 | 0.2% |
| 18 | Arizona | 118,001 | 1.7% |
| 32 | Arkansas | 54,602 | 0.8% |
| 2 | California | 756,661 | 11.1% |
| 13 | Colorado | 155,142 | 2.3% |
| 33 | Connecticut | 54,378 | 0.8% |
| 43 | Delaware | 24,444 | 0.4% |
| 1 | Florida | 788,677 | 11.5% |
| 6 | Georgia | 223,828 | 3.3% |
| 41 | Hawaii | 28,025 | 0.4% |
| 37 | Idaho | 35,491 | 0.5% |
| 5 | Illinois | 340,166 | 5.0% |
| 19 | Indiana | 113,522 | 1.7% |
| 31 | Iowa | 62,383 | 0.9% |
| 34 | Kansas | 51,886 | 0.8% |
| 30 | Kentucky | 67,582 | 1.0% |
| 23 | Louisiana | 83,061 | 1.2% |
| 39 | Maine | 30,929 | 0.5% |
| 17 | Maryland | 126,230 | 1.8% |
| 14 | Massachusetts | 144,366 | 2.1% |
| 9 | Michigan | 193,909 | 2.8% |
| 16 | Minnesota | 130,236 | 1.9% |
| 36 | Mississippi | 40,975 | 0.6% |
| 20 | Missouri | 101,199 | 1.5% |
| 38 | Montana | 34,360 | 0.5% |
| 35 | Nebraska | 43,647 | 0.6% |
| 27 | Nevada | 71,507 | 1.0% |
| 44 | New Hampshire | 22,573 | 0.3% |
| 8 | New Jersey | 200,689 | 2.9% |
| 40 | New Mexico | 30,360 | 0.4% |
| 3 | New York | 655,238 | 9.6% |
| 10 | North Carolina | 193,621 | 2.8% |
| 49 | North Dakota | 15,000 | 0.2% |
| 11 | Ohio | 179,393 | 2.6% |
| 25 | Oklahoma | 73,083 | 1.1% |
| 24 | Oregon | 76,720 | 1.1% |
| 7 | Pennsylvania | 223,637 | 3.3% |
| 42 | Rhode Island | 24,957 | 0.4% |
| 22 | South Carolina | 85,557 | 1.3% |
| 46 | South Dakota | 18,540 | 0.3% |
| 29 | Tennessee | 68,085 | 1.0% |
| 4 | Texas | 437,278 | 6.4% |
| 26 | Utah | 71,799 | 1.0% |
| 48 | Vermont | 16,413 | 0.2% |
| 12 | Virginia | 165,245 | 2.4% |
| 15 | Washington | 136,437 | 2.0% |
| 45 | West Virginia | 20,409 | 0.3% |
| 21 | Wisconsin | 94,561 | 1.4% |
| 47 | Wyoming | 17,823 | 0.3% |

RANK ORDER

| RANK | STATE | RETURNS | % of USA |
|------|-------|---------|----------|
| 1 | Florida | 788,677 | 11.5% |
| 2 | California | 756,661 | 11.1% |
| 3 | New York | 655,238 | 9.6% |
| 4 | Texas | 437,278 | 6.4% |
| 5 | Illinois | 340,166 | 5.0% |
| 6 | Georgia | 223,828 | 3.3% |
| 7 | Pennsylvania | 223,637 | 3.3% |
| 8 | New Jersey | 200,689 | 2.9% |
| 9 | Michigan | 193,909 | 2.8% |
| 10 | North Carolina | 193,621 | 2.8% |
| 11 | Ohio | 179,393 | 2.6% |
| 12 | Virginia | 165,245 | 2.4% |
| 13 | Colorado | 155,142 | 2.3% |
| 14 | Massachusetts | 144,366 | 2.1% |
| 15 | Washington | 136,437 | 2.0% |
| 16 | Minnesota | 130,236 | 1.9% |
| 17 | Maryland | 126,230 | 1.8% |
| 18 | Arizona | 118,001 | 1.7% |
| 19 | Indiana | 113,522 | 1.7% |
| 20 | Missouri | 101,199 | 1.5% |
| 21 | Wisconsin | 94,561 | 1.4% |
| 22 | South Carolina | 85,557 | 1.3% |
| 23 | Louisiana | 83,061 | 1.2% |
| 24 | Oregon | 76,720 | 1.1% |
| 25 | Oklahoma | 73,083 | 1.1% |
| 26 | Utah | 71,799 | 1.0% |
| 27 | Nevada | 71,507 | 1.0% |
| 28 | Alabama | 70,056 | 1.0% |
| 29 | Tennessee | 68,085 | 1.0% |
| 30 | Kentucky | 67,582 | 1.0% |
| 31 | Iowa | 62,383 | 0.9% |
| 32 | Arkansas | 54,602 | 0.8% |
| 33 | Connecticut | 54,378 | 0.8% |
| 34 | Kansas | 51,886 | 0.8% |
| 35 | Nebraska | 43,647 | 0.6% |
| 36 | Mississippi | 40,975 | 0.6% |
| 37 | Idaho | 35,491 | 0.5% |
| 38 | Montana | 34,360 | 0.5% |
| 39 | Maine | 30,929 | 0.5% |
| 40 | New Mexico | 30,360 | 0.4% |
| 41 | Hawaii | 28,025 | 0.4% |
| 42 | Rhode Island | 24,957 | 0.4% |
| 43 | Delaware | 24,444 | 0.4% |
| 44 | New Hampshire | 22,573 | 0.3% |
| 45 | West Virginia | 20,409 | 0.3% |
| 46 | South Dakota | 18,540 | 0.3% |
| 47 | Wyoming | 17,823 | 0.3% |
| 48 | Vermont | 16,413 | 0.2% |
| 49 | North Dakota | 15,000 | 0.2% |
| 50 | Alaska | 12,340 | 0.2% |
| | District of Columbia | 16,788 | 0.2% |

Source: U.S. Department of the Treasury, Internal Revenue Service
"Fiscal Year 2012 IRS Data Book" (http://www.irs.gov/uac/SOI-Tax-Stats-IRS-Data-Book)
*Total includes returns from international sources and other miscellaneous returns not shown separately.

# Federal Tax Refunds in 2012

## National Total = 123,358,811 Refunds*

ALPHA ORDER

| RANK | STATE | REFUNDS | % of USA |
|---|---|---|---|
| 23 | Alabama | 1,804,690 | 1.5% |
| 47 | Alaska | 308,862 | 0.3% |
| 20 | Arizona | 2,283,380 | 1.9% |
| 34 | Arkansas | 1,049,181 | 0.9% |
| 1 | California | 13,862,370 | 11.2% |
| 22 | Colorado | 1,962,632 | 1.6% |
| 27 | Connecticut | 1,464,462 | 1.2% |
| 45 | Delaware | 374,282 | 0.3% |
| 3 | Florida | 8,389,372 | 6.8% |
| 9 | Georgia | 3,908,253 | 3.2% |
| 41 | Hawaii | 550,994 | 0.4% |
| 40 | Idaho | 554,643 | 0.4% |
| 6 | Illinois | 5,295,743 | 4.3% |
| 15 | Indiana | 2,626,268 | 2.1% |
| 30 | Iowa | 1,171,417 | 0.9% |
| 33 | Kansas | 1,089,736 | 0.9% |
| 26 | Kentucky | 1,634,618 | 1.3% |
| 24 | Louisiana | 1,753,536 | 1.4% |
| 42 | Maine | 531,900 | 0.4% |
| 17 | Maryland | 2,386,855 | 1.9% |
| 14 | Massachusetts | 2,693,489 | 2.2% |
| 8 | Michigan | 3,925,143 | 3.2% |
| 21 | Minnesota | 2,118,566 | 1.7% |
| 31 | Mississippi | 1,119,145 | 0.9% |
| 18 | Missouri | 2,300,059 | 1.9% |
| 44 | Montana | 384,348 | 0.3% |
| 37 | Nebraska | 723,006 | 0.6% |
| 32 | Nevada | 1,111,970 | 0.9% |
| 39 | New Hampshire | 574,120 | 0.5% |
| 10 | New Jersey | 3,631,643 | 2.9% |
| 36 | New Mexico | 771,191 | 0.6% |
| 4 | New York | 7,949,259 | 6.4% |
| 11 | North Carolina | 3,589,629 | 2.9% |
| 48 | North Dakota | 272,606 | 0.2% |
| 7 | Ohio | 4,740,122 | 3.8% |
| 29 | Oklahoma | 1,353,063 | 1.1% |
| 28 | Oregon | 1,409,483 | 1.1% |
| 5 | Pennsylvania | 5,297,935 | 4.3% |
| 43 | Rhode Island | 448,757 | 0.4% |
| 25 | South Carolina | 1,753,491 | 1.4% |
| 46 | South Dakota | 337,431 | 0.3% |
| 16 | Tennessee | 2,544,287 | 2.1% |
| 2 | Texas | 9,893,591 | 8.0% |
| 35 | Utah | 1,005,036 | 0.8% |
| 49 | Vermont | 266,367 | 0.2% |
| 12 | Virginia | 3,210,945 | 2.6% |
| 13 | Washington | 2,706,375 | 2.2% |
| 38 | West Virginia | 697,819 | 0.6% |
| 19 | Wisconsin | 2,299,788 | 1.9% |
| 50 | Wyoming | 247,976 | 0.2% |

RANK ORDER

| RANK | STATE | REFUNDS | % of USA |
|---|---|---|---|
| 1 | California | 13,862,370 | 11.2% |
| 2 | Texas | 9,893,591 | 8.0% |
| 3 | Florida | 8,389,372 | 6.8% |
| 4 | New York | 7,949,259 | 6.4% |
| 5 | Pennsylvania | 5,297,935 | 4.3% |
| 6 | Illinois | 5,295,743 | 4.3% |
| 7 | Ohio | 4,740,122 | 3.8% |
| 8 | Michigan | 3,925,143 | 3.2% |
| 9 | Georgia | 3,908,253 | 3.2% |
| 10 | New Jersey | 3,631,643 | 2.9% |
| 11 | North Carolina | 3,589,629 | 2.9% |
| 12 | Virginia | 3,210,945 | 2.6% |
| 13 | Washington | 2,706,375 | 2.2% |
| 14 | Massachusetts | 2,693,489 | 2.2% |
| 15 | Indiana | 2,626,268 | 2.1% |
| 16 | Tennessee | 2,544,287 | 2.1% |
| 17 | Maryland | 2,386,855 | 1.9% |
| 18 | Missouri | 2,300,059 | 1.9% |
| 19 | Wisconsin | 2,299,788 | 1.9% |
| 20 | Arizona | 2,283,380 | 1.9% |
| 21 | Minnesota | 2,118,566 | 1.7% |
| 22 | Colorado | 1,962,632 | 1.6% |
| 23 | Alabama | 1,804,690 | 1.5% |
| 24 | Louisiana | 1,753,536 | 1.4% |
| 25 | South Carolina | 1,753,491 | 1.4% |
| 26 | Kentucky | 1,634,618 | 1.3% |
| 27 | Connecticut | 1,464,462 | 1.2% |
| 28 | Oregon | 1,409,483 | 1.1% |
| 29 | Oklahoma | 1,353,063 | 1.1% |
| 30 | Iowa | 1,171,417 | 0.9% |
| 31 | Mississippi | 1,119,145 | 0.9% |
| 32 | Nevada | 1,111,970 | 0.9% |
| 33 | Kansas | 1,089,736 | 0.9% |
| 34 | Arkansas | 1,049,181 | 0.9% |
| 35 | Utah | 1,005,036 | 0.8% |
| 36 | New Mexico | 771,191 | 0.6% |
| 37 | Nebraska | 723,006 | 0.6% |
| 38 | West Virginia | 697,819 | 0.6% |
| 39 | New Hampshire | 574,120 | 0.5% |
| 40 | Idaho | 554,643 | 0.4% |
| 41 | Hawaii | 550,994 | 0.4% |
| 42 | Maine | 531,900 | 0.4% |
| 43 | Rhode Island | 448,757 | 0.4% |
| 44 | Montana | 384,348 | 0.3% |
| 45 | Delaware | 374,282 | 0.3% |
| 46 | South Dakota | 337,431 | 0.3% |
| 47 | Alaska | 308,862 | 0.3% |
| 48 | North Dakota | 272,606 | 0.2% |
| 49 | Vermont | 266,367 | 0.2% |
| 50 | Wyoming | 247,976 | 0.2% |
| | District of Columbia | 278,935 | 0.2% |

Source: U.S. Department of the Treasury, Internal Revenue Service
"Fiscal Year 2012 IRS Data Book" (http://www.irs.gov/uac/SOI-Tax-Stats-IRS-Data-Book)
*Total includes refunds to international sources and other miscellaneous refunds not shown separately.

# Value of Federal Tax Refunds in 2012

## National Total = $373,428,754,000*

ALPHA ORDER

| RANK | STATE | REFUNDS | % of USA |
|---|---|---|---|
| 24 | Alabama | $5,289,399,000 | 1.4% |
| 47 | Alaska | 811,368,000 | 0.2% |
| 21 | Arizona | 6,290,211,000 | 1.7% |
| 35 | Arkansas | 2,931,984,000 | 0.8% |
| 1 | California | 41,894,334,000 | 11.2% |
| 23 | Colorado | 5,625,018,000 | 1.5% |
| 18 | Connecticut | 6,593,434,000 | 1.8% |
| 29 | Delaware | 3,888,671,000 | 1.0% |
| 4 | Florida | 23,865,014,000 | 6.4% |
| 9 | Georgia | 12,022,713,000 | 3.2% |
| 42 | Hawaii | 1,433,423,000 | 0.4% |
| 43 | Idaho | 1,387,668,000 | 0.4% |
| 5 | Illinois | 16,767,195,000 | 4.5% |
| 17 | Indiana | 7,087,659,000 | 1.9% |
| 34 | Iowa | 2,977,650,000 | 0.8% |
| 36 | Kansas | 2,862,001,000 | 0.8% |
| 28 | Kentucky | 4,430,116,000 | 1.2% |
| 25 | Louisiana | 5,287,798,000 | 1.4% |
| 44 | Maine | 1,343,896,000 | 0.4% |
| 16 | Maryland | 7,257,470,000 | 1.9% |
| 13 | Massachusetts | 8,674,056,000 | 2.3% |
| 10 | Michigan | 10,792,947,000 | 2.9% |
| 19 | Minnesota | 6,557,810,000 | 1.8% |
| 31 | Mississippi | 3,332,747,000 | 0.9% |
| 20 | Missouri | 6,442,756,000 | 1.7% |
| 45 | Montana | 862,743,000 | 0.2% |
| 38 | Nebraska | 1,880,669,000 | 0.5% |
| 32 | Nevada | 3,141,754,000 | 0.8% |
| 41 | New Hampshire | 1,488,585,000 | 0.4% |
| 8 | New Jersey | 12,258,226,000 | 3.3% |
| 37 | New Mexico | 1,975,230,000 | 0.5% |
| 3 | New York | 28,481,035,000 | 7.6% |
| 11 | North Carolina | 10,066,606,000 | 2.7% |
| 48 | North Dakota | 700,946,000 | 0.2% |
| 7 | Ohio | 13,063,147,000 | 3.5% |
| 27 | Oklahoma | 4,444,247,000 | 1.2% |
| 30 | Oregon | 3,572,129,000 | 1.0% |
| 6 | Pennsylvania | 14,766,611,000 | 4.0% |
| 40 | Rhode Island | 1,522,007,000 | 0.4% |
| 26 | South Carolina | 4,467,036,000 | 1.2% |
| 46 | South Dakota | 836,521,000 | 0.2% |
| 14 | Tennessee | 8,081,139,000 | 2.2% |
| 2 | Texas | 33,464,687,000 | 9.0% |
| 33 | Utah | 3,004,212,000 | 0.8% |
| 49 | Vermont | 671,390,000 | 0.2% |
| 12 | Virginia | 9,593,063,000 | 2.6% |
| 15 | Washington | 7,475,082,000 | 2.0% |
| 39 | West Virginia | 1,793,899,000 | 0.5% |
| 22 | Wisconsin | 5,947,952,000 | 1.6% |
| 50 | Wyoming | 668,210,000 | 0.2% |

RANK ORDER

| RANK | STATE | REFUNDS | % of USA |
|---|---|---|---|
| 1 | California | $41,894,334,000 | 11.2% |
| 2 | Texas | 33,464,687,000 | 9.0% |
| 3 | New York | 28,481,035,000 | 7.6% |
| 4 | Florida | 23,865,014,000 | 6.4% |
| 5 | Illinois | 16,767,195,000 | 4.5% |
| 6 | Pennsylvania | 14,766,611,000 | 4.0% |
| 7 | Ohio | 13,063,147,000 | 3.5% |
| 8 | New Jersey | 12,258,226,000 | 3.3% |
| 9 | Georgia | 12,022,713,000 | 3.2% |
| 10 | Michigan | 10,792,947,000 | 2.9% |
| 11 | North Carolina | 10,066,606,000 | 2.7% |
| 12 | Virginia | 9,593,063,000 | 2.6% |
| 13 | Massachusetts | 8,674,056,000 | 2.3% |
| 14 | Tennessee | 8,081,139,000 | 2.2% |
| 15 | Washington | 7,475,082,000 | 2.0% |
| 16 | Maryland | 7,257,470,000 | 1.9% |
| 17 | Indiana | 7,087,659,000 | 1.9% |
| 18 | Connecticut | 6,593,434,000 | 1.8% |
| 19 | Minnesota | 6,557,810,000 | 1.8% |
| 20 | Missouri | 6,442,756,000 | 1.7% |
| 21 | Arizona | 6,290,211,000 | 1.7% |
| 22 | Wisconsin | 5,947,952,000 | 1.6% |
| 23 | Colorado | 5,625,018,000 | 1.5% |
| 24 | Alabama | 5,289,399,000 | 1.4% |
| 25 | Louisiana | 5,287,798,000 | 1.4% |
| 26 | South Carolina | 4,467,036,000 | 1.2% |
| 27 | Oklahoma | 4,444,247,000 | 1.2% |
| 28 | Kentucky | 4,430,116,000 | 1.2% |
| 29 | Delaware | 3,888,671,000 | 1.0% |
| 30 | Oregon | 3,572,129,000 | 1.0% |
| 31 | Mississippi | 3,332,747,000 | 0.9% |
| 32 | Nevada | 3,141,754,000 | 0.8% |
| 33 | Utah | 3,004,212,000 | 0.8% |
| 34 | Iowa | 2,977,650,000 | 0.8% |
| 35 | Arkansas | 2,931,984,000 | 0.8% |
| 36 | Kansas | 2,862,001,000 | 0.8% |
| 37 | New Mexico | 1,975,230,000 | 0.5% |
| 38 | Nebraska | 1,880,669,000 | 0.5% |
| 39 | West Virginia | 1,793,899,000 | 0.5% |
| 40 | Rhode Island | 1,522,007,000 | 0.4% |
| 41 | New Hampshire | 1,488,585,000 | 0.4% |
| 42 | Hawaii | 1,433,423,000 | 0.4% |
| 43 | Idaho | 1,387,668,000 | 0.4% |
| 44 | Maine | 1,343,896,000 | 0.4% |
| 45 | Montana | 862,743,000 | 0.2% |
| 46 | South Dakota | 836,521,000 | 0.2% |
| 47 | Alaska | 811,368,000 | 0.2% |
| 48 | North Dakota | 700,946,000 | 0.2% |
| 49 | Vermont | 671,390,000 | 0.2% |
| 50 | Wyoming | 668,210,000 | 0.2% |
| | District of Columbia | 833,947,000 | 0.2% |

Source: U.S. Department of the Treasury, Internal Revenue Service
"Fiscal Year 2012 IRS Data Book" (http://www.irs.gov/uac/SOI-Tax-Stats-IRS-Data-Book)
*Total includes refunds to international sources and other miscellaneous refunds not shown separately.

# Average Value of Federal Tax Refunds in 2012

## National Average = $3,027*

ALPHA ORDER

| RANK | STATE | AVERAGE REFUND |
|------|-------|----------------|
| 19 | Alabama | $2,931 |
| 34 | Alaska | 2,627 |
| 29 | Arizona | 2,755 |
| 25 | Arkansas | 2,795 |
| 14 | California | 3,022 |
| 20 | Colorado | 2,866 |
| 2 | Connecticut | 4,502 |
| 1 | Delaware | 10,390 |
| 21 | Florida | 2,845 |
| 12 | Georgia | 3,076 |
| 36 | Hawaii | 2,602 |
| 48 | Idaho | 2,502 |
| 10 | Illinois | 3,166 |
| 32 | Indiana | 2,699 |
| 44 | Iowa | 2,542 |
| 35 | Kansas | 2,626 |
| 31 | Kentucky | 2,710 |
| 15 | Louisiana | 3,016 |
| 46 | Maine | 2,527 |
| 13 | Maryland | 3,041 |
| 8 | Massachusetts | 3,220 |
| 30 | Michigan | 2,750 |
| 11 | Minnesota | 3,095 |
| 18 | Mississippi | 2,978 |
| 24 | Missouri | 2,801 |
| 50 | Montana | 2,245 |
| 37 | Nebraska | 2,601 |
| 22 | Nevada | 2,825 |
| 38 | New Hampshire | 2,593 |
| 6 | New Jersey | 3,375 |
| 42 | New Mexico | 2,561 |
| 3 | New York | 3,583 |
| 23 | North Carolina | 2,804 |
| 40 | North Dakota | 2,571 |
| 28 | Ohio | 2,756 |
| 7 | Oklahoma | 3,285 |
| 45 | Oregon | 2,534 |
| 26 | Pennsylvania | 2,787 |
| 4 | Rhode Island | 3,392 |
| 43 | South Carolina | 2,548 |
| 49 | South Dakota | 2,479 |
| 9 | Tennessee | 3,176 |
| 5 | Texas | 3,382 |
| 16 | Utah | 2,989 |
| 47 | Vermont | 2,521 |
| 17 | Virginia | 2,988 |
| 27 | Washington | 2,762 |
| 40 | West Virginia | 2,571 |
| 39 | Wisconsin | 2,586 |
| 33 | Wyoming | 2,695 |

RANK ORDER

| RANK | STATE | AVERAGE REFUND |
|------|-------|----------------|
| 1 | Delaware | $10,390 |
| 2 | Connecticut | 4,502 |
| 3 | New York | 3,583 |
| 4 | Rhode Island | 3,392 |
| 5 | Texas | 3,382 |
| 6 | New Jersey | 3,375 |
| 7 | Oklahoma | 3,285 |
| 8 | Massachusetts | 3,220 |
| 9 | Tennessee | 3,176 |
| 10 | Illinois | 3,166 |
| 11 | Minnesota | 3,095 |
| 12 | Georgia | 3,076 |
| 13 | Maryland | 3,041 |
| 14 | California | 3,022 |
| 15 | Louisiana | 3,016 |
| 16 | Utah | 2,989 |
| 17 | Virginia | 2,988 |
| 18 | Mississippi | 2,978 |
| 19 | Alabama | 2,931 |
| 20 | Colorado | 2,866 |
| 21 | Florida | 2,845 |
| 22 | Nevada | 2,825 |
| 23 | North Carolina | 2,804 |
| 24 | Missouri | 2,801 |
| 25 | Arkansas | 2,795 |
| 26 | Pennsylvania | 2,787 |
| 27 | Washington | 2,762 |
| 28 | Ohio | 2,756 |
| 29 | Arizona | 2,755 |
| 30 | Michigan | 2,750 |
| 31 | Kentucky | 2,710 |
| 32 | Indiana | 2,699 |
| 33 | Wyoming | 2,695 |
| 34 | Alaska | 2,627 |
| 35 | Kansas | 2,626 |
| 36 | Hawaii | 2,602 |
| 37 | Nebraska | 2,601 |
| 38 | New Hampshire | 2,593 |
| 39 | Wisconsin | 2,586 |
| 40 | North Dakota | 2,571 |
| 40 | West Virginia | 2,571 |
| 42 | New Mexico | 2,561 |
| 43 | South Carolina | 2,548 |
| 44 | Iowa | 2,542 |
| 45 | Oregon | 2,534 |
| 46 | Maine | 2,527 |
| 47 | Vermont | 2,521 |
| 48 | Idaho | 2,502 |
| 49 | South Dakota | 2,479 |
| 50 | Montana | 2,245 |
| | District of Columbia | 2,990 |

Source: CQ Press using data from U.S. Department of the Treasury, Internal Revenue Service
"Fiscal Year 2012 IRS Data Book" (http://www.irs.gov/uac/SOI-Tax-Stats-IRS-Data-Book)
*National average includes refunds to international sources and other miscellaneous refunds not shown separately.

# Value of Federal Individual Income Tax Refunds in 2012

## National Total = $322,666,998,000*

ALPHA ORDER

| RANK | STATE | REFUNDS | % of USA |
|------|-------|---------|----------|
| 21 | Alabama | $4,929,830,000 | 1.5% |
| 47 | Alaska | 765,027,000 | 0.2% |
| 18 | Arizona | 5,784,097,000 | 1.8% |
| 33 | Arkansas | 2,680,057,000 | 0.8% |
| 1 | California | 37,102,177,000 | 11.5% |
| 24 | Colorado | 4,886,442,000 | 1.5% |
| 26 | Connecticut | 4,190,561,000 | 1.3% |
| 44 | Delaware | 918,221,000 | 0.3% |
| 3 | Florida | 22,760,604,000 | 7.1% |
| 9 | Georgia | 10,472,192,000 | 3.2% |
| 40 | Hawaii | 1,326,139,000 | 0.4% |
| 41 | Idaho | 1,282,373,000 | 0.4% |
| 5 | Illinois | 14,713,626,000 | 4.6% |
| 16 | Indiana | 6,568,931,000 | 2.0% |
| 32 | Iowa | 2,763,798,000 | 0.9% |
| 34 | Kansas | 2,623,951,000 | 0.8% |
| 27 | Kentucky | 4,149,368,000 | 1.3% |
| 22 | Louisiana | 4,912,424,000 | 1.5% |
| 42 | Maine | 1,152,149,000 | 0.4% |
| 17 | Maryland | 6,392,264,000 | 2.0% |
| 13 | Massachusetts | 6,993,226,000 | 2.2% |
| 10 | Michigan | 9,439,101,000 | 2.9% |
| 23 | Minnesota | 4,896,523,000 | 1.5% |
| 29 | Mississippi | 3,135,297,000 | 1.0% |
| 19 | Missouri | 5,601,452,000 | 1.7% |
| 45 | Montana | 820,375,000 | 0.3% |
| 38 | Nebraska | 1,671,329,000 | 0.5% |
| 31 | Nevada | 2,977,230,000 | 0.9% |
| 39 | New Hampshire | 1,385,507,000 | 0.4% |
| 8 | New Jersey | 10,513,293,000 | 3.3% |
| 36 | New Mexico | 1,899,656,000 | 0.6% |
| 4 | New York | 22,683,218,000 | 7.0% |
| 11 | North Carolina | 8,975,090,000 | 2.8% |
| 49 | North Dakota | 624,362,000 | 0.2% |
| 7 | Ohio | 11,277,078,000 | 3.5% |
| 28 | Oklahoma | 3,476,301,000 | 1.1% |
| 30 | Oregon | 3,127,983,000 | 1.0% |
| 6 | Pennsylvania | 12,971,622,000 | 4.0% |
| 43 | Rhode Island | 1,106,239,000 | 0.3% |
| 25 | South Carolina | 4,292,094,000 | 1.3% |
| 46 | South Dakota | 775,476,000 | 0.2% |
| 15 | Tennessee | 6,611,272,000 | 2.0% |
| 2 | Texas | 28,522,439,000 | 8.8% |
| 35 | Utah | 2,599,157,000 | 0.8% |
| 50 | Vermont | 574,037,000 | 0.2% |
| 12 | Virginia | 8,352,177,000 | 2.6% |
| 14 | Washington | 6,842,995,000 | 2.1% |
| 37 | West Virginia | 1,712,175,000 | 0.5% |
| 20 | Wisconsin | 5,206,458,000 | 1.6% |
| 48 | Wyoming | 626,865,000 | 0.2% |

RANK ORDER

| RANK | STATE | REFUNDS | % of USA |
|------|-------|---------|----------|
| 1 | California | $37,102,177,000 | 11.5% |
| 2 | Texas | 28,522,439,000 | 8.8% |
| 3 | Florida | 22,760,604,000 | 7.1% |
| 4 | New York | 22,683,218,000 | 7.0% |
| 5 | Illinois | 14,713,626,000 | 4.6% |
| 6 | Pennsylvania | 12,971,622,000 | 4.0% |
| 7 | Ohio | 11,277,078,000 | 3.5% |
| 8 | New Jersey | 10,513,293,000 | 3.3% |
| 9 | Georgia | 10,472,192,000 | 3.2% |
| 10 | Michigan | 9,439,101,000 | 2.9% |
| 11 | North Carolina | 8,975,090,000 | 2.8% |
| 12 | Virginia | 8,352,177,000 | 2.6% |
| 13 | Massachusetts | 6,993,226,000 | 2.2% |
| 14 | Washington | 6,842,995,000 | 2.1% |
| 15 | Tennessee | 6,611,272,000 | 2.0% |
| 16 | Indiana | 6,568,931,000 | 2.0% |
| 17 | Maryland | 6,392,264,000 | 2.0% |
| 18 | Arizona | 5,784,097,000 | 1.8% |
| 19 | Missouri | 5,601,452,000 | 1.7% |
| 20 | Wisconsin | 5,206,458,000 | 1.6% |
| 21 | Alabama | 4,929,830,000 | 1.5% |
| 22 | Louisiana | 4,912,424,000 | 1.5% |
| 23 | Minnesota | 4,896,523,000 | 1.5% |
| 24 | Colorado | 4,886,442,000 | 1.5% |
| 25 | South Carolina | 4,292,094,000 | 1.3% |
| 26 | Connecticut | 4,190,561,000 | 1.3% |
| 27 | Kentucky | 4,149,368,000 | 1.3% |
| 28 | Oklahoma | 3,476,301,000 | 1.1% |
| 29 | Mississippi | 3,135,297,000 | 1.0% |
| 30 | Oregon | 3,127,983,000 | 1.0% |
| 31 | Nevada | 2,977,230,000 | 0.9% |
| 32 | Iowa | 2,763,798,000 | 0.9% |
| 33 | Arkansas | 2,680,057,000 | 0.8% |
| 34 | Kansas | 2,623,951,000 | 0.8% |
| 35 | Utah | 2,599,157,000 | 0.8% |
| 36 | New Mexico | 1,899,656,000 | 0.6% |
| 37 | West Virginia | 1,712,175,000 | 0.5% |
| 38 | Nebraska | 1,671,329,000 | 0.5% |
| 39 | New Hampshire | 1,385,507,000 | 0.4% |
| 40 | Hawaii | 1,326,139,000 | 0.4% |
| 41 | Idaho | 1,282,373,000 | 0.4% |
| 42 | Maine | 1,152,149,000 | 0.4% |
| 43 | Rhode Island | 1,106,239,000 | 0.3% |
| 44 | Delaware | 918,221,000 | 0.3% |
| 45 | Montana | 820,375,000 | 0.3% |
| 46 | South Dakota | 775,476,000 | 0.2% |
| 47 | Alaska | 765,027,000 | 0.2% |
| 48 | Wyoming | 626,865,000 | 0.2% |
| 49 | North Dakota | 624,362,000 | 0.2% |
| 50 | Vermont | 574,037,000 | 0.2% |
|  | District of Columbia | 726,932,000 | 0.2% |

Source: U.S. Department of the Treasury, Internal Revenue Service
    "Fiscal Year 2012 IRS Data Book" (http://www.irs.gov/uac/SOI-Tax-Stats-IRS-Data-Book)
*Total includes refunds to international sources and other miscellaneous refunds not shown separately.

# Average Value of Federal Individual Income Tax Refunds in 2012

## National Average = $2,674*

ALPHA ORDER

| RANK | STATE | AVERAGE REFUND |
|---|---|---|
| 8 | Alabama | $2,788 |
| 24 | Alaska | 2,554 |
| 23 | Arizona | 2,581 |
| 20 | Arkansas | 2,618 |
| 10 | California | 2,733 |
| 25 | Colorado | 2,553 |
| 3 | Connecticut | 2,925 |
| 28 | Delaware | 2,526 |
| 9 | Florida | 2,772 |
| 13 | Georgia | 2,728 |
| 37 | Hawaii | 2,469 |
| 42 | Idaho | 2,384 |
| 7 | Illinois | 2,838 |
| 27 | Indiana | 2,545 |
| 39 | Iowa | 2,421 |
| 35 | Kansas | 2,473 |
| 22 | Kentucky | 2,586 |
| 5 | Louisiana | 2,874 |
| 50 | Maine | 2,216 |
| 10 | Maryland | 2,733 |
| 16 | Massachusetts | 2,652 |
| 38 | Michigan | 2,454 |
| 45 | Minnesota | 2,365 |
| 6 | Mississippi | 2,867 |
| 34 | Missouri | 2,492 |
| 48 | Montana | 2,222 |
| 44 | Nebraska | 2,380 |
| 12 | Nevada | 2,730 |
| 36 | New Hampshire | 2,471 |
| 1 | New Jersey | 2,957 |
| 29 | New Mexico | 2,520 |
| 4 | New York | 2,919 |
| 26 | North Carolina | 2,549 |
| 43 | North Dakota | 2,381 |
| 39 | Ohio | 2,421 |
| 18 | Oklahoma | 2,638 |
| 47 | Oregon | 2,275 |
| 33 | Pennsylvania | 2,494 |
| 30 | Rhode Island | 2,515 |
| 32 | South Carolina | 2,500 |
| 41 | South Dakota | 2,385 |
| 15 | Tennessee | 2,654 |
| 2 | Texas | 2,955 |
| 17 | Utah | 2,649 |
| 49 | Vermont | 2,221 |
| 14 | Virginia | 2,656 |
| 21 | Washington | 2,597 |
| 31 | West Virginia | 2,506 |
| 46 | Wisconsin | 2,313 |
| 19 | Wyoming | 2,633 |

RANK ORDER

| RANK | STATE | AVERAGE REFUND |
|---|---|---|
| 1 | New Jersey | $2,957 |
| 2 | Texas | 2,955 |
| 3 | Connecticut | 2,925 |
| 4 | New York | 2,919 |
| 5 | Louisiana | 2,874 |
| 6 | Mississippi | 2,867 |
| 7 | Illinois | 2,838 |
| 8 | Alabama | 2,788 |
| 9 | Florida | 2,772 |
| 10 | California | 2,733 |
| 10 | Maryland | 2,733 |
| 12 | Nevada | 2,730 |
| 13 | Georgia | 2,728 |
| 14 | Virginia | 2,656 |
| 15 | Tennessee | 2,654 |
| 16 | Massachusetts | 2,652 |
| 17 | Utah | 2,649 |
| 18 | Oklahoma | 2,638 |
| 19 | Wyoming | 2,633 |
| 20 | Arkansas | 2,618 |
| 21 | Washington | 2,597 |
| 22 | Kentucky | 2,586 |
| 23 | Arizona | 2,581 |
| 24 | Alaska | 2,554 |
| 25 | Colorado | 2,553 |
| 26 | North Carolina | 2,549 |
| 27 | Indiana | 2,545 |
| 28 | Delaware | 2,526 |
| 29 | New Mexico | 2,520 |
| 30 | Rhode Island | 2,515 |
| 31 | West Virginia | 2,506 |
| 32 | South Carolina | 2,500 |
| 33 | Pennsylvania | 2,494 |
| 34 | Missouri | 2,492 |
| 35 | Kansas | 2,473 |
| 36 | New Hampshire | 2,471 |
| 37 | Hawaii | 2,469 |
| 38 | Michigan | 2,454 |
| 39 | Iowa | 2,421 |
| 39 | Ohio | 2,421 |
| 41 | South Dakota | 2,385 |
| 42 | Idaho | 2,384 |
| 43 | North Dakota | 2,381 |
| 44 | Nebraska | 2,380 |
| 45 | Minnesota | 2,365 |
| 46 | Wisconsin | 2,313 |
| 47 | Oregon | 2,275 |
| 48 | Montana | 2,222 |
| 49 | Vermont | 2,221 |
| 50 | Maine | 2,216 |
| | District of Columbia | 2,674 |

Source: CQ Press using data from U.S. Department of the Treasury, Internal Revenue Service
"Fiscal Year 2012 IRS Data Book" (http://www.irs.gov/uac/SOI-Tax-Stats-IRS-Data-Book)
*National average includes refunds to international sources and other miscellaneous refunds not shown separately.

# Value of Federal Business Income Tax Refunds in 2012

## National Total = $43,970,393,000*

ALPHA ORDER

| RANK | STATE | REFUNDS | % of USA |
|------|-------|---------|----------|
| 28 | Alabama | $321,437,000 | 0.7% |
| 48 | Alaska | 31,412,000 | 0.1% |
| 25 | Arizona | 406,589,000 | 0.9% |
| 32 | Arkansas | 214,902,000 | 0.5% |
| 3 | California | 4,124,217,000 | 9.4% |
| 21 | Colorado | 644,095,000 | 1.5% |
| 5 | Connecticut | 2,274,714,000 | 5.2% |
| 4 | Delaware | 2,788,966,000 | 6.3% |
| 18 | Florida | 773,984,000 | 1.8% |
| 12 | Georgia | 1,382,782,000 | 3.1% |
| 40 | Hawaii | 91,421,000 | 0.2% |
| 41 | Idaho | 90,762,000 | 0.2% |
| 6 | Illinois | 1,655,613,000 | 3.8% |
| 24 | Indiana | 441,851,000 | 1.0% |
| 34 | Iowa | 183,375,000 | 0.4% |
| 33 | Kansas | 189,154,000 | 0.4% |
| 31 | Kentucky | 220,675,000 | 0.5% |
| 29 | Louisiana | 302,873,000 | 0.7% |
| 35 | Maine | 179,652,000 | 0.4% |
| 19 | Maryland | 764,633,000 | 1.7% |
| 11 | Massachusetts | 1,482,065,000 | 3.4% |
| 15 | Michigan | 1,090,473,000 | 2.5% |
| 9 | Minnesota | 1,523,973,000 | 3.5% |
| 36 | Mississippi | 167,362,000 | 0.4% |
| 20 | Missouri | 709,395,000 | 1.6% |
| 49 | Montana | 30,137,000 | 0.1% |
| 37 | Nebraska | 161,251,000 | 0.4% |
| 39 | Nevada | 110,656,000 | 0.3% |
| 43 | New Hampshire | 79,270,000 | 0.2% |
| 10 | New Jersey | 1,519,885,000 | 3.5% |
| 46 | New Mexico | 52,379,000 | 0.1% |
| 1 | New York | 4,994,691,000 | 11.4% |
| 16 | North Carolina | 985,125,000 | 2.2% |
| 44 | North Dakota | 64,312,000 | 0.1% |
| 8 | Ohio | 1,560,233,000 | 3.5% |
| 17 | Oklahoma | 824,731,000 | 1.9% |
| 26 | Oregon | 406,585,000 | 0.9% |
| 7 | Pennsylvania | 1,591,304,000 | 3.6% |
| 27 | Rhode Island | 392,497,000 | 0.9% |
| 38 | South Carolina | 145,403,000 | 0.3% |
| 47 | South Dakota | 37,280,000 | 0.1% |
| 13 | Tennessee | 1,322,440,000 | 3.0% |
| 2 | Texas | 4,385,589,000 | 10.0% |
| 30 | Utah | 291,146,000 | 0.7% |
| 42 | Vermont | 90,535,000 | 0.2% |
| 14 | Virginia | 1,124,912,000 | 2.6% |
| 23 | Washington | 520,547,000 | 1.2% |
| 45 | West Virginia | 64,244,000 | 0.1% |
| 22 | Wisconsin | 632,066,000 | 1.4% |
| 50 | Wyoming | 22,176,000 | 0.1% |

RANK ORDER

| RANK | STATE | REFUNDS | % of USA |
|------|-------|---------|----------|
| 1 | New York | $4,994,691,000 | 11.4% |
| 2 | Texas | 4,385,589,000 | 10.0% |
| 3 | California | 4,124,217,000 | 9.4% |
| 4 | Delaware | 2,788,966,000 | 6.3% |
| 5 | Connecticut | 2,274,714,000 | 5.2% |
| 6 | Illinois | 1,655,613,000 | 3.8% |
| 7 | Pennsylvania | 1,591,304,000 | 3.6% |
| 8 | Ohio | 1,560,233,000 | 3.5% |
| 9 | Minnesota | 1,523,973,000 | 3.5% |
| 10 | New Jersey | 1,519,885,000 | 3.5% |
| 11 | Massachusetts | 1,482,065,000 | 3.4% |
| 12 | Georgia | 1,382,782,000 | 3.1% |
| 13 | Tennessee | 1,322,440,000 | 3.0% |
| 14 | Virginia | 1,124,912,000 | 2.6% |
| 15 | Michigan | 1,090,473,000 | 2.5% |
| 16 | North Carolina | 985,125,000 | 2.2% |
| 17 | Oklahoma | 824,731,000 | 1.9% |
| 18 | Florida | 773,984,000 | 1.8% |
| 19 | Maryland | 764,633,000 | 1.7% |
| 20 | Missouri | 709,395,000 | 1.6% |
| 21 | Colorado | 644,095,000 | 1.5% |
| 22 | Wisconsin | 632,066,000 | 1.4% |
| 23 | Washington | 520,547,000 | 1.2% |
| 24 | Indiana | 441,851,000 | 1.0% |
| 25 | Arizona | 406,589,000 | 0.9% |
| 26 | Oregon | 406,585,000 | 0.9% |
| 27 | Rhode Island | 392,497,000 | 0.9% |
| 28 | Alabama | 321,437,000 | 0.7% |
| 29 | Louisiana | 302,873,000 | 0.7% |
| 30 | Utah | 291,146,000 | 0.7% |
| 31 | Kentucky | 220,675,000 | 0.5% |
| 32 | Arkansas | 214,902,000 | 0.5% |
| 33 | Kansas | 189,154,000 | 0.4% |
| 34 | Iowa | 183,375,000 | 0.4% |
| 35 | Maine | 179,652,000 | 0.4% |
| 36 | Mississippi | 167,362,000 | 0.4% |
| 37 | Nebraska | 161,251,000 | 0.4% |
| 38 | South Carolina | 145,403,000 | 0.3% |
| 39 | Nevada | 110,656,000 | 0.3% |
| 40 | Hawaii | 91,421,000 | 0.2% |
| 41 | Idaho | 90,762,000 | 0.2% |
| 42 | Vermont | 90,535,000 | 0.2% |
| 43 | New Hampshire | 79,270,000 | 0.2% |
| 44 | North Dakota | 64,312,000 | 0.1% |
| 45 | West Virginia | 64,244,000 | 0.1% |
| 46 | New Mexico | 52,379,000 | 0.1% |
| 47 | South Dakota | 37,280,000 | 0.1% |
| 48 | Alaska | 31,412,000 | 0.1% |
| 49 | Montana | 30,137,000 | 0.1% |
| 50 | Wyoming | 22,176,000 | 0.1% |
|  | District of Columbia | 72,274,000 | 0.2% |

Source: U.S. Department of the Treasury, Internal Revenue Service
   "Fiscal Year 2012 IRS Data Book" (http://www.irs.gov/uac/SOI-Tax-Stats-IRS-Data-Book)
*Total includes refunds to international sources and other miscellaneous refunds not shown separately.   Includes taxes on corporation income (Form 1120 series) and unrelated business income from tax-exempt organizations.

# Average Value of Federal Business Income Tax Refunds in 2012

## National Average = $98,720*

ALPHA ORDER

| RANK | STATE | AVERAGE REFUND |
|---|---|---|
| 25 | Alabama | $69,111 |
| 42 | Alaska | 31,163 |
| 30 | Arizona | 62,475 |
| 29 | Arkansas | 63,244 |
| 23 | California | 71,213 |
| 18 | Colorado | 83,768 |
| 2 | Connecticut | 479,695 |
| 1 | Delaware | 1,536,620 |
| 44 | Florida | 27,230 |
| 11 | Georgia | 120,399 |
| 41 | Hawaii | 32,066 |
| 36 | Idaho | 41,749 |
| 17 | Illinois | 87,962 |
| 26 | Indiana | 64,826 |
| 45 | Iowa | 27,034 |
| 40 | Kansas | 33,850 |
| 31 | Kentucky | 52,818 |
| 33 | Louisiana | 49,240 |
| 20 | Maine | 78,076 |
| 15 | Maryland | 96,740 |
| 6 | Massachusetts | 165,835 |
| 22 | Michigan | 72,722 |
| 8 | Minnesota | 151,368 |
| 34 | Mississippi | 47,438 |
| 19 | Missouri | 79,743 |
| 50 | Montana | 9,023 |
| 35 | Nebraska | 43,370 |
| 46 | Nevada | 25,782 |
| 37 | New Hampshire | 37,216 |
| 10 | New Jersey | 122,938 |
| 47 | New Mexico | 22,176 |
| 5 | New York | 173,012 |
| 16 | North Carolina | 89,794 |
| 38 | North Dakota | 36,940 |
| 12 | Ohio | 105,958 |
| 7 | Oklahoma | 161,112 |
| 28 | Oregon | 63,618 |
| 14 | Pennsylvania | 100,158 |
| 3 | Rhode Island | 301,689 |
| 43 | South Carolina | 30,832 |
| 48 | South Dakota | 16,945 |
| 4 | Tennessee | 206,955 |
| 9 | Texas | 127,019 |
| 21 | Utah | 78,013 |
| 24 | Vermont | 70,730 |
| 13 | Virginia | 101,289 |
| 32 | Washington | 51,074 |
| 39 | West Virginia | 36,774 |
| 27 | Wisconsin | 64,300 |
| 49 | Wyoming | 13,825 |

RANK ORDER

| RANK | STATE | AVERAGE REFUND |
|---|---|---|
| 1 | Delaware | $1,536,620 |
| 2 | Connecticut | 479,695 |
| 3 | Rhode Island | 301,689 |
| 4 | Tennessee | 206,955 |
| 5 | New York | 173,012 |
| 6 | Massachusetts | 165,835 |
| 7 | Oklahoma | 161,112 |
| 8 | Minnesota | 151,368 |
| 9 | Texas | 127,019 |
| 10 | New Jersey | 122,938 |
| 11 | Georgia | 120,399 |
| 12 | Ohio | 105,958 |
| 13 | Virginia | 101,289 |
| 14 | Pennsylvania | 100,158 |
| 15 | Maryland | 96,740 |
| 16 | North Carolina | 89,794 |
| 17 | Illinois | 87,962 |
| 18 | Colorado | 83,768 |
| 19 | Missouri | 79,743 |
| 20 | Maine | 78,076 |
| 21 | Utah | 78,013 |
| 22 | Michigan | 72,722 |
| 23 | California | 71,213 |
| 24 | Vermont | 70,730 |
| 25 | Alabama | 69,111 |
| 26 | Indiana | 64,826 |
| 27 | Wisconsin | 64,300 |
| 28 | Oregon | 63,618 |
| 29 | Arkansas | 63,244 |
| 30 | Arizona | 62,475 |
| 31 | Kentucky | 52,818 |
| 32 | Washington | 51,074 |
| 33 | Louisiana | 49,240 |
| 34 | Mississippi | 47,438 |
| 35 | Nebraska | 43,370 |
| 36 | Idaho | 41,749 |
| 37 | New Hampshire | 37,216 |
| 38 | North Dakota | 36,940 |
| 39 | West Virginia | 36,774 |
| 40 | Kansas | 33,850 |
| 41 | Hawaii | 32,066 |
| 42 | Alaska | 31,163 |
| 43 | South Carolina | 30,832 |
| 44 | Florida | 27,230 |
| 45 | Iowa | 27,034 |
| 46 | Nevada | 25,782 |
| 47 | New Mexico | 22,176 |
| 48 | South Dakota | 16,945 |
| 49 | Wyoming | 13,825 |
| 50 | Montana | 9,023 |

District of Columbia    57,912

Source: CQ Press using data from U.S. Department of the Treasury, Internal Revenue Service
"Fiscal Year 2012 IRS Data Book" (http://www.irs.gov/uac/SOI-Tax-Stats-IRS-Data-Book)
*National average includes refunds to international sources and other miscellaneous refunds not shown separately.

# Per Capita Federal Economic Stimulus Funds as of 2013

## National Per Capita = $860*

| RANK | STATE | PER CAPITA |
|---|---|---|
| 37 | Alabama | $752 |
| 1 | Alaska | 3,151 |
| 9 | Arizona | 1,160 |
| 32 | Arkansas | 789 |
| 24 | California | 903 |
| 14 | Colorado | 1,069 |
| 44 | Connecticut | 706 |
| 18 | Delaware | 1,019 |
| 50 | Florida | 564 |
| 46 | Georgia | 701 |
| 17 | Hawaii | 1,034 |
| 15 | Idaho | 1,056 |
| 21 | Illinois | 932 |
| 47 | Indiana | 687 |
| 40 | Iowa | 734 |
| 30 | Kansas | 803 |
| 29 | Kentucky | 814 |
| 42 | Louisiana | 721 |
| 13 | Maine | 1,093 |
| 8 | Maryland | 1,184 |
| 12 | Massachusetts | 1,141 |
| 25 | Michigan | 875 |
| 38 | Minnesota | 740 |
| 23 | Mississippi | 909 |
| 28 | Missouri | 816 |
| 5 | Montana | 1,504 |
| 43 | Nebraska | 714 |
| 16 | Nevada | 1,040 |
| 39 | New Hampshire | 739 |
| 49 | New Jersey | 632 |
| 6 | New Mexico | 1,304 |
| 26 | New York | 874 |
| 35 | North Carolina | 774 |
| 4 | North Dakota | 1,519 |
| 33 | Ohio | 787 |
| 31 | Oklahoma | 794 |
| 27 | Oregon | 829 |
| 41 | Pennsylvania | 729 |
| 9 | Rhode Island | 1,160 |
| 19 | South Carolina | 976 |
| 3 | South Dakota | 1,599 |
| 22 | Tennessee | 916 |
| 48 | Texas | 651 |
| 36 | Utah | 762 |
| 2 | Vermont | 1,678 |
| 34 | Virginia | 780 |
| 7 | Washington | 1,206 |
| 20 | West Virginia | 973 |
| 45 | Wisconsin | 704 |
| 11 | Wyoming | 1,142 |

| RANK | STATE | PER CAPITA |
|---|---|---|
| 1 | Alaska | $3,151 |
| 2 | Vermont | 1,678 |
| 3 | South Dakota | 1,599 |
| 4 | North Dakota | 1,519 |
| 5 | Montana | 1,504 |
| 6 | New Mexico | 1,304 |
| 7 | Washington | 1,206 |
| 8 | Maryland | 1,184 |
| 9 | Arizona | 1,160 |
| 9 | Rhode Island | 1,160 |
| 11 | Wyoming | 1,142 |
| 12 | Massachusetts | 1,141 |
| 13 | Maine | 1,093 |
| 14 | Colorado | 1,069 |
| 15 | Idaho | 1,056 |
| 16 | Nevada | 1,040 |
| 17 | Hawaii | 1,034 |
| 18 | Delaware | 1,019 |
| 19 | South Carolina | 976 |
| 20 | West Virginia | 973 |
| 21 | Illinois | 932 |
| 22 | Tennessee | 916 |
| 23 | Mississippi | 909 |
| 24 | California | 903 |
| 25 | Michigan | 875 |
| 26 | New York | 874 |
| 27 | Oregon | 829 |
| 28 | Missouri | 816 |
| 29 | Kentucky | 814 |
| 30 | Kansas | 803 |
| 31 | Oklahoma | 794 |
| 32 | Arkansas | 789 |
| 33 | Ohio | 787 |
| 34 | Virginia | 780 |
| 35 | North Carolina | 774 |
| 36 | Utah | 762 |
| 37 | Alabama | 752 |
| 38 | Minnesota | 740 |
| 39 | New Hampshire | 739 |
| 40 | Iowa | 734 |
| 41 | Pennsylvania | 729 |
| 42 | Louisiana | 721 |
| 43 | Nebraska | 714 |
| 44 | Connecticut | 706 |
| 45 | Wisconsin | 704 |
| 46 | Georgia | 701 |
| 47 | Indiana | 687 |
| 48 | Texas | 651 |
| 49 | New Jersey | 632 |
| 50 | Florida | 564 |
| | District of Columbia | 9,257 |

Source: CQ Press using data from Recovery Accountability and Transparency Board
  "Funding Awarded by State "
    (http://www.recovery.gov/arra/Pages/TextView.aspx?data=recipientFundingAwardedByState)
*Funds awarded from February 17, 2009 to December 31, 2013.  Updated as of January 30, 2014.

# Federal Government Expenditures in 2012

## National Total = $3,160,300,000,000*

ALPHA ORDER

| RANK | STATE | EXPENDITURES | % of USA |
|------|-------|--------------|----------|
| 21 | Alabama | $45,500,000,000 | 1.4% |
| 46 | Alaska | 7,000,000,000 | 0.2% |
| 18 | Arizona | 51,000,000,000 | 1.6% |
| 34 | Arkansas | 19,600,000,000 | 0.6% |
| 3 | California | 258,900,000,000 | 8.2% |
| 24 | Colorado | 33,600,000,000 | 1.1% |
| 22 | Connecticut | 39,300,000,000 | 1.2% |
| 41 | Delaware | 10,900,000,000 | 0.3% |
| 1 | Florida | 528,400,000,000 | 16.7% |
| 13 | Georgia | 68,300,000,000 | 2.2% |
| 33 | Hawaii | 20,200,000,000 | 0.6% |
| 42 | Idaho | 10,400,000,000 | 0.3% |
| 12 | Illinois | 69,500,000,000 | 2.2% |
| 23 | Indiana | 34,100,000,000 | 1.1% |
| 32 | Iowa | 20,500,000,000 | 0.6% |
| 36 | Kansas | 15,500,000,000 | 0.5% |
| 24 | Kentucky | 33,600,000,000 | 1.1% |
| 5 | Louisiana | 116,000,000,000 | 3.7% |
| 40 | Maine | 11,000,000,000 | 0.3% |
| 14 | Maryland | 63,600,000,000 | 2.0% |
| 16 | Massachusetts | 57,800,000,000 | 1.8% |
| 15 | Michigan | 60,500,000,000 | 1.9% |
| 28 | Minnesota | 27,600,000,000 | 0.9% |
| 26 | Mississippi | 32,100,000,000 | 1.0% |
| 19 | Missouri | 48,100,000,000 | 1.5% |
| 47 | Montana | 6,700,000,000 | 0.2% |
| 39 | Nebraska | 11,300,000,000 | 0.4% |
| 35 | Nevada | 15,800,000,000 | 0.5% |
| 44 | New Hampshire | 9,400,000,000 | 0.3% |
| 8 | New Jersey | 94,200,000,000 | 3.0% |
| 31 | New Mexico | 21,600,000,000 | 0.7% |
| 4 | New York | 151,700,000,000 | 4.8% |
| 9 | North Carolina | 81,900,000,000 | 2.6% |
| 45 | North Dakota | 8,000,000,000 | 0.3% |
| 11 | Ohio | 70,900,000,000 | 2.2% |
| 30 | Oklahoma | 24,000,000,000 | 0.8% |
| 29 | Oregon | 26,800,000,000 | 0.8% |
| 7 | Pennsylvania | 95,300,000,000 | 3.0% |
| 43 | Rhode Island | 10,000,000,000 | 0.3% |
| 10 | South Carolina | 74,100,000,000 | 2.3% |
| 48 | South Dakota | 6,000,000,000 | 0.2% |
| 20 | Tennessee | 47,900,000,000 | 1.5% |
| 2 | Texas | 277,000,000,000 | 8.8% |
| 38 | Utah | 13,100,000,000 | 0.4% |
| 49 | Vermont | 5,000,000,000 | 0.2% |
| 6 | Virginia | 112,100,000,000 | 3.5% |
| 17 | Washington | 53,100,000,000 | 1.7% |
| 37 | West Virginia | 14,400,000,000 | 0.5% |
| 27 | Wisconsin | 28,400,000,000 | 0.9% |
| 50 | Wyoming | 3,500,000,000 | 0.1% |

RANK ORDER

| RANK | STATE | EXPENDITURES | % of USA |
|------|-------|--------------|----------|
| 1 | Florida | $528,400,000,000 | 16.7% |
| 2 | Texas | 277,000,000,000 | 8.8% |
| 3 | California | 258,900,000,000 | 8.2% |
| 4 | New York | 151,700,000,000 | 4.8% |
| 5 | Louisiana | 116,000,000,000 | 3.7% |
| 6 | Virginia | 112,100,000,000 | 3.5% |
| 7 | Pennsylvania | 95,300,000,000 | 3.0% |
| 8 | New Jersey | 94,200,000,000 | 3.0% |
| 9 | North Carolina | 81,900,000,000 | 2.6% |
| 10 | South Carolina | 74,100,000,000 | 2.3% |
| 11 | Ohio | 70,900,000,000 | 2.2% |
| 12 | Illinois | 69,500,000,000 | 2.2% |
| 13 | Georgia | 68,300,000,000 | 2.2% |
| 14 | Maryland | 63,600,000,000 | 2.0% |
| 15 | Michigan | 60,500,000,000 | 1.9% |
| 16 | Massachusetts | 57,800,000,000 | 1.8% |
| 17 | Washington | 53,100,000,000 | 1.7% |
| 18 | Arizona | 51,000,000,000 | 1.6% |
| 19 | Missouri | 48,100,000,000 | 1.5% |
| 20 | Tennessee | 47,900,000,000 | 1.5% |
| 21 | Alabama | 45,500,000,000 | 1.4% |
| 22 | Connecticut | 39,300,000,000 | 1.2% |
| 23 | Indiana | 34,100,000,000 | 1.1% |
| 24 | Colorado | 33,600,000,000 | 1.1% |
| 24 | Kentucky | 33,600,000,000 | 1.1% |
| 26 | Mississippi | 32,100,000,000 | 1.0% |
| 27 | Wisconsin | 28,400,000,000 | 0.9% |
| 28 | Minnesota | 27,600,000,000 | 0.9% |
| 29 | Oregon | 26,800,000,000 | 0.8% |
| 30 | Oklahoma | 24,000,000,000 | 0.8% |
| 31 | New Mexico | 21,600,000,000 | 0.7% |
| 32 | Iowa | 20,500,000,000 | 0.6% |
| 33 | Hawaii | 20,200,000,000 | 0.6% |
| 34 | Arkansas | 19,600,000,000 | 0.6% |
| 35 | Nevada | 15,800,000,000 | 0.5% |
| 36 | Kansas | 15,500,000,000 | 0.5% |
| 37 | West Virginia | 14,400,000,000 | 0.5% |
| 38 | Utah | 13,100,000,000 | 0.4% |
| 39 | Nebraska | 11,300,000,000 | 0.4% |
| 40 | Maine | 11,000,000,000 | 0.3% |
| 41 | Delaware | 10,900,000,000 | 0.3% |
| 42 | Idaho | 10,400,000,000 | 0.3% |
| 43 | Rhode Island | 10,000,000,000 | 0.3% |
| 44 | New Hampshire | 9,400,000,000 | 0.3% |
| 45 | North Dakota | 8,000,000,000 | 0.3% |
| 46 | Alaska | 7,000,000,000 | 0.2% |
| 47 | Montana | 6,700,000,000 | 0.2% |
| 48 | South Dakota | 6,000,000,000 | 0.2% |
| 49 | Vermont | 5,000,000,000 | 0.2% |
| 50 | Wyoming | 3,500,000,000 | 0.1% |
| | District of Columbia | 23,700,000,000 | 0.7% |

Source: U.S. Office of Management and Budget, USAspending.gov
"Prime Award Spending Data Summary" (http://www.usaspending.gov/explore, as of January 31, 2014)
*Total includes $28,775,900,000 in U.S. territories and $162,624,100,000 in expenditures not distributed by state. Expenditures allocated based on place of performance of a contract. Includes Contracts, Grants, Direct Payments, Insurance, and "Other." This source replaces a previous data series by the U.S. Census and definitions differ.

# Per Capita Federal Government Expenditures in 2012

## National Per Capita = $9,459*

| ALPHA ORDER | | | | RANK ORDER | | |
|---|---|---|---|---|---|---|
| RANK | STATE | PER CAPITA | | RANK | STATE | PER CAPITA |
| 16 | Alabama | $9,445 | | 1 | Florida | $27,349 |
| 14 | Alaska | 9,585 | | 2 | Louisiana | 25,206 |
| 22 | Arizona | 7,785 | | 3 | South Carolina | 15,688 |
| 36 | Arkansas | 6,644 | | 4 | Hawaii | 14,531 |
| 33 | California | 6,813 | | 5 | Virginia | 13,693 |
| 38 | Colorado | 6,475 | | 6 | Delaware | 11,886 |
| 8 | Connecticut | 10,942 | | 7 | North Dakota | 11,407 |
| 6 | Delaware | 11,886 | | 8 | Connecticut | 10,942 |
| 1 | Florida | 27,349 | | 9 | Maryland | 10,807 |
| 31 | Georgia | 6,888 | | 10 | Mississippi | 10,749 |
| 4 | Hawaii | 14,531 | | 11 | Texas | 10,629 |
| 37 | Idaho | 6,518 | | 12 | New Jersey | 10,623 |
| 45 | Illinois | 5,401 | | 13 | New Mexico | 10,367 |
| 47 | Indiana | 5,216 | | 14 | Alaska | 9,585 |
| 34 | Iowa | 6,667 | | 15 | Rhode Island | 9,521 |
| 46 | Kansas | 5,372 | | 16 | Alabama | 9,445 |
| 26 | Kentucky | 7,672 | | 17 | Massachusetts | 8,698 |
| 2 | Louisiana | 25,206 | | 18 | North Carolina | 8,401 |
| 19 | Maine | 8,280 | | 19 | Maine | 8,280 |
| 9 | Maryland | 10,807 | | 20 | Vermont | 7,988 |
| 17 | Massachusetts | 8,698 | | 21 | Missouri | 7,984 |
| 41 | Michigan | 6,122 | | 22 | Arizona | 7,785 |
| 48 | Minnesota | 5,130 | | 23 | West Virginia | 7,756 |
| 10 | Mississippi | 10,749 | | 24 | New York | 7,749 |
| 21 | Missouri | 7,984 | | 25 | Washington | 7,701 |
| 35 | Montana | 6,663 | | 26 | Kentucky | 7,672 |
| 42 | Nebraska | 6,090 | | 27 | Pennsylvania | 7,466 |
| 44 | Nevada | 5,736 | | 28 | Tennessee | 7,421 |
| 30 | New Hampshire | 7,112 | | 29 | South Dakota | 7,194 |
| 12 | New Jersey | 10,623 | | 30 | New Hampshire | 7,112 |
| 13 | New Mexico | 10,367 | | 31 | Georgia | 6,888 |
| 24 | New York | 7,749 | | 32 | Oregon | 6,872 |
| 18 | North Carolina | 8,401 | | 33 | California | 6,813 |
| 7 | North Dakota | 11,407 | | 34 | Iowa | 6,667 |
| 40 | Ohio | 6,137 | | 35 | Montana | 6,663 |
| 39 | Oklahoma | 6,290 | | 36 | Arkansas | 6,644 |
| 32 | Oregon | 6,872 | | 37 | Idaho | 6,518 |
| 27 | Pennsylvania | 7,466 | | 38 | Colorado | 6,475 |
| 15 | Rhode Island | 9,521 | | 39 | Oklahoma | 6,290 |
| 3 | South Carolina | 15,688 | | 40 | Ohio | 6,137 |
| 29 | South Dakota | 7,194 | | 41 | Michigan | 6,122 |
| 28 | Tennessee | 7,421 | | 42 | Nebraska | 6,090 |
| 11 | Texas | 10,629 | | 43 | Wyoming | 6,070 |
| 50 | Utah | 4,589 | | 44 | Nevada | 5,736 |
| 20 | Vermont | 7,988 | | 45 | Illinois | 5,401 |
| 5 | Virginia | 13,693 | | 46 | Kansas | 5,372 |
| 25 | Washington | 7,701 | | 47 | Indiana | 5,216 |
| 23 | West Virginia | 7,756 | | 48 | Minnesota | 5,130 |
| 49 | Wisconsin | 4,961 | | 49 | Wisconsin | 4,961 |
| 43 | Wyoming | 6,070 | | 50 | Utah | 4,589 |
| | | | | | District of Columbia | 37,416 |

Source: CQ Press using data from U.S. Office of Management and Budget, USAspending.gov
"Prime Award Spending Data Summary" (http://www.usaspending.gov/explore, as of January 31, 2014)
*National per capita excludes expenditures and population for territories and undistributed amounts. Expenditures allocated based on place of performance of a contract. Includes Contracts, Grants, Direct Payments, Insurance, and "Other." This source replaces a previous data series by the U.S. Census and definitions differ.

# Federal Government Grants in 2012

## National Total = $539,500,000,000*

ALPHA ORDER

| RANK | STATE | EXPENDITURES | % of USA |
|------|-------|-------------|----------|
| 21 | Alabama | $7,100,000,000 | 1.3% |
| 36 | Alaska | 2,300,000,000 | 0.4% |
| 14 | Arizona | 9,500,000,000 | 1.8% |
| 28 | Arkansas | 4,900,000,000 | 0.9% |
| 1 | California | 51,500,000,000 | 9.5% |
| 26 | Colorado | 5,400,000,000 | 1.0% |
| 23 | Connecticut | 6,300,000,000 | 1.2% |
| 47 | Delaware | 1,500,000,000 | 0.3% |
| 6 | Florida | 18,200,000,000 | 3.4% |
| 11 | Georgia | 11,400,000,000 | 2.1% |
| 42 | Hawaii | 1,700,000,000 | 0.3% |
| 42 | Idaho | 1,700,000,000 | 0.3% |
| 9 | Illinois | 14,000,000,000 | 2.6% |
| 32 | Indiana | 3,800,000,000 | 0.7% |
| 30 | Iowa | 4,400,000,000 | 0.8% |
| 36 | Kansas | 2,300,000,000 | 0.4% |
| 18 | Kentucky | 8,100,000,000 | 1.5% |
| 16 | Louisiana | 9,000,000,000 | 1.7% |
| 35 | Maine | 2,600,000,000 | 0.5% |
| 19 | Maryland | 8,000,000,000 | 1.5% |
| 10 | Massachusetts | 12,300,000,000 | 2.3% |
| 8 | Michigan | 14,900,000,000 | 2.8% |
| 24 | Minnesota | 5,900,000,000 | 1.1% |
| 40 | Mississippi | 2,100,000,000 | 0.4% |
| 16 | Missouri | 9,000,000,000 | 1.7% |
| 42 | Montana | 1,700,000,000 | 0.3% |
| 39 | Nebraska | 2,200,000,000 | 0.4% |
| 36 | Nevada | 2,300,000,000 | 0.4% |
| 48 | New Hampshire | 1,300,000,000 | 0.2% |
| 13 | New Jersey | 10,800,000,000 | 2.0% |
| 27 | New Mexico | 5,000,000,000 | 0.9% |
| 2 | New York | 42,700,000,000 | 7.9% |
| 7 | North Carolina | 15,700,000,000 | 2.9% |
| 45 | North Dakota | 1,600,000,000 | 0.3% |
| 4 | Ohio | 20,000,000,000 | 3.7% |
| 25 | Oklahoma | 5,500,000,000 | 1.0% |
| 29 | Oregon | 4,600,000,000 | 0.9% |
| 5 | Pennsylvania | 19,900,000,000 | 3.7% |
| 40 | Rhode Island | 2,100,000,000 | 0.4% |
| 22 | South Carolina | 6,800,000,000 | 1.3% |
| 48 | South Dakota | 1,300,000,000 | 0.2% |
| 12 | Tennessee | 11,200,000,000 | 2.1% |
| 3 | Texas | 31,000,000,000 | 5.7% |
| 34 | Utah | 2,900,000,000 | 0.5% |
| 45 | Vermont | 1,600,000,000 | 0.3% |
| 20 | Virginia | 7,600,000,000 | 1.4% |
| 15 | Washington | 9,200,000,000 | 1.7% |
| 33 | West Virginia | 3,100,000,000 | 0.6% |
| 31 | Wisconsin | 4,200,000,000 | 0.8% |
| 50 | Wyoming | 964,200,000 | 0.2% |

RANK ORDER

| RANK | STATE | EXPENDITURES | % of USA |
|------|-------|-------------|----------|
| 1 | California | $51,500,000,000 | 9.5% |
| 2 | New York | 42,700,000,000 | 7.9% |
| 3 | Texas | 31,000,000,000 | 5.7% |
| 4 | Ohio | 20,000,000,000 | 3.7% |
| 5 | Pennsylvania | 19,900,000,000 | 3.7% |
| 6 | Florida | 18,200,000,000 | 3.4% |
| 7 | North Carolina | 15,700,000,000 | 2.9% |
| 8 | Michigan | 14,900,000,000 | 2.8% |
| 9 | Illinois | 14,000,000,000 | 2.6% |
| 10 | Massachusetts | 12,300,000,000 | 2.3% |
| 11 | Georgia | 11,400,000,000 | 2.1% |
| 12 | Tennessee | 11,200,000,000 | 2.1% |
| 13 | New Jersey | 10,800,000,000 | 2.0% |
| 14 | Arizona | 9,500,000,000 | 1.8% |
| 15 | Washington | 9,200,000,000 | 1.7% |
| 16 | Louisiana | 9,000,000,000 | 1.7% |
| 16 | Missouri | 9,000,000,000 | 1.7% |
| 18 | Kentucky | 8,100,000,000 | 1.5% |
| 19 | Maryland | 8,000,000,000 | 1.5% |
| 20 | Virginia | 7,600,000,000 | 1.4% |
| 21 | Alabama | 7,100,000,000 | 1.3% |
| 22 | South Carolina | 6,800,000,000 | 1.3% |
| 23 | Connecticut | 6,300,000,000 | 1.2% |
| 24 | Minnesota | 5,900,000,000 | 1.1% |
| 25 | Oklahoma | 5,500,000,000 | 1.0% |
| 26 | Colorado | 5,400,000,000 | 1.0% |
| 27 | New Mexico | 5,000,000,000 | 0.9% |
| 28 | Arkansas | 4,900,000,000 | 0.9% |
| 29 | Oregon | 4,600,000,000 | 0.9% |
| 30 | Iowa | 4,400,000,000 | 0.8% |
| 31 | Wisconsin | 4,200,000,000 | 0.8% |
| 32 | Indiana | 3,800,000,000 | 0.7% |
| 33 | West Virginia | 3,100,000,000 | 0.6% |
| 34 | Utah | 2,900,000,000 | 0.5% |
| 35 | Maine | 2,600,000,000 | 0.5% |
| 36 | Alaska | 2,300,000,000 | 0.4% |
| 36 | Kansas | 2,300,000,000 | 0.4% |
| 36 | Nevada | 2,300,000,000 | 0.4% |
| 39 | Nebraska | 2,200,000,000 | 0.4% |
| 40 | Mississippi | 2,100,000,000 | 0.4% |
| 40 | Rhode Island | 2,100,000,000 | 0.4% |
| 42 | Hawaii | 1,700,000,000 | 0.3% |
| 42 | Idaho | 1,700,000,000 | 0.3% |
| 42 | Montana | 1,700,000,000 | 0.3% |
| 45 | North Dakota | 1,600,000,000 | 0.3% |
| 45 | Vermont | 1,600,000,000 | 0.3% |
| 47 | Delaware | 1,500,000,000 | 0.3% |
| 48 | New Hampshire | 1,300,000,000 | 0.2% |
| 48 | South Dakota | 1,300,000,000 | 0.2% |
| 50 | Wyoming | 964,200,000 | 0.2% |
| | District of Columbia | 3,200,000,000 | 0.6% |

Source: U.S. Office of Management and Budget, USAspending.gov
   "Prime Award Spending Data Summary" (http://www.usaspending.gov/explore, as of January 31, 2014)
*Total includes $6,937,500,000 in U.S. territories and $96,198,300,000 in expenditures not distributed by state. Expenditures allocated based on place of performance of a contract. Includes funds awarded to a non-federal entity for a defined public or private purpose in which services are not rendered to the federal government. This source replaces a previous data series by the U.S. Census and definitions differ.

# Per Capita Expenditures for Federal Government Grants in 2012

## National Per Capita = $1,390*

ALPHA ORDER

| RANK | STATE | PER CAPITA | | RANK | STATE | PER CAPITA |
|---|---|---|---|---|---|---|
| 24 | Alabama | $1,474 | | 1 | Alaska | $3,149 |
| 1 | Alaska | 3,149 | | 2 | Vermont | 2,556 |
| 25 | Arizona | 1,450 | | 3 | New Mexico | 2,400 |
| 17 | Arkansas | 1,661 | | 4 | North Dakota | 2,281 |
| 30 | California | 1,355 | | 5 | New York | 2,181 |
| 41 | Colorado | 1,041 | | 6 | Rhode Island | 1,999 |
| 11 | Connecticut | 1,754 | | 7 | Maine | 1,957 |
| 18 | Delaware | 1,636 | | 8 | Louisiana | 1,956 |
| 44 | Florida | 942 | | 9 | Massachusetts | 1,851 |
| 37 | Georgia | 1,150 | | 10 | Kentucky | 1,849 |
| 32 | Hawaii | 1,223 | | 11 | Connecticut | 1,754 |
| 40 | Idaho | 1,065 | | 12 | Tennessee | 1,735 |
| 39 | Illinois | 1,088 | | 13 | Ohio | 1,731 |
| 50 | Indiana | 581 | | 14 | Montana | 1,691 |
| 28 | Iowa | 1,431 | | 15 | Wyoming | 1,672 |
| 47 | Kansas | 797 | | 16 | West Virginia | 1,670 |
| 10 | Kentucky | 1,849 | | 17 | Arkansas | 1,661 |
| 8 | Louisiana | 1,956 | | 18 | Delaware | 1,636 |
| 7 | Maine | 1,957 | | 19 | North Carolina | 1,611 |
| 29 | Maryland | 1,359 | | 20 | Pennsylvania | 1,559 |
| 9 | Massachusetts | 1,851 | | 20 | South Dakota | 1,559 |
| 22 | Michigan | 1,508 | | 22 | Michigan | 1,508 |
| 38 | Minnesota | 1,097 | | 23 | Missouri | 1,494 |
| 49 | Mississippi | 703 | | 24 | Alabama | 1,474 |
| 23 | Missouri | 1,494 | | 25 | Arizona | 1,450 |
| 14 | Montana | 1,691 | | 26 | Oklahoma | 1,441 |
| 35 | Nebraska | 1,186 | | 27 | South Carolina | 1,440 |
| 46 | Nevada | 835 | | 28 | Iowa | 1,431 |
| 43 | New Hampshire | 984 | | 29 | Maryland | 1,359 |
| 33 | New Jersey | 1,218 | | 30 | California | 1,355 |
| 3 | New Mexico | 2,400 | | 31 | Washington | 1,334 |
| 5 | New York | 2,181 | | 32 | Hawaii | 1,223 |
| 19 | North Carolina | 1,611 | | 33 | New Jersey | 1,218 |
| 4 | North Dakota | 2,281 | | 34 | Texas | 1,190 |
| 13 | Ohio | 1,731 | | 35 | Nebraska | 1,186 |
| 26 | Oklahoma | 1,441 | | 36 | Oregon | 1,180 |
| 36 | Oregon | 1,180 | | 37 | Georgia | 1,150 |
| 20 | Pennsylvania | 1,559 | | 38 | Minnesota | 1,097 |
| 6 | Rhode Island | 1,999 | | 39 | Illinois | 1,088 |
| 27 | South Carolina | 1,440 | | 40 | Idaho | 1,065 |
| 20 | South Dakota | 1,559 | | 41 | Colorado | 1,041 |
| 12 | Tennessee | 1,735 | | 42 | Utah | 1,016 |
| 34 | Texas | 1,190 | | 43 | New Hampshire | 984 |
| 42 | Utah | 1,016 | | 44 | Florida | 942 |
| 2 | Vermont | 2,556 | | 45 | Virginia | 928 |
| 45 | Virginia | 928 | | 46 | Nevada | 835 |
| 31 | Washington | 1,334 | | 47 | Kansas | 797 |
| 16 | West Virginia | 1,670 | | 48 | Wisconsin | 734 |
| 48 | Wisconsin | 734 | | 49 | Mississippi | 703 |
| 15 | Wyoming | 1,672 | | 50 | Indiana | 581 |

RANK ORDER

District of Columbia     5,052

Source: CQ Press using data from U.S. Office of Management and Budget, USAspending.gov
"Prime Award Spending Data Summary" (http://www.usaspending.gov/explore, as of January 31, 2014)
*National per capita excludes expenditures and population for territories and undistributed amounts. Expenditures allocated based on place of performance of a contract. Includes funds awarded to a non-federal entity for a defined public or private purpose in which services are not rendered to the federal government. This source replaces a previous data series by the U.S. Census and definitions differ.

# Federal Government Procurement Contract Awards in 2012

## National Total = $517,500,000,000*

ALPHA ORDER

| RANK | STATE | EXPENDITURES | % of USA |
|------|-------|--------------|----------|
| 14 | Alabama | $10,700,000,000 | 2.1% |
| 34 | Alaska | 2,400,000,000 | 0.5% |
| 9 | Arizona | 14,200,000,000 | 2.7% |
| 41 | Arkansas | 1,100,000,000 | 0.2% |
| 2 | California | 51,900,000,000 | 10.0% |
| 12 | Colorado | 11,100,000,000 | 2.1% |
| 11 | Connecticut | 13,000,000,000 | 2.5% |
| 48 | Delaware | 527,700,000 | 0.1% |
| 6 | Florida | 15,400,000,000 | 3.0% |
| 17 | Georgia | 7,900,000,000 | 1.5% |
| 32 | Hawaii | 2,800,000,000 | 0.5% |
| 34 | Idaho | 2,400,000,000 | 0.5% |
| 13 | Illinois | 10,900,000,000 | 2.1% |
| 27 | Indiana | 3,700,000,000 | 0.7% |
| 38 | Iowa | 1,700,000,000 | 0.3% |
| 36 | Kansas | 2,100,000,000 | 0.4% |
| 22 | Kentucky | 6,500,000,000 | 1.3% |
| 26 | Louisiana | 4,300,000,000 | 0.8% |
| 38 | Maine | 1,700,000,000 | 0.3% |
| 4 | Maryland | 27,300,000,000 | 5.3% |
| 7 | Massachusetts | 15,100,000,000 | 2.9% |
| 23 | Michigan | 6,300,000,000 | 1.2% |
| 33 | Minnesota | 2,700,000,000 | 0.5% |
| 21 | Mississippi | 6,600,000,000 | 1.3% |
| 7 | Missouri | 15,100,000,000 | 2.9% |
| 47 | Montana | 573,200,000 | 0.1% |
| 41 | Nebraska | 1,100,000,000 | 0.2% |
| 31 | Nevada | 2,900,000,000 | 0.6% |
| 37 | New Hampshire | 1,900,000,000 | 0.4% |
| 20 | New Jersey | 6,900,000,000 | 1.3% |
| 19 | New Mexico | 7,200,000,000 | 1.4% |
| 15 | New York | 10,500,000,000 | 2.0% |
| 25 | North Carolina | 5,400,000,000 | 1.0% |
| 44 | North Dakota | 866,300,000 | 0.2% |
| 18 | Ohio | 7,400,000,000 | 1.4% |
| 30 | Oklahoma | 3,100,000,000 | 0.6% |
| 40 | Oregon | 1,500,000,000 | 0.3% |
| 5 | Pennsylvania | 18,800,000,000 | 3.6% |
| 45 | Rhode Island | 713,400,000 | 0.1% |
| 23 | South Carolina | 6,300,000,000 | 1.2% |
| 46 | South Dakota | 642,300,000 | 0.1% |
| 16 | Tennessee | 8,600,000,000 | 1.7% |
| 3 | Texas | 38,200,000,000 | 7.4% |
| 28 | Utah | 3,400,000,000 | 0.7% |
| 49 | Vermont | 408,500,000 | 0.1% |
| 1 | Virginia | 55,200,000,000 | 10.7% |
| 10 | Washington | 13,200,000,000 | 2.6% |
| 41 | West Virginia | 1,100,000,000 | 0.2% |
| 29 | Wisconsin | 3,200,000,000 | 0.6% |
| 50 | Wyoming | 348,000,000 | 0.1% |

RANK ORDER

| RANK | STATE | EXPENDITURES | % of USA |
|------|-------|--------------|----------|
| 1 | Virginia | $55,200,000,000 | 10.7% |
| 2 | California | 51,900,000,000 | 10.0% |
| 3 | Texas | 38,200,000,000 | 7.4% |
| 4 | Maryland | 27,300,000,000 | 5.3% |
| 5 | Pennsylvania | 18,800,000,000 | 3.6% |
| 6 | Florida | 15,400,000,000 | 3.0% |
| 7 | Massachusetts | 15,100,000,000 | 2.9% |
| 7 | Missouri | 15,100,000,000 | 2.9% |
| 9 | Arizona | 14,200,000,000 | 2.7% |
| 10 | Washington | 13,200,000,000 | 2.6% |
| 11 | Connecticut | 13,000,000,000 | 2.5% |
| 12 | Colorado | 11,100,000,000 | 2.1% |
| 13 | Illinois | 10,900,000,000 | 2.1% |
| 14 | Alabama | 10,700,000,000 | 2.1% |
| 15 | New York | 10,500,000,000 | 2.0% |
| 16 | Tennessee | 8,600,000,000 | 1.7% |
| 17 | Georgia | 7,900,000,000 | 1.5% |
| 18 | Ohio | 7,400,000,000 | 1.4% |
| 19 | New Mexico | 7,200,000,000 | 1.4% |
| 20 | New Jersey | 6,900,000,000 | 1.3% |
| 21 | Mississippi | 6,600,000,000 | 1.3% |
| 22 | Kentucky | 6,500,000,000 | 1.3% |
| 23 | Michigan | 6,300,000,000 | 1.2% |
| 23 | South Carolina | 6,300,000,000 | 1.2% |
| 25 | North Carolina | 5,400,000,000 | 1.0% |
| 26 | Louisiana | 4,300,000,000 | 0.8% |
| 27 | Indiana | 3,700,000,000 | 0.7% |
| 28 | Utah | 3,400,000,000 | 0.7% |
| 29 | Wisconsin | 3,200,000,000 | 0.6% |
| 30 | Oklahoma | 3,100,000,000 | 0.6% |
| 31 | Nevada | 2,900,000,000 | 0.6% |
| 32 | Hawaii | 2,800,000,000 | 0.5% |
| 33 | Minnesota | 2,700,000,000 | 0.5% |
| 34 | Alaska | 2,400,000,000 | 0.5% |
| 34 | Idaho | 2,400,000,000 | 0.5% |
| 36 | Kansas | 2,100,000,000 | 0.4% |
| 37 | New Hampshire | 1,900,000,000 | 0.4% |
| 38 | Iowa | 1,700,000,000 | 0.3% |
| 38 | Maine | 1,700,000,000 | 0.3% |
| 40 | Oregon | 1,500,000,000 | 0.3% |
| 41 | Arkansas | 1,100,000,000 | 0.2% |
| 41 | Nebraska | 1,100,000,000 | 0.2% |
| 41 | West Virginia | 1,100,000,000 | 0.2% |
| 44 | North Dakota | 866,300,000 | 0.2% |
| 45 | Rhode Island | 713,400,000 | 0.1% |
| 46 | South Dakota | 642,300,000 | 0.1% |
| 47 | Montana | 573,200,000 | 0.1% |
| 48 | Delaware | 527,700,000 | 0.1% |
| 49 | Vermont | 408,500,000 | 0.1% |
| 50 | Wyoming | 348,000,000 | 0.1% |
| | District of Columbia | 18,700,000,000 | 3.6% |

Source: U.S. Office of Management and Budget, USAspending.gov
"Prime Award Spending Data Summary" (http://www.usaspending.gov/explore, as of January 31, 2014)
*Total includes $1,318,500,000 in U.S. territories and $60,602,100,000 in expenditures not distributed by state. Expenditures allocated based on place of performance of a contract. Does not include grants, co-operative agreements, or contracts under grants. This source replaces a previous data series by the U.S. Census and definitions differ.

# Per Capita Expenditures for Federal Government Procurement Contract Awards in 2012
## National Per Capita = $1,451*

ALPHA ORDER

| RANK | STATE | PER CAPITA |
|---|---|---|
| 8 | Alabama | $2,221 |
| 5 | Alaska | 3,286 |
| 10 | Arizona | 2,168 |
| 50 | Arkansas | 373 |
| 19 | California | 1,366 |
| 11 | Colorado | 2,139 |
| 3 | Connecticut | 3,619 |
| 41 | Delaware | 575 |
| 29 | Florida | 797 |
| 29 | Georgia | 797 |
| 12 | Hawaii | 2,014 |
| 14 | Idaho | 1,504 |
| 27 | Illinois | 847 |
| 43 | Indiana | 566 |
| 46 | Iowa | 553 |
| 33 | Kansas | 728 |
| 15 | Kentucky | 1,484 |
| 26 | Louisiana | 934 |
| 22 | Maine | 1,280 |
| 2 | Maryland | 4,639 |
| 7 | Massachusetts | 2,272 |
| 37 | Michigan | 637 |
| 48 | Minnesota | 502 |
| 9 | Mississippi | 2,210 |
| 6 | Missouri | 2,506 |
| 42 | Montana | 570 |
| 39 | Nebraska | 593 |
| 25 | Nevada | 1,053 |
| 18 | New Hampshire | 1,438 |
| 31 | New Jersey | 778 |
| 4 | New Mexico | 3,456 |
| 47 | New York | 536 |
| 45 | North Carolina | 554 |
| 23 | North Dakota | 1,235 |
| 36 | Ohio | 641 |
| 28 | Oklahoma | 812 |
| 49 | Oregon | 385 |
| 16 | Pennsylvania | 1,473 |
| 34 | Rhode Island | 679 |
| 20 | South Carolina | 1,334 |
| 32 | South Dakota | 770 |
| 21 | Tennessee | 1,332 |
| 17 | Texas | 1,466 |
| 24 | Utah | 1,191 |
| 35 | Vermont | 653 |
| 1 | Virginia | 6,743 |
| 13 | Washington | 1,914 |
| 40 | West Virginia | 592 |
| 44 | Wisconsin | 559 |
| 38 | Wyoming | 604 |

RANK ORDER

| RANK | STATE | PER CAPITA |
|---|---|---|
| 1 | Virginia | $6,743 |
| 2 | Maryland | 4,639 |
| 3 | Connecticut | 3,619 |
| 4 | New Mexico | 3,456 |
| 5 | Alaska | 3,286 |
| 6 | Missouri | 2,506 |
| 7 | Massachusetts | 2,272 |
| 8 | Alabama | 2,221 |
| 9 | Mississippi | 2,210 |
| 10 | Arizona | 2,168 |
| 11 | Colorado | 2,139 |
| 12 | Hawaii | 2,014 |
| 13 | Washington | 1,914 |
| 14 | Idaho | 1,504 |
| 15 | Kentucky | 1,484 |
| 16 | Pennsylvania | 1,473 |
| 17 | Texas | 1,466 |
| 18 | New Hampshire | 1,438 |
| 19 | California | 1,366 |
| 20 | South Carolina | 1,334 |
| 21 | Tennessee | 1,332 |
| 22 | Maine | 1,280 |
| 23 | North Dakota | 1,235 |
| 24 | Utah | 1,191 |
| 25 | Nevada | 1,053 |
| 26 | Louisiana | 934 |
| 27 | Illinois | 847 |
| 28 | Oklahoma | 812 |
| 29 | Florida | 797 |
| 29 | Georgia | 797 |
| 31 | New Jersey | 778 |
| 32 | South Dakota | 770 |
| 33 | Kansas | 728 |
| 34 | Rhode Island | 679 |
| 35 | Vermont | 653 |
| 36 | Ohio | 641 |
| 37 | Michigan | 637 |
| 38 | Wyoming | 604 |
| 39 | Nebraska | 593 |
| 40 | West Virginia | 592 |
| 41 | Delaware | 575 |
| 42 | Montana | 570 |
| 43 | Indiana | 566 |
| 44 | Wisconsin | 559 |
| 45 | North Carolina | 554 |
| 46 | Iowa | 553 |
| 47 | New York | 536 |
| 48 | Minnesota | 502 |
| 49 | Oregon | 385 |
| 50 | Arkansas | 373 |

District of Columbia 29,522

Source: CQ Press using data from U.S. Office of Management and Budget, USAspending.gov
"Prime Award Spending Data Summary" (http://www.usaspending.gov/explore, as of January 31, 2014)
*National per capita excludes expenditures and population for territories and undistributed amounts. Expenditures allocated based on place of performance of a contract. Does not include grants, co-operative agreements, or contracts under grants. This source replaces a previous data series by the U.S. Census and definitions differ.

# Federal Government Direct Payments to Individuals in 2012

## National Total = $959,600,000,000*

ALPHA ORDER

| RANK | STATE | EXPENDITURES | % of USA |
|---|---|---|---|
| 20 | Alabama | $17,800,000,000 | 1.9% |
| 50 | Alaska | 1,600,000,000 | 0.2% |
| 15 | Arizona | 20,600,000,000 | 2.1% |
| 30 | Arkansas | 10,900,000,000 | 1.1% |
| 1 | California | 90,100,000,000 | 9.4% |
| 26 | Colorado | 13,000,000,000 | 1.4% |
| 29 | Connecticut | 11,000,000,000 | 1.1% |
| 45 | Delaware | 3,100,000,000 | 0.3% |
| 2 | Florida | 66,900,000,000 | 7.0% |
| 10 | Georgia | 27,300,000,000 | 2.8% |
| 42 | Hawaii | 4,000,000,000 | 0.4% |
| 40 | Idaho | 4,800,000,000 | 0.5% |
| 7 | Illinois | 36,200,000,000 | 3.8% |
| 14 | Indiana | 21,300,000,000 | 2.2% |
| 31 | Iowa | 10,800,000,000 | 1.1% |
| 33 | Kansas | 9,100,000,000 | 0.9% |
| 23 | Kentucky | 15,500,000,000 | 1.6% |
| 25 | Louisiana | 13,400,000,000 | 1.4% |
| 39 | Maine | 5,000,000,000 | 0.5% |
| 24 | Maryland | 15,400,000,000 | 1.6% |
| 18 | Massachusetts | 19,700,000,000 | 2.1% |
| 8 | Michigan | 35,200,000,000 | 3.7% |
| 22 | Minnesota | 16,100,000,000 | 1.7% |
| 32 | Mississippi | 10,100,000,000 | 1.1% |
| 17 | Missouri | 20,100,000,000 | 2.1% |
| 44 | Montana | 3,500,000,000 | 0.4% |
| 37 | Nebraska | 5,900,000,000 | 0.6% |
| 35 | Nevada | 7,300,000,000 | 0.8% |
| 41 | New Hampshire | 4,400,000,000 | 0.5% |
| 11 | New Jersey | 26,500,000,000 | 2.8% |
| 36 | New Mexico | 6,400,000,000 | 0.7% |
| 4 | New York | 58,700,000,000 | 6.1% |
| 9 | North Carolina | 31,400,000,000 | 3.3% |
| 47 | North Dakota | 2,200,000,000 | 0.2% |
| 6 | Ohio | 36,500,000,000 | 3.8% |
| 28 | Oklahoma | 12,500,000,000 | 1.3% |
| 26 | Oregon | 13,000,000,000 | 1.4% |
| 5 | Pennsylvania | 44,300,000,000 | 4.6% |
| 43 | Rhode Island | 3,600,000,000 | 0.4% |
| 21 | South Carolina | 16,600,000,000 | 1.7% |
| 46 | South Dakota | 2,800,000,000 | 0.3% |
| 13 | Tennessee | 21,700,000,000 | 2.3% |
| 3 | Texas | 62,100,000,000 | 6.5% |
| 37 | Utah | 5,900,000,000 | 0.6% |
| 47 | Vermont | 2,200,000,000 | 0.2% |
| 12 | Virginia | 23,700,000,000 | 2.5% |
| 16 | Washington | 20,400,000,000 | 2.1% |
| 34 | West Virginia | 7,700,000,000 | 0.8% |
| 19 | Wisconsin | 18,400,000,000 | 1.9% |
| 49 | Wyoming | 1,700,000,000 | 0.2% |

RANK ORDER

| RANK | STATE | EXPENDITURES | % of USA |
|---|---|---|---|
| 1 | California | $90,100,000,000 | 9.4% |
| 2 | Florida | 66,900,000,000 | 7.0% |
| 3 | Texas | 62,100,000,000 | 6.5% |
| 4 | New York | 58,700,000,000 | 6.1% |
| 5 | Pennsylvania | 44,300,000,000 | 4.6% |
| 6 | Ohio | 36,500,000,000 | 3.8% |
| 7 | Illinois | 36,200,000,000 | 3.8% |
| 8 | Michigan | 35,200,000,000 | 3.7% |
| 9 | North Carolina | 31,400,000,000 | 3.3% |
| 10 | Georgia | 27,300,000,000 | 2.8% |
| 11 | New Jersey | 26,500,000,000 | 2.8% |
| 12 | Virginia | 23,700,000,000 | 2.5% |
| 13 | Tennessee | 21,700,000,000 | 2.3% |
| 14 | Indiana | 21,300,000,000 | 2.2% |
| 15 | Arizona | 20,600,000,000 | 2.1% |
| 16 | Washington | 20,400,000,000 | 2.1% |
| 17 | Missouri | 20,100,000,000 | 2.1% |
| 18 | Massachusetts | 19,700,000,000 | 2.1% |
| 19 | Wisconsin | 18,400,000,000 | 1.9% |
| 20 | Alabama | 17,800,000,000 | 1.9% |
| 21 | South Carolina | 16,600,000,000 | 1.7% |
| 22 | Minnesota | 16,100,000,000 | 1.7% |
| 23 | Kentucky | 15,500,000,000 | 1.6% |
| 24 | Maryland | 15,400,000,000 | 1.6% |
| 25 | Louisiana | 13,400,000,000 | 1.4% |
| 26 | Colorado | 13,000,000,000 | 1.4% |
| 26 | Oregon | 13,000,000,000 | 1.4% |
| 28 | Oklahoma | 12,500,000,000 | 1.3% |
| 29 | Connecticut | 11,000,000,000 | 1.1% |
| 30 | Arkansas | 10,900,000,000 | 1.1% |
| 31 | Iowa | 10,800,000,000 | 1.1% |
| 32 | Mississippi | 10,100,000,000 | 1.1% |
| 33 | Kansas | 9,100,000,000 | 0.9% |
| 34 | West Virginia | 7,700,000,000 | 0.8% |
| 35 | Nevada | 7,300,000,000 | 0.8% |
| 36 | New Mexico | 6,400,000,000 | 0.7% |
| 37 | Nebraska | 5,900,000,000 | 0.6% |
| 37 | Utah | 5,900,000,000 | 0.6% |
| 39 | Maine | 5,000,000,000 | 0.5% |
| 40 | Idaho | 4,800,000,000 | 0.5% |
| 41 | New Hampshire | 4,400,000,000 | 0.5% |
| 42 | Hawaii | 4,000,000,000 | 0.4% |
| 43 | Rhode Island | 3,600,000,000 | 0.4% |
| 44 | Montana | 3,500,000,000 | 0.4% |
| 45 | Delaware | 3,100,000,000 | 0.3% |
| 46 | South Dakota | 2,800,000,000 | 0.3% |
| 47 | North Dakota | 2,200,000,000 | 0.2% |
| 47 | Vermont | 2,200,000,000 | 0.2% |
| 49 | Wyoming | 1,700,000,000 | 0.2% |
| 50 | Alaska | 1,600,000,000 | 0.2% |
| | District of Columbia | 1,400,000,000 | 0.1% |

Source: U.S. Office of Management and Budget, USAspending.gov
"Prime Award Spending Data Summary" (http://www.usaspending.gov/explore, as of January 31, 2014)
*Total includes $14,495,491,700 in U.S. territories and $5,304,508,300 in expenditures not distributed by state. Expenditures allocated based on place of performance of a contract. Includes funds paid to individuals who have been assessed as needing services, in lieu of social service provisions, generally for the large entitlement programs such as Social Security, Unemployment Insurance, and Federal Pell Grants. This source replaces a previous data series by the U.S. Census and definitions differ.

# Per Capita Federal Government Direct Payments to Individuals in 2012

## National Per Capita = $2,994*

| RANK | STATE | PER CAPITA | | RANK | STATE | PER CAPITA |
|---|---|---|---|---|---|---|
| | ALPHA ORDER | | | | RANK ORDER | |
| 3 | Alabama | $3,695 | | 1 | West Virginia | $4,147 |
| 49 | Alaska | 2,191 | | 2 | Maine | 3,764 |
| 28 | Arizona | 3,144 | | 3 | Alabama | 3,695 |
| 3 | Arkansas | 3,695 | | 3 | Arkansas | 3,695 |
| 48 | California | 2,371 | | 5 | Michigan | 3,562 |
| 46 | Colorado | 2,505 | | 6 | Kentucky | 3,539 |
| 31 | Connecticut | 3,063 | | 7 | Vermont | 3,515 |
| 15 | Delaware | 3,380 | | 8 | South Carolina | 3,514 |
| 12 | Florida | 3,463 | | 9 | Iowa | 3,512 |
| 43 | Georgia | 2,753 | | 10 | Montana | 3,481 |
| 41 | Hawaii | 2,878 | | 11 | Pennsylvania | 3,471 |
| 32 | Idaho | 3,008 | | 12 | Florida | 3,463 |
| 42 | Illinois | 2,813 | | 13 | Rhode Island | 3,428 |
| 22 | Indiana | 3,258 | | 14 | Mississippi | 3,382 |
| 9 | Iowa | 3,512 | | 15 | Delaware | 3,380 |
| 27 | Kansas | 3,154 | | 16 | Tennessee | 3,362 |
| 6 | Kentucky | 3,539 | | 17 | South Dakota | 3,357 |
| 39 | Louisiana | 2,912 | | 18 | Missouri | 3,336 |
| 2 | Maine | 3,764 | | 19 | Oregon | 3,334 |
| 45 | Maryland | 2,617 | | 20 | New Hampshire | 3,329 |
| 36 | Massachusetts | 2,964 | | 21 | Oklahoma | 3,276 |
| 5 | Michigan | 3,562 | | 22 | Indiana | 3,258 |
| 34 | Minnesota | 2,993 | | 23 | North Carolina | 3,221 |
| 14 | Mississippi | 3,382 | | 24 | Wisconsin | 3,214 |
| 18 | Missouri | 3,336 | | 25 | Nebraska | 3,180 |
| 10 | Montana | 3,481 | | 26 | Ohio | 3,159 |
| 25 | Nebraska | 3,180 | | 27 | Kansas | 3,154 |
| 44 | Nevada | 2,650 | | 28 | Arizona | 3,144 |
| 20 | New Hampshire | 3,329 | | 29 | North Dakota | 3,137 |
| 35 | New Jersey | 2,988 | | 30 | New Mexico | 3,072 |
| 30 | New Mexico | 3,072 | | 31 | Connecticut | 3,063 |
| 33 | New York | 2,999 | | 32 | Idaho | 3,008 |
| 23 | North Carolina | 3,221 | | 33 | New York | 2,999 |
| 29 | North Dakota | 3,137 | | 34 | Minnesota | 2,993 |
| 26 | Ohio | 3,159 | | 35 | New Jersey | 2,988 |
| 21 | Oklahoma | 3,276 | | 36 | Massachusetts | 2,964 |
| 19 | Oregon | 3,334 | | 37 | Washington | 2,959 |
| 11 | Pennsylvania | 3,471 | | 38 | Wyoming | 2,948 |
| 13 | Rhode Island | 3,428 | | 39 | Louisiana | 2,912 |
| 8 | South Carolina | 3,514 | | 40 | Virginia | 2,895 |
| 17 | South Dakota | 3,357 | | 41 | Hawaii | 2,878 |
| 16 | Tennessee | 3,362 | | 42 | Illinois | 2,813 |
| 47 | Texas | 2,383 | | 43 | Georgia | 2,753 |
| 50 | Utah | 2,067 | | 44 | Nevada | 2,650 |
| 7 | Vermont | 3,515 | | 45 | Maryland | 2,617 |
| 40 | Virginia | 2,895 | | 46 | Colorado | 2,505 |
| 37 | Washington | 2,959 | | 47 | Texas | 2,383 |
| 1 | West Virginia | 4,147 | | 48 | California | 2,371 |
| 24 | Wisconsin | 3,214 | | 49 | Alaska | 2,191 |
| 38 | Wyoming | 2,948 | | 50 | Utah | 2,067 |
| | | | | | District of Columbia | 2,210 |

Source: CQ Press using data from U.S. Office of Management and Budget, USAspending.gov
"Prime Award Spending Data Summary" (http://www.usaspending.gov/explore, as of January 31, 2014)
*National per capita excludes expenditures and population for territories and undistributed amounts. Expenditures allocated based on place of performance of a contract. Includes funds paid to individuals who have been assessed as needing services, in lieu of social service provisions, generally for the large entitlement programs such as Social Security, Unemployment Insurance, and Federal Pell Grants. This source replaces a previous data series by the U.S. Census and definitions differ.

# Federal Government Insurance Payments in 2012

## National Total = $1,138,000,000,000*

ALPHA ORDER

| RANK | STATE | EXPENDITURES | % of USA |
|---|---|---|---|
| 17 | Alabama | $9,800,000,000 | 0.9% |
| 49 | Alaska | 622,000,000 | 0.1% |
| 22 | Arizona | 6,600,000,000 | 0.6% |
| 37 | Arkansas | 2,700,000,000 | 0.2% |
| 4 | California | 65,100,000,000 | 5.7% |
| 26 | Colorado | 4,100,000,000 | 0.4% |
| 18 | Connecticut | 8,900,000,000 | 0.8% |
| 24 | Delaware | 5,800,000,000 | 0.5% |
| 1 | Florida | 427,500,000,000 | 37.6% |
| 10 | Georgia | 21,500,000,000 | 1.9% |
| 14 | Hawaii | 11,600,000,000 | 1.0% |
| 44 | Idaho | 1,500,000,000 | 0.1% |
| 19 | Illinois | 8,200,000,000 | 0.7% |
| 25 | Indiana | 5,100,000,000 | 0.4% |
| 30 | Iowa | 3,400,000,000 | 0.3% |
| 41 | Kansas | 2,000,000,000 | 0.2% |
| 31 | Kentucky | 3,200,000,000 | 0.3% |
| 3 | Louisiana | 89,200,000,000 | 7.8% |
| 42 | Maine | 1,700,000,000 | 0.1% |
| 12 | Maryland | 12,900,000,000 | 1.1% |
| 15 | Massachusetts | 10,600,000,000 | 0.9% |
| 27 | Michigan | 3,900,000,000 | 0.3% |
| 36 | Minnesota | 2,800,000,000 | 0.2% |
| 11 | Mississippi | 13,200,000,000 | 1.2% |
| 28 | Missouri | 3,800,000,000 | 0.3% |
| 47 | Montana | 919,200,000 | 0.1% |
| 40 | Nebraska | 2,100,000,000 | 0.2% |
| 31 | Nevada | 3,200,000,000 | 0.3% |
| 42 | New Hampshire | 1,700,000,000 | 0.1% |
| 5 | New Jersey | 50,000,000,000 | 4.4% |
| 34 | New Mexico | 2,900,000,000 | 0.3% |
| 7 | New York | 39,700,000,000 | 3.5% |
| 8 | North Carolina | 29,300,000,000 | 2.6% |
| 31 | North Dakota | 3,200,000,000 | 0.3% |
| 21 | Ohio | 6,700,000,000 | 0.6% |
| 34 | Oklahoma | 2,900,000,000 | 0.3% |
| 20 | Oregon | 7,500,000,000 | 0.7% |
| 13 | Pennsylvania | 12,600,000,000 | 1.1% |
| 29 | Rhode Island | 3,600,000,000 | 0.3% |
| 6 | South Carolina | 44,300,000,000 | 3.9% |
| 45 | South Dakota | 1,100,000,000 | 0.1% |
| 23 | Tennessee | 6,300,000,000 | 0.6% |
| 2 | Texas | 145,700,000,000 | 12.8% |
| 46 | Utah | 941,000,000 | 0.1% |
| 48 | Vermont | 756,800,000 | 0.1% |
| 9 | Virginia | 25,500,000,000 | 2.2% |
| 16 | Washington | 10,400,000,000 | 0.9% |
| 39 | West Virginia | 2,400,000,000 | 0.2% |
| 38 | Wisconsin | 2,500,000,000 | 0.2% |
| 50 | Wyoming | 470,700,000 | 0.0% |

RANK ORDER

| RANK | STATE | EXPENDITURES | % of USA |
|---|---|---|---|
| 1 | Florida | $427,500,000,000 | 37.6% |
| 2 | Texas | 145,700,000,000 | 12.8% |
| 3 | Louisiana | 89,200,000,000 | 7.8% |
| 4 | California | 65,100,000,000 | 5.7% |
| 5 | New Jersey | 50,000,000,000 | 4.4% |
| 6 | South Carolina | 44,300,000,000 | 3.9% |
| 7 | New York | 39,700,000,000 | 3.5% |
| 8 | North Carolina | 29,300,000,000 | 2.6% |
| 9 | Virginia | 25,500,000,000 | 2.2% |
| 10 | Georgia | 21,500,000,000 | 1.9% |
| 11 | Mississippi | 13,200,000,000 | 1.2% |
| 12 | Maryland | 12,900,000,000 | 1.1% |
| 13 | Pennsylvania | 12,600,000,000 | 1.1% |
| 14 | Hawaii | 11,600,000,000 | 1.0% |
| 15 | Massachusetts | 10,600,000,000 | 0.9% |
| 16 | Washington | 10,400,000,000 | 0.9% |
| 17 | Alabama | 9,800,000,000 | 0.9% |
| 18 | Connecticut | 8,900,000,000 | 0.8% |
| 19 | Illinois | 8,200,000,000 | 0.7% |
| 20 | Oregon | 7,500,000,000 | 0.7% |
| 21 | Ohio | 6,700,000,000 | 0.6% |
| 22 | Arizona | 6,600,000,000 | 0.6% |
| 23 | Tennessee | 6,300,000,000 | 0.6% |
| 24 | Delaware | 5,800,000,000 | 0.5% |
| 25 | Indiana | 5,100,000,000 | 0.4% |
| 26 | Colorado | 4,100,000,000 | 0.4% |
| 27 | Michigan | 3,900,000,000 | 0.3% |
| 28 | Missouri | 3,800,000,000 | 0.3% |
| 29 | Rhode Island | 3,600,000,000 | 0.3% |
| 30 | Iowa | 3,400,000,000 | 0.3% |
| 31 | Kentucky | 3,200,000,000 | 0.3% |
| 31 | Nevada | 3,200,000,000 | 0.3% |
| 31 | North Dakota | 3,200,000,000 | 0.3% |
| 34 | New Mexico | 2,900,000,000 | 0.3% |
| 34 | Oklahoma | 2,900,000,000 | 0.3% |
| 36 | Minnesota | 2,800,000,000 | 0.2% |
| 37 | Arkansas | 2,700,000,000 | 0.2% |
| 38 | Wisconsin | 2,500,000,000 | 0.2% |
| 39 | West Virginia | 2,400,000,000 | 0.2% |
| 40 | Nebraska | 2,100,000,000 | 0.2% |
| 41 | Kansas | 2,000,000,000 | 0.2% |
| 42 | Maine | 1,700,000,000 | 0.1% |
| 42 | New Hampshire | 1,700,000,000 | 0.1% |
| 44 | Idaho | 1,500,000,000 | 0.1% |
| 45 | South Dakota | 1,100,000,000 | 0.1% |
| 46 | Utah | 941,000,000 | 0.1% |
| 47 | Montana | 919,200,000 | 0.1% |
| 48 | Vermont | 756,800,000 | 0.1% |
| 49 | Alaska | 622,000,000 | 0.1% |
| 50 | Wyoming | 470,700,000 | 0.0% |
| | District of Columbia | 344,700,000 | 0.0% |

Source: U.S. Office of Management and Budget, USAspending.gov
    "Prime Award Spending Data Summary" (http://www.usaspending.gov/explore, as of January 31, 2014)
*Total includes $5,022,199,100 in U.S. territories in expenditures not distributed by state. Expenditures allocated based on place of performance of a contract. Includes financial assistance provided to assure reimbursement for losses sustained under specified conditions. Coverage may be provided directly by the federal government or through private carriers and may or may not involve the payment of premiums. This source replaces a previous data series by the U.S. Census and definitions differ.

# Per Capita Federal Government Insurance Payments in 2012

## National Per Capita = $3,609*

| ALPHA ORDER | | | | RANK ORDER | | |
|---|---|---|---|---|---|---|
| RANK | STATE | PER CAPITA | | RANK | STATE | PER CAPITA |
| 16 | Alabama | $2,034 | | 1 | Florida | $22,126 |
| 37 | Alaska | 852 | | 2 | Louisiana | 19,382 |
| 31 | Arizona | 1,007 | | 3 | South Carolina | 9,379 |
| 35 | Arkansas | 915 | | 4 | Hawaii | 8,345 |
| 19 | California | 1,713 | | 5 | Delaware | 6,325 |
| 39 | Colorado | 790 | | 6 | New Jersey | 5,638 |
| 13 | Connecticut | 2,478 | | 7 | Texas | 5,591 |
| 5 | Delaware | 6,325 | | 8 | North Dakota | 4,563 |
| 1 | Florida | 22,126 | | 9 | Mississippi | 4,420 |
| 15 | Georgia | 2,168 | | 10 | Rhode Island | 3,428 |
| 4 | Hawaii | 8,345 | | 11 | Virginia | 3,115 |
| 34 | Idaho | 940 | | 12 | North Carolina | 3,006 |
| 44 | Illinois | 637 | | 13 | Connecticut | 2,478 |
| 40 | Indiana | 780 | | 14 | Maryland | 2,192 |
| 30 | Iowa | 1,106 | | 15 | Georgia | 2,168 |
| 43 | Kansas | 693 | | 16 | Alabama | 2,034 |
| 42 | Kentucky | 731 | | 17 | New York | 2,028 |
| 2 | Louisiana | 19,382 | | 18 | Oregon | 1,923 |
| 26 | Maine | 1,280 | | 19 | California | 1,713 |
| 14 | Maryland | 2,192 | | 20 | Massachusetts | 1,595 |
| 20 | Massachusetts | 1,595 | | 21 | Washington | 1,508 |
| 49 | Michigan | 395 | | 22 | New Mexico | 1,392 |
| 47 | Minnesota | 520 | | 23 | South Dakota | 1,319 |
| 9 | Mississippi | 4,420 | | 24 | West Virginia | 1,293 |
| 45 | Missouri | 631 | | 25 | New Hampshire | 1,286 |
| 36 | Montana | 914 | | 26 | Maine | 1,280 |
| 29 | Nebraska | 1,132 | | 27 | Vermont | 1,209 |
| 28 | Nevada | 1,162 | | 28 | Nevada | 1,162 |
| 25 | New Hampshire | 1,286 | | 29 | Nebraska | 1,132 |
| 6 | New Jersey | 5,638 | | 30 | Iowa | 1,106 |
| 22 | New Mexico | 1,392 | | 31 | Arizona | 1,007 |
| 17 | New York | 2,028 | | 32 | Pennsylvania | 987 |
| 12 | North Carolina | 3,006 | | 33 | Tennessee | 976 |
| 8 | North Dakota | 4,563 | | 34 | Idaho | 940 |
| 46 | Ohio | 580 | | 35 | Arkansas | 915 |
| 41 | Oklahoma | 760 | | 36 | Montana | 914 |
| 18 | Oregon | 1,923 | | 37 | Alaska | 852 |
| 32 | Pennsylvania | 987 | | 38 | Wyoming | 816 |
| 10 | Rhode Island | 3,428 | | 39 | Colorado | 790 |
| 3 | South Carolina | 9,379 | | 40 | Indiana | 780 |
| 23 | South Dakota | 1,319 | | 41 | Oklahoma | 760 |
| 33 | Tennessee | 976 | | 42 | Kentucky | 731 |
| 7 | Texas | 5,591 | | 43 | Kansas | 693 |
| 50 | Utah | 330 | | 44 | Illinois | 637 |
| 27 | Vermont | 1,209 | | 45 | Missouri | 631 |
| 11 | Virginia | 3,115 | | 46 | Ohio | 580 |
| 21 | Washington | 1,508 | | 47 | Minnesota | 520 |
| 24 | West Virginia | 1,293 | | 48 | Wisconsin | 437 |
| 48 | Wisconsin | 437 | | 49 | Michigan | 395 |
| 38 | Wyoming | 816 | | 50 | Utah | 330 |

District of Columbia     544

Source: CQ Press using data from U.S. Office of Management and Budget, USAspending.gov
   "Prime Award Spending Data Summary" (http://www.usaspending.gov/explore, as of January 31, 2014)
*National per capita excludes expenditures and population for territories. Expenditures allocated based on place of performance
of a contract. Includes financial assistance provided to assure reimbursement for losses sustained under specified conditions.
Coverage may be provided directly by the federal government or through private carriers and may or may not involve the
payment of premiums. This source replaces a previous data series by the U.S. Census and definitions differ.

# Federal Government Loans, Guarantees, and Other Expenditures in 2012

## National Total = $5,700,000,000*

ALPHA ORDER

| RANK | STATE | EXPENDITURES | % of USA |
|------|-------|-------------:|---------:|
| 18 | Alabama | $107,200,000 | 1.9% |
| 44 | Alaska | 19,000,000 | 0.3% |
| 17 | Arizona | 111,400,000 | 2.0% |
| 22 | Arkansas | 101,200,000 | 1.8% |
| 2 | California | 391,300,000 | 6.9% |
| 30 | Colorado | 63,600,000 | 1.1% |
| 34 | Connecticut | 46,200,000 | 0.8% |
| 46 | Delaware | 15,100,000 | 0.3% |
| 1 | Florida | 396,100,000 | 6.9% |
| 7 | Georgia | 198,800,000 | 3.5% |
| 42 | Hawaii | 21,277,700 | 0.4% |
| 37 | Idaho | 43,200,000 | 0.8% |
| 6 | Illinois | 200,300,000 | 3.5% |
| 13 | Indiana | 139,800,000 | 2.5% |
| 24 | Iowa | 97,700,000 | 1.7% |
| 31 | Kansas | 56,700,000 | 1.0% |
| 14 | Kentucky | 125,200,000 | 2.2% |
| 20 | Louisiana | 105,200,000 | 1.8% |
| 35 | Maine | 44,400,000 | 0.8% |
| 27 | Maryland | 82,600,000 | 1.4% |
| 26 | Massachusetts | 88,300,000 | 1.5% |
| 9 | Michigan | 167,100,000 | 2.9% |
| 16 | Minnesota | 113,000,000 | 2.0% |
| 19 | Mississippi | 106,100,000 | 1.9% |
| 12 | Missouri | 142,100,000 | 2.5% |
| 40 | Montana | 32,400,000 | 0.6% |
| 32 | Nebraska | 55,500,000 | 1.0% |
| 25 | Nevada | 96,400,000 | 1.7% |
| 41 | New Hampshire | 31,300,000 | 0.5% |
| 28 | New Jersey | 73,200,000 | 1.3% |
| 33 | New Mexico | 51,800,000 | 0.9% |
| 3 | New York | 268,100,000 | 4.7% |
| 4 | North Carolina | 249,500,000 | 4.4% |
| 39 | North Dakota | 34,600,000 | 0.6% |
| 5 | Ohio | 244,000,000 | 4.3% |
| 23 | Oklahoma | 101,100,000 | 1.8% |
| 8 | Oregon | 193,000,000 | 3.4% |
| 50 | Pennsylvania | (218,800,000) | |
| 43 | Rhode Island | 19,330,300 | 0.3% |
| 21 | South Carolina | 102,300,000 | 1.8% |
| 36 | South Dakota | 44,000,000 | 0.8% |
| 10 | Tennessee | 144,600,000 | 2.5% |
| 48 | Texas | (10,600,000) | |
| 38 | Utah | 38,300,000 | 0.7% |
| 47 | Vermont | 15,000,000 | 0.3% |
| 11 | Virginia | 143,000,000 | 2.5% |
| 49 | Washington | (214,800,000) | |
| 29 | West Virginia | 66,900,000 | 1.2% |
| 15 | Wisconsin | 119,700,000 | 2.1% |
| 45 | Wyoming | 18,300,000 | 0.3% |

RANK ORDER

| RANK | STATE | EXPENDITURES | % of USA |
|------|-------|-------------:|---------:|
| 1 | Florida | $396,100,000 | 6.9% |
| 2 | California | 391,300,000 | 6.9% |
| 3 | New York | 268,100,000 | 4.7% |
| 4 | North Carolina | 249,500,000 | 4.4% |
| 5 | Ohio | 244,000,000 | 4.3% |
| 6 | Illinois | 200,300,000 | 3.5% |
| 7 | Georgia | 198,800,000 | 3.5% |
| 8 | Oregon | 193,000,000 | 3.4% |
| 9 | Michigan | 167,100,000 | 2.9% |
| 10 | Tennessee | 144,600,000 | 2.5% |
| 11 | Virginia | 143,000,000 | 2.5% |
| 12 | Missouri | 142,100,000 | 2.5% |
| 13 | Indiana | 139,800,000 | 2.5% |
| 14 | Kentucky | 125,200,000 | 2.2% |
| 15 | Wisconsin | 119,700,000 | 2.1% |
| 16 | Minnesota | 113,000,000 | 2.0% |
| 17 | Arizona | 111,400,000 | 2.0% |
| 18 | Alabama | 107,200,000 | 1.9% |
| 19 | Mississippi | 106,100,000 | 1.9% |
| 20 | Louisiana | 105,200,000 | 1.8% |
| 21 | South Carolina | 102,300,000 | 1.8% |
| 22 | Arkansas | 101,200,000 | 1.8% |
| 23 | Oklahoma | 101,100,000 | 1.8% |
| 24 | Iowa | 97,700,000 | 1.7% |
| 25 | Nevada | 96,400,000 | 1.7% |
| 26 | Massachusetts | 88,300,000 | 1.5% |
| 27 | Maryland | 82,600,000 | 1.4% |
| 28 | New Jersey | 73,200,000 | 1.3% |
| 29 | West Virginia | 66,900,000 | 1.2% |
| 30 | Colorado | 63,600,000 | 1.1% |
| 31 | Kansas | 56,700,000 | 1.0% |
| 32 | Nebraska | 55,500,000 | 1.0% |
| 33 | New Mexico | 51,800,000 | 0.9% |
| 34 | Connecticut | 46,200,000 | 0.8% |
| 35 | Maine | 44,400,000 | 0.8% |
| 36 | South Dakota | 44,000,000 | 0.8% |
| 37 | Idaho | 43,200,000 | 0.8% |
| 38 | Utah | 38,300,000 | 0.7% |
| 39 | North Dakota | 34,600,000 | 0.6% |
| 40 | Montana | 32,400,000 | 0.6% |
| 41 | New Hampshire | 31,300,000 | 0.5% |
| 42 | Hawaii | 21,277,700 | 0.4% |
| 43 | Rhode Island | 19,330,300 | 0.3% |
| 44 | Alaska | 19,000,000 | 0.3% |
| 45 | Wyoming | 18,300,000 | 0.3% |
| 46 | Delaware | 15,100,000 | 0.3% |
| 47 | Vermont | 15,000,000 | 0.3% |
| 48 | Texas | (10,600,000) | |
| 49 | Washington | (214,800,000) | |
| 50 | Pennsylvania | (218,800,000) | |
| | District of Columbia | 8,000,000 | 0.1% |

Source: U.S. Office of Management and Budget, USAspending.gov
"Prime Award Spending Data Summary" (http://www.usaspending.gov/explore, as of January 31, 2014)
*Total includes $1,066,882,500 in U.S. territories and -$55,890,500 in expenditures not distributed by state. Expenditures allocated based on place of performance of a contract. Loans are awards where a Federal agency provides funds to a non-Federal recipient that require repayment. Includes cost of loan and is net of repayments. "Other" represents all other reimbursable, indirect, contingent, intangible financial assistance. This source replaces a previous data series by the U.S. Census and definitions differ.

# Per Capita Federal Government Loans, Guarantees, and Other Expenditures in 2012
## National Per Capita = $15*

| RANK | STATE | PER CAPITA |
|---|---|---|
| 23 | Alabama | $22 |
| 15 | Alaska | 26 |
| 34 | Arizona | 17 |
| 7 | Arkansas | 34 |
| 46 | California | 10 |
| 45 | Colorado | 12 |
| 42 | Connecticut | 13 |
| 37 | Delaware | 16 |
| 26 | Florida | 21 |
| 31 | Georgia | 20 |
| 39 | Hawaii | 15 |
| 14 | Idaho | 27 |
| 37 | Illinois | 16 |
| 26 | Indiana | 21 |
| 9 | Iowa | 32 |
| 31 | Kansas | 20 |
| 13 | Kentucky | 29 |
| 22 | Louisiana | 23 |
| 8 | Maine | 33 |
| 40 | Maryland | 14 |
| 42 | Massachusetts | 13 |
| 34 | Michigan | 17 |
| 26 | Minnesota | 21 |
| 4 | Mississippi | 36 |
| 19 | Missouri | 24 |
| 9 | Montana | 32 |
| 12 | Nebraska | 30 |
| 6 | Nevada | 35 |
| 19 | New Hampshire | 24 |
| 47 | New Jersey | 8 |
| 18 | New Mexico | 25 |
| 40 | New York | 14 |
| 15 | North Carolina | 26 |
| 2 | North Dakota | 49 |
| 26 | Ohio | 21 |
| 15 | Oklahoma | 26 |
| 2 | Oregon | 49 |
| 49 | Pennsylvania | (17) |
| 33 | Rhode Island | 18 |
| 23 | South Carolina | 22 |
| 1 | South Dakota | 53 |
| 23 | Tennessee | 22 |
| 48 | Texas | 0 |
| 42 | Utah | 13 |
| 19 | Vermont | 24 |
| 34 | Virginia | 17 |
| 50 | Washington | (31) |
| 4 | West Virginia | 36 |
| 26 | Wisconsin | 21 |
| 9 | Wyoming | 32 |

| RANK | STATE | PER CAPITA |
|---|---|---|
| 1 | South Dakota | $53 |
| 2 | North Dakota | 49 |
| 2 | Oregon | 49 |
| 4 | Mississippi | 36 |
| 4 | West Virginia | 36 |
| 6 | Nevada | 35 |
| 7 | Arkansas | 34 |
| 8 | Maine | 33 |
| 9 | Iowa | 32 |
| 9 | Montana | 32 |
| 9 | Wyoming | 32 |
| 12 | Nebraska | 30 |
| 13 | Kentucky | 29 |
| 14 | Idaho | 27 |
| 15 | Alaska | 26 |
| 15 | North Carolina | 26 |
| 15 | Oklahoma | 26 |
| 18 | New Mexico | 25 |
| 19 | Missouri | 24 |
| 19 | New Hampshire | 24 |
| 19 | Vermont | 24 |
| 22 | Louisiana | 23 |
| 23 | Alabama | 22 |
| 23 | South Carolina | 22 |
| 23 | Tennessee | 22 |
| 26 | Florida | 21 |
| 26 | Indiana | 21 |
| 26 | Minnesota | 21 |
| 26 | Ohio | 21 |
| 26 | Wisconsin | 21 |
| 31 | Georgia | 20 |
| 31 | Kansas | 20 |
| 33 | Rhode Island | 18 |
| 34 | Arizona | 17 |
| 34 | Michigan | 17 |
| 34 | Virginia | 17 |
| 37 | Delaware | 16 |
| 37 | Illinois | 16 |
| 39 | Hawaii | 15 |
| 40 | Maryland | 14 |
| 40 | New York | 14 |
| 42 | Connecticut | 13 |
| 42 | Massachusetts | 13 |
| 42 | Utah | 13 |
| 45 | Colorado | 12 |
| 46 | California | 10 |
| 47 | New Jersey | 8 |
| 48 | Texas | 0 |
| 49 | Pennsylvania | (17) |
| 50 | Washington | (31) |
| | District of Columbia | 13 |

Source: CQ Press using data from U.S. Office of Management and Budget, USAspending.gov
"Prime Award Spending Data Summary" (http://www.usaspending.gov/explore, as of January 31, 2014)
*National per capita excludes expenditures and population for territories and undistributed amounts. Expenditures allocated based on place of performance of a contract. Loans are awards where a Federal agency provides funds to a non-Federal recipient that require repayment. Includes cost of loan and is net of repayments. "Other" represents all other reimbursable, indirect, contingent, intangible financial assistance. This source replaces a previous data series by the U.S. Census and definitions differ.

# Federal Civilian Employees in 2012

## National Total = 1,850,311 Employees*

ALPHA ORDER

| RANK | STATE | EMPLOYEES | % of USA |
|---|---|---|---|
| 13 | Alabama | 38,986 | 2.1% |
| 36 | Alaska | 11,170 | 0.6% |
| 14 | Arizona | 37,320 | 2.0% |
| 35 | Arkansas | 12,864 | 0.7% |
| 1 | California | 150,762 | 8.1% |
| 16 | Colorado | 36,282 | 2.0% |
| 41 | Connecticut | 7,762 | 0.4% |
| 50 | Delaware | 3,031 | 0.2% |
| 5 | Florida | 82,915 | 4.5% |
| 6 | Georgia | 71,486 | 3.9% |
| 23 | Hawaii | 23,446 | 1.3% |
| 43 | Idaho | 7,388 | 0.4% |
| 11 | Illinois | 45,801 | 2.5% |
| 26 | Indiana | 22,007 | 1.2% |
| 42 | Iowa | 7,715 | 0.4% |
| 33 | Kansas | 15,515 | 0.8% |
| 24 | Kentucky | 23,198 | 1.3% |
| 28 | Louisiana | 19,307 | 1.0% |
| 39 | Maine | 9,873 | 0.5% |
| 4 | Maryland | 119,816 | 6.5% |
| 21 | Massachusetts | 24,926 | 1.3% |
| 18 | Michigan | 27,693 | 1.5% |
| 32 | Minnesota | 15,864 | 0.9% |
| 30 | Mississippi | 17,088 | 0.9% |
| 17 | Missouri | 32,933 | 1.8% |
| 40 | Montana | 8,637 | 0.5% |
| 38 | Nebraska | 9,979 | 0.5% |
| 37 | Nevada | 11,102 | 0.6% |
| 49 | New Hampshire | 4,069 | 0.2% |
| 22 | New Jersey | 24,806 | 1.3% |
| 25 | New Mexico | 23,032 | 1.2% |
| 8 | New York | 62,011 | 3.4% |
| 12 | North Carolina | 39,886 | 2.2% |
| 46 | North Dakota | 5,409 | 0.3% |
| 10 | Ohio | 48,422 | 2.6% |
| 15 | Oklahoma | 36,382 | 2.0% |
| 31 | Oregon | 16,857 | 0.9% |
| 7 | Pennsylvania | 63,137 | 3.4% |
| 45 | Rhode Island | 6,245 | 0.3% |
| 27 | South Carolina | 20,198 | 1.1% |
| 44 | South Dakota | 7,261 | 0.4% |
| 20 | Tennessee | 25,140 | 1.4% |
| 3 | Texas | 131,580 | 7.1% |
| 19 | Utah | 25,508 | 1.4% |
| 48 | Vermont | 4,234 | 0.2% |
| 2 | Virginia | 144,753 | 7.8% |
| 9 | Washington | 50,300 | 2.7% |
| 29 | West Virginia | 18,093 | 1.0% |
| 34 | Wisconsin | 13,455 | 0.7% |
| 47 | Wyoming | 4,818 | 0.3% |

RANK ORDER

| RANK | STATE | EMPLOYEES | % of USA |
|---|---|---|---|
| 1 | California | 150,762 | 8.1% |
| 2 | Virginia | 144,753 | 7.8% |
| 3 | Texas | 131,580 | 7.1% |
| 4 | Maryland | 119,816 | 6.5% |
| 5 | Florida | 82,915 | 4.5% |
| 6 | Georgia | 71,486 | 3.9% |
| 7 | Pennsylvania | 63,137 | 3.4% |
| 8 | New York | 62,011 | 3.4% |
| 9 | Washington | 50,300 | 2.7% |
| 10 | Ohio | 48,422 | 2.6% |
| 11 | Illinois | 45,801 | 2.5% |
| 12 | North Carolina | 39,886 | 2.2% |
| 13 | Alabama | 38,986 | 2.1% |
| 14 | Arizona | 37,320 | 2.0% |
| 15 | Oklahoma | 36,382 | 2.0% |
| 16 | Colorado | 36,282 | 2.0% |
| 17 | Missouri | 32,933 | 1.8% |
| 18 | Michigan | 27,693 | 1.5% |
| 19 | Utah | 25,508 | 1.4% |
| 20 | Tennessee | 25,140 | 1.4% |
| 21 | Massachusetts | 24,926 | 1.3% |
| 22 | New Jersey | 24,806 | 1.3% |
| 23 | Hawaii | 23,446 | 1.3% |
| 24 | Kentucky | 23,198 | 1.3% |
| 25 | New Mexico | 23,032 | 1.2% |
| 26 | Indiana | 22,007 | 1.2% |
| 27 | South Carolina | 20,198 | 1.1% |
| 28 | Louisiana | 19,307 | 1.0% |
| 29 | West Virginia | 18,093 | 1.0% |
| 30 | Mississippi | 17,088 | 0.9% |
| 31 | Oregon | 16,857 | 0.9% |
| 32 | Minnesota | 15,864 | 0.9% |
| 33 | Kansas | 15,515 | 0.8% |
| 34 | Wisconsin | 13,455 | 0.7% |
| 35 | Arkansas | 12,864 | 0.7% |
| 36 | Alaska | 11,170 | 0.6% |
| 37 | Nevada | 11,102 | 0.6% |
| 38 | Nebraska | 9,979 | 0.5% |
| 39 | Maine | 9,873 | 0.5% |
| 40 | Montana | 8,637 | 0.5% |
| 41 | Connecticut | 7,762 | 0.4% |
| 42 | Iowa | 7,715 | 0.4% |
| 43 | Idaho | 7,388 | 0.4% |
| 44 | South Dakota | 7,261 | 0.4% |
| 45 | Rhode Island | 6,245 | 0.3% |
| 46 | North Dakota | 5,409 | 0.3% |
| 47 | Wyoming | 4,818 | 0.3% |
| 48 | Vermont | 4,234 | 0.2% |
| 49 | New Hampshire | 4,069 | 0.2% |
| 50 | Delaware | 3,031 | 0.2% |
| | District of Columbia | 143,537 | 7.8% |

Source: U.S. Office of Personnel Management
"Common Characteristics of the Government" (http://www.opm.gov/feddata/)
*Head count based on place of employment. There were an average of 2,782,467 federal civilian employees in 2012. Excludes
Central Intelligence Agency, Defense Intelligence Agency, and National Security Agency.

# Rate of Federal Civilian Employees in 2012

## National Rate = 59 Employees per 10,000 Population*

ALPHA ORDER

| RANK | STATE | RATE |
|------|-------|------|
| 12 | Alabama | 81 |
| 4 | Alaska | 153 |
| 20 | Arizona | 57 |
| 29 | Arkansas | 44 |
| 36 | California | 40 |
| 17 | Colorado | 70 |
| 50 | Connecticut | 22 |
| 42 | Delaware | 33 |
| 30 | Florida | 43 |
| 16 | Georgia | 72 |
| 3 | Hawaii | 168 |
| 28 | Idaho | 46 |
| 40 | Illinois | 36 |
| 41 | Indiana | 34 |
| 48 | Iowa | 25 |
| 23 | Kansas | 54 |
| 25 | Kentucky | 53 |
| 33 | Louisiana | 42 |
| 14 | Maine | 74 |
| 1 | Maryland | 204 |
| 39 | Massachusetts | 38 |
| 46 | Michigan | 28 |
| 45 | Minnesota | 29 |
| 20 | Mississippi | 57 |
| 22 | Missouri | 55 |
| 10 | Montana | 86 |
| 23 | Nebraska | 54 |
| 36 | Nevada | 40 |
| 44 | New Hampshire | 31 |
| 46 | New Jersey | 28 |
| 5 | New Mexico | 110 |
| 43 | New York | 32 |
| 35 | North Carolina | 41 |
| 13 | North Dakota | 77 |
| 33 | Ohio | 42 |
| 7 | Oklahoma | 95 |
| 30 | Oregon | 43 |
| 27 | Pennsylvania | 49 |
| 19 | Rhode Island | 59 |
| 30 | South Carolina | 43 |
| 9 | South Dakota | 87 |
| 38 | Tennessee | 39 |
| 26 | Texas | 50 |
| 8 | Utah | 89 |
| 18 | Vermont | 68 |
| 2 | Virginia | 177 |
| 15 | Washington | 73 |
| 6 | West Virginia | 98 |
| 49 | Wisconsin | 23 |
| 11 | Wyoming | 84 |

RANK ORDER

| RANK | STATE | RATE |
|------|-------|------|
| 1 | Maryland | 204 |
| 2 | Virginia | 177 |
| 3 | Hawaii | 168 |
| 4 | Alaska | 153 |
| 5 | New Mexico | 110 |
| 6 | West Virginia | 98 |
| 7 | Oklahoma | 95 |
| 8 | Utah | 89 |
| 9 | South Dakota | 87 |
| 10 | Montana | 86 |
| 11 | Wyoming | 84 |
| 12 | Alabama | 81 |
| 13 | North Dakota | 77 |
| 14 | Maine | 74 |
| 15 | Washington | 73 |
| 16 | Georgia | 72 |
| 17 | Colorado | 70 |
| 18 | Vermont | 68 |
| 19 | Rhode Island | 59 |
| 20 | Arizona | 57 |
| 20 | Mississippi | 57 |
| 22 | Missouri | 55 |
| 23 | Kansas | 54 |
| 23 | Nebraska | 54 |
| 25 | Kentucky | 53 |
| 26 | Texas | 50 |
| 27 | Pennsylvania | 49 |
| 28 | Idaho | 46 |
| 29 | Arkansas | 44 |
| 30 | Florida | 43 |
| 30 | Oregon | 43 |
| 30 | South Carolina | 43 |
| 33 | Louisiana | 42 |
| 33 | Ohio | 42 |
| 35 | North Carolina | 41 |
| 36 | California | 40 |
| 36 | Nevada | 40 |
| 38 | Tennessee | 39 |
| 39 | Massachusetts | 38 |
| 40 | Illinois | 36 |
| 41 | Indiana | 34 |
| 42 | Delaware | 33 |
| 43 | New York | 32 |
| 44 | New Hampshire | 31 |
| 45 | Minnesota | 29 |
| 46 | Michigan | 28 |
| 46 | New Jersey | 28 |
| 48 | Iowa | 25 |
| 49 | Wisconsin | 23 |
| 50 | Connecticut | 22 |

| District of Columbia | 2,270 |
|----------------------|-------|

Source: CQ Press using data from U.S. Office of Personnel Management
   "Common Characteristics of the Government" (http://www.opm.gov/feddata/)
*Head count based on place of employment.  There were an average of 2,782,467 federal civilian employees in 2012.  Excludes Central Intelligence Agency, Defense Intelligence Agency, and National Security Agency.

# X. Government Finances: State and Local

*(Continued)*

*(Continued)*

# State and Local Government Total Revenue in 2011

## National Total = $3,433,535,571,000*

| ALPHA ORDER | | | | | RANK ORDER | | | |
|---|---|---|---|---|---|---|---|---|
| RANK | STATE | REVENUE | % of USA | | RANK | STATE | REVENUE | % of USA |
| 28 | Alabama | $40,658,127,000 | 1.2% | | 1 | California | $519,381,834,000 | 15.1% |
| 39 | Alaska | 18,444,157,000 | 0.5% | | 2 | New York | 323,769,304,000 | 9.4% |
| 19 | Arizona | 58,722,643,000 | 1.7% | | 3 | Texas | 224,474,606,000 | 6.5% |
| 33 | Arkansas | 27,841,110,000 | 0.8% | | 4 | Florida | 181,173,802,000 | 5.3% |
| 1 | California | 519,381,834,000 | 15.1% | | 5 | Pennsylvania | 134,309,794,000 | 3.9% |
| 22 | Colorado | 53,015,083,000 | 1.5% | | 6 | Illinois | 133,625,891,000 | 3.9% |
| 26 | Connecticut | 42,151,373,000 | 1.2% | | 7 | Ohio | 131,659,008,000 | 3.8% |
| 45 | Delaware | 11,200,911,000 | 0.3% | | 8 | New Jersey | 105,224,674,000 | 3.1% |
| 4 | Florida | 181,173,802,000 | 5.3% | | 9 | Michigan | 93,406,207,000 | 2.7% |
| 11 | Georgia | 85,077,189,000 | 2.5% | | 10 | North Carolina | 93,302,012,000 | 2.7% |
| 40 | Hawaii | 15,958,833,000 | 0.5% | | 11 | Georgia | 85,077,189,000 | 2.5% |
| 41 | Idaho | 14,096,854,000 | 0.4% | | 12 | Massachusetts | 82,041,677,000 | 2.4% |
| 6 | Illinois | 133,625,891,000 | 3.9% | | 13 | Washington | 77,839,836,000 | 2.3% |
| 21 | Indiana | 56,855,910,000 | 1.7% | | 14 | Virginia | 76,354,585,000 | 2.2% |
| 30 | Iowa | 34,540,917,000 | 1.0% | | 15 | Minnesota | 63,624,439,000 | 1.9% |
| 32 | Kansas | 28,561,910,000 | 0.8% | | 16 | Maryland | 62,842,897,000 | 1.8% |
| 27 | Kentucky | 40,787,680,000 | 1.2% | | 17 | Wisconsin | 62,693,308,000 | 1.8% |
| 23 | Louisiana | 49,138,661,000 | 1.4% | | 18 | Tennessee | 60,326,708,000 | 1.8% |
| 42 | Maine | 13,985,949,000 | 0.4% | | 19 | Arizona | 58,722,643,000 | 1.7% |
| 16 | Maryland | 62,842,897,000 | 1.8% | | 20 | Missouri | 57,095,221,000 | 1.7% |
| 12 | Massachusetts | 82,041,677,000 | 2.4% | | 21 | Indiana | 56,855,910,000 | 1.7% |
| 9 | Michigan | 93,406,207,000 | 2.7% | | 22 | Colorado | 53,015,083,000 | 1.5% |
| 15 | Minnesota | 63,624,439,000 | 1.9% | | 23 | Louisiana | 49,138,661,000 | 1.4% |
| 31 | Mississippi | 31,412,414,000 | 0.9% | | 24 | Oregon | 47,046,783,000 | 1.4% |
| 20 | Missouri | 57,095,221,000 | 1.7% | | 25 | South Carolina | 45,778,673,000 | 1.3% |
| 46 | Montana | 10,234,859,000 | 0.3% | | 26 | Connecticut | 42,151,373,000 | 1.2% |
| 37 | Nebraska | 21,652,714,000 | 0.6% | | 27 | Kentucky | 40,787,680,000 | 1.2% |
| 34 | Nevada | 25,913,959,000 | 0.8% | | 28 | Alabama | 40,658,127,000 | 1.2% |
| 44 | New Hampshire | 12,218,517,000 | 0.4% | | 29 | Oklahoma | 35,378,005,000 | 1.0% |
| 8 | New Jersey | 105,224,674,000 | 3.1% | | 30 | Iowa | 34,540,917,000 | 1.0% |
| 36 | New Mexico | 24,272,770,000 | 0.7% | | 31 | Mississippi | 31,412,414,000 | 0.9% |
| 2 | New York | 323,769,304,000 | 9.4% | | 32 | Kansas | 28,561,910,000 | 0.8% |
| 10 | North Carolina | 93,302,012,000 | 2.7% | | 33 | Arkansas | 27,841,110,000 | 0.8% |
| 48 | North Dakota | 9,645,315,000 | 0.3% | | 34 | Nevada | 25,913,959,000 | 0.8% |
| 7 | Ohio | 131,659,008,000 | 3.8% | | 35 | Utah | 25,187,556,000 | 0.7% |
| 29 | Oklahoma | 35,378,005,000 | 1.0% | | 36 | New Mexico | 24,272,770,000 | 0.7% |
| 24 | Oregon | 47,046,783,000 | 1.4% | | 37 | Nebraska | 21,652,714,000 | 0.6% |
| 5 | Pennsylvania | 134,309,794,000 | 3.9% | | 38 | West Virginia | 18,738,643,000 | 0.5% |
| 43 | Rhode Island | 12,742,033,000 | 0.4% | | 39 | Alaska | 18,444,157,000 | 0.5% |
| 25 | South Carolina | 45,778,673,000 | 1.3% | | 40 | Hawaii | 15,958,833,000 | 0.5% |
| 49 | South Dakota | 8,463,415,000 | 0.2% | | 41 | Idaho | 14,096,854,000 | 0.4% |
| 18 | Tennessee | 60,326,708,000 | 1.8% | | 42 | Maine | 13,985,949,000 | 0.4% |
| 3 | Texas | 224,474,606,000 | 6.5% | | 43 | Rhode Island | 12,742,033,000 | 0.4% |
| 35 | Utah | 25,187,556,000 | 0.7% | | 44 | New Hampshire | 12,218,517,000 | 0.4% |
| 50 | Vermont | 7,580,598,000 | 0.2% | | 45 | Delaware | 11,200,911,000 | 0.3% |
| 14 | Virginia | 76,354,585,000 | 2.2% | | 46 | Montana | 10,234,859,000 | 0.3% |
| 13 | Washington | 77,839,836,000 | 2.3% | | 47 | Wyoming | 10,208,346,000 | 0.3% |
| 38 | West Virginia | 18,738,643,000 | 0.5% | | 48 | North Dakota | 9,645,315,000 | 0.3% |
| 17 | Wisconsin | 62,693,308,000 | 1.8% | | 49 | South Dakota | 8,463,415,000 | 0.2% |
| 47 | Wyoming | 10,208,346,000 | 0.3% | | 50 | Vermont | 7,580,598,000 | 0.2% |
| | | | | | | District of Columbia | 12,877,861,000 | 0.4% |

Source: U.S. Bureau of the Census, Governments Division
   "2011 State and Local Government Finances" (http://www.census.gov/govs/local/)
*Total revenue includes all money received from external sources. This includes taxes, intergovernmental transfers and insurance trust revenue, and revenue from government owned utilities and other commercial or auxiliary enterprise.

# Per Capita State and Local Government Revenue in 2011

## National Per Capita = $11,019*

ALPHA ORDER

| RANK | STATE | PER CAPITA |
|---|---|---|
| 50 | Alabama | $8,464 |
| 1 | Alaska | 25,480 |
| 44 | Arizona | 9,080 |
| 37 | Arkansas | 9,474 |
| 5 | California | 13,783 |
| 27 | Colorado | 10,362 |
| 14 | Connecticut | 11,752 |
| 7 | Delaware | 12,334 |
| 36 | Florida | 9,494 |
| 49 | Georgia | 8,670 |
| 16 | Hawaii | 11,580 |
| 46 | Idaho | 8,901 |
| 26 | Illinois | 10,391 |
| 48 | Indiana | 8,725 |
| 19 | Iowa | 11,273 |
| 31 | Kansas | 9,951 |
| 42 | Kentucky | 9,340 |
| 22 | Louisiana | 10,741 |
| 25 | Maine | 10,527 |
| 21 | Maryland | 10,762 |
| 6 | Massachusetts | 12,417 |
| 38 | Michigan | 9,457 |
| 12 | Minnesota | 11,898 |
| 23 | Mississippi | 10,550 |
| 35 | Missouri | 9,502 |
| 29 | Montana | 10,259 |
| 13 | Nebraska | 11,754 |
| 34 | Nevada | 9,527 |
| 43 | New Hampshire | 9,272 |
| 11 | New Jersey | 11,910 |
| 15 | New Mexico | 11,677 |
| 3 | New York | 16,602 |
| 33 | North Carolina | 9,667 |
| 4 | North Dakota | 14,086 |
| 17 | Ohio | 11,408 |
| 41 | Oklahoma | 9,349 |
| 8 | Oregon | 12,162 |
| 24 | Pennsylvania | 10,539 |
| 9 | Rhode Island | 12,128 |
| 32 | South Carolina | 9,796 |
| 28 | South Dakota | 10,276 |
| 39 | Tennessee | 9,426 |
| 47 | Texas | 8,758 |
| 45 | Utah | 8,950 |
| 10 | Vermont | 12,098 |
| 40 | Virginia | 9,421 |
| 17 | Washington | 11,408 |
| 30 | West Virginia | 10,102 |
| 20 | Wisconsin | 10,980 |
| 2 | Wyoming | 17,993 |

RANK ORDER

| RANK | STATE | PER CAPITA |
|---|---|---|
| 1 | Alaska | $25,480 |
| 2 | Wyoming | 17,993 |
| 3 | New York | 16,602 |
| 4 | North Dakota | 14,086 |
| 5 | California | 13,783 |
| 6 | Massachusetts | 12,417 |
| 7 | Delaware | 12,334 |
| 8 | Oregon | 12,162 |
| 9 | Rhode Island | 12,128 |
| 10 | Vermont | 12,098 |
| 11 | New Jersey | 11,910 |
| 12 | Minnesota | 11,898 |
| 13 | Nebraska | 11,754 |
| 14 | Connecticut | 11,752 |
| 15 | New Mexico | 11,677 |
| 16 | Hawaii | 11,580 |
| 17 | Ohio | 11,408 |
| 17 | Washington | 11,408 |
| 19 | Iowa | 11,273 |
| 20 | Wisconsin | 10,980 |
| 21 | Maryland | 10,762 |
| 22 | Louisiana | 10,741 |
| 23 | Mississippi | 10,550 |
| 24 | Pennsylvania | 10,539 |
| 25 | Maine | 10,527 |
| 26 | Illinois | 10,391 |
| 27 | Colorado | 10,362 |
| 28 | South Dakota | 10,276 |
| 29 | Montana | 10,259 |
| 30 | West Virginia | 10,102 |
| 31 | Kansas | 9,951 |
| 32 | South Carolina | 9,796 |
| 33 | North Carolina | 9,667 |
| 34 | Nevada | 9,527 |
| 35 | Missouri | 9,502 |
| 36 | Florida | 9,494 |
| 37 | Arkansas | 9,474 |
| 38 | Michigan | 9,457 |
| 39 | Tennessee | 9,426 |
| 40 | Virginia | 9,421 |
| 41 | Oklahoma | 9,349 |
| 42 | Kentucky | 9,340 |
| 43 | New Hampshire | 9,272 |
| 44 | Arizona | 9,080 |
| 45 | Utah | 8,950 |
| 46 | Idaho | 8,901 |
| 47 | Texas | 8,758 |
| 48 | Indiana | 8,725 |
| 49 | Georgia | 8,670 |
| 50 | Alabama | 8,464 |

| District of Columbia | 20,804 |
|---|---|

Source: CQ Press using data from U.S. Bureau of the Census, Governments Division
    "2011 State and Local Government Finances" (http://www.census.gov/govs/local/)
*Total revenue includes all money received from external sources. This includes taxes, intergovernmental transfers and insurance trust revenue, and revenue from government owned utilities and other commercial or auxiliary enterprise.

# State and Local Government Revenue from the Federal Government in 2011

## National Total = $645,961,684,000

ALPHA ORDER

| RANK | STATE | REVENUE | % of USA |
|------|-------|---------|----------|
| 23 | Alabama | $9,590,191,000 | 1.5% |
| 40 | Alaska | 3,360,673,000 | 0.5% |
| 14 | Arizona | 13,025,856,000 | 2.0% |
| 33 | Arkansas | 6,723,216,000 | 1.0% |
| 1 | California | 75,876,661,000 | 11.7% |
| 30 | Colorado | 7,445,767,000 | 1.2% |
| 31 | Connecticut | 7,201,164,000 | 1.1% |
| 50 | Delaware | 1,899,144,000 | 0.3% |
| 4 | Florida | 32,023,819,000 | 5.0% |
| 10 | Georgia | 16,552,641,000 | 2.6% |
| 41 | Hawaii | 3,180,863,000 | 0.5% |
| 42 | Idaho | 2,987,651,000 | 0.5% |
| 7 | Illinois | 22,527,224,000 | 3.5% |
| 19 | Indiana | 11,538,049,000 | 1.8% |
| 29 | Iowa | 7,524,475,000 | 1.2% |
| 34 | Kansas | 5,158,672,000 | 0.8% |
| 24 | Kentucky | 9,414,784,000 | 1.5% |
| 13 | Louisiana | 13,649,946,000 | 2.1% |
| 38 | Maine | 3,399,180,000 | 0.5% |
| 17 | Maryland | 12,452,869,000 | 1.9% |
| 11 | Massachusetts | 15,518,145,000 | 2.4% |
| 8 | Michigan | 21,859,003,000 | 3.4% |
| 22 | Minnesota | 10,576,654,000 | 1.6% |
| 25 | Mississippi | 9,322,736,000 | 1.4% |
| 16 | Missouri | 12,526,052,000 | 1.9% |
| 44 | Montana | 2,669,071,000 | 0.4% |
| 37 | Nebraska | 3,747,101,000 | 0.6% |
| 39 | Nevada | 3,367,932,000 | 0.5% |
| 46 | New Hampshire | 2,128,172,000 | 0.3% |
| 12 | New Jersey | 15,246,954,000 | 2.4% |
| 32 | New Mexico | 6,744,161,000 | 1.0% |
| 2 | New York | 59,816,881,000 | 9.3% |
| 9 | North Carolina | 17,989,311,000 | 2.8% |
| 49 | North Dakota | 1,903,346,000 | 0.3% |
| 6 | Ohio | 26,041,221,000 | 4.0% |
| 28 | Oklahoma | 8,199,932,000 | 1.3% |
| 26 | Oregon | 8,748,975,000 | 1.4% |
| 5 | Pennsylvania | 27,103,241,000 | 4.2% |
| 43 | Rhode Island | 2,889,426,000 | 0.4% |
| 27 | South Carolina | 8,725,520,000 | 1.4% |
| 48 | South Dakota | 2,054,905,000 | 0.3% |
| 15 | Tennessee | 13,013,643,000 | 2.0% |
| 3 | Texas | 46,737,257,000 | 7.2% |
| 35 | Utah | 5,046,312,000 | 0.8% |
| 47 | Vermont | 2,116,754,000 | 0.3% |
| 20 | Virginia | 11,511,209,000 | 1.8% |
| 18 | Washington | 12,385,327,000 | 1.9% |
| 36 | West Virginia | 4,945,437,000 | 0.8% |
| 21 | Wisconsin | 11,023,893,000 | 1.7% |
| 45 | Wyoming | 2,353,678,000 | 0.4% |

RANK ORDER

| RANK | STATE | REVENUE | % of USA |
|------|-------|---------|----------|
| 1 | California | $75,876,661,000 | 11.7% |
| 2 | New York | 59,816,881,000 | 9.3% |
| 3 | Texas | 46,737,257,000 | 7.2% |
| 4 | Florida | 32,023,819,000 | 5.0% |
| 5 | Pennsylvania | 27,103,241,000 | 4.2% |
| 6 | Ohio | 26,041,221,000 | 4.0% |
| 7 | Illinois | 22,527,224,000 | 3.5% |
| 8 | Michigan | 21,859,003,000 | 3.4% |
| 9 | North Carolina | 17,989,311,000 | 2.8% |
| 10 | Georgia | 16,552,641,000 | 2.6% |
| 11 | Massachusetts | 15,518,145,000 | 2.4% |
| 12 | New Jersey | 15,246,954,000 | 2.4% |
| 13 | Louisiana | 13,649,946,000 | 2.1% |
| 14 | Arizona | 13,025,856,000 | 2.0% |
| 15 | Tennessee | 13,013,643,000 | 2.0% |
| 16 | Missouri | 12,526,052,000 | 1.9% |
| 17 | Maryland | 12,452,869,000 | 1.9% |
| 18 | Washington | 12,385,327,000 | 1.9% |
| 19 | Indiana | 11,538,049,000 | 1.8% |
| 20 | Virginia | 11,511,209,000 | 1.8% |
| 21 | Wisconsin | 11,023,893,000 | 1.7% |
| 22 | Minnesota | 10,576,654,000 | 1.6% |
| 23 | Alabama | 9,590,191,000 | 1.5% |
| 24 | Kentucky | 9,414,784,000 | 1.5% |
| 25 | Mississippi | 9,322,736,000 | 1.4% |
| 26 | Oregon | 8,748,975,000 | 1.4% |
| 27 | South Carolina | 8,725,520,000 | 1.4% |
| 28 | Oklahoma | 8,199,932,000 | 1.3% |
| 29 | Iowa | 7,524,475,000 | 1.2% |
| 30 | Colorado | 7,445,767,000 | 1.2% |
| 31 | Connecticut | 7,201,164,000 | 1.1% |
| 32 | New Mexico | 6,744,161,000 | 1.0% |
| 33 | Arkansas | 6,723,216,000 | 1.0% |
| 34 | Kansas | 5,158,672,000 | 0.8% |
| 35 | Utah | 5,046,312,000 | 0.8% |
| 36 | West Virginia | 4,945,437,000 | 0.8% |
| 37 | Nebraska | 3,747,101,000 | 0.6% |
| 38 | Maine | 3,399,180,000 | 0.5% |
| 39 | Nevada | 3,367,932,000 | 0.5% |
| 40 | Alaska | 3,360,673,000 | 0.5% |
| 41 | Hawaii | 3,180,863,000 | 0.5% |
| 42 | Idaho | 2,987,651,000 | 0.5% |
| 43 | Rhode Island | 2,889,426,000 | 0.4% |
| 44 | Montana | 2,669,071,000 | 0.4% |
| 45 | Wyoming | 2,353,678,000 | 0.4% |
| 46 | New Hampshire | 2,128,172,000 | 0.3% |
| 47 | Vermont | 2,116,754,000 | 0.3% |
| 48 | South Dakota | 2,054,905,000 | 0.3% |
| 49 | North Dakota | 1,903,346,000 | 0.3% |
| 50 | Delaware | 1,899,144,000 | 0.3% |
| | District of Columbia | 4,116,590,000 | 0.6% |

Source: U.S. Bureau of the Census, Governments Division
"2011 State and Local Government Finances" (http://www.census.gov/govs/local/)

# Per Capita State and Local Government Revenue
## from the Federal Government in 2011
## National Per Capita = $2,073

ALPHA ORDER

| RANK | STATE | PER CAPITA |
|---|---|---|
| 32 | Alabama | $1,996 |
| 1 | Alaska | 4,643 |
| 29 | Arizona | 2,014 |
| 17 | Arkansas | 2,288 |
| 29 | California | 2,014 |
| 48 | Colorado | 1,455 |
| 31 | Connecticut | 2,008 |
| 25 | Delaware | 2,091 |
| 46 | Florida | 1,678 |
| 45 | Georgia | 1,687 |
| 16 | Hawaii | 2,308 |
| 35 | Idaho | 1,886 |
| 43 | Illinois | 1,752 |
| 42 | Indiana | 1,771 |
| 14 | Iowa | 2,456 |
| 40 | Kansas | 1,797 |
| 22 | Kentucky | 2,156 |
| 7 | Louisiana | 2,984 |
| 12 | Maine | 2,559 |
| 23 | Maryland | 2,132 |
| 15 | Massachusetts | 2,349 |
| 20 | Michigan | 2,213 |
| 33 | Minnesota | 1,978 |
| 5 | Mississippi | 3,131 |
| 26 | Missouri | 2,085 |
| 10 | Montana | 2,675 |
| 27 | Nebraska | 2,034 |
| 50 | Nevada | 1,238 |
| 47 | New Hampshire | 1,615 |
| 44 | New Jersey | 1,726 |
| 4 | New Mexico | 3,244 |
| 6 | New York | 3,067 |
| 37 | North Carolina | 1,864 |
| 8 | North Dakota | 2,780 |
| 19 | Ohio | 2,256 |
| 21 | Oklahoma | 2,167 |
| 18 | Oregon | 2,262 |
| 24 | Pennsylvania | 2,127 |
| 9 | Rhode Island | 2,750 |
| 36 | South Carolina | 1,867 |
| 13 | South Dakota | 2,495 |
| 28 | Tennessee | 2,033 |
| 38 | Texas | 1,823 |
| 41 | Utah | 1,793 |
| 3 | Vermont | 3,378 |
| 49 | Virginia | 1,420 |
| 39 | Washington | 1,815 |
| 11 | West Virginia | 2,666 |
| 34 | Wisconsin | 1,931 |
| 2 | Wyoming | 4,149 |

RANK ORDER

| RANK | STATE | PER CAPITA |
|---|---|---|
| 1 | Alaska | $4,643 |
| 2 | Wyoming | 4,149 |
| 3 | Vermont | 3,378 |
| 4 | New Mexico | 3,244 |
| 5 | Mississippi | 3,131 |
| 6 | New York | 3,067 |
| 7 | Louisiana | 2,984 |
| 8 | North Dakota | 2,780 |
| 9 | Rhode Island | 2,750 |
| 10 | Montana | 2,675 |
| 11 | West Virginia | 2,666 |
| 12 | Maine | 2,559 |
| 13 | South Dakota | 2,495 |
| 14 | Iowa | 2,456 |
| 15 | Massachusetts | 2,349 |
| 16 | Hawaii | 2,308 |
| 17 | Arkansas | 2,288 |
| 18 | Oregon | 2,262 |
| 19 | Ohio | 2,256 |
| 20 | Michigan | 2,213 |
| 21 | Oklahoma | 2,167 |
| 22 | Kentucky | 2,156 |
| 23 | Maryland | 2,132 |
| 24 | Pennsylvania | 2,127 |
| 25 | Delaware | 2,091 |
| 26 | Missouri | 2,085 |
| 27 | Nebraska | 2,034 |
| 28 | Tennessee | 2,033 |
| 29 | Arizona | 2,014 |
| 29 | California | 2,014 |
| 31 | Connecticut | 2,008 |
| 32 | Alabama | 1,996 |
| 33 | Minnesota | 1,978 |
| 34 | Wisconsin | 1,931 |
| 35 | Idaho | 1,886 |
| 36 | South Carolina | 1,867 |
| 37 | North Carolina | 1,864 |
| 38 | Texas | 1,823 |
| 39 | Washington | 1,815 |
| 40 | Kansas | 1,797 |
| 41 | Utah | 1,793 |
| 42 | Indiana | 1,771 |
| 43 | Illinois | 1,752 |
| 44 | New Jersey | 1,726 |
| 45 | Georgia | 1,687 |
| 46 | Florida | 1,678 |
| 47 | New Hampshire | 1,615 |
| 48 | Colorado | 1,455 |
| 49 | Virginia | 1,420 |
| 50 | Nevada | 1,238 |
| | District of Columbia | 6,650 |

Source: CQ Press using data from U.S. Bureau of the Census, Governments Division
"2011 State and Local Government Finances" (http://www.census.gov/govs/local/)

# Percent of State and Local Government Revenue
## from the Federal Government in 2011
## National Percent = 18.8%*

ALPHA ORDER

| RANK | STATE | PERCENT |
|------|-------|---------|
| 10 | Alabama | 23.6 |
| 35 | Alaska | 18.2 |
| 16 | Arizona | 22.2 |
| 9 | Arkansas | 24.1 |
| 47 | California | 14.6 |
| 49 | Colorado | 14.0 |
| 41 | Connecticut | 17.1 |
| 42 | Delaware | 17.0 |
| 37 | Florida | 17.7 |
| 29 | Georgia | 19.5 |
| 25 | Hawaii | 19.9 |
| 20 | Idaho | 21.2 |
| 43 | Illinois | 16.9 |
| 22 | Indiana | 20.3 |
| 18 | Iowa | 21.8 |
| 36 | Kansas | 18.1 |
| 13 | Kentucky | 23.1 |
| 3 | Louisiana | 27.8 |
| 7 | Maine | 24.3 |
| 26 | Maryland | 19.8 |
| 32 | Massachusetts | 18.9 |
| 11 | Michigan | 23.4 |
| 44 | Minnesota | 16.6 |
| 1 | Mississippi | 29.7 |
| 17 | Missouri | 21.9 |
| 6 | Montana | 26.1 |
| 40 | Nebraska | 17.3 |
| 50 | Nevada | 13.0 |
| 39 | New Hampshire | 17.4 |
| 48 | New Jersey | 14.5 |
| 3 | New Mexico | 27.8 |
| 34 | New York | 18.5 |
| 30 | North Carolina | 19.3 |
| 28 | North Dakota | 19.7 |
| 26 | Ohio | 19.8 |
| 12 | Oklahoma | 23.2 |
| 33 | Oregon | 18.6 |
| 23 | Pennsylvania | 20.2 |
| 15 | Rhode Island | 22.7 |
| 31 | South Carolina | 19.1 |
| 7 | South Dakota | 24.3 |
| 19 | Tennessee | 21.6 |
| 21 | Texas | 20.8 |
| 24 | Utah | 20.0 |
| 2 | Vermont | 27.9 |
| 46 | Virginia | 15.1 |
| 45 | Washington | 15.9 |
| 5 | West Virginia | 26.4 |
| 38 | Wisconsin | 17.6 |
| 13 | Wyoming | 23.1 |

RANK ORDER

| RANK | STATE | PERCENT |
|------|-------|---------|
| 1 | Mississippi | 29.7 |
| 2 | Vermont | 27.9 |
| 3 | Louisiana | 27.8 |
| 3 | New Mexico | 27.8 |
| 5 | West Virginia | 26.4 |
| 6 | Montana | 26.1 |
| 7 | Maine | 24.3 |
| 7 | South Dakota | 24.3 |
| 9 | Arkansas | 24.1 |
| 10 | Alabama | 23.6 |
| 11 | Michigan | 23.4 |
| 12 | Oklahoma | 23.2 |
| 13 | Kentucky | 23.1 |
| 13 | Wyoming | 23.1 |
| 15 | Rhode Island | 22.7 |
| 16 | Arizona | 22.2 |
| 17 | Missouri | 21.9 |
| 18 | Iowa | 21.8 |
| 19 | Tennessee | 21.6 |
| 20 | Idaho | 21.2 |
| 21 | Texas | 20.8 |
| 22 | Indiana | 20.3 |
| 23 | Pennsylvania | 20.2 |
| 24 | Utah | 20.0 |
| 25 | Hawaii | 19.9 |
| 26 | Maryland | 19.8 |
| 26 | Ohio | 19.8 |
| 28 | North Dakota | 19.7 |
| 29 | Georgia | 19.5 |
| 30 | North Carolina | 19.3 |
| 31 | South Carolina | 19.1 |
| 32 | Massachusetts | 18.9 |
| 33 | Oregon | 18.6 |
| 34 | New York | 18.5 |
| 35 | Alaska | 18.2 |
| 36 | Kansas | 18.1 |
| 37 | Florida | 17.7 |
| 38 | Wisconsin | 17.6 |
| 39 | New Hampshire | 17.4 |
| 40 | Nebraska | 17.3 |
| 41 | Connecticut | 17.1 |
| 42 | Delaware | 17.0 |
| 43 | Illinois | 16.9 |
| 44 | Minnesota | 16.6 |
| 45 | Washington | 15.9 |
| 46 | Virginia | 15.1 |
| 47 | California | 14.6 |
| 48 | New Jersey | 14.5 |
| 49 | Colorado | 14.0 |
| 50 | Nevada | 13.0 |
| | District of Columbia | 32.0 |

Source: CQ Press using data from U.S. Bureau of the Census, Governments Division
"2011 State and Local Government Finances" (http://www.census.gov/govs/local/)
*As a percent of total revenue.

# State and Local Government Own Source Revenue in 2011

## National Total = $1,966,815,199,000*

ALPHA ORDER

| RANK | STATE | REVENUE | % of USA |
|---|---|---|---|
| 26 | Alabama | $24,983,377,000 | 1.3% |
| 36 | Alaska | 12,458,955,000 | 0.6% |
| 20 | Arizona | 30,987,666,000 | 1.6% |
| 34 | Arkansas | 14,820,451,000 | 0.8% |
| 1 | California | 268,224,294,000 | 13.6% |
| 19 | Colorado | 34,058,466,000 | 1.7% |
| 23 | Connecticut | 27,739,815,000 | 1.4% |
| 45 | Delaware | 6,965,208,000 | 0.4% |
| 4 | Florida | 106,851,087,000 | 5.4% |
| 13 | Georgia | 47,551,004,000 | 2.4% |
| 40 | Hawaii | 9,731,812,000 | 0.5% |
| 42 | Idaho | 7,772,507,000 | 0.4% |
| 5 | Illinois | 79,558,403,000 | 4.0% |
| 18 | Indiana | 35,759,783,000 | 1.8% |
| 29 | Iowa | 20,042,046,000 | 1.0% |
| 31 | Kansas | 18,379,745,000 | 0.9% |
| 28 | Kentucky | 22,225,736,000 | 1.1% |
| 24 | Louisiana | 26,920,095,000 | 1.4% |
| 41 | Maine | 8,079,918,000 | 0.4% |
| 15 | Maryland | 38,661,990,000 | 2.0% |
| 11 | Massachusetts | 49,379,348,000 | 2.5% |
| 9 | Michigan | 56,352,420,000 | 2.9% |
| 16 | Minnesota | 38,215,621,000 | 1.9% |
| 32 | Mississippi | 15,448,529,000 | 0.8% |
| 21 | Missouri | 29,785,399,000 | 1.5% |
| 48 | Montana | 5,272,157,000 | 0.3% |
| 38 | Nebraska | 11,645,121,000 | 0.6% |
| 35 | Nevada | 14,511,065,000 | 0.7% |
| 43 | New Hampshire | 7,670,223,000 | 0.4% |
| 7 | New Jersey | 69,591,556,000 | 3.5% |
| 37 | New Mexico | 12,053,657,000 | 0.6% |
| 2 | New York | 190,882,845,000 | 9.7% |
| 10 | North Carolina | 53,023,022,000 | 2.7% |
| 46 | North Dakota | 6,447,656,000 | 0.3% |
| 8 | Ohio | 67,646,836,000 | 3.4% |
| 30 | Oklahoma | 19,557,046,000 | 1.0% |
| 27 | Oregon | 23,025,353,000 | 1.2% |
| 6 | Pennsylvania | 79,525,919,000 | 4.0% |
| 44 | Rhode Island | 7,241,946,000 | 0.4% |
| 25 | South Carolina | 26,609,197,000 | 1.4% |
| 50 | South Dakota | 4,147,634,000 | 0.2% |
| 22 | Tennessee | 29,634,638,000 | 1.5% |
| 3 | Texas | 135,218,244,000 | 6.9% |
| 33 | Utah | 15,069,235,000 | 0.8% |
| 49 | Vermont | 4,347,785,000 | 0.2% |
| 12 | Virginia | 49,175,882,000 | 2.5% |
| 14 | Washington | 43,604,806,000 | 2.2% |
| 39 | West Virginia | 10,844,014,000 | 0.6% |
| 17 | Wisconsin | 36,232,114,000 | 1.8% |
| 47 | Wyoming | 6,226,129,000 | 0.3% |

RANK ORDER

| RANK | STATE | REVENUE | % of USA |
|---|---|---|---|
| 1 | California | $268,224,294,000 | 13.6% |
| 2 | New York | 190,882,845,000 | 9.7% |
| 3 | Texas | 135,218,244,000 | 6.9% |
| 4 | Florida | 106,851,087,000 | 5.4% |
| 5 | Illinois | 79,558,403,000 | 4.0% |
| 6 | Pennsylvania | 79,525,919,000 | 4.0% |
| 7 | New Jersey | 69,591,556,000 | 3.5% |
| 8 | Ohio | 67,646,836,000 | 3.4% |
| 9 | Michigan | 56,352,420,000 | 2.9% |
| 10 | North Carolina | 53,023,022,000 | 2.7% |
| 11 | Massachusetts | 49,379,348,000 | 2.5% |
| 12 | Virginia | 49,175,882,000 | 2.5% |
| 13 | Georgia | 47,551,004,000 | 2.4% |
| 14 | Washington | 43,604,806,000 | 2.2% |
| 15 | Maryland | 38,661,990,000 | 2.0% |
| 16 | Minnesota | 38,215,621,000 | 1.9% |
| 17 | Wisconsin | 36,232,114,000 | 1.8% |
| 18 | Indiana | 35,759,783,000 | 1.8% |
| 19 | Colorado | 34,058,466,000 | 1.7% |
| 20 | Arizona | 30,987,666,000 | 1.6% |
| 21 | Missouri | 29,785,399,000 | 1.5% |
| 22 | Tennessee | 29,634,638,000 | 1.5% |
| 23 | Connecticut | 27,739,815,000 | 1.4% |
| 24 | Louisiana | 26,920,095,000 | 1.4% |
| 25 | South Carolina | 26,609,197,000 | 1.4% |
| 26 | Alabama | 24,983,377,000 | 1.3% |
| 27 | Oregon | 23,025,353,000 | 1.2% |
| 28 | Kentucky | 22,225,736,000 | 1.1% |
| 29 | Iowa | 20,042,046,000 | 1.0% |
| 30 | Oklahoma | 19,557,046,000 | 1.0% |
| 31 | Kansas | 18,379,745,000 | 0.9% |
| 32 | Mississippi | 15,448,529,000 | 0.8% |
| 33 | Utah | 15,069,235,000 | 0.8% |
| 34 | Arkansas | 14,820,451,000 | 0.8% |
| 35 | Nevada | 14,511,065,000 | 0.7% |
| 36 | Alaska | 12,458,955,000 | 0.6% |
| 37 | New Mexico | 12,053,657,000 | 0.6% |
| 38 | Nebraska | 11,645,121,000 | 0.6% |
| 39 | West Virginia | 10,844,014,000 | 0.6% |
| 40 | Hawaii | 9,731,812,000 | 0.5% |
| 41 | Maine | 8,079,918,000 | 0.4% |
| 42 | Idaho | 7,772,507,000 | 0.4% |
| 43 | New Hampshire | 7,670,223,000 | 0.4% |
| 44 | Rhode Island | 7,241,946,000 | 0.4% |
| 45 | Delaware | 6,965,208,000 | 0.4% |
| 46 | North Dakota | 6,447,656,000 | 0.3% |
| 47 | Wyoming | 6,226,129,000 | 0.3% |
| 48 | Montana | 5,272,157,000 | 0.3% |
| 49 | Vermont | 4,347,785,000 | 0.2% |
| 50 | South Dakota | 4,147,634,000 | 0.2% |
| | District of Columbia | 6,657,444,000 | 0.3% |

Source: U.S. Bureau of the Census, Governments Division
"2011 State and Local Government Finances" (http://www.census.gov/govs/local/)
*Own source revenue includes taxes, current charges, and miscellaneous general revenue. Excluded are intergovernmental transfers, insurance trust revenue, and revenue from government owned utilities and other commercial or auxiliary enterprise.

# Per Capita State and Local Government Own Source Revenue in 2011

## National Per Capita = $6,312*

ALPHA ORDER

| RANK | STATE | PER CAPITA |
|------|-------|------------|
| 40 | Alabama | $5,201 |
| 1 | Alaska | 17,212 |
| 49 | Arizona | 4,791 |
| 44 | Arkansas | 5,043 |
| 10 | California | 7,118 |
| 14 | Colorado | 6,657 |
| 6 | Connecticut | 7,734 |
| 7 | Delaware | 7,670 |
| 33 | Florida | 5,599 |
| 48 | Georgia | 4,846 |
| 11 | Hawaii | 7,062 |
| 47 | Idaho | 4,908 |
| 22 | Illinois | 6,187 |
| 35 | Indiana | 5,488 |
| 16 | Iowa | 6,541 |
| 17 | Kansas | 6,403 |
| 43 | Kentucky | 5,090 |
| 26 | Louisiana | 5,884 |
| 23 | Maine | 6,082 |
| 15 | Maryland | 6,621 |
| 8 | Massachusetts | 7,474 |
| 31 | Michigan | 5,706 |
| 9 | Minnesota | 7,147 |
| 41 | Mississippi | 5,188 |
| 46 | Missouri | 4,957 |
| 38 | Montana | 5,284 |
| 20 | Nebraska | 6,321 |
| 37 | Nevada | 5,335 |
| 29 | New Hampshire | 5,820 |
| 5 | New Jersey | 7,877 |
| 30 | New Mexico | 5,799 |
| 3 | New York | 9,788 |
| 34 | North Carolina | 5,494 |
| 4 | North Dakota | 9,416 |
| 27 | Ohio | 5,861 |
| 42 | Oklahoma | 5,168 |
| 25 | Oregon | 5,952 |
| 21 | Pennsylvania | 6,240 |
| 13 | Rhode Island | 6,893 |
| 32 | South Carolina | 5,694 |
| 45 | South Dakota | 5,036 |
| 50 | Tennessee | 4,631 |
| 39 | Texas | 5,275 |
| 36 | Utah | 5,354 |
| 12 | Vermont | 6,939 |
| 24 | Virginia | 6,068 |
| 18 | Washington | 6,391 |
| 28 | West Virginia | 5,846 |
| 19 | Wisconsin | 6,346 |
| 2 | Wyoming | 10,974 |

RANK ORDER

| RANK | STATE | PER CAPITA |
|------|-------|------------|
| 1 | Alaska | $17,212 |
| 2 | Wyoming | 10,974 |
| 3 | New York | 9,788 |
| 4 | North Dakota | 9,416 |
| 5 | New Jersey | 7,877 |
| 6 | Connecticut | 7,734 |
| 7 | Delaware | 7,670 |
| 8 | Massachusetts | 7,474 |
| 9 | Minnesota | 7,147 |
| 10 | California | 7,118 |
| 11 | Hawaii | 7,062 |
| 12 | Vermont | 6,939 |
| 13 | Rhode Island | 6,893 |
| 14 | Colorado | 6,657 |
| 15 | Maryland | 6,621 |
| 16 | Iowa | 6,541 |
| 17 | Kansas | 6,403 |
| 18 | Washington | 6,391 |
| 19 | Wisconsin | 6,346 |
| 20 | Nebraska | 6,321 |
| 21 | Pennsylvania | 6,240 |
| 22 | Illinois | 6,187 |
| 23 | Maine | 6,082 |
| 24 | Virginia | 6,068 |
| 25 | Oregon | 5,952 |
| 26 | Louisiana | 5,884 |
| 27 | Ohio | 5,861 |
| 28 | West Virginia | 5,846 |
| 29 | New Hampshire | 5,820 |
| 30 | New Mexico | 5,799 |
| 31 | Michigan | 5,706 |
| 32 | South Carolina | 5,694 |
| 33 | Florida | 5,599 |
| 34 | North Carolina | 5,494 |
| 35 | Indiana | 5,488 |
| 36 | Utah | 5,354 |
| 37 | Nevada | 5,335 |
| 38 | Montana | 5,284 |
| 39 | Texas | 5,275 |
| 40 | Alabama | 5,201 |
| 41 | Mississippi | 5,188 |
| 42 | Oklahoma | 5,168 |
| 43 | Kentucky | 5,090 |
| 44 | Arkansas | 5,043 |
| 45 | South Dakota | 5,036 |
| 46 | Missouri | 4,957 |
| 47 | Idaho | 4,908 |
| 48 | Georgia | 4,846 |
| 49 | Arizona | 4,791 |
| 50 | Tennessee | 4,631 |

District of Columbia 10,755

Source: CQ Press using data from U.S. Bureau of the Census, Governments Division
"2011 State and Local Government Finances" (http://www.census.gov/govs/local/)
*Own source revenue includes taxes, current charges, and miscellaneous general revenue. Excluded are intergovernmental transfers, insurance trust revenue, and revenue from government owned utilities and other commercial or auxiliary enterprise.

# State and Local Government Tax Revenue in 2011

## National Total = $1,338,436,677,000

| RANK | STATE | REVENUE | % of USA | | RANK | STATE | REVENUE | % of USA |
|------|-------|---------|----------|---|------|-------|---------|----------|
| 27 | Alabama | $13,878,574,000 | 1.0% | | 1 | California | $185,218,208,000 | 13.8% |
| 37 | Alaska | 7,292,155,000 | 0.5% | | 2 | New York | 144,733,996,000 | 10.8% |
| 21 | Arizona | 21,655,498,000 | 1.6% | | 3 | Texas | 90,778,181,000 | 6.8% |
| 33 | Arkansas | 9,949,704,000 | 0.7% | | 4 | Florida | 65,259,273,000 | 4.9% |
| 1 | California | 185,218,208,000 | 13.8% | | 5 | Illinois | 59,551,953,000 | 4.4% |
| 20 | Colorado | 21,791,868,000 | 1.6% | | 6 | Pennsylvania | 55,770,938,000 | 4.2% |
| 19 | Connecticut | 22,762,680,000 | 1.7% | | 7 | New Jersey | 53,149,940,000 | 4.0% |
| 46 | Delaware | 4,072,252,000 | 0.3% | | 8 | Ohio | 45,123,778,000 | 3.4% |
| 4 | Florida | 65,259,273,000 | 4.9% | | 9 | Michigan | 36,102,277,000 | 2.7% |
| 13 | Georgia | 31,132,743,000 | 2.3% | | 10 | Massachusetts | 35,841,109,000 | 2.7% |
| 40 | Hawaii | 6,572,749,000 | 0.5% | | 11 | North Carolina | 33,710,615,000 | 2.5% |
| 44 | Idaho | 4,711,409,000 | 0.4% | | 12 | Virginia | 32,152,972,000 | 2.4% |
| 5 | Illinois | 59,551,953,000 | 4.4% | | 13 | Georgia | 31,132,743,000 | 2.3% |
| 18 | Indiana | 23,152,483,000 | 1.7% | | 14 | Maryland | 29,037,074,000 | 2.2% |
| 29 | Iowa | 12,649,129,000 | 0.9% | | 15 | Washington | 28,409,657,000 | 2.1% |
| 31 | Kansas | 11,756,882,000 | 0.9% | | 16 | Minnesota | 26,822,750,000 | 2.0% |
| 25 | Kentucky | 14,556,418,000 | 1.1% | | 17 | Wisconsin | 25,605,386,000 | 1.9% |
| 24 | Louisiana | 16,612,385,000 | 1.2% | | 18 | Indiana | 23,152,483,000 | 1.7% |
| 41 | Maine | 6,054,014,000 | 0.5% | | 19 | Connecticut | 22,762,680,000 | 1.7% |
| 14 | Maryland | 29,037,074,000 | 2.2% | | 20 | Colorado | 21,791,868,000 | 1.6% |
| 10 | Massachusetts | 35,841,109,000 | 2.7% | | 21 | Arizona | 21,655,498,000 | 1.6% |
| 9 | Michigan | 36,102,277,000 | 2.7% | | 22 | Missouri | 19,641,850,000 | 1.5% |
| 16 | Minnesota | 26,822,750,000 | 2.0% | | 23 | Tennessee | 19,077,703,000 | 1.4% |
| 34 | Mississippi | 9,269,168,000 | 0.7% | | 24 | Louisiana | 16,612,385,000 | 1.2% |
| 22 | Missouri | 19,641,850,000 | 1.5% | | 25 | Kentucky | 14,556,418,000 | 1.1% |
| 48 | Montana | 3,434,612,000 | 0.3% | | 26 | Oregon | 14,110,679,000 | 1.1% |
| 36 | Nebraska | 7,800,549,000 | 0.6% | | 27 | Alabama | 13,878,574,000 | 1.0% |
| 32 | Nevada | 10,214,320,000 | 0.8% | | 28 | South Carolina | 13,743,802,000 | 1.0% |
| 42 | New Hampshire | 5,311,294,000 | 0.4% | | 29 | Iowa | 12,649,129,000 | 0.9% |
| 7 | New Jersey | 53,149,940,000 | 4.0% | | 30 | Oklahoma | 12,010,585,000 | 0.9% |
| 38 | New Mexico | 7,249,589,000 | 0.5% | | 31 | Kansas | 11,756,882,000 | 0.9% |
| 2 | New York | 144,733,996,000 | 10.8% | | 32 | Nevada | 10,214,320,000 | 0.8% |
| 11 | North Carolina | 33,710,615,000 | 2.5% | | 33 | Arkansas | 9,949,704,000 | 0.7% |
| 45 | North Dakota | 4,709,350,000 | 0.4% | | 34 | Mississippi | 9,269,168,000 | 0.7% |
| 8 | Ohio | 45,123,778,000 | 3.4% | | 35 | Utah | 9,057,134,000 | 0.7% |
| 30 | Oklahoma | 12,010,585,000 | 0.9% | | 36 | Nebraska | 7,800,549,000 | 0.6% |
| 26 | Oregon | 14,110,679,000 | 1.1% | | 37 | Alaska | 7,292,155,000 | 0.5% |
| 6 | Pennsylvania | 55,770,938,000 | 4.2% | | 38 | New Mexico | 7,249,589,000 | 0.5% |
| 43 | Rhode Island | 5,080,343,000 | 0.4% | | 39 | West Virginia | 6,975,261,000 | 0.5% |
| 28 | South Carolina | 13,743,802,000 | 1.0% | | 40 | Hawaii | 6,572,749,000 | 0.5% |
| 50 | South Dakota | 2,699,154,000 | 0.2% | | 41 | Maine | 6,054,014,000 | 0.5% |
| 23 | Tennessee | 19,077,703,000 | 1.4% | | 42 | New Hampshire | 5,311,294,000 | 0.4% |
| 3 | Texas | 90,778,181,000 | 6.8% | | 43 | Rhode Island | 5,080,343,000 | 0.4% |
| 35 | Utah | 9,057,134,000 | 0.7% | | 44 | Idaho | 4,711,409,000 | 0.4% |
| 49 | Vermont | 3,140,119,000 | 0.2% | | 45 | North Dakota | 4,709,350,000 | 0.4% |
| 12 | Virginia | 32,152,972,000 | 2.4% | | 46 | Delaware | 4,072,252,000 | 0.3% |
| 15 | Washington | 28,409,657,000 | 2.1% | | 47 | Wyoming | 3,673,312,000 | 0.3% |
| 39 | West Virginia | 6,975,261,000 | 0.5% | | 48 | Montana | 3,434,612,000 | 0.3% |
| 17 | Wisconsin | 25,605,386,000 | 1.9% | | 49 | Vermont | 3,140,119,000 | 0.2% |
| 47 | Wyoming | 3,673,312,000 | 0.3% | | 50 | South Dakota | 2,699,154,000 | 0.2% |
| | | | | | | District of Columbia | 5,368,803,000 | 0.4% |

ALPHA ORDER

RANK ORDER

Source: U.S. Bureau of the Census, Governments Division
"2011 State and Local Government Finances" (http://www.census.gov/govs/local/)

# Per Capita State and Local Government Tax Revenue in 2011

## National Per Capita = $4,296

ALPHA ORDER

| RANK | STATE | PER CAPITA |
|---|---|---|
| 50 | Alabama | $2,889 |
| 1 | Alaska | 10,074 |
| 39 | Arizona | 3,348 |
| 38 | Arkansas | 3,386 |
| 11 | California | 4,915 |
| 19 | Colorado | 4,259 |
| 5 | Connecticut | 6,346 |
| 16 | Delaware | 4,484 |
| 37 | Florida | 3,420 |
| 45 | Georgia | 3,173 |
| 13 | Hawaii | 4,769 |
| 48 | Idaho | 2,975 |
| 14 | Illinois | 4,631 |
| 32 | Indiana | 3,553 |
| 22 | Iowa | 4,128 |
| 23 | Kansas | 4,096 |
| 40 | Kentucky | 3,333 |
| 31 | Louisiana | 3,631 |
| 15 | Maine | 4,557 |
| 10 | Maryland | 4,972 |
| 7 | Massachusetts | 5,425 |
| 29 | Michigan | 3,655 |
| 8 | Minnesota | 5,016 |
| 46 | Mississippi | 3,113 |
| 42 | Missouri | 3,269 |
| 36 | Montana | 3,443 |
| 20 | Nebraska | 4,234 |
| 28 | Nevada | 3,755 |
| 24 | New Hampshire | 4,030 |
| 6 | New Jersey | 6,016 |
| 35 | New Mexico | 3,488 |
| 2 | New York | 7,422 |
| 34 | North Carolina | 3,493 |
| 3 | North Dakota | 6,878 |
| 26 | Ohio | 3,910 |
| 44 | Oklahoma | 3,174 |
| 30 | Oregon | 3,648 |
| 18 | Pennsylvania | 4,376 |
| 12 | Rhode Island | 4,835 |
| 49 | South Carolina | 2,941 |
| 41 | South Dakota | 3,277 |
| 47 | Tennessee | 2,981 |
| 33 | Texas | 3,542 |
| 43 | Utah | 3,218 |
| 9 | Vermont | 5,011 |
| 25 | Virginia | 3,967 |
| 21 | Washington | 4,164 |
| 27 | West Virginia | 3,760 |
| 16 | Wisconsin | 4,484 |
| 4 | Wyoming | 6,474 |

RANK ORDER

| RANK | STATE | PER CAPITA |
|---|---|---|
| 1 | Alaska | $10,074 |
| 2 | New York | 7,422 |
| 3 | North Dakota | 6,878 |
| 4 | Wyoming | 6,474 |
| 5 | Connecticut | 6,346 |
| 6 | New Jersey | 6,016 |
| 7 | Massachusetts | 5,425 |
| 8 | Minnesota | 5,016 |
| 9 | Vermont | 5,011 |
| 10 | Maryland | 4,972 |
| 11 | California | 4,915 |
| 12 | Rhode Island | 4,835 |
| 13 | Hawaii | 4,769 |
| 14 | Illinois | 4,631 |
| 15 | Maine | 4,557 |
| 16 | Delaware | 4,484 |
| 16 | Wisconsin | 4,484 |
| 18 | Pennsylvania | 4,376 |
| 19 | Colorado | 4,259 |
| 20 | Nebraska | 4,234 |
| 21 | Washington | 4,164 |
| 22 | Iowa | 4,128 |
| 23 | Kansas | 4,096 |
| 24 | New Hampshire | 4,030 |
| 25 | Virginia | 3,967 |
| 26 | Ohio | 3,910 |
| 27 | West Virginia | 3,760 |
| 28 | Nevada | 3,755 |
| 29 | Michigan | 3,655 |
| 30 | Oregon | 3,648 |
| 31 | Louisiana | 3,631 |
| 32 | Indiana | 3,553 |
| 33 | Texas | 3,542 |
| 34 | North Carolina | 3,493 |
| 35 | New Mexico | 3,488 |
| 36 | Montana | 3,443 |
| 37 | Florida | 3,420 |
| 38 | Arkansas | 3,386 |
| 39 | Arizona | 3,348 |
| 40 | Kentucky | 3,333 |
| 41 | South Dakota | 3,277 |
| 42 | Missouri | 3,269 |
| 43 | Utah | 3,218 |
| 44 | Oklahoma | 3,174 |
| 45 | Georgia | 3,173 |
| 46 | Mississippi | 3,113 |
| 47 | Tennessee | 2,981 |
| 48 | Idaho | 2,975 |
| 49 | South Carolina | 2,941 |
| 50 | Alabama | 2,889 |

District of Columbia    8,673

Source: CQ Press using data from U.S. Bureau of the Census, Governments Division
"2011 State and Local Government Finances" (http://www.census.gov/govs/local/)

# Percent of State and Local Government Revenue from Taxes in 2011

## National Percent = 39.0%

| ALPHA ORDER | | | | RANK ORDER | | |
|---|---|---|---|---|---|---|
| RANK | STATE | PERCENT | | RANK | STATE | PERCENT |
| 40 | Alabama | 34.1 | | 1 | Connecticut | 54.0 |
| 21 | Alaska | 39.5 | | 2 | New Jersey | 50.5 |
| 25 | Arizona | 36.9 | | 3 | North Dakota | 48.8 |
| 35 | Arkansas | 35.7 | | 4 | Maryland | 46.2 |
| 35 | California | 35.7 | | 5 | New York | 44.7 |
| 16 | Colorado | 41.1 | | 6 | Illinois | 44.6 |
| 1 | Connecticut | 54.0 | | 7 | Massachusetts | 43.7 |
| 29 | Delaware | 36.4 | | 8 | New Hampshire | 43.5 |
| 31 | Florida | 36.0 | | 9 | Maine | 43.3 |
| 26 | Georgia | 36.6 | | 10 | Minnesota | 42.2 |
| 14 | Hawaii | 41.2 | | 11 | Virginia | 42.1 |
| 44 | Idaho | 33.4 | | 12 | Pennsylvania | 41.5 |
| 6 | Illinois | 44.6 | | 13 | Vermont | 41.4 |
| 18 | Indiana | 40.7 | | 14 | Hawaii | 41.2 |
| 26 | Iowa | 36.6 | | 14 | Kansas | 41.2 |
| 14 | Kansas | 41.2 | | 16 | Colorado | 41.1 |
| 35 | Kentucky | 35.7 | | 17 | Wisconsin | 40.8 |
| 42 | Louisiana | 33.8 | | 18 | Indiana | 40.7 |
| 9 | Maine | 43.3 | | 19 | Texas | 40.4 |
| 4 | Maryland | 46.2 | | 20 | Rhode Island | 39.9 |
| 7 | Massachusetts | 43.7 | | 21 | Alaska | 39.5 |
| 23 | Michigan | 38.7 | | 22 | Nevada | 39.4 |
| 10 | Minnesota | 42.2 | | 23 | Michigan | 38.7 |
| 50 | Mississippi | 29.5 | | 24 | West Virginia | 37.2 |
| 38 | Missouri | 34.4 | | 25 | Arizona | 36.9 |
| 43 | Montana | 33.6 | | 26 | Georgia | 36.6 |
| 31 | Nebraska | 36.0 | | 26 | Iowa | 36.6 |
| 22 | Nevada | 39.4 | | 28 | Washington | 36.5 |
| 8 | New Hampshire | 43.5 | | 29 | Delaware | 36.4 |
| 2 | New Jersey | 50.5 | | 30 | North Carolina | 36.1 |
| 49 | New Mexico | 29.9 | | 31 | Florida | 36.0 |
| 5 | New York | 44.7 | | 31 | Nebraska | 36.0 |
| 30 | North Carolina | 36.1 | | 31 | Utah | 36.0 |
| 3 | North Dakota | 48.8 | | 31 | Wyoming | 36.0 |
| 39 | Ohio | 34.3 | | 35 | Arkansas | 35.7 |
| 41 | Oklahoma | 33.9 | | 35 | California | 35.7 |
| 47 | Oregon | 30.0 | | 35 | Kentucky | 35.7 |
| 12 | Pennsylvania | 41.5 | | 38 | Missouri | 34.4 |
| 20 | Rhode Island | 39.9 | | 39 | Ohio | 34.3 |
| 47 | South Carolina | 30.0 | | 40 | Alabama | 34.1 |
| 45 | South Dakota | 31.9 | | 41 | Oklahoma | 33.9 |
| 46 | Tennessee | 31.6 | | 42 | Louisiana | 33.8 |
| 19 | Texas | 40.4 | | 43 | Montana | 33.6 |
| 31 | Utah | 36.0 | | 44 | Idaho | 33.4 |
| 13 | Vermont | 41.4 | | 45 | South Dakota | 31.9 |
| 11 | Virginia | 42.1 | | 46 | Tennessee | 31.6 |
| 28 | Washington | 36.5 | | 47 | Oregon | 30.0 |
| 24 | West Virginia | 37.2 | | 47 | South Carolina | 30.0 |
| 17 | Wisconsin | 40.8 | | 49 | New Mexico | 29.9 |
| 31 | Wyoming | 36.0 | | 50 | Mississippi | 29.5 |
| | | | | | District of Columbia | 41.7 |

Source: CQ Press using data from U.S. Bureau of the Census, Governments Division
"2011 State and Local Government Finances" (http://www.census.gov/govs/local/)

# State and Local Government Tax Revenue
## as a Percent of Personal Income in 2011
## National Percent = 10.3% of Personal Income*

ALPHA ORDER

ALPHA ORDER

| RANK | STATE | PERCENT | | RANK | STATE | PERCENT |
|------|-------|---------|---|------|-------|---------|
| 48 | Alabama | 8.3 | | 1 | Alaska | 22.1 |
| 1 | Alaska | 22.1 | | 2 | North Dakota | 14.6 |
| 36 | Arizona | 9.5 | | 3 | New York | 14.5 |
| 23 | Arkansas | 10.0 | | 4 | Wyoming | 13.5 |
| 8 | California | 11.3 | | 5 | Vermont | 12.1 |
| 30 | Colorado | 9.7 | | 6 | Maine | 11.9 |
| 13 | Connecticut | 11.0 | | 7 | New Jersey | 11.5 |
| 15 | Delaware | 10.8 | | 8 | California | 11.3 |
| 44 | Florida | 8.6 | | 8 | Minnesota | 11.3 |
| 40 | Georgia | 8.8 | | 8 | West Virginia | 11.3 |
| 12 | Hawaii | 11.1 | | 8 | Wisconsin | 11.3 |
| 39 | Idaho | 9.0 | | 12 | Hawaii | 11.1 |
| 16 | Illinois | 10.6 | | 13 | Connecticut | 11.0 |
| 23 | Indiana | 10.0 | | 13 | Rhode Island | 11.0 |
| 23 | Iowa | 10.0 | | 15 | Delaware | 10.8 |
| 23 | Kansas | 10.0 | | 16 | Illinois | 10.6 |
| 28 | Kentucky | 9.8 | | 17 | Ohio | 10.3 |
| 38 | Louisiana | 9.4 | | 17 | Pennsylvania | 10.3 |
| 6 | Maine | 11.9 | | 19 | Massachusetts | 10.2 |
| 28 | Maryland | 9.8 | | 19 | New Mexico | 10.2 |
| 19 | Massachusetts | 10.2 | | 21 | Michigan | 10.1 |
| 21 | Michigan | 10.1 | | 21 | Nevada | 10.1 |
| 8 | Minnesota | 11.3 | | 23 | Arkansas | 10.0 |
| 30 | Mississippi | 9.7 | | 23 | Indiana | 10.0 |
| 44 | Missouri | 8.6 | | 23 | Iowa | 10.0 |
| 34 | Montana | 9.6 | | 23 | Kansas | 10.0 |
| 23 | Nebraska | 10.0 | | 23 | Nebraska | 10.0 |
| 21 | Nevada | 10.1 | | 28 | Kentucky | 9.8 |
| 40 | New Hampshire | 8.8 | | 28 | Maryland | 9.8 |
| 7 | New Jersey | 11.5 | | 30 | Colorado | 9.7 |
| 19 | New Mexico | 10.2 | | 30 | Mississippi | 9.7 |
| 3 | New York | 14.5 | | 30 | North Carolina | 9.7 |
| 30 | North Carolina | 9.7 | | 30 | Oregon | 9.7 |
| 2 | North Dakota | 14.6 | | 34 | Montana | 9.6 |
| 17 | Ohio | 10.3 | | 34 | Utah | 9.6 |
| 47 | Oklahoma | 8.4 | | 36 | Arizona | 9.5 |
| 30 | Oregon | 9.7 | | 36 | Washington | 9.5 |
| 17 | Pennsylvania | 10.3 | | 38 | Louisiana | 9.4 |
| 13 | Rhode Island | 11.0 | | 39 | Idaho | 9.0 |
| 40 | South Carolina | 8.8 | | 40 | Georgia | 8.8 |
| 50 | South Dakota | 7.4 | | 40 | New Hampshire | 8.8 |
| 49 | Tennessee | 8.1 | | 40 | South Carolina | 8.8 |
| 40 | Texas | 8.8 | | 40 | Texas | 8.8 |
| 34 | Utah | 9.6 | | 44 | Florida | 8.6 |
| 5 | Vermont | 12.1 | | 44 | Missouri | 8.6 |
| 44 | Virginia | 8.6 | | 44 | Virginia | 8.6 |
| 36 | Washington | 9.5 | | 47 | Oklahoma | 8.4 |
| 8 | West Virginia | 11.3 | | 48 | Alabama | 8.3 |
| 8 | Wisconsin | 11.3 | | 49 | Tennessee | 8.1 |
| 4 | Wyoming | 13.5 | | 50 | South Dakota | 7.4 |
| | | | | | District of Columbia | 11.8 |

Source: CQ Press using data from Bureau of Economic Analysis and U.S. Census Bureau
  "Annual State Personal Income" (http://www.bea.gov/iTable/index_regional.cfm) and
  "2011 State and Local Government Finances" (http://www.census.gov/govs/local/)
*The personal income total used for this table is the sum of state estimates. This total differs from the national income and product accounts (NIPA) estimate of personal income because it omits the earnings of federal civilian and military personnel stationed abroad and of U.S. residents employed abroad temporarily by private U.S. firms.

# State and Local Government General Sales Tax Revenue in 2011

## National Total = $301,370,080,000*

| ALPHA ORDER | | | | | RANK ORDER | | | |
|---|---|---|---|---|---|---|---|---|
| RANK | STATE | REVENUE | % of USA | | RANK | STATE | REVENUE | % of USA |
| 23 | Alabama | $3,973,861,000 | 1.3% | | 1 | California | $40,101,659,000 | 13.3% |
| 46 | Alaska | 334,183,000 | 0.1% | | 2 | Texas | 27,251,830,000 | 9.0% |
| 12 | Arizona | 8,219,119,000 | 2.7% | | 3 | New York | 24,007,985,000 | 8.0% |
| 26 | Arkansas | 3,650,422,000 | 1.2% | | 4 | Florida | 21,123,834,000 | 7.0% |
| 1 | California | 40,101,659,000 | 13.3% | | 5 | Washington | 12,914,466,000 | 4.3% |
| 17 | Colorado | 5,223,887,000 | 1.7% | | 6 | Pennsylvania | 9,586,705,000 | 3.2% |
| 28 | Connecticut | 3,252,123,000 | 1.1% | | 7 | Ohio | 9,501,144,000 | 3.2% |
| 47 | Delaware | 0 | 0.0% | | 8 | Michigan | 9,477,156,000 | 3.1% |
| 4 | Florida | 21,123,834,000 | 7.0% | | 9 | Illinois | 9,089,870,000 | 3.0% |
| 10 | Georgia | 8,543,263,000 | 2.8% | | 10 | Georgia | 8,543,263,000 | 2.8% |
| 35 | Hawaii | 2,495,807,000 | 0.8% | | 11 | North Carolina | 8,277,295,000 | 2.7% |
| 39 | Idaho | 1,187,070,000 | 0.4% | | 12 | Arizona | 8,219,119,000 | 2.7% |
| 9 | Illinois | 9,089,870,000 | 3.0% | | 13 | New Jersey | 8,144,397,000 | 2.7% |
| 16 | Indiana | 6,269,721,000 | 2.1% | | 14 | Tennessee | 8,142,474,000 | 2.7% |
| 32 | Iowa | 2,902,001,000 | 1.0% | | 15 | Louisiana | 6,555,162,000 | 2.2% |
| 27 | Kansas | 3,285,008,000 | 1.1% | | 16 | Indiana | 6,269,721,000 | 2.1% |
| 33 | Kentucky | 2,896,252,000 | 1.0% | | 17 | Colorado | 5,223,887,000 | 1.7% |
| 15 | Louisiana | 6,555,162,000 | 2.2% | | 18 | Missouri | 4,953,603,000 | 1.6% |
| 42 | Maine | 1,010,241,000 | 0.3% | | 19 | Massachusetts | 4,920,521,000 | 1.6% |
| 25 | Maryland | 3,896,700,000 | 1.3% | | 20 | Minnesota | 4,762,431,000 | 1.6% |
| 19 | Massachusetts | 4,920,521,000 | 1.6% | | 21 | Virginia | 4,477,825,000 | 1.5% |
| 8 | Michigan | 9,477,156,000 | 3.1% | | 22 | Wisconsin | 4,437,614,000 | 1.5% |
| 20 | Minnesota | 4,762,431,000 | 1.6% | | 23 | Alabama | 3,973,861,000 | 1.3% |
| 31 | Mississippi | 2,969,375,000 | 1.0% | | 24 | Oklahoma | 3,919,090,000 | 1.3% |
| 18 | Missouri | 4,953,603,000 | 1.6% | | 25 | Maryland | 3,896,700,000 | 1.3% |
| 47 | Montana | 0 | 0.0% | | 26 | Arkansas | 3,650,422,000 | 1.2% |
| 37 | Nebraska | 1,690,657,000 | 0.6% | | 27 | Kansas | 3,285,008,000 | 1.1% |
| 29 | Nevada | 3,237,683,000 | 1.1% | | 28 | Connecticut | 3,252,123,000 | 1.1% |
| 47 | New Hampshire | 0 | 0.0% | | 29 | Nevada | 3,237,683,000 | 1.1% |
| 13 | New Jersey | 8,144,397,000 | 2.7% | | 30 | South Carolina | 3,149,831,000 | 1.0% |
| 34 | New Mexico | 2,797,554,000 | 0.9% | | 31 | Mississippi | 2,969,375,000 | 1.0% |
| 3 | New York | 24,007,985,000 | 8.0% | | 32 | Iowa | 2,902,001,000 | 1.0% |
| 11 | North Carolina | 8,277,295,000 | 2.7% | | 33 | Kentucky | 2,896,252,000 | 1.0% |
| 43 | North Dakota | 902,874,000 | 0.3% | | 34 | New Mexico | 2,797,554,000 | 0.9% |
| 7 | Ohio | 9,501,144,000 | 3.2% | | 35 | Hawaii | 2,495,807,000 | 0.8% |
| 24 | Oklahoma | 3,919,090,000 | 1.3% | | 36 | Utah | 2,441,482,000 | 0.8% |
| 47 | Oregon | 0 | 0.0% | | 37 | Nebraska | 1,690,657,000 | 0.6% |
| 6 | Pennsylvania | 9,586,705,000 | 3.2% | | 38 | West Virginia | 1,210,255,000 | 0.4% |
| 44 | Rhode Island | 824,507,000 | 0.3% | | 39 | Idaho | 1,187,070,000 | 0.4% |
| 30 | South Carolina | 3,149,831,000 | 1.0% | | 40 | South Dakota | 1,097,373,000 | 0.4% |
| 40 | South Dakota | 1,097,373,000 | 0.4% | | 41 | Wyoming | 1,047,557,000 | 0.3% |
| 14 | Tennessee | 8,142,474,000 | 2.7% | | 42 | Maine | 1,010,241,000 | 0.3% |
| 2 | Texas | 27,251,830,000 | 9.0% | | 43 | North Dakota | 902,874,000 | 0.3% |
| 36 | Utah | 2,441,482,000 | 0.8% | | 44 | Rhode Island | 824,507,000 | 0.3% |
| 45 | Vermont | 335,012,000 | 0.1% | | 45 | Vermont | 335,012,000 | 0.1% |
| 21 | Virginia | 4,477,825,000 | 1.5% | | 46 | Alaska | 334,183,000 | 0.1% |
| 5 | Washington | 12,914,466,000 | 4.3% | | 47 | Delaware | 0 | 0.0% |
| 38 | West Virginia | 1,210,255,000 | 0.4% | | 47 | Montana | 0 | 0.0% |
| 22 | Wisconsin | 4,437,614,000 | 1.5% | | 47 | New Hampshire | 0 | 0.0% |
| 41 | Wyoming | 1,047,557,000 | 0.3% | | 47 | Oregon | 0 | 0.0% |
| | | | | | | District of Columbia | 881,201,000 | 0.3% |

Source: U.S. Bureau of the Census, Governments Division
    "2011 State and Local Government Finances" (http://www.census.gov/govs/local/)
*Does not include special sales taxes such as those on sale of alcohol, gasoline, or tobacco.

# Per Capita State and Local Government General Sales Tax Revenue in 2011

## National Per Capita = $967*

| ALPHA ORDER | | | | RANK ORDER | | |
|---|---|---|---|---|---|---|
| RANK | STATE | PER CAPITA | | RANK | STATE | PER CAPITA |
| 30 | Alabama | $827 | | 1 | Washington | $1,893 |
| 46 | Alaska | 462 | | 2 | Wyoming | 1,846 |
| 9 | Arizona | 1,271 | | 3 | Hawaii | 1,811 |
| 10 | Arkansas | 1,242 | | 4 | Louisiana | 1,433 |
| 15 | California | 1,064 | | 5 | New Mexico | 1,346 |
| 18 | Colorado | 1,021 | | 6 | South Dakota | 1,332 |
| 25 | Connecticut | 907 | | 7 | North Dakota | 1,319 |
| 47 | Delaware | 0 | | 8 | Tennessee | 1,272 |
| 14 | Florida | 1,107 | | 9 | Arizona | 1,271 |
| 27 | Georgia | 871 | | 10 | Arkansas | 1,242 |
| 3 | Hawaii | 1,811 | | 11 | New York | 1,231 |
| 37 | Idaho | 750 | | 12 | Nevada | 1,190 |
| 39 | Illinois | 707 | | 13 | Kansas | 1,144 |
| 20 | Indiana | 962 | | 14 | Florida | 1,107 |
| 22 | Iowa | 947 | | 15 | California | 1,064 |
| 13 | Kansas | 1,144 | | 16 | Texas | 1,063 |
| 42 | Kentucky | 663 | | 17 | Oklahoma | 1,036 |
| 4 | Louisiana | 1,433 | | 18 | Colorado | 1,021 |
| 35 | Maine | 760 | | 19 | Mississippi | 997 |
| 41 | Maryland | 667 | | 20 | Indiana | 962 |
| 38 | Massachusetts | 745 | | 21 | Michigan | 960 |
| 21 | Michigan | 960 | | 22 | Iowa | 947 |
| 26 | Minnesota | 891 | | 23 | New Jersey | 922 |
| 19 | Mississippi | 997 | | 24 | Nebraska | 918 |
| 31 | Missouri | 824 | | 25 | Connecticut | 907 |
| 47 | Montana | 0 | | 26 | Minnesota | 891 |
| 24 | Nebraska | 918 | | 27 | Georgia | 871 |
| 12 | Nevada | 1,190 | | 28 | Utah | 868 |
| 47 | New Hampshire | 0 | | 29 | North Carolina | 858 |
| 23 | New Jersey | 922 | | 30 | Alabama | 827 |
| 5 | New Mexico | 1,346 | | 31 | Missouri | 824 |
| 11 | New York | 1,231 | | 32 | Ohio | 823 |
| 29 | North Carolina | 858 | | 33 | Rhode Island | 785 |
| 7 | North Dakota | 1,319 | | 34 | Wisconsin | 777 |
| 32 | Ohio | 823 | | 35 | Maine | 760 |
| 17 | Oklahoma | 1,036 | | 36 | Pennsylvania | 752 |
| 47 | Oregon | 0 | | 37 | Idaho | 750 |
| 36 | Pennsylvania | 752 | | 38 | Massachusetts | 745 |
| 33 | Rhode Island | 785 | | 39 | Illinois | 707 |
| 40 | South Carolina | 674 | | 40 | South Carolina | 674 |
| 6 | South Dakota | 1,332 | | 41 | Maryland | 667 |
| 8 | Tennessee | 1,272 | | 42 | Kentucky | 663 |
| 16 | Texas | 1,063 | | 43 | West Virginia | 652 |
| 28 | Utah | 868 | | 44 | Virginia | 553 |
| 45 | Vermont | 535 | | 45 | Vermont | 535 |
| 44 | Virginia | 553 | | 46 | Alaska | 462 |
| 1 | Washington | 1,893 | | 47 | Delaware | 0 |
| 43 | West Virginia | 652 | | 47 | Montana | 0 |
| 34 | Wisconsin | 777 | | 47 | New Hampshire | 0 |
| 2 | Wyoming | 1,846 | | 47 | Oregon | 0 |
| | | | | | District of Columbia | 1,424 |

Source: CQ Press using data from U.S. Bureau of the Census, Governments Division
   "2011 State and Local Government Finances" (http://www.census.gov/govs/local/)
*Does not include special sales taxes such as those on sale of alcohol, gasoline, or tobacco.

# State and Local Government Property Tax Revenue in 2011

## National Total = $443,259,172,000

ALPHA ORDER

| RANK | STATE | REVENUE | % of USA |
|------|-------|---------|----------|
| 33 | Alabama | $2,588,390,000 | 0.6% |
| 40 | Alaska | 1,492,499,000 | 0.3% |
| 20 | Arizona | 7,104,412,000 | 1.6% |
| 39 | Arkansas | 1,812,948,000 | 0.4% |
| 1 | California | 53,506,490,000 | 12.1% |
| 18 | Colorado | 8,320,119,000 | 1.9% |
| 14 | Connecticut | 9,229,775,000 | 2.1% |
| 50 | Delaware | 666,240,000 | 0.2% |
| 4 | Florida | 25,934,924,000 | 5.9% |
| 12 | Georgia | 10,349,138,000 | 2.3% |
| 46 | Hawaii | 1,324,771,000 | 0.3% |
| 43 | Idaho | 1,367,956,000 | 0.3% |
| 6 | Illinois | 24,172,045,000 | 5.5% |
| 21 | Indiana | 6,313,350,000 | 1.4% |
| 26 | Iowa | 4,369,466,000 | 1.0% |
| 27 | Kansas | 3,915,805,000 | 0.9% |
| 31 | Kentucky | 3,003,461,000 | 0.7% |
| 28 | Louisiana | 3,536,943,000 | 0.8% |
| 36 | Maine | 2,400,881,000 | 0.5% |
| 17 | Maryland | 8,425,357,000 | 1.9% |
| 9 | Massachusetts | 13,286,932,000 | 3.0% |
| 8 | Michigan | 13,568,841,000 | 3.1% |
| 19 | Minnesota | 8,179,949,000 | 1.8% |
| 35 | Mississippi | 2,546,095,000 | 0.6% |
| 22 | Missouri | 5,877,847,000 | 1.3% |
| 45 | Montana | 1,339,480,000 | 0.3% |
| 32 | Nebraska | 2,874,399,000 | 0.6% |
| 30 | Nevada | 3,010,793,000 | 0.7% |
| 29 | New Hampshire | 3,317,013,000 | 0.7% |
| 5 | New Jersey | 25,513,862,000 | 5.8% |
| 44 | New Mexico | 1,365,810,000 | 0.3% |
| 2 | New York | 45,420,289,000 | 10.2% |
| 16 | North Carolina | 8,640,184,000 | 1.9% |
| 49 | North Dakota | 730,146,000 | 0.2% |
| 10 | Ohio | 13,159,029,000 | 3.0% |
| 38 | Oklahoma | 2,223,834,000 | 0.5% |
| 24 | Oregon | 5,054,454,000 | 1.1% |
| 7 | Pennsylvania | 16,610,320,000 | 3.7% |
| 37 | Rhode Island | 2,273,300,000 | 0.5% |
| 25 | South Carolina | 4,804,227,000 | 1.1% |
| 48 | South Dakota | 980,962,000 | 0.2% |
| 23 | Tennessee | 5,101,115,000 | 1.2% |
| 3 | Texas | 39,596,363,000 | 8.9% |
| 34 | Utah | 2,550,899,000 | 0.6% |
| 42 | Vermont | 1,375,819,000 | 0.3% |
| 11 | Virginia | 11,103,895,000 | 2.5% |
| 15 | Washington | 8,674,647,000 | 2.0% |
| 41 | West Virginia | 1,428,863,000 | 0.3% |
| 13 | Wisconsin | 9,827,091,000 | 2.2% |
| 47 | Wyoming | 1,230,548,000 | 0.3% |

RANK ORDER

| RANK | STATE | REVENUE | % of USA |
|------|-------|---------|----------|
| 1 | California | $53,506,490,000 | 12.1% |
| 2 | New York | 45,420,289,000 | 10.2% |
| 3 | Texas | 39,596,363,000 | 8.9% |
| 4 | Florida | 25,934,924,000 | 5.9% |
| 5 | New Jersey | 25,513,862,000 | 5.8% |
| 6 | Illinois | 24,172,045,000 | 5.5% |
| 7 | Pennsylvania | 16,610,320,000 | 3.7% |
| 8 | Michigan | 13,568,841,000 | 3.1% |
| 9 | Massachusetts | 13,286,932,000 | 3.0% |
| 10 | Ohio | 13,159,029,000 | 3.0% |
| 11 | Virginia | 11,103,895,000 | 2.5% |
| 12 | Georgia | 10,349,138,000 | 2.3% |
| 13 | Wisconsin | 9,827,091,000 | 2.2% |
| 14 | Connecticut | 9,229,775,000 | 2.1% |
| 15 | Washington | 8,674,647,000 | 2.0% |
| 16 | North Carolina | 8,640,184,000 | 1.9% |
| 17 | Maryland | 8,425,357,000 | 1.9% |
| 18 | Colorado | 8,320,119,000 | 1.9% |
| 19 | Minnesota | 8,179,949,000 | 1.8% |
| 20 | Arizona | 7,104,412,000 | 1.6% |
| 21 | Indiana | 6,313,350,000 | 1.4% |
| 22 | Missouri | 5,877,847,000 | 1.3% |
| 23 | Tennessee | 5,101,115,000 | 1.2% |
| 24 | Oregon | 5,054,454,000 | 1.1% |
| 25 | South Carolina | 4,804,227,000 | 1.1% |
| 26 | Iowa | 4,369,466,000 | 1.0% |
| 27 | Kansas | 3,915,805,000 | 0.9% |
| 28 | Louisiana | 3,536,943,000 | 0.8% |
| 29 | New Hampshire | 3,317,013,000 | 0.7% |
| 30 | Nevada | 3,010,793,000 | 0.7% |
| 31 | Kentucky | 3,003,461,000 | 0.7% |
| 32 | Nebraska | 2,874,399,000 | 0.6% |
| 33 | Alabama | 2,588,390,000 | 0.6% |
| 34 | Utah | 2,550,899,000 | 0.6% |
| 35 | Mississippi | 2,546,095,000 | 0.6% |
| 36 | Maine | 2,400,881,000 | 0.5% |
| 37 | Rhode Island | 2,273,300,000 | 0.5% |
| 38 | Oklahoma | 2,223,834,000 | 0.5% |
| 39 | Arkansas | 1,812,948,000 | 0.4% |
| 40 | Alaska | 1,492,499,000 | 0.3% |
| 41 | West Virginia | 1,428,863,000 | 0.3% |
| 42 | Vermont | 1,375,819,000 | 0.3% |
| 43 | Idaho | 1,367,956,000 | 0.3% |
| 44 | New Mexico | 1,365,810,000 | 0.3% |
| 45 | Montana | 1,339,480,000 | 0.3% |
| 46 | Hawaii | 1,324,771,000 | 0.3% |
| 47 | Wyoming | 1,230,548,000 | 0.3% |
| 48 | South Dakota | 980,962,000 | 0.2% |
| 49 | North Dakota | 730,146,000 | 0.2% |
| 50 | Delaware | 666,240,000 | 0.2% |
| | District of Columbia | 1,757,196,000 | 0.4% |

Source: U.S. Bureau of the Census, Governments Division
"2011 State and Local Government Finances" (http://www.census.gov/govs/local/)

# Per Capita State and Local Government Property Tax Revenue in 2011

## National Per Capita = $1,423

ALPHA ORDER

| RANK | STATE | PER CAPITA |
|------|-------|-----------|
| 50 | Alabama | $539 |
| 8 | Alaska | 2,062 |
| 31 | Arizona | 1,099 |
| 48 | Arkansas | 617 |
| 19 | California | 1,420 |
| 13 | Colorado | 1,626 |
| 2 | Connecticut | 2,573 |
| 45 | Delaware | 734 |
| 23 | Florida | 1,359 |
| 33 | Georgia | 1,055 |
| 37 | Hawaii | 961 |
| 40 | Idaho | 864 |
| 10 | Illinois | 1,880 |
| 36 | Indiana | 969 |
| 18 | Iowa | 1,426 |
| 22 | Kansas | 1,364 |
| 46 | Kentucky | 688 |
| 43 | Louisiana | 773 |
| 11 | Maine | 1,807 |
| 17 | Maryland | 1,443 |
| 9 | Massachusetts | 2,011 |
| 20 | Michigan | 1,374 |
| 16 | Minnesota | 1,530 |
| 41 | Mississippi | 855 |
| 35 | Missouri | 978 |
| 24 | Montana | 1,343 |
| 14 | Nebraska | 1,560 |
| 30 | Nevada | 1,107 |
| 3 | New Hampshire | 2,517 |
| 1 | New Jersey | 2,888 |
| 47 | New Mexico | 657 |
| 4 | New York | 2,329 |
| 39 | North Carolina | 895 |
| 32 | North Dakota | 1,066 |
| 29 | Ohio | 1,140 |
| 49 | Oklahoma | 588 |
| 25 | Oregon | 1,307 |
| 26 | Pennsylvania | 1,303 |
| 7 | Rhode Island | 2,164 |
| 34 | South Carolina | 1,028 |
| 28 | South Dakota | 1,191 |
| 42 | Tennessee | 797 |
| 15 | Texas | 1,545 |
| 38 | Utah | 906 |
| 5 | Vermont | 2,196 |
| 21 | Virginia | 1,370 |
| 27 | Washington | 1,271 |
| 44 | West Virginia | 770 |
| 12 | Wisconsin | 1,721 |
| 6 | Wyoming | 2,169 |

RANK ORDER

| RANK | STATE | PER CAPITA |
|------|-------|-----------|
| 1 | New Jersey | $2,888 |
| 2 | Connecticut | 2,573 |
| 3 | New Hampshire | 2,517 |
| 4 | New York | 2,329 |
| 5 | Vermont | 2,196 |
| 6 | Wyoming | 2,169 |
| 7 | Rhode Island | 2,164 |
| 8 | Alaska | 2,062 |
| 9 | Massachusetts | 2,011 |
| 10 | Illinois | 1,880 |
| 11 | Maine | 1,807 |
| 12 | Wisconsin | 1,721 |
| 13 | Colorado | 1,626 |
| 14 | Nebraska | 1,560 |
| 15 | Texas | 1,545 |
| 16 | Minnesota | 1,530 |
| 17 | Maryland | 1,443 |
| 18 | Iowa | 1,426 |
| 19 | California | 1,420 |
| 20 | Michigan | 1,374 |
| 21 | Virginia | 1,370 |
| 22 | Kansas | 1,364 |
| 23 | Florida | 1,359 |
| 24 | Montana | 1,343 |
| 25 | Oregon | 1,307 |
| 26 | Pennsylvania | 1,303 |
| 27 | Washington | 1,271 |
| 28 | South Dakota | 1,191 |
| 29 | Ohio | 1,140 |
| 30 | Nevada | 1,107 |
| 31 | Arizona | 1,099 |
| 32 | North Dakota | 1,066 |
| 33 | Georgia | 1,055 |
| 34 | South Carolina | 1,028 |
| 35 | Missouri | 978 |
| 36 | Indiana | 969 |
| 37 | Hawaii | 961 |
| 38 | Utah | 906 |
| 39 | North Carolina | 895 |
| 40 | Idaho | 864 |
| 41 | Mississippi | 855 |
| 42 | Tennessee | 797 |
| 43 | Louisiana | 773 |
| 44 | West Virginia | 770 |
| 45 | Delaware | 734 |
| 46 | Kentucky | 688 |
| 47 | New Mexico | 657 |
| 48 | Arkansas | 617 |
| 49 | Oklahoma | 588 |
| 50 | Alabama | 539 |
| | District of Columbia | 2,839 |

Source: CQ Press using data from U.S. Bureau of the Census, Governments Division
"2011 State and Local Government Finances" (http://www.census.gov/govs/local/)

# State and Local Government Property Tax as a Percent of State and Local Government Total Revenue in 2011
## National Percent = 12.9%

ALPHA ORDER

ALPHA ORDER

| RANK | STATE | PERCENT |
|---|---|---|
| 47 | Alabama | 6.4 |
| 40 | Alaska | 8.1 |
| 24 | Arizona | 12.1 |
| 46 | Arkansas | 6.5 |
| 32 | California | 10.3 |
| 10 | Colorado | 15.7 |
| 3 | Connecticut | 21.9 |
| 49 | Delaware | 5.9 |
| 14 | Florida | 14.3 |
| 23 | Georgia | 12.2 |
| 39 | Hawaii | 8.3 |
| 36 | Idaho | 9.7 |
| 4 | Illinois | 18.1 |
| 28 | Indiana | 11.1 |
| 21 | Iowa | 12.7 |
| 16 | Kansas | 13.7 |
| 44 | Kentucky | 7.4 |
| 45 | Louisiana | 7.2 |
| 8 | Maine | 17.2 |
| 17 | Maryland | 13.4 |
| 9 | Massachusetts | 16.2 |
| 12 | Michigan | 14.5 |
| 20 | Minnesota | 12.9 |
| 40 | Mississippi | 8.1 |
| 32 | Missouri | 10.3 |
| 19 | Montana | 13.1 |
| 18 | Nebraska | 13.3 |
| 26 | Nevada | 11.6 |
| 1 | New Hampshire | 27.1 |
| 2 | New Jersey | 24.2 |
| 50 | New Mexico | 5.6 |
| 15 | New York | 14.0 |
| 37 | North Carolina | 9.3 |
| 42 | North Dakota | 7.6 |
| 35 | Ohio | 10.0 |
| 48 | Oklahoma | 6.3 |
| 30 | Oregon | 10.7 |
| 22 | Pennsylvania | 12.4 |
| 6 | Rhode Island | 17.8 |
| 31 | South Carolina | 10.5 |
| 26 | South Dakota | 11.6 |
| 38 | Tennessee | 8.5 |
| 7 | Texas | 17.6 |
| 34 | Utah | 10.1 |
| 4 | Vermont | 18.1 |
| 12 | Virginia | 14.5 |
| 28 | Washington | 11.1 |
| 42 | West Virginia | 7.6 |
| 10 | Wisconsin | 15.7 |
| 24 | Wyoming | 12.1 |

RANK ORDER

| RANK | STATE | PERCENT |
|---|---|---|
| 1 | New Hampshire | 27.1 |
| 2 | New Jersey | 24.2 |
| 3 | Connecticut | 21.9 |
| 4 | Illinois | 18.1 |
| 4 | Vermont | 18.1 |
| 6 | Rhode Island | 17.8 |
| 7 | Texas | 17.6 |
| 8 | Maine | 17.2 |
| 9 | Massachusetts | 16.2 |
| 10 | Colorado | 15.7 |
| 10 | Wisconsin | 15.7 |
| 12 | Michigan | 14.5 |
| 12 | Virginia | 14.5 |
| 14 | Florida | 14.3 |
| 15 | New York | 14.0 |
| 16 | Kansas | 13.7 |
| 17 | Maryland | 13.4 |
| 18 | Nebraska | 13.3 |
| 19 | Montana | 13.1 |
| 20 | Minnesota | 12.9 |
| 21 | Iowa | 12.7 |
| 22 | Pennsylvania | 12.4 |
| 23 | Georgia | 12.2 |
| 24 | Arizona | 12.1 |
| 24 | Wyoming | 12.1 |
| 26 | Nevada | 11.6 |
| 26 | South Dakota | 11.6 |
| 28 | Indiana | 11.1 |
| 28 | Washington | 11.1 |
| 30 | Oregon | 10.7 |
| 31 | South Carolina | 10.5 |
| 32 | California | 10.3 |
| 32 | Missouri | 10.3 |
| 34 | Utah | 10.1 |
| 35 | Ohio | 10.0 |
| 36 | Idaho | 9.7 |
| 37 | North Carolina | 9.3 |
| 38 | Tennessee | 8.5 |
| 39 | Hawaii | 8.3 |
| 40 | Alaska | 8.1 |
| 40 | Mississippi | 8.1 |
| 42 | North Dakota | 7.6 |
| 42 | West Virginia | 7.6 |
| 44 | Kentucky | 7.4 |
| 45 | Louisiana | 7.2 |
| 46 | Arkansas | 6.5 |
| 47 | Alabama | 6.4 |
| 48 | Oklahoma | 6.3 |
| 49 | Delaware | 5.9 |
| 50 | New Mexico | 5.6 |

| District of Columbia | 13.6 |
|---|---|

Source: CQ Press using data from U.S. Bureau of the Census, Governments Division
"2011 State and Local Government Finances" (http://www.census.gov/govs/local/)

# State and Local Government Property Tax Revenue as a Percent of State and Local Government Own Source Revenue in 2011
## National Percent = 22.5%*

ALPHA ORDER

| RANK | STATE | PERCENT |
|---|---|---|
| 49 | Alabama | 10.4 |
| 45 | Alaska | 12.0 |
| 18 | Arizona | 22.9 |
| 44 | Arkansas | 12.2 |
| 28 | California | 19.9 |
| 13 | Colorado | 24.4 |
| 3 | Connecticut | 33.3 |
| 50 | Delaware | 9.6 |
| 14 | Florida | 24.3 |
| 21 | Georgia | 21.8 |
| 40 | Hawaii | 13.6 |
| 35 | Idaho | 17.6 |
| 6 | Illinois | 30.4 |
| 34 | Indiana | 17.7 |
| 21 | Iowa | 21.8 |
| 25 | Kansas | 21.3 |
| 41 | Kentucky | 13.5 |
| 43 | Louisiana | 13.1 |
| 7 | Maine | 29.7 |
| 21 | Maryland | 21.8 |
| 10 | Massachusetts | 26.9 |
| 15 | Michigan | 24.1 |
| 24 | Minnesota | 21.4 |
| 38 | Mississippi | 16.5 |
| 31 | Missouri | 19.7 |
| 11 | Montana | 25.4 |
| 12 | Nebraska | 24.7 |
| 27 | Nevada | 20.7 |
| 1 | New Hampshire | 43.2 |
| 2 | New Jersey | 36.7 |
| 47 | New Mexico | 11.3 |
| 16 | New York | 23.8 |
| 39 | North Carolina | 16.3 |
| 47 | North Dakota | 11.3 |
| 32 | Ohio | 19.5 |
| 46 | Oklahoma | 11.4 |
| 20 | Oregon | 22.0 |
| 26 | Pennsylvania | 20.9 |
| 5 | Rhode Island | 31.4 |
| 33 | South Carolina | 18.1 |
| 17 | South Dakota | 23.7 |
| 36 | Tennessee | 17.2 |
| 8 | Texas | 29.3 |
| 37 | Utah | 16.9 |
| 4 | Vermont | 31.6 |
| 19 | Virginia | 22.6 |
| 28 | Washington | 19.9 |
| 42 | West Virginia | 13.2 |
| 9 | Wisconsin | 27.1 |
| 30 | Wyoming | 19.8 |

RANK ORDER

| RANK | STATE | PERCENT |
|---|---|---|
| 1 | New Hampshire | 43.2 |
| 2 | New Jersey | 36.7 |
| 3 | Connecticut | 33.3 |
| 4 | Vermont | 31.6 |
| 5 | Rhode Island | 31.4 |
| 6 | Illinois | 30.4 |
| 7 | Maine | 29.7 |
| 8 | Texas | 29.3 |
| 9 | Wisconsin | 27.1 |
| 10 | Massachusetts | 26.9 |
| 11 | Montana | 25.4 |
| 12 | Nebraska | 24.7 |
| 13 | Colorado | 24.4 |
| 14 | Florida | 24.3 |
| 15 | Michigan | 24.1 |
| 16 | New York | 23.8 |
| 17 | South Dakota | 23.7 |
| 18 | Arizona | 22.9 |
| 19 | Virginia | 22.6 |
| 20 | Oregon | 22.0 |
| 21 | Georgia | 21.8 |
| 21 | Iowa | 21.8 |
| 21 | Maryland | 21.8 |
| 24 | Minnesota | 21.4 |
| 25 | Kansas | 21.3 |
| 26 | Pennsylvania | 20.9 |
| 27 | Nevada | 20.7 |
| 28 | California | 19.9 |
| 28 | Washington | 19.9 |
| 30 | Wyoming | 19.8 |
| 31 | Missouri | 19.7 |
| 32 | Ohio | 19.5 |
| 33 | South Carolina | 18.1 |
| 34 | Indiana | 17.7 |
| 35 | Idaho | 17.6 |
| 36 | Tennessee | 17.2 |
| 37 | Utah | 16.9 |
| 38 | Mississippi | 16.5 |
| 39 | North Carolina | 16.3 |
| 40 | Hawaii | 13.6 |
| 41 | Kentucky | 13.5 |
| 42 | West Virginia | 13.2 |
| 43 | Louisiana | 13.1 |
| 44 | Arkansas | 12.2 |
| 45 | Alaska | 12.0 |
| 46 | Oklahoma | 11.4 |
| 47 | New Mexico | 11.3 |
| 47 | North Dakota | 11.3 |
| 49 | Alabama | 10.4 |
| 50 | Delaware | 9.6 |

District of Columbia — 26.4

Source: CQ Press using data from U.S. Bureau of the Census, Governments Division
"2011 State and Local Government Finances" (http://www.census.gov/govs/local/)
*Own source revenue includes taxes, current charges, and miscellaneous general revenue. Excluded are intergovernmental transfers, insurance trust revenue, and revenue from government owned utilities and other commercial or auxiliary enterprise.

# State and Local Tax Burden as a Percent of Income in 2010

## National Percent = 9.9% of Income*

ALPHA ORDER

| RANK | STATE | PERCENT |
|---|---|---|
| 42 | Alabama | 8.2 |
| 50 | Alaska | 7.0 |
| 39 | Arizona | 8.4 |
| 15 | Arkansas | 10.0 |
| 4 | California | 11.2 |
| 32 | Colorado | 9.1 |
| 3 | Connecticut | 12.3 |
| 27 | Delaware | 9.3 |
| 27 | Florida | 9.3 |
| 33 | Georgia | 9.0 |
| 13 | Hawaii | 10.1 |
| 25 | Idaho | 9.4 |
| 10 | Illinois | 10.2 |
| 23 | Indiana | 9.6 |
| 23 | Iowa | 9.6 |
| 19 | Kansas | 9.7 |
| 25 | Kentucky | 9.4 |
| 46 | Louisiana | 7.8 |
| 9 | Maine | 10.3 |
| 10 | Maryland | 10.2 |
| 8 | Massachusetts | 10.4 |
| 18 | Michigan | 9.8 |
| 7 | Minnesota | 10.8 |
| 36 | Mississippi | 8.7 |
| 33 | Missouri | 9.0 |
| 38 | Montana | 8.6 |
| 19 | Nebraska | 9.7 |
| 42 | Nevada | 8.2 |
| 44 | New Hampshire | 8.1 |
| 2 | New Jersey | 12.4 |
| 39 | New Mexico | 8.4 |
| 1 | New York | 12.8 |
| 17 | North Carolina | 9.9 |
| 35 | North Dakota | 8.9 |
| 19 | Ohio | 9.7 |
| 36 | Oklahoma | 8.7 |
| 15 | Oregon | 10.0 |
| 10 | Pennsylvania | 10.2 |
| 6 | Rhode Island | 10.9 |
| 39 | South Carolina | 8.4 |
| 49 | South Dakota | 7.6 |
| 48 | Tennessee | 7.7 |
| 45 | Texas | 7.9 |
| 27 | Utah | 9.3 |
| 13 | Vermont | 10.1 |
| 27 | Virginia | 9.3 |
| 27 | Washington | 9.3 |
| 19 | West Virginia | 9.7 |
| 5 | Wisconsin | 11.1 |
| 46 | Wyoming | 7.8 |

RANK ORDER

| RANK | STATE | PERCENT |
|---|---|---|
| 1 | New York | 12.8 |
| 2 | New Jersey | 12.4 |
| 3 | Connecticut | 12.3 |
| 4 | California | 11.2 |
| 5 | Wisconsin | 11.1 |
| 6 | Rhode Island | 10.9 |
| 7 | Minnesota | 10.8 |
| 8 | Massachusetts | 10.4 |
| 9 | Maine | 10.3 |
| 10 | Illinois | 10.2 |
| 10 | Maryland | 10.2 |
| 10 | Pennsylvania | 10.2 |
| 13 | Hawaii | 10.1 |
| 13 | Vermont | 10.1 |
| 15 | Arkansas | 10.0 |
| 15 | Oregon | 10.0 |
| 17 | North Carolina | 9.9 |
| 18 | Michigan | 9.8 |
| 19 | Kansas | 9.7 |
| 19 | Nebraska | 9.7 |
| 19 | Ohio | 9.7 |
| 19 | West Virginia | 9.7 |
| 23 | Indiana | 9.6 |
| 23 | Iowa | 9.6 |
| 25 | Idaho | 9.4 |
| 25 | Kentucky | 9.4 |
| 27 | Delaware | 9.3 |
| 27 | Florida | 9.3 |
| 27 | Utah | 9.3 |
| 27 | Virginia | 9.3 |
| 27 | Washington | 9.3 |
| 32 | Colorado | 9.1 |
| 33 | Georgia | 9.0 |
| 33 | Missouri | 9.0 |
| 35 | North Dakota | 8.9 |
| 36 | Mississippi | 8.7 |
| 36 | Oklahoma | 8.7 |
| 38 | Montana | 8.6 |
| 39 | Arizona | 8.4 |
| 39 | New Mexico | 8.4 |
| 39 | South Carolina | 8.4 |
| 42 | Alabama | 8.2 |
| 42 | Nevada | 8.2 |
| 44 | New Hampshire | 8.1 |
| 45 | Texas | 7.9 |
| 46 | Louisiana | 7.8 |
| 46 | Wyoming | 7.8 |
| 48 | Tennessee | 7.7 |
| 49 | South Dakota | 7.6 |
| 50 | Alaska | 7.0 |

| District of Columbia | 9.2 |
|---|---|

Source: The Tax Foundation
   "State and Local Tax Burdens: All States, One Year, 1977-2010" (www.taxfoundation.org/research/show/336.html)
*All state and local taxes.

# State and Local Government Total Expenditures in 2011

## National Total = $3,162,628,274,000*

ALPHA ORDER

| RANK | STATE | EXPENDITURES | % of USA |
|------|-------|-------------:|---------:|
| 25 | Alabama | $42,161,028,000 | 1.3% |
| 39 | Alaska | 14,687,040,000 | 0.5% |
| 20 | Arizona | 52,533,819,000 | 1.7% |
| 34 | Arkansas | 23,768,782,000 | 0.8% |
| 1 | California | 457,591,036,000 | 14.5% |
| 21 | Colorado | 51,576,659,000 | 1.6% |
| 26 | Connecticut | 40,675,690,000 | 1.3% |
| 45 | Delaware | 9,897,809,000 | 0.3% |
| 4 | Florida | 164,062,212,000 | 5.2% |
| 11 | Georgia | 78,093,549,000 | 2.5% |
| 40 | Hawaii | 14,389,261,000 | 0.5% |
| 42 | Idaho | 12,065,995,000 | 0.4% |
| 6 | Illinois | 130,777,103,000 | 4.1% |
| 19 | Indiana | 52,682,140,000 | 1.7% |
| 30 | Iowa | 30,324,897,000 | 1.0% |
| 32 | Kansas | 26,534,127,000 | 0.8% |
| 28 | Kentucky | 39,062,585,000 | 1.2% |
| 23 | Louisiana | 48,756,593,000 | 1.5% |
| 41 | Maine | 12,615,776,000 | 0.4% |
| 15 | Maryland | 57,612,277,000 | 1.8% |
| 12 | Massachusetts | 75,734,282,000 | 2.4% |
| 9 | Michigan | 89,817,860,000 | 2.8% |
| 17 | Minnesota | 55,683,581,000 | 1.8% |
| 31 | Mississippi | 27,307,717,000 | 0.9% |
| 22 | Missouri | 49,876,922,000 | 1.6% |
| 46 | Montana | 9,293,762,000 | 0.3% |
| 37 | Nebraska | 19,527,121,000 | 0.6% |
| 35 | Nevada | 23,268,683,000 | 0.7% |
| 43 | New Hampshire | 11,637,435,000 | 0.4% |
| 8 | New Jersey | 101,255,553,000 | 3.2% |
| 36 | New Mexico | 22,415,452,000 | 0.7% |
| 2 | New York | 300,324,433,000 | 9.5% |
| 10 | North Carolina | 80,849,495,000 | 2.6% |
| 48 | North Dakota | 7,137,121,000 | 0.2% |
| 7 | Ohio | 116,246,959,000 | 3.7% |
| 29 | Oklahoma | 30,717,191,000 | 1.0% |
| 27 | Oregon | 39,932,203,000 | 1.3% |
| 5 | Pennsylvania | 132,879,459,000 | 4.2% |
| 44 | Rhode Island | 11,465,758,000 | 0.4% |
| 24 | South Carolina | 42,784,130,000 | 1.4% |
| 49 | South Dakota | 7,013,644,000 | 0.2% |
| 18 | Tennessee | 55,155,159,000 | 1.7% |
| 3 | Texas | 221,029,984,000 | 7.0% |
| 33 | Utah | 24,927,890,000 | 0.8% |
| 50 | Vermont | 6,922,191,000 | 0.2% |
| 14 | Virginia | 69,225,717,000 | 2.2% |
| 13 | Washington | 74,904,561,000 | 2.4% |
| 38 | West Virginia | 16,400,370,000 | 0.5% |
| 16 | Wisconsin | 56,696,015,000 | 1.8% |
| 47 | Wyoming | 8,687,958,000 | 0.3% |

RANK ORDER

| RANK | STATE | EXPENDITURES | % of USA |
|------|-------|-------------:|---------:|
| 1 | California | $457,591,036,000 | 14.5% |
| 2 | New York | 300,324,433,000 | 9.5% |
| 3 | Texas | 221,029,984,000 | 7.0% |
| 4 | Florida | 164,062,212,000 | 5.2% |
| 5 | Pennsylvania | 132,879,459,000 | 4.2% |
| 6 | Illinois | 130,777,103,000 | 4.1% |
| 7 | Ohio | 116,246,959,000 | 3.7% |
| 8 | New Jersey | 101,255,553,000 | 3.2% |
| 9 | Michigan | 89,817,860,000 | 2.8% |
| 10 | North Carolina | 80,849,495,000 | 2.6% |
| 11 | Georgia | 78,093,549,000 | 2.5% |
| 12 | Massachusetts | 75,734,282,000 | 2.4% |
| 13 | Washington | 74,904,561,000 | 2.4% |
| 14 | Virginia | 69,225,717,000 | 2.2% |
| 15 | Maryland | 57,612,277,000 | 1.8% |
| 16 | Wisconsin | 56,696,015,000 | 1.8% |
| 17 | Minnesota | 55,683,581,000 | 1.8% |
| 18 | Tennessee | 55,155,159,000 | 1.7% |
| 19 | Indiana | 52,682,140,000 | 1.7% |
| 20 | Arizona | 52,533,819,000 | 1.7% |
| 21 | Colorado | 51,576,659,000 | 1.6% |
| 22 | Missouri | 49,876,922,000 | 1.6% |
| 23 | Louisiana | 48,756,593,000 | 1.5% |
| 24 | South Carolina | 42,784,130,000 | 1.4% |
| 25 | Alabama | 42,161,028,000 | 1.3% |
| 26 | Connecticut | 40,675,690,000 | 1.3% |
| 27 | Oregon | 39,932,203,000 | 1.3% |
| 28 | Kentucky | 39,062,585,000 | 1.2% |
| 29 | Oklahoma | 30,717,191,000 | 1.0% |
| 30 | Iowa | 30,324,897,000 | 1.0% |
| 31 | Mississippi | 27,307,717,000 | 0.9% |
| 32 | Kansas | 26,534,127,000 | 0.8% |
| 33 | Utah | 24,927,890,000 | 0.8% |
| 34 | Arkansas | 23,768,782,000 | 0.8% |
| 35 | Nevada | 23,268,683,000 | 0.7% |
| 36 | New Mexico | 22,415,452,000 | 0.7% |
| 37 | Nebraska | 19,527,121,000 | 0.6% |
| 38 | West Virginia | 16,400,370,000 | 0.5% |
| 39 | Alaska | 14,687,040,000 | 0.5% |
| 40 | Hawaii | 14,389,261,000 | 0.5% |
| 41 | Maine | 12,615,776,000 | 0.4% |
| 42 | Idaho | 12,065,995,000 | 0.4% |
| 43 | New Hampshire | 11,637,435,000 | 0.4% |
| 44 | Rhode Island | 11,465,758,000 | 0.4% |
| 45 | Delaware | 9,897,809,000 | 0.3% |
| 46 | Montana | 9,293,762,000 | 0.3% |
| 47 | Wyoming | 8,687,958,000 | 0.3% |
| 48 | North Dakota | 7,137,121,000 | 0.2% |
| 49 | South Dakota | 7,013,644,000 | 0.2% |
| 50 | Vermont | 6,922,191,000 | 0.2% |
| | District of Columbia | 13,641,290,000 | 0.4% |

Source: U.S. Bureau of the Census, Governments Division
   "2011 State and Local Government Finances" (http://www.census.gov/govs/local/)
*Total expenditures includes all money paid other than for retirement of debt and extension of loans.  Includes payments from all sources of funds including current revenues and proceeds from borrowing and prior year fund balances.  Includes intergovernmental transfers and expenditures for government owned utilities and other commercial or auxiliary enterprise, and insurance trust expenditures.

# Per Capita State and Local Government Total Expenditures in 2011

## National Per Capita = $10,150*

| ALPHA ORDER | | | | RANK ORDER | | |
|---|---|---|---|---|---|---|
| RANK | STATE | PER CAPITA | | RANK | STATE | PER CAPITA |
| 36 | Alabama | $8,777 | | 1 | Alaska | $20,290 |
| 1 | Alaska | 20,290 | | 2 | New York | 15,400 |
| 45 | Arizona | 8,123 | | 3 | Wyoming | 15,313 |
| 47 | Arkansas | 8,089 | | 4 | California | 12,143 |
| 4 | California | 12,143 | | 5 | Massachusetts | 11,463 |
| 21 | Colorado | 10,081 | | 6 | New Jersey | 11,461 |
| 7 | Connecticut | 11,341 | | 7 | Connecticut | 11,341 |
| 11 | Delaware | 10,899 | | 8 | Vermont | 11,047 |
| 39 | Florida | 8,598 | | 9 | Washington | 10,978 |
| 49 | Georgia | 7,959 | | 10 | Rhode Island | 10,913 |
| 15 | Hawaii | 10,441 | | 11 | Delaware | 10,899 |
| 50 | Idaho | 7,619 | | 12 | New Mexico | 10,784 |
| 20 | Illinois | 10,169 | | 13 | Louisiana | 10,658 |
| 48 | Indiana | 8,085 | | 14 | Nebraska | 10,600 |
| 24 | Iowa | 9,897 | | 15 | Hawaii | 10,441 |
| 28 | Kansas | 9,244 | | 16 | Pennsylvania | 10,427 |
| 32 | Kentucky | 8,945 | | 17 | North Dakota | 10,423 |
| 13 | Louisiana | 10,658 | | 18 | Minnesota | 10,413 |
| 26 | Maine | 9,496 | | 19 | Oregon | 10,323 |
| 25 | Maryland | 9,866 | | 20 | Illinois | 10,169 |
| 5 | Massachusetts | 11,463 | | 21 | Colorado | 10,081 |
| 31 | Michigan | 9,094 | | 22 | Ohio | 10,073 |
| 18 | Minnesota | 10,413 | | 23 | Wisconsin | 9,930 |
| 29 | Mississippi | 9,171 | | 24 | Iowa | 9,897 |
| 44 | Missouri | 8,300 | | 25 | Maryland | 9,866 |
| 27 | Montana | 9,315 | | 26 | Maine | 9,496 |
| 14 | Nebraska | 10,600 | | 27 | Montana | 9,315 |
| 40 | Nevada | 8,555 | | 28 | Kansas | 9,244 |
| 35 | New Hampshire | 8,831 | | 29 | Mississippi | 9,171 |
| 6 | New Jersey | 11,461 | | 30 | South Carolina | 9,155 |
| 12 | New Mexico | 10,784 | | 31 | Michigan | 9,094 |
| 2 | New York | 15,400 | | 32 | Kentucky | 8,945 |
| 43 | North Carolina | 8,377 | | 33 | Utah | 8,857 |
| 17 | North Dakota | 10,423 | | 34 | West Virginia | 8,842 |
| 22 | Ohio | 10,073 | | 35 | New Hampshire | 8,831 |
| 46 | Oklahoma | 8,117 | | 36 | Alabama | 8,777 |
| 19 | Oregon | 10,323 | | 37 | Texas | 8,623 |
| 16 | Pennsylvania | 10,427 | | 38 | Tennessee | 8,618 |
| 10 | Rhode Island | 10,913 | | 39 | Florida | 8,598 |
| 30 | South Carolina | 9,155 | | 40 | Nevada | 8,555 |
| 42 | South Dakota | 8,516 | | 41 | Virginia | 8,542 |
| 38 | Tennessee | 8,618 | | 42 | South Dakota | 8,516 |
| 37 | Texas | 8,623 | | 43 | North Carolina | 8,377 |
| 33 | Utah | 8,857 | | 44 | Missouri | 8,300 |
| 8 | Vermont | 11,047 | | 45 | Arizona | 8,123 |
| 41 | Virginia | 8,542 | | 46 | Oklahoma | 8,117 |
| 9 | Washington | 10,978 | | 47 | Arkansas | 8,089 |
| 34 | West Virginia | 8,842 | | 48 | Indiana | 8,085 |
| 23 | Wisconsin | 9,930 | | 49 | Georgia | 7,959 |
| 3 | Wyoming | 15,313 | | 50 | Idaho | 7,619 |
| | | | | | District of Columbia | 22,037 |

Source: CQ Press using data from U.S. Bureau of the Census, Governments Division
"2011 State and Local Government Finances" (http://www.census.gov/govs/local/)
*Total expenditures includes all money paid other than for retirement of debt and extension of loans. Includes payments from all sources of funds including current revenues and proceeds from borrowing and prior year fund balances. Includes intergovernmental transfers and expenditures for government owned utilities and other commercial or auxiliary enterprise, and insurance trust expenditures.

# State and Local Government Direct General Expenditures in 2011

## National Total = $2,583,100,739,000*

| RANK | STATE | EXPENDITURES | % of USA |
|------|-------|-------------|----------|
| 25 | Alabama | $35,385,191,000 | 1.4% |
| 39 | Alaska | 12,790,477,000 | 0.5% |
| 20 | Arizona | 42,684,746,000 | 1.7% |
| 33 | Arkansas | 20,784,517,000 | 0.8% |
| 1 | California | 353,674,626,000 | 13.7% |
| 23 | Colorado | 41,285,551,000 | 1.6% |
| 26 | Connecticut | 33,366,550,000 | 1.3% |
| 45 | Delaware | 8,586,127,000 | 0.3% |
| 4 | Florida | 137,974,357,000 | 5.3% |
| 11 | Georgia | 64,037,873,000 | 2.5% |
| 40 | Hawaii | 12,205,684,000 | 0.5% |
| 42 | Idaho | 10,488,457,000 | 0.4% |
| 6 | Illinois | 104,305,704,000 | 4.0% |
| 18 | Indiana | 45,838,359,000 | 1.8% |
| 29 | Iowa | 26,457,162,000 | 1.0% |
| 32 | Kansas | 22,966,622,000 | 0.9% |
| 27 | Kentucky | 32,329,416,000 | 1.3% |
| 19 | Louisiana | 42,827,115,000 | 1.7% |
| 41 | Maine | 11,353,942,000 | 0.4% |
| 15 | Maryland | 49,842,519,000 | 1.9% |
| 12 | Massachusetts | 61,545,455,000 | 2.4% |
| 9 | Michigan | 73,705,470,000 | 2.9% |
| 17 | Minnesota | 47,241,100,000 | 1.8% |
| 31 | Mississippi | 23,831,060,000 | 0.9% |
| 22 | Missouri | 41,478,542,000 | 1.6% |
| 46 | Montana | 8,112,395,000 | 0.3% |
| 37 | Nebraska | 14,523,597,000 | 0.6% |
| 36 | Nevada | 18,694,662,000 | 0.7% |
| 43 | New Hampshire | 10,237,502,000 | 0.4% |
| 8 | New Jersey | 81,559,227,000 | 3.2% |
| 35 | New Mexico | 19,440,075,000 | 0.8% |
| 2 | New York | 235,261,859,000 | 9.1% |
| 10 | North Carolina | 67,309,269,000 | 2.6% |
| 48 | North Dakota | 6,426,326,000 | 0.2% |
| 7 | Ohio | 94,278,105,000 | 3.6% |
| 30 | Oklahoma | 25,758,613,000 | 1.0% |
| 28 | Oregon | 31,797,518,000 | 1.2% |
| 5 | Pennsylvania | 108,685,034,000 | 4.2% |
| 44 | Rhode Island | 9,230,061,000 | 0.4% |
| 24 | South Carolina | 35,579,527,000 | 1.4% |
| 50 | South Dakota | 6,165,418,000 | 0.2% |
| 21 | Tennessee | 42,056,487,000 | 1.6% |
| 3 | Texas | 185,643,845,000 | 7.2% |
| 34 | Utah | 20,369,821,000 | 0.8% |
| 49 | Vermont | 6,173,633,000 | 0.2% |
| 13 | Virginia | 60,912,146,000 | 2.4% |
| 14 | Washington | 57,776,930,000 | 2.2% |
| 38 | West Virginia | 14,466,087,000 | 0.6% |
| 16 | Wisconsin | 47,713,578,000 | 1.8% |
| 47 | Wyoming | 7,556,910,000 | 0.3% |

| RANK | STATE | EXPENDITURES | % of USA |
|------|-------|-------------|----------|
| 1 | California | $353,674,626,000 | 13.7% |
| 2 | New York | 235,261,859,000 | 9.1% |
| 3 | Texas | 185,643,845,000 | 7.2% |
| 4 | Florida | 137,974,357,000 | 5.3% |
| 5 | Pennsylvania | 108,685,034,000 | 4.2% |
| 6 | Illinois | 104,305,704,000 | 4.0% |
| 7 | Ohio | 94,278,105,000 | 3.6% |
| 8 | New Jersey | 81,559,227,000 | 3.2% |
| 9 | Michigan | 73,705,470,000 | 2.9% |
| 10 | North Carolina | 67,309,269,000 | 2.6% |
| 11 | Georgia | 64,037,873,000 | 2.5% |
| 12 | Massachusetts | 61,545,455,000 | 2.4% |
| 13 | Virginia | 60,912,146,000 | 2.4% |
| 14 | Washington | 57,776,930,000 | 2.2% |
| 15 | Maryland | 49,842,519,000 | 1.9% |
| 16 | Wisconsin | 47,713,578,000 | 1.8% |
| 17 | Minnesota | 47,241,100,000 | 1.8% |
| 18 | Indiana | 45,838,359,000 | 1.8% |
| 19 | Louisiana | 42,827,115,000 | 1.7% |
| 20 | Arizona | 42,684,746,000 | 1.7% |
| 21 | Tennessee | 42,056,487,000 | 1.6% |
| 22 | Missouri | 41,478,542,000 | 1.6% |
| 23 | Colorado | 41,285,551,000 | 1.6% |
| 24 | South Carolina | 35,579,527,000 | 1.4% |
| 25 | Alabama | 35,385,191,000 | 1.4% |
| 26 | Connecticut | 33,366,550,000 | 1.3% |
| 27 | Kentucky | 32,329,416,000 | 1.3% |
| 28 | Oregon | 31,797,518,000 | 1.2% |
| 29 | Iowa | 26,457,162,000 | 1.0% |
| 30 | Oklahoma | 25,758,613,000 | 1.0% |
| 31 | Mississippi | 23,831,060,000 | 0.9% |
| 32 | Kansas | 22,966,622,000 | 0.9% |
| 33 | Arkansas | 20,784,517,000 | 0.8% |
| 34 | Utah | 20,369,821,000 | 0.8% |
| 35 | New Mexico | 19,440,075,000 | 0.8% |
| 36 | Nevada | 18,694,662,000 | 0.7% |
| 37 | Nebraska | 14,523,597,000 | 0.6% |
| 38 | West Virginia | 14,466,087,000 | 0.6% |
| 39 | Alaska | 12,790,477,000 | 0.5% |
| 40 | Hawaii | 12,205,684,000 | 0.5% |
| 41 | Maine | 11,353,942,000 | 0.4% |
| 42 | Idaho | 10,488,457,000 | 0.4% |
| 43 | New Hampshire | 10,237,502,000 | 0.4% |
| 44 | Rhode Island | 9,230,061,000 | 0.4% |
| 45 | Delaware | 8,586,127,000 | 0.3% |
| 46 | Montana | 8,112,395,000 | 0.3% |
| 47 | Wyoming | 7,556,910,000 | 0.3% |
| 48 | North Dakota | 6,426,326,000 | 0.2% |
| 49 | Vermont | 6,173,633,000 | 0.2% |
| 50 | South Dakota | 6,165,418,000 | 0.2% |
| | District of Columbia | 10,385,492,000 | 0.4% |

Source: U.S. Bureau of the Census, Governments Division
"2011 State and Local Government Finances" (http://www.census.gov/govs/local/)
*Direct general expenditures include expenditures for current operations, assistance and subsidies, interest on debt, and capital outlay. Excludes intergovernmental transfers, expenditures for government owned utilities and other commercial or auxiliary enterprise, and insurance trust expenditures.

# Per Capita State and Local Government Direct General Expenditures in 2011

## National Per Capita = $8,290*

| ALPHA ORDER | | | RANK ORDER | | |
|---|---|---|---|---|---|
| RANK | STATE | PER CAPITA | RANK | STATE | PER CAPITA |
| 37 | Alabama | $7,366 | 1 | Alaska | $17,670 |
| 1 | Alaska | 17,670 | 2 | Wyoming | 13,320 |
| 48 | Arizona | 6,600 | 3 | New York | 12,064 |
| 41 | Arkansas | 7,073 | 4 | Vermont | 9,853 |
| 6 | California | 9,385 | 5 | Delaware | 9,455 |
| 26 | Colorado | 8,069 | 6 | California | 9,385 |
| 11 | Connecticut | 9,303 | 6 | North Dakota | 9,385 |
| 5 | Delaware | 9,455 | 8 | Louisiana | 9,362 |
| 40 | Florida | 7,231 | 9 | New Mexico | 9,352 |
| 50 | Georgia | 6,526 | 10 | Massachusetts | 9,315 |
| 13 | Hawaii | 8,857 | 11 | Connecticut | 9,303 |
| 47 | Idaho | 6,623 | 12 | New Jersey | 9,232 |
| 25 | Illinois | 8,111 | 13 | Hawaii | 8,857 |
| 42 | Indiana | 7,034 | 14 | Minnesota | 8,835 |
| 16 | Iowa | 8,635 | 15 | Rhode Island | 8,785 |
| 28 | Kansas | 8,001 | 16 | Iowa | 8,635 |
| 36 | Kentucky | 7,403 | 17 | Maine | 8,546 |
| 8 | Louisiana | 9,362 | 18 | Maryland | 8,535 |
| 17 | Maine | 8,546 | 19 | Pennsylvania | 8,528 |
| 18 | Maryland | 8,535 | 20 | Washington | 8,468 |
| 10 | Massachusetts | 9,315 | 21 | Wisconsin | 8,356 |
| 35 | Michigan | 7,462 | 22 | Oregon | 8,220 |
| 14 | Minnesota | 8,835 | 23 | Ohio | 8,169 |
| 27 | Mississippi | 8,004 | 24 | Montana | 8,131 |
| 44 | Missouri | 6,903 | 25 | Illinois | 8,111 |
| 24 | Montana | 8,131 | 26 | Colorado | 8,069 |
| 29 | Nebraska | 7,884 | 27 | Mississippi | 8,004 |
| 45 | Nevada | 6,873 | 28 | Kansas | 8,001 |
| 31 | New Hampshire | 7,769 | 29 | Nebraska | 7,884 |
| 12 | New Jersey | 9,232 | 30 | West Virginia | 7,799 |
| 9 | New Mexico | 9,352 | 31 | New Hampshire | 7,769 |
| 3 | New York | 12,064 | 32 | South Carolina | 7,613 |
| 43 | North Carolina | 6,974 | 33 | Virginia | 7,516 |
| 6 | North Dakota | 9,385 | 34 | South Dakota | 7,486 |
| 23 | Ohio | 8,169 | 35 | Michigan | 7,462 |
| 46 | Oklahoma | 6,807 | 36 | Kentucky | 7,403 |
| 22 | Oregon | 8,220 | 37 | Alabama | 7,366 |
| 19 | Pennsylvania | 8,528 | 38 | Texas | 7,243 |
| 15 | Rhode Island | 8,785 | 39 | Utah | 7,238 |
| 32 | South Carolina | 7,613 | 40 | Florida | 7,231 |
| 34 | South Dakota | 7,486 | 41 | Arkansas | 7,073 |
| 49 | Tennessee | 6,572 | 42 | Indiana | 7,034 |
| 38 | Texas | 7,243 | 43 | North Carolina | 6,974 |
| 39 | Utah | 7,238 | 44 | Missouri | 6,903 |
| 4 | Vermont | 9,853 | 45 | Nevada | 6,873 |
| 33 | Virginia | 7,516 | 46 | Oklahoma | 6,807 |
| 20 | Washington | 8,468 | 47 | Idaho | 6,623 |
| 30 | West Virginia | 7,799 | 48 | Arizona | 6,600 |
| 21 | Wisconsin | 8,356 | 49 | Tennessee | 6,572 |
| 2 | Wyoming | 13,320 | 50 | Georgia | 6,526 |
| | | | | District of Columbia | 16,777 |

Source: CQ Press using data from U.S. Bureau of the Census, Governments Division
"2011 State and Local Government Finances" (http://www.census.gov/govs/local/)
*Direct general expenditures include expenditures for current operations, assistance and subsidies, interest on debt, and capital outlay. Excludes intergovernmental transfers, expenditures for government owned utilities and other commercial or auxiliary enterprise, and insurance trust expenditures.

# State and Local Government Debt Outstanding in 2011

## National Total = $2,907,756,031,000*

ALPHA ORDER

| RANK | STATE | DEBT | % of USA |
|------|-------|------|----------|
| 28 | Alabama | $29,315,372,000 | 1.0% |
| 42 | Alaska | 10,197,865,000 | 0.4% |
| 16 | Arizona | 50,926,194,000 | 1.8% |
| 36 | Arkansas | 13,543,811,000 | 0.5% |
| 1 | California | 418,832,878,000 | 14.4% |
| 14 | Colorado | 52,186,187,000 | 1.8% |
| 23 | Connecticut | 41,490,174,000 | 1.4% |
| 44 | Delaware | 8,277,935,000 | 0.3% |
| 4 | Florida | 151,903,834,000 | 5.2% |
| 13 | Georgia | 54,367,087,000 | 1.9% |
| 37 | Hawaii | 13,377,007,000 | 0.5% |
| 45 | Idaho | 6,230,994,000 | 0.2% |
| 5 | Illinois | 145,485,105,000 | 5.0% |
| 17 | Indiana | 49,405,141,000 | 1.7% |
| 33 | Iowa | 18,327,971,000 | 0.6% |
| 30 | Kansas | 27,124,892,000 | 0.9% |
| 22 | Kentucky | 42,167,519,000 | 1.5% |
| 25 | Louisiana | 38,621,989,000 | 1.3% |
| 43 | Maine | 8,983,385,000 | 0.3% |
| 20 | Maryland | 44,603,401,000 | 1.5% |
| 8 | Massachusetts | 92,558,199,000 | 3.2% |
| 11 | Michigan | 73,842,390,000 | 2.5% |
| 18 | Minnesota | 46,761,005,000 | 1.6% |
| 35 | Mississippi | 14,186,468,000 | 0.5% |
| 19 | Missouri | 46,105,095,000 | 1.6% |
| 46 | Montana | 5,976,760,000 | 0.2% |
| 38 | Nebraska | 12,941,977,000 | 0.4% |
| 29 | Nevada | 27,708,291,000 | 1.0% |
| 40 | New Hampshire | 11,237,885,000 | 0.4% |
| 7 | New Jersey | 102,259,634,000 | 3.5% |
| 34 | New Mexico | 16,648,925,000 | 0.6% |
| 2 | New York | 334,622,001,000 | 11.5% |
| 15 | North Carolina | 51,187,426,000 | 1.8% |
| 49 | North Dakota | 4,425,916,000 | 0.2% |
| 9 | Ohio | 77,533,373,000 | 2.7% |
| 32 | Oklahoma | 19,202,119,000 | 0.7% |
| 27 | Oregon | 34,753,649,000 | 1.2% |
| 6 | Pennsylvania | 123,483,715,000 | 4.2% |
| 39 | Rhode Island | 11,939,950,000 | 0.4% |
| 24 | South Carolina | 41,054,098,000 | 1.4% |
| 47 | South Dakota | 5,734,814,000 | 0.2% |
| 26 | Tennessee | 38,303,352,000 | 1.3% |
| 3 | Texas | 258,240,642,000 | 8.9% |
| 31 | Utah | 20,133,390,000 | 0.7% |
| 48 | Vermont | 4,729,149,000 | 0.2% |
| 12 | Virginia | 63,816,250,000 | 2.2% |
| 10 | Washington | 74,091,088,000 | 2.5% |
| 41 | West Virginia | 10,991,723,000 | 0.4% |
| 21 | Wisconsin | 44,271,580,000 | 1.5% |
| 50 | Wyoming | 2,369,891,000 | 0.1% |

RANK ORDER

| RANK | STATE | DEBT | % of USA |
|------|-------|------|----------|
| 1 | California | $418,832,878,000 | 14.4% |
| 2 | New York | 334,622,001,000 | 11.5% |
| 3 | Texas | 258,240,642,000 | 8.9% |
| 4 | Florida | 151,903,834,000 | 5.2% |
| 5 | Illinois | 145,485,105,000 | 5.0% |
| 6 | Pennsylvania | 123,483,715,000 | 4.2% |
| 7 | New Jersey | 102,259,634,000 | 3.5% |
| 8 | Massachusetts | 92,558,199,000 | 3.2% |
| 9 | Ohio | 77,533,373,000 | 2.7% |
| 10 | Washington | 74,091,088,000 | 2.5% |
| 11 | Michigan | 73,842,390,000 | 2.5% |
| 12 | Virginia | 63,816,250,000 | 2.2% |
| 13 | Georgia | 54,367,087,000 | 1.9% |
| 14 | Colorado | 52,186,187,000 | 1.8% |
| 15 | North Carolina | 51,187,426,000 | 1.8% |
| 16 | Arizona | 50,926,194,000 | 1.8% |
| 17 | Indiana | 49,405,141,000 | 1.7% |
| 18 | Minnesota | 46,761,005,000 | 1.6% |
| 19 | Missouri | 46,105,095,000 | 1.6% |
| 20 | Maryland | 44,603,401,000 | 1.5% |
| 21 | Wisconsin | 44,271,580,000 | 1.5% |
| 22 | Kentucky | 42,167,519,000 | 1.5% |
| 23 | Connecticut | 41,490,174,000 | 1.4% |
| 24 | South Carolina | 41,054,098,000 | 1.4% |
| 25 | Louisiana | 38,621,989,000 | 1.3% |
| 26 | Tennessee | 38,303,352,000 | 1.3% |
| 27 | Oregon | 34,753,649,000 | 1.2% |
| 28 | Alabama | 29,315,372,000 | 1.0% |
| 29 | Nevada | 27,708,291,000 | 1.0% |
| 30 | Kansas | 27,124,892,000 | 0.9% |
| 31 | Utah | 20,133,390,000 | 0.7% |
| 32 | Oklahoma | 19,202,119,000 | 0.7% |
| 33 | Iowa | 18,327,971,000 | 0.6% |
| 34 | New Mexico | 16,648,925,000 | 0.6% |
| 35 | Mississippi | 14,186,468,000 | 0.5% |
| 36 | Arkansas | 13,543,811,000 | 0.5% |
| 37 | Hawaii | 13,377,007,000 | 0.5% |
| 38 | Nebraska | 12,941,977,000 | 0.4% |
| 39 | Rhode Island | 11,939,950,000 | 0.4% |
| 40 | New Hampshire | 11,237,885,000 | 0.4% |
| 41 | West Virginia | 10,991,723,000 | 0.4% |
| 42 | Alaska | 10,197,865,000 | 0.4% |
| 43 | Maine | 8,983,385,000 | 0.3% |
| 44 | Delaware | 8,277,935,000 | 0.3% |
| 45 | Idaho | 6,230,994,000 | 0.2% |
| 46 | Montana | 5,976,760,000 | 0.2% |
| 47 | South Dakota | 5,734,814,000 | 0.2% |
| 48 | Vermont | 4,729,149,000 | 0.2% |
| 49 | North Dakota | 4,425,916,000 | 0.2% |
| 50 | Wyoming | 2,369,891,000 | 0.1% |
| | District of Columbia | 11,276,535,000 | 0.4% |

Source: U.S. Bureau of the Census, Governments Division
"2011 State and Local Government Finances" (http://www.census.gov/govs/local/)
*Includes short-term, long-term, full faith and credit, nonguaranteed, and public debt for private purposes.

# Per Capita State and Local Government Debt Outstanding in 2011

## National Per Capita = $9,332*

| RANK | STATE | PER CAPITA | | RANK | STATE | PER CAPITA |
|------|-------|-----------|---|------|-------|-----------|
| | **ALPHA ORDER** | | | | **RANK ORDER** | |
| 39 | Alabama | $6,103 | | 1 | New York | $17,159 |
| 2 | Alaska | 14,088 | | 2 | Alaska | 14,088 |
| 25 | Arizona | 7,874 | | 3 | Massachusetts | 14,009 |
| 48 | Arkansas | 4,609 | | 4 | New Jersey | 11,575 |
| 8 | California | 11,114 | | 5 | Connecticut | 11,568 |
| 10 | Colorado | 10,200 | | 6 | Rhode Island | 11,364 |
| 5 | Connecticut | 11,568 | | 7 | Illinois | 11,313 |
| 17 | Delaware | 9,115 | | 8 | California | 11,114 |
| 24 | Florida | 7,960 | | 9 | Washington | 10,859 |
| 44 | Georgia | 5,541 | | 10 | Colorado | 10,200 |
| 13 | Hawaii | 9,707 | | 11 | Nevada | 10,187 |
| 50 | Idaho | 3,934 | | 12 | Texas | 10,075 |
| 7 | Illinois | 11,313 | | 13 | Hawaii | 9,707 |
| 30 | Indiana | 7,582 | | 14 | Pennsylvania | 9,690 |
| 42 | Iowa | 5,982 | | 15 | Kentucky | 9,656 |
| 16 | Kansas | 9,450 | | 16 | Kansas | 9,450 |
| 15 | Kentucky | 9,656 | | 17 | Delaware | 9,115 |
| 22 | Louisiana | 8,442 | | 18 | Oregon | 8,984 |
| 36 | Maine | 6,762 | | 19 | South Carolina | 8,785 |
| 29 | Maryland | 7,638 | | 20 | Minnesota | 8,745 |
| 3 | Massachusetts | 14,009 | | 21 | New Hampshire | 8,528 |
| 32 | Michigan | 7,476 | | 22 | Louisiana | 8,442 |
| 20 | Minnesota | 8,745 | | 23 | New Mexico | 8,009 |
| 47 | Mississippi | 4,765 | | 24 | Florida | 7,960 |
| 28 | Missouri | 7,673 | | 25 | Arizona | 7,874 |
| 40 | Montana | 5,991 | | 25 | Virginia | 7,874 |
| 34 | Nebraska | 7,025 | | 27 | Wisconsin | 7,754 |
| 11 | Nevada | 10,187 | | 28 | Missouri | 7,673 |
| 21 | New Hampshire | 8,528 | | 29 | Maryland | 7,638 |
| 4 | New Jersey | 11,575 | | 30 | Indiana | 7,582 |
| 23 | New Mexico | 8,009 | | 31 | Vermont | 7,547 |
| 1 | New York | 17,159 | | 32 | Michigan | 7,476 |
| 45 | North Carolina | 5,304 | | 33 | Utah | 7,154 |
| 38 | North Dakota | 6,464 | | 34 | Nebraska | 7,025 |
| 37 | Ohio | 6,718 | | 35 | South Dakota | 6,963 |
| 46 | Oklahoma | 5,074 | | 36 | Maine | 6,762 |
| 18 | Oregon | 8,984 | | 37 | Ohio | 6,718 |
| 14 | Pennsylvania | 9,690 | | 38 | North Dakota | 6,464 |
| 6 | Rhode Island | 11,364 | | 39 | Alabama | 6,103 |
| 19 | South Carolina | 8,785 | | 40 | Montana | 5,991 |
| 35 | South Dakota | 6,963 | | 41 | Tennessee | 5,985 |
| 41 | Tennessee | 5,985 | | 42 | Iowa | 5,982 |
| 12 | Texas | 10,075 | | 43 | West Virginia | 5,926 |
| 33 | Utah | 7,154 | | 44 | Georgia | 5,541 |
| 31 | Vermont | 7,547 | | 45 | North Carolina | 5,304 |
| 25 | Virginia | 7,874 | | 46 | Oklahoma | 5,074 |
| 9 | Washington | 10,859 | | 47 | Mississippi | 4,765 |
| 43 | West Virginia | 5,926 | | 48 | Arkansas | 4,609 |
| 27 | Wisconsin | 7,754 | | 49 | Wyoming | 4,177 |
| 49 | Wyoming | 4,177 | | 50 | Idaho | 3,934 |
| | | | | | District of Columbia | 18,217 |

Source: CQ Press using data from U.S. Bureau of the Census, Governments Division
"2011 State and Local Government Finances" (http://www.census.gov/govs/local/)
*Includes short-term, long-term, full faith and credit, nonguaranteed, and public debt for private purposes.

# State and Local Government Full-Time Equivalent Employees in 2011

## National Total = 16,358,439 FTE Employees*

ALPHA ORDER

| RANK | STATE | EMPLOYEES | % of USA |
|---|---|---|---|
| 19 | Alabama | 284,778 | 1.7% |
| 44 | Alaska | 54,743 | 0.3% |
| 22 | Arizona | 280,795 | 1.7% |
| 31 | Arkansas | 189,608 | 1.2% |
| 1 | California | 1,752,070 | 10.7% |
| 24 | Colorado | 270,166 | 1.7% |
| 32 | Connecticut | 185,209 | 1.1% |
| 46 | Delaware | 49,751 | 0.3% |
| 4 | Florida | 888,159 | 5.4% |
| 9 | Georgia | 509,276 | 3.1% |
| 41 | Hawaii | 73,669 | 0.5% |
| 39 | Idaho | 78,569 | 0.5% |
| 5 | Illinois | 626,921 | 3.8% |
| 14 | Indiana | 329,503 | 2.0% |
| 33 | Iowa | 177,268 | 1.1% |
| 29 | Kansas | 196,847 | 1.2% |
| 26 | Kentucky | 246,859 | 1.5% |
| 21 | Louisiana | 281,597 | 1.7% |
| 40 | Maine | 75,370 | 0.5% |
| 18 | Maryland | 307,031 | 1.9% |
| 16 | Massachusetts | 320,738 | 2.0% |
| 11 | Michigan | 456,578 | 2.8% |
| 23 | Minnesota | 277,179 | 1.7% |
| 30 | Mississippi | 191,995 | 1.2% |
| 17 | Missouri | 317,310 | 1.9% |
| 43 | Montana | 57,874 | 0.4% |
| 36 | Nebraska | 120,974 | 0.7% |
| 37 | Nevada | 114,307 | 0.7% |
| 42 | New Hampshire | 72,273 | 0.4% |
| 10 | New Jersey | 488,114 | 3.0% |
| 35 | New Mexico | 125,664 | 0.8% |
| 3 | New York | 1,175,681 | 7.2% |
| 8 | North Carolina | 556,065 | 3.4% |
| 49 | North Dakota | 45,047 | 0.3% |
| 6 | Ohio | 594,695 | 3.6% |
| 27 | Oklahoma | 214,757 | 1.3% |
| 28 | Oregon | 197,299 | 1.2% |
| 7 | Pennsylvania | 591,926 | 3.6% |
| 47 | Rhode Island | 49,746 | 0.3% |
| 25 | South Carolina | 253,574 | 1.6% |
| 48 | South Dakota | 45,851 | 0.3% |
| 15 | Tennessee | 327,457 | 2.0% |
| 2 | Texas | 1,450,198 | 8.9% |
| 34 | Utah | 147,591 | 0.9% |
| 50 | Vermont | 39,649 | 0.2% |
| 12 | Virginia | 438,837 | 2.7% |
| 13 | Washington | 346,367 | 2.1% |
| 38 | West Virginia | 103,701 | 0.6% |
| 20 | Wisconsin | 283,568 | 1.7% |
| 45 | Wyoming | 52,732 | 0.3% |

RANK ORDER

| RANK | STATE | EMPLOYEES | % of USA |
|---|---|---|---|
| 1 | California | 1,752,070 | 10.7% |
| 2 | Texas | 1,450,198 | 8.9% |
| 3 | New York | 1,175,681 | 7.2% |
| 4 | Florida | 888,159 | 5.4% |
| 5 | Illinois | 626,921 | 3.8% |
| 6 | Ohio | 594,695 | 3.6% |
| 7 | Pennsylvania | 591,926 | 3.6% |
| 8 | North Carolina | 556,065 | 3.4% |
| 9 | Georgia | 509,276 | 3.1% |
| 10 | New Jersey | 488,114 | 3.0% |
| 11 | Michigan | 456,578 | 2.8% |
| 12 | Virginia | 438,837 | 2.7% |
| 13 | Washington | 346,367 | 2.1% |
| 14 | Indiana | 329,503 | 2.0% |
| 15 | Tennessee | 327,457 | 2.0% |
| 16 | Massachusetts | 320,738 | 2.0% |
| 17 | Missouri | 317,310 | 1.9% |
| 18 | Maryland | 307,031 | 1.9% |
| 19 | Alabama | 284,778 | 1.7% |
| 20 | Wisconsin | 283,568 | 1.7% |
| 21 | Louisiana | 281,597 | 1.7% |
| 22 | Arizona | 280,795 | 1.7% |
| 23 | Minnesota | 277,179 | 1.7% |
| 24 | Colorado | 270,166 | 1.7% |
| 25 | South Carolina | 253,574 | 1.6% |
| 26 | Kentucky | 246,859 | 1.5% |
| 27 | Oklahoma | 214,757 | 1.3% |
| 28 | Oregon | 197,299 | 1.2% |
| 29 | Kansas | 196,847 | 1.2% |
| 30 | Mississippi | 191,995 | 1.2% |
| 31 | Arkansas | 189,608 | 1.2% |
| 32 | Connecticut | 185,209 | 1.1% |
| 33 | Iowa | 177,268 | 1.1% |
| 34 | Utah | 147,591 | 0.9% |
| 35 | New Mexico | 125,664 | 0.8% |
| 36 | Nebraska | 120,974 | 0.7% |
| 37 | Nevada | 114,307 | 0.7% |
| 38 | West Virginia | 103,701 | 0.6% |
| 39 | Idaho | 78,569 | 0.5% |
| 40 | Maine | 75,370 | 0.5% |
| 41 | Hawaii | 73,669 | 0.5% |
| 42 | New Hampshire | 72,273 | 0.4% |
| 43 | Montana | 57,874 | 0.4% |
| 44 | Alaska | 54,743 | 0.3% |
| 45 | Wyoming | 52,732 | 0.3% |
| 46 | Delaware | 49,751 | 0.3% |
| 47 | Rhode Island | 49,746 | 0.3% |
| 48 | South Dakota | 45,851 | 0.3% |
| 49 | North Dakota | 45,047 | 0.3% |
| 50 | Vermont | 39,649 | 0.2% |
| | District of Columbia | 42,502 | 0.3% |

Source: U.S. Bureau of the Census, Governments Division
   "Government Employment and Payroll" (http://www.census.gov/govs/apes/index.html)
*As of March 2011.

# Rate of State and Local Government Full-Time Equivalent Employees in 2011

## National Rate = 525 State/Local Government Employees per 10,000 Population*

| ALPHA ORDER | | | RANK ORDER | | |
|---|---|---|---|---|---|
| RANK | STATE | RATE | RANK | STATE | RATE |
| 12 | Alabama | 593 | 1 | Wyoming | 929 |
| 2 | Alaska | 756 | 2 | Alaska | 756 |
| 49 | Arizona | 434 | 3 | Kansas | 686 |
| 6 | Arkansas | 645 | 4 | North Dakota | 658 |
| 45 | California | 465 | 5 | Nebraska | 657 |
| 28 | Colorado | 528 | 6 | Arkansas | 645 |
| 34 | Connecticut | 516 | 6 | Mississippi | 645 |
| 23 | Delaware | 548 | 8 | Vermont | 633 |
| 45 | Florida | 465 | 9 | Louisiana | 616 |
| 32 | Georgia | 519 | 10 | New Mexico | 605 |
| 27 | Hawaii | 535 | 11 | New York | 603 |
| 41 | Idaho | 496 | 12 | Alabama | 593 |
| 42 | Illinois | 488 | 13 | Montana | 580 |
| 39 | Indiana | 506 | 14 | Iowa | 579 |
| 14 | Iowa | 579 | 15 | North Carolina | 576 |
| 3 | Kansas | 686 | 16 | Oklahoma | 568 |
| 19 | Kentucky | 565 | 17 | Maine | 567 |
| 9 | Louisiana | 616 | 18 | Texas | 566 |
| 17 | Maine | 567 | 19 | Kentucky | 565 |
| 30 | Maryland | 526 | 20 | West Virginia | 559 |
| 43 | Massachusetts | 485 | 21 | South Dakota | 557 |
| 48 | Michigan | 462 | 22 | New Jersey | 552 |
| 33 | Minnesota | 518 | 23 | Delaware | 548 |
| 6 | Mississippi | 645 | 23 | New Hampshire | 548 |
| 28 | Missouri | 528 | 25 | South Carolina | 543 |
| 13 | Montana | 580 | 26 | Virginia | 541 |
| 5 | Nebraska | 657 | 27 | Hawaii | 535 |
| 50 | Nevada | 420 | 28 | Colorado | 528 |
| 23 | New Hampshire | 548 | 28 | Missouri | 528 |
| 22 | New Jersey | 552 | 30 | Maryland | 526 |
| 10 | New Mexico | 605 | 31 | Utah | 524 |
| 11 | New York | 603 | 32 | Georgia | 519 |
| 15 | North Carolina | 576 | 33 | Minnesota | 518 |
| 4 | North Dakota | 658 | 34 | Connecticut | 516 |
| 35 | Ohio | 515 | 35 | Ohio | 515 |
| 16 | Oklahoma | 568 | 36 | Tennessee | 512 |
| 37 | Oregon | 510 | 37 | Oregon | 510 |
| 47 | Pennsylvania | 464 | 38 | Washington | 508 |
| 44 | Rhode Island | 473 | 39 | Indiana | 506 |
| 25 | South Carolina | 543 | 40 | Wisconsin | 497 |
| 21 | South Dakota | 557 | 41 | Idaho | 496 |
| 36 | Tennessee | 512 | 42 | Illinois | 488 |
| 18 | Texas | 566 | 43 | Massachusetts | 485 |
| 31 | Utah | 524 | 44 | Rhode Island | 473 |
| 8 | Vermont | 633 | 45 | California | 465 |
| 26 | Virginia | 541 | 45 | Florida | 465 |
| 38 | Washington | 508 | 47 | Pennsylvania | 464 |
| 20 | West Virginia | 559 | 48 | Michigan | 462 |
| 40 | Wisconsin | 497 | 49 | Arizona | 434 |
| 1 | Wyoming | 929 | 50 | Nevada | 420 |
| | | | | District of Columbia | 687 |

Source: CQ Press using data from U.S. Bureau of the Census, Governments Division
"Government Employment and Payroll" (http://www.census.gov/govs/apes/index.html)
*As of March 2011.

# Average Annual Earnings of Full-Time State and Local Government Employees in 2011
## National Average = $53,298*

ALPHA ORDER

| RANK | STATE | SALARY |
|------|-------|--------|
| 42 | Alabama | $42,444 |
| 7 | Alaska | 62,117 |
| 22 | Arizona | 50,073 |
| 50 | Arkansas | 37,416 |
| 1 | California | 71,155 |
| 16 | Colorado | 53,587 |
| 4 | Connecticut | 65,097 |
| 19 | Delaware | 52,757 |
| 28 | Florida | 47,694 |
| 39 | Georgia | 42,793 |
| 21 | Hawaii | 50,681 |
| 37 | Idaho | 43,392 |
| 11 | Illinois | 59,046 |
| 33 | Indiana | 45,362 |
| 18 | Iowa | 52,832 |
| 38 | Kansas | 43,077 |
| 46 | Kentucky | 40,279 |
| 35 | Louisiana | 43,720 |
| 48 | Maine | 38,812 |
| 9 | Maryland | 60,063 |
| 10 | Massachusetts | 59,996 |
| 12 | Michigan | 58,263 |
| 13 | Minnesota | 57,451 |
| 49 | Mississippi | 38,235 |
| 40 | Missouri | 42,624 |
| 32 | Montana | 45,483 |
| 27 | Nebraska | 47,996 |
| 8 | Nevada | 60,683 |
| 24 | New Hampshire | 48,937 |
| 2 | New Jersey | 67,550 |
| 36 | New Mexico | 43,651 |
| 3 | New York | 65,897 |
| 34 | North Carolina | 43,941 |
| 30 | North Dakota | 46,209 |
| 20 | Ohio | 52,280 |
| 47 | Oklahoma | 40,046 |
| 15 | Oregon | 54,279 |
| 17 | Pennsylvania | 53,512 |
| 6 | Rhode Island | 62,718 |
| 41 | South Carolina | 42,497 |
| 44 | South Dakota | 40,763 |
| 43 | Tennessee | 40,917 |
| 31 | Texas | 45,867 |
| 29 | Utah | 46,521 |
| 25 | Vermont | 48,501 |
| 26 | Virginia | 48,175 |
| 5 | Washington | 64,986 |
| 45 | West Virginia | 40,364 |
| 14 | Wisconsin | 54,529 |
| 23 | Wyoming | 49,658 |

RANK ORDER

| RANK | STATE | SALARY |
|------|-------|--------|
| 1 | California | $71,155 |
| 2 | New Jersey | 67,550 |
| 3 | New York | 65,897 |
| 4 | Connecticut | 65,097 |
| 5 | Washington | 64,986 |
| 6 | Rhode Island | 62,718 |
| 7 | Alaska | 62,117 |
| 8 | Nevada | 60,683 |
| 9 | Maryland | 60,063 |
| 10 | Massachusetts | 59,996 |
| 11 | Illinois | 59,046 |
| 12 | Michigan | 58,263 |
| 13 | Minnesota | 57,451 |
| 14 | Wisconsin | 54,529 |
| 15 | Oregon | 54,279 |
| 16 | Colorado | 53,587 |
| 17 | Pennsylvania | 53,512 |
| 18 | Iowa | 52,832 |
| 19 | Delaware | 52,757 |
| 20 | Ohio | 52,280 |
| 21 | Hawaii | 50,681 |
| 22 | Arizona | 50,073 |
| 23 | Wyoming | 49,658 |
| 24 | New Hampshire | 48,937 |
| 25 | Vermont | 48,501 |
| 26 | Virginia | 48,175 |
| 27 | Nebraska | 47,996 |
| 28 | Florida | 47,694 |
| 29 | Utah | 46,521 |
| 30 | North Dakota | 46,209 |
| 31 | Texas | 45,867 |
| 32 | Montana | 45,483 |
| 33 | Indiana | 45,362 |
| 34 | North Carolina | 43,941 |
| 35 | Louisiana | 43,720 |
| 36 | New Mexico | 43,651 |
| 37 | Idaho | 43,392 |
| 38 | Kansas | 43,077 |
| 39 | Georgia | 42,793 |
| 40 | Missouri | 42,624 |
| 41 | South Carolina | 42,497 |
| 42 | Alabama | 42,444 |
| 43 | Tennessee | 40,917 |
| 44 | South Dakota | 40,763 |
| 45 | West Virginia | 40,364 |
| 46 | Kentucky | 40,279 |
| 47 | Oklahoma | 40,046 |
| 48 | Maine | 38,812 |
| 49 | Mississippi | 38,235 |
| 50 | Arkansas | 37,416 |
| | District of Columbia | 72,821 |

Source: CQ Press using data from U.S. Bureau of the Census, Governments Division
"Government Employment and Payroll" (http://www.census.gov/govs/apes/index.html)
*March 2011 full-time payroll (multiplied by 12) divided by full-time employees.

# State Government Total Revenue in 2011

## National Total = $2,265,212,581,000*

| RANK | STATE | REVENUE | % of USA |
|------|-------|---------|----------|
| 28 | Alabama | $26,305,162,000 | 1.2% |
| 38 | Alaska | 14,920,900,000 | 0.7% |
| 20 | Arizona | 38,028,534,000 | 1.7% |
| 32 | Arkansas | 22,785,157,000 | 1.0% |
| 1 | California | 334,311,421,000 | 14.8% |
| 26 | Colorado | 29,488,801,000 | 1.3% |
| 27 | Connecticut | 28,904,574,000 | 1.3% |
| 44 | Delaware | 9,349,728,000 | 0.4% |
| 4 | Florida | 106,166,255,000 | 4.7% |
| 12 | Georgia | 52,294,783,000 | 2.3% |
| 39 | Hawaii | 12,931,811,000 | 0.6% |
| 42 | Idaho | 10,476,454,000 | 0.5% |
| 7 | Illinois | 80,685,183,000 | 3.6% |
| 18 | Indiana | 38,894,976,000 | 1.7% |
| 30 | Iowa | 24,088,747,000 | 1.1% |
| 34 | Kansas | 18,582,208,000 | 0.8% |
| 25 | Kentucky | 31,051,859,000 | 1.4% |
| 23 | Louisiana | 33,974,652,000 | 1.5% |
| 41 | Maine | 10,611,116,000 | 0.5% |
| 17 | Maryland | 41,737,483,000 | 1.8% |
| 11 | Massachusetts | 56,634,466,000 | 2.5% |
| 9 | Michigan | 64,429,901,000 | 2.8% |
| 15 | Minnesota | 45,684,189,000 | 2.0% |
| 31 | Mississippi | 23,441,796,000 | 1.0% |
| 19 | Missouri | 38,606,945,000 | 1.7% |
| 46 | Montana | 7,950,510,000 | 0.4% |
| 40 | Nebraska | 11,523,401,000 | 0.5% |
| 35 | Nevada | 17,597,124,000 | 0.8% |
| 45 | New Hampshire | 8,542,308,000 | 0.4% |
| 8 | New Jersey | 70,798,018,000 | 3.1% |
| 33 | New Mexico | 19,771,493,000 | 0.9% |
| 2 | New York | 205,546,377,000 | 9.1% |
| 10 | North Carolina | 63,194,017,000 | 2.8% |
| 47 | North Dakota | 7,805,674,000 | 0.3% |
| 5 | Ohio | 96,872,947,000 | 4.3% |
| 29 | Oklahoma | 26,234,738,000 | 1.2% |
| 21 | Oregon | 34,797,285,000 | 1.5% |
| 6 | Pennsylvania | 91,705,305,000 | 4.0% |
| 43 | Rhode Island | 9,388,083,000 | 0.4% |
| 24 | South Carolina | 31,733,200,000 | 1.4% |
| 50 | South Dakota | 6,017,179,000 | 0.3% |
| 22 | Tennessee | 34,653,154,000 | 1.5% |
| 3 | Texas | 134,302,447,000 | 5.9% |
| 36 | Utah | 16,984,797,000 | 0.7% |
| 49 | Vermont | 6,506,203,000 | 0.3% |
| 13 | Virginia | 50,781,571,000 | 2.2% |
| 14 | Washington | 50,420,289,000 | 2.2% |
| 37 | West Virginia | 15,397,630,000 | 0.7% |
| 16 | Wisconsin | 44,807,389,000 | 2.0% |
| 48 | Wyoming | 7,494,341,000 | 0.3% |

| RANK | STATE | REVENUE | % of USA |
|------|-------|---------|----------|
| 1 | California | $334,311,421,000 | 14.8% |
| 2 | New York | 205,546,377,000 | 9.1% |
| 3 | Texas | 134,302,447,000 | 5.9% |
| 4 | Florida | 106,166,255,000 | 4.7% |
| 5 | Ohio | 96,872,947,000 | 4.3% |
| 6 | Pennsylvania | 91,705,305,000 | 4.0% |
| 7 | Illinois | 80,685,183,000 | 3.6% |
| 8 | New Jersey | 70,798,018,000 | 3.1% |
| 9 | Michigan | 64,429,901,000 | 2.8% |
| 10 | North Carolina | 63,194,017,000 | 2.8% |
| 11 | Massachusetts | 56,634,466,000 | 2.5% |
| 12 | Georgia | 52,294,783,000 | 2.3% |
| 13 | Virginia | 50,781,571,000 | 2.2% |
| 14 | Washington | 50,420,289,000 | 2.2% |
| 15 | Minnesota | 45,684,189,000 | 2.0% |
| 16 | Wisconsin | 44,807,389,000 | 2.0% |
| 17 | Maryland | 41,737,483,000 | 1.8% |
| 18 | Indiana | 38,894,976,000 | 1.7% |
| 19 | Missouri | 38,606,945,000 | 1.7% |
| 20 | Arizona | 38,028,534,000 | 1.7% |
| 21 | Oregon | 34,797,285,000 | 1.5% |
| 22 | Tennessee | 34,653,154,000 | 1.5% |
| 23 | Louisiana | 33,974,652,000 | 1.5% |
| 24 | South Carolina | 31,733,200,000 | 1.4% |
| 25 | Kentucky | 31,051,859,000 | 1.4% |
| 26 | Colorado | 29,488,801,000 | 1.3% |
| 27 | Connecticut | 28,904,574,000 | 1.3% |
| 28 | Alabama | 26,305,162,000 | 1.2% |
| 29 | Oklahoma | 26,234,738,000 | 1.2% |
| 30 | Iowa | 24,088,747,000 | 1.1% |
| 31 | Mississippi | 23,441,796,000 | 1.0% |
| 32 | Arkansas | 22,785,157,000 | 1.0% |
| 33 | New Mexico | 19,771,493,000 | 0.9% |
| 34 | Kansas | 18,582,208,000 | 0.8% |
| 35 | Nevada | 17,597,124,000 | 0.8% |
| 36 | Utah | 16,984,797,000 | 0.7% |
| 37 | West Virginia | 15,397,630,000 | 0.7% |
| 38 | Alaska | 14,920,900,000 | 0.7% |
| 39 | Hawaii | 12,931,811,000 | 0.6% |
| 40 | Nebraska | 11,523,401,000 | 0.5% |
| 41 | Maine | 10,611,116,000 | 0.5% |
| 42 | Idaho | 10,476,454,000 | 0.5% |
| 43 | Rhode Island | 9,388,083,000 | 0.4% |
| 44 | Delaware | 9,349,728,000 | 0.4% |
| 45 | New Hampshire | 8,542,308,000 | 0.4% |
| 46 | Montana | 7,950,510,000 | 0.4% |
| 47 | North Dakota | 7,805,674,000 | 0.3% |
| 48 | Wyoming | 7,494,341,000 | 0.3% |
| 49 | Vermont | 6,506,203,000 | 0.3% |
| 50 | South Dakota | 6,017,179,000 | 0.3% |
| | District of Columbia** | NA | NA |

Source: U.S. Bureau of the Census, Governments Division
"2011 State and Local Government Finances" (http://www.census.gov/govs/local/)
*Total revenue includes all money received from external sources. This includes taxes, intergovernmental transfers and insurance trust revenue, and revenue from government owned utilities and other commercial or auxiliary enterprise.
**Not applicable.

# Per Capita State Government Total Revenue in 2011

## National Per Capita = $7,284*

ALPHA ORDER

| RANK | STATE | PER CAPITA |
|------|-------|-----------|
| 47 | Alabama | $5,476 |
| 1 | Alaska | 20,613 |
| 44 | Arizona | 5,880 |
| 23 | Arkansas | 7,754 |
| 11 | California | 8,871 |
| 45 | Colorado | 5,764 |
| 16 | Connecticut | 8,059 |
| 6 | Delaware | 10,296 |
| 46 | Florida | 5,564 |
| 49 | Georgia | 5,329 |
| 8 | Hawaii | 9,384 |
| 32 | Idaho | 6,615 |
| 39 | Illinois | 6,274 |
| 43 | Indiana | 5,969 |
| 21 | Iowa | 7,862 |
| 36 | Kansas | 6,474 |
| 29 | Kentucky | 7,111 |
| 24 | Louisiana | 7,427 |
| 18 | Maine | 7,987 |
| 28 | Maryland | 7,147 |
| 12 | Massachusetts | 8,572 |
| 34 | Michigan | 6,523 |
| 13 | Minnesota | 8,543 |
| 20 | Mississippi | 7,873 |
| 38 | Missouri | 6,425 |
| 19 | Montana | 7,969 |
| 41 | Nebraska | 6,255 |
| 37 | Nevada | 6,469 |
| 35 | New Hampshire | 6,482 |
| 17 | New Jersey | 8,014 |
| 7 | New Mexico | 9,512 |
| 4 | New York | 10,540 |
| 33 | North Carolina | 6,548 |
| 3 | North Dakota | 11,399 |
| 14 | Ohio | 8,394 |
| 30 | Oklahoma | 6,933 |
| 9 | Oregon | 8,996 |
| 27 | Pennsylvania | 7,196 |
| 10 | Rhode Island | 8,936 |
| 31 | South Carolina | 6,790 |
| 26 | South Dakota | 7,306 |
| 48 | Tennessee | 5,415 |
| 50 | Texas | 5,240 |
| 42 | Utah | 6,035 |
| 5 | Vermont | 10,383 |
| 40 | Virginia | 6,266 |
| 25 | Washington | 7,389 |
| 15 | West Virginia | 8,301 |
| 22 | Wisconsin | 7,847 |
| 2 | Wyoming | 13,209 |

RANK ORDER

| RANK | STATE | PER CAPITA |
|------|-------|-----------|
| 1 | Alaska | $20,613 |
| 2 | Wyoming | 13,209 |
| 3 | North Dakota | 11,399 |
| 4 | New York | 10,540 |
| 5 | Vermont | 10,383 |
| 6 | Delaware | 10,296 |
| 7 | New Mexico | 9,512 |
| 8 | Hawaii | 9,384 |
| 9 | Oregon | 8,996 |
| 10 | Rhode Island | 8,936 |
| 11 | California | 8,871 |
| 12 | Massachusetts | 8,572 |
| 13 | Minnesota | 8,543 |
| 14 | Ohio | 8,394 |
| 15 | West Virginia | 8,301 |
| 16 | Connecticut | 8,059 |
| 17 | New Jersey | 8,014 |
| 18 | Maine | 7,987 |
| 19 | Montana | 7,969 |
| 20 | Mississippi | 7,873 |
| 21 | Iowa | 7,862 |
| 22 | Wisconsin | 7,847 |
| 23 | Arkansas | 7,754 |
| 24 | Louisiana | 7,427 |
| 25 | Washington | 7,389 |
| 26 | South Dakota | 7,306 |
| 27 | Pennsylvania | 7,196 |
| 28 | Maryland | 7,147 |
| 29 | Kentucky | 7,111 |
| 30 | Oklahoma | 6,933 |
| 31 | South Carolina | 6,790 |
| 32 | Idaho | 6,615 |
| 33 | North Carolina | 6,548 |
| 34 | Michigan | 6,523 |
| 35 | New Hampshire | 6,482 |
| 36 | Kansas | 6,474 |
| 37 | Nevada | 6,469 |
| 38 | Missouri | 6,425 |
| 39 | Illinois | 6,274 |
| 40 | Virginia | 6,266 |
| 41 | Nebraska | 6,255 |
| 42 | Utah | 6,035 |
| 43 | Indiana | 5,969 |
| 44 | Arizona | 5,880 |
| 45 | Colorado | 5,764 |
| 46 | Florida | 5,564 |
| 47 | Alabama | 5,476 |
| 48 | Tennessee | 5,415 |
| 49 | Georgia | 5,329 |
| 50 | Texas | 5,240 |

District of Columbia**                     NA

Source: CQ Press using data from U.S. Bureau of the Census, Governments Division
   "2011 State and Local Government Finances" (http://www.census.gov/govs/local/)
*Total revenue includes all money received from external sources. This includes taxes, intergovernmental transfers and
insurance trust revenue, and revenue from government owned utilities and other commercial or auxiliary enterprise.
**Not applicable.

# State Government Intergovernmental Revenue in 2011

## National Total = $592,997,583,000*

ALPHA ORDER

| RANK | STATE | REVENUE | % of USA |
|---|---|---|---|
| 24 | Alabama | $8,881,520,000 | 1.5% |
| 39 | Alaska | 3,040,677,000 | 0.5% |
| 14 | Arizona | 12,360,358,000 | 2.1% |
| 32 | Arkansas | 6,313,263,000 | 1.1% |
| 1 | California | 68,508,784,000 | 11.6% |
| 33 | Colorado | 6,248,609,000 | 1.1% |
| 30 | Connecticut | 6,561,366,000 | 1.1% |
| 48 | Delaware | 1,890,925,000 | 0.3% |
| 4 | Florida | 27,804,346,000 | 4.7% |
| 10 | Georgia | 15,266,487,000 | 2.6% |
| 40 | Hawaii | 2,918,445,000 | 0.5% |
| 42 | Idaho | 2,804,663,000 | 0.5% |
| 8 | Illinois | 19,586,991,000 | 3.3% |
| 19 | Indiana | 10,858,319,000 | 1.8% |
| 29 | Iowa | 7,043,992,000 | 1.2% |
| 34 | Kansas | 4,940,903,000 | 0.8% |
| 23 | Kentucky | 9,025,194,000 | 1.5% |
| 13 | Louisiana | 12,532,918,000 | 2.1% |
| 38 | Maine | 3,241,435,000 | 0.5% |
| 17 | Maryland | 11,335,533,000 | 1.9% |
| 12 | Massachusetts | 14,136,989,000 | 2.4% |
| 7 | Michigan | 19,914,367,000 | 3.4% |
| 22 | Minnesota | 9,819,493,000 | 1.7% |
| 25 | Mississippi | 8,726,548,000 | 1.5% |
| 16 | Missouri | 12,015,114,000 | 2.0% |
| 44 | Montana | 2,414,552,000 | 0.4% |
| 37 | Nebraska | 3,401,587,000 | 0.6% |
| 41 | Nevada | 2,826,846,000 | 0.5% |
| 46 | New Hampshire | 2,158,531,000 | 0.4% |
| 11 | New Jersey | 14,792,596,000 | 2.5% |
| 31 | New Mexico | 6,364,080,000 | 1.1% |
| 2 | New York | 60,200,009,000 | 10.2% |
| 9 | North Carolina | 16,048,794,000 | 2.7% |
| 50 | North Dakota | 1,737,078,000 | 0.3% |
| 5 | Ohio | 24,133,257,000 | 4.1% |
| 27 | Oklahoma | 7,873,706,000 | 1.3% |
| 28 | Oregon | 7,608,740,000 | 1.3% |
| 6 | Pennsylvania | 23,842,639,000 | 4.0% |
| 43 | Rhode Island | 2,731,772,000 | 0.5% |
| 26 | South Carolina | 8,689,743,000 | 1.5% |
| 49 | South Dakota | 1,878,950,000 | 0.3% |
| 15 | Tennessee | 12,116,843,000 | 2.0% |
| 3 | Texas | 42,858,907,000 | 7.2% |
| 36 | Utah | 4,364,882,000 | 0.7% |
| 47 | Vermont | 2,035,378,000 | 0.3% |
| 21 | Virginia | 10,512,522,000 | 1.8% |
| 18 | Washington | 10,944,017,000 | 1.8% |
| 35 | West Virginia | 4,748,528,000 | 0.8% |
| 20 | Wisconsin | 10,535,845,000 | 1.8% |
| 45 | Wyoming | 2,400,542,000 | 0.4% |

RANK ORDER

| RANK | STATE | REVENUE | % of USA |
|---|---|---|---|
| 1 | California | $68,508,784,000 | 11.6% |
| 2 | New York | 60,200,009,000 | 10.2% |
| 3 | Texas | 42,858,907,000 | 7.2% |
| 4 | Florida | 27,804,346,000 | 4.7% |
| 5 | Ohio | 24,133,257,000 | 4.1% |
| 6 | Pennsylvania | 23,842,639,000 | 4.0% |
| 7 | Michigan | 19,914,367,000 | 3.4% |
| 8 | Illinois | 19,586,991,000 | 3.3% |
| 9 | North Carolina | 16,048,794,000 | 2.7% |
| 10 | Georgia | 15,266,487,000 | 2.6% |
| 11 | New Jersey | 14,792,596,000 | 2.5% |
| 12 | Massachusetts | 14,136,989,000 | 2.4% |
| 13 | Louisiana | 12,532,918,000 | 2.1% |
| 14 | Arizona | 12,360,358,000 | 2.1% |
| 15 | Tennessee | 12,116,843,000 | 2.0% |
| 16 | Missouri | 12,015,114,000 | 2.0% |
| 17 | Maryland | 11,335,533,000 | 1.9% |
| 18 | Washington | 10,944,017,000 | 1.8% |
| 19 | Indiana | 10,858,319,000 | 1.8% |
| 20 | Wisconsin | 10,535,845,000 | 1.8% |
| 21 | Virginia | 10,512,522,000 | 1.8% |
| 22 | Minnesota | 9,819,493,000 | 1.7% |
| 23 | Kentucky | 9,025,194,000 | 1.5% |
| 24 | Alabama | 8,881,520,000 | 1.5% |
| 25 | Mississippi | 8,726,548,000 | 1.5% |
| 26 | South Carolina | 8,689,743,000 | 1.5% |
| 27 | Oklahoma | 7,873,706,000 | 1.3% |
| 28 | Oregon | 7,608,740,000 | 1.3% |
| 29 | Iowa | 7,043,992,000 | 1.2% |
| 30 | Connecticut | 6,561,366,000 | 1.1% |
| 31 | New Mexico | 6,364,080,000 | 1.1% |
| 32 | Arkansas | 6,313,263,000 | 1.1% |
| 33 | Colorado | 6,248,609,000 | 1.1% |
| 34 | Kansas | 4,940,903,000 | 0.8% |
| 35 | West Virginia | 4,748,528,000 | 0.8% |
| 36 | Utah | 4,364,882,000 | 0.7% |
| 37 | Nebraska | 3,401,587,000 | 0.6% |
| 38 | Maine | 3,241,435,000 | 0.5% |
| 39 | Alaska | 3,040,677,000 | 0.5% |
| 40 | Hawaii | 2,918,445,000 | 0.5% |
| 41 | Nevada | 2,826,846,000 | 0.5% |
| 42 | Idaho | 2,804,663,000 | 0.5% |
| 43 | Rhode Island | 2,731,772,000 | 0.5% |
| 44 | Montana | 2,414,552,000 | 0.4% |
| 45 | Wyoming | 2,400,542,000 | 0.4% |
| 46 | New Hampshire | 2,158,531,000 | 0.4% |
| 47 | Vermont | 2,035,378,000 | 0.3% |
| 48 | Delaware | 1,890,925,000 | 0.3% |
| 49 | South Dakota | 1,878,950,000 | 0.3% |
| 50 | North Dakota | 1,737,078,000 | 0.3% |
|  | District of Columbia** | NA | NA |

Source: U.S. Bureau of the Census, Governments Division
   "2011 State and Local Government Finances" (http://www.census.gov/govs/local/)
*Includes revenue from federal and local government sources.
**Not applicable.

# Per Capita State Government Intergovernmental Revenue in 2011

## National Per Capita = $1,907*

ALPHA ORDER

| RANK | STATE | PER CAPITA |
|------|-------|-----------|
| 30 | Alabama | $1,849 |
| 2 | Alaska | 4,201 |
| 26 | Arizona | 1,911 |
| 15 | Arkansas | 2,148 |
| 35 | California | 1,818 |
| 49 | Colorado | 1,221 |
| 34 | Connecticut | 1,829 |
| 19 | Delaware | 2,082 |
| 47 | Florida | 1,457 |
| 44 | Georgia | 1,556 |
| 17 | Hawaii | 2,118 |
| 36 | Idaho | 1,771 |
| 46 | Illinois | 1,523 |
| 40 | Indiana | 1,666 |
| 13 | Iowa | 2,299 |
| 37 | Kansas | 1,721 |
| 21 | Kentucky | 2,067 |
| 7 | Louisiana | 2,740 |
| 11 | Maine | 2,440 |
| 25 | Maryland | 1,941 |
| 16 | Massachusetts | 2,140 |
| 22 | Michigan | 2,016 |
| 33 | Minnesota | 1,836 |
| 6 | Mississippi | 2,931 |
| 23 | Missouri | 2,000 |
| 12 | Montana | 2,420 |
| 31 | Nebraska | 1,846 |
| 50 | Nevada | 1,039 |
| 42 | New Hampshire | 1,638 |
| 38 | New Jersey | 1,674 |
| 5 | New Mexico | 3,062 |
| 4 | New York | 3,087 |
| 41 | North Carolina | 1,663 |
| 10 | North Dakota | 2,537 |
| 18 | Ohio | 2,091 |
| 20 | Oklahoma | 2,081 |
| 24 | Oregon | 1,967 |
| 28 | Pennsylvania | 1,871 |
| 8 | Rhode Island | 2,600 |
| 29 | South Carolina | 1,859 |
| 14 | South Dakota | 2,281 |
| 27 | Tennessee | 1,893 |
| 39 | Texas | 1,672 |
| 45 | Utah | 1,551 |
| 3 | Vermont | 3,248 |
| 48 | Virginia | 1,297 |
| 43 | Washington | 1,604 |
| 9 | West Virginia | 2,560 |
| 32 | Wisconsin | 1,845 |
| 1 | Wyoming | 4,231 |

RANK ORDER

| RANK | STATE | PER CAPITA |
|------|-------|-----------|
| 1 | Wyoming | $4,231 |
| 2 | Alaska | 4,201 |
| 3 | Vermont | 3,248 |
| 4 | New York | 3,087 |
| 5 | New Mexico | 3,062 |
| 6 | Mississippi | 2,931 |
| 7 | Louisiana | 2,740 |
| 8 | Rhode Island | 2,600 |
| 9 | West Virginia | 2,560 |
| 10 | North Dakota | 2,537 |
| 11 | Maine | 2,440 |
| 12 | Montana | 2,420 |
| 13 | Iowa | 2,299 |
| 14 | South Dakota | 2,281 |
| 15 | Arkansas | 2,148 |
| 16 | Massachusetts | 2,140 |
| 17 | Hawaii | 2,118 |
| 18 | Ohio | 2,091 |
| 19 | Delaware | 2,082 |
| 20 | Oklahoma | 2,081 |
| 21 | Kentucky | 2,067 |
| 22 | Michigan | 2,016 |
| 23 | Missouri | 2,000 |
| 24 | Oregon | 1,967 |
| 25 | Maryland | 1,941 |
| 26 | Arizona | 1,911 |
| 27 | Tennessee | 1,893 |
| 28 | Pennsylvania | 1,871 |
| 29 | South Carolina | 1,859 |
| 30 | Alabama | 1,849 |
| 31 | Nebraska | 1,846 |
| 32 | Wisconsin | 1,845 |
| 33 | Minnesota | 1,836 |
| 34 | Connecticut | 1,829 |
| 35 | California | 1,818 |
| 36 | Idaho | 1,771 |
| 37 | Kansas | 1,721 |
| 38 | New Jersey | 1,674 |
| 39 | Texas | 1,672 |
| 40 | Indiana | 1,666 |
| 41 | North Carolina | 1,663 |
| 42 | New Hampshire | 1,638 |
| 43 | Washington | 1,604 |
| 44 | Georgia | 1,556 |
| 45 | Utah | 1,551 |
| 46 | Illinois | 1,523 |
| 47 | Florida | 1,457 |
| 48 | Virginia | 1,297 |
| 49 | Colorado | 1,221 |
| 50 | Nevada | 1,039 |

District of Columbia**          NA

Source: CQ Press using data from U.S. Bureau of the Census, Governments Division
"2011 State and Local Government Finances" (http://www.census.gov/govs/local/)
*Includes revenue from federal and local government sources.
**Not applicable.

# State Government Own Source Revenue in 2011

## National Total = $1,061,315,859,000*

| RANK | STATE | REVENUE | % of USA |
|------|-------|---------|----------|
| 26 | Alabama | $14,395,261,000 | 1.4% |
| 33 | Alaska | 9,624,998,000 | 0.9% |
| 20 | Arizona | 16,105,419,000 | 1.5% |
| 30 | Arkansas | 11,117,905,000 | 1.0% |
| 1 | California | 142,927,463,000 | 13.5% |
| 23 | Colorado | 14,856,336,000 | 1.4% |
| 19 | Connecticut | 16,923,583,000 | 1.6% |
| 41 | Delaware | 5,662,509,000 | 0.5% |
| 4 | Florida | 47,486,660,000 | 4.5% |
| 15 | Georgia | 21,901,338,000 | 2.1% |
| 39 | Hawaii | 7,285,231,000 | 0.7% |
| 44 | Idaho | 4,539,438,000 | 0.4% |
| 6 | Illinois | 39,788,077,000 | 3.7% |
| 18 | Indiana | 20,591,592,000 | 1.9% |
| 31 | Iowa | 11,053,370,000 | 1.0% |
| 32 | Kansas | 10,047,317,000 | 0.9% |
| 24 | Kentucky | 14,543,181,000 | 1.4% |
| 25 | Louisiana | 14,406,106,000 | 1.4% |
| 42 | Maine | 5,007,698,000 | 0.5% |
| 16 | Maryland | 21,684,192,000 | 2.0% |
| 10 | Massachusetts | 30,758,571,000 | 2.9% |
| 9 | Michigan | 34,802,577,000 | 3.3% |
| 14 | Minnesota | 23,632,196,000 | 2.2% |
| 35 | Mississippi | 8,916,360,000 | 0.8% |
| 22 | Missouri | 15,067,790,000 | 1.4% |
| 49 | Montana | 3,354,033,000 | 0.3% |
| 40 | Nebraska | 5,987,566,000 | 0.6% |
| 38 | Nevada | 7,617,002,000 | 0.7% |
| 46 | New Hampshire | 4,114,855,000 | 0.4% |
| 8 | New Jersey | 36,883,804,000 | 3.5% |
| 36 | New Mexico | 8,490,181,000 | 0.8% |
| 2 | New York | 88,640,813,000 | 8.4% |
| 11 | North Carolina | 29,803,864,000 | 2.8% |
| 43 | North Dakota | 4,946,010,000 | 0.5% |
| 7 | Ohio | 37,707,073,000 | 3.6% |
| 29 | Oklahoma | 12,325,729,000 | 1.2% |
| 28 | Oregon | 13,214,540,000 | 1.2% |
| 5 | Pennsylvania | 45,656,641,000 | 4.3% |
| 45 | Rhode Island | 4,425,487,000 | 0.4% |
| 27 | South Carolina | 14,101,763,000 | 1.3% |
| 50 | South Dakota | 2,245,368,000 | 0.2% |
| 21 | Tennessee | 15,375,775,000 | 1.4% |
| 3 | Texas | 64,288,789,000 | 6.1% |
| 34 | Utah | 9,469,719,000 | 0.9% |
| 48 | Vermont | 3,592,519,000 | 0.3% |
| 12 | Virginia | 28,681,524,000 | 2.7% |
| 13 | Washington | 24,048,996,000 | 2.3% |
| 37 | West Virginia | 7,965,706,000 | 0.8% |
| 17 | Wisconsin | 21,597,017,000 | 2.0% |
| 47 | Wyoming | 3,655,917,000 | 0.3% |

| RANK | STATE | REVENUE | % of USA |
|------|-------|---------|----------|
| 1 | California | $142,927,463,000 | 13.5% |
| 2 | New York | 88,640,813,000 | 8.4% |
| 3 | Texas | 64,288,789,000 | 6.1% |
| 4 | Florida | 47,486,660,000 | 4.5% |
| 5 | Pennsylvania | 45,656,641,000 | 4.3% |
| 6 | Illinois | 39,788,077,000 | 3.7% |
| 7 | Ohio | 37,707,073,000 | 3.6% |
| 8 | New Jersey | 36,883,804,000 | 3.5% |
| 9 | Michigan | 34,802,577,000 | 3.3% |
| 10 | Massachusetts | 30,758,571,000 | 2.9% |
| 11 | North Carolina | 29,803,864,000 | 2.8% |
| 12 | Virginia | 28,681,524,000 | 2.7% |
| 13 | Washington | 24,048,996,000 | 2.3% |
| 14 | Minnesota | 23,632,196,000 | 2.2% |
| 15 | Georgia | 21,901,338,000 | 2.1% |
| 16 | Maryland | 21,684,192,000 | 2.0% |
| 17 | Wisconsin | 21,597,017,000 | 2.0% |
| 18 | Indiana | 20,591,592,000 | 1.9% |
| 19 | Connecticut | 16,923,583,000 | 1.6% |
| 20 | Arizona | 16,105,419,000 | 1.5% |
| 21 | Tennessee | 15,375,775,000 | 1.4% |
| 22 | Missouri | 15,067,790,000 | 1.4% |
| 23 | Colorado | 14,856,336,000 | 1.4% |
| 24 | Kentucky | 14,543,181,000 | 1.4% |
| 25 | Louisiana | 14,406,106,000 | 1.4% |
| 26 | Alabama | 14,395,261,000 | 1.4% |
| 27 | South Carolina | 14,101,763,000 | 1.3% |
| 28 | Oregon | 13,214,540,000 | 1.2% |
| 29 | Oklahoma | 12,325,729,000 | 1.2% |
| 30 | Arkansas | 11,117,905,000 | 1.0% |
| 31 | Iowa | 11,053,370,000 | 1.0% |
| 32 | Kansas | 10,047,317,000 | 0.9% |
| 33 | Alaska | 9,624,998,000 | 0.9% |
| 34 | Utah | 9,469,719,000 | 0.9% |
| 35 | Mississippi | 8,916,360,000 | 0.8% |
| 36 | New Mexico | 8,490,181,000 | 0.8% |
| 37 | West Virginia | 7,965,706,000 | 0.8% |
| 38 | Nevada | 7,617,002,000 | 0.7% |
| 39 | Hawaii | 7,285,231,000 | 0.7% |
| 40 | Nebraska | 5,987,566,000 | 0.6% |
| 41 | Delaware | 5,662,509,000 | 0.5% |
| 42 | Maine | 5,007,698,000 | 0.5% |
| 43 | North Dakota | 4,946,010,000 | 0.5% |
| 44 | Idaho | 4,539,438,000 | 0.4% |
| 45 | Rhode Island | 4,425,487,000 | 0.4% |
| 46 | New Hampshire | 4,114,855,000 | 0.4% |
| 47 | Wyoming | 3,655,917,000 | 0.3% |
| 48 | Vermont | 3,592,519,000 | 0.3% |
| 49 | Montana | 3,354,033,000 | 0.3% |
| 50 | South Dakota | 2,245,368,000 | 0.2% |
| | District of Columbia** | NA | NA |

Source: U.S. Bureau of the Census, Governments Division
"2011 State and Local Government Finances" (http://www.census.gov/govs/local/)
*Own source revenue includes taxes, current charges, and miscellaneous general revenue. Excluded are intergovernmental transfers, insurance trust revenue, and revenue from government owned utilities and other commercial or auxiliary enterprise.
**Not applicable.

# Per Capita State Government Own Source Revenue in 2011

## National Per Capita = $3,413*

ALPHA ORDER

| RANK | STATE | PER CAPITA |
|---|---|---|
| 39 | Alabama | $2,997 |
| 1 | Alaska | 13,297 |
| 47 | Arizona | 2,490 |
| 16 | Arkansas | 3,783 |
| 15 | California | 3,793 |
| 41 | Colorado | 2,904 |
| 7 | Connecticut | 4,718 |
| 4 | Delaware | 6,235 |
| 48 | Florida | 2,489 |
| 50 | Georgia | 2,232 |
| 6 | Hawaii | 5,286 |
| 42 | Idaho | 2,866 |
| 36 | Illinois | 3,094 |
| 33 | Indiana | 3,160 |
| 20 | Iowa | 3,607 |
| 25 | Kansas | 3,500 |
| 29 | Kentucky | 3,330 |
| 34 | Louisiana | 3,149 |
| 18 | Maine | 3,769 |
| 19 | Maryland | 3,713 |
| 8 | Massachusetts | 4,655 |
| 24 | Michigan | 3,524 |
| 10 | Minnesota | 4,419 |
| 40 | Mississippi | 2,995 |
| 45 | Missouri | 2,508 |
| 28 | Montana | 3,362 |
| 32 | Nebraska | 3,250 |
| 43 | Nevada | 2,800 |
| 35 | New Hampshire | 3,123 |
| 13 | New Jersey | 4,175 |
| 14 | New Mexico | 4,084 |
| 9 | New York | 4,545 |
| 37 | North Carolina | 3,088 |
| 2 | North Dakota | 7,223 |
| 30 | Ohio | 3,267 |
| 31 | Oklahoma | 3,257 |
| 26 | Oregon | 3,416 |
| 21 | Pennsylvania | 3,583 |
| 12 | Rhode Island | 4,212 |
| 38 | South Carolina | 3,017 |
| 44 | South Dakota | 2,726 |
| 49 | Tennessee | 2,403 |
| 45 | Texas | 2,508 |
| 27 | Utah | 3,365 |
| 5 | Vermont | 5,733 |
| 22 | Virginia | 3,539 |
| 23 | Washington | 3,525 |
| 11 | West Virginia | 4,294 |
| 17 | Wisconsin | 3,782 |
| 3 | Wyoming | 6,444 |

RANK ORDER

| RANK | STATE | PER CAPITA |
|---|---|---|
| 1 | Alaska | $13,297 |
| 2 | North Dakota | 7,223 |
| 3 | Wyoming | 6,444 |
| 4 | Delaware | 6,235 |
| 5 | Vermont | 5,733 |
| 6 | Hawaii | 5,286 |
| 7 | Connecticut | 4,718 |
| 8 | Massachusetts | 4,655 |
| 9 | New York | 4,545 |
| 10 | Minnesota | 4,419 |
| 11 | West Virginia | 4,294 |
| 12 | Rhode Island | 4,212 |
| 13 | New Jersey | 4,175 |
| 14 | New Mexico | 4,084 |
| 15 | California | 3,793 |
| 16 | Arkansas | 3,783 |
| 17 | Wisconsin | 3,782 |
| 18 | Maine | 3,769 |
| 19 | Maryland | 3,713 |
| 20 | Iowa | 3,607 |
| 21 | Pennsylvania | 3,583 |
| 22 | Virginia | 3,539 |
| 23 | Washington | 3,525 |
| 24 | Michigan | 3,524 |
| 25 | Kansas | 3,500 |
| 26 | Oregon | 3,416 |
| 27 | Utah | 3,365 |
| 28 | Montana | 3,362 |
| 29 | Kentucky | 3,330 |
| 30 | Ohio | 3,267 |
| 31 | Oklahoma | 3,257 |
| 32 | Nebraska | 3,250 |
| 33 | Indiana | 3,160 |
| 34 | Louisiana | 3,149 |
| 35 | New Hampshire | 3,123 |
| 36 | Illinois | 3,094 |
| 37 | North Carolina | 3,088 |
| 38 | South Carolina | 3,017 |
| 39 | Alabama | 2,997 |
| 40 | Mississippi | 2,995 |
| 41 | Colorado | 2,904 |
| 42 | Idaho | 2,866 |
| 43 | Nevada | 2,800 |
| 44 | South Dakota | 2,726 |
| 45 | Missouri | 2,508 |
| 45 | Texas | 2,508 |
| 47 | Arizona | 2,490 |
| 48 | Florida | 2,489 |
| 49 | Tennessee | 2,403 |
| 50 | Georgia | 2,232 |

| District of Columbia** | NA |
|---|---|

Source: CQ Press using data from U.S. Bureau of the Census, Governments Division
   "2011 State and Local Government Finances" (http://www.census.gov/govs/local/)
*Own source revenue includes taxes, current charges, and miscellaneous general revenue. Excluded are intergovernmental transfers, insurance trust revenue, and revenue from government owned utilities and other commercial or auxiliary enterprise.
**Not applicable.

# Profits of State Lotteries in 2012

## National Total = $19,409,080,000*

ALPHA ORDER

| RANK | STATE | PROFITS | % of USA |
|---|---|---|---|
| NA | Alabama** | NA | NA |
| NA | Alaska** | NA | NA |
| 25 | Arizona | 164,700,000 | 0.8% |
| 32 | Arkansas | 97,500,000 | 0.5% |
| 3 | California | 1,320,000,000 | 6.8% |
| 30 | Colorado | 123,200,000 | 0.6% |
| 19 | Connecticut | 310,000,000 | 1.6% |
| 22 | Delaware | 271,330,000 | 1.4% |
| 2 | Florida | 1,321,600,000 | 6.8% |
| 7 | Georgia | 901,300,000 | 4.6% |
| NA | Hawaii** | NA | NA |
| 38 | Idaho | 41,500,000 | 0.2% |
| 11 | Illinois | 708,500,000 | 3.7% |
| 24 | Indiana | 210,840,000 | 1.1% |
| 33 | Iowa | 78,730,000 | 0.4% |
| 34 | Kansas | 72,000,000 | 0.4% |
| 23 | Kentucky | 216,400,000 | 1.1% |
| 26 | Louisiana | 156,900,000 | 0.8% |
| 37 | Maine | 54,300,000 | 0.3% |
| 12 | Maryland | 683,070,000 | 3.5% |
| 8 | Massachusetts | 833,900,000 | 4.3% |
| 10 | Michigan | 770,000,000 | 4.0% |
| 29 | Minnesota | 123,650,000 | 0.6% |
| NA | Mississippi** | NA | NA |
| 21 | Missouri | 280,000,000 | 1.4% |
| 42 | Montana | 13,100,000 | 0.1% |
| 40 | Nebraska | 36,080,000 | 0.2% |
| NA | Nevada** | NA | NA |
| 36 | New Hampshire | 66,770,000 | 0.3% |
| 6 | New Jersey | 950,000,000 | 4.9% |
| 39 | New Mexico | 41,300,000 | 0.2% |
| 1 | New York | 2,887,990,000 | 14.9% |
| 16 | North Carolina | 456,760,000 | 2.4% |
| 43 | North Dakota | 7,620,000 | 0.0% |
| 9 | Ohio | 771,030,000 | 4.0% |
| 35 | Oklahoma | 69,990,000 | 0.4% |
| 14 | Oregon | 526,600,000 | 2.7% |
| 5 | Pennsylvania | 1,060,890,000 | 5.5% |
| 17 | Rhode Island | 377,700,000 | 1.9% |
| 20 | South Carolina | 297,740,000 | 1.5% |
| 31 | South Dakota | 100,400,000 | 0.5% |
| 18 | Tennessee | 323,400,000 | 1.7% |
| 4 | Texas | 1,156,560,000 | 6.0% |
| NA | Utah** | NA | NA |
| 41 | Vermont | 22,300,000 | 0.1% |
| 15 | Virginia | 487,060,000 | 2.5% |
| 28 | Washington | 138,000,000 | 0.7% |
| 13 | West Virginia | 662,980,000 | 3.4% |
| 27 | Wisconsin | 149,900,000 | 0.8% |
| NA | Wyoming** | NA | NA |

RANK ORDER

| RANK | STATE | PROFITS | % of USA |
|---|---|---|---|
| 1 | New York | $2,887,990,000 | 14.9% |
| 2 | Florida | 1,321,600,000 | 6.8% |
| 3 | California | 1,320,000,000 | 6.8% |
| 4 | Texas | 1,156,560,000 | 6.0% |
| 5 | Pennsylvania | 1,060,890,000 | 5.5% |
| 6 | New Jersey | 950,000,000 | 4.9% |
| 7 | Georgia | 901,300,000 | 4.6% |
| 8 | Massachusetts | 833,900,000 | 4.3% |
| 9 | Ohio | 771,030,000 | 4.0% |
| 10 | Michigan | 770,000,000 | 4.0% |
| 11 | Illinois | 708,500,000 | 3.7% |
| 12 | Maryland | 683,070,000 | 3.5% |
| 13 | West Virginia | 662,980,000 | 3.4% |
| 14 | Oregon | 526,600,000 | 2.7% |
| 15 | Virginia | 487,060,000 | 2.5% |
| 16 | North Carolina | 456,760,000 | 2.4% |
| 17 | Rhode Island | 377,700,000 | 1.9% |
| 18 | Tennessee | 323,400,000 | 1.7% |
| 19 | Connecticut | 310,000,000 | 1.6% |
| 20 | South Carolina | 297,740,000 | 1.5% |
| 21 | Missouri | 280,000,000 | 1.4% |
| 22 | Delaware | 271,330,000 | 1.4% |
| 23 | Kentucky | 216,400,000 | 1.1% |
| 24 | Indiana | 210,840,000 | 1.1% |
| 25 | Arizona | 164,700,000 | 0.8% |
| 26 | Louisiana | 156,900,000 | 0.8% |
| 27 | Wisconsin | 149,900,000 | 0.8% |
| 28 | Washington | 138,000,000 | 0.7% |
| 29 | Minnesota | 123,650,000 | 0.6% |
| 30 | Colorado | 123,200,000 | 0.6% |
| 31 | South Dakota | 100,400,000 | 0.5% |
| 32 | Arkansas | 97,500,000 | 0.5% |
| 33 | Iowa | 78,730,000 | 0.4% |
| 34 | Kansas | 72,000,000 | 0.4% |
| 35 | Oklahoma | 69,990,000 | 0.4% |
| 36 | New Hampshire | 66,770,000 | 0.3% |
| 37 | Maine | 54,300,000 | 0.3% |
| 38 | Idaho | 41,500,000 | 0.2% |
| 39 | New Mexico | 41,300,000 | 0.2% |
| 40 | Nebraska | 36,080,000 | 0.2% |
| 41 | Vermont | 22,300,000 | 0.1% |
| 42 | Montana | 13,100,000 | 0.1% |
| 43 | North Dakota | 7,620,000 | 0.0% |
| NA | Alabama** | NA | NA |
| NA | Alaska** | NA | NA |
| NA | Hawaii** | NA | NA |
| NA | Mississippi** | NA | NA |
| NA | Nevada** | NA | NA |
| NA | Utah** | NA | NA |
| NA | Wyoming** | NA | NA |
| | District of Columbia | 65,500,000 | 0.3% |

Source: North American Association of State and Provincial Lotteries, Willoughby Hills, OH

"Lottery Sales and Profits" (http://www.naspl.org/index.cfm?fuseaction=content&menuid=17&pageid=1025)

*Reported profits for fiscal year 2012 on sales of $68,778,740,000. National total does not include profits for Puerto Rico.

**No lottery as of fiscal year 2012.

# Per Capita Profits of State Lotteries in 2012

## National Per Capita = $65.18*

ALPHA ORDER

| RANK | STATE | PER CAPITA |
|------|-------|------------|
| NA | Alabama** | NA |
| NA | Alaska** | NA |
| 34 | Arizona | 25.13 |
| 29 | Arkansas | 33.06 |
| 27 | California | 34.70 |
| 36 | Colorado | 23.75 |
| 11 | Connecticut | 86.34 |
| 3 | Delaware | 295.86 |
| 14 | Florida | 68.41 |
| 10 | Georgia | 90.86 |
| NA | Hawaii** | NA |
| 32 | Idaho | 26.01 |
| 18 | Illinois | 55.03 |
| 30 | Indiana | 32.25 |
| 33 | Iowa | 25.61 |
| 35 | Kansas | 24.95 |
| 21 | Kentucky | 49.40 |
| 28 | Louisiana | 34.09 |
| 25 | Maine | 40.85 |
| 8 | Maryland | 116.08 |
| 6 | Massachusetts | 125.47 |
| 13 | Michigan | 77.91 |
| 37 | Minnesota | 22.99 |
| NA | Mississippi** | NA |
| 23 | Missouri | 46.50 |
| 42 | Montana | 13.03 |
| 40 | Nebraska | 19.44 |
| NA | Nevada** | NA |
| 19 | New Hampshire | 50.56 |
| 9 | New Jersey | 107.17 |
| 39 | New Mexico | 19.80 |
| 4 | New York | 147.57 |
| 22 | North Carolina | 46.84 |
| 43 | North Dakota | 10.89 |
| 15 | Ohio | 66.79 |
| 41 | Oklahoma | 18.35 |
| 5 | Oregon | 135.05 |
| 12 | Pennsylvania | 83.12 |
| 1 | Rhode Island | 359.61 |
| 16 | South Carolina | 63.03 |
| 7 | South Dakota | 120.48 |
| 20 | Tennessee | 50.09 |
| 24 | Texas | 44.38 |
| NA | Utah** | NA |
| 26 | Vermont | 35.62 |
| 17 | Virginia | 59.50 |
| 38 | Washington | 20.01 |
| 2 | West Virginia | 357.32 |
| 31 | Wisconsin | 26.18 |
| NA | Wyoming** | NA |

RANK ORDER

| RANK | STATE | PER CAPITA |
|------|-------|------------|
| 1 | Rhode Island | $359.61 |
| 2 | West Virginia | 357.32 |
| 3 | Delaware | 295.86 |
| 4 | New York | 147.57 |
| 5 | Oregon | 135.05 |
| 6 | Massachusetts | 125.47 |
| 7 | South Dakota | 120.48 |
| 8 | Maryland | 116.08 |
| 9 | New Jersey | 107.17 |
| 10 | Georgia | 90.86 |
| 11 | Connecticut | 86.34 |
| 12 | Pennsylvania | 83.12 |
| 13 | Michigan | 77.91 |
| 14 | Florida | 68.41 |
| 15 | Ohio | 66.79 |
| 16 | South Carolina | 63.03 |
| 17 | Virginia | 59.50 |
| 18 | Illinois | 55.03 |
| 19 | New Hampshire | 50.56 |
| 20 | Tennessee | 50.09 |
| 21 | Kentucky | 49.40 |
| 22 | North Carolina | 46.84 |
| 23 | Missouri | 46.50 |
| 24 | Texas | 44.38 |
| 25 | Maine | 40.85 |
| 26 | Vermont | 35.62 |
| 27 | California | 34.70 |
| 28 | Louisiana | 34.09 |
| 29 | Arkansas | 33.06 |
| 30 | Indiana | 32.25 |
| 31 | Wisconsin | 26.18 |
| 32 | Idaho | 26.01 |
| 33 | Iowa | 25.61 |
| 34 | Arizona | 25.13 |
| 35 | Kansas | 24.95 |
| 36 | Colorado | 23.75 |
| 37 | Minnesota | 22.99 |
| 38 | Washington | 20.01 |
| 39 | New Mexico | 19.80 |
| 40 | Nebraska | 19.44 |
| 41 | Oklahoma | 18.35 |
| 42 | Montana | 13.03 |
| 43 | North Dakota | 10.89 |
| NA | Alabama** | NA |
| NA | Alaska** | NA |
| NA | Hawaii** | NA |
| NA | Mississippi** | NA |
| NA | Nevada** | NA |
| NA | Utah** | NA |
| NA | Wyoming** | NA |

District of Columbia     103.59

Source: CQ Press using data from North American Association of State and Provincial Lotteries, Willoughby Hills, OH
"Lottery Sales and Profits" (http://www.naspl.org/index.cfm?fuseaction=content&menuid=17&pageid=1025)
*For fiscal year 2012. National rate is based on population of states with a lottery.
**No lottery as of fiscal year 2012.

# Projected vs. Actual State Tax Collections in 2013

## National Percent = 103.1% of Projected Taxes*

ALPHA ORDER

| RANK | STATE | PERCENT |
|---|---|---|
| 18 | Alabama | 103.7 |
| 50 | Alaska | 77.3 |
| 24 | Arizona | 102.7 |
| 3 | Arkansas | 115.9 |
| 26 | California | 102.6 |
| 4 | Colorado | 114.1 |
| 45 | Connecticut | 99.7 |
| 14 | Delaware | 105.2 |
| 37 | Florida | 101.2 |
| 22 | Georgia | 103.0 |
| 7 | Hawaii | 107.7 |
| 20 | Idaho | 103.3 |
| 8 | Illinois | 107.6 |
| 34 | Indiana | 101.6 |
| 16 | Iowa | 105.0 |
| 35 | Kansas | 101.4 |
| 30 | Kentucky | 102.1 |
| 40 | Louisiana | 100.7 |
| 38 | Maine | 101.1 |
| 36 | Maryland | 101.3 |
| 43 | Massachusetts | 99.8 |
| 31 | Michigan | 102.0 |
| 6 | Minnesota | 107.8 |
| 12 | Mississippi | 106.7 |
| 13 | Missouri | 106.3 |
| 11 | Montana | 107.3 |
| 10 | Nebraska | 107.5 |
| 8 | Nevada | 107.6 |
| 5 | New Hampshire | 108.1 |
| 47 | New Jersey | 98.7 |
| 48 | New Mexico | 97.9 |
| 41 | New York | 100.0 |
| 28 | North Carolina | 102.3 |
| 1 | North Dakota | 182.0 |
| 24 | Ohio | 102.7 |
| 14 | Oklahoma | 105.2 |
| 39 | Oregon | 100.9 |
| 42 | Pennsylvania | 99.9 |
| 43 | Rhode Island | 99.8 |
| 17 | South Carolina | 104.7 |
| 33 | South Dakota | 101.7 |
| 19 | Tennessee | 103.5 |
| 2 | Texas | 118.7 |
| 22 | Utah | 103.0 |
| 20 | Vermont | 103.3 |
| 27 | Virginia | 102.4 |
| 49 | Washington | 92.6 |
| 46 | West Virginia | 98.9 |
| 29 | Wisconsin | 102.2 |
| 32 | Wyoming | 101.8 |

RANK ORDER

| RANK | STATE | PERCENT |
|---|---|---|
| 1 | North Dakota | 182.0 |
| 2 | Texas | 118.7 |
| 3 | Arkansas | 115.9 |
| 4 | Colorado | 114.1 |
| 5 | New Hampshire | 108.1 |
| 6 | Minnesota | 107.8 |
| 7 | Hawaii | 107.7 |
| 8 | Illinois | 107.6 |
| 8 | Nevada | 107.6 |
| 10 | Nebraska | 107.5 |
| 11 | Montana | 107.3 |
| 12 | Mississippi | 106.7 |
| 13 | Missouri | 106.3 |
| 14 | Delaware | 105.2 |
| 14 | Oklahoma | 105.2 |
| 16 | Iowa | 105.0 |
| 17 | South Carolina | 104.7 |
| 18 | Alabama | 103.7 |
| 19 | Tennessee | 103.5 |
| 20 | Idaho | 103.3 |
| 20 | Vermont | 103.3 |
| 22 | Georgia | 103.0 |
| 22 | Utah | 103.0 |
| 24 | Arizona | 102.7 |
| 24 | Ohio | 102.7 |
| 26 | California | 102.6 |
| 27 | Virginia | 102.4 |
| 28 | North Carolina | 102.3 |
| 29 | Wisconsin | 102.2 |
| 30 | Kentucky | 102.1 |
| 31 | Michigan | 102.0 |
| 32 | Wyoming | 101.8 |
| 33 | South Dakota | 101.7 |
| 34 | Indiana | 101.6 |
| 35 | Kansas | 101.4 |
| 36 | Maryland | 101.3 |
| 37 | Florida | 101.2 |
| 38 | Maine | 101.1 |
| 39 | Oregon | 100.9 |
| 40 | Louisiana | 100.7 |
| 41 | New York | 100.0 |
| 42 | Pennsylvania | 99.9 |
| 43 | Massachusetts | 99.8 |
| 43 | Rhode Island | 99.8 |
| 45 | Connecticut | 99.7 |
| 46 | West Virginia | 98.9 |
| 47 | New Jersey | 98.7 |
| 48 | New Mexico | 97.9 |
| 49 | Washington | 92.6 |
| 50 | Alaska | 77.3 |

District of Columbia**          NA

Source: CQ Press using data from National Association of State Budget Officers
"The Fiscal Survey of States" (Fall 2013, http://www.nasbo.org)

*For fiscal year 2013. This table compares sales, personal, and corporate income tax collections projected in adopting budgets with the amount collected.

**Not available.

# State Government Tax Revenue in 2012

## National Total = $794,570,079,000

| RANK | STATE | REVENUE | % of USA |
|------|-------|---------|----------|
| 25 | Alabama | $9,052,880,000 | 1.1% |
| 33 | Alaska | 7,049,398,000 | 0.9% |
| 20 | Arizona | 12,973,265,000 | 1.6% |
| 29 | Arkansas | 8,287,744,000 | 1.0% |
| 1 | California | 112,372,263,000 | 14.1% |
| 24 | Colorado | 10,250,628,000 | 1.3% |
| 18 | Connecticut | 15,419,556,000 | 1.9% |
| 44 | Delaware | 3,360,235,000 | 0.4% |
| 5 | Florida | 32,997,012,000 | 4.2% |
| 16 | Georgia | 16,576,903,000 | 2.1% |
| 38 | Hawaii | 5,516,146,000 | 0.7% |
| 43 | Idaho | 3,374,304,000 | 0.4% |
| 4 | Illinois | 36,437,803,000 | 4.6% |
| 17 | Indiana | 15,704,680,000 | 2.0% |
| 31 | Iowa | 7,832,388,000 | 1.0% |
| 32 | Kansas | 7,418,341,000 | 0.9% |
| 23 | Kentucky | 10,472,861,000 | 1.3% |
| 26 | Louisiana | 8,994,053,000 | 1.1% |
| 42 | Maine | 3,777,130,000 | 0.5% |
| 15 | Maryland | 17,064,468,000 | 2.1% |
| 10 | Massachusetts | 22,805,644,000 | 2.9% |
| 9 | Michigan | 23,968,760,000 | 3.0% |
| 12 | Minnesota | 20,560,540,000 | 2.6% |
| 34 | Mississippi | 6,953,362,000 | 0.9% |
| 22 | Missouri | 10,800,741,000 | 1.4% |
| 48 | Montana | 2,459,324,000 | 0.3% |
| 41 | Nebraska | 4,358,328,000 | 0.5% |
| 35 | Nevada | 6,775,112,000 | 0.9% |
| 49 | New Hampshire | 2,206,329,000 | 0.3% |
| 7 | New Jersey | 27,456,175,000 | 3.5% |
| 40 | New Mexico | 5,088,335,000 | 0.6% |
| 2 | New York | 71,545,745,000 | 9.0% |
| 11 | North Carolina | 22,713,357,000 | 2.9% |
| 37 | North Dakota | 5,620,036,000 | 0.7% |
| 8 | Ohio | 25,924,024,000 | 3.3% |
| 27 | Oklahoma | 8,826,132,000 | 1.1% |
| 28 | Oregon | 8,699,626,000 | 1.1% |
| 6 | Pennsylvania | 32,949,917,000 | 4.1% |
| 45 | Rhode Island | 2,805,287,000 | 0.4% |
| 30 | South Carolina | 8,036,482,000 | 1.0% |
| 50 | South Dakota | 1,521,477,000 | 0.2% |
| 21 | Tennessee | 11,982,345,000 | 1.5% |
| 3 | Texas | 48,596,548,000 | 6.1% |
| 36 | Utah | 5,809,953,000 | 0.7% |
| 46 | Vermont | 2,757,370,000 | 0.3% |
| 13 | Virginia | 18,137,586,000 | 2.3% |
| 14 | Washington | 17,624,715,000 | 2.2% |
| 39 | West Virginia | 5,355,809,000 | 0.7% |
| 19 | Wisconsin | 14,747,971,000 | 1.9% |
| 47 | Wyoming | 2,550,991,000 | 0.3% |

| RANK | STATE | REVENUE | % of USA |
|------|-------|---------|----------|
| 1 | California | $112,372,263,000 | 14.1% |
| 2 | New York | 71,545,745,000 | 9.0% |
| 3 | Texas | 48,596,548,000 | 6.1% |
| 4 | Illinois | 36,437,803,000 | 4.6% |
| 5 | Florida | 32,997,012,000 | 4.2% |
| 6 | Pennsylvania | 32,949,917,000 | 4.1% |
| 7 | New Jersey | 27,456,175,000 | 3.5% |
| 8 | Ohio | 25,924,024,000 | 3.3% |
| 9 | Michigan | 23,968,760,000 | 3.0% |
| 10 | Massachusetts | 22,805,644,000 | 2.9% |
| 11 | North Carolina | 22,713,357,000 | 2.9% |
| 12 | Minnesota | 20,560,540,000 | 2.6% |
| 13 | Virginia | 18,137,586,000 | 2.3% |
| 14 | Washington | 17,624,715,000 | 2.2% |
| 15 | Maryland | 17,064,468,000 | 2.1% |
| 16 | Georgia | 16,576,903,000 | 2.1% |
| 17 | Indiana | 15,704,680,000 | 2.0% |
| 18 | Connecticut | 15,419,556,000 | 1.9% |
| 19 | Wisconsin | 14,747,971,000 | 1.9% |
| 20 | Arizona | 12,973,265,000 | 1.6% |
| 21 | Tennessee | 11,982,345,000 | 1.5% |
| 22 | Missouri | 10,800,741,000 | 1.4% |
| 23 | Kentucky | 10,472,861,000 | 1.3% |
| 24 | Colorado | 10,250,628,000 | 1.3% |
| 25 | Alabama | 9,052,880,000 | 1.1% |
| 26 | Louisiana | 8,994,053,000 | 1.1% |
| 27 | Oklahoma | 8,826,132,000 | 1.1% |
| 28 | Oregon | 8,699,626,000 | 1.1% |
| 29 | Arkansas | 8,287,744,000 | 1.0% |
| 30 | South Carolina | 8,036,482,000 | 1.0% |
| 31 | Iowa | 7,832,388,000 | 1.0% |
| 32 | Kansas | 7,418,341,000 | 0.9% |
| 33 | Alaska | 7,049,398,000 | 0.9% |
| 34 | Mississippi | 6,953,362,000 | 0.9% |
| 35 | Nevada | 6,775,112,000 | 0.9% |
| 36 | Utah | 5,809,953,000 | 0.7% |
| 37 | North Dakota | 5,620,036,000 | 0.7% |
| 38 | Hawaii | 5,516,146,000 | 0.7% |
| 39 | West Virginia | 5,355,809,000 | 0.7% |
| 40 | New Mexico | 5,088,335,000 | 0.6% |
| 41 | Nebraska | 4,358,328,000 | 0.5% |
| 42 | Maine | 3,777,130,000 | 0.5% |
| 43 | Idaho | 3,374,304,000 | 0.4% |
| 44 | Delaware | 3,360,235,000 | 0.4% |
| 45 | Rhode Island | 2,805,287,000 | 0.4% |
| 46 | Vermont | 2,757,370,000 | 0.3% |
| 47 | Wyoming | 2,550,991,000 | 0.3% |
| 48 | Montana | 2,459,324,000 | 0.3% |
| 49 | New Hampshire | 2,206,329,000 | 0.3% |
| 50 | South Dakota | 1,521,477,000 | 0.2% |
| | District of Columbia* | NA | NA |

Source: U.S. Bureau of the Census, Governments Division
   "2012 State Government Tax Collections" (http://www.census.gov/govs/statetax/)
*Not applicable.

# Per Capita State Government Tax Revenue in 2012

## National Per Capita = $2,536

ALPHA ORDER

| RANK | STATE | PER CAPITA |
|------|-------|------------|
| 42 | Alabama | $1,877 |
| 1 | Alaska | 9,638 |
| 39 | Arizona | 1,980 |
| 17 | Arkansas | 2,810 |
| 12 | California | 2,954 |
| 40 | Colorado | 1,976 |
| 5 | Connecticut | 4,295 |
| 8 | Delaware | 3,664 |
| 47 | Florida | 1,708 |
| 49 | Georgia | 1,671 |
| 6 | Hawaii | 3,962 |
| 37 | Idaho | 2,115 |
| 16 | Illinois | 2,830 |
| 28 | Indiana | 2,402 |
| 23 | Iowa | 2,548 |
| 21 | Kansas | 2,571 |
| 29 | Kentucky | 2,391 |
| 41 | Louisiana | 1,954 |
| 15 | Maine | 2,842 |
| 13 | Maryland | 2,900 |
| 10 | Massachusetts | 3,431 |
| 27 | Michigan | 2,425 |
| 7 | Minnesota | 3,822 |
| 31 | Mississippi | 2,329 |
| 46 | Missouri | 1,794 |
| 25 | Montana | 2,447 |
| 30 | Nebraska | 2,349 |
| 24 | Nevada | 2,456 |
| 49 | New Hampshire | 1,671 |
| 11 | New Jersey | 3,097 |
| 26 | New Mexico | 2,440 |
| 9 | New York | 3,656 |
| 31 | North Carolina | 2,329 |
| 2 | North Dakota | 8,033 |
| 34 | Ohio | 2,246 |
| 33 | Oklahoma | 2,314 |
| 35 | Oregon | 2,231 |
| 19 | Pennsylvania | 2,582 |
| 18 | Rhode Island | 2,671 |
| 48 | South Carolina | 1,701 |
| 45 | South Dakota | 1,826 |
| 44 | Tennessee | 1,856 |
| 43 | Texas | 1,865 |
| 38 | Utah | 2,035 |
| 4 | Vermont | 4,405 |
| 36 | Virginia | 2,216 |
| 22 | Washington | 2,555 |
| 14 | West Virginia | 2,887 |
| 20 | Wisconsin | 2,575 |
| 3 | Wyoming | 4,426 |

RANK ORDER

| RANK | STATE | PER CAPITA |
|------|-------|------------|
| 1 | Alaska | $9,638 |
| 2 | North Dakota | 8,033 |
| 3 | Wyoming | 4,426 |
| 4 | Vermont | 4,405 |
| 5 | Connecticut | 4,295 |
| 6 | Hawaii | 3,962 |
| 7 | Minnesota | 3,822 |
| 8 | Delaware | 3,664 |
| 9 | New York | 3,656 |
| 10 | Massachusetts | 3,431 |
| 11 | New Jersey | 3,097 |
| 12 | California | 2,954 |
| 13 | Maryland | 2,900 |
| 14 | West Virginia | 2,887 |
| 15 | Maine | 2,842 |
| 16 | Illinois | 2,830 |
| 17 | Arkansas | 2,810 |
| 18 | Rhode Island | 2,671 |
| 19 | Pennsylvania | 2,582 |
| 20 | Wisconsin | 2,575 |
| 21 | Kansas | 2,571 |
| 22 | Washington | 2,555 |
| 23 | Iowa | 2,548 |
| 24 | Nevada | 2,456 |
| 25 | Montana | 2,447 |
| 26 | New Mexico | 2,440 |
| 27 | Michigan | 2,425 |
| 28 | Indiana | 2,402 |
| 29 | Kentucky | 2,391 |
| 30 | Nebraska | 2,349 |
| 31 | Mississippi | 2,329 |
| 31 | North Carolina | 2,329 |
| 33 | Oklahoma | 2,314 |
| 34 | Ohio | 2,246 |
| 35 | Oregon | 2,231 |
| 36 | Virginia | 2,216 |
| 37 | Idaho | 2,115 |
| 38 | Utah | 2,035 |
| 39 | Arizona | 1,980 |
| 40 | Colorado | 1,976 |
| 41 | Louisiana | 1,954 |
| 42 | Alabama | 1,877 |
| 43 | Texas | 1,865 |
| 44 | Tennessee | 1,856 |
| 45 | South Dakota | 1,826 |
| 46 | Missouri | 1,794 |
| 47 | Florida | 1,708 |
| 48 | South Carolina | 1,701 |
| 49 | Georgia | 1,671 |
| 49 | New Hampshire | 1,671 |
| | District of Columbia* | NA |

Source: CQ Press using data from U.S. Bureau of the Census, Governments Division
"2012 State Government Tax Collections" (http://www.census.gov/govs/statetax/)
*Not applicable.

# State Government Tax Revenue as a Percent of Personal Income in 2012

## National Percent = 5.9% of Personal Income*

ALPHA ORDER

| RANK | STATE | PERCENT |
|------|-------|---------|
| 39 | Alabama | 5.3 |
| 1 | Alaska | 20.6 |
| 37 | Arizona | 5.5 |
| 9 | Arkansas | 8.1 |
| 16 | California | 6.6 |
| 47 | Colorado | 4.4 |
| 10 | Connecticut | 7.3 |
| 6 | Delaware | 8.7 |
| 48 | Florida | 4.2 |
| 45 | Georgia | 4.5 |
| 5 | Hawaii | 9.0 |
| 22 | Idaho | 6.3 |
| 22 | Illinois | 6.3 |
| 18 | Indiana | 6.5 |
| 27 | Iowa | 6.0 |
| 26 | Kansas | 6.1 |
| 15 | Kentucky | 6.8 |
| 40 | Louisiana | 5.0 |
| 11 | Maine | 7.2 |
| 35 | Maryland | 5.6 |
| 22 | Massachusetts | 6.3 |
| 18 | Michigan | 6.5 |
| 8 | Minnesota | 8.3 |
| 12 | Mississippi | 7.0 |
| 44 | Missouri | 4.6 |
| 18 | Montana | 6.5 |
| 38 | Nebraska | 5.4 |
| 16 | Nevada | 6.6 |
| 50 | New Hampshire | 3.5 |
| 32 | New Jersey | 5.8 |
| 12 | New Mexico | 7.0 |
| 12 | New York | 7.0 |
| 22 | North Carolina | 6.3 |
| 2 | North Dakota | 15.5 |
| 34 | Ohio | 5.7 |
| 28 | Oklahoma | 5.9 |
| 32 | Oregon | 5.8 |
| 28 | Pennsylvania | 5.9 |
| 28 | Rhode Island | 5.9 |
| 40 | South Carolina | 5.0 |
| 48 | South Dakota | 4.2 |
| 42 | Tennessee | 4.9 |
| 45 | Texas | 4.5 |
| 28 | Utah | 5.9 |
| 3 | Vermont | 10.2 |
| 43 | Virginia | 4.7 |
| 35 | Washington | 5.6 |
| 7 | West Virginia | 8.4 |
| 21 | Wisconsin | 6.4 |
| 4 | Wyoming | 9.1 |

RANK ORDER

| RANK | STATE | PERCENT |
|------|-------|---------|
| 1 | Alaska | 20.6 |
| 2 | North Dakota | 15.5 |
| 3 | Vermont | 10.2 |
| 4 | Wyoming | 9.1 |
| 5 | Hawaii | 9.0 |
| 6 | Delaware | 8.7 |
| 7 | West Virginia | 8.4 |
| 8 | Minnesota | 8.3 |
| 9 | Arkansas | 8.1 |
| 10 | Connecticut | 7.3 |
| 11 | Maine | 7.2 |
| 12 | Mississippi | 7.0 |
| 12 | New Mexico | 7.0 |
| 12 | New York | 7.0 |
| 15 | Kentucky | 6.8 |
| 16 | California | 6.6 |
| 16 | Nevada | 6.6 |
| 18 | Indiana | 6.5 |
| 18 | Michigan | 6.5 |
| 18 | Montana | 6.5 |
| 21 | Wisconsin | 6.4 |
| 22 | Idaho | 6.3 |
| 22 | Illinois | 6.3 |
| 22 | Massachusetts | 6.3 |
| 22 | North Carolina | 6.3 |
| 26 | Kansas | 6.1 |
| 27 | Iowa | 6.0 |
| 28 | Oklahoma | 5.9 |
| 28 | Pennsylvania | 5.9 |
| 28 | Rhode Island | 5.9 |
| 28 | Utah | 5.9 |
| 32 | New Jersey | 5.8 |
| 32 | Oregon | 5.8 |
| 34 | Ohio | 5.7 |
| 35 | Maryland | 5.6 |
| 35 | Washington | 5.6 |
| 37 | Arizona | 5.5 |
| 38 | Nebraska | 5.4 |
| 39 | Alabama | 5.3 |
| 40 | Louisiana | 5.0 |
| 40 | South Carolina | 5.0 |
| 42 | Tennessee | 4.9 |
| 43 | Virginia | 4.7 |
| 44 | Missouri | 4.6 |
| 45 | Georgia | 4.5 |
| 45 | Texas | 4.5 |
| 47 | Colorado | 4.4 |
| 48 | Florida | 4.2 |
| 48 | South Dakota | 4.2 |
| 50 | New Hampshire | 3.5 |

District of Columbia**  NA

Source: CQ Press using data from U.S. Bureau of the Census, Governments Division
    "2012 State Government Tax Collections" (http://www.census.gov/govs/statetax/) and
    U.S. Department of Commerce, Bureau of Economic Analysis
    "Annual State Personal Income" (http://www.bea.gov/iTable/index.cfm)
*National figure does not include personal income or taxes from the District of Columbia.
**Not applicable.

# State Government Individual Income Tax Revenue in 2012

## National Total = $280,359,640,000

ALPHA ORDER

| RANK | STATE | REVENUE | % of USA |
|------|-------|---------|----------|
| 24 | Alabama | $3,017,437,000 | 1.1% |
| 44 | Alaska | 0 | 0.0% |
| 22 | Arizona | 3,093,904,000 | 1.1% |
| 29 | Arkansas | 2,401,902,000 | 0.9% |
| 1 | California | 55,024,435,000 | 19.6% |
| 18 | Colorado | 4,875,627,000 | 1.7% |
| 12 | Connecticut | 7,371,189,000 | 2.6% |
| 35 | Delaware | 1,311,589,000 | 0.5% |
| 44 | Florida | 0 | 0.0% |
| 10 | Georgia | 8,142,371,000 | 2.9% |
| 32 | Hawaii | 1,540,746,000 | 0.5% |
| 36 | Idaho | 1,213,335,000 | 0.4% |
| 3 | Illinois | 15,692,351,000 | 5.6% |
| 19 | Indiana | 4,765,566,000 | 1.7% |
| 23 | Iowa | 3,029,709,000 | 1.1% |
| 25 | Kansas | 2,891,743,000 | 1.0% |
| 20 | Kentucky | 3,512,075,000 | 1.3% |
| 27 | Louisiana | 2,474,606,000 | 0.9% |
| 34 | Maine | 1,441,926,000 | 0.5% |
| 13 | Maryland | 7,116,605,000 | 2.5% |
| 4 | Massachusetts | 11,933,452,000 | 4.3% |
| 14 | Michigan | 6,827,913,000 | 2.4% |
| 11 | Minnesota | 7,988,084,000 | 2.8% |
| 33 | Mississippi | 1,501,267,000 | 0.5% |
| 17 | Missouri | 5,131,686,000 | 1.8% |
| 39 | Montana | 900,180,000 | 0.3% |
| 30 | Nebraska | 1,838,344,000 | 0.7% |
| 44 | Nevada | 0 | 0.0% |
| 43 | New Hampshire | 81,557,000 | 0.0% |
| 5 | New Jersey | 11,128,418,000 | 4.0% |
| 37 | New Mexico | 1,150,468,000 | 0.4% |
| 2 | New York | 38,771,968,000 | 13.8% |
| 6 | North Carolina | 10,383,796,000 | 3.7% |
| 41 | North Dakota | 432,527,000 | 0.2% |
| 9 | Ohio | 9,029,657,000 | 3.2% |
| 26 | Oklahoma | 2,774,376,000 | 1.0% |
| 16 | Oregon | 5,825,797,000 | 2.1% |
| 8 | Pennsylvania | 10,102,113,000 | 3.6% |
| 38 | Rhode Island | 1,064,447,000 | 0.4% |
| 21 | South Carolina | 3,096,834,000 | 1.1% |
| 44 | South Dakota | 0 | 0.0% |
| 42 | Tennessee | 182,251,000 | 0.1% |
| 44 | Texas | 0 | 0.0% |
| 28 | Utah | 2,466,495,000 | 0.9% |
| 40 | Vermont | 598,450,000 | 0.2% |
| 7 | Virginia | 10,216,148,000 | 3.6% |
| 44 | Washington | 0 | 0.0% |
| 31 | West Virginia | 1,755,746,000 | 0.6% |
| 15 | Wisconsin | 6,260,550,000 | 2.2% |
| 44 | Wyoming | 0 | 0.0% |

RANK ORDER

| RANK | STATE | REVENUE | % of USA |
|------|-------|---------|----------|
| 1 | California | $55,024,435,000 | 19.6% |
| 2 | New York | 38,771,968,000 | 13.8% |
| 3 | Illinois | 15,692,351,000 | 5.6% |
| 4 | Massachusetts | 11,933,452,000 | 4.3% |
| 5 | New Jersey | 11,128,418,000 | 4.0% |
| 6 | North Carolina | 10,383,796,000 | 3.7% |
| 7 | Virginia | 10,216,148,000 | 3.6% |
| 8 | Pennsylvania | 10,102,113,000 | 3.6% |
| 9 | Ohio | 9,029,657,000 | 3.2% |
| 10 | Georgia | 8,142,371,000 | 2.9% |
| 11 | Minnesota | 7,988,084,000 | 2.8% |
| 12 | Connecticut | 7,371,189,000 | 2.6% |
| 13 | Maryland | 7,116,605,000 | 2.5% |
| 14 | Michigan | 6,827,913,000 | 2.4% |
| 15 | Wisconsin | 6,260,550,000 | 2.2% |
| 16 | Oregon | 5,825,797,000 | 2.1% |
| 17 | Missouri | 5,131,686,000 | 1.8% |
| 18 | Colorado | 4,875,627,000 | 1.7% |
| 19 | Indiana | 4,765,566,000 | 1.7% |
| 20 | Kentucky | 3,512,075,000 | 1.3% |
| 21 | South Carolina | 3,096,834,000 | 1.1% |
| 22 | Arizona | 3,093,904,000 | 1.1% |
| 23 | Iowa | 3,029,709,000 | 1.1% |
| 24 | Alabama | 3,017,437,000 | 1.1% |
| 25 | Kansas | 2,891,743,000 | 1.0% |
| 26 | Oklahoma | 2,774,376,000 | 1.0% |
| 27 | Louisiana | 2,474,606,000 | 0.9% |
| 28 | Utah | 2,466,495,000 | 0.9% |
| 29 | Arkansas | 2,401,902,000 | 0.9% |
| 30 | Nebraska | 1,838,344,000 | 0.7% |
| 31 | West Virginia | 1,755,746,000 | 0.6% |
| 32 | Hawaii | 1,540,746,000 | 0.5% |
| 33 | Mississippi | 1,501,267,000 | 0.5% |
| 34 | Maine | 1,441,926,000 | 0.5% |
| 35 | Delaware | 1,311,589,000 | 0.5% |
| 36 | Idaho | 1,213,335,000 | 0.4% |
| 37 | New Mexico | 1,150,468,000 | 0.4% |
| 38 | Rhode Island | 1,064,447,000 | 0.4% |
| 39 | Montana | 900,180,000 | 0.3% |
| 40 | Vermont | 598,450,000 | 0.2% |
| 41 | North Dakota | 432,527,000 | 0.2% |
| 42 | Tennessee | 182,251,000 | 0.1% |
| 43 | New Hampshire | 81,557,000 | 0.0% |
| 44 | Alaska | 0 | 0.0% |
| 44 | Florida | 0 | 0.0% |
| 44 | Nevada | 0 | 0.0% |
| 44 | South Dakota | 0 | 0.0% |
| 44 | Texas | 0 | 0.0% |
| 44 | Washington | 0 | 0.0% |
| 44 | Wyoming | 0 | 0.0% |
| | District of Columbia* | NA | NA |

Source: U.S. Bureau of the Census, Governments Division
     "2012 State Government Tax Collections" (http://www.census.gov/govs/statetax/)
*Not applicable.

# Per Capita State Government Individual Income Tax Revenue in 2012

## National Per Capita = $895

ALPHA ORDER

ALPHA ORDER

| RANK | STATE | PER CAPITA |
|---|---|---|
| 36 | Alabama | $626 |
| 44 | Alaska | 0 |
| 41 | Arizona | 472 |
| 27 | Arkansas | 814 |
| 6 | California | 1,446 |
| 22 | Colorado | 940 |
| 1 | Connecticut | 2,053 |
| 7 | Delaware | 1,430 |
| 44 | Florida | 0 |
| 26 | Georgia | 821 |
| 12 | Hawaii | 1,107 |
| 31 | Idaho | 760 |
| 10 | Illinois | 1,219 |
| 32 | Indiana | 729 |
| 19 | Iowa | 986 |
| 17 | Kansas | 1,002 |
| 28 | Kentucky | 802 |
| 39 | Louisiana | 538 |
| 14 | Maine | 1,085 |
| 11 | Maryland | 1,209 |
| 3 | Massachusetts | 1,796 |
| 34 | Michigan | 691 |
| 5 | Minnesota | 1,485 |
| 40 | Mississippi | 503 |
| 25 | Missouri | 852 |
| 23 | Montana | 896 |
| 18 | Nebraska | 991 |
| 44 | Nevada | 0 |
| 42 | New Hampshire | 62 |
| 8 | New Jersey | 1,255 |
| 38 | New Mexico | 552 |
| 2 | New York | 1,981 |
| 15 | North Carolina | 1,065 |
| 37 | North Dakota | 618 |
| 30 | Ohio | 782 |
| 33 | Oklahoma | 727 |
| 4 | Oregon | 1,494 |
| 29 | Pennsylvania | 791 |
| 16 | Rhode Island | 1,013 |
| 35 | South Carolina | 656 |
| 44 | South Dakota | 0 |
| 43 | Tennessee | 28 |
| 44 | Texas | 0 |
| 24 | Utah | 864 |
| 20 | Vermont | 956 |
| 9 | Virginia | 1,248 |
| 44 | Washington | 0 |
| 21 | West Virginia | 946 |
| 13 | Wisconsin | 1,093 |
| 44 | Wyoming | 0 |

RANK ORDER

| RANK | STATE | PER CAPITA |
|---|---|---|
| 1 | Connecticut | $2,053 |
| 2 | New York | 1,981 |
| 3 | Massachusetts | 1,796 |
| 4 | Oregon | 1,494 |
| 5 | Minnesota | 1,485 |
| 6 | California | 1,446 |
| 7 | Delaware | 1,430 |
| 8 | New Jersey | 1,255 |
| 9 | Virginia | 1,248 |
| 10 | Illinois | 1,219 |
| 11 | Maryland | 1,209 |
| 12 | Hawaii | 1,107 |
| 13 | Wisconsin | 1,093 |
| 14 | Maine | 1,085 |
| 15 | North Carolina | 1,065 |
| 16 | Rhode Island | 1,013 |
| 17 | Kansas | 1,002 |
| 18 | Nebraska | 991 |
| 19 | Iowa | 986 |
| 20 | Vermont | 956 |
| 21 | West Virginia | 946 |
| 22 | Colorado | 940 |
| 23 | Montana | 896 |
| 24 | Utah | 864 |
| 25 | Missouri | 852 |
| 26 | Georgia | 821 |
| 27 | Arkansas | 814 |
| 28 | Kentucky | 802 |
| 29 | Pennsylvania | 791 |
| 30 | Ohio | 782 |
| 31 | Idaho | 760 |
| 32 | Indiana | 729 |
| 33 | Oklahoma | 727 |
| 34 | Michigan | 691 |
| 35 | South Carolina | 656 |
| 36 | Alabama | 626 |
| 37 | North Dakota | 618 |
| 38 | New Mexico | 552 |
| 39 | Louisiana | 538 |
| 40 | Mississippi | 503 |
| 41 | Arizona | 472 |
| 42 | New Hampshire | 62 |
| 43 | Tennessee | 28 |
| 44 | Alaska | 0 |
| 44 | Florida | 0 |
| 44 | Nevada | 0 |
| 44 | South Dakota | 0 |
| 44 | Texas | 0 |
| 44 | Washington | 0 |
| 44 | Wyoming | 0 |
| | District of Columbia* | NA |

Source: CQ Press using data from U.S. Bureau of the Census, Governments Division
"2012 State Government Tax Collections" (http://www.census.gov/govs/statetax/)
*Not applicable.

# State Government Corporation Net Income Tax Revenue in 2012

## National Total = $41,741,281,000

ALPHA ORDER

| RANK | STATE | REVENUE | % of USA |
|---|---|---|---|
| 26 | Alabama | $413,253,000 | 1.0% |
| 15 | Alaska | 663,144,000 | 1.6% |
| 16 | Arizona | 647,809,000 | 1.6% |
| 27 | Arkansas | 404,083,000 | 1.0% |
| 1 | California | 7,949,000,000 | 19.0% |
| 22 | Colorado | 492,224,000 | 1.2% |
| 17 | Connecticut | 625,320,000 | 1.5% |
| 33 | Delaware | 262,378,000 | 0.6% |
| 4 | Florida | 2,003,490,000 | 4.8% |
| 19 | Georgia | 590,676,000 | 1.4% |
| 45 | Hawaii | 80,256,000 | 0.2% |
| 40 | Idaho | 188,589,000 | 0.5% |
| 3 | Illinois | 3,494,539,000 | 8.4% |
| 11 | Indiana | 958,800,000 | 2.3% |
| 25 | Iowa | 425,776,000 | 1.0% |
| 29 | Kansas | 317,578,000 | 0.8% |
| 20 | Kentucky | 575,164,000 | 1.4% |
| 31 | Louisiana | 290,389,000 | 0.7% |
| 37 | Maine | 232,118,000 | 0.6% |
| 13 | Maryland | 880,356,000 | 2.1% |
| 5 | Massachusetts | 2,001,780,000 | 4.8% |
| 18 | Michigan | 608,829,000 | 1.5% |
| 10 | Minnesota | 1,066,022,000 | 2.6% |
| 28 | Mississippi | 395,678,000 | 0.9% |
| 30 | Missouri | 301,681,000 | 0.7% |
| 41 | Montana | 132,361,000 | 0.3% |
| 36 | Nebraska | 234,296,000 | 0.6% |
| 47 | Nevada | 0 | 0.0% |
| 21 | New Hampshire | 521,309,000 | 1.2% |
| 6 | New Jersey | 1,929,133,000 | 4.6% |
| 32 | New Mexico | 281,047,000 | 0.7% |
| 2 | New York | 4,567,889,000 | 10.9% |
| 9 | North Carolina | 1,220,072,000 | 2.9% |
| 38 | North Dakota | 215,622,000 | 0.5% |
| 43 | Ohio | 117,446,000 | 0.3% |
| 23 | Oklahoma | 446,009,000 | 1.1% |
| 24 | Oregon | 433,126,000 | 1.0% |
| 7 | Pennsylvania | 1,837,374,000 | 4.4% |
| 42 | Rhode Island | 122,197,000 | 0.3% |
| 35 | South Carolina | 252,904,000 | 0.6% |
| 46 | South Dakota | 59,837,000 | 0.1% |
| 8 | Tennessee | 1,225,890,000 | 2.9% |
| 47 | Texas | 0 | 0.0% |
| 34 | Utah | 258,578,000 | 0.6% |
| 44 | Vermont | 96,579,000 | 0.2% |
| 14 | Virginia | 838,790,000 | 2.0% |
| 47 | Washington | 0 | 0.0% |
| 39 | West Virginia | 192,385,000 | 0.5% |
| 12 | Wisconsin | 889,505,000 | 2.1% |
| 47 | Wyoming | 0 | 0.0% |

RANK ORDER

| RANK | STATE | REVENUE | % of USA |
|---|---|---|---|
| 1 | California | $7,949,000,000 | 19.0% |
| 2 | New York | 4,567,889,000 | 10.9% |
| 3 | Illinois | 3,494,539,000 | 8.4% |
| 4 | Florida | 2,003,490,000 | 4.8% |
| 5 | Massachusetts | 2,001,780,000 | 4.8% |
| 6 | New Jersey | 1,929,133,000 | 4.6% |
| 7 | Pennsylvania | 1,837,374,000 | 4.4% |
| 8 | Tennessee | 1,225,890,000 | 2.9% |
| 9 | North Carolina | 1,220,072,000 | 2.9% |
| 10 | Minnesota | 1,066,022,000 | 2.6% |
| 11 | Indiana | 958,800,000 | 2.3% |
| 12 | Wisconsin | 889,505,000 | 2.1% |
| 13 | Maryland | 880,356,000 | 2.1% |
| 14 | Virginia | 838,790,000 | 2.0% |
| 15 | Alaska | 663,144,000 | 1.6% |
| 16 | Arizona | 647,809,000 | 1.6% |
| 17 | Connecticut | 625,320,000 | 1.5% |
| 18 | Michigan | 608,829,000 | 1.5% |
| 19 | Georgia | 590,676,000 | 1.4% |
| 20 | Kentucky | 575,164,000 | 1.4% |
| 21 | New Hampshire | 521,309,000 | 1.2% |
| 22 | Colorado | 492,224,000 | 1.2% |
| 23 | Oklahoma | 446,009,000 | 1.1% |
| 24 | Oregon | 433,126,000 | 1.0% |
| 25 | Iowa | 425,776,000 | 1.0% |
| 26 | Alabama | 413,253,000 | 1.0% |
| 27 | Arkansas | 404,083,000 | 1.0% |
| 28 | Mississippi | 395,678,000 | 0.9% |
| 29 | Kansas | 317,578,000 | 0.8% |
| 30 | Missouri | 301,681,000 | 0.7% |
| 31 | Louisiana | 290,389,000 | 0.7% |
| 32 | New Mexico | 281,047,000 | 0.7% |
| 33 | Delaware | 262,378,000 | 0.6% |
| 34 | Utah | 258,578,000 | 0.6% |
| 35 | South Carolina | 252,904,000 | 0.6% |
| 36 | Nebraska | 234,296,000 | 0.6% |
| 37 | Maine | 232,118,000 | 0.6% |
| 38 | North Dakota | 215,622,000 | 0.5% |
| 39 | West Virginia | 192,385,000 | 0.5% |
| 40 | Idaho | 188,589,000 | 0.5% |
| 41 | Montana | 132,361,000 | 0.3% |
| 42 | Rhode Island | 122,197,000 | 0.3% |
| 43 | Ohio | 117,446,000 | 0.3% |
| 44 | Vermont | 96,579,000 | 0.2% |
| 45 | Hawaii | 80,256,000 | 0.2% |
| 46 | South Dakota | 59,837,000 | 0.1% |
| 47 | Nevada | 0 | 0.0% |
| 47 | Texas | 0 | 0.0% |
| 47 | Washington | 0 | 0.0% |
| 47 | Wyoming | 0 | 0.0% |
| | District of Columbia* | NA | NA |

Source: U.S. Bureau of the Census, Governments Division
"2012 State Government Tax Collections" (http://www.census.gov/govs/statetax/)
*Not applicable.

# Per Capita State Government Corporation Net Income Tax Revenue in 2012

## National Per Capita = $133

ALPHA ORDER

| RANK | STATE | PER CAPITA |
|------|-------|-----------|
| 38 | Alabama | $86 |
| 1 | Alaska | 907 |
| 35 | Arizona | 99 |
| 20 | Arkansas | 137 |
| 9 | California | 209 |
| 36 | Colorado | 95 |
| 13 | Connecticut | 174 |
| 5 | Delaware | 286 |
| 32 | Florida | 104 |
| 42 | Georgia | 60 |
| 43 | Hawaii | 58 |
| 27 | Idaho | 118 |
| 6 | Illinois | 271 |
| 17 | Indiana | 147 |
| 19 | Iowa | 139 |
| 31 | Kansas | 110 |
| 24 | Kentucky | 131 |
| 40 | Louisiana | 63 |
| 12 | Maine | 175 |
| 16 | Maryland | 150 |
| 4 | Massachusetts | 301 |
| 41 | Michigan | 62 |
| 10 | Minnesota | 198 |
| 22 | Mississippi | 133 |
| 45 | Missouri | 50 |
| 23 | Montana | 132 |
| 25 | Nebraska | 126 |
| 47 | Nevada | 0 |
| 2 | New Hampshire | 395 |
| 8 | New Jersey | 218 |
| 21 | New Mexico | 135 |
| 7 | New York | 233 |
| 26 | North Carolina | 125 |
| 3 | North Dakota | 308 |
| 46 | Ohio | 10 |
| 28 | Oklahoma | 117 |
| 30 | Oregon | 111 |
| 18 | Pennsylvania | 144 |
| 29 | Rhode Island | 116 |
| 44 | South Carolina | 54 |
| 39 | South Dakota | 72 |
| 11 | Tennessee | 190 |
| 47 | Texas | 0 |
| 37 | Utah | 91 |
| 15 | Vermont | 154 |
| 34 | Virginia | 102 |
| 47 | Washington | 0 |
| 32 | West Virginia | 104 |
| 14 | Wisconsin | 155 |
| 47 | Wyoming | 0 |

RANK ORDER

| RANK | STATE | PER CAPITA |
|------|-------|-----------|
| 1 | Alaska | $907 |
| 2 | New Hampshire | 395 |
| 3 | North Dakota | 308 |
| 4 | Massachusetts | 301 |
| 5 | Delaware | 286 |
| 6 | Illinois | 271 |
| 7 | New York | 233 |
| 8 | New Jersey | 218 |
| 9 | California | 209 |
| 10 | Minnesota | 198 |
| 11 | Tennessee | 190 |
| 12 | Maine | 175 |
| 13 | Connecticut | 174 |
| 14 | Wisconsin | 155 |
| 15 | Vermont | 154 |
| 16 | Maryland | 150 |
| 17 | Indiana | 147 |
| 18 | Pennsylvania | 144 |
| 19 | Iowa | 139 |
| 20 | Arkansas | 137 |
| 21 | New Mexico | 135 |
| 22 | Mississippi | 133 |
| 23 | Montana | 132 |
| 24 | Kentucky | 131 |
| 25 | Nebraska | 126 |
| 26 | North Carolina | 125 |
| 27 | Idaho | 118 |
| 28 | Oklahoma | 117 |
| 29 | Rhode Island | 116 |
| 30 | Oregon | 111 |
| 31 | Kansas | 110 |
| 32 | Florida | 104 |
| 32 | West Virginia | 104 |
| 34 | Virginia | 102 |
| 35 | Arizona | 99 |
| 36 | Colorado | 95 |
| 37 | Utah | 91 |
| 38 | Alabama | 86 |
| 39 | South Dakota | 72 |
| 40 | Louisiana | 63 |
| 41 | Michigan | 62 |
| 42 | Georgia | 60 |
| 43 | Hawaii | 58 |
| 44 | South Carolina | 54 |
| 45 | Missouri | 50 |
| 46 | Ohio | 10 |
| 47 | Nevada | 0 |
| 47 | Texas | 0 |
| 47 | Washington | 0 |
| 47 | Wyoming | 0 |

District of Columbia*  NA

Source: CQ Press using data from U.S. Bureau of the Census, Governments Division
  "2012 State Government Tax Collections" (http://www.census.gov/govs/statetax/)
*Not applicable.

# State Government General Sales Tax Revenue in 2012

## National Total = $242,697,113,000*

ALPHA ORDER

ALPHA ORDER

| RANK | STATE | REVENUE | % of USA |
|------|-------|---------|----------|
| 34 | Alabama | $2,274,658,000 | 0.9% |
| 46 | Alaska | 0 | 0.0% |
| 13 | Arizona | 6,210,756,000 | 2.6% |
| 29 | Arkansas | 2,809,416,000 | 1.2% |
| 1 | California | 28,536,238,000 | 11.8% |
| 33 | Colorado | 2,302,333,000 | 0.9% |
| 20 | Connecticut | 3,758,881,000 | 1.5% |
| 46 | Delaware | 0 | 0.0% |
| 3 | Florida | 19,403,788,000 | 8.0% |
| 15 | Georgia | 5,303,524,000 | 2.2% |
| 30 | Hawaii | 2,697,951,000 | 1.1% |
| 39 | Idaho | 1,224,656,000 | 0.5% |
| 10 | Illinois | 8,034,466,000 | 3.3% |
| 11 | Indiana | 6,621,954,000 | 2.7% |
| 31 | Iowa | 2,423,160,000 | 1.0% |
| 27 | Kansas | 2,825,880,000 | 1.2% |
| 25 | Kentucky | 3,052,236,000 | 1.3% |
| 28 | Louisiana | 2,815,919,000 | 1.2% |
| 41 | Maine | 1,064,342,000 | 0.4% |
| 18 | Maryland | 4,076,578,000 | 1.7% |
| 16 | Massachusetts | 5,079,105,000 | 2.1% |
| 6 | Michigan | 9,565,702,000 | 3.9% |
| 17 | Minnesota | 4,942,140,000 | 2.0% |
| 24 | Mississippi | 3,072,243,000 | 1.3% |
| 23 | Missouri | 3,103,410,000 | 1.3% |
| 46 | Montana | 0 | 0.0% |
| 37 | Nebraska | 1,456,625,000 | 0.6% |
| 22 | Nevada | 3,433,958,000 | 1.4% |
| 46 | New Hampshire | 0 | 0.0% |
| 9 | New Jersey | 8,099,549,000 | 3.3% |
| 35 | New Mexico | 1,990,535,000 | 0.8% |
| 4 | New York | 11,904,357,000 | 4.9% |
| 14 | North Carolina | 5,573,658,000 | 2.3% |
| 40 | North Dakota | 1,122,783,000 | 0.5% |
| 8 | Ohio | 8,272,728,000 | 3.4% |
| 32 | Oklahoma | 2,415,964,000 | 1.0% |
| 46 | Oregon | 0 | 0.0% |
| 7 | Pennsylvania | 9,166,842,000 | 3.8% |
| 43 | Rhode Island | 839,414,000 | 0.3% |
| 26 | South Carolina | 2,926,177,000 | 1.2% |
| 44 | South Dakota | 838,240,000 | 0.3% |
| 12 | Tennessee | 6,512,362,000 | 2.7% |
| 2 | Texas | 24,500,909,000 | 10.1% |
| 36 | Utah | 1,857,035,000 | 0.8% |
| 45 | Vermont | 342,085,000 | 0.1% |
| 21 | Virginia | 3,487,343,000 | 1.4% |
| 5 | Washington | 10,614,137,000 | 4.4% |
| 38 | West Virginia | 1,277,328,000 | 0.5% |
| 19 | Wisconsin | 3,871,581,000 | 1.6% |
| 42 | Wyoming | 994,167,000 | 0.4% |

RANK ORDER

| RANK | STATE | REVENUE | % of USA |
|------|-------|---------|----------|
| 1 | California | $28,536,238,000 | 11.8% |
| 2 | Texas | 24,500,909,000 | 10.1% |
| 3 | Florida | 19,403,788,000 | 8.0% |
| 4 | New York | 11,904,357,000 | 4.9% |
| 5 | Washington | 10,614,137,000 | 4.4% |
| 6 | Michigan | 9,565,702,000 | 3.9% |
| 7 | Pennsylvania | 9,166,842,000 | 3.8% |
| 8 | Ohio | 8,272,728,000 | 3.4% |
| 9 | New Jersey | 8,099,549,000 | 3.3% |
| 10 | Illinois | 8,034,466,000 | 3.3% |
| 11 | Indiana | 6,621,954,000 | 2.7% |
| 12 | Tennessee | 6,512,362,000 | 2.7% |
| 13 | Arizona | 6,210,756,000 | 2.6% |
| 14 | North Carolina | 5,573,658,000 | 2.3% |
| 15 | Georgia | 5,303,524,000 | 2.2% |
| 16 | Massachusetts | 5,079,105,000 | 2.1% |
| 17 | Minnesota | 4,942,140,000 | 2.0% |
| 18 | Maryland | 4,076,578,000 | 1.7% |
| 19 | Wisconsin | 3,871,581,000 | 1.6% |
| 20 | Connecticut | 3,758,881,000 | 1.5% |
| 21 | Virginia | 3,487,343,000 | 1.4% |
| 22 | Nevada | 3,433,958,000 | 1.4% |
| 23 | Missouri | 3,103,410,000 | 1.3% |
| 24 | Mississippi | 3,072,243,000 | 1.3% |
| 25 | Kentucky | 3,052,236,000 | 1.3% |
| 26 | South Carolina | 2,926,177,000 | 1.2% |
| 27 | Kansas | 2,825,880,000 | 1.2% |
| 28 | Louisiana | 2,815,919,000 | 1.2% |
| 29 | Arkansas | 2,809,416,000 | 1.2% |
| 30 | Hawaii | 2,697,951,000 | 1.1% |
| 31 | Iowa | 2,423,160,000 | 1.0% |
| 32 | Oklahoma | 2,415,964,000 | 1.0% |
| 33 | Colorado | 2,302,333,000 | 0.9% |
| 34 | Alabama | 2,274,658,000 | 0.9% |
| 35 | New Mexico | 1,990,535,000 | 0.8% |
| 36 | Utah | 1,857,035,000 | 0.8% |
| 37 | Nebraska | 1,456,625,000 | 0.6% |
| 38 | West Virginia | 1,277,328,000 | 0.5% |
| 39 | Idaho | 1,224,656,000 | 0.5% |
| 40 | North Dakota | 1,122,783,000 | 0.5% |
| 41 | Maine | 1,064,342,000 | 0.4% |
| 42 | Wyoming | 994,167,000 | 0.4% |
| 43 | Rhode Island | 839,414,000 | 0.3% |
| 44 | South Dakota | 838,240,000 | 0.3% |
| 45 | Vermont | 342,085,000 | 0.1% |
| 46 | Alaska | 0 | 0.0% |
| 46 | Delaware | 0 | 0.0% |
| 46 | Montana | 0 | 0.0% |
| 46 | New Hampshire | 0 | 0.0% |
| 46 | Oregon | 0 | 0.0% |
| | District of Columbia** | NA | NA |

Source: U.S. Bureau of the Census, Governments Division

"2012 State Government Tax Collections" (http://www.census.gov/govs/statetax/)

*Does not include special sales taxes such as those on sale of alcohol, gasoline, or tobacco.

**Not applicable.

# Per Capita State Government General Sales Tax Revenue in 2012

## National Per Capita = $775*

| ALPHA ORDER | | | | RANK ORDER | | |
|---|---|---|---|---|---|---|
| RANK | STATE | PER CAPITA | | RANK | STATE | PER CAPITA |
| 43 | Alabama | $472 | | 1 | Hawaii | $1,938 |
| 46 | Alaska | 0 | | 2 | Wyoming | 1,725 |
| 16 | Arizona | 948 | | 3 | North Dakota | 1,605 |
| 15 | Arkansas | 953 | | 4 | Washington | 1,539 |
| 26 | California | 750 | | 5 | Nevada | 1,245 |
| 44 | Colorado | 444 | | 6 | Connecticut | 1,047 |
| 6 | Connecticut | 1,047 | | 7 | Mississippi | 1,029 |
| 46 | Delaware | 0 | | 8 | Indiana | 1,013 |
| 11 | Florida | 1,004 | | 9 | Tennessee | 1,009 |
| 41 | Georgia | 535 | | 10 | South Dakota | 1,006 |
| 1 | Hawaii | 1,938 | | 11 | Florida | 1,004 |
| 24 | Idaho | 767 | | 12 | Kansas | 979 |
| 35 | Illinois | 624 | | 13 | Michigan | 968 |
| 8 | Indiana | 1,013 | | 14 | New Mexico | 954 |
| 22 | Iowa | 788 | | 15 | Arkansas | 953 |
| 12 | Kansas | 979 | | 16 | Arizona | 948 |
| 29 | Kentucky | 697 | | 17 | Texas | 940 |
| 37 | Louisiana | 612 | | 18 | Minnesota | 919 |
| 20 | Maine | 801 | | 19 | New Jersey | 914 |
| 30 | Maryland | 693 | | 20 | Maine | 801 |
| 25 | Massachusetts | 764 | | 21 | Rhode Island | 799 |
| 13 | Michigan | 968 | | 22 | Iowa | 788 |
| 18 | Minnesota | 919 | | 23 | Nebraska | 785 |
| 7 | Mississippi | 1,029 | | 24 | Idaho | 767 |
| 42 | Missouri | 515 | | 25 | Massachusetts | 764 |
| 46 | Montana | 0 | | 26 | California | 750 |
| 23 | Nebraska | 785 | | 27 | Pennsylvania | 718 |
| 5 | Nevada | 1,245 | | 28 | Ohio | 717 |
| 46 | New Hampshire | 0 | | 29 | Kentucky | 697 |
| 19 | New Jersey | 914 | | 30 | Maryland | 693 |
| 14 | New Mexico | 954 | | 31 | West Virginia | 688 |
| 38 | New York | 608 | | 32 | Wisconsin | 676 |
| 39 | North Carolina | 572 | | 33 | Utah | 650 |
| 3 | North Dakota | 1,605 | | 34 | Oklahoma | 633 |
| 28 | Ohio | 717 | | 35 | Illinois | 624 |
| 34 | Oklahoma | 633 | | 36 | South Carolina | 619 |
| 46 | Oregon | 0 | | 37 | Louisiana | 612 |
| 27 | Pennsylvania | 718 | | 38 | New York | 608 |
| 21 | Rhode Island | 799 | | 39 | North Carolina | 572 |
| 36 | South Carolina | 619 | | 40 | Vermont | 546 |
| 10 | South Dakota | 1,006 | | 41 | Georgia | 535 |
| 9 | Tennessee | 1,009 | | 42 | Missouri | 515 |
| 17 | Texas | 940 | | 43 | Alabama | 472 |
| 33 | Utah | 650 | | 44 | Colorado | 444 |
| 40 | Vermont | 546 | | 45 | Virginia | 426 |
| 45 | Virginia | 426 | | 46 | Alaska | 0 |
| 4 | Washington | 1,539 | | 46 | Delaware | 0 |
| 31 | West Virginia | 688 | | 46 | Montana | 0 |
| 32 | Wisconsin | 676 | | 46 | New Hampshire | 0 |
| 2 | Wyoming | 1,725 | | 46 | Oregon | 0 |
| | | | | District of Columbia** | | NA |

Source: CQ Press using data from U.S. Bureau of the Census, Governments Division
   "2012 State Government Tax Collections" (http://www.census.gov/govs/statetax/)
*Does not include special sales taxes such as those on sale of alcohol, gasoline, or tobacco.
**Not applicable.

# State Government Motor Fuels Sales Tax Revenue in 2012

## National Total = $39,914,893,000

ALPHA ORDER

| RANK | STATE | REVENUE | % of USA |
|---|---|---|---|
| 24 | Alabama | $541,499,000 | 1.4% |
| 50 | Alaska | 40,980,000 | 0.1% |
| 11 | Arizona | 896,983,000 | 2.2% |
| 29 | Arkansas | 467,055,000 | 1.2% |
| 1 | California | 5,544,530,000 | 13.9% |
| 22 | Colorado | 630,573,000 | 1.6% |
| 28 | Connecticut | 487,104,000 | 1.2% |
| 46 | Delaware | 112,908,000 | 0.3% |
| 3 | Florida | 2,273,685,000 | 5.7% |
| 13 | Georgia | 880,987,000 | 2.2% |
| 48 | Hawaii | 93,349,000 | 0.2% |
| 39 | Idaho | 236,769,000 | 0.6% |
| 8 | Illinois | 1,290,266,000 | 3.2% |
| 18 | Indiana | 783,897,000 | 2.0% |
| 31 | Iowa | 440,161,000 | 1.1% |
| 32 | Kansas | 435,049,000 | 1.1% |
| 17 | Kentucky | 790,229,000 | 2.0% |
| 23 | Louisiana | 575,063,000 | 1.4% |
| 38 | Maine | 242,124,000 | 0.6% |
| 19 | Maryland | 733,410,000 | 1.8% |
| 21 | Massachusetts | 668,112,000 | 1.7% |
| 10 | Michigan | 973,502,000 | 2.4% |
| 15 | Minnesota | 849,218,000 | 2.1% |
| 33 | Mississippi | 417,048,000 | 1.0% |
| 20 | Missouri | 708,064,000 | 1.8% |
| 41 | Montana | 211,992,000 | 0.5% |
| 36 | Nebraska | 299,764,000 | 0.8% |
| 37 | Nevada | 291,400,000 | 0.7% |
| 43 | New Hampshire | 143,794,000 | 0.4% |
| 25 | New Jersey | 539,714,000 | 1.4% |
| 40 | New Mexico | 234,796,000 | 0.6% |
| 7 | New York | 1,604,727,000 | 4.0% |
| 5 | North Carolina | 1,861,838,000 | 4.7% |
| 42 | North Dakota | 204,573,000 | 0.5% |
| 6 | Ohio | 1,684,209,000 | 4.2% |
| 30 | Oklahoma | 444,636,000 | 1.1% |
| 26 | Oregon | 533,420,000 | 1.3% |
| 4 | Pennsylvania | 2,073,677,000 | 5.2% |
| 45 | Rhode Island | 117,663,000 | 0.3% |
| 27 | South Carolina | 531,615,000 | 1.3% |
| 44 | South Dakota | 136,431,000 | 0.3% |
| 16 | Tennessee | 837,787,000 | 2.1% |
| 2 | Texas | 3,178,419,000 | 8.0% |
| 35 | Utah | 372,212,000 | 0.9% |
| 47 | Vermont | 108,177,000 | 0.3% |
| 14 | Virginia | 866,243,000 | 2.2% |
| 9 | Washington | 1,177,987,000 | 3.0% |
| 34 | West Virginia | 387,040,000 | 1.0% |
| 12 | Wisconsin | 893,771,000 | 2.2% |
| 49 | Wyoming | 66,443,000 | 0.2% |

RANK ORDER

| RANK | STATE | REVENUE | % of USA |
|---|---|---|---|
| 1 | California | $5,544,530,000 | 13.9% |
| 2 | Texas | 3,178,419,000 | 8.0% |
| 3 | Florida | 2,273,685,000 | 5.7% |
| 4 | Pennsylvania | 2,073,677,000 | 5.2% |
| 5 | North Carolina | 1,861,838,000 | 4.7% |
| 6 | Ohio | 1,684,209,000 | 4.2% |
| 7 | New York | 1,604,727,000 | 4.0% |
| 8 | Illinois | 1,290,266,000 | 3.2% |
| 9 | Washington | 1,177,987,000 | 3.0% |
| 10 | Michigan | 973,502,000 | 2.4% |
| 11 | Arizona | 896,983,000 | 2.2% |
| 12 | Wisconsin | 893,771,000 | 2.2% |
| 13 | Georgia | 880,987,000 | 2.2% |
| 14 | Virginia | 866,243,000 | 2.2% |
| 15 | Minnesota | 849,218,000 | 2.1% |
| 16 | Tennessee | 837,787,000 | 2.1% |
| 17 | Kentucky | 790,229,000 | 2.0% |
| 18 | Indiana | 783,897,000 | 2.0% |
| 19 | Maryland | 733,410,000 | 1.8% |
| 20 | Missouri | 708,064,000 | 1.8% |
| 21 | Massachusetts | 668,112,000 | 1.7% |
| 22 | Colorado | 630,573,000 | 1.6% |
| 23 | Louisiana | 575,063,000 | 1.4% |
| 24 | Alabama | 541,499,000 | 1.4% |
| 25 | New Jersey | 539,714,000 | 1.4% |
| 26 | Oregon | 533,420,000 | 1.3% |
| 27 | South Carolina | 531,615,000 | 1.3% |
| 28 | Connecticut | 487,104,000 | 1.2% |
| 29 | Arkansas | 467,055,000 | 1.2% |
| 30 | Oklahoma | 444,636,000 | 1.1% |
| 31 | Iowa | 440,161,000 | 1.1% |
| 32 | Kansas | 435,049,000 | 1.1% |
| 33 | Mississippi | 417,048,000 | 1.0% |
| 34 | West Virginia | 387,040,000 | 1.0% |
| 35 | Utah | 372,212,000 | 0.9% |
| 36 | Nebraska | 299,764,000 | 0.8% |
| 37 | Nevada | 291,400,000 | 0.7% |
| 38 | Maine | 242,124,000 | 0.6% |
| 39 | Idaho | 236,769,000 | 0.6% |
| 40 | New Mexico | 234,796,000 | 0.6% |
| 41 | Montana | 211,992,000 | 0.5% |
| 42 | North Dakota | 204,573,000 | 0.5% |
| 43 | New Hampshire | 143,794,000 | 0.4% |
| 44 | South Dakota | 136,431,000 | 0.3% |
| 45 | Rhode Island | 117,663,000 | 0.3% |
| 46 | Delaware | 112,908,000 | 0.3% |
| 47 | Vermont | 108,177,000 | 0.3% |
| 48 | Hawaii | 93,349,000 | 0.2% |
| 49 | Wyoming | 66,443,000 | 0.2% |
| 50 | Alaska | 40,980,000 | 0.1% |
| | District of Columbia* | NA | NA |

Source: U.S. Bureau of the Census, Governments Division
   "2012 State Government Tax Collections" (http://www.census.gov/govs/statetax/)
*Not applicable.

# Per Capita State Government Motor Fuel Sales Tax Revenue in 2012

## National Per Capita = $127

ALPHA ORDER

| RANK | STATE | PER CAPITA |
|------|-------|------------|
| 38 | Alabama | $112 |
| 50 | Alaska | 56 |
| 21 | Arizona | 137 |
| 12 | Arkansas | 158 |
| 17 | California | 146 |
| 29 | Colorado | 122 |
| 23 | Connecticut | 136 |
| 28 | Delaware | 123 |
| 32 | Florida | 118 |
| 46 | Georgia | 89 |
| 48 | Hawaii | 67 |
| 16 | Idaho | 148 |
| 44 | Illinois | 100 |
| 31 | Indiana | 120 |
| 19 | Iowa | 143 |
| 15 | Kansas | 151 |
| 6 | Kentucky | 180 |
| 26 | Louisiana | 125 |
| 5 | Maine | 182 |
| 26 | Maryland | 125 |
| 43 | Massachusetts | 101 |
| 45 | Michigan | 98 |
| 12 | Minnesota | 158 |
| 20 | Mississippi | 140 |
| 32 | Missouri | 118 |
| 2 | Montana | 211 |
| 10 | Nebraska | 162 |
| 41 | Nevada | 106 |
| 40 | New Hampshire | 109 |
| 49 | New Jersey | 61 |
| 36 | New Mexico | 113 |
| 47 | New York | 82 |
| 4 | North Carolina | 191 |
| 1 | North Dakota | 292 |
| 17 | Ohio | 146 |
| 34 | Oklahoma | 117 |
| 21 | Oregon | 137 |
| 10 | Pennsylvania | 162 |
| 38 | Rhode Island | 112 |
| 36 | South Carolina | 113 |
| 9 | South Dakota | 164 |
| 24 | Tennessee | 130 |
| 29 | Texas | 122 |
| 24 | Utah | 130 |
| 7 | Vermont | 173 |
| 41 | Virginia | 106 |
| 8 | Washington | 171 |
| 3 | West Virginia | 209 |
| 14 | Wisconsin | 156 |
| 35 | Wyoming | 115 |

RANK ORDER

| RANK | STATE | PER CAPITA |
|------|-------|------------|
| 1 | North Dakota | $292 |
| 2 | Montana | 211 |
| 3 | West Virginia | 209 |
| 4 | North Carolina | 191 |
| 5 | Maine | 182 |
| 6 | Kentucky | 180 |
| 7 | Vermont | 173 |
| 8 | Washington | 171 |
| 9 | South Dakota | 164 |
| 10 | Nebraska | 162 |
| 10 | Pennsylvania | 162 |
| 12 | Arkansas | 158 |
| 12 | Minnesota | 158 |
| 14 | Wisconsin | 156 |
| 15 | Kansas | 151 |
| 16 | Idaho | 148 |
| 17 | California | 146 |
| 17 | Ohio | 146 |
| 19 | Iowa | 143 |
| 20 | Mississippi | 140 |
| 21 | Arizona | 137 |
| 21 | Oregon | 137 |
| 23 | Connecticut | 136 |
| 24 | Tennessee | 130 |
| 24 | Utah | 130 |
| 26 | Louisiana | 125 |
| 26 | Maryland | 125 |
| 28 | Delaware | 123 |
| 29 | Colorado | 122 |
| 29 | Texas | 122 |
| 31 | Indiana | 120 |
| 32 | Florida | 118 |
| 32 | Missouri | 118 |
| 34 | Oklahoma | 117 |
| 35 | Wyoming | 115 |
| 36 | New Mexico | 113 |
| 36 | South Carolina | 113 |
| 38 | Alabama | 112 |
| 38 | Rhode Island | 112 |
| 40 | New Hampshire | 109 |
| 41 | Nevada | 106 |
| 41 | Virginia | 106 |
| 43 | Massachusetts | 101 |
| 44 | Illinois | 100 |
| 45 | Michigan | 98 |
| 46 | Georgia | 89 |
| 47 | New York | 82 |
| 48 | Hawaii | 67 |
| 49 | New Jersey | 61 |
| 50 | Alaska | 56 |
| | District of Columbia* | NA |

Source: CQ Press using data from U.S. Bureau of the Census, Governments Division
   "2012 State Government Tax Collections" (http://www.census.gov/govs/statetax/)
*Not applicable.

# State Tax Rates on Gasoline in 2013

## National Median = 23.00 Cents per Gallon*

<u>ALPHA ORDER</u>

| RANK | STATE | CENTS PER GALLON |
|---|---|---|
| 40 | Alabama | 18.00 |
| 50 | Alaska | 8.00 |
| 36 | Arizona | 19.00 |
| 28 | Arkansas | 21.80 |
| 1 | California | 43.00 |
| 26 | Colorado | 22.00 |
| 19 | Connecticut | 25.00 |
| 24 | Delaware | 23.00 |
| 46 | Florida | 16.90 |
| 35 | Georgia | 19.50 |
| 44 | Hawaii | 17.00 |
| 16 | Idaho | 26.00 |
| 32 | Illinois | 20.10 |
| 40 | Indiana | 18.00 |
| 26 | Iowa | 22.00 |
| 18 | Kansas | 25.03 |
| 10 | Kentucky | 29.90 |
| 31 | Louisiana | 20.13 |
| 8 | Maine | 30.00 |
| 23 | Maryland | 23.50 |
| 30 | Massachusetts | 21.00 |
| 36 | Michigan | 19.00 |
| 11 | Minnesota | 28.60 |
| 39 | Mississippi | 18.40 |
| 43 | Missouri | 17.30 |
| 13 | Montana | 27.00 |
| 17 | Nebraska | 25.50 |
| 22 | Nevada | 23.81 |
| 34 | New Hampshire | 19.63 |
| 48 | New Jersey | 14.50 |
| 38 | New Mexico | 18.88 |
| 15 | New York | 26.60 |
| 2 | North Carolina | 37.75 |
| 24 | North Dakota | 23.00 |
| 12 | Ohio | 28.00 |
| 44 | Oklahoma | 17.00 |
| 8 | Oregon | 30.00 |
| 7 | Pennsylvania | 31.20 |
| 5 | Rhode Island | 33.00 |
| 47 | South Carolina | 16.75 |
| 21 | South Dakota | 24.00 |
| 29 | Tennessee | 21.40 |
| 33 | Texas | 20.00 |
| 20 | Utah | 24.50 |
| 14 | Vermont | 26.68 |
| 42 | Virginia | 17.50 |
| 3 | Washington | 37.50 |
| 4 | West Virginia | 34.70 |
| 6 | Wisconsin | 32.90 |
| 49 | Wyoming | 14.00 |

<u>RANK ORDER</u>

| RANK | STATE | CENTS PER GALLON |
|---|---|---|
| 1 | California | 43.00 |
| 2 | North Carolina | 37.75 |
| 3 | Washington | 37.50 |
| 4 | West Virginia | 34.70 |
| 5 | Rhode Island | 33.00 |
| 6 | Wisconsin | 32.90 |
| 7 | Pennsylvania | 31.20 |
| 8 | Maine | 30.00 |
| 8 | Oregon | 30.00 |
| 10 | Kentucky | 29.90 |
| 11 | Minnesota | 28.60 |
| 12 | Ohio | 28.00 |
| 13 | Montana | 27.00 |
| 14 | Vermont | 26.68 |
| 15 | New York | 26.60 |
| 16 | Idaho | 26.00 |
| 17 | Nebraska | 25.50 |
| 18 | Kansas | 25.03 |
| 19 | Connecticut | 25.00 |
| 20 | Utah | 24.50 |
| 21 | South Dakota | 24.00 |
| 22 | Nevada | 23.81 |
| 23 | Maryland | 23.50 |
| 24 | Delaware | 23.00 |
| 24 | North Dakota | 23.00 |
| 26 | Colorado | 22.00 |
| 26 | Iowa | 22.00 |
| 28 | Arkansas | 21.80 |
| 29 | Tennessee | 21.40 |
| 30 | Massachusetts | 21.00 |
| 31 | Louisiana | 20.13 |
| 32 | Illinois | 20.10 |
| 33 | Texas | 20.00 |
| 34 | New Hampshire | 19.63 |
| 35 | Georgia | 19.50 |
| 36 | Arizona | 19.00 |
| 36 | Michigan | 19.00 |
| 38 | New Mexico | 18.88 |
| 39 | Mississippi | 18.40 |
| 40 | Alabama | 18.00 |
| 40 | Indiana | 18.00 |
| 42 | Virginia | 17.50 |
| 43 | Missouri | 17.30 |
| 44 | Hawaii | 17.00 |
| 44 | Oklahoma | 17.00 |
| 46 | Florida | 16.90 |
| 47 | South Carolina | 16.75 |
| 48 | New Jersey | 14.50 |
| 49 | Wyoming | 14.00 |
| 50 | Alaska | 8.00 |
| | District of Columbia | 23.50 |

Source: Federation of Tax Administrators
"Motor Fuel Excise Tax Rates" (http://www.taxadmin.org/fta/rate/tax_stru.html)
*As of January 1, 2013. Federal gasoline tax rate is an additional 18.4 cents per gallon. Many states also allow additional local option taxes on gasoline.

# State Government Motor Vehicle and Operators' License Tax Revenue in 2012

## National Total = $25,221,629,000

ALPHA ORDER

| RANK | STATE | REVENUE | % of USA |
|------|-------|---------|----------|
| 26 | Alabama | $223,554,000 | 0.9% |
| 48 | Alaska | 58,196,000 | 0.2% |
| 32 | Arizona | 176,112,000 | 0.7% |
| 35 | Arkansas | 171,699,000 | 0.7% |
| 1 | California | 3,836,019,000 | 15.2% |
| 19 | Colorado | 486,730,000 | 1.9% |
| 25 | Connecticut | 252,631,000 | 1.0% |
| 50 | Delaware | 55,071,000 | 0.2% |
| 4 | Florida | 1,655,169,000 | 6.6% |
| 22 | Georgia | 355,328,000 | 1.4% |
| 27 | Hawaii | 206,651,000 | 0.8% |
| 38 | Idaho | 139,276,000 | 0.6% |
| 3 | Illinois | 1,725,176,000 | 6.8% |
| 13 | Indiana | 541,803,000 | 2.1% |
| 15 | Iowa | 529,008,000 | 2.1% |
| 28 | Kansas | 206,015,000 | 0.8% |
| 29 | Kentucky | 204,452,000 | 0.8% |
| 37 | Louisiana | 144,192,000 | 0.6% |
| 41 | Maine | 109,795,000 | 0.4% |
| 21 | Maryland | 470,200,000 | 1.9% |
| 20 | Massachusetts | 475,451,000 | 1.9% |
| 6 | Michigan | 972,814,000 | 3.9% |
| 11 | Minnesota | 676,531,000 | 2.7% |
| 33 | Mississippi | 174,886,000 | 0.7% |
| 24 | Missouri | 285,327,000 | 1.1% |
| 36 | Montana | 151,851,000 | 0.6% |
| 39 | Nebraska | 128,406,000 | 0.5% |
| 30 | Nevada | 182,876,000 | 0.7% |
| 43 | New Hampshire | 106,866,000 | 0.4% |
| 12 | New Jersey | 658,291,000 | 2.6% |
| 44 | New Mexico | 96,393,000 | 0.4% |
| 5 | New York | 1,550,829,000 | 6.1% |
| 9 | North Carolina | 692,597,000 | 2.7% |
| 40 | North Dakota | 110,521,000 | 0.4% |
| 8 | Ohio | 796,006,000 | 3.2% |
| 10 | Oklahoma | 680,189,000 | 2.7% |
| 16 | Oregon | 506,605,000 | 2.0% |
| 7 | Pennsylvania | 900,338,000 | 3.6% |
| 49 | Rhode Island | 57,518,000 | 0.2% |
| 31 | South Carolina | 179,150,000 | 0.7% |
| 46 | South Dakota | 68,502,000 | 0.3% |
| 23 | Tennessee | 308,737,000 | 1.2% |
| 2 | Texas | 1,963,629,000 | 7.8% |
| 34 | Utah | 173,156,000 | 0.7% |
| 45 | Vermont | 72,257,000 | 0.3% |
| 18 | Virginia | 491,933,000 | 2.0% |
| 14 | Washington | 540,761,000 | 2.1% |
| 42 | West Virginia | 107,649,000 | 0.4% |
| 17 | Wisconsin | 496,592,000 | 2.0% |
| 47 | Wyoming | 67,891,000 | 0.3% |

RANK ORDER

| RANK | STATE | REVENUE | % of USA |
|------|-------|---------|----------|
| 1 | California | $3,836,019,000 | 15.2% |
| 2 | Texas | 1,963,629,000 | 7.8% |
| 3 | Illinois | 1,725,176,000 | 6.8% |
| 4 | Florida | 1,655,169,000 | 6.6% |
| 5 | New York | 1,550,829,000 | 6.1% |
| 6 | Michigan | 972,814,000 | 3.9% |
| 7 | Pennsylvania | 900,338,000 | 3.6% |
| 8 | Ohio | 796,006,000 | 3.2% |
| 9 | North Carolina | 692,597,000 | 2.7% |
| 10 | Oklahoma | 680,189,000 | 2.7% |
| 11 | Minnesota | 676,531,000 | 2.7% |
| 12 | New Jersey | 658,291,000 | 2.6% |
| 13 | Indiana | 541,803,000 | 2.1% |
| 14 | Washington | 540,761,000 | 2.1% |
| 15 | Iowa | 529,008,000 | 2.1% |
| 16 | Oregon | 506,605,000 | 2.0% |
| 17 | Wisconsin | 496,592,000 | 2.0% |
| 18 | Virginia | 491,933,000 | 2.0% |
| 19 | Colorado | 486,730,000 | 1.9% |
| 20 | Massachusetts | 475,451,000 | 1.9% |
| 21 | Maryland | 470,200,000 | 1.9% |
| 22 | Georgia | 355,328,000 | 1.4% |
| 23 | Tennessee | 308,737,000 | 1.2% |
| 24 | Missouri | 285,327,000 | 1.1% |
| 25 | Connecticut | 252,631,000 | 1.0% |
| 26 | Alabama | 223,554,000 | 0.9% |
| 27 | Hawaii | 206,651,000 | 0.8% |
| 28 | Kansas | 206,015,000 | 0.8% |
| 29 | Kentucky | 204,452,000 | 0.8% |
| 30 | Nevada | 182,876,000 | 0.7% |
| 31 | South Carolina | 179,150,000 | 0.7% |
| 32 | Arizona | 176,112,000 | 0.7% |
| 33 | Mississippi | 174,886,000 | 0.7% |
| 34 | Utah | 173,156,000 | 0.7% |
| 35 | Arkansas | 171,699,000 | 0.7% |
| 36 | Montana | 151,851,000 | 0.6% |
| 37 | Louisiana | 144,192,000 | 0.6% |
| 38 | Idaho | 139,276,000 | 0.6% |
| 39 | Nebraska | 128,406,000 | 0.5% |
| 40 | North Dakota | 110,521,000 | 0.4% |
| 41 | Maine | 109,795,000 | 0.4% |
| 42 | West Virginia | 107,649,000 | 0.4% |
| 43 | New Hampshire | 106,866,000 | 0.4% |
| 44 | New Mexico | 96,393,000 | 0.4% |
| 45 | Vermont | 72,257,000 | 0.3% |
| 46 | South Dakota | 68,502,000 | 0.3% |
| 47 | Wyoming | 67,891,000 | 0.3% |
| 48 | Alaska | 58,196,000 | 0.2% |
| 49 | Rhode Island | 57,518,000 | 0.2% |
| 50 | Delaware | 55,071,000 | 0.2% |
| | District of Columbia* | NA | NA |

Source: U.S. Bureau of the Census, Governments Division
"2012 State Government Tax Collections" (http://www.census.gov/govs/statetax/)
*Not applicable.

# Per Capita State Government Motor Vehicle and Operators' License Tax Revenue in 2012
## National Per Capita = $80.51

ALPHA ORDER

| RANK | STATE | PER CAPITA |
|------|-------|-----------|
| 45 | Alabama | $46.36 |
| 22 | Alaska | 79.56 |
| 50 | Arizona | 26.87 |
| 39 | Arkansas | 58.22 |
| 11 | California | 100.84 |
| 13 | Colorado | 93.83 |
| 31 | Connecticut | 70.36 |
| 37 | Delaware | 60.05 |
| 16 | Florida | 85.68 |
| 48 | Georgia | 35.82 |
| 5 | Hawaii | 148.42 |
| 14 | Idaho | 87.28 |
| 6 | Illinois | 133.99 |
| 17 | Indiana | 82.88 |
| 2 | Iowa | 172.08 |
| 28 | Kansas | 71.39 |
| 44 | Kentucky | 46.67 |
| 49 | Louisiana | 31.33 |
| 18 | Maine | 82.60 |
| 21 | Maryland | 79.90 |
| 27 | Massachusetts | 71.54 |
| 12 | Michigan | 98.43 |
| 8 | Minnesota | 125.77 |
| 38 | Mississippi | 58.59 |
| 43 | Missouri | 47.38 |
| 4 | Montana | 151.07 |
| 32 | Nebraska | 69.20 |
| 34 | Nevada | 66.29 |
| 20 | New Hampshire | 80.92 |
| 26 | New Jersey | 74.26 |
| 46 | New Mexico | 46.22 |
| 23 | New York | 79.24 |
| 29 | North Carolina | 71.02 |
| 3 | North Dakota | 157.97 |
| 33 | Ohio | 68.95 |
| 1 | Oklahoma | 178.30 |
| 7 | Oregon | 129.92 |
| 30 | Pennsylvania | 70.54 |
| 41 | Rhode Island | 54.76 |
| 47 | South Carolina | 37.93 |
| 19 | South Dakota | 82.20 |
| 42 | Tennessee | 47.82 |
| 25 | Texas | 75.35 |
| 35 | Utah | 60.64 |
| 10 | Vermont | 115.42 |
| 36 | Virginia | 60.10 |
| 24 | Washington | 78.41 |
| 40 | West Virginia | 58.02 |
| 15 | Wisconsin | 86.72 |
| 9 | Wyoming | 117.78 |

RANK ORDER

| RANK | STATE | PER CAPITA |
|------|-------|-----------|
| 1 | Oklahoma | $178.30 |
| 2 | Iowa | 172.08 |
| 3 | North Dakota | 157.97 |
| 4 | Montana | 151.07 |
| 5 | Hawaii | 148.42 |
| 6 | Illinois | 133.99 |
| 7 | Oregon | 129.92 |
| 8 | Minnesota | 125.77 |
| 9 | Wyoming | 117.78 |
| 10 | Vermont | 115.42 |
| 11 | California | 100.84 |
| 12 | Michigan | 98.43 |
| 13 | Colorado | 93.83 |
| 14 | Idaho | 87.28 |
| 15 | Wisconsin | 86.72 |
| 16 | Florida | 85.68 |
| 17 | Indiana | 82.88 |
| 18 | Maine | 82.60 |
| 19 | South Dakota | 82.20 |
| 20 | New Hampshire | 80.92 |
| 21 | Maryland | 79.90 |
| 22 | Alaska | 79.56 |
| 23 | New York | 79.24 |
| 24 | Washington | 78.41 |
| 25 | Texas | 75.35 |
| 26 | New Jersey | 74.26 |
| 27 | Massachusetts | 71.54 |
| 28 | Kansas | 71.39 |
| 29 | North Carolina | 71.02 |
| 30 | Pennsylvania | 70.54 |
| 31 | Connecticut | 70.36 |
| 32 | Nebraska | 69.20 |
| 33 | Ohio | 68.95 |
| 34 | Nevada | 66.29 |
| 35 | Utah | 60.64 |
| 36 | Virginia | 60.10 |
| 37 | Delaware | 60.05 |
| 38 | Mississippi | 58.59 |
| 39 | Arkansas | 58.22 |
| 40 | West Virginia | 58.02 |
| 41 | Rhode Island | 54.76 |
| 42 | Tennessee | 47.82 |
| 43 | Missouri | 47.38 |
| 44 | Kentucky | 46.67 |
| 45 | Alabama | 46.36 |
| 46 | New Mexico | 46.22 |
| 47 | South Carolina | 37.93 |
| 48 | Georgia | 35.82 |
| 49 | Louisiana | 31.33 |
| 50 | Arizona | 26.87 |
| | District of Columbia* | NA |

Source: CQ Press using data from U.S. Bureau of the Census, Governments Division
  "2012 State Government Tax Collections" (http://www.census.gov/govs/statetax/)
*Not applicable.

# State Government Tobacco Product Sales Tax Revenue in 2012

## National Total = $17,086,174,000

ALPHA ORDER

| RANK | STATE | REVENUE | % of USA |
|---|---|---|---|
| 33 | Alabama | $126,151,000 | 0.7% |
| 44 | Alaska | 67,382,000 | 0.4% |
| 17 | Arizona | 319,467,000 | 1.9% |
| 23 | Arkansas | 246,976,000 | 1.4% |
| 5 | California | 895,677,000 | 5.2% |
| 27 | Colorado | 203,399,000 | 1.2% |
| 14 | Connecticut | 418,231,000 | 2.4% |
| 36 | Delaware | 120,850,000 | 0.7% |
| 16 | Florida | 381,485,000 | 2.2% |
| 24 | Georgia | 227,146,000 | 1.3% |
| 35 | Hawaii | 121,971,000 | 0.7% |
| 46 | Idaho | 48,461,000 | 0.3% |
| 8 | Illinois | 606,422,000 | 3.5% |
| 12 | Indiana | 465,200,000 | 2.7% |
| 25 | Iowa | 225,499,000 | 1.3% |
| 39 | Kansas | 103,639,000 | 0.6% |
| 21 | Kentucky | 276,544,000 | 1.6% |
| 31 | Louisiana | 133,194,000 | 0.8% |
| 30 | Maine | 139,729,000 | 0.8% |
| 15 | Maryland | 411,427,000 | 2.4% |
| 10 | Massachusetts | 573,759,000 | 3.4% |
| 4 | Michigan | 951,319,000 | 5.6% |
| 13 | Minnesota | 421,545,000 | 2.5% |
| 29 | Mississippi | 157,433,000 | 0.9% |
| 38 | Missouri | 104,918,000 | 0.6% |
| 41 | Montana | 87,148,000 | 0.5% |
| 47 | Nebraska | 33,725,000 | 0.2% |
| 40 | Nevada | 102,644,000 | 0.6% |
| 26 | New Hampshire | 215,161,000 | 1.3% |
| 7 | New Jersey | 792,066,000 | 4.6% |
| 43 | New Mexico | 74,800,000 | 0.4% |
| 1 | New York | 1,631,995,000 | 9.6% |
| 18 | North Carolina | 294,754,000 | 1.7% |
| 48 | North Dakota | 28,240,000 | 0.2% |
| 6 | Ohio | 843,180,000 | 4.9% |
| 19 | Oklahoma | 292,973,000 | 1.7% |
| 22 | Oregon | 255,652,000 | 1.5% |
| 3 | Pennsylvania | 1,118,961,000 | 6.5% |
| 32 | Rhode Island | 130,811,000 | 0.8% |
| 49 | South Carolina | 26,247,000 | 0.2% |
| 45 | South Dakota | 60,372,000 | 0.4% |
| 20 | Tennessee | 279,017,000 | 1.6% |
| 2 | Texas | 1,469,712,000 | 8.6% |
| 34 | Utah | 123,988,000 | 0.7% |
| 42 | Vermont | 80,230,000 | 0.5% |
| 28 | Virginia | 192,441,000 | 1.1% |
| 11 | Washington | 470,765,000 | 2.8% |
| 37 | West Virginia | 109,618,000 | 0.6% |
| 9 | Wisconsin | 597,866,000 | 3.5% |
| 50 | Wyoming | 25,984,000 | 0.2% |

RANK ORDER

| RANK | STATE | REVENUE | % of USA |
|---|---|---|---|
| 1 | New York | $1,631,995,000 | 9.6% |
| 2 | Texas | 1,469,712,000 | 8.6% |
| 3 | Pennsylvania | 1,118,961,000 | 6.5% |
| 4 | Michigan | 951,319,000 | 5.6% |
| 5 | California | 895,677,000 | 5.2% |
| 6 | Ohio | 843,180,000 | 4.9% |
| 7 | New Jersey | 792,066,000 | 4.6% |
| 8 | Illinois | 606,422,000 | 3.5% |
| 9 | Wisconsin | 597,866,000 | 3.5% |
| 10 | Massachusetts | 573,759,000 | 3.4% |
| 11 | Washington | 470,765,000 | 2.8% |
| 12 | Indiana | 465,200,000 | 2.7% |
| 13 | Minnesota | 421,545,000 | 2.5% |
| 14 | Connecticut | 418,231,000 | 2.4% |
| 15 | Maryland | 411,427,000 | 2.4% |
| 16 | Florida | 381,485,000 | 2.2% |
| 17 | Arizona | 319,467,000 | 1.9% |
| 18 | North Carolina | 294,754,000 | 1.7% |
| 19 | Oklahoma | 292,973,000 | 1.7% |
| 20 | Tennessee | 279,017,000 | 1.6% |
| 21 | Kentucky | 276,544,000 | 1.6% |
| 22 | Oregon | 255,652,000 | 1.5% |
| 23 | Arkansas | 246,976,000 | 1.4% |
| 24 | Georgia | 227,146,000 | 1.3% |
| 25 | Iowa | 225,499,000 | 1.3% |
| 26 | New Hampshire | 215,161,000 | 1.3% |
| 27 | Colorado | 203,399,000 | 1.2% |
| 28 | Virginia | 192,441,000 | 1.1% |
| 29 | Mississippi | 157,433,000 | 0.9% |
| 30 | Maine | 139,729,000 | 0.8% |
| 31 | Louisiana | 133,194,000 | 0.8% |
| 32 | Rhode Island | 130,811,000 | 0.8% |
| 33 | Alabama | 126,151,000 | 0.7% |
| 34 | Utah | 123,988,000 | 0.7% |
| 35 | Hawaii | 121,971,000 | 0.7% |
| 36 | Delaware | 120,850,000 | 0.7% |
| 37 | West Virginia | 109,618,000 | 0.6% |
| 38 | Missouri | 104,918,000 | 0.6% |
| 39 | Kansas | 103,639,000 | 0.6% |
| 40 | Nevada | 102,644,000 | 0.6% |
| 41 | Montana | 87,148,000 | 0.5% |
| 42 | Vermont | 80,230,000 | 0.5% |
| 43 | New Mexico | 74,800,000 | 0.4% |
| 44 | Alaska | 67,382,000 | 0.4% |
| 45 | South Dakota | 60,372,000 | 0.4% |
| 46 | Idaho | 48,461,000 | 0.3% |
| 47 | Nebraska | 33,725,000 | 0.2% |
| 48 | North Dakota | 28,240,000 | 0.2% |
| 49 | South Carolina | 26,247,000 | 0.2% |
| 50 | Wyoming | 25,984,000 | 0.2% |
| | District of Columbia* | NA | NA |

Source: U.S. Bureau of the Census, Governments Division
"2012 State Government Tax Collections" (http://www.census.gov/govs/statetax/)
*Not applicable.

# Per Capita State Government Tobacco Sales Tax Revenue in 2012

## National Per Capita = $54.54

ALPHA ORDER

| RANK | STATE | PER CAPITA |
|------|-------|------------|
| 43 | Alabama | $26.16 |
| 9 | Alaska | 92.12 |
| 30 | Arizona | 48.75 |
| 15 | Arkansas | 83.75 |
| 44 | California | 23.54 |
| 36 | Colorado | 39.21 |
| 5 | Connecticut | 116.49 |
| 2 | Delaware | 131.78 |
| 47 | Florida | 19.75 |
| 46 | Georgia | 22.90 |
| 12 | Hawaii | 87.60 |
| 40 | Idaho | 30.37 |
| 31 | Illinois | 47.10 |
| 22 | Indiana | 71.16 |
| 19 | Iowa | 73.35 |
| 38 | Kansas | 35.91 |
| 26 | Kentucky | 63.13 |
| 42 | Louisiana | 28.94 |
| 6 | Maine | 105.12 |
| 23 | Maryland | 69.92 |
| 14 | Massachusetts | 86.33 |
| 8 | Michigan | 96.25 |
| 17 | Minnesota | 78.37 |
| 29 | Mississippi | 52.74 |
| 49 | Missouri | 17.42 |
| 13 | Montana | 86.70 |
| 48 | Nebraska | 18.18 |
| 37 | Nevada | 37.20 |
| 1 | New Hampshire | 162.91 |
| 10 | New Jersey | 89.35 |
| 39 | New Mexico | 35.87 |
| 16 | New York | 83.39 |
| 41 | North Carolina | 30.22 |
| 35 | North Dakota | 40.36 |
| 20 | Ohio | 73.04 |
| 18 | Oklahoma | 76.80 |
| 25 | Oregon | 65.56 |
| 11 | Pennsylvania | 87.67 |
| 4 | Rhode Island | 124.55 |
| 50 | South Carolina | 5.56 |
| 21 | South Dakota | 72.44 |
| 34 | Tennessee | 43.22 |
| 28 | Texas | 56.40 |
| 33 | Utah | 43.42 |
| 3 | Vermont | 128.16 |
| 45 | Virginia | 23.51 |
| 24 | Washington | 68.26 |
| 27 | West Virginia | 59.08 |
| 7 | Wisconsin | 104.41 |
| 32 | Wyoming | 45.08 |

RANK ORDER

| RANK | STATE | PER CAPITA |
|------|-------|------------|
| 1 | New Hampshire | $162.91 |
| 2 | Delaware | 131.78 |
| 3 | Vermont | 128.16 |
| 4 | Rhode Island | 124.55 |
| 5 | Connecticut | 116.49 |
| 6 | Maine | 105.12 |
| 7 | Wisconsin | 104.41 |
| 8 | Michigan | 96.25 |
| 9 | Alaska | 92.12 |
| 10 | New Jersey | 89.35 |
| 11 | Pennsylvania | 87.67 |
| 12 | Hawaii | 87.60 |
| 13 | Montana | 86.70 |
| 14 | Massachusetts | 86.33 |
| 15 | Arkansas | 83.75 |
| 16 | New York | 83.39 |
| 17 | Minnesota | 78.37 |
| 18 | Oklahoma | 76.80 |
| 19 | Iowa | 73.35 |
| 20 | Ohio | 73.04 |
| 21 | South Dakota | 72.44 |
| 22 | Indiana | 71.16 |
| 23 | Maryland | 69.92 |
| 24 | Washington | 68.26 |
| 25 | Oregon | 65.56 |
| 26 | Kentucky | 63.13 |
| 27 | West Virginia | 59.08 |
| 28 | Texas | 56.40 |
| 29 | Mississippi | 52.74 |
| 30 | Arizona | 48.75 |
| 31 | Illinois | 47.10 |
| 32 | Wyoming | 45.08 |
| 33 | Utah | 43.42 |
| 34 | Tennessee | 43.22 |
| 35 | North Dakota | 40.36 |
| 36 | Colorado | 39.21 |
| 37 | Nevada | 37.20 |
| 38 | Kansas | 35.91 |
| 39 | New Mexico | 35.87 |
| 40 | Idaho | 30.37 |
| 41 | North Carolina | 30.22 |
| 42 | Louisiana | 28.94 |
| 43 | Alabama | 26.16 |
| 44 | California | 23.54 |
| 45 | Virginia | 23.51 |
| 46 | Georgia | 22.90 |
| 47 | Florida | 19.75 |
| 48 | Nebraska | 18.18 |
| 49 | Missouri | 17.42 |
| 50 | South Carolina | 5.56 |
| | District of Columbia* | NA |

Source: CQ Press using data from U.S. Bureau of the Census, Governments Division
   "2012 State Government Tax Collections" (http://www.census.gov/govs/statetax/)
*Not applicable.

# State Tax on a Pack of Cigarettes in 2014

## National Median = $1.36 per Pack*

ALPHA ORDER

| RANK | STATE | TAX PER PACK |
|---|---|---|
| 46 | Alabama | $0.43 |
| 11 | Alaska | 2.00 |
| 11 | Arizona | 2.00 |
| 29 | Arkansas | 1.15 |
| 32 | California | 0.87 |
| 33 | Colorado | 0.84 |
| 4 | Connecticut | 3.40 |
| 21 | Delaware | 1.60 |
| 26 | Florida | 1.34 |
| 47 | Georgia | 0.37 |
| 5 | Hawaii | 3.20 |
| 41 | Idaho | 0.57 |
| 16 | Illinois | 1.98 |
| 31 | Indiana | 1.00 |
| 25 | Iowa | 1.36 |
| 35 | Kansas | 0.79 |
| 39 | Kentucky | 0.60 |
| 48 | Louisiana | 0.36 |
| 11 | Maine | 2.00 |
| 11 | Maryland | 2.00 |
| 2 | Massachusetts | 3.51 |
| 11 | Michigan | 2.00 |
| 7 | Minnesota | 2.83 |
| 36 | Mississippi | 0.68 |
| 50 | Missouri | 0.17 |
| 18 | Montana | 1.70 |
| 37 | Nebraska | 0.64 |
| 34 | Nevada | 0.80 |
| 17 | New Hampshire | 1.78 |
| 8 | New Jersey | 2.70 |
| 20 | New Mexico | 1.66 |
| 1 | New York | 4.35 |
| 44 | North Carolina | 0.45 |
| 45 | North Dakota | 0.44 |
| 28 | Ohio | 1.25 |
| 30 | Oklahoma | 1.03 |
| 27 | Oregon | 1.31 |
| 21 | Pennsylvania | 1.60 |
| 3 | Rhode Island | 3.50 |
| 41 | South Carolina | 0.57 |
| 23 | South Dakota | 1.53 |
| 38 | Tennessee | 0.62 |
| 24 | Texas | 1.41 |
| 18 | Utah | 1.70 |
| 9 | Vermont | 2.62 |
| 49 | Virginia | 0.30 |
| 6 | Washington | 3.03 |
| 43 | West Virginia | 0.55 |
| 10 | Wisconsin | 2.52 |
| 39 | Wyoming | 0.60 |

RANK ORDER

| RANK | STATE | TAX PER PACK |
|---|---|---|
| 1 | New York | $4.35 |
| 2 | Massachusetts | 3.51 |
| 3 | Rhode Island | 3.50 |
| 4 | Connecticut | 3.40 |
| 5 | Hawaii | 3.20 |
| 6 | Washington | 3.03 |
| 7 | Minnesota | 2.83 |
| 8 | New Jersey | 2.70 |
| 9 | Vermont | 2.62 |
| 10 | Wisconsin | 2.52 |
| 11 | Alaska | 2.00 |
| 11 | Arizona | 2.00 |
| 11 | Maine | 2.00 |
| 11 | Maryland | 2.00 |
| 11 | Michigan | 2.00 |
| 16 | Illinois | 1.98 |
| 17 | New Hampshire | 1.78 |
| 18 | Montana | 1.70 |
| 18 | Utah | 1.70 |
| 20 | New Mexico | 1.66 |
| 21 | Delaware | 1.60 |
| 21 | Pennsylvania | 1.60 |
| 23 | South Dakota | 1.53 |
| 24 | Texas | 1.41 |
| 25 | Iowa | 1.36 |
| 26 | Florida | 1.34 |
| 27 | Oregon | 1.31 |
| 28 | Ohio | 1.25 |
| 29 | Arkansas | 1.15 |
| 30 | Oklahoma | 1.03 |
| 31 | Indiana | 1.00 |
| 32 | California | 0.87 |
| 33 | Colorado | 0.84 |
| 34 | Nevada | 0.80 |
| 35 | Kansas | 0.79 |
| 36 | Mississippi | 0.68 |
| 37 | Nebraska | 0.64 |
| 38 | Tennessee | 0.62 |
| 39 | Kentucky | 0.60 |
| 39 | Wyoming | 0.60 |
| 41 | Idaho | 0.57 |
| 41 | South Carolina | 0.57 |
| 43 | West Virginia | 0.55 |
| 44 | North Carolina | 0.45 |
| 45 | North Dakota | 0.44 |
| 46 | Alabama | 0.43 |
| 47 | Georgia | 0.37 |
| 48 | Louisiana | 0.36 |
| 49 | Virginia | 0.30 |
| 50 | Missouri | 0.17 |
| | District of Columbia | 2.50 |

Source: Federation of Tax Administrators
   "State Excise Tax Rates on Cigarettes" (http://www.taxadmin.org/FTA/rate/tax_stru.html)
*As of January 1, 2014.  Many states also allow additional local option taxes on cigarettes.

# State Government Alcoholic Beverage Sales Tax Revenue in 2012

## National Total = $6,018,645,000

ALPHA ORDER

| RANK | STATE | REVENUE | % of USA |
|------|-------|---------|----------|
| 11 | Alabama | $173,251,000 | 2.9% |
| 34 | Alaska | 40,230,000 | 0.7% |
| 23 | Arizona | 68,379,000 | 1.1% |
| 28 | Arkansas | 48,803,000 | 0.8% |
| 4 | California | 346,000,000 | 5.7% |
| 35 | Colorado | 38,817,000 | 0.6% |
| 24 | Connecticut | 60,595,000 | 1.0% |
| 41 | Delaware | 17,654,000 | 0.3% |
| 2 | Florida | 527,016,000 | 8.8% |
| 10 | Georgia | 175,051,000 | 2.9% |
| 27 | Hawaii | 48,854,000 | 0.8% |
| 49 | Idaho | 8,099,000 | 0.1% |
| 7 | Illinois | 279,270,000 | 4.6% |
| 30 | Indiana | 44,155,000 | 0.7% |
| 45 | Iowa | 14,727,000 | 0.2% |
| 17 | Kansas | 118,202,000 | 2.0% |
| 16 | Kentucky | 118,253,000 | 2.0% |
| 25 | Louisiana | 56,869,000 | 0.9% |
| 42 | Maine | 17,352,000 | 0.3% |
| 38 | Maryland | 31,010,000 | 0.5% |
| 22 | Massachusetts | 77,861,000 | 1.3% |
| 13 | Michigan | 149,159,000 | 2.5% |
| 21 | Minnesota | 79,389,000 | 1.3% |
| 31 | Mississippi | 42,183,000 | 0.7% |
| 36 | Missouri | 34,341,000 | 0.6% |
| 37 | Montana | 34,019,000 | 0.6% |
| 39 | Nebraska | 28,472,000 | 0.5% |
| 32 | Nevada | 41,695,000 | 0.7% |
| 47 | New Hampshire | 9,723,000 | 0.2% |
| 14 | New Jersey | 135,304,000 | 2.2% |
| 33 | New Mexico | 40,574,000 | 0.7% |
| 8 | New York | 238,932,000 | 4.0% |
| 6 | North Carolina | 322,970,000 | 5.4% |
| 48 | North Dakota | 8,463,000 | 0.1% |
| 19 | Ohio | 98,113,000 | 1.6% |
| 18 | Oklahoma | 103,831,000 | 1.7% |
| 43 | Oregon | 17,322,000 | 0.3% |
| 5 | Pennsylvania | 324,024,000 | 5.4% |
| 46 | Rhode Island | 12,785,000 | 0.2% |
| 12 | South Carolina | 153,951,000 | 2.6% |
| 44 | South Dakota | 15,449,000 | 0.3% |
| 15 | Tennessee | 133,055,000 | 2.2% |
| 1 | Texas | 937,614,000 | 15.6% |
| 29 | Utah | 45,823,000 | 0.8% |
| 40 | Vermont | 22,403,000 | 0.4% |
| 9 | Virginia | 190,796,000 | 3.2% |
| 3 | Washington | 349,164,000 | 5.8% |
| 20 | West Virginia | 87,240,000 | 1.4% |
| 26 | Wisconsin | 49,661,000 | 0.8% |
| 50 | Wyoming | 1,742,000 | 0.0% |

RANK ORDER

| RANK | STATE | REVENUE | % of USA |
|------|-------|---------|----------|
| 1 | Texas | $937,614,000 | 15.6% |
| 2 | Florida | 527,016,000 | 8.8% |
| 3 | Washington | 349,164,000 | 5.8% |
| 4 | California | 346,000,000 | 5.7% |
| 5 | Pennsylvania | 324,024,000 | 5.4% |
| 6 | North Carolina | 322,970,000 | 5.4% |
| 7 | Illinois | 279,270,000 | 4.6% |
| 8 | New York | 238,932,000 | 4.0% |
| 9 | Virginia | 190,796,000 | 3.2% |
| 10 | Georgia | 175,051,000 | 2.9% |
| 11 | Alabama | 173,251,000 | 2.9% |
| 12 | South Carolina | 153,951,000 | 2.6% |
| 13 | Michigan | 149,159,000 | 2.5% |
| 14 | New Jersey | 135,304,000 | 2.2% |
| 15 | Tennessee | 133,055,000 | 2.2% |
| 16 | Kentucky | 118,253,000 | 2.0% |
| 17 | Kansas | 118,202,000 | 2.0% |
| 18 | Oklahoma | 103,831,000 | 1.7% |
| 19 | Ohio | 98,113,000 | 1.6% |
| 20 | West Virginia | 87,240,000 | 1.4% |
| 21 | Minnesota | 79,389,000 | 1.3% |
| 22 | Massachusetts | 77,861,000 | 1.3% |
| 23 | Arizona | 68,379,000 | 1.1% |
| 24 | Connecticut | 60,595,000 | 1.0% |
| 25 | Louisiana | 56,869,000 | 0.9% |
| 26 | Wisconsin | 49,661,000 | 0.8% |
| 27 | Hawaii | 48,854,000 | 0.8% |
| 28 | Arkansas | 48,803,000 | 0.8% |
| 29 | Utah | 45,823,000 | 0.8% |
| 30 | Indiana | 44,155,000 | 0.7% |
| 31 | Mississippi | 42,183,000 | 0.7% |
| 32 | Nevada | 41,695,000 | 0.7% |
| 33 | New Mexico | 40,574,000 | 0.7% |
| 34 | Alaska | 40,230,000 | 0.7% |
| 35 | Colorado | 38,817,000 | 0.6% |
| 36 | Missouri | 34,341,000 | 0.6% |
| 37 | Montana | 34,019,000 | 0.6% |
| 38 | Maryland | 31,010,000 | 0.5% |
| 39 | Nebraska | 28,472,000 | 0.5% |
| 40 | Vermont | 22,403,000 | 0.4% |
| 41 | Delaware | 17,654,000 | 0.3% |
| 42 | Maine | 17,352,000 | 0.3% |
| 43 | Oregon | 17,322,000 | 0.3% |
| 44 | South Dakota | 15,449,000 | 0.3% |
| 45 | Iowa | 14,727,000 | 0.2% |
| 46 | Rhode Island | 12,785,000 | 0.2% |
| 47 | New Hampshire | 9,723,000 | 0.2% |
| 48 | North Dakota | 8,463,000 | 0.1% |
| 49 | Idaho | 8,099,000 | 0.1% |
| 50 | Wyoming | 1,742,000 | 0.0% |
| | District of Columbia* | NA | NA |

Source: U.S. Bureau of the Census, Governments Division
"2012 State Government Tax Collections" (http://www.census.gov/govs/statetax/)
*Not applicable.

# Per Capita State Government Alcoholic Beverage Sales Tax Revenue in 2012

## National Per Capita = $19.21

ALPHA ORDER

| RANK | STATE | PER CAPITA |
|---|---|---|
| 6 | Alabama | $35.93 |
| 1 | Alaska | 55.00 |
| 38 | Arizona | 10.43 |
| 24 | Arkansas | 16.55 |
| 39 | California | 9.10 |
| 42 | Colorado | 7.48 |
| 23 | Connecticut | 16.88 |
| 20 | Delaware | 19.25 |
| 12 | Florida | 27.28 |
| 22 | Georgia | 17.65 |
| 8 | Hawaii | 35.09 |
| 47 | Idaho | 5.08 |
| 17 | Illinois | 21.69 |
| 44 | Indiana | 6.75 |
| 48 | Iowa | 4.79 |
| 4 | Kansas | 40.96 |
| 14 | Kentucky | 27.00 |
| 33 | Louisiana | 12.36 |
| 32 | Maine | 13.05 |
| 46 | Maryland | 5.27 |
| 37 | Massachusetts | 11.72 |
| 29 | Michigan | 15.09 |
| 30 | Minnesota | 14.76 |
| 31 | Mississippi | 14.13 |
| 45 | Missouri | 5.70 |
| 9 | Montana | 33.85 |
| 26 | Nebraska | 15.34 |
| 28 | Nevada | 15.11 |
| 43 | New Hampshire | 7.36 |
| 27 | New Jersey | 15.26 |
| 19 | New Mexico | 19.45 |
| 34 | New York | 12.21 |
| 10 | North Carolina | 33.12 |
| 36 | North Dakota | 12.10 |
| 41 | Ohio | 8.50 |
| 13 | Oklahoma | 27.22 |
| 49 | Oregon | 4.44 |
| 15 | Pennsylvania | 25.39 |
| 35 | Rhode Island | 12.17 |
| 11 | South Carolina | 32.59 |
| 21 | South Dakota | 18.54 |
| 18 | Tennessee | 20.61 |
| 5 | Texas | 35.98 |
| 25 | Utah | 16.05 |
| 7 | Vermont | 35.79 |
| 16 | Virginia | 23.31 |
| 2 | Washington | 50.63 |
| 3 | West Virginia | 47.02 |
| 40 | Wisconsin | 8.67 |
| 50 | Wyoming | 3.02 |

RANK ORDER

| RANK | STATE | PER CAPITA |
|---|---|---|
| 1 | Alaska | $55.00 |
| 2 | Washington | 50.63 |
| 3 | West Virginia | 47.02 |
| 4 | Kansas | 40.96 |
| 5 | Texas | 35.98 |
| 6 | Alabama | 35.93 |
| 7 | Vermont | 35.79 |
| 8 | Hawaii | 35.09 |
| 9 | Montana | 33.85 |
| 10 | North Carolina | 33.12 |
| 11 | South Carolina | 32.59 |
| 12 | Florida | 27.28 |
| 13 | Oklahoma | 27.22 |
| 14 | Kentucky | 27.00 |
| 15 | Pennsylvania | 25.39 |
| 16 | Virginia | 23.31 |
| 17 | Illinois | 21.69 |
| 18 | Tennessee | 20.61 |
| 19 | New Mexico | 19.45 |
| 20 | Delaware | 19.25 |
| 21 | South Dakota | 18.54 |
| 22 | Georgia | 17.65 |
| 23 | Connecticut | 16.88 |
| 24 | Arkansas | 16.55 |
| 25 | Utah | 16.05 |
| 26 | Nebraska | 15.34 |
| 27 | New Jersey | 15.26 |
| 28 | Nevada | 15.11 |
| 29 | Michigan | 15.09 |
| 30 | Minnesota | 14.76 |
| 31 | Mississippi | 14.13 |
| 32 | Maine | 13.05 |
| 33 | Louisiana | 12.36 |
| 34 | New York | 12.21 |
| 35 | Rhode Island | 12.17 |
| 36 | North Dakota | 12.10 |
| 37 | Massachusetts | 11.72 |
| 38 | Arizona | 10.43 |
| 39 | California | 9.10 |
| 40 | Wisconsin | 8.67 |
| 41 | Ohio | 8.50 |
| 42 | Colorado | 7.48 |
| 43 | New Hampshire | 7.36 |
| 44 | Indiana | 6.75 |
| 45 | Missouri | 5.70 |
| 46 | Maryland | 5.27 |
| 47 | Idaho | 5.08 |
| 48 | Iowa | 4.79 |
| 49 | Oregon | 4.44 |
| 50 | Wyoming | 3.02 |
| | District of Columbia* | NA |

Source: CQ Press using data from U.S. Bureau of the Census, Governments Division
   "2012 State Government Tax Collections" (http://www.census.gov/govs/statetax/)
*Not applicable.

# State Government Total Expenditures in 2011

## National Total = $2,004,325,002,000*

ALPHA ORDER

| RANK | STATE | EXPENDITURES | % of USA |
|---|---|---|---|
| 27 | Alabama | $28,061,237,000 | 1.4% |
| 39 | Alaska | 11,320,127,000 | 0.6% |
| 20 | Arizona | 32,875,412,000 | 1.6% |
| 32 | Arkansas | 18,861,507,000 | 0.9% |
| 1 | California | 282,524,665,000 | 14.1% |
| 25 | Colorado | 28,413,134,000 | 1.4% |
| 26 | Connecticut | 28,094,106,000 | 1.4% |
| 44 | Delaware | 7,936,467,000 | 0.4% |
| 5 | Florida | 84,633,065,000 | 4.2% |
| 14 | Georgia | 44,750,297,000 | 2.2% |
| 38 | Hawaii | 11,475,771,000 | 0.6% |
| 42 | Idaho | 8,733,485,000 | 0.4% |
| 7 | Illinois | 74,655,351,000 | 3.7% |
| 18 | Indiana | 35,261,522,000 | 1.8% |
| 31 | Iowa | 19,937,080,000 | 1.0% |
| 34 | Kansas | 16,686,643,000 | 0.8% |
| 23 | Kentucky | 29,369,940,000 | 1.5% |
| 19 | Louisiana | 33,396,449,000 | 1.7% |
| 41 | Maine | 9,099,085,000 | 0.5% |
| 17 | Maryland | 37,672,576,000 | 1.9% |
| 11 | Massachusetts | 52,550,586,000 | 2.6% |
| 9 | Michigan | 63,108,508,000 | 3.1% |
| 16 | Minnesota | 38,488,350,000 | 1.9% |
| 30 | Mississippi | 20,157,417,000 | 1.0% |
| 22 | Missouri | 30,646,880,000 | 1.5% |
| 46 | Montana | 7,105,366,000 | 0.4% |
| 40 | Nebraska | 9,356,473,000 | 0.5% |
| 36 | Nevada | 13,203,265,000 | 0.7% |
| 45 | New Hampshire | 7,638,166,000 | 0.4% |
| 8 | New Jersey | 67,114,331,000 | 3.3% |
| 33 | New Mexico | 17,865,171,000 | 0.9% |
| 2 | New York | 184,009,243,000 | 9.2% |
| 10 | North Carolina | 53,088,745,000 | 2.6% |
| 49 | North Dakota | 5,515,725,000 | 0.3% |
| 6 | Ohio | 79,201,570,000 | 4.0% |
| 29 | Oklahoma | 22,377,598,000 | 1.1% |
| 28 | Oregon | 27,336,568,000 | 1.4% |
| 4 | Pennsylvania | 90,791,525,000 | 4.5% |
| 43 | Rhode Island | 8,270,898,000 | 0.4% |
| 24 | South Carolina | 29,352,302,000 | 1.5% |
| 50 | South Dakota | 4,498,447,000 | 0.2% |
| 21 | Tennessee | 30,841,226,000 | 1.5% |
| 3 | Texas | 125,939,778,000 | 6.3% |
| 35 | Utah | 16,682,581,000 | 0.8% |
| 47 | Vermont | 5,853,842,000 | 0.3% |
| 13 | Virginia | 45,549,347,000 | 2.3% |
| 12 | Washington | 45,999,749,000 | 2.3% |
| 37 | West Virginia | 13,000,033,000 | 0.6% |
| 15 | Wisconsin | 39,349,832,000 | 2.0% |
| 48 | Wyoming | 5,673,561,000 | 0.3% |

RANK ORDER

| RANK | STATE | EXPENDITURES | % of USA |
|---|---|---|---|
| 1 | California | $282,524,665,000 | 14.1% |
| 2 | New York | 184,009,243,000 | 9.2% |
| 3 | Texas | 125,939,778,000 | 6.3% |
| 4 | Pennsylvania | 90,791,525,000 | 4.5% |
| 5 | Florida | 84,633,065,000 | 4.2% |
| 6 | Ohio | 79,201,570,000 | 4.0% |
| 7 | Illinois | 74,655,351,000 | 3.7% |
| 8 | New Jersey | 67,114,331,000 | 3.3% |
| 9 | Michigan | 63,108,508,000 | 3.1% |
| 10 | North Carolina | 53,088,745,000 | 2.6% |
| 11 | Massachusetts | 52,550,586,000 | 2.6% |
| 12 | Washington | 45,999,749,000 | 2.3% |
| 13 | Virginia | 45,549,347,000 | 2.3% |
| 14 | Georgia | 44,750,297,000 | 2.2% |
| 15 | Wisconsin | 39,349,832,000 | 2.0% |
| 16 | Minnesota | 38,488,350,000 | 1.9% |
| 17 | Maryland | 37,672,576,000 | 1.9% |
| 18 | Indiana | 35,261,522,000 | 1.8% |
| 19 | Louisiana | 33,396,449,000 | 1.7% |
| 20 | Arizona | 32,875,412,000 | 1.6% |
| 21 | Tennessee | 30,841,226,000 | 1.5% |
| 22 | Missouri | 30,646,880,000 | 1.5% |
| 23 | Kentucky | 29,369,940,000 | 1.5% |
| 24 | South Carolina | 29,352,302,000 | 1.5% |
| 25 | Colorado | 28,413,134,000 | 1.4% |
| 26 | Connecticut | 28,094,106,000 | 1.4% |
| 27 | Alabama | 28,061,237,000 | 1.4% |
| 28 | Oregon | 27,336,568,000 | 1.4% |
| 29 | Oklahoma | 22,377,598,000 | 1.1% |
| 30 | Mississippi | 20,157,417,000 | 1.0% |
| 31 | Iowa | 19,937,080,000 | 1.0% |
| 32 | Arkansas | 18,861,507,000 | 0.9% |
| 33 | New Mexico | 17,865,171,000 | 0.9% |
| 34 | Kansas | 16,686,643,000 | 0.8% |
| 35 | Utah | 16,682,581,000 | 0.8% |
| 36 | Nevada | 13,203,265,000 | 0.7% |
| 37 | West Virginia | 13,000,033,000 | 0.6% |
| 38 | Hawaii | 11,475,771,000 | 0.6% |
| 39 | Alaska | 11,320,127,000 | 0.6% |
| 40 | Nebraska | 9,356,473,000 | 0.5% |
| 41 | Maine | 9,099,085,000 | 0.5% |
| 42 | Idaho | 8,733,485,000 | 0.4% |
| 43 | Rhode Island | 8,270,898,000 | 0.4% |
| 44 | Delaware | 7,936,467,000 | 0.4% |
| 45 | New Hampshire | 7,638,166,000 | 0.4% |
| 46 | Montana | 7,105,366,000 | 0.4% |
| 47 | Vermont | 5,853,842,000 | 0.3% |
| 48 | Wyoming | 5,673,561,000 | 0.3% |
| 49 | North Dakota | 5,515,725,000 | 0.3% |
| 50 | South Dakota | 4,498,447,000 | 0.2% |
| | District of Columbia** | NA | NA |

Source: U.S. Bureau of the Census, Governments Division
   "2011 State and Local Government Finances" (http://www.census.gov/govs/local/)
*Total expenditures includes all money paid other than for retirement of debt and extension of loans. Includes payments from all sources of funds including current revenues and proceeds from borrowing and prior year fund balances. Includes intergovernmental transfers and expenditures for government owned utilities and other commercial or auxiliary enterprise, and insurance trust expenditures. **Not applicable.

# Per Capita State Government Total Expenditures in 2011

## National Per Capita = $6,445*

ALPHA ORDER

| RANK | STATE | PER CAPITA |
|------|-------|-----------|
| 33 | Alabama | $5,842 |
| 1 | Alaska | 15,639 |
| 44 | Arizona | 5,083 |
| 28 | Arkansas | 6,419 |
| 13 | California | 7,497 |
| 38 | Colorado | 5,553 |
| 11 | Connecticut | 7,833 |
| 5 | Delaware | 8,739 |
| 50 | Florida | 4,435 |
| 49 | Georgia | 4,561 |
| 7 | Hawaii | 8,327 |
| 39 | Idaho | 5,514 |
| 35 | Illinois | 5,805 |
| 42 | Indiana | 5,411 |
| 26 | Iowa | 6,507 |
| 34 | Kansas | 5,813 |
| 25 | Kentucky | 6,726 |
| 14 | Louisiana | 7,300 |
| 22 | Maine | 6,849 |
| 27 | Maryland | 6,451 |
| 9 | Massachusetts | 7,954 |
| 29 | Michigan | 6,390 |
| 15 | Minnesota | 7,198 |
| 23 | Mississippi | 6,770 |
| 43 | Missouri | 5,100 |
| 17 | Montana | 7,122 |
| 45 | Nebraska | 5,079 |
| 47 | Nevada | 4,854 |
| 36 | New Hampshire | 5,796 |
| 12 | New Jersey | 7,597 |
| 6 | New Mexico | 8,595 |
| 3 | New York | 9,436 |
| 40 | North Carolina | 5,501 |
| 8 | North Dakota | 8,055 |
| 21 | Ohio | 6,863 |
| 32 | Oklahoma | 5,913 |
| 18 | Oregon | 7,067 |
| 16 | Pennsylvania | 7,124 |
| 10 | Rhode Island | 7,872 |
| 30 | South Carolina | 6,281 |
| 41 | South Dakota | 5,462 |
| 48 | Tennessee | 4,819 |
| 46 | Texas | 4,913 |
| 31 | Utah | 5,928 |
| 4 | Vermont | 9,342 |
| 37 | Virginia | 5,620 |
| 24 | Washington | 6,742 |
| 19 | West Virginia | 7,008 |
| 20 | Wisconsin | 6,892 |
| 2 | Wyoming | 10,000 |

RANK ORDER

| RANK | STATE | PER CAPITA |
|------|-------|-----------|
| 1 | Alaska | $15,639 |
| 2 | Wyoming | 10,000 |
| 3 | New York | 9,436 |
| 4 | Vermont | 9,342 |
| 5 | Delaware | 8,739 |
| 6 | New Mexico | 8,595 |
| 7 | Hawaii | 8,327 |
| 8 | North Dakota | 8,055 |
| 9 | Massachusetts | 7,954 |
| 10 | Rhode Island | 7,872 |
| 11 | Connecticut | 7,833 |
| 12 | New Jersey | 7,597 |
| 13 | California | 7,497 |
| 14 | Louisiana | 7,300 |
| 15 | Minnesota | 7,198 |
| 16 | Pennsylvania | 7,124 |
| 17 | Montana | 7,122 |
| 18 | Oregon | 7,067 |
| 19 | West Virginia | 7,008 |
| 20 | Wisconsin | 6,892 |
| 21 | Ohio | 6,863 |
| 22 | Maine | 6,849 |
| 23 | Mississippi | 6,770 |
| 24 | Washington | 6,742 |
| 25 | Kentucky | 6,726 |
| 26 | Iowa | 6,507 |
| 27 | Maryland | 6,451 |
| 28 | Arkansas | 6,419 |
| 29 | Michigan | 6,390 |
| 30 | South Carolina | 6,281 |
| 31 | Utah | 5,928 |
| 32 | Oklahoma | 5,913 |
| 33 | Alabama | 5,842 |
| 34 | Kansas | 5,813 |
| 35 | Illinois | 5,805 |
| 36 | New Hampshire | 5,796 |
| 37 | Virginia | 5,620 |
| 38 | Colorado | 5,553 |
| 39 | Idaho | 5,514 |
| 40 | North Carolina | 5,501 |
| 41 | South Dakota | 5,462 |
| 42 | Indiana | 5,411 |
| 43 | Missouri | 5,100 |
| 44 | Arizona | 5,083 |
| 45 | Nebraska | 5,079 |
| 46 | Texas | 4,913 |
| 47 | Nevada | 4,854 |
| 48 | Tennessee | 4,819 |
| 49 | Georgia | 4,561 |
| 50 | Florida | 4,435 |
| | District of Columbia** | NA |

Source: CQ Press using data from U.S. Bureau of the Census, Governments Division
"2011 State and Local Government Finances" (http://www.census.gov/govs/local/)
*Total expenditures includes all money paid other than for retirement of debt and extension of loans. Includes payments from all sources of funds including current revenues and proceeds from borrowing and prior year fund balances. Includes intergovernmental transfers and expenditures for government owned utilities and other commercial or auxiliary enterprise, and insurance trust expenditures. **Not applicable.

# State Government Direct General Expenditures in 2011

## National Total = $1,158,125,621,000*

ALPHA ORDER

| RANK | STATE | EXPENDITURES | % of USA |
|------|-------|--------------|----------|
| 26 | Alabama | $17,489,681,000 | 1.5% |
| 38 | Alaska | 8,233,111,000 | 0.7% |
| 23 | Arizona | 19,454,708,000 | 1.7% |
| 32 | Arkansas | 11,707,930,000 | 1.0% |
| 1 | California | 135,802,688,000 | 11.7% |
| 27 | Colorado | 15,939,368,000 | 1.4% |
| 25 | Connecticut | 17,763,271,000 | 1.5% |
| 42 | Delaware | 5,764,611,000 | 0.5% |
| 5 | Florida | 52,259,669,000 | 4.5% |
| 14 | Georgia | 26,810,367,000 | 2.3% |
| 36 | Hawaii | 9,755,259,000 | 0.8% |
| 43 | Idaho | 5,368,437,000 | 0.5% |
| 6 | Illinois | 43,793,443,000 | 3.8% |
| 18 | Indiana | 21,637,009,000 | 1.9% |
| 31 | Iowa | 12,067,286,000 | 1.0% |
| 35 | Kansas | 10,318,064,000 | 0.9% |
| 22 | Kentucky | 19,607,046,000 | 1.7% |
| 17 | Louisiana | 22,554,788,000 | 1.9% |
| 39 | Maine | 6,703,456,000 | 0.6% |
| 15 | Maryland | 24,181,403,000 | 2.1% |
| 9 | Massachusetts | 34,354,818,000 | 3.0% |
| 10 | Michigan | 32,323,402,000 | 2.8% |
| 19 | Minnesota | 21,568,056,000 | 1.9% |
| 30 | Mississippi | 12,293,075,000 | 1.1% |
| 21 | Missouri | 19,824,240,000 | 1.7% |
| 46 | Montana | 4,729,095,000 | 0.4% |
| 40 | Nebraska | 6,310,373,000 | 0.5% |
| 41 | Nevada | 6,085,569,000 | 0.5% |
| 45 | New Hampshire | 5,184,468,000 | 0.4% |
| 8 | New Jersey | 37,565,232,000 | 3.2% |
| 34 | New Mexico | 11,268,727,000 | 1.0% |
| 2 | New York | 86,379,987,000 | 7.5% |
| 11 | North Carolina | 30,701,730,000 | 2.7% |
| 48 | North Dakota | 3,731,468,000 | 0.3% |
| 7 | Ohio | 42,501,306,000 | 3.7% |
| 29 | Oklahoma | 14,533,770,000 | 1.3% |
| 28 | Oregon | 15,336,841,000 | 1.3% |
| 4 | Pennsylvania | 53,513,356,000 | 4.6% |
| 44 | Rhode Island | 5,333,920,000 | 0.5% |
| 24 | South Carolina | 18,073,794,000 | 1.6% |
| 49 | South Dakota | 3,287,711,000 | 0.3% |
| 20 | Tennessee | 20,460,980,000 | 1.8% |
| 3 | Texas | 78,933,692,000 | 6.8% |
| 33 | Utah | 11,602,054,000 | 1.0% |
| 47 | Vermont | 3,837,768,000 | 0.3% |
| 12 | Virginia | 28,861,034,000 | 2.5% |
| 13 | Washington | 27,541,976,000 | 2.4% |
| 37 | West Virginia | 8,912,094,000 | 0.8% |
| 16 | Wisconsin | 22,611,704,000 | 2.0% |
| 50 | Wyoming | 3,251,786,000 | 0.3% |

RANK ORDER

| RANK | STATE | EXPENDITURES | % of USA |
|------|-------|--------------|----------|
| 1 | California | $135,802,688,000 | 11.7% |
| 2 | New York | 86,379,987,000 | 7.5% |
| 3 | Texas | 78,933,692,000 | 6.8% |
| 4 | Pennsylvania | 53,513,356,000 | 4.6% |
| 5 | Florida | 52,259,669,000 | 4.5% |
| 6 | Illinois | 43,793,443,000 | 3.8% |
| 7 | Ohio | 42,501,306,000 | 3.7% |
| 8 | New Jersey | 37,565,232,000 | 3.2% |
| 9 | Massachusetts | 34,354,818,000 | 3.0% |
| 10 | Michigan | 32,323,402,000 | 2.8% |
| 11 | North Carolina | 30,701,730,000 | 2.7% |
| 12 | Virginia | 28,861,034,000 | 2.5% |
| 13 | Washington | 27,541,976,000 | 2.4% |
| 14 | Georgia | 26,810,367,000 | 2.3% |
| 15 | Maryland | 24,181,403,000 | 2.1% |
| 16 | Wisconsin | 22,611,704,000 | 2.0% |
| 17 | Louisiana | 22,554,788,000 | 1.9% |
| 18 | Indiana | 21,637,009,000 | 1.9% |
| 19 | Minnesota | 21,568,056,000 | 1.9% |
| 20 | Tennessee | 20,460,980,000 | 1.8% |
| 21 | Missouri | 19,824,240,000 | 1.7% |
| 22 | Kentucky | 19,607,046,000 | 1.7% |
| 23 | Arizona | 19,454,708,000 | 1.7% |
| 24 | South Carolina | 18,073,794,000 | 1.6% |
| 25 | Connecticut | 17,763,271,000 | 1.5% |
| 26 | Alabama | 17,489,681,000 | 1.5% |
| 27 | Colorado | 15,939,368,000 | 1.4% |
| 28 | Oregon | 15,336,841,000 | 1.3% |
| 29 | Oklahoma | 14,533,770,000 | 1.3% |
| 30 | Mississippi | 12,293,075,000 | 1.1% |
| 31 | Iowa | 12,067,286,000 | 1.0% |
| 32 | Arkansas | 11,707,930,000 | 1.0% |
| 33 | Utah | 11,602,054,000 | 1.0% |
| 34 | New Mexico | 11,268,727,000 | 1.0% |
| 35 | Kansas | 10,318,064,000 | 0.9% |
| 36 | Hawaii | 9,755,259,000 | 0.8% |
| 37 | West Virginia | 8,912,094,000 | 0.8% |
| 38 | Alaska | 8,233,111,000 | 0.7% |
| 39 | Maine | 6,703,456,000 | 0.6% |
| 40 | Nebraska | 6,310,373,000 | 0.5% |
| 41 | Nevada | 6,085,569,000 | 0.5% |
| 42 | Delaware | 5,764,611,000 | 0.5% |
| 43 | Idaho | 5,368,437,000 | 0.5% |
| 44 | Rhode Island | 5,333,920,000 | 0.5% |
| 45 | New Hampshire | 5,184,468,000 | 0.4% |
| 46 | Montana | 4,729,095,000 | 0.4% |
| 47 | Vermont | 3,837,768,000 | 0.3% |
| 48 | North Dakota | 3,731,468,000 | 0.3% |
| 49 | South Dakota | 3,287,711,000 | 0.3% |
| 50 | Wyoming | 3,251,786,000 | 0.3% |
| | District of Columbia** | NA | NA |

Source: U.S. Bureau of the Census, Governments Division
"2011 State and Local Government Finances" (http://www.census.gov/govs/local/)
*Direct general expenditures include expenditures for current operations, assistance and subsidies, interest on debt, and capital outlay. Excludes intergovernmental transfers, expenditures for government owned utilities and other commercial or auxiliary enterprise, and insurance trust expenditures.
**Not applicable.

# Per Capita State Government Direct General Expenditures in 2011

## National Per Capita = $3,724*

| ALPHA ORDER | | | | RANK ORDER | | |
|---|---|---|---|---|---|---|
| RANK | STATE | PER CAPITA | | RANK | STATE | PER CAPITA |
| 33 | Alabama | $3,641 | | 1 | Alaska | $11,374 |
| 1 | Alaska | 11,374 | | 2 | Hawaii | 7,079 |
| 47 | Arizona | 3,008 | | 3 | Delaware | 6,348 |
| 25 | Arkansas | 3,984 | | 4 | Vermont | 6,125 |
| 34 | California | 3,604 | | 5 | Wyoming | 5,731 |
| 45 | Colorado | 3,115 | | 6 | North Dakota | 5,449 |
| 11 | Connecticut | 4,953 | | 7 | New Mexico | 5,421 |
| 3 | Delaware | 6,348 | | 8 | Massachusetts | 5,200 |
| 48 | Florida | 2,739 | | 9 | Rhode Island | 5,077 |
| 49 | Georgia | 2,732 | | 10 | Maine | 5,046 |
| 2 | Hawaii | 7,079 | | 11 | Connecticut | 4,953 |
| 39 | Idaho | 3,390 | | 12 | Louisiana | 4,930 |
| 38 | Illinois | 3,405 | | 13 | West Virginia | 4,805 |
| 40 | Indiana | 3,320 | | 14 | Montana | 4,740 |
| 28 | Iowa | 3,938 | | 15 | Kentucky | 4,490 |
| 35 | Kansas | 3,595 | | 16 | New York | 4,429 |
| 15 | Kentucky | 4,490 | | 17 | New Jersey | 4,252 |
| 12 | Louisiana | 4,930 | | 18 | Pennsylvania | 4,199 |
| 10 | Maine | 5,046 | | 19 | Maryland | 4,141 |
| 19 | Maryland | 4,141 | | 20 | Mississippi | 4,129 |
| 8 | Massachusetts | 5,200 | | 21 | Utah | 4,122 |
| 42 | Michigan | 3,273 | | 22 | Washington | 4,036 |
| 23 | Minnesota | 4,033 | | 23 | Minnesota | 4,033 |
| 20 | Mississippi | 4,129 | | 24 | South Dakota | 3,992 |
| 41 | Missouri | 3,299 | | 25 | Arkansas | 3,984 |
| 14 | Montana | 4,740 | | 26 | Oregon | 3,965 |
| 37 | Nebraska | 3,425 | | 27 | Wisconsin | 3,960 |
| 50 | Nevada | 2,237 | | 28 | Iowa | 3,938 |
| 29 | New Hampshire | 3,934 | | 29 | New Hampshire | 3,934 |
| 17 | New Jersey | 4,252 | | 30 | South Carolina | 3,867 |
| 7 | New Mexico | 5,421 | | 31 | Oklahoma | 3,841 |
| 16 | New York | 4,429 | | 32 | Ohio | 3,683 |
| 44 | North Carolina | 3,181 | | 33 | Alabama | 3,641 |
| 6 | North Dakota | 5,449 | | 34 | California | 3,604 |
| 32 | Ohio | 3,683 | | 35 | Kansas | 3,595 |
| 31 | Oklahoma | 3,841 | | 36 | Virginia | 3,561 |
| 26 | Oregon | 3,965 | | 37 | Nebraska | 3,425 |
| 18 | Pennsylvania | 4,199 | | 38 | Illinois | 3,405 |
| 9 | Rhode Island | 5,077 | | 39 | Idaho | 3,390 |
| 30 | South Carolina | 3,867 | | 40 | Indiana | 3,320 |
| 24 | South Dakota | 3,992 | | 41 | Missouri | 3,299 |
| 43 | Tennessee | 3,197 | | 42 | Michigan | 3,273 |
| 46 | Texas | 3,080 | | 43 | Tennessee | 3,197 |
| 21 | Utah | 4,122 | | 44 | North Carolina | 3,181 |
| 4 | Vermont | 6,125 | | 45 | Colorado | 3,115 |
| 36 | Virginia | 3,561 | | 46 | Texas | 3,080 |
| 22 | Washington | 4,036 | | 47 | Arizona | 3,008 |
| 13 | West Virginia | 4,805 | | 48 | Florida | 2,739 |
| 27 | Wisconsin | 3,960 | | 49 | Georgia | 2,732 |
| 5 | Wyoming | 5,731 | | 50 | Nevada | 2,237 |

District of Columbia**          NA

Source: CQ Press using data from U.S. Bureau of the Census, Governments Division
   "2011 State and Local Government Finances" (http://www.census.gov/govs/local/)
*Direct general expenditures include expenditures for current operations, assistance and subsidies, interest on debt, and capital outlay. Excludes intergovernmental transfers, expenditures for government owned utilities and other commercial or auxiliary enterprise, and insurance trust expenditures.
**Not applicable.

# State Government Debt Outstanding in 2011

## National Total = $1,132,814,566,000*

ALPHA ORDER

| RANK | STATE | DEBT | % of USA |
|---|---|---|---|
| 29 | Alabama | $9,067,280,000 | 0.8% |
| 38 | Alaska | 6,417,682,000 | 0.6% |
| 23 | Arizona | 14,163,076,000 | 1.3% |
| 45 | Arkansas | 3,748,749,000 | 0.3% |
| 1 | California | 149,670,954,000 | 13.2% |
| 20 | Colorado | 16,335,260,000 | 1.4% |
| 11 | Connecticut | 30,523,708,000 | 2.7% |
| 41 | Delaware | 5,807,957,000 | 0.5% |
| 7 | Florida | 43,471,755,000 | 3.8% |
| 25 | Georgia | 13,402,568,000 | 1.2% |
| 32 | Hawaii | 7,912,833,000 | 0.7% |
| 44 | Idaho | 3,928,080,000 | 0.3% |
| 4 | Illinois | 64,801,423,000 | 5.7% |
| 16 | Indiana | 22,144,251,000 | 2.0% |
| 33 | Iowa | 7,573,811,000 | 0.7% |
| 36 | Kansas | 6,893,030,000 | 0.6% |
| 22 | Kentucky | 14,751,471,000 | 1.3% |
| 19 | Louisiana | 18,447,200,000 | 1.6% |
| 39 | Maine | 5,904,221,000 | 0.5% |
| 14 | Maryland | 25,250,138,000 | 2.2% |
| 3 | Massachusetts | 74,315,823,000 | 6.6% |
| 9 | Michigan | 30,975,273,000 | 2.7% |
| 26 | Minnesota | 12,896,921,000 | 1.1% |
| 37 | Mississippi | 6,768,371,000 | 0.6% |
| 17 | Missouri | 20,682,303,000 | 1.8% |
| 42 | Montana | 4,266,731,000 | 0.4% |
| 48 | Nebraska | 2,345,750,000 | 0.2% |
| 43 | Nevada | 4,201,115,000 | 0.4% |
| 30 | New Hampshire | 8,450,218,000 | 0.7% |
| 5 | New Jersey | 64,004,651,000 | 5.7% |
| 31 | New Mexico | 8,118,832,000 | 0.7% |
| 2 | New York | 134,928,505,000 | 11.9% |
| 18 | North Carolina | 18,556,175,000 | 1.6% |
| 49 | North Dakota | 2,060,516,000 | 0.2% |
| 10 | Ohio | 30,974,275,000 | 2.7% |
| 27 | Oklahoma | 10,254,716,000 | 0.9% |
| 24 | Oregon | 14,069,253,000 | 1.2% |
| 6 | Pennsylvania | 45,267,281,000 | 4.0% |
| 28 | Rhode Island | 9,173,572,000 | 0.8% |
| 21 | South Carolina | 15,341,040,000 | 1.4% |
| 46 | South Dakota | 3,544,772,000 | 0.3% |
| 40 | Tennessee | 5,899,369,000 | 0.5% |
| 8 | Texas | 38,530,338,000 | 3.4% |
| 35 | Utah | 7,205,779,000 | 0.6% |
| 47 | Vermont | 3,485,346,000 | 0.3% |
| 13 | Virginia | 26,479,450,000 | 2.3% |
| 12 | Washington | 28,153,562,000 | 2.5% |
| 34 | West Virginia | 7,406,254,000 | 0.7% |
| 15 | Wisconsin | 22,878,524,000 | 2.0% |
| 50 | Wyoming | 1,364,404,000 | 0.1% |

RANK ORDER

| RANK | STATE | DEBT | % of USA |
|---|---|---|---|
| 1 | California | $149,670,954,000 | 13.2% |
| 2 | New York | 134,928,505,000 | 11.9% |
| 3 | Massachusetts | 74,315,823,000 | 6.6% |
| 4 | Illinois | 64,801,423,000 | 5.7% |
| 5 | New Jersey | 64,004,651,000 | 5.7% |
| 6 | Pennsylvania | 45,267,281,000 | 4.0% |
| 7 | Florida | 43,471,755,000 | 3.8% |
| 8 | Texas | 38,530,338,000 | 3.4% |
| 9 | Michigan | 30,975,273,000 | 2.7% |
| 10 | Ohio | 30,974,275,000 | 2.7% |
| 11 | Connecticut | 30,523,708,000 | 2.7% |
| 12 | Washington | 28,153,562,000 | 2.5% |
| 13 | Virginia | 26,479,450,000 | 2.3% |
| 14 | Maryland | 25,250,138,000 | 2.2% |
| 15 | Wisconsin | 22,878,524,000 | 2.0% |
| 16 | Indiana | 22,144,251,000 | 2.0% |
| 17 | Missouri | 20,682,303,000 | 1.8% |
| 18 | North Carolina | 18,556,175,000 | 1.6% |
| 19 | Louisiana | 18,447,200,000 | 1.6% |
| 20 | Colorado | 16,335,260,000 | 1.4% |
| 21 | South Carolina | 15,341,040,000 | 1.4% |
| 22 | Kentucky | 14,751,471,000 | 1.3% |
| 23 | Arizona | 14,163,076,000 | 1.3% |
| 24 | Oregon | 14,069,253,000 | 1.2% |
| 25 | Georgia | 13,402,568,000 | 1.2% |
| 26 | Minnesota | 12,896,921,000 | 1.1% |
| 27 | Oklahoma | 10,254,716,000 | 0.9% |
| 28 | Rhode Island | 9,173,572,000 | 0.8% |
| 29 | Alabama | 9,067,280,000 | 0.8% |
| 30 | New Hampshire | 8,450,218,000 | 0.7% |
| 31 | New Mexico | 8,118,832,000 | 0.7% |
| 32 | Hawaii | 7,912,833,000 | 0.7% |
| 33 | Iowa | 7,573,811,000 | 0.7% |
| 34 | West Virginia | 7,406,254,000 | 0.7% |
| 35 | Utah | 7,205,779,000 | 0.6% |
| 36 | Kansas | 6,893,030,000 | 0.6% |
| 37 | Mississippi | 6,768,371,000 | 0.6% |
| 38 | Alaska | 6,417,682,000 | 0.6% |
| 39 | Maine | 5,904,221,000 | 0.5% |
| 40 | Tennessee | 5,899,369,000 | 0.5% |
| 41 | Delaware | 5,807,957,000 | 0.5% |
| 42 | Montana | 4,266,731,000 | 0.4% |
| 43 | Nevada | 4,201,115,000 | 0.4% |
| 44 | Idaho | 3,928,080,000 | 0.3% |
| 45 | Arkansas | 3,748,749,000 | 0.3% |
| 46 | South Dakota | 3,544,772,000 | 0.3% |
| 47 | Vermont | 3,485,346,000 | 0.3% |
| 48 | Nebraska | 2,345,750,000 | 0.2% |
| 49 | North Dakota | 2,060,516,000 | 0.2% |
| 50 | Wyoming | 1,364,404,000 | 0.1% |
| | District of Columbia** | NA | NA |

Source: U.S. Bureau of the Census, Governments Division
   "2011 State and Local Government Finances" (http://www.census.gov/govs/local/)
*Includes short-term, long-term, full faith and credit, nonguaranteed, and public debt for private purposes.
**Not applicable.

# Per Capita State Government Debt Outstanding in 2011

## National Per Capita = $3,643*

| ALPHA ORDER | | | | RANK ORDER | | |
|---|---|---|---|---|---|---|
| RANK | STATE | PER CAPITA | | RANK | STATE | PER CAPITA |
| 44 | Alabama | $1,888 | | 1 | Massachusetts | $11,248 |
| 2 | Alaska | 8,866 | | 2 | Alaska | 8,866 |
| 42 | Arizona | 2,190 | | 3 | Rhode Island | 8,731 |
| 48 | Arkansas | 1,276 | | 4 | Connecticut | 8,510 |
| 20 | California | 3,972 | | 5 | New Jersey | 7,245 |
| 29 | Colorado | 3,193 | | 6 | New York | 6,919 |
| 4 | Connecticut | 8,510 | | 7 | New Hampshire | 6,412 |
| 8 | Delaware | 6,395 | | 8 | Delaware | 6,395 |
| 40 | Florida | 2,278 | | 9 | Hawaii | 5,742 |
| 47 | Georgia | 1,366 | | 10 | Vermont | 5,562 |
| 9 | Hawaii | 5,742 | | 11 | Illinois | 5,039 |
| 35 | Idaho | 2,480 | | 12 | Maine | 4,444 |
| 11 | Illinois | 5,039 | | 13 | Maryland | 4,324 |
| 25 | Indiana | 3,398 | | 14 | South Dakota | 4,304 |
| 36 | Iowa | 2,472 | | 15 | Montana | 4,277 |
| 39 | Kansas | 2,401 | | 16 | Washington | 4,126 |
| 26 | Kentucky | 3,378 | | 17 | Louisiana | 4,032 |
| 17 | Louisiana | 4,032 | | 18 | Wisconsin | 4,007 |
| 12 | Maine | 4,444 | | 19 | West Virginia | 3,993 |
| 13 | Maryland | 4,324 | | 20 | California | 3,972 |
| 1 | Massachusetts | 11,248 | | 21 | New Mexico | 3,906 |
| 30 | Michigan | 3,136 | | 22 | Oregon | 3,637 |
| 37 | Minnesota | 2,412 | | 23 | Pennsylvania | 3,552 |
| 41 | Mississippi | 2,273 | | 24 | Missouri | 3,442 |
| 24 | Missouri | 3,442 | | 25 | Indiana | 3,398 |
| 15 | Montana | 4,277 | | 26 | Kentucky | 3,378 |
| 49 | Nebraska | 1,273 | | 27 | South Carolina | 3,283 |
| 45 | Nevada | 1,545 | | 28 | Virginia | 3,267 |
| 7 | New Hampshire | 6,412 | | 29 | Colorado | 3,193 |
| 5 | New Jersey | 7,245 | | 30 | Michigan | 3,136 |
| 21 | New Mexico | 3,906 | | 31 | North Dakota | 3,009 |
| 6 | New York | 6,919 | | 32 | Oklahoma | 2,710 |
| 43 | North Carolina | 1,923 | | 33 | Ohio | 2,684 |
| 31 | North Dakota | 3,009 | | 34 | Utah | 2,560 |
| 33 | Ohio | 2,684 | | 35 | Idaho | 2,480 |
| 32 | Oklahoma | 2,710 | | 36 | Iowa | 2,472 |
| 22 | Oregon | 3,637 | | 37 | Minnesota | 2,412 |
| 23 | Pennsylvania | 3,552 | | 38 | Wyoming | 2,405 |
| 3 | Rhode Island | 8,731 | | 39 | Kansas | 2,401 |
| 27 | South Carolina | 3,283 | | 40 | Florida | 2,278 |
| 14 | South Dakota | 4,304 | | 41 | Mississippi | 2,273 |
| 50 | Tennessee | 922 | | 42 | Arizona | 2,190 |
| 46 | Texas | 1,503 | | 43 | North Carolina | 1,923 |
| 34 | Utah | 2,560 | | 44 | Alabama | 1,888 |
| 10 | Vermont | 5,562 | | 45 | Nevada | 1,545 |
| 28 | Virginia | 3,267 | | 46 | Texas | 1,503 |
| 16 | Washington | 4,126 | | 47 | Georgia | 1,366 |
| 19 | West Virginia | 3,993 | | 48 | Arkansas | 1,276 |
| 18 | Wisconsin | 4,007 | | 49 | Nebraska | 1,273 |
| 38 | Wyoming | 2,405 | | 50 | Tennessee | 922 |
| | | | | | District of Columbia** | NA |

Source: CQ Press using data from U.S. Bureau of the Census, Governments Division
   "2011 State and Local Government Finances" (http://www.census.gov/govs/local/)
*Includes short-term, long-term, full faith and credit, nonguaranteed, and public debt for private purposes.
**Not applicable.

# State Government Full-Time Equivalent Employees in 2011

## National Total = 4,359,380 FTE Employees*

ALPHA ORDER

| RANK | STATE | EMPLOYEES | % of USA |
|---|---|---|---|
| 16 | Alabama | 89,768 | 2.1% |
| 40 | Alaska | 26,747 | 0.6% |
| 26 | Arizona | 68,786 | 1.6% |
| 29 | Arkansas | 62,562 | 1.4% |
| 1 | California | 407,321 | 9.3% |
| 24 | Colorado | 72,113 | 1.7% |
| 30 | Connecticut | 62,090 | 1.4% |
| 41 | Delaware | 26,215 | 0.6% |
| 4 | Florida | 184,237 | 4.2% |
| 12 | Georgia | 123,627 | 2.8% |
| 31 | Hawaii | 58,142 | 1.3% |
| 42 | Idaho | 21,773 | 0.5% |
| 10 | Illinois | 131,153 | 3.0% |
| 15 | Indiana | 89,796 | 2.1% |
| 34 | Iowa | 50,378 | 1.2% |
| 36 | Kansas | 43,555 | 1.0% |
| 21 | Kentucky | 81,493 | 1.9% |
| 20 | Louisiana | 84,402 | 1.9% |
| 43 | Maine | 21,354 | 0.5% |
| 18 | Maryland | 86,714 | 2.0% |
| 14 | Massachusetts | 92,033 | 2.1% |
| 8 | Michigan | 144,921 | 3.3% |
| 22 | Minnesota | 79,672 | 1.8% |
| 32 | Mississippi | 57,656 | 1.3% |
| 17 | Missouri | 87,361 | 2.0% |
| 44 | Montana | 20,795 | 0.5% |
| 38 | Nebraska | 32,065 | 0.7% |
| 39 | Nevada | 28,121 | 0.6% |
| 45 | New Hampshire | 19,394 | 0.4% |
| 7 | New Jersey | 146,801 | 3.4% |
| 35 | New Mexico | 46,794 | 1.1% |
| 3 | New York | 243,647 | 5.6% |
| 6 | North Carolina | 154,364 | 3.5% |
| 47 | North Dakota | 18,592 | 0.4% |
| 9 | Ohio | 139,049 | 3.2% |
| 27 | Oklahoma | 68,339 | 1.6% |
| 28 | Oregon | 65,542 | 1.5% |
| 5 | Pennsylvania | 168,548 | 3.9% |
| 46 | Rhode Island | 18,900 | 0.4% |
| 23 | South Carolina | 77,342 | 1.8% |
| 48 | South Dakota | 14,458 | 0.3% |
| 19 | Tennessee | 86,215 | 2.0% |
| 2 | Texas | 318,370 | 7.3% |
| 33 | Utah | 53,501 | 1.2% |
| 49 | Vermont | 14,419 | 0.3% |
| 11 | Virginia | 124,930 | 2.9% |
| 13 | Washington | 121,136 | 2.8% |
| 37 | West Virginia | 39,882 | 0.9% |
| 25 | Wisconsin | 70,891 | 1.6% |
| 50 | Wyoming | 13,416 | 0.3% |

RANK ORDER

| RANK | STATE | EMPLOYEES | % of USA |
|---|---|---|---|
| 1 | California | 407,321 | 9.3% |
| 2 | Texas | 318,370 | 7.3% |
| 3 | New York | 243,647 | 5.6% |
| 4 | Florida | 184,237 | 4.2% |
| 5 | Pennsylvania | 168,548 | 3.9% |
| 6 | North Carolina | 154,364 | 3.5% |
| 7 | New Jersey | 146,801 | 3.4% |
| 8 | Michigan | 144,921 | 3.3% |
| 9 | Ohio | 139,049 | 3.2% |
| 10 | Illinois | 131,153 | 3.0% |
| 11 | Virginia | 124,930 | 2.9% |
| 12 | Georgia | 123,627 | 2.8% |
| 13 | Washington | 121,136 | 2.8% |
| 14 | Massachusetts | 92,033 | 2.1% |
| 15 | Indiana | 89,796 | 2.1% |
| 16 | Alabama | 89,768 | 2.1% |
| 17 | Missouri | 87,361 | 2.0% |
| 18 | Maryland | 86,714 | 2.0% |
| 19 | Tennessee | 86,215 | 2.0% |
| 20 | Louisiana | 84,402 | 1.9% |
| 21 | Kentucky | 81,493 | 1.9% |
| 22 | Minnesota | 79,672 | 1.8% |
| 23 | South Carolina | 77,342 | 1.8% |
| 24 | Colorado | 72,113 | 1.7% |
| 25 | Wisconsin | 70,891 | 1.6% |
| 26 | Arizona | 68,786 | 1.6% |
| 27 | Oklahoma | 68,339 | 1.6% |
| 28 | Oregon | 65,542 | 1.5% |
| 29 | Arkansas | 62,562 | 1.4% |
| 30 | Connecticut | 62,090 | 1.4% |
| 31 | Hawaii | 58,142 | 1.3% |
| 32 | Mississippi | 57,656 | 1.3% |
| 33 | Utah | 53,501 | 1.2% |
| 34 | Iowa | 50,378 | 1.2% |
| 35 | New Mexico | 46,794 | 1.1% |
| 36 | Kansas | 43,555 | 1.0% |
| 37 | West Virginia | 39,882 | 0.9% |
| 38 | Nebraska | 32,065 | 0.7% |
| 39 | Nevada | 28,121 | 0.6% |
| 40 | Alaska | 26,747 | 0.6% |
| 41 | Delaware | 26,215 | 0.6% |
| 42 | Idaho | 21,773 | 0.5% |
| 43 | Maine | 21,354 | 0.5% |
| 44 | Montana | 20,795 | 0.5% |
| 45 | New Hampshire | 19,394 | 0.4% |
| 46 | Rhode Island | 18,900 | 0.4% |
| 47 | North Dakota | 18,592 | 0.4% |
| 48 | South Dakota | 14,458 | 0.3% |
| 49 | Vermont | 14,419 | 0.3% |
| 50 | Wyoming | 13,416 | 0.3% |
| | District of Columbia** | NA | NA |

Source: U.S. Bureau of the Census, Governments Division
"Government Employment and Payroll" (http://www.census.gov/govs/apes/index.html)
*As of March 2011.
**Not applicable.

# Rate of State Government Full-Time Equivalent Employees in 2011

## National Rate = 140 State Government Employees per 10,000 Population*

ALPHA ORDER

| RANK | STATE | RATE |
|------|-------|------|
| 13 | Alabama | 187 |
| 2 | Alaska | 370 |
| 47 | Arizona | 106 |
| 9 | Arkansas | 213 |
| 46 | California | 108 |
| 35 | Colorado | 141 |
| 21 | Connecticut | 173 |
| 3 | Delaware | 289 |
| 50 | Florida | 97 |
| 41 | Georgia | 126 |
| 1 | Hawaii | 422 |
| 38 | Idaho | 137 |
| 49 | Illinois | 102 |
| 37 | Indiana | 138 |
| 25 | Iowa | 164 |
| 29 | Kansas | 152 |
| 13 | Kentucky | 187 |
| 15 | Louisiana | 184 |
| 26 | Maine | 161 |
| 31 | Maryland | 148 |
| 36 | Massachusetts | 139 |
| 32 | Michigan | 147 |
| 30 | Minnesota | 149 |
| 11 | Mississippi | 194 |
| 34 | Missouri | 145 |
| 10 | Montana | 208 |
| 20 | Nebraska | 174 |
| 48 | Nevada | 103 |
| 32 | New Hampshire | 147 |
| 23 | New Jersey | 166 |
| 7 | New Mexico | 225 |
| 42 | New York | 125 |
| 27 | North Carolina | 160 |
| 4 | North Dakota | 272 |
| 45 | Ohio | 120 |
| 16 | Oklahoma | 181 |
| 22 | Oregon | 169 |
| 40 | Pennsylvania | 132 |
| 17 | Rhode Island | 180 |
| 24 | South Carolina | 165 |
| 19 | South Dakota | 176 |
| 39 | Tennessee | 135 |
| 43 | Texas | 124 |
| 12 | Utah | 190 |
| 6 | Vermont | 230 |
| 28 | Virginia | 154 |
| 18 | Washington | 178 |
| 8 | West Virginia | 215 |
| 43 | Wisconsin | 124 |
| 5 | Wyoming | 236 |

RANK ORDER

| RANK | STATE | RATE |
|------|-------|------|
| 1 | Hawaii | 422 |
| 2 | Alaska | 370 |
| 3 | Delaware | 289 |
| 4 | North Dakota | 272 |
| 5 | Wyoming | 236 |
| 6 | Vermont | 230 |
| 7 | New Mexico | 225 |
| 8 | West Virginia | 215 |
| 9 | Arkansas | 213 |
| 10 | Montana | 208 |
| 11 | Mississippi | 194 |
| 12 | Utah | 190 |
| 13 | Alabama | 187 |
| 13 | Kentucky | 187 |
| 15 | Louisiana | 184 |
| 16 | Oklahoma | 181 |
| 17 | Rhode Island | 180 |
| 18 | Washington | 178 |
| 19 | South Dakota | 176 |
| 20 | Nebraska | 174 |
| 21 | Connecticut | 173 |
| 22 | Oregon | 169 |
| 23 | New Jersey | 166 |
| 24 | South Carolina | 165 |
| 25 | Iowa | 164 |
| 26 | Maine | 161 |
| 27 | North Carolina | 160 |
| 28 | Virginia | 154 |
| 29 | Kansas | 152 |
| 30 | Minnesota | 149 |
| 31 | Maryland | 148 |
| 32 | Michigan | 147 |
| 32 | New Hampshire | 147 |
| 34 | Missouri | 145 |
| 35 | Colorado | 141 |
| 36 | Massachusetts | 139 |
| 37 | Indiana | 138 |
| 38 | Idaho | 137 |
| 39 | Tennessee | 135 |
| 40 | Pennsylvania | 132 |
| 41 | Georgia | 126 |
| 42 | New York | 125 |
| 43 | Texas | 124 |
| 43 | Wisconsin | 124 |
| 45 | Ohio | 120 |
| 46 | California | 108 |
| 47 | Arizona | 106 |
| 48 | Nevada | 103 |
| 49 | Illinois | 102 |
| 50 | Florida | 97 |

| District of Columbia** | NA |
|------------------------|-----|

Source: CQ Press using data from U.S. Bureau of the Census, Governments Division
    "Government Employment and Payroll" (http://www.census.gov/govs/apes/index.html)
*Full-time equivalent as of March 2011.
**Not applicable.

# Average Annual Earnings of Full-Time State Government Employees in 2011

## National Average = $56,825*

ALPHA ORDER

| RANK | STATE | SALARY |
|------|-------|--------|
| 32 | Alabama | $50,063 |
| 9 | Alaska | 63,739 |
| 24 | Arizona | 53,211 |
| 41 | Arkansas | 47,277 |
| 1 | California | 73,928 |
| 14 | Colorado | 60,525 |
| 3 | Connecticut | 70,388 |
| 30 | Delaware | 50,887 |
| 44 | Florida | 46,595 |
| 43 | Georgia | 46,883 |
| 37 | Hawaii | 48,286 |
| 22 | Idaho | 54,121 |
| 8 | Illinois | 65,179 |
| 33 | Indiana | 49,893 |
| 5 | Iowa | 67,310 |
| 31 | Kansas | 50,741 |
| 45 | Kentucky | 46,401 |
| 27 | Louisiana | 51,754 |
| 34 | Maine | 49,875 |
| 17 | Maryland | 56,434 |
| 11 | Massachusetts | 61,316 |
| 10 | Michigan | 63,650 |
| 7 | Minnesota | 65,246 |
| 48 | Mississippi | 44,281 |
| 50 | Missouri | 42,588 |
| 35 | Montana | 49,516 |
| 36 | Nebraska | 49,505 |
| 16 | Nevada | 58,272 |
| 19 | New Hampshire | 55,803 |
| 2 | New Jersey | 71,159 |
| 40 | New Mexico | 47,527 |
| 4 | New York | 68,145 |
| 39 | North Carolina | 47,560 |
| 28 | North Dakota | 51,063 |
| 13 | Ohio | 60,583 |
| 42 | Oklahoma | 46,962 |
| 20 | Oregon | 55,469 |
| 18 | Pennsylvania | 56,240 |
| 6 | Rhode Island | 65,796 |
| 46 | South Carolina | 45,592 |
| 38 | South Dakota | 47,650 |
| 47 | Tennessee | 44,620 |
| 25 | Texas | 52,705 |
| 23 | Utah | 53,250 |
| 21 | Vermont | 55,304 |
| 26 | Virginia | 52,481 |
| 12 | Washington | 61,028 |
| 49 | West Virginia | 43,421 |
| 15 | Wisconsin | 60,039 |
| 29 | Wyoming | 50,973 |

RANK ORDER

| RANK | STATE | SALARY |
|------|-------|--------|
| 1 | California | $73,928 |
| 2 | New Jersey | 71,159 |
| 3 | Connecticut | 70,388 |
| 4 | New York | 68,145 |
| 5 | Iowa | 67,310 |
| 6 | Rhode Island | 65,796 |
| 7 | Minnesota | 65,246 |
| 8 | Illinois | 65,179 |
| 9 | Alaska | 63,739 |
| 10 | Michigan | 63,650 |
| 11 | Massachusetts | 61,316 |
| 12 | Washington | 61,028 |
| 13 | Ohio | 60,583 |
| 14 | Colorado | 60,525 |
| 15 | Wisconsin | 60,039 |
| 16 | Nevada | 58,272 |
| 17 | Maryland | 56,434 |
| 18 | Pennsylvania | 56,240 |
| 19 | New Hampshire | 55,803 |
| 20 | Oregon | 55,469 |
| 21 | Vermont | 55,304 |
| 22 | Idaho | 54,121 |
| 23 | Utah | 53,250 |
| 24 | Arizona | 53,211 |
| 25 | Texas | 52,705 |
| 26 | Virginia | 52,481 |
| 27 | Louisiana | 51,754 |
| 28 | North Dakota | 51,063 |
| 29 | Wyoming | 50,973 |
| 30 | Delaware | 50,887 |
| 31 | Kansas | 50,741 |
| 32 | Alabama | 50,063 |
| 33 | Indiana | 49,893 |
| 34 | Maine | 49,875 |
| 35 | Montana | 49,516 |
| 36 | Nebraska | 49,505 |
| 37 | Hawaii | 48,286 |
| 38 | South Dakota | 47,650 |
| 39 | North Carolina | 47,560 |
| 40 | New Mexico | 47,527 |
| 41 | Arkansas | 47,277 |
| 42 | Oklahoma | 46,962 |
| 43 | Georgia | 46,883 |
| 44 | Florida | 46,595 |
| 45 | Kentucky | 46,401 |
| 46 | South Carolina | 45,592 |
| 47 | Tennessee | 44,620 |
| 48 | Mississippi | 44,281 |
| 49 | West Virginia | 43,421 |
| 50 | Missouri | 42,588 |

District of Columbia**   NA

Source: CQ Press using data from U.S. Bureau of the Census, Governments Division
   "Government Employment and Payroll" (http://www.census.gov/govs/apes/index.html)
*March 2011 full-time payroll (multiplied by 12) divided by full-time employees.
**Not applicable.

# Local Government Total Revenue in 2011

## National Total = $1,669,420,996,000*

<table>
<tr><td colspan="4">ALPHA ORDER</td><td colspan="4">RANK ORDER</td></tr>
<tr><td>RANK</td><td>STATE</td><td>REVENUE</td><td>% of USA</td><td>RANK</td><td>STATE</td><td>REVENUE</td><td>% of USA</td></tr>
<tr><td>24</td><td>Alabama</td><td>$20,705,515,000</td><td>1.2%</td><td>1</td><td>California</td><td>$278,013,471,000</td><td>16.7%</td></tr>
<tr><td>41</td><td>Alaska</td><td>5,246,497,000</td><td>0.3%</td><td>2</td><td>New York</td><td>176,178,833,000</td><td>10.6%</td></tr>
<tr><td>17</td><td>Arizona</td><td>28,806,773,000</td><td>1.7%</td><td>3</td><td>Texas</td><td>121,552,443,000</td><td>7.3%</td></tr>
<tr><td>36</td><td>Arkansas</td><td>9,832,080,000</td><td>0.6%</td><td>4</td><td>Florida</td><td>95,465,342,000</td><td>5.7%</td></tr>
<tr><td>1</td><td>California</td><td>278,013,471,000</td><td>16.7%</td><td>5</td><td>Illinois</td><td>71,336,467,000</td><td>4.3%</td></tr>
<tr><td>16</td><td>Colorado</td><td>29,736,610,000</td><td>1.8%</td><td>6</td><td>Pennsylvania</td><td>63,998,283,000</td><td>3.8%</td></tr>
<tr><td>27</td><td>Connecticut</td><td>17,624,161,000</td><td>1.1%</td><td>7</td><td>Ohio</td><td>55,419,558,000</td><td>3.3%</td></tr>
<tr><td>48</td><td>Delaware</td><td>3,221,109,000</td><td>0.2%</td><td>8</td><td>Michigan</td><td>47,631,914,000</td><td>2.9%</td></tr>
<tr><td>4</td><td>Florida</td><td>95,465,342,000</td><td>5.7%</td><td>9</td><td>New Jersey</td><td>46,411,965,000</td><td>2.8%</td></tr>
<tr><td>10</td><td>Georgia</td><td>44,066,127,000</td><td>2.6%</td><td>10</td><td>Georgia</td><td>44,066,127,000</td><td>2.6%</td></tr>
<tr><td>46</td><td>Hawaii</td><td>3,271,098,000</td><td>0.2%</td><td>11</td><td>North Carolina</td><td>42,852,468,000</td><td>2.6%</td></tr>
<tr><td>38</td><td>Idaho</td><td>5,666,197,000</td><td>0.3%</td><td>12</td><td>Washington</td><td>38,165,146,000</td><td>2.3%</td></tr>
<tr><td>5</td><td>Illinois</td><td>71,336,467,000</td><td>4.3%</td><td>13</td><td>Virginia</td><td>36,459,561,000</td><td>2.2%</td></tr>
<tr><td>21</td><td>Indiana</td><td>27,354,430,000</td><td>1.6%</td><td>14</td><td>Massachusetts</td><td>34,068,076,000</td><td>2.0%</td></tr>
<tr><td>28</td><td>Iowa</td><td>15,240,763,000</td><td>0.9%</td><td>15</td><td>Tennessee</td><td>32,412,749,000</td><td>1.9%</td></tr>
<tr><td>30</td><td>Kansas</td><td>13,972,569,000</td><td>0.8%</td><td>16</td><td>Colorado</td><td>29,736,610,000</td><td>1.8%</td></tr>
<tr><td>29</td><td>Kentucky</td><td>14,563,516,000</td><td>0.9%</td><td>17</td><td>Arizona</td><td>28,806,773,000</td><td>1.7%</td></tr>
<tr><td>23</td><td>Louisiana</td><td>21,949,574,000</td><td>1.3%</td><td>18</td><td>Minnesota</td><td>28,652,509,000</td><td>1.7%</td></tr>
<tr><td>42</td><td>Maine</td><td>4,775,680,000</td><td>0.3%</td><td>19</td><td>Maryland</td><td>28,584,801,000</td><td>1.7%</td></tr>
<tr><td>19</td><td>Maryland</td><td>28,584,801,000</td><td>1.7%</td><td>20</td><td>Wisconsin</td><td>27,805,037,000</td><td>1.7%</td></tr>
<tr><td>14</td><td>Massachusetts</td><td>34,068,076,000</td><td>2.0%</td><td>21</td><td>Indiana</td><td>27,354,430,000</td><td>1.6%</td></tr>
<tr><td>8</td><td>Michigan</td><td>47,631,914,000</td><td>2.9%</td><td>22</td><td>Missouri</td><td>25,149,616,000</td><td>1.5%</td></tr>
<tr><td>18</td><td>Minnesota</td><td>28,652,509,000</td><td>1.7%</td><td>23</td><td>Louisiana</td><td>21,949,574,000</td><td>1.3%</td></tr>
<tr><td>33</td><td>Mississippi</td><td>12,712,805,000</td><td>0.8%</td><td>24</td><td>Alabama</td><td>20,705,515,000</td><td>1.2%</td></tr>
<tr><td>22</td><td>Missouri</td><td>25,149,616,000</td><td>1.5%</td><td>25</td><td>South Carolina</td><td>19,352,896,000</td><td>1.2%</td></tr>
<tr><td>45</td><td>Montana</td><td>3,512,643,000</td><td>0.2%</td><td>26</td><td>Oregon</td><td>17,945,906,000</td><td>1.1%</td></tr>
<tr><td>34</td><td>Nebraska</td><td>12,467,736,000</td><td>0.7%</td><td>27</td><td>Connecticut</td><td>17,624,161,000</td><td>1.1%</td></tr>
<tr><td>32</td><td>Nevada</td><td>12,892,864,000</td><td>0.8%</td><td>28</td><td>Iowa</td><td>15,240,763,000</td><td>0.9%</td></tr>
<tr><td>40</td><td>New Hampshire</td><td>5,399,050,000</td><td>0.3%</td><td>29</td><td>Kentucky</td><td>14,563,516,000</td><td>0.9%</td></tr>
<tr><td>9</td><td>New Jersey</td><td>46,411,965,000</td><td>2.8%</td><td>30</td><td>Kansas</td><td>13,972,569,000</td><td>0.8%</td></tr>
<tr><td>37</td><td>New Mexico</td><td>8,542,927,000</td><td>0.5%</td><td>31</td><td>Oklahoma</td><td>13,295,347,000</td><td>0.8%</td></tr>
<tr><td>2</td><td>New York</td><td>176,178,833,000</td><td>10.6%</td><td>32</td><td>Nevada</td><td>12,892,864,000</td><td>0.8%</td></tr>
<tr><td>11</td><td>North Carolina</td><td>42,852,468,000</td><td>2.6%</td><td>33</td><td>Mississippi</td><td>12,712,805,000</td><td>0.8%</td></tr>
<tr><td>49</td><td>North Dakota</td><td>2,850,102,000</td><td>0.2%</td><td>34</td><td>Nebraska</td><td>12,467,736,000</td><td>0.7%</td></tr>
<tr><td>7</td><td>Ohio</td><td>55,419,558,000</td><td>3.3%</td><td>35</td><td>Utah</td><td>11,026,526,000</td><td>0.7%</td></tr>
<tr><td>31</td><td>Oklahoma</td><td>13,295,347,000</td><td>0.8%</td><td>36</td><td>Arkansas</td><td>9,832,080,000</td><td>0.6%</td></tr>
<tr><td>26</td><td>Oregon</td><td>17,945,906,000</td><td>1.1%</td><td>37</td><td>New Mexico</td><td>8,542,927,000</td><td>0.5%</td></tr>
<tr><td>6</td><td>Pennsylvania</td><td>63,998,283,000</td><td>3.8%</td><td>38</td><td>Idaho</td><td>5,666,197,000</td><td>0.3%</td></tr>
<tr><td>44</td><td>Rhode Island</td><td>4,426,503,000</td><td>0.3%</td><td>39</td><td>West Virginia</td><td>5,465,978,000</td><td>0.3%</td></tr>
<tr><td>25</td><td>South Carolina</td><td>19,352,896,000</td><td>1.2%</td><td>40</td><td>New Hampshire</td><td>5,399,050,000</td><td>0.3%</td></tr>
<tr><td>47</td><td>South Dakota</td><td>3,261,447,000</td><td>0.2%</td><td>41</td><td>Alaska</td><td>5,246,497,000</td><td>0.3%</td></tr>
<tr><td>15</td><td>Tennessee</td><td>32,412,749,000</td><td>1.9%</td><td>42</td><td>Maine</td><td>4,775,680,000</td><td>0.3%</td></tr>
<tr><td>3</td><td>Texas</td><td>121,552,443,000</td><td>7.3%</td><td>43</td><td>Wyoming</td><td>4,621,793,000</td><td>0.3%</td></tr>
<tr><td>35</td><td>Utah</td><td>11,026,526,000</td><td>0.7%</td><td>44</td><td>Rhode Island</td><td>4,426,503,000</td><td>0.3%</td></tr>
<tr><td>50</td><td>Vermont</td><td>2,577,674,000</td><td>0.2%</td><td>45</td><td>Montana</td><td>3,512,643,000</td><td>0.2%</td></tr>
<tr><td>13</td><td>Virginia</td><td>36,459,561,000</td><td>2.2%</td><td>46</td><td>Hawaii</td><td>3,271,098,000</td><td>0.2%</td></tr>
<tr><td>12</td><td>Washington</td><td>38,165,146,000</td><td>2.3%</td><td>47</td><td>South Dakota</td><td>3,261,447,000</td><td>0.2%</td></tr>
<tr><td>39</td><td>West Virginia</td><td>5,465,978,000</td><td>0.3%</td><td>48</td><td>Delaware</td><td>3,221,109,000</td><td>0.2%</td></tr>
<tr><td>20</td><td>Wisconsin</td><td>27,805,037,000</td><td>1.7%</td><td>49</td><td>North Dakota</td><td>2,850,102,000</td><td>0.2%</td></tr>
<tr><td>43</td><td>Wyoming</td><td>4,621,793,000</td><td>0.3%</td><td>50</td><td>Vermont</td><td>2,577,674,000</td><td>0.2%</td></tr>
<tr><td></td><td></td><td></td><td></td><td></td><td>District of Columbia</td><td>12,877,861,000</td><td>0.8%</td></tr>
</table>

Source: U.S. Bureau of the Census, Governments Division
"2011 State and Local Government Finances" (http://www.census.gov/govs/local/)
*Total revenue includes all money received from external sources. This includes taxes, intergovernmental transfers and insurance trust revenue, and revenue from government owned utilities and other commercial or auxiliary enterprise.

# Per Capita Local Government Total Revenue in 2011

## National Per Capita = $5,358*

ALPHA ORDER

RANK ORDER

| RANK | STATE | PER CAPITA | RANK | STATE | PER CAPITA |
|---|---|---|---|---|---|
| 30 | Alabama | $4,310 | 1 | New York | $9,034 |
| 4 | Alaska | 7,248 | 2 | Wyoming | 8,146 |
| 28 | Arizona | 4,454 | 3 | California | 7,378 |
| 47 | Arkansas | 3,346 | 4 | Alaska | 7,248 |
| 3 | California | 7,378 | 5 | Nebraska | 6,768 |
| 6 | Colorado | 5,812 | 6 | Colorado | 5,812 |
| 16 | Connecticut | 4,914 | 7 | Washington | 5,593 |
| 44 | Delaware | 3,547 | 8 | Illinois | 5,547 |
| 14 | Florida | 5,003 | 9 | Minnesota | 5,358 |
| 27 | Georgia | 4,491 | 10 | New Jersey | 5,253 |
| 50 | Hawaii | 2,374 | 11 | Massachusetts | 5,156 |
| 43 | Idaho | 3,578 | 12 | Tennessee | 5,065 |
| 8 | Illinois | 5,547 | 13 | Pennsylvania | 5,022 |
| 33 | Indiana | 4,198 | 14 | Florida | 5,003 |
| 15 | Iowa | 4,974 | 15 | Iowa | 4,974 |
| 19 | Kansas | 4,868 | 16 | Connecticut | 4,914 |
| 48 | Kentucky | 3,335 | 17 | Maryland | 4,895 |
| 22 | Louisiana | 4,798 | 18 | Wisconsin | 4,870 |
| 42 | Maine | 3,595 | 19 | Kansas | 4,868 |
| 17 | Maryland | 4,895 | 20 | Michigan | 4,823 |
| 11 | Massachusetts | 5,156 | 21 | Ohio | 4,802 |
| 20 | Michigan | 4,823 | 22 | Louisiana | 4,798 |
| 9 | Minnesota | 5,358 | 23 | Texas | 4,742 |
| 31 | Mississippi | 4,270 | 24 | Nevada | 4,740 |
| 34 | Missouri | 4,185 | 25 | Oregon | 4,639 |
| 45 | Montana | 3,521 | 26 | Virginia | 4,499 |
| 5 | Nebraska | 6,768 | 27 | Georgia | 4,491 |
| 24 | Nevada | 4,740 | 28 | Arizona | 4,454 |
| 39 | New Hampshire | 4,097 | 29 | North Carolina | 4,440 |
| 10 | New Jersey | 5,253 | 30 | Alabama | 4,310 |
| 38 | New Mexico | 4,110 | 31 | Mississippi | 4,270 |
| 1 | New York | 9,034 | 32 | Rhode Island | 4,213 |
| 29 | North Carolina | 4,440 | 33 | Indiana | 4,198 |
| 35 | North Dakota | 4,162 | 34 | Missouri | 4,185 |
| 21 | Ohio | 4,802 | 35 | North Dakota | 4,162 |
| 46 | Oklahoma | 3,513 | 36 | South Carolina | 4,141 |
| 25 | Oregon | 4,639 | 37 | Vermont | 4,114 |
| 13 | Pennsylvania | 5,022 | 38 | New Mexico | 4,110 |
| 32 | Rhode Island | 4,213 | 39 | New Hampshire | 4,097 |
| 36 | South Carolina | 4,141 | 40 | South Dakota | 3,960 |
| 40 | South Dakota | 3,960 | 41 | Utah | 3,918 |
| 12 | Tennessee | 5,065 | 42 | Maine | 3,595 |
| 23 | Texas | 4,742 | 43 | Idaho | 3,578 |
| 41 | Utah | 3,918 | 44 | Delaware | 3,547 |
| 37 | Vermont | 4,114 | 45 | Montana | 3,521 |
| 26 | Virginia | 4,499 | 46 | Oklahoma | 3,513 |
| 7 | Washington | 5,593 | 47 | Arkansas | 3,346 |
| 49 | West Virginia | 2,947 | 48 | Kentucky | 3,335 |
| 18 | Wisconsin | 4,870 | 49 | West Virginia | 2,947 |
| 2 | Wyoming | 8,146 | 50 | Hawaii | 2,374 |

District of Columbia 20,804

Source: CQ Press using data from U.S. Bureau of the Census, Governments Division
    "2011 State and Local Government Finances" (http://www.census.gov/govs/local/)
*Total revenue includes all money received from external sources.  This includes taxes, intergovernmental transfers and insurance trust revenue, and revenue from government owned utilities and other commercial or auxiliary enterprise.

# Local Government Revenue from the Federal Government in 2011

## National Total = $72,558,179,000

ALPHA ORDER

| RANK | STATE | REVENUE | % of USA |
|---|---|---|---|
| 18 | Alabama | $1,092,738,000 | 1.5% |
| 37 | Alaska | 325,774,000 | 0.4% |
| 20 | Arizona | 966,667,000 | 1.3% |
| 35 | Arkansas | 418,010,000 | 0.6% |
| 1 | California | 11,294,779,000 | 15.6% |
| 15 | Colorado | 1,273,529,000 | 1.8% |
| 30 | Connecticut | 649,087,000 | 0.9% |
| 50 | Delaware | 72,859,000 | 0.1% |
| 3 | Florida | 4,668,556,000 | 6.4% |
| 12 | Georgia | 1,564,413,000 | 2.2% |
| 40 | Hawaii | 269,656,000 | 0.4% |
| 45 | Idaho | 192,896,000 | 0.3% |
| 6 | Illinois | 3,308,226,000 | 4.6% |
| 24 | Indiana | 746,230,000 | 1.0% |
| 28 | Iowa | 702,499,000 | 1.0% |
| 38 | Kansas | 287,588,000 | 0.4% |
| 32 | Kentucky | 553,167,000 | 0.8% |
| 16 | Louisiana | 1,212,434,000 | 1.7% |
| 47 | Maine | 170,877,000 | 0.2% |
| 14 | Maryland | 1,475,705,000 | 2.0% |
| 11 | Massachusetts | 1,675,224,000 | 2.3% |
| 9 | Michigan | 2,146,529,000 | 3.0% |
| 22 | Minnesota | 920,989,000 | 1.3% |
| 25 | Mississippi | 715,484,000 | 1.0% |
| 23 | Missouri | 822,576,000 | 1.1% |
| 41 | Montana | 262,117,000 | 0.4% |
| 36 | Nebraska | 394,065,000 | 0.5% |
| 26 | Nevada | 711,502,000 | 1.0% |
| 46 | New Hampshire | 185,191,000 | 0.3% |
| 19 | New Jersey | 1,091,886,000 | 1.5% |
| 31 | New Mexico | 568,921,000 | 0.8% |
| 2 | New York | 6,103,031,000 | 8.4% |
| 8 | North Carolina | 2,278,463,000 | 3.1% |
| 43 | North Dakota | 202,381,000 | 0.3% |
| 7 | Ohio | 2,471,660,000 | 3.4% |
| 34 | Oklahoma | 444,374,000 | 0.6% |
| 17 | Oregon | 1,159,929,000 | 1.6% |
| 5 | Pennsylvania | 3,489,115,000 | 4.8% |
| 44 | Rhode Island | 201,554,000 | 0.3% |
| 33 | South Carolina | 490,917,000 | 0.7% |
| 42 | South Dakota | 204,469,000 | 0.3% |
| 21 | Tennessee | 964,360,000 | 1.3% |
| 4 | Texas | 4,518,628,000 | 6.2% |
| 29 | Utah | 686,826,000 | 0.9% |
| 49 | Vermont | 91,220,000 | 0.1% |
| 13 | Virginia | 1,513,802,000 | 2.1% |
| 10 | Washington | 1,748,567,000 | 2.4% |
| 39 | West Virginia | 277,153,000 | 0.4% |
| 27 | Wisconsin | 705,359,000 | 1.0% |
| 48 | Wyoming | 149,607,000 | 0.2% |

RANK ORDER

| RANK | STATE | REVENUE | % of USA |
|---|---|---|---|
| 1 | California | $11,294,779,000 | 15.6% |
| 2 | New York | 6,103,031,000 | 8.4% |
| 3 | Florida | 4,668,556,000 | 6.4% |
| 4 | Texas | 4,518,628,000 | 6.2% |
| 5 | Pennsylvania | 3,489,115,000 | 4.8% |
| 6 | Illinois | 3,308,226,000 | 4.6% |
| 7 | Ohio | 2,471,660,000 | 3.4% |
| 8 | North Carolina | 2,278,463,000 | 3.1% |
| 9 | Michigan | 2,146,529,000 | 3.0% |
| 10 | Washington | 1,748,567,000 | 2.4% |
| 11 | Massachusetts | 1,675,224,000 | 2.3% |
| 12 | Georgia | 1,564,413,000 | 2.2% |
| 13 | Virginia | 1,513,802,000 | 2.1% |
| 14 | Maryland | 1,475,705,000 | 2.0% |
| 15 | Colorado | 1,273,529,000 | 1.8% |
| 16 | Louisiana | 1,212,434,000 | 1.7% |
| 17 | Oregon | 1,159,929,000 | 1.6% |
| 18 | Alabama | 1,092,738,000 | 1.5% |
| 19 | New Jersey | 1,091,886,000 | 1.5% |
| 20 | Arizona | 966,667,000 | 1.3% |
| 21 | Tennessee | 964,360,000 | 1.3% |
| 22 | Minnesota | 920,989,000 | 1.3% |
| 23 | Missouri | 822,576,000 | 1.1% |
| 24 | Indiana | 746,230,000 | 1.0% |
| 25 | Mississippi | 715,484,000 | 1.0% |
| 26 | Nevada | 711,502,000 | 1.0% |
| 27 | Wisconsin | 705,359,000 | 1.0% |
| 28 | Iowa | 702,499,000 | 1.0% |
| 29 | Utah | 686,826,000 | 0.9% |
| 30 | Connecticut | 649,087,000 | 0.9% |
| 31 | New Mexico | 568,921,000 | 0.8% |
| 32 | Kentucky | 553,167,000 | 0.8% |
| 33 | South Carolina | 490,917,000 | 0.7% |
| 34 | Oklahoma | 444,374,000 | 0.6% |
| 35 | Arkansas | 418,010,000 | 0.6% |
| 36 | Nebraska | 394,065,000 | 0.5% |
| 37 | Alaska | 325,774,000 | 0.4% |
| 38 | Kansas | 287,588,000 | 0.4% |
| 39 | West Virginia | 277,153,000 | 0.4% |
| 40 | Hawaii | 269,656,000 | 0.4% |
| 41 | Montana | 262,117,000 | 0.4% |
| 42 | South Dakota | 204,469,000 | 0.3% |
| 43 | North Dakota | 202,381,000 | 0.3% |
| 44 | Rhode Island | 201,554,000 | 0.3% |
| 45 | Idaho | 192,896,000 | 0.3% |
| 46 | New Hampshire | 185,191,000 | 0.3% |
| 47 | Maine | 170,877,000 | 0.2% |
| 48 | Wyoming | 149,607,000 | 0.2% |
| 49 | Vermont | 91,220,000 | 0.1% |
| 50 | Delaware | 72,859,000 | 0.1% |
| | District of Columbia | 4,116,590,000 | 5.7% |

Source: U.S. Bureau of the Census, Governments Division
   "2011 State and Local Government Finances" (http://www.census.gov/govs/local/)

# Per Capita Local Government Revenue from the Federal Government in 2011

## National Per Capita = $233

ALPHA ORDER

| RANK | STATE | PER CAPITA |
|------|-------|------------|
| 23 | Alabama | $227 |
| 1 | Alaska | 450 |
| 35 | Arizona | 149 |
| 38 | Arkansas | 142 |
| 3 | California | 300 |
| 16 | Colorado | 249 |
| 30 | Connecticut | 181 |
| 50 | Delaware | 80 |
| 18 | Florida | 245 |
| 33 | Georgia | 159 |
| 27 | Hawaii | 196 |
| 45 | Idaho | 122 |
| 12 | Illinois | 257 |
| 47 | Indiana | 115 |
| 22 | Iowa | 229 |
| 49 | Kansas | 100 |
| 42 | Kentucky | 127 |
| 8 | Louisiana | 265 |
| 41 | Maine | 129 |
| 15 | Maryland | 253 |
| 14 | Massachusetts | 254 |
| 24 | Michigan | 217 |
| 32 | Minnesota | 172 |
| 20 | Mississippi | 240 |
| 40 | Missouri | 137 |
| 10 | Montana | 263 |
| 25 | Nebraska | 214 |
| 11 | Nevada | 262 |
| 39 | New Hampshire | 141 |
| 43 | New Jersey | 124 |
| 6 | New Mexico | 274 |
| 2 | New York | 313 |
| 21 | North Carolina | 236 |
| 5 | North Dakota | 296 |
| 25 | Ohio | 214 |
| 46 | Oklahoma | 117 |
| 3 | Oregon | 300 |
| 6 | Pennsylvania | 274 |
| 28 | Rhode Island | 192 |
| 48 | South Carolina | 105 |
| 17 | South Dakota | 248 |
| 34 | Tennessee | 151 |
| 31 | Texas | 176 |
| 19 | Utah | 244 |
| 37 | Vermont | 146 |
| 29 | Virginia | 187 |
| 13 | Washington | 256 |
| 35 | West Virginia | 149 |
| 43 | Wisconsin | 124 |
| 9 | Wyoming | 264 |

RANK ORDER

| RANK | STATE | PER CAPITA |
|------|-------|------------|
| 1 | Alaska | $450 |
| 2 | New York | 313 |
| 3 | California | 300 |
| 3 | Oregon | 300 |
| 5 | North Dakota | 296 |
| 6 | New Mexico | 274 |
| 6 | Pennsylvania | 274 |
| 8 | Louisiana | 265 |
| 9 | Wyoming | 264 |
| 10 | Montana | 263 |
| 11 | Nevada | 262 |
| 12 | Illinois | 257 |
| 13 | Washington | 256 |
| 14 | Massachusetts | 254 |
| 15 | Maryland | 253 |
| 16 | Colorado | 249 |
| 17 | South Dakota | 248 |
| 18 | Florida | 245 |
| 19 | Utah | 244 |
| 20 | Mississippi | 240 |
| 21 | North Carolina | 236 |
| 22 | Iowa | 229 |
| 23 | Alabama | 227 |
| 24 | Michigan | 217 |
| 25 | Nebraska | 214 |
| 25 | Ohio | 214 |
| 27 | Hawaii | 196 |
| 28 | Rhode Island | 192 |
| 29 | Virginia | 187 |
| 30 | Connecticut | 181 |
| 31 | Texas | 176 |
| 32 | Minnesota | 172 |
| 33 | Georgia | 159 |
| 34 | Tennessee | 151 |
| 35 | Arizona | 149 |
| 35 | West Virginia | 149 |
| 37 | Vermont | 146 |
| 38 | Arkansas | 142 |
| 39 | New Hampshire | 141 |
| 40 | Missouri | 137 |
| 41 | Maine | 129 |
| 42 | Kentucky | 127 |
| 43 | New Jersey | 124 |
| 43 | Wisconsin | 124 |
| 45 | Idaho | 122 |
| 46 | Oklahoma | 117 |
| 47 | Indiana | 115 |
| 48 | South Carolina | 105 |
| 49 | Kansas | 100 |
| 50 | Delaware | 80 |
| | District of Columbia | 6,650 |

Source: CQ Press using data from U.S. Bureau of the Census, Governments Division
"2011 State and Local Government Finances" (http://www.census.gov/govs/local/)

# Local Government Own Source Revenue in 2011

## National Total = $905,499,340,000*

| ALPHA ORDER | | | | | RANK ORDER | | | |
|---|---|---|---|---|---|---|---|---|
| RANK | STATE | REVENUE | % of USA | | RANK | STATE | REVENUE | % of USA |
| 26 | Alabama | $10,588,116,000 | 1.2% | | 1 | California | $125,296,831,000 | 13.8% |
| 42 | Alaska | 2,833,957,000 | 0.3% | | 2 | New York | 102,242,032,000 | 11.3% |
| 18 | Arizona | 14,882,247,000 | 1.6% | | 3 | Texas | 70,929,455,000 | 7.8% |
| 36 | Arkansas | 3,702,546,000 | 0.4% | | 4 | Florida | 59,364,427,000 | 6.6% |
| 1 | California | 125,296,831,000 | 13.8% | | 5 | Illinois | 39,770,326,000 | 4.4% |
| 14 | Colorado | 19,202,130,000 | 2.1% | | 6 | Pennsylvania | 33,869,278,000 | 3.7% |
| 25 | Connecticut | 10,816,232,000 | 1.2% | | 7 | New Jersey | 32,707,752,000 | 3.6% |
| 49 | Delaware | 1,302,699,000 | 0.1% | | 8 | Ohio | 29,939,763,000 | 3.3% |
| 4 | Florida | 59,364,427,000 | 6.6% | | 9 | Georgia | 25,649,666,000 | 2.8% |
| 9 | Georgia | 25,649,666,000 | 2.8% | | 10 | North Carolina | 23,219,158,000 | 2.6% |
| 45 | Hawaii | 2,446,581,000 | 0.3% | | 11 | Michigan | 21,549,843,000 | 2.4% |
| 39 | Idaho | 3,233,069,000 | 0.4% | | 12 | Virginia | 20,494,358,000 | 2.3% |
| 5 | Illinois | 39,770,326,000 | 4.4% | | 13 | Washington | 19,555,810,000 | 2.2% |
| 17 | Indiana | 15,168,191,000 | 1.7% | | 14 | Colorado | 19,202,130,000 | 2.1% |
| 28 | Iowa | 8,988,676,000 | 1.0% | | 15 | Massachusetts | 18,620,777,000 | 2.1% |
| 29 | Kansas | 8,332,428,000 | 0.9% | | 16 | Maryland | 16,977,798,000 | 1.9% |
| 30 | Kentucky | 7,682,555,000 | 0.8% | | 17 | Indiana | 15,168,191,000 | 1.7% |
| 23 | Louisiana | 12,513,989,000 | 1.4% | | 18 | Arizona | 14,882,247,000 | 1.6% |
| 40 | Maine | 3,072,220,000 | 0.3% | | 19 | Missouri | 14,717,609,000 | 1.6% |
| 16 | Maryland | 16,977,798,000 | 1.9% | | 20 | Wisconsin | 14,635,097,000 | 1.6% |
| 15 | Massachusetts | 18,620,777,000 | 2.1% | | 21 | Minnesota | 14,583,425,000 | 1.6% |
| 11 | Michigan | 21,549,843,000 | 2.4% | | 22 | Tennessee | 14,258,863,000 | 1.6% |
| 21 | Minnesota | 14,583,425,000 | 1.6% | | 23 | Louisiana | 12,513,989,000 | 1.4% |
| 33 | Mississippi | 6,532,169,000 | 0.7% | | 24 | South Carolina | 12,507,434,000 | 1.4% |
| 19 | Missouri | 14,717,609,000 | 1.6% | | 25 | Connecticut | 10,816,232,000 | 1.2% |
| 46 | Montana | 1,918,124,000 | 0.2% | | 26 | Alabama | 10,588,116,000 | 1.2% |
| 34 | Nebraska | 5,657,555,000 | 0.6% | | 27 | Oregon | 9,810,813,000 | 1.1% |
| 32 | Nevada | 6,894,063,000 | 0.8% | | 28 | Iowa | 8,988,676,000 | 1.0% |
| 38 | New Hampshire | 3,555,368,000 | 0.4% | | 29 | Kansas | 8,332,428,000 | 0.9% |
| 7 | New Jersey | 32,707,752,000 | 3.6% | | 30 | Kentucky | 7,682,555,000 | 0.8% |
| 37 | New Mexico | 3,563,476,000 | 0.4% | | 31 | Oklahoma | 7,231,317,000 | 0.8% |
| 2 | New York | 102,242,032,000 | 11.3% | | 32 | Nevada | 6,894,063,000 | 0.8% |
| 10 | North Carolina | 23,219,158,000 | 2.6% | | 33 | Mississippi | 6,532,169,000 | 0.7% |
| 48 | North Dakota | 1,501,646,000 | 0.2% | | 34 | Nebraska | 5,657,555,000 | 0.6% |
| 8 | Ohio | 29,939,763,000 | 3.3% | | 35 | Utah | 5,599,516,000 | 0.6% |
| 31 | Oklahoma | 7,231,317,000 | 0.8% | | 36 | Arkansas | 3,702,546,000 | 0.4% |
| 27 | Oregon | 9,810,813,000 | 1.1% | | 37 | New Mexico | 3,563,476,000 | 0.4% |
| 6 | Pennsylvania | 33,869,278,000 | 3.7% | | 38 | New Hampshire | 3,555,368,000 | 0.4% |
| 43 | Rhode Island | 2,816,459,000 | 0.3% | | 39 | Idaho | 3,233,069,000 | 0.4% |
| 24 | South Carolina | 12,507,434,000 | 1.4% | | 40 | Maine | 3,072,220,000 | 0.3% |
| 47 | South Dakota | 1,902,266,000 | 0.2% | | 41 | West Virginia | 2,878,308,000 | 0.3% |
| 22 | Tennessee | 14,258,863,000 | 1.6% | | 42 | Alaska | 2,833,957,000 | 0.3% |
| 3 | Texas | 70,929,455,000 | 7.8% | | 43 | Rhode Island | 2,816,459,000 | 0.3% |
| 35 | Utah | 5,599,516,000 | 0.6% | | 44 | Wyoming | 2,570,212,000 | 0.3% |
| 50 | Vermont | 755,266,000 | 0.1% | | 45 | Hawaii | 2,446,581,000 | 0.3% |
| 12 | Virginia | 20,494,358,000 | 2.3% | | 46 | Montana | 1,918,124,000 | 0.2% |
| 13 | Washington | 19,555,810,000 | 2.2% | | 47 | South Dakota | 1,902,266,000 | 0.2% |
| 41 | West Virginia | 2,878,308,000 | 0.3% | | 48 | North Dakota | 1,501,646,000 | 0.2% |
| 20 | Wisconsin | 14,635,097,000 | 1.6% | | 49 | Delaware | 1,302,699,000 | 0.1% |
| 44 | Wyoming | 2,570,212,000 | 0.3% | | 50 | Vermont | 755,266,000 | 0.1% |
| | | | | | | District of Columbia | 6,657,444,000 | 0.7% |

Source: U.S. Bureau of the Census, Governments Division
"2011 State and Local Government Finances" (http://www.census.gov/govs/local/)
*Own source revenue includes taxes, current charges, and miscellaneous general revenue. Excluded are intergovernmental transfers, insurance trust revenue, and revenue from government owned utilities and other commercial or auxiliary enterprise.

# Per Capita Local Government Own Source Revenue in 2011

## National Per Capita = $2,906*

ALPHA ORDER

| RANK | STATE | PER CAPITA |
|---|---|---|
| 36 | Alabama | $2,204 |
| 3 | Alaska | 3,915 |
| 34 | Arizona | 2,301 |
| 49 | Arkansas | 1,260 |
| 6 | California | 3,325 |
| 4 | Colorado | 3,753 |
| 10 | Connecticut | 3,016 |
| 48 | Delaware | 1,434 |
| 7 | Florida | 3,111 |
| 23 | Georgia | 2,614 |
| 44 | Hawaii | 1,775 |
| 40 | Idaho | 2,041 |
| 8 | Illinois | 3,093 |
| 31 | Indiana | 2,328 |
| 11 | Iowa | 2,934 |
| 13 | Kansas | 2,903 |
| 45 | Kentucky | 1,759 |
| 17 | Louisiana | 2,735 |
| 32 | Maine | 2,312 |
| 12 | Maryland | 2,907 |
| 15 | Massachusetts | 2,818 |
| 39 | Michigan | 2,182 |
| 18 | Minnesota | 2,727 |
| 37 | Mississippi | 2,194 |
| 29 | Missouri | 2,449 |
| 42 | Montana | 1,923 |
| 9 | Nebraska | 3,071 |
| 27 | Nevada | 2,535 |
| 19 | New Hampshire | 2,698 |
| 5 | New Jersey | 3,702 |
| 46 | New Mexico | 1,714 |
| 1 | New York | 5,243 |
| 30 | North Carolina | 2,406 |
| 38 | North Dakota | 2,193 |
| 24 | Ohio | 2,594 |
| 43 | Oklahoma | 1,911 |
| 26 | Oregon | 2,536 |
| 22 | Pennsylvania | 2,658 |
| 20 | Rhode Island | 2,681 |
| 21 | South Carolina | 2,676 |
| 33 | South Dakota | 2,310 |
| 35 | Tennessee | 2,228 |
| 16 | Texas | 2,767 |
| 41 | Utah | 1,990 |
| 50 | Vermont | 1,205 |
| 28 | Virginia | 2,529 |
| 14 | Washington | 2,866 |
| 47 | West Virginia | 1,552 |
| 25 | Wisconsin | 2,563 |
| 2 | Wyoming | 4,530 |

RANK ORDER

| RANK | STATE | PER CAPITA |
|---|---|---|
| 1 | New York | $5,243 |
| 2 | Wyoming | 4,530 |
| 3 | Alaska | 3,915 |
| 4 | Colorado | 3,753 |
| 5 | New Jersey | 3,702 |
| 6 | California | 3,325 |
| 7 | Florida | 3,111 |
| 8 | Illinois | 3,093 |
| 9 | Nebraska | 3,071 |
| 10 | Connecticut | 3,016 |
| 11 | Iowa | 2,934 |
| 12 | Maryland | 2,907 |
| 13 | Kansas | 2,903 |
| 14 | Washington | 2,866 |
| 15 | Massachusetts | 2,818 |
| 16 | Texas | 2,767 |
| 17 | Louisiana | 2,735 |
| 18 | Minnesota | 2,727 |
| 19 | New Hampshire | 2,698 |
| 20 | Rhode Island | 2,681 |
| 21 | South Carolina | 2,676 |
| 22 | Pennsylvania | 2,658 |
| 23 | Georgia | 2,614 |
| 24 | Ohio | 2,594 |
| 25 | Wisconsin | 2,563 |
| 26 | Oregon | 2,536 |
| 27 | Nevada | 2,535 |
| 28 | Virginia | 2,529 |
| 29 | Missouri | 2,449 |
| 30 | North Carolina | 2,406 |
| 31 | Indiana | 2,328 |
| 32 | Maine | 2,312 |
| 33 | South Dakota | 2,310 |
| 34 | Arizona | 2,301 |
| 35 | Tennessee | 2,228 |
| 36 | Alabama | 2,204 |
| 37 | Mississippi | 2,194 |
| 38 | North Dakota | 2,193 |
| 39 | Michigan | 2,182 |
| 40 | Idaho | 2,041 |
| 41 | Utah | 1,990 |
| 42 | Montana | 1,923 |
| 43 | Oklahoma | 1,911 |
| 44 | Hawaii | 1,775 |
| 45 | Kentucky | 1,759 |
| 46 | New Mexico | 1,714 |
| 47 | West Virginia | 1,552 |
| 48 | Delaware | 1,434 |
| 49 | Arkansas | 1,260 |
| 50 | Vermont | 1,205 |
| | District of Columbia | 10,755 |

Source: CQ Press using data from U.S. Bureau of the Census, Governments Division
   "2011 State and Local Government Finances" (http://www.census.gov/govs/local/)
*Own source revenue includes taxes, current charges, and miscellaneous general revenue. Excluded are intergovernmental transfers, insurance trust revenue, and revenue from government owned utilities and other commercial or auxiliary enterprise.

# Local Government Tax Revenue in 2011

## National Total = $578,177,391,000

ALPHA ORDER

| RANK | STATE | REVENUE | % of USA |
|------|-------|---------|----------|
| 28 | Alabama | $5,243,047,000 | 0.9% |
| 42 | Alaska | 1,754,476,000 | 0.3% |
| 19 | Arizona | 9,390,279,000 | 1.6% |
| 40 | Arkansas | 1,996,880,000 | 0.3% |
| 2 | California | 68,522,924,000 | 11.9% |
| 14 | Colorado | 12,324,184,000 | 2.1% |
| 20 | Connecticut | 9,353,756,000 | 1.6% |
| 49 | Delaware | 810,658,000 | 0.1% |
| 4 | Florida | 32,700,603,000 | 5.7% |
| 9 | Georgia | 15,129,493,000 | 2.6% |
| 43 | Hawaii | 1,715,020,000 | 0.3% |
| 44 | Idaho | 1,449,687,000 | 0.3% |
| 5 | Illinois | 28,945,752,000 | 5.0% |
| 21 | Indiana | 8,243,067,000 | 1.4% |
| 27 | Iowa | 5,412,653,000 | 0.9% |
| 29 | Kansas | 4,959,381,000 | 0.9% |
| 30 | Kentucky | 4,357,618,000 | 0.8% |
| 24 | Louisiana | 7,746,964,000 | 1.3% |
| 37 | Maine | 2,378,204,000 | 0.4% |
| 12 | Maryland | 13,013,566,000 | 2.3% |
| 11 | Massachusetts | 13,753,911,000 | 2.4% |
| 13 | Michigan | 12,572,577,000 | 2.2% |
| 23 | Minnesota | 7,869,831,000 | 1.4% |
| 36 | Mississippi | 2,719,389,000 | 0.5% |
| 18 | Missouri | 9,531,932,000 | 1.6% |
| 47 | Montana | 1,131,096,000 | 0.2% |
| 33 | Nebraska | 3,647,436,000 | 0.6% |
| 32 | Nevada | 3,882,192,000 | 0.7% |
| 35 | New Hampshire | 2,970,133,000 | 0.5% |
| 6 | New Jersey | 25,967,187,000 | 4.5% |
| 38 | New Mexico | 2,364,663,000 | 0.4% |
| 1 | New York | 76,788,844,000 | 13.3% |
| 15 | North Carolina | 11,310,041,000 | 2.0% |
| 48 | North Dakota | 887,003,000 | 0.2% |
| 8 | Ohio | 20,105,645,000 | 3.5% |
| 31 | Oklahoma | 4,234,439,000 | 0.7% |
| 26 | Oregon | 5,991,950,000 | 1.0% |
| 7 | Pennsylvania | 23,418,652,000 | 4.1% |
| 39 | Rhode Island | 2,325,842,000 | 0.4% |
| 25 | South Carolina | 6,056,306,000 | 1.0% |
| 45 | South Dakota | 1,319,547,000 | 0.2% |
| 22 | Tennessee | 7,869,998,000 | 1.4% |
| 3 | Texas | 47,632,085,000 | 8.2% |
| 34 | Utah | 3,581,230,000 | 0.6% |
| 50 | Vermont | 452,193,000 | 0.1% |
| 10 | Virginia | 14,743,900,000 | 2.6% |
| 16 | Washington | 10,998,624,000 | 1.9% |
| 41 | West Virginia | 1,764,336,000 | 0.3% |
| 17 | Wisconsin | 10,258,059,000 | 1.8% |
| 46 | Wyoming | 1,211,335,000 | 0.2% |

RANK ORDER

| RANK | STATE | REVENUE | % of USA |
|------|-------|---------|----------|
| 1 | New York | $76,788,844,000 | 13.3% |
| 2 | California | 68,522,924,000 | 11.9% |
| 3 | Texas | 47,632,085,000 | 8.2% |
| 4 | Florida | 32,700,603,000 | 5.7% |
| 5 | Illinois | 28,945,752,000 | 5.0% |
| 6 | New Jersey | 25,967,187,000 | 4.5% |
| 7 | Pennsylvania | 23,418,652,000 | 4.1% |
| 8 | Ohio | 20,105,645,000 | 3.5% |
| 9 | Georgia | 15,129,493,000 | 2.6% |
| 10 | Virginia | 14,743,900,000 | 2.6% |
| 11 | Massachusetts | 13,753,911,000 | 2.4% |
| 12 | Maryland | 13,013,566,000 | 2.3% |
| 13 | Michigan | 12,572,577,000 | 2.2% |
| 14 | Colorado | 12,324,184,000 | 2.1% |
| 15 | North Carolina | 11,310,041,000 | 2.0% |
| 16 | Washington | 10,998,624,000 | 1.9% |
| 17 | Wisconsin | 10,258,059,000 | 1.8% |
| 18 | Missouri | 9,531,932,000 | 1.6% |
| 19 | Arizona | 9,390,279,000 | 1.6% |
| 20 | Connecticut | 9,353,756,000 | 1.6% |
| 21 | Indiana | 8,243,067,000 | 1.4% |
| 22 | Tennessee | 7,869,998,000 | 1.4% |
| 23 | Minnesota | 7,869,831,000 | 1.4% |
| 24 | Louisiana | 7,746,964,000 | 1.3% |
| 25 | South Carolina | 6,056,306,000 | 1.0% |
| 26 | Oregon | 5,991,950,000 | 1.0% |
| 27 | Iowa | 5,412,653,000 | 0.9% |
| 28 | Alabama | 5,243,047,000 | 0.9% |
| 29 | Kansas | 4,959,381,000 | 0.9% |
| 30 | Kentucky | 4,357,618,000 | 0.8% |
| 31 | Oklahoma | 4,234,439,000 | 0.7% |
| 32 | Nevada | 3,882,192,000 | 0.7% |
| 33 | Nebraska | 3,647,436,000 | 0.6% |
| 34 | Utah | 3,581,230,000 | 0.6% |
| 35 | New Hampshire | 2,970,133,000 | 0.5% |
| 36 | Mississippi | 2,719,389,000 | 0.5% |
| 37 | Maine | 2,378,204,000 | 0.4% |
| 38 | New Mexico | 2,364,663,000 | 0.4% |
| 39 | Rhode Island | 2,325,842,000 | 0.4% |
| 40 | Arkansas | 1,996,880,000 | 0.3% |
| 41 | West Virginia | 1,764,336,000 | 0.3% |
| 42 | Alaska | 1,754,476,000 | 0.3% |
| 43 | Hawaii | 1,715,020,000 | 0.3% |
| 44 | Idaho | 1,449,687,000 | 0.3% |
| 45 | South Dakota | 1,319,547,000 | 0.2% |
| 46 | Wyoming | 1,211,335,000 | 0.2% |
| 47 | Montana | 1,131,096,000 | 0.2% |
| 48 | North Dakota | 887,003,000 | 0.2% |
| 49 | Delaware | 810,658,000 | 0.1% |
| 50 | Vermont | 452,193,000 | 0.1% |
| | District of Columbia | 5,368,803,000 | 0.9% |

Source: U.S. Bureau of the Census, Governments Division
"2011 State and Local Government Finances" (http://www.census.gov/govs/local/)

# Per Capita Local Government Tax Revenue in 2011

## National Per Capita = $1,856

ALPHA ORDER

| RANK | STATE | PER CAPITA |
|---|---|---|
| 43 | Alabama | $1,091 |
| 4 | Alaska | 2,424 |
| 30 | Arizona | 1,452 |
| 50 | Arkansas | 680 |
| 16 | California | 1,818 |
| 5 | Colorado | 2,409 |
| 3 | Connecticut | 2,608 |
| 48 | Delaware | 893 |
| 22 | Florida | 1,714 |
| 28 | Georgia | 1,542 |
| 37 | Hawaii | 1,244 |
| 46 | Idaho | 915 |
| 7 | Illinois | 2,251 |
| 36 | Indiana | 1,265 |
| 19 | Iowa | 1,766 |
| 21 | Kansas | 1,728 |
| 44 | Kentucky | 998 |
| 23 | Louisiana | 1,693 |
| 18 | Maine | 1,790 |
| 8 | Maryland | 2,229 |
| 11 | Massachusetts | 2,082 |
| 34 | Michigan | 1,273 |
| 29 | Minnesota | 1,472 |
| 47 | Mississippi | 913 |
| 26 | Missouri | 1,586 |
| 41 | Montana | 1,134 |
| 12 | Nebraska | 1,980 |
| 31 | Nevada | 1,427 |
| 6 | New Hampshire | 2,254 |
| 2 | New Jersey | 2,939 |
| 40 | New Mexico | 1,138 |
| 1 | New York | 3,938 |
| 39 | North Carolina | 1,172 |
| 33 | North Dakota | 1,295 |
| 20 | Ohio | 1,742 |
| 42 | Oklahoma | 1,119 |
| 27 | Oregon | 1,549 |
| 14 | Pennsylvania | 1,838 |
| 9 | Rhode Island | 2,214 |
| 32 | South Carolina | 1,296 |
| 25 | South Dakota | 1,602 |
| 38 | Tennessee | 1,230 |
| 13 | Texas | 1,858 |
| 35 | Utah | 1,272 |
| 49 | Vermont | 722 |
| 15 | Virginia | 1,819 |
| 24 | Washington | 1,612 |
| 45 | West Virginia | 951 |
| 17 | Wisconsin | 1,797 |
| 10 | Wyoming | 2,135 |

RANK ORDER

| RANK | STATE | PER CAPITA |
|---|---|---|
| 1 | New York | $3,938 |
| 2 | New Jersey | 2,939 |
| 3 | Connecticut | 2,608 |
| 4 | Alaska | 2,424 |
| 5 | Colorado | 2,409 |
| 6 | New Hampshire | 2,254 |
| 7 | Illinois | 2,251 |
| 8 | Maryland | 2,229 |
| 9 | Rhode Island | 2,214 |
| 10 | Wyoming | 2,135 |
| 11 | Massachusetts | 2,082 |
| 12 | Nebraska | 1,980 |
| 13 | Texas | 1,858 |
| 14 | Pennsylvania | 1,838 |
| 15 | Virginia | 1,819 |
| 16 | California | 1,818 |
| 17 | Wisconsin | 1,797 |
| 18 | Maine | 1,790 |
| 19 | Iowa | 1,766 |
| 20 | Ohio | 1,742 |
| 21 | Kansas | 1,728 |
| 22 | Florida | 1,714 |
| 23 | Louisiana | 1,693 |
| 24 | Washington | 1,612 |
| 25 | South Dakota | 1,602 |
| 26 | Missouri | 1,586 |
| 27 | Oregon | 1,549 |
| 28 | Georgia | 1,542 |
| 29 | Minnesota | 1,472 |
| 30 | Arizona | 1,452 |
| 31 | Nevada | 1,427 |
| 32 | South Carolina | 1,296 |
| 33 | North Dakota | 1,295 |
| 34 | Michigan | 1,273 |
| 35 | Utah | 1,272 |
| 36 | Indiana | 1,265 |
| 37 | Hawaii | 1,244 |
| 38 | Tennessee | 1,230 |
| 39 | North Carolina | 1,172 |
| 40 | New Mexico | 1,138 |
| 41 | Montana | 1,134 |
| 42 | Oklahoma | 1,119 |
| 43 | Alabama | 1,091 |
| 44 | Kentucky | 998 |
| 45 | West Virginia | 951 |
| 46 | Idaho | 915 |
| 47 | Mississippi | 913 |
| 48 | Delaware | 893 |
| 49 | Vermont | 722 |
| 50 | Arkansas | 680 |
| | District of Columbia | 8,673 |

Source: CQ Press using data from U.S. Bureau of the Census, Governments Division
"2011 State and Local Government Finances" (http://www.census.gov/govs/local/)

# Local Government Total Expenditures in 2011

## National Total = $1,664,493,675,000*

ALPHA ORDER

ALPHA ORDER

| RANK | STATE | EXPENDITURES | % of USA |
|------|-------|-------------|----------|
| 24 | Alabama | $20,930,846,000 | 1.3% |
| 41 | Alaska | 5,089,936,000 | 0.3% |
| 17 | Arizona | 28,490,919,000 | 1.7% |
| 36 | Arkansas | 10,068,451,000 | 0.6% |
| 1 | California | 264,385,783,000 | 15.9% |
| 16 | Colorado | 29,540,236,000 | 1.8% |
| 27 | Connecticut | 17,072,375,000 | 1.0% |
| 47 | Delaware | 3,255,320,000 | 0.2% |
| 4 | Florida | 99,516,831,000 | 6.0% |
| 10 | Georgia | 43,986,680,000 | 2.6% |
| 48 | Hawaii | 3,121,124,000 | 0.2% |
| 39 | Idaho | 5,370,342,000 | 0.3% |
| 5 | Illinois | 71,832,853,000 | 4.3% |
| 21 | Indiana | 26,666,866,000 | 1.6% |
| 28 | Iowa | 15,638,247,000 | 0.9% |
| 30 | Kansas | 14,054,702,000 | 0.8% |
| 29 | Kentucky | 14,773,793,000 | 0.9% |
| 23 | Louisiana | 21,950,803,000 | 1.3% |
| 42 | Maine | 4,815,473,000 | 0.3% |
| 19 | Maryland | 28,162,561,000 | 1.7% |
| 14 | Massachusetts | 32,680,752,000 | 2.0% |
| 8 | Michigan | 46,803,227,000 | 2.8% |
| 18 | Minnesota | 28,396,919,000 | 1.7% |
| 34 | Mississippi | 12,404,929,000 | 0.7% |
| 22 | Missouri | 25,095,876,000 | 1.5% |
| 45 | Montana | 3,541,586,000 | 0.2% |
| 33 | Nebraska | 12,433,533,000 | 0.7% |
| 31 | Nevada | 13,997,084,000 | 0.8% |
| 40 | New Hampshire | 5,249,410,000 | 0.3% |
| 9 | New Jersey | 45,696,118,000 | 2.7% |
| 37 | New Mexico | 8,909,817,000 | 0.5% |
| 2 | New York | 183,668,748,000 | 11.0% |
| 11 | North Carolina | 41,540,149,000 | 2.5% |
| 49 | North Dakota | 2,927,586,000 | 0.2% |
| 7 | Ohio | 55,973,542,000 | 3.4% |
| 32 | Oklahoma | 12,760,087,000 | 0.8% |
| 26 | Oregon | 18,374,983,000 | 1.1% |
| 6 | Pennsylvania | 61,901,587,000 | 3.7% |
| 44 | Rhode Island | 4,248,226,000 | 0.3% |
| 25 | South Carolina | 19,048,447,000 | 1.1% |
| 46 | South Dakota | 3,290,451,000 | 0.2% |
| 15 | Tennessee | 31,413,686,000 | 1.9% |
| 3 | Texas | 125,844,891,000 | 7.6% |
| 35 | Utah | 11,386,104,000 | 0.7% |
| 50 | Vermont | 2,621,864,000 | 0.2% |
| 13 | Virginia | 35,200,193,000 | 2.1% |
| 12 | Washington | 38,311,888,000 | 2.3% |
| 38 | West Virginia | 5,937,445,000 | 0.4% |
| 20 | Wisconsin | 27,807,304,000 | 1.7% |
| 43 | Wyoming | 4,661,812,000 | 0.3% |

RANK ORDER

| RANK | STATE | EXPENDITURES | % of USA |
|------|-------|-------------|----------|
| 1 | California | $264,385,783,000 | 15.9% |
| 2 | New York | 183,668,748,000 | 11.0% |
| 3 | Texas | 125,844,891,000 | 7.6% |
| 4 | Florida | 99,516,831,000 | 6.0% |
| 5 | Illinois | 71,832,853,000 | 4.3% |
| 6 | Pennsylvania | 61,901,587,000 | 3.7% |
| 7 | Ohio | 55,973,542,000 | 3.4% |
| 8 | Michigan | 46,803,227,000 | 2.8% |
| 9 | New Jersey | 45,696,118,000 | 2.7% |
| 10 | Georgia | 43,986,680,000 | 2.6% |
| 11 | North Carolina | 41,540,149,000 | 2.5% |
| 12 | Washington | 38,311,888,000 | 2.3% |
| 13 | Virginia | 35,200,193,000 | 2.1% |
| 14 | Massachusetts | 32,680,752,000 | 2.0% |
| 15 | Tennessee | 31,413,686,000 | 1.9% |
| 16 | Colorado | 29,540,236,000 | 1.8% |
| 17 | Arizona | 28,490,919,000 | 1.7% |
| 18 | Minnesota | 28,396,919,000 | 1.7% |
| 19 | Maryland | 28,162,561,000 | 1.7% |
| 20 | Wisconsin | 27,807,304,000 | 1.7% |
| 21 | Indiana | 26,666,866,000 | 1.6% |
| 22 | Missouri | 25,095,876,000 | 1.5% |
| 23 | Louisiana | 21,950,803,000 | 1.3% |
| 24 | Alabama | 20,930,846,000 | 1.3% |
| 25 | South Carolina | 19,048,447,000 | 1.1% |
| 26 | Oregon | 18,374,983,000 | 1.1% |
| 27 | Connecticut | 17,072,375,000 | 1.0% |
| 28 | Iowa | 15,638,247,000 | 0.9% |
| 29 | Kentucky | 14,773,793,000 | 0.9% |
| 30 | Kansas | 14,054,702,000 | 0.8% |
| 31 | Nevada | 13,997,084,000 | 0.8% |
| 32 | Oklahoma | 12,760,087,000 | 0.8% |
| 33 | Nebraska | 12,433,533,000 | 0.7% |
| 34 | Mississippi | 12,404,929,000 | 0.7% |
| 35 | Utah | 11,386,104,000 | 0.7% |
| 36 | Arkansas | 10,068,451,000 | 0.6% |
| 37 | New Mexico | 8,909,817,000 | 0.5% |
| 38 | West Virginia | 5,937,445,000 | 0.4% |
| 39 | Idaho | 5,370,342,000 | 0.3% |
| 40 | New Hampshire | 5,249,410,000 | 0.3% |
| 41 | Alaska | 5,089,936,000 | 0.3% |
| 42 | Maine | 4,815,473,000 | 0.3% |
| 43 | Wyoming | 4,661,812,000 | 0.3% |
| 44 | Rhode Island | 4,248,226,000 | 0.3% |
| 45 | Montana | 3,541,586,000 | 0.2% |
| 46 | South Dakota | 3,290,451,000 | 0.2% |
| 47 | Delaware | 3,255,320,000 | 0.2% |
| 48 | Hawaii | 3,121,124,000 | 0.2% |
| 49 | North Dakota | 2,927,586,000 | 0.2% |
| 50 | Vermont | 2,621,864,000 | 0.2% |
| | District of Columbia | 13,641,290,000 | 0.8% |

Source: U.S. Bureau of the Census, Governments Division
   "2011 State and Local Government Finances" (http://www.census.gov/govs/local/)
*Total expenditures includes all money paid other than for retirement of debt and extension of loans. Includes payments from all sources of funds including current revenues and proceeds from borrowing and prior year fund balances. Includes intergovernmental transfers and expenditures for government owned utilities and other commercial or auxiliary enterprise and insurance trust expenditures.

# Per Capita Local Government Total Expenditures in 2011

## National Per Capita = $5,342*

| ALPHA ORDER | | | | RANK ORDER | | |
|---|---|---|---|---|---|---|
| RANK | STATE | PER CAPITA | | RANK | STATE | PER CAPITA |
| 28 | Alabama | $4,357 | | 1 | New York | $9,418 |
| 3 | Alaska | 7,032 | | 2 | Wyoming | 8,217 |
| 27 | Arizona | 4,405 | | 3 | Alaska | 7,032 |
| 45 | Arkansas | 3,426 | | 4 | California | 7,016 |
| 4 | California | 7,016 | | 5 | Nebraska | 6,749 |
| 6 | Colorado | 5,774 | | 6 | Colorado | 5,774 |
| 23 | Connecticut | 4,760 | | 7 | Washington | 5,615 |
| 43 | Delaware | 3,585 | | 8 | Illinois | 5,586 |
| 10 | Florida | 5,215 | | 9 | Minnesota | 5,311 |
| 26 | Georgia | 4,483 | | 10 | Florida | 5,215 |
| 50 | Hawaii | 2,265 | | 11 | New Jersey | 5,172 |
| 46 | Idaho | 3,391 | | 12 | Nevada | 5,146 |
| 8 | Illinois | 5,586 | | 13 | Iowa | 5,104 |
| 36 | Indiana | 4,092 | | 14 | Massachusetts | 4,946 |
| 13 | Iowa | 5,104 | | 15 | Texas | 4,910 |
| 17 | Kansas | 4,896 | | 16 | Tennessee | 4,909 |
| 47 | Kentucky | 3,383 | | 17 | Kansas | 4,896 |
| 22 | Louisiana | 4,798 | | 18 | Wisconsin | 4,870 |
| 42 | Maine | 3,625 | | 19 | Pennsylvania | 4,857 |
| 21 | Maryland | 4,823 | | 20 | Ohio | 4,850 |
| 14 | Massachusetts | 4,946 | | 21 | Maryland | 4,823 |
| 25 | Michigan | 4,739 | | 22 | Louisiana | 4,798 |
| 9 | Minnesota | 5,311 | | 23 | Connecticut | 4,760 |
| 35 | Mississippi | 4,166 | | 24 | Oregon | 4,750 |
| 34 | Missouri | 4,176 | | 25 | Michigan | 4,739 |
| 44 | Montana | 3,550 | | 26 | Georgia | 4,483 |
| 5 | Nebraska | 6,749 | | 27 | Arizona | 4,405 |
| 12 | Nevada | 5,146 | | 28 | Alabama | 4,357 |
| 41 | New Hampshire | 3,983 | | 29 | Virginia | 4,343 |
| 11 | New Jersey | 5,172 | | 30 | North Carolina | 4,304 |
| 31 | New Mexico | 4,286 | | 31 | New Mexico | 4,286 |
| 1 | New York | 9,418 | | 32 | North Dakota | 4,275 |
| 30 | North Carolina | 4,304 | | 33 | Vermont | 4,184 |
| 32 | North Dakota | 4,275 | | 34 | Missouri | 4,176 |
| 20 | Ohio | 4,850 | | 35 | Mississippi | 4,166 |
| 48 | Oklahoma | 3,372 | | 36 | Indiana | 4,092 |
| 24 | Oregon | 4,750 | | 37 | South Carolina | 4,076 |
| 19 | Pennsylvania | 4,857 | | 38 | Utah | 4,046 |
| 39 | Rhode Island | 4,043 | | 39 | Rhode Island | 4,043 |
| 37 | South Carolina | 4,076 | | 40 | South Dakota | 3,995 |
| 40 | South Dakota | 3,995 | | 41 | New Hampshire | 3,983 |
| 16 | Tennessee | 4,909 | | 42 | Maine | 3,625 |
| 15 | Texas | 4,910 | | 43 | Delaware | 3,585 |
| 38 | Utah | 4,046 | | 44 | Montana | 3,550 |
| 33 | Vermont | 4,184 | | 45 | Arkansas | 3,426 |
| 29 | Virginia | 4,343 | | 46 | Idaho | 3,391 |
| 7 | Washington | 5,615 | | 47 | Kentucky | 3,383 |
| 49 | West Virginia | 3,201 | | 48 | Oklahoma | 3,372 |
| 18 | Wisconsin | 4,870 | | 49 | West Virginia | 3,201 |
| 2 | Wyoming | 8,217 | | 50 | Hawaii | 2,265 |
| | | | | District of Columbia | | 22,037 |

Source: CQ Press using data from U.S. Bureau of the Census, Governments Division
"2011 State and Local Government Finances" (http://www.census.gov/govs/local/)
*Total expenditures includes all money paid other than for retirement of debt and extension of loans. Includes payments from all sources of funds including current revenues and proceeds from borrowing and prior year fund balances. Includes intergovernmental transfers and expenditures for government owned utilities and other commercial or auxiliary enterprise and insurance trust expenditures.

# Local Government Direct General Expenditures in 2011

## National Total = $1,424,975,118,000*

ALPHA ORDER

RANK ORDER

| RANK | STATE | EXPENDITURES | % of USA | | RANK | STATE | EXPENDITURES | % of USA |
|------|-------|-------------|----------|---|------|-------|-------------|----------|
| 24 | Alabama | $17,895,510,000 | 1.3% | | 1 | California | $217,871,938,000 | 15.3% |
| 42 | Alaska | 4,557,366,000 | 0.3% | | 2 | New York | 148,881,872,000 | 10.4% |
| 20 | Arizona | 23,230,038,000 | 1.6% | | 3 | Texas | 106,710,153,000 | 7.5% |
| 34 | Arkansas | 9,076,587,000 | 0.6% | | 4 | Florida | 85,714,688,000 | 6.0% |
| 1 | California | 217,871,938,000 | 15.3% | | 5 | Illinois | 60,512,261,000 | 4.2% |
| 17 | Colorado | 25,346,183,000 | 1.8% | | 6 | Pennsylvania | 55,171,678,000 | 3.9% |
| 27 | Connecticut | 15,603,279,000 | 1.1% | | 7 | Ohio | 51,776,799,000 | 3.6% |
| 47 | Delaware | 2,821,516,000 | 0.2% | | 8 | New Jersey | 43,993,995,000 | 3.1% |
| 4 | Florida | 85,714,688,000 | 6.0% | | 9 | Michigan | 41,382,068,000 | 2.9% |
| 10 | Georgia | 37,227,506,000 | 2.6% | | 10 | Georgia | 37,227,506,000 | 2.6% |
| 49 | Hawaii | 2,450,425,000 | 0.2% | | 11 | North Carolina | 36,607,539,000 | 2.6% |
| 39 | Idaho | 5,120,020,000 | 0.4% | | 12 | Virginia | 32,051,112,000 | 2.2% |
| 5 | Illinois | 60,512,261,000 | 4.2% | | 13 | Washington | 30,234,954,000 | 2.1% |
| 19 | Indiana | 24,201,350,000 | 1.7% | | 14 | Massachusetts | 27,190,637,000 | 1.9% |
| 28 | Iowa | 14,389,876,000 | 1.0% | | 15 | Minnesota | 25,673,044,000 | 1.8% |
| 30 | Kansas | 12,648,558,000 | 0.9% | | 16 | Maryland | 25,661,116,000 | 1.8% |
| 29 | Kentucky | 12,722,370,000 | 0.9% | | 17 | Colorado | 25,346,183,000 | 1.8% |
| 23 | Louisiana | 20,272,327,000 | 1.4% | | 18 | Wisconsin | 25,101,874,000 | 1.8% |
| 41 | Maine | 4,650,486,000 | 0.3% | | 19 | Indiana | 24,201,350,000 | 1.7% |
| 16 | Maryland | 25,661,116,000 | 1.8% | | 20 | Arizona | 23,230,038,000 | 1.6% |
| 14 | Massachusetts | 27,190,637,000 | 1.9% | | 21 | Missouri | 21,654,302,000 | 1.5% |
| 9 | Michigan | 41,382,068,000 | 2.9% | | 22 | Tennessee | 21,595,507,000 | 1.5% |
| 15 | Minnesota | 25,673,044,000 | 1.8% | | 23 | Louisiana | 20,272,327,000 | 1.4% |
| 32 | Mississippi | 11,537,985,000 | 0.8% | | 24 | Alabama | 17,895,510,000 | 1.3% |
| 21 | Missouri | 21,654,302,000 | 1.5% | | 25 | South Carolina | 17,505,733,000 | 1.2% |
| 45 | Montana | 3,383,300,000 | 0.2% | | 26 | Oregon | 16,460,677,000 | 1.2% |
| 36 | Nebraska | 8,213,224,000 | 0.6% | | 27 | Connecticut | 15,603,279,000 | 1.1% |
| 31 | Nevada | 12,609,093,000 | 0.9% | | 28 | Iowa | 14,389,876,000 | 1.0% |
| 40 | New Hampshire | 5,053,034,000 | 0.4% | | 29 | Kentucky | 12,722,370,000 | 0.9% |
| 8 | New Jersey | 43,993,995,000 | 3.1% | | 30 | Kansas | 12,648,558,000 | 0.9% |
| 37 | New Mexico | 8,171,348,000 | 0.6% | | 31 | Nevada | 12,609,093,000 | 0.9% |
| 2 | New York | 148,881,872,000 | 10.4% | | 32 | Mississippi | 11,537,985,000 | 0.8% |
| 11 | North Carolina | 36,607,539,000 | 2.6% | | 33 | Oklahoma | 11,224,843,000 | 0.8% |
| 48 | North Dakota | 2,694,858,000 | 0.2% | | 34 | Arkansas | 9,076,587,000 | 0.6% |
| 7 | Ohio | 51,776,799,000 | 3.6% | | 35 | Utah | 8,767,767,000 | 0.6% |
| 33 | Oklahoma | 11,224,843,000 | 0.8% | | 36 | Nebraska | 8,213,224,000 | 0.6% |
| 26 | Oregon | 16,460,677,000 | 1.2% | | 37 | New Mexico | 8,171,348,000 | 0.6% |
| 6 | Pennsylvania | 55,171,678,000 | 3.9% | | 38 | West Virginia | 5,553,993,000 | 0.4% |
| 44 | Rhode Island | 3,896,141,000 | 0.3% | | 39 | Idaho | 5,120,020,000 | 0.4% |
| 25 | South Carolina | 17,505,733,000 | 1.2% | | 40 | New Hampshire | 5,053,034,000 | 0.4% |
| 46 | South Dakota | 2,877,707,000 | 0.2% | | 41 | Maine | 4,650,486,000 | 0.3% |
| 22 | Tennessee | 21,595,507,000 | 1.5% | | 42 | Alaska | 4,557,366,000 | 0.3% |
| 3 | Texas | 106,710,153,000 | 7.5% | | 43 | Wyoming | 4,305,124,000 | 0.3% |
| 35 | Utah | 8,767,767,000 | 0.6% | | 44 | Rhode Island | 3,896,141,000 | 0.3% |
| 50 | Vermont | 2,335,865,000 | 0.2% | | 45 | Montana | 3,383,300,000 | 0.2% |
| 12 | Virginia | 32,051,112,000 | 2.2% | | 46 | South Dakota | 2,877,707,000 | 0.2% |
| 13 | Washington | 30,234,954,000 | 2.1% | | 47 | Delaware | 2,821,516,000 | 0.2% |
| 38 | West Virginia | 5,553,993,000 | 0.4% | | 48 | North Dakota | 2,694,858,000 | 0.2% |
| 18 | Wisconsin | 25,101,874,000 | 1.8% | | 49 | Hawaii | 2,450,425,000 | 0.2% |
| 43 | Wyoming | 4,305,124,000 | 0.3% | | 50 | Vermont | 2,335,865,000 | 0.2% |
| | | | | | | District of Columbia | 10,385,492,000 | 0.7% |

Source: U.S. Bureau of the Census, Governments Division
"2011 State and Local Government Finances" (http://www.census.gov/govs/local/)
*Direct general expenditures include expenditures for current operations, assistance and subsidies, interest on debt, and capital outlay. Excludes intergovernmental transfers, expenditures for government owned utilities and other commercial or auxiliary enterprise, and insurance trust expenditures.

# Per Capita Local Government Direct General Expenditures in 2011

## National Per Capita = $4,573*

| RANK | STATE | PER CAPITA |
|------|-------|------------|
| 34 | Alabama | $3,725 |
| 3 | Alaska | 6,296 |
| 38 | Arizona | 3,592 |
| 46 | Arkansas | 3,089 |
| 4 | California | 5,782 |
| 6 | Colorado | 4,954 |
| 19 | Connecticut | 4,350 |
| 45 | Delaware | 3,107 |
| 11 | Florida | 4,492 |
| 30 | Georgia | 3,794 |
| 50 | Hawaii | 1,778 |
| 43 | Idaho | 3,233 |
| 8 | Illinois | 4,706 |
| 35 | Indiana | 3,714 |
| 9 | Iowa | 4,696 |
| 16 | Kansas | 4,407 |
| 49 | Kentucky | 2,913 |
| 14 | Louisiana | 4,431 |
| 39 | Maine | 3,500 |
| 18 | Maryland | 4,394 |
| 24 | Massachusetts | 4,115 |
| 22 | Michigan | 4,190 |
| 7 | Minnesota | 4,801 |
| 28 | Mississippi | 3,875 |
| 37 | Missouri | 3,604 |
| 41 | Montana | 3,391 |
| 13 | Nebraska | 4,458 |
| 10 | Nevada | 4,636 |
| 29 | New Hampshire | 3,834 |
| 5 | New Jersey | 4,980 |
| 27 | New Mexico | 3,931 |
| 1 | New York | 7,634 |
| 31 | North Carolina | 3,793 |
| 26 | North Dakota | 3,936 |
| 12 | Ohio | 4,486 |
| 48 | Oklahoma | 2,966 |
| 21 | Oregon | 4,255 |
| 20 | Pennsylvania | 4,329 |
| 36 | Rhode Island | 3,708 |
| 32 | South Carolina | 3,746 |
| 40 | South Dakota | 3,494 |
| 42 | Tennessee | 3,374 |
| 23 | Texas | 4,163 |
| 44 | Utah | 3,115 |
| 33 | Vermont | 3,728 |
| 25 | Virginia | 3,955 |
| 14 | Washington | 4,431 |
| 47 | West Virginia | 2,994 |
| 17 | Wisconsin | 4,396 |
| 2 | Wyoming | 7,588 |

| RANK | STATE | PER CAPITA |
|------|-------|------------|
| 1 | New York | $7,634 |
| 2 | Wyoming | 7,588 |
| 3 | Alaska | 6,296 |
| 4 | California | 5,782 |
| 5 | New Jersey | 4,980 |
| 6 | Colorado | 4,954 |
| 7 | Minnesota | 4,801 |
| 8 | Illinois | 4,706 |
| 9 | Iowa | 4,696 |
| 10 | Nevada | 4,636 |
| 11 | Florida | 4,492 |
| 12 | Ohio | 4,486 |
| 13 | Nebraska | 4,458 |
| 14 | Louisiana | 4,431 |
| 14 | Washington | 4,431 |
| 16 | Kansas | 4,407 |
| 17 | Wisconsin | 4,396 |
| 18 | Maryland | 4,394 |
| 19 | Connecticut | 4,350 |
| 20 | Pennsylvania | 4,329 |
| 21 | Oregon | 4,255 |
| 22 | Michigan | 4,190 |
| 23 | Texas | 4,163 |
| 24 | Massachusetts | 4,115 |
| 25 | Virginia | 3,955 |
| 26 | North Dakota | 3,936 |
| 27 | New Mexico | 3,931 |
| 28 | Mississippi | 3,875 |
| 29 | New Hampshire | 3,834 |
| 30 | Georgia | 3,794 |
| 31 | North Carolina | 3,793 |
| 32 | South Carolina | 3,746 |
| 33 | Vermont | 3,728 |
| 34 | Alabama | 3,725 |
| 35 | Indiana | 3,714 |
| 36 | Rhode Island | 3,708 |
| 37 | Missouri | 3,604 |
| 38 | Arizona | 3,592 |
| 39 | Maine | 3,500 |
| 40 | South Dakota | 3,494 |
| 41 | Montana | 3,391 |
| 42 | Tennessee | 3,374 |
| 43 | Idaho | 3,233 |
| 44 | Utah | 3,115 |
| 45 | Delaware | 3,107 |
| 46 | Arkansas | 3,089 |
| 47 | West Virginia | 2,994 |
| 48 | Oklahoma | 2,966 |
| 49 | Kentucky | 2,913 |
| 50 | Hawaii | 1,778 |

| | District of Columbia | 16,777 |

Source: CQ Press using data from U.S. Bureau of the Census, Governments Division
"2011 State and Local Government Finances" (http://www.census.gov/govs/local/)
*Direct general expenditures include expenditures for current operations, assistance and subsidies, interest on debt, and capital outlay. Excludes intergovernmental transfers, expenditures for government owned utilities and other commercial or auxiliary enterprise, and insurance trust expenditures.

# Local Government Debt Outstanding in 2011

## National Total = $1,774,941,465,000*

ALPHA ORDER

| RANK | STATE | DEBT | % of USA |
|---|---|---|---|
| 25 | Alabama | $20,248,092,000 | 1.1% |
| 39 | Alaska | 3,780,183,000 | 0.2% |
| 13 | Arizona | 36,763,118,000 | 2.1% |
| 34 | Arkansas | 9,795,062,000 | 0.6% |
| 1 | California | 269,161,924,000 | 15.2% |
| 14 | Colorado | 35,850,927,000 | 2.0% |
| 31 | Connecticut | 10,966,466,000 | 0.6% |
| 44 | Delaware | 2,469,978,000 | 0.1% |
| 4 | Florida | 108,432,079,000 | 6.1% |
| 10 | Georgia | 40,964,519,000 | 2.3% |
| 38 | Hawaii | 5,464,174,000 | 0.3% |
| 46 | Idaho | 2,302,914,000 | 0.1% |
| 5 | Illinois | 80,683,682,000 | 4.5% |
| 19 | Indiana | 27,260,890,000 | 1.5% |
| 32 | Iowa | 10,754,160,000 | 0.6% |
| 26 | Kansas | 20,231,862,000 | 1.1% |
| 18 | Kentucky | 27,416,048,000 | 1.5% |
| 27 | Louisiana | 20,174,789,000 | 1.1% |
| 41 | Maine | 3,079,164,000 | 0.2% |
| 28 | Maryland | 19,353,263,000 | 1.1% |
| 29 | Massachusetts | 18,242,376,000 | 1.0% |
| 9 | Michigan | 42,867,117,000 | 2.4% |
| 15 | Minnesota | 33,864,084,000 | 1.9% |
| 37 | Mississippi | 7,418,097,000 | 0.4% |
| 21 | Missouri | 25,422,792,000 | 1.4% |
| 48 | Montana | 1,710,029,000 | 0.1% |
| 33 | Nebraska | 10,596,227,000 | 0.6% |
| 22 | Nevada | 23,507,176,000 | 1.3% |
| 42 | New Hampshire | 2,787,667,000 | 0.2% |
| 11 | New Jersey | 38,254,983,000 | 2.2% |
| 36 | New Mexico | 8,530,093,000 | 0.5% |
| 3 | New York | 199,693,496,000 | 11.3% |
| 16 | North Carolina | 32,631,251,000 | 1.8% |
| 45 | North Dakota | 2,365,400,000 | 0.1% |
| 7 | Ohio | 46,559,098,000 | 2.6% |
| 35 | Oklahoma | 8,947,403,000 | 0.5% |
| 24 | Oregon | 20,684,396,000 | 1.2% |
| 6 | Pennsylvania | 78,216,434,000 | 4.4% |
| 43 | Rhode Island | 2,766,378,000 | 0.2% |
| 20 | South Carolina | 25,713,058,000 | 1.4% |
| 47 | South Dakota | 2,190,042,000 | 0.1% |
| 17 | Tennessee | 32,403,983,000 | 1.8% |
| 2 | Texas | 219,710,304,000 | 12.4% |
| 30 | Utah | 12,927,611,000 | 0.7% |
| 49 | Vermont | 1,243,803,000 | 0.1% |
| 12 | Virginia | 37,336,800,000 | 2.1% |
| 8 | Washington | 45,937,526,000 | 2.6% |
| 40 | West Virginia | 3,585,469,000 | 0.2% |
| 23 | Wisconsin | 21,393,056,000 | 1.2% |
| 50 | Wyoming | 1,005,487,000 | 0.1% |

RANK ORDER

| RANK | STATE | DEBT | % of USA |
|---|---|---|---|
| 1 | California | $269,161,924,000 | 15.2% |
| 2 | Texas | 219,710,304,000 | 12.4% |
| 3 | New York | 199,693,496,000 | 11.3% |
| 4 | Florida | 108,432,079,000 | 6.1% |
| 5 | Illinois | 80,683,682,000 | 4.5% |
| 6 | Pennsylvania | 78,216,434,000 | 4.4% |
| 7 | Ohio | 46,559,098,000 | 2.6% |
| 8 | Washington | 45,937,526,000 | 2.6% |
| 9 | Michigan | 42,867,117,000 | 2.4% |
| 10 | Georgia | 40,964,519,000 | 2.3% |
| 11 | New Jersey | 38,254,983,000 | 2.2% |
| 12 | Virginia | 37,336,800,000 | 2.1% |
| 13 | Arizona | 36,763,118,000 | 2.1% |
| 14 | Colorado | 35,850,927,000 | 2.0% |
| 15 | Minnesota | 33,864,084,000 | 1.9% |
| 16 | North Carolina | 32,631,251,000 | 1.8% |
| 17 | Tennessee | 32,403,983,000 | 1.8% |
| 18 | Kentucky | 27,416,048,000 | 1.5% |
| 19 | Indiana | 27,260,890,000 | 1.5% |
| 20 | South Carolina | 25,713,058,000 | 1.4% |
| 21 | Missouri | 25,422,792,000 | 1.4% |
| 22 | Nevada | 23,507,176,000 | 1.3% |
| 23 | Wisconsin | 21,393,056,000 | 1.2% |
| 24 | Oregon | 20,684,396,000 | 1.2% |
| 25 | Alabama | 20,248,092,000 | 1.1% |
| 26 | Kansas | 20,231,862,000 | 1.1% |
| 27 | Louisiana | 20,174,789,000 | 1.1% |
| 28 | Maryland | 19,353,263,000 | 1.1% |
| 29 | Massachusetts | 18,242,376,000 | 1.0% |
| 30 | Utah | 12,927,611,000 | 0.7% |
| 31 | Connecticut | 10,966,466,000 | 0.6% |
| 32 | Iowa | 10,754,160,000 | 0.6% |
| 33 | Nebraska | 10,596,227,000 | 0.6% |
| 34 | Arkansas | 9,795,062,000 | 0.6% |
| 35 | Oklahoma | 8,947,403,000 | 0.5% |
| 36 | New Mexico | 8,530,093,000 | 0.5% |
| 37 | Mississippi | 7,418,097,000 | 0.4% |
| 38 | Hawaii | 5,464,174,000 | 0.3% |
| 39 | Alaska | 3,780,183,000 | 0.2% |
| 40 | West Virginia | 3,585,469,000 | 0.2% |
| 41 | Maine | 3,079,164,000 | 0.2% |
| 42 | New Hampshire | 2,787,667,000 | 0.2% |
| 43 | Rhode Island | 2,766,378,000 | 0.2% |
| 44 | Delaware | 2,469,978,000 | 0.1% |
| 45 | North Dakota | 2,365,400,000 | 0.1% |
| 46 | Idaho | 2,302,914,000 | 0.1% |
| 47 | South Dakota | 2,190,042,000 | 0.1% |
| 48 | Montana | 1,710,029,000 | 0.1% |
| 49 | Vermont | 1,243,803,000 | 0.1% |
| 50 | Wyoming | 1,005,487,000 | 0.1% |
| | District of Columbia | 11,276,535,000 | 0.6% |

Source: U.S. Bureau of the Census, Governments Division
    "2011 State and Local Government Finances" (http://www.census.gov/govs/local/)
*Includes short-term, long-term, full faith and credit, nonguaranteed, and public debt for private purposes.

# Per Capita Local Government Debt Outstanding in 2011

## National Per Capita = $5,696*

ALPHA ORDER

| RANK | STATE | PER CAPITA |
|------|-------|------------|
| 25 | Alabama | $4,215 |
| 17 | Alaska | 5,222 |
| 13 | Arizona | 5,684 |
| 35 | Arkansas | 3,333 |
| 4 | California | 7,143 |
| 6 | Colorado | 7,007 |
| 37 | Connecticut | 3,058 |
| 39 | Delaware | 2,720 |
| 14 | Florida | 5,682 |
| 27 | Georgia | 4,175 |
| 30 | Hawaii | 3,965 |
| 50 | Idaho | 1,454 |
| 10 | Illinois | 6,274 |
| 26 | Indiana | 4,183 |
| 32 | Iowa | 3,510 |
| 5 | Kansas | 7,048 |
| 9 | Kentucky | 6,278 |
| 21 | Louisiana | 4,410 |
| 44 | Maine | 2,318 |
| 36 | Maryland | 3,314 |
| 38 | Massachusetts | 2,761 |
| 22 | Michigan | 4,340 |
| 8 | Minnesota | 6,333 |
| 42 | Mississippi | 2,491 |
| 24 | Missouri | 4,231 |
| 49 | Montana | 1,714 |
| 12 | Nebraska | 5,752 |
| 2 | Nevada | 8,642 |
| 45 | New Hampshire | 2,115 |
| 23 | New Jersey | 4,330 |
| 28 | New Mexico | 4,104 |
| 1 | New York | 10,240 |
| 34 | North Carolina | 3,381 |
| 33 | North Dakota | 3,454 |
| 29 | Ohio | 4,034 |
| 43 | Oklahoma | 2,364 |
| 16 | Oregon | 5,347 |
| 11 | Pennsylvania | 6,138 |
| 41 | Rhode Island | 2,633 |
| 15 | South Carolina | 5,502 |
| 40 | South Dakota | 2,659 |
| 18 | Tennessee | 5,063 |
| 3 | Texas | 8,572 |
| 20 | Utah | 4,593 |
| 46 | Vermont | 1,985 |
| 19 | Virginia | 4,607 |
| 7 | Washington | 6,732 |
| 47 | West Virginia | 1,933 |
| 31 | Wisconsin | 3,747 |
| 48 | Wyoming | 1,772 |

RANK ORDER

| RANK | STATE | PER CAPITA |
|------|-------|------------|
| 1 | New York | $10,240 |
| 2 | Nevada | 8,642 |
| 3 | Texas | 8,572 |
| 4 | California | 7,143 |
| 5 | Kansas | 7,048 |
| 6 | Colorado | 7,007 |
| 7 | Washington | 6,732 |
| 8 | Minnesota | 6,333 |
| 9 | Kentucky | 6,278 |
| 10 | Illinois | 6,274 |
| 11 | Pennsylvania | 6,138 |
| 12 | Nebraska | 5,752 |
| 13 | Arizona | 5,684 |
| 14 | Florida | 5,682 |
| 15 | South Carolina | 5,502 |
| 16 | Oregon | 5,347 |
| 17 | Alaska | 5,222 |
| 18 | Tennessee | 5,063 |
| 19 | Virginia | 4,607 |
| 20 | Utah | 4,593 |
| 21 | Louisiana | 4,410 |
| 22 | Michigan | 4,340 |
| 23 | New Jersey | 4,330 |
| 24 | Missouri | 4,231 |
| 25 | Alabama | 4,215 |
| 26 | Indiana | 4,183 |
| 27 | Georgia | 4,175 |
| 28 | New Mexico | 4,104 |
| 29 | Ohio | 4,034 |
| 30 | Hawaii | 3,965 |
| 31 | Wisconsin | 3,747 |
| 32 | Iowa | 3,510 |
| 33 | North Dakota | 3,454 |
| 34 | North Carolina | 3,381 |
| 35 | Arkansas | 3,333 |
| 36 | Maryland | 3,314 |
| 37 | Connecticut | 3,058 |
| 38 | Massachusetts | 2,761 |
| 39 | Delaware | 2,720 |
| 40 | South Dakota | 2,659 |
| 41 | Rhode Island | 2,633 |
| 42 | Mississippi | 2,491 |
| 43 | Oklahoma | 2,364 |
| 44 | Maine | 2,318 |
| 45 | New Hampshire | 2,115 |
| 46 | Vermont | 1,985 |
| 47 | West Virginia | 1,933 |
| 48 | Wyoming | 1,772 |
| 49 | Montana | 1,714 |
| 50 | Idaho | 1,454 |

District of Columbia 18,217

Source: CQ Press using data from U.S. Bureau of the Census, Governments Division
"2011 State and Local Government Finances" (http://www.census.gov/govs/local/)
*Includes short-term, long-term, full faith and credit, nonguaranteed, and public debt for private purposes.

# Local Government Full-Time Equivalent Employees in 2011

## National Total = 11,999,059 FTE Employees*

ALPHA ORDER

| RANK | STATE | EMPLOYEES | % of USA |
|------|-------|-----------|----------|
| 24 | Alabama | 195,010 | 1.6% |
| 46 | Alaska | 27,996 | 0.2% |
| 20 | Arizona | 212,009 | 1.8% |
| 31 | Arkansas | 127,046 | 1.1% |
| 1 | California | 1,344,749 | 11.2% |
| 21 | Colorado | 198,053 | 1.7% |
| 33 | Connecticut | 123,119 | 1.0% |
| 49 | Delaware | 23,536 | 0.2% |
| 4 | Florida | 703,922 | 5.9% |
| 9 | Georgia | 385,649 | 3.2% |
| 50 | Hawaii | 15,527 | 0.1% |
| 39 | Idaho | 56,796 | 0.5% |
| 5 | Illinois | 495,768 | 4.1% |
| 14 | Indiana | 239,707 | 2.0% |
| 32 | Iowa | 126,890 | 1.1% |
| 27 | Kansas | 153,292 | 1.3% |
| 26 | Kentucky | 165,366 | 1.4% |
| 23 | Louisiana | 197,195 | 1.6% |
| 40 | Maine | 54,016 | 0.5% |
| 18 | Maryland | 220,317 | 1.8% |
| 16 | Massachusetts | 228,705 | 1.9% |
| 12 | Michigan | 311,657 | 2.6% |
| 22 | Minnesota | 197,507 | 1.6% |
| 29 | Mississippi | 134,339 | 1.1% |
| 15 | Missouri | 229,949 | 1.9% |
| 43 | Montana | 37,079 | 0.3% |
| 35 | Nebraska | 88,909 | 0.7% |
| 36 | Nevada | 86,186 | 0.7% |
| 41 | New Hampshire | 52,879 | 0.4% |
| 10 | New Jersey | 341,313 | 2.8% |
| 37 | New Mexico | 78,870 | 0.7% |
| 3 | New York | 932,034 | 7.8% |
| 8 | North Carolina | 401,701 | 3.3% |
| 47 | North Dakota | 26,455 | 0.2% |
| 6 | Ohio | 455,646 | 3.8% |
| 28 | Oklahoma | 146,418 | 1.2% |
| 30 | Oregon | 131,757 | 1.1% |
| 7 | Pennsylvania | 423,378 | 3.5% |
| 45 | Rhode Island | 30,846 | 0.3% |
| 25 | South Carolina | 176,232 | 1.5% |
| 44 | South Dakota | 31,393 | 0.3% |
| 13 | Tennessee | 241,242 | 2.0% |
| 2 | Texas | 1,131,828 | 9.4% |
| 34 | Utah | 94,090 | 0.8% |
| 48 | Vermont | 25,230 | 0.2% |
| 11 | Virginia | 313,907 | 2.6% |
| 17 | Washington | 225,231 | 1.9% |
| 38 | West Virginia | 63,819 | 0.5% |
| 19 | Wisconsin | 212,677 | 1.8% |
| 42 | Wyoming | 39,316 | 0.3% |

RANK ORDER

| RANK | STATE | EMPLOYEES | % of USA |
|------|-------|-----------|----------|
| 1 | California | 1,344,749 | 11.2% |
| 2 | Texas | 1,131,828 | 9.4% |
| 3 | New York | 932,034 | 7.8% |
| 4 | Florida | 703,922 | 5.9% |
| 5 | Illinois | 495,768 | 4.1% |
| 6 | Ohio | 455,646 | 3.8% |
| 7 | Pennsylvania | 423,378 | 3.5% |
| 8 | North Carolina | 401,701 | 3.3% |
| 9 | Georgia | 385,649 | 3.2% |
| 10 | New Jersey | 341,313 | 2.8% |
| 11 | Virginia | 313,907 | 2.6% |
| 12 | Michigan | 311,657 | 2.6% |
| 13 | Tennessee | 241,242 | 2.0% |
| 14 | Indiana | 239,707 | 2.0% |
| 15 | Missouri | 229,949 | 1.9% |
| 16 | Massachusetts | 228,705 | 1.9% |
| 17 | Washington | 225,231 | 1.9% |
| 18 | Maryland | 220,317 | 1.8% |
| 19 | Wisconsin | 212,677 | 1.8% |
| 20 | Arizona | 212,009 | 1.8% |
| 21 | Colorado | 198,053 | 1.7% |
| 22 | Minnesota | 197,507 | 1.6% |
| 23 | Louisiana | 197,195 | 1.6% |
| 24 | Alabama | 195,010 | 1.6% |
| 25 | South Carolina | 176,232 | 1.5% |
| 26 | Kentucky | 165,366 | 1.4% |
| 27 | Kansas | 153,292 | 1.3% |
| 28 | Oklahoma | 146,418 | 1.2% |
| 29 | Mississippi | 134,339 | 1.1% |
| 30 | Oregon | 131,757 | 1.1% |
| 31 | Arkansas | 127,046 | 1.1% |
| 32 | Iowa | 126,890 | 1.1% |
| 33 | Connecticut | 123,119 | 1.0% |
| 34 | Utah | 94,090 | 0.8% |
| 35 | Nebraska | 88,909 | 0.7% |
| 36 | Nevada | 86,186 | 0.7% |
| 37 | New Mexico | 78,870 | 0.7% |
| 38 | West Virginia | 63,819 | 0.5% |
| 39 | Idaho | 56,796 | 0.5% |
| 40 | Maine | 54,016 | 0.5% |
| 41 | New Hampshire | 52,879 | 0.4% |
| 42 | Wyoming | 39,316 | 0.3% |
| 43 | Montana | 37,079 | 0.3% |
| 44 | South Dakota | 31,393 | 0.3% |
| 45 | Rhode Island | 30,846 | 0.3% |
| 46 | Alaska | 27,996 | 0.2% |
| 47 | North Dakota | 26,455 | 0.2% |
| 48 | Vermont | 25,230 | 0.2% |
| 49 | Delaware | 23,536 | 0.2% |
| 50 | Hawaii | 15,527 | 0.1% |
| | District of Columbia | 42,502 | 0.4% |

Source: U.S. Bureau of the Census, Governments Division
   "Government Employment and Payroll" (http://www.census.gov/govs/apes/index.html)
*As of March 2011.

# Rate of Local Government Full-Time Equivalent Employees in 2011

## National Rate = 385 Local Government Employees per 10,000 Population*

| ALPHA ORDER | | | RANK ORDER | | |
|---|---|---|---|---|---|
| RANK | STATE | RATE | RANK | STATE | RATE |
| 12 | Alabama | 406 | 1 | Wyoming | 693 |
| 17 | Alaska | 387 | 2 | Kansas | 534 |
| 45 | Arizona | 328 | 3 | Nebraska | 483 |
| 7 | Arkansas | 432 | 4 | New York | 478 |
| 37 | California | 357 | 5 | Mississippi | 451 |
| 17 | Colorado | 387 | 6 | Texas | 442 |
| 40 | Connecticut | 343 | 7 | Arkansas | 432 |
| 49 | Delaware | 259 | 8 | Louisiana | 431 |
| 33 | Florida | 369 | 9 | North Carolina | 416 |
| 16 | Georgia | 393 | 10 | Iowa | 414 |
| 50 | Hawaii | 113 | 11 | Maine | 407 |
| 36 | Idaho | 359 | 12 | Alabama | 406 |
| 21 | Illinois | 386 | 13 | Vermont | 403 |
| 35 | Indiana | 368 | 14 | New Hampshire | 401 |
| 10 | Iowa | 414 | 15 | Ohio | 395 |
| 2 | Kansas | 534 | 16 | Georgia | 393 |
| 26 | Kentucky | 379 | 17 | Alaska | 387 |
| 8 | Louisiana | 431 | 17 | Colorado | 387 |
| 11 | Maine | 407 | 17 | Oklahoma | 387 |
| 28 | Maryland | 377 | 17 | Virginia | 387 |
| 38 | Massachusetts | 346 | 21 | Illinois | 386 |
| 47 | Michigan | 316 | 21 | New Jersey | 386 |
| 33 | Minnesota | 369 | 21 | North Dakota | 386 |
| 5 | Mississippi | 451 | 24 | Missouri | 383 |
| 24 | Missouri | 383 | 25 | South Dakota | 381 |
| 31 | Montana | 372 | 26 | Kentucky | 379 |
| 3 | Nebraska | 483 | 26 | New Mexico | 379 |
| 46 | Nevada | 317 | 28 | Maryland | 377 |
| 14 | New Hampshire | 401 | 28 | South Carolina | 377 |
| 21 | New Jersey | 386 | 28 | Tennessee | 377 |
| 26 | New Mexico | 379 | 31 | Montana | 372 |
| 4 | New York | 478 | 31 | Wisconsin | 372 |
| 9 | North Carolina | 416 | 33 | Florida | 369 |
| 21 | North Dakota | 386 | 33 | Minnesota | 369 |
| 15 | Ohio | 395 | 35 | Indiana | 368 |
| 17 | Oklahoma | 387 | 36 | Idaho | 359 |
| 41 | Oregon | 341 | 37 | California | 357 |
| 43 | Pennsylvania | 332 | 38 | Massachusetts | 346 |
| 48 | Rhode Island | 294 | 39 | West Virginia | 344 |
| 28 | South Carolina | 377 | 40 | Connecticut | 343 |
| 25 | South Dakota | 381 | 41 | Oregon | 341 |
| 28 | Tennessee | 377 | 42 | Utah | 334 |
| 6 | Texas | 442 | 43 | Pennsylvania | 332 |
| 42 | Utah | 334 | 44 | Washington | 330 |
| 13 | Vermont | 403 | 45 | Arizona | 328 |
| 17 | Virginia | 387 | 46 | Nevada | 317 |
| 44 | Washington | 330 | 47 | Michigan | 316 |
| 39 | West Virginia | 344 | 48 | Rhode Island | 294 |
| 31 | Wisconsin | 372 | 49 | Delaware | 259 |
| 1 | Wyoming | 693 | 50 | Hawaii | 113 |
| | | | | District of Columbia | 687 |

Source: CQ Press using data from U.S. Bureau of the Census, Governments Division
"Government Employment and Payroll" (http://www.census.gov/govs/apes/index.html)
*Full-time equivalent as of March 2011.

# Average Annual Earnings of Full-Time Local Government Employees in 2011

## National Average = $52,061*

ALPHA ORDER

| RANK | STATE | SALARY |
|------|-------|--------|
| 43 | Alabama | $39,132 |
| 9 | Alaska | 60,536 |
| 22 | Arizona | 49,116 |
| 50 | Arkansas | 32,755 |
| 1 | California | 70,351 |
| 19 | Colorado | 51,357 |
| 5 | Connecticut | 62,529 |
| 14 | Delaware | 54,878 |
| 23 | Florida | 47,978 |
| 36 | Georgia | 41,540 |
| 11 | Hawaii | 59,163 |
| 42 | Idaho | 39,464 |
| 12 | Illinois | 57,569 |
| 30 | Indiana | 43,781 |
| 25 | Iowa | 47,307 |
| 39 | Kansas | 40,918 |
| 46 | Kentucky | 37,420 |
| 40 | Louisiana | 40,364 |
| 49 | Maine | 34,636 |
| 6 | Maryland | 61,506 |
| 10 | Massachusetts | 59,479 |
| 13 | Michigan | 55,824 |
| 15 | Minnesota | 54,296 |
| 48 | Mississippi | 35,679 |
| 34 | Missouri | 42,638 |
| 31 | Montana | 43,346 |
| 24 | Nebraska | 47,493 |
| 7 | Nevada | 61,497 |
| 27 | New Hampshire | 46,563 |
| 3 | New Jersey | 65,985 |
| 37 | New Mexico | 41,456 |
| 4 | New York | 65,304 |
| 35 | North Carolina | 42,608 |
| 32 | North Dakota | 42,750 |
| 20 | Ohio | 49,910 |
| 47 | Oklahoma | 37,044 |
| 16 | Oregon | 53,655 |
| 18 | Pennsylvania | 52,495 |
| 8 | Rhode Island | 60,863 |
| 38 | South Carolina | 41,176 |
| 45 | South Dakota | 37,595 |
| 41 | Tennessee | 39,660 |
| 29 | Texas | 44,031 |
| 33 | Utah | 42,663 |
| 28 | Vermont | 44,367 |
| 26 | Virginia | 46,588 |
| 2 | Washington | 67,134 |
| 44 | West Virginia | 38,486 |
| 17 | Wisconsin | 52,783 |
| 21 | Wyoming | 49,167 |

RANK ORDER

| RANK | STATE | SALARY |
|------|-------|--------|
| 1 | California | $70,351 |
| 2 | Washington | 67,134 |
| 3 | New Jersey | 65,985 |
| 4 | New York | 65,304 |
| 5 | Connecticut | 62,529 |
| 6 | Maryland | 61,506 |
| 7 | Nevada | 61,497 |
| 8 | Rhode Island | 60,863 |
| 9 | Alaska | 60,536 |
| 10 | Massachusetts | 59,479 |
| 11 | Hawaii | 59,163 |
| 12 | Illinois | 57,569 |
| 13 | Michigan | 55,824 |
| 14 | Delaware | 54,878 |
| 15 | Minnesota | 54,296 |
| 16 | Oregon | 53,655 |
| 17 | Wisconsin | 52,783 |
| 18 | Pennsylvania | 52,495 |
| 19 | Colorado | 51,357 |
| 20 | Ohio | 49,910 |
| 21 | Wyoming | 49,167 |
| 22 | Arizona | 49,116 |
| 23 | Florida | 47,978 |
| 24 | Nebraska | 47,493 |
| 25 | Iowa | 47,307 |
| 26 | Virginia | 46,588 |
| 27 | New Hampshire | 46,563 |
| 28 | Vermont | 44,367 |
| 29 | Texas | 44,031 |
| 30 | Indiana | 43,781 |
| 31 | Montana | 43,346 |
| 32 | North Dakota | 42,750 |
| 33 | Utah | 42,663 |
| 34 | Missouri | 42,638 |
| 35 | North Carolina | 42,608 |
| 36 | Georgia | 41,540 |
| 37 | New Mexico | 41,456 |
| 38 | South Carolina | 41,176 |
| 39 | Kansas | 40,918 |
| 40 | Louisiana | 40,364 |
| 41 | Tennessee | 39,660 |
| 42 | Idaho | 39,464 |
| 43 | Alabama | 39,132 |
| 44 | West Virginia | 38,486 |
| 45 | South Dakota | 37,595 |
| 46 | Kentucky | 37,420 |
| 47 | Oklahoma | 37,044 |
| 48 | Mississippi | 35,679 |
| 49 | Maine | 34,636 |
| 50 | Arkansas | 32,755 |
| | District of Columbia | 72,821 |

Source: CQ Press using data from U.S. Bureau of the Census, Governments Division
"Government Employment and Payroll" (http://www.census.gov/govs/apes/index.html)
*March 2011 full-time payroll (multiplied by 12) divided by full-time employees.

# XI. Health

# Average Annual Single Coverage Health Insurance Premium per Enrolled Employee in 2012
## National Average = $5,384*

ALPHA ORDER

| RANK | STATE | PREMIUM |
|---|---|---|
| 45 | Alabama | $4,961 |
| 1 | Alaska | 7,420 |
| 31 | Arizona | 5,196 |
| 49 | Arkansas | 4,459 |
| 18 | California | 5,422 |
| 30 | Colorado | 5,275 |
| 4 | Connecticut | 5,934 |
| 14 | Delaware | 5,583 |
| 32 | Florida | 5,179 |
| 34 | Georgia | 5,159 |
| 41 | Hawaii | 5,076 |
| 50 | Idaho | 4,439 |
| 20 | Illinois | 5,404 |
| 16 | Indiana | 5,504 |
| 36 | Iowa | 5,141 |
| 44 | Kansas | 4,968 |
| 21 | Kentucky | 5,397 |
| 23 | Louisiana | 5,381 |
| 10 | Maine | 5,692 |
| 29 | Maryland | 5,302 |
| 2 | Massachusetts | 6,121 |
| 26 | Michigan | 5,365 |
| 27 | Minnesota | 5,338 |
| 48 | Mississippi | 4,713 |
| 35 | Missouri | 5,150 |
| 13 | Montana | 5,585 |
| 38 | Nebraska | 5,101 |
| 46 | Nevada | 4,949 |
| 11 | New Hampshire | 5,688 |
| 8 | New Jersey | 5,837 |
| 43 | New Mexico | 5,035 |
| 3 | New York | 6,033 |
| 12 | North Carolina | 5,632 |
| 24 | North Dakota | 5,377 |
| 40 | Ohio | 5,081 |
| 47 | Oklahoma | 4,851 |
| 17 | Oregon | 5,460 |
| 22 | Pennsylvania | 5,385 |
| 6 | Rhode Island | 5,870 |
| 39 | South Carolina | 5,098 |
| 19 | South Dakota | 5,409 |
| 42 | Tennessee | 5,067 |
| 37 | Texas | 5,124 |
| 33 | Utah | 5,162 |
| 15 | Vermont | 5,580 |
| 28 | Virginia | 5,309 |
| 25 | Washington | 5,368 |
| 5 | West Virginia | 5,884 |
| 9 | Wisconsin | 5,737 |
| 7 | Wyoming | 5,861 |

RANK ORDER

| RANK | STATE | PREMIUM |
|---|---|---|
| 1 | Alaska | $7,420 |
| 2 | Massachusetts | 6,121 |
| 3 | New York | 6,033 |
| 4 | Connecticut | 5,934 |
| 5 | West Virginia | 5,884 |
| 6 | Rhode Island | 5,870 |
| 7 | Wyoming | 5,861 |
| 8 | New Jersey | 5,837 |
| 9 | Wisconsin | 5,737 |
| 10 | Maine | 5,692 |
| 11 | New Hampshire | 5,688 |
| 12 | North Carolina | 5,632 |
| 13 | Montana | 5,585 |
| 14 | Delaware | 5,583 |
| 15 | Vermont | 5,580 |
| 16 | Indiana | 5,504 |
| 17 | Oregon | 5,460 |
| 18 | California | 5,422 |
| 19 | South Dakota | 5,409 |
| 20 | Illinois | 5,404 |
| 21 | Kentucky | 5,397 |
| 22 | Pennsylvania | 5,385 |
| 23 | Louisiana | 5,381 |
| 24 | North Dakota | 5,377 |
| 25 | Washington | 5,368 |
| 26 | Michigan | 5,365 |
| 27 | Minnesota | 5,338 |
| 28 | Virginia | 5,309 |
| 29 | Maryland | 5,302 |
| 30 | Colorado | 5,275 |
| 31 | Arizona | 5,196 |
| 32 | Florida | 5,179 |
| 33 | Utah | 5,162 |
| 34 | Georgia | 5,159 |
| 35 | Missouri | 5,150 |
| 36 | Iowa | 5,141 |
| 37 | Texas | 5,124 |
| 38 | Nebraska | 5,101 |
| 39 | South Carolina | 5,098 |
| 40 | Ohio | 5,081 |
| 41 | Hawaii | 5,076 |
| 42 | Tennessee | 5,067 |
| 43 | New Mexico | 5,035 |
| 44 | Kansas | 4,968 |
| 45 | Alabama | 4,961 |
| 46 | Nevada | 4,949 |
| 47 | Oklahoma | 4,851 |
| 48 | Mississippi | 4,713 |
| 49 | Arkansas | 4,459 |
| 50 | Idaho | 4,439 |
| | District of Columbia | 5,581 |

Source: U.S. Department of Health and Human Services, Agency for Healthcare Research and Quality
"Private-Sector Data by Firm Size and State" (Table II Series, Medical Expenditures Panel Survey)
(http://www.meps.ahrq.gov/mepsweb/survey_comp/Insurance.jsp)
*Enrolled employees at private-sector establishments that offer health insurance coverage.

# Average Annual Family Coverage Health Insurance Premium per Enrolled Employee in 2012
## National Average = $15,473*

| ALPHA ORDER | | | | RANK ORDER | | |
|---|---|---|---|---|---|---|
| RANK | STATE | PREMIUM | | RANK | STATE | PREMIUM |
| 50 | Alabama | $12,764 | | 1 | Alaska | $17,902 |
| 1 | Alaska | 17,902 | | 2 | Massachusetts | 17,129 |
| 27 | Arizona | 15,250 | | 3 | New Jersey | 16,947 |
| 48 | Arkansas | 13,295 | | 4 | New York | 16,924 |
| 11 | California | 15,898 | | 5 | Connecticut | 16,891 |
| 10 | Colorado | 16,037 | | 6 | New Hampshire | 16,372 |
| 5 | Connecticut | 16,891 | | 7 | Washington | 16,291 |
| 18 | Delaware | 15,599 | | 8 | Wisconsin | 16,248 |
| 21 | Florida | 15,471 | | 9 | Maine | 16,203 |
| 36 | Georgia | 14,646 | | 10 | Colorado | 16,037 |
| 34 | Hawaii | 14,722 | | 11 | California | 15,898 |
| 45 | Idaho | 14,057 | | 12 | New Mexico | 15,880 |
| 14 | Illinois | 15,753 | | 13 | Rhode Island | 15,863 |
| 22 | Indiana | 15,461 | | 14 | Illinois | 15,753 |
| 42 | Iowa | 14,310 | | 15 | Kentucky | 15,734 |
| 46 | Kansas | 13,750 | | 16 | West Virginia | 15,640 |
| 15 | Kentucky | 15,734 | | 17 | North Carolina | 15,606 |
| 30 | Louisiana | 15,091 | | 18 | Delaware | 15,599 |
| 9 | Maine | 16,203 | | 19 | Wyoming | 15,598 |
| 28 | Maryland | 15,239 | | 20 | Oregon | 15,487 |
| 2 | Massachusetts | 17,129 | | 21 | Florida | 15,471 |
| 40 | Michigan | 14,397 | | 22 | Indiana | 15,461 |
| 24 | Minnesota | 15,408 | | 23 | Ohio | 15,455 |
| 44 | Mississippi | 14,172 | | 24 | Minnesota | 15,408 |
| 32 | Missouri | 14,986 | | 25 | Virginia | 15,376 |
| 35 | Montana | 14,704 | | 26 | Pennsylvania | 15,369 |
| 39 | Nebraska | 14,472 | | 27 | Arizona | 15,250 |
| 49 | Nevada | 12,904 | | 28 | Maryland | 15,239 |
| 6 | New Hampshire | 16,372 | | 29 | Vermont | 15,093 |
| 3 | New Jersey | 16,947 | | 30 | Louisiana | 15,091 |
| 12 | New Mexico | 15,880 | | 31 | South Dakota | 14,999 |
| 4 | New York | 16,924 | | 32 | Missouri | 14,986 |
| 17 | North Carolina | 15,606 | | 33 | Tennessee | 14,888 |
| 41 | North Dakota | 14,348 | | 34 | Hawaii | 14,722 |
| 23 | Ohio | 15,455 | | 35 | Montana | 14,704 |
| 47 | Oklahoma | 13,554 | | 36 | Georgia | 14,646 |
| 20 | Oregon | 15,487 | | 37 | Texas | 14,616 |
| 26 | Pennsylvania | 15,369 | | 38 | Utah | 14,558 |
| 13 | Rhode Island | 15,863 | | 39 | Nebraska | 14,472 |
| 43 | South Carolina | 14,285 | | 40 | Michigan | 14,397 |
| 31 | South Dakota | 14,999 | | 41 | North Dakota | 14,348 |
| 33 | Tennessee | 14,888 | | 42 | Iowa | 14,310 |
| 37 | Texas | 14,616 | | 43 | South Carolina | 14,285 |
| 38 | Utah | 14,558 | | 44 | Mississippi | 14,172 |
| 29 | Vermont | 15,093 | | 45 | Idaho | 14,057 |
| 25 | Virginia | 15,376 | | 46 | Kansas | 13,750 |
| 7 | Washington | 16,291 | | 47 | Oklahoma | 13,554 |
| 16 | West Virginia | 15,640 | | 48 | Arkansas | 13,295 |
| 8 | Wisconsin | 16,248 | | 49 | Nevada | 12,904 |
| 19 | Wyoming | 15,598 | | 50 | Alabama | 12,764 |
| | | | | | District of Columbia | 17,206 |

Source: U.S. Department of Health and Human Services, Agency for Healthcare Research and Quality
   "Private-Sector Data by Firm Size and State" (Table II Series, Medical Expenditures Panel Survey)
   (http://www.meps.ahrq.gov/mepsweb/survey_comp/Insurance.jsp)
*Enrolled employees at private-sector establishments that offer health insurance coverage.

# Percent of Private-Sector Establishments That Offer Health Insurance: 2012

## National Percent = 50.1%

| ALPHA ORDER | | | | RANK ORDER | | |
|---|---|---|---|---|---|---|
| RANK | STATE | PERCENT | | RANK | STATE | PERCENT |
| 16 | Alabama | 52.4 | | 1 | Hawaii | 84.1 |
| 47 | Alaska | 40.3 | | 2 | Massachusetts | 58.6 |
| 38 | Arizona | 46.0 | | 3 | New Jersey | 57.9 |
| 31 | Arkansas | 47.5 | | 4 | Pennsylvania | 57.7 |
| 17 | California | 51.3 | | 5 | Maryland | 56.8 |
| 33 | Colorado | 47.2 | | 6 | Ohio | 56.4 |
| 8 | Connecticut | 55.8 | | 7 | Nevada | 56.2 |
| 9 | Delaware | 54.5 | | 8 | Connecticut | 55.8 |
| 43 | Florida | 44.7 | | 9 | Delaware | 54.5 |
| 30 | Georgia | 47.7 | | 10 | Kentucky | 54.4 |
| 1 | Hawaii | 84.1 | | 11 | New Hampshire | 54.1 |
| 48 | Idaho | 39.1 | | 12 | Rhode Island | 53.4 |
| 39 | Illinois | 45.8 | | 13 | New York | 53.0 |
| 41 | Indiana | 44.9 | | 14 | Missouri | 52.7 |
| 19 | Iowa | 50.7 | | 15 | Kansas | 52.6 |
| 15 | Kansas | 52.6 | | 16 | Alabama | 52.4 |
| 10 | Kentucky | 54.4 | | 17 | California | 51.3 |
| 44 | Louisiana | 44.2 | | 18 | Vermont | 50.8 |
| 32 | Maine | 47.4 | | 19 | Iowa | 50.7 |
| 5 | Maryland | 56.8 | | 19 | Oklahoma | 50.7 |
| 2 | Massachusetts | 58.6 | | 21 | Minnesota | 50.1 |
| 29 | Michigan | 48.2 | | 22 | West Virginia | 50.0 |
| 21 | Minnesota | 50.1 | | 23 | Oregon | 49.9 |
| 28 | Mississippi | 48.3 | | 24 | Tennessee | 49.8 |
| 14 | Missouri | 52.7 | | 25 | Wisconsin | 49.6 |
| 49 | Montana | 39.0 | | 26 | Washington | 49.3 |
| 50 | Nebraska | 36.9 | | 27 | Virginia | 48.7 |
| 7 | Nevada | 56.2 | | 28 | Mississippi | 48.3 |
| 11 | New Hampshire | 54.1 | | 29 | Michigan | 48.2 |
| 3 | New Jersey | 57.9 | | 30 | Georgia | 47.7 |
| 37 | New Mexico | 46.2 | | 31 | Arkansas | 47.5 |
| 13 | New York | 53.0 | | 32 | Maine | 47.4 |
| 34 | North Carolina | 46.5 | | 33 | Colorado | 47.2 |
| 42 | North Dakota | 44.8 | | 34 | North Carolina | 46.5 |
| 6 | Ohio | 56.4 | | 34 | South Carolina | 46.5 |
| 19 | Oklahoma | 50.7 | | 34 | Texas | 46.5 |
| 23 | Oregon | 49.9 | | 37 | New Mexico | 46.2 |
| 4 | Pennsylvania | 57.7 | | 38 | Arizona | 46.0 |
| 12 | Rhode Island | 53.4 | | 39 | Illinois | 45.8 |
| 34 | South Carolina | 46.5 | | 40 | South Dakota | 45.0 |
| 40 | South Dakota | 45.0 | | 41 | Indiana | 44.9 |
| 24 | Tennessee | 49.8 | | 42 | North Dakota | 44.8 |
| 34 | Texas | 46.5 | | 43 | Florida | 44.7 |
| 45 | Utah | 43.3 | | 44 | Louisiana | 44.2 |
| 18 | Vermont | 50.8 | | 45 | Utah | 43.3 |
| 27 | Virginia | 48.7 | | 46 | Wyoming | 41.2 |
| 26 | Washington | 49.3 | | 47 | Alaska | 40.3 |
| 22 | West Virginia | 50.0 | | 48 | Idaho | 39.1 |
| 25 | Wisconsin | 49.6 | | 49 | Montana | 39.0 |
| 46 | Wyoming | 41.2 | | 50 | Nebraska | 36.9 |
| | | | | | District of Columbia | 66.0 |

Source: U.S. Department of Health and Human Services, Agency for Healthcare Research and Quality
"Private-Sector Data by Firm Size and State" (Table II Series, Medical Expenditures Panel Survey)
(http://www.meps.ahrq.gov/mepsweb/survey_comp/Insurance.jsp)

# Persons Not Covered by Health Insurance in 2012

## National Total = 47,951,000 Uninsured

ALPHA ORDER

| RANK | STATE | UNINSURED | % of USA |
|---|---|---|---|
| 20 | Alabama | 711,000 | 1.5% |
| 42 | Alaska | 134,000 | 0.3% |
| 11 | Arizona | 1,198,000 | 2.5% |
| 28 | Arkansas | 535,000 | 1.1% |
| 1 | California | 6,787,000 | 14.2% |
| 21 | Colorado | 705,000 | 1.5% |
| 35 | Connecticut | 284,000 | 0.6% |
| 47 | Delaware | 97,000 | 0.2% |
| 3 | Florida | 4,116,000 | 8.6% |
| 5 | Georgia | 1,856,000 | 3.9% |
| 46 | Hawaii | 105,000 | 0.2% |
| 38 | Idaho | 253,000 | 0.5% |
| 6 | Illinois | 1,732,000 | 3.6% |
| 16 | Indiana | 849,000 | 1.8% |
| 34 | Iowa | 306,000 | 0.6% |
| 33 | Kansas | 358,000 | 0.7% |
| 22 | Kentucky | 682,000 | 1.4% |
| 17 | Louisiana | 819,000 | 1.7% |
| 44 | Maine | 126,000 | 0.3% |
| 19 | Maryland | 733,000 | 1.5% |
| 36 | Massachusetts | 272,000 | 0.6% |
| 12 | Michigan | 1,060,000 | 2.2% |
| 31 | Minnesota | 443,000 | 0.9% |
| 30 | Mississippi | 444,000 | 0.9% |
| 18 | Missouri | 794,000 | 1.7% |
| 40 | Montana | 181,000 | 0.4% |
| 39 | Nebraska | 245,000 | 0.5% |
| 24 | Nevada | 642,000 | 1.3% |
| 41 | New Hampshire | 157,000 | 0.3% |
| 10 | New Jersey | 1,223,000 | 2.6% |
| 29 | New Mexico | 453,000 | 0.9% |
| 4 | New York | 2,185,000 | 4.6% |
| 7 | North Carolina | 1,658,000 | 3.5% |
| 49 | North Dakota | 80,000 | 0.2% |
| 9 | Ohio | 1,402,000 | 2.9% |
| 25 | Oklahoma | 640,000 | 1.3% |
| 26 | Oregon | 597,000 | 1.2% |
| 8 | Pennsylvania | 1,521,000 | 3.2% |
| 43 | Rhode Island | 128,000 | 0.3% |
| 23 | South Carolina | 665,000 | 1.4% |
| 45 | South Dakota | 119,000 | 0.2% |
| 15 | Tennessee | 892,000 | 1.9% |
| 2 | Texas | 6,426,000 | 13.4% |
| 32 | Utah | 411,000 | 0.9% |
| 50 | Vermont | 43,000 | 0.1% |
| 13 | Virginia | 998,000 | 2.1% |
| 14 | Washington | 933,000 | 1.9% |
| 37 | West Virginia | 264,000 | 0.6% |
| 27 | Wisconsin | 550,000 | 1.1% |
| 48 | Wyoming | 89,000 | 0.2% |

RANK ORDER

| RANK | STATE | UNINSURED | % of USA |
|---|---|---|---|
| 1 | California | 6,787,000 | 14.2% |
| 2 | Texas | 6,426,000 | 13.4% |
| 3 | Florida | 4,116,000 | 8.6% |
| 4 | New York | 2,185,000 | 4.6% |
| 5 | Georgia | 1,856,000 | 3.9% |
| 6 | Illinois | 1,732,000 | 3.6% |
| 7 | North Carolina | 1,658,000 | 3.5% |
| 8 | Pennsylvania | 1,521,000 | 3.2% |
| 9 | Ohio | 1,402,000 | 2.9% |
| 10 | New Jersey | 1,223,000 | 2.6% |
| 11 | Arizona | 1,198,000 | 2.5% |
| 12 | Michigan | 1,060,000 | 2.2% |
| 13 | Virginia | 998,000 | 2.1% |
| 14 | Washington | 933,000 | 1.9% |
| 15 | Tennessee | 892,000 | 1.9% |
| 16 | Indiana | 849,000 | 1.8% |
| 17 | Louisiana | 819,000 | 1.7% |
| 18 | Missouri | 794,000 | 1.7% |
| 19 | Maryland | 733,000 | 1.5% |
| 20 | Alabama | 711,000 | 1.5% |
| 21 | Colorado | 705,000 | 1.5% |
| 22 | Kentucky | 682,000 | 1.4% |
| 23 | South Carolina | 665,000 | 1.4% |
| 24 | Nevada | 642,000 | 1.3% |
| 25 | Oklahoma | 640,000 | 1.3% |
| 26 | Oregon | 597,000 | 1.2% |
| 27 | Wisconsin | 550,000 | 1.1% |
| 28 | Arkansas | 535,000 | 1.1% |
| 29 | New Mexico | 453,000 | 0.9% |
| 30 | Mississippi | 444,000 | 0.9% |
| 31 | Minnesota | 443,000 | 0.9% |
| 32 | Utah | 411,000 | 0.9% |
| 33 | Kansas | 358,000 | 0.7% |
| 34 | Iowa | 306,000 | 0.6% |
| 35 | Connecticut | 284,000 | 0.6% |
| 36 | Massachusetts | 272,000 | 0.6% |
| 37 | West Virginia | 264,000 | 0.6% |
| 38 | Idaho | 253,000 | 0.5% |
| 39 | Nebraska | 245,000 | 0.5% |
| 40 | Montana | 181,000 | 0.4% |
| 41 | New Hampshire | 157,000 | 0.3% |
| 42 | Alaska | 134,000 | 0.3% |
| 43 | Rhode Island | 128,000 | 0.3% |
| 44 | Maine | 126,000 | 0.3% |
| 45 | South Dakota | 119,000 | 0.2% |
| 46 | Hawaii | 105,000 | 0.2% |
| 47 | Delaware | 97,000 | 0.2% |
| 48 | Wyoming | 89,000 | 0.2% |
| 49 | North Dakota | 80,000 | 0.2% |
| 50 | Vermont | 43,000 | 0.1% |
|  | District of Columbia | 50,000 | 0.1% |

Source: U.S. Bureau of the Census
"Income, Poverty, and Health Insurance Coverage: 2012"
(http://www.census.gov/hhes/www/hlthins/data/incpovhlth/index.html)

# Percent of Population Not Covered by Health Insurance in 2012

## National Percent = 15.8% of Population*

| ALPHA ORDER | | | | RANK ORDER | | |
|---|---|---|---|---|---|---|
| RANK | STATE | PERCENT | | RANK | STATE | PERCENT |
| 21 | Alabama | 14.4 | | 1 | Texas | 24.3 |
| 8 | Alaska | 18.4 | | 2 | Nevada | 22.5 |
| 9 | Arizona | 18.2 | | 3 | New Mexico | 21.0 |
| 11 | Arkansas | 18.1 | | 4 | Florida | 20.7 |
| 7 | California | 19.0 | | 5 | Louisiana | 19.7 |
| 25 | Colorado | 14.1 | | 6 | Georgia | 19.3 |
| 46 | Connecticut | 9.3 | | 7 | California | 19.0 |
| 43 | Delaware | 10.7 | | 8 | Alaska | 18.4 |
| 4 | Florida | 20.7 | | 9 | Arizona | 18.2 |
| 6 | Georgia | 19.3 | | 9 | Montana | 18.2 |
| 49 | Hawaii | 7.8 | | 11 | Arkansas | 18.1 |
| 14 | Idaho | 17.3 | | 12 | South Carolina | 17.9 |
| 21 | Illinois | 14.4 | | 13 | Mississippi | 17.5 |
| 34 | Indiana | 12.9 | | 14 | Idaho | 17.3 |
| 42 | Iowa | 10.8 | | 15 | Oklahoma | 17.1 |
| 34 | Kansas | 12.9 | | 16 | North Carolina | 16.9 |
| 19 | Kentucky | 15.0 | | 17 | Wyoming | 16.8 |
| 5 | Louisiana | 19.7 | | 18 | Oregon | 15.1 |
| 45 | Maine | 9.6 | | 19 | Kentucky | 15.0 |
| 32 | Maryland | 13.0 | | 19 | New Jersey | 15.0 |
| 50 | Massachusetts | 4.3 | | 21 | Alabama | 14.4 |
| 37 | Michigan | 12.1 | | 21 | Illinois | 14.4 |
| 47 | Minnesota | 9.1 | | 23 | Utah | 14.3 |
| 13 | Mississippi | 17.5 | | 23 | West Virginia | 14.3 |
| 26 | Missouri | 14.0 | | 25 | Colorado | 14.1 |
| 9 | Montana | 18.2 | | 26 | Missouri | 14.0 |
| 32 | Nebraska | 13.0 | | 26 | Washington | 14.0 |
| 2 | Nevada | 22.5 | | 28 | Tennessee | 13.9 |
| 39 | New Hampshire | 11.6 | | 29 | South Dakota | 13.5 |
| 19 | New Jersey | 15.0 | | 30 | Virginia | 13.3 |
| 3 | New Mexico | 21.0 | | 31 | Ohio | 13.2 |
| 34 | New York | 12.9 | | 32 | Maryland | 13.0 |
| 16 | North Carolina | 16.9 | | 32 | Nebraska | 13.0 |
| 40 | North Dakota | 11.3 | | 34 | Indiana | 12.9 |
| 31 | Ohio | 13.2 | | 34 | Kansas | 12.9 |
| 15 | Oklahoma | 17.1 | | 34 | New York | 12.9 |
| 18 | Oregon | 15.1 | | 37 | Michigan | 12.1 |
| 41 | Pennsylvania | 11.2 | | 38 | Rhode Island | 12.0 |
| 38 | Rhode Island | 12.0 | | 39 | New Hampshire | 11.6 |
| 12 | South Carolina | 17.9 | | 40 | North Dakota | 11.3 |
| 29 | South Dakota | 13.5 | | 41 | Pennsylvania | 11.2 |
| 28 | Tennessee | 13.9 | | 42 | Iowa | 10.8 |
| 1 | Texas | 24.3 | | 43 | Delaware | 10.7 |
| 23 | Utah | 14.3 | | 44 | Wisconsin | 9.8 |
| 48 | Vermont | 8.3 | | 45 | Maine | 9.6 |
| 30 | Virginia | 13.3 | | 46 | Connecticut | 9.3 |
| 26 | Washington | 14.0 | | 47 | Minnesota | 9.1 |
| 23 | West Virginia | 14.3 | | 48 | Vermont | 8.3 |
| 44 | Wisconsin | 9.8 | | 49 | Hawaii | 7.8 |
| 17 | Wyoming | 16.8 | | 50 | Massachusetts | 4.3 |
| | | | | District of Columbia | | 9.7 |

Source: U.S. Bureau of the Census
"Income, Poverty, and Health Insurance Coverage: 2012"
(http://www.census.gov/hhes/www/hlthins/data/incpovhlth/index.html)
*Three-year average for 2010 through 2012.

# Percent of Population Lacking Access to Primary Care in 2013

## National Percent = 10.9% of Population*

ALPHA ORDER

| RANK | STATE | PERCENT |
|------|-------|---------|
| 9 | Alabama | 19.5 |
| 11 | Alaska | 17.7 |
| 10 | Arizona | 18.6 |
| 31 | Arkansas | 8.7 |
| 34 | California | 8.3 |
| 25 | Colorado | 10.8 |
| 29 | Connecticut | 9.5 |
| 27 | Delaware | 9.7 |
| 13 | Florida | 16.4 |
| 23 | Georgia | 11.8 |
| 45 | Hawaii | 2.5 |
| 12 | Idaho | 17.4 |
| 14 | Illinois | 16.2 |
| 32 | Indiana | 8.6 |
| 19 | Iowa | 12.3 |
| 17 | Kansas | 13.0 |
| 30 | Kentucky | 9.0 |
| 3 | Louisiana | 24.4 |
| 43 | Maine | 3.2 |
| 28 | Maryland | 9.6 |
| 42 | Massachusetts | 3.4 |
| 26 | Michigan | 9.9 |
| 41 | Minnesota | 4.6 |
| 1 | Mississippi | 34.3 |
| 4 | Missouri | 23.4 |
| 15 | Montana | 15.9 |
| 47 | Nebraska | 1.2 |
| 21 | Nevada | 11.9 |
| 46 | New Hampshire | 2.3 |
| 49 | New Jersey | 0.1 |
| 2 | New Mexico | 30.8 |
| 24 | New York | 11.4 |
| 39 | North Carolina | 6.7 |
| 6 | North Dakota | 20.3 |
| 40 | Ohio | 4.9 |
| 5 | Oklahoma | 23.2 |
| 21 | Oregon | 11.9 |
| 43 | Pennsylvania | 3.2 |
| 50 | Rhode Island | 0.0 |
| 16 | South Carolina | 13.7 |
| 7 | South Dakota | 20.2 |
| 38 | Tennessee | 7.0 |
| 20 | Texas | 12.0 |
| 36 | Utah | 7.6 |
| 48 | Vermont | 1.0 |
| 37 | Virginia | 7.4 |
| 18 | Washington | 12.7 |
| 35 | West Virginia | 8.1 |
| 32 | Wisconsin | 8.6 |
| 7 | Wyoming | 20.2 |

RANK ORDER

| RANK | STATE | PERCENT |
|------|-------|---------|
| 1 | Mississippi | 34.3 |
| 2 | New Mexico | 30.8 |
| 3 | Louisiana | 24.4 |
| 4 | Missouri | 23.4 |
| 5 | Oklahoma | 23.2 |
| 6 | North Dakota | 20.3 |
| 7 | South Dakota | 20.2 |
| 7 | Wyoming | 20.2 |
| 9 | Alabama | 19.5 |
| 10 | Arizona | 18.6 |
| 11 | Alaska | 17.7 |
| 12 | Idaho | 17.4 |
| 13 | Florida | 16.4 |
| 14 | Illinois | 16.2 |
| 15 | Montana | 15.9 |
| 16 | South Carolina | 13.7 |
| 17 | Kansas | 13.0 |
| 18 | Washington | 12.7 |
| 19 | Iowa | 12.3 |
| 20 | Texas | 12.0 |
| 21 | Nevada | 11.9 |
| 21 | Oregon | 11.9 |
| 23 | Georgia | 11.8 |
| 24 | New York | 11.4 |
| 25 | Colorado | 10.8 |
| 26 | Michigan | 9.9 |
| 27 | Delaware | 9.7 |
| 28 | Maryland | 9.6 |
| 29 | Connecticut | 9.5 |
| 30 | Kentucky | 9.0 |
| 31 | Arkansas | 8.7 |
| 32 | Indiana | 8.6 |
| 32 | Wisconsin | 8.6 |
| 34 | California | 8.3 |
| 35 | West Virginia | 8.1 |
| 36 | Utah | 7.6 |
| 37 | Virginia | 7.4 |
| 38 | Tennessee | 7.0 |
| 39 | North Carolina | 6.7 |
| 40 | Ohio | 4.9 |
| 41 | Minnesota | 4.6 |
| 42 | Massachusetts | 3.4 |
| 43 | Maine | 3.2 |
| 43 | Pennsylvania | 3.2 |
| 45 | Hawaii | 2.5 |
| 46 | New Hampshire | 2.3 |
| 47 | Nebraska | 1.2 |
| 48 | Vermont | 1.0 |
| 49 | New Jersey | 0.1 |
| 50 | Rhode Island | 0.0 |

District of Columbia        24.9

Source: CQ Press using data from U.S. Department of Health and Human Services, Division of Shortage Designation
   "State Population and HPSA Designation Population Statistics" (as of January 9, 2013)
      (http://datawarehouse.hrsa.gov/hpsadetail.aspx)
*Percent of population considered under-served by primary medical practitioners (Family and General Practice doctors, Internists,
Ob/Gyns, and Pediatricians). An under-served population does not have primary medical care within reasonable economic and
geographic bounds.

# Physicians in 2012

## National Total = 1,012,546 Physicians*

ALPHA ORDER

ALPHA ORDER

| RANK | STATE | PHYSICIANS | % of USA |
|---|---|---|---|
| 27 | Alabama | 12,051 | 1.2% |
| 49 | Alaska | 1,913 | 0.2% |
| 18 | Arizona | 17,867 | 1.8% |
| 32 | Arkansas | 7,050 | 0.7% |
| 1 | California | 123,474 | 12.2% |
| 21 | Colorado | 16,632 | 1.6% |
| 23 | Connecticut | 15,987 | 1.6% |
| 46 | Delaware | 2,706 | 0.3% |
| 4 | Florida | 60,644 | 6.0% |
| 14 | Georgia | 25,784 | 2.5% |
| 38 | Hawaii | 5,099 | 0.5% |
| 43 | Idaho | 3,262 | 0.3% |
| 6 | Illinois | 43,179 | 4.3% |
| 22 | Indiana | 16,498 | 1.6% |
| 33 | Iowa | 6,943 | 0.7% |
| 30 | Kansas | 7,821 | 0.8% |
| 28 | Kentucky | 11,747 | 1.2% |
| 24 | Louisiana | 14,326 | 1.4% |
| 42 | Maine | 4,567 | 0.5% |
| 12 | Maryland | 28,478 | 2.8% |
| 8 | Massachusetts | 36,578 | 3.6% |
| 10 | Michigan | 30,430 | 3.0% |
| 17 | Minnesota | 19,003 | 1.9% |
| 34 | Mississippi | 6,341 | 0.6% |
| 20 | Missouri | 17,424 | 1.7% |
| 45 | Montana | 2,760 | 0.3% |
| 37 | Nebraska | 5,326 | 0.5% |
| 35 | Nevada | 6,153 | 0.6% |
| 41 | New Hampshire | 4,724 | 0.5% |
| 9 | New Jersey | 32,097 | 3.2% |
| 36 | New Mexico | 6,036 | 0.6% |
| 2 | New York | 89,947 | 8.9% |
| 11 | North Carolina | 29,122 | 2.9% |
| 48 | North Dakota | 1,987 | 0.2% |
| 7 | Ohio | 37,406 | 3.7% |
| 29 | Oklahoma | 7,930 | 0.8% |
| 25 | Oregon | 13,665 | 1.3% |
| 5 | Pennsylvania | 46,186 | 4.6% |
| 40 | Rhode Island | 4,741 | 0.5% |
| 26 | South Carolina | 12,780 | 1.3% |
| 47 | South Dakota | 2,226 | 0.2% |
| 16 | Tennessee | 19,823 | 2.0% |
| 3 | Texas | 64,708 | 6.4% |
| 31 | Utah | 7,103 | 0.7% |
| 44 | Vermont | 2,856 | 0.3% |
| 13 | Virginia | 26,549 | 2.6% |
| 15 | Washington | 22,661 | 2.2% |
| 39 | West Virginia | 5,049 | 0.5% |
| 19 | Wisconsin | 17,787 | 1.8% |
| 50 | Wyoming | 1,285 | 0.1% |

RANK ORDER

| RANK | STATE | PHYSICIANS | % of USA |
|---|---|---|---|
| 1 | California | 123,474 | 12.2% |
| 2 | New York | 89,947 | 8.9% |
| 3 | Texas | 64,708 | 6.4% |
| 4 | Florida | 60,644 | 6.0% |
| 5 | Pennsylvania | 46,186 | 4.6% |
| 6 | Illinois | 43,179 | 4.3% |
| 7 | Ohio | 37,406 | 3.7% |
| 8 | Massachusetts | 36,578 | 3.6% |
| 9 | New Jersey | 32,097 | 3.2% |
| 10 | Michigan | 30,430 | 3.0% |
| 11 | North Carolina | 29,122 | 2.9% |
| 12 | Maryland | 28,478 | 2.8% |
| 13 | Virginia | 26,549 | 2.6% |
| 14 | Georgia | 25,784 | 2.5% |
| 15 | Washington | 22,661 | 2.2% |
| 16 | Tennessee | 19,823 | 2.0% |
| 17 | Minnesota | 19,003 | 1.9% |
| 18 | Arizona | 17,867 | 1.8% |
| 19 | Wisconsin | 17,787 | 1.8% |
| 20 | Missouri | 17,424 | 1.7% |
| 21 | Colorado | 16,632 | 1.6% |
| 22 | Indiana | 16,498 | 1.6% |
| 23 | Connecticut | 15,987 | 1.6% |
| 24 | Louisiana | 14,326 | 1.4% |
| 25 | Oregon | 13,665 | 1.3% |
| 26 | South Carolina | 12,780 | 1.3% |
| 27 | Alabama | 12,051 | 1.2% |
| 28 | Kentucky | 11,747 | 1.2% |
| 29 | Oklahoma | 7,930 | 0.8% |
| 30 | Kansas | 7,821 | 0.8% |
| 31 | Utah | 7,103 | 0.7% |
| 32 | Arkansas | 7,050 | 0.7% |
| 33 | Iowa | 6,943 | 0.7% |
| 34 | Mississippi | 6,341 | 0.6% |
| 35 | Nevada | 6,153 | 0.6% |
| 36 | New Mexico | 6,036 | 0.6% |
| 37 | Nebraska | 5,326 | 0.5% |
| 38 | Hawaii | 5,099 | 0.5% |
| 39 | West Virginia | 5,049 | 0.5% |
| 40 | Rhode Island | 4,741 | 0.5% |
| 41 | New Hampshire | 4,724 | 0.5% |
| 42 | Maine | 4,567 | 0.5% |
| 43 | Idaho | 3,262 | 0.3% |
| 44 | Vermont | 2,856 | 0.3% |
| 45 | Montana | 2,760 | 0.3% |
| 46 | Delaware | 2,706 | 0.3% |
| 47 | South Dakota | 2,226 | 0.2% |
| 48 | North Dakota | 1,987 | 0.2% |
| 49 | Alaska | 1,913 | 0.2% |
| 50 | Wyoming | 1,285 | 0.1% |
| | District of Columbia | 5,835 | 0.6% |

Source: American Medical Association (Chicago, Illinois)
"Physician Characteristics and Distribution in the U.S." (2014 Edition)
*As of December 31, 2012.  Total does not include 14,242 physicians in the U.S. territories and possessions, at APOs and FPOs, or whose addresses are unknown.

# Rate of Physicians in 2012

## National Rate = 323 Physicians per 100,000 Population*

| ALPHA ORDER | | | | RANK ORDER | | |
|---|---|---|---|---|---|---|
| RANK | STATE | RATE | | RANK | STATE | RATE |
| 41 | Alabama | 250 | | 1 | Massachusetts | 550 |
| 38 | Alaska | 262 | | 2 | Maryland | 484 |
| 32 | Arizona | 273 | | 3 | New York | 459 |
| 44 | Arkansas | 239 | | 4 | Vermont | 456 |
| 16 | California | 325 | | 5 | Rhode Island | 451 |
| 19 | Colorado | 320 | | 6 | Connecticut | 445 |
| 6 | Connecticut | 445 | | 7 | Hawaii | 367 |
| 26 | Delaware | 295 | | 8 | New Jersey | 362 |
| 20 | Florida | 314 | | 8 | Pennsylvania | 362 |
| 39 | Georgia | 260 | | 10 | New Hampshire | 357 |
| 7 | Hawaii | 367 | | 11 | Minnesota | 353 |
| 50 | Idaho | 204 | | 12 | Oregon | 350 |
| 14 | Illinois | 336 | | 13 | Maine | 344 |
| 40 | Indiana | 252 | | 14 | Illinois | 336 |
| 45 | Iowa | 226 | | 15 | Washington | 329 |
| 34 | Kansas | 271 | | 16 | California | 325 |
| 36 | Kentucky | 268 | | 17 | Ohio | 324 |
| 21 | Louisiana | 311 | | 17 | Virginia | 324 |
| 13 | Maine | 344 | | 19 | Colorado | 320 |
| 2 | Maryland | 484 | | 20 | Florida | 314 |
| 1 | Massachusetts | 550 | | 21 | Louisiana | 311 |
| 23 | Michigan | 308 | | 21 | Wisconsin | 311 |
| 11 | Minnesota | 353 | | 23 | Michigan | 308 |
| 48 | Mississippi | 212 | | 24 | Tennessee | 307 |
| 28 | Missouri | 289 | | 25 | North Carolina | 299 |
| 31 | Montana | 274 | | 26 | Delaware | 295 |
| 29 | Nebraska | 287 | | 27 | New Mexico | 290 |
| 46 | Nevada | 223 | | 28 | Missouri | 289 |
| 10 | New Hampshire | 357 | | 29 | Nebraska | 287 |
| 8 | New Jersey | 362 | | 30 | North Dakota | 283 |
| 27 | New Mexico | 290 | | 31 | Montana | 274 |
| 3 | New York | 459 | | 32 | Arizona | 273 |
| 25 | North Carolina | 299 | | 33 | West Virginia | 272 |
| 30 | North Dakota | 283 | | 34 | Kansas | 271 |
| 17 | Ohio | 324 | | 34 | South Carolina | 271 |
| 49 | Oklahoma | 208 | | 36 | Kentucky | 268 |
| 12 | Oregon | 350 | | 37 | South Dakota | 267 |
| 8 | Pennsylvania | 362 | | 38 | Alaska | 262 |
| 5 | Rhode Island | 451 | | 39 | Georgia | 260 |
| 34 | South Carolina | 271 | | 40 | Indiana | 252 |
| 37 | South Dakota | 267 | | 41 | Alabama | 250 |
| 24 | Tennessee | 307 | | 42 | Utah | 249 |
| 43 | Texas | 248 | | 43 | Texas | 248 |
| 42 | Utah | 249 | | 44 | Arkansas | 239 |
| 4 | Vermont | 456 | | 45 | Iowa | 226 |
| 17 | Virginia | 324 | | 46 | Nevada | 223 |
| 15 | Washington | 329 | | 46 | Wyoming | 223 |
| 33 | West Virginia | 272 | | 48 | Mississippi | 212 |
| 21 | Wisconsin | 311 | | 49 | Oklahoma | 208 |
| 46 | Wyoming | 223 | | 50 | Idaho | 204 |
| | | | | District of Columbia | | 921 |

Source: CQ Press using data from American Medical Association (Chicago, Illinois)
   "Physician Characteristics and Distribution in the U.S." (2014 Edition)
*As of December 31, 2012. National rate does not include physicians in the U.S. territories and possessions, at APOs and FPOs, or whose addresses are unknown.

# Rate of Registered Nurses in 2012

## National Rate = 839 Nurses per 100,000 Population*

| RANK | STATE | RATE | | RANK | STATE | RATE |
|------|-------|------|---|------|-------|------|
| 22 | Alabama | 908 | | 1 | South Dakota | 1,322 |
| 39 | Alaska | 733 | | 2 | Massachusetts | 1,197 |
| 46 | Arizona | 696 | | 3 | Rhode Island | 1,127 |
| 34 | Arkansas | 796 | | 4 | Missouri | 1,083 |
| 47 | California | 658 | | 5 | North Dakota | 1,081 |
| 33 | Colorado | 797 | | 6 | Maine | 1,073 |
| 15 | Connecticut | 969 | | 7 | Delaware | 1,053 |
| 7 | Delaware | 1,053 | | 8 | Iowa | 1,046 |
| 30 | Florida | 847 | | 9 | Ohio | 1,043 |
| 48 | Georgia | 647 | | 10 | Minnesota | 1,021 |
| 40 | Hawaii | 724 | | 11 | Vermont | 1,008 |
| 42 | Idaho | 716 | | 12 | Nebraska | 1,002 |
| 24 | Illinois | 892 | | 13 | Pennsylvania | 981 |
| 23 | Indiana | 894 | | 14 | Kentucky | 980 |
| 8 | Iowa | 1,046 | | 15 | Connecticut | 969 |
| 21 | Kansas | 914 | | 16 | Wisconsin | 954 |
| 14 | Kentucky | 980 | | 17 | New Hampshire | 948 |
| 27 | Louisiana | 873 | | 18 | Mississippi | 944 |
| 6 | Maine | 1,073 | | 19 | West Virginia | 939 |
| 35 | Maryland | 775 | | 20 | Michigan | 916 |
| 2 | Massachusetts | 1,197 | | 21 | Kansas | 914 |
| 20 | Michigan | 916 | | 22 | Alabama | 908 |
| 10 | Minnesota | 1,021 | | 23 | Indiana | 894 |
| 18 | Mississippi | 944 | | 24 | Illinois | 892 |
| 4 | Missouri | 1,083 | | 25 | South Carolina | 886 |
| 32 | Montana | 835 | | 26 | North Carolina | 885 |
| 12 | Nebraska | 1,002 | | 27 | Louisiana | 873 |
| 50 | Nevada | 610 | | 28 | Tennessee | 861 |
| 17 | New Hampshire | 948 | | 29 | New York | 853 |
| 31 | New Jersey | 842 | | 30 | Florida | 847 |
| 44 | New Mexico | 709 | | 31 | New Jersey | 842 |
| 29 | New York | 853 | | 32 | Montana | 835 |
| 26 | North Carolina | 885 | | 33 | Colorado | 797 |
| 5 | North Dakota | 1,081 | | 34 | Arkansas | 796 |
| 9 | Ohio | 1,043 | | 35 | Maryland | 775 |
| 45 | Oklahoma | 704 | | 36 | Wyoming | 773 |
| 38 | Oregon | 740 | | 37 | Washington | 741 |
| 13 | Pennsylvania | 981 | | 38 | Oregon | 740 |
| 3 | Rhode Island | 1,127 | | 39 | Alaska | 733 |
| 25 | South Carolina | 886 | | 40 | Hawaii | 724 |
| 1 | South Dakota | 1,322 | | 41 | Texas | 719 |
| 28 | Tennessee | 861 | | 42 | Idaho | 716 |
| 41 | Texas | 719 | | 42 | Virginia | 716 |
| 49 | Utah | 628 | | 44 | New Mexico | 709 |
| 11 | Vermont | 1,008 | | 45 | Oklahoma | 704 |
| 42 | Virginia | 716 | | 46 | Arizona | 696 |
| 37 | Washington | 741 | | 47 | California | 658 |
| 19 | West Virginia | 939 | | 48 | Georgia | 647 |
| 16 | Wisconsin | 954 | | 49 | Utah | 628 |
| 36 | Wyoming | 773 | | 50 | Nevada | 610 |

RANK ORDER (header, above right table)

District of Columbia 1,786

Source: CQ Press using data from U.S. Department of Labor, Bureau of Labor Statistics
   "Occupational Employment and Wages, 2012" (http://www.bls.gov/oes/)
*Does not include self-employed.

# Rate of Dentists in 2011

## National Rate = 62 Dentists per 100,000 Population*

ALPHA ORDER

| RANK | STATE | RATE |
|------|-------|------|
| 48 | Alabama | 44 |
| 3 | Alaska | 81 |
| 28 | Arizona | 55 |
| 49 | Arkansas | 42 |
| 7 | California | 78 |
| 11 | Colorado | 69 |
| 5 | Connecticut | 79 |
| 43 | Delaware | 48 |
| 28 | Florida | 55 |
| 45 | Georgia | 47 |
| 5 | Hawaii | 79 |
| 22 | Idaho | 59 |
| 12 | Illinois | 68 |
| 40 | Indiana | 49 |
| 25 | Iowa | 56 |
| 33 | Kansas | 52 |
| 25 | Kentucky | 56 |
| 37 | Louisiana | 50 |
| 35 | Maine | 51 |
| 8 | Maryland | 75 |
| 1 | Massachusetts | 86 |
| 17 | Michigan | 62 |
| 17 | Minnesota | 62 |
| 49 | Mississippi | 42 |
| 37 | Missouri | 50 |
| 17 | Montana | 62 |
| 16 | Nebraska | 63 |
| 30 | Nevada | 54 |
| 14 | New Hampshire | 65 |
| 2 | New Jersey | 83 |
| 40 | New Mexico | 49 |
| 4 | New York | 80 |
| 45 | North Carolina | 47 |
| 25 | North Dakota | 56 |
| 30 | Ohio | 54 |
| 37 | Oklahoma | 50 |
| 10 | Oregon | 71 |
| 15 | Pennsylvania | 64 |
| 22 | Rhode Island | 59 |
| 43 | South Carolina | 48 |
| 30 | South Dakota | 54 |
| 35 | Tennessee | 51 |
| 40 | Texas | 49 |
| 13 | Utah | 67 |
| 21 | Vermont | 60 |
| 17 | Virginia | 62 |
| 9 | Washington | 72 |
| 45 | West Virginia | 47 |
| 24 | Wisconsin | 58 |
| 33 | Wyoming | 52 |

RANK ORDER

| RANK | STATE | RATE |
|------|-------|------|
| 1 | Massachusetts | 86 |
| 2 | New Jersey | 83 |
| 3 | Alaska | 81 |
| 4 | New York | 80 |
| 5 | Connecticut | 79 |
| 5 | Hawaii | 79 |
| 7 | California | 78 |
| 8 | Maryland | 75 |
| 9 | Washington | 72 |
| 10 | Oregon | 71 |
| 11 | Colorado | 69 |
| 12 | Illinois | 68 |
| 13 | Utah | 67 |
| 14 | New Hampshire | 65 |
| 15 | Pennsylvania | 64 |
| 16 | Nebraska | 63 |
| 17 | Michigan | 62 |
| 17 | Minnesota | 62 |
| 17 | Montana | 62 |
| 17 | Virginia | 62 |
| 21 | Vermont | 60 |
| 22 | Idaho | 59 |
| 22 | Rhode Island | 59 |
| 24 | Wisconsin | 58 |
| 25 | Iowa | 56 |
| 25 | Kentucky | 56 |
| 25 | North Dakota | 56 |
| 28 | Arizona | 55 |
| 28 | Florida | 55 |
| 30 | Nevada | 54 |
| 30 | Ohio | 54 |
| 30 | South Dakota | 54 |
| 33 | Kansas | 52 |
| 33 | Wyoming | 52 |
| 35 | Maine | 51 |
| 35 | Tennessee | 51 |
| 37 | Louisiana | 50 |
| 37 | Missouri | 50 |
| 37 | Oklahoma | 50 |
| 40 | Indiana | 49 |
| 40 | New Mexico | 49 |
| 40 | Texas | 49 |
| 43 | Delaware | 48 |
| 43 | South Carolina | 48 |
| 45 | Georgia | 47 |
| 45 | North Carolina | 47 |
| 45 | West Virginia | 47 |
| 48 | Alabama | 44 |
| 49 | Arkansas | 42 |
| 49 | Mississippi | 42 |
| | District of Columbia | 108 |

Source: American Dental Association
   "Dentist Supply in the US: 1993 - 2011" (http://www.ada.org/1443.aspx)
*Professionally active dentists.  National figure includes 36 dentists for whom state is not known.

# Community Hospitals in 2012

## National Total = 4,999 Hospitals*

| RANK | STATE | HOSPITALS | % of USA |
|---|---|---|---|
| 22 | Alabama | 97 | 1.9% |
| 47 | Alaska | 23 | 0.5% |
| 30 | Arizona | 72 | 1.4% |
| 26 | Arkansas | 83 | 1.7% |
| 2 | California | 349 | 7.0% |
| 28 | Colorado | 82 | 1.6% |
| 43 | Connecticut | 34 | 0.7% |
| 50 | Delaware | 7 | 0.1% |
| 3 | Florida | 216 | 4.3% |
| 9 | Georgia | 148 | 3.0% |
| 45 | Hawaii | 24 | 0.5% |
| 39 | Idaho | 40 | 0.8% |
| 5 | Illinois | 188 | 3.8% |
| 14 | Indiana | 124 | 2.5% |
| 17 | Iowa | 118 | 2.4% |
| 12 | Kansas | 131 | 2.6% |
| 20 | Kentucky | 106 | 2.1% |
| 14 | Louisiana | 124 | 2.5% |
| 41 | Maine | 37 | 0.7% |
| 35 | Maryland | 50 | 1.0% |
| 26 | Massachusetts | 83 | 1.7% |
| 8 | Michigan | 151 | 3.0% |
| 10 | Minnesota | 133 | 2.7% |
| 21 | Mississippi | 98 | 2.0% |
| 16 | Missouri | 123 | 2.5% |
| 36 | Montana | 48 | 1.0% |
| 24 | Nebraska | 89 | 1.8% |
| 40 | Nevada | 38 | 0.8% |
| 44 | New Hampshire | 28 | 0.6% |
| 29 | New Jersey | 77 | 1.5% |
| 41 | New Mexico | 37 | 0.7% |
| 7 | New York | 178 | 3.6% |
| 17 | North Carolina | 118 | 2.4% |
| 38 | North Dakota | 44 | 0.9% |
| 6 | Ohio | 185 | 3.7% |
| 19 | Oklahoma | 117 | 2.3% |
| 32 | Oregon | 58 | 1.2% |
| 4 | Pennsylvania | 192 | 3.8% |
| 49 | Rhode Island | 11 | 0.2% |
| 31 | South Carolina | 67 | 1.3% |
| 34 | South Dakota | 54 | 1.1% |
| 11 | Tennessee | 132 | 2.6% |
| 1 | Texas | 425 | 8.5% |
| 37 | Utah | 47 | 0.9% |
| 48 | Vermont | 14 | 0.3% |
| 23 | Virginia | 94 | 1.9% |
| 25 | Washington | 87 | 1.7% |
| 33 | West Virginia | 55 | 1.1% |
| 13 | Wisconsin | 128 | 2.6% |
| 45 | Wyoming | 24 | 0.5% |

| RANK | STATE | HOSPITALS | % of USA |
|---|---|---|---|
| 1 | Texas | 425 | 8.5% |
| 2 | California | 349 | 7.0% |
| 3 | Florida | 216 | 4.3% |
| 4 | Pennsylvania | 192 | 3.8% |
| 5 | Illinois | 188 | 3.8% |
| 6 | Ohio | 185 | 3.7% |
| 7 | New York | 178 | 3.6% |
| 8 | Michigan | 151 | 3.0% |
| 9 | Georgia | 148 | 3.0% |
| 10 | Minnesota | 133 | 2.7% |
| 11 | Tennessee | 132 | 2.6% |
| 12 | Kansas | 131 | 2.6% |
| 13 | Wisconsin | 128 | 2.6% |
| 14 | Indiana | 124 | 2.5% |
| 14 | Louisiana | 124 | 2.5% |
| 16 | Missouri | 123 | 2.5% |
| 17 | Iowa | 118 | 2.4% |
| 17 | North Carolina | 118 | 2.4% |
| 19 | Oklahoma | 117 | 2.3% |
| 20 | Kentucky | 106 | 2.1% |
| 21 | Mississippi | 98 | 2.0% |
| 22 | Alabama | 97 | 1.9% |
| 23 | Virginia | 94 | 1.9% |
| 24 | Nebraska | 89 | 1.8% |
| 25 | Washington | 87 | 1.7% |
| 26 | Arkansas | 83 | 1.7% |
| 26 | Massachusetts | 83 | 1.7% |
| 28 | Colorado | 82 | 1.6% |
| 29 | New Jersey | 77 | 1.5% |
| 30 | Arizona | 72 | 1.4% |
| 31 | South Carolina | 67 | 1.3% |
| 32 | Oregon | 58 | 1.2% |
| 33 | West Virginia | 55 | 1.1% |
| 34 | South Dakota | 54 | 1.1% |
| 35 | Maryland | 50 | 1.0% |
| 36 | Montana | 48 | 1.0% |
| 37 | Utah | 47 | 0.9% |
| 38 | North Dakota | 44 | 0.9% |
| 39 | Idaho | 40 | 0.8% |
| 40 | Nevada | 38 | 0.8% |
| 41 | Maine | 37 | 0.7% |
| 41 | New Mexico | 37 | 0.7% |
| 43 | Connecticut | 34 | 0.7% |
| 44 | New Hampshire | 28 | 0.6% |
| 45 | Hawaii | 24 | 0.5% |
| 45 | Wyoming | 24 | 0.5% |
| 47 | Alaska | 23 | 0.5% |
| 48 | Vermont | 14 | 0.3% |
| 49 | Rhode Island | 11 | 0.2% |
| 50 | Delaware | 7 | 0.1% |
| | District of Columbia | 11 | 0.2% |

Source: American Hospital Association (Chicago, IL)
"Hospital Statistics" (2014 edition)

*Community hospitals are all nonfederal, short-term general, and special hospitals whose facilities and services are available to the public.

# Rate of Community Hospitals in 2012

## National Rate = 1.6 Community Hospitals per 100,000 Population*

| ALPHA ORDER | | | RANK ORDER | | |
|---|---|---|---|---|---|
| RANK | STATE | RATE | RANK | STATE | RATE |
| 21 | Alabama | 2.0 | 1 | South Dakota | 6.5 |
| 9 | Alaska | 3.1 | 2 | North Dakota | 6.3 |
| 41 | Arizona | 1.1 | 3 | Montana | 4.8 |
| 12 | Arkansas | 2.8 | 3 | Nebraska | 4.8 |
| 45 | California | 0.9 | 5 | Kansas | 4.5 |
| 27 | Colorado | 1.6 | 6 | Wyoming | 4.2 |
| 45 | Connecticut | 0.9 | 7 | Iowa | 3.8 |
| 49 | Delaware | 0.8 | 8 | Mississippi | 3.3 |
| 41 | Florida | 1.1 | 9 | Alaska | 3.1 |
| 31 | Georgia | 1.5 | 9 | Oklahoma | 3.1 |
| 26 | Hawaii | 1.7 | 11 | West Virginia | 3.0 |
| 15 | Idaho | 2.5 | 12 | Arkansas | 2.8 |
| 31 | Illinois | 1.5 | 12 | Maine | 2.8 |
| 24 | Indiana | 1.9 | 14 | Louisiana | 2.7 |
| 7 | Iowa | 3.8 | 15 | Idaho | 2.5 |
| 5 | Kansas | 4.5 | 15 | Minnesota | 2.5 |
| 17 | Kentucky | 2.4 | 17 | Kentucky | 2.4 |
| 14 | Louisiana | 2.7 | 18 | Vermont | 2.2 |
| 12 | Maine | 2.8 | 18 | Wisconsin | 2.2 |
| 49 | Maryland | 0.8 | 20 | New Hampshire | 2.1 |
| 39 | Massachusetts | 1.2 | 21 | Alabama | 2.0 |
| 31 | Michigan | 1.5 | 21 | Missouri | 2.0 |
| 15 | Minnesota | 2.5 | 21 | Tennessee | 2.0 |
| 8 | Mississippi | 3.3 | 24 | Indiana | 1.9 |
| 21 | Missouri | 2.0 | 25 | New Mexico | 1.8 |
| 3 | Montana | 4.8 | 26 | Hawaii | 1.7 |
| 3 | Nebraska | 4.8 | 27 | Colorado | 1.6 |
| 36 | Nevada | 1.4 | 27 | Ohio | 1.6 |
| 20 | New Hampshire | 2.1 | 27 | Texas | 1.6 |
| 45 | New Jersey | 0.9 | 27 | Utah | 1.6 |
| 25 | New Mexico | 1.8 | 31 | Georgia | 1.5 |
| 45 | New York | 0.9 | 31 | Illinois | 1.5 |
| 39 | North Carolina | 1.2 | 31 | Michigan | 1.5 |
| 2 | North Dakota | 6.3 | 31 | Oregon | 1.5 |
| 27 | Ohio | 1.6 | 31 | Pennsylvania | 1.5 |
| 9 | Oklahoma | 3.1 | 36 | Nevada | 1.4 |
| 31 | Oregon | 1.5 | 36 | South Carolina | 1.4 |
| 31 | Pennsylvania | 1.5 | 38 | Washington | 1.3 |
| 44 | Rhode Island | 1.0 | 39 | Massachusetts | 1.2 |
| 36 | South Carolina | 1.4 | 39 | North Carolina | 1.2 |
| 1 | South Dakota | 6.5 | 41 | Arizona | 1.1 |
| 21 | Tennessee | 2.0 | 41 | Florida | 1.1 |
| 27 | Texas | 1.6 | 41 | Virginia | 1.1 |
| 27 | Utah | 1.6 | 44 | Rhode Island | 1.0 |
| 18 | Vermont | 2.2 | 45 | California | 0.9 |
| 41 | Virginia | 1.1 | 45 | Connecticut | 0.9 |
| 38 | Washington | 1.3 | 45 | New Jersey | 0.9 |
| 11 | West Virginia | 3.0 | 45 | New York | 0.9 |
| 18 | Wisconsin | 2.2 | 49 | Delaware | 0.8 |
| 6 | Wyoming | 4.2 | 49 | Maryland | 0.8 |
| | | | District of Columbia | | 1.7 |

Source: CQ Press using data from American Hospital Association (Chicago, IL)
    "Hospital Statistics" (2014 edition)
*Community hospitals are all nonfederal, short-term general, and special hospitals whose facilities and services are available to the public.

# Births in 2012

## National Total = 3,952,841 Live Births*

ALPHA ORDER

| RANK | STATE | BIRTHS | % of USA |
|---|---|---|---|
| 24 | Alabama | 58,448 | 1.5% |
| 45 | Alaska | 11,187 | 0.3% |
| 14 | Arizona | 86,441 | 2.2% |
| 33 | Arkansas | 38,347 | 1.0% |
| 1 | California | 503,755 | 12.7% |
| 22 | Colorado | 65,187 | 1.6% |
| 34 | Connecticut | 36,539 | 0.9% |
| 46 | Delaware | 11,023 | 0.3% |
| 4 | Florida | 213,148 | 5.4% |
| 8 | Georgia | 130,280 | 3.3% |
| 40 | Hawaii | 18,980 | 0.5% |
| 38 | Idaho | 22,963 | 0.6% |
| 5 | Illinois | 159,160 | 4.0% |
| 15 | Indiana | 83,227 | 2.1% |
| 31 | Iowa | 38,702 | 1.0% |
| 30 | Kansas | 40,341 | 1.0% |
| 26 | Kentucky | 55,758 | 1.4% |
| 23 | Louisiana | 62,642 | 1.6% |
| 41 | Maine | 12,798 | 0.3% |
| 18 | Maryland | 72,883 | 1.8% |
| 19 | Massachusetts | 72,439 | 1.8% |
| 10 | Michigan | 113,091 | 2.9% |
| 20 | Minnesota | 68,772 | 1.7% |
| 32 | Mississippi | 38,669 | 1.0% |
| 17 | Missouri | 75,446 | 1.9% |
| 43 | Montana | 12,118 | 0.3% |
| 37 | Nebraska | 25,942 | 0.7% |
| 35 | Nevada | 34,911 | 0.9% |
| 42 | New Hampshire | 12,352 | 0.3% |
| 11 | New Jersey | 104,230 | 2.6% |
| 36 | New Mexico | 27,068 | 0.7% |
| 3 | New York | 240,916 | 6.1% |
| 9 | North Carolina | 119,831 | 3.0% |
| 48 | North Dakota | 10,106 | 0.3% |
| 7 | Ohio | 138,483 | 3.5% |
| 27 | Oklahoma | 52,751 | 1.3% |
| 29 | Oregon | 45,067 | 1.1% |
| 6 | Pennsylvania | 142,514 | 3.6% |
| 47 | Rhode Island | 10,926 | 0.3% |
| 25 | South Carolina | 57,155 | 1.4% |
| 44 | South Dakota | 12,104 | 0.3% |
| 16 | Tennessee | 80,371 | 2.0% |
| 2 | Texas | 382,727 | 9.7% |
| 28 | Utah | 51,465 | 1.3% |
| 50 | Vermont | 6,009 | 0.2% |
| 12 | Virginia | 103,013 | 2.6% |
| 13 | Washington | 87,463 | 2.2% |
| 39 | West Virginia | 20,827 | 0.5% |
| 21 | Wisconsin | 67,295 | 1.7% |
| 49 | Wyoming | 7,572 | 0.2% |

RANK ORDER

| RANK | STATE | BIRTHS | % of USA |
|---|---|---|---|
| 1 | California | 503,755 | 12.7% |
| 2 | Texas | 382,727 | 9.7% |
| 3 | New York | 240,916 | 6.1% |
| 4 | Florida | 213,148 | 5.4% |
| 5 | Illinois | 159,160 | 4.0% |
| 6 | Pennsylvania | 142,514 | 3.6% |
| 7 | Ohio | 138,483 | 3.5% |
| 8 | Georgia | 130,280 | 3.3% |
| 9 | North Carolina | 119,831 | 3.0% |
| 10 | Michigan | 113,091 | 2.9% |
| 11 | New Jersey | 104,230 | 2.6% |
| 12 | Virginia | 103,013 | 2.6% |
| 13 | Washington | 87,463 | 2.2% |
| 14 | Arizona | 86,441 | 2.2% |
| 15 | Indiana | 83,227 | 2.1% |
| 16 | Tennessee | 80,371 | 2.0% |
| 17 | Missouri | 75,446 | 1.9% |
| 18 | Maryland | 72,883 | 1.8% |
| 19 | Massachusetts | 72,439 | 1.8% |
| 20 | Minnesota | 68,772 | 1.7% |
| 21 | Wisconsin | 67,295 | 1.7% |
| 22 | Colorado | 65,187 | 1.6% |
| 23 | Louisiana | 62,642 | 1.6% |
| 24 | Alabama | 58,448 | 1.5% |
| 25 | South Carolina | 57,155 | 1.4% |
| 26 | Kentucky | 55,758 | 1.4% |
| 27 | Oklahoma | 52,751 | 1.3% |
| 28 | Utah | 51,465 | 1.3% |
| 29 | Oregon | 45,067 | 1.1% |
| 30 | Kansas | 40,341 | 1.0% |
| 31 | Iowa | 38,702 | 1.0% |
| 32 | Mississippi | 38,669 | 1.0% |
| 33 | Arkansas | 38,347 | 1.0% |
| 34 | Connecticut | 36,539 | 0.9% |
| 35 | Nevada | 34,911 | 0.9% |
| 36 | New Mexico | 27,068 | 0.7% |
| 37 | Nebraska | 25,942 | 0.7% |
| 38 | Idaho | 22,963 | 0.6% |
| 39 | West Virginia | 20,827 | 0.5% |
| 40 | Hawaii | 18,980 | 0.5% |
| 41 | Maine | 12,798 | 0.3% |
| 42 | New Hampshire | 12,352 | 0.3% |
| 43 | Montana | 12,118 | 0.3% |
| 44 | South Dakota | 12,104 | 0.3% |
| 45 | Alaska | 11,187 | 0.3% |
| 46 | Delaware | 11,023 | 0.3% |
| 47 | Rhode Island | 10,926 | 0.3% |
| 48 | North Dakota | 10,106 | 0.3% |
| 49 | Wyoming | 7,572 | 0.2% |
| 50 | Vermont | 6,009 | 0.2% |
| | District of Columbia | 9,399 | 0.2% |

Source: U.S. Department of Health and Human Services, National Center for Health Statistics
"National Vital Statistics Reports" (Vol. 62, No. 9, December 30, 2013, http://www.cdc.gov/nchs/births.htm)
*Final data by state of residence.

# Birth Rate in 2012

## National Rate = 12.6 Live Births per 1,000 Population*

| ALPHA ORDER | | | | RANK ORDER | | |
|---|---|---|---|---|---|---|
| RANK | STATE | RATE | | RANK | STATE | RATE |
| 33 | Alabama | 12.1 | | 1 | Utah | 18.0 |
| 2 | Alaska | 15.3 | | 2 | Alaska | 15.3 |
| 12 | Arizona | 13.2 | | 3 | Texas | 14.7 |
| 16 | Arkansas | 13.0 | | 4 | South Dakota | 14.5 |
| 12 | California | 13.2 | | 5 | Idaho | 14.4 |
| 24 | Colorado | 12.6 | | 5 | North Dakota | 14.4 |
| 47 | Connecticut | 10.2 | | 7 | Kansas | 14.0 |
| 36 | Delaware | 12.0 | | 7 | Nebraska | 14.0 |
| 44 | Florida | 11.0 | | 9 | Oklahoma | 13.8 |
| 14 | Georgia | 13.1 | | 10 | Hawaii | 13.6 |
| 10 | Hawaii | 13.6 | | 10 | Louisiana | 13.6 |
| 5 | Idaho | 14.4 | | 12 | Arizona | 13.2 |
| 28 | Illinois | 12.4 | | 12 | California | 13.2 |
| 20 | Indiana | 12.7 | | 14 | Georgia | 13.1 |
| 24 | Iowa | 12.6 | | 14 | Wyoming | 13.1 |
| 7 | Kansas | 14.0 | | 16 | Arkansas | 13.0 |
| 20 | Kentucky | 12.7 | | 16 | Mississippi | 13.0 |
| 10 | Louisiana | 13.6 | | 16 | New Mexico | 13.0 |
| 48 | Maine | 9.6 | | 19 | Minnesota | 12.8 |
| 28 | Maryland | 12.4 | | 20 | Indiana | 12.7 |
| 45 | Massachusetts | 10.9 | | 20 | Kentucky | 12.7 |
| 41 | Michigan | 11.4 | | 20 | Nevada | 12.7 |
| 19 | Minnesota | 12.8 | | 20 | Washington | 12.7 |
| 16 | Mississippi | 13.0 | | 24 | Colorado | 12.6 |
| 27 | Missouri | 12.5 | | 24 | Iowa | 12.6 |
| 33 | Montana | 12.1 | | 24 | Virginia | 12.6 |
| 7 | Nebraska | 14.0 | | 27 | Missouri | 12.5 |
| 20 | Nevada | 12.7 | | 28 | Illinois | 12.4 |
| 50 | New Hampshire | 9.4 | | 28 | Maryland | 12.4 |
| 38 | New Jersey | 11.8 | | 28 | Tennessee | 12.4 |
| 16 | New Mexico | 13.0 | | 31 | New York | 12.3 |
| 31 | New York | 12.3 | | 31 | North Carolina | 12.3 |
| 31 | North Carolina | 12.3 | | 33 | Alabama | 12.1 |
| 5 | North Dakota | 14.4 | | 33 | Montana | 12.1 |
| 36 | Ohio | 12.0 | | 33 | South Carolina | 12.1 |
| 9 | Oklahoma | 13.8 | | 36 | Delaware | 12.0 |
| 40 | Oregon | 11.6 | | 36 | Ohio | 12.0 |
| 42 | Pennsylvania | 11.2 | | 38 | New Jersey | 11.8 |
| 46 | Rhode Island | 10.4 | | 38 | Wisconsin | 11.8 |
| 33 | South Carolina | 12.1 | | 40 | Oregon | 11.6 |
| 4 | South Dakota | 14.5 | | 41 | Michigan | 11.4 |
| 28 | Tennessee | 12.4 | | 42 | Pennsylvania | 11.2 |
| 3 | Texas | 14.7 | | 42 | West Virginia | 11.2 |
| 1 | Utah | 18.0 | | 44 | Florida | 11.0 |
| 48 | Vermont | 9.6 | | 45 | Massachusetts | 10.9 |
| 24 | Virginia | 12.6 | | 46 | Rhode Island | 10.4 |
| 20 | Washington | 12.7 | | 47 | Connecticut | 10.2 |
| 42 | West Virginia | 11.2 | | 48 | Maine | 9.6 |
| 38 | Wisconsin | 11.8 | | 48 | Vermont | 9.6 |
| 14 | Wyoming | 13.1 | | 50 | New Hampshire | 9.4 |
| | | | | | District of Columbia | 14.9 |

Source: U.S. Department of Health and Human Services, National Center for Health Statistics
   "National Vital Statistics Reports" (Vol. 62, No. 9, December 30, 2013, http://www.cdc.gov/nchs/births.htm)
*Final data by state of residence.

# Births of Low Birthweight as a Percent of All Births in 2011

## National Percent = 8.1% of Live Births*

ALPHA ORDER

| RANK | STATE | PERCENT |
|------|-------|---------|
| 3 | Alabama | 9.9 |
| 50 | Alaska | 6.0 |
| 37 | Arizona | 7.0 |
| 7 | Arkansas | 9.1 |
| 39 | California | 6.8 |
| 13 | Colorado | 8.7 |
| 30 | Connecticut | 7.7 |
| 19 | Delaware | 8.4 |
| 13 | Florida | 8.7 |
| 6 | Georgia | 9.4 |
| 21 | Hawaii | 8.2 |
| 47 | Idaho | 6.1 |
| 21 | Illinois | 8.2 |
| 25 | Indiana | 8.1 |
| 44 | Iowa | 6.5 |
| 33 | Kansas | 7.2 |
| 7 | Kentucky | 9.1 |
| 2 | Louisiana | 10.9 |
| 40 | Maine | 6.7 |
| 11 | Maryland | 8.9 |
| 31 | Massachusetts | 7.6 |
| 20 | Michigan | 8.3 |
| 45 | Minnesota | 6.4 |
| 1 | Mississippi | 11.8 |
| 29 | Missouri | 7.9 |
| 33 | Montana | 7.2 |
| 43 | Nebraska | 6.6 |
| 21 | Nevada | 8.2 |
| 36 | New Hampshire | 7.1 |
| 16 | New Jersey | 8.5 |
| 12 | New Mexico | 8.8 |
| 25 | New York | 8.1 |
| 9 | North Carolina | 9.0 |
| 40 | North Dakota | 6.7 |
| 15 | Ohio | 8.6 |
| 16 | Oklahoma | 8.5 |
| 47 | Oregon | 6.1 |
| 21 | Pennsylvania | 8.2 |
| 32 | Rhode Island | 7.4 |
| 3 | South Carolina | 9.9 |
| 46 | South Dakota | 6.3 |
| 9 | Tennessee | 9.0 |
| 16 | Texas | 8.5 |
| 38 | Utah | 6.9 |
| 40 | Vermont | 6.7 |
| 28 | Virginia | 8.0 |
| 47 | Washington | 6.1 |
| 5 | West Virginia | 9.6 |
| 33 | Wisconsin | 7.2 |
| 25 | Wyoming | 8.1 |

RANK ORDER

| RANK | STATE | PERCENT |
|------|-------|---------|
| 1 | Mississippi | 11.8 |
| 2 | Louisiana | 10.9 |
| 3 | Alabama | 9.9 |
| 3 | South Carolina | 9.9 |
| 5 | West Virginia | 9.6 |
| 6 | Georgia | 9.4 |
| 7 | Arkansas | 9.1 |
| 7 | Kentucky | 9.1 |
| 9 | North Carolina | 9.0 |
| 9 | Tennessee | 9.0 |
| 11 | Maryland | 8.9 |
| 12 | New Mexico | 8.8 |
| 13 | Colorado | 8.7 |
| 13 | Florida | 8.7 |
| 15 | Ohio | 8.6 |
| 16 | New Jersey | 8.5 |
| 16 | Oklahoma | 8.5 |
| 16 | Texas | 8.5 |
| 19 | Delaware | 8.4 |
| 20 | Michigan | 8.3 |
| 21 | Hawaii | 8.2 |
| 21 | Illinois | 8.2 |
| 21 | Nevada | 8.2 |
| 21 | Pennsylvania | 8.2 |
| 25 | Indiana | 8.1 |
| 25 | New York | 8.1 |
| 25 | Wyoming | 8.1 |
| 28 | Virginia | 8.0 |
| 29 | Missouri | 7.9 |
| 30 | Connecticut | 7.7 |
| 31 | Massachusetts | 7.6 |
| 32 | Rhode Island | 7.4 |
| 33 | Kansas | 7.2 |
| 33 | Montana | 7.2 |
| 33 | Wisconsin | 7.2 |
| 36 | New Hampshire | 7.1 |
| 37 | Arizona | 7.0 |
| 38 | Utah | 6.9 |
| 39 | California | 6.8 |
| 40 | Maine | 6.7 |
| 40 | North Dakota | 6.7 |
| 40 | Vermont | 6.7 |
| 43 | Nebraska | 6.6 |
| 44 | Iowa | 6.5 |
| 45 | Minnesota | 6.4 |
| 46 | South Dakota | 6.3 |
| 47 | Idaho | 6.1 |
| 47 | Oregon | 6.1 |
| 47 | Washington | 6.1 |
| 50 | Alaska | 6.0 |
| | District of Columbia | 10.4 |

Source: U.S. Department of Health and Human Services, National Center for Health Statistics
   "National Vital Statistics Reports" (Vol. 62, No. 1, June 2013, http://www.cdc.gov/nchs/births.htm)
*Final data by state of residence.  Births of less than 2,500 grams (5 pounds 8 ounces).

# Births to Teenage Mothers as a Percent of All Births in 2011

## National Percent = 8.3% of Live Births*

ALPHA ORDER

| RANK | STATE | PERCENT |
|------|-------|---------|
| 8 | Alabama | 11.1 |
| 26 | Alaska | 7.7 |
| 12 | Arizona | 9.8 |
| 3 | Arkansas | 12.5 |
| 28 | California | 7.6 |
| 31 | Colorado | 7.3 |
| 45 | Connecticut | 5.4 |
| 24 | Delaware | 8.0 |
| 24 | Florida | 8.0 |
| 12 | Georgia | 9.8 |
| 42 | Hawaii | 6.3 |
| 32 | Idaho | 7.1 |
| 22 | Illinois | 8.1 |
| 14 | Indiana | 9.5 |
| 33 | Iowa | 7.0 |
| 18 | Kansas | 8.8 |
| 9 | Kentucky | 11.0 |
| 6 | Louisiana | 11.3 |
| 35 | Maine | 6.8 |
| 38 | Maryland | 6.6 |
| 50 | Massachusetts | 4.8 |
| 20 | Michigan | 8.5 |
| 46 | Minnesota | 5.1 |
| 1 | Mississippi | 13.5 |
| 16 | Missouri | 9.1 |
| 26 | Montana | 7.7 |
| 37 | Nebraska | 6.7 |
| 19 | Nevada | 8.7 |
| 49 | New Hampshire | 4.9 |
| 46 | New Jersey | 5.1 |
| 2 | New Mexico | 12.6 |
| 44 | New York | 5.7 |
| 15 | North Carolina | 9.2 |
| 35 | North Dakota | 6.8 |
| 17 | Ohio | 8.9 |
| 5 | Oklahoma | 11.5 |
| 34 | Oregon | 6.9 |
| 28 | Pennsylvania | 7.6 |
| 28 | Rhode Island | 7.6 |
| 11 | South Carolina | 10.5 |
| 22 | South Dakota | 8.1 |
| 10 | Tennessee | 10.7 |
| 6 | Texas | 11.3 |
| 48 | Utah | 5.0 |
| 43 | Vermont | 6.2 |
| 40 | Virginia | 6.4 |
| 40 | Washington | 6.4 |
| 4 | West Virginia | 11.9 |
| 38 | Wisconsin | 6.6 |
| 21 | Wyoming | 8.4 |

RANK ORDER

| RANK | STATE | PERCENT |
|------|-------|---------|
| 1 | Mississippi | 13.5 |
| 2 | New Mexico | 12.6 |
| 3 | Arkansas | 12.5 |
| 4 | West Virginia | 11.9 |
| 5 | Oklahoma | 11.5 |
| 6 | Louisiana | 11.3 |
| 6 | Texas | 11.3 |
| 8 | Alabama | 11.1 |
| 9 | Kentucky | 11.0 |
| 10 | Tennessee | 10.7 |
| 11 | South Carolina | 10.5 |
| 12 | Arizona | 9.8 |
| 12 | Georgia | 9.8 |
| 14 | Indiana | 9.5 |
| 15 | North Carolina | 9.2 |
| 16 | Missouri | 9.1 |
| 17 | Ohio | 8.9 |
| 18 | Kansas | 8.8 |
| 19 | Nevada | 8.7 |
| 20 | Michigan | 8.5 |
| 21 | Wyoming | 8.4 |
| 22 | Illinois | 8.1 |
| 22 | South Dakota | 8.1 |
| 24 | Delaware | 8.0 |
| 24 | Florida | 8.0 |
| 26 | Alaska | 7.7 |
| 26 | Montana | 7.7 |
| 28 | California | 7.6 |
| 28 | Pennsylvania | 7.6 |
| 28 | Rhode Island | 7.6 |
| 31 | Colorado | 7.3 |
| 32 | Idaho | 7.1 |
| 33 | Iowa | 7.0 |
| 34 | Oregon | 6.9 |
| 35 | Maine | 6.8 |
| 35 | North Dakota | 6.8 |
| 37 | Nebraska | 6.7 |
| 38 | Maryland | 6.6 |
| 38 | Wisconsin | 6.6 |
| 40 | Virginia | 6.4 |
| 40 | Washington | 6.4 |
| 42 | Hawaii | 6.3 |
| 43 | Vermont | 6.2 |
| 44 | New York | 5.7 |
| 45 | Connecticut | 5.4 |
| 46 | Minnesota | 5.1 |
| 46 | New Jersey | 5.1 |
| 48 | Utah | 5.0 |
| 49 | New Hampshire | 4.9 |
| 50 | Massachusetts | 4.8 |

| | District of Columbia | 9.5 |

Source: CQ Press using data from U.S. Department of Health and Human Services, Centers for Disease Control and Prevention
"National Vital Statistics Reports" (Vol. 61, No. 1, August 2012, http://www.cdc.gov/nchs/births.htm) and
"CDC Wonder" (http://wonder.cdc.gov)
*Final data. Live births to women 15 to 19 years old by state of residence.

# Births to Unmarried Women as a Percent of All Births in 2011

## National Percent = 40.7% of Live Births*

| ALPHA ORDER | | | RANK ORDER | | |
|---|---|---|---|---|---|
| RANK | STATE | PERCENT | RANK | STATE | PERCENT |
| 17 | Alabama | 42.1 | 1 | Mississippi | 54.4 |
| 35 | Alaska | 36.8 | 2 | Louisiana | 52.9 |
| 9 | Arizona | 44.7 | 3 | New Mexico | 51.3 |
| 8 | Arkansas | 44.9 | 4 | Delaware | 48.6 |
| 26 | California | 40.4 | 5 | Florida | 47.6 |
| 49 | Colorado | 23.7 | 6 | South Carolina | 47.1 |
| 31 | Connecticut | 38.0 | 7 | Georgia | 45.4 |
| 4 | Delaware | 48.6 | 8 | Arkansas | 44.9 |
| 5 | Florida | 47.6 | 9 | Arizona | 44.7 |
| 7 | Georgia | 45.4 | 10 | Rhode Island | 44.5 |
| 32 | Hawaii | 37.5 | 11 | Nevada | 44.2 |
| 48 | Idaho | 26.8 | 12 | Tennessee | 44.1 |
| 28 | Illinois | 40.0 | 13 | West Virginia | 43.9 |
| 15 | Indiana | 42.7 | 14 | Ohio | 43.4 |
| 43 | Iowa | 33.8 | 15 | Indiana | 42.7 |
| 33 | Kansas | 37.3 | 16 | Michigan | 42.3 |
| 22 | Kentucky | 41.5 | 17 | Alabama | 42.1 |
| 2 | Louisiana | 52.9 | 18 | Texas | 42.0 |
| 19 | Maine | 41.8 | 19 | Maine | 41.8 |
| 23 | Maryland | 41.2 | 19 | Oklahoma | 41.8 |
| 40 | Massachusetts | 34.7 | 21 | Pennsylvania | 41.7 |
| 16 | Michigan | 42.3 | 22 | Kentucky | 41.5 |
| 47 | Minnesota | 32.7 | 23 | Maryland | 41.2 |
| 1 | Mississippi | 54.4 | 24 | New York | 41.1 |
| 27 | Missouri | 40.1 | 25 | North Carolina | 40.9 |
| 36 | Montana | 36.5 | 26 | California | 40.4 |
| 45 | Nebraska | 33.2 | 27 | Missouri | 40.1 |
| 11 | Nevada | 44.2 | 28 | Illinois | 40.0 |
| 41 | New Hampshire | 34.5 | 29 | Vermont | 39.5 |
| 37 | New Jersey | 35.9 | 30 | South Dakota | 38.9 |
| 3 | New Mexico | 51.3 | 31 | Connecticut | 38.0 |
| 24 | New York | 41.1 | 32 | Hawaii | 37.5 |
| 25 | North Carolina | 40.9 | 33 | Kansas | 37.3 |
| 44 | North Dakota | 33.4 | 34 | Wisconsin | 36.9 |
| 14 | Ohio | 43.4 | 35 | Alaska | 36.8 |
| 19 | Oklahoma | 41.8 | 36 | Montana | 36.5 |
| 38 | Oregon | 35.7 | 37 | New Jersey | 35.9 |
| 21 | Pennsylvania | 41.7 | 38 | Oregon | 35.7 |
| 10 | Rhode Island | 44.5 | 39 | Virginia | 35.5 |
| 6 | South Carolina | 47.1 | 40 | Massachusetts | 34.7 |
| 30 | South Dakota | 38.9 | 41 | New Hampshire | 34.5 |
| 12 | Tennessee | 44.1 | 41 | Wyoming | 34.5 |
| 18 | Texas | 42.0 | 43 | Iowa | 33.8 |
| 50 | Utah | 18.7 | 44 | North Dakota | 33.4 |
| 29 | Vermont | 39.5 | 45 | Nebraska | 33.2 |
| 39 | Virginia | 35.5 | 46 | Washington | 32.8 |
| 46 | Washington | 32.8 | 47 | Minnesota | 32.7 |
| 13 | West Virginia | 43.9 | 48 | Idaho | 26.8 |
| 34 | Wisconsin | 36.9 | 49 | Colorado | 23.7 |
| 41 | Wyoming | 34.5 | 50 | Utah | 18.7 |
| | | | | District of Columbia | 53.6 |

Source: U.S. Department of Health and Human Services, National Center for Health Statistics
"National Vital Statistics Reports" (Vol. 62, No. 1, June 2013, http://www.cdc.gov/nchs/births.htm)
*Final data by state of residence.

# Percent of Women Receiving Late or No Prenatal Care in 2011

## National Percent = 6.0% of Women*

<table>
<tr><td colspan="3">ALPHA ORDER</td><td colspan="3">RANK ORDER</td></tr>
<tr><td>RANK</td><td>STATE</td><td>PERCENT</td><td>RANK</td><td>STATE</td><td>PERCENT</td></tr>
<tr><td>NA</td><td>Alabama**</td><td>NA</td><td>1</td><td>Nevada</td><td>11.5</td></tr>
<tr><td>NA</td><td>Alaska**</td><td>NA</td><td>2</td><td>Texas</td><td>10.4</td></tr>
<tr><td>NA</td><td>Arizona**</td><td>NA</td><td>3</td><td>Maryland</td><td>8.4</td></tr>
<tr><td>NA</td><td>Arkansas**</td><td>NA</td><td>4</td><td>New Mexico</td><td>8.3</td></tr>
<tr><td>35</td><td>California</td><td>3.4</td><td>5</td><td>Oklahoma</td><td>8.2</td></tr>
<tr><td>11</td><td>Colorado</td><td>6.7</td><td>6</td><td>Delaware</td><td>7.4</td></tr>
<tr><td>NA</td><td>Connecticut**</td><td>NA</td><td>7</td><td>Georgia</td><td>7.3</td></tr>
<tr><td>6</td><td>Delaware</td><td>7.4</td><td>8</td><td>North Dakota</td><td>7.2</td></tr>
<tr><td>19</td><td>Florida</td><td>5.5</td><td>8</td><td>South Carolina</td><td>7.2</td></tr>
<tr><td>7</td><td>Georgia</td><td>7.3</td><td>10</td><td>Tennessee</td><td>6.9</td></tr>
<tr><td>NA</td><td>Hawaii**</td><td>NA</td><td>11</td><td>Colorado</td><td>6.7</td></tr>
<tr><td>24</td><td>Idaho</td><td>4.8</td><td>12</td><td>Pennsylvania</td><td>6.6</td></tr>
<tr><td>24</td><td>Illinois</td><td>4.8</td><td>13</td><td>Indiana</td><td>6.4</td></tr>
<tr><td>13</td><td>Indiana</td><td>6.4</td><td>13</td><td>Washington</td><td>6.4</td></tr>
<tr><td>34</td><td>Iowa</td><td>3.7</td><td>15</td><td>South Dakota</td><td>6.1</td></tr>
<tr><td>26</td><td>Kansas</td><td>4.6</td><td>15</td><td>Wyoming</td><td>6.1</td></tr>
<tr><td>20</td><td>Kentucky</td><td>5.4</td><td>17</td><td>Louisiana</td><td>6.0</td></tr>
<tr><td>17</td><td>Louisiana</td><td>6.0</td><td>18</td><td>Ohio</td><td>5.6</td></tr>
<tr><td>NA</td><td>Maine**</td><td>NA</td><td>19</td><td>Florida</td><td>5.5</td></tr>
<tr><td>3</td><td>Maryland</td><td>8.4</td><td>20</td><td>Kentucky</td><td>5.4</td></tr>
<tr><td>NA</td><td>Massachusetts**</td><td>NA</td><td>20</td><td>Montana</td><td>5.4</td></tr>
<tr><td>28</td><td>Michigan</td><td>4.5</td><td>20</td><td>New York</td><td>5.4</td></tr>
<tr><td>NA</td><td>Minnesota**</td><td>NA</td><td>20</td><td>North Carolina</td><td>5.4</td></tr>
<tr><td>NA</td><td>Mississippi**</td><td>NA</td><td>24</td><td>Idaho</td><td>4.8</td></tr>
<tr><td>26</td><td>Missouri</td><td>4.6</td><td>24</td><td>Illinois</td><td>4.8</td></tr>
<tr><td>20</td><td>Montana</td><td>5.4</td><td>26</td><td>Kansas</td><td>4.6</td></tr>
<tr><td>28</td><td>Nebraska</td><td>4.5</td><td>26</td><td>Missouri</td><td>4.6</td></tr>
<tr><td>1</td><td>Nevada</td><td>11.5</td><td>28</td><td>Michigan</td><td>4.5</td></tr>
<tr><td>33</td><td>New Hampshire</td><td>3.8</td><td>28</td><td>Nebraska</td><td>4.5</td></tr>
<tr><td>NA</td><td>New Jersey**</td><td>NA</td><td>30</td><td>Oregon</td><td>4.4</td></tr>
<tr><td>4</td><td>New Mexico</td><td>8.3</td><td>31</td><td>Utah</td><td>4.0</td></tr>
<tr><td>20</td><td>New York</td><td>5.4</td><td>32</td><td>Wisconsin</td><td>3.9</td></tr>
<tr><td>20</td><td>North Carolina</td><td>5.4</td><td>33</td><td>New Hampshire</td><td>3.8</td></tr>
<tr><td>8</td><td>North Dakota</td><td>7.2</td><td>34</td><td>Iowa</td><td>3.7</td></tr>
<tr><td>18</td><td>Ohio</td><td>5.6</td><td>35</td><td>California</td><td>3.4</td></tr>
<tr><td>5</td><td>Oklahoma</td><td>8.2</td><td>36</td><td>Vermont</td><td>2.4</td></tr>
<tr><td>30</td><td>Oregon</td><td>4.4</td><td>NA</td><td>Alabama**</td><td>NA</td></tr>
<tr><td>12</td><td>Pennsylvania</td><td>6.6</td><td>NA</td><td>Alaska**</td><td>NA</td></tr>
<tr><td>NA</td><td>Rhode Island**</td><td>NA</td><td>NA</td><td>Arizona**</td><td>NA</td></tr>
<tr><td>8</td><td>South Carolina</td><td>7.2</td><td>NA</td><td>Arkansas**</td><td>NA</td></tr>
<tr><td>15</td><td>South Dakota</td><td>6.1</td><td>NA</td><td>Connecticut**</td><td>NA</td></tr>
<tr><td>10</td><td>Tennessee</td><td>6.9</td><td>NA</td><td>Hawaii**</td><td>NA</td></tr>
<tr><td>2</td><td>Texas</td><td>10.4</td><td>NA</td><td>Maine**</td><td>NA</td></tr>
<tr><td>31</td><td>Utah</td><td>4.0</td><td>NA</td><td>Massachusetts**</td><td>NA</td></tr>
<tr><td>36</td><td>Vermont</td><td>2.4</td><td>NA</td><td>Minnesota**</td><td>NA</td></tr>
<tr><td>NA</td><td>Virginia**</td><td>NA</td><td>NA</td><td>Mississippi**</td><td>NA</td></tr>
<tr><td>13</td><td>Washington</td><td>6.4</td><td>NA</td><td>New Jersey**</td><td>NA</td></tr>
<tr><td>NA</td><td>West Virginia**</td><td>NA</td><td>NA</td><td>Rhode Island**</td><td>NA</td></tr>
<tr><td>32</td><td>Wisconsin</td><td>3.9</td><td>NA</td><td>Virginia**</td><td>NA</td></tr>
<tr><td>15</td><td>Wyoming</td><td>6.1</td><td>NA</td><td>West Virginia**</td><td>NA</td></tr>
<tr><td></td><td></td><td></td><td></td><td>District of Columbia</td><td>9.2</td></tr>
</table>

Source: CQ Press using data from U.S. Department of Health and Human Services, Centers for Disease Control and Prevention
"CDC Wonder" (http://wonder.cdc.gov)

*Final data by state of residence. "Late" means care begun in third trimester. National figure is for reporting states only.

**Not available.

# Reported Legal Abortions in 2010

## Reporting States' Total = 765,651 Abortions*

ALPHA ORDER

| RANK | STATE | ABORTIONS | % of USA |
|---|---|---|---|
| 19 | Alabama | 10,280 | 1.3% |
| 42 | Alaska | 1,715 | 0.2% |
| 17 | Arizona | 11,438 | 1.5% |
| 32 | Arkansas | 4,532 | 0.6% |
| NA | California** | NA | NA |
| 18 | Colorado | 11,210 | 1.5% |
| 15 | Connecticut | 13,438 | 1.8% |
| 31 | Delaware | 4,666 | 0.6% |
| 2 | Florida | 79,908 | 10.4% |
| 6 | Georgia | 34,585 | 4.5% |
| 36 | Hawaii | 3,064 | 0.4% |
| 43 | Idaho | 1,510 | 0.2% |
| 4 | Illinois | 41,859 | 5.5% |
| 20 | Indiana | 10,048 | 1.3% |
| 29 | Iowa | 5,399 | 0.7% |
| 23 | Kansas | 8,333 | 1.1% |
| 34 | Kentucky | 3,929 | 0.5% |
| 22 | Louisiana | 8,872 | 1.2% |
| 38 | Maine | 2,311 | 0.3% |
| NA | Maryland** | NA | NA |
| 13 | Massachusetts | 20,802 | 2.7% |
| 11 | Michigan | 23,307 | 3.0% |
| 16 | Minnesota | 11,505 | 1.5% |
| 39 | Mississippi | 2,297 | 0.3% |
| 27 | Missouri | 6,163 | 0.8% |
| 40 | Montana | 2,160 | 0.3% |
| 37 | Nebraska | 2,464 | 0.3% |
| 25 | Nevada | 7,787 | 1.0% |
| NA | New Hampshire** | NA | NA |
| 8 | New Jersey | 28,217 | 3.7% |
| 30 | New Mexico | 4,779 | 0.6% |
| 1 | New York | 115,724 | 15.1% |
| 7 | North Carolina | 30,952 | 4.0% |
| 45 | North Dakota | 1,291 | 0.2% |
| 9 | Ohio | 28,123 | 3.7% |
| 28 | Oklahoma | 6,097 | 0.8% |
| 21 | Oregon | 9,990 | 1.3% |
| 5 | Pennsylvania | 36,778 | 4.8% |
| 33 | Rhode Island | 4,181 | 0.5% |
| 26 | South Carolina | 6,464 | 0.8% |
| 46 | South Dakota | 737 | 0.1% |
| 14 | Tennessee | 16,373 | 2.1% |
| 3 | Texas | 77,463 | 10.1% |
| 35 | Utah | 3,780 | 0.5% |
| 44 | Vermont | 1,333 | 0.2% |
| 10 | Virginia | 25,943 | 3.4% |
| 12 | Washington | 21,124 | 2.8% |
| 41 | West Virginia | 1,999 | 0.3% |
| 24 | Wisconsin | 7,825 | 1.0% |
| NA | Wyoming** | NA | NA |

RANK ORDER

| RANK | STATE | ABORTIONS | % of USA |
|---|---|---|---|
| 1 | New York | 115,724 | 15.1% |
| 2 | Florida | 79,908 | 10.4% |
| 3 | Texas | 77,463 | 10.1% |
| 4 | Illinois | 41,859 | 5.5% |
| 5 | Pennsylvania | 36,778 | 4.8% |
| 6 | Georgia | 34,585 | 4.5% |
| 7 | North Carolina | 30,952 | 4.0% |
| 8 | New Jersey | 28,217 | 3.7% |
| 9 | Ohio | 28,123 | 3.7% |
| 10 | Virginia | 25,943 | 3.4% |
| 11 | Michigan | 23,307 | 3.0% |
| 12 | Washington | 21,124 | 2.8% |
| 13 | Massachusetts | 20,802 | 2.7% |
| 14 | Tennessee | 16,373 | 2.1% |
| 15 | Connecticut | 13,438 | 1.8% |
| 16 | Minnesota | 11,505 | 1.5% |
| 17 | Arizona | 11,438 | 1.5% |
| 18 | Colorado | 11,210 | 1.5% |
| 19 | Alabama | 10,280 | 1.3% |
| 20 | Indiana | 10,048 | 1.3% |
| 21 | Oregon | 9,990 | 1.3% |
| 22 | Louisiana | 8,872 | 1.2% |
| 23 | Kansas | 8,333 | 1.1% |
| 24 | Wisconsin | 7,825 | 1.0% |
| 25 | Nevada | 7,787 | 1.0% |
| 26 | South Carolina | 6,464 | 0.8% |
| 27 | Missouri | 6,163 | 0.8% |
| 28 | Oklahoma | 6,097 | 0.8% |
| 29 | Iowa | 5,399 | 0.7% |
| 30 | New Mexico | 4,779 | 0.6% |
| 31 | Delaware | 4,666 | 0.6% |
| 32 | Arkansas | 4,532 | 0.6% |
| 33 | Rhode Island | 4,181 | 0.5% |
| 34 | Kentucky | 3,929 | 0.5% |
| 35 | Utah | 3,780 | 0.5% |
| 36 | Hawaii | 3,064 | 0.4% |
| 37 | Nebraska | 2,464 | 0.3% |
| 38 | Maine | 2,311 | 0.3% |
| 39 | Mississippi | 2,297 | 0.3% |
| 40 | Montana | 2,160 | 0.3% |
| 41 | West Virginia | 1,999 | 0.3% |
| 42 | Alaska | 1,715 | 0.2% |
| 43 | Idaho | 1,510 | 0.2% |
| 44 | Vermont | 1,333 | 0.2% |
| 45 | North Dakota | 1,291 | 0.2% |
| 46 | South Dakota | 737 | 0.1% |
| NA | California** | NA | NA |
| NA | Maryland** | NA | NA |
| NA | New Hampshire** | NA | NA |
| NA | Wyoming** | NA | NA |
|  | District of Columbia | 2,896 | 0.4% |

Source: U.S. Department of Health and Human Services, Centers for Disease Control and Prevention
"Abortion Surveillance-United States, 2010" (MMWR, Vol. 62, No. SS-8, 11/29/13, www.cdc.gov/mmwr/mmwr_ss/ss_pvol.html)
*By state of occurrence. Total is for reporting states only.
**Not reported.

# Reported Legal Abortions per 1,000 Live Births in 2010

## Reporting States' Ratio = 228 Abortions per 1,000 Live Births*

| ALPHA ORDER | | | RANK ORDER | | |
|---|---|---|---|---|---|
| RANK | STATE | RATIO | RANK | STATE | RATIO |
| 25 | Alabama | 171 | 1 | New York | 474 |
| 29 | Alaska | 150 | 2 | Delaware | 411 |
| 33 | Arizona | 131 | 3 | Rhode Island | 374 |
| 35 | Arkansas | 118 | 4 | Florida | 372 |
| NA | California** | NA | 5 | Connecticut | 356 |
| 26 | Colorado | 169 | 6 | Massachusetts | 285 |
| 5 | Connecticut | 356 | 7 | New Jersey | 264 |
| 2 | Delaware | 411 | 8 | Georgia | 258 |
| 4 | Florida | 372 | 9 | Pennsylvania | 257 |
| 8 | Georgia | 258 | 10 | Illinois | 253 |
| 28 | Hawaii | 161 | 10 | North Carolina | 253 |
| 44 | Idaho | 65 | 12 | Virginia | 252 |
| 10 | Illinois | 253 | 13 | Washington | 244 |
| 34 | Indiana | 120 | 14 | Oregon | 219 |
| 32 | Iowa | 139 | 15 | Nevada | 217 |
| 18 | Kansas | 205 | 16 | Vermont | 214 |
| 43 | Kentucky | 70 | 17 | Tennessee | 206 |
| 30 | Louisiana | 142 | 18 | Kansas | 205 |
| 23 | Maine | 178 | 19 | Michigan | 203 |
| NA | Maryland** | NA | 20 | Ohio | 202 |
| 6 | Massachusetts | 285 | 21 | Texas | 201 |
| 19 | Michigan | 203 | 22 | Montana | 179 |
| 27 | Minnesota | 168 | 23 | Maine | 178 |
| 46 | Mississippi | 57 | 24 | New Mexico | 172 |
| 41 | Missouri | 80 | 25 | Alabama | 171 |
| 22 | Montana | 179 | 26 | Colorado | 169 |
| 40 | Nebraska | 95 | 27 | Minnesota | 168 |
| 15 | Nevada | 217 | 28 | Hawaii | 161 |
| NA | New Hampshire** | NA | 29 | Alaska | 150 |
| 7 | New Jersey | 264 | 30 | Louisiana | 142 |
| 24 | New Mexico | 172 | 30 | North Dakota | 142 |
| 1 | New York | 474 | 32 | Iowa | 139 |
| 10 | North Carolina | 253 | 33 | Arizona | 131 |
| 30 | North Dakota | 142 | 34 | Indiana | 120 |
| 20 | Ohio | 202 | 35 | Arkansas | 118 |
| 36 | Oklahoma | 115 | 36 | Oklahoma | 115 |
| 14 | Oregon | 219 | 37 | Wisconsin | 114 |
| 9 | Pennsylvania | 257 | 38 | South Carolina | 111 |
| 3 | Rhode Island | 374 | 39 | West Virginia | 98 |
| 38 | South Carolina | 111 | 40 | Nebraska | 95 |
| 45 | South Dakota | 62 | 41 | Missouri | 80 |
| 17 | Tennessee | 206 | 42 | Utah | 72 |
| 21 | Texas | 201 | 43 | Kentucky | 70 |
| 42 | Utah | 72 | 44 | Idaho | 65 |
| 16 | Vermont | 214 | 45 | South Dakota | 62 |
| 12 | Virginia | 252 | 46 | Mississippi | 57 |
| 13 | Washington | 244 | NA | California** | NA |
| 39 | West Virginia | 98 | NA | Maryland** | NA |
| 37 | Wisconsin | 114 | NA | New Hampshire** | NA |
| NA | Wyoming** | NA | NA | Wyoming** | NA |

District of Columbia    316

Source: U.S. Department of Health and Human Services, Centers for Disease Control and Prevention
    "Abortion Surveillance-United States, 2010" (MMWR, Vol. 62, No. SS-8, 11/29/13, www.cdc.gov/mmwr/mmwr_ss/ss_pvol.html)
*By state of occurrence.  National figure is for reporting states only.
**Not reported.

# Infant Deaths in 2010

## National Total = 24,586 Infant Deaths*

ALPHA ORDER

| RANK | STATE | DEATHS | % of USA |
|---|---|---|---|
| 14 | Alabama | 523 | 2.1% |
| 49 | Alaska | 43 | 0.2% |
| 15 | Arizona | 522 | 2.1% |
| 29 | Arkansas | 282 | 1.1% |
| 1 | California | 2,420 | 9.8% |
| 23 | Colorado | 392 | 1.6% |
| 34 | Connecticut | 199 | 0.8% |
| 41 | Delaware | 87 | 0.4% |
| 3 | Florida | 1,403 | 5.7% |
| 8 | Georgia | 860 | 3.5% |
| 39 | Hawaii | 117 | 0.5% |
| 40 | Idaho | 112 | 0.5% |
| 5 | Illinois | 1,118 | 4.5% |
| 12 | Indiana | 640 | 2.6% |
| 35 | Iowa | 189 | 0.8% |
| 31 | Kansas | 253 | 1.0% |
| 26 | Kentucky | 379 | 1.5% |
| 19 | Louisiana | 474 | 1.9% |
| 45 | Maine | 70 | 0.3% |
| 18 | Maryland | 498 | 2.0% |
| 27 | Massachusetts | 323 | 1.3% |
| 10 | Michigan | 817 | 3.3% |
| 28 | Minnesota | 308 | 1.3% |
| 25 | Mississippi | 387 | 1.6% |
| 17 | Missouri | 507 | 2.1% |
| 44 | Montana | 71 | 0.3% |
| 38 | Nebraska | 136 | 0.6% |
| 33 | Nevada | 201 | 0.8% |
| 47 | New Hampshire | 51 | 0.2% |
| 16 | New Jersey | 514 | 2.1% |
| 36 | New Mexico | 157 | 0.6% |
| 4 | New York | 1,243 | 5.1% |
| 9 | North Carolina | 858 | 3.5% |
| 46 | North Dakota | 62 | 0.3% |
| 6 | Ohio | 1,072 | 4.4% |
| 21 | Oklahoma | 404 | 1.6% |
| 32 | Oregon | 225 | 0.9% |
| 7 | Pennsylvania | 1,039 | 4.2% |
| 43 | Rhode Island | 79 | 0.3% |
| 20 | South Carolina | 430 | 1.7% |
| 42 | South Dakota | 82 | 0.3% |
| 13 | Tennessee | 630 | 2.6% |
| 2 | Texas | 2,368 | 9.6% |
| 30 | Utah | 254 | 1.0% |
| 50 | Vermont | 26 | 0.1% |
| 11 | Virginia | 700 | 2.8% |
| 24 | Washington | 389 | 1.6% |
| 37 | West Virginia | 149 | 0.6% |
| 22 | Wisconsin | 400 | 1.6% |
| 47 | Wyoming | 51 | 0.2% |

RANK ORDER

| RANK | STATE | DEATHS | % of USA |
|---|---|---|---|
| 1 | California | 2,420 | 9.8% |
| 2 | Texas | 2,368 | 9.6% |
| 3 | Florida | 1,403 | 5.7% |
| 4 | New York | 1,243 | 5.1% |
| 5 | Illinois | 1,118 | 4.5% |
| 6 | Ohio | 1,072 | 4.4% |
| 7 | Pennsylvania | 1,039 | 4.2% |
| 8 | Georgia | 860 | 3.5% |
| 9 | North Carolina | 858 | 3.5% |
| 10 | Michigan | 817 | 3.3% |
| 11 | Virginia | 700 | 2.8% |
| 12 | Indiana | 640 | 2.6% |
| 13 | Tennessee | 630 | 2.6% |
| 14 | Alabama | 523 | 2.1% |
| 15 | Arizona | 522 | 2.1% |
| 16 | New Jersey | 514 | 2.1% |
| 17 | Missouri | 507 | 2.1% |
| 18 | Maryland | 498 | 2.0% |
| 19 | Louisiana | 474 | 1.9% |
| 20 | South Carolina | 430 | 1.7% |
| 21 | Oklahoma | 404 | 1.6% |
| 22 | Wisconsin | 400 | 1.6% |
| 23 | Colorado | 392 | 1.6% |
| 24 | Washington | 389 | 1.6% |
| 25 | Mississippi | 387 | 1.6% |
| 26 | Kentucky | 379 | 1.5% |
| 27 | Massachusetts | 323 | 1.3% |
| 28 | Minnesota | 308 | 1.3% |
| 29 | Arkansas | 282 | 1.1% |
| 30 | Utah | 254 | 1.0% |
| 31 | Kansas | 253 | 1.0% |
| 32 | Oregon | 225 | 0.9% |
| 33 | Nevada | 201 | 0.8% |
| 34 | Connecticut | 199 | 0.8% |
| 35 | Iowa | 189 | 0.8% |
| 36 | New Mexico | 157 | 0.6% |
| 37 | West Virginia | 149 | 0.6% |
| 38 | Nebraska | 136 | 0.6% |
| 39 | Hawaii | 117 | 0.5% |
| 40 | Idaho | 112 | 0.5% |
| 41 | Delaware | 87 | 0.4% |
| 42 | South Dakota | 82 | 0.3% |
| 43 | Rhode Island | 79 | 0.3% |
| 44 | Montana | 71 | 0.3% |
| 45 | Maine | 70 | 0.3% |
| 46 | North Dakota | 62 | 0.3% |
| 47 | New Hampshire | 51 | 0.2% |
| 47 | Wyoming | 51 | 0.2% |
| 49 | Alaska | 43 | 0.2% |
| 50 | Vermont | 26 | 0.1% |
| | District of Columbia | 72 | 0.3% |

Source: U.S. Department of Health and Human Services, National Center for Health Statistics
   "National Vital Statistics Reports" (Vol. 61, No. 4, May 8, 2013, http://www.cdc.gov/nchs/deaths.htm)
*Final data. Deaths of infants under 1 year old by state of residence.

# Infant Mortality Rate in 2010

## National Rate = 6.2 Infant Deaths per 1,000 Live Births*

ALPHA ORDER

| RANK | STATE | RATE |
|---|---|---|
| 2 | Alabama | 8.7 |
| 50 | Alaska | 3.8 |
| 29 | Arizona | 6.0 |
| 10 | Arkansas | 7.3 |
| 44 | California | 4.7 |
| 30 | Colorado | 5.9 |
| 36 | Connecticut | 5.3 |
| 5 | Delaware | 7.7 |
| 24 | Florida | 6.5 |
| 25 | Georgia | 6.4 |
| 27 | Hawaii | 6.2 |
| 42 | Idaho | 4.8 |
| 20 | Illinois | 6.8 |
| 6 | Indiana | 7.6 |
| 40 | Iowa | 4.9 |
| 26 | Kansas | 6.2 |
| 19 | Kentucky | 6.8 |
| 7 | Louisiana | 7.6 |
| 35 | Maine | 5.4 |
| 21 | Maryland | 6.8 |
| 47 | Massachusetts | 4.4 |
| 13 | Michigan | 7.1 |
| 46 | Minnesota | 4.5 |
| 1 | Mississippi | 9.7 |
| 23 | Missouri | 6.6 |
| 31 | Montana | 5.9 |
| 37 | Nebraska | 5.3 |
| 34 | Nevada | 5.6 |
| 49 | New Hampshire | 4.0 |
| 43 | New Jersey | 4.8 |
| 33 | New Mexico | 5.6 |
| 38 | New York | 5.1 |
| 15 | North Carolina | 7.0 |
| 17 | North Dakota | 6.8 |
| 4 | Ohio | 7.7 |
| 8 | Oklahoma | 7.6 |
| 39 | Oregon | 4.9 |
| 12 | Pennsylvania | 7.3 |
| 14 | Rhode Island | 7.1 |
| 9 | South Carolina | 7.4 |
| 16 | South Dakota | 6.9 |
| 3 | Tennessee | 7.9 |
| 28 | Texas | 6.1 |
| 41 | Utah | 4.9 |
| 48 | Vermont | 4.2 |
| 18 | Virginia | 6.8 |
| 45 | Washington | 4.5 |
| 11 | West Virginia | 7.3 |
| 32 | Wisconsin | 5.8 |
| 21 | Wyoming | 6.8 |

RANK ORDER

| RANK | STATE | RATE |
|---|---|---|
| 1 | Mississippi | 9.7 |
| 2 | Alabama | 8.7 |
| 3 | Tennessee | 7.9 |
| 4 | Ohio | 7.7 |
| 5 | Delaware | 7.7 |
| 6 | Indiana | 7.6 |
| 7 | Louisiana | 7.6 |
| 8 | Oklahoma | 7.6 |
| 9 | South Carolina | 7.4 |
| 10 | Arkansas | 7.3 |
| 11 | West Virginia | 7.3 |
| 12 | Pennsylvania | 7.3 |
| 13 | Michigan | 7.1 |
| 14 | Rhode Island | 7.1 |
| 15 | North Carolina | 7.0 |
| 16 | South Dakota | 6.9 |
| 17 | North Dakota | 6.8 |
| 18 | Virginia | 6.8 |
| 19 | Kentucky | 6.8 |
| 20 | Illinois | 6.8 |
| 21 | Maryland | 6.8 |
| 21 | Wyoming | 6.8 |
| 23 | Missouri | 6.6 |
| 24 | Florida | 6.5 |
| 25 | Georgia | 6.4 |
| 26 | Kansas | 6.2 |
| 27 | Hawaii | 6.2 |
| 28 | Texas | 6.1 |
| 29 | Arizona | 6.0 |
| 30 | Colorado | 5.9 |
| 31 | Montana | 5.9 |
| 32 | Wisconsin | 5.8 |
| 33 | New Mexico | 5.6 |
| 34 | Nevada | 5.6 |
| 35 | Maine | 5.4 |
| 36 | Connecticut | 5.3 |
| 37 | Nebraska | 5.3 |
| 38 | New York | 5.1 |
| 39 | Oregon | 4.9 |
| 40 | Iowa | 4.9 |
| 41 | Utah | 4.9 |
| 42 | Idaho | 4.8 |
| 43 | New Jersey | 4.8 |
| 44 | California | 4.7 |
| 45 | Washington | 4.5 |
| 46 | Minnesota | 4.5 |
| 47 | Massachusetts | 4.4 |
| 48 | Vermont | 4.2 |
| 49 | New Hampshire | 4.0 |
| 50 | Alaska | 3.8 |
| | District of Columbia | 7.9 |

Source: U.S. Department of Health and Human Services, National Center for Health Statistics
"National Vital Statistics Reports" (Vol. 61, No. 4, May 8, 2013, http://www.cdc.gov/nchs/deaths.htm)
*Final data.  Deaths of infants under 1 year old by state of residence.

# Deaths in 2011

## National Total = 2,513,171 Deaths*

ALPHA ORDER

| RANK | STATE | DEATHS | % of USA |
|---|---|---|---|
| 18 | Alabama | 48,683 | 1.9% |
| 50 | Alaska | 3,849 | 0.2% |
| 20 | Arizona | 48,381 | 1.9% |
| 29 | Arkansas | 29,632 | 1.2% |
| 1 | California | 238,993 | 9.5% |
| 28 | Colorado | 32,563 | 1.3% |
| 30 | Connecticut | 29,548 | 1.2% |
| 45 | Delaware | 7,840 | 0.3% |
| 2 | Florida | 173,961 | 6.9% |
| 11 | Georgia | 70,401 | 2.8% |
| 42 | Hawaii | 9,921 | 0.4% |
| 40 | Idaho | 12,026 | 0.5% |
| 7 | Illinois | 101,898 | 4.1% |
| 14 | Indiana | 58,195 | 2.3% |
| 32 | Iowa | 28,184 | 1.1% |
| 33 | Kansas | 25,119 | 1.0% |
| 22 | Kentucky | 42,624 | 1.7% |
| 24 | Louisiana | 40,680 | 1.6% |
| 39 | Maine | 13,031 | 0.5% |
| 21 | Maryland | 43,750 | 1.7% |
| 16 | Massachusetts | 53,699 | 2.1% |
| 8 | Michigan | 89,496 | 3.6% |
| 25 | Minnesota | 39,822 | 1.6% |
| 31 | Mississippi | 29,278 | 1.2% |
| 15 | Missouri | 55,813 | 2.2% |
| 44 | Montana | 9,117 | 0.4% |
| 37 | Nebraska | 15,477 | 0.6% |
| 35 | Nevada | 20,340 | 0.8% |
| 41 | New Hampshire | 10,821 | 0.4% |
| 10 | New Jersey | 70,553 | 2.8% |
| 36 | New Mexico | 16,434 | 0.7% |
| 4 | New York | 148,903 | 5.9% |
| 9 | North Carolina | 79,875 | 3.2% |
| 47 | North Dakota | 5,964 | 0.2% |
| 6 | Ohio | 111,444 | 4.4% |
| 26 | Oklahoma | 37,142 | 1.5% |
| 27 | Oregon | 32,786 | 1.3% |
| 5 | Pennsylvania | 128,290 | 5.1% |
| 43 | Rhode Island | 9,585 | 0.4% |
| 23 | South Carolina | 42,093 | 1.7% |
| 46 | South Dakota | 7,313 | 0.3% |
| 13 | Tennessee | 60,544 | 2.4% |
| 3 | Texas | 168,643 | 6.7% |
| 38 | Utah | 15,265 | 0.6% |
| 48 | Vermont | 5,434 | 0.2% |
| 12 | Virginia | 60,807 | 2.4% |
| 17 | Washington | 49,692 | 2.0% |
| 34 | West Virginia | 21,868 | 0.9% |
| 19 | Wisconsin | 48,419 | 1.9% |
| 49 | Wyoming | 4,387 | 0.2% |

RANK ORDER

| RANK | STATE | DEATHS | % of USA |
|---|---|---|---|
| 1 | California | 238,993 | 9.5% |
| 2 | Florida | 173,961 | 6.9% |
| 3 | Texas | 168,643 | 6.7% |
| 4 | New York | 148,903 | 5.9% |
| 5 | Pennsylvania | 128,290 | 5.1% |
| 6 | Ohio | 111,444 | 4.4% |
| 7 | Illinois | 101,898 | 4.1% |
| 8 | Michigan | 89,496 | 3.6% |
| 9 | North Carolina | 79,875 | 3.2% |
| 10 | New Jersey | 70,553 | 2.8% |
| 11 | Georgia | 70,401 | 2.8% |
| 12 | Virginia | 60,807 | 2.4% |
| 13 | Tennessee | 60,544 | 2.4% |
| 14 | Indiana | 58,195 | 2.3% |
| 15 | Missouri | 55,813 | 2.2% |
| 16 | Massachusetts | 53,699 | 2.1% |
| 17 | Washington | 49,692 | 2.0% |
| 18 | Alabama | 48,683 | 1.9% |
| 19 | Wisconsin | 48,419 | 1.9% |
| 20 | Arizona | 48,381 | 1.9% |
| 21 | Maryland | 43,750 | 1.7% |
| 22 | Kentucky | 42,624 | 1.7% |
| 23 | South Carolina | 42,093 | 1.7% |
| 24 | Louisiana | 40,680 | 1.6% |
| 25 | Minnesota | 39,822 | 1.6% |
| 26 | Oklahoma | 37,142 | 1.5% |
| 27 | Oregon | 32,786 | 1.3% |
| 28 | Colorado | 32,563 | 1.3% |
| 29 | Arkansas | 29,632 | 1.2% |
| 30 | Connecticut | 29,548 | 1.2% |
| 31 | Mississippi | 29,278 | 1.2% |
| 32 | Iowa | 28,184 | 1.1% |
| 33 | Kansas | 25,119 | 1.0% |
| 34 | West Virginia | 21,868 | 0.9% |
| 35 | Nevada | 20,340 | 0.8% |
| 36 | New Mexico | 16,434 | 0.7% |
| 37 | Nebraska | 15,477 | 0.6% |
| 38 | Utah | 15,265 | 0.6% |
| 39 | Maine | 13,031 | 0.5% |
| 40 | Idaho | 12,026 | 0.5% |
| 41 | New Hampshire | 10,821 | 0.4% |
| 42 | Hawaii | 9,921 | 0.4% |
| 43 | Rhode Island | 9,585 | 0.4% |
| 44 | Montana | 9,117 | 0.4% |
| 45 | Delaware | 7,840 | 0.3% |
| 46 | South Dakota | 7,313 | 0.3% |
| 47 | North Dakota | 5,964 | 0.2% |
| 48 | Vermont | 5,434 | 0.2% |
| 49 | Wyoming | 4,387 | 0.2% |
| 50 | Alaska | 3,849 | 0.2% |
| | District of Columbia | 4,589 | 0.2% |

Source: U.S. Department of Health and Human Services, National Center for Health Statistics
"National Vital Statistics Reports" (Vol. 61, No. 6, October 10, 2012, http://www.cdc.gov/nchs/deaths.htm)
*Preliminary data by state of residence.

# Age-Adjusted Death Rate in 2011

## National Rate = 740.6 Deaths per 100,000 Population*

ALPHA ORDER

| RANK | STATE | RATE |
|------|-------|------|
| 3 | Alabama | 933.7 |
| 25 | Alaska | 747.9 |
| 42 | Arizona | 688.9 |
| 6 | Arkansas | 894.6 |
| 49 | California | 638.8 |
| 43 | Colorado | 677.8 |
| 47 | Connecticut | 660.9 |
| 19 | Delaware | 763.4 |
| 44 | Florida | 677.1 |
| 13 | Georgia | 806.2 |
| 50 | Hawaii | 584.8 |
| 26 | Idaho | 744.9 |
| 28 | Illinois | 737.3 |
| 10 | Indiana | 825.0 |
| 30 | Iowa | 722.7 |
| 18 | Kansas | 767.2 |
| 4 | Kentucky | 910.3 |
| 7 | Louisiana | 882.1 |
| 23 | Maine | 749.5 |
| 34 | Maryland | 715.9 |
| 45 | Massachusetts | 676.1 |
| 16 | Michigan | 784.2 |
| 48 | Minnesota | 659.2 |
| 1 | Mississippi | 956.2 |
| 12 | Missouri | 811.4 |
| 20 | Montana | 760.7 |
| 33 | Nebraska | 719.8 |
| 15 | Nevada | 789.6 |
| 36 | New Hampshire | 710.0 |
| 40 | New Jersey | 690.6 |
| 24 | New Mexico | 748.0 |
| 46 | New York | 664.2 |
| 14 | North Carolina | 790.8 |
| 39 | North Dakota | 697.3 |
| 11 | Ohio | 822.0 |
| 5 | Oklahoma | 910.1 |
| 29 | Oregon | 724.1 |
| 17 | Pennsylvania | 776.1 |
| 37 | Rhode Island | 707.6 |
| 9 | South Carolina | 839.9 |
| 32 | South Dakota | 720.4 |
| 8 | Tennessee | 879.1 |
| 22 | Texas | 751.6 |
| 38 | Utah | 699.0 |
| 35 | Vermont | 711.0 |
| 27 | Virginia | 741.6 |
| 41 | Washington | 690.4 |
| 2 | West Virginia | 953.3 |
| 31 | Wisconsin | 721.3 |
| 21 | Wyoming | 754.6 |

RANK ORDER

| RANK | STATE | RATE |
|------|-------|------|
| 1 | Mississippi | 956.2 |
| 2 | West Virginia | 953.3 |
| 3 | Alabama | 933.7 |
| 4 | Kentucky | 910.3 |
| 5 | Oklahoma | 910.1 |
| 6 | Arkansas | 894.6 |
| 7 | Louisiana | 882.1 |
| 8 | Tennessee | 879.1 |
| 9 | South Carolina | 839.9 |
| 10 | Indiana | 825.0 |
| 11 | Ohio | 822.0 |
| 12 | Missouri | 811.4 |
| 13 | Georgia | 806.2 |
| 14 | North Carolina | 790.8 |
| 15 | Nevada | 789.6 |
| 16 | Michigan | 784.2 |
| 17 | Pennsylvania | 776.1 |
| 18 | Kansas | 767.2 |
| 19 | Delaware | 763.4 |
| 20 | Montana | 760.7 |
| 21 | Wyoming | 754.6 |
| 22 | Texas | 751.6 |
| 23 | Maine | 749.5 |
| 24 | New Mexico | 748.0 |
| 25 | Alaska | 747.9 |
| 26 | Idaho | 744.9 |
| 27 | Virginia | 741.6 |
| 28 | Illinois | 737.3 |
| 29 | Oregon | 724.1 |
| 30 | Iowa | 722.7 |
| 31 | Wisconsin | 721.3 |
| 32 | South Dakota | 720.4 |
| 33 | Nebraska | 719.8 |
| 34 | Maryland | 715.9 |
| 35 | Vermont | 711.0 |
| 36 | New Hampshire | 710.0 |
| 37 | Rhode Island | 707.6 |
| 38 | Utah | 699.0 |
| 39 | North Dakota | 697.3 |
| 40 | New Jersey | 690.6 |
| 41 | Washington | 690.4 |
| 42 | Arizona | 688.9 |
| 43 | Colorado | 677.8 |
| 44 | Florida | 677.1 |
| 45 | Massachusetts | 676.1 |
| 46 | New York | 664.2 |
| 47 | Connecticut | 660.9 |
| 48 | Minnesota | 659.2 |
| 49 | California | 638.8 |
| 50 | Hawaii | 584.8 |
| | District of Columbia | 756.0 |

Source: U.S. Department of Health and Human Services, National Center for Health Statistics
    "National Vital Statistics Reports" (Vol. 61, No. 6, October 10, 2012, http://www.cdc.gov/nchs/deaths.htm)
*Preliminary data by state of residence. Age-adjusted rates eliminate the distorting effects of the aging of the population. Rates
based on the year 2000 standard population.

# Estimated Deaths by Cancer in 2013

## National Estimated Total = 580,350 Deaths

ALPHA ORDER

| RANK | STATE | DEATHS | % of USA |
|---|---|---|---|
| 21 | Alabama | 10,430 | 1.8% |
| 49 | Alaska | 980 | 0.2% |
| 19 | Arizona | 11,210 | 1.9% |
| 30 | Arkansas | 6,650 | 1.1% |
| 1 | California | 57,290 | 9.9% |
| 28 | Colorado | 7,350 | 1.3% |
| 29 | Connecticut | 6,890 | 1.2% |
| 45 | Delaware | 1,940 | 0.3% |
| 2 | Florida | 42,370 | 7.3% |
| 11 | Georgia | 16,010 | 2.8% |
| 42 | Hawaii | 2,400 | 0.4% |
| 41 | Idaho | 2,660 | 0.5% |
| 7 | Illinois | 24,000 | 4.1% |
| 14 | Indiana | 13,250 | 2.3% |
| 31 | Iowa | 6,420 | 1.1% |
| 33 | Kansas | 5,430 | 0.9% |
| 22 | Kentucky | 9,970 | 1.7% |
| 25 | Louisiana | 9,040 | 1.6% |
| 38 | Maine | 3,240 | 0.6% |
| 20 | Maryland | 10,480 | 1.8% |
| 15 | Massachusetts | 12,840 | 2.2% |
| 8 | Michigan | 20,570 | 3.5% |
| 24 | Minnesota | 9,610 | 1.7% |
| 32 | Mississippi | 6,300 | 1.1% |
| 16 | Missouri | 12,730 | 2.2% |
| 44 | Montana | 2,000 | 0.3% |
| 37 | Nebraska | 3,440 | 0.6% |
| 34 | Nevada | 4,760 | 0.8% |
| 40 | Ncw Hampshire | 2,680 | 0.5% |
| 10 | New Jersey | 16,410 | 2.8% |
| 36 | New Mexico | 3,540 | 0.6% |
| 4 | New York | 34,240 | 5.9% |
| 9 | North Carolina | 18,620 | 3.2% |
| 48 | North Dakota | 1,280 | 0.2% |
| 6 | Ohio | 25,130 | 4.3% |
| 26 | Oklahoma | 7,850 | 1.4% |
| 27 | Oregon | 7,820 | 1.3% |
| 5 | Pennsylvania | 28,680 | 4.9% |
| 43 | Rhode Island | 2,140 | 0.4% |
| 23 | South Carolina | 9,800 | 1.7% |
| 46 | South Dakota | 1,590 | 0.3% |
| 13 | Tennessee | 14,080 | 2.4% |
| 3 | Texas | 37,180 | 6.4% |
| 39 | Utah | 2,790 | 0.5% |
| 47 | Vermont | 1,300 | 0.2% |
| 12 | Virginia | 14,720 | 2.5% |
| 17 | Washington | 12,390 | 2.1% |
| 35 | West Virginia | 4,660 | 0.8% |
| 18 | Wisconsin | 11,220 | 1.9% |
| 50 | Wyoming | 950 | 0.2% |

RANK ORDER

| RANK | STATE | DEATHS | % of USA |
|---|---|---|---|
| 1 | California | 57,290 | 9.9% |
| 2 | Florida | 42,370 | 7.3% |
| 3 | Texas | 37,180 | 6.4% |
| 4 | New York | 34,240 | 5.9% |
| 5 | Pennsylvania | 28,680 | 4.9% |
| 6 | Ohio | 25,130 | 4.3% |
| 7 | Illinois | 24,000 | 4.1% |
| 8 | Michigan | 20,570 | 3.5% |
| 9 | North Carolina | 18,620 | 3.2% |
| 10 | New Jersey | 16,410 | 2.8% |
| 11 | Georgia | 16,010 | 2.8% |
| 12 | Virginia | 14,720 | 2.5% |
| 13 | Tennessee | 14,080 | 2.4% |
| 14 | Indiana | 13,250 | 2.3% |
| 15 | Massachusetts | 12,840 | 2.2% |
| 16 | Missouri | 12,730 | 2.2% |
| 17 | Washington | 12,390 | 2.1% |
| 18 | Wisconsin | 11,220 | 1.9% |
| 19 | Arizona | 11,210 | 1.9% |
| 20 | Maryland | 10,480 | 1.8% |
| 21 | Alabama | 10,430 | 1.8% |
| 22 | Kentucky | 9,970 | 1.7% |
| 23 | South Carolina | 9,800 | 1.7% |
| 24 | Minnesota | 9,610 | 1.7% |
| 25 | Louisiana | 9,040 | 1.6% |
| 26 | Oklahoma | 7,850 | 1.4% |
| 27 | Oregon | 7,820 | 1.3% |
| 28 | Colorado | 7,350 | 1.3% |
| 29 | Connecticut | 6,890 | 1.2% |
| 30 | Arkansas | 6,650 | 1.1% |
| 31 | Iowa | 6,420 | 1.1% |
| 32 | Mississippi | 6,300 | 1.1% |
| 33 | Kansas | 5,430 | 0.9% |
| 34 | Nevada | 4,760 | 0.8% |
| 35 | West Virginia | 4,660 | 0.8% |
| 36 | New Mexico | 3,540 | 0.6% |
| 37 | Nebraska | 3,440 | 0.6% |
| 38 | Maine | 3,240 | 0.6% |
| 39 | Utah | 2,790 | 0.5% |
| 40 | New Hampshire | 2,680 | 0.5% |
| 41 | Idaho | 2,660 | 0.5% |
| 42 | Hawaii | 2,400 | 0.4% |
| 43 | Rhode Island | 2,140 | 0.4% |
| 44 | Montana | 2,000 | 0.3% |
| 45 | Delaware | 1,940 | 0.3% |
| 46 | South Dakota | 1,590 | 0.3% |
| 47 | Vermont | 1,300 | 0.2% |
| 48 | North Dakota | 1,280 | 0.2% |
| 49 | Alaska | 980 | 0.2% |
| 50 | Wyoming | 950 | 0.2% |
| | District of Columbia | 1,030 | 0.2% |

Source: American Cancer Society
"Cancer Facts & Figures 2013" (Copyright 2013, American Cancer Society, www.cancer.org/Research/CancerFactsFigures/)

# Estimated Death Rate by Cancer in 2013

## National Estimated Rate = 184.9 Deaths per 100,000 Population*

ALPHA ORDER

| RANK | STATE | RATE |
|------|-------|------|
| 9 | Alabama | 216.3 |
| 49 | Alaska | 134.0 |
| 41 | Arizona | 171.1 |
| 4 | Arkansas | 225.5 |
| 46 | California | 150.6 |
| 48 | Colorado | 141.7 |
| 26 | Connecticut | 191.9 |
| 10 | Delaware | 211.5 |
| 6 | Florida | 219.3 |
| 45 | Georgia | 161.4 |
| 40 | Hawaii | 172.4 |
| 43 | Idaho | 166.7 |
| 30 | Illinois | 186.4 |
| 20 | Indiana | 202.7 |
| 13 | Iowa | 208.8 |
| 29 | Kansas | 188.2 |
| 3 | Kentucky | 227.6 |
| 23 | Louisiana | 196.4 |
| 2 | Maine | 243.8 |
| 37 | Maryland | 178.1 |
| 25 | Massachusetts | 193.2 |
| 14 | Michigan | 208.1 |
| 36 | Minnesota | 178.7 |
| 12 | Mississippi | 211.1 |
| 11 | Missouri | 211.4 |
| 22 | Montana | 199.0 |
| 31 | Nebraska | 185.4 |
| 39 | Nevada | 172.5 |
| 19 | New Hampshire | 202.9 |
| 32 | New Jersey | 185.1 |
| 42 | New Mexico | 169.7 |
| 38 | New York | 175.0 |
| 27 | North Carolina | 190.9 |
| 33 | North Dakota | 183.0 |
| 8 | Ohio | 217.7 |
| 17 | Oklahoma | 205.8 |
| 21 | Oregon | 200.5 |
| 5 | Pennsylvania | 224.7 |
| 18 | Rhode Island | 203.8 |
| 16 | South Carolina | 207.5 |
| 28 | South Dakota | 190.8 |
| 7 | Tennessee | 218.1 |
| 47 | Texas | 142.7 |
| 50 | Utah | 97.7 |
| 15 | Vermont | 207.7 |
| 34 | Virginia | 179.8 |
| 35 | Washington | 179.6 |
| 1 | West Virginia | 251.2 |
| 24 | Wisconsin | 195.9 |
| 44 | Wyoming | 164.8 |

RANK ORDER

| RANK | STATE | RATE |
|------|-------|------|
| 1 | West Virginia | 251.2 |
| 2 | Maine | 243.8 |
| 3 | Kentucky | 227.6 |
| 4 | Arkansas | 225.5 |
| 5 | Pennsylvania | 224.7 |
| 6 | Florida | 219.3 |
| 7 | Tennessee | 218.1 |
| 8 | Ohio | 217.7 |
| 9 | Alabama | 216.3 |
| 10 | Delaware | 211.5 |
| 11 | Missouri | 211.4 |
| 12 | Mississippi | 211.1 |
| 13 | Iowa | 208.8 |
| 14 | Michigan | 208.1 |
| 15 | Vermont | 207.7 |
| 16 | South Carolina | 207.5 |
| 17 | Oklahoma | 205.8 |
| 18 | Rhode Island | 203.8 |
| 19 | New Hampshire | 202.9 |
| 20 | Indiana | 202.7 |
| 21 | Oregon | 200.5 |
| 22 | Montana | 199.0 |
| 23 | Louisiana | 196.4 |
| 24 | Wisconsin | 195.9 |
| 25 | Massachusetts | 193.2 |
| 26 | Connecticut | 191.9 |
| 27 | North Carolina | 190.9 |
| 28 | South Dakota | 190.8 |
| 29 | Kansas | 188.2 |
| 30 | Illinois | 186.4 |
| 31 | Nebraska | 185.4 |
| 32 | New Jersey | 185.1 |
| 33 | North Dakota | 183.0 |
| 34 | Virginia | 179.8 |
| 35 | Washington | 179.6 |
| 36 | Minnesota | 178.7 |
| 37 | Maryland | 178.1 |
| 38 | New York | 175.0 |
| 39 | Nevada | 172.5 |
| 40 | Hawaii | 172.4 |
| 41 | Arizona | 171.1 |
| 42 | New Mexico | 169.7 |
| 43 | Idaho | 166.7 |
| 44 | Wyoming | 164.8 |
| 45 | Georgia | 161.4 |
| 46 | California | 150.6 |
| 47 | Texas | 142.7 |
| 48 | Colorado | 141.7 |
| 49 | Alaska | 134.0 |
| 50 | Utah | 97.7 |
| | District of Columbia | 162.9 |

Source: CQ Press using data from American Cancer Society
   "Cancer Facts & Figures 2013" (Copyright 2013, American Cancer Society, www.cancer.org/Research/CancerFactsFigures/)
*Rates calculated using 2012 Census resident population estimates.  Not age-adjusted.

# Estimated New Cancer Cases in 2013

## National Estimated Total = 1,660,290 New Cases*

ALPHA ORDER

| RANK | STATE | CASES | % of USA |
|------|-------|-------|----------|
| 23 | Alabama | 27,080 | 1.6% |
| 49 | Alaska | 3,290 | 0.2% |
| 17 | Arizona | 34,010 | 2.0% |
| 31 | Arkansas | 16,330 | 1.0% |
| 1 | California | 171,330 | 10.3% |
| 26 | Colorado | 23,410 | 1.4% |
| 28 | Connecticut | 21,180 | 1.3% |
| 45 | Delaware | 5,370 | 0.3% |
| 2 | Florida | 118,320 | 7.1% |
| 11 | Georgia | 49,280 | 3.0% |
| 42 | Hawaii | 6,650 | 0.4% |
| 41 | Idaho | 7,670 | 0.5% |
| 7 | Illinois | 66,090 | 4.0% |
| 16 | Indiana | 35,550 | 2.1% |
| 30 | Iowa | 17,480 | 1.1% |
| 33 | Kansas | 14,370 | 0.9% |
| 24 | Kentucky | 25,100 | 1.5% |
| 25 | Louisiana | 24,930 | 1.5% |
| 38 | Maine | 9,190 | 0.6% |
| 20 | Maryland | 30,680 | 1.8% |
| 13 | Massachusetts | 38,250 | 2.3% |
| 8 | Michigan | 57,560 | 3.5% |
| 21 | Minnesota | 28,410 | 1.7% |
| 32 | Mississippi | 15,830 | 1.0% |
| 18 | Missouri | 33,950 | 2.0% |
| 44 | Montana | 5,450 | 0.3% |
| 39 | Nebraska | 9,060 | 0.5% |
| 34 | Nevada | 13,830 | 0.8% |
| 40 | New Hampshire | 8,470 | 0.5% |
| 10 | New Jersey | 49,440 | 3.0% |
| 37 | New Mexico | 10,090 | 0.6% |
| 4 | New York | 108,760 | 6.6% |
| 9 | North Carolina | 53,200 | 3.2% |
| 48 | North Dakota | 3,510 | 0.2% |
| 6 | Ohio | 66,610 | 4.0% |
| 29 | Oklahoma | 20,160 | 1.2% |
| 27 | Oregon | 21,720 | 1.3% |
| 5 | Pennsylvania | 79,560 | 4.8% |
| 43 | Rhode Island | 6,280 | 0.4% |
| 22 | South Carolina | 27,620 | 1.7% |
| 46 | South Dakota | 4,570 | 0.3% |
| 15 | Tennessee | 36,580 | 2.2% |
| 3 | Texas | 112,230 | 6.8% |
| 36 | Utah | 10,810 | 0.7% |
| 47 | Vermont | 4,200 | 0.3% |
| 12 | Virginia | 40,870 | 2.5% |
| 14 | Washington | 37,290 | 2.2% |
| 35 | West Virginia | 11,450 | 0.7% |
| 19 | Wisconsin | 31,590 | 1.9% |
| 50 | Wyoming | 2,700 | 0.2% |

RANK ORDER

| RANK | STATE | CASES | % of USA |
|------|-------|-------|----------|
| 1 | California | 171,330 | 10.3% |
| 2 | Florida | 118,320 | 7.1% |
| 3 | Texas | 112,230 | 6.8% |
| 4 | New York | 108,760 | 6.6% |
| 5 | Pennsylvania | 79,560 | 4.8% |
| 6 | Ohio | 66,610 | 4.0% |
| 7 | Illinois | 66,090 | 4.0% |
| 8 | Michigan | 57,560 | 3.5% |
| 9 | North Carolina | 53,200 | 3.2% |
| 10 | New Jersey | 49,440 | 3.0% |
| 11 | Georgia | 49,280 | 3.0% |
| 12 | Virginia | 40,870 | 2.5% |
| 13 | Massachusetts | 38,250 | 2.3% |
| 14 | Washington | 37,290 | 2.2% |
| 15 | Tennessee | 36,580 | 2.2% |
| 16 | Indiana | 35,550 | 2.1% |
| 17 | Arizona | 34,010 | 2.0% |
| 18 | Missouri | 33,950 | 2.0% |
| 19 | Wisconsin | 31,590 | 1.9% |
| 20 | Maryland | 30,680 | 1.8% |
| 21 | Minnesota | 28,410 | 1.7% |
| 22 | South Carolina | 27,620 | 1.7% |
| 23 | Alabama | 27,080 | 1.6% |
| 24 | Kentucky | 25,100 | 1.5% |
| 25 | Louisiana | 24,930 | 1.5% |
| 26 | Colorado | 23,410 | 1.4% |
| 27 | Oregon | 21,720 | 1.3% |
| 28 | Connecticut | 21,180 | 1.3% |
| 29 | Oklahoma | 20,160 | 1.2% |
| 30 | Iowa | 17,480 | 1.1% |
| 31 | Arkansas | 16,330 | 1.0% |
| 32 | Mississippi | 15,830 | 1.0% |
| 33 | Kansas | 14,370 | 0.9% |
| 34 | Nevada | 13,830 | 0.8% |
| 35 | West Virginia | 11,450 | 0.7% |
| 36 | Utah | 10,810 | 0.7% |
| 37 | New Mexico | 10,090 | 0.6% |
| 38 | Maine | 9,190 | 0.6% |
| 39 | Nebraska | 9,060 | 0.5% |
| 40 | New Hampshire | 8,470 | 0.5% |
| 41 | Idaho | 7,670 | 0.5% |
| 42 | Hawaii | 6,650 | 0.4% |
| 43 | Rhode Island | 6,280 | 0.4% |
| 44 | Montana | 5,450 | 0.3% |
| 45 | Delaware | 5,370 | 0.3% |
| 46 | South Dakota | 4,570 | 0.3% |
| 47 | Vermont | 4,200 | 0.3% |
| 48 | North Dakota | 3,510 | 0.2% |
| 49 | Alaska | 3,290 | 0.2% |
| 50 | Wyoming | 2,700 | 0.2% |
| | District of Columbia | 2,920 | 0.2% |

Source: American Cancer Society
    "Cancer Facts & Figures 2013" (Copyright 2013, American Cancer Society, www.cancer.org/Research/CancerFactsFigures/)
*These estimates are offered as a rough guide and should not be regarded as definitive. They are calculated by the American Cancer Society using a model based on 1995-2009 incidence data. Totals do not include basal and squamous cell skin cancers or in situ carcinomas except urinary bladder.

# Estimated Rate of New Cancer Cases in 2013

## National Estimated Rate = 528.9 New Cases per 100,000 Population*

ALPHA ORDER

| RANK | STATE | RATE |
|------|-------|------|
| 18 | Alabama | 561.6 |
| 48 | Alaska | 449.8 |
| 34 | Arizona | 519.0 |
| 22 | Arkansas | 553.7 |
| 47 | California | 450.4 |
| 46 | Colorado | 451.3 |
| 8 | Connecticut | 589.9 |
| 9 | Delaware | 585.5 |
| 6 | Florida | 612.5 |
| 40 | Georgia | 496.8 |
| 44 | Hawaii | 477.6 |
| 43 | Idaho | 480.7 |
| 35 | Illinois | 513.3 |
| 26 | Indiana | 543.8 |
| 15 | Iowa | 568.6 |
| 39 | Kansas | 497.9 |
| 14 | Kentucky | 573.0 |
| 28 | Louisiana | 541.7 |
| 1 | Maine | 691.4 |
| 33 | Maryland | 521.4 |
| 13 | Massachusetts | 575.5 |
| 11 | Michigan | 582.4 |
| 32 | Minnesota | 528.2 |
| 30 | Mississippi | 530.3 |
| 17 | Missouri | 563.8 |
| 27 | Montana | 542.2 |
| 41 | Nebraska | 488.3 |
| 37 | Nevada | 501.3 |
| 3 | New Hampshire | 641.3 |
| 19 | New Jersey | 557.7 |
| 42 | New Mexico | 483.8 |
| 21 | New York | 555.7 |
| 25 | North Carolina | 545.5 |
| 36 | North Dakota | 501.7 |
| 12 | Ohio | 577.0 |
| 31 | Oklahoma | 528.5 |
| 20 | Oregon | 557.0 |
| 4 | Pennsylvania | 623.3 |
| 7 | Rhode Island | 597.9 |
| 10 | South Carolina | 584.7 |
| 24 | South Dakota | 548.4 |
| 16 | Tennessee | 566.6 |
| 49 | Texas | 430.7 |
| 50 | Utah | 378.6 |
| 2 | Vermont | 670.9 |
| 38 | Virginia | 499.3 |
| 29 | Washington | 540.7 |
| 5 | West Virginia | 617.1 |
| 23 | Wisconsin | 551.7 |
| 45 | Wyoming | 468.4 |

RANK ORDER

| RANK | STATE | RATE |
|------|-------|------|
| 1 | Maine | 691.4 |
| 2 | Vermont | 670.9 |
| 3 | New Hampshire | 641.3 |
| 4 | Pennsylvania | 623.3 |
| 5 | West Virginia | 617.1 |
| 6 | Florida | 612.5 |
| 7 | Rhode Island | 597.9 |
| 8 | Connecticut | 589.9 |
| 9 | Delaware | 585.5 |
| 10 | South Carolina | 584.7 |
| 11 | Michigan | 582.4 |
| 12 | Ohio | 577.0 |
| 13 | Massachusetts | 575.5 |
| 14 | Kentucky | 573.0 |
| 15 | Iowa | 568.6 |
| 16 | Tennessee | 566.6 |
| 17 | Missouri | 563.8 |
| 18 | Alabama | 561.6 |
| 19 | New Jersey | 557.7 |
| 20 | Oregon | 557.0 |
| 21 | New York | 555.7 |
| 22 | Arkansas | 553.7 |
| 23 | Wisconsin | 551.7 |
| 24 | South Dakota | 548.4 |
| 25 | North Carolina | 545.5 |
| 26 | Indiana | 543.8 |
| 27 | Montana | 542.2 |
| 28 | Louisiana | 541.7 |
| 29 | Washington | 540.7 |
| 30 | Mississippi | 530.3 |
| 31 | Oklahoma | 528.5 |
| 32 | Minnesota | 528.2 |
| 33 | Maryland | 521.4 |
| 34 | Arizona | 519.0 |
| 35 | Illinois | 513.3 |
| 36 | North Dakota | 501.7 |
| 37 | Nevada | 501.3 |
| 38 | Virginia | 499.3 |
| 39 | Kansas | 497.9 |
| 40 | Georgia | 496.8 |
| 41 | Nebraska | 488.3 |
| 42 | New Mexico | 483.8 |
| 43 | Idaho | 480.7 |
| 44 | Hawaii | 477.6 |
| 45 | Wyoming | 468.4 |
| 46 | Colorado | 451.3 |
| 47 | California | 450.4 |
| 48 | Alaska | 449.8 |
| 49 | Texas | 430.7 |
| 50 | Utah | 378.6 |
|  | District of Columbia | 461.8 |

Source: CQ Press using data from American Cancer Society
    "Cancer Facts & Figures 2013" (Copyright 2013, American Cancer Society, www.cancer.org/Research/CancerFactsFigures/)
*These estimates are offered as a rough guide and should not be regarded as definitive.  They are calculated by the American Cancer Society using a model based on 1995-2009 incidence data.  Totals do not include basal and squamous cell skin cancers or in situ carcinomas except urinary bladder.  Rates calculated using 2012 Census resident population estimates.

# Deaths by Accidents in 2010

## National Total = 120,859 Deaths*

ALPHA ORDER

| RANK | STATE | DEATHS | % of USA |
|------|-------|--------|----------|
| 20 | Alabama | 2,394 | 2.0% |
| 46 | Alaska | 366 | 0.3% |
| 12 | Arizona | 3,018 | 2.5% |
| 29 | Arkansas | 1,461 | 1.2% |
| 1 | California | 10,435 | 8.6% |
| 23 | Colorado | 2,106 | 1.7% |
| 31 | Connecticut | 1,337 | 1.1% |
| 47 | Delaware | 357 | 0.3% |
| 3 | Florida | 8,875 | 7.3% |
| 10 | Georgia | 3,745 | 3.1% |
| 44 | Hawaii | 432 | 0.4% |
| 39 | Idaho | 654 | 0.5% |
| 8 | Illinois | 3,997 | 3.3% |
| 16 | Indiana | 2,534 | 2.1% |
| 33 | Iowa | 1,273 | 1.1% |
| 32 | Kansas | 1,317 | 1.1% |
| 14 | Kentucky | 2,632 | 2.2% |
| 26 | Louisiana | 1,999 | 1.7% |
| 41 | Maine | 540 | 0.4% |
| 30 | Maryland | 1,446 | 1.2% |
| 25 | Massachusetts | 2,060 | 1.7% |
| 9 | Michigan | 3,770 | 3.1% |
| 24 | Minnesota | 2,103 | 1.7% |
| 27 | Mississippi | 1,685 | 1.4% |
| 13 | Missouri | 2,975 | 2.5% |
| 40 | Montana | 548 | 0.5% |
| 38 | Nebraska | 700 | 0.6% |
| 36 | Nevada | 1,088 | 0.9% |
| 42 | New Hampshire | 517 | 0.4% |
| 19 | New Jersey | 2,486 | 2.1% |
| 35 | New Mexico | 1,233 | 1.0% |
| 6 | New York | 5,004 | 4.1% |
| 7 | North Carolina | 4,144 | 3.4% |
| 50 | North Dakota | 285 | 0.2% |
| 5 | Ohio | 5,124 | 4.2% |
| 21 | Oklahoma | 2,288 | 1.9% |
| 28 | Oregon | 1,566 | 1.3% |
| 4 | Pennsylvania | 5,751 | 4.8% |
| 43 | Rhode Island | 475 | 0.4% |
| 22 | South Carolina | 2,274 | 1.9% |
| 45 | South Dakota | 393 | 0.3% |
| 11 | Tennessee | 3,539 | 2.9% |
| 2 | Texas | 9,212 | 7.6% |
| 37 | Utah | 970 | 0.8% |
| 49 | Vermont | 298 | 0.2% |
| 17 | Virginia | 2,527 | 2.1% |
| 15 | Washington | 2,609 | 2.2% |
| 34 | West Virginia | 1,234 | 1.0% |
| 18 | Wisconsin | 2,525 | 2.1% |
| 48 | Wyoming | 346 | 0.3% |

RANK ORDER

| RANK | STATE | DEATHS | % of USA |
|------|-------|--------|----------|
| 1 | California | 10,435 | 8.6% |
| 2 | Texas | 9,212 | 7.6% |
| 3 | Florida | 8,875 | 7.3% |
| 4 | Pennsylvania | 5,751 | 4.8% |
| 5 | Ohio | 5,124 | 4.2% |
| 6 | New York | 5,004 | 4.1% |
| 7 | North Carolina | 4,144 | 3.4% |
| 8 | Illinois | 3,997 | 3.3% |
| 9 | Michigan | 3,770 | 3.1% |
| 10 | Georgia | 3,745 | 3.1% |
| 11 | Tennessee | 3,539 | 2.9% |
| 12 | Arizona | 3,018 | 2.5% |
| 13 | Missouri | 2,975 | 2.5% |
| 14 | Kentucky | 2,632 | 2.2% |
| 15 | Washington | 2,609 | 2.2% |
| 16 | Indiana | 2,534 | 2.1% |
| 17 | Virginia | 2,527 | 2.1% |
| 18 | Wisconsin | 2,525 | 2.1% |
| 19 | New Jersey | 2,486 | 2.1% |
| 20 | Alabama | 2,394 | 2.0% |
| 21 | Oklahoma | 2,288 | 1.9% |
| 22 | South Carolina | 2,274 | 1.9% |
| 23 | Colorado | 2,106 | 1.7% |
| 24 | Minnesota | 2,103 | 1.7% |
| 25 | Massachusetts | 2,060 | 1.7% |
| 26 | Louisiana | 1,999 | 1.7% |
| 27 | Mississippi | 1,685 | 1.4% |
| 28 | Oregon | 1,566 | 1.3% |
| 29 | Arkansas | 1,461 | 1.2% |
| 30 | Maryland | 1,446 | 1.2% |
| 31 | Connecticut | 1,337 | 1.1% |
| 32 | Kansas | 1,317 | 1.1% |
| 33 | Iowa | 1,273 | 1.1% |
| 34 | West Virginia | 1,234 | 1.0% |
| 35 | New Mexico | 1,233 | 1.0% |
| 36 | Nevada | 1,088 | 0.9% |
| 37 | Utah | 970 | 0.8% |
| 38 | Nebraska | 700 | 0.6% |
| 39 | Idaho | 654 | 0.5% |
| 40 | Montana | 548 | 0.5% |
| 41 | Maine | 540 | 0.4% |
| 42 | New Hampshire | 517 | 0.4% |
| 43 | Rhode Island | 475 | 0.4% |
| 44 | Hawaii | 432 | 0.4% |
| 45 | South Dakota | 393 | 0.3% |
| 46 | Alaska | 366 | 0.3% |
| 47 | Delaware | 357 | 0.3% |
| 48 | Wyoming | 346 | 0.3% |
| 49 | Vermont | 298 | 0.2% |
| 50 | North Dakota | 285 | 0.2% |
|  | District of Columbia | 212 | 0.2% |

Source: U.S. Department of Health and Human Services, National Center for Health Statistics
"National Vital Statistics Reports" (Vol. 61, No. 4, May 8, 2013, http://www.cdc.gov/nchs/deaths.htm)
*Final data by state of residence. Includes motor vehicle deaths, poisoning, falls, drowning, and other accidents.

# Age-Adjusted Death Rate by Accidents in 2010

## National Rate = 38.0 Deaths per 100,000 Population*

ALPHA ORDER

| RANK | STATE | RATE |
|---|---|---|
| 10 | Alabama | 49.6 |
| 6 | Alaska | 58.7 |
| 14 | Arizona | 46.7 |
| 11 | Arkansas | 49.4 |
| 47 | California | 27.8 |
| 18 | Colorado | 43.5 |
| 42 | Connecticut | 33.6 |
| 30 | Delaware | 39.2 |
| 20 | Florida | 43.1 |
| 27 | Georgia | 40.7 |
| 45 | Hawaii | 29.6 |
| 23 | Idaho | 42.1 |
| 44 | Illinois | 30.4 |
| 33 | Indiana | 38.5 |
| 36 | Iowa | 37.2 |
| 17 | Kansas | 44.0 |
| 3 | Kentucky | 60.5 |
| 16 | Louisiana | 44.4 |
| 39 | Maine | 36.5 |
| 49 | Maryland | 24.7 |
| 46 | Massachusetts | 28.5 |
| 40 | Michigan | 36.2 |
| 38 | Minnesota | 36.7 |
| 7 | Mississippi | 56.8 |
| 13 | Missouri | 47.9 |
| 9 | Montana | 53.2 |
| 41 | Nebraska | 35.8 |
| 24 | Nevada | 41.3 |
| 36 | New Hampshire | 37.2 |
| 48 | New Jersey | 26.7 |
| 2 | New Mexico | 60.7 |
| 50 | New York | 24.2 |
| 19 | North Carolina | 43.2 |
| 32 | North Dakota | 38.8 |
| 22 | Ohio | 42.4 |
| 4 | Oklahoma | 60.3 |
| 34 | Oregon | 37.8 |
| 25 | Pennsylvania | 41.1 |
| 29 | Rhode Island | 40.0 |
| 12 | South Carolina | 48.9 |
| 15 | South Dakota | 44.5 |
| 8 | Tennessee | 54.9 |
| 31 | Texas | 39.0 |
| 28 | Utah | 40.6 |
| 21 | Vermont | 42.7 |
| 43 | Virginia | 31.6 |
| 35 | Washington | 37.6 |
| 1 | West Virginia | 63.7 |
| 26 | Wisconsin | 40.8 |
| 5 | Wyoming | 59.8 |

RANK ORDER

| RANK | STATE | RATE |
|---|---|---|
| 1 | West Virginia | 63.7 |
| 2 | New Mexico | 60.7 |
| 3 | Kentucky | 60.5 |
| 4 | Oklahoma | 60.3 |
| 5 | Wyoming | 59.8 |
| 6 | Alaska | 58.7 |
| 7 | Mississippi | 56.8 |
| 8 | Tennessee | 54.9 |
| 9 | Montana | 53.2 |
| 10 | Alabama | 49.6 |
| 11 | Arkansas | 49.4 |
| 12 | South Carolina | 48.9 |
| 13 | Missouri | 47.9 |
| 14 | Arizona | 46.7 |
| 15 | South Dakota | 44.5 |
| 16 | Louisiana | 44.4 |
| 17 | Kansas | 44.0 |
| 18 | Colorado | 43.5 |
| 19 | North Carolina | 43.2 |
| 20 | Florida | 43.1 |
| 21 | Vermont | 42.7 |
| 22 | Ohio | 42.4 |
| 23 | Idaho | 42.1 |
| 24 | Nevada | 41.3 |
| 25 | Pennsylvania | 41.1 |
| 26 | Wisconsin | 40.8 |
| 27 | Georgia | 40.7 |
| 28 | Utah | 40.6 |
| 29 | Rhode Island | 40.0 |
| 30 | Delaware | 39.2 |
| 31 | Texas | 39.0 |
| 32 | North Dakota | 38.8 |
| 33 | Indiana | 38.5 |
| 34 | Oregon | 37.8 |
| 35 | Washington | 37.6 |
| 36 | Iowa | 37.2 |
| 36 | New Hampshire | 37.2 |
| 38 | Minnesota | 36.7 |
| 39 | Maine | 36.5 |
| 40 | Michigan | 36.2 |
| 41 | Nebraska | 35.8 |
| 42 | Connecticut | 33.6 |
| 43 | Virginia | 31.6 |
| 44 | Illinois | 30.4 |
| 45 | Hawaii | 29.6 |
| 46 | Massachusetts | 28.5 |
| 47 | California | 27.8 |
| 48 | New Jersey | 26.7 |
| 49 | Maryland | 24.7 |
| 50 | New York | 24.2 |

| District of Columbia | 35.1 |
|---|---|

Source: U.S. Department of Health and Human Services, National Center for Health Statistics
"National Vital Statistics Reports" (Vol. 61, No. 4, May 8, 2013, http://www.cdc.gov/nchs/deaths.htm)
*Final data by state of residence. Includes motor vehicle deaths, poisoning, falls, drowning, and other accidents. Age-adjusted rates based on the year 2000 standard population.

# Deaths by Cerebrovascular Diseases in 2010

## National Total = 129,476 Deaths*

ALPHA ORDER

| RANK | STATE | DEATHS | % of USA |
|------|-------|--------|----------|
| 16 | Alabama | 2,619 | 2.0% |
| 50 | Alaska | 167 | 0.1% |
| 23 | Arizona | 2,138 | 1.7% |
| 28 | Arkansas | 1,741 | 1.3% |
| 1 | California | 13,662 | 10.6% |
| 29 | Colorado | 1,607 | 1.2% |
| 33 | Connecticut | 1,349 | 1.0% |
| 46 | Delaware | 407 | 0.3% |
| 3 | Florida | 8,432 | 6.5% |
| 10 | Georgia | 3,762 | 2.9% |
| 40 | Hawaii | 605 | 0.5% |
| 39 | Idaho | 642 | 0.5% |
| 7 | Illinois | 5,349 | 4.1% |
| 14 | Indiana | 3,082 | 2.4% |
| 30 | Iowa | 1,537 | 1.2% |
| 32 | Kansas | 1,370 | 1.1% |
| 24 | Kentucky | 1,992 | 1.5% |
| 26 | Louisiana | 1,977 | 1.5% |
| 41 | Maine | 602 | 0.5% |
| 21 | Maryland | 2,279 | 1.8% |
| 19 | Massachusetts | 2,516 | 1.9% |
| 8 | Michigan | 4,474 | 3.5% |
| 22 | Minnesota | 2,167 | 1.7% |
| 31 | Mississippi | 1,520 | 1.2% |
| 15 | Missouri | 3,001 | 2.3% |
| 43 | Montana | 494 | 0.4% |
| 35 | Nebraska | 876 | 0.7% |
| 37 | Nevada | 796 | 0.6% |
| 42 | New Hampshire | 500 | 0.4% |
| 11 | New Jersey | 3,402 | 2.6% |
| 36 | New Mexico | 806 | 0.6% |
| 5 | New York | 6,213 | 4.8% |
| 9 | North Carolina | 4,298 | 3.3% |
| 47 | North Dakota | 382 | 0.3% |
| 6 | Ohio | 5,755 | 4.4% |
| 25 | Oklahoma | 1,980 | 1.5% |
| 27 | Oregon | 1,793 | 1.4% |
| 4 | Pennsylvania | 6,701 | 5.2% |
| 44 | Rhode Island | 431 | 0.3% |
| 20 | South Carolina | 2,293 | 1.8% |
| 45 | South Dakota | 416 | 0.3% |
| 13 | Tennessee | 3,205 | 2.5% |
| 2 | Texas | 9,180 | 7.1% |
| 38 | Utah | 739 | 0.6% |
| 48 | Vermont | 265 | 0.2% |
| 12 | Virginia | 3,293 | 2.5% |
| 18 | Washington | 2,548 | 2.0% |
| 34 | West Virginia | 1,104 | 0.9% |
| 17 | Wisconsin | 2,609 | 2.0% |
| 49 | Wyoming | 204 | 0.2% |

RANK ORDER

| RANK | STATE | DEATHS | % of USA |
|------|-------|--------|----------|
| 1 | California | 13,662 | 10.6% |
| 2 | Texas | 9,180 | 7.1% |
| 3 | Florida | 8,432 | 6.5% |
| 4 | Pennsylvania | 6,701 | 5.2% |
| 5 | New York | 6,213 | 4.8% |
| 6 | Ohio | 5,755 | 4.4% |
| 7 | Illinois | 5,349 | 4.1% |
| 8 | Michigan | 4,474 | 3.5% |
| 9 | North Carolina | 4,298 | 3.3% |
| 10 | Georgia | 3,762 | 2.9% |
| 11 | New Jersey | 3,402 | 2.6% |
| 12 | Virginia | 3,293 | 2.5% |
| 13 | Tennessee | 3,205 | 2.5% |
| 14 | Indiana | 3,082 | 2.4% |
| 15 | Missouri | 3,001 | 2.3% |
| 16 | Alabama | 2,619 | 2.0% |
| 17 | Wisconsin | 2,609 | 2.0% |
| 18 | Washington | 2,548 | 2.0% |
| 19 | Massachusetts | 2,516 | 1.9% |
| 20 | South Carolina | 2,293 | 1.8% |
| 21 | Maryland | 2,279 | 1.8% |
| 22 | Minnesota | 2,167 | 1.7% |
| 23 | Arizona | 2,138 | 1.7% |
| 24 | Kentucky | 1,992 | 1.5% |
| 25 | Oklahoma | 1,980 | 1.5% |
| 26 | Louisiana | 1,977 | 1.5% |
| 27 | Oregon | 1,793 | 1.4% |
| 28 | Arkansas | 1,741 | 1.3% |
| 29 | Colorado | 1,607 | 1.2% |
| 30 | Iowa | 1,537 | 1.2% |
| 31 | Mississippi | 1,520 | 1.2% |
| 32 | Kansas | 1,370 | 1.1% |
| 33 | Connecticut | 1,349 | 1.0% |
| 34 | West Virginia | 1,104 | 0.9% |
| 35 | Nebraska | 876 | 0.7% |
| 36 | New Mexico | 806 | 0.6% |
| 37 | Nevada | 796 | 0.6% |
| 38 | Utah | 739 | 0.6% |
| 39 | Idaho | 642 | 0.5% |
| 40 | Hawaii | 605 | 0.5% |
| 41 | Maine | 602 | 0.5% |
| 42 | New Hampshire | 500 | 0.4% |
| 43 | Montana | 494 | 0.4% |
| 44 | Rhode Island | 431 | 0.3% |
| 45 | South Dakota | 416 | 0.3% |
| 46 | Delaware | 407 | 0.3% |
| 47 | North Dakota | 382 | 0.3% |
| 48 | Vermont | 265 | 0.2% |
| 49 | Wyoming | 204 | 0.2% |
| 50 | Alaska | 167 | 0.1% |
| | District of Columbia | 196 | 0.2% |

Source: U.S. Department of Health and Human Services, National Center for Health Statistics
"National Vital Statistics Reports" (Vol. 61, No. 4, May 8, 2013, http://www.cdc.gov/nchs/deaths.htm)
*Final data by state of residence. Cerebrovascular diseases include stroke and other disorders of the blood vessels of the brain.

# Age-Adjusted Death Rate by Cerebrovascular Diseases in 2010

## National Rate = 39.1 Deaths per 100,000 Population*

| ALPHA ORDER | | | RANK ORDER | | |
|---|---|---|---|---|---|
| RANK | STATE | RATE | RANK | STATE | RATE |
| 2 | Alabama | 51.6 | 1 | Arkansas | 53.8 |
| 21 | Alaska | 40.9 | 2 | Alabama | 51.6 |
| 46 | Arizona | 31.9 | 3 | Mississippi | 51.2 |
| 1 | Arkansas | 53.8 | 4 | Oklahoma | 50.0 |
| 32 | California | 38.1 | 5 | Tennessee | 48.7 |
| 37 | Colorado | 36.1 | 6 | South Carolina | 47.9 |
| 49 | Connecticut | 29.4 | 7 | West Virginia | 47.8 |
| 22 | Delaware | 40.7 | 8 | Georgia | 46.3 |
| 45 | Florida | 32.8 | 9 | Louisiana | 44.9 |
| 8 | Georgia | 46.3 | 10 | North Carolina | 44.7 |
| 39 | Hawaii | 35.8 | 11 | Indiana | 44.5 |
| 18 | Idaho | 42.0 | 12 | Texas | 44.4 |
| 28 | Illinois | 39.2 | 13 | Kentucky | 44.1 |
| 11 | Indiana | 44.5 | 14 | Missouri | 44.0 |
| 33 | Iowa | 38.0 | 15 | North Dakota | 42.9 |
| 20 | Kansas | 41.2 | 16 | Ohio | 42.6 |
| 13 | Kentucky | 44.1 | 17 | Virginia | 42.1 |
| 9 | Louisiana | 44.9 | 18 | Idaho | 42.0 |
| 41 | Maine | 34.5 | 19 | Montana | 41.8 |
| 29 | Maryland | 38.8 | 20 | Kansas | 41.2 |
| 48 | Massachusetts | 31.3 | 21 | Alaska | 40.9 |
| 26 | Michigan | 39.5 | 22 | Delaware | 40.7 |
| 37 | Minnesota | 36.1 | 23 | Nebraska | 40.5 |
| 3 | Mississippi | 51.2 | 24 | Oregon | 40.1 |
| 14 | Missouri | 44.0 | 25 | South Dakota | 39.9 |
| 19 | Montana | 41.8 | 26 | Michigan | 39.5 |
| 23 | Nebraska | 40.5 | 27 | Pennsylvania | 39.3 |
| 43 | Nevada | 33.3 | 28 | Illinois | 39.2 |
| 42 | New Hampshire | 33.5 | 29 | Maryland | 38.8 |
| 43 | New Jersey | 33.3 | 30 | Wisconsin | 38.7 |
| 31 | New Mexico | 38.4 | 31 | New Mexico | 38.4 |
| 50 | New York | 27.9 | 32 | California | 38.1 |
| 10 | North Carolina | 44.7 | 33 | Iowa | 38.0 |
| 15 | North Dakota | 42.9 | 34 | Wyoming | 37.2 |
| 16 | Ohio | 42.6 | 35 | Utah | 37.1 |
| 4 | Oklahoma | 50.0 | 36 | Washington | 37.0 |
| 24 | Oregon | 40.1 | 37 | Colorado | 36.1 |
| 27 | Pennsylvania | 39.3 | 37 | Minnesota | 36.1 |
| 47 | Rhode Island | 31.4 | 39 | Hawaii | 35.8 |
| 6 | South Carolina | 47.9 | 40 | Vermont | 35.3 |
| 25 | South Dakota | 39.9 | 41 | Maine | 34.5 |
| 5 | Tennessee | 48.7 | 42 | New Hampshire | 33.5 |
| 12 | Texas | 44.4 | 43 | Nevada | 33.3 |
| 35 | Utah | 37.1 | 43 | New Jersey | 33.3 |
| 40 | Vermont | 35.3 | 45 | Florida | 32.8 |
| 17 | Virginia | 42.1 | 46 | Arizona | 31.9 |
| 36 | Washington | 37.0 | 47 | Rhode Island | 31.4 |
| 7 | West Virginia | 47.8 | 48 | Massachusetts | 31.3 |
| 30 | Wisconsin | 38.7 | 49 | Connecticut | 29.4 |
| 34 | Wyoming | 37.2 | 50 | New York | 27.9 |
| | | | | District of Columbia | 32.7 |

Source: U.S. Department of Health and Human Services, National Center for Health Statistics
   "National Vital Statistics Reports" (Vol. 61, No. 4, May 8, 2013, http://www.cdc.gov/nchs/deaths.htm)
*Final data by state of residence. Cerebrovascular diseases include stroke and other disorders of the blood vessels of the brain.
Age-adjusted rates based on the year 2000 standard population.

# Deaths by Diseases of the Heart in 2010

## National Total = 597,689 Deaths*

ALPHA ORDER

| RANK | STATE | DEATHS | % of USA |
|------|-------|--------|----------|
| 16 | Alabama | 12,083 | 2.0% |
| 50 | Alaska | 707 | 0.1% |
| 22 | Arizona | 9,954 | 1.7% |
| 27 | Arkansas | 7,274 | 1.2% |
| 1 | California | 58,641 | 9.8% |
| 32 | Colorado | 6,038 | 1.0% |
| 29 | Connecticut | 7,127 | 1.2% |
| 45 | Delaware | 1,776 | 0.3% |
| 3 | Florida | 41,737 | 7.0% |
| 11 | Georgia | 15,987 | 2.7% |
| 43 | Hawaii | 2,239 | 0.4% |
| 40 | Idaho | 2,495 | 0.4% |
| 7 | Illinois | 24,959 | 4.2% |
| 15 | Indiana | 13,388 | 2.2% |
| 30 | Iowa | 6,880 | 1.2% |
| 33 | Kansas | 5,433 | 0.9% |
| 23 | Kentucky | 9,662 | 1.6% |
| 21 | Louisiana | 10,282 | 1.7% |
| 39 | Maine | 2,628 | 0.4% |
| 19 | Maryland | 10,915 | 1.8% |
| 17 | Massachusetts | 12,043 | 2.0% |
| 8 | Michigan | 23,326 | 3.9% |
| 28 | Minnesota | 7,185 | 1.2% |
| 26 | Mississippi | 7,542 | 1.3% |
| 13 | Missouri | 13,840 | 2.3% |
| 44 | Montana | 1,849 | 0.3% |
| 36 | Nebraska | 3,355 | 0.6% |
| 35 | Nevada | 4,811 | 0.8% |
| 42 | New Hampshire | 2,290 | 0.4% |
| 9 | New Jersey | 18,730 | 3.1% |
| 37 | New Mexico | 3,224 | 0.5% |
| 2 | New York | 44,981 | 7.5% |
| 10 | North Carolina | 17,154 | 2.9% |
| 47 | North Dakota | 1,395 | 0.2% |
| 6 | Ohio | 26,164 | 4.4% |
| 24 | Oklahoma | 9,426 | 1.6% |
| 31 | Oregon | 6,198 | 1.0% |
| 5 | Pennsylvania | 31,556 | 5.3% |
| 41 | Rhode Island | 2,322 | 0.4% |
| 25 | South Carolina | 9,295 | 1.6% |
| 46 | South Dakota | 1,616 | 0.3% |
| 12 | Tennessee | 14,582 | 2.4% |
| 4 | Texas | 38,253 | 6.4% |
| 38 | Utah | 2,889 | 0.5% |
| 48 | Vermont | 1,172 | 0.2% |
| 14 | Virginia | 13,404 | 2.2% |
| 20 | Washington | 10,602 | 1.8% |
| 34 | West Virginia | 4,897 | 0.8% |
| 18 | Wisconsin | 11,115 | 1.9% |
| 49 | Wyoming | 962 | 0.2% |

RANK ORDER

| RANK | STATE | DEATHS | % of USA |
|------|-------|--------|----------|
| 1 | California | 58,641 | 9.8% |
| 2 | New York | 44,981 | 7.5% |
| 3 | Florida | 41,737 | 7.0% |
| 4 | Texas | 38,253 | 6.4% |
| 5 | Pennsylvania | 31,556 | 5.3% |
| 6 | Ohio | 26,164 | 4.4% |
| 7 | Illinois | 24,959 | 4.2% |
| 8 | Michigan | 23,326 | 3.9% |
| 9 | New Jersey | 18,730 | 3.1% |
| 10 | North Carolina | 17,154 | 2.9% |
| 11 | Georgia | 15,987 | 2.7% |
| 12 | Tennessee | 14,582 | 2.4% |
| 13 | Missouri | 13,840 | 2.3% |
| 14 | Virginia | 13,404 | 2.2% |
| 15 | Indiana | 13,388 | 2.2% |
| 16 | Alabama | 12,083 | 2.0% |
| 17 | Massachusetts | 12,043 | 2.0% |
| 18 | Wisconsin | 11,115 | 1.9% |
| 19 | Maryland | 10,915 | 1.8% |
| 20 | Washington | 10,602 | 1.8% |
| 21 | Louisiana | 10,282 | 1.7% |
| 22 | Arizona | 9,954 | 1.7% |
| 23 | Kentucky | 9,662 | 1.6% |
| 24 | Oklahoma | 9,426 | 1.6% |
| 25 | South Carolina | 9,295 | 1.6% |
| 26 | Mississippi | 7,542 | 1.3% |
| 27 | Arkansas | 7,274 | 1.2% |
| 28 | Minnesota | 7,185 | 1.2% |
| 29 | Connecticut | 7,127 | 1.2% |
| 30 | Iowa | 6,880 | 1.2% |
| 31 | Oregon | 6,198 | 1.0% |
| 32 | Colorado | 6,038 | 1.0% |
| 33 | Kansas | 5,433 | 0.9% |
| 34 | West Virginia | 4,897 | 0.8% |
| 35 | Nevada | 4,811 | 0.8% |
| 36 | Nebraska | 3,355 | 0.6% |
| 37 | New Mexico | 3,224 | 0.5% |
| 38 | Utah | 2,889 | 0.5% |
| 39 | Maine | 2,628 | 0.4% |
| 40 | Idaho | 2,495 | 0.4% |
| 41 | Rhode Island | 2,322 | 0.4% |
| 42 | New Hampshire | 2,290 | 0.4% |
| 43 | Hawaii | 2,239 | 0.4% |
| 44 | Montana | 1,849 | 0.3% |
| 45 | Delaware | 1,776 | 0.3% |
| 46 | South Dakota | 1,616 | 0.3% |
| 47 | North Dakota | 1,395 | 0.2% |
| 48 | Vermont | 1,172 | 0.2% |
| 49 | Wyoming | 962 | 0.2% |
| 50 | Alaska | 707 | 0.1% |
|  | District of Columbia | 1,306 | 0.2% |

Source: U.S. Department of Health and Human Services, National Center for Health Statistics
"National Vital Statistics Reports" (Vol. 61, No. 4, May 8, 2013, http://www.cdc.gov/nchs/deaths.htm)
*Final data by state of residence.

# Age-Adjusted Death Rate by Diseases of the Heart in 2010

## National Rate = 179.1 Deaths per 100,000 Population*

ALPHA ORDER

| RANK | STATE | RATE |
|---|---|---|
| 2 | Alabama | 236.0 |
| 40 | Alaska | 151.5 |
| 45 | Arizona | 146.7 |
| 5 | Arkansas | 222.5 |
| 31 | California | 161.9 |
| 49 | Colorado | 132.8 |
| 34 | Connecticut | 155.7 |
| 22 | Delaware | 175.7 |
| 30 | Florida | 162.3 |
| 13 | Georgia | 192.6 |
| 48 | Hawaii | 134.7 |
| 32 | Idaho | 159.3 |
| 20 | Illinois | 181.7 |
| 15 | Indiana | 191.8 |
| 24 | Iowa | 173.3 |
| 29 | Kansas | 164.9 |
| 8 | Kentucky | 210.1 |
| 4 | Louisiana | 229.4 |
| 43 | Maine | 151.1 |
| 18 | Maryland | 182.2 |
| 44 | Massachusetts | 150.0 |
| 9 | Michigan | 204.2 |
| 50 | Minnesota | 119.4 |
| 1 | Mississippi | 251.1 |
| 10 | Missouri | 201.8 |
| 36 | Montana | 154.2 |
| 36 | Nebraska | 154.2 |
| 12 | Nevada | 197.3 |
| 39 | New Hampshire | 152.7 |
| 19 | New Jersey | 182.0 |
| 42 | New Mexico | 151.2 |
| 11 | New York | 199.9 |
| 23 | North Carolina | 174.9 |
| 33 | North Dakota | 158.0 |
| 14 | Ohio | 192.4 |
| 3 | Oklahoma | 235.2 |
| 47 | Oregon | 137.9 |
| 17 | Pennsylvania | 187.0 |
| 27 | Rhode Island | 167.1 |
| 16 | South Carolina | 189.9 |
| 35 | South Dakota | 155.2 |
| 6 | Tennessee | 217.4 |
| 21 | Texas | 181.1 |
| 46 | Utah | 143.2 |
| 38 | Vermont | 153.6 |
| 26 | Virginia | 168.5 |
| 40 | Washington | 151.5 |
| 7 | West Virginia | 211.2 |
| 28 | Wisconsin | 165.1 |
| 25 | Wyoming | 169.8 |

RANK ORDER

| RANK | STATE | RATE |
|---|---|---|
| 1 | Mississippi | 251.1 |
| 2 | Alabama | 236.0 |
| 3 | Oklahoma | 235.2 |
| 4 | Louisiana | 229.4 |
| 5 | Arkansas | 222.5 |
| 6 | Tennessee | 217.4 |
| 7 | West Virginia | 211.2 |
| 8 | Kentucky | 210.1 |
| 9 | Michigan | 204.2 |
| 10 | Missouri | 201.8 |
| 11 | New York | 199.9 |
| 12 | Nevada | 197.3 |
| 13 | Georgia | 192.6 |
| 14 | Ohio | 192.4 |
| 15 | Indiana | 191.8 |
| 16 | South Carolina | 189.9 |
| 17 | Pennsylvania | 187.0 |
| 18 | Maryland | 182.2 |
| 19 | New Jersey | 182.0 |
| 20 | Illinois | 181.7 |
| 21 | Texas | 181.1 |
| 22 | Delaware | 175.7 |
| 23 | North Carolina | 174.9 |
| 24 | Iowa | 173.3 |
| 25 | Wyoming | 169.8 |
| 26 | Virginia | 168.5 |
| 27 | Rhode Island | 167.1 |
| 28 | Wisconsin | 165.1 |
| 29 | Kansas | 164.9 |
| 30 | Florida | 162.3 |
| 31 | California | 161.9 |
| 32 | Idaho | 159.3 |
| 33 | North Dakota | 158.0 |
| 34 | Connecticut | 155.7 |
| 35 | South Dakota | 155.2 |
| 36 | Montana | 154.2 |
| 36 | Nebraska | 154.2 |
| 38 | Vermont | 153.6 |
| 39 | New Hampshire | 152.7 |
| 40 | Alaska | 151.5 |
| 40 | Washington | 151.5 |
| 42 | New Mexico | 151.2 |
| 43 | Maine | 151.1 |
| 44 | Massachusetts | 150.0 |
| 45 | Arizona | 146.7 |
| 46 | Utah | 143.2 |
| 47 | Oregon | 137.9 |
| 48 | Hawaii | 134.7 |
| 49 | Colorado | 132.8 |
| 50 | Minnesota | 119.4 |
| | District of Columbia | 222.4 |

Source: U.S. Department of Health and Human Services, National Center for Health Statistics
   "National Vital Statistics Reports" (Vol. 61, No. 4, May 8, 2013, http://www.cdc.gov/nchs/deaths.htm)
*Final data by state of residence. Age-adjusted rates based on the year 2000 standard population.

# Deaths by Suicide in 2010

## National Total = 38,364 Suicides*

| ALPHA ORDER | | | | | RANK ORDER | | | |
|---|---|---|---|---|---|---|---|---|
| RANK | STATE | DEATHS | % of USA | | RANK | STATE | DEATHS | % of USA |
| 21 | Alabama | 679 | 1.8% | | 1 | California | 3,913 | 10.2% |
| 44 | Alaska | 164 | 0.4% | | 2 | Texas | 2,891 | 7.5% |
| 11 | Arizona | 1,093 | 2.8% | | 3 | Florida | 2,789 | 7.3% |
| 31 | Arkansas | 447 | 1.2% | | 4 | Pennsylvania | 1,576 | 4.1% |
| 1 | California | 3,913 | 10.2% | | 5 | New York | 1,547 | 4.0% |
| 15 | Colorado | 865 | 2.3% | | 6 | Ohio | 1,439 | 3.8% |
| 36 | Connecticut | 353 | 0.9% | | 7 | Michigan | 1,263 | 3.3% |
| 48 | Delaware | 106 | 0.3% | | 8 | Illinois | 1,178 | 3.1% |
| 3 | Florida | 2,789 | 7.3% | | 9 | North Carolina | 1,174 | 3.1% |
| 10 | Georgia | 1,133 | 3.0% | | 10 | Georgia | 1,133 | 3.0% |
| 40 | Hawaii | 207 | 0.5% | | 11 | Arizona | 1,093 | 2.8% |
| 37 | Idaho | 290 | 0.8% | | 12 | Virginia | 963 | 2.5% |
| 8 | Illinois | 1,178 | 3.1% | | 13 | Washington | 957 | 2.5% |
| 16 | Indiana | 864 | 2.3% | | 14 | Tennessee | 943 | 2.5% |
| 35 | Iowa | 372 | 1.0% | | 15 | Colorado | 865 | 2.3% |
| 33 | Kansas | 401 | 1.0% | | 16 | Indiana | 864 | 2.3% |
| 23 | Kentucky | 631 | 1.6% | | 17 | Missouri | 856 | 2.2% |
| 27 | Louisiana | 557 | 1.5% | | 18 | Wisconsin | 793 | 2.1% |
| 43 | Maine | 186 | 0.5% | | 19 | New Jersey | 719 | 1.9% |
| 29 | Maryland | 502 | 1.3% | | 20 | Oregon | 685 | 1.8% |
| 26 | Massachusetts | 598 | 1.6% | | 21 | Alabama | 679 | 1.8% |
| 7 | Michigan | 1,263 | 3.3% | | 22 | South Carolina | 637 | 1.7% |
| 25 | Minnesota | 606 | 1.6% | | 23 | Kentucky | 631 | 1.6% |
| 34 | Mississippi | 388 | 1.0% | | 24 | Oklahoma | 618 | 1.6% |
| 17 | Missouri | 856 | 2.2% | | 25 | Minnesota | 606 | 1.6% |
| 39 | Montana | 227 | 0.6% | | 26 | Massachusetts | 598 | 1.6% |
| 42 | Nebraska | 193 | 0.5% | | 27 | Louisiana | 557 | 1.5% |
| 28 | Nevada | 547 | 1.4% | | 28 | Nevada | 547 | 1.4% |
| 41 | New Hampshire | 196 | 0.5% | | 29 | Maryland | 502 | 1.3% |
| 19 | New Jersey | 719 | 1.9% | | 30 | Utah | 473 | 1.2% |
| 32 | New Mexico | 413 | 1.1% | | 31 | Arkansas | 447 | 1.2% |
| 5 | New York | 1,547 | 4.0% | | 32 | New Mexico | 413 | 1.1% |
| 9 | North Carolina | 1,174 | 3.1% | | 33 | Kansas | 401 | 1.0% |
| 48 | North Dakota | 106 | 0.3% | | 34 | Mississippi | 388 | 1.0% |
| 6 | Ohio | 1,439 | 3.8% | | 35 | Iowa | 372 | 1.0% |
| 24 | Oklahoma | 618 | 1.6% | | 36 | Connecticut | 353 | 0.9% |
| 20 | Oregon | 685 | 1.8% | | 37 | Idaho | 290 | 0.8% |
| 4 | Pennsylvania | 1,576 | 4.1% | | 38 | West Virginia | 279 | 0.7% |
| 47 | Rhode Island | 129 | 0.3% | | 39 | Montana | 227 | 0.6% |
| 22 | South Carolina | 637 | 1.7% | | 40 | Hawaii | 207 | 0.5% |
| 45 | South Dakota | 140 | 0.4% | | 41 | New Hampshire | 196 | 0.5% |
| 14 | Tennessee | 943 | 2.5% | | 42 | Nebraska | 193 | 0.5% |
| 2 | Texas | 2,891 | 7.5% | | 43 | Maine | 186 | 0.5% |
| 30 | Utah | 473 | 1.2% | | 44 | Alaska | 164 | 0.4% |
| 48 | Vermont | 106 | 0.3% | | 45 | South Dakota | 140 | 0.4% |
| 12 | Virginia | 963 | 2.5% | | 46 | Wyoming | 131 | 0.3% |
| 13 | Washington | 957 | 2.5% | | 47 | Rhode Island | 129 | 0.3% |
| 38 | West Virginia | 279 | 0.7% | | 48 | Delaware | 106 | 0.3% |
| 18 | Wisconsin | 793 | 2.1% | | 48 | North Dakota | 106 | 0.3% |
| 46 | Wyoming | 131 | 0.3% | | 48 | Vermont | 106 | 0.3% |
| | | | | | District of Columbia | | 41 | 0.1% |

Source: U.S. Department of Health and Human Services, National Center for Health Statistics
"National Vital Statistics Reports" (Vol. 61, No. 4, May 8, 2013, http://www.cdc.gov/nchs/deaths.htm)
*Final data by state of residence. Also referred to as "Intentional self-harm."

# Age-Adjusted Death Rate by Suicide in 2010

## National Rate = 12.1 Deaths per 100,000 Population*

ALPHA ORDER

| RANK | STATE | RATE |
|---|---|---|
| 21 | Alabama | 14.0 |
| 1 | Alaska | 22.8 |
| 10 | Arizona | 17.0 |
| 15 | Arkansas | 15.5 |
| 44 | California | 10.3 |
| 11 | Colorado | 16.8 |
| 45 | Connecticut | 9.4 |
| 41 | Delaware | 11.3 |
| 25 | Florida | 13.7 |
| 38 | Georgia | 11.7 |
| 16 | Hawaii | 15.0 |
| 6 | Idaho | 18.8 |
| 46 | Illinois | 9.0 |
| 29 | Indiana | 13.1 |
| 35 | Iowa | 12.1 |
| 23 | Kansas | 13.9 |
| 18 | Kentucky | 14.2 |
| 32 | Louisiana | 12.3 |
| 28 | Maine | 13.2 |
| 48 | Maryland | 8.3 |
| 47 | Massachusetts | 8.8 |
| 31 | Michigan | 12.5 |
| 42 | Minnesota | 11.2 |
| 30 | Mississippi | 13.0 |
| 21 | Missouri | 14.0 |
| 3 | Montana | 21.8 |
| 43 | Nebraska | 10.4 |
| 5 | Nevada | 19.8 |
| 19 | New Hampshire | 14.1 |
| 49 | New Jersey | 7.7 |
| 4 | New Mexico | 20.1 |
| 49 | New York | 7.7 |
| 36 | North Carolina | 12.0 |
| 14 | North Dakota | 15.6 |
| 34 | Ohio | 12.2 |
| 12 | Oklahoma | 16.5 |
| 9 | Oregon | 17.1 |
| 37 | Pennsylvania | 11.9 |
| 32 | Rhode Island | 12.3 |
| 26 | South Carolina | 13.5 |
| 8 | South Dakota | 17.5 |
| 17 | Tennessee | 14.6 |
| 38 | Texas | 11.7 |
| 7 | Utah | 18.3 |
| 13 | Vermont | 15.7 |
| 38 | Virginia | 11.7 |
| 23 | Washington | 13.9 |
| 19 | West Virginia | 14.1 |
| 27 | Wisconsin | 13.4 |
| 2 | Wyoming | 22.4 |

RANK ORDER

| RANK | STATE | RATE |
|---|---|---|
| 1 | Alaska | 22.8 |
| 2 | Wyoming | 22.4 |
| 3 | Montana | 21.8 |
| 4 | New Mexico | 20.1 |
| 5 | Nevada | 19.8 |
| 6 | Idaho | 18.8 |
| 7 | Utah | 18.3 |
| 8 | South Dakota | 17.5 |
| 9 | Oregon | 17.1 |
| 10 | Arizona | 17.0 |
| 11 | Colorado | 16.8 |
| 12 | Oklahoma | 16.5 |
| 13 | Vermont | 15.7 |
| 14 | North Dakota | 15.6 |
| 15 | Arkansas | 15.5 |
| 16 | Hawaii | 15.0 |
| 17 | Tennessee | 14.6 |
| 18 | Kentucky | 14.2 |
| 19 | New Hampshire | 14.1 |
| 19 | West Virginia | 14.1 |
| 21 | Alabama | 14.0 |
| 21 | Missouri | 14.0 |
| 23 | Kansas | 13.9 |
| 23 | Washington | 13.9 |
| 25 | Florida | 13.7 |
| 26 | South Carolina | 13.5 |
| 27 | Wisconsin | 13.4 |
| 28 | Maine | 13.2 |
| 29 | Indiana | 13.1 |
| 30 | Mississippi | 13.0 |
| 31 | Michigan | 12.5 |
| 32 | Louisiana | 12.3 |
| 32 | Rhode Island | 12.3 |
| 34 | Ohio | 12.2 |
| 35 | Iowa | 12.1 |
| 36 | North Carolina | 12.0 |
| 37 | Pennsylvania | 11.9 |
| 38 | Georgia | 11.7 |
| 38 | Texas | 11.7 |
| 38 | Virginia | 11.7 |
| 41 | Delaware | 11.3 |
| 42 | Minnesota | 11.2 |
| 43 | Nebraska | 10.4 |
| 44 | California | 10.3 |
| 45 | Connecticut | 9.4 |
| 46 | Illinois | 9.0 |
| 47 | Massachusetts | 8.8 |
| 48 | Maryland | 8.3 |
| 49 | New Jersey | 7.7 |
| 49 | New York | 7.7 |
| | District of Columbia | 6.9 |

Source: U.S. Department of Health and Human Services, National Center for Health Statistics
"National Vital Statistics Reports" (Vol. 61, No. 4, May 8, 2013, http://www.cdc.gov/nchs/deaths.htm)
*Final data by state of residence. Also referred to as "Intentional self-harm." Age-adjusted rates based on the year 2000 standard population.

# Deaths by AIDS in 2010

## National Total = 8,369 Deaths*

| ALPHA ORDER | | | |
|---|---|---|---|
| RANK | STATE | DEATHS | % of USA |
| 14 | Alabama | 153 | 1.8% |
| 48 | Alaska | 6 | 0.1% |
| 21 | Arizona | 102 | 1.2% |
| 26 | Arkansas | 64 | 0.8% |
| 4 | California | 742 | 8.9% |
| 25 | Colorado | 67 | 0.8% |
| 23 | Connecticut | 83 | 1.0% |
| 33 | Delaware | 46 | 0.5% |
| 1 | Florida | 1,068 | 12.8% |
| 5 | Georgia | 495 | 5.9% |
| 39 | Hawaii | 13 | 0.2% |
| 43 | Idaho | 9 | 0.1% |
| 9 | Illinois | 300 | 3.6% |
| 22 | Indiana | 91 | 1.1% |
| 37 | Iowa | 15 | 0.2% |
| 35 | Kansas | 27 | 0.3% |
| 28 | Kentucky | 53 | 0.6% |
| 11 | Louisiana | 225 | 2.7% |
| 43 | Maine | 9 | 0.1% |
| 8 | Maryland | 316 | 3.8% |
| 18 | Massachusetts | 120 | 1.4% |
| 15 | Michigan | 150 | 1.8% |
| 31 | Minnesota | 48 | 0.6% |
| 19 | Mississippi | 118 | 1.4% |
| 20 | Missouri | 105 | 1.3% |
| 46 | Montana | 7 | 0.1% |
| 41 | Nebraska | 12 | 0.1% |
| 27 | Nevada | 60 | 0.7% |
| 43 | New Hampshire | 9 | 0.1% |
| 6 | New Jersey | 378 | 4.5% |
| 34 | New Mexico | 33 | 0.4% |
| 2 | New York | 990 | 11.8% |
| 7 | North Carolina | 328 | 3.9% |
| 50 | North Dakota | 2 | 0.0% |
| 17 | Ohio | 138 | 1.6% |
| 30 | Oklahoma | 50 | 0.6% |
| 32 | Oregon | 47 | 0.6% |
| 10 | Pennsylvania | 266 | 3.2% |
| 36 | Rhode Island | 20 | 0.2% |
| 13 | South Carolina | 184 | 2.2% |
| 42 | South Dakota | 10 | 0.1% |
| 12 | Tennessee | 207 | 2.5% |
| 3 | Texas | 773 | 9.2% |
| 39 | Utah | 13 | 0.2% |
| 46 | Vermont | 7 | 0.1% |
| 16 | Virginia | 142 | 1.7% |
| 24 | Washington | 76 | 0.9% |
| 38 | West Virginia | 14 | 0.2% |
| 29 | Wisconsin | 51 | 0.6% |
| 48 | Wyoming | 6 | 0.1% |

| RANK ORDER | | | |
|---|---|---|---|
| RANK | STATE | DEATHS | % of USA |
| 1 | Florida | 1,068 | 12.8% |
| 2 | New York | 990 | 11.8% |
| 3 | Texas | 773 | 9.2% |
| 4 | California | 742 | 8.9% |
| 5 | Georgia | 495 | 5.9% |
| 6 | New Jersey | 378 | 4.5% |
| 7 | North Carolina | 328 | 3.9% |
| 8 | Maryland | 316 | 3.8% |
| 9 | Illinois | 300 | 3.6% |
| 10 | Pennsylvania | 266 | 3.2% |
| 11 | Louisiana | 225 | 2.7% |
| 12 | Tennessee | 207 | 2.5% |
| 13 | South Carolina | 184 | 2.2% |
| 14 | Alabama | 153 | 1.8% |
| 15 | Michigan | 150 | 1.8% |
| 16 | Virginia | 142 | 1.7% |
| 17 | Ohio | 138 | 1.6% |
| 18 | Massachusetts | 120 | 1.4% |
| 19 | Mississippi | 118 | 1.4% |
| 20 | Missouri | 105 | 1.3% |
| 21 | Arizona | 102 | 1.2% |
| 22 | Indiana | 91 | 1.1% |
| 23 | Connecticut | 83 | 1.0% |
| 24 | Washington | 76 | 0.9% |
| 25 | Colorado | 67 | 0.8% |
| 26 | Arkansas | 64 | 0.8% |
| 27 | Nevada | 60 | 0.7% |
| 28 | Kentucky | 53 | 0.6% |
| 29 | Wisconsin | 51 | 0.6% |
| 30 | Oklahoma | 50 | 0.6% |
| 31 | Minnesota | 48 | 0.6% |
| 32 | Oregon | 47 | 0.6% |
| 33 | Delaware | 46 | 0.5% |
| 34 | New Mexico | 33 | 0.4% |
| 35 | Kansas | 27 | 0.3% |
| 36 | Rhode Island | 20 | 0.2% |
| 37 | Iowa | 15 | 0.2% |
| 38 | West Virginia | 14 | 0.2% |
| 39 | Hawaii | 13 | 0.2% |
| 39 | Utah | 13 | 0.2% |
| 41 | Nebraska | 12 | 0.1% |
| 42 | South Dakota | 10 | 0.1% |
| 43 | Idaho | 9 | 0.1% |
| 43 | Maine | 9 | 0.1% |
| 43 | New Hampshire | 9 | 0.1% |
| 46 | Montana | 7 | 0.1% |
| 46 | Vermont | 7 | 0.1% |
| 48 | Alaska | 6 | 0.1% |
| 48 | Wyoming | 6 | 0.1% |
| 50 | North Dakota | 2 | 0.0% |
| | District of Columbia | 121 | 1.4% |

Source: U.S. Department of Health and Human Services, National Center for Health Statistics
"National Vital Statistics Reports" (Vol. 61, No. 4, May 8, 2013, http://www.cdc.gov/nchs/deaths.htm)
*Final data by state of residence. AIDS is Acquired Immunodeficiency Syndrome. It is a specific group of diseases or conditions which are indicative of severe immunosuppression related to infection with the Human Immunodeficiency Virus (HIV).

# Age-Adjusted Death Rate by AIDS in 2010

## National Rate = 2.6 Deaths per 100,000 Population*

ALPHA ORDER

| RANK | STATE | RATE |
|------|-------|------|
| 11 | Alabama | 3.2 |
| NA | Alaska** | NA |
| 23 | Arizona | 1.6 |
| 15 | Arkansas | 2.2 |
| 18 | California | 1.9 |
| 29 | Colorado | 1.2 |
| 17 | Connecticut | 2.0 |
| 5 | Delaware | 4.9 |
| 1 | Florida | 5.4 |
| 2 | Georgia | 5.0 |
| NA | Hawaii** | NA |
| NA | Idaho** | NA |
| 14 | Illinois | 2.3 |
| 26 | Indiana | 1.5 |
| NA | Iowa** | NA |
| 34 | Kansas | 0.9 |
| 29 | Kentucky | 1.2 |
| 2 | Louisiana | 5.0 |
| NA | Maine** | NA |
| 2 | Maryland | 5.0 |
| 23 | Massachusetts | 1.6 |
| 26 | Michigan | 1.5 |
| 34 | Minnesota | 0.9 |
| 7 | Mississippi | 4.2 |
| 20 | Missouri | 1.8 |
| NA | Montana** | NA |
| NA | Nebraska** | NA |
| 15 | Nevada | 2.2 |
| NA | New Hampshire** | NA |
| 8 | New Jersey | 3.9 |
| 23 | New Mexico | 1.6 |
| 6 | New York | 4.7 |
| 10 | North Carolina | 3.3 |
| NA | North Dakota** | NA |
| 32 | Ohio | 1.1 |
| 28 | Oklahoma | 1.4 |
| 29 | Oregon | 1.2 |
| 18 | Pennsylvania | 1.9 |
| 20 | Rhode Island | 1.8 |
| 8 | South Carolina | 3.9 |
| NA | South Dakota** | NA |
| 11 | Tennessee | 3.2 |
| 11 | Texas | 3.2 |
| NA | Utah** | NA |
| NA | Vermont** | NA |
| 22 | Virginia | 1.7 |
| 33 | Washington | 1.0 |
| NA | West Virginia** | NA |
| 36 | Wisconsin | 0.8 |
| NA | Wyoming** | NA |

RANK ORDER

| RANK | STATE | RATE |
|------|-------|------|
| 1 | Florida | 5.4 |
| 2 | Georgia | 5.0 |
| 2 | Louisiana | 5.0 |
| 2 | Maryland | 5.0 |
| 5 | Delaware | 4.9 |
| 6 | New York | 4.7 |
| 7 | Mississippi | 4.2 |
| 8 | New Jersey | 3.9 |
| 8 | South Carolina | 3.9 |
| 10 | North Carolina | 3.3 |
| 11 | Alabama | 3.2 |
| 11 | Tennessee | 3.2 |
| 11 | Texas | 3.2 |
| 14 | Illinois | 2.3 |
| 15 | Arkansas | 2.2 |
| 15 | Nevada | 2.2 |
| 17 | Connecticut | 2.0 |
| 18 | California | 1.9 |
| 18 | Pennsylvania | 1.9 |
| 20 | Missouri | 1.8 |
| 20 | Rhode Island | 1.8 |
| 22 | Virginia | 1.7 |
| 23 | Arizona | 1.6 |
| 23 | Massachusetts | 1.6 |
| 23 | New Mexico | 1.6 |
| 26 | Indiana | 1.5 |
| 26 | Michigan | 1.5 |
| 28 | Oklahoma | 1.4 |
| 29 | Colorado | 1.2 |
| 29 | Kentucky | 1.2 |
| 29 | Oregon | 1.2 |
| 32 | Ohio | 1.1 |
| 33 | Washington | 1.0 |
| 34 | Kansas | 0.9 |
| 34 | Minnesota | 0.9 |
| 36 | Wisconsin | 0.8 |
| NA | Alaska** | NA |
| NA | Hawaii** | NA |
| NA | Idaho** | NA |
| NA | Iowa** | NA |
| NA | Maine** | NA |
| NA | Montana** | NA |
| NA | Nebraska** | NA |
| NA | New Hampshire** | NA |
| NA | North Dakota** | NA |
| NA | South Dakota** | NA |
| NA | Utah** | NA |
| NA | Vermont** | NA |
| NA | West Virginia** | NA |
| NA | Wyoming** | NA |

| | | |
|---|---|---|
| | District of Columbia | 20.4 |

Source: U.S. Department of Health and Human Services, National Center for Health Statistics
"National Vital Statistics Reports" (Vol. 61, No. 4, May 8, 2013, http://www.cdc.gov/nchs/deaths.htm)
*Final data by state of residence. AIDS is Acquired Immunodeficiency Syndrome. It is a specific group of diseases or conditions which are indicative of severe immunosuppression related to infection with the Human Immunodeficiency Virus (HIV). Age-adjusted rates based on the year 2000 standard population.
**Insufficient data to determine a reliable rate.

# Adult Per Capita Alcohol Consumption in 2011

## National Per Capita = 2.6 Gallons Consumed per Adult 21 Years and Older*

ALPHA ORDER

| RANK | STATE | PER CAPITA |
|------|-------|------------|
| 42 | Alabama | 2.2 |
| 6 | Alaska | 3.3 |
| 22 | Arizona | 2.7 |
| 49 | Arkansas | 1.9 |
| 27 | California | 2.6 |
| 9 | Colorado | 3.1 |
| 22 | Connecticut | 2.7 |
| 2 | Delaware | 4.0 |
| 16 | Florida | 2.8 |
| 42 | Georgia | 2.2 |
| 16 | Hawaii | 2.8 |
| 11 | Idaho | 3.0 |
| 22 | Illinois | 2.7 |
| 39 | Indiana | 2.3 |
| 27 | Iowa | 2.6 |
| 42 | Kansas | 2.2 |
| 48 | Kentucky | 2.0 |
| 13 | Louisiana | 2.9 |
| 16 | Maine | 2.8 |
| 33 | Maryland | 2.5 |
| 13 | Massachusetts | 2.9 |
| 27 | Michigan | 2.6 |
| 16 | Minnesota | 2.8 |
| 33 | Mississippi | 2.5 |
| 16 | Missouri | 2.8 |
| 7 | Montana | 3.2 |
| 27 | Nebraska | 2.6 |
| 3 | Nevada | 3.8 |
| 1 | New Hampshire | 5.3 |
| 22 | New Jersey | 2.7 |
| 22 | New Mexico | 2.7 |
| 37 | New York | 2.4 |
| 39 | North Carolina | 2.3 |
| 4 | North Dakota | 3.6 |
| 42 | Ohio | 2.2 |
| 42 | Oklahoma | 2.2 |
| 16 | Oregon | 2.8 |
| 33 | Pennsylvania | 2.5 |
| 11 | Rhode Island | 3.0 |
| 27 | South Carolina | 2.6 |
| 9 | South Dakota | 3.1 |
| 39 | Tennessee | 2.3 |
| 27 | Texas | 2.6 |
| 50 | Utah | 1.6 |
| 7 | Vermont | 3.2 |
| 37 | Virginia | 2.4 |
| 33 | Washington | 2.5 |
| 47 | West Virginia | 2.1 |
| 5 | Wisconsin | 3.4 |
| 13 | Wyoming | 2.9 |

RANK ORDER

| RANK | STATE | PER CAPITA |
|------|-------|------------|
| 1 | New Hampshire | 5.3 |
| 2 | Delaware | 4.0 |
| 3 | Nevada | 3.8 |
| 4 | North Dakota | 3.6 |
| 5 | Wisconsin | 3.4 |
| 6 | Alaska | 3.3 |
| 7 | Montana | 3.2 |
| 7 | Vermont | 3.2 |
| 9 | Colorado | 3.1 |
| 9 | South Dakota | 3.1 |
| 11 | Idaho | 3.0 |
| 11 | Rhode Island | 3.0 |
| 13 | Louisiana | 2.9 |
| 13 | Massachusetts | 2.9 |
| 13 | Wyoming | 2.9 |
| 16 | Florida | 2.8 |
| 16 | Hawaii | 2.8 |
| 16 | Maine | 2.8 |
| 16 | Minnesota | 2.8 |
| 16 | Missouri | 2.8 |
| 16 | Oregon | 2.8 |
| 22 | Arizona | 2.7 |
| 22 | Connecticut | 2.7 |
| 22 | Illinois | 2.7 |
| 22 | New Jersey | 2.7 |
| 22 | New Mexico | 2.7 |
| 27 | California | 2.6 |
| 27 | Iowa | 2.6 |
| 27 | Michigan | 2.6 |
| 27 | Nebraska | 2.6 |
| 27 | South Carolina | 2.6 |
| 27 | Texas | 2.6 |
| 33 | Maryland | 2.5 |
| 33 | Mississippi | 2.5 |
| 33 | Pennsylvania | 2.5 |
| 33 | Washington | 2.5 |
| 37 | New York | 2.4 |
| 37 | Virginia | 2.4 |
| 39 | Indiana | 2.3 |
| 39 | North Carolina | 2.3 |
| 39 | Tennessee | 2.3 |
| 42 | Alabama | 2.2 |
| 42 | Georgia | 2.2 |
| 42 | Kansas | 2.2 |
| 42 | Ohio | 2.2 |
| 42 | Oklahoma | 2.2 |
| 47 | West Virginia | 2.1 |
| 48 | Kentucky | 2.0 |
| 49 | Arkansas | 1.9 |
| 50 | Utah | 1.6 |

| District of Columbia | 4.3 |

Source: CQ Press using data from U.S. Dept of Health and Human Services, National Institute on Alcohol Abuse and Alcoholism
"Apparent Per Capita Alcohol Consumption, 1977-2011" (http://pubs.niaaa.nih.gov/publications/surveillance97/CONS11.htm)
*This is apparent consumption of actual alcohol, not entire volume of an alcoholic beverage (for example, wine is roughly 11% absolute alcohol content). Apparent consumption is based on several sources which together approximate sales but do not actually measure consumption. Accordingly, figures for some states may be skewed by purchases by nonresidents.

# Percent of Adults Who Smoke: 2012

## National Median = 19.6% of Adults*

| ALPHA ORDER | | | | RANK ORDER | | |
|---|---|---|---|---|---|---|
| RANK | STATE | PERCENT | | RANK | STATE | PERCENT |
| 9 | Alabama | 23.8 | | 1 | Kentucky | 28.3 |
| 19 | Alaska | 20.5 | | 2 | West Virginia | 28.2 |
| 41 | Arizona | 17.1 | | 3 | Arkansas | 25.0 |
| 3 | Arkansas | 25.0 | | 4 | Tennessee | 24.9 |
| 49 | California | 12.6 | | 5 | Louisiana | 24.8 |
| 35 | Colorado | 17.7 | | 6 | Indiana | 24.0 |
| 47 | Connecticut | 16.0 | | 6 | Mississippi | 24.0 |
| 23 | Delaware | 19.7 | | 8 | Missouri | 23.9 |
| 35 | Florida | 17.7 | | 9 | Alabama | 23.8 |
| 20 | Georgia | 20.4 | | 10 | Michigan | 23.3 |
| 48 | Hawaii | 14.6 | | 10 | Ohio | 23.3 |
| 43 | Idaho | 16.4 | | 10 | Oklahoma | 23.3 |
| 30 | Illinois | 18.6 | | 13 | South Carolina | 22.5 |
| 6 | Indiana | 24.0 | | 14 | South Dakota | 22.0 |
| 32 | Iowa | 18.1 | | 15 | Wyoming | 21.8 |
| 26 | Kansas | 19.4 | | 16 | Pennsylvania | 21.4 |
| 1 | Kentucky | 28.3 | | 17 | North Dakota | 21.2 |
| 5 | Louisiana | 24.8 | | 18 | North Carolina | 20.9 |
| 22 | Maine | 20.3 | | 19 | Alaska | 20.5 |
| 45 | Maryland | 16.2 | | 20 | Georgia | 20.4 |
| 43 | Massachusetts | 16.4 | | 20 | Wisconsin | 20.4 |
| 10 | Michigan | 23.3 | | 22 | Maine | 20.3 |
| 29 | Minnesota | 18.8 | | 23 | Delaware | 19.7 |
| 6 | Mississippi | 24.0 | | 23 | Montana | 19.7 |
| 8 | Missouri | 23.9 | | 23 | Nebraska | 19.7 |
| 23 | Montana | 19.7 | | 26 | Kansas | 19.4 |
| 23 | Nebraska | 19.7 | | 27 | New Mexico | 19.3 |
| 32 | Nevada | 18.1 | | 28 | Virginia | 19.0 |
| 39 | New Hampshire | 17.2 | | 29 | Minnesota | 18.8 |
| 38 | New Jersey | 17.3 | | 30 | Illinois | 18.6 |
| 27 | New Mexico | 19.3 | | 31 | Texas | 18.2 |
| 45 | New York | 16.2 | | 32 | Iowa | 18.1 |
| 18 | North Carolina | 20.9 | | 32 | Nevada | 18.1 |
| 17 | North Dakota | 21.2 | | 34 | Oregon | 17.9 |
| 10 | Ohio | 23.3 | | 35 | Colorado | 17.7 |
| 10 | Oklahoma | 23.3 | | 35 | Florida | 17.7 |
| 34 | Oregon | 17.9 | | 37 | Rhode Island | 17.4 |
| 16 | Pennsylvania | 21.4 | | 38 | New Jersey | 17.3 |
| 37 | Rhode Island | 17.4 | | 39 | New Hampshire | 17.2 |
| 13 | South Carolina | 22.5 | | 39 | Washington | 17.2 |
| 14 | South Dakota | 22.0 | | 41 | Arizona | 17.1 |
| 4 | Tennessee | 24.9 | | 42 | Vermont | 16.5 |
| 31 | Texas | 18.2 | | 43 | Idaho | 16.4 |
| 50 | Utah | 10.6 | | 43 | Massachusetts | 16.4 |
| 42 | Vermont | 16.5 | | 45 | Maryland | 16.2 |
| 28 | Virginia | 19.0 | | 45 | New York | 16.2 |
| 39 | Washington | 17.2 | | 47 | Connecticut | 16.0 |
| 2 | West Virginia | 28.2 | | 48 | Hawaii | 14.6 |
| 20 | Wisconsin | 20.4 | | 49 | California | 12.6 |
| 15 | Wyoming | 21.8 | | 50 | Utah | 10.6 |
| | | | | | District of Columbia | 19.6 |

Source: U.S. Department of Health and Human Services, Centers for Disease Control and Prevention
   "2012 Behavioral Risk Factor Surveillance Summary Prevalence Data" (http://apps.nccd.cdc.gov/brfss/)
*Persons 18 and older who have smoked more than 100 cigarettes during their lifetime and who currently smoke every day or some days.

# Percent of Adults Overweight or Obese: 2012

## National Median = 63.4% of Adults*

| ALPHA ORDER | | | | RANK ORDER | | |
|---|---|---|---|---|---|---|
| RANK | STATE | PERCENT | | RANK | STATE | PERCENT |
| 5 | Alabama | 67.8 | | 1 | Louisiana | 69.5 |
| 23 | Alaska | 64.8 | | 2 | Mississippi | 68.9 |
| 40 | Arizona | 62.0 | | 3 | Arkansas | 68.7 |
| 3 | Arkansas | 68.7 | | 4 | West Virginia | 68.3 |
| 45 | California | 60.3 | | 5 | Alabama | 67.8 |
| 50 | Colorado | 55.7 | | 5 | Oklahoma | 67.8 |
| 36 | Connecticut | 62.3 | | 7 | Kentucky | 66.9 |
| 11 | Delaware | 66.0 | | 8 | Wisconsin | 66.5 |
| 38 | Florida | 62.1 | | 9 | North Dakota | 66.3 |
| 25 | Georgia | 64.6 | | 10 | South Carolina | 66.1 |
| 49 | Hawaii | 56.1 | | 11 | Delaware | 66.0 |
| 34 | Idaho | 62.6 | | 11 | South Dakota | 66.0 |
| 27 | Illinois | 63.9 | | 13 | North Carolina | 65.9 |
| 17 | Indiana | 65.5 | | 14 | Missouri | 65.8 |
| 24 | Iowa | 64.7 | | 15 | Michigan | 65.7 |
| 16 | Kansas | 65.6 | | 16 | Kansas | 65.6 |
| 7 | Kentucky | 66.9 | | 17 | Indiana | 65.5 |
| 1 | Louisiana | 69.5 | | 18 | Ohio | 65.3 |
| 26 | Maine | 64.2 | | 18 | Tennessee | 65.3 |
| 28 | Maryland | 63.8 | | 20 | Texas | 65.1 |
| 47 | Massachusetts | 58.8 | | 21 | Nebraska | 65.0 |
| 15 | Michigan | 65.7 | | 21 | Pennsylvania | 65.0 |
| 31 | Minnesota | 63.0 | | 23 | Alaska | 64.8 |
| 2 | Mississippi | 68.9 | | 24 | Iowa | 64.7 |
| 14 | Missouri | 65.8 | | 25 | Georgia | 64.6 |
| 42 | Montana | 61.3 | | 26 | Maine | 64.2 |
| 21 | Nebraska | 65.0 | | 27 | Illinois | 63.9 |
| 35 | Nevada | 62.5 | | 28 | Maryland | 63.8 |
| 38 | New Hampshire | 62.1 | | 29 | Virginia | 63.6 |
| 41 | New Jersey | 61.6 | | 30 | Wyoming | 63.3 |
| 33 | New Mexico | 62.8 | | 31 | Minnesota | 63.0 |
| 44 | New York | 60.6 | | 32 | Rhode Island | 62.9 |
| 13 | North Carolina | 65.9 | | 33 | New Mexico | 62.8 |
| 9 | North Dakota | 66.3 | | 34 | Idaho | 62.6 |
| 18 | Ohio | 65.3 | | 35 | Nevada | 62.5 |
| 5 | Oklahoma | 67.8 | | 36 | Connecticut | 62.3 |
| 43 | Oregon | 61.1 | | 37 | Washington | 62.2 |
| 21 | Pennsylvania | 65.0 | | 38 | Florida | 62.1 |
| 32 | Rhode Island | 62.9 | | 38 | New Hampshire | 62.1 |
| 10 | South Carolina | 66.1 | | 40 | Arizona | 62.0 |
| 11 | South Dakota | 66.0 | | 41 | New Jersey | 61.6 |
| 18 | Tennessee | 65.3 | | 42 | Montana | 61.3 |
| 20 | Texas | 65.1 | | 43 | Oregon | 61.1 |
| 48 | Utah | 57.8 | | 44 | New York | 60.6 |
| 45 | Vermont | 60.3 | | 45 | California | 60.3 |
| 29 | Virginia | 63.6 | | 45 | Vermont | 60.3 |
| 37 | Washington | 62.2 | | 47 | Massachusetts | 58.8 |
| 4 | West Virginia | 68.3 | | 48 | Utah | 57.8 |
| 8 | Wisconsin | 66.5 | | 49 | Hawaii | 56.1 |
| 30 | Wyoming | 63.3 | | 50 | Colorado | 55.7 |
| | | | | | District of Columbia | 51.9 |

Source: CQ Press using data from U.S. Department of Health and Human Services, Centers for Disease Control and Prevention "2012 Behavioral Risk Factor Surveillance Summary Prevalence Data" (http://apps.nccd.cdc.gov/brfss/)

*Persons 18 and older. Overweight is defined as a Body Mass Index (BMI) of 25.0 to 29.9 regardless of sex. Obese is a BMI of 30.0 or greater. BMI is a ratio of height to weight. As an example, a person 5' 8" and weighing 165 pounds has a BMI of 25. The same height at 197 pounds has a BMI of 30. See http://www.cdc.gov/healthyweight/assessing/bmi/index.html.

# Percent of Children Aged 19 to 35 Months Fully Immunized in 2012

## National Percent = 68.4%*

| ALPHA ORDER | | | RANK ORDER | | |
|---|---|---|---|---|---|
| RANK | STATE | PERCENT | RANK | STATE | PERCENT |
| 21 | Alabama | 71.3 | 1 | Hawaii | 80.2 |
| 50 | Alaska | 59.5 | 2 | New Hampshire | 80.1 |
| 29 | Arizona | 67.5 | 3 | Mississippi | 77.5 |
| 36 | Arkansas | 66.4 | 4 | Connecticut | 77.1 |
| 32 | California | 66.8 | 5 | North Carolina | 75.4 |
| 18 | Colorado | 71.7 | 6 | Wisconsin | 75.2 |
| 4 | Connecticut | 77.1 | 7 | Iowa | 74.8 |
| 12 | Delaware | 72.6 | 8 | Georgia | 74.7 |
| 24 | Florida | 68.6 | 9 | Massachusetts | 73.5 |
| 8 | Georgia | 74.7 | 10 | Tennessee | 73.1 |
| 1 | Hawaii | 80.2 | 11 | Utah | 73.0 |
| 46 | Idaho | 63.0 | 12 | Delaware | 72.6 |
| 25 | Illinois | 68.5 | 12 | Maine | 72.6 |
| 47 | Indiana | 61.4 | 12 | Nebraska | 72.6 |
| 7 | Iowa | 74.8 | 15 | Rhode Island | 72.5 |
| 40 | Kansas | 65.0 | 16 | North Dakota | 72.2 |
| 28 | Kentucky | 68.2 | 17 | South Carolina | 71.8 |
| 25 | Louisiana | 68.5 | 18 | Colorado | 71.7 |
| 12 | Maine | 72.6 | 19 | New Mexico | 71.6 |
| 31 | Maryland | 67.1 | 20 | New Jersey | 71.5 |
| 9 | Massachusetts | 73.5 | 21 | Alabama | 71.3 |
| 22 | Michigan | 70.5 | 22 | Michigan | 70.5 |
| 37 | Minnesota | 66.2 | 23 | Virginia | 69.8 |
| 3 | Mississippi | 77.5 | 24 | Florida | 68.6 |
| 42 | Missouri | 63.9 | 25 | Illinois | 68.5 |
| 35 | Montana | 66.5 | 25 | Louisiana | 68.5 |
| 12 | Nebraska | 72.6 | 27 | Pennsylvania | 68.3 |
| 38 | Nevada | 65.3 | 28 | Kentucky | 68.2 |
| 2 | New Hampshire | 80.1 | 29 | Arizona | 67.5 |
| 20 | New Jersey | 71.5 | 30 | Wyoming | 67.2 |
| 19 | New Mexico | 71.6 | 31 | Maryland | 67.1 |
| 43 | New York | 63.7 | 32 | California | 66.8 |
| 5 | North Carolina | 75.4 | 32 | Ohio | 66.8 |
| 16 | North Dakota | 72.2 | 34 | Oregon | 66.7 |
| 32 | Ohio | 66.8 | 35 | Montana | 66.5 |
| 48 | Oklahoma | 61.0 | 36 | Arkansas | 66.4 |
| 34 | Oregon | 66.7 | 37 | Minnesota | 66.2 |
| 27 | Pennsylvania | 68.3 | 38 | Nevada | 65.3 |
| 15 | Rhode Island | 72.5 | 39 | Washington | 65.2 |
| 17 | South Carolina | 71.8 | 40 | Kansas | 65.0 |
| 44 | South Dakota | 63.6 | 41 | Texas | 64.8 |
| 10 | Tennessee | 73.1 | 42 | Missouri | 63.9 |
| 41 | Texas | 64.8 | 43 | New York | 63.7 |
| 11 | Utah | 73.0 | 44 | South Dakota | 63.6 |
| 45 | Vermont | 63.2 | 45 | Vermont | 63.2 |
| 23 | Virginia | 69.8 | 46 | Idaho | 63.0 |
| 39 | Washington | 65.2 | 47 | Indiana | 61.4 |
| 49 | West Virginia | 60.8 | 48 | Oklahoma | 61.0 |
| 6 | Wisconsin | 75.2 | 49 | West Virginia | 60.8 |
| 30 | Wyoming | 67.2 | 50 | Alaska | 59.5 |

| | | |
|---|---|---|
| | District of Columbia | 73.4 |

Source: U.S. Department of Health and Human Services, Centers for Disease Control and Prevention
    "State Vaccination Coverage Levels" (MMWR, Vol. 62, No. 36, September 13, 2013, http://www.cdc.gov/mmwr/)
*Fully immunized (4:3:1:3:3:1:4 series) children received four doses of DTP/DT/DTaP (Diphtheria, Tetanus, Pertussis [Whooping Cough], Acellular Pertussis), three doses of OPV (Oral Poliovirus Vaccine), one dose of MCV (Measles-Containing Vaccine), three doses of Hib (Haemophilus influenzae type b), three doses of Hepatitis B vaccine, one dose of Varicella (chickenpox) vaccine, and four doses of PCV (pneumococcal conjugate vaccine).  This differs from previous "fully" immunized tables.

# XII. Households and Housing

# Households in 2012

## National Total = 115,969,540 Households*

| ALPHA ORDER | | | | | RANK ORDER | | | |
|---|---|---|---|---|---|---|---|---|
| RANK | STATE | HOUSEHOLDS | % of USA | | RANK | STATE | HOUSEHOLDS | % of USA |
| 23 | Alabama | 1,845,169 | 1.6% | | 1 | California | 12,552,658 | 10.8% |
| 49 | Alaska | 251,651 | 0.2% | | 2 | Texas | 8,970,959 | 7.7% |
| 17 | Arizona | 2,392,168 | 2.1% | | 3 | New York | 7,238,922 | 6.2% |
| 31 | Arkansas | 1,143,859 | 1.0% | | 4 | Florida | 7,197,943 | 6.2% |
| 1 | California | 12,552,658 | 10.8% | | 5 | Pennsylvania | 4,958,249 | 4.3% |
| 22 | Colorado | 1,996,088 | 1.7% | | 6 | Illinois | 4,770,194 | 4.1% |
| 29 | Connecticut | 1,357,812 | 1.2% | | 7 | Ohio | 4,554,672 | 3.9% |
| 45 | Delaware | 340,308 | 0.3% | | 8 | Michigan | 3,819,068 | 3.3% |
| 4 | Florida | 7,197,943 | 6.2% | | 9 | North Carolina | 3,731,325 | 3.2% |
| 10 | Georgia | 3,532,908 | 3.0% | | 10 | Georgia | 3,532,908 | 3.0% |
| 42 | Hawaii | 447,748 | 0.4% | | 11 | New Jersey | 3,198,799 | 2.8% |
| 39 | Idaho | 583,106 | 0.5% | | 12 | Virginia | 3,038,967 | 2.6% |
| 6 | Illinois | 4,770,194 | 4.1% | | 13 | Washington | 2,636,817 | 2.3% |
| 16 | Indiana | 2,480,077 | 2.1% | | 14 | Massachusetts | 2,522,394 | 2.2% |
| 30 | Iowa | 1,227,048 | 1.1% | | 15 | Tennessee | 2,480,090 | 2.1% |
| 32 | Kansas | 1,113,911 | 1.0% | | 16 | Indiana | 2,480,077 | 2.1% |
| 26 | Kentucky | 1,707,004 | 1.5% | | 17 | Arizona | 2,392,168 | 2.1% |
| 25 | Louisiana | 1,719,473 | 1.5% | | 18 | Missouri | 2,359,135 | 2.0% |
| 40 | Maine | 554,543 | 0.5% | | 19 | Wisconsin | 2,288,362 | 2.0% |
| 20 | Maryland | 2,157,717 | 1.9% | | 20 | Maryland | 2,157,717 | 1.9% |
| 14 | Massachusetts | 2,522,394 | 2.2% | | 21 | Minnesota | 2,111,943 | 1.8% |
| 8 | Michigan | 3,819,068 | 3.3% | | 22 | Colorado | 1,996,088 | 1.7% |
| 21 | Minnesota | 2,111,943 | 1.8% | | 23 | Alabama | 1,845,169 | 1.6% |
| 33 | Mississippi | 1,090,521 | 0.9% | | 24 | South Carolina | 1,787,340 | 1.5% |
| 18 | Missouri | 2,359,135 | 2.0% | | 25 | Louisiana | 1,719,473 | 1.5% |
| 44 | Montana | 408,938 | 0.4% | | 26 | Kentucky | 1,707,004 | 1.5% |
| 38 | Nebraska | 733,570 | 0.6% | | 27 | Oregon | 1,516,957 | 1.3% |
| 34 | Nevada | 1,006,605 | 0.9% | | 28 | Oklahoma | 1,446,667 | 1.2% |
| 41 | New Hampshire | 519,137 | 0.4% | | 29 | Connecticut | 1,357,812 | 1.2% |
| 11 | New Jersey | 3,198,799 | 2.8% | | 30 | Iowa | 1,227,048 | 1.1% |
| 36 | New Mexico | 764,996 | 0.7% | | 31 | Arkansas | 1,143,859 | 1.0% |
| 3 | New York | 7,238,922 | 6.2% | | 32 | Kansas | 1,113,911 | 1.0% |
| 9 | North Carolina | 3,731,325 | 3.2% | | 33 | Mississippi | 1,090,521 | 0.9% |
| 47 | North Dakota | 290,944 | 0.3% | | 34 | Nevada | 1,006,605 | 0.9% |
| 7 | Ohio | 4,554,672 | 3.9% | | 35 | Utah | 895,691 | 0.8% |
| 28 | Oklahoma | 1,446,667 | 1.2% | | 36 | New Mexico | 764,996 | 0.7% |
| 27 | Oregon | 1,516,957 | 1.3% | | 37 | West Virginia | 741,544 | 0.6% |
| 5 | Pennsylvania | 4,958,249 | 4.3% | | 38 | Nebraska | 733,570 | 0.6% |
| 43 | Rhode Island | 413,083 | 0.4% | | 39 | Idaho | 583,106 | 0.5% |
| 24 | South Carolina | 1,787,340 | 1.5% | | 40 | Maine | 554,543 | 0.5% |
| 46 | South Dakota | 323,765 | 0.3% | | 41 | New Hampshire | 519,137 | 0.4% |
| 15 | Tennessee | 2,480,090 | 2.1% | | 42 | Hawaii | 447,748 | 0.4% |
| 2 | Texas | 8,970,959 | 7.7% | | 43 | Rhode Island | 413,083 | 0.4% |
| 35 | Utah | 895,691 | 0.8% | | 44 | Montana | 408,938 | 0.4% |
| 48 | Vermont | 258,520 | 0.2% | | 45 | Delaware | 340,308 | 0.3% |
| 12 | Virginia | 3,038,967 | 2.6% | | 46 | South Dakota | 323,765 | 0.3% |
| 13 | Washington | 2,636,817 | 2.3% | | 47 | North Dakota | 290,944 | 0.3% |
| 37 | West Virginia | 741,544 | 0.6% | | 48 | Vermont | 258,520 | 0.2% |
| 19 | Wisconsin | 2,288,362 | 2.0% | | 49 | Alaska | 251,651 | 0.2% |
| 50 | Wyoming | 223,513 | 0.2% | | 50 | Wyoming | 223,513 | 0.2% |
| | | | | | | District of Columbia | 266,662 | 0.2% |

Source: U.S. Bureau of the Census

"2012 American Community Survey-Table S2501" (http://www.census.gov/acs/www/index.html)

*A household includes all persons who occupy a housing unit.  A household consists of a single family, one person living alone, two or more families living together, or any other group of related or unrelated persons who share living arrangements.

# Persons per Household in 2012

## National Rate = 2.64 Persons per Household*

| ALPHA ORDER | | | | RANK ORDER | | |
|---|---|---|---|---|---|---|
| RANK | STATE | PERSONS | | RANK | STATE | PERSONS |
| 25 | Alabama | 2.55 | | 1 | Utah | 3.14 |
| 5 | Alaska | 2.80 | | 2 | Hawaii | 3.01 |
| 10 | Arizona | 2.68 | | 3 | California | 2.97 |
| 33 | Arkansas | 2.51 | | 4 | Texas | 2.84 |
| 3 | California | 2.97 | | 5 | Alaska | 2.80 |
| 27 | Colorado | 2.54 | | 6 | Georgia | 2.73 |
| 21 | Connecticut | 2.56 | | 7 | New Jersey | 2.71 |
| 15 | Delaware | 2.62 | | 8 | Nevada | 2.70 |
| 15 | Florida | 2.62 | | 9 | Idaho | 2.69 |
| 6 | Georgia | 2.73 | | 10 | Arizona | 2.68 |
| 2 | Hawaii | 3.01 | | 11 | New Mexico | 2.67 |
| 9 | Idaho | 2.69 | | 12 | Maryland | 2.66 |
| 14 | Illinois | 2.64 | | 13 | Mississippi | 2.65 |
| 21 | Indiana | 2.56 | | 14 | Illinois | 2.64 |
| 46 | Iowa | 2.42 | | 15 | Delaware | 2.62 |
| 31 | Kansas | 2.52 | | 15 | Florida | 2.62 |
| 35 | Kentucky | 2.49 | | 15 | New York | 2.62 |
| 19 | Louisiana | 2.60 | | 18 | Virginia | 2.61 |
| 48 | Maine | 2.33 | | 19 | Louisiana | 2.60 |
| 12 | Maryland | 2.66 | | 20 | South Carolina | 2.57 |
| 27 | Massachusetts | 2.54 | | 21 | Connecticut | 2.56 |
| 30 | Michigan | 2.53 | | 21 | Indiana | 2.56 |
| 37 | Minnesota | 2.48 | | 21 | Oklahoma | 2.56 |
| 13 | Mississippi | 2.65 | | 21 | Washington | 2.56 |
| 37 | Missouri | 2.48 | | 25 | Alabama | 2.55 |
| 47 | Montana | 2.39 | | 25 | North Carolina | 2.55 |
| 42 | Nebraska | 2.46 | | 27 | Colorado | 2.54 |
| 8 | Nevada | 2.70 | | 27 | Massachusetts | 2.54 |
| 39 | New Hampshire | 2.47 | | 27 | Tennessee | 2.54 |
| 7 | New Jersey | 2.71 | | 30 | Michigan | 2.53 |
| 11 | New Mexico | 2.67 | | 31 | Kansas | 2.52 |
| 15 | New York | 2.62 | | 31 | Wyoming | 2.52 |
| 25 | North Carolina | 2.55 | | 33 | Arkansas | 2.51 |
| 49 | North Dakota | 2.32 | | 33 | Oregon | 2.51 |
| 39 | Ohio | 2.47 | | 35 | Kentucky | 2.49 |
| 21 | Oklahoma | 2.56 | | 35 | Pennsylvania | 2.49 |
| 33 | Oregon | 2.51 | | 37 | Minnesota | 2.48 |
| 35 | Pennsylvania | 2.49 | | 37 | Missouri | 2.48 |
| 43 | Rhode Island | 2.44 | | 39 | New Hampshire | 2.47 |
| 20 | South Carolina | 2.57 | | 39 | Ohio | 2.47 |
| 39 | South Dakota | 2.47 | | 39 | South Dakota | 2.47 |
| 27 | Tennessee | 2.54 | | 42 | Nebraska | 2.46 |
| 4 | Texas | 2.84 | | 43 | Rhode Island | 2.44 |
| 1 | Utah | 3.14 | | 43 | West Virginia | 2.44 |
| 49 | Vermont | 2.32 | | 43 | Wisconsin | 2.44 |
| 18 | Virginia | 2.61 | | 46 | Iowa | 2.42 |
| 21 | Washington | 2.56 | | 47 | Montana | 2.39 |
| 43 | West Virginia | 2.44 | | 48 | Maine | 2.33 |
| 43 | Wisconsin | 2.44 | | 49 | North Dakota | 2.32 |
| 31 | Wyoming | 2.52 | | 49 | Vermont | 2.32 |
| | | | | | District of Columbia | 2.22 |

Source: U.S. Bureau of the Census
   "2012 American Community Survey-Table R1105" (http://www.census.gov/acs/www/index.html)
*A household includes all persons who occupy a housing unit.  A household consists of a single family, one person living alone, two or more families living together, or any other group of related or unrelated persons who share living arrangements.

# Percent of Households with One Person in 2012

## National Percent = 27.8% of Households*

ALPHA ORDER

| RANK | STATE | PERCENT |
|------|-------|---------|
| 17 | Alabama | 28.9 |
| 42 | Alaska | 26.7 |
| 36 | Arizona | 27.5 |
| 16 | Arkansas | 29.0 |
| 47 | California | 24.4 |
| 24 | Colorado | 28.2 |
| 33 | Connecticut | 27.8 |
| 40 | Delaware | 27.1 |
| 8 | Florida | 29.6 |
| 41 | Georgia | 26.8 |
| 48 | Hawaii | 24.0 |
| 48 | Idaho | 24.0 |
| 20 | Illinois | 28.8 |
| 29 | Indiana | 27.9 |
| 21 | Iowa | 28.6 |
| 17 | Kansas | 28.9 |
| 29 | Kentucky | 27.9 |
| 12 | Louisiana | 29.3 |
| 10 | Maine | 29.5 |
| 36 | Maryland | 27.5 |
| 17 | Massachusetts | 28.9 |
| 14 | Michigan | 29.2 |
| 28 | Minnesota | 28.0 |
| 36 | Mississippi | 27.5 |
| 10 | Missouri | 29.5 |
| 7 | Montana | 29.7 |
| 12 | Nebraska | 29.3 |
| 39 | Nevada | 27.4 |
| 44 | New Hampshire | 26.1 |
| 45 | New Jersey | 25.8 |
| 21 | New Mexico | 28.6 |
| 5 | New York | 30.0 |
| 29 | North Carolina | 27.9 |
| 1 | North Dakota | 32.3 |
| 3 | Ohio | 30.3 |
| 24 | Oklahoma | 28.2 |
| 34 | Oregon | 27.7 |
| 8 | Pennsylvania | 29.6 |
| 5 | Rhode Island | 30.0 |
| 35 | South Carolina | 27.6 |
| 3 | South Dakota | 30.3 |
| 23 | Tennessee | 28.5 |
| 46 | Texas | 25.2 |
| 50 | Utah | 19.8 |
| 29 | Vermont | 27.9 |
| 43 | Virginia | 26.6 |
| 24 | Washington | 28.2 |
| 2 | West Virginia | 31.1 |
| 14 | Wisconsin | 29.2 |
| 27 | Wyoming | 28.1 |

RANK ORDER

| RANK | STATE | PERCENT |
|------|-------|---------|
| 1 | North Dakota | 32.3 |
| 2 | West Virginia | 31.1 |
| 3 | Ohio | 30.3 |
| 3 | South Dakota | 30.3 |
| 5 | New York | 30.0 |
| 5 | Rhode Island | 30.0 |
| 7 | Montana | 29.7 |
| 8 | Florida | 29.6 |
| 8 | Pennsylvania | 29.6 |
| 10 | Maine | 29.5 |
| 10 | Missouri | 29.5 |
| 12 | Louisiana | 29.3 |
| 12 | Nebraska | 29.3 |
| 14 | Michigan | 29.2 |
| 14 | Wisconsin | 29.2 |
| 16 | Arkansas | 29.0 |
| 17 | Alabama | 28.9 |
| 17 | Kansas | 28.9 |
| 17 | Massachusetts | 28.9 |
| 20 | Illinois | 28.8 |
| 21 | Iowa | 28.6 |
| 21 | New Mexico | 28.6 |
| 23 | Tennessee | 28.5 |
| 24 | Colorado | 28.2 |
| 24 | Oklahoma | 28.2 |
| 24 | Washington | 28.2 |
| 27 | Wyoming | 28.1 |
| 28 | Minnesota | 28.0 |
| 29 | Indiana | 27.9 |
| 29 | Kentucky | 27.9 |
| 29 | North Carolina | 27.9 |
| 29 | Vermont | 27.9 |
| 33 | Connecticut | 27.8 |
| 34 | Oregon | 27.7 |
| 35 | South Carolina | 27.6 |
| 36 | Arizona | 27.5 |
| 36 | Maryland | 27.5 |
| 36 | Mississippi | 27.5 |
| 39 | Nevada | 27.4 |
| 40 | Delaware | 27.1 |
| 41 | Georgia | 26.8 |
| 42 | Alaska | 26.7 |
| 43 | Virginia | 26.6 |
| 44 | New Hampshire | 26.1 |
| 45 | New Jersey | 25.8 |
| 46 | Texas | 25.2 |
| 47 | California | 24.4 |
| 48 | Hawaii | 24.0 |
| 48 | Idaho | 24.0 |
| 50 | Utah | 19.8 |
| | District of Columbia | 45.8 |

Source: U.S. Bureau of the Census

"2012 American Community Survey-Table S2501" (http://www.census.gov/acs/www/index.html)

*A household includes all persons who occupy a housing unit. A household consists of a single family, one person living alone, two or more families living together, or any other group of related or unrelated persons who share living arrangements.

# Percent of Households Headed by Married Couples in 2012

## National Percent = 48.1% of Households*

ALPHA ORDER

| RANK | STATE | PERCENT |
|------|-------|---------|
| 35 | Alabama | 47.9 |
| 18 | Alaska | 49.0 |
| 41 | Arizona | 46.9 |
| 21 | Arkansas | 48.8 |
| 25 | California | 48.6 |
| 21 | Colorado | 48.8 |
| 24 | Connecticut | 48.7 |
| 33 | Delaware | 48.0 |
| 44 | Florida | 46.1 |
| 35 | Georgia | 47.9 |
| 5 | Hawaii | 51.2 |
| 2 | Idaho | 55.3 |
| 33 | Illinois | 48.0 |
| 14 | Indiana | 49.6 |
| 7 | Iowa | 51.0 |
| 10 | Kansas | 50.6 |
| 19 | Kentucky | 48.9 |
| 50 | Louisiana | 43.3 |
| 21 | Maine | 48.8 |
| 39 | Maryland | 47.2 |
| 43 | Massachusetts | 46.5 |
| 37 | Michigan | 47.7 |
| 6 | Minnesota | 51.1 |
| 47 | Mississippi | 44.1 |
| 37 | Missouri | 47.7 |
| 11 | Montana | 50.3 |
| 11 | Nebraska | 50.3 |
| 46 | Nevada | 44.2 |
| 3 | New Hampshire | 51.8 |
| 8 | New Jersey | 50.8 |
| 45 | New Mexico | 45.4 |
| 49 | New York | 43.5 |
| 29 | North Carolina | 48.1 |
| 29 | North Dakota | 48.1 |
| 42 | Ohio | 46.8 |
| 26 | Oklahoma | 48.5 |
| 29 | Oregon | 48.1 |
| 29 | Pennsylvania | 48.1 |
| 48 | Rhode Island | 43.7 |
| 40 | South Carolina | 47.0 |
| 16 | South Dakota | 49.3 |
| 27 | Tennessee | 48.4 |
| 13 | Texas | 50.1 |
| 1 | Utah | 60.6 |
| 19 | Vermont | 48.9 |
| 9 | Virginia | 50.7 |
| 15 | Washington | 49.4 |
| 27 | West Virginia | 48.4 |
| 17 | Wisconsin | 49.2 |
| 4 | Wyoming | 51.6 |

RANK ORDER

| RANK | STATE | PERCENT |
|------|-------|---------|
| 1 | Utah | 60.6 |
| 2 | Idaho | 55.3 |
| 3 | New Hampshire | 51.8 |
| 4 | Wyoming | 51.6 |
| 5 | Hawaii | 51.2 |
| 6 | Minnesota | 51.1 |
| 7 | Iowa | 51.0 |
| 8 | New Jersey | 50.8 |
| 9 | Virginia | 50.7 |
| 10 | Kansas | 50.6 |
| 11 | Montana | 50.3 |
| 11 | Nebraska | 50.3 |
| 13 | Texas | 50.1 |
| 14 | Indiana | 49.6 |
| 15 | Washington | 49.4 |
| 16 | South Dakota | 49.3 |
| 17 | Wisconsin | 49.2 |
| 18 | Alaska | 49.0 |
| 19 | Kentucky | 48.9 |
| 19 | Vermont | 48.9 |
| 21 | Arkansas | 48.8 |
| 21 | Colorado | 48.8 |
| 21 | Maine | 48.8 |
| 24 | Connecticut | 48.7 |
| 25 | California | 48.6 |
| 26 | Oklahoma | 48.5 |
| 27 | Tennessee | 48.4 |
| 27 | West Virginia | 48.4 |
| 29 | North Carolina | 48.1 |
| 29 | North Dakota | 48.1 |
| 29 | Oregon | 48.1 |
| 29 | Pennsylvania | 48.1 |
| 33 | Delaware | 48.0 |
| 33 | Illinois | 48.0 |
| 35 | Alabama | 47.9 |
| 35 | Georgia | 47.9 |
| 37 | Michigan | 47.7 |
| 37 | Missouri | 47.7 |
| 39 | Maryland | 47.2 |
| 40 | South Carolina | 47.0 |
| 41 | Arizona | 46.9 |
| 42 | Ohio | 46.8 |
| 43 | Massachusetts | 46.5 |
| 44 | Florida | 46.1 |
| 45 | New Mexico | 45.4 |
| 46 | Nevada | 44.2 |
| 47 | Mississippi | 44.1 |
| 48 | Rhode Island | 43.7 |
| 49 | New York | 43.5 |
| 50 | Louisiana | 43.3 |
| | District of Columbia | 23.3 |

Source: U.S. Bureau of the Census
   "2012 American Community Survey-Table R1101" (http://www.census.gov/acs/www/index.html)
*A household includes all persons who occupy a housing unit.  A household consists of a single family, one person living alone,
two or more families living together, or any other group of related or unrelated persons who share living arrangements.

# Percent of Households Headed by Single Mothers in 2012

## National Percent = 7.3% of Households*

ALPHA ORDER

| RANK | STATE | PERCENT |
|------|-------|---------|
| 8 | Alabama | 8.1 |
| 8 | Alaska | 8.1 |
| 17 | Arizona | 7.3 |
| 17 | Arkansas | 7.3 |
| 22 | California | 7.2 |
| 33 | Colorado | 6.4 |
| 15 | Connecticut | 7.4 |
| 22 | Delaware | 7.2 |
| 26 | Florida | 7.1 |
| 3 | Georgia | 8.8 |
| 49 | Hawaii | 5.4 |
| 40 | Idaho | 6.2 |
| 26 | Illinois | 7.1 |
| 17 | Indiana | 7.3 |
| 39 | Iowa | 6.3 |
| 33 | Kansas | 6.4 |
| 13 | Kentucky | 7.5 |
| 2 | Louisiana | 9.6 |
| 41 | Maine | 6.0 |
| 13 | Maryland | 7.5 |
| 29 | Massachusetts | 7.0 |
| 17 | Michigan | 7.3 |
| 33 | Minnesota | 6.4 |
| 1 | Mississippi | 10.6 |
| 22 | Missouri | 7.2 |
| 50 | Montana | 5.1 |
| 32 | Nebraska | 6.5 |
| 7 | Nevada | 8.3 |
| 45 | New Hampshire | 5.8 |
| 26 | New Jersey | 7.1 |
| 5 | New Mexico | 8.4 |
| 12 | New York | 7.6 |
| 11 | North Carolina | 7.8 |
| 48 | North Dakota | 5.5 |
| 15 | Ohio | 7.4 |
| 17 | Oklahoma | 7.3 |
| 33 | Oregon | 6.4 |
| 33 | Pennsylvania | 6.4 |
| 10 | Rhode Island | 7.9 |
| 4 | South Carolina | 8.7 |
| 30 | South Dakota | 6.9 |
| 22 | Tennessee | 7.2 |
| 5 | Texas | 8.4 |
| 47 | Utah | 5.7 |
| 45 | Vermont | 5.8 |
| 31 | Virginia | 6.6 |
| 41 | Washington | 6.0 |
| 43 | West Virginia | 5.9 |
| 33 | Wisconsin | 6.4 |
| 43 | Wyoming | 5.9 |

RANK ORDER

| RANK | STATE | PERCENT |
|------|-------|---------|
| 1 | Mississippi | 10.6 |
| 2 | Louisiana | 9.6 |
| 3 | Georgia | 8.8 |
| 4 | South Carolina | 8.7 |
| 5 | New Mexico | 8.4 |
| 5 | Texas | 8.4 |
| 7 | Nevada | 8.3 |
| 8 | Alabama | 8.1 |
| 8 | Alaska | 8.1 |
| 10 | Rhode Island | 7.9 |
| 11 | North Carolina | 7.8 |
| 12 | New York | 7.6 |
| 13 | Kentucky | 7.5 |
| 13 | Maryland | 7.5 |
| 15 | Connecticut | 7.4 |
| 15 | Ohio | 7.4 |
| 17 | Arizona | 7.3 |
| 17 | Arkansas | 7.3 |
| 17 | Indiana | 7.3 |
| 17 | Michigan | 7.3 |
| 17 | Oklahoma | 7.3 |
| 22 | California | 7.2 |
| 22 | Delaware | 7.2 |
| 22 | Missouri | 7.2 |
| 22 | Tennessee | 7.2 |
| 26 | Florida | 7.1 |
| 26 | Illinois | 7.1 |
| 26 | New Jersey | 7.1 |
| 29 | Massachusetts | 7.0 |
| 30 | South Dakota | 6.9 |
| 31 | Virginia | 6.6 |
| 32 | Nebraska | 6.5 |
| 33 | Colorado | 6.4 |
| 33 | Kansas | 6.4 |
| 33 | Minnesota | 6.4 |
| 33 | Oregon | 6.4 |
| 33 | Pennsylvania | 6.4 |
| 33 | Wisconsin | 6.4 |
| 39 | Iowa | 6.3 |
| 40 | Idaho | 6.2 |
| 41 | Maine | 6.0 |
| 41 | Washington | 6.0 |
| 43 | West Virginia | 5.9 |
| 43 | Wyoming | 5.9 |
| 45 | New Hampshire | 5.8 |
| 45 | Vermont | 5.8 |
| 47 | Utah | 5.7 |
| 48 | North Dakota | 5.5 |
| 49 | Hawaii | 5.4 |
| 50 | Montana | 5.1 |

District of Columbia     7.5

Source: U.S. Bureau of the Census
    "2012 American Community Survey-Table CP02" (http://www.census.gov/acs/www/index.html)
*No spouse present in household with children under 18 years old.  A household includes all persons who occupy a housing unit.
A household consists of a single family, one person living alone, two or more families living together, or any other group of
related or unrelated persons who share living arrangements.

# Percent of Households Headed by Single Fathers in 2012

## National Percent = 2.3% of Households*

| ALPHA ORDER | | | | RANK ORDER | | |
|---|---|---|---|---|---|---|
| RANK | STATE | PERCENT | | RANK | STATE | PERCENT |
| 50 | Alabama | 1.6 | | 1 | Nevada | 3.2 |
| 4 | Alaska | 2.9 | | 2 | New Mexico | 3.1 |
| 4 | Arizona | 2.9 | | 3 | Wyoming | 3.0 |
| 34 | Arkansas | 2.2 | | 4 | Alaska | 2.9 |
| 6 | California | 2.8 | | 4 | Arizona | 2.9 |
| 19 | Colorado | 2.4 | | 6 | California | 2.8 |
| 37 | Connecticut | 2.1 | | 7 | Montana | 2.7 |
| 13 | Delaware | 2.5 | | 8 | Idaho | 2.6 |
| 37 | Florida | 2.1 | | 8 | Kansas | 2.6 |
| 34 | Georgia | 2.2 | | 8 | Louisiana | 2.6 |
| 48 | Hawaii | 1.7 | | 8 | Nebraska | 2.6 |
| 8 | Idaho | 2.6 | | 8 | Oklahoma | 2.6 |
| 37 | Illinois | 2.1 | | 13 | Delaware | 2.5 |
| 13 | Indiana | 2.5 | | 13 | Indiana | 2.5 |
| 13 | Iowa | 2.5 | | 13 | Iowa | 2.5 |
| 8 | Kansas | 2.6 | | 13 | Oregon | 2.5 |
| 19 | Kentucky | 2.4 | | 13 | Texas | 2.5 |
| 8 | Louisiana | 2.6 | | 13 | Wisconsin | 2.5 |
| 19 | Maine | 2.4 | | 19 | Colorado | 2.4 |
| 25 | Maryland | 2.3 | | 19 | Kentucky | 2.4 |
| 48 | Massachusetts | 1.7 | | 19 | Maine | 2.4 |
| 37 | Michigan | 2.1 | | 19 | Mississippi | 2.4 |
| 25 | Minnesota | 2.3 | | 19 | South Dakota | 2.4 |
| 19 | Mississippi | 2.4 | | 19 | Washington | 2.4 |
| 25 | Missouri | 2.3 | | 25 | Maryland | 2.3 |
| 7 | Montana | 2.7 | | 25 | Minnesota | 2.3 |
| 8 | Nebraska | 2.6 | | 25 | Missouri | 2.3 |
| 1 | Nevada | 3.2 | | 25 | New Hampshire | 2.3 |
| 25 | New Hampshire | 2.3 | | 25 | North Carolina | 2.3 |
| 45 | New Jersey | 2.0 | | 25 | North Dakota | 2.3 |
| 2 | New Mexico | 3.1 | | 25 | Ohio | 2.3 |
| 37 | New York | 2.1 | | 25 | Tennessee | 2.3 |
| 25 | North Carolina | 2.3 | | 25 | Utah | 2.3 |
| 25 | North Dakota | 2.3 | | 34 | Arkansas | 2.2 |
| 25 | Ohio | 2.3 | | 34 | Georgia | 2.2 |
| 8 | Oklahoma | 2.6 | | 34 | Vermont | 2.2 |
| 13 | Oregon | 2.5 | | 37 | Connecticut | 2.1 |
| 37 | Pennsylvania | 2.1 | | 37 | Florida | 2.1 |
| 45 | Rhode Island | 2.0 | | 37 | Illinois | 2.1 |
| 37 | South Carolina | 2.1 | | 37 | Michigan | 2.1 |
| 19 | South Dakota | 2.4 | | 37 | New York | 2.1 |
| 25 | Tennessee | 2.3 | | 37 | Pennsylvania | 2.1 |
| 13 | Texas | 2.5 | | 37 | South Carolina | 2.1 |
| 25 | Utah | 2.3 | | 37 | Virginia | 2.1 |
| 34 | Vermont | 2.2 | | 45 | New Jersey | 2.0 |
| 37 | Virginia | 2.1 | | 45 | Rhode Island | 2.0 |
| 19 | Washington | 2.4 | | 45 | West Virginia | 2.0 |
| 45 | West Virginia | 2.0 | | 48 | Hawaii | 1.7 |
| 13 | Wisconsin | 2.5 | | 48 | Massachusetts | 1.7 |
| 3 | Wyoming | 3.0 | | 50 | Alabama | 1.6 |
| | | | | District of Columbia | | 1.2 |

Source: U.S. Bureau of the Census
    "2012 American Community Survey-Table CP02" (http://www.census.gov/acs/www/index.html)
*No spouse present in household with children under 18 years old.  A household includes all persons who occupy a housing unit.
A household consists of a single family, one person living alone, two or more families living together, or any other group of
related or unrelated persons who share living arrangements.

# Housing Units in 2012

## National Total = 132,452,249 Housing Units*

| ALPHA ORDER | | | | | RANK ORDER | | | |
|---|---|---|---|---|---|---|---|---|
| RANK | STATE | HOUSING UNITS | % of USA | | RANK | STATE | HOUSING UNITS | % of USA |
| 23 | Alabama | 2,189,567 | 1.7% | | 1 | California | 13,708,197 | 10.3% |
| 49 | Alaska | 307,628 | 0.2% | | 2 | Texas | 10,154,835 | 7.7% |
| 14 | Arizona | 2,871,486 | 2.2% | | 3 | Florida | 9,031,530 | 6.8% |
| 31 | Arkansas | 1,328,225 | 1.0% | | 4 | New York | 8,123,585 | 6.1% |
| 1 | California | 13,708,197 | 10.3% | | 5 | Pennsylvania | 5,572,765 | 4.2% |
| 22 | Colorado | 2,230,536 | 1.7% | | 6 | Illinois | 5,290,149 | 4.0% |
| 29 | Connecticut | 1,488,002 | 1.1% | | 7 | Ohio | 5,128,846 | 3.9% |
| 45 | Delaware | 410,308 | 0.3% | | 8 | Michigan | 4,525,081 | 3.4% |
| 3 | Florida | 9,031,530 | 6.8% | | 9 | North Carolina | 4,375,400 | 3.3% |
| 10 | Georgia | 4,107,554 | 3.1% | | 10 | Georgia | 4,107,554 | 3.1% |
| 42 | Hawaii | 524,387 | 0.4% | | 11 | New Jersey | 3,574,763 | 2.7% |
| 40 | Idaho | 673,048 | 0.5% | | 12 | Virginia | 3,398,389 | 2.6% |
| 6 | Illinois | 5,290,149 | 4.0% | | 13 | Washington | 2,914,775 | 2.2% |
| 17 | Indiana | 2,808,430 | 2.1% | | 14 | Arizona | 2,871,486 | 2.2% |
| 30 | Iowa | 1,345,711 | 1.0% | | 15 | Tennessee | 2,834,808 | 2.1% |
| 33 | Kansas | 1,238,703 | 0.9% | | 16 | Massachusetts | 2,810,394 | 2.1% |
| 26 | Kentucky | 1,937,321 | 1.5% | | 17 | Indiana | 2,808,430 | 2.1% |
| 25 | Louisiana | 1,987,059 | 1.5% | | 18 | Missouri | 2,720,087 | 2.1% |
| 39 | Maine | 724,187 | 0.5% | | 19 | Wisconsin | 2,632,625 | 2.0% |
| 20 | Maryland | 2,395,635 | 1.8% | | 20 | Maryland | 2,395,635 | 1.8% |
| 16 | Massachusetts | 2,810,394 | 2.1% | | 21 | Minnesota | 2,361,074 | 1.8% |
| 8 | Michigan | 4,525,081 | 3.4% | | 22 | Colorado | 2,230,536 | 1.7% |
| 21 | Minnesota | 2,361,074 | 1.8% | | 23 | Alabama | 2,189,567 | 1.7% |
| 32 | Mississippi | 1,283,897 | 1.0% | | 24 | South Carolina | 2,156,768 | 1.6% |
| 18 | Missouri | 2,720,087 | 2.1% | | 25 | Louisiana | 1,987,059 | 1.5% |
| 43 | Montana | 486,161 | 0.4% | | 26 | Kentucky | 1,937,321 | 1.5% |
| 38 | Nebraska | 804,274 | 0.6% | | 27 | Oregon | 1,682,531 | 1.3% |
| 34 | Nevada | 1,182,842 | 0.9% | | 28 | Oklahoma | 1,677,646 | 1.3% |
| 41 | New Hampshire | 617,005 | 0.5% | | 29 | Connecticut | 1,488,002 | 1.1% |
| 11 | New Jersey | 3,574,763 | 2.7% | | 30 | Iowa | 1,345,711 | 1.0% |
| 36 | New Mexico | 906,838 | 0.7% | | 31 | Arkansas | 1,328,225 | 1.0% |
| 4 | New York | 8,123,585 | 6.1% | | 32 | Mississippi | 1,283,897 | 1.0% |
| 9 | North Carolina | 4,375,400 | 3.3% | | 33 | Kansas | 1,238,703 | 0.9% |
| 47 | North Dakota | 329,249 | 0.2% | | 34 | Nevada | 1,182,842 | 0.9% |
| 7 | Ohio | 5,128,846 | 3.9% | | 35 | Utah | 996,777 | 0.8% |
| 28 | Oklahoma | 1,677,646 | 1.3% | | 36 | New Mexico | 906,838 | 0.7% |
| 27 | Oregon | 1,682,531 | 1.3% | | 37 | West Virginia | 882,800 | 0.7% |
| 5 | Pennsylvania | 5,572,765 | 4.2% | | 38 | Nebraska | 804,274 | 0.6% |
| 44 | Rhode Island | 462,618 | 0.3% | | 39 | Maine | 724,187 | 0.5% |
| 24 | South Carolina | 2,156,768 | 1.6% | | 40 | Idaho | 673,048 | 0.5% |
| 46 | South Dakota | 368,247 | 0.3% | | 41 | New Hampshire | 617,005 | 0.5% |
| 15 | Tennessee | 2,834,808 | 2.1% | | 42 | Hawaii | 524,387 | 0.4% |
| 2 | Texas | 10,154,835 | 7.7% | | 43 | Montana | 486,161 | 0.4% |
| 35 | Utah | 996,777 | 0.8% | | 44 | Rhode Island | 462,618 | 0.3% |
| 48 | Vermont | 324,052 | 0.2% | | 45 | Delaware | 410,308 | 0.3% |
| 12 | Virginia | 3,398,389 | 2.6% | | 46 | South Dakota | 368,247 | 0.3% |
| 13 | Washington | 2,914,775 | 2.2% | | 47 | North Dakota | 329,249 | 0.2% |
| 37 | West Virginia | 882,800 | 0.7% | | 48 | Vermont | 324,052 | 0.2% |
| 19 | Wisconsin | 2,632,625 | 2.0% | | 49 | Alaska | 307,628 | 0.2% |
| 50 | Wyoming | 265,207 | 0.2% | | 50 | Wyoming | 265,207 | 0.2% |
| | | | | | | District of Columbia | 300,247 | 0.2% |

Source: U.S. Bureau of the Census
    "2012 American Community Survey-Table B25001" (http://www.census.gov/acs/www/index.html)
*A housing unit is a house, an apartment, a mobile home, a group of rooms, or a single room that is occupied (or if vacant, is intended for occupancy) as separate living quarters. Separate living quarters are those in which the occupants live and eat separately from any other persons in the building and which have direct access from the outside of the building or through a common hall.

# Housing Units per Square Mile in 2012

## National Average = 37.4 Housing Units*

### ALPHA ORDER

| RANK | STATE | RATE |
|------|-------|------|
| 26 | Alabama | 43.1 |
| 50 | Alaska | 0.5 |
| 34 | Arizona | 25.3 |
| 33 | Arkansas | 25.5 |
| 13 | California | 87.9 |
| 38 | Colorado | 21.5 |
| 4 | Connecticut | 307.1 |
| 6 | Delaware | 210.0 |
| 8 | Florida | 167.5 |
| 19 | Georgia | 70.9 |
| 15 | Hawaii | 81.6 |
| 44 | Idaho | 8.1 |
| 11 | Illinois | 95.2 |
| 17 | Indiana | 78.3 |
| 36 | Iowa | 24.1 |
| 40 | Kansas | 15.1 |
| 22 | Kentucky | 48.8 |
| 24 | Louisiana | 45.6 |
| 37 | Maine | 23.5 |
| 5 | Maryland | 245.1 |
| 3 | Massachusetts | 358.5 |
| 16 | Michigan | 79.7 |
| 31 | Minnesota | 29.7 |
| 32 | Mississippi | 27.4 |
| 27 | Missouri | 39.5 |
| 48 | Montana | 3.3 |
| 43 | Nebraska | 10.5 |
| 42 | Nevada | 10.8 |
| 20 | New Hampshire | 68.8 |
| 1 | New Jersey | 482.0 |
| 45 | New Mexico | 7.5 |
| 7 | New York | 172.1 |
| 12 | North Carolina | 89.8 |
| 47 | North Dakota | 4.8 |
| 9 | Ohio | 125.3 |
| 35 | Oklahoma | 24.4 |
| 39 | Oregon | 17.5 |
| 10 | Pennsylvania | 124.3 |
| 2 | Rhode Island | 442.7 |
| 18 | South Carolina | 71.6 |
| 46 | South Dakota | 4.9 |
| 20 | Tennessee | 68.8 |
| 28 | Texas | 38.8 |
| 41 | Utah | 12.1 |
| 30 | Vermont | 35.0 |
| 14 | Virginia | 85.8 |
| 25 | Washington | 43.8 |
| 29 | West Virginia | 36.7 |
| 23 | Wisconsin | 48.5 |
| 49 | Wyoming | 2.7 |

### RANK ORDER

| RANK | STATE | RATE |
|------|-------|------|
| 1 | New Jersey | 482.0 |
| 2 | Rhode Island | 442.7 |
| 3 | Massachusetts | 358.5 |
| 4 | Connecticut | 307.1 |
| 5 | Maryland | 245.1 |
| 6 | Delaware | 210.0 |
| 7 | New York | 172.1 |
| 8 | Florida | 167.5 |
| 9 | Ohio | 125.3 |
| 10 | Pennsylvania | 124.3 |
| 11 | Illinois | 95.2 |
| 12 | North Carolina | 89.8 |
| 13 | California | 87.9 |
| 14 | Virginia | 85.8 |
| 15 | Hawaii | 81.6 |
| 16 | Michigan | 79.7 |
| 17 | Indiana | 78.3 |
| 18 | South Carolina | 71.6 |
| 19 | Georgia | 70.9 |
| 20 | New Hampshire | 68.8 |
| 20 | Tennessee | 68.8 |
| 22 | Kentucky | 48.8 |
| 23 | Wisconsin | 48.5 |
| 24 | Louisiana | 45.6 |
| 25 | Washington | 43.8 |
| 26 | Alabama | 43.1 |
| 27 | Missouri | 39.5 |
| 28 | Texas | 38.8 |
| 29 | West Virginia | 36.7 |
| 30 | Vermont | 35.0 |
| 31 | Minnesota | 29.7 |
| 32 | Mississippi | 27.4 |
| 33 | Arkansas | 25.5 |
| 34 | Arizona | 25.3 |
| 35 | Oklahoma | 24.4 |
| 36 | Iowa | 24.1 |
| 37 | Maine | 23.5 |
| 38 | Colorado | 21.5 |
| 39 | Oregon | 17.5 |
| 40 | Kansas | 15.1 |
| 41 | Utah | 12.1 |
| 42 | Nevada | 10.8 |
| 43 | Nebraska | 10.5 |
| 44 | Idaho | 8.1 |
| 45 | New Mexico | 7.5 |
| 46 | South Dakota | 4.9 |
| 47 | North Dakota | 4.8 |
| 48 | Montana | 3.3 |
| 49 | Wyoming | 2.7 |
| 50 | Alaska | 0.5 |

District of Columbia    4,922.1

Source: CQ Press using data from U.S. Bureau of the Census
   "2012 American Community Survey-Table B25001" (http://www.census.gov/acs/www/index.html)
*Based on land area.  A housing unit is a house, an apartment, a mobile home, a group of rooms, or a single room that is occupied (or if vacant, is intended for occupancy) as separate living quarters.  Separate living quarters are those in which the occupants live and eat separately from any other persons in the building and which have direct access from the outside of the building or through a common hall.

# Percent of Housing Units That Are Owner-Occupied in 2012

## National Percent = 63.9% of Housing Units*

ALPHA ORDER

| RANK | STATE | PERCENT |
|---|---|---|
| 13 | Alabama | 68.8 |
| 40 | Alaska | 63.4 |
| 41 | Arizona | 62.6 |
| 31 | Arkansas | 66.2 |
| 49 | California | 54.0 |
| 38 | Colorado | 64.0 |
| 23 | Connecticut | 66.9 |
| 8 | Delaware | 70.8 |
| 34 | Florida | 65.6 |
| 39 | Georgia | 63.7 |
| 47 | Hawaii | 56.9 |
| 14 | Idaho | 68.4 |
| 25 | Illinois | 66.6 |
| 10 | Indiana | 69.4 |
| 2 | Iowa | 71.9 |
| 27 | Kansas | 66.4 |
| 22 | Kentucky | 67.0 |
| 33 | Louisiana | 65.7 |
| 3 | Maine | 71.4 |
| 26 | Maryland | 66.5 |
| 44 | Massachusetts | 62.2 |
| 5 | Michigan | 71.1 |
| 3 | Minnesota | 71.4 |
| 15 | Mississippi | 68.2 |
| 18 | Missouri | 67.5 |
| 20 | Montana | 67.1 |
| 29 | Nebraska | 66.3 |
| 48 | Nevada | 54.9 |
| 7 | New Hampshire | 70.9 |
| 36 | New Jersey | 65.1 |
| 17 | New Mexico | 67.7 |
| 50 | New York | 53.7 |
| 35 | North Carolina | 65.4 |
| 37 | North Dakota | 65.0 |
| 29 | Ohio | 66.3 |
| 27 | Oklahoma | 66.4 |
| 45 | Oregon | 61.6 |
| 12 | Pennsylvania | 68.9 |
| 46 | Rhode Island | 60.0 |
| 16 | South Carolina | 68.1 |
| 20 | South Dakota | 67.1 |
| 24 | Tennessee | 66.7 |
| 42 | Texas | 62.3 |
| 9 | Utah | 69.6 |
| 6 | Vermont | 71.0 |
| 31 | Virginia | 66.2 |
| 42 | Washington | 62.3 |
| 1 | West Virginia | 72.0 |
| 19 | Wisconsin | 67.3 |
| 11 | Wyoming | 69.0 |

RANK ORDER

| RANK | STATE | PERCENT |
|---|---|---|
| 1 | West Virginia | 72.0 |
| 2 | Iowa | 71.9 |
| 3 | Maine | 71.4 |
| 3 | Minnesota | 71.4 |
| 5 | Michigan | 71.1 |
| 6 | Vermont | 71.0 |
| 7 | New Hampshire | 70.9 |
| 8 | Delaware | 70.8 |
| 9 | Utah | 69.6 |
| 10 | Indiana | 69.4 |
| 11 | Wyoming | 69.0 |
| 12 | Pennsylvania | 68.9 |
| 13 | Alabama | 68.8 |
| 14 | Idaho | 68.4 |
| 15 | Mississippi | 68.2 |
| 16 | South Carolina | 68.1 |
| 17 | New Mexico | 67.7 |
| 18 | Missouri | 67.5 |
| 19 | Wisconsin | 67.3 |
| 20 | Montana | 67.1 |
| 20 | South Dakota | 67.1 |
| 22 | Kentucky | 67.0 |
| 23 | Connecticut | 66.9 |
| 24 | Tennessee | 66.7 |
| 25 | Illinois | 66.6 |
| 26 | Maryland | 66.5 |
| 27 | Kansas | 66.4 |
| 27 | Oklahoma | 66.4 |
| 29 | Nebraska | 66.3 |
| 29 | Ohio | 66.3 |
| 31 | Arkansas | 66.2 |
| 31 | Virginia | 66.2 |
| 33 | Louisiana | 65.7 |
| 34 | Florida | 65.6 |
| 35 | North Carolina | 65.4 |
| 36 | New Jersey | 65.1 |
| 37 | North Dakota | 65.0 |
| 38 | Colorado | 64.0 |
| 39 | Georgia | 63.7 |
| 40 | Alaska | 63.4 |
| 41 | Arizona | 62.6 |
| 42 | Texas | 62.3 |
| 42 | Washington | 62.3 |
| 44 | Massachusetts | 62.2 |
| 45 | Oregon | 61.6 |
| 46 | Rhode Island | 60.0 |
| 47 | Hawaii | 56.9 |
| 48 | Nevada | 54.9 |
| 49 | California | 54.0 |
| 50 | New York | 53.7 |
| | District of Columbia | 41.5 |

Source: U.S. Bureau of the Census
"2012 American Community Survey-Table R2512" (http://www.census.gov/acs/www/index.html)
*For occupied housing units.

# New Housing Units Authorized in 2013

## National Total = 976,369 Units*

ALPHA ORDER

| RANK | STATE | UNITS | % of USA |
|---|---|---|---|
| 29 | Alabama | 10,954 | 1.1% |
| 49 | Alaska | 1,081 | 0.1% |
| 11 | Arizona | 23,765 | 2.4% |
| 36 | Arkansas | 6,548 | 0.7% |
| 3 | California | 79,028 | 8.1% |
| 9 | Colorado | 27,296 | 2.8% |
| 37 | Connecticut | 5,762 | 0.6% |
| 41 | Delaware | 4,875 | 0.5% |
| 2 | Florida | 87,432 | 9.0% |
| 5 | Georgia | 34,721 | 3.6% |
| 43 | Hawaii | 3,866 | 0.4% |
| 33 | Idaho | 8,847 | 0.9% |
| 21 | Illinois | 15,348 | 1.6% |
| 17 | Indiana | 18,029 | 1.8% |
| 30 | Iowa | 10,826 | 1.1% |
| 34 | Kansas | 7,985 | 0.8% |
| 31 | Kentucky | 8,885 | 0.9% |
| 25 | Louisiana | 13,964 | 1.4% |
| 44 | Maine | 3,212 | 0.3% |
| 16 | Maryland | 18,138 | 1.9% |
| 23 | Massachusetts | 14,538 | 1.5% |
| 19 | Michigan | 15,934 | 1.6% |
| 18 | Minnesota | 16,524 | 1.7% |
| 39 | Mississippi | 5,298 | 0.5% |
| 27 | Missouri | 12,799 | 1.3% |
| 42 | Montana | 4,103 | 0.4% |
| 35 | Nebraska | 7,863 | 0.8% |
| 28 | Nevada | 11,232 | 1.2% |
| 45 | New Hampshire | 2,662 | 0.3% |
| 10 | New Jersey | 24,270 | 2.5% |
| 40 | New Mexico | 4,987 | 0.5% |
| 6 | New York | 32,938 | 3.4% |
| 4 | North Carolina | 50,787 | 5.2% |
| 32 | North Dakota | 8,855 | 0.9% |
| 15 | Ohio | 21,310 | 2.2% |
| 26 | Oklahoma | 13,417 | 1.4% |
| 22 | Oregon | 14,969 | 1.5% |
| 14 | Pennsylvania | 22,116 | 2.3% |
| 50 | Rhode Island | 915 | 0.1% |
| 12 | South Carolina | 23,637 | 2.4% |
| 38 | South Dakota | 5,390 | 0.6% |
| 13 | Tennessee | 23,036 | 2.4% |
| 1 | Texas | 146,372 | 15.0% |
| 20 | Utah | 15,602 | 1.6% |
| 48 | Vermont | 1,455 | 0.1% |
| 8 | Virginia | 31,367 | 3.2% |
| 7 | Washington | 31,664 | 3.2% |
| 46 | West Virginia | 2,335 | 0.2% |
| 24 | Wisconsin | 13,984 | 1.4% |
| 47 | Wyoming | 2,193 | 0.2% |

RANK ORDER

| RANK | STATE | UNITS | % of USA |
|---|---|---|---|
| 1 | Texas | 146,372 | 15.0% |
| 2 | Florida | 87,432 | 9.0% |
| 3 | California | 79,028 | 8.1% |
| 4 | North Carolina | 50,787 | 5.2% |
| 5 | Georgia | 34,721 | 3.6% |
| 6 | New York | 32,938 | 3.4% |
| 7 | Washington | 31,664 | 3.2% |
| 8 | Virginia | 31,367 | 3.2% |
| 9 | Colorado | 27,296 | 2.8% |
| 10 | New Jersey | 24,270 | 2.5% |
| 11 | Arizona | 23,765 | 2.4% |
| 12 | South Carolina | 23,637 | 2.4% |
| 13 | Tennessee | 23,036 | 2.4% |
| 14 | Pennsylvania | 22,116 | 2.3% |
| 15 | Ohio | 21,310 | 2.2% |
| 16 | Maryland | 18,138 | 1.9% |
| 17 | Indiana | 18,029 | 1.8% |
| 18 | Minnesota | 16,524 | 1.7% |
| 19 | Michigan | 15,934 | 1.6% |
| 20 | Utah | 15,602 | 1.6% |
| 21 | Illinois | 15,348 | 1.6% |
| 22 | Oregon | 14,969 | 1.5% |
| 23 | Massachusetts | 14,538 | 1.5% |
| 24 | Wisconsin | 13,984 | 1.4% |
| 25 | Louisiana | 13,964 | 1.4% |
| 26 | Oklahoma | 13,417 | 1.4% |
| 27 | Missouri | 12,799 | 1.3% |
| 28 | Nevada | 11,232 | 1.2% |
| 29 | Alabama | 10,954 | 1.1% |
| 30 | Iowa | 10,826 | 1.1% |
| 31 | Kentucky | 8,885 | 0.9% |
| 32 | North Dakota | 8,855 | 0.9% |
| 33 | Idaho | 8,847 | 0.9% |
| 34 | Kansas | 7,985 | 0.8% |
| 35 | Nebraska | 7,863 | 0.8% |
| 36 | Arkansas | 6,548 | 0.7% |
| 37 | Connecticut | 5,762 | 0.6% |
| 38 | South Dakota | 5,390 | 0.6% |
| 39 | Mississippi | 5,298 | 0.5% |
| 40 | New Mexico | 4,987 | 0.5% |
| 41 | Delaware | 4,875 | 0.5% |
| 42 | Montana | 4,103 | 0.4% |
| 43 | Hawaii | 3,866 | 0.4% |
| 44 | Maine | 3,212 | 0.3% |
| 45 | New Hampshire | 2,662 | 0.3% |
| 46 | West Virginia | 2,335 | 0.2% |
| 47 | Wyoming | 2,193 | 0.2% |
| 48 | Vermont | 1,455 | 0.1% |
| 49 | Alaska | 1,081 | 0.1% |
| 50 | Rhode Island | 915 | 0.1% |
| | District of Columbia | 3,255 | 0.3% |

Source: U.S. Bureau of the Census
    "Building Permits Survey" (http://www.census.gov/construction/bps/statemonthly.html)
*Preliminary and unadjusted year-to-date monthly data as of December 2013.  Includes single and multifamily privately owned units.  All places issuing building permits for privately-owned residential structures. More than 98 percent of all privately-owned residential buildings constructed are in permit-issuing places.

# Value of New Housing Units Authorized in 2013

## National Total = $175,155,053,000*

ALPHA ORDER

| RANK | STATE | VALUE | % of USA |
|------|-------|-------|----------|
| 29 | Alabama | $1,952,195,000 | 1.1% |
| 48 | Alaska | 258,950,000 | 0.1% |
| 8 | Arizona | 5,149,389,000 | 2.9% |
| 37 | Arkansas | 1,086,972,000 | 0.6% |
| 3 | California | 17,976,515,000 | 10.3% |
| 6 | Colorado | 5,897,200,000 | 3.4% |
| 36 | Connecticut | 1,126,179,000 | 0.6% |
| 43 | Delaware | 592,117,000 | 0.3% |
| 2 | Florida | 18,319,434,000 | 10.5% |
| 7 | Georgia | 5,444,945,000 | 3.1% |
| 38 | Hawaii | 1,018,149,000 | 0.6% |
| 31 | Idaho | 1,640,654,000 | 0.9% |
| 20 | Illinois | 3,127,597,000 | 1.8% |
| 21 | Indiana | 3,110,635,000 | 1.8% |
| 28 | Iowa | 1,965,720,000 | 1.1% |
| 32 | Kansas | 1,399,345,000 | 0.8% |
| 34 | Kentucky | 1,164,228,000 | 0.7% |
| 24 | Louisiana | 2,516,033,000 | 1.4% |
| 45 | Maine | 568,327,000 | 0.3% |
| 22 | Maryland | 2,852,125,000 | 1.6% |
| 14 | Massachusetts | 3,698,244,000 | 2.1% |
| 17 | Michigan | 3,240,632,000 | 1.9% |
| 15 | Minnesota | 3,548,356,000 | 2.0% |
| 40 | Mississippi | 798,400,000 | 0.5% |
| 27 | Missouri | 2,104,251,000 | 1.2% |
| 42 | Montana | 633,425,000 | 0.4% |
| 33 | Nebraska | 1,268,495,000 | 0.7% |
| 30 | Nevada | 1,758,328,000 | 1.0% |
| 44 | New Hampshire | 586,185,000 | 0.3% |
| 18 | New Jersey | 3,233,931,000 | 1.8% |
| 39 | New Mexico | 819,180,000 | 0.5% |
| 10 | New York | 4,665,631,000 | 2.7% |
| 4 | North Carolina | 8,089,818,000 | 4.6% |
| 35 | North Dakota | 1,146,830,000 | 0.7% |
| 16 | Ohio | 3,508,940,000 | 2.0% |
| 26 | Oklahoma | 2,272,276,000 | 1.3% |
| 23 | Oregon | 2,763,563,000 | 1.6% |
| 12 | Pennsylvania | 3,873,436,000 | 2.2% |
| 50 | Rhode Island | 173,522,000 | 0.1% |
| 11 | South Carolina | 4,618,515,000 | 2.6% |
| 41 | South Dakota | 726,924,000 | 0.4% |
| 13 | Tennessee | 3,699,763,000 | 2.1% |
| 1 | Texas | 22,263,422,000 | 12.7% |
| 19 | Utah | 3,198,777,000 | 1.8% |
| 49 | Vermont | 256,873,000 | 0.1% |
| 9 | Virginia | 4,818,065,000 | 2.8% |
| 5 | Washington | 6,612,131,000 | 3.8% |
| 47 | West Virginia | 363,585,000 | 0.2% |
| 25 | Wisconsin | 2,458,079,000 | 1.4% |
| 46 | Wyoming | 508,876,000 | 0.3% |

RANK ORDER

| RANK | STATE | VALUE | % of USA |
|------|-------|-------|----------|
| 1 | Texas | $22,263,422,000 | 12.7% |
| 2 | Florida | 18,319,434,000 | 10.5% |
| 3 | California | 17,976,515,000 | 10.3% |
| 4 | North Carolina | 8,089,818,000 | 4.6% |
| 5 | Washington | 6,612,131,000 | 3.8% |
| 6 | Colorado | 5,897,200,000 | 3.4% |
| 7 | Georgia | 5,444,945,000 | 3.1% |
| 8 | Arizona | 5,149,389,000 | 2.9% |
| 9 | Virginia | 4,818,065,000 | 2.8% |
| 10 | New York | 4,665,631,000 | 2.7% |
| 11 | South Carolina | 4,618,515,000 | 2.6% |
| 12 | Pennsylvania | 3,873,436,000 | 2.2% |
| 13 | Tennessee | 3,699,763,000 | 2.1% |
| 14 | Massachusetts | 3,698,244,000 | 2.1% |
| 15 | Minnesota | 3,548,356,000 | 2.0% |
| 16 | Ohio | 3,508,940,000 | 2.0% |
| 17 | Michigan | 3,240,632,000 | 1.9% |
| 18 | New Jersey | 3,233,931,000 | 1.8% |
| 19 | Utah | 3,198,777,000 | 1.8% |
| 20 | Illinois | 3,127,597,000 | 1.8% |
| 21 | Indiana | 3,110,635,000 | 1.8% |
| 22 | Maryland | 2,852,125,000 | 1.6% |
| 23 | Oregon | 2,763,563,000 | 1.6% |
| 24 | Louisiana | 2,516,033,000 | 1.4% |
| 25 | Wisconsin | 2,458,079,000 | 1.4% |
| 26 | Oklahoma | 2,272,276,000 | 1.3% |
| 27 | Missouri | 2,104,251,000 | 1.2% |
| 28 | Iowa | 1,965,720,000 | 1.1% |
| 29 | Alabama | 1,952,195,000 | 1.1% |
| 30 | Nevada | 1,758,328,000 | 1.0% |
| 31 | Idaho | 1,640,654,000 | 0.9% |
| 32 | Kansas | 1,399,345,000 | 0.8% |
| 33 | Nebraska | 1,268,495,000 | 0.7% |
| 34 | Kentucky | 1,164,228,000 | 0.7% |
| 35 | North Dakota | 1,146,830,000 | 0.7% |
| 36 | Connecticut | 1,126,179,000 | 0.6% |
| 37 | Arkansas | 1,086,972,000 | 0.6% |
| 38 | Hawaii | 1,018,149,000 | 0.6% |
| 39 | New Mexico | 819,180,000 | 0.5% |
| 40 | Mississippi | 798,400,000 | 0.5% |
| 41 | South Dakota | 726,924,000 | 0.4% |
| 42 | Montana | 633,425,000 | 0.4% |
| 43 | Delaware | 592,117,000 | 0.3% |
| 44 | New Hampshire | 586,185,000 | 0.3% |
| 45 | Maine | 568,327,000 | 0.3% |
| 46 | Wyoming | 508,876,000 | 0.3% |
| 47 | West Virginia | 363,585,000 | 0.2% |
| 48 | Alaska | 258,950,000 | 0.1% |
| 49 | Vermont | 256,873,000 | 0.1% |
| 50 | Rhode Island | 173,522,000 | 0.1% |
| | District of Columbia | 279,888,000 | 0.2% |

Source: U.S. Bureau of the Census
   "Building Permits Survey" (http://www.census.gov/construction/bps/statemonthly.html)
*Preliminary and unadjusted year-to-date monthly data as of December 2013. Includes single and multifamily privately owned units. All places issuing building permits for privately-owned residential structures. More than 98 percent of all privately-owned residential buildings constructed are in permit-issuing places.

# Average Value of New Housing Units in 2013

## National Average = $179,394 per Unit*

ALPHA ORDER

| RANK | STATE | VALUE |
|---|---|---|
| 22 | Alabama | $178,218 |
| 3 | Alaska | 239,547 |
| 7 | Arizona | 216,680 |
| 30 | Arkansas | 166,001 |
| 5 | California | 227,470 |
| 8 | Colorado | 216,046 |
| 15 | Connecticut | 195,449 |
| 50 | Delaware | 121,460 |
| 10 | Florida | 209,528 |
| 38 | Georgia | 156,820 |
| 1 | Hawaii | 263,360 |
| 18 | Idaho | 185,447 |
| 13 | Illinois | 203,779 |
| 28 | Indiana | 172,535 |
| 20 | Iowa | 181,574 |
| 26 | Kansas | 175,247 |
| 48 | Kentucky | 131,033 |
| 21 | Louisiana | 180,180 |
| 23 | Maine | 176,939 |
| 37 | Maryland | 157,246 |
| 2 | Massachusetts | 254,385 |
| 14 | Michigan | 203,378 |
| 9 | Minnesota | 214,740 |
| 44 | Mississippi | 150,698 |
| 32 | Missouri | 164,407 |
| 41 | Montana | 154,381 |
| 34 | Nebraska | 161,325 |
| 39 | Nevada | 156,546 |
| 6 | New Hampshire | 220,205 |
| 47 | New Jersey | 133,248 |
| 33 | New Mexico | 164,263 |
| 45 | New York | 141,649 |
| 36 | North Carolina | 159,289 |
| 49 | North Dakota | 129,512 |
| 31 | Ohio | 164,662 |
| 29 | Oklahoma | 169,358 |
| 19 | Oregon | 184,619 |
| 27 | Pennsylvania | 175,142 |
| 17 | Rhode Island | 189,642 |
| 16 | South Carolina | 195,393 |
| 46 | South Dakota | 134,865 |
| 35 | Tennessee | 160,608 |
| 43 | Texas | 152,102 |
| 12 | Utah | 205,024 |
| 24 | Vermont | 176,545 |
| 42 | Virginia | 153,603 |
| 11 | Washington | 208,822 |
| 40 | West Virginia | 155,711 |
| 25 | Wisconsin | 175,778 |
| 4 | Wyoming | 232,046 |

RANK ORDER

| RANK | STATE | VALUE |
|---|---|---|
| 1 | Hawaii | $263,360 |
| 2 | Massachusetts | 254,385 |
| 3 | Alaska | 239,547 |
| 4 | Wyoming | 232,046 |
| 5 | California | 227,470 |
| 6 | New Hampshire | 220,205 |
| 7 | Arizona | 216,680 |
| 8 | Colorado | 216,046 |
| 9 | Minnesota | 214,740 |
| 10 | Florida | 209,528 |
| 11 | Washington | 208,822 |
| 12 | Utah | 205,024 |
| 13 | Illinois | 203,779 |
| 14 | Michigan | 203,378 |
| 15 | Connecticut | 195,449 |
| 16 | South Carolina | 195,393 |
| 17 | Rhode Island | 189,642 |
| 18 | Idaho | 185,447 |
| 19 | Oregon | 184,619 |
| 20 | Iowa | 181,574 |
| 21 | Louisiana | 180,180 |
| 22 | Alabama | 178,218 |
| 23 | Maine | 176,939 |
| 24 | Vermont | 176,545 |
| 25 | Wisconsin | 175,778 |
| 26 | Kansas | 175,247 |
| 27 | Pennsylvania | 175,142 |
| 28 | Indiana | 172,535 |
| 29 | Oklahoma | 169,358 |
| 30 | Arkansas | 166,001 |
| 31 | Ohio | 164,662 |
| 32 | Missouri | 164,407 |
| 33 | New Mexico | 164,263 |
| 34 | Nebraska | 161,325 |
| 35 | Tennessee | 160,608 |
| 36 | North Carolina | 159,289 |
| 37 | Maryland | 157,246 |
| 38 | Georgia | 156,820 |
| 39 | Nevada | 156,546 |
| 40 | West Virginia | 155,711 |
| 41 | Montana | 154,381 |
| 42 | Virginia | 153,603 |
| 43 | Texas | 152,102 |
| 44 | Mississippi | 150,698 |
| 45 | New York | 141,649 |
| 46 | South Dakota | 134,865 |
| 47 | New Jersey | 133,248 |
| 48 | Kentucky | 131,033 |
| 49 | North Dakota | 129,512 |
| 50 | Delaware | 121,460 |
| | District of Columbia | 85,987 |

Source: CQ Press using data from U.S. Bureau of the Census
   "Building Permits Survey" (http://www.census.gov/construction/bps/statemonthly.html)
*Preliminary and unadjusted year-to-date monthly data as of December 2013. Includes single and multifamily privately owned units. All places issuing building permits for privately-owned residential structures. More than 98 percent of all privately-owned residential buildings constructed are in permit-issuing places.

# Median Value of Owner-Occupied Housing in 2012

## National Median = $171,900*

ALPHA ORDER

| RANK | STATE | MEDIAN |
|------|-------|--------|
| 43 | Alabama | $123,200 |
| 8 | Alaska | 245,100 |
| 27 | Arizona | 151,500 |
| 48 | Arkansas | 107,600 |
| 2 | California | 349,400 |
| 12 | Colorado | 234,900 |
| 7 | Connecticut | 267,800 |
| 14 | Delaware | 226,900 |
| 30 | Florida | 148,200 |
| 32 | Georgia | 142,300 |
| 1 | Hawaii | 496,600 |
| 26 | Idaho | 154,500 |
| 22 | Illinois | 170,600 |
| 44 | Indiana | 122,700 |
| 42 | Iowa | 126,300 |
| 38 | Kansas | 130,100 |
| 45 | Kentucky | 120,800 |
| 33 | Louisiana | 139,500 |
| 21 | Maine | 172,300 |
| 6 | Maryland | 279,900 |
| 3 | Massachusetts | 323,800 |
| 46 | Michigan | 115,700 |
| 20 | Minnesota | 178,400 |
| 50 | Mississippi | 99,800 |
| 36 | Missouri | 135,000 |
| 19 | Montana | 184,800 |
| 40 | Nebraska | 128,300 |
| 28 | Nevada | 150,700 |
| 11 | New Hampshire | 236,000 |
| 4 | New Jersey | 311,600 |
| 25 | New Mexico | 157,500 |
| 5 | New York | 280,900 |
| 29 | North Carolina | 150,100 |
| 31 | North Dakota | 142,500 |
| 41 | Ohio | 127,600 |
| 47 | Oklahoma | 114,300 |
| 15 | Oregon | 223,900 |
| 24 | Pennsylvania | 163,800 |
| 13 | Rhode Island | 234,600 |
| 35 | South Carolina | 135,500 |
| 37 | South Dakota | 134,300 |
| 34 | Tennessee | 137,800 |
| 39 | Texas | 129,200 |
| 17 | Utah | 199,700 |
| 16 | Vermont | 216,900 |
| 10 | Virginia | 237,800 |
| 9 | Washington | 243,000 |
| 49 | West Virginia | 100,400 |
| 23 | Wisconsin | 165,200 |
| 18 | Wyoming | 187,400 |

RANK ORDER

| RANK | STATE | MEDIAN |
|------|-------|--------|
| 1 | Hawaii | $496,600 |
| 2 | California | 349,400 |
| 3 | Massachusetts | 323,800 |
| 4 | New Jersey | 311,600 |
| 5 | New York | 280,900 |
| 6 | Maryland | 279,900 |
| 7 | Connecticut | 267,800 |
| 8 | Alaska | 245,100 |
| 9 | Washington | 243,000 |
| 10 | Virginia | 237,800 |
| 11 | New Hampshire | 236,000 |
| 12 | Colorado | 234,900 |
| 13 | Rhode Island | 234,600 |
| 14 | Delaware | 226,900 |
| 15 | Oregon | 223,900 |
| 16 | Vermont | 216,900 |
| 17 | Utah | 199,700 |
| 18 | Wyoming | 187,400 |
| 19 | Montana | 184,800 |
| 20 | Minnesota | 178,400 |
| 21 | Maine | 172,300 |
| 22 | Illinois | 170,600 |
| 23 | Wisconsin | 165,200 |
| 24 | Pennsylvania | 163,800 |
| 25 | New Mexico | 157,500 |
| 26 | Idaho | 154,500 |
| 27 | Arizona | 151,500 |
| 28 | Nevada | 150,700 |
| 29 | North Carolina | 150,100 |
| 30 | Florida | 148,200 |
| 31 | North Dakota | 142,500 |
| 32 | Georgia | 142,300 |
| 33 | Louisiana | 139,500 |
| 34 | Tennessee | 137,800 |
| 35 | South Carolina | 135,500 |
| 36 | Missouri | 135,000 |
| 37 | South Dakota | 134,300 |
| 38 | Kansas | 130,100 |
| 39 | Texas | 129,200 |
| 40 | Nebraska | 128,300 |
| 41 | Ohio | 127,600 |
| 42 | Iowa | 126,300 |
| 43 | Alabama | 123,200 |
| 44 | Indiana | 122,700 |
| 45 | Kentucky | 120,800 |
| 46 | Michigan | 115,700 |
| 47 | Oklahoma | 114,300 |
| 48 | Arkansas | 107,600 |
| 49 | West Virginia | 100,400 |
| 50 | Mississippi | 99,800 |
| | District of Columbia | 460,700 |

Source: U.S. Bureau of the Census
"2012 American Community Survey-Table R2510" (http://www.census.gov/acs/www/index.html)
*Housing units with a mortgage.

# Percent Change in House Prices: 2012 to 2013

## National Percent Change = 8.4% Increase*

ALPHA ORDER

| RANK | STATE | PERCENT CHANGE |
|---|---|---|
| 29 | Alabama | 5.0 |
| 43 | Alaska | 3.1 |
| 3 | Arizona | 15.2 |
| 41 | Arkansas | 3.8 |
| 2 | California | 22.8 |
| 11 | Colorado | 10.3 |
| 47 | Connecticut | 2.3 |
| 46 | Delaware | 2.4 |
| 4 | Florida | 12.0 |
| 9 | Georgia | 11.2 |
| 10 | Hawaii | 10.7 |
| 12 | Idaho | 9.6 |
| 35 | Illinois | 4.3 |
| 27 | Indiana | 5.3 |
| 37 | Iowa | 4.1 |
| 40 | Kansas | 3.9 |
| 34 | Kentucky | 4.5 |
| 39 | Louisiana | 4.0 |
| 32 | Maine | 4.7 |
| 14 | Maryland | 7.2 |
| 22 | Massachusetts | 6.2 |
| 8 | Michigan | 11.4 |
| 13 | Minnesota | 8.9 |
| 50 | Mississippi | 1.3 |
| 25 | Missouri | 5.8 |
| 16 | Montana | 6.8 |
| 28 | Nebraska | 5.2 |
| 1 | Nevada | 25.2 |
| 23 | New Hampshire | 5.9 |
| 42 | New Jersey | 3.3 |
| 48 | New Mexico | 2.1 |
| 44 | New York | 3.0 |
| 19 | North Carolina | 6.6 |
| 16 | North Dakota | 6.8 |
| 35 | Ohio | 4.3 |
| 37 | Oklahoma | 4.1 |
| 7 | Oregon | 11.5 |
| 30 | Pennsylvania | 4.8 |
| 19 | Rhode Island | 6.6 |
| 21 | South Carolina | 6.3 |
| 26 | South Dakota | 5.7 |
| 18 | Tennessee | 6.7 |
| 15 | Texas | 7.1 |
| 6 | Utah | 11.8 |
| 45 | Vermont | 2.7 |
| 30 | Virginia | 4.8 |
| 5 | Washington | 11.9 |
| 23 | West Virginia | 5.9 |
| 33 | Wisconsin | 4.6 |
| 49 | Wyoming | 2.0 |

RANK ORDER

| RANK | STATE | PERCENT CHANGE |
|---|---|---|
| 1 | Nevada | 25.2 |
| 2 | California | 22.8 |
| 3 | Arizona | 15.2 |
| 4 | Florida | 12.0 |
| 5 | Washington | 11.9 |
| 6 | Utah | 11.8 |
| 7 | Oregon | 11.5 |
| 8 | Michigan | 11.4 |
| 9 | Georgia | 11.2 |
| 10 | Hawaii | 10.7 |
| 11 | Colorado | 10.3 |
| 12 | Idaho | 9.6 |
| 13 | Minnesota | 8.9 |
| 14 | Maryland | 7.2 |
| 15 | Texas | 7.1 |
| 16 | Montana | 6.8 |
| 16 | North Dakota | 6.8 |
| 18 | Tennessee | 6.7 |
| 19 | North Carolina | 6.6 |
| 19 | Rhode Island | 6.6 |
| 21 | South Carolina | 6.3 |
| 22 | Massachusetts | 6.2 |
| 23 | New Hampshire | 5.9 |
| 23 | West Virginia | 5.9 |
| 25 | Missouri | 5.8 |
| 26 | South Dakota | 5.7 |
| 27 | Indiana | 5.3 |
| 28 | Nebraska | 5.2 |
| 29 | Alabama | 5.0 |
| 30 | Pennsylvania | 4.8 |
| 30 | Virginia | 4.8 |
| 32 | Maine | 4.7 |
| 33 | Wisconsin | 4.6 |
| 34 | Kentucky | 4.5 |
| 35 | Illinois | 4.3 |
| 35 | Ohio | 4.3 |
| 37 | Iowa | 4.1 |
| 37 | Oklahoma | 4.1 |
| 39 | Louisiana | 4.0 |
| 40 | Kansas | 3.9 |
| 41 | Arkansas | 3.8 |
| 42 | New Jersey | 3.3 |
| 43 | Alaska | 3.1 |
| 44 | New York | 3.0 |
| 45 | Vermont | 2.7 |
| 46 | Delaware | 2.4 |
| 47 | Connecticut | 2.3 |
| 48 | New Mexico | 2.1 |
| 49 | Wyoming | 2.0 |
| 50 | Mississippi | 1.3 |
| | District of Columbia | 11.8 |

Source: Federal Housing Finance Agency
"State HPI Summary" (http://www.fhfa.gov/Default.aspx?Page=215&Type=summary)
*Single-family house prices. As of September 30, 2013.

# Percent Change in House Prices: 2009 to 2013

## National Percent Change = 0.2% Increase*

ALPHA ORDER

| RANK | STATE | PERCENT CHANGE |
|------|-------|----------------|
| 34 | Alabama | (4.3) |
| 9 | Alaska | 5.6 |
| 42 | Arizona | (7.9) |
| 19 | Arkansas | 1.2 |
| 4 | California | 10.3 |
| 2 | Colorado | 13.5 |
| 44 | Connecticut | (8.8) |
| 45 | Delaware | (9.1) |
| 39 | Florida | (6.3) |
| 38 | Georgia | (5.9) |
| 18 | Hawaii | 1.5 |
| 46 | Idaho | (9.9) |
| 49 | Illinois | (10.5) |
| 14 | Indiana | 2.8 |
| 11 | Iowa | 5.0 |
| 17 | Kansas | 1.8 |
| 15 | Kentucky | 2.7 |
| 12 | Louisiana | 4.9 |
| 33 | Maine | (4.0) |
| 37 | Maryland | (5.2) |
| 13 | Massachusetts | 3.0 |
| 9 | Michigan | 5.6 |
| 24 | Minnesota | (0.5) |
| 30 | Mississippi | (3.5) |
| 26 | Missouri | (1.1) |
| 20 | Montana | 0.8 |
| 6 | Nebraska | 8.2 |
| 50 | Nevada | (15.4) |
| 36 | New Hampshire | (4.8) |
| 47 | New Jersey | (10.1) |
| 48 | New Mexico | (10.4) |
| 29 | New York | (3.3) |
| 31 | North Carolina | (3.9) |
| 1 | North Dakota | 27.1 |
| 26 | Ohio | (1.1) |
| 7 | Oklahoma | 6.2 |
| 40 | Oregon | (7.1) |
| 25 | Pennsylvania | (0.7) |
| 41 | Rhode Island | (7.3) |
| 31 | South Carolina | (3.9) |
| 5 | South Dakota | 8.6 |
| 20 | Tennessee | 0.8 |
| 3 | Texas | 11.2 |
| 28 | Utah | (3.1) |
| 16 | Vermont | 2.1 |
| 22 | Virginia | 0.0 |
| 43 | Washington | (8.2) |
| 8 | West Virginia | 5.8 |
| 35 | Wisconsin | (4.7) |
| 22 | Wyoming | 0.0 |

RANK ORDER

| RANK | STATE | PERCENT CHANGE |
|------|-------|----------------|
| 1 | North Dakota | 27.1 |
| 2 | Colorado | 13.5 |
| 3 | Texas | 11.2 |
| 4 | California | 10.3 |
| 5 | South Dakota | 8.6 |
| 6 | Nebraska | 8.2 |
| 7 | Oklahoma | 6.2 |
| 8 | West Virginia | 5.8 |
| 9 | Alaska | 5.6 |
| 9 | Michigan | 5.6 |
| 11 | Iowa | 5.0 |
| 12 | Louisiana | 4.9 |
| 13 | Massachusetts | 3.0 |
| 14 | Indiana | 2.8 |
| 15 | Kentucky | 2.7 |
| 16 | Vermont | 2.1 |
| 17 | Kansas | 1.8 |
| 18 | Hawaii | 1.5 |
| 19 | Arkansas | 1.2 |
| 20 | Montana | 0.8 |
| 20 | Tennessee | 0.8 |
| 22 | Virginia | 0.0 |
| 22 | Wyoming | 0.0 |
| 24 | Minnesota | (0.5) |
| 25 | Pennsylvania | (0.7) |
| 26 | Missouri | (1.1) |
| 26 | Ohio | (1.1) |
| 28 | Utah | (3.1) |
| 29 | New York | (3.3) |
| 30 | Mississippi | (3.5) |
| 31 | North Carolina | (3.9) |
| 31 | South Carolina | (3.9) |
| 33 | Maine | (4.0) |
| 34 | Alabama | (4.3) |
| 35 | Wisconsin | (4.7) |
| 36 | New Hampshire | (4.8) |
| 37 | Maryland | (5.2) |
| 38 | Georgia | (5.9) |
| 39 | Florida | (6.3) |
| 40 | Oregon | (7.1) |
| 41 | Rhode Island | (7.3) |
| 42 | Arizona | (7.9) |
| 43 | Washington | (8.2) |
| 44 | Connecticut | (8.8) |
| 45 | Delaware | (9.1) |
| 46 | Idaho | (9.9) |
| 47 | New Jersey | (10.1) |
| 48 | New Mexico | (10.4) |
| 49 | Illinois | (10.5) |
| 50 | Nevada | (15.4) |

| | | |
|---|---|---|
| | District of Columbia | 28.1 |

Source: Federal Housing Finance Agency
"State HPI Summary" (http://www.fhfa.gov/Default.aspx?Page=215&Type=summary)
*Single-family house prices. As of September 30, 2013.

# Existing Home Sales in 2011

## National Total = 4,880,000 Homes*

ALPHA ORDER

| RANK | STATE | HOMES | % of USA |
|------|-------|-------|----------|
| 24 | Alabama | 72,000 | 1.5% |
| 43 | Alaska | 19,600 | 0.4% |
| 8 | Arizona | 163,600 | 3.4% |
| 28 | Arkansas | 63,200 | 1.3% |
| 1 | California | 475,600 | 9.7% |
| 18 | Colorado | 88,000 | 1.8% |
| 34 | Connecticut | 40,800 | 0.8% |
| 48 | Delaware | 10,800 | 0.2% |
| 3 | Florida | 385,600 | 7.9% |
| 6 | Georgia | 182,400 | 3.7% |
| 42 | Hawaii | 20,000 | 0.4% |
| 35 | Idaho | 38,000 | 0.8% |
| 7 | Illinois | 169,200 | 3.5% |
| 17 | Indiana | 94,400 | 1.9% |
| 30 | Iowa | 53,200 | 1.1% |
| 32 | Kansas | 50,000 | 1.0% |
| 27 | Kentucky | 68,000 | 1.4% |
| 29 | Louisiana | 58,000 | 1.2% |
| 40 | Maine | 21,200 | 0.4% |
| 25 | Maryland | 70,400 | 1.4% |
| 16 | Massachusetts | 96,400 | 2.0% |
| 10 | Michigan | 144,000 | 3.0% |
| 22 | Minnesota | 76,400 | 1.6% |
| 33 | Mississippi | 44,000 | 0.9% |
| 19 | Missouri | 87,600 | 1.8% |
| 41 | Montana | 20,800 | 0.4% |
| 36 | Nebraska | 33,200 | 0.7% |
| 12 | Nevada | 106,000 | 2.2% |
| 43 | New Hampshire | 19,600 | 0.4% |
| 14 | New Jersey | 101,400 | 2.1% |
| 38 | New Mexico | 28,400 | 0.6% |
| 5 | New York | 226,800 | 4.6% |
| 11 | North Carolina | 129,200 | 2.6% |
| 47 | North Dakota | 12,800 | 0.3% |
| 4 | Ohio | 232,000 | 4.8% |
| 23 | Oklahoma | 74,800 | 1.5% |
| 30 | Oregon | 53,200 | 1.1% |
| 9 | Pennsylvania | 155,200 | 3.2% |
| 46 | Rhode Island | 13,200 | 0.3% |
| 26 | South Carolina | 69,600 | 1.4% |
| 45 | South Dakota | 15,200 | 0.3% |
| 15 | Tennessee | 99,600 | 2.0% |
| 2 | Texas | 426,400 | 8.7% |
| 37 | Utah | 30,400 | 0.6% |
| 48 | Vermont | 10,800 | 0.2% |
| 12 | Virginia | 106,000 | 2.2% |
| 20 | Washington | 82,300 | 1.7% |
| 39 | West Virginia | 27,200 | 0.6% |
| 21 | Wisconsin | 77,200 | 1.6% |
| 50 | Wyoming | 8,000 | 0.2% |

RANK ORDER

| RANK | STATE | HOMES | % of USA |
|------|-------|-------|----------|
| 1 | California | 475,600 | 9.7% |
| 2 | Texas | 426,400 | 8.7% |
| 3 | Florida | 385,600 | 7.9% |
| 4 | Ohio | 232,000 | 4.8% |
| 5 | New York | 226,800 | 4.6% |
| 6 | Georgia | 182,400 | 3.7% |
| 7 | Illinois | 169,200 | 3.5% |
| 8 | Arizona | 163,600 | 3.4% |
| 9 | Pennsylvania | 155,200 | 3.2% |
| 10 | Michigan | 144,000 | 3.0% |
| 11 | North Carolina | 129,200 | 2.6% |
| 12 | Nevada | 106,000 | 2.2% |
| 12 | Virginia | 106,000 | 2.2% |
| 14 | New Jersey | 101,400 | 2.1% |
| 15 | Tennessee | 99,600 | 2.0% |
| 16 | Massachusetts | 96,400 | 2.0% |
| 17 | Indiana | 94,400 | 1.9% |
| 18 | Colorado | 88,000 | 1.8% |
| 19 | Missouri | 87,600 | 1.8% |
| 20 | Washington | 82,300 | 1.7% |
| 21 | Wisconsin | 77,200 | 1.6% |
| 22 | Minnesota | 76,400 | 1.6% |
| 23 | Oklahoma | 74,800 | 1.5% |
| 24 | Alabama | 72,000 | 1.5% |
| 25 | Maryland | 70,400 | 1.4% |
| 26 | South Carolina | 69,600 | 1.4% |
| 27 | Kentucky | 68,000 | 1.4% |
| 28 | Arkansas | 63,200 | 1.3% |
| 29 | Louisiana | 58,000 | 1.2% |
| 30 | Iowa | 53,200 | 1.1% |
| 30 | Oregon | 53,200 | 1.1% |
| 32 | Kansas | 50,000 | 1.0% |
| 33 | Mississippi | 44,000 | 0.9% |
| 34 | Connecticut | 40,800 | 0.8% |
| 35 | Idaho | 38,000 | 0.8% |
| 36 | Nebraska | 33,200 | 0.7% |
| 37 | Utah | 30,400 | 0.6% |
| 38 | New Mexico | 28,400 | 0.6% |
| 39 | West Virginia | 27,200 | 0.6% |
| 40 | Maine | 21,200 | 0.4% |
| 41 | Montana | 20,800 | 0.4% |
| 42 | Hawaii | 20,000 | 0.4% |
| 43 | Alaska | 19,600 | 0.4% |
| 43 | New Hampshire | 19,600 | 0.4% |
| 45 | South Dakota | 15,200 | 0.3% |
| 46 | Rhode Island | 13,200 | 0.3% |
| 47 | North Dakota | 12,800 | 0.3% |
| 48 | Delaware | 10,800 | 0.2% |
| 48 | Vermont | 10,800 | 0.2% |
| 50 | Wyoming | 8,000 | 0.2% |
| | District of Columbia | 8,400 | 0.2% |

Source: National Association of Realtors®, Economics and Research Division
   "Existing Home Sales" (http://www.realtor.org/research/research/metroprice)
*Seasonally adjusted preliminary data as of September 2011. Includes existing houses, apartment condos, and co-ops. Excludes new construction. National Association of Realtors has ceased publication of this data.

# Percent Change in Existing Home Sales: 2010 to 2011

## National Percent Change = 17.0% Increase*

<u>ALPHA ORDER</u>

| RANK | STATE | PERCENT CHANGE |
|------|-------|----------------|
| 41 | Alabama | 12.5 |
| 30 | Alaska | 16.7 |
| 14 | Arizona | 22.5 |
| 34 | Arkansas | 16.2 |
| 47 | California | 7.4 |
| 22 | Colorado | 20.2 |
| 47 | Connecticut | 7.4 |
| 7 | Delaware | 28.6 |
| 44 | Florida | 10.6 |
| 16 | Georgia | 22.3 |
| 49 | Hawaii | 6.4 |
| 4 | Idaho | 33.8 |
| 23 | Illinois | 19.8 |
| 26 | Indiana | 18.6 |
| 5 | Iowa | 33.0 |
| 14 | Kansas | 22.5 |
| 32 | Kentucky | 16.4 |
| 21 | Louisiana | 20.8 |
| 40 | Maine | 12.8 |
| 45 | Maryland | 10.0 |
| 42 | Massachusetts | 12.1 |
| 29 | Michigan | 17.3 |
| 11 | Minnesota | 23.2 |
| 38 | Mississippi | 13.4 |
| 19 | Missouri | 21.0 |
| 20 | Montana | 20.9 |
| 3 | Nebraska | 36.1 |
| 24 | Nevada | 19.4 |
| 30 | New Hampshire | 16.7 |
| 39 | New Jersey | 13.0 |
| 32 | New Mexico | 16.4 |
| 36 | New York | 14.5 |
| 28 | North Carolina | 18.3 |
| 1 | North Dakota | 39.1 |
| 13 | Ohio | 22.6 |
| 9 | Oklahoma | 27.2 |
| 12 | Oregon | 23.1 |
| 35 | Pennsylvania | 15.1 |
| 37 | Rhode Island | 13.8 |
| 25 | South Carolina | 19.2 |
| 10 | South Dakota | 26.7 |
| 18 | Tennessee | 21.5 |
| 27 | Texas | 18.4 |
| 2 | Utah | 38.2 |
| 7 | Vermont | 28.6 |
| 50 | Virginia | 3.5 |
| 17 | Washington | 21.7 |
| 46 | West Virginia | 9.7 |
| 6 | Wisconsin | 29.5 |
| 43 | Wyoming | 11.1 |

<u>RANK ORDER</u>

| RANK | STATE | PERCENT CHANGE |
|------|-------|----------------|
| 1 | North Dakota | 39.1 |
| 2 | Utah | 38.2 |
| 3 | Nebraska | 36.1 |
| 4 | Idaho | 33.8 |
| 5 | Iowa | 33.0 |
| 6 | Wisconsin | 29.5 |
| 7 | Delaware | 28.6 |
| 7 | Vermont | 28.6 |
| 9 | Oklahoma | 27.2 |
| 10 | South Dakota | 26.7 |
| 11 | Minnesota | 23.2 |
| 12 | Oregon | 23.1 |
| 13 | Ohio | 22.6 |
| 14 | Arizona | 22.5 |
| 14 | Kansas | 22.5 |
| 16 | Georgia | 22.3 |
| 17 | Washington | 21.7 |
| 18 | Tennessee | 21.5 |
| 19 | Missouri | 21.0 |
| 20 | Montana | 20.9 |
| 21 | Louisiana | 20.8 |
| 22 | Colorado | 20.2 |
| 23 | Illinois | 19.8 |
| 24 | Nevada | 19.4 |
| 25 | South Carolina | 19.2 |
| 26 | Indiana | 18.6 |
| 27 | Texas | 18.4 |
| 28 | North Carolina | 18.3 |
| 29 | Michigan | 17.3 |
| 30 | Alaska | 16.7 |
| 30 | New Hampshire | 16.7 |
| 32 | Kentucky | 16.4 |
| 32 | New Mexico | 16.4 |
| 34 | Arkansas | 16.2 |
| 35 | Pennsylvania | 15.1 |
| 36 | New York | 14.5 |
| 37 | Rhode Island | 13.8 |
| 38 | Mississippi | 13.4 |
| 39 | New Jersey | 13.0 |
| 40 | Maine | 12.8 |
| 41 | Alabama | 12.5 |
| 42 | Massachusetts | 12.1 |
| 43 | Wyoming | 11.1 |
| 44 | Florida | 10.6 |
| 45 | Maryland | 10.0 |
| 46 | West Virginia | 9.7 |
| 47 | California | 7.4 |
| 47 | Connecticut | 7.4 |
| 49 | Hawaii | 6.4 |
| 50 | Virginia | 3.5 |
| | District of Columbia | 5.0 |

Source: National Association of Realtors®, Economics and Research Division
   "Existing Home Sales" (http://www.realtor.org/research/research/metroprice)
*Seasonally adjusted preliminary data as of September 2011.  Includes existing houses, apartment condos, and co-ops.  Excludes new construction.  National Association of Realtors has ceased publication of this data.

# Percent of Owner-Occupied Housing Units with a Mortgage in 2012

## National Percent = 65.7% with Mortgages

ALPHA ORDER

| RANK | STATE | PERCENT |
|------|-------|---------|
| 41 | Alabama | 58.3 |
| 26 | Alaska | 65.2 |
| 22 | Arizona | 66.2 |
| 44 | Arkansas | 57.6 |
| 2 | California | 73.9 |
| 2 | Colorado | 73.9 |
| 10 | Connecticut | 70.7 |
| 12 | Delaware | 69.7 |
| 36 | Florida | 61.1 |
| 13 | Georgia | 69.4 |
| 18 | Hawaii | 67.8 |
| 18 | Idaho | 67.8 |
| 18 | Illinois | 67.8 |
| 17 | Indiana | 68.0 |
| 35 | Iowa | 61.8 |
| 32 | Kansas | 62.5 |
| 39 | Kentucky | 60.8 |
| 47 | Louisiana | 55.5 |
| 29 | Maine | 63.9 |
| 1 | Maryland | 75.2 |
| 6 | Massachusetts | 71.5 |
| 30 | Michigan | 63.6 |
| 14 | Minnesota | 68.7 |
| 49 | Mississippi | 52.9 |
| 28 | Missouri | 64.1 |
| 42 | Montana | 57.9 |
| 31 | Nebraska | 63.1 |
| 5 | Nevada | 71.7 |
| 15 | New Hampshire | 68.5 |
| 11 | New Jersey | 70.1 |
| 40 | New Mexico | 58.4 |
| 27 | New York | 64.4 |
| 23 | North Carolina | 66.0 |
| 48 | North Dakota | 53.5 |
| 24 | Ohio | 65.9 |
| 43 | Oklahoma | 57.8 |
| 16 | Oregon | 68.3 |
| 33 | Pennsylvania | 62.1 |
| 6 | Rhode Island | 71.5 |
| 36 | South Carolina | 61.1 |
| 46 | South Dakota | 57.4 |
| 34 | Tennessee | 61.9 |
| 36 | Texas | 61.1 |
| 4 | Utah | 72.9 |
| 25 | Vermont | 65.6 |
| 8 | Virginia | 71.4 |
| 9 | Washington | 70.8 |
| 50 | West Virginia | 48.3 |
| 21 | Wisconsin | 66.4 |
| 45 | Wyoming | 57.5 |

RANK ORDER

| RANK | STATE | PERCENT |
|------|-------|---------|
| 1 | Maryland | 75.2 |
| 2 | California | 73.9 |
| 2 | Colorado | 73.9 |
| 4 | Utah | 72.9 |
| 5 | Nevada | 71.7 |
| 6 | Massachusetts | 71.5 |
| 6 | Rhode Island | 71.5 |
| 8 | Virginia | 71.4 |
| 9 | Washington | 70.8 |
| 10 | Connecticut | 70.7 |
| 11 | New Jersey | 70.1 |
| 12 | Delaware | 69.7 |
| 13 | Georgia | 69.4 |
| 14 | Minnesota | 68.7 |
| 15 | New Hampshire | 68.5 |
| 16 | Oregon | 68.3 |
| 17 | Indiana | 68.0 |
| 18 | Hawaii | 67.8 |
| 18 | Idaho | 67.8 |
| 18 | Illinois | 67.8 |
| 21 | Wisconsin | 66.4 |
| 22 | Arizona | 66.2 |
| 23 | North Carolina | 66.0 |
| 24 | Ohio | 65.9 |
| 25 | Vermont | 65.6 |
| 26 | Alaska | 65.2 |
| 27 | New York | 64.4 |
| 28 | Missouri | 64.1 |
| 29 | Maine | 63.9 |
| 30 | Michigan | 63.6 |
| 31 | Nebraska | 63.1 |
| 32 | Kansas | 62.5 |
| 33 | Pennsylvania | 62.1 |
| 34 | Tennessee | 61.9 |
| 35 | Iowa | 61.8 |
| 36 | Florida | 61.1 |
| 36 | South Carolina | 61.1 |
| 36 | Texas | 61.1 |
| 39 | Kentucky | 60.8 |
| 40 | New Mexico | 58.4 |
| 41 | Alabama | 58.3 |
| 42 | Montana | 57.9 |
| 43 | Oklahoma | 57.8 |
| 44 | Arkansas | 57.6 |
| 45 | Wyoming | 57.5 |
| 46 | South Dakota | 57.4 |
| 47 | Louisiana | 55.5 |
| 48 | North Dakota | 53.5 |
| 49 | Mississippi | 52.9 |
| 50 | West Virginia | 48.3 |

| District of Columbia | 78.7 |

Source: CQ Press using data from U.S. Bureau of the Census
"2012 American Community Survey-Table B25027" (http://www.census.gov/acs/www/index.html)

# Median Monthly Mortgage Payment in 2012

## National Median = $1,460*

| ALPHA ORDER | | | RANK ORDER | | |
|---|---|---|---|---|---|
| RANK | STATE | MEDIAN | RANK | STATE | MEDIAN |
| 45 | Alabama | $1,104 | 1 | New Jersey | $2,342 |
| 8 | Alaska | 1,831 | 2 | Hawaii | 2,244 |
| 26 | Arizona | 1,320 | 3 | California | 2,119 |
| 49 | Arkansas | 975 | 4 | Connecticut | 2,027 |
| 3 | California | 2,119 | 5 | Massachusetts | 2,010 |
| 14 | Colorado | 1,551 | 6 | New York | 1,967 |
| 4 | Connecticut | 2,027 | 7 | Maryland | 1,918 |
| 16 | Delaware | 1,517 | 8 | Alaska | 1,831 |
| 20 | Florida | 1,425 | 9 | New Hampshire | 1,828 |
| 25 | Georgia | 1,331 | 10 | Rhode Island | 1,774 |
| 2 | Hawaii | 2,244 | 11 | Washington | 1,715 |
| 38 | Idaho | 1,174 | 12 | Virginia | 1,670 |
| 13 | Illinois | 1,618 | 13 | Illinois | 1,618 |
| 47 | Indiana | 1,069 | 14 | Colorado | 1,551 |
| 43 | Iowa | 1,140 | 15 | Oregon | 1,544 |
| 29 | Kansas | 1,250 | 16 | Delaware | 1,517 |
| 46 | Kentucky | 1,084 | 17 | Vermont | 1,478 |
| 41 | Louisiana | 1,148 | 18 | Minnesota | 1,465 |
| 27 | Maine | 1,300 | 19 | Nevada | 1,433 |
| 7 | Maryland | 1,918 | 20 | Florida | 1,425 |
| 5 | Massachusetts | 2,010 | 21 | Utah | 1,396 |
| 30 | Michigan | 1,233 | 22 | Pennsylvania | 1,382 |
| 18 | Minnesota | 1,465 | 23 | Wisconsin | 1,376 |
| 48 | Mississippi | 1,031 | 24 | Texas | 1,374 |
| 37 | Missouri | 1,176 | 25 | Georgia | 1,331 |
| 30 | Montana | 1,233 | 26 | Arizona | 1,320 |
| 32 | Nebraska | 1,229 | 27 | Maine | 1,300 |
| 19 | Nevada | 1,433 | 28 | Wyoming | 1,297 |
| 9 | New Hampshire | 1,828 | 29 | Kansas | 1,250 |
| 1 | New Jersey | 2,342 | 30 | Michigan | 1,233 |
| 36 | New Mexico | 1,193 | 30 | Montana | 1,233 |
| 6 | New York | 1,967 | 32 | Nebraska | 1,229 |
| 34 | North Carolina | 1,209 | 33 | Ohio | 1,215 |
| 35 | North Dakota | 1,205 | 34 | North Carolina | 1,209 |
| 33 | Ohio | 1,215 | 35 | North Dakota | 1,205 |
| 44 | Oklahoma | 1,111 | 36 | New Mexico | 1,193 |
| 15 | Oregon | 1,544 | 37 | Missouri | 1,176 |
| 22 | Pennsylvania | 1,382 | 38 | Idaho | 1,174 |
| 10 | Rhode Island | 1,774 | 38 | South Dakota | 1,174 |
| 40 | South Carolina | 1,155 | 40 | South Carolina | 1,155 |
| 38 | South Dakota | 1,174 | 41 | Louisiana | 1,148 |
| 42 | Tennessee | 1,143 | 42 | Tennessee | 1,143 |
| 24 | Texas | 1,374 | 43 | Iowa | 1,140 |
| 21 | Utah | 1,396 | 44 | Oklahoma | 1,111 |
| 17 | Vermont | 1,478 | 45 | Alabama | 1,104 |
| 12 | Virginia | 1,670 | 46 | Kentucky | 1,084 |
| 11 | Washington | 1,715 | 47 | Indiana | 1,069 |
| 50 | West Virginia | 931 | 48 | Mississippi | 1,031 |
| 23 | Wisconsin | 1,376 | 49 | Arkansas | 975 |
| 28 | Wyoming | 1,297 | 50 | West Virginia | 931 |
| | | | | District of Columbia | 2,262 |

Source: U.S. Bureau of the Census
"2012 American Community Survey-Table R2511" (http://www.census.gov/acs/www/index.html)
*Monthly housing costs for owner-occupied housing.

# Percent of Home Owners Spending 30% or More of Household Income on Housing Costs in 2012
## National Percent = 33.7% of Home Owners*

ALPHA ORDER

| RANK | STATE | PERCENT |
|------|-------|---------|
| 36 | Alabama | 28.1 |
| 26 | Alaska | 31.5 |
| 16 | Arizona | 33.4 |
| 42 | Arkansas | 25.3 |
| 2 | California | 45.5 |
| 22 | Colorado | 32.1 |
| 7 | Connecticut | 38.7 |
| 19 | Delaware | 33.1 |
| 4 | Florida | 42.9 |
| 20 | Georgia | 32.5 |
| 1 | Hawaii | 47.9 |
| 20 | Idaho | 32.5 |
| 13 | Illinois | 35.1 |
| 46 | Indiana | 23.7 |
| 49 | Iowa | 22.3 |
| 43 | Kansas | 25.0 |
| 40 | Kentucky | 26.1 |
| 35 | Louisiana | 28.5 |
| 15 | Maine | 34.4 |
| 18 | Maryland | 33.2 |
| 13 | Massachusetts | 35.1 |
| 29 | Michigan | 30.4 |
| 39 | Minnesota | 26.9 |
| 23 | Mississippi | 31.7 |
| 37 | Missouri | 27.7 |
| 23 | Montana | 31.7 |
| 45 | Nebraska | 24.2 |
| 6 | Nevada | 39.1 |
| 9 | New Hampshire | 37.8 |
| 3 | New Jersey | 43.7 |
| 16 | New Mexico | 33.4 |
| 5 | New York | 39.3 |
| 29 | North Carolina | 30.4 |
| 50 | North Dakota | 17.3 |
| 38 | Ohio | 27.2 |
| 41 | Oklahoma | 26.0 |
| 8 | Oregon | 37.9 |
| 31 | Pennsylvania | 30.1 |
| 9 | Rhode Island | 37.8 |
| 32 | South Carolina | 30.0 |
| 47 | South Dakota | 23.2 |
| 28 | Tennessee | 30.5 |
| 34 | Texas | 29.0 |
| 23 | Utah | 31.7 |
| 12 | Vermont | 35.8 |
| 27 | Virginia | 31.3 |
| 11 | Washington | 36.6 |
| 48 | West Virginia | 22.4 |
| 33 | Wisconsin | 29.8 |
| 44 | Wyoming | 24.4 |

RANK ORDER

| RANK | STATE | PERCENT |
|------|-------|---------|
| 1 | Hawaii | 47.9 |
| 2 | California | 45.5 |
| 3 | New Jersey | 43.7 |
| 4 | Florida | 42.9 |
| 5 | New York | 39.3 |
| 6 | Nevada | 39.1 |
| 7 | Connecticut | 38.7 |
| 8 | Oregon | 37.9 |
| 9 | New Hampshire | 37.8 |
| 9 | Rhode Island | 37.8 |
| 11 | Washington | 36.6 |
| 12 | Vermont | 35.8 |
| 13 | Illinois | 35.1 |
| 13 | Massachusetts | 35.1 |
| 15 | Maine | 34.4 |
| 16 | Arizona | 33.4 |
| 16 | New Mexico | 33.4 |
| 18 | Maryland | 33.2 |
| 19 | Delaware | 33.1 |
| 20 | Georgia | 32.5 |
| 20 | Idaho | 32.5 |
| 22 | Colorado | 32.1 |
| 23 | Mississippi | 31.7 |
| 23 | Montana | 31.7 |
| 23 | Utah | 31.7 |
| 26 | Alaska | 31.5 |
| 27 | Virginia | 31.3 |
| 28 | Tennessee | 30.5 |
| 29 | Michigan | 30.4 |
| 29 | North Carolina | 30.4 |
| 31 | Pennsylvania | 30.1 |
| 32 | South Carolina | 30.0 |
| 33 | Wisconsin | 29.8 |
| 34 | Texas | 29.0 |
| 35 | Louisiana | 28.5 |
| 36 | Alabama | 28.1 |
| 37 | Missouri | 27.7 |
| 38 | Ohio | 27.2 |
| 39 | Minnesota | 26.9 |
| 40 | Kentucky | 26.1 |
| 41 | Oklahoma | 26.0 |
| 42 | Arkansas | 25.3 |
| 43 | Kansas | 25.0 |
| 44 | Wyoming | 24.4 |
| 45 | Nebraska | 24.2 |
| 46 | Indiana | 23.7 |
| 47 | South Dakota | 23.2 |
| 48 | West Virginia | 22.4 |
| 49 | Iowa | 22.3 |
| 50 | North Dakota | 17.3 |

| | District of Columbia | 31.9 |

Source: U.S. Bureau of the Census
   "2012 American Community Survey-Table R2513" (http://www.census.gov/acs/www/index.html)
*For owner-occupied housing units with a mortgage.

# Median Annual Real Estate Taxes in 2012

## National Median = $2,075*

| | ALPHA ORDER | | | | RANK ORDER | |
|---|---|---|---|---|---|---|
| RANK | STATE | MEDIAN | | RANK | STATE | MEDIAN |
| 50 | Alabama | $535 | | 1 | New Jersey | $7,183 |
| 12 | Alaska | 2,904 | | 2 | Connecticut | 5,075 |
| 35 | Arizona | 1,327 | | 3 | New Hampshire | 4,987 |
| 47 | Arkansas | 671 | | 4 | New York | 4,402 |
| 11 | California | 2,945 | | 5 | Illinois | 3,939 |
| 29 | Colorado | 1,478 | | 6 | Rhode Island | 3,842 |
| 2 | Connecticut | 5,075 | | 7 | Massachusetts | 3,821 |
| 38 | Delaware | 1,191 | | 8 | Vermont | 3,652 |
| 27 | Florida | 1,643 | | 9 | Wisconsin | 3,223 |
| 32 | Georgia | 1,390 | | 10 | Maryland | 3,066 |
| 33 | Hawaii | 1,377 | | 11 | California | 2,945 |
| 37 | Idaho | 1,194 | | 12 | Alaska | 2,904 |
| 5 | Illinois | 3,939 | | 13 | Washington | 2,759 |
| 41 | Indiana | 1,053 | | 14 | Oregon | 2,474 |
| 23 | Iowa | 1,834 | | 15 | Texas | 2,473 |
| 24 | Kansas | 1,805 | | 16 | Pennsylvania | 2,448 |
| 43 | Kentucky | 1,015 | | 17 | Nebraska | 2,399 |
| 48 | Louisiana | 653 | | 18 | Minnesota | 2,186 |
| 19 | Maine | 2,127 | | 19 | Maine | 2,127 |
| 10 | Maryland | 3,066 | | 20 | Michigan | 2,114 |
| 7 | Massachusetts | 3,821 | | 21 | Ohio | 1,979 |
| 20 | Michigan | 2,114 | | 22 | Virginia | 1,884 |
| 18 | Minnesota | 2,186 | | 23 | Iowa | 1,834 |
| 45 | Mississippi | 771 | | 24 | Kansas | 1,805 |
| 34 | Missouri | 1,359 | | 25 | South Dakota | 1,797 |
| 28 | Montana | 1,609 | | 26 | North Dakota | 1,737 |
| 17 | Nebraska | 2,399 | | 27 | Florida | 1,643 |
| 30 | Nevada | 1,460 | | 28 | Montana | 1,609 |
| 3 | New Hampshire | 4,987 | | 29 | Colorado | 1,478 |
| 1 | New Jersey | 7,183 | | 30 | Nevada | 1,460 |
| 39 | New Mexico | 1,163 | | 31 | Utah | 1,431 |
| 4 | New York | 4,402 | | 32 | Georgia | 1,390 |
| 36 | North Carolina | 1,286 | | 33 | Hawaii | 1,377 |
| 26 | North Dakota | 1,737 | | 34 | Missouri | 1,359 |
| 21 | Ohio | 1,979 | | 35 | Arizona | 1,327 |
| 44 | Oklahoma | 982 | | 36 | North Carolina | 1,286 |
| 14 | Oregon | 2,474 | | 37 | Idaho | 1,194 |
| 16 | Pennsylvania | 2,448 | | 38 | Delaware | 1,191 |
| 6 | Rhode Island | 3,842 | | 39 | New Mexico | 1,163 |
| 46 | South Carolina | 765 | | 40 | Wyoming | 1,149 |
| 25 | South Dakota | 1,797 | | 41 | Indiana | 1,053 |
| 42 | Tennessee | 1,018 | | 42 | Tennessee | 1,018 |
| 15 | Texas | 2,473 | | 43 | Kentucky | 1,015 |
| 31 | Utah | 1,431 | | 44 | Oklahoma | 982 |
| 8 | Vermont | 3,652 | | 45 | Mississippi | 771 |
| 22 | Virginia | 1,884 | | 46 | South Carolina | 765 |
| 13 | Washington | 2,759 | | 47 | Arkansas | 671 |
| 49 | West Virginia | 587 | | 48 | Louisiana | 653 |
| 9 | Wisconsin | 3,223 | | 49 | West Virginia | 587 |
| 40 | Wyoming | 1,149 | | 50 | Alabama | 535 |
| | | | | | District of Columbia | 2,635 |

Source: U.S. Bureau of the Census
"2012 American Community Survey-Table B25103" (http://www.census.gov/acs/www/index.html)
*For owner-occupied housing units with or without mortgages.

# Homeownership Rate in 2012

## National Rate = 65.4%*

ALPHA ORDER

| RANK | STATE | RATE |
|------|-------|------|
| 11 | Alabama | 71.9 |
| 43 | Alaska | 63.7 |
| 39 | Arizona | 65.3 |
| 37 | Arkansas | 66.0 |
| 49 | California | 54.5 |
| 39 | Colorado | 65.3 |
| 20 | Connecticut | 68.8 |
| 6 | Delaware | 73.4 |
| 31 | Florida | 67.0 |
| 41 | Georgia | 64.3 |
| 47 | Hawaii | 57.2 |
| 8 | Idaho | 73.0 |
| 32 | Illinois | 66.8 |
| 9 | Indiana | 72.1 |
| 17 | Iowa | 70.2 |
| 45 | Kansas | 63.2 |
| 22 | Kentucky | 68.7 |
| 22 | Louisiana | 68.7 |
| 5 | Maine | 74.1 |
| 24 | Maryland | 68.5 |
| 38 | Massachusetts | 65.8 |
| 2 | Michigan | 74.8 |
| 10 | Minnesota | 72.0 |
| 4 | Mississippi | 74.2 |
| 15 | Missouri | 70.8 |
| 27 | Montana | 67.8 |
| 18 | Nebraska | 69.3 |
| 48 | Nevada | 55.7 |
| 2 | New Hampshire | 74.8 |
| 34 | New Jersey | 66.6 |
| 32 | New Mexico | 66.8 |
| 50 | New York | 53.6 |
| 30 | North Carolina | 67.2 |
| 35 | North Dakota | 66.2 |
| 25 | Ohio | 67.9 |
| 20 | Oklahoma | 68.8 |
| 36 | Oregon | 66.1 |
| 14 | Pennsylvania | 71.0 |
| 46 | Rhode Island | 62.1 |
| 12 | South Carolina | 71.5 |
| 19 | South Dakota | 69.2 |
| 25 | Tennessee | 67.9 |
| 41 | Texas | 64.3 |
| 13 | Utah | 71.1 |
| 6 | Vermont | 73.4 |
| 27 | Virginia | 67.8 |
| 44 | Washington | 63.5 |
| 1 | West Virginia | 75.8 |
| 29 | Wisconsin | 67.5 |
| 16 | Wyoming | 70.3 |

RANK ORDER

| RANK | STATE | RATE |
|------|-------|------|
| 1 | West Virginia | 75.8 |
| 2 | Michigan | 74.8 |
| 2 | New Hampshire | 74.8 |
| 4 | Mississippi | 74.2 |
| 5 | Maine | 74.1 |
| 6 | Delaware | 73.4 |
| 6 | Vermont | 73.4 |
| 8 | Idaho | 73.0 |
| 9 | Indiana | 72.1 |
| 10 | Minnesota | 72.0 |
| 11 | Alabama | 71.9 |
| 12 | South Carolina | 71.5 |
| 13 | Utah | 71.1 |
| 14 | Pennsylvania | 71.0 |
| 15 | Missouri | 70.8 |
| 16 | Wyoming | 70.3 |
| 17 | Iowa | 70.2 |
| 18 | Nebraska | 69.3 |
| 19 | South Dakota | 69.2 |
| 20 | Connecticut | 68.8 |
| 20 | Oklahoma | 68.8 |
| 22 | Kentucky | 68.7 |
| 22 | Louisiana | 68.7 |
| 24 | Maryland | 68.5 |
| 25 | Ohio | 67.9 |
| 25 | Tennessee | 67.9 |
| 27 | Montana | 67.8 |
| 27 | Virginia | 67.8 |
| 29 | Wisconsin | 67.5 |
| 30 | North Carolina | 67.2 |
| 31 | Florida | 67.0 |
| 32 | Illinois | 66.8 |
| 32 | New Mexico | 66.8 |
| 34 | New Jersey | 66.6 |
| 35 | North Dakota | 66.2 |
| 36 | Oregon | 66.1 |
| 37 | Arkansas | 66.0 |
| 38 | Massachusetts | 65.8 |
| 39 | Arizona | 65.3 |
| 39 | Colorado | 65.3 |
| 41 | Georgia | 64.3 |
| 41 | Texas | 64.3 |
| 43 | Alaska | 63.7 |
| 44 | Washington | 63.5 |
| 45 | Kansas | 63.2 |
| 46 | Rhode Island | 62.1 |
| 47 | Hawaii | 57.2 |
| 48 | Nevada | 55.7 |
| 49 | California | 54.5 |
| 50 | New York | 53.6 |
| | District of Columbia | 45.0 |

Source: U.S. Bureau of the Census
   "Housing Vacancies and Homeownership, Annual Statistics: 2012"
      (http://www.census.gov/housing/hvs/data/ann12ind.html)
*Percent of households occupied by the owner.

# Percent of Housing Units That Are Renter-Occupied in 2012

## National Percent = 36.1% of Housing Units*

| ALPHA ORDER | | | | RANK ORDER | | |
|---|---|---|---|---|---|---|
| RANK | STATE | PERCENT | | RANK | STATE | PERCENT |
| 38 | Alabama | 31.2 | | 1 | New York | 46.3 |
| 11 | Alaska | 36.6 | | 2 | California | 46.0 |
| 10 | Arizona | 37.4 | | 3 | Nevada | 45.1 |
| 19 | Arkansas | 33.8 | | 4 | Hawaii | 43.1 |
| 2 | California | 46.0 | | 5 | Rhode Island | 40.0 |
| 13 | Colorado | 36.0 | | 6 | Oregon | 38.4 |
| 28 | Connecticut | 33.1 | | 7 | Massachusetts | 37.8 |
| 43 | Delaware | 29.2 | | 8 | Texas | 37.7 |
| 17 | Florida | 34.4 | | 8 | Washington | 37.7 |
| 12 | Georgia | 36.3 | | 10 | Arizona | 37.4 |
| 4 | Hawaii | 43.1 | | 11 | Alaska | 36.6 |
| 37 | Idaho | 31.6 | | 12 | Georgia | 36.3 |
| 26 | Illinois | 33.4 | | 13 | Colorado | 36.0 |
| 41 | Indiana | 30.6 | | 14 | North Dakota | 35.0 |
| 49 | Iowa | 28.1 | | 15 | New Jersey | 34.9 |
| 23 | Kansas | 33.6 | | 16 | North Carolina | 34.6 |
| 29 | Kentucky | 33.0 | | 17 | Florida | 34.4 |
| 18 | Louisiana | 34.3 | | 18 | Louisiana | 34.3 |
| 47 | Maine | 28.6 | | 19 | Arkansas | 33.8 |
| 25 | Maryland | 33.5 | | 19 | Virginia | 33.8 |
| 7 | Massachusetts | 37.8 | | 21 | Nebraska | 33.7 |
| 46 | Michigan | 28.9 | | 21 | Ohio | 33.7 |
| 47 | Minnesota | 28.6 | | 23 | Kansas | 33.6 |
| 36 | Mississippi | 31.8 | | 23 | Oklahoma | 33.6 |
| 33 | Missouri | 32.5 | | 25 | Maryland | 33.5 |
| 30 | Montana | 32.9 | | 26 | Illinois | 33.4 |
| 21 | Nebraska | 33.7 | | 27 | Tennessee | 33.3 |
| 3 | Nevada | 45.1 | | 28 | Connecticut | 33.1 |
| 44 | New Hampshire | 29.1 | | 29 | Kentucky | 33.0 |
| 15 | New Jersey | 34.9 | | 30 | Montana | 32.9 |
| 34 | New Mexico | 32.3 | | 30 | South Dakota | 32.9 |
| 1 | New York | 46.3 | | 32 | Wisconsin | 32.7 |
| 16 | North Carolina | 34.6 | | 33 | Missouri | 32.5 |
| 14 | North Dakota | 35.0 | | 34 | New Mexico | 32.3 |
| 21 | Ohio | 33.7 | | 35 | South Carolina | 31.9 |
| 23 | Oklahoma | 33.6 | | 36 | Mississippi | 31.8 |
| 6 | Oregon | 38.4 | | 37 | Idaho | 31.6 |
| 39 | Pennsylvania | 31.1 | | 38 | Alabama | 31.2 |
| 5 | Rhode Island | 40.0 | | 39 | Pennsylvania | 31.1 |
| 35 | South Carolina | 31.9 | | 40 | Wyoming | 31.0 |
| 30 | South Dakota | 32.9 | | 41 | Indiana | 30.6 |
| 27 | Tennessee | 33.3 | | 42 | Utah | 30.4 |
| 8 | Texas | 37.7 | | 43 | Delaware | 29.2 |
| 42 | Utah | 30.4 | | 44 | New Hampshire | 29.1 |
| 45 | Vermont | 29.0 | | 45 | Vermont | 29.0 |
| 19 | Virginia | 33.8 | | 46 | Michigan | 28.9 |
| 8 | Washington | 37.7 | | 47 | Maine | 28.6 |
| 50 | West Virginia | 28.0 | | 47 | Minnesota | 28.6 |
| 32 | Wisconsin | 32.7 | | 49 | Iowa | 28.1 |
| 40 | Wyoming | 31.0 | | 50 | West Virginia | 28.0 |
| | | | | | District of Columbia | 58.5 |

Source: U.S. Bureau of the Census
   "2012 American Community Survey-Table R2512" (http://www.census.gov/acs/www/index.html)
*For occupied housing units.

# Median Monthly Rental Payment in 2012

## National Median = $884*

ALPHA ORDER

| RANK | STATE | MEDIAN |
|------|-------|--------|
| 41 | Alabama | $689 |
| 5 | Alaska | 1,120 |
| 16 | Arizona | 888 |
| 48 | Arkansas | 640 |
| 2 | California | 1,200 |
| 15 | Colorado | 934 |
| 9 | Connecticut | 1,019 |
| 11 | Delaware | 960 |
| 12 | Florida | 954 |
| 22 | Georgia | 837 |
| 1 | Hawaii | 1,379 |
| 38 | Idaho | 702 |
| 18 | Illinois | 868 |
| 35 | Indiana | 715 |
| 45 | Iowa | 661 |
| 36 | Kansas | 711 |
| 49 | Kentucky | 636 |
| 30 | Louisiana | 747 |
| 31 | Maine | 744 |
| 3 | Maryland | 1,170 |
| 8 | Massachusetts | 1,036 |
| 29 | Michigan | 748 |
| 24 | Minnesota | 813 |
| 44 | Mississippi | 666 |
| 37 | Missouri | 706 |
| 43 | Montana | 681 |
| 40 | Nebraska | 692 |
| 14 | Nevada | 944 |
| 10 | New Hampshire | 967 |
| 4 | New Jersey | 1,148 |
| 28 | New Mexico | 753 |
| 6 | New York | 1,079 |
| 26 | North Carolina | 756 |
| 47 | North Dakota | 644 |
| 39 | Ohio | 700 |
| 42 | Oklahoma | 686 |
| 19 | Oregon | 862 |
| 25 | Pennsylvania | 798 |
| 17 | Rhode Island | 878 |
| 27 | South Carolina | 754 |
| 46 | South Dakota | 651 |
| 34 | Tennessee | 730 |
| 23 | Texas | 831 |
| 21 | Utah | 851 |
| 20 | Vermont | 860 |
| 7 | Virginia | 1,068 |
| 12 | Washington | 954 |
| 50 | West Virginia | 607 |
| 32 | Wisconsin | 743 |
| 33 | Wyoming | 742 |

RANK ORDER

| RANK | STATE | MEDIAN |
|------|-------|--------|
| 1 | Hawaii | $1,379 |
| 2 | California | 1,200 |
| 3 | Maryland | 1,170 |
| 4 | New Jersey | 1,148 |
| 5 | Alaska | 1,120 |
| 6 | New York | 1,079 |
| 7 | Virginia | 1,068 |
| 8 | Massachusetts | 1,036 |
| 9 | Connecticut | 1,019 |
| 10 | New Hampshire | 967 |
| 11 | Delaware | 960 |
| 12 | Florida | 954 |
| 12 | Washington | 954 |
| 14 | Nevada | 944 |
| 15 | Colorado | 934 |
| 16 | Arizona | 888 |
| 17 | Rhode Island | 878 |
| 18 | Illinois | 868 |
| 19 | Oregon | 862 |
| 20 | Vermont | 860 |
| 21 | Utah | 851 |
| 22 | Georgia | 837 |
| 23 | Texas | 831 |
| 24 | Minnesota | 813 |
| 25 | Pennsylvania | 798 |
| 26 | North Carolina | 756 |
| 27 | South Carolina | 754 |
| 28 | New Mexico | 753 |
| 29 | Michigan | 748 |
| 30 | Louisiana | 747 |
| 31 | Maine | 744 |
| 32 | Wisconsin | 743 |
| 33 | Wyoming | 742 |
| 34 | Tennessee | 730 |
| 35 | Indiana | 715 |
| 36 | Kansas | 711 |
| 37 | Missouri | 706 |
| 38 | Idaho | 702 |
| 39 | Ohio | 700 |
| 40 | Nebraska | 692 |
| 41 | Alabama | 689 |
| 42 | Oklahoma | 686 |
| 43 | Montana | 681 |
| 44 | Mississippi | 666 |
| 45 | Iowa | 661 |
| 46 | South Dakota | 651 |
| 47 | North Dakota | 644 |
| 48 | Arkansas | 640 |
| 49 | Kentucky | 636 |
| 50 | West Virginia | 607 |
| | District of Columbia | 1,235 |

Source: U.S. Bureau of the Census
   "2012 American Community Survey-Table R2514" (http://www.census.gov/acs/www/index.html)
*Monthly housing costs for renter-occupied housing.

# Percent of Renters Spending 30% or More of Household Income on Rent and Utilities in 2012
## National Percent = 48.1% of Renters

ALPHA ORDER

| RANK | STATE | PERCENT |
|---|---|---|
| 40 | Alabama | 42.6 |
| 38 | Alaska | 44.3 |
| 13 | Arizona | 47.7 |
| 41 | Arkansas | 42.5 |
| 1 | California | 54.6 |
| 9 | Colorado | 48.6 |
| 8 | Connecticut | 49.6 |
| 30 | Delaware | 45.6 |
| 2 | Florida | 54.2 |
| 13 | Georgia | 47.7 |
| 5 | Hawaii | 50.3 |
| 28 | Idaho | 45.8 |
| 17 | Illinois | 47.0 |
| 31 | Indiana | 45.4 |
| 44 | Iowa | 41.5 |
| 45 | Kansas | 40.9 |
| 39 | Kentucky | 42.7 |
| 29 | Louisiana | 45.7 |
| 16 | Maine | 47.2 |
| 11 | Maryland | 48.0 |
| 19 | Massachusetts | 46.8 |
| 7 | Michigan | 49.8 |
| 33 | Minnesota | 45.3 |
| 35 | Mississippi | 45.2 |
| 20 | Missouri | 46.4 |
| 43 | Montana | 42.3 |
| 46 | Nebraska | 39.4 |
| 9 | Nevada | 48.6 |
| 24 | New Hampshire | 46.1 |
| 3 | New Jersey | 51.3 |
| 25 | New Mexico | 46.0 |
| 4 | New York | 50.4 |
| 36 | North Carolina | 44.8 |
| 50 | North Dakota | 31.7 |
| 31 | Ohio | 45.4 |
| 42 | Oklahoma | 42.4 |
| 6 | Oregon | 50.0 |
| 26 | Pennsylvania | 45.9 |
| 12 | Rhode Island | 47.8 |
| 23 | South Carolina | 46.3 |
| 49 | South Dakota | 36.7 |
| 33 | Tennessee | 45.3 |
| 37 | Texas | 44.5 |
| 20 | Utah | 46.4 |
| 18 | Vermont | 46.9 |
| 20 | Virginia | 46.4 |
| 13 | Washington | 47.7 |
| 47 | West Virginia | 38.9 |
| 26 | Wisconsin | 45.9 |
| 48 | Wyoming | 38.8 |

RANK ORDER

| RANK | STATE | PERCENT |
|---|---|---|
| 1 | California | 54.6 |
| 2 | Florida | 54.2 |
| 3 | New Jersey | 51.3 |
| 4 | New York | 50.4 |
| 5 | Hawaii | 50.3 |
| 6 | Oregon | 50.0 |
| 7 | Michigan | 49.8 |
| 8 | Connecticut | 49.6 |
| 9 | Colorado | 48.6 |
| 9 | Nevada | 48.6 |
| 11 | Maryland | 48.0 |
| 12 | Rhode Island | 47.8 |
| 13 | Arizona | 47.7 |
| 13 | Georgia | 47.7 |
| 13 | Washington | 47.7 |
| 16 | Maine | 47.2 |
| 17 | Illinois | 47.0 |
| 18 | Vermont | 46.9 |
| 19 | Massachusetts | 46.8 |
| 20 | Missouri | 46.4 |
| 20 | Utah | 46.4 |
| 20 | Virginia | 46.4 |
| 23 | South Carolina | 46.3 |
| 24 | New Hampshire | 46.1 |
| 25 | New Mexico | 46.0 |
| 26 | Pennsylvania | 45.9 |
| 26 | Wisconsin | 45.9 |
| 28 | Idaho | 45.8 |
| 29 | Louisiana | 45.7 |
| 30 | Delaware | 45.6 |
| 31 | Indiana | 45.4 |
| 31 | Ohio | 45.4 |
| 33 | Minnesota | 45.3 |
| 33 | Tennessee | 45.3 |
| 35 | Mississippi | 45.2 |
| 36 | North Carolina | 44.8 |
| 37 | Texas | 44.5 |
| 38 | Alaska | 44.3 |
| 39 | Kentucky | 42.7 |
| 40 | Alabama | 42.6 |
| 41 | Arkansas | 42.5 |
| 42 | Oklahoma | 42.4 |
| 43 | Montana | 42.3 |
| 44 | Iowa | 41.5 |
| 45 | Kansas | 40.9 |
| 46 | Nebraska | 39.4 |
| 47 | West Virginia | 38.9 |
| 48 | Wyoming | 38.8 |
| 49 | South Dakota | 36.7 |
| 50 | North Dakota | 31.7 |
| | District of Columbia | 45.8 |

Source: U.S. Bureau of the Census
"2012 American Community Survey-Table R2515" (http://www.census.gov/acs/www/index.html)

# State and Local Government Expenditures
## for Housing and Community Development in 2011
## National Total = $56,121,299,000*

ALPHA ORDER

| RANK | STATE | EXPENDITURES | % of USA |
|---|---|---|---|
| 25 | Alabama | $603,227,000 | 1.1% |
| 28 | Alaska | 383,675,000 | 0.7% |
| 23 | Arizona | 634,630,000 | 1.1% |
| 36 | Arkansas | 257,379,000 | 0.5% |
| 1 | California | 10,189,560,000 | 18.2% |
| 22 | Colorado | 719,777,000 | 1.3% |
| 20 | Connecticut | 876,813,000 | 1.6% |
| 43 | Delaware | 165,953,000 | 0.3% |
| 3 | Florida | 3,329,648,000 | 5.9% |
| 12 | Georgia | 1,363,359,000 | 2.4% |
| 38 | Hawaii | 231,268,000 | 0.4% |
| 45 | Idaho | 147,308,000 | 0.3% |
| 7 | Illinois | 2,328,735,000 | 4.1% |
| 15 | Indiana | 1,209,742,000 | 2.2% |
| 34 | Iowa | 301,554,000 | 0.5% |
| 35 | Kansas | 290,710,000 | 0.5% |
| 27 | Kentucky | 448,476,000 | 0.8% |
| 9 | Louisiana | 1,650,521,000 | 2.9% |
| 33 | Maine | 319,752,000 | 0.6% |
| 14 | Maryland | 1,305,031,000 | 2.3% |
| 8 | Massachusetts | 2,151,517,000 | 3.8% |
| 13 | Michigan | 1,348,458,000 | 2.4% |
| 19 | Minnesota | 948,748,000 | 1.7% |
| 31 | Mississippi | 349,881,000 | 0.6% |
| 21 | Missouri | 742,371,000 | 1.3% |
| 46 | Montana | 147,243,000 | 0.3% |
| 42 | Nebraska | 175,634,000 | 0.3% |
| 37 | Nevada | 251,414,000 | 0.4% |
| 39 | New Hampshire | 230,916,000 | 0.4% |
| 10 | New Jersey | 1,558,752,000 | 2.8% |
| 41 | New Mexico | 215,746,000 | 0.4% |
| 2 | New York | 5,533,718,000 | 9.9% |
| 17 | North Carolina | 1,111,134,000 | 2.0% |
| 49 | North Dakota | 91,863,000 | 0.2% |
| 4 | Ohio | 2,458,002,000 | 4.4% |
| 30 | Oklahoma | 358,501,000 | 0.6% |
| 24 | Oregon | 622,443,000 | 1.1% |
| 6 | Pennsylvania | 2,331,851,000 | 4.2% |
| 40 | Rhode Island | 225,342,000 | 0.4% |
| 26 | South Carolina | 569,312,000 | 1.0% |
| 48 | South Dakota | 111,662,000 | 0.2% |
| 16 | Tennessee | 1,175,533,000 | 2.1% |
| 5 | Texas | 2,447,832,000 | 4.4% |
| 29 | Utah | 364,834,000 | 0.7% |
| 47 | Vermont | 141,596,000 | 0.3% |
| 18 | Virginia | 978,208,000 | 1.7% |
| 11 | Washington | 1,546,020,000 | 2.8% |
| 44 | West Virginia | 150,252,000 | 0.3% |
| 32 | Wisconsin | 338,518,000 | 0.6% |
| 50 | Wyoming | 27,464,000 | 0.0% |

RANK ORDER

| RANK | STATE | EXPENDITURES | % of USA |
|---|---|---|---|
| 1 | California | $10,189,560,000 | 18.2% |
| 2 | New York | 5,533,718,000 | 9.9% |
| 3 | Florida | 3,329,648,000 | 5.9% |
| 4 | Ohio | 2,458,002,000 | 4.4% |
| 5 | Texas | 2,447,832,000 | 4.4% |
| 6 | Pennsylvania | 2,331,851,000 | 4.2% |
| 7 | Illinois | 2,328,735,000 | 4.1% |
| 8 | Massachusetts | 2,151,517,000 | 3.8% |
| 9 | Louisiana | 1,650,521,000 | 2.9% |
| 10 | New Jersey | 1,558,752,000 | 2.8% |
| 11 | Washington | 1,546,020,000 | 2.8% |
| 12 | Georgia | 1,363,359,000 | 2.4% |
| 13 | Michigan | 1,348,458,000 | 2.4% |
| 14 | Maryland | 1,305,031,000 | 2.3% |
| 15 | Indiana | 1,209,742,000 | 2.2% |
| 16 | Tennessee | 1,175,533,000 | 2.1% |
| 17 | North Carolina | 1,111,134,000 | 2.0% |
| 18 | Virginia | 978,208,000 | 1.7% |
| 19 | Minnesota | 948,748,000 | 1.7% |
| 20 | Connecticut | 876,813,000 | 1.6% |
| 21 | Missouri | 742,371,000 | 1.3% |
| 22 | Colorado | 719,777,000 | 1.3% |
| 23 | Arizona | 634,630,000 | 1.1% |
| 24 | Oregon | 622,443,000 | 1.1% |
| 25 | Alabama | 603,227,000 | 1.1% |
| 26 | South Carolina | 569,312,000 | 1.0% |
| 27 | Kentucky | 448,476,000 | 0.8% |
| 28 | Alaska | 383,675,000 | 0.7% |
| 29 | Utah | 364,834,000 | 0.7% |
| 30 | Oklahoma | 358,501,000 | 0.6% |
| 31 | Mississippi | 349,881,000 | 0.6% |
| 32 | Wisconsin | 338,518,000 | 0.6% |
| 33 | Maine | 319,752,000 | 0.6% |
| 34 | Iowa | 301,554,000 | 0.5% |
| 35 | Kansas | 290,710,000 | 0.5% |
| 36 | Arkansas | 257,379,000 | 0.5% |
| 37 | Nevada | 251,414,000 | 0.4% |
| 38 | Hawaii | 231,268,000 | 0.4% |
| 39 | New Hampshire | 230,916,000 | 0.4% |
| 40 | Rhode Island | 225,342,000 | 0.4% |
| 41 | New Mexico | 215,746,000 | 0.4% |
| 42 | Nebraska | 175,634,000 | 0.3% |
| 43 | Delaware | 165,953,000 | 0.3% |
| 44 | West Virginia | 150,252,000 | 0.3% |
| 45 | Idaho | 147,308,000 | 0.3% |
| 46 | Montana | 147,243,000 | 0.3% |
| 47 | Vermont | 141,596,000 | 0.3% |
| 48 | South Dakota | 111,662,000 | 0.2% |
| 49 | North Dakota | 91,863,000 | 0.2% |
| 50 | Wyoming | 27,464,000 | 0.0% |
| | District of Columbia | 659,416,000 | 1.2% |

Source: U.S. Bureau of the Census, Governments Division
   "2011 State and Local Government Finances" (http://www.census.gov/govs/local/)
*Direct general expenditures.

# Per Capita State and Local Government Expenditures
## for Housing and Community Development in 2011
## National Per Capita = $180*

ALPHA ORDER

| RANK | STATE | PER CAPITA |
|---|---|---|
| 31 | Alabama | $126 |
| 1 | Alaska | 530 |
| 40 | Arizona | 98 |
| 47 | Arkansas | 88 |
| 5 | California | 270 |
| 25 | Colorado | 141 |
| 6 | Connecticut | 244 |
| 15 | Delaware | 183 |
| 21 | Florida | 174 |
| 26 | Georgia | 139 |
| 22 | Hawaii | 168 |
| 45 | Idaho | 93 |
| 17 | Illinois | 181 |
| 13 | Indiana | 186 |
| 40 | Iowa | 98 |
| 39 | Kansas | 101 |
| 38 | Kentucky | 103 |
| 2 | Louisiana | 361 |
| 7 | Maine | 241 |
| 10 | Maryland | 223 |
| 3 | Massachusetts | 326 |
| 27 | Michigan | 137 |
| 18 | Minnesota | 177 |
| 35 | Mississippi | 118 |
| 32 | Missouri | 124 |
| 24 | Montana | 148 |
| 42 | Nebraska | 95 |
| 46 | Nevada | 92 |
| 20 | New Hampshire | 175 |
| 19 | New Jersey | 176 |
| 37 | New Mexico | 104 |
| 4 | New York | 284 |
| 36 | North Carolina | 115 |
| 29 | North Dakota | 134 |
| 12 | Ohio | 213 |
| 42 | Oklahoma | 95 |
| 23 | Oregon | 161 |
| 15 | Pennsylvania | 183 |
| 11 | Rhode Island | 214 |
| 33 | South Carolina | 122 |
| 28 | South Dakota | 136 |
| 14 | Tennessee | 184 |
| 42 | Texas | 95 |
| 30 | Utah | 130 |
| 9 | Vermont | 226 |
| 34 | Virginia | 121 |
| 8 | Washington | 227 |
| 48 | West Virginia | 81 |
| 49 | Wisconsin | 59 |
| 50 | Wyoming | 48 |

RANK ORDER

| RANK | STATE | PER CAPITA |
|---|---|---|
| 1 | Alaska | $530 |
| 2 | Louisiana | 361 |
| 3 | Massachusetts | 326 |
| 4 | New York | 284 |
| 5 | California | 270 |
| 6 | Connecticut | 244 |
| 7 | Maine | 241 |
| 8 | Washington | 227 |
| 9 | Vermont | 226 |
| 10 | Maryland | 223 |
| 11 | Rhode Island | 214 |
| 12 | Ohio | 213 |
| 13 | Indiana | 186 |
| 14 | Tennessee | 184 |
| 15 | Delaware | 183 |
| 15 | Pennsylvania | 183 |
| 17 | Illinois | 181 |
| 18 | Minnesota | 177 |
| 19 | New Jersey | 176 |
| 20 | New Hampshire | 175 |
| 21 | Florida | 174 |
| 22 | Hawaii | 168 |
| 23 | Oregon | 161 |
| 24 | Montana | 148 |
| 25 | Colorado | 141 |
| 26 | Georgia | 139 |
| 27 | Michigan | 137 |
| 28 | South Dakota | 136 |
| 29 | North Dakota | 134 |
| 30 | Utah | 130 |
| 31 | Alabama | 126 |
| 32 | Missouri | 124 |
| 33 | South Carolina | 122 |
| 34 | Virginia | 121 |
| 35 | Mississippi | 118 |
| 36 | North Carolina | 115 |
| 37 | New Mexico | 104 |
| 38 | Kentucky | 103 |
| 39 | Kansas | 101 |
| 40 | Arizona | 98 |
| 40 | Iowa | 98 |
| 42 | Nebraska | 95 |
| 42 | Oklahoma | 95 |
| 42 | Texas | 95 |
| 45 | Idaho | 93 |
| 46 | Nevada | 92 |
| 47 | Arkansas | 88 |
| 48 | West Virginia | 81 |
| 49 | Wisconsin | 59 |
| 50 | Wyoming | 48 |

| District of Columbia | 1,065 |
|---|---|

Source: CQ Press using data from U.S. Bureau of the Census, Governments Division
"2011 State and Local Government Finances" (http://www.census.gov/govs/local/)
*Direct general expenditures.

# State & Local Government Spending for Housing and Community Development as a Percent of All State and Local Government Expenditures in 2011
## National Percent = 2.2%*

ALPHA ORDER

| RANK | STATE | PERCENT |
|------|-------|---------|
| 30 | Alabama | 1.7 |
| 3 | Alaska | 3.0 |
| 35 | Arizona | 1.5 |
| 44 | Arkansas | 1.2 |
| 4 | California | 2.9 |
| 30 | Colorado | 1.7 |
| 8 | Connecticut | 2.6 |
| 22 | Delaware | 1.9 |
| 12 | Florida | 2.4 |
| 18 | Georgia | 2.1 |
| 22 | Hawaii | 1.9 |
| 37 | Idaho | 1.4 |
| 17 | Illinois | 2.2 |
| 8 | Indiana | 2.6 |
| 46 | Iowa | 1.1 |
| 41 | Kansas | 1.3 |
| 37 | Kentucky | 1.4 |
| 1 | Louisiana | 3.9 |
| 5 | Maine | 2.8 |
| 8 | Maryland | 2.6 |
| 2 | Massachusetts | 3.5 |
| 25 | Michigan | 1.8 |
| 20 | Minnesota | 2.0 |
| 35 | Mississippi | 1.5 |
| 25 | Missouri | 1.8 |
| 25 | Montana | 1.8 |
| 44 | Nebraska | 1.2 |
| 41 | Nevada | 1.3 |
| 15 | New Hampshire | 2.3 |
| 22 | New Jersey | 1.9 |
| 46 | New Mexico | 1.1 |
| 12 | New York | 2.4 |
| 30 | North Carolina | 1.7 |
| 37 | North Dakota | 1.4 |
| 8 | Ohio | 2.6 |
| 37 | Oklahoma | 1.4 |
| 20 | Oregon | 2.0 |
| 18 | Pennsylvania | 2.1 |
| 12 | Rhode Island | 2.4 |
| 33 | South Carolina | 1.6 |
| 25 | South Dakota | 1.8 |
| 5 | Tennessee | 2.8 |
| 41 | Texas | 1.3 |
| 25 | Utah | 1.8 |
| 15 | Vermont | 2.3 |
| 33 | Virginia | 1.6 |
| 7 | Washington | 2.7 |
| 48 | West Virginia | 1.0 |
| 49 | Wisconsin | 0.7 |
| 50 | Wyoming | 0.4 |

RANK ORDER

| RANK | STATE | PERCENT |
|------|-------|---------|
| 1 | Louisiana | 3.9 |
| 2 | Massachusetts | 3.5 |
| 3 | Alaska | 3.0 |
| 4 | California | 2.9 |
| 5 | Maine | 2.8 |
| 5 | Tennessee | 2.8 |
| 7 | Washington | 2.7 |
| 8 | Connecticut | 2.6 |
| 8 | Indiana | 2.6 |
| 8 | Maryland | 2.6 |
| 8 | Ohio | 2.6 |
| 12 | Florida | 2.4 |
| 12 | New York | 2.4 |
| 12 | Rhode Island | 2.4 |
| 15 | New Hampshire | 2.3 |
| 15 | Vermont | 2.3 |
| 17 | Illinois | 2.2 |
| 18 | Georgia | 2.1 |
| 18 | Pennsylvania | 2.1 |
| 20 | Minnesota | 2.0 |
| 20 | Oregon | 2.0 |
| 22 | Delaware | 1.9 |
| 22 | Hawaii | 1.9 |
| 22 | New Jersey | 1.9 |
| 25 | Michigan | 1.8 |
| 25 | Missouri | 1.8 |
| 25 | Montana | 1.8 |
| 25 | South Dakota | 1.8 |
| 25 | Utah | 1.8 |
| 30 | Alabama | 1.7 |
| 30 | Colorado | 1.7 |
| 30 | North Carolina | 1.7 |
| 33 | South Carolina | 1.6 |
| 33 | Virginia | 1.6 |
| 35 | Arizona | 1.5 |
| 35 | Mississippi | 1.5 |
| 37 | Idaho | 1.4 |
| 37 | Kentucky | 1.4 |
| 37 | North Dakota | 1.4 |
| 37 | Oklahoma | 1.4 |
| 41 | Kansas | 1.3 |
| 41 | Nevada | 1.3 |
| 41 | Texas | 1.3 |
| 44 | Arkansas | 1.2 |
| 44 | Nebraska | 1.2 |
| 46 | Iowa | 1.1 |
| 46 | New Mexico | 1.1 |
| 48 | West Virginia | 1.0 |
| 49 | Wisconsin | 0.7 |
| 50 | Wyoming | 0.4 |

District of Columbia    6.3

Source: CQ Press using data from U.S. Bureau of the Census, Governments Division
   "2011 State and Local Government Finances" (http://www.census.gov/govs/local/)
*As a percent of direct general expenditures.

# XIII. Population

# Apportionment Population in 2010

## National Total = 309,183,463*

ALPHA ORDER

| RANK | STATE | POPULATION | % of USA |
|---|---|---|---|
| 23 | Alabama | 4,802,982 | 1.6% |
| 47 | Alaska | 721,523 | 0.2% |
| 16 | Arizona | 6,412,700 | 2.1% |
| 32 | Arkansas | 2,926,229 | 0.9% |
| 1 | California | 37,341,989 | 12.1% |
| 22 | Colorado | 5,044,930 | 1.6% |
| 29 | Connecticut | 3,581,628 | 1.2% |
| 45 | Delaware | 900,877 | 0.3% |
| 4 | Florida | 18,900,773 | 6.1% |
| 9 | Georgia | 9,727,566 | 3.1% |
| 40 | Hawaii | 1,366,862 | 0.4% |
| 39 | Idaho | 1,573,499 | 0.5% |
| 5 | Illinois | 12,864,380 | 4.2% |
| 15 | Indiana | 6,501,582 | 2.1% |
| 30 | Iowa | 3,053,787 | 1.0% |
| 33 | Kansas | 2,863,813 | 0.9% |
| 26 | Kentucky | 4,350,606 | 1.4% |
| 25 | Louisiana | 4,553,962 | 1.5% |
| 41 | Maine | 1,333,074 | 0.4% |
| 19 | Maryland | 5,789,929 | 1.9% |
| 14 | Massachusetts | 6,559,644 | 2.1% |
| 8 | Michigan | 9,911,626 | 3.2% |
| 21 | Minnesota | 5,314,879 | 1.7% |
| 31 | Mississippi | 2,978,240 | 1.0% |
| 18 | Missouri | 6,011,478 | 1.9% |
| 44 | Montana | 994,416 | 0.3% |
| 38 | Nebraska | 1,831,825 | 0.6% |
| 35 | Nevada | 2,709,432 | 0.9% |
| 42 | New Hampshire | 1,321,445 | 0.4% |
| 11 | New Jersey | 8,807,501 | 2.8% |
| 36 | New Mexico | 2,067,273 | 0.7% |
| 3 | New York | 19,421,055 | 6.3% |
| 10 | North Carolina | 9,565,781 | 3.1% |
| 48 | North Dakota | 675,905 | 0.2% |
| 7 | Ohio | 11,568,495 | 3.7% |
| 28 | Oklahoma | 3,764,882 | 1.2% |
| 27 | Oregon | 3,848,606 | 1.2% |
| 6 | Pennsylvania | 12,734,905 | 4.1% |
| 43 | Rhode Island | 1,055,247 | 0.3% |
| 24 | South Carolina | 4,645,975 | 1.5% |
| 46 | South Dakota | 819,761 | 0.3% |
| 17 | Tennessee | 6,375,431 | 2.1% |
| 2 | Texas | 25,268,418 | 8.2% |
| 34 | Utah | 2,770,765 | 0.9% |
| 49 | Vermont | 630,337 | 0.2% |
| 12 | Virginia | 8,037,736 | 2.6% |
| 13 | Washington | 6,753,369 | 2.2% |
| 37 | West Virginia | 1,859,815 | 0.6% |
| 20 | Wisconsin | 5,698,230 | 1.8% |
| 50 | Wyoming | 568,300 | 0.2% |

RANK ORDER

| RANK | STATE | POPULATION | % of USA |
|---|---|---|---|
| 1 | California | 37,341,989 | 12.1% |
| 2 | Texas | 25,268,418 | 8.2% |
| 3 | New York | 19,421,055 | 6.3% |
| 4 | Florida | 18,900,773 | 6.1% |
| 5 | Illinois | 12,864,380 | 4.2% |
| 6 | Pennsylvania | 12,734,905 | 4.1% |
| 7 | Ohio | 11,568,495 | 3.7% |
| 8 | Michigan | 9,911,626 | 3.2% |
| 9 | Georgia | 9,727,566 | 3.1% |
| 10 | North Carolina | 9,565,781 | 3.1% |
| 11 | New Jersey | 8,807,501 | 2.8% |
| 12 | Virginia | 8,037,736 | 2.6% |
| 13 | Washington | 6,753,369 | 2.2% |
| 14 | Massachusetts | 6,559,644 | 2.1% |
| 15 | Indiana | 6,501,582 | 2.1% |
| 16 | Arizona | 6,412,700 | 2.1% |
| 17 | Tennessee | 6,375,431 | 2.1% |
| 18 | Missouri | 6,011,478 | 1.9% |
| 19 | Maryland | 5,789,929 | 1.9% |
| 20 | Wisconsin | 5,698,230 | 1.8% |
| 21 | Minnesota | 5,314,879 | 1.7% |
| 22 | Colorado | 5,044,930 | 1.6% |
| 23 | Alabama | 4,802,982 | 1.6% |
| 24 | South Carolina | 4,645,975 | 1.5% |
| 25 | Louisiana | 4,553,962 | 1.5% |
| 26 | Kentucky | 4,350,606 | 1.4% |
| 27 | Oregon | 3,848,606 | 1.2% |
| 28 | Oklahoma | 3,764,882 | 1.2% |
| 29 | Connecticut | 3,581,628 | 1.2% |
| 30 | Iowa | 3,053,787 | 1.0% |
| 31 | Mississippi | 2,978,240 | 1.0% |
| 32 | Arkansas | 2,926,229 | 0.9% |
| 33 | Kansas | 2,863,813 | 0.9% |
| 34 | Utah | 2,770,765 | 0.9% |
| 35 | Nevada | 2,709,432 | 0.9% |
| 36 | New Mexico | 2,067,273 | 0.7% |
| 37 | West Virginia | 1,859,815 | 0.6% |
| 38 | Nebraska | 1,831,825 | 0.6% |
| 39 | Idaho | 1,573,499 | 0.5% |
| 40 | Hawaii | 1,366,862 | 0.4% |
| 41 | Maine | 1,333,074 | 0.4% |
| 42 | New Hampshire | 1,321,445 | 0.4% |
| 43 | Rhode Island | 1,055,247 | 0.3% |
| 44 | Montana | 994,416 | 0.3% |
| 45 | Delaware | 900,877 | 0.3% |
| 46 | South Dakota | 819,761 | 0.3% |
| 47 | Alaska | 721,523 | 0.2% |
| 48 | North Dakota | 675,905 | 0.2% |
| 49 | Vermont | 630,337 | 0.2% |
| 50 | Wyoming | 568,300 | 0.2% |
| | District of Columbia** | NA | NA |

Source: U.S. Bureau of the Census
    "Congressional Apportionment" (http://www.census.gov/population/apportionment/)
*Apportionment population includes the resident population for the 50 states, as ascertained by the Twenty-Third Decennial Census under Title 13, United States Code, and counts of overseas U.S. military and federal civilian employees (and their dependents living with them) allocated to their home state, as reported by the employing federal agencies. The apportionment population excludes the population of the District of Columbia. **Not applicable.

# Population in 2013

## National Total = 316,128,839*

ALPHA ORDER

| RANK | STATE | POPULATION | % of USA |
|---|---|---|---|
| 23 | Alabama | 4,833,722 | 1.5% |
| 47 | Alaska | 735,132 | 0.2% |
| 15 | Arizona | 6,626,624 | 2.1% |
| 32 | Arkansas | 2,959,373 | 0.9% |
| 1 | California | 38,332,521 | 12.1% |
| 22 | Colorado | 5,268,367 | 1.7% |
| 29 | Connecticut | 3,596,080 | 1.1% |
| 45 | Delaware | 925,749 | 0.3% |
| 4 | Florida | 19,552,860 | 6.2% |
| 8 | Georgia | 9,992,167 | 3.2% |
| 40 | Hawaii | 1,404,054 | 0.4% |
| 39 | Idaho | 1,612,136 | 0.5% |
| 5 | Illinois | 12,882,135 | 4.1% |
| 16 | Indiana | 6,570,902 | 2.1% |
| 30 | Iowa | 3,090,416 | 1.0% |
| 34 | Kansas | 2,893,957 | 0.9% |
| 26 | Kentucky | 4,395,295 | 1.4% |
| 25 | Louisiana | 4,625,470 | 1.5% |
| 41 | Maine | 1,328,302 | 0.4% |
| 19 | Maryland | 5,928,814 | 1.9% |
| 14 | Massachusetts | 6,692,824 | 2.1% |
| 9 | Michigan | 9,895,622 | 3.1% |
| 21 | Minnesota | 5,420,380 | 1.7% |
| 31 | Mississippi | 2,991,207 | 0.9% |
| 18 | Missouri | 6,044,171 | 1.9% |
| 44 | Montana | 1,015,165 | 0.3% |
| 37 | Nebraska | 1,868,516 | 0.6% |
| 35 | Nevada | 2,790,136 | 0.9% |
| 42 | New Hampshire | 1,323,459 | 0.4% |
| 11 | New Jersey | 8,899,339 | 2.8% |
| 36 | New Mexico | 2,085,287 | 0.7% |
| 3 | New York | 19,651,127 | 6.2% |
| 10 | North Carolina | 9,848,060 | 3.1% |
| 48 | North Dakota | 723,393 | 0.2% |
| 7 | Ohio | 11,570,808 | 3.7% |
| 28 | Oklahoma | 3,850,568 | 1.2% |
| 27 | Oregon | 3,930,065 | 1.2% |
| 6 | Pennsylvania | 12,773,801 | 4.0% |
| 43 | Rhode Island | 1,051,511 | 0.3% |
| 24 | South Carolina | 4,774,839 | 1.5% |
| 46 | South Dakota | 844,877 | 0.3% |
| 17 | Tennessee | 6,495,978 | 2.1% |
| 2 | Texas | 26,448,193 | 8.4% |
| 33 | Utah | 2,900,872 | 0.9% |
| 49 | Vermont | 626,630 | 0.2% |
| 12 | Virginia | 8,260,405 | 2.6% |
| 13 | Washington | 6,971,406 | 2.2% |
| 38 | West Virginia | 1,854,304 | 0.6% |
| 20 | Wisconsin | 5,742,713 | 1.8% |
| 50 | Wyoming | 582,658 | 0.2% |

RANK ORDER

| RANK | STATE | POPULATION | % of USA |
|---|---|---|---|
| 1 | California | 38,332,521 | 12.1% |
| 2 | Texas | 26,448,193 | 8.4% |
| 3 | New York | 19,651,127 | 6.2% |
| 4 | Florida | 19,552,860 | 6.2% |
| 5 | Illinois | 12,882,135 | 4.1% |
| 6 | Pennsylvania | 12,773,801 | 4.0% |
| 7 | Ohio | 11,570,808 | 3.7% |
| 8 | Georgia | 9,992,167 | 3.2% |
| 9 | Michigan | 9,895,622 | 3.1% |
| 10 | North Carolina | 9,848,060 | 3.1% |
| 11 | New Jersey | 8,899,339 | 2.8% |
| 12 | Virginia | 8,260,405 | 2.6% |
| 13 | Washington | 6,971,406 | 2.2% |
| 14 | Massachusetts | 6,692,824 | 2.1% |
| 15 | Arizona | 6,626,624 | 2.1% |
| 16 | Indiana | 6,570,902 | 2.1% |
| 17 | Tennessee | 6,495,978 | 2.1% |
| 18 | Missouri | 6,044,171 | 1.9% |
| 19 | Maryland | 5,928,814 | 1.9% |
| 20 | Wisconsin | 5,742,713 | 1.8% |
| 21 | Minnesota | 5,420,380 | 1.7% |
| 22 | Colorado | 5,268,367 | 1.7% |
| 23 | Alabama | 4,833,722 | 1.5% |
| 24 | South Carolina | 4,774,839 | 1.5% |
| 25 | Louisiana | 4,625,470 | 1.5% |
| 26 | Kentucky | 4,395,295 | 1.4% |
| 27 | Oregon | 3,930,065 | 1.2% |
| 28 | Oklahoma | 3,850,568 | 1.2% |
| 29 | Connecticut | 3,596,080 | 1.1% |
| 30 | Iowa | 3,090,416 | 1.0% |
| 31 | Mississippi | 2,991,207 | 0.9% |
| 32 | Arkansas | 2,959,373 | 0.9% |
| 33 | Utah | 2,900,872 | 0.9% |
| 34 | Kansas | 2,893,957 | 0.9% |
| 35 | Nevada | 2,790,136 | 0.9% |
| 36 | New Mexico | 2,085,287 | 0.7% |
| 37 | Nebraska | 1,868,516 | 0.6% |
| 38 | West Virginia | 1,854,304 | 0.6% |
| 39 | Idaho | 1,612,136 | 0.5% |
| 40 | Hawaii | 1,404,054 | 0.4% |
| 41 | Maine | 1,328,302 | 0.4% |
| 42 | New Hampshire | 1,323,459 | 0.4% |
| 43 | Rhode Island | 1,051,511 | 0.3% |
| 44 | Montana | 1,015,165 | 0.3% |
| 45 | Delaware | 925,749 | 0.3% |
| 46 | South Dakota | 844,877 | 0.3% |
| 47 | Alaska | 735,132 | 0.2% |
| 48 | North Dakota | 723,393 | 0.2% |
| 49 | Vermont | 626,630 | 0.2% |
| 50 | Wyoming | 582,658 | 0.2% |
| | District of Columbia | 646,449 | 0.2% |

Source: U.S. Bureau of the Census
  "Population Estimates" (December 2013, http://www.census.gov/popest/data/index.html)
*Resident population estimate as of July 1, 2013.

# Population in 2012

## National Total = 313,873,685*

ALPHA ORDER

| RANK | STATE | POPULATION | % of USA |
|---|---|---|---|
| 23 | Alabama | 4,817,528 | 1.5% |
| 47 | Alaska | 730,307 | 0.2% |
| 15 | Arizona | 6,551,149 | 2.1% |
| 32 | Arkansas | 2,949,828 | 0.9% |
| 1 | California | 37,999,878 | 12.1% |
| 22 | Colorado | 5,189,458 | 1.7% |
| 29 | Connecticut | 3,591,765 | 1.1% |
| 45 | Delaware | 917,053 | 0.3% |
| 4 | Florida | 19,320,749 | 6.2% |
| 8 | Georgia | 9,915,646 | 3.2% |
| 40 | Hawaii | 1,390,090 | 0.4% |
| 39 | Idaho | 1,595,590 | 0.5% |
| 5 | Illinois | 12,868,192 | 4.1% |
| 16 | Indiana | 6,537,782 | 2.1% |
| 30 | Iowa | 3,075,039 | 1.0% |
| 33 | Kansas | 2,885,398 | 0.9% |
| 26 | Kentucky | 4,379,730 | 1.4% |
| 25 | Louisiana | 4,602,134 | 1.5% |
| 41 | Maine | 1,328,501 | 0.4% |
| 19 | Maryland | 5,884,868 | 1.9% |
| 14 | Massachusetts | 6,645,303 | 2.1% |
| 9 | Michigan | 9,882,519 | 3.1% |
| 21 | Minnesota | 5,379,646 | 1.7% |
| 31 | Mississippi | 2,986,450 | 1.0% |
| 18 | Missouri | 6,024,522 | 1.9% |
| 44 | Montana | 1,005,494 | 0.3% |
| 38 | Nebraska | 1,855,350 | 0.6% |
| 35 | Nevada | 2,754,354 | 0.9% |
| 42 | New Hampshire | 1,321,617 | 0.4% |
| 11 | New Jersey | 8,867,749 | 2.8% |
| 36 | New Mexico | 2,083,540 | 0.7% |
| 3 | New York | 19,576,125 | 6.2% |
| 10 | North Carolina | 9,748,364 | 3.1% |
| 48 | North Dakota | 701,345 | 0.2% |
| 7 | Ohio | 11,553,031 | 3.7% |
| 28 | Oklahoma | 3,815,780 | 1.2% |
| 27 | Oregon | 3,899,801 | 1.2% |
| 6 | Pennsylvania | 12,764,475 | 4.1% |
| 43 | Rhode Island | 1,050,304 | 0.3% |
| 24 | South Carolina | 4,723,417 | 1.5% |
| 46 | South Dakota | 834,047 | 0.3% |
| 17 | Tennessee | 6,454,914 | 2.1% |
| 2 | Texas | 26,060,796 | 8.3% |
| 34 | Utah | 2,854,871 | 0.9% |
| 49 | Vermont | 625,953 | 0.2% |
| 12 | Virginia | 8,186,628 | 2.6% |
| 13 | Washington | 6,895,318 | 2.2% |
| 37 | West Virginia | 1,856,680 | 0.6% |
| 20 | Wisconsin | 5,724,554 | 1.8% |
| 50 | Wyoming | 576,626 | 0.2% |

RANK ORDER

| RANK | STATE | POPULATION | % of USA |
|---|---|---|---|
| 1 | California | 37,999,878 | 12.1% |
| 2 | Texas | 26,060,796 | 8.3% |
| 3 | New York | 19,576,125 | 6.2% |
| 4 | Florida | 19,320,749 | 6.2% |
| 5 | Illinois | 12,868,192 | 4.1% |
| 6 | Pennsylvania | 12,764,475 | 4.1% |
| 7 | Ohio | 11,553,031 | 3.7% |
| 8 | Georgia | 9,915,646 | 3.2% |
| 9 | Michigan | 9,882,519 | 3.1% |
| 10 | North Carolina | 9,748,364 | 3.1% |
| 11 | New Jersey | 8,867,749 | 2.8% |
| 12 | Virginia | 8,186,628 | 2.6% |
| 13 | Washington | 6,895,318 | 2.2% |
| 14 | Massachusetts | 6,645,303 | 2.1% |
| 15 | Arizona | 6,551,149 | 2.1% |
| 16 | Indiana | 6,537,782 | 2.1% |
| 17 | Tennessee | 6,454,914 | 2.1% |
| 18 | Missouri | 6,024,522 | 1.9% |
| 19 | Maryland | 5,884,868 | 1.9% |
| 20 | Wisconsin | 5,724,554 | 1.8% |
| 21 | Minnesota | 5,379,646 | 1.7% |
| 22 | Colorado | 5,189,458 | 1.7% |
| 23 | Alabama | 4,817,528 | 1.5% |
| 24 | South Carolina | 4,723,417 | 1.5% |
| 25 | Louisiana | 4,602,134 | 1.5% |
| 26 | Kentucky | 4,379,730 | 1.4% |
| 27 | Oregon | 3,899,801 | 1.2% |
| 28 | Oklahoma | 3,815,780 | 1.2% |
| 29 | Connecticut | 3,591,765 | 1.1% |
| 30 | Iowa | 3,075,039 | 1.0% |
| 31 | Mississippi | 2,986,450 | 1.0% |
| 32 | Arkansas | 2,949,828 | 0.9% |
| 33 | Kansas | 2,885,398 | 0.9% |
| 34 | Utah | 2,854,871 | 0.9% |
| 35 | Nevada | 2,754,354 | 0.9% |
| 36 | New Mexico | 2,083,540 | 0.7% |
| 37 | West Virginia | 1,856,680 | 0.6% |
| 38 | Nebraska | 1,855,350 | 0.6% |
| 39 | Idaho | 1,595,590 | 0.5% |
| 40 | Hawaii | 1,390,090 | 0.4% |
| 41 | Maine | 1,328,501 | 0.4% |
| 42 | New Hampshire | 1,321,617 | 0.4% |
| 43 | Rhode Island | 1,050,304 | 0.3% |
| 44 | Montana | 1,005,494 | 0.3% |
| 45 | Delaware | 917,053 | 0.3% |
| 46 | South Dakota | 834,047 | 0.3% |
| 47 | Alaska | 730,307 | 0.2% |
| 48 | North Dakota | 701,345 | 0.2% |
| 49 | Vermont | 625,953 | 0.2% |
| 50 | Wyoming | 576,626 | 0.2% |
|  | District of Columbia | 633,427 | 0.2% |

Source: U.S. Bureau of the Census
 "Population Estimates" (December 2013, http://www.census.gov/popest/data/index.html)
*Resident population. Revised estimates of July 1, 2013.

# Numerical Population Change: 2012 to 2013

## National Total = 2,255,154 Increase*

ALPHA ORDER

| RANK | STATE | GAIN/LOSS | % of USA |
|------|-------|-----------|----------|
| 28 | Alabama | 16,194 | 0.7% |
| 42 | Alaska | 4,825 | 0.2% |
| 8 | Arizona | 75,475 | 3.3% |
| 37 | Arkansas | 9,545 | 0.4% |
| 2 | California | 332,643 | 14.8% |
| 5 | Colorado | 78,909 | 3.5% |
| 44 | Connecticut | 4,315 | 0.2% |
| 39 | Delaware | 8,696 | 0.4% |
| 3 | Florida | 232,111 | 10.3% |
| 6 | Georgia | 76,521 | 3.4% |
| 31 | Hawaii | 13,964 | 0.6% |
| 27 | Idaho | 16,546 | 0.7% |
| 32 | Illinois | 13,943 | 0.6% |
| 19 | Indiana | 33,120 | 1.5% |
| 30 | Iowa | 15,377 | 0.7% |
| 40 | Kansas | 8,559 | 0.4% |
| 29 | Kentucky | 15,565 | 0.7% |
| 22 | Louisiana | 23,336 | 1.0% |
| 49 | Maine | (199) | |
| 14 | Maryland | 43,946 | 1.9% |
| 12 | Massachusetts | 47,521 | 2.1% |
| 34 | Michigan | 13,103 | 0.6% |
| 16 | Minnesota | 40,734 | 1.8% |
| 43 | Mississippi | 4,757 | 0.2% |
| 24 | Missouri | 19,649 | 0.9% |
| 36 | Montana | 9,671 | 0.4% |
| 33 | Nebraska | 13,166 | 0.6% |
| 17 | Nevada | 35,782 | 1.6% |
| 45 | New Hampshire | 1,842 | 0.1% |
| 20 | New Jersey | 31,590 | 1.4% |
| 46 | New Mexico | 1,747 | 0.1% |
| 9 | New York | 75,002 | 3.3% |
| 4 | North Carolina | 99,696 | 4.4% |
| 23 | North Dakota | 22,048 | 1.0% |
| 26 | Ohio | 17,777 | 0.8% |
| 18 | Oklahoma | 34,788 | 1.5% |
| 21 | Oregon | 30,264 | 1.3% |
| 38 | Pennsylvania | 9,326 | 0.4% |
| 47 | Rhode Island | 1,207 | 0.1% |
| 11 | South Carolina | 51,422 | 2.3% |
| 35 | South Dakota | 10,830 | 0.5% |
| 15 | Tennessee | 41,064 | 1.8% |
| 1 | Texas | 387,397 | 17.2% |
| 13 | Utah | 46,001 | 2.0% |
| 48 | Vermont | 677 | 0.0% |
| 10 | Virginia | 73,777 | 3.3% |
| 7 | Washington | 76,088 | 3.4% |
| 50 | West Virginia | (2,376) | |
| 25 | Wisconsin | 18,159 | 0.8% |
| 41 | Wyoming | 6,032 | 0.3% |

RANK ORDER

| RANK | STATE | GAIN/LOSS | % of USA |
|------|-------|-----------|----------|
| 1 | Texas | 387,397 | 17.2% |
| 2 | California | 332,643 | 14.8% |
| 3 | Florida | 232,111 | 10.3% |
| 4 | North Carolina | 99,696 | 4.4% |
| 5 | Colorado | 78,909 | 3.5% |
| 6 | Georgia | 76,521 | 3.4% |
| 7 | Washington | 76,088 | 3.4% |
| 8 | Arizona | 75,475 | 3.3% |
| 9 | New York | 75,002 | 3.3% |
| 10 | Virginia | 73,777 | 3.3% |
| 11 | South Carolina | 51,422 | 2.3% |
| 12 | Massachusetts | 47,521 | 2.1% |
| 13 | Utah | 46,001 | 2.0% |
| 14 | Maryland | 43,946 | 1.9% |
| 15 | Tennessee | 41,064 | 1.8% |
| 16 | Minnesota | 40,734 | 1.8% |
| 17 | Nevada | 35,782 | 1.6% |
| 18 | Oklahoma | 34,788 | 1.5% |
| 19 | Indiana | 33,120 | 1.5% |
| 20 | New Jersey | 31,590 | 1.4% |
| 21 | Oregon | 30,264 | 1.3% |
| 22 | Louisiana | 23,336 | 1.0% |
| 23 | North Dakota | 22,048 | 1.0% |
| 24 | Missouri | 19,649 | 0.9% |
| 25 | Wisconsin | 18,159 | 0.8% |
| 26 | Ohio | 17,777 | 0.8% |
| 27 | Idaho | 16,546 | 0.7% |
| 28 | Alabama | 16,194 | 0.7% |
| 29 | Kentucky | 15,565 | 0.7% |
| 30 | Iowa | 15,377 | 0.7% |
| 31 | Hawaii | 13,964 | 0.6% |
| 32 | Illinois | 13,943 | 0.6% |
| 33 | Nebraska | 13,166 | 0.6% |
| 34 | Michigan | 13,103 | 0.6% |
| 35 | South Dakota | 10,830 | 0.5% |
| 36 | Montana | 9,671 | 0.4% |
| 37 | Arkansas | 9,545 | 0.4% |
| 38 | Pennsylvania | 9,326 | 0.4% |
| 39 | Delaware | 8,696 | 0.4% |
| 40 | Kansas | 8,559 | 0.4% |
| 41 | Wyoming | 6,032 | 0.3% |
| 42 | Alaska | 4,825 | 0.2% |
| 43 | Mississippi | 4,757 | 0.2% |
| 44 | Connecticut | 4,315 | 0.2% |
| 45 | New Hampshire | 1,842 | 0.1% |
| 46 | New Mexico | 1,747 | 0.1% |
| 47 | Rhode Island | 1,207 | 0.1% |
| 48 | Vermont | 677 | 0.0% |
| 49 | Maine | (199) | |
| 50 | West Virginia | (2,376) | |
| | District of Columbia | 13,022 | 0.6% |

Source: CQ Press using data from U.S. Bureau of the Census
 "Population Estimates" (December 2013, http://www.census.gov/popest/data/index.html)
*Resident population from July 1, 2012 to July 1, 2013.

# Percent Change in Population: 2012 to 2013

## National Percent Change = 0.7% Increase*

ALPHA ORDER

| RANK | STATE | PERCENT CHANGE |
|------|-------|----------------|
| 34 | Alabama | 0.3 |
| 23 | Alaska | 0.7 |
| 7 | Arizona | 1.2 |
| 34 | Arkansas | 0.3 |
| 16 | California | 0.9 |
| 3 | Colorado | 1.5 |
| 41 | Connecticut | 0.1 |
| 16 | Delaware | 0.9 |
| 7 | Florida | 1.2 |
| 20 | Georgia | 0.8 |
| 11 | Hawaii | 1.0 |
| 11 | Idaho | 1.0 |
| 41 | Illinois | 0.1 |
| 28 | Indiana | 0.5 |
| 28 | Iowa | 0.5 |
| 34 | Kansas | 0.3 |
| 31 | Kentucky | 0.4 |
| 28 | Louisiana | 0.5 |
| 49 | Maine | 0.0 |
| 23 | Maryland | 0.7 |
| 23 | Massachusetts | 0.7 |
| 41 | Michigan | 0.1 |
| 20 | Minnesota | 0.8 |
| 39 | Mississippi | 0.2 |
| 34 | Missouri | 0.3 |
| 11 | Montana | 1.0 |
| 23 | Nebraska | 0.7 |
| 5 | Nevada | 1.3 |
| 41 | New Hampshire | 0.1 |
| 31 | New Jersey | 0.4 |
| 41 | New Mexico | 0.1 |
| 31 | New York | 0.4 |
| 11 | North Carolina | 1.0 |
| 1 | North Dakota | 3.1 |
| 39 | Ohio | 0.2 |
| 16 | Oklahoma | 0.9 |
| 20 | Oregon | 0.8 |
| 41 | Pennsylvania | 0.1 |
| 41 | Rhode Island | 0.1 |
| 9 | South Carolina | 1.1 |
| 5 | South Dakota | 1.3 |
| 27 | Tennessee | 0.6 |
| 3 | Texas | 1.5 |
| 2 | Utah | 1.6 |
| 41 | Vermont | 0.1 |
| 16 | Virginia | 0.9 |
| 9 | Washington | 1.1 |
| 50 | West Virginia | (0.1) |
| 34 | Wisconsin | 0.3 |
| 11 | Wyoming | 1.0 |

RANK ORDER

| RANK | STATE | PERCENT CHANGE |
|------|-------|----------------|
| 1 | North Dakota | 3.1 |
| 2 | Utah | 1.6 |
| 3 | Colorado | 1.5 |
| 3 | Texas | 1.5 |
| 5 | Nevada | 1.3 |
| 5 | South Dakota | 1.3 |
| 7 | Arizona | 1.2 |
| 7 | Florida | 1.2 |
| 9 | South Carolina | 1.1 |
| 9 | Washington | 1.1 |
| 11 | Hawaii | 1.0 |
| 11 | Idaho | 1.0 |
| 11 | Montana | 1.0 |
| 11 | North Carolina | 1.0 |
| 11 | Wyoming | 1.0 |
| 16 | California | 0.9 |
| 16 | Delaware | 0.9 |
| 16 | Oklahoma | 0.9 |
| 16 | Virginia | 0.9 |
| 20 | Georgia | 0.8 |
| 20 | Minnesota | 0.8 |
| 20 | Oregon | 0.8 |
| 23 | Alaska | 0.7 |
| 23 | Maryland | 0.7 |
| 23 | Massachusetts | 0.7 |
| 23 | Nebraska | 0.7 |
| 27 | Tennessee | 0.6 |
| 28 | Indiana | 0.5 |
| 28 | Iowa | 0.5 |
| 28 | Louisiana | 0.5 |
| 31 | Kentucky | 0.4 |
| 31 | New Jersey | 0.4 |
| 31 | New York | 0.4 |
| 34 | Alabama | 0.3 |
| 34 | Arkansas | 0.3 |
| 34 | Kansas | 0.3 |
| 34 | Missouri | 0.3 |
| 34 | Wisconsin | 0.3 |
| 39 | Mississippi | 0.2 |
| 39 | Ohio | 0.2 |
| 41 | Connecticut | 0.1 |
| 41 | Illinois | 0.1 |
| 41 | Michigan | 0.1 |
| 41 | New Hampshire | 0.1 |
| 41 | New Mexico | 0.1 |
| 41 | Pennsylvania | 0.1 |
| 41 | Rhode Island | 0.1 |
| 41 | Vermont | 0.1 |
| 49 | Maine | 0.0 |
| 50 | West Virginia | (0.1) |

| | District of Columbia | 2.1 |

Source: CQ Press using data from U.S. Bureau of the Census
   "Population Estimates" (December 2013, http://www.census.gov/popest/data/index.html)
*Resident population from July 1, 2012 to July 1, 2013.

# Population in 2010 Census

## National Total = 308,745,538*

ALPHA ORDER

| RANK | STATE | POPULATION | % of USA |
|------|-------|-----------|----------|
| 23 | Alabama | 4,779,736 | 1.5% |
| 47 | Alaska | 710,231 | 0.2% |
| 16 | Arizona | 6,392,017 | 2.1% |
| 32 | Arkansas | 2,915,918 | 0.9% |
| 1 | California | 37,253,956 | 12.1% |
| 22 | Colorado | 5,029,196 | 1.6% |
| 29 | Connecticut | 3,574,097 | 1.2% |
| 45 | Delaware | 897,934 | 0.3% |
| 4 | Florida | 18,801,310 | 6.1% |
| 9 | Georgia | 9,687,653 | 3.1% |
| 40 | Hawaii | 1,360,301 | 0.4% |
| 39 | Idaho | 1,567,582 | 0.5% |
| 5 | Illinois | 12,830,632 | 4.2% |
| 15 | Indiana | 6,483,802 | 2.1% |
| 30 | Iowa | 3,046,355 | 1.0% |
| 33 | Kansas | 2,853,118 | 0.9% |
| 26 | Kentucky | 4,339,367 | 1.4% |
| 25 | Louisiana | 4,533,372 | 1.5% |
| 41 | Maine | 1,328,361 | 0.4% |
| 19 | Maryland | 5,773,552 | 1.9% |
| 14 | Massachusetts | 6,547,629 | 2.1% |
| 8 | Michigan | 9,883,640 | 3.2% |
| 21 | Minnesota | 5,303,925 | 1.7% |
| 31 | Mississippi | 2,967,297 | 1.0% |
| 18 | Missouri | 5,988,927 | 1.9% |
| 44 | Montana | 989,415 | 0.3% |
| 38 | Nebraska | 1,826,341 | 0.6% |
| 35 | Nevada | 2,700,551 | 0.9% |
| 42 | New Hampshire | 1,316,470 | 0.4% |
| 11 | New Jersey | 8,791,894 | 2.8% |
| 36 | New Mexico | 2,059,179 | 0.7% |
| 3 | New York | 19,378,102 | 6.3% |
| 10 | North Carolina | 9,535,483 | 3.1% |
| 48 | North Dakota | 672,591 | 0.2% |
| 7 | Ohio | 11,536,504 | 3.7% |
| 28 | Oklahoma | 3,751,351 | 1.2% |
| 27 | Oregon | 3,831,074 | 1.2% |
| 6 | Pennsylvania | 12,702,379 | 4.1% |
| 43 | Rhode Island | 1,052,567 | 0.3% |
| 24 | South Carolina | 4,625,364 | 1.5% |
| 46 | South Dakota | 814,180 | 0.3% |
| 17 | Tennessee | 6,346,105 | 2.1% |
| 2 | Texas | 25,145,561 | 8.1% |
| 34 | Utah | 2,763,885 | 0.9% |
| 49 | Vermont | 625,741 | 0.2% |
| 12 | Virginia | 8,001,024 | 2.6% |
| 13 | Washington | 6,724,540 | 2.2% |
| 37 | West Virginia | 1,852,994 | 0.6% |
| 20 | Wisconsin | 5,686,986 | 1.8% |
| 50 | Wyoming | 563,626 | 0.2% |

RANK ORDER

| RANK | STATE | POPULATION | % of USA |
|------|-------|-----------|----------|
| 1 | California | 37,253,956 | 12.1% |
| 2 | Texas | 25,145,561 | 8.1% |
| 3 | New York | 19,378,102 | 6.3% |
| 4 | Florida | 18,801,310 | 6.1% |
| 5 | Illinois | 12,830,632 | 4.2% |
| 6 | Pennsylvania | 12,702,379 | 4.1% |
| 7 | Ohio | 11,536,504 | 3.7% |
| 8 | Michigan | 9,883,640 | 3.2% |
| 9 | Georgia | 9,687,653 | 3.1% |
| 10 | North Carolina | 9,535,483 | 3.1% |
| 11 | New Jersey | 8,791,894 | 2.8% |
| 12 | Virginia | 8,001,024 | 2.6% |
| 13 | Washington | 6,724,540 | 2.2% |
| 14 | Massachusetts | 6,547,629 | 2.1% |
| 15 | Indiana | 6,483,802 | 2.1% |
| 16 | Arizona | 6,392,017 | 2.1% |
| 17 | Tennessee | 6,346,105 | 2.1% |
| 18 | Missouri | 5,988,927 | 1.9% |
| 19 | Maryland | 5,773,552 | 1.9% |
| 20 | Wisconsin | 5,686,986 | 1.8% |
| 21 | Minnesota | 5,303,925 | 1.7% |
| 22 | Colorado | 5,029,196 | 1.6% |
| 23 | Alabama | 4,779,736 | 1.5% |
| 24 | South Carolina | 4,625,364 | 1.5% |
| 25 | Louisiana | 4,533,372 | 1.5% |
| 26 | Kentucky | 4,339,367 | 1.4% |
| 27 | Oregon | 3,831,074 | 1.2% |
| 28 | Oklahoma | 3,751,351 | 1.2% |
| 29 | Connecticut | 3,574,097 | 1.2% |
| 30 | Iowa | 3,046,355 | 1.0% |
| 31 | Mississippi | 2,967,297 | 1.0% |
| 32 | Arkansas | 2,915,918 | 0.9% |
| 33 | Kansas | 2,853,118 | 0.9% |
| 34 | Utah | 2,763,885 | 0.9% |
| 35 | Nevada | 2,700,551 | 0.9% |
| 36 | New Mexico | 2,059,179 | 0.7% |
| 37 | West Virginia | 1,852,994 | 0.6% |
| 38 | Nebraska | 1,826,341 | 0.6% |
| 39 | Idaho | 1,567,582 | 0.5% |
| 40 | Hawaii | 1,360,301 | 0.4% |
| 41 | Maine | 1,328,361 | 0.4% |
| 42 | New Hampshire | 1,316,470 | 0.4% |
| 43 | Rhode Island | 1,052,567 | 0.3% |
| 44 | Montana | 989,415 | 0.3% |
| 45 | Delaware | 897,934 | 0.3% |
| 46 | South Dakota | 814,180 | 0.3% |
| 47 | Alaska | 710,231 | 0.2% |
| 48 | North Dakota | 672,591 | 0.2% |
| 49 | Vermont | 625,741 | 0.2% |
| 50 | Wyoming | 563,626 | 0.2% |
| | District of Columbia | 601,723 | 0.2% |

Source: U.S. Bureau of the Census
   "First 2010 Census Results" (http://www.census.gov/2010census/news/press-kits/apportionment/apport.html)
*Resident population as of April 2010 Census.

# Projected State Population in 2030

## National Total = 363,584,435*

ALPHA ORDER

| RANK | STATE | POPULATION | % of USA |
|------|-------|-----------:|---------:|
| 24 | Alabama | 4,874,243 | 1.3% |
| 46 | Alaska | 867,674 | 0.2% |
| 10 | Arizona | 10,712,397 | 2.9% |
| 32 | Arkansas | 3,240,208 | 0.9% |
| 1 | California | 46,444,861 | 12.8% |
| 22 | Colorado | 5,792,357 | 1.6% |
| 30 | Connecticut | 3,688,630 | 1.0% |
| 45 | Delaware | 1,012,658 | 0.3% |
| 3 | Florida | 28,685,769 | 7.9% |
| 8 | Georgia | 12,017,838 | 3.3% |
| 41 | Hawaii | 1,466,046 | 0.4% |
| 37 | Idaho | 1,969,624 | 0.5% |
| 5 | Illinois | 13,432,892 | 3.7% |
| 18 | Indiana | 6,810,108 | 1.9% |
| 34 | Iowa | 2,955,172 | 0.8% |
| 35 | Kansas | 2,940,084 | 0.8% |
| 27 | Kentucky | 4,554,998 | 1.3% |
| 26 | Louisiana | 4,802,633 | 1.3% |
| 42 | Maine | 1,411,097 | 0.4% |
| 16 | Maryland | 7,022,251 | 1.9% |
| 17 | Massachusetts | 7,012,009 | 1.9% |
| 11 | Michigan | 10,694,172 | 2.9% |
| 20 | Minnesota | 6,306,130 | 1.7% |
| 33 | Mississippi | 3,092,410 | 0.9% |
| 19 | Missouri | 6,430,173 | 1.8% |
| 44 | Montana | 1,044,898 | 0.3% |
| 38 | Nebraska | 1,820,247 | 0.5% |
| 28 | Nevada | 4,282,102 | 1.2% |
| 40 | New Hampshire | 1,646,471 | 0.5% |
| 13 | New Jersey | 9,802,440 | 2.7% |
| 36 | New Mexico | 2,099,708 | 0.6% |
| 4 | New York | 19,477,429 | 5.4% |
| 7 | North Carolina | 12,227,739 | 3.4% |
| 49 | North Dakota | 606,566 | 0.2% |
| 9 | Ohio | 11,550,528 | 3.2% |
| 29 | Oklahoma | 3,913,251 | 1.1% |
| 25 | Oregon | 4,833,918 | 1.3% |
| 6 | Pennsylvania | 12,768,184 | 3.5% |
| 43 | Rhode Island | 1,152,941 | 0.3% |
| 23 | South Carolina | 5,148,569 | 1.4% |
| 47 | South Dakota | 800,462 | 0.2% |
| 15 | Tennessee | 7,380,634 | 2.0% |
| 2 | Texas | 33,317,744 | 9.2% |
| 31 | Utah | 3,485,367 | 1.0% |
| 48 | Vermont | 711,867 | 0.2% |
| 12 | Virginia | 9,825,019 | 2.7% |
| 14 | Washington | 8,624,801 | 2.4% |
| 39 | West Virginia | 1,719,959 | 0.5% |
| 21 | Wisconsin | 6,150,764 | 1.7% |
| 50 | Wyoming | 522,979 | 0.1% |

RANK ORDER

| RANK | STATE | POPULATION | % of USA |
|------|-------|-----------:|---------:|
| 1 | California | 46,444,861 | 12.8% |
| 2 | Texas | 33,317,744 | 9.2% |
| 3 | Florida | 28,685,769 | 7.9% |
| 4 | New York | 19,477,429 | 5.4% |
| 5 | Illinois | 13,432,892 | 3.7% |
| 6 | Pennsylvania | 12,768,184 | 3.5% |
| 7 | North Carolina | 12,227,739 | 3.4% |
| 8 | Georgia | 12,017,838 | 3.3% |
| 9 | Ohio | 11,550,528 | 3.2% |
| 10 | Arizona | 10,712,397 | 2.9% |
| 11 | Michigan | 10,694,172 | 2.9% |
| 12 | Virginia | 9,825,019 | 2.7% |
| 13 | New Jersey | 9,802,440 | 2.7% |
| 14 | Washington | 8,624,801 | 2.4% |
| 15 | Tennessee | 7,380,634 | 2.0% |
| 16 | Maryland | 7,022,251 | 1.9% |
| 17 | Massachusetts | 7,012,009 | 1.9% |
| 18 | Indiana | 6,810,108 | 1.9% |
| 19 | Missouri | 6,430,173 | 1.8% |
| 20 | Minnesota | 6,306,130 | 1.7% |
| 21 | Wisconsin | 6,150,764 | 1.7% |
| 22 | Colorado | 5,792,357 | 1.6% |
| 23 | South Carolina | 5,148,569 | 1.4% |
| 24 | Alabama | 4,874,243 | 1.3% |
| 25 | Oregon | 4,833,918 | 1.3% |
| 26 | Louisiana | 4,802,633 | 1.3% |
| 27 | Kentucky | 4,554,998 | 1.3% |
| 28 | Nevada | 4,282,102 | 1.2% |
| 29 | Oklahoma | 3,913,251 | 1.1% |
| 30 | Connecticut | 3,688,630 | 1.0% |
| 31 | Utah | 3,485,367 | 1.0% |
| 32 | Arkansas | 3,240,208 | 0.9% |
| 33 | Mississippi | 3,092,410 | 0.9% |
| 34 | Iowa | 2,955,172 | 0.8% |
| 35 | Kansas | 2,940,084 | 0.8% |
| 36 | New Mexico | 2,099,708 | 0.6% |
| 37 | Idaho | 1,969,624 | 0.5% |
| 38 | Nebraska | 1,820,247 | 0.5% |
| 39 | West Virginia | 1,719,959 | 0.5% |
| 40 | New Hampshire | 1,646,471 | 0.5% |
| 41 | Hawaii | 1,466,046 | 0.4% |
| 42 | Maine | 1,411,097 | 0.4% |
| 43 | Rhode Island | 1,152,941 | 0.3% |
| 44 | Montana | 1,044,898 | 0.3% |
| 45 | Delaware | 1,012,658 | 0.3% |
| 46 | Alaska | 867,674 | 0.2% |
| 47 | South Dakota | 800,462 | 0.2% |
| 48 | Vermont | 711,867 | 0.2% |
| 49 | North Dakota | 606,566 | 0.2% |
| 50 | Wyoming | 522,979 | 0.1% |
| | District of Columbia | 433,414 | 0.1% |

Source: U.S. Bureau of the Census
"State Interim Population Projections: 2004-2030"
(http://www.census.gov/population/www/projections/projectionsagesex.html)
*Based on 2000 Census.

# Population per Square Mile in 2013

## National Rate = 89.5 Persons per Square Mile*

ALPHA ORDER

| RANK | STATE | RATE |
|---|---|---|
| 27 | Alabama | 95.4 |
| 50 | Alaska | 1.3 |
| 33 | Arizona | 58.3 |
| 34 | Arkansas | 56.9 |
| 11 | California | 246.1 |
| 37 | Colorado | 50.8 |
| 4 | Connecticut | 743.0 |
| 6 | Delaware | 475.0 |
| 8 | Florida | 364.8 |
| 18 | Georgia | 173.8 |
| 13 | Hawaii | 218.4 |
| 44 | Idaho | 19.5 |
| 12 | Illinois | 232.0 |
| 16 | Indiana | 183.4 |
| 36 | Iowa | 55.3 |
| 40 | Kansas | 35.4 |
| 22 | Kentucky | 111.3 |
| 23 | Louisiana | 107.1 |
| 38 | Maine | 43.1 |
| 5 | Maryland | 610.9 |
| 3 | Massachusetts | 857.9 |
| 17 | Michigan | 175.1 |
| 30 | Minnesota | 68.1 |
| 32 | Mississippi | 63.8 |
| 28 | Missouri | 88.0 |
| 48 | Montana | 7.0 |
| 43 | Nebraska | 24.3 |
| 42 | Nevada | 25.4 |
| 21 | New Hampshire | 147.8 |
| 1 | New Jersey | 1,210.1 |
| 45 | New Mexico | 17.2 |
| 7 | New York | 417.0 |
| 15 | North Carolina | 202.6 |
| 47 | North Dakota | 10.5 |
| 10 | Ohio | 283.2 |
| 35 | Oklahoma | 56.1 |
| 39 | Oregon | 40.9 |
| 9 | Pennsylvania | 285.5 |
| 2 | Rhode Island | 1,016.9 |
| 19 | South Carolina | 158.8 |
| 46 | South Dakota | 11.1 |
| 20 | Tennessee | 157.5 |
| 26 | Texas | 101.2 |
| 41 | Utah | 35.3 |
| 31 | Vermont | 68.0 |
| 14 | Virginia | 209.2 |
| 25 | Washington | 104.9 |
| 29 | West Virginia | 77.1 |
| 24 | Wisconsin | 106.0 |
| 49 | Wyoming | 6.0 |

RANK ORDER

| RANK | STATE | RATE |
|---|---|---|
| 1 | New Jersey | 1,210.1 |
| 2 | Rhode Island | 1,016.9 |
| 3 | Massachusetts | 857.9 |
| 4 | Connecticut | 743.0 |
| 5 | Maryland | 610.9 |
| 6 | Delaware | 475.0 |
| 7 | New York | 417.0 |
| 8 | Florida | 364.8 |
| 9 | Pennsylvania | 285.5 |
| 10 | Ohio | 283.2 |
| 11 | California | 246.1 |
| 12 | Illinois | 232.0 |
| 13 | Hawaii | 218.4 |
| 14 | Virginia | 209.2 |
| 15 | North Carolina | 202.6 |
| 16 | Indiana | 183.4 |
| 17 | Michigan | 175.1 |
| 18 | Georgia | 173.8 |
| 19 | South Carolina | 158.8 |
| 20 | Tennessee | 157.5 |
| 21 | New Hampshire | 147.8 |
| 22 | Kentucky | 111.3 |
| 23 | Louisiana | 107.1 |
| 24 | Wisconsin | 106.0 |
| 25 | Washington | 104.9 |
| 26 | Texas | 101.2 |
| 27 | Alabama | 95.4 |
| 28 | Missouri | 88.0 |
| 29 | West Virginia | 77.1 |
| 30 | Minnesota | 68.1 |
| 31 | Vermont | 68.0 |
| 32 | Mississippi | 63.8 |
| 33 | Arizona | 58.3 |
| 34 | Arkansas | 56.9 |
| 35 | Oklahoma | 56.1 |
| 36 | Iowa | 55.3 |
| 37 | Colorado | 50.8 |
| 38 | Maine | 43.1 |
| 39 | Oregon | 40.9 |
| 40 | Kansas | 35.4 |
| 41 | Utah | 35.3 |
| 42 | Nevada | 25.4 |
| 43 | Nebraska | 24.3 |
| 44 | Idaho | 19.5 |
| 45 | New Mexico | 17.2 |
| 46 | South Dakota | 11.1 |
| 47 | North Dakota | 10.5 |
| 48 | Montana | 7.0 |
| 49 | Wyoming | 6.0 |
| 50 | Alaska | 1.3 |
| | District of Columbia | 10,597.5 |

Source: CQ Press using data from U.S. Bureau of the Census
"Population Estimates" (December 2013, http://www.census.gov/popest/data/index.html)
*Resident population. Based on land area of states.

# Male Population in 2012

## National Total = 154,492,067 Males

ALPHA ORDER

| RANK | STATE | MALES | % of USA |
|------|-------|-------|----------|
| 23 | Alabama | 2,338,557 | 1.5% |
| 47 | Alaska | 381,238 | 0.2% |
| 14 | Arizona | 3,258,483 | 2.1% |
| 32 | Arkansas | 1,448,490 | 0.9% |
| 1 | California | 18,918,564 | 12.2% |
| 22 | Colorado | 2,603,705 | 1.7% |
| 29 | Connecticut | 1,749,916 | 1.1% |
| 45 | Delaware | 444,358 | 0.3% |
| 4 | Florida | 9,447,827 | 6.1% |
| 8 | Georgia | 4,851,024 | 3.1% |
| 40 | Hawaii | 701,965 | 0.5% |
| 39 | Idaho | 798,612 | 0.5% |
| 5 | Illinois | 6,319,455 | 4.1% |
| 16 | Indiana | 3,218,190 | 2.1% |
| 30 | Iowa | 1,524,488 | 1.0% |
| 34 | Kansas | 1,435,281 | 0.9% |
| 26 | Kentucky | 2,157,711 | 1.4% |
| 25 | Louisiana | 2,252,050 | 1.5% |
| 42 | Maine | 650,278 | 0.4% |
| 19 | Maryland | 2,850,403 | 1.8% |
| 15 | Massachusetts | 3,220,373 | 2.1% |
| 9 | Michigan | 4,850,511 | 3.1% |
| 21 | Minnesota | 2,672,169 | 1.7% |
| 31 | Mississippi | 1,449,291 | 0.9% |
| 18 | Missouri | 2,951,036 | 1.9% |
| 44 | Montana | 504,949 | 0.3% |
| 37 | Nebraska | 922,302 | 0.6% |
| 35 | Nevada | 1,391,207 | 0.9% |
| 41 | New Hampshire | 652,237 | 0.4% |
| 11 | New Jersey | 4,323,685 | 2.8% |
| 36 | New Mexico | 1,032,707 | 0.7% |
| 3 | New York | 9,489,217 | 6.1% |
| 10 | North Carolina | 4,752,898 | 3.1% |
| 48 | North Dakota | 355,742 | 0.2% |
| 7 | Ohio | 5,642,620 | 3.7% |
| 28 | Oklahoma | 1,889,825 | 1.2% |
| 27 | Oregon | 1,930,712 | 1.2% |
| 6 | Pennsylvania | 6,230,177 | 4.0% |
| 43 | Rhode Island | 508,276 | 0.3% |
| 24 | South Carolina | 2,297,213 | 1.5% |
| 46 | South Dakota | 418,316 | 0.3% |
| 17 | Tennessee | 3,148,763 | 2.0% |
| 2 | Texas | 12,947,734 | 8.4% |
| 33 | Utah | 1,435,860 | 0.9% |
| 49 | Vermont | 308,778 | 0.2% |
| 12 | Virginia | 4,021,525 | 2.6% |
| 13 | Washington | 3,441,550 | 2.2% |
| 38 | West Virginia | 915,405 | 0.6% |
| 20 | Wisconsin | 2,843,072 | 1.8% |
| 50 | Wyoming | 294,281 | 0.2% |

RANK ORDER

| RANK | STATE | MALES | % of USA |
|------|-------|-------|----------|
| 1 | California | 18,918,564 | 12.2% |
| 2 | Texas | 12,947,734 | 8.4% |
| 3 | New York | 9,489,217 | 6.1% |
| 4 | Florida | 9,447,827 | 6.1% |
| 5 | Illinois | 6,319,455 | 4.1% |
| 6 | Pennsylvania | 6,230,177 | 4.0% |
| 7 | Ohio | 5,642,620 | 3.7% |
| 8 | Georgia | 4,851,024 | 3.1% |
| 9 | Michigan | 4,850,511 | 3.1% |
| 10 | North Carolina | 4,752,898 | 3.1% |
| 11 | New Jersey | 4,323,685 | 2.8% |
| 12 | Virginia | 4,021,525 | 2.6% |
| 13 | Washington | 3,441,550 | 2.2% |
| 14 | Arizona | 3,258,483 | 2.1% |
| 15 | Massachusetts | 3,220,373 | 2.1% |
| 16 | Indiana | 3,218,190 | 2.1% |
| 17 | Tennessee | 3,148,763 | 2.0% |
| 18 | Missouri | 2,951,036 | 1.9% |
| 19 | Maryland | 2,850,403 | 1.8% |
| 20 | Wisconsin | 2,843,072 | 1.8% |
| 21 | Minnesota | 2,672,169 | 1.7% |
| 22 | Colorado | 2,603,705 | 1.7% |
| 23 | Alabama | 2,338,557 | 1.5% |
| 24 | South Carolina | 2,297,213 | 1.5% |
| 25 | Louisiana | 2,252,050 | 1.5% |
| 26 | Kentucky | 2,157,711 | 1.4% |
| 27 | Oregon | 1,930,712 | 1.2% |
| 28 | Oklahoma | 1,889,825 | 1.2% |
| 29 | Connecticut | 1,749,916 | 1.1% |
| 30 | Iowa | 1,524,488 | 1.0% |
| 31 | Mississippi | 1,449,291 | 0.9% |
| 32 | Arkansas | 1,448,490 | 0.9% |
| 33 | Utah | 1,435,860 | 0.9% |
| 34 | Kansas | 1,435,281 | 0.9% |
| 35 | Nevada | 1,391,207 | 0.9% |
| 36 | New Mexico | 1,032,707 | 0.7% |
| 37 | Nebraska | 922,302 | 0.6% |
| 38 | West Virginia | 915,405 | 0.6% |
| 39 | Idaho | 798,612 | 0.5% |
| 40 | Hawaii | 701,965 | 0.5% |
| 41 | New Hampshire | 652,237 | 0.4% |
| 42 | Maine | 650,278 | 0.4% |
| 43 | Rhode Island | 508,276 | 0.3% |
| 44 | Montana | 504,949 | 0.3% |
| 45 | Delaware | 444,358 | 0.3% |
| 46 | South Dakota | 418,316 | 0.3% |
| 47 | Alaska | 381,238 | 0.2% |
| 48 | North Dakota | 355,742 | 0.2% |
| 49 | Vermont | 308,778 | 0.2% |
| 50 | Wyoming | 294,281 | 0.2% |
| | District of Columbia | 299,041 | 0.2% |

Source: U.S. Bureau of the Census
"State Characteristics: Vintage 2012" (http://www.census.gov/popest/data/state/asrh/2012/index.html)

# Female Population in 2012

## National Total = 159,421,973 Females

ALPHA ORDER

| RANK | STATE | FEMALES | % of USA |
|------|-------|---------|----------|
| 23 | Alabama | 2,483,466 | 1.6% |
| 47 | Alaska | 350,211 | 0.2% |
| 17 | Arizona | 3,294,772 | 2.1% |
| 32 | Arkansas | 1,500,641 | 0.9% |
| 1 | California | 19,122,866 | 12.0% |
| 22 | Colorado | 2,583,877 | 1.6% |
| 29 | Connecticut | 1,840,431 | 1.2% |
| 45 | Delaware | 472,734 | 0.3% |
| 4 | Florida | 9,869,741 | 6.2% |
| 8 | Georgia | 5,068,921 | 3.2% |
| 40 | Hawaii | 690,348 | 0.4% |
| 39 | Idaho | 797,116 | 0.5% |
| 5 | Illinois | 6,555,800 | 4.1% |
| 15 | Indiana | 3,319,144 | 2.1% |
| 30 | Iowa | 1,549,698 | 1.0% |
| 33 | Kansas | 1,450,624 | 0.9% |
| 26 | Kentucky | 2,222,704 | 1.4% |
| 25 | Louisiana | 2,349,843 | 1.5% |
| 41 | Maine | 678,914 | 0.4% |
| 19 | Maryland | 3,034,160 | 1.9% |
| 14 | Massachusetts | 3,425,771 | 2.1% |
| 9 | Michigan | 5,032,849 | 3.2% |
| 21 | Minnesota | 2,706,970 | 1.7% |
| 31 | Mississippi | 1,535,635 | 1.0% |
| 18 | Missouri | 3,070,952 | 1.9% |
| 44 | Montana | 500,192 | 0.3% |
| 38 | Nebraska | 933,223 | 0.6% |
| 35 | Nevada | 1,367,724 | 0.9% |
| 42 | New Hampshire | 668,481 | 0.4% |
| 11 | New Jersey | 4,540,905 | 2.8% |
| 36 | New Mexico | 1,052,831 | 0.7% |
| 3 | New York | 10,081,044 | 6.3% |
| 10 | North Carolina | 4,999,175 | 3.1% |
| 48 | North Dakota | 343,886 | 0.2% |
| 7 | Ohio | 5,901,605 | 3.7% |
| 28 | Oklahoma | 1,924,995 | 1.2% |
| 27 | Oregon | 1,968,641 | 1.2% |
| 6 | Pennsylvania | 6,533,359 | 4.1% |
| 43 | Rhode Island | 542,016 | 0.3% |
| 24 | South Carolina | 2,426,510 | 1.5% |
| 46 | South Dakota | 415,038 | 0.3% |
| 16 | Tennessee | 3,307,480 | 2.1% |
| 2 | Texas | 13,111,469 | 8.2% |
| 34 | Utah | 1,419,427 | 0.9% |
| 49 | Vermont | 317,233 | 0.2% |
| 12 | Virginia | 4,164,342 | 2.6% |
| 13 | Washington | 3,455,462 | 2.2% |
| 37 | West Virginia | 940,008 | 0.6% |
| 20 | Wisconsin | 2,883,326 | 1.8% |
| 50 | Wyoming | 282,131 | 0.2% |

RANK ORDER

| RANK | STATE | FEMALES | % of USA |
|------|-------|---------|----------|
| 1 | California | 19,122,866 | 12.0% |
| 2 | Texas | 13,111,469 | 8.2% |
| 3 | New York | 10,081,044 | 6.3% |
| 4 | Florida | 9,869,741 | 6.2% |
| 5 | Illinois | 6,555,800 | 4.1% |
| 6 | Pennsylvania | 6,533,359 | 4.1% |
| 7 | Ohio | 5,901,605 | 3.7% |
| 8 | Georgia | 5,068,921 | 3.2% |
| 9 | Michigan | 5,032,849 | 3.2% |
| 10 | North Carolina | 4,999,175 | 3.1% |
| 11 | New Jersey | 4,540,905 | 2.8% |
| 12 | Virginia | 4,164,342 | 2.6% |
| 13 | Washington | 3,455,462 | 2.2% |
| 14 | Massachusetts | 3,425,771 | 2.1% |
| 15 | Indiana | 3,319,144 | 2.1% |
| 16 | Tennessee | 3,307,480 | 2.1% |
| 17 | Arizona | 3,294,772 | 2.1% |
| 18 | Missouri | 3,070,952 | 1.9% |
| 19 | Maryland | 3,034,160 | 1.9% |
| 20 | Wisconsin | 2,883,326 | 1.8% |
| 21 | Minnesota | 2,706,970 | 1.7% |
| 22 | Colorado | 2,583,877 | 1.6% |
| 23 | Alabama | 2,483,466 | 1.6% |
| 24 | South Carolina | 2,426,510 | 1.5% |
| 25 | Louisiana | 2,349,843 | 1.5% |
| 26 | Kentucky | 2,222,704 | 1.4% |
| 27 | Oregon | 1,968,641 | 1.2% |
| 28 | Oklahoma | 1,924,995 | 1.2% |
| 29 | Connecticut | 1,840,431 | 1.2% |
| 30 | Iowa | 1,549,698 | 1.0% |
| 31 | Mississippi | 1,535,635 | 1.0% |
| 32 | Arkansas | 1,500,641 | 0.9% |
| 33 | Kansas | 1,450,624 | 0.9% |
| 34 | Utah | 1,419,427 | 0.9% |
| 35 | Nevada | 1,367,724 | 0.9% |
| 36 | New Mexico | 1,052,831 | 0.7% |
| 37 | West Virginia | 940,008 | 0.6% |
| 38 | Nebraska | 933,223 | 0.6% |
| 39 | Idaho | 797,116 | 0.5% |
| 40 | Hawaii | 690,348 | 0.4% |
| 41 | Maine | 678,914 | 0.4% |
| 42 | New Hampshire | 668,481 | 0.4% |
| 43 | Rhode Island | 542,016 | 0.3% |
| 44 | Montana | 500,192 | 0.3% |
| 45 | Delaware | 472,734 | 0.3% |
| 46 | South Dakota | 415,038 | 0.3% |
| 47 | Alaska | 350,211 | 0.2% |
| 48 | North Dakota | 343,886 | 0.2% |
| 49 | Vermont | 317,233 | 0.2% |
| 50 | Wyoming | 282,131 | 0.2% |
| | District of Columbia | 333,282 | 0.2% |

Source: U.S. Bureau of the Census
"State Characteristics: Vintage 2012" (http://www.census.gov/popest/data/state/asrh/2012/index.html)

# Male to Female Ratio in 2012

## National Ratio = 96.9 Males per 100 Females

| ALPHA ORDER | | | | RANK ORDER | | |
|---|---|---|---|---|---|---|
| RANK | STATE | RATIO | | RANK | STATE | RATIO |
| 45 | Alabama | 94.2 | | 1 | Alaska | 108.9 |
| 1 | Alaska | 108.9 | | 2 | Wyoming | 104.3 |
| 12 | Arizona | 98.9 | | 3 | North Dakota | 103.4 |
| 29 | Arkansas | 96.5 | | 4 | Hawaii | 101.7 |
| 12 | California | 98.9 | | 4 | Nevada | 101.7 |
| 8 | Colorado | 100.8 | | 6 | Utah | 101.2 |
| 41 | Connecticut | 95.1 | | 7 | Montana | 101.0 |
| 47 | Delaware | 94.0 | | 8 | Colorado | 100.8 |
| 35 | Florida | 95.7 | | 8 | South Dakota | 100.8 |
| 35 | Georgia | 95.7 | | 10 | Idaho | 100.2 |
| 4 | Hawaii | 101.7 | | 11 | Washington | 99.6 |
| 10 | Idaho | 100.2 | | 12 | Arizona | 98.9 |
| 30 | Illinois | 96.4 | | 12 | California | 98.9 |
| 27 | Indiana | 97.0 | | 12 | Kansas | 98.9 |
| 19 | Iowa | 98.4 | | 15 | Nebraska | 98.8 |
| 12 | Kansas | 98.9 | | 15 | Texas | 98.8 |
| 26 | Kentucky | 97.1 | | 17 | Minnesota | 98.7 |
| 33 | Louisiana | 95.8 | | 18 | Wisconsin | 98.6 |
| 33 | Maine | 95.8 | | 19 | Iowa | 98.4 |
| 49 | Maryland | 93.9 | | 20 | Oklahoma | 98.2 |
| 47 | Massachusetts | 94.0 | | 21 | New Mexico | 98.1 |
| 30 | Michigan | 96.4 | | 21 | Oregon | 98.1 |
| 17 | Minnesota | 98.7 | | 23 | New Hampshire | 97.6 |
| 44 | Mississippi | 94.4 | | 24 | West Virginia | 97.4 |
| 32 | Missouri | 96.1 | | 25 | Vermont | 97.3 |
| 7 | Montana | 101.0 | | 26 | Kentucky | 97.1 |
| 15 | Nebraska | 98.8 | | 27 | Indiana | 97.0 |
| 4 | Nevada | 101.7 | | 28 | Virginia | 96.6 |
| 23 | New Hampshire | 97.6 | | 29 | Arkansas | 96.5 |
| 39 | New Jersey | 95.2 | | 30 | Illinois | 96.4 |
| 21 | New Mexico | 98.1 | | 30 | Michigan | 96.4 |
| 46 | New York | 94.1 | | 32 | Missouri | 96.1 |
| 41 | North Carolina | 95.1 | | 33 | Louisiana | 95.8 |
| 3 | North Dakota | 103.4 | | 33 | Maine | 95.8 |
| 37 | Ohio | 95.6 | | 35 | Florida | 95.7 |
| 20 | Oklahoma | 98.2 | | 35 | Georgia | 95.7 |
| 21 | Oregon | 98.1 | | 37 | Ohio | 95.6 |
| 38 | Pennsylvania | 95.4 | | 38 | Pennsylvania | 95.4 |
| 50 | Rhode Island | 93.8 | | 39 | New Jersey | 95.2 |
| 43 | South Carolina | 94.7 | | 39 | Tennessee | 95.2 |
| 8 | South Dakota | 100.8 | | 41 | Connecticut | 95.1 |
| 39 | Tennessee | 95.2 | | 41 | North Carolina | 95.1 |
| 15 | Texas | 98.8 | | 43 | South Carolina | 94.7 |
| 6 | Utah | 101.2 | | 44 | Mississippi | 94.4 |
| 25 | Vermont | 97.3 | | 45 | Alabama | 94.2 |
| 28 | Virginia | 96.6 | | 46 | New York | 94.1 |
| 11 | Washington | 99.6 | | 47 | Delaware | 94.0 |
| 24 | West Virginia | 97.4 | | 47 | Massachusetts | 94.0 |
| 18 | Wisconsin | 98.6 | | 49 | Maryland | 93.9 |
| 2 | Wyoming | 104.3 | | 50 | Rhode Island | 93.8 |
| | | | | | District of Columbia | 89.7 |

Source: CQ Press using data from U.S. Bureau of the Census
    "State Characteristics: Vintage 2012" (http://www.census.gov/popest/data/state/asrh/2012/index.html)

# White Population in 2012

## National Total = 244,495,567*

ALPHA ORDER

| RANK | STATE | POPULATION | % of USA |
|------|-------|-----------:|----------|
| 25 | Alabama | 3,373,844 | 1.4% |
| 49 | Alaska | 493,430 | 0.2% |
| 16 | Arizona | 5,522,144 | 2.3% |
| 33 | Arkansas | 2,359,569 | 1.0% |
| 1 | California | 28,033,826 | 11.5% |
| 21 | Colorado | 4,572,022 | 1.9% |
| 27 | Connecticut | 2,942,335 | 1.2% |
| 45 | Delaware | 654,352 | 0.3% |
| 3 | Florida | 15,120,082 | 6.2% |
| 11 | Georgia | 6,231,978 | 2.5% |
| 50 | Hawaii | 363,544 | 0.1% |
| 39 | Idaho | 1,497,404 | 0.6% |
| 6 | Illinois | 10,028,832 | 4.1% |
| 13 | Indiana | 5,659,668 | 2.3% |
| 30 | Iowa | 2,851,533 | 1.2% |
| 32 | Kansas | 2,517,663 | 1.0% |
| 22 | Kentucky | 3,882,987 | 1.6% |
| 28 | Louisiana | 2,930,137 | 1.2% |
| 40 | Maine | 1,266,849 | 0.5% |
| 23 | Maryland | 3,579,276 | 1.5% |
| 15 | Massachusetts | 5,560,222 | 2.3% |
| 8 | Michigan | 7,920,263 | 3.2% |
| 20 | Minnesota | 4,654,134 | 1.9% |
| 35 | Mississippi | 1,788,664 | 0.7% |
| 19 | Missouri | 5,049,604 | 2.1% |
| 43 | Montana | 901,340 | 0.4% |
| 38 | Nebraska | 1,668,779 | 0.7% |
| 34 | Nevada | 2,128,047 | 0.9% |
| 41 | New Hampshire | 1,247,076 | 0.5% |
| 10 | New Jersey | 6,538,430 | 2.7% |
| 37 | New Mexico | 1,735,255 | 0.7% |
| 4 | New York | 13,930,819 | 5.7% |
| 9 | North Carolina | 7,013,116 | 2.9% |
| 46 | North Dakota | 630,215 | 0.3% |
| 7 | Ohio | 9,630,901 | 3.9% |
| 29 | Oklahoma | 2,881,880 | 1.2% |
| 24 | Oregon | 3,444,767 | 1.4% |
| 5 | Pennsylvania | 10,655,948 | 4.4% |
| 42 | Rhode Island | 902,439 | 0.4% |
| 26 | South Carolina | 3,229,346 | 1.3% |
| 44 | South Dakota | 718,352 | 0.3% |
| 17 | Tennessee | 5,117,456 | 2.1% |
| 2 | Texas | 21,001,450 | 8.6% |
| 31 | Utah | 2,620,788 | 1.1% |
| 47 | Vermont | 597,050 | 0.2% |
| 12 | Virginia | 5,818,810 | 2.4% |
| 14 | Washington | 5,625,335 | 2.3% |
| 36 | West Virginia | 1,743,721 | 0.7% |
| 18 | Wisconsin | 5,052,112 | 2.1% |
| 48 | Wyoming | 536,450 | 0.2% |

RANK ORDER

| RANK | STATE | POPULATION | % of USA |
|------|-------|-----------:|----------|
| 1 | California | 28,033,826 | 11.5% |
| 2 | Texas | 21,001,450 | 8.6% |
| 3 | Florida | 15,120,082 | 6.2% |
| 4 | New York | 13,930,819 | 5.7% |
| 5 | Pennsylvania | 10,655,948 | 4.4% |
| 6 | Illinois | 10,028,832 | 4.1% |
| 7 | Ohio | 9,630,901 | 3.9% |
| 8 | Michigan | 7,920,263 | 3.2% |
| 9 | North Carolina | 7,013,116 | 2.9% |
| 10 | New Jersey | 6,538,430 | 2.7% |
| 11 | Georgia | 6,231,978 | 2.5% |
| 12 | Virginia | 5,818,810 | 2.4% |
| 13 | Indiana | 5,659,668 | 2.3% |
| 14 | Washington | 5,625,335 | 2.3% |
| 15 | Massachusetts | 5,560,222 | 2.3% |
| 16 | Arizona | 5,522,144 | 2.3% |
| 17 | Tennessee | 5,117,456 | 2.1% |
| 18 | Wisconsin | 5,052,112 | 2.1% |
| 19 | Missouri | 5,049,604 | 2.1% |
| 20 | Minnesota | 4,654,134 | 1.9% |
| 21 | Colorado | 4,572,022 | 1.9% |
| 22 | Kentucky | 3,882,987 | 1.6% |
| 23 | Maryland | 3,579,276 | 1.5% |
| 24 | Oregon | 3,444,767 | 1.4% |
| 25 | Alabama | 3,373,844 | 1.4% |
| 26 | South Carolina | 3,229,346 | 1.3% |
| 27 | Connecticut | 2,942,335 | 1.2% |
| 28 | Louisiana | 2,930,137 | 1.2% |
| 29 | Oklahoma | 2,881,880 | 1.2% |
| 30 | Iowa | 2,851,533 | 1.2% |
| 31 | Utah | 2,620,788 | 1.1% |
| 32 | Kansas | 2,517,663 | 1.0% |
| 33 | Arkansas | 2,359,569 | 1.0% |
| 34 | Nevada | 2,128,047 | 0.9% |
| 35 | Mississippi | 1,788,664 | 0.7% |
| 36 | West Virginia | 1,743,721 | 0.7% |
| 37 | New Mexico | 1,735,255 | 0.7% |
| 38 | Nebraska | 1,668,779 | 0.7% |
| 39 | Idaho | 1,497,404 | 0.6% |
| 40 | Maine | 1,266,849 | 0.5% |
| 41 | New Hampshire | 1,247,076 | 0.5% |
| 42 | Rhode Island | 902,439 | 0.4% |
| 43 | Montana | 901,340 | 0.4% |
| 44 | South Dakota | 718,352 | 0.3% |
| 45 | Delaware | 654,352 | 0.3% |
| 46 | North Dakota | 630,215 | 0.3% |
| 47 | Vermont | 597,050 | 0.2% |
| 48 | Wyoming | 536,450 | 0.2% |
| 49 | Alaska | 493,430 | 0.2% |
| 50 | Hawaii | 363,544 | 0.1% |
| | District of Columbia | 271,323 | 0.1% |

Source: U.S. Bureau of the Census

"State Characteristics: Vintage 2012" (http://www.census.gov/popest/data/state/asrh/2012/index.html)

*Those who identified themselves as one race. "White" is defined by Census as a person having origins in any of the original peoples of Europe, North Africa, or the Middle East. There are 197,705,655 non-Hispanic whites. Census states "Race is a self-identification data item in which respondents choose the race or races with which they most closely identify."

# Percent of Population White in 2012

## National Percent = 77.9%*

| ALPHA ORDER | | | RANK ORDER | | |
|---|---|---|---|---|---|
| RANK | STATE | PERCENT | RANK | STATE | PERCENT |
| 43 | Alabama | 70.0 | 1 | Vermont | 95.4 |
| 45 | Alaska | 67.5 | 2 | Maine | 95.3 |
| 21 | Arizona | 84.3 | 3 | New Hampshire | 94.4 |
| 31 | Arkansas | 80.0 | 4 | West Virginia | 94.0 |
| 38 | California | 73.7 | 5 | Idaho | 93.8 |
| 15 | Colorado | 88.1 | 6 | Wyoming | 93.1 |
| 27 | Connecticut | 82.0 | 7 | Iowa | 92.8 |
| 40 | Delaware | 71.4 | 8 | Utah | 91.8 |
| 33 | Florida | 78.3 | 9 | North Dakota | 90.1 |
| 47 | Georgia | 62.8 | 10 | Nebraska | 89.9 |
| 50 | Hawaii | 26.1 | 11 | Montana | 89.7 |
| 5 | Idaho | 93.8 | 12 | Kentucky | 88.6 |
| 34 | Illinois | 77.9 | 13 | Oregon | 88.3 |
| 17 | Indiana | 86.6 | 14 | Wisconsin | 88.2 |
| 7 | Iowa | 92.8 | 15 | Colorado | 88.1 |
| 16 | Kansas | 87.2 | 16 | Kansas | 87.2 |
| 12 | Kentucky | 88.6 | 17 | Indiana | 86.6 |
| 46 | Louisiana | 63.7 | 18 | Minnesota | 86.5 |
| 2 | Maine | 95.3 | 19 | South Dakota | 86.2 |
| 48 | Maryland | 60.8 | 20 | Rhode Island | 85.9 |
| 23 | Massachusetts | 83.7 | 21 | Arizona | 84.3 |
| 30 | Michigan | 80.1 | 22 | Missouri | 83.9 |
| 18 | Minnesota | 86.5 | 23 | Massachusetts | 83.7 |
| 49 | Mississippi | 59.9 | 24 | Pennsylvania | 83.5 |
| 22 | Missouri | 83.9 | 25 | Ohio | 83.4 |
| 11 | Montana | 89.7 | 26 | New Mexico | 83.2 |
| 10 | Nebraska | 89.9 | 27 | Connecticut | 82.0 |
| 35 | Nevada | 77.1 | 28 | Washington | 81.6 |
| 3 | New Hampshire | 94.4 | 29 | Texas | 80.6 |
| 37 | New Jersey | 73.8 | 30 | Michigan | 80.1 |
| 26 | New Mexico | 83.2 | 31 | Arkansas | 80.0 |
| 41 | New York | 71.2 | 32 | Tennessee | 79.3 |
| 39 | North Carolina | 71.9 | 33 | Florida | 78.3 |
| 9 | North Dakota | 90.1 | 34 | Illinois | 77.9 |
| 25 | Ohio | 83.4 | 35 | Nevada | 77.1 |
| 36 | Oklahoma | 75.5 | 36 | Oklahoma | 75.5 |
| 13 | Oregon | 88.3 | 37 | New Jersey | 73.8 |
| 24 | Pennsylvania | 83.5 | 38 | California | 73.7 |
| 20 | Rhode Island | 85.9 | 39 | North Carolina | 71.9 |
| 44 | South Carolina | 68.4 | 40 | Delaware | 71.4 |
| 19 | South Dakota | 86.2 | 41 | New York | 71.2 |
| 32 | Tennessee | 79.3 | 42 | Virginia | 71.1 |
| 29 | Texas | 80.6 | 43 | Alabama | 70.0 |
| 8 | Utah | 91.8 | 44 | South Carolina | 68.4 |
| 1 | Vermont | 95.4 | 45 | Alaska | 67.5 |
| 42 | Virginia | 71.1 | 46 | Louisiana | 63.7 |
| 28 | Washington | 81.6 | 47 | Georgia | 62.8 |
| 4 | West Virginia | 94.0 | 48 | Maryland | 60.8 |
| 14 | Wisconsin | 88.2 | 49 | Mississippi | 59.9 |
| 6 | Wyoming | 93.1 | 50 | Hawaii | 26.1 |
| | | | | District of Columbia | 42.9 |

Source: CQ Press using data from U.S. Bureau of the Census
    "State Characteristics: Vintage 2012" (http://www.census.gov/popest/data/state/asrh/2012/index.html)
*Those who identified themselves as one race. "White" is defined by Census as a person having origins in any of the original peoples of Europe, North Africa, or the Middle East. Non-Hispanic whites comprise 63.0% of the total population. Census states "Race is a self-identification data item in which respondents choose the race or races with which they most closely identify."

# Black Population in 2012

## National Total = 41,204,793*

ALPHA ORDER

| RANK | STATE | POPULATION | % of USA |
|------|-------|-----------|----------|
| 16 | Alabama | 1,279,805 | 3.1% |
| 42 | Alaska | 27,373 | 0.1% |
| 26 | Arizona | 297,985 | 0.7% |
| 22 | Arkansas | 459,739 | 1.1% |
| 5 | California | 2,515,716 | 6.1% |
| 31 | Colorado | 225,390 | 0.5% |
| 23 | Connecticut | 401,496 | 1.0% |
| 32 | Delaware | 202,090 | 0.5% |
| 3 | Florida | 3,206,350 | 7.8% |
| 4 | Georgia | 3,091,904 | 7.5% |
| 41 | Hawaii | 29,905 | 0.1% |
| 46 | Idaho | 12,037 | 0.0% |
| 7 | Illinois | 1,900,578 | 4.6% |
| 20 | Indiana | 616,199 | 1.5% |
| 34 | Iowa | 97,080 | 0.2% |
| 33 | Kansas | 178,820 | 0.4% |
| 25 | Kentucky | 354,119 | 0.9% |
| 10 | Louisiana | 1,491,433 | 3.6% |
| 44 | Maine | 17,603 | 0.0% |
| 8 | Maryland | 1,766,990 | 4.3% |
| 21 | Massachusetts | 525,799 | 1.3% |
| 13 | Michigan | 1,415,107 | 3.4% |
| 27 | Minnesota | 297,962 | 0.7% |
| 17 | Mississippi | 1,116,367 | 2.7% |
| 19 | Missouri | 706,079 | 1.7% |
| 50 | Montana | 5,679 | 0.0% |
| 35 | Nebraska | 88,758 | 0.2% |
| 30 | Nevada | 244,462 | 0.6% |
| 43 | New Hampshire | 18,374 | 0.0% |
| 15 | New Jersey | 1,298,879 | 3.2% |
| 39 | New Mexico | 51,087 | 0.1% |
| 1 | New York | 3,422,914 | 8.3% |
| 6 | North Carolina | 2,147,599 | 5.2% |
| 47 | North Dakota | 10,547 | 0.0% |
| 12 | Ohio | 1,439,598 | 3.5% |
| 28 | Oklahoma | 291,551 | 0.7% |
| 36 | Oregon | 77,564 | 0.2% |
| 11 | Pennsylvania | 1,456,977 | 3.5% |
| 37 | Rhode Island | 77,123 | 0.2% |
| 14 | South Carolina | 1,322,528 | 3.2% |
| 45 | South Dakota | 13,939 | 0.0% |
| 18 | Tennessee | 1,097,978 | 2.7% |
| 2 | Texas | 3,216,242 | 7.8% |
| 40 | Utah | 36,717 | 0.1% |
| 49 | Vermont | 6,879 | 0.0% |
| 9 | Virginia | 1,612,713 | 3.9% |
| 29 | Washington | 268,660 | 0.7% |
| 38 | West Virginia | 65,787 | 0.2% |
| 24 | Wisconsin | 373,275 | 0.9% |
| 48 | Wyoming | 8,555 | 0.0% |

RANK ORDER

| RANK | STATE | POPULATION | % of USA |
|------|-------|-----------|----------|
| 1 | New York | 3,422,914 | 8.3% |
| 2 | Texas | 3,216,242 | 7.8% |
| 3 | Florida | 3,206,350 | 7.8% |
| 4 | Georgia | 3,091,904 | 7.5% |
| 5 | California | 2,515,716 | 6.1% |
| 6 | North Carolina | 2,147,599 | 5.2% |
| 7 | Illinois | 1,900,578 | 4.6% |
| 8 | Maryland | 1,766,990 | 4.3% |
| 9 | Virginia | 1,612,713 | 3.9% |
| 10 | Louisiana | 1,491,433 | 3.6% |
| 11 | Pennsylvania | 1,456,977 | 3.5% |
| 12 | Ohio | 1,439,598 | 3.5% |
| 13 | Michigan | 1,415,107 | 3.4% |
| 14 | South Carolina | 1,322,528 | 3.2% |
| 15 | New Jersey | 1,298,879 | 3.2% |
| 16 | Alabama | 1,279,805 | 3.1% |
| 17 | Mississippi | 1,116,367 | 2.7% |
| 18 | Tennessee | 1,097,978 | 2.7% |
| 19 | Missouri | 706,079 | 1.7% |
| 20 | Indiana | 616,199 | 1.5% |
| 21 | Massachusetts | 525,799 | 1.3% |
| 22 | Arkansas | 459,739 | 1.1% |
| 23 | Connecticut | 401,496 | 1.0% |
| 24 | Wisconsin | 373,275 | 0.9% |
| 25 | Kentucky | 354,119 | 0.9% |
| 26 | Arizona | 297,985 | 0.7% |
| 27 | Minnesota | 297,962 | 0.7% |
| 28 | Oklahoma | 291,551 | 0.7% |
| 29 | Washington | 268,660 | 0.7% |
| 30 | Nevada | 244,462 | 0.6% |
| 31 | Colorado | 225,390 | 0.5% |
| 32 | Delaware | 202,090 | 0.5% |
| 33 | Kansas | 178,820 | 0.4% |
| 34 | Iowa | 97,080 | 0.2% |
| 35 | Nebraska | 88,758 | 0.2% |
| 36 | Oregon | 77,564 | 0.2% |
| 37 | Rhode Island | 77,123 | 0.2% |
| 38 | West Virginia | 65,787 | 0.2% |
| 39 | New Mexico | 51,087 | 0.1% |
| 40 | Utah | 36,717 | 0.1% |
| 41 | Hawaii | 29,905 | 0.1% |
| 42 | Alaska | 27,373 | 0.1% |
| 43 | New Hampshire | 18,374 | 0.0% |
| 44 | Maine | 17,603 | 0.0% |
| 45 | South Dakota | 13,939 | 0.0% |
| 46 | Idaho | 12,037 | 0.0% |
| 47 | North Dakota | 10,547 | 0.0% |
| 48 | Wyoming | 8,555 | 0.0% |
| 49 | Vermont | 6,879 | 0.0% |
| 50 | Montana | 5,679 | 0.0% |
|  | District of Columbia | 316,482 | 0.8% |

Source: U.S. Bureau of the Census
"State Characteristics: Vintage 2012" (http://www.census.gov/popest/data/state/asrh/2012/index.html)
*Those who identified themselves as one race. "Black" is defined by Census as a person having origins in any of the Black racial groups of Africa. Census states "Race is a self-identification data item in which respondents choose the race or races with which they most closely identify."

# Percent of Population Black in 2012

## National Percent = 13.1%*

ALPHA ORDER

| RANK | STATE | PERCENT |
|------|-------|---------|
| 6 | Alabama | 26.5 |
| 36 | Alaska | 3.7 |
| 33 | Arizona | 4.5 |
| 13 | Arkansas | 15.6 |
| 28 | California | 6.6 |
| 34 | Colorado | 4.3 |
| 21 | Connecticut | 11.2 |
| 7 | Delaware | 22.0 |
| 12 | Florida | 16.6 |
| 3 | Georgia | 31.2 |
| 40 | Hawaii | 2.1 |
| 49 | Idaho | 0.8 |
| 14 | Illinois | 14.8 |
| 22 | Indiana | 9.4 |
| 38 | Iowa | 3.2 |
| 30 | Kansas | 6.2 |
| 24 | Kentucky | 8.1 |
| 2 | Louisiana | 32.4 |
| 46 | Maine | 1.3 |
| 4 | Maryland | 30.0 |
| 25 | Massachusetts | 7.9 |
| 16 | Michigan | 14.3 |
| 31 | Minnesota | 5.5 |
| 1 | Mississippi | 37.4 |
| 19 | Missouri | 11.7 |
| 50 | Montana | 0.6 |
| 32 | Nebraska | 4.8 |
| 23 | Nevada | 8.9 |
| 45 | New Hampshire | 1.4 |
| 15 | New Jersey | 14.7 |
| 39 | New Mexico | 2.4 |
| 10 | New York | 17.5 |
| 7 | North Carolina | 22.0 |
| 43 | North Dakota | 1.5 |
| 17 | Ohio | 12.5 |
| 26 | Oklahoma | 7.6 |
| 41 | Oregon | 2.0 |
| 20 | Pennsylvania | 11.4 |
| 27 | Rhode Island | 7.3 |
| 5 | South Carolina | 28.0 |
| 42 | South Dakota | 1.7 |
| 11 | Tennessee | 17.0 |
| 18 | Texas | 12.3 |
| 46 | Utah | 1.3 |
| 48 | Vermont | 1.1 |
| 9 | Virginia | 19.7 |
| 35 | Washington | 3.9 |
| 37 | West Virginia | 3.5 |
| 29 | Wisconsin | 6.5 |
| 43 | Wyoming | 1.5 |

RANK ORDER

| RANK | STATE | PERCENT |
|------|-------|---------|
| 1 | Mississippi | 37.4 |
| 2 | Louisiana | 32.4 |
| 3 | Georgia | 31.2 |
| 4 | Maryland | 30.0 |
| 5 | South Carolina | 28.0 |
| 6 | Alabama | 26.5 |
| 7 | Delaware | 22.0 |
| 7 | North Carolina | 22.0 |
| 9 | Virginia | 19.7 |
| 10 | New York | 17.5 |
| 11 | Tennessee | 17.0 |
| 12 | Florida | 16.6 |
| 13 | Arkansas | 15.6 |
| 14 | Illinois | 14.8 |
| 15 | New Jersey | 14.7 |
| 16 | Michigan | 14.3 |
| 17 | Ohio | 12.5 |
| 18 | Texas | 12.3 |
| 19 | Missouri | 11.7 |
| 20 | Pennsylvania | 11.4 |
| 21 | Connecticut | 11.2 |
| 22 | Indiana | 9.4 |
| 23 | Nevada | 8.9 |
| 24 | Kentucky | 8.1 |
| 25 | Massachusetts | 7.9 |
| 26 | Oklahoma | 7.6 |
| 27 | Rhode Island | 7.3 |
| 28 | California | 6.6 |
| 29 | Wisconsin | 6.5 |
| 30 | Kansas | 6.2 |
| 31 | Minnesota | 5.5 |
| 32 | Nebraska | 4.8 |
| 33 | Arizona | 4.5 |
| 34 | Colorado | 4.3 |
| 35 | Washington | 3.9 |
| 36 | Alaska | 3.7 |
| 37 | West Virginia | 3.5 |
| 38 | Iowa | 3.2 |
| 39 | New Mexico | 2.4 |
| 40 | Hawaii | 2.1 |
| 41 | Oregon | 2.0 |
| 42 | South Dakota | 1.7 |
| 43 | North Dakota | 1.5 |
| 43 | Wyoming | 1.5 |
| 45 | New Hampshire | 1.4 |
| 46 | Maine | 1.3 |
| 46 | Utah | 1.3 |
| 48 | Vermont | 1.1 |
| 49 | Idaho | 0.8 |
| 50 | Montana | 0.6 |
| | District of Columbia | 50.1 |

Source: CQ Press using data from U.S. Bureau of the Census
   "State Characteristics: Vintage 2012" (http://www.census.gov/popest/data/state/asrh/2012/index.html)
*Those who identified themselves as one race. "Black" is defined by Census as a person having origins in any of the Black racial groups of Africa.  Census states "Race is a self-identification data item in which respondents choose the race or races with which they most closely identify."

# Hispanic Population in 2012

## National Total = 53,027,708*

ALPHA ORDER

| RANK | STATE | POPULATION | % of USA |
|---|---|---|---|
| 33 | Alabama | 196,032 | 0.4% |
| 43 | Alaska | 44,869 | 0.1% |
| 6 | Arizona | 1,976,106 | 3.7% |
| 32 | Arkansas | 199,693 | 0.4% |
| 1 | California | 14,537,666 | 27.4% |
| 8 | Colorado | 1,088,744 | 2.1% |
| 18 | Connecticut | 510,645 | 1.0% |
| 41 | Delaware | 78,813 | 0.1% |
| 3 | Florida | 4,484,199 | 8.5% |
| 10 | Georgia | 909,902 | 1.7% |
| 39 | Hawaii | 131,744 | 0.2% |
| 34 | Idaho | 185,160 | 0.3% |
| 5 | Illinois | 2,101,208 | 4.0% |
| 21 | Indiana | 412,609 | 0.8% |
| 36 | Iowa | 162,894 | 0.3% |
| 26 | Kansas | 317,061 | 0.6% |
| 37 | Kentucky | 142,028 | 0.3% |
| 31 | Louisiana | 208,325 | 0.4% |
| 48 | Maine | 18,599 | 0.0% |
| 17 | Maryland | 512,010 | 1.0% |
| 16 | Massachusetts | 674,073 | 1.3% |
| 20 | Michigan | 456,330 | 0.9% |
| 28 | Minnesota | 264,359 | 0.5% |
| 40 | Mississippi | 85,260 | 0.2% |
| 30 | Missouri | 225,314 | 0.4% |
| 45 | Montana | 31,552 | 0.1% |
| 35 | Nebraska | 179,970 | 0.3% |
| 14 | Nevada | 752,049 | 1.4% |
| 44 | New Hampshire | 40,042 | 0.1% |
| 7 | New Jersey | 1,641,398 | 3.1% |
| 9 | New Mexico | 979,722 | 1.8% |
| 4 | New York | 3,552,781 | 6.7% |
| 11 | North Carolina | 850,853 | 1.6% |
| 49 | North Dakota | 17,230 | 0.0% |
| 23 | Ohio | 377,119 | 0.7% |
| 24 | Oklahoma | 356,300 | 0.7% |
| 19 | Oregon | 474,157 | 0.9% |
| 13 | Pennsylvania | 781,202 | 1.5% |
| 38 | Rhode Island | 138,549 | 0.3% |
| 29 | South Carolina | 249,712 | 0.5% |
| 46 | South Dakota | 25,715 | 0.0% |
| 27 | Tennessee | 312,732 | 0.6% |
| 2 | Texas | 9,960,900 | 18.8% |
| 22 | Utah | 379,436 | 0.7% |
| 50 | Vermont | 10,057 | 0.0% |
| 15 | Virginia | 687,496 | 1.3% |
| 12 | Washington | 807,599 | 1.5% |
| 47 | West Virginia | 24,530 | 0.0% |
| 25 | Wisconsin | 355,468 | 0.7% |
| 42 | Wyoming | 54,770 | 0.1% |

RANK ORDER

| RANK | STATE | POPULATION | % of USA |
|---|---|---|---|
| 1 | California | 14,537,666 | 27.4% |
| 2 | Texas | 9,960,900 | 18.8% |
| 3 | Florida | 4,484,199 | 8.5% |
| 4 | New York | 3,552,781 | 6.7% |
| 5 | Illinois | 2,101,208 | 4.0% |
| 6 | Arizona | 1,976,106 | 3.7% |
| 7 | New Jersey | 1,641,398 | 3.1% |
| 8 | Colorado | 1,088,744 | 2.1% |
| 9 | New Mexico | 979,722 | 1.8% |
| 10 | Georgia | 909,902 | 1.7% |
| 11 | North Carolina | 850,853 | 1.6% |
| 12 | Washington | 807,599 | 1.5% |
| 13 | Pennsylvania | 781,202 | 1.5% |
| 14 | Nevada | 752,049 | 1.4% |
| 15 | Virginia | 687,496 | 1.3% |
| 16 | Massachusetts | 674,073 | 1.3% |
| 17 | Maryland | 512,010 | 1.0% |
| 18 | Connecticut | 510,645 | 1.0% |
| 19 | Oregon | 474,157 | 0.9% |
| 20 | Michigan | 456,330 | 0.9% |
| 21 | Indiana | 412,609 | 0.8% |
| 22 | Utah | 379,436 | 0.7% |
| 23 | Ohio | 377,119 | 0.7% |
| 24 | Oklahoma | 356,300 | 0.7% |
| 25 | Wisconsin | 355,468 | 0.7% |
| 26 | Kansas | 317,061 | 0.6% |
| 27 | Tennessee | 312,732 | 0.6% |
| 28 | Minnesota | 264,359 | 0.5% |
| 29 | South Carolina | 249,712 | 0.5% |
| 30 | Missouri | 225,314 | 0.4% |
| 31 | Louisiana | 208,325 | 0.4% |
| 32 | Arkansas | 199,693 | 0.4% |
| 33 | Alabama | 196,032 | 0.4% |
| 34 | Idaho | 185,160 | 0.3% |
| 35 | Nebraska | 179,970 | 0.3% |
| 36 | Iowa | 162,894 | 0.3% |
| 37 | Kentucky | 142,028 | 0.3% |
| 38 | Rhode Island | 138,549 | 0.3% |
| 39 | Hawaii | 131,744 | 0.2% |
| 40 | Mississippi | 85,260 | 0.2% |
| 41 | Delaware | 78,813 | 0.1% |
| 42 | Wyoming | 54,770 | 0.1% |
| 43 | Alaska | 44,869 | 0.1% |
| 44 | New Hampshire | 40,042 | 0.1% |
| 45 | Montana | 31,552 | 0.1% |
| 46 | South Dakota | 25,715 | 0.0% |
| 47 | West Virginia | 24,530 | 0.0% |
| 48 | Maine | 18,599 | 0.0% |
| 49 | North Dakota | 17,230 | 0.0% |
| 50 | Vermont | 10,057 | 0.0% |
| | District of Columbia | 62,726 | 0.1% |

Source: U.S. Bureau of the Census
"State Characteristics: Vintage 2012" (http://www.census.gov/popest/data/state/asrh/2012/index.html)
*Persons of Hispanic origin may be of any race. Census states "Race is a self-identification data item in which respondents choose the race or races with which they most closely identify."

# Percent of Population Hispanic in 2012

## National Percent = 16.9%*

ALPHA ORDER

| RANK | STATE | PERCENT |
|------|-------|---------|
| 39 | Alabama | 4.1 |
| 31 | Alaska | 6.1 |
| 4 | Arizona | 30.2 |
| 28 | Arkansas | 6.8 |
| 2 | California | 38.2 |
| 7 | Colorado | 21.0 |
| 11 | Connecticut | 14.2 |
| 26 | Delaware | 8.6 |
| 6 | Florida | 23.2 |
| 23 | Georgia | 9.2 |
| 20 | Hawaii | 9.5 |
| 16 | Idaho | 11.6 |
| 10 | Illinois | 16.3 |
| 29 | Indiana | 6.3 |
| 33 | Iowa | 5.3 |
| 17 | Kansas | 11.0 |
| 42 | Kentucky | 3.2 |
| 38 | Louisiana | 4.5 |
| 49 | Maine | 1.4 |
| 24 | Maryland | 8.7 |
| 18 | Massachusetts | 10.1 |
| 37 | Michigan | 4.6 |
| 35 | Minnesota | 4.9 |
| 46 | Mississippi | 2.9 |
| 40 | Missouri | 3.7 |
| 43 | Montana | 3.1 |
| 19 | Nebraska | 9.7 |
| 5 | Nevada | 27.3 |
| 45 | New Hampshire | 3.0 |
| 8 | New Jersey | 18.5 |
| 1 | New Mexico | 47.0 |
| 9 | New York | 18.2 |
| 24 | North Carolina | 8.7 |
| 47 | North Dakota | 2.5 |
| 41 | Ohio | 3.3 |
| 22 | Oklahoma | 9.3 |
| 14 | Oregon | 12.2 |
| 31 | Pennsylvania | 6.1 |
| 13 | Rhode Island | 13.2 |
| 33 | South Carolina | 5.3 |
| 43 | South Dakota | 3.1 |
| 36 | Tennessee | 4.8 |
| 2 | Texas | 38.2 |
| 12 | Utah | 13.3 |
| 48 | Vermont | 1.6 |
| 27 | Virginia | 8.4 |
| 15 | Washington | 11.7 |
| 50 | West Virginia | 1.3 |
| 30 | Wisconsin | 6.2 |
| 20 | Wyoming | 9.5 |

RANK ORDER

| RANK | STATE | PERCENT |
|------|-------|---------|
| 1 | New Mexico | 47.0 |
| 2 | California | 38.2 |
| 2 | Texas | 38.2 |
| 4 | Arizona | 30.2 |
| 5 | Nevada | 27.3 |
| 6 | Florida | 23.2 |
| 7 | Colorado | 21.0 |
| 8 | New Jersey | 18.5 |
| 9 | New York | 18.2 |
| 10 | Illinois | 16.3 |
| 11 | Connecticut | 14.2 |
| 12 | Utah | 13.3 |
| 13 | Rhode Island | 13.2 |
| 14 | Oregon | 12.2 |
| 15 | Washington | 11.7 |
| 16 | Idaho | 11.6 |
| 17 | Kansas | 11.0 |
| 18 | Massachusetts | 10.1 |
| 19 | Nebraska | 9.7 |
| 20 | Hawaii | 9.5 |
| 20 | Wyoming | 9.5 |
| 22 | Oklahoma | 9.3 |
| 23 | Georgia | 9.2 |
| 24 | Maryland | 8.7 |
| 24 | North Carolina | 8.7 |
| 26 | Delaware | 8.6 |
| 27 | Virginia | 8.4 |
| 28 | Arkansas | 6.8 |
| 29 | Indiana | 6.3 |
| 30 | Wisconsin | 6.2 |
| 31 | Alaska | 6.1 |
| 31 | Pennsylvania | 6.1 |
| 33 | Iowa | 5.3 |
| 33 | South Carolina | 5.3 |
| 35 | Minnesota | 4.9 |
| 36 | Tennessee | 4.8 |
| 37 | Michigan | 4.6 |
| 38 | Louisiana | 4.5 |
| 39 | Alabama | 4.1 |
| 40 | Missouri | 3.7 |
| 41 | Ohio | 3.3 |
| 42 | Kentucky | 3.2 |
| 43 | Montana | 3.1 |
| 43 | South Dakota | 3.1 |
| 45 | New Hampshire | 3.0 |
| 46 | Mississippi | 2.9 |
| 47 | North Dakota | 2.5 |
| 48 | Vermont | 1.6 |
| 49 | Maine | 1.4 |
| 50 | West Virginia | 1.3 |
| | District of Columbia | 9.9 |

Source: CQ Press using data from U.S. Bureau of the Census
"State Characteristics: Vintage 2012" (http://www.census.gov/popest/data/state/asrh/2012/index.html)
*Persons of Hispanic origin may be of any race. Census states "Race is a self-identification data item in which respondents choose the race or races with which they most closely identify."

# Asian Population in 2012

## National Total = 16,145,821*

| ALPHA ORDER | | | | | RANK ORDER | | | |
|---|---|---|---|---|---|---|---|---|
| RANK | STATE | POPULATION | % of USA | | RANK | STATE | POPULATION | % of USA |
| 33 | Alabama | 59,602 | 0.4% | | 1 | California | 5,294,255 | 32.8% |
| 35 | Alaska | 41,986 | 0.3% | | 2 | New York | 1,566,191 | 9.7% |
| 19 | Arizona | 204,840 | 1.3% | | 3 | Texas | 1,095,443 | 6.8% |
| 36 | Arkansas | 41,338 | 0.3% | | 4 | New Jersey | 794,923 | 4.9% |
| 1 | California | 5,294,255 | 32.8% | | 5 | Illinois | 638,108 | 4.0% |
| 21 | Colorado | 155,031 | 1.0% | | 6 | Hawaii | 532,599 | 3.3% |
| 22 | Connecticut | 150,529 | 0.9% | | 7 | Washington | 531,395 | 3.3% |
| 40 | Delaware | 32,141 | 0.2% | | 8 | Florida | 511,960 | 3.2% |
| 8 | Florida | 511,960 | 3.2% | | 9 | Virginia | 487,505 | 3.0% |
| 13 | Georgia | 351,734 | 2.2% | | 10 | Massachusetts | 387,770 | 2.4% |
| 6 | Hawaii | 532,599 | 3.3% | | 11 | Pennsylvania | 383,917 | 2.4% |
| 43 | Idaho | 21,899 | 0.1% | | 12 | Maryland | 352,347 | 2.2% |
| 5 | Illinois | 638,108 | 4.0% | | 13 | Georgia | 351,734 | 2.2% |
| 24 | Indiana | 116,029 | 0.7% | | 14 | Michigan | 259,806 | 1.6% |
| 32 | Iowa | 60,004 | 0.4% | | 15 | North Carolina | 238,933 | 1.5% |
| 28 | Kansas | 74,598 | 0.5% | | 16 | Minnesota | 235,120 | 1.5% |
| 34 | Kentucky | 55,336 | 0.3% | | 17 | Nevada | 217,264 | 1.3% |
| 27 | Louisiana | 77,252 | 0.5% | | 18 | Ohio | 210,865 | 1.3% |
| 44 | Maine | 14,810 | 0.1% | | 19 | Arizona | 204,840 | 1.3% |
| 12 | Maryland | 352,347 | 2.2% | | 20 | Oregon | 156,077 | 1.0% |
| 10 | Massachusetts | 387,770 | 2.4% | | 21 | Colorado | 155,031 | 1.0% |
| 14 | Michigan | 259,806 | 1.6% | | 22 | Connecticut | 150,529 | 0.9% |
| 16 | Minnesota | 235,120 | 1.5% | | 23 | Wisconsin | 140,885 | 0.9% |
| 42 | Mississippi | 28,255 | 0.2% | | 24 | Indiana | 116,029 | 0.7% |
| 25 | Missouri | 107,092 | 0.7% | | 25 | Missouri | 107,092 | 0.7% |
| 49 | Montana | 7,315 | 0.0% | | 26 | Tennessee | 102,862 | 0.6% |
| 37 | Nebraska | 36,467 | 0.2% | | 27 | Louisiana | 77,252 | 0.5% |
| 17 | Nevada | 217,264 | 1.3% | | 28 | Kansas | 74,598 | 0.5% |
| 41 | New Hampshire | 31,126 | 0.2% | | 29 | Oklahoma | 72,539 | 0.4% |
| 4 | New Jersey | 794,923 | 4.9% | | 30 | South Carolina | 67,529 | 0.4% |
| 39 | New Mexico | 33,665 | 0.2% | | 31 | Utah | 63,857 | 0.4% |
| 2 | New York | 1,566,191 | 9.7% | | 32 | Iowa | 60,004 | 0.4% |
| 15 | North Carolina | 238,933 | 1.5% | | 33 | Alabama | 59,602 | 0.4% |
| 48 | North Dakota | 7,840 | 0.0% | | 34 | Kentucky | 55,336 | 0.3% |
| 18 | Ohio | 210,865 | 1.3% | | 35 | Alaska | 41,986 | 0.3% |
| 29 | Oklahoma | 72,539 | 0.4% | | 36 | Arkansas | 41,338 | 0.3% |
| 20 | Oregon | 156,077 | 1.0% | | 37 | Nebraska | 36,467 | 0.2% |
| 11 | Pennsylvania | 383,917 | 2.4% | | 38 | Rhode Island | 33,852 | 0.2% |
| 38 | Rhode Island | 33,852 | 0.2% | | 39 | New Mexico | 33,665 | 0.2% |
| 30 | South Carolina | 67,529 | 0.4% | | 40 | Delaware | 32,141 | 0.2% |
| 46 | South Dakota | 9,005 | 0.1% | | 41 | New Hampshire | 31,126 | 0.2% |
| 26 | Tennessee | 102,862 | 0.6% | | 42 | Mississippi | 28,255 | 0.2% |
| 3 | Texas | 1,095,443 | 6.8% | | 43 | Idaho | 21,899 | 0.1% |
| 31 | Utah | 63,857 | 0.4% | | 44 | Maine | 14,810 | 0.1% |
| 47 | Vermont | 8,912 | 0.1% | | 45 | West Virginia | 13,796 | 0.1% |
| 9 | Virginia | 487,505 | 3.0% | | 46 | South Dakota | 9,005 | 0.1% |
| 7 | Washington | 531,395 | 3.3% | | 47 | Vermont | 8,912 | 0.1% |
| 45 | West Virginia | 13,796 | 0.1% | | 48 | North Dakota | 7,840 | 0.0% |
| 23 | Wisconsin | 140,885 | 0.9% | | 49 | Montana | 7,315 | 0.0% |
| 50 | Wyoming | 5,183 | 0.0% | | 50 | Wyoming | 5,183 | 0.0% |
| | | | | | | District of Columbia | 24,034 | 0.1% |

Source: U.S. Bureau of the Census
"State Characteristics: Vintage 2012" (http://www.census.gov/popest/data/state/asrh/2012/index.html)
*Those who identified themselves as one race. Census states "Race is a self-identification data item in which respondents choose the race or races with which they most closely identify."

# Percent of Population Asian in 2012

## National Percent = 5.1%*

ALPHA ORDER

| RANK | STATE | PERCENT |
|---|---|---|
| 43 | Alabama | 1.2 |
| 10 | Alaska | 5.7 |
| 19 | Arizona | 3.1 |
| 38 | Arkansas | 1.4 |
| 2 | California | 13.9 |
| 20 | Colorado | 3.0 |
| 13 | Connecticut | 4.2 |
| 16 | Delaware | 3.5 |
| 22 | Florida | 2.7 |
| 16 | Georgia | 3.5 |
| 1 | Hawaii | 38.3 |
| 38 | Idaho | 1.4 |
| 11 | Illinois | 5.0 |
| 32 | Indiana | 1.8 |
| 29 | Iowa | 2.0 |
| 23 | Kansas | 2.6 |
| 42 | Kentucky | 1.3 |
| 35 | Louisiana | 1.7 |
| 44 | Maine | 1.1 |
| 7 | Maryland | 6.0 |
| 9 | Massachusetts | 5.8 |
| 23 | Michigan | 2.6 |
| 12 | Minnesota | 4.4 |
| 47 | Mississippi | 0.9 |
| 32 | Missouri | 1.8 |
| 49 | Montana | 0.7 |
| 29 | Nebraska | 2.0 |
| 5 | Nevada | 7.9 |
| 27 | New Hampshire | 2.4 |
| 3 | New Jersey | 9.0 |
| 36 | New Mexico | 1.6 |
| 4 | New York | 8.0 |
| 25 | North Carolina | 2.5 |
| 44 | North Dakota | 1.1 |
| 32 | Ohio | 1.8 |
| 31 | Oklahoma | 1.9 |
| 15 | Oregon | 4.0 |
| 20 | Pennsylvania | 3.0 |
| 18 | Rhode Island | 3.2 |
| 38 | South Carolina | 1.4 |
| 44 | South Dakota | 1.1 |
| 36 | Tennessee | 1.6 |
| 13 | Texas | 4.2 |
| 28 | Utah | 2.2 |
| 38 | Vermont | 1.4 |
| 7 | Virginia | 6.0 |
| 6 | Washington | 7.7 |
| 49 | West Virginia | 0.7 |
| 25 | Wisconsin | 2.5 |
| 47 | Wyoming | 0.9 |

RANK ORDER

| RANK | STATE | PERCENT |
|---|---|---|
| 1 | Hawaii | 38.3 |
| 2 | California | 13.9 |
| 3 | New Jersey | 9.0 |
| 4 | New York | 8.0 |
| 5 | Nevada | 7.9 |
| 6 | Washington | 7.7 |
| 7 | Maryland | 6.0 |
| 7 | Virginia | 6.0 |
| 9 | Massachusetts | 5.8 |
| 10 | Alaska | 5.7 |
| 11 | Illinois | 5.0 |
| 12 | Minnesota | 4.4 |
| 13 | Connecticut | 4.2 |
| 13 | Texas | 4.2 |
| 15 | Oregon | 4.0 |
| 16 | Delaware | 3.5 |
| 16 | Georgia | 3.5 |
| 18 | Rhode Island | 3.2 |
| 19 | Arizona | 3.1 |
| 20 | Colorado | 3.0 |
| 20 | Pennsylvania | 3.0 |
| 22 | Florida | 2.7 |
| 23 | Kansas | 2.6 |
| 23 | Michigan | 2.6 |
| 25 | North Carolina | 2.5 |
| 25 | Wisconsin | 2.5 |
| 27 | New Hampshire | 2.4 |
| 28 | Utah | 2.2 |
| 29 | Iowa | 2.0 |
| 29 | Nebraska | 2.0 |
| 31 | Oklahoma | 1.9 |
| 32 | Indiana | 1.8 |
| 32 | Missouri | 1.8 |
| 32 | Ohio | 1.8 |
| 35 | Louisiana | 1.7 |
| 36 | New Mexico | 1.6 |
| 36 | Tennessee | 1.6 |
| 38 | Arkansas | 1.4 |
| 38 | Idaho | 1.4 |
| 38 | South Carolina | 1.4 |
| 38 | Vermont | 1.4 |
| 42 | Kentucky | 1.3 |
| 43 | Alabama | 1.2 |
| 44 | Maine | 1.1 |
| 44 | North Dakota | 1.1 |
| 44 | South Dakota | 1.1 |
| 47 | Mississippi | 0.9 |
| 47 | Wyoming | 0.9 |
| 49 | Montana | 0.7 |
| 49 | West Virginia | 0.7 |

| | | |
|---|---|---|
| | District of Columbia | 3.8 |

Source: CQ Press using data from U.S. Bureau of the Census
   "State Characteristics: Vintage 2012" (http://www.census.gov/popest/data/state/asrh/2012/index.html)
*Those who identified themselves as one race. Census states "Race is a self-identification data item in which respondents choose the race or races with which they most closely identify."

# American Indian Population in 2012

## National Total = 3,857,495*

ALPHA ORDER

| RANK | STATE | POPULATION | % of USA |
|------|-------|-----------:|---------:|
| 28 | Alabama | 33,579 | 0.9% |
| 9 | Alaska | 108,249 | 2.8% |
| 2 | Arizona | 345,622 | 9.0% |
| 33 | Arkansas | 27,647 | 0.7% |
| 1 | California | 639,740 | 16.6% |
| 11 | Colorado | 81,688 | 2.1% |
| 39 | Connecticut | 17,688 | 0.5% |
| 46 | Delaware | 6,161 | 0.2% |
| 10 | Florida | 95,218 | 2.5% |
| 20 | Georgia | 50,539 | 1.3% |
| 47 | Hawaii | 5,507 | 0.1% |
| 35 | Idaho | 26,684 | 0.7% |
| 12 | Illinois | 75,948 | 2.0% |
| 36 | Indiana | 25,494 | 0.7% |
| 42 | Iowa | 14,179 | 0.4% |
| 27 | Kansas | 33,909 | 0.9% |
| 43 | Kentucky | 12,429 | 0.3% |
| 26 | Louisiana | 34,249 | 0.9% |
| 45 | Maine | 8,859 | 0.2% |
| 29 | Maryland | 32,275 | 0.8% |
| 31 | Massachusetts | 31,172 | 0.8% |
| 14 | Michigan | 69,751 | 1.8% |
| 15 | Minnesota | 68,961 | 1.8% |
| 40 | Mississippi | 17,501 | 0.5% |
| 30 | Missouri | 31,631 | 0.8% |
| 17 | Montana | 65,164 | 1.7% |
| 38 | Nebraska | 24,281 | 0.6% |
| 21 | Nevada | 44,571 | 1.2% |
| 49 | New Hampshire | 3,633 | 0.1% |
| 19 | New Jersey | 52,255 | 1.4% |
| 5 | New Mexico | 213,081 | 5.5% |
| 6 | New York | 186,613 | 4.8% |
| 7 | North Carolina | 150,965 | 3.9% |
| 25 | North Dakota | 38,283 | 1.0% |
| 32 | Ohio | 30,606 | 0.8% |
| 3 | Oklahoma | 341,844 | 8.9% |
| 16 | Oregon | 68,955 | 1.8% |
| 24 | Pennsylvania | 41,680 | 1.1% |
| 44 | Rhode Island | 9,358 | 0.2% |
| 37 | South Carolina | 25,254 | 0.7% |
| 13 | South Dakota | 74,223 | 1.9% |
| 34 | Tennessee | 27,247 | 0.7% |
| 4 | Texas | 265,563 | 6.9% |
| 23 | Utah | 42,049 | 1.1% |
| 50 | Vermont | 2,280 | 0.1% |
| 22 | Virginia | 43,768 | 1.1% |
| 8 | Washington | 126,526 | 3.3% |
| 48 | West Virginia | 4,104 | 0.1% |
| 18 | Wisconsin | 62,021 | 1.6% |
| 41 | Wyoming | 15,003 | 0.4% |

RANK ORDER

| RANK | STATE | POPULATION | % of USA |
|------|-------|-----------:|---------:|
| 1 | California | 639,740 | 16.6% |
| 2 | Arizona | 345,622 | 9.0% |
| 3 | Oklahoma | 341,844 | 8.9% |
| 4 | Texas | 265,563 | 6.9% |
| 5 | New Mexico | 213,081 | 5.5% |
| 6 | New York | 186,613 | 4.8% |
| 7 | North Carolina | 150,965 | 3.9% |
| 8 | Washington | 126,526 | 3.3% |
| 9 | Alaska | 108,249 | 2.8% |
| 10 | Florida | 95,218 | 2.5% |
| 11 | Colorado | 81,688 | 2.1% |
| 12 | Illinois | 75,948 | 2.0% |
| 13 | South Dakota | 74,223 | 1.9% |
| 14 | Michigan | 69,751 | 1.8% |
| 15 | Minnesota | 68,961 | 1.8% |
| 16 | Oregon | 68,955 | 1.8% |
| 17 | Montana | 65,164 | 1.7% |
| 18 | Wisconsin | 62,021 | 1.6% |
| 19 | New Jersey | 52,255 | 1.4% |
| 20 | Georgia | 50,539 | 1.3% |
| 21 | Nevada | 44,571 | 1.2% |
| 22 | Virginia | 43,768 | 1.1% |
| 23 | Utah | 42,049 | 1.1% |
| 24 | Pennsylvania | 41,680 | 1.1% |
| 25 | North Dakota | 38,283 | 1.0% |
| 26 | Louisiana | 34,249 | 0.9% |
| 27 | Kansas | 33,909 | 0.9% |
| 28 | Alabama | 33,579 | 0.9% |
| 29 | Maryland | 32,275 | 0.8% |
| 30 | Missouri | 31,631 | 0.8% |
| 31 | Massachusetts | 31,172 | 0.8% |
| 32 | Ohio | 30,606 | 0.8% |
| 33 | Arkansas | 27,647 | 0.7% |
| 34 | Tennessee | 27,247 | 0.7% |
| 35 | Idaho | 26,684 | 0.7% |
| 36 | Indiana | 25,494 | 0.7% |
| 37 | South Carolina | 25,254 | 0.7% |
| 38 | Nebraska | 24,281 | 0.6% |
| 39 | Connecticut | 17,688 | 0.5% |
| 40 | Mississippi | 17,501 | 0.5% |
| 41 | Wyoming | 15,003 | 0.4% |
| 42 | Iowa | 14,179 | 0.4% |
| 43 | Kentucky | 12,429 | 0.3% |
| 44 | Rhode Island | 9,358 | 0.2% |
| 45 | Maine | 8,859 | 0.2% |
| 46 | Delaware | 6,161 | 0.2% |
| 47 | Hawaii | 5,507 | 0.1% |
| 48 | West Virginia | 4,104 | 0.1% |
| 49 | New Hampshire | 3,633 | 0.1% |
| 50 | Vermont | 2,280 | 0.1% |
| | District of Columbia | 3,488 | 0.1% |

Source: U.S. Bureau of the Census
   "State Characteristics: Vintage 2012" (http://www.census.gov/popest/data/state/asrh/2012/index.html)
*Those who identified themselves as one race. Includes Alaska Native populations. Census states "Race is a self-identification data item in which respondents choose the race or races with which they most closely identify."

# Percent of Population American Indian in 2012

## National Percent = 1.2%*

ALPHA ORDER

| RANK | STATE | PERCENT |
|------|-------|---------|
| 25 | Alabama | 0.7 |
| 1 | Alaska | 14.8 |
| 7 | Arizona | 5.3 |
| 23 | Arkansas | 0.9 |
| 11 | California | 1.7 |
| 13 | Colorado | 1.6 |
| 33 | Connecticut | 0.5 |
| 25 | Delaware | 0.7 |
| 33 | Florida | 0.5 |
| 33 | Georgia | 0.5 |
| 42 | Hawaii | 0.4 |
| 11 | Idaho | 1.7 |
| 30 | Illinois | 0.6 |
| 42 | Indiana | 0.4 |
| 33 | Iowa | 0.5 |
| 19 | Kansas | 1.2 |
| 46 | Kentucky | 0.3 |
| 25 | Louisiana | 0.7 |
| 25 | Maine | 0.7 |
| 33 | Maryland | 0.5 |
| 33 | Massachusetts | 0.5 |
| 25 | Michigan | 0.7 |
| 17 | Minnesota | 1.3 |
| 30 | Mississippi | 0.6 |
| 33 | Missouri | 0.5 |
| 5 | Montana | 6.5 |
| 17 | Nebraska | 1.3 |
| 13 | Nevada | 1.6 |
| 46 | New Hampshire | 0.3 |
| 30 | New Jersey | 0.6 |
| 2 | New Mexico | 10.2 |
| 21 | New York | 1.0 |
| 15 | North Carolina | 1.5 |
| 6 | North Dakota | 5.5 |
| 46 | Ohio | 0.3 |
| 3 | Oklahoma | 9.0 |
| 9 | Oregon | 1.8 |
| 46 | Pennsylvania | 0.3 |
| 23 | Rhode Island | 0.9 |
| 33 | South Carolina | 0.5 |
| 4 | South Dakota | 8.9 |
| 42 | Tennessee | 0.4 |
| 21 | Texas | 1.0 |
| 15 | Utah | 1.5 |
| 42 | Vermont | 0.4 |
| 33 | Virginia | 0.5 |
| 9 | Washington | 1.8 |
| 50 | West Virginia | 0.2 |
| 20 | Wisconsin | 1.1 |
| 8 | Wyoming | 2.6 |

RANK ORDER

| RANK | STATE | PERCENT |
|------|-------|---------|
| 1 | Alaska | 14.8 |
| 2 | New Mexico | 10.2 |
| 3 | Oklahoma | 9.0 |
| 4 | South Dakota | 8.9 |
| 5 | Montana | 6.5 |
| 6 | North Dakota | 5.5 |
| 7 | Arizona | 5.3 |
| 8 | Wyoming | 2.6 |
| 9 | Oregon | 1.8 |
| 9 | Washington | 1.8 |
| 11 | California | 1.7 |
| 11 | Idaho | 1.7 |
| 13 | Colorado | 1.6 |
| 13 | Nevada | 1.6 |
| 15 | North Carolina | 1.5 |
| 15 | Utah | 1.5 |
| 17 | Minnesota | 1.3 |
| 17 | Nebraska | 1.3 |
| 19 | Kansas | 1.2 |
| 20 | Wisconsin | 1.1 |
| 21 | New York | 1.0 |
| 21 | Texas | 1.0 |
| 23 | Arkansas | 0.9 |
| 23 | Rhode Island | 0.9 |
| 25 | Alabama | 0.7 |
| 25 | Delaware | 0.7 |
| 25 | Louisiana | 0.7 |
| 25 | Maine | 0.7 |
| 25 | Michigan | 0.7 |
| 30 | Illinois | 0.6 |
| 30 | Mississippi | 0.6 |
| 30 | New Jersey | 0.6 |
| 33 | Connecticut | 0.5 |
| 33 | Florida | 0.5 |
| 33 | Georgia | 0.5 |
| 33 | Iowa | 0.5 |
| 33 | Maryland | 0.5 |
| 33 | Massachusetts | 0.5 |
| 33 | Missouri | 0.5 |
| 33 | South Carolina | 0.5 |
| 33 | Virginia | 0.5 |
| 42 | Hawaii | 0.4 |
| 42 | Indiana | 0.4 |
| 42 | Tennessee | 0.4 |
| 42 | Vermont | 0.4 |
| 46 | Kentucky | 0.3 |
| 46 | New Hampshire | 0.3 |
| 46 | Ohio | 0.3 |
| 46 | Pennsylvania | 0.3 |
| 50 | West Virginia | 0.2 |
| | District of Columbia | 0.6 |

Source: CQ Press using data from U.S. Bureau of the Census
"State Characteristics: Vintage 2012" (http://www.census.gov/popest/data/state/asrh/2012/index.html)
*Those who identified themselves as one race. Includes Alaska Native populations. Census states "Race is a self-identification data item in which respondents choose the race or races with which they most closely identify."

# Native Hawaiian or Other Pacific Islander Population in 2012

## National Total = 707,228*

### ALPHA ORDER

| RANK | STATE | POPULATION | % of USA |
|---|---|---|---|
| 26 | Alabama | 5,270 | 0.7% |
| 15 | Alaska | 8,558 | 1.2% |
| 9 | Arizona | 16,922 | 2.4% |
| 20 | Arkansas | 7,495 | 1.1% |
| 1 | California | 187,855 | 26.6% |
| 13 | Colorado | 9,231 | 1.3% |
| 30 | Connecticut | 3,641 | 0.5% |
| 43 | Delaware | 766 | 0.1% |
| 7 | Florida | 20,454 | 2.9% |
| 11 | Georgia | 11,061 | 1.6% |
| 2 | Hawaii | 140,112 | 19.8% |
| 35 | Idaho | 2,916 | 0.4% |
| 17 | Illinois | 7,877 | 1.1% |
| 28 | Indiana | 3,769 | 0.5% |
| 38 | Iowa | 2,634 | 0.4% |
| 34 | Kansas | 2,953 | 0.4% |
| 31 | Kentucky | 3,441 | 0.5% |
| 36 | Louisiana | 2,781 | 0.4% |
| 48 | Maine | 513 | 0.1% |
| 24 | Maryland | 5,674 | 0.8% |
| 21 | Massachusetts | 6,304 | 0.9% |
| 29 | Michigan | 3,720 | 0.5% |
| 33 | Minnesota | 3,206 | 0.5% |
| 40 | Mississippi | 1,715 | 0.2% |
| 18 | Missouri | 7,821 | 1.1% |
| 42 | Montana | 774 | 0.1% |
| 39 | Nebraska | 2,163 | 0.3% |
| 8 | Nevada | 20,121 | 2.8% |
| 45 | New Hampshire | 596 | 0.1% |
| 16 | New Jersey | 8,228 | 1.2% |
| 32 | New Mexico | 3,327 | 0.5% |
| 6 | New York | 25,101 | 3.5% |
| 12 | North Carolina | 10,834 | 1.5% |
| 49 | North Dakota | 475 | 0.1% |
| 25 | Ohio | 5,597 | 0.8% |
| 22 | Oklahoma | 5,976 | 0.8% |
| 10 | Oregon | 15,848 | 2.2% |
| 19 | Pennsylvania | 7,723 | 1.1% |
| 41 | Rhode Island | 1,648 | 0.2% |
| 27 | South Carolina | 4,104 | 0.6% |
| 44 | South Dakota | 608 | 0.1% |
| 23 | Tennessee | 5,788 | 0.8% |
| 4 | Texas | 33,980 | 4.8% |
| 5 | Utah | 27,563 | 3.9% |
| 50 | Vermont | 203 | 0.0% |
| 14 | Virginia | 8,830 | 1.2% |
| 3 | Washington | 46,143 | 6.5% |
| 47 | West Virginia | 563 | 0.1% |
| 37 | Wisconsin | 2,640 | 0.4% |
| 46 | Wyoming | 575 | 0.1% |

### RANK ORDER

| RANK | STATE | POPULATION | % of USA |
|---|---|---|---|
| 1 | California | 187,855 | 26.6% |
| 2 | Hawaii | 140,112 | 19.8% |
| 3 | Washington | 46,143 | 6.5% |
| 4 | Texas | 33,980 | 4.8% |
| 5 | Utah | 27,563 | 3.9% |
| 6 | New York | 25,101 | 3.5% |
| 7 | Florida | 20,454 | 2.9% |
| 8 | Nevada | 20,121 | 2.8% |
| 9 | Arizona | 16,922 | 2.4% |
| 10 | Oregon | 15,848 | 2.2% |
| 11 | Georgia | 11,061 | 1.6% |
| 12 | North Carolina | 10,834 | 1.5% |
| 13 | Colorado | 9,231 | 1.3% |
| 14 | Virginia | 8,830 | 1.2% |
| 15 | Alaska | 8,558 | 1.2% |
| 16 | New Jersey | 8,228 | 1.2% |
| 17 | Illinois | 7,877 | 1.1% |
| 18 | Missouri | 7,821 | 1.1% |
| 19 | Pennsylvania | 7,723 | 1.1% |
| 20 | Arkansas | 7,495 | 1.1% |
| 21 | Massachusetts | 6,304 | 0.9% |
| 22 | Oklahoma | 5,976 | 0.8% |
| 23 | Tennessee | 5,788 | 0.8% |
| 24 | Maryland | 5,674 | 0.8% |
| 25 | Ohio | 5,597 | 0.8% |
| 26 | Alabama | 5,270 | 0.7% |
| 27 | South Carolina | 4,104 | 0.6% |
| 28 | Indiana | 3,769 | 0.5% |
| 29 | Michigan | 3,720 | 0.5% |
| 30 | Connecticut | 3,641 | 0.5% |
| 31 | Kentucky | 3,441 | 0.5% |
| 32 | New Mexico | 3,327 | 0.5% |
| 33 | Minnesota | 3,206 | 0.5% |
| 34 | Kansas | 2,953 | 0.4% |
| 35 | Idaho | 2,916 | 0.4% |
| 36 | Louisiana | 2,781 | 0.4% |
| 37 | Wisconsin | 2,640 | 0.4% |
| 38 | Iowa | 2,634 | 0.4% |
| 39 | Nebraska | 2,163 | 0.3% |
| 40 | Mississippi | 1,715 | 0.2% |
| 41 | Rhode Island | 1,648 | 0.2% |
| 42 | Montana | 774 | 0.1% |
| 43 | Delaware | 766 | 0.1% |
| 44 | South Dakota | 608 | 0.1% |
| 45 | New Hampshire | 596 | 0.1% |
| 46 | Wyoming | 575 | 0.1% |
| 47 | West Virginia | 563 | 0.1% |
| 48 | Maine | 513 | 0.1% |
| 49 | North Dakota | 475 | 0.1% |
| 50 | Vermont | 203 | 0.0% |
|  | District of Columbia | 1,131 | 0.2% |

Source: U.S. Bureau of the Census
     "State Characteristics: Vintage 2012" (http://www.census.gov/popest/data/state/asrh/2012/index.html)
*Those who identified themselves as one race.  Census states "Race is a self-identification data item in which respondents choose the race or races with which they most closely identify."

# Percent of Population Native Hawaiian or Other Pacific Islander in 2012

## National Percent = 0.2%*

ALPHA ORDER

| RANK | STATE | PERCENT | | RANK | STATE | PERCENT |
|------|-------|---------|--|------|-------|---------|
| 15 | Alabama | 0.1 | | 1 | Hawaii | 10.1 |
| 2 | Alaska | 1.2 | | 2 | Alaska | 1.2 |
| 8 | Arizona | 0.3 | | 3 | Utah | 1.0 |
| 8 | Arkansas | 0.3 | | 4 | Nevada | 0.7 |
| 6 | California | 0.5 | | 4 | Washington | 0.7 |
| 10 | Colorado | 0.2 | | 6 | California | 0.5 |
| 15 | Connecticut | 0.1 | | 7 | Oregon | 0.4 |
| 15 | Delaware | 0.1 | | 8 | Arizona | 0.3 |
| 15 | Florida | 0.1 | | 8 | Arkansas | 0.3 |
| 15 | Georgia | 0.1 | | 10 | Colorado | 0.2 |
| 1 | Hawaii | 10.1 | | 10 | Idaho | 0.2 |
| 10 | Idaho | 0.2 | | 10 | New Mexico | 0.2 |
| 15 | Illinois | 0.1 | | 10 | Oklahoma | 0.2 |
| 15 | Indiana | 0.1 | | 10 | Rhode Island | 0.2 |
| 15 | Iowa | 0.1 | | 15 | Alabama | 0.1 |
| 15 | Kansas | 0.1 | | 15 | Connecticut | 0.1 |
| 15 | Kentucky | 0.1 | | 15 | Delaware | 0.1 |
| 15 | Louisiana | 0.1 | | 15 | Florida | 0.1 |
| 44 | Maine | 0.0 | | 15 | Georgia | 0.1 |
| 15 | Maryland | 0.1 | | 15 | Illinois | 0.1 |
| 15 | Massachusetts | 0.1 | | 15 | Indiana | 0.1 |
| 44 | Michigan | 0.0 | | 15 | Iowa | 0.1 |
| 15 | Minnesota | 0.1 | | 15 | Kansas | 0.1 |
| 15 | Mississippi | 0.1 | | 15 | Kentucky | 0.1 |
| 15 | Missouri | 0.1 | | 15 | Louisiana | 0.1 |
| 15 | Montana | 0.1 | | 15 | Maryland | 0.1 |
| 15 | Nebraska | 0.1 | | 15 | Massachusetts | 0.1 |
| 4 | Nevada | 0.7 | | 15 | Minnesota | 0.1 |
| 44 | New Hampshire | 0.0 | | 15 | Mississippi | 0.1 |
| 15 | New Jersey | 0.1 | | 15 | Missouri | 0.1 |
| 10 | New Mexico | 0.2 | | 15 | Montana | 0.1 |
| 15 | New York | 0.1 | | 15 | Nebraska | 0.1 |
| 15 | North Carolina | 0.1 | | 15 | New Jersey | 0.1 |
| 15 | North Dakota | 0.1 | | 15 | New York | 0.1 |
| 44 | Ohio | 0.0 | | 15 | North Carolina | 0.1 |
| 10 | Oklahoma | 0.2 | | 15 | North Dakota | 0.1 |
| 7 | Oregon | 0.4 | | 15 | Pennsylvania | 0.1 |
| 15 | Pennsylvania | 0.1 | | 15 | South Carolina | 0.1 |
| 10 | Rhode Island | 0.2 | | 15 | South Dakota | 0.1 |
| 15 | South Carolina | 0.1 | | 15 | Tennessee | 0.1 |
| 15 | South Dakota | 0.1 | | 15 | Texas | 0.1 |
| 15 | Tennessee | 0.1 | | 15 | Virginia | 0.1 |
| 15 | Texas | 0.1 | | 15 | Wyoming | 0.1 |
| 3 | Utah | 1.0 | | 44 | Maine | 0.0 |
| 44 | Vermont | 0.0 | | 44 | Michigan | 0.0 |
| 15 | Virginia | 0.1 | | 44 | New Hampshire | 0.0 |
| 4 | Washington | 0.7 | | 44 | Ohio | 0.0 |
| 44 | West Virginia | 0.0 | | 44 | Vermont | 0.0 |
| 44 | Wisconsin | 0.0 | | 44 | West Virginia | 0.0 |
| 15 | Wyoming | 0.1 | | 44 | Wisconsin | 0.0 |
| | | | | | District of Columbia | 0.2 |

Source: CQ Press using data from U.S. Bureau of the Census
   "State Characteristics: Vintage 2012" (http://www.census.gov/popest/data/state/asrh/2012/index.html)
*Those who identified themselves as one race. Census states "Race is a self-identification data item in which respondents choose the race or races with which they most closely identify."

# Non-Hispanic White Population in 2012

## National Total = 197,705,655*

| RANK | STATE | POPULATION | % of USA |
|---|---|---|---|
| 23 | Alabama | 3,210,178 | 1.6% |
| 49 | Alaska | 461,208 | 0.2% |
| 21 | Arizona | 3,739,038 | 1.9% |
| 33 | Arkansas | 2,180,732 | 1.1% |
| 1 | California | 14,971,342 | 7.6% |
| 22 | Colorado | 3,608,087 | 1.8% |
| 30 | Connecticut | 2,522,870 | 1.3% |
| 46 | Delaware | 592,014 | 0.3% |
| 4 | Florida | 11,008,396 | 5.6% |
| 10 | Georgia | 5,469,942 | 2.8% |
| 50 | Hawaii | 318,118 | 0.2% |
| 38 | Idaho | 1,331,650 | 0.7% |
| 7 | Illinois | 8,114,559 | 4.1% |
| 11 | Indiana | 5,295,511 | 2.7% |
| 28 | Iowa | 2,705,594 | 1.4% |
| 32 | Kansas | 2,235,436 | 1.1% |
| 20 | Kentucky | 3,761,002 | 1.9% |
| 27 | Louisiana | 2,755,571 | 1.4% |
| 39 | Maine | 1,251,365 | 0.6% |
| 24 | Maryland | 3,170,288 | 1.6% |
| 14 | Massachusetts | 5,037,923 | 2.5% |
| 8 | Michigan | 7,533,928 | 3.8% |
| 19 | Minnesota | 4,429,871 | 2.2% |
| 35 | Mississippi | 1,720,045 | 0.9% |
| 16 | Missouri | 4,856,485 | 2.5% |
| 41 | Montana | 876,823 | 0.4% |
| 36 | Nebraska | 1,510,296 | 0.8% |
| 37 | Nevada | 1,458,379 | 0.7% |
| 40 | New Hampshire | 1,213,106 | 0.6% |
| 13 | New Jersey | 5,161,886 | 2.6% |
| 42 | New Mexico | 830,454 | 0.4% |
| 3 | New York | 11,272,085 | 5.7% |
| 9 | North Carolina | 6,309,775 | 3.2% |
| 45 | North Dakota | 616,336 | 0.3% |
| 6 | Ohio | 9,321,104 | 4.7% |
| 29 | Oklahoma | 2,588,845 | 1.3% |
| 25 | Oregon | 3,033,807 | 1.5% |
| 5 | Pennsylvania | 10,054,425 | 5.1% |
| 43 | Rhode Island | 797,099 | 0.4% |
| 26 | South Carolina | 3,021,140 | 1.5% |
| 44 | South Dakota | 698,668 | 0.4% |
| 17 | Tennessee | 4,848,546 | 2.5% |
| 2 | Texas | 11,583,831 | 5.9% |
| 31 | Utah | 2,281,568 | 1.2% |
| 47 | Vermont | 588,677 | 0.3% |
| 12 | Virginia | 5,245,511 | 2.7% |
| 15 | Washington | 4,935,687 | 2.5% |
| 34 | West Virginia | 1,722,801 | 0.9% |
| 18 | Wisconsin | 4,741,504 | 2.4% |
| 48 | Wyoming | 487,822 | 0.2% |

| RANK | STATE | POPULATION | % of USA |
|---|---|---|---|
| 1 | California | 14,971,342 | 7.6% |
| 2 | Texas | 11,583,831 | 5.9% |
| 3 | New York | 11,272,085 | 5.7% |
| 4 | Florida | 11,008,396 | 5.6% |
| 5 | Pennsylvania | 10,054,425 | 5.1% |
| 6 | Ohio | 9,321,104 | 4.7% |
| 7 | Illinois | 8,114,559 | 4.1% |
| 8 | Michigan | 7,533,928 | 3.8% |
| 9 | North Carolina | 6,309,775 | 3.2% |
| 10 | Georgia | 5,469,942 | 2.8% |
| 11 | Indiana | 5,295,511 | 2.7% |
| 12 | Virginia | 5,245,511 | 2.7% |
| 13 | New Jersey | 5,161,886 | 2.6% |
| 14 | Massachusetts | 5,037,923 | 2.5% |
| 15 | Washington | 4,935,687 | 2.5% |
| 16 | Missouri | 4,856,485 | 2.5% |
| 17 | Tennessee | 4,848,546 | 2.5% |
| 18 | Wisconsin | 4,741,504 | 2.4% |
| 19 | Minnesota | 4,429,871 | 2.2% |
| 20 | Kentucky | 3,761,002 | 1.9% |
| 21 | Arizona | 3,739,038 | 1.9% |
| 22 | Colorado | 3,608,087 | 1.8% |
| 23 | Alabama | 3,210,178 | 1.6% |
| 24 | Maryland | 3,170,288 | 1.6% |
| 25 | Oregon | 3,033,807 | 1.5% |
| 26 | South Carolina | 3,021,140 | 1.5% |
| 27 | Louisiana | 2,755,571 | 1.4% |
| 28 | Iowa | 2,705,594 | 1.4% |
| 29 | Oklahoma | 2,588,845 | 1.3% |
| 30 | Connecticut | 2,522,870 | 1.3% |
| 31 | Utah | 2,281,568 | 1.2% |
| 32 | Kansas | 2,235,436 | 1.1% |
| 33 | Arkansas | 2,180,732 | 1.1% |
| 34 | West Virginia | 1,722,801 | 0.9% |
| 35 | Mississippi | 1,720,045 | 0.9% |
| 36 | Nebraska | 1,510,296 | 0.8% |
| 37 | Nevada | 1,458,379 | 0.7% |
| 38 | Idaho | 1,331,650 | 0.7% |
| 39 | Maine | 1,251,365 | 0.6% |
| 40 | New Hampshire | 1,213,106 | 0.6% |
| 41 | Montana | 876,823 | 0.4% |
| 42 | New Mexico | 830,454 | 0.4% |
| 43 | Rhode Island | 797,099 | 0.4% |
| 44 | South Dakota | 698,668 | 0.4% |
| 45 | North Dakota | 616,336 | 0.3% |
| 46 | Delaware | 592,014 | 0.3% |
| 47 | Vermont | 588,677 | 0.3% |
| 48 | Wyoming | 487,822 | 0.2% |
| 49 | Alaska | 461,208 | 0.2% |
| 50 | Hawaii | 318,118 | 0.2% |
| | District of Columbia | 224,327 | 0.1% |

Source: U.S. Bureau of the Census

"State Characteristics: Vintage 2012" (http://www.census.gov/popest/data/state/asrh/2012/index.html)

*Those who identified themselves as one race. "White" is defined by Census as a person having origins in any of the original peoples of Europe, North Africa, or the Middle East. This is a subset of the 244,495,567 white population. There are 6,237,796 non-Hispanics identified as one of the other five race categories. Persons of Hispanic origin may be of any race. Census states "Race is a self-identification data item in which respondents choose the race or races with which they most closely identify."

# Percent of Population Non-Hispanic White in 2012

## National Percent = 63.0%*

<table>
<tr><th colspan="3">ALPHA ORDER</th><th colspan="3">RANK ORDER</th></tr>
<tr><th>RANK</th><th>STATE</th><th>PERCENT</th><th>RANK</th><th>STATE</th><th>PERCENT</th></tr>
<tr><td>31</td><td>Alabama</td><td>66.6</td><td>1</td><td>Maine</td><td>94.1</td></tr>
<tr><td>36</td><td>Alaska</td><td>63.1</td><td>2</td><td>Vermont</td><td>94.0</td></tr>
<tr><td>42</td><td>Arizona</td><td>57.1</td><td>3</td><td>West Virginia</td><td>92.9</td></tr>
<tr><td>26</td><td>Arkansas</td><td>73.9</td><td>4</td><td>New Hampshire</td><td>91.9</td></tr>
<tr><td>49</td><td>California</td><td>39.4</td><td>5</td><td>North Dakota</td><td>88.1</td></tr>
<tr><td>29</td><td>Colorado</td><td>69.6</td><td>6</td><td>Iowa</td><td>88.0</td></tr>
<tr><td>28</td><td>Connecticut</td><td>70.3</td><td>7</td><td>Montana</td><td>87.2</td></tr>
<tr><td>33</td><td>Delaware</td><td>64.6</td><td>8</td><td>Kentucky</td><td>85.9</td></tr>
<tr><td>43</td><td>Florida</td><td>57.0</td><td>9</td><td>Wyoming</td><td>84.6</td></tr>
<tr><td>44</td><td>Georgia</td><td>55.1</td><td>10</td><td>South Dakota</td><td>83.8</td></tr>
<tr><td>50</td><td>Hawaii</td><td>22.8</td><td>11</td><td>Idaho</td><td>83.5</td></tr>
<tr><td>11</td><td>Idaho</td><td>83.5</td><td>12</td><td>Wisconsin</td><td>82.8</td></tr>
<tr><td>37</td><td>Illinois</td><td>63.0</td><td>13</td><td>Minnesota</td><td>82.4</td></tr>
<tr><td>15</td><td>Indiana</td><td>81.0</td><td>14</td><td>Nebraska</td><td>81.4</td></tr>
<tr><td>6</td><td>Iowa</td><td>88.0</td><td>15</td><td>Indiana</td><td>81.0</td></tr>
<tr><td>21</td><td>Kansas</td><td>77.5</td><td>16</td><td>Ohio</td><td>80.7</td></tr>
<tr><td>8</td><td>Kentucky</td><td>85.9</td><td>17</td><td>Missouri</td><td>80.6</td></tr>
<tr><td>38</td><td>Louisiana</td><td>59.9</td><td>18</td><td>Utah</td><td>79.9</td></tr>
<tr><td>1</td><td>Maine</td><td>94.1</td><td>19</td><td>Pennsylvania</td><td>78.8</td></tr>
<tr><td>45</td><td>Maryland</td><td>53.9</td><td>20</td><td>Oregon</td><td>77.8</td></tr>
<tr><td>24</td><td>Massachusetts</td><td>75.8</td><td>21</td><td>Kansas</td><td>77.5</td></tr>
<tr><td>22</td><td>Michigan</td><td>76.2</td><td>22</td><td>Michigan</td><td>76.2</td></tr>
<tr><td>13</td><td>Minnesota</td><td>82.4</td><td>23</td><td>Rhode Island</td><td>75.9</td></tr>
<tr><td>40</td><td>Mississippi</td><td>57.6</td><td>24</td><td>Massachusetts</td><td>75.8</td></tr>
<tr><td>17</td><td>Missouri</td><td>80.6</td><td>25</td><td>Tennessee</td><td>75.1</td></tr>
<tr><td>7</td><td>Montana</td><td>87.2</td><td>26</td><td>Arkansas</td><td>73.9</td></tr>
<tr><td>14</td><td>Nebraska</td><td>81.4</td><td>27</td><td>Washington</td><td>71.6</td></tr>
<tr><td>46</td><td>Nevada</td><td>52.9</td><td>28</td><td>Connecticut</td><td>70.3</td></tr>
<tr><td>4</td><td>New Hampshire</td><td>91.9</td><td>29</td><td>Colorado</td><td>69.6</td></tr>
<tr><td>39</td><td>New Jersey</td><td>58.2</td><td>30</td><td>Oklahoma</td><td>67.9</td></tr>
<tr><td>48</td><td>New Mexico</td><td>39.8</td><td>31</td><td>Alabama</td><td>66.6</td></tr>
<tr><td>40</td><td>New York</td><td>57.6</td><td>32</td><td>North Carolina</td><td>64.7</td></tr>
<tr><td>32</td><td>North Carolina</td><td>64.7</td><td>33</td><td>Delaware</td><td>64.6</td></tr>
<tr><td>5</td><td>North Dakota</td><td>88.1</td><td>34</td><td>Virginia</td><td>64.1</td></tr>
<tr><td>16</td><td>Ohio</td><td>80.7</td><td>35</td><td>South Carolina</td><td>64.0</td></tr>
<tr><td>30</td><td>Oklahoma</td><td>67.9</td><td>36</td><td>Alaska</td><td>63.1</td></tr>
<tr><td>20</td><td>Oregon</td><td>77.8</td><td>37</td><td>Illinois</td><td>63.0</td></tr>
<tr><td>19</td><td>Pennsylvania</td><td>78.8</td><td>38</td><td>Louisiana</td><td>59.9</td></tr>
<tr><td>23</td><td>Rhode Island</td><td>75.9</td><td>39</td><td>New Jersey</td><td>58.2</td></tr>
<tr><td>35</td><td>South Carolina</td><td>64.0</td><td>40</td><td>Mississippi</td><td>57.6</td></tr>
<tr><td>10</td><td>South Dakota</td><td>83.8</td><td>40</td><td>New York</td><td>57.6</td></tr>
<tr><td>25</td><td>Tennessee</td><td>75.1</td><td>42</td><td>Arizona</td><td>57.1</td></tr>
<tr><td>47</td><td>Texas</td><td>44.5</td><td>43</td><td>Florida</td><td>57.0</td></tr>
<tr><td>18</td><td>Utah</td><td>79.9</td><td>44</td><td>Georgia</td><td>55.1</td></tr>
<tr><td>2</td><td>Vermont</td><td>94.0</td><td>45</td><td>Maryland</td><td>53.9</td></tr>
<tr><td>34</td><td>Virginia</td><td>64.1</td><td>46</td><td>Nevada</td><td>52.9</td></tr>
<tr><td>27</td><td>Washington</td><td>71.6</td><td>47</td><td>Texas</td><td>44.5</td></tr>
<tr><td>3</td><td>West Virginia</td><td>92.9</td><td>48</td><td>New Mexico</td><td>39.8</td></tr>
<tr><td>12</td><td>Wisconsin</td><td>82.8</td><td>49</td><td>California</td><td>39.4</td></tr>
<tr><td>9</td><td>Wyoming</td><td>84.6</td><td>50</td><td>Hawaii</td><td>22.8</td></tr>
<tr><td></td><td></td><td></td><td></td><td>District of Columbia</td><td>35.5</td></tr>
</table>

Source: CQ Press using data from U.S. Bureau of the Census
"State Characteristics: Vintage 2012" (http://www.census.gov/popest/data/state/asrh/2012/index.html)
*Those who identified themselves as one race. "White" is defined by Census as a person having origins in any of the original peoples of Europe, North Africa, or the Middle East. This non-Hispanic white subset is 80.1% of the total white population. Persons of Hispanic origin may be of any race. Census states "Race is a self-identification data item in which respondents choose the race or races with which they most closely identify."

# Multiple Race Population in 2012

## National Total = 7,503,136*

ALPHA ORDER

| RANK | STATE | POPULATION | % of USA |
|------|-------|-----------:|---------:|
| 31 | Alabama | 69,923 | 0.9% |
| 35 | Alaska | 51,853 | 0.7% |
| 16 | Arizona | 165,742 | 2.2% |
| 34 | Arkansas | 53,343 | 0.7% |
| 1 | California | 1,370,038 | 18.3% |
| 18 | Colorado | 144,220 | 1.9% |
| 29 | Connecticut | 74,658 | 1.0% |
| 44 | Delaware | 21,582 | 0.3% |
| 4 | Florida | 363,504 | 4.8% |
| 14 | Georgia | 182,729 | 2.4% |
| 5 | Hawaii | 320,646 | 4.3% |
| 39 | Idaho | 34,788 | 0.5% |
| 8 | Illinois | 223,912 | 3.0% |
| 23 | Indiana | 116,175 | 1.5% |
| 37 | Iowa | 48,756 | 0.6% |
| 27 | Kansas | 77,962 | 1.0% |
| 30 | Kentucky | 72,103 | 1.0% |
| 32 | Louisiana | 66,041 | 0.9% |
| 45 | Maine | 20,558 | 0.3% |
| 17 | Maryland | 148,001 | 2.0% |
| 20 | Massachusetts | 134,877 | 1.8% |
| 11 | Michigan | 214,713 | 2.9% |
| 22 | Minnesota | 119,756 | 1.6% |
| 40 | Mississippi | 32,424 | 0.4% |
| 21 | Missouri | 119,761 | 1.6% |
| 43 | Montana | 24,869 | 0.3% |
| 38 | Nebraska | 35,077 | 0.5% |
| 25 | Nevada | 104,466 | 1.4% |
| 46 | New Hampshire | 19,913 | 0.3% |
| 15 | New Jersey | 171,875 | 2.3% |
| 36 | New Mexico | 49,123 | 0.7% |
| 3 | New York | 438,623 | 5.8% |
| 13 | North Carolina | 190,626 | 2.5% |
| 48 | North Dakota | 12,268 | 0.2% |
| 7 | Ohio | 226,658 | 3.0% |
| 9 | Oklahoma | 221,030 | 2.9% |
| 19 | Oregon | 136,142 | 1.8% |
| 10 | Pennsylvania | 217,291 | 2.9% |
| 42 | Rhode Island | 25,872 | 0.3% |
| 28 | South Carolina | 74,962 | 1.0% |
| 47 | South Dakota | 17,227 | 0.2% |
| 24 | Tennessee | 104,912 | 1.4% |
| 2 | Texas | 446,525 | 6.0% |
| 33 | Utah | 64,313 | 0.9% |
| 49 | Vermont | 10,687 | 0.1% |
| 12 | Virginia | 214,241 | 2.9% |
| 6 | Washington | 298,953 | 4.0% |
| 41 | West Virginia | 27,442 | 0.4% |
| 26 | Wisconsin | 95,465 | 1.3% |
| 50 | Wyoming | 10,646 | 0.1% |

RANK ORDER

| RANK | STATE | POPULATION | % of USA |
|------|-------|-----------:|---------:|
| 1 | California | 1,370,038 | 18.3% |
| 2 | Texas | 446,525 | 6.0% |
| 3 | New York | 438,623 | 5.8% |
| 4 | Florida | 363,504 | 4.8% |
| 5 | Hawaii | 320,646 | 4.3% |
| 6 | Washington | 298,953 | 4.0% |
| 7 | Ohio | 226,658 | 3.0% |
| 8 | Illinois | 223,912 | 3.0% |
| 9 | Oklahoma | 221,030 | 2.9% |
| 10 | Pennsylvania | 217,291 | 2.9% |
| 11 | Michigan | 214,713 | 2.9% |
| 12 | Virginia | 214,241 | 2.9% |
| 13 | North Carolina | 190,626 | 2.5% |
| 14 | Georgia | 182,729 | 2.4% |
| 15 | New Jersey | 171,875 | 2.3% |
| 16 | Arizona | 165,742 | 2.2% |
| 17 | Maryland | 148,001 | 2.0% |
| 18 | Colorado | 144,220 | 1.9% |
| 19 | Oregon | 136,142 | 1.8% |
| 20 | Massachusetts | 134,877 | 1.8% |
| 21 | Missouri | 119,761 | 1.6% |
| 22 | Minnesota | 119,756 | 1.6% |
| 23 | Indiana | 116,175 | 1.5% |
| 24 | Tennessee | 104,912 | 1.4% |
| 25 | Nevada | 104,466 | 1.4% |
| 26 | Wisconsin | 95,465 | 1.3% |
| 27 | Kansas | 77,962 | 1.0% |
| 28 | South Carolina | 74,962 | 1.0% |
| 29 | Connecticut | 74,658 | 1.0% |
| 30 | Kentucky | 72,103 | 1.0% |
| 31 | Alabama | 69,923 | 0.9% |
| 32 | Louisiana | 66,041 | 0.9% |
| 33 | Utah | 64,313 | 0.9% |
| 34 | Arkansas | 53,343 | 0.7% |
| 35 | Alaska | 51,853 | 0.7% |
| 36 | New Mexico | 49,123 | 0.7% |
| 37 | Iowa | 48,756 | 0.6% |
| 38 | Nebraska | 35,077 | 0.5% |
| 39 | Idaho | 34,788 | 0.5% |
| 40 | Mississippi | 32,424 | 0.4% |
| 41 | West Virginia | 27,442 | 0.4% |
| 42 | Rhode Island | 25,872 | 0.3% |
| 43 | Montana | 24,869 | 0.3% |
| 44 | Delaware | 21,582 | 0.3% |
| 45 | Maine | 20,558 | 0.3% |
| 46 | New Hampshire | 19,913 | 0.3% |
| 47 | South Dakota | 17,227 | 0.2% |
| 48 | North Dakota | 12,268 | 0.2% |
| 49 | Vermont | 10,687 | 0.1% |
| 50 | Wyoming | 10,646 | 0.1% |
| | District of Columbia | 15,865 | 0.2% |

Source: U.S. Bureau of the Census
    "State Characteristics: Vintage 2012" (http://www.census.gov/popest/data/state/asrh/2012/index.html)
*This includes those who identified themselves as two or more races. This is the population who did not identify themselves as one race (White, Black, American Indian/Native Alaska Native, Asian, or Native Hawaiian or Other Pacific Islander) but as a member of multiple racial groups. Census states "Race is a self-identification data item in which respondents choose the race or races with which they most closely identify."

# Percent of Population Multiple Races in 2012

## National Percent = 2.4%*

| ALPHA ORDER | | | | RANK ORDER | | |
|---|---|---|---|---|---|---|
| RANK | STATE | PERCENT | | RANK | STATE | PERCENT |
| 45 | Alabama | 1.5 | | 1 | Hawaii | 23.0 |
| 2 | Alaska | 7.1 | | 2 | Alaska | 7.1 |
| 11 | Arizona | 2.5 | | 3 | Oklahoma | 5.8 |
| 31 | Arkansas | 1.8 | | 4 | Washington | 4.3 |
| 6 | California | 3.6 | | 5 | Nevada | 3.8 |
| 8 | Colorado | 2.8 | | 6 | California | 3.6 |
| 22 | Connecticut | 2.1 | | 7 | Oregon | 3.5 |
| 15 | Delaware | 2.4 | | 8 | Colorado | 2.8 |
| 28 | Florida | 1.9 | | 9 | Kansas | 2.7 |
| 31 | Georgia | 1.8 | | 10 | Virginia | 2.6 |
| 1 | Hawaii | 23.0 | | 11 | Arizona | 2.5 |
| 18 | Idaho | 2.2 | | 11 | Maryland | 2.5 |
| 36 | Illinois | 1.7 | | 11 | Montana | 2.5 |
| 31 | Indiana | 1.8 | | 11 | Rhode Island | 2.5 |
| 41 | Iowa | 1.6 | | 15 | Delaware | 2.4 |
| 9 | Kansas | 2.7 | | 15 | New Mexico | 2.4 |
| 41 | Kentucky | 1.6 | | 17 | Utah | 2.3 |
| 49 | Louisiana | 1.4 | | 18 | Idaho | 2.2 |
| 45 | Maine | 1.5 | | 18 | Michigan | 2.2 |
| 11 | Maryland | 2.5 | | 18 | Minnesota | 2.2 |
| 24 | Massachusetts | 2.0 | | 18 | New York | 2.2 |
| 18 | Michigan | 2.2 | | 22 | Connecticut | 2.1 |
| 18 | Minnesota | 2.2 | | 22 | South Dakota | 2.1 |
| 50 | Mississippi | 1.1 | | 24 | Massachusetts | 2.0 |
| 24 | Missouri | 2.0 | | 24 | Missouri | 2.0 |
| 11 | Montana | 2.5 | | 24 | North Carolina | 2.0 |
| 28 | Nebraska | 1.9 | | 24 | Ohio | 2.0 |
| 5 | Nevada | 3.8 | | 28 | Florida | 1.9 |
| 45 | New Hampshire | 1.5 | | 28 | Nebraska | 1.9 |
| 28 | New Jersey | 1.9 | | 28 | New Jersey | 1.9 |
| 15 | New Mexico | 2.4 | | 31 | Arkansas | 1.8 |
| 18 | New York | 2.2 | | 31 | Georgia | 1.8 |
| 24 | North Carolina | 2.0 | | 31 | Indiana | 1.8 |
| 31 | North Dakota | 1.8 | | 31 | North Dakota | 1.8 |
| 24 | Ohio | 2.0 | | 31 | Wyoming | 1.8 |
| 3 | Oklahoma | 5.8 | | 36 | Illinois | 1.7 |
| 7 | Oregon | 3.5 | | 36 | Pennsylvania | 1.7 |
| 36 | Pennsylvania | 1.7 | | 36 | Texas | 1.7 |
| 11 | Rhode Island | 2.5 | | 36 | Vermont | 1.7 |
| 41 | South Carolina | 1.6 | | 36 | Wisconsin | 1.7 |
| 22 | South Dakota | 2.1 | | 41 | Iowa | 1.6 |
| 41 | Tennessee | 1.6 | | 41 | Kentucky | 1.6 |
| 36 | Texas | 1.7 | | 41 | South Carolina | 1.6 |
| 17 | Utah | 2.3 | | 41 | Tennessee | 1.6 |
| 36 | Vermont | 1.7 | | 45 | Alabama | 1.5 |
| 10 | Virginia | 2.6 | | 45 | Maine | 1.5 |
| 4 | Washington | 4.3 | | 45 | New Hampshire | 1.5 |
| 45 | West Virginia | 1.5 | | 45 | West Virginia | 1.5 |
| 36 | Wisconsin | 1.7 | | 49 | Louisiana | 1.4 |
| 31 | Wyoming | 1.8 | | 50 | Mississippi | 1.1 |
| | | | | | District of Columbia | 2.5 |

Source: CQ Press using data from U.S. Bureau of the Census
    "State Characteristics: Vintage 2012" (http://www.census.gov/popest/data/state/asrh/2012/index.html)
*This includes those who identified themselves as two or more races.  This is the population who did not identify themselves as one race (White, Black, American Indian/Native Alaska Native, Asian, or Native Hawaiian or Other Pacific Islander) but as a member of multiple racial groups.  Census states "Race is a self-identification data item in which respondents choose the race or races with which they most closely identify."

# Median Age in 2012

## National Median = 37.4 Years Old

| ALPHA ORDER | | | RANK ORDER | | |
|---|---|---|---|---|---|
| **RANK** | **STATE** | **MEDIAN AGE** | **RANK** | **STATE** | **MEDIAN AGE** |
| 21 | Alabama | 38.2 | 1 | Maine | 43.5 |
| 49 | Alaska | 33.7 | 2 | Vermont | 42.3 |
| 37 | Arizona | 36.5 | 3 | New Hampshire | 42.0 |
| 27 | Arkansas | 37.6 | 4 | West Virginia | 41.7 |
| 46 | California | 35.5 | 5 | Florida | 41.3 |
| 38 | Colorado | 36.3 | 6 | Connecticut | 40.5 |
| 6 | Connecticut | 40.5 | 6 | Pennsylvania | 40.5 |
| 13 | Delaware | 39.2 | 8 | Montana | 40.1 |
| 5 | Florida | 41.3 | 9 | Rhode Island | 39.8 |
| 45 | Georgia | 35.7 | 10 | Michigan | 39.4 |
| 18 | Hawaii | 38.3 | 11 | Massachusetts | 39.3 |
| 47 | Idaho | 35.2 | 11 | New Jersey | 39.3 |
| 32 | Illinois | 37.0 | 13 | Delaware | 39.2 |
| 31 | Indiana | 37.2 | 13 | Ohio | 39.2 |
| 22 | Iowa | 38.1 | 15 | Wisconsin | 38.9 |
| 43 | Kansas | 36.0 | 16 | Oregon | 38.8 |
| 18 | Kentucky | 38.3 | 17 | South Carolina | 38.4 |
| 44 | Louisiana | 35.9 | 18 | Hawaii | 38.3 |
| 1 | Maine | 43.5 | 18 | Kentucky | 38.3 |
| 22 | Maryland | 38.1 | 18 | Tennessee | 38.3 |
| 11 | Massachusetts | 39.3 | 21 | Alabama | 38.2 |
| 10 | Michigan | 39.4 | 22 | Iowa | 38.1 |
| 27 | Minnesota | 37.6 | 22 | Maryland | 38.1 |
| 38 | Mississippi | 36.3 | 22 | Missouri | 38.1 |
| 22 | Missouri | 38.1 | 22 | New York | 38.1 |
| 8 | Montana | 40.1 | 26 | North Carolina | 37.8 |
| 40 | Nebraska | 36.2 | 27 | Arkansas | 37.6 |
| 33 | Nevada | 36.9 | 27 | Minnesota | 37.6 |
| 3 | New Hampshire | 42.0 | 27 | Virginia | 37.6 |
| 11 | New Jersey | 39.3 | 30 | Washington | 37.5 |
| 36 | New Mexico | 36.8 | 31 | Indiana | 37.2 |
| 22 | New York | 38.1 | 32 | Illinois | 37.0 |
| 26 | North Carolina | 37.8 | 33 | Nevada | 36.9 |
| 42 | North Dakota | 36.1 | 33 | South Dakota | 36.9 |
| 13 | Ohio | 39.2 | 33 | Wyoming | 36.9 |
| 40 | Oklahoma | 36.2 | 36 | New Mexico | 36.8 |
| 16 | Oregon | 38.8 | 37 | Arizona | 36.5 |
| 6 | Pennsylvania | 40.5 | 38 | Colorado | 36.3 |
| 9 | Rhode Island | 39.8 | 38 | Mississippi | 36.3 |
| 17 | South Carolina | 38.4 | 40 | Nebraska | 36.2 |
| 33 | South Dakota | 36.9 | 40 | Oklahoma | 36.2 |
| 18 | Tennessee | 38.3 | 42 | North Dakota | 36.1 |
| 48 | Texas | 33.9 | 43 | Kansas | 36.0 |
| 50 | Utah | 29.9 | 44 | Louisiana | 35.9 |
| 2 | Vermont | 42.3 | 45 | Georgia | 35.7 |
| 27 | Virginia | 37.6 | 46 | California | 35.5 |
| 30 | Washington | 37.5 | 47 | Idaho | 35.2 |
| 4 | West Virginia | 41.7 | 48 | Texas | 33.9 |
| 15 | Wisconsin | 38.9 | 49 | Alaska | 33.7 |
| 33 | Wyoming | 36.9 | 50 | Utah | 29.9 |
| | | | | District of Columbia | 33.6 |

Source: U.S. Bureau of the Census
   "State Characteristics: Vintage 2012" (http://www.census.gov/popest/data/state/asrh/2012/index.html)

# Population under 5 Years Old in 2012

## National Total = 19,999,344

ALPHA ORDER

| RANK | STATE | POPULATION | % of USA |
|---|---|---|---|
| 24 | Alabama | 305,267 | 1.5% |
| 47 | Alaska | 54,791 | 0.3% |
| 14 | Arizona | 439,633 | 2.2% |
| 33 | Arkansas | 194,019 | 1.0% |
| 1 | California | 2,541,497 | 12.7% |
| 22 | Colorado | 337,568 | 1.7% |
| 34 | Connecticut | 193,456 | 1.0% |
| 45 | Delaware | 56,279 | 0.3% |
| 4 | Florida | 1,071,463 | 5.4% |
| 8 | Georgia | 675,032 | 3.4% |
| 40 | Hawaii | 89,149 | 0.4% |
| 38 | Idaho | 115,972 | 0.6% |
| 5 | Illinois | 816,278 | 4.1% |
| 15 | Indiana | 425,503 | 2.1% |
| 32 | Iowa | 196,366 | 1.0% |
| 31 | Kansas | 203,267 | 1.0% |
| 26 | Kentucky | 279,535 | 1.4% |
| 23 | Louisiana | 314,766 | 1.6% |
| 41 | Maine | 66,904 | 0.3% |
| 19 | Maryland | 365,224 | 1.8% |
| 18 | Massachusetts | 365,557 | 1.8% |
| 10 | Michigan | 575,714 | 2.9% |
| 21 | Minnesota | 348,338 | 1.7% |
| 30 | Mississippi | 203,828 | 1.0% |
| 17 | Missouri | 379,246 | 1.9% |
| 43 | Montana | 60,964 | 0.3% |
| 37 | Nebraska | 132,268 | 0.7% |
| 35 | Nevada | 183,301 | 0.9% |
| 42 | New Hampshire | 65,953 | 0.3% |
| 11 | New Jersey | 527,649 | 2.6% |
| 36 | New Mexico | 143,536 | 0.7% |
| 3 | New York | 1,167,185 | 5.8% |
| 9 | North Carolina | 619,940 | 3.1% |
| 48 | North Dakota | 46,109 | 0.2% |
| 7 | Ohio | 694,870 | 3.5% |
| 27 | Oklahoma | 261,958 | 1.3% |
| 29 | Oregon | 232,516 | 1.2% |
| 6 | Pennsylvania | 719,703 | 3.6% |
| 46 | Rhode Island | 55,068 | 0.3% |
| 25 | South Carolina | 296,401 | 1.5% |
| 44 | South Dakota | 59,202 | 0.3% |
| 16 | Tennessee | 403,976 | 2.0% |
| 2 | Texas | 1,941,845 | 9.7% |
| 28 | Utah | 257,848 | 1.3% |
| 50 | Vermont | 30,521 | 0.2% |
| 12 | Virginia | 509,602 | 2.5% |
| 13 | Washington | 443,157 | 2.2% |
| 39 | West Virginia | 103,071 | 0.5% |
| 20 | Wisconsin | 350,581 | 1.8% |
| 49 | Wyoming | 38,592 | 0.2% |

RANK ORDER

| RANK | STATE | POPULATION | % of USA |
|---|---|---|---|
| 1 | California | 2,541,497 | 12.7% |
| 2 | Texas | 1,941,845 | 9.7% |
| 3 | New York | 1,167,185 | 5.8% |
| 4 | Florida | 1,071,463 | 5.4% |
| 5 | Illinois | 816,278 | 4.1% |
| 6 | Pennsylvania | 719,703 | 3.6% |
| 7 | Ohio | 694,870 | 3.5% |
| 8 | Georgia | 675,032 | 3.4% |
| 9 | North Carolina | 619,940 | 3.1% |
| 10 | Michigan | 575,714 | 2.9% |
| 11 | New Jersey | 527,649 | 2.6% |
| 12 | Virginia | 509,602 | 2.5% |
| 13 | Washington | 443,157 | 2.2% |
| 14 | Arizona | 439,633 | 2.2% |
| 15 | Indiana | 425,503 | 2.1% |
| 16 | Tennessee | 403,976 | 2.0% |
| 17 | Missouri | 379,246 | 1.9% |
| 18 | Massachusetts | 365,557 | 1.8% |
| 19 | Maryland | 365,224 | 1.8% |
| 20 | Wisconsin | 350,581 | 1.8% |
| 21 | Minnesota | 348,338 | 1.7% |
| 22 | Colorado | 337,568 | 1.7% |
| 23 | Louisiana | 314,766 | 1.6% |
| 24 | Alabama | 305,267 | 1.5% |
| 25 | South Carolina | 296,401 | 1.5% |
| 26 | Kentucky | 279,535 | 1.4% |
| 27 | Oklahoma | 261,958 | 1.3% |
| 28 | Utah | 257,848 | 1.3% |
| 29 | Oregon | 232,516 | 1.2% |
| 30 | Mississippi | 203,828 | 1.0% |
| 31 | Kansas | 203,267 | 1.0% |
| 32 | Iowa | 196,366 | 1.0% |
| 33 | Arkansas | 194,019 | 1.0% |
| 34 | Connecticut | 193,456 | 1.0% |
| 35 | Nevada | 183,301 | 0.9% |
| 36 | New Mexico | 143,536 | 0.7% |
| 37 | Nebraska | 132,268 | 0.7% |
| 38 | Idaho | 115,972 | 0.6% |
| 39 | West Virginia | 103,071 | 0.5% |
| 40 | Hawaii | 89,149 | 0.4% |
| 41 | Maine | 66,904 | 0.3% |
| 42 | New Hampshire | 65,953 | 0.3% |
| 43 | Montana | 60,964 | 0.3% |
| 44 | South Dakota | 59,202 | 0.3% |
| 45 | Delaware | 56,279 | 0.3% |
| 46 | Rhode Island | 55,068 | 0.3% |
| 47 | Alaska | 54,791 | 0.3% |
| 48 | North Dakota | 46,109 | 0.2% |
| 49 | Wyoming | 38,592 | 0.2% |
| 50 | Vermont | 30,521 | 0.2% |
| | District of Columbia | 38,876 | 0.2% |

Source: U.S. Bureau of the Census
"State Characteristics: Vintage 2012" (http://www.census.gov/popest/data/state/asrh/2012/index.html)

# Percent of Population under 5 Years Old in 2012

## National Percent = 6.4% of Population

ALPHA ORDER

| RANK | STATE | PERCENT |
|---|---|---|
| 27 | Alabama | 6.3 |
| 2 | Alaska | 7.5 |
| 13 | Arizona | 6.7 |
| 16 | Arkansas | 6.6 |
| 13 | California | 6.7 |
| 19 | Colorado | 6.5 |
| 46 | Connecticut | 5.4 |
| 34 | Delaware | 6.1 |
| 44 | Florida | 5.5 |
| 10 | Georgia | 6.8 |
| 22 | Hawaii | 6.4 |
| 4 | Idaho | 7.3 |
| 27 | Illinois | 6.3 |
| 19 | Indiana | 6.5 |
| 22 | Iowa | 6.4 |
| 7 | Kansas | 7.0 |
| 22 | Kentucky | 6.4 |
| 10 | Louisiana | 6.8 |
| 48 | Maine | 5.0 |
| 32 | Maryland | 6.2 |
| 44 | Massachusetts | 5.5 |
| 41 | Michigan | 5.8 |
| 19 | Minnesota | 6.5 |
| 10 | Mississippi | 6.8 |
| 27 | Missouri | 6.3 |
| 34 | Montana | 6.1 |
| 5 | Nebraska | 7.1 |
| 16 | Nevada | 6.6 |
| 48 | New Hampshire | 5.0 |
| 37 | New Jersey | 6.0 |
| 8 | New Mexico | 6.9 |
| 37 | New York | 6.0 |
| 22 | North Carolina | 6.4 |
| 16 | North Dakota | 6.6 |
| 37 | Ohio | 6.0 |
| 8 | Oklahoma | 6.9 |
| 37 | Oregon | 6.0 |
| 42 | Pennsylvania | 5.6 |
| 47 | Rhode Island | 5.2 |
| 27 | South Carolina | 6.3 |
| 5 | South Dakota | 7.1 |
| 27 | Tennessee | 6.3 |
| 2 | Texas | 7.5 |
| 1 | Utah | 9.0 |
| 50 | Vermont | 4.9 |
| 32 | Virginia | 6.2 |
| 22 | Washington | 6.4 |
| 42 | West Virginia | 5.6 |
| 34 | Wisconsin | 6.1 |
| 13 | Wyoming | 6.7 |

RANK ORDER

| RANK | STATE | PERCENT |
|---|---|---|
| 1 | Utah | 9.0 |
| 2 | Alaska | 7.5 |
| 2 | Texas | 7.5 |
| 4 | Idaho | 7.3 |
| 5 | Nebraska | 7.1 |
| 5 | South Dakota | 7.1 |
| 7 | Kansas | 7.0 |
| 8 | New Mexico | 6.9 |
| 8 | Oklahoma | 6.9 |
| 10 | Georgia | 6.8 |
| 10 | Louisiana | 6.8 |
| 10 | Mississippi | 6.8 |
| 13 | Arizona | 6.7 |
| 13 | California | 6.7 |
| 13 | Wyoming | 6.7 |
| 16 | Arkansas | 6.6 |
| 16 | Nevada | 6.6 |
| 16 | North Dakota | 6.6 |
| 19 | Colorado | 6.5 |
| 19 | Indiana | 6.5 |
| 19 | Minnesota | 6.5 |
| 22 | Hawaii | 6.4 |
| 22 | Iowa | 6.4 |
| 22 | Kentucky | 6.4 |
| 22 | North Carolina | 6.4 |
| 22 | Washington | 6.4 |
| 27 | Alabama | 6.3 |
| 27 | Illinois | 6.3 |
| 27 | Missouri | 6.3 |
| 27 | South Carolina | 6.3 |
| 27 | Tennessee | 6.3 |
| 32 | Maryland | 6.2 |
| 32 | Virginia | 6.2 |
| 34 | Delaware | 6.1 |
| 34 | Montana | 6.1 |
| 34 | Wisconsin | 6.1 |
| 37 | New Jersey | 6.0 |
| 37 | New York | 6.0 |
| 37 | Ohio | 6.0 |
| 37 | Oregon | 6.0 |
| 41 | Michigan | 5.8 |
| 42 | Pennsylvania | 5.6 |
| 42 | West Virginia | 5.6 |
| 44 | Florida | 5.5 |
| 44 | Massachusetts | 5.5 |
| 46 | Connecticut | 5.4 |
| 47 | Rhode Island | 5.2 |
| 48 | Maine | 5.0 |
| 48 | New Hampshire | 5.0 |
| 50 | Vermont | 4.9 |
| | District of Columbia | 6.1 |

Source: CQ Press using data from U.S. Bureau of the Census
"State Characteristics: Vintage 2012" (http://www.census.gov/popest/data/state/asrh/2012/index.html)

# Population 5 to 17 Years Old in 2012

## National Total = 53,728,744

ALPHA ORDER

| RANK | STATE | POPULATION | % of USA |
|---|---|---|---|
| 23 | Alabama | 819,139 | 1.5% |
| 47 | Alaska | 132,309 | 0.2% |
| 13 | Arizona | 1,181,261 | 2.2% |
| 34 | Arkansas | 516,862 | 1.0% |
| 1 | California | 6,698,722 | 12.5% |
| 22 | Colorado | 893,790 | 1.7% |
| 30 | Connecticut | 600,102 | 1.1% |
| 45 | Delaware | 148,771 | 0.3% |
| 4 | Florida | 2,931,017 | 5.5% |
| 8 | Georgia | 1,815,093 | 3.4% |
| 40 | Hawaii | 213,862 | 0.4% |
| 38 | Idaho | 310,681 | 0.6% |
| 5 | Illinois | 2,247,787 | 4.2% |
| 14 | Indiana | 1,165,974 | 2.2% |
| 32 | Iowa | 526,587 | 1.0% |
| 33 | Kansas | 521,037 | 1.0% |
| 26 | Kentucky | 738,703 | 1.4% |
| 24 | Louisiana | 803,037 | 1.5% |
| 42 | Maine | 199,014 | 0.4% |
| 19 | Maryland | 978,576 | 1.8% |
| 17 | Massachusetts | 1,035,858 | 1.9% |
| 9 | Michigan | 1,691,156 | 3.1% |
| 21 | Minnesota | 927,810 | 1.7% |
| 31 | Mississippi | 541,505 | 1.0% |
| 18 | Missouri | 1,024,229 | 1.9% |
| 44 | Montana | 161,016 | 0.3% |
| 37 | Nebraska | 331,137 | 0.6% |
| 35 | Nevada | 480,282 | 0.9% |
| 41 | New Hampshire | 208,887 | 0.4% |
| 11 | New Jersey | 1,498,735 | 2.8% |
| 36 | New Mexico | 370,906 | 0.7% |
| 3 | New York | 3,095,969 | 5.8% |
| 10 | North Carolina | 1,666,588 | 3.1% |
| 48 | North Dakota | 108,499 | 0.2% |
| 7 | Ohio | 1,968,804 | 3.7% |
| 27 | Oklahoma | 675,405 | 1.3% |
| 29 | Oregon | 628,108 | 1.2% |
| 6 | Pennsylvania | 2,019,683 | 3.8% |
| 43 | Rhode Island | 161,406 | 0.3% |
| 25 | South Carolina | 783,689 | 1.5% |
| 46 | South Dakota | 144,967 | 0.3% |
| 16 | Tennessee | 1,090,040 | 2.0% |
| 2 | Texas | 5,043,794 | 9.4% |
| 28 | Utah | 630,124 | 1.2% |
| 50 | Vermont | 93,430 | 0.2% |
| 12 | Virginia | 1,347,135 | 2.5% |
| 15 | Washington | 1,141,810 | 2.1% |
| 39 | West Virginia | 280,970 | 0.5% |
| 20 | Wisconsin | 966,976 | 1.8% |
| 49 | Wyoming | 96,898 | 0.2% |

RANK ORDER

| RANK | STATE | POPULATION | % of USA |
|---|---|---|---|
| 1 | California | 6,698,722 | 12.5% |
| 2 | Texas | 5,043,794 | 9.4% |
| 3 | New York | 3,095,969 | 5.8% |
| 4 | Florida | 2,931,017 | 5.5% |
| 5 | Illinois | 2,247,787 | 4.2% |
| 6 | Pennsylvania | 2,019,683 | 3.8% |
| 7 | Ohio | 1,968,804 | 3.7% |
| 8 | Georgia | 1,815,093 | 3.4% |
| 9 | Michigan | 1,691,156 | 3.1% |
| 10 | North Carolina | 1,666,588 | 3.1% |
| 11 | New Jersey | 1,498,735 | 2.8% |
| 12 | Virginia | 1,347,135 | 2.5% |
| 13 | Arizona | 1,181,261 | 2.2% |
| 14 | Indiana | 1,165,974 | 2.2% |
| 15 | Washington | 1,141,810 | 2.1% |
| 16 | Tennessee | 1,090,040 | 2.0% |
| 17 | Massachusetts | 1,035,858 | 1.9% |
| 18 | Missouri | 1,024,229 | 1.9% |
| 19 | Maryland | 978,576 | 1.8% |
| 20 | Wisconsin | 966,976 | 1.8% |
| 21 | Minnesota | 927,810 | 1.7% |
| 22 | Colorado | 893,790 | 1.7% |
| 23 | Alabama | 819,139 | 1.5% |
| 24 | Louisiana | 803,037 | 1.5% |
| 25 | South Carolina | 783,689 | 1.5% |
| 26 | Kentucky | 738,703 | 1.4% |
| 27 | Oklahoma | 675,405 | 1.3% |
| 28 | Utah | 630,124 | 1.2% |
| 29 | Oregon | 628,108 | 1.2% |
| 30 | Connecticut | 600,102 | 1.1% |
| 31 | Mississippi | 541,505 | 1.0% |
| 32 | Iowa | 526,587 | 1.0% |
| 33 | Kansas | 521,037 | 1.0% |
| 34 | Arkansas | 516,862 | 1.0% |
| 35 | Nevada | 480,282 | 0.9% |
| 36 | New Mexico | 370,906 | 0.7% |
| 37 | Nebraska | 331,137 | 0.6% |
| 38 | Idaho | 310,681 | 0.6% |
| 39 | West Virginia | 280,970 | 0.5% |
| 40 | Hawaii | 213,862 | 0.4% |
| 41 | New Hampshire | 208,887 | 0.4% |
| 42 | Maine | 199,014 | 0.4% |
| 43 | Rhode Island | 161,406 | 0.3% |
| 44 | Montana | 161,016 | 0.3% |
| 45 | Delaware | 148,771 | 0.3% |
| 46 | South Dakota | 144,967 | 0.3% |
| 47 | Alaska | 132,309 | 0.2% |
| 48 | North Dakota | 108,499 | 0.2% |
| 49 | Wyoming | 96,898 | 0.2% |
| 50 | Vermont | 93,430 | 0.2% |
| | District of Columbia | 70,604 | 0.1% |

Source: CQ Press using data from U.S. Bureau of the Census
"State Characteristics: Vintage 2012" (http://www.census.gov/popest/data/state/asrh/2012/index.html)

# Percent of Population 5 to 17 Years Old in 2012

## National Percent = 17.1% of Population

ALPHA ORDER

| RANK | STATE | PERCENT |
|------|-------|---------|
| 25 | Alabama | 17.0 |
| 5 | Alaska | 18.1 |
| 8 | Arizona | 18.0 |
| 14 | Arkansas | 17.5 |
| 13 | California | 17.6 |
| 19 | Colorado | 17.2 |
| 32 | Connecticut | 16.7 |
| 37 | Delaware | 16.2 |
| 47 | Florida | 15.2 |
| 4 | Georgia | 18.3 |
| 45 | Hawaii | 15.4 |
| 2 | Idaho | 19.5 |
| 14 | Illinois | 17.5 |
| 9 | Indiana | 17.8 |
| 21 | Iowa | 17.1 |
| 5 | Kansas | 18.1 |
| 27 | Kentucky | 16.9 |
| 14 | Louisiana | 17.5 |
| 49 | Maine | 15.0 |
| 33 | Maryland | 16.6 |
| 43 | Massachusetts | 15.6 |
| 21 | Michigan | 17.1 |
| 19 | Minnesota | 17.2 |
| 5 | Mississippi | 18.1 |
| 25 | Missouri | 17.0 |
| 39 | Montana | 16.0 |
| 9 | Nebraska | 17.8 |
| 17 | Nevada | 17.4 |
| 40 | New Hampshire | 15.8 |
| 27 | New Jersey | 16.9 |
| 9 | New Mexico | 17.8 |
| 40 | New York | 15.8 |
| 21 | North Carolina | 17.1 |
| 44 | North Dakota | 15.5 |
| 21 | Ohio | 17.1 |
| 12 | Oklahoma | 17.7 |
| 38 | Oregon | 16.1 |
| 40 | Pennsylvania | 15.8 |
| 45 | Rhode Island | 15.4 |
| 33 | South Carolina | 16.6 |
| 17 | South Dakota | 17.4 |
| 27 | Tennessee | 16.9 |
| 3 | Texas | 19.4 |
| 1 | Utah | 22.1 |
| 50 | Vermont | 14.9 |
| 36 | Virginia | 16.5 |
| 33 | Washington | 16.6 |
| 48 | West Virginia | 15.1 |
| 27 | Wisconsin | 16.9 |
| 31 | Wyoming | 16.8 |

RANK ORDER

| RANK | STATE | PERCENT |
|------|-------|---------|
| 1 | Utah | 22.1 |
| 2 | Idaho | 19.5 |
| 3 | Texas | 19.4 |
| 4 | Georgia | 18.3 |
| 5 | Alaska | 18.1 |
| 5 | Kansas | 18.1 |
| 5 | Mississippi | 18.1 |
| 8 | Arizona | 18.0 |
| 9 | Indiana | 17.8 |
| 9 | Nebraska | 17.8 |
| 9 | New Mexico | 17.8 |
| 12 | Oklahoma | 17.7 |
| 13 | California | 17.6 |
| 14 | Arkansas | 17.5 |
| 14 | Illinois | 17.5 |
| 14 | Louisiana | 17.5 |
| 17 | Nevada | 17.4 |
| 17 | South Dakota | 17.4 |
| 19 | Colorado | 17.2 |
| 19 | Minnesota | 17.2 |
| 21 | Iowa | 17.1 |
| 21 | Michigan | 17.1 |
| 21 | North Carolina | 17.1 |
| 21 | Ohio | 17.1 |
| 25 | Alabama | 17.0 |
| 25 | Missouri | 17.0 |
| 27 | Kentucky | 16.9 |
| 27 | New Jersey | 16.9 |
| 27 | Tennessee | 16.9 |
| 27 | Wisconsin | 16.9 |
| 31 | Wyoming | 16.8 |
| 32 | Connecticut | 16.7 |
| 33 | Maryland | 16.6 |
| 33 | South Carolina | 16.6 |
| 33 | Washington | 16.6 |
| 36 | Virginia | 16.5 |
| 37 | Delaware | 16.2 |
| 38 | Oregon | 16.1 |
| 39 | Montana | 16.0 |
| 40 | New Hampshire | 15.8 |
| 40 | New York | 15.8 |
| 40 | Pennsylvania | 15.8 |
| 43 | Massachusetts | 15.6 |
| 44 | North Dakota | 15.5 |
| 45 | Hawaii | 15.4 |
| 45 | Rhode Island | 15.4 |
| 47 | Florida | 15.2 |
| 48 | West Virginia | 15.1 |
| 49 | Maine | 15.0 |
| 50 | Vermont | 14.9 |
| | District of Columbia | 11.2 |

Source: CQ Press using data from U.S. Bureau of the Census
"State Characteristics: Vintage 2012" (http://www.census.gov/popest/data/state/asrh/2012/index.html)

# Population 18 Years Old and Older in 2012

## National Total = 240,185,952

ALPHA ORDER

| RANK | STATE | POPULATION | % of USA |
|---|---|---|---|
| 23 | Alabama | 3,697,617 | 1.5% |
| 48 | Alaska | 544,349 | 0.2% |
| 17 | Arizona | 4,932,361 | 2.1% |
| 32 | Arkansas | 2,238,250 | 0.9% |
| 1 | California | 28,801,211 | 12.0% |
| 22 | Colorado | 3,956,224 | 1.6% |
| 29 | Connecticut | 2,796,789 | 1.2% |
| 45 | Delaware | 712,042 | 0.3% |
| 3 | Florida | 15,315,088 | 6.4% |
| 10 | Georgia | 7,429,820 | 3.1% |
| 40 | Hawaii | 1,089,302 | 0.5% |
| 39 | Idaho | 1,169,075 | 0.5% |
| 6 | Illinois | 9,811,190 | 4.1% |
| 16 | Indiana | 4,945,857 | 2.1% |
| 30 | Iowa | 2,351,233 | 1.0% |
| 33 | Kansas | 2,161,601 | 0.9% |
| 26 | Kentucky | 3,362,177 | 1.4% |
| 25 | Louisiana | 3,484,090 | 1.5% |
| 41 | Maine | 1,063,274 | 0.4% |
| 19 | Maryland | 4,540,763 | 1.9% |
| 14 | Massachusetts | 5,244,729 | 2.2% |
| 8 | Michigan | 7,616,490 | 3.2% |
| 21 | Minnesota | 4,102,991 | 1.7% |
| 31 | Mississippi | 2,239,593 | 0.9% |
| 18 | Missouri | 4,618,513 | 1.9% |
| 44 | Montana | 783,161 | 0.3% |
| 38 | Nebraska | 1,392,120 | 0.6% |
| 34 | Nevada | 2,095,348 | 0.9% |
| 42 | New Hampshire | 1,045,878 | 0.4% |
| 11 | New Jersey | 6,838,206 | 2.8% |
| 36 | New Mexico | 1,571,096 | 0.7% |
| 4 | New York | 15,307,107 | 6.4% |
| 9 | North Carolina | 7,465,545 | 3.1% |
| 47 | North Dakota | 545,020 | 0.2% |
| 7 | Ohio | 8,880,551 | 3.7% |
| 28 | Oklahoma | 2,877,457 | 1.2% |
| 27 | Oregon | 3,038,729 | 1.3% |
| 5 | Pennsylvania | 10,024,150 | 4.2% |
| 43 | Rhode Island | 833,818 | 0.3% |
| 24 | South Carolina | 3,643,633 | 1.5% |
| 46 | South Dakota | 629,185 | 0.3% |
| 15 | Tennessee | 4,962,227 | 2.1% |
| 2 | Texas | 19,073,564 | 7.9% |
| 35 | Utah | 1,967,315 | 0.8% |
| 49 | Vermont | 502,060 | 0.2% |
| 12 | Virginia | 6,329,130 | 2.6% |
| 13 | Washington | 5,312,045 | 2.2% |
| 37 | West Virginia | 1,471,372 | 0.6% |
| 20 | Wisconsin | 4,408,841 | 1.8% |
| 50 | Wyoming | 440,922 | 0.2% |

RANK ORDER

| RANK | STATE | POPULATION | % of USA |
|---|---|---|---|
| 1 | California | 28,801,211 | 12.0% |
| 2 | Texas | 19,073,564 | 7.9% |
| 3 | Florida | 15,315,088 | 6.4% |
| 4 | New York | 15,307,107 | 6.4% |
| 5 | Pennsylvania | 10,024,150 | 4.2% |
| 6 | Illinois | 9,811,190 | 4.1% |
| 7 | Ohio | 8,880,551 | 3.7% |
| 8 | Michigan | 7,616,490 | 3.2% |
| 9 | North Carolina | 7,465,545 | 3.1% |
| 10 | Georgia | 7,429,820 | 3.1% |
| 11 | New Jersey | 6,838,206 | 2.8% |
| 12 | Virginia | 6,329,130 | 2.6% |
| 13 | Washington | 5,312,045 | 2.2% |
| 14 | Massachusetts | 5,244,729 | 2.2% |
| 15 | Tennessee | 4,962,227 | 2.1% |
| 16 | Indiana | 4,945,857 | 2.1% |
| 17 | Arizona | 4,932,361 | 2.1% |
| 18 | Missouri | 4,618,513 | 1.9% |
| 19 | Maryland | 4,540,763 | 1.9% |
| 20 | Wisconsin | 4,408,841 | 1.8% |
| 21 | Minnesota | 4,102,991 | 1.7% |
| 22 | Colorado | 3,956,224 | 1.6% |
| 23 | Alabama | 3,697,617 | 1.5% |
| 24 | South Carolina | 3,643,633 | 1.5% |
| 25 | Louisiana | 3,484,090 | 1.5% |
| 26 | Kentucky | 3,362,177 | 1.4% |
| 27 | Oregon | 3,038,729 | 1.3% |
| 28 | Oklahoma | 2,877,457 | 1.2% |
| 29 | Connecticut | 2,796,789 | 1.2% |
| 30 | Iowa | 2,351,233 | 1.0% |
| 31 | Mississippi | 2,239,593 | 0.9% |
| 32 | Arkansas | 2,238,250 | 0.9% |
| 33 | Kansas | 2,161,601 | 0.9% |
| 34 | Nevada | 2,095,348 | 0.9% |
| 35 | Utah | 1,967,315 | 0.8% |
| 36 | New Mexico | 1,571,096 | 0.7% |
| 37 | West Virginia | 1,471,372 | 0.6% |
| 38 | Nebraska | 1,392,120 | 0.6% |
| 39 | Idaho | 1,169,075 | 0.5% |
| 40 | Hawaii | 1,089,302 | 0.5% |
| 41 | Maine | 1,063,274 | 0.4% |
| 42 | New Hampshire | 1,045,878 | 0.4% |
| 43 | Rhode Island | 833,818 | 0.3% |
| 44 | Montana | 783,161 | 0.3% |
| 45 | Delaware | 712,042 | 0.3% |
| 46 | South Dakota | 629,185 | 0.3% |
| 47 | North Dakota | 545,020 | 0.2% |
| 48 | Alaska | 544,349 | 0.2% |
| 49 | Vermont | 502,060 | 0.2% |
| 50 | Wyoming | 440,922 | 0.2% |
| | District of Columbia | 522,843 | 0.2% |

Source: U.S. Bureau of the Census
"State Characteristics: Vintage 2012" (http://www.census.gov/popest/data/state/asrh/2012/index.html)

# Percent of Population 18 Years Old and Older in 2012

## National Percent = 76.5% of Population

ALPHA ORDER

| RANK | STATE | PERCENT |
|------|-------|---------|
| 26 | Alabama | 76.7 |
| 47 | Alaska | 74.4 |
| 41 | Arizona | 75.3 |
| 34 | Arkansas | 75.9 |
| 36 | California | 75.7 |
| 31 | Colorado | 76.3 |
| 11 | Connecticut | 77.9 |
| 15 | Delaware | 77.6 |
| 4 | Florida | 79.3 |
| 45 | Georgia | 74.9 |
| 9 | Hawaii | 78.2 |
| 48 | Idaho | 73.3 |
| 33 | Illinois | 76.2 |
| 36 | Indiana | 75.7 |
| 29 | Iowa | 76.5 |
| 45 | Kansas | 74.9 |
| 25 | Kentucky | 76.8 |
| 36 | Louisiana | 75.7 |
| 2 | Maine | 80.0 |
| 17 | Maryland | 77.2 |
| 7 | Massachusetts | 78.9 |
| 18 | Michigan | 77.1 |
| 31 | Minnesota | 76.3 |
| 43 | Mississippi | 75.0 |
| 26 | Missouri | 76.7 |
| 11 | Montana | 77.9 |
| 43 | Nebraska | 75.0 |
| 34 | Nevada | 75.9 |
| 6 | New Hampshire | 79.2 |
| 18 | New Jersey | 77.1 |
| 41 | New Mexico | 75.3 |
| 9 | New York | 78.2 |
| 28 | North Carolina | 76.6 |
| 11 | North Dakota | 77.9 |
| 23 | Ohio | 76.9 |
| 40 | Oklahoma | 75.4 |
| 11 | Oregon | 77.9 |
| 8 | Pennsylvania | 78.5 |
| 3 | Rhode Island | 79.4 |
| 18 | South Carolina | 77.1 |
| 39 | South Dakota | 75.5 |
| 23 | Tennessee | 76.9 |
| 49 | Texas | 73.2 |
| 50 | Utah | 68.9 |
| 1 | Vermont | 80.2 |
| 16 | Virginia | 77.3 |
| 21 | Washington | 77.0 |
| 4 | West Virginia | 79.3 |
| 21 | Wisconsin | 77.0 |
| 29 | Wyoming | 76.5 |

RANK ORDER

| RANK | STATE | PERCENT |
|------|-------|---------|
| 1 | Vermont | 80.2 |
| 2 | Maine | 80.0 |
| 3 | Rhode Island | 79.4 |
| 4 | Florida | 79.3 |
| 4 | West Virginia | 79.3 |
| 6 | New Hampshire | 79.2 |
| 7 | Massachusetts | 78.9 |
| 8 | Pennsylvania | 78.5 |
| 9 | Hawaii | 78.2 |
| 9 | New York | 78.2 |
| 11 | Connecticut | 77.9 |
| 11 | Montana | 77.9 |
| 11 | North Dakota | 77.9 |
| 11 | Oregon | 77.9 |
| 15 | Delaware | 77.6 |
| 16 | Virginia | 77.3 |
| 17 | Maryland | 77.2 |
| 18 | Michigan | 77.1 |
| 18 | New Jersey | 77.1 |
| 18 | South Carolina | 77.1 |
| 21 | Washington | 77.0 |
| 21 | Wisconsin | 77.0 |
| 23 | Ohio | 76.9 |
| 23 | Tennessee | 76.9 |
| 25 | Kentucky | 76.8 |
| 26 | Alabama | 76.7 |
| 26 | Missouri | 76.7 |
| 28 | North Carolina | 76.6 |
| 29 | Iowa | 76.5 |
| 29 | Wyoming | 76.5 |
| 31 | Colorado | 76.3 |
| 31 | Minnesota | 76.3 |
| 33 | Illinois | 76.2 |
| 34 | Arkansas | 75.9 |
| 34 | Nevada | 75.9 |
| 36 | California | 75.7 |
| 36 | Indiana | 75.7 |
| 36 | Louisiana | 75.7 |
| 39 | South Dakota | 75.5 |
| 40 | Oklahoma | 75.4 |
| 41 | Arizona | 75.3 |
| 41 | New Mexico | 75.3 |
| 43 | Mississippi | 75.0 |
| 43 | Nebraska | 75.0 |
| 45 | Georgia | 74.9 |
| 45 | Kansas | 74.9 |
| 47 | Alaska | 74.4 |
| 48 | Idaho | 73.3 |
| 49 | Texas | 73.2 |
| 50 | Utah | 68.9 |
| | District of Columbia | 82.7 |

Source: CQ Press using data from U.S. Bureau of the Census
"State Characteristics: Vintage 2012" (http://www.census.gov/popest/data/state/asrh/2012/index.html)

# Population 18 to 24 Years Old in 2012

## National Total = 31,359,915

ALPHA ORDER

| RANK | STATE | POPULATION | % of USA |
|---|---|---|---|
| 23 | Alabama | 484,941 | 1.5% |
| 48 | Alaska | 79,667 | 0.3% |
| 16 | Arizona | 652,951 | 2.1% |
| 34 | Arkansas | 286,692 | 0.9% |
| 1 | California | 4,021,243 | 12.8% |
| 21 | Colorado | 506,670 | 1.6% |
| 29 | Connecticut | 337,068 | 1.1% |
| 45 | Delaware | 93,661 | 0.3% |
| 4 | Florida | 1,790,985 | 5.7% |
| 8 | Georgia | 1,016,282 | 3.2% |
| 40 | Hawaii | 136,870 | 0.4% |
| 39 | Idaho | 156,847 | 0.5% |
| 6 | Illinois | 1,254,647 | 4.0% |
| 15 | Indiana | 662,480 | 2.1% |
| 31 | Iowa | 314,290 | 1.0% |
| 33 | Kansas | 296,942 | 0.9% |
| 26 | Kentucky | 423,887 | 1.4% |
| 25 | Louisiana | 475,856 | 1.5% |
| 43 | Maine | 115,693 | 0.4% |
| 19 | Maryland | 567,740 | 1.8% |
| 13 | Massachusetts | 685,561 | 2.2% |
| 9 | Michigan | 998,675 | 3.2% |
| 22 | Minnesota | 506,376 | 1.6% |
| 32 | Mississippi | 311,121 | 1.0% |
| 18 | Missouri | 593,526 | 1.9% |
| 44 | Montana | 98,514 | 0.3% |
| 37 | Nebraska | 185,681 | 0.6% |
| 35 | Nevada | 254,747 | 0.8% |
| 41 | New Hampshire | 125,753 | 0.4% |
| 12 | New Jersey | 785,211 | 2.5% |
| 36 | New Mexico | 207,225 | 0.7% |
| 3 | New York | 1,997,646 | 6.4% |
| 10 | North Carolina | 972,162 | 3.1% |
| 46 | North Dakota | 87,393 | 0.3% |
| 7 | Ohio | 1,108,674 | 3.5% |
| 27 | Oklahoma | 391,504 | 1.2% |
| 28 | Oregon | 365,004 | 1.2% |
| 5 | Pennsylvania | 1,263,768 | 4.0% |
| 42 | Rhode Island | 120,461 | 0.4% |
| 24 | South Carolina | 484,411 | 1.5% |
| 47 | South Dakota | 83,612 | 0.3% |
| 17 | Tennessee | 624,228 | 2.0% |
| 2 | Texas | 2,683,024 | 8.6% |
| 30 | Utah | 326,987 | 1.0% |
| 49 | Vermont | 66,323 | 0.2% |
| 11 | Virginia | 823,193 | 2.6% |
| 14 | Washington | 667,879 | 2.1% |
| 38 | West Virginia | 171,139 | 0.5% |
| 20 | Wisconsin | 554,069 | 1.8% |
| 50 | Wyoming | 58,144 | 0.2% |

RANK ORDER

| RANK | STATE | POPULATION | % of USA |
|---|---|---|---|
| 1 | California | 4,021,243 | 12.8% |
| 2 | Texas | 2,683,024 | 8.6% |
| 3 | New York | 1,997,646 | 6.4% |
| 4 | Florida | 1,790,985 | 5.7% |
| 5 | Pennsylvania | 1,263,768 | 4.0% |
| 6 | Illinois | 1,254,647 | 4.0% |
| 7 | Ohio | 1,108,674 | 3.5% |
| 8 | Georgia | 1,016,282 | 3.2% |
| 9 | Michigan | 998,675 | 3.2% |
| 10 | North Carolina | 972,162 | 3.1% |
| 11 | Virginia | 823,193 | 2.6% |
| 12 | New Jersey | 785,211 | 2.5% |
| 13 | Massachusetts | 685,561 | 2.2% |
| 14 | Washington | 667,879 | 2.1% |
| 15 | Indiana | 662,480 | 2.1% |
| 16 | Arizona | 652,951 | 2.1% |
| 17 | Tennessee | 624,228 | 2.0% |
| 18 | Missouri | 593,526 | 1.9% |
| 19 | Maryland | 567,740 | 1.8% |
| 20 | Wisconsin | 554,069 | 1.8% |
| 21 | Colorado | 506,670 | 1.6% |
| 22 | Minnesota | 506,376 | 1.6% |
| 23 | Alabama | 484,941 | 1.5% |
| 24 | South Carolina | 484,411 | 1.5% |
| 25 | Louisiana | 475,856 | 1.5% |
| 26 | Kentucky | 423,887 | 1.4% |
| 27 | Oklahoma | 391,504 | 1.2% |
| 28 | Oregon | 365,004 | 1.2% |
| 29 | Connecticut | 337,068 | 1.1% |
| 30 | Utah | 326,987 | 1.0% |
| 31 | Iowa | 314,290 | 1.0% |
| 32 | Mississippi | 311,121 | 1.0% |
| 33 | Kansas | 296,942 | 0.9% |
| 34 | Arkansas | 286,692 | 0.9% |
| 35 | Nevada | 254,747 | 0.8% |
| 36 | New Mexico | 207,225 | 0.7% |
| 37 | Nebraska | 185,681 | 0.6% |
| 38 | West Virginia | 171,139 | 0.5% |
| 39 | Idaho | 156,847 | 0.5% |
| 40 | Hawaii | 136,870 | 0.4% |
| 41 | New Hampshire | 125,753 | 0.4% |
| 42 | Rhode Island | 120,461 | 0.4% |
| 43 | Maine | 115,693 | 0.4% |
| 44 | Montana | 98,514 | 0.3% |
| 45 | Delaware | 93,661 | 0.3% |
| 46 | North Dakota | 87,393 | 0.3% |
| 47 | South Dakota | 83,612 | 0.3% |
| 48 | Alaska | 79,667 | 0.3% |
| 49 | Vermont | 66,323 | 0.2% |
| 50 | Wyoming | 58,144 | 0.2% |
| | District of Columbia | 82,492 | 0.3% |

Source: CQ Press using data from U.S. Bureau of the Census
"State Characteristics: Vintage 2012" (http://www.census.gov/popest/data/state/asrh/2012/index.html)

# Percent of Population 18 to 24 Years Old in 2012

## National Percent = 10.0% of Population

ALPHA ORDER

| RANK | STATE | PERCENT |
|------|-------|---------|
| 18 | Alabama | 10.1 |
| 4 | Alaska | 10.9 |
| 23 | Arizona | 10.0 |
| 34 | Arkansas | 9.7 |
| 5 | California | 10.6 |
| 30 | Colorado | 9.8 |
| 43 | Connecticut | 9.4 |
| 14 | Delaware | 10.2 |
| 46 | Florida | 9.3 |
| 14 | Georgia | 10.2 |
| 30 | Hawaii | 9.8 |
| 30 | Idaho | 9.8 |
| 34 | Illinois | 9.7 |
| 18 | Indiana | 10.1 |
| 14 | Iowa | 10.2 |
| 8 | Kansas | 10.3 |
| 34 | Kentucky | 9.7 |
| 8 | Louisiana | 10.3 |
| 50 | Maine | 8.7 |
| 40 | Maryland | 9.6 |
| 8 | Massachusetts | 10.3 |
| 18 | Michigan | 10.1 |
| 43 | Minnesota | 9.4 |
| 7 | Mississippi | 10.4 |
| 27 | Missouri | 9.9 |
| 30 | Montana | 9.8 |
| 23 | Nebraska | 10.0 |
| 47 | Nevada | 9.2 |
| 42 | New Hampshire | 9.5 |
| 49 | New Jersey | 8.9 |
| 27 | New Mexico | 9.9 |
| 14 | New York | 10.2 |
| 23 | North Carolina | 10.0 |
| 1 | North Dakota | 12.5 |
| 40 | Ohio | 9.6 |
| 8 | Oklahoma | 10.3 |
| 43 | Oregon | 9.4 |
| 27 | Pennsylvania | 9.9 |
| 2 | Rhode Island | 11.5 |
| 8 | South Carolina | 10.3 |
| 23 | South Dakota | 10.0 |
| 34 | Tennessee | 9.7 |
| 8 | Texas | 10.3 |
| 2 | Utah | 11.5 |
| 5 | Vermont | 10.6 |
| 18 | Virginia | 10.1 |
| 34 | Washington | 9.7 |
| 47 | West Virginia | 9.2 |
| 34 | Wisconsin | 9.7 |
| 18 | Wyoming | 10.1 |

RANK ORDER

| RANK | STATE | PERCENT |
|------|-------|---------|
| 1 | North Dakota | 12.5 |
| 2 | Rhode Island | 11.5 |
| 2 | Utah | 11.5 |
| 4 | Alaska | 10.9 |
| 5 | California | 10.6 |
| 5 | Vermont | 10.6 |
| 7 | Mississippi | 10.4 |
| 8 | Kansas | 10.3 |
| 8 | Louisiana | 10.3 |
| 8 | Massachusetts | 10.3 |
| 8 | Oklahoma | 10.3 |
| 8 | South Carolina | 10.3 |
| 8 | Texas | 10.3 |
| 14 | Delaware | 10.2 |
| 14 | Georgia | 10.2 |
| 14 | Iowa | 10.2 |
| 14 | New York | 10.2 |
| 18 | Alabama | 10.1 |
| 18 | Indiana | 10.1 |
| 18 | Michigan | 10.1 |
| 18 | Virginia | 10.1 |
| 18 | Wyoming | 10.1 |
| 23 | Arizona | 10.0 |
| 23 | Nebraska | 10.0 |
| 23 | North Carolina | 10.0 |
| 23 | South Dakota | 10.0 |
| 27 | Missouri | 9.9 |
| 27 | New Mexico | 9.9 |
| 27 | Pennsylvania | 9.9 |
| 30 | Colorado | 9.8 |
| 30 | Hawaii | 9.8 |
| 30 | Idaho | 9.8 |
| 30 | Montana | 9.8 |
| 34 | Arkansas | 9.7 |
| 34 | Illinois | 9.7 |
| 34 | Kentucky | 9.7 |
| 34 | Tennessee | 9.7 |
| 34 | Washington | 9.7 |
| 34 | Wisconsin | 9.7 |
| 40 | Maryland | 9.6 |
| 40 | Ohio | 9.6 |
| 42 | New Hampshire | 9.5 |
| 43 | Connecticut | 9.4 |
| 43 | Minnesota | 9.4 |
| 43 | Oregon | 9.4 |
| 46 | Florida | 9.3 |
| 47 | Nevada | 9.2 |
| 47 | West Virginia | 9.2 |
| 49 | New Jersey | 8.9 |
| 50 | Maine | 8.7 |

| District of Columbia | | 13.0 |

Source: CQ Press using data from U.S. Bureau of the Census
   "State Characteristics: Vintage 2012" (http://www.census.gov/popest/data/state/asrh/2012/index.html)

# Population 25 to 44 Years Old in 2012

## National Total = 82,825,741

ALPHA ORDER

| RANK | STATE | POPULATION | % of USA |
|---|---|---|---|
| 23 | Alabama | 1,224,424 | 1.5% |
| 47 | Alaska | 203,103 | 0.2% |
| 15 | Arizona | 1,704,005 | 2.1% |
| 34 | Arkansas | 747,881 | 0.9% |
| 1 | California | 10,644,074 | 12.9% |
| 20 | Colorado | 1,469,016 | 1.8% |
| 29 | Connecticut | 892,999 | 1.1% |
| 45 | Delaware | 227,779 | 0.3% |
| 4 | Florida | 4,804,301 | 5.8% |
| 8 | Georgia | 2,744,780 | 3.3% |
| 40 | Hawaii | 374,049 | 0.5% |
| 39 | Idaho | 404,451 | 0.5% |
| 5 | Illinois | 3,480,142 | 4.2% |
| 17 | Indiana | 1,661,297 | 2.0% |
| 33 | Iowa | 749,469 | 0.9% |
| 35 | Kansas | 730,489 | 0.9% |
| 26 | Kentucky | 1,133,798 | 1.4% |
| 24 | Louisiana | 1,212,463 | 1.5% |
| 42 | Maine | 309,665 | 0.4% |
| 18 | Maryland | 1,577,257 | 1.9% |
| 14 | Massachusetts | 1,745,608 | 2.1% |
| 10 | Michigan | 2,399,581 | 2.9% |
| 22 | Minnesota | 1,404,314 | 1.7% |
| 32 | Mississippi | 758,556 | 0.9% |
| 19 | Missouri | 1,522,521 | 1.8% |
| 44 | Montana | 239,194 | 0.3% |
| 37 | Nebraska | 472,662 | 0.6% |
| 31 | Nevada | 771,724 | 0.9% |
| 41 | New Hampshire | 316,659 | 0.4% |
| 11 | New Jersey | 2,332,643 | 2.8% |
| 36 | New Mexico | 522,485 | 0.6% |
| 3 | New York | 5,296,680 | 6.4% |
| 9 | North Carolina | 2,579,838 | 3.1% |
| 48 | North Dakota | 175,862 | 0.2% |
| 7 | Ohio | 2,862,615 | 3.5% |
| 28 | Oklahoma | 983,633 | 1.2% |
| 27 | Oregon | 1,038,829 | 1.3% |
| 6 | Pennsylvania | 3,126,423 | 3.8% |
| 43 | Rhode Island | 260,131 | 0.3% |
| 25 | South Carolina | 1,200,302 | 1.4% |
| 46 | South Dakota | 204,168 | 0.2% |
| 16 | Tennessee | 1,685,981 | 2.0% |
| 2 | Texas | 7,300,015 | 8.8% |
| 30 | Utah | 801,747 | 1.0% |
| 50 | Vermont | 145,199 | 0.2% |
| 12 | Virginia | 2,235,331 | 2.7% |
| 13 | Washington | 1,886,869 | 2.3% |
| 38 | West Virginia | 452,561 | 0.5% |
| 21 | Wisconsin | 1,433,567 | 1.7% |
| 49 | Wyoming | 149,367 | 0.2% |

RANK ORDER

| RANK | STATE | POPULATION | % of USA |
|---|---|---|---|
| 1 | California | 10,644,074 | 12.9% |
| 2 | Texas | 7,300,015 | 8.8% |
| 3 | New York | 5,296,680 | 6.4% |
| 4 | Florida | 4,804,301 | 5.8% |
| 5 | Illinois | 3,480,142 | 4.2% |
| 6 | Pennsylvania | 3,126,423 | 3.8% |
| 7 | Ohio | 2,862,615 | 3.5% |
| 8 | Georgia | 2,744,780 | 3.3% |
| 9 | North Carolina | 2,579,838 | 3.1% |
| 10 | Michigan | 2,399,581 | 2.9% |
| 11 | New Jersey | 2,332,643 | 2.8% |
| 12 | Virginia | 2,235,331 | 2.7% |
| 13 | Washington | 1,886,869 | 2.3% |
| 14 | Massachusetts | 1,745,608 | 2.1% |
| 15 | Arizona | 1,704,005 | 2.1% |
| 16 | Tennessee | 1,685,981 | 2.0% |
| 17 | Indiana | 1,661,297 | 2.0% |
| 18 | Maryland | 1,577,257 | 1.9% |
| 19 | Missouri | 1,522,521 | 1.8% |
| 20 | Colorado | 1,469,016 | 1.8% |
| 21 | Wisconsin | 1,433,567 | 1.7% |
| 22 | Minnesota | 1,404,314 | 1.7% |
| 23 | Alabama | 1,224,424 | 1.5% |
| 24 | Louisiana | 1,212,463 | 1.5% |
| 25 | South Carolina | 1,200,302 | 1.4% |
| 26 | Kentucky | 1,133,798 | 1.4% |
| 27 | Oregon | 1,038,829 | 1.3% |
| 28 | Oklahoma | 983,633 | 1.2% |
| 29 | Connecticut | 892,999 | 1.1% |
| 30 | Utah | 801,747 | 1.0% |
| 31 | Nevada | 771,724 | 0.9% |
| 32 | Mississippi | 758,556 | 0.9% |
| 33 | Iowa | 749,469 | 0.9% |
| 34 | Arkansas | 747,881 | 0.9% |
| 35 | Kansas | 730,489 | 0.9% |
| 36 | New Mexico | 522,485 | 0.6% |
| 37 | Nebraska | 472,662 | 0.6% |
| 38 | West Virginia | 452,561 | 0.5% |
| 39 | Idaho | 404,451 | 0.5% |
| 40 | Hawaii | 374,049 | 0.5% |
| 41 | New Hampshire | 316,659 | 0.4% |
| 42 | Maine | 309,665 | 0.4% |
| 43 | Rhode Island | 260,131 | 0.3% |
| 44 | Montana | 239,194 | 0.3% |
| 45 | Delaware | 227,779 | 0.3% |
| 46 | South Dakota | 204,168 | 0.2% |
| 47 | Alaska | 203,103 | 0.2% |
| 48 | North Dakota | 175,862 | 0.2% |
| 49 | Wyoming | 149,367 | 0.2% |
| 50 | Vermont | 145,199 | 0.2% |
| | District of Columbia | 225,234 | 0.3% |

Source: CQ Press using data from U.S. Bureau of the Census
"State Characteristics: Vintage 2012" (http://www.census.gov/popest/data/state/asrh/2012/index.html)

# Percent of Population 25 to 44 Years Old in 2012

## National Percent = 26.4% of Population

ALPHA ORDER

| RANK | STATE | PERCENT |
|------|-------|---------|
| 26 | Alabama | 25.4 |
| 6 | Alaska | 27.8 |
| 21 | Arizona | 26.0 |
| 26 | Arkansas | 25.4 |
| 3 | California | 28.0 |
| 1 | Colorado | 28.3 |
| 37 | Connecticut | 24.9 |
| 39 | Delaware | 24.8 |
| 37 | Florida | 24.9 |
| 7 | Georgia | 27.7 |
| 12 | Hawaii | 26.9 |
| 31 | Idaho | 25.3 |
| 11 | Illinois | 27.0 |
| 26 | Indiana | 25.4 |
| 44 | Iowa | 24.4 |
| 31 | Kansas | 25.3 |
| 22 | Kentucky | 25.9 |
| 16 | Louisiana | 26.3 |
| 49 | Maine | 23.3 |
| 13 | Maryland | 26.8 |
| 16 | Massachusetts | 26.3 |
| 46 | Michigan | 24.3 |
| 19 | Minnesota | 26.1 |
| 26 | Mississippi | 25.4 |
| 31 | Missouri | 25.3 |
| 48 | Montana | 23.8 |
| 25 | Nebraska | 25.5 |
| 3 | Nevada | 28.0 |
| 47 | New Hampshire | 24.0 |
| 16 | New Jersey | 26.3 |
| 34 | New Mexico | 25.1 |
| 10 | New York | 27.1 |
| 15 | North Carolina | 26.5 |
| 34 | North Dakota | 25.1 |
| 39 | Ohio | 24.8 |
| 24 | Oklahoma | 25.8 |
| 14 | Oregon | 26.6 |
| 42 | Pennsylvania | 24.5 |
| 39 | Rhode Island | 24.8 |
| 26 | South Carolina | 25.4 |
| 42 | South Dakota | 24.5 |
| 19 | Tennessee | 26.1 |
| 3 | Texas | 28.0 |
| 2 | Utah | 28.1 |
| 50 | Vermont | 23.2 |
| 9 | Virginia | 27.3 |
| 8 | Washington | 27.4 |
| 44 | West Virginia | 24.4 |
| 36 | Wisconsin | 25.0 |
| 22 | Wyoming | 25.9 |

RANK ORDER

| RANK | STATE | PERCENT |
|------|-------|---------|
| 1 | Colorado | 28.3 |
| 2 | Utah | 28.1 |
| 3 | California | 28.0 |
| 3 | Nevada | 28.0 |
| 3 | Texas | 28.0 |
| 6 | Alaska | 27.8 |
| 7 | Georgia | 27.7 |
| 8 | Washington | 27.4 |
| 9 | Virginia | 27.3 |
| 10 | New York | 27.1 |
| 11 | Illinois | 27.0 |
| 12 | Hawaii | 26.9 |
| 13 | Maryland | 26.8 |
| 14 | Oregon | 26.6 |
| 15 | North Carolina | 26.5 |
| 16 | Louisiana | 26.3 |
| 16 | Massachusetts | 26.3 |
| 16 | New Jersey | 26.3 |
| 19 | Minnesota | 26.1 |
| 19 | Tennessee | 26.1 |
| 21 | Arizona | 26.0 |
| 22 | Kentucky | 25.9 |
| 22 | Wyoming | 25.9 |
| 24 | Oklahoma | 25.8 |
| 25 | Nebraska | 25.5 |
| 26 | Alabama | 25.4 |
| 26 | Arkansas | 25.4 |
| 26 | Indiana | 25.4 |
| 26 | Mississippi | 25.4 |
| 26 | South Carolina | 25.4 |
| 31 | Idaho | 25.3 |
| 31 | Kansas | 25.3 |
| 31 | Missouri | 25.3 |
| 34 | New Mexico | 25.1 |
| 34 | North Dakota | 25.1 |
| 36 | Wisconsin | 25.0 |
| 37 | Connecticut | 24.9 |
| 37 | Florida | 24.9 |
| 39 | Delaware | 24.8 |
| 39 | Ohio | 24.8 |
| 39 | Rhode Island | 24.8 |
| 42 | Pennsylvania | 24.5 |
| 42 | South Dakota | 24.5 |
| 44 | Iowa | 24.4 |
| 44 | West Virginia | 24.4 |
| 46 | Michigan | 24.3 |
| 47 | New Hampshire | 24.0 |
| 48 | Montana | 23.8 |
| 49 | Maine | 23.3 |
| 50 | Vermont | 23.2 |

District of Columbia   35.6

Source: CQ Press using data from U.S. Bureau of the Census
"State Characteristics: Vintage 2012" (http://www.census.gov/popest/data/state/asrh/2012/index.html)

# Population 45 to 64 Years Old in 2012

## National Total = 82,854,940

ALPHA ORDER

| RANK | STATE | POPULATION | % of USA |
|---|---|---|---|
| 23 | Alabama | 1,288,872 | 1.6% |
| 47 | Alaska | 199,082 | 0.2% |
| 19 | Arizona | 1,603,872 | 1.9% |
| 32 | Arkansas | 761,087 | 0.9% |
| 1 | California | 9,535,809 | 11.5% |
| 22 | Colorado | 1,367,297 | 1.7% |
| 28 | Connecticut | 1,034,010 | 1.2% |
| 45 | Delaware | 250,128 | 0.3% |
| 4 | Florida | 5,210,087 | 6.3% |
| 10 | Georgia | 2,529,059 | 3.1% |
| 42 | Hawaii | 367,582 | 0.4% |
| 41 | Idaho | 395,199 | 0.5% |
| 6 | Illinois | 3,381,964 | 4.1% |
| 16 | Indiana | 1,732,932 | 2.1% |
| 30 | Iowa | 817,169 | 1.0% |
| 33 | Kansas | 739,901 | 0.9% |
| 26 | Kentucky | 1,189,839 | 1.4% |
| 25 | Louisiana | 1,200,566 | 1.4% |
| 39 | Maine | 411,540 | 0.5% |
| 17 | Maryland | 1,632,747 | 2.0% |
| 13 | Massachusetts | 1,855,066 | 2.2% |
| 8 | Michigan | 2,775,520 | 3.3% |
| 21 | Minnesota | 1,462,534 | 1.8% |
| 31 | Mississippi | 765,841 | 0.9% |
| 18 | Missouri | 1,619,285 | 2.0% |
| 44 | Montana | 287,164 | 0.3% |
| 38 | Nebraska | 476,423 | 0.6% |
| 34 | Nevada | 707,963 | 0.9% |
| 40 | New Hampshire | 409,663 | 0.5% |
| 11 | New Jersey | 2,469,797 | 3.0% |
| 36 | New Mexico | 546,553 | 0.7% |
| 3 | New York | 5,255,209 | 6.3% |
| 9 | North Carolina | 2,565,676 | 3.1% |
| 49 | North Dakota | 181,099 | 0.2% |
| 7 | Ohio | 3,204,140 | 3.9% |
| 29 | Oklahoma | 968,073 | 1.2% |
| 27 | Oregon | 1,053,277 | 1.3% |
| 5 | Pennsylvania | 3,591,098 | 4.3% |
| 43 | Rhode Island | 294,597 | 0.4% |
| 24 | South Carolina | 1,263,461 | 1.5% |
| 46 | South Dakota | 219,222 | 0.3% |
| 15 | Tennessee | 1,733,511 | 2.1% |
| 2 | Texas | 6,251,230 | 7.5% |
| 35 | Utah | 567,162 | 0.7% |
| 48 | Vermont | 192,094 | 0.2% |
| 12 | Virginia | 2,208,101 | 2.7% |
| 14 | Washington | 1,848,880 | 2.2% |
| 37 | West Virginia | 535,723 | 0.6% |
| 20 | Wisconsin | 1,596,705 | 1.9% |
| 50 | Wyoming | 157,903 | 0.2% |

RANK ORDER

| RANK | STATE | POPULATION | % of USA |
|---|---|---|---|
| 1 | California | 9,535,809 | 11.5% |
| 2 | Texas | 6,251,230 | 7.5% |
| 3 | New York | 5,255,209 | 6.3% |
| 4 | Florida | 5,210,087 | 6.3% |
| 5 | Pennsylvania | 3,591,098 | 4.3% |
| 6 | Illinois | 3,381,964 | 4.1% |
| 7 | Ohio | 3,204,140 | 3.9% |
| 8 | Michigan | 2,775,520 | 3.3% |
| 9 | North Carolina | 2,565,676 | 3.1% |
| 10 | Georgia | 2,529,059 | 3.1% |
| 11 | New Jersey | 2,469,797 | 3.0% |
| 12 | Virginia | 2,208,101 | 2.7% |
| 13 | Massachusetts | 1,855,066 | 2.2% |
| 14 | Washington | 1,848,880 | 2.2% |
| 15 | Tennessee | 1,733,511 | 2.1% |
| 16 | Indiana | 1,732,932 | 2.1% |
| 17 | Maryland | 1,632,747 | 2.0% |
| 18 | Missouri | 1,619,285 | 2.0% |
| 19 | Arizona | 1,603,872 | 1.9% |
| 20 | Wisconsin | 1,596,705 | 1.9% |
| 21 | Minnesota | 1,462,534 | 1.8% |
| 22 | Colorado | 1,367,297 | 1.7% |
| 23 | Alabama | 1,288,872 | 1.6% |
| 24 | South Carolina | 1,263,461 | 1.5% |
| 25 | Louisiana | 1,200,566 | 1.4% |
| 26 | Kentucky | 1,189,839 | 1.4% |
| 27 | Oregon | 1,053,277 | 1.3% |
| 28 | Connecticut | 1,034,010 | 1.2% |
| 29 | Oklahoma | 968,073 | 1.2% |
| 30 | Iowa | 817,169 | 1.0% |
| 31 | Mississippi | 765,841 | 0.9% |
| 32 | Arkansas | 761,087 | 0.9% |
| 33 | Kansas | 739,901 | 0.9% |
| 34 | Nevada | 707,963 | 0.9% |
| 35 | Utah | 567,162 | 0.7% |
| 36 | New Mexico | 546,553 | 0.7% |
| 37 | West Virginia | 535,723 | 0.6% |
| 38 | Nebraska | 476,423 | 0.6% |
| 39 | Maine | 411,540 | 0.5% |
| 40 | New Hampshire | 409,663 | 0.5% |
| 41 | Idaho | 395,199 | 0.5% |
| 42 | Hawaii | 367,582 | 0.4% |
| 43 | Rhode Island | 294,597 | 0.4% |
| 44 | Montana | 287,164 | 0.3% |
| 45 | Delaware | 250,128 | 0.3% |
| 46 | South Dakota | 219,222 | 0.3% |
| 47 | Alaska | 199,082 | 0.2% |
| 48 | Vermont | 192,094 | 0.2% |
| 49 | North Dakota | 181,099 | 0.2% |
| 50 | Wyoming | 157,903 | 0.2% |
| | District of Columbia | 143,228 | 0.2% |

Source: U.S. Bureau of the Census
"State Characteristics: Vintage 2012" (http://www.census.gov/popest/data/state/asrh/2012/index.html)

# Percent of Population 45 to 64 Years Old in 2012

## National Percent = 26.4% of Population

ALPHA ORDER

| RANK | STATE | PERCENT |
|------|-------|---------|
| 27 | Alabama | 26.7 |
| 17 | Alaska | 27.2 |
| 48 | Arizona | 24.5 |
| 39 | Arkansas | 25.8 |
| 46 | California | 25.1 |
| 31 | Colorado | 26.4 |
| 5 | Connecticut | 28.8 |
| 16 | Delaware | 27.3 |
| 20 | Florida | 27.0 |
| 44 | Georgia | 25.5 |
| 31 | Hawaii | 26.4 |
| 47 | Idaho | 24.8 |
| 33 | Illinois | 26.3 |
| 30 | Indiana | 26.5 |
| 29 | Iowa | 26.6 |
| 43 | Kansas | 25.6 |
| 17 | Kentucky | 27.2 |
| 37 | Louisiana | 26.1 |
| 1 | Maine | 31.0 |
| 14 | Maryland | 27.7 |
| 10 | Massachusetts | 27.9 |
| 7 | Michigan | 28.1 |
| 17 | Minnesota | 27.2 |
| 40 | Mississippi | 25.7 |
| 23 | Missouri | 26.9 |
| 6 | Montana | 28.6 |
| 40 | Nebraska | 25.7 |
| 40 | Nevada | 25.7 |
| 1 | New Hampshire | 31.0 |
| 10 | New Jersey | 27.9 |
| 36 | New Mexico | 26.2 |
| 23 | New York | 26.9 |
| 33 | North Carolina | 26.3 |
| 38 | North Dakota | 25.9 |
| 13 | Ohio | 27.8 |
| 45 | Oklahoma | 25.4 |
| 20 | Oregon | 27.0 |
| 7 | Pennsylvania | 28.1 |
| 9 | Rhode Island | 28.0 |
| 27 | South Carolina | 26.7 |
| 33 | South Dakota | 26.3 |
| 23 | Tennessee | 26.9 |
| 49 | Texas | 24.0 |
| 50 | Utah | 19.9 |
| 3 | Vermont | 30.7 |
| 20 | Virginia | 27.0 |
| 26 | Washington | 26.8 |
| 4 | West Virginia | 28.9 |
| 10 | Wisconsin | 27.9 |
| 15 | Wyoming | 27.4 |

RANK ORDER

| RANK | STATE | PERCENT |
|------|-------|---------|
| 1 | Maine | 31.0 |
| 1 | New Hampshire | 31.0 |
| 3 | Vermont | 30.7 |
| 4 | West Virginia | 28.9 |
| 5 | Connecticut | 28.8 |
| 6 | Montana | 28.6 |
| 7 | Michigan | 28.1 |
| 7 | Pennsylvania | 28.1 |
| 9 | Rhode Island | 28.0 |
| 10 | Massachusetts | 27.9 |
| 10 | New Jersey | 27.9 |
| 10 | Wisconsin | 27.9 |
| 13 | Ohio | 27.8 |
| 14 | Maryland | 27.7 |
| 15 | Wyoming | 27.4 |
| 16 | Delaware | 27.3 |
| 17 | Alaska | 27.2 |
| 17 | Kentucky | 27.2 |
| 17 | Minnesota | 27.2 |
| 20 | Florida | 27.0 |
| 20 | Oregon | 27.0 |
| 20 | Virginia | 27.0 |
| 23 | Missouri | 26.9 |
| 23 | New York | 26.9 |
| 23 | Tennessee | 26.9 |
| 26 | Washington | 26.8 |
| 27 | Alabama | 26.7 |
| 27 | South Carolina | 26.7 |
| 29 | Iowa | 26.6 |
| 30 | Indiana | 26.5 |
| 31 | Colorado | 26.4 |
| 31 | Hawaii | 26.4 |
| 33 | Illinois | 26.3 |
| 33 | North Carolina | 26.3 |
| 33 | South Dakota | 26.3 |
| 36 | New Mexico | 26.2 |
| 37 | Louisiana | 26.1 |
| 38 | North Dakota | 25.9 |
| 39 | Arkansas | 25.8 |
| 40 | Mississippi | 25.7 |
| 40 | Nebraska | 25.7 |
| 40 | Nevada | 25.7 |
| 43 | Kansas | 25.6 |
| 44 | Georgia | 25.5 |
| 45 | Oklahoma | 25.4 |
| 46 | California | 25.1 |
| 47 | Idaho | 24.8 |
| 48 | Arizona | 24.5 |
| 49 | Texas | 24.0 |
| 50 | Utah | 19.9 |
| | District of Columbia | 22.7 |

Source: CQ Press using data from U.S. Bureau of the Census
  "State Characteristics: Vintage 2012" (http://www.census.gov/popest/data/state/asrh/2012/index.html)

# Population 65 Years Old and Older in 2012

## National Total = 43,145,356

| RANK | STATE | POPULATION | % of USA |
|---|---|---|---|
| 22 | Alabama | 699,380 | 1.6% |
| 50 | Alaska | 62,497 | 0.1% |
| 13 | Arizona | 971,533 | 2.3% |
| 31 | Arkansas | 442,590 | 1.0% |
| 1 | California | 4,600,085 | 10.7% |
| 25 | Colorado | 613,241 | 1.4% |
| 29 | Connecticut | 532,712 | 1.2% |
| 45 | Delaware | 140,474 | 0.3% |
| 2 | Florida | 3,509,715 | 8.1% |
| 11 | Georgia | 1,139,699 | 2.6% |
| 41 | Hawaii | 210,801 | 0.5% |
| 40 | Idaho | 212,578 | 0.5% |
| 7 | Illinois | 1,694,437 | 3.9% |
| 17 | Indiana | 889,148 | 2.1% |
| 30 | Iowa | 470,305 | 1.1% |
| 33 | Kansas | 394,269 | 0.9% |
| 24 | Kentucky | 614,653 | 1.4% |
| 26 | Louisiana | 595,205 | 1.4% |
| 39 | Maine | 226,376 | 0.5% |
| 20 | Maryland | 763,019 | 1.8% |
| 14 | Massachusetts | 958,494 | 2.2% |
| 8 | Michigan | 1,442,714 | 3.3% |
| 21 | Minnesota | 729,767 | 1.7% |
| 32 | Mississippi | 404,075 | 0.9% |
| 18 | Missouri | 883,181 | 2.0% |
| 44 | Montana | 158,289 | 0.4% |
| 38 | Nebraska | 257,354 | 0.6% |
| 34 | Nevada | 360,914 | 0.8% |
| 42 | New Hampshire | 193,803 | 0.4% |
| 10 | New Jersey | 1,250,555 | 2.9% |
| 36 | New Mexico | 294,833 | 0.7% |
| 4 | New York | 2,757,572 | 6.4% |
| 9 | North Carolina | 1,347,869 | 3.1% |
| 47 | North Dakota | 100,666 | 0.2% |
| 6 | Ohio | 1,705,122 | 4.0% |
| 28 | Oklahoma | 534,247 | 1.2% |
| 27 | Oregon | 581,619 | 1.3% |
| 5 | Pennsylvania | 2,042,861 | 4.7% |
| 43 | Rhode Island | 158,629 | 0.4% |
| 23 | South Carolina | 695,459 | 1.6% |
| 46 | South Dakota | 122,183 | 0.3% |
| 15 | Tennessee | 918,507 | 2.1% |
| 3 | Texas | 2,839,295 | 6.6% |
| 37 | Utah | 271,419 | 0.6% |
| 48 | Vermont | 98,444 | 0.2% |
| 12 | Virginia | 1,062,505 | 2.5% |
| 16 | Washington | 908,417 | 2.1% |
| 35 | West Virginia | 311,949 | 0.7% |
| 19 | Wisconsin | 824,500 | 1.9% |
| 49 | Wyoming | 75,508 | 0.2% |

| RANK | STATE | POPULATION | % of USA |
|---|---|---|---|
| 1 | California | 4,600,085 | 10.7% |
| 2 | Florida | 3,509,715 | 8.1% |
| 3 | Texas | 2,839,295 | 6.6% |
| 4 | New York | 2,757,572 | 6.4% |
| 5 | Pennsylvania | 2,042,861 | 4.7% |
| 6 | Ohio | 1,705,122 | 4.0% |
| 7 | Illinois | 1,694,437 | 3.9% |
| 8 | Michigan | 1,442,714 | 3.3% |
| 9 | North Carolina | 1,347,869 | 3.1% |
| 10 | New Jersey | 1,250,555 | 2.9% |
| 11 | Georgia | 1,139,699 | 2.6% |
| 12 | Virginia | 1,062,505 | 2.5% |
| 13 | Arizona | 971,533 | 2.3% |
| 14 | Massachusetts | 958,494 | 2.2% |
| 15 | Tennessee | 918,507 | 2.1% |
| 16 | Washington | 908,417 | 2.1% |
| 17 | Indiana | 889,148 | 2.1% |
| 18 | Missouri | 883,181 | 2.0% |
| 19 | Wisconsin | 824,500 | 1.9% |
| 20 | Maryland | 763,019 | 1.8% |
| 21 | Minnesota | 729,767 | 1.7% |
| 22 | Alabama | 699,380 | 1.6% |
| 23 | South Carolina | 695,459 | 1.6% |
| 24 | Kentucky | 614,653 | 1.4% |
| 25 | Colorado | 613,241 | 1.4% |
| 26 | Louisiana | 595,205 | 1.4% |
| 27 | Oregon | 581,619 | 1.3% |
| 28 | Oklahoma | 534,247 | 1.2% |
| 29 | Connecticut | 532,712 | 1.2% |
| 30 | Iowa | 470,305 | 1.1% |
| 31 | Arkansas | 442,590 | 1.0% |
| 32 | Mississippi | 404,075 | 0.9% |
| 33 | Kansas | 394,269 | 0.9% |
| 34 | Nevada | 360,914 | 0.8% |
| 35 | West Virginia | 311,949 | 0.7% |
| 36 | New Mexico | 294,833 | 0.7% |
| 37 | Utah | 271,419 | 0.6% |
| 38 | Nebraska | 257,354 | 0.6% |
| 39 | Maine | 226,376 | 0.5% |
| 40 | Idaho | 212,578 | 0.5% |
| 41 | Hawaii | 210,801 | 0.5% |
| 42 | New Hampshire | 193,803 | 0.4% |
| 43 | Rhode Island | 158,629 | 0.4% |
| 44 | Montana | 158,289 | 0.4% |
| 45 | Delaware | 140,474 | 0.3% |
| 46 | South Dakota | 122,183 | 0.3% |
| 47 | North Dakota | 100,666 | 0.2% |
| 48 | Vermont | 98,444 | 0.2% |
| 49 | Wyoming | 75,508 | 0.2% |
| 50 | Alaska | 62,497 | 0.1% |
|  | District of Columbia | 71,889 | 0.2% |

Source: U.S. Bureau of the Census
"State Characteristics: Vintage 2012" (http://www.census.gov/popest/data/state/asrh/2012/index.html)

# Percent of Population 65 Years Old and Older in 2012

## National Percent = 13.7% of Population

| RANK | STATE | PERCENT |
|------|-------|---------|
| 21 | Alabama | 14.5 |
| 50 | Alaska | 8.5 |
| 13 | Arizona | 14.8 |
| 11 | Arkansas | 15.0 |
| 45 | California | 12.1 |
| 46 | Colorado | 11.8 |
| 13 | Connecticut | 14.8 |
| 7 | Delaware | 15.3 |
| 1 | Florida | 18.2 |
| 47 | Georgia | 11.5 |
| 9 | Hawaii | 15.1 |
| 37 | Idaho | 13.3 |
| 38 | Illinois | 13.2 |
| 34 | Indiana | 13.6 |
| 7 | Iowa | 15.3 |
| 33 | Kansas | 13.7 |
| 29 | Kentucky | 14.0 |
| 44 | Louisiana | 12.9 |
| 2 | Maine | 17.0 |
| 42 | Maryland | 13.0 |
| 22 | Massachusetts | 14.4 |
| 20 | Michigan | 14.6 |
| 34 | Minnesota | 13.6 |
| 36 | Mississippi | 13.5 |
| 16 | Missouri | 14.7 |
| 5 | Montana | 15.7 |
| 31 | Nebraska | 13.9 |
| 40 | Nevada | 13.1 |
| 16 | New Hampshire | 14.7 |
| 26 | New Jersey | 14.1 |
| 26 | New Mexico | 14.1 |
| 26 | New York | 14.1 |
| 32 | North Carolina | 13.8 |
| 22 | North Dakota | 14.4 |
| 13 | Ohio | 14.8 |
| 29 | Oklahoma | 14.0 |
| 12 | Oregon | 14.9 |
| 4 | Pennsylvania | 16.0 |
| 9 | Rhode Island | 15.1 |
| 16 | South Carolina | 14.7 |
| 16 | South Dakota | 14.7 |
| 25 | Tennessee | 14.2 |
| 48 | Texas | 10.9 |
| 49 | Utah | 9.5 |
| 5 | Vermont | 15.7 |
| 42 | Virginia | 13.0 |
| 38 | Washington | 13.2 |
| 3 | West Virginia | 16.8 |
| 22 | Wisconsin | 14.4 |
| 40 | Wyoming | 13.1 |

| RANK | STATE | PERCENT |
|------|-------|---------|
| 1 | Florida | 18.2 |
| 2 | Maine | 17.0 |
| 3 | West Virginia | 16.8 |
| 4 | Pennsylvania | 16.0 |
| 5 | Montana | 15.7 |
| 5 | Vermont | 15.7 |
| 7 | Delaware | 15.3 |
| 7 | Iowa | 15.3 |
| 9 | Hawaii | 15.1 |
| 9 | Rhode Island | 15.1 |
| 11 | Arkansas | 15.0 |
| 12 | Oregon | 14.9 |
| 13 | Arizona | 14.8 |
| 13 | Connecticut | 14.8 |
| 13 | Ohio | 14.8 |
| 16 | Missouri | 14.7 |
| 16 | New Hampshire | 14.7 |
| 16 | South Carolina | 14.7 |
| 16 | South Dakota | 14.7 |
| 20 | Michigan | 14.6 |
| 21 | Alabama | 14.5 |
| 22 | Massachusetts | 14.4 |
| 22 | North Dakota | 14.4 |
| 22 | Wisconsin | 14.4 |
| 25 | Tennessee | 14.2 |
| 26 | New Jersey | 14.1 |
| 26 | New Mexico | 14.1 |
| 26 | New York | 14.1 |
| 29 | Kentucky | 14.0 |
| 29 | Oklahoma | 14.0 |
| 31 | Nebraska | 13.9 |
| 32 | North Carolina | 13.8 |
| 33 | Kansas | 13.7 |
| 34 | Indiana | 13.6 |
| 34 | Minnesota | 13.6 |
| 36 | Mississippi | 13.5 |
| 37 | Idaho | 13.3 |
| 38 | Illinois | 13.2 |
| 38 | Washington | 13.2 |
| 40 | Nevada | 13.1 |
| 40 | Wyoming | 13.1 |
| 42 | Maryland | 13.0 |
| 42 | Virginia | 13.0 |
| 44 | Louisiana | 12.9 |
| 45 | California | 12.1 |
| 46 | Colorado | 11.8 |
| 47 | Georgia | 11.5 |
| 48 | Texas | 10.9 |
| 49 | Utah | 9.5 |
| 50 | Alaska | 8.5 |
| | District of Columbia | 11.4 |

Source: CQ Press using data from U.S. Bureau of the Census
"State Characteristics: Vintage 2012" (http://www.census.gov/popest/data/state/asrh/2012/index.html)

# Population 85 Years Old and Older in 2012

## National Total = 5,887,300

| ALPHA ORDER | | | | RANK ORDER | | | |
|---|---|---|---|---|---|---|---|
| RANK | STATE | POPULATION | % of USA | RANK | STATE | POPULATION | % of USA |
| 24 | Alabama | 80,104 | 1.4% | 1 | California | 654,281 | 11.1% |
| 50 | Alaska | 5,373 | 0.1% | 2 | Florida | 482,753 | 8.2% |
| 18 | Arizona | 114,425 | 1.9% | 3 | New York | 414,385 | 7.0% |
| 32 | Arkansas | 53,920 | 0.9% | 4 | Texas | 335,632 | 5.7% |
| 1 | California | 654,281 | 11.1% | 5 | Pennsylvania | 322,052 | 5.5% |
| 26 | Colorado | 76,510 | 1.3% | 6 | Illinois | 247,838 | 4.2% |
| 22 | Connecticut | 88,168 | 1.5% | 7 | Ohio | 243,513 | 4.1% |
| 47 | Delaware | 16,820 | 0.3% | 8 | Michigan | 203,914 | 3.5% |
| 2 | Florida | 482,753 | 8.2% | 9 | New Jersey | 189,119 | 3.2% |
| 15 | Georgia | 123,483 | 2.1% | 10 | North Carolina | 159,872 | 2.7% |
| 38 | Hawaii | 34,623 | 0.6% | 11 | Massachusetts | 153,113 | 2.6% |
| 42 | Idaho | 26,610 | 0.5% | 12 | Virginia | 132,220 | 2.2% |
| 6 | Illinois | 247,838 | 4.2% | 13 | Washington | 124,598 | 2.1% |
| 16 | Indiana | 121,927 | 2.1% | 14 | Wisconsin | 124,180 | 2.1% |
| 25 | Iowa | 77,372 | 1.3% | 15 | Georgia | 123,483 | 2.1% |
| 31 | Kansas | 62,168 | 1.1% | 16 | Indiana | 121,927 | 2.1% |
| 28 | Kentucky | 72,971 | 1.2% | 17 | Missouri | 120,285 | 2.0% |
| 29 | Louisiana | 70,740 | 1.2% | 18 | Arizona | 114,425 | 1.9% |
| 40 | Maine | 30,473 | 0.5% | 19 | Minnesota | 112,619 | 1.9% |
| 21 | Maryland | 105,808 | 1.8% | 20 | Tennessee | 106,389 | 1.8% |
| 11 | Massachusetts | 153,113 | 2.6% | 21 | Maryland | 105,808 | 1.8% |
| 8 | Michigan | 203,914 | 3.5% | 22 | Connecticut | 88,168 | 1.5% |
| 19 | Minnesota | 112,619 | 1.9% | 23 | Oregon | 82,133 | 1.4% |
| 33 | Mississippi | 47,229 | 0.8% | 24 | Alabama | 80,104 | 1.4% |
| 17 | Missouri | 120,285 | 2.0% | 25 | Iowa | 77,372 | 1.3% |
| 44 | Montana | 21,081 | 0.4% | 26 | Colorado | 76,510 | 1.3% |
| 34 | Nebraska | 40,950 | 0.7% | 27 | South Carolina | 76,103 | 1.3% |
| 37 | Nevada | 34,744 | 0.6% | 28 | Kentucky | 72,971 | 1.2% |
| 43 | New Hampshire | 26,414 | 0.4% | 29 | Louisiana | 70,740 | 1.2% |
| 9 | New Jersey | 189,119 | 3.2% | 30 | Oklahoma | 65,560 | 1.1% |
| 36 | New Mexico | 34,877 | 0.6% | 31 | Kansas | 62,168 | 1.1% |
| 3 | New York | 414,385 | 7.0% | 32 | Arkansas | 53,920 | 0.9% |
| 10 | North Carolina | 159,872 | 2.7% | 33 | Mississippi | 47,229 | 0.8% |
| 46 | North Dakota | 17,330 | 0.3% | 34 | Nebraska | 40,950 | 0.7% |
| 7 | Ohio | 243,513 | 4.1% | 35 | West Virginia | 37,733 | 0.6% |
| 30 | Oklahoma | 65,560 | 1.1% | 36 | New Mexico | 34,877 | 0.6% |
| 23 | Oregon | 82,133 | 1.4% | 37 | Nevada | 34,744 | 0.6% |
| 5 | Pennsylvania | 322,052 | 5.5% | 38 | Hawaii | 34,623 | 0.6% |
| 41 | Rhode Island | 27,564 | 0.5% | 39 | Utah | 33,457 | 0.6% |
| 27 | South Carolina | 76,103 | 1.3% | 40 | Maine | 30,473 | 0.5% |
| 45 | South Dakota | 20,171 | 0.3% | 41 | Rhode Island | 27,564 | 0.5% |
| 20 | Tennessee | 106,389 | 1.8% | 42 | Idaho | 26,610 | 0.5% |
| 4 | Texas | 335,632 | 5.7% | 43 | New Hampshire | 26,414 | 0.4% |
| 39 | Utah | 33,457 | 0.6% | 44 | Montana | 21,081 | 0.4% |
| 48 | Vermont | 13,502 | 0.2% | 45 | South Dakota | 20,171 | 0.3% |
| 12 | Virginia | 132,220 | 2.2% | 46 | North Dakota | 17,330 | 0.3% |
| 13 | Washington | 124,598 | 2.1% | 47 | Delaware | 16,820 | 0.3% |
| 35 | West Virginia | 37,733 | 0.6% | 48 | Vermont | 13,502 | 0.2% |
| 14 | Wisconsin | 124,180 | 2.1% | 49 | Wyoming | 9,221 | 0.2% |
| 49 | Wyoming | 9,221 | 0.2% | 50 | Alaska | 5,373 | 0.1% |
| | | | | | District of Columbia | 11,003 | 0.2% |

Source: U.S. Bureau of the Census
    "State Characteristics: Vintage 2012" (http://www.census.gov/popest/data/state/asrh/2012/index.html)

# Percent of Population 85 Years Old and Older in 2012

## National Percent = 1.9% of Population

ALPHA ORDER

| RANK | STATE | PERCENT |
|------|-------|---------|
| 31 | Alabama | 1.7 |
| 50 | Alaska | 0.7 |
| 31 | Arizona | 1.7 |
| 27 | Arkansas | 1.8 |
| 31 | California | 1.7 |
| 44 | Colorado | 1.5 |
| 2 | Connecticut | 2.5 |
| 27 | Delaware | 1.8 |
| 2 | Florida | 2.5 |
| 48 | Georgia | 1.2 |
| 2 | Hawaii | 2.5 |
| 31 | Idaho | 1.7 |
| 25 | Illinois | 1.9 |
| 25 | Indiana | 1.9 |
| 2 | Iowa | 2.5 |
| 11 | Kansas | 2.2 |
| 31 | Kentucky | 1.7 |
| 44 | Louisiana | 1.5 |
| 9 | Maine | 2.3 |
| 27 | Maryland | 1.8 |
| 9 | Massachusetts | 2.3 |
| 15 | Michigan | 2.1 |
| 15 | Minnesota | 2.1 |
| 38 | Mississippi | 1.6 |
| 22 | Missouri | 2.0 |
| 15 | Montana | 2.1 |
| 11 | Nebraska | 2.2 |
| 46 | Nevada | 1.3 |
| 22 | New Hampshire | 2.0 |
| 15 | New Jersey | 2.1 |
| 31 | New Mexico | 1.7 |
| 15 | New York | 2.1 |
| 38 | North Carolina | 1.6 |
| 2 | North Dakota | 2.5 |
| 15 | Ohio | 2.1 |
| 31 | Oklahoma | 1.7 |
| 15 | Oregon | 2.1 |
| 2 | Pennsylvania | 2.5 |
| 1 | Rhode Island | 2.6 |
| 38 | South Carolina | 1.6 |
| 8 | South Dakota | 2.4 |
| 38 | Tennessee | 1.6 |
| 46 | Texas | 1.3 |
| 48 | Utah | 1.2 |
| 11 | Vermont | 2.2 |
| 38 | Virginia | 1.6 |
| 27 | Washington | 1.8 |
| 22 | West Virginia | 2.0 |
| 11 | Wisconsin | 2.2 |
| 38 | Wyoming | 1.6 |

RANK ORDER

| RANK | STATE | PERCENT |
|------|-------|---------|
| 1 | Rhode Island | 2.6 |
| 2 | Connecticut | 2.5 |
| 2 | Florida | 2.5 |
| 2 | Hawaii | 2.5 |
| 2 | Iowa | 2.5 |
| 2 | North Dakota | 2.5 |
| 2 | Pennsylvania | 2.5 |
| 8 | South Dakota | 2.4 |
| 9 | Maine | 2.3 |
| 9 | Massachusetts | 2.3 |
| 11 | Kansas | 2.2 |
| 11 | Nebraska | 2.2 |
| 11 | Vermont | 2.2 |
| 11 | Wisconsin | 2.2 |
| 15 | Michigan | 2.1 |
| 15 | Minnesota | 2.1 |
| 15 | Montana | 2.1 |
| 15 | New Jersey | 2.1 |
| 15 | New York | 2.1 |
| 15 | Ohio | 2.1 |
| 15 | Oregon | 2.1 |
| 22 | Missouri | 2.0 |
| 22 | New Hampshire | 2.0 |
| 22 | West Virginia | 2.0 |
| 25 | Illinois | 1.9 |
| 25 | Indiana | 1.9 |
| 27 | Arkansas | 1.8 |
| 27 | Delaware | 1.8 |
| 27 | Maryland | 1.8 |
| 27 | Washington | 1.8 |
| 31 | Alabama | 1.7 |
| 31 | Arizona | 1.7 |
| 31 | California | 1.7 |
| 31 | Idaho | 1.7 |
| 31 | Kentucky | 1.7 |
| 31 | New Mexico | 1.7 |
| 31 | Oklahoma | 1.7 |
| 38 | Mississippi | 1.6 |
| 38 | North Carolina | 1.6 |
| 38 | South Carolina | 1.6 |
| 38 | Tennessee | 1.6 |
| 38 | Virginia | 1.6 |
| 38 | Wyoming | 1.6 |
| 44 | Colorado | 1.5 |
| 44 | Louisiana | 1.5 |
| 46 | Nevada | 1.3 |
| 46 | Texas | 1.3 |
| 48 | Georgia | 1.2 |
| 48 | Utah | 1.2 |
| 50 | Alaska | 0.7 |
|  | District of Columbia | 1.7 |

Source: CQ Press using data from U.S. Bureau of the Census
"State Characteristics: Vintage 2012" (http://www.census.gov/popest/data/state/asrh/2012/index.html)

# Percent of Native Population Born in Their State of Residence in 2012

## National Percent = 67.6%

ALPHA ORDER

| RANK | STATE | PERCENT |
|------|-------|---------|
| 13 | Alabama | 72.7 |
| 48 | Alaska | 43.5 |
| 45 | Arizona | 44.4 |
| 28 | Arkansas | 64.3 |
| 9 | California | 74.6 |
| 44 | Colorado | 46.6 |
| 30 | Connecticut | 64.0 |
| 43 | Delaware | 49.1 |
| 47 | Florida | 44.3 |
| 33 | Georgia | 61.1 |
| 25 | Hawaii | 66.2 |
| 42 | Idaho | 50.3 |
| 6 | Illinois | 77.8 |
| 16 | Indiana | 71.7 |
| 8 | Iowa | 74.9 |
| 31 | Kansas | 63.5 |
| 15 | Kentucky | 72.1 |
| 3 | Louisiana | 81.6 |
| 21 | Maine | 67.6 |
| 37 | Maryland | 55.2 |
| 11 | Massachusetts | 74.1 |
| 2 | Michigan | 81.7 |
| 10 | Minnesota | 74.2 |
| 12 | Mississippi | 73.5 |
| 19 | Missouri | 69.2 |
| 39 | Montana | 54.2 |
| 18 | Nebraska | 69.6 |
| 50 | Nevada | 30.9 |
| 45 | New Hampshire | 44.4 |
| 24 | New Jersey | 66.8 |
| 35 | New Mexico | 58.8 |
| 1 | New York | 82.1 |
| 32 | North Carolina | 62.8 |
| 20 | North Dakota | 68.8 |
| 5 | Ohio | 78.1 |
| 27 | Oklahoma | 64.5 |
| 41 | Oregon | 50.7 |
| 4 | Pennsylvania | 78.5 |
| 23 | Rhode Island | 67.1 |
| 33 | South Carolina | 61.1 |
| 25 | South Dakota | 66.2 |
| 28 | Tennessee | 64.3 |
| 14 | Texas | 72.4 |
| 22 | Utah | 67.5 |
| 40 | Vermont | 53.7 |
| 36 | Virginia | 55.8 |
| 38 | Washington | 54.7 |
| 17 | West Virginia | 70.6 |
| 7 | Wisconsin | 75.0 |
| 49 | Wyoming | 42.0 |

RANK ORDER

| RANK | STATE | PERCENT |
|------|-------|---------|
| 1 | New York | 82.1 |
| 2 | Michigan | 81.7 |
| 3 | Louisiana | 81.6 |
| 4 | Pennsylvania | 78.5 |
| 5 | Ohio | 78.1 |
| 6 | Illinois | 77.8 |
| 7 | Wisconsin | 75.0 |
| 8 | Iowa | 74.9 |
| 9 | California | 74.6 |
| 10 | Minnesota | 74.2 |
| 11 | Massachusetts | 74.1 |
| 12 | Mississippi | 73.5 |
| 13 | Alabama | 72.7 |
| 14 | Texas | 72.4 |
| 15 | Kentucky | 72.1 |
| 16 | Indiana | 71.7 |
| 17 | West Virginia | 70.6 |
| 18 | Nebraska | 69.6 |
| 19 | Missouri | 69.2 |
| 20 | North Dakota | 68.8 |
| 21 | Maine | 67.6 |
| 22 | Utah | 67.5 |
| 23 | Rhode Island | 67.1 |
| 24 | New Jersey | 66.8 |
| 25 | Hawaii | 66.2 |
| 25 | South Dakota | 66.2 |
| 27 | Oklahoma | 64.5 |
| 28 | Arkansas | 64.3 |
| 28 | Tennessee | 64.3 |
| 30 | Connecticut | 64.0 |
| 31 | Kansas | 63.5 |
| 32 | North Carolina | 62.8 |
| 33 | Georgia | 61.1 |
| 33 | South Carolina | 61.1 |
| 35 | New Mexico | 58.8 |
| 36 | Virginia | 55.8 |
| 37 | Maryland | 55.2 |
| 38 | Washington | 54.7 |
| 39 | Montana | 54.2 |
| 40 | Vermont | 53.7 |
| 41 | Oregon | 50.7 |
| 42 | Idaho | 50.3 |
| 43 | Delaware | 49.1 |
| 44 | Colorado | 46.6 |
| 45 | Arizona | 44.4 |
| 45 | New Hampshire | 44.4 |
| 47 | Florida | 44.3 |
| 48 | Alaska | 43.5 |
| 49 | Wyoming | 42.0 |
| 50 | Nevada | 30.9 |

| | District of Columbia | 43.3 |

Source: U.S. Bureau of the Census

"2012 American Community Survey-Table R0601" (http://www.census.gov/acs/www/index.html)

# Domestic Migration of Population: 2012 to 2013

## National Net Migration = 0 People*

ALPHA ORDER

| RANK | STATE | NET MIGRATION |
|---|---|---|
| 21 | Alabama | 451 |
| 35 | Alaska | (4,006) |
| 6 | Arizona | 26,417 |
| 29 | Arkansas | (2,031) |
| 48 | California | (49,259) |
| 4 | Colorado | 36,284 |
| 43 | Connecticut | (17,224) |
| 18 | Delaware | 3,010 |
| 2 | Florida | 91,484 |
| 36 | Georgia | (6,347) |
| 27 | Hawaii | (1,457) |
| 16 | Idaho | 4,579 |
| 49 | Illinois | (67,313) |
| 25 | Indiana | (1,179) |
| 20 | Iowa | 671 |
| 42 | Kansas | (12,557) |
| 30 | Kentucky | (2,290) |
| 32 | Louisiana | (2,492) |
| 26 | Maine | (1,423) |
| 40 | Maryland | (8,525) |
| 33 | Massachusetts | (2,833) |
| 45 | Michigan | (28,539) |
| 24 | Minnesota | (1,147) |
| 37 | Mississippi | (7,038) |
| 38 | Missouri | (7,612) |
| 14 | Montana | 5,467 |
| 23 | Nebraska | (695) |
| 10 | Nevada | 12,854 |
| 31 | New Hampshire | (2,355) |
| 47 | New Jersey | (45,035) |
| 41 | New Mexico | (10,526) |
| 50 | New York | (104,470) |
| 3 | North Carolina | 37,240 |
| 8 | North Dakota | 16,961 |
| 44 | Ohio | (23,094) |
| 9 | Oklahoma | 14,268 |
| 12 | Oregon | 10,215 |
| 46 | Pennsylvania | (30,718) |
| 34 | Rhode Island | (3,922) |
| 5 | South Carolina | 29,324 |
| 15 | South Dakota | 4,762 |
| 11 | Tennessee | 12,649 |
| 1 | Texas | 113,528 |
| 13 | Utah | 5,567 |
| 22 | Vermont | (653) |
| 17 | Virginia | 3,099 |
| 7 | Washington | 17,027 |
| 28 | West Virginia | (1,894) |
| 39 | Wisconsin | (8,158) |
| 19 | Wyoming | 2,616 |

RANK ORDER

| RANK | STATE | NET MIGRATION |
|---|---|---|
| 1 | Texas | 113,528 |
| 2 | Florida | 91,484 |
| 3 | North Carolina | 37,240 |
| 4 | Colorado | 36,284 |
| 5 | South Carolina | 29,324 |
| 6 | Arizona | 26,417 |
| 7 | Washington | 17,027 |
| 8 | North Dakota | 16,961 |
| 9 | Oklahoma | 14,268 |
| 10 | Nevada | 12,854 |
| 11 | Tennessee | 12,649 |
| 12 | Oregon | 10,215 |
| 13 | Utah | 5,567 |
| 14 | Montana | 5,467 |
| 15 | South Dakota | 4,762 |
| 16 | Idaho | 4,579 |
| 17 | Virginia | 3,099 |
| 18 | Delaware | 3,010 |
| 19 | Wyoming | 2,616 |
| 20 | Iowa | 671 |
| 21 | Alabama | 451 |
| 22 | Vermont | (653) |
| 23 | Nebraska | (695) |
| 24 | Minnesota | (1,147) |
| 25 | Indiana | (1,179) |
| 26 | Maine | (1,423) |
| 27 | Hawaii | (1,457) |
| 28 | West Virginia | (1,894) |
| 29 | Arkansas | (2,031) |
| 30 | Kentucky | (2,290) |
| 31 | New Hampshire | (2,355) |
| 32 | Louisiana | (2,492) |
| 33 | Massachusetts | (2,833) |
| 34 | Rhode Island | (3,922) |
| 35 | Alaska | (4,006) |
| 36 | Georgia | (6,347) |
| 37 | Mississippi | (7,038) |
| 38 | Missouri | (7,612) |
| 39 | Wisconsin | (8,158) |
| 40 | Maryland | (8,525) |
| 41 | New Mexico | (10,526) |
| 42 | Kansas | (12,557) |
| 43 | Connecticut | (17,224) |
| 44 | Ohio | (23,094) |
| 45 | Michigan | (28,539) |
| 46 | Pennsylvania | (30,718) |
| 47 | New Jersey | (45,035) |
| 48 | California | (49,259) |
| 49 | Illinois | (67,313) |
| 50 | New York | (104,470) |
| | District of Columbia | 6,319 |

Source: U.S. Bureau of the Census

"Components of Population Change" (http://www.census.gov/popest/data/datasets.html)
*From July 1, 2012 to June 30, 2013. Includes armed forces residing in each state. Net Domestic Migration is the difference between domestic inmigration to an area and domestic outmigration from it during the period. Domestic inmigration and outmigration consist of moves where both the origins and destinations are within the United States (excluding Puerto Rico).

# Net International Migration: 2012 to 2013

## National Net = 843,145 Immigrants*

ALPHA ORDER

RANK ORDER

| RANK | STATE | IMMIGRANTS | % of USA |
|------|-------|-----------:|---------:|
| 30 | Alabama | 5,256 | 0.6% |
| 40 | Alaska | 1,828 | 0.2% |
| 18 | Arizona | 10,864 | 1.3% |
| 37 | Arkansas | 2,965 | 0.4% |
| 1 | California | 123,217 | 14.6% |
| 20 | Colorado | 8,573 | 1.0% |
| 16 | Connecticut | 15,702 | 1.9% |
| 38 | Delaware | 2,422 | 0.3% |
| 3 | Florida | 99,454 | 11.8% |
| 11 | Georgia | 22,343 | 2.6% |
| 24 | Hawaii | 7,459 | 0.9% |
| 43 | Idaho | 1,563 | 0.2% |
| 8 | Illinois | 27,751 | 3.3% |
| 19 | Indiana | 9,404 | 1.1% |
| 34 | Iowa | 4,143 | 0.5% |
| 31 | Kansas | 5,105 | 0.6% |
| 29 | Kentucky | 5,569 | 0.7% |
| 25 | Louisiana | 6,695 | 0.8% |
| 45 | Maine | 1,042 | 0.1% |
| 10 | Maryland | 24,944 | 3.0% |
| 6 | Massachusetts | 31,349 | 3.7% |
| 14 | Michigan | 17,488 | 2.1% |
| 17 | Minnesota | 12,208 | 1.4% |
| 39 | Mississippi | 2,232 | 0.3% |
| 23 | Missouri | 7,462 | 0.9% |
| 48 | Montana | 725 | 0.1% |
| 36 | Nebraska | 3,214 | 0.4% |
| 22 | Nevada | 7,463 | 0.9% |
| 41 | New Hampshire | 1,781 | 0.2% |
| 5 | New Jersey | 46,373 | 5.5% |
| 42 | New Mexico | 1,717 | 0.2% |
| 2 | New York | 101,778 | 12.1% |
| 13 | North Carolina | 20,545 | 2.4% |
| 44 | North Dakota | 1,090 | 0.1% |
| 15 | Ohio | 15,708 | 1.9% |
| 32 | Oklahoma | 4,756 | 0.6% |
| 27 | Oregon | 6,375 | 0.8% |
| 9 | Pennsylvania | 24,996 | 3.0% |
| 35 | Rhode Island | 3,688 | 0.4% |
| 26 | South Carolina | 6,513 | 0.8% |
| 46 | South Dakota | 1,040 | 0.1% |
| 21 | Tennessee | 8,155 | 1.0% |
| 4 | Texas | 64,187 | 7.6% |
| 33 | Utah | 4,353 | 0.5% |
| 49 | Vermont | 464 | 0.1% |
| 7 | Virginia | 29,762 | 3.5% |
| 12 | Washington | 21,384 | 2.5% |
| 47 | West Virginia | 981 | 0.1% |
| 28 | Wisconsin | 5,876 | 0.7% |
| 50 | Wyoming | 325 | 0.0% |

| RANK | STATE | IMMIGRANTS | % of USA |
|------|-------|-----------:|---------:|
| 1 | California | 123,217 | 14.6% |
| 2 | New York | 101,778 | 12.1% |
| 3 | Florida | 99,454 | 11.8% |
| 4 | Texas | 64,187 | 7.6% |
| 5 | New Jersey | 46,373 | 5.5% |
| 6 | Massachusetts | 31,349 | 3.7% |
| 7 | Virginia | 29,762 | 3.5% |
| 8 | Illinois | 27,751 | 3.3% |
| 9 | Pennsylvania | 24,996 | 3.0% |
| 10 | Maryland | 24,944 | 3.0% |
| 11 | Georgia | 22,343 | 2.6% |
| 12 | Washington | 21,384 | 2.5% |
| 13 | North Carolina | 20,545 | 2.4% |
| 14 | Michigan | 17,488 | 2.1% |
| 15 | Ohio | 15,708 | 1.9% |
| 16 | Connecticut | 15,702 | 1.9% |
| 17 | Minnesota | 12,208 | 1.4% |
| 18 | Arizona | 10,864 | 1.3% |
| 19 | Indiana | 9,404 | 1.1% |
| 20 | Colorado | 8,573 | 1.0% |
| 21 | Tennessee | 8,155 | 1.0% |
| 22 | Nevada | 7,463 | 0.9% |
| 23 | Missouri | 7,462 | 0.9% |
| 24 | Hawaii | 7,459 | 0.9% |
| 25 | Louisiana | 6,695 | 0.8% |
| 26 | South Carolina | 6,513 | 0.8% |
| 27 | Oregon | 6,375 | 0.8% |
| 28 | Wisconsin | 5,876 | 0.7% |
| 29 | Kentucky | 5,569 | 0.7% |
| 30 | Alabama | 5,256 | 0.6% |
| 31 | Kansas | 5,105 | 0.6% |
| 32 | Oklahoma | 4,756 | 0.6% |
| 33 | Utah | 4,353 | 0.5% |
| 34 | Iowa | 4,143 | 0.5% |
| 35 | Rhode Island | 3,688 | 0.4% |
| 36 | Nebraska | 3,214 | 0.4% |
| 37 | Arkansas | 2,965 | 0.4% |
| 38 | Delaware | 2,422 | 0.3% |
| 39 | Mississippi | 2,232 | 0.3% |
| 40 | Alaska | 1,828 | 0.2% |
| 41 | New Hampshire | 1,781 | 0.2% |
| 42 | New Mexico | 1,717 | 0.2% |
| 43 | Idaho | 1,563 | 0.2% |
| 44 | North Dakota | 1,090 | 0.1% |
| 45 | Maine | 1,042 | 0.1% |
| 46 | South Dakota | 1,040 | 0.1% |
| 47 | West Virginia | 981 | 0.1% |
| 48 | Montana | 725 | 0.1% |
| 49 | Vermont | 464 | 0.1% |
| 50 | Wyoming | 325 | 0.0% |
| | District of Columbia | 2,858 | 0.3% |

Source: U.S. Bureau of the Census

"Components of Population Change" (http://www.census.gov/popest/data/datasets.html)

*From July 1, 2012 to June 30, 2013. Net International Migration is the difference between migration to an area from outside the United States (immigration) and migration from the area to outside the United States (emigration) during the period. Includes legal immigration and estimates of undocumented immigration.

# Percent of Population Foreign Born in 2012

## National Percent = 13.0% of Population*

<u>ALPHA ORDER</u>

| RANK | STATE | PERCENT |
|------|-------|---------|
| 43 | Alabama | 3.4 |
| 23 | Alaska | 7.2 |
| 12 | Arizona | 13.4 |
| 37 | Arkansas | 4.4 |
| 1 | California | 27.1 |
| 16 | Colorado | 9.8 |
| 11 | Connecticut | 13.8 |
| 20 | Delaware | 8.5 |
| 4 | Florida | 19.4 |
| 18 | Georgia | 9.5 |
| 6 | Hawaii | 18.1 |
| 27 | Idaho | 6.1 |
| 10 | Illinois | 13.9 |
| 34 | Indiana | 4.6 |
| 35 | Iowa | 4.5 |
| 25 | Kansas | 6.5 |
| 45 | Kentucky | 3.1 |
| 41 | Louisiana | 3.7 |
| 42 | Maine | 3.5 |
| 9 | Maryland | 14.3 |
| 8 | Massachusetts | 15.0 |
| 27 | Michigan | 6.1 |
| 23 | Minnesota | 7.2 |
| 48 | Mississippi | 2.0 |
| 40 | Missouri | 3.8 |
| 49 | Montana | 1.8 |
| 26 | Nebraska | 6.4 |
| 5 | Nevada | 19.2 |
| 31 | New Hampshire | 5.4 |
| 3 | New Jersey | 21.2 |
| 19 | New Mexico | 9.2 |
| 2 | New York | 22.6 |
| 22 | North Carolina | 7.7 |
| 46 | North Dakota | 2.8 |
| 39 | Ohio | 3.9 |
| 30 | Oklahoma | 5.6 |
| 17 | Oregon | 9.6 |
| 29 | Pennsylvania | 6.0 |
| 13 | Rhode Island | 13.3 |
| 33 | South Carolina | 4.7 |
| 47 | South Dakota | 2.7 |
| 35 | Tennessee | 4.5 |
| 7 | Texas | 16.4 |
| 21 | Utah | 8.4 |
| 38 | Vermont | 4.1 |
| 15 | Virginia | 11.6 |
| 13 | Washington | 13.3 |
| 50 | West Virginia | 1.4 |
| 32 | Wisconsin | 4.8 |
| 43 | Wyoming | 3.4 |

<u>RANK ORDER</u>

| RANK | STATE | PERCENT |
|------|-------|---------|
| 1 | California | 27.1 |
| 2 | New York | 22.6 |
| 3 | New Jersey | 21.2 |
| 4 | Florida | 19.4 |
| 5 | Nevada | 19.2 |
| 6 | Hawaii | 18.1 |
| 7 | Texas | 16.4 |
| 8 | Massachusetts | 15.0 |
| 9 | Maryland | 14.3 |
| 10 | Illinois | 13.9 |
| 11 | Connecticut | 13.8 |
| 12 | Arizona | 13.4 |
| 13 | Rhode Island | 13.3 |
| 13 | Washington | 13.3 |
| 15 | Virginia | 11.6 |
| 16 | Colorado | 9.8 |
| 17 | Oregon | 9.6 |
| 18 | Georgia | 9.5 |
| 19 | New Mexico | 9.2 |
| 20 | Delaware | 8.5 |
| 21 | Utah | 8.4 |
| 22 | North Carolina | 7.7 |
| 23 | Alaska | 7.2 |
| 23 | Minnesota | 7.2 |
| 25 | Kansas | 6.5 |
| 26 | Nebraska | 6.4 |
| 27 | Idaho | 6.1 |
| 27 | Michigan | 6.1 |
| 29 | Pennsylvania | 6.0 |
| 30 | Oklahoma | 5.6 |
| 31 | New Hampshire | 5.4 |
| 32 | Wisconsin | 4.8 |
| 33 | South Carolina | 4.7 |
| 34 | Indiana | 4.6 |
| 35 | Iowa | 4.5 |
| 35 | Tennessee | 4.5 |
| 37 | Arkansas | 4.4 |
| 38 | Vermont | 4.1 |
| 39 | Ohio | 3.9 |
| 40 | Missouri | 3.8 |
| 41 | Louisiana | 3.7 |
| 42 | Maine | 3.5 |
| 43 | Alabama | 3.4 |
| 43 | Wyoming | 3.4 |
| 45 | Kentucky | 3.1 |
| 46 | North Dakota | 2.8 |
| 47 | South Dakota | 2.7 |
| 48 | Mississippi | 2.0 |
| 49 | Montana | 1.8 |
| 50 | West Virginia | 1.4 |
| | District of Columbia | 14.3 |

Source: U.S. Bureau of the Census
   "2012 American Community Survey-Table R0501" (http://www.census.gov/acs/www/index.html)
*"Foreign born" are persons not born in the United States, Puerto Rico, a U.S. Island Area, or abroad of American parent or parents.

# Percent of Population Speaking a Language
## Other than English at Home in 2012
## National Percent = 21.0%*

ALPHA ORDER

| RANK | STATE | PERCENT |
|---|---|---|
| 46 | Alabama | 5.1 |
| 17 | Alaska | 16.6 |
| 8 | Arizona | 27.1 |
| 39 | Arkansas | 6.9 |
| 1 | California | 44.3 |
| 16 | Colorado | 17.0 |
| 12 | Connecticut | 22.2 |
| 22 | Delaware | 12.9 |
| 7 | Florida | 27.9 |
| 21 | Georgia | 13.4 |
| 9 | Hawaii | 25.1 |
| 28 | Idaho | 10.4 |
| 10 | Illinois | 22.6 |
| 32 | Indiana | 8.5 |
| 36 | Iowa | 7.2 |
| 23 | Kansas | 11.2 |
| 47 | Kentucky | 4.9 |
| 33 | Louisiana | 8.4 |
| 37 | Maine | 7.1 |
| 15 | Maryland | 17.2 |
| 11 | Massachusetts | 22.3 |
| 30 | Michigan | 9.4 |
| 26 | Minnesota | 10.9 |
| 49 | Mississippi | 3.6 |
| 43 | Missouri | 6.0 |
| 48 | Montana | 4.3 |
| 23 | Nebraska | 11.2 |
| 6 | Nevada | 30.2 |
| 34 | New Hampshire | 7.9 |
| 4 | New Jersey | 30.4 |
| 2 | New Mexico | 35.4 |
| 4 | New York | 30.4 |
| 25 | North Carolina | 11.1 |
| 44 | North Dakota | 5.8 |
| 40 | Ohio | 6.7 |
| 29 | Oklahoma | 9.7 |
| 19 | Oregon | 14.7 |
| 27 | Pennsylvania | 10.6 |
| 13 | Rhode Island | 20.9 |
| 38 | South Carolina | 7.0 |
| 42 | South Dakota | 6.3 |
| 40 | Tennessee | 6.7 |
| 3 | Texas | 35.2 |
| 19 | Utah | 14.7 |
| 45 | Vermont | 5.4 |
| 18 | Virginia | 15.5 |
| 14 | Washington | 19.3 |
| 50 | West Virginia | 2.4 |
| 31 | Wisconsin | 8.8 |
| 35 | Wyoming | 7.6 |

RANK ORDER

| RANK | STATE | PERCENT |
|---|---|---|
| 1 | California | 44.3 |
| 2 | New Mexico | 35.4 |
| 3 | Texas | 35.2 |
| 4 | New Jersey | 30.4 |
| 4 | New York | 30.4 |
| 6 | Nevada | 30.2 |
| 7 | Florida | 27.9 |
| 8 | Arizona | 27.1 |
| 9 | Hawaii | 25.1 |
| 10 | Illinois | 22.6 |
| 11 | Massachusetts | 22.3 |
| 12 | Connecticut | 22.2 |
| 13 | Rhode Island | 20.9 |
| 14 | Washington | 19.3 |
| 15 | Maryland | 17.2 |
| 16 | Colorado | 17.0 |
| 17 | Alaska | 16.6 |
| 18 | Virginia | 15.5 |
| 19 | Oregon | 14.7 |
| 19 | Utah | 14.7 |
| 21 | Georgia | 13.4 |
| 22 | Delaware | 12.9 |
| 23 | Kansas | 11.2 |
| 23 | Nebraska | 11.2 |
| 25 | North Carolina | 11.1 |
| 26 | Minnesota | 10.9 |
| 27 | Pennsylvania | 10.6 |
| 28 | Idaho | 10.4 |
| 29 | Oklahoma | 9.7 |
| 30 | Michigan | 9.4 |
| 31 | Wisconsin | 8.8 |
| 32 | Indiana | 8.5 |
| 33 | Louisiana | 8.4 |
| 34 | New Hampshire | 7.9 |
| 35 | Wyoming | 7.6 |
| 36 | Iowa | 7.2 |
| 37 | Maine | 7.1 |
| 38 | South Carolina | 7.0 |
| 39 | Arkansas | 6.9 |
| 40 | Ohio | 6.7 |
| 40 | Tennessee | 6.7 |
| 42 | South Dakota | 6.3 |
| 43 | Missouri | 6.0 |
| 44 | North Dakota | 5.8 |
| 45 | Vermont | 5.4 |
| 46 | Alabama | 5.1 |
| 47 | Kentucky | 4.9 |
| 48 | Montana | 4.3 |
| 49 | Mississippi | 3.6 |
| 50 | West Virginia | 2.4 |

| | | |
|---|---|---|
| | District of Columbia | 16.6 |

Source: U.S. Bureau of the Census
  "2012 American Community Survey-Table R1601" (http://www.census.gov/acs/www/index.html)
*Population five years old and older.

# Percent of Population Speaking Spanish at Home in 2012

## National Percent = 13.0%*

| ALPHA ORDER | | | | RANK ORDER | | |
|---|---|---|---|---|---|---|
| RANK | STATE | PERCENT | | RANK | STATE | PERCENT |
| 37 | Alabama | 3.2 | | 1 | Texas | 29.8 |
| 36 | Alaska | 3.5 | | 2 | California | 29.0 |
| 5 | Arizona | 20.8 | | 3 | New Mexico | 27.8 |
| 27 | Arkansas | 5.0 | | 4 | Nevada | 21.1 |
| 2 | California | 29.0 | | 5 | Arizona | 20.8 |
| 10 | Colorado | 11.9 | | 6 | Florida | 20.5 |
| 11 | Connecticut | 11.2 | | 7 | New Jersey | 15.7 |
| 22 | Delaware | 7.1 | | 8 | New York | 15.0 |
| 6 | Florida | 20.5 | | 9 | Illinois | 13.1 |
| 17 | Georgia | 7.9 | | 10 | Colorado | 11.9 |
| 45 | Hawaii | 1.8 | | 11 | Connecticut | 11.2 |
| 18 | Idaho | 7.7 | | 12 | Rhode Island | 11.1 |
| 9 | Illinois | 13.1 | | 13 | Utah | 10.0 |
| 29 | Indiana | 4.6 | | 14 | Oregon | 8.6 |
| 32 | Iowa | 3.9 | | 15 | Washington | 8.5 |
| 19 | Kansas | 7.5 | | 16 | Massachusetts | 8.4 |
| 39 | Kentucky | 2.5 | | 17 | Georgia | 7.9 |
| 35 | Louisiana | 3.6 | | 18 | Idaho | 7.7 |
| 50 | Maine | 1.0 | | 19 | Kansas | 7.5 |
| 22 | Maryland | 7.1 | | 20 | Nebraska | 7.4 |
| 16 | Massachusetts | 8.4 | | 20 | North Carolina | 7.4 |
| 38 | Michigan | 3.1 | | 22 | Delaware | 7.1 |
| 32 | Minnesota | 3.9 | | 22 | Maryland | 7.1 |
| 42 | Mississippi | 2.2 | | 24 | Virginia | 6.7 |
| 39 | Missouri | 2.5 | | 25 | Oklahoma | 6.6 |
| 47 | Montana | 1.5 | | 26 | Wyoming | 5.4 |
| 20 | Nebraska | 7.4 | | 27 | Arkansas | 5.0 |
| 4 | Nevada | 21.1 | | 28 | Wisconsin | 4.7 |
| 43 | New Hampshire | 2.0 | | 29 | Indiana | 4.6 |
| 7 | New Jersey | 15.7 | | 29 | Pennsylvania | 4.6 |
| 3 | New Mexico | 27.8 | | 31 | South Carolina | 4.5 |
| 8 | New York | 15.0 | | 32 | Iowa | 3.9 |
| 20 | North Carolina | 7.4 | | 32 | Minnesota | 3.9 |
| 46 | North Dakota | 1.6 | | 32 | Tennessee | 3.9 |
| 41 | Ohio | 2.3 | | 35 | Louisiana | 3.6 |
| 25 | Oklahoma | 6.6 | | 36 | Alaska | 3.5 |
| 14 | Oregon | 8.6 | | 37 | Alabama | 3.2 |
| 29 | Pennsylvania | 4.6 | | 38 | Michigan | 3.1 |
| 12 | Rhode Island | 11.1 | | 39 | Kentucky | 2.5 |
| 31 | South Carolina | 4.5 | | 39 | Missouri | 2.5 |
| 44 | South Dakota | 1.9 | | 41 | Ohio | 2.3 |
| 32 | Tennessee | 3.9 | | 42 | Mississippi | 2.2 |
| 1 | Texas | 29.8 | | 43 | New Hampshire | 2.0 |
| 13 | Utah | 10.0 | | 44 | South Dakota | 1.9 |
| 48 | Vermont | 1.1 | | 45 | Hawaii | 1.8 |
| 24 | Virginia | 6.7 | | 46 | North Dakota | 1.6 |
| 15 | Washington | 8.5 | | 47 | Montana | 1.5 |
| 48 | West Virginia | 1.1 | | 48 | Vermont | 1.1 |
| 28 | Wisconsin | 4.7 | | 48 | West Virginia | 1.1 |
| 26 | Wyoming | 5.4 | | 50 | Maine | 1.0 |
| | | | | District of Columbia | | 8.0 |

Source: U.S. Bureau of the Census
   "2012 American Community Survey-Table R1602" (http://www.census.gov/acs/www/index.html)
*Population five years old and older.

# Marriages in 2011

## National Total = 2,118,000 Marriages*

ALPHA ORDER

| RANK | STATE | MARRIAGES | % of USA |
|------|-------|-----------|----------|
| 17 | Alabama | 40,300 | 1.9% |
| 46 | Alaska | 5,600 | 0.3% |
| 19 | Arizona | 37,000 | 1.7% |
| 25 | Arkansas | 30,600 | 1.4% |
| 1 | California | 218,600 | 10.3% |
| 21 | Colorado | 35,800 | 1.7% |
| 34 | Connecticut | 19,700 | 0.9% |
| 48 | Delaware | 4,700 | 0.2% |
| 3 | Florida | 141,000 | 6.7% |
| 9 | Georgia | 64,800 | 3.1% |
| 31 | Hawaii | 24,200 | 1.1% |
| 38 | Idaho | 13,600 | 0.6% |
| 6 | Illinois | 72,100 | 3.4% |
| 14 | Indiana | 44,300 | 2.1% |
| 33 | Iowa | 20,500 | 1.0% |
| 35 | Kansas | 18,100 | 0.9% |
| 24 | Kentucky | 32,800 | 1.5% |
| 28 | Louisiana | 29,300 | 1.4% |
| 41 | Maine | 9,600 | 0.5% |
| 22 | Maryland | 33,800 | 1.6% |
| 20 | Massachusetts | 36,200 | 1.7% |
| 12 | Michigan | 56,300 | 2.7% |
| 27 | Minnesota | 29,900 | 1.4% |
| 37 | Mississippi | 14,600 | 0.7% |
| 18 | Missouri | 39,700 | 1.9% |
| 43 | Montana | 7,800 | 0.4% |
| 40 | Nebraska | 12,200 | 0.6% |
| 5 | Nevada | 100,500 | 4.7% |
| 42 | New Hampshire | 9,400 | 0.4% |
| 15 | New Jersey | 42,300 | 2.0% |
| 36 | New Mexico | 16,700 | 0.8% |
| 4 | New York | 134,300 | 6.3% |
| 10 | North Carolina | 64,700 | 3.1% |
| 49 | North Dakota | 4,600 | 0.2% |
| 7 | Ohio | 68,100 | 3.2% |
| 29 | Oklahoma | 26,200 | 1.2% |
| 30 | Oregon | 25,600 | 1.2% |
| 8 | Pennsylvania | 67,500 | 3.2% |
| 44 | Rhode Island | 6,300 | 0.3% |
| 23 | South Carolina | 33,700 | 1.6% |
| 45 | South Dakota | 6,200 | 0.3% |
| 11 | Tennessee | 57,600 | 2.7% |
| 2 | Texas | 182,300 | 8.6% |
| 31 | Utah | 24,200 | 1.1% |
| 47 | Vermont | 5,200 | 0.2% |
| 13 | Virginia | 55,100 | 2.6% |
| 16 | Washington | 41,700 | 2.0% |
| 39 | West Virginia | 13,400 | 0.6% |
| 26 | Wisconsin | 30,300 | 1.4% |
| 50 | Wyoming | 4,400 | 0.2% |

RANK ORDER

| RANK | STATE | MARRIAGES | % of USA |
|------|-------|-----------|----------|
| 1 | California | 218,600 | 10.3% |
| 2 | Texas | 182,300 | 8.6% |
| 3 | Florida | 141,000 | 6.7% |
| 4 | New York | 134,300 | 6.3% |
| 5 | Nevada | 100,500 | 4.7% |
| 6 | Illinois | 72,100 | 3.4% |
| 7 | Ohio | 68,100 | 3.2% |
| 8 | Pennsylvania | 67,500 | 3.2% |
| 9 | Georgia | 64,800 | 3.1% |
| 10 | North Carolina | 64,700 | 3.1% |
| 11 | Tennessee | 57,600 | 2.7% |
| 12 | Michigan | 56,300 | 2.7% |
| 13 | Virginia | 55,100 | 2.6% |
| 14 | Indiana | 44,300 | 2.1% |
| 15 | New Jersey | 42,300 | 2.0% |
| 16 | Washington | 41,700 | 2.0% |
| 17 | Alabama | 40,300 | 1.9% |
| 18 | Missouri | 39,700 | 1.9% |
| 19 | Arizona | 37,000 | 1.7% |
| 20 | Massachusetts | 36,200 | 1.7% |
| 21 | Colorado | 35,800 | 1.7% |
| 22 | Maryland | 33,800 | 1.6% |
| 23 | South Carolina | 33,700 | 1.6% |
| 24 | Kentucky | 32,800 | 1.5% |
| 25 | Arkansas | 30,600 | 1.4% |
| 26 | Wisconsin | 30,300 | 1.4% |
| 27 | Minnesota | 29,900 | 1.4% |
| 28 | Louisiana | 29,300 | 1.4% |
| 29 | Oklahoma | 26,200 | 1.2% |
| 30 | Oregon | 25,600 | 1.2% |
| 31 | Hawaii | 24,200 | 1.1% |
| 31 | Utah | 24,200 | 1.1% |
| 33 | Iowa | 20,500 | 1.0% |
| 34 | Connecticut | 19,700 | 0.9% |
| 35 | Kansas | 18,100 | 0.9% |
| 36 | New Mexico | 16,700 | 0.8% |
| 37 | Mississippi | 14,600 | 0.7% |
| 38 | Idaho | 13,600 | 0.6% |
| 39 | West Virginia | 13,400 | 0.6% |
| 40 | Nebraska | 12,200 | 0.6% |
| 41 | Maine | 9,600 | 0.5% |
| 42 | New Hampshire | 9,400 | 0.4% |
| 43 | Montana | 7,800 | 0.4% |
| 44 | Rhode Island | 6,300 | 0.3% |
| 45 | South Dakota | 6,200 | 0.3% |
| 46 | Alaska | 5,600 | 0.3% |
| 47 | Vermont | 5,200 | 0.2% |
| 48 | Delaware | 4,700 | 0.2% |
| 49 | North Dakota | 4,600 | 0.2% |
| 50 | Wyoming | 4,400 | 0.2% |
| | District of Columbia | 5,400 | 0.3% |

Source: CQ Press using data from U.S. Department of Health and Human Services, National Center for Health Statistics
"National Vital Statistics System, Marriages and Divorces" (http://www.cdc.gov/nchs/mardiv.htm)
*Provisional estimates by state of occurrence.

# Marriage Rate in 2011

## National Rate = 6.8 Marriages per 1,000 Population*

ALPHA ORDER

| RANK | STATE | RATE |
|---|---|---|
| 7 | Alabama | 8.4 |
| 10 | Alaska | 7.8 |
| 40 | Arizona | 5.7 |
| 3 | Arkansas | 10.4 |
| 38 | California | 5.8 |
| 21 | Colorado | 7.0 |
| 44 | Connecticut | 5.5 |
| 48 | Delaware | 5.2 |
| 15 | Florida | 7.4 |
| 29 | Georgia | 6.6 |
| 2 | Hawaii | 17.6 |
| 5 | Idaho | 8.6 |
| 42 | Illinois | 5.6 |
| 24 | Indiana | 6.8 |
| 26 | Iowa | 6.7 |
| 34 | Kansas | 6.3 |
| 13 | Kentucky | 7.5 |
| 33 | Louisiana | 6.4 |
| 16 | Maine | 7.2 |
| 38 | Maryland | 5.8 |
| 44 | Massachusetts | 5.5 |
| 40 | Michigan | 5.7 |
| 42 | Minnesota | 5.6 |
| 49 | Mississippi | 4.9 |
| 29 | Missouri | 6.6 |
| 10 | Montana | 7.8 |
| 29 | Nebraska | 6.6 |
| 1 | Nevada | 36.9 |
| 19 | New Hampshire | 7.1 |
| 50 | New Jersey | 4.8 |
| 9 | New Mexico | 8.0 |
| 22 | New York | 6.9 |
| 26 | North Carolina | 6.7 |
| 26 | North Dakota | 6.7 |
| 37 | Ohio | 5.9 |
| 22 | Oklahoma | 6.9 |
| 29 | Oregon | 6.6 |
| 46 | Pennsylvania | 5.3 |
| 36 | Rhode Island | 6.0 |
| 16 | South Carolina | 7.2 |
| 13 | South Dakota | 7.5 |
| 4 | Tennessee | 9.0 |
| 19 | Texas | 7.1 |
| 5 | Utah | 8.6 |
| 8 | Vermont | 8.3 |
| 24 | Virginia | 6.8 |
| 35 | Washington | 6.1 |
| 16 | West Virginia | 7.2 |
| 46 | Wisconsin | 5.3 |
| 10 | Wyoming | 7.8 |

RANK ORDER

| RANK | STATE | RATE |
|---|---|---|
| 1 | Nevada | 36.9 |
| 2 | Hawaii | 17.6 |
| 3 | Arkansas | 10.4 |
| 4 | Tennessee | 9.0 |
| 5 | Idaho | 8.6 |
| 5 | Utah | 8.6 |
| 7 | Alabama | 8.4 |
| 8 | Vermont | 8.3 |
| 9 | New Mexico | 8.0 |
| 10 | Alaska | 7.8 |
| 10 | Montana | 7.8 |
| 10 | Wyoming | 7.8 |
| 13 | Kentucky | 7.5 |
| 13 | South Dakota | 7.5 |
| 15 | Florida | 7.4 |
| 16 | Maine | 7.2 |
| 16 | South Carolina | 7.2 |
| 16 | West Virginia | 7.2 |
| 19 | New Hampshire | 7.1 |
| 19 | Texas | 7.1 |
| 21 | Colorado | 7.0 |
| 22 | New York | 6.9 |
| 22 | Oklahoma | 6.9 |
| 24 | Indiana | 6.8 |
| 24 | Virginia | 6.8 |
| 26 | Iowa | 6.7 |
| 26 | North Carolina | 6.7 |
| 26 | North Dakota | 6.7 |
| 29 | Georgia | 6.6 |
| 29 | Missouri | 6.6 |
| 29 | Nebraska | 6.6 |
| 29 | Oregon | 6.6 |
| 33 | Louisiana | 6.4 |
| 34 | Kansas | 6.3 |
| 35 | Washington | 6.1 |
| 36 | Rhode Island | 6.0 |
| 37 | Ohio | 5.9 |
| 38 | California | 5.8 |
| 38 | Maryland | 5.8 |
| 40 | Arizona | 5.7 |
| 40 | Michigan | 5.7 |
| 42 | Illinois | 5.6 |
| 42 | Minnesota | 5.6 |
| 44 | Connecticut | 5.5 |
| 44 | Massachusetts | 5.5 |
| 46 | Pennsylvania | 5.3 |
| 46 | Wisconsin | 5.3 |
| 48 | Delaware | 5.2 |
| 49 | Mississippi | 4.9 |
| 50 | New Jersey | 4.8 |
| | District of Columbia | 8.7 |

Source: U.S. Department of Health and Human Services, National Center for Health Statistics
  "National Vital Statistics System, Marriages and Divorces" (http://www.cdc.gov/nchs/mardiv.htm)
*Provisional data by state of occurrence.

# Estimated Median Age of Men at First Marriage in 2012

## National Median = 29.1 Years*

| ALPHA ORDER | | | | RANK ORDER | | |
|---|---|---|---|---|---|---|
| RANK | STATE | AGE | | RANK | STATE | AGE |
| 38 | Alabama | 27.7 | | 1 | Rhode Island | 31.6 |
| 21 | Alaska | 28.7 | | 2 | New York | 30.9 |
| 19 | Arizona | 28.8 | | 3 | Massachusetts | 30.7 |
| 45 | Arkansas | 26.9 | | 4 | New Jersey | 30.6 |
| 7 | California | 30.0 | | 4 | Vermont | 30.6 |
| 32 | Colorado | 28.1 | | 6 | Connecticut | 30.3 |
| 6 | Connecticut | 30.3 | | 7 | California | 30.0 |
| 10 | Delaware | 29.7 | | 8 | Florida | 29.9 |
| 8 | Florida | 29.9 | | 9 | Pennsylvania | 29.8 |
| 16 | Georgia | 29.0 | | 10 | Delaware | 29.7 |
| 26 | Hawaii | 28.4 | | 10 | Illinois | 29.7 |
| 49 | Idaho | 26.3 | | 10 | Maryland | 29.7 |
| 10 | Illinois | 29.7 | | 10 | New Hampshire | 29.7 |
| 35 | Indiana | 27.8 | | 14 | Michigan | 29.5 |
| 39 | Iowa | 27.6 | | 15 | Oregon | 29.1 |
| 44 | Kansas | 27.0 | | 16 | Georgia | 29.0 |
| 40 | Kentucky | 27.3 | | 16 | Ohio | 29.0 |
| 18 | Louisiana | 28.9 | | 18 | Louisiana | 28.9 |
| 21 | Maine | 28.7 | | 19 | Arizona | 28.8 |
| 10 | Maryland | 29.7 | | 19 | Minnesota | 28.8 |
| 3 | Massachusetts | 30.7 | | 21 | Alaska | 28.7 |
| 14 | Michigan | 29.5 | | 21 | Maine | 28.7 |
| 19 | Minnesota | 28.8 | | 21 | Virginia | 28.7 |
| 26 | Mississippi | 28.4 | | 24 | Wisconsin | 28.6 |
| 35 | Missouri | 27.8 | | 25 | Montana | 28.5 |
| 25 | Montana | 28.5 | | 26 | Hawaii | 28.4 |
| 40 | Nebraska | 27.3 | | 26 | Mississippi | 28.4 |
| 26 | Nevada | 28.4 | | 26 | Nevada | 28.4 |
| 10 | New Hampshire | 29.7 | | 29 | North Carolina | 28.3 |
| 4 | New Jersey | 30.6 | | 29 | South Carolina | 28.3 |
| 45 | New Mexico | 26.9 | | 29 | South Dakota | 28.3 |
| 2 | New York | 30.9 | | 32 | Colorado | 28.1 |
| 29 | North Carolina | 28.3 | | 32 | Washington | 28.1 |
| 40 | North Dakota | 27.3 | | 34 | Tennessee | 27.9 |
| 16 | Ohio | 29.0 | | 35 | Indiana | 27.8 |
| 48 | Oklahoma | 26.6 | | 35 | Missouri | 27.8 |
| 15 | Oregon | 29.1 | | 35 | Texas | 27.8 |
| 9 | Pennsylvania | 29.8 | | 38 | Alabama | 27.7 |
| 1 | Rhode Island | 31.6 | | 39 | Iowa | 27.6 |
| 29 | South Carolina | 28.3 | | 40 | Kentucky | 27.3 |
| 29 | South Dakota | 28.3 | | 40 | Nebraska | 27.3 |
| 34 | Tennessee | 27.9 | | 40 | North Dakota | 27.3 |
| 35 | Texas | 27.8 | | 43 | West Virginia | 27.1 |
| 50 | Utah | 26.2 | | 44 | Kansas | 27.0 |
| 4 | Vermont | 30.6 | | 45 | Arkansas | 26.9 |
| 21 | Virginia | 28.7 | | 45 | New Mexico | 26.9 |
| 32 | Washington | 28.1 | | 45 | Wyoming | 26.9 |
| 43 | West Virginia | 27.1 | | 48 | Oklahoma | 26.6 |
| 24 | Wisconsin | 28.6 | | 49 | Idaho | 26.3 |
| 45 | Wyoming | 26.9 | | 50 | Utah | 26.2 |
| | | | | | District of Columbia | 30.2 |

Source: U.S. Bureau of the Census
    "2012 American Community Survey-Table R1204" (http://www.census.gov/acs/www/index.html)
*The median age at first marriage is calculated indirectly by estimating the proportion of young people who will marry during their lifetime, calculating one-half of this proportion, and determining the age (at the time of the survey) of people at this half-way mark. It does not represent the actual median age of the population who married during the calendar year.

# Estimated Median Age of Women at First Marriage in 2012

## National Median = 27.1 Years*

ALPHA ORDER

| RANK | STATE | AGE |
|------|-------|-----|
| 38 | Alabama | 26.0 |
| 45 | Alaska | 25.5 |
| 15 | Arizona | 27.3 |
| 47 | Arkansas | 25.2 |
| 9 | California | 27.9 |
| 27 | Colorado | 26.5 |
| 5 | Connecticut | 28.7 |
| 12 | Delaware | 27.6 |
| 10 | Florida | 27.8 |
| 21 | Georgia | 26.8 |
| 20 | Hawaii | 26.9 |
| 49 | Idaho | 24.4 |
| 7 | Illinois | 28.2 |
| 31 | Indiana | 26.3 |
| 34 | Iowa | 26.1 |
| 41 | Kansas | 25.7 |
| 44 | Kentucky | 25.6 |
| 16 | Louisiana | 27.1 |
| 29 | Maine | 26.4 |
| 8 | Maryland | 28.1 |
| 3 | Massachusetts | 29.2 |
| 14 | Michigan | 27.5 |
| 25 | Minnesota | 26.6 |
| 29 | Mississippi | 26.4 |
| 27 | Missouri | 26.5 |
| 34 | Montana | 26.1 |
| 39 | Nebraska | 25.8 |
| 21 | Nevada | 26.8 |
| 16 | New Hampshire | 27.1 |
| 6 | New Jersey | 28.4 |
| 31 | New Mexico | 26.3 |
| 2 | New York | 29.3 |
| 25 | North Carolina | 26.6 |
| 39 | North Dakota | 25.8 |
| 16 | Ohio | 27.1 |
| 46 | Oklahoma | 25.3 |
| 12 | Oregon | 27.6 |
| 11 | Pennsylvania | 27.7 |
| 1 | Rhode Island | 29.5 |
| 21 | South Carolina | 26.8 |
| 41 | South Dakota | 25.7 |
| 34 | Tennessee | 26.1 |
| 34 | Texas | 26.1 |
| 50 | Utah | 24.1 |
| 4 | Vermont | 28.8 |
| 21 | Virginia | 26.8 |
| 31 | Washington | 26.3 |
| 41 | West Virginia | 25.7 |
| 19 | Wisconsin | 27.0 |
| 48 | Wyoming | 25.0 |

RANK ORDER

| RANK | STATE | AGE |
|------|-------|-----|
| 1 | Rhode Island | 29.5 |
| 2 | New York | 29.3 |
| 3 | Massachusetts | 29.2 |
| 4 | Vermont | 28.8 |
| 5 | Connecticut | 28.7 |
| 6 | New Jersey | 28.4 |
| 7 | Illinois | 28.2 |
| 8 | Maryland | 28.1 |
| 9 | California | 27.9 |
| 10 | Florida | 27.8 |
| 11 | Pennsylvania | 27.7 |
| 12 | Delaware | 27.6 |
| 12 | Oregon | 27.6 |
| 14 | Michigan | 27.5 |
| 15 | Arizona | 27.3 |
| 16 | Louisiana | 27.1 |
| 16 | New Hampshire | 27.1 |
| 16 | Ohio | 27.1 |
| 19 | Wisconsin | 27.0 |
| 20 | Hawaii | 26.9 |
| 21 | Georgia | 26.8 |
| 21 | Nevada | 26.8 |
| 21 | South Carolina | 26.8 |
| 21 | Virginia | 26.8 |
| 25 | Minnesota | 26.6 |
| 25 | North Carolina | 26.6 |
| 27 | Colorado | 26.5 |
| 27 | Missouri | 26.5 |
| 29 | Maine | 26.4 |
| 29 | Mississippi | 26.4 |
| 31 | Indiana | 26.3 |
| 31 | New Mexico | 26.3 |
| 31 | Washington | 26.3 |
| 34 | Iowa | 26.1 |
| 34 | Montana | 26.1 |
| 34 | Tennessee | 26.1 |
| 34 | Texas | 26.1 |
| 38 | Alabama | 26.0 |
| 39 | Nebraska | 25.8 |
| 39 | North Dakota | 25.8 |
| 41 | Kansas | 25.7 |
| 41 | South Dakota | 25.7 |
| 41 | West Virginia | 25.7 |
| 44 | Kentucky | 25.6 |
| 45 | Alaska | 25.5 |
| 46 | Oklahoma | 25.3 |
| 47 | Arkansas | 25.2 |
| 48 | Wyoming | 25.0 |
| 49 | Idaho | 24.4 |
| 50 | Utah | 24.1 |
| | District of Columbia | 29.8 |

Source: U.S. Bureau of the Census
    "2012 American Community Survey-Table R1205" (http://www.census.gov/acs/www/index.html)
*The median age at first marriage is calculated indirectly by estimating the proportion of young people who will marry during their lifetime, calculating one-half of this proportion, and determining the age (at the time of the survey) of people at this half-way mark.  It does not represent the actual median age of the population who married during the calendar year.

# Ratio of Unmarried Men to Unmarried Women in 2012

## National Ratio = 110.9 Unmarried Men for Every 100 Unmarried Women*

ALPHA ORDER

| RANK | STATE | RATIO |
|------|-------|-------|
| 43 | Alabama | 106.8 |
| 1 | Alaska | 138.1 |
| 15 | Arizona | 114.1 |
| 25 | Arkansas | 111.6 |
| 13 | California | 114.7 |
| 7 | Colorado | 119.0 |
| 41 | Connecticut | 107.4 |
| 47 | Delaware | 105.0 |
| 28 | Florida | 110.7 |
| 40 | Georgia | 107.5 |
| 3 | Hawaii | 124.9 |
| 13 | Idaho | 114.7 |
| 35 | Illinois | 108.8 |
| 32 | Indiana | 109.7 |
| 18 | Iowa | 113.7 |
| 9 | Kansas | 116.9 |
| 23 | Kentucky | 112.1 |
| 39 | Louisiana | 108.0 |
| 42 | Maine | 107.2 |
| 48 | Maryland | 104.3 |
| 48 | Massachusetts | 104.3 |
| 31 | Michigan | 110.1 |
| 20 | Minnesota | 112.9 |
| 50 | Mississippi | 103.1 |
| 37 | Missouri | 108.5 |
| 5 | Montana | 120.3 |
| 10 | Nebraska | 116.1 |
| 8 | Nevada | 117.2 |
| 24 | New Hampshire | 111.9 |
| 26 | New Jersey | 111.5 |
| 29 | New Mexico | 110.5 |
| 43 | New York | 106.8 |
| 34 | North Carolina | 109.2 |
| 2 | North Dakota | 125.9 |
| 35 | Ohio | 108.8 |
| 12 | Oklahoma | 114.9 |
| 22 | Oregon | 112.6 |
| 33 | Pennsylvania | 109.4 |
| 45 | Rhode Island | 106.3 |
| 46 | South Carolina | 105.2 |
| 6 | South Dakota | 119.4 |
| 38 | Tennessee | 108.4 |
| 20 | Texas | 112.9 |
| 15 | Utah | 114.1 |
| 30 | Vermont | 110.3 |
| 27 | Virginia | 111.4 |
| 11 | Washington | 115.1 |
| 17 | West Virginia | 113.8 |
| 19 | Wisconsin | 113.0 |
| 4 | Wyoming | 122.2 |

RANK ORDER

| RANK | STATE | RATIO |
|------|-------|-------|
| 1 | Alaska | 138.1 |
| 2 | North Dakota | 125.9 |
| 3 | Hawaii | 124.9 |
| 4 | Wyoming | 122.2 |
| 5 | Montana | 120.3 |
| 6 | South Dakota | 119.4 |
| 7 | Colorado | 119.0 |
| 8 | Nevada | 117.2 |
| 9 | Kansas | 116.9 |
| 10 | Nebraska | 116.1 |
| 11 | Washington | 115.1 |
| 12 | Oklahoma | 114.9 |
| 13 | California | 114.7 |
| 13 | Idaho | 114.7 |
| 15 | Arizona | 114.1 |
| 15 | Utah | 114.1 |
| 17 | West Virginia | 113.8 |
| 18 | Iowa | 113.7 |
| 19 | Wisconsin | 113.0 |
| 20 | Minnesota | 112.9 |
| 20 | Texas | 112.9 |
| 22 | Oregon | 112.6 |
| 23 | Kentucky | 112.1 |
| 24 | New Hampshire | 111.9 |
| 25 | Arkansas | 111.6 |
| 26 | New Jersey | 111.5 |
| 27 | Virginia | 111.4 |
| 28 | Florida | 110.7 |
| 29 | New Mexico | 110.5 |
| 30 | Vermont | 110.3 |
| 31 | Michigan | 110.1 |
| 32 | Indiana | 109.7 |
| 33 | Pennsylvania | 109.4 |
| 34 | North Carolina | 109.2 |
| 35 | Illinois | 108.8 |
| 35 | Ohio | 108.8 |
| 37 | Missouri | 108.5 |
| 38 | Tennessee | 108.4 |
| 39 | Louisiana | 108.0 |
| 40 | Georgia | 107.5 |
| 41 | Connecticut | 107.4 |
| 42 | Maine | 107.2 |
| 43 | Alabama | 106.8 |
| 43 | New York | 106.8 |
| 45 | Rhode Island | 106.3 |
| 46 | South Carolina | 105.2 |
| 47 | Delaware | 105.0 |
| 48 | Maryland | 104.3 |
| 48 | Massachusetts | 104.3 |
| 50 | Mississippi | 103.1 |
| | District of Columbia | 90.2 |

Source: U.S. Bureau of the Census
"2012 American Community Survey-Table R1203" (http://www.census.gov/acs/www/index.html)
*Population 15 to 44 years old.

# Divorces in 2011

## Reporting States' Total = 877,000 Divorces*

ALPHA ORDER

| RANK | STATE | DIVORCES | % of USA |
|------|-------|----------|----------|
| 16 | Alabama | 20,700 | 2.4% |
| 38 | Alaska | 3,500 | 0.4% |
| 13 | Arizona | 25,300 | 2.9% |
| 22 | Arkansas | 15,600 | 1.8% |
| NA | California** | NA | NA |
| 15 | Colorado | 22,500 | 2.6% |
| 28 | Connecticut | 11,100 | 1.3% |
| 40 | Delaware | 3,300 | 0.4% |
| 1 | Florida | 85,800 | 9.8% |
| NA | Georgia** | NA | NA |
| NA | Hawaii** | NA | NA |
| 31 | Idaho | 7,800 | 0.9% |
| 8 | Illinois | 33,500 | 3.8% |
| NA | Indiana** | NA | NA |
| 32 | Iowa | 7,400 | 0.8% |
| 27 | Kansas | 11,200 | 1.3% |
| 18 | Kentucky | 19,200 | 2.2% |
| NA | Louisiana** | NA | NA |
| 35 | Maine | 5,600 | 0.6% |
| 20 | Maryland | 16,900 | 1.9% |
| 19 | Massachusetts | 17,800 | 2.0% |
| 7 | Michigan | 33,600 | 3.8% |
| NA | Minnesota** | NA | NA |
| 26 | Mississippi | 11,900 | 1.4% |
| 14 | Missouri | 23,400 | 2.7% |
| 37 | Montana | 4,000 | 0.5% |
| 34 | Nebraska | 6,400 | 0.7% |
| 23 | Nevada | 15,300 | 1.7% |
| 36 | New Hampshire | 5,000 | 0.6% |
| 12 | New Jersey | 25,600 | 2.9% |
| 33 | New Mexico | 6,900 | 0.8% |
| 3 | New York | 56,400 | 6.4% |
| 5 | North Carolina | 35,700 | 4.1% |
| 44 | North Dakota | 1,800 | 0.2% |
| 4 | Ohio | 39,300 | 4.5% |
| 17 | Oklahoma | 19,700 | 2.2% |
| 25 | Oregon | 14,700 | 1.7% |
| 5 | Pennsylvania | 35,700 | 4.1% |
| 39 | Rhode Island | 3,400 | 0.4% |
| 24 | South Carolina | 15,000 | 1.7% |
| 41 | South Dakota | 2,700 | 0.3% |
| 11 | Tennessee | 27,500 | 3.1% |
| 2 | Texas | 82,200 | 9.4% |
| 29 | Utah | 10,400 | 1.2% |
| 43 | Vermont | 2,300 | 0.3% |
| 9 | Virginia | 30,800 | 3.5% |
| 10 | Washington | 28,000 | 3.2% |
| 30 | West Virginia | 9,600 | 1.1% |
| 21 | Wisconsin | 16,600 | 1.9% |
| 41 | Wyoming | 2,700 | 0.3% |

RANK ORDER

| RANK | STATE | DIVORCES | % of USA |
|------|-------|----------|----------|
| 1 | Florida | 85,800 | 9.8% |
| 2 | Texas | 82,200 | 9.4% |
| 3 | New York | 56,400 | 6.4% |
| 4 | Ohio | 39,300 | 4.5% |
| 5 | North Carolina | 35,700 | 4.1% |
| 5 | Pennsylvania | 35,700 | 4.1% |
| 7 | Michigan | 33,600 | 3.8% |
| 8 | Illinois | 33,500 | 3.8% |
| 9 | Virginia | 30,800 | 3.5% |
| 10 | Washington | 28,000 | 3.2% |
| 11 | Tennessee | 27,500 | 3.1% |
| 12 | New Jersey | 25,600 | 2.9% |
| 13 | Arizona | 25,300 | 2.9% |
| 14 | Missouri | 23,400 | 2.7% |
| 15 | Colorado | 22,500 | 2.6% |
| 16 | Alabama | 20,700 | 2.4% |
| 17 | Oklahoma | 19,700 | 2.2% |
| 18 | Kentucky | 19,200 | 2.2% |
| 19 | Massachusetts | 17,800 | 2.0% |
| 20 | Maryland | 16,900 | 1.9% |
| 21 | Wisconsin | 16,600 | 1.9% |
| 22 | Arkansas | 15,600 | 1.8% |
| 23 | Nevada | 15,300 | 1.7% |
| 24 | South Carolina | 15,000 | 1.7% |
| 25 | Oregon | 14,700 | 1.7% |
| 26 | Mississippi | 11,900 | 1.4% |
| 27 | Kansas | 11,200 | 1.3% |
| 28 | Connecticut | 11,100 | 1.3% |
| 29 | Utah | 10,400 | 1.2% |
| 30 | West Virginia | 9,600 | 1.1% |
| 31 | Idaho | 7,800 | 0.9% |
| 32 | Iowa | 7,400 | 0.8% |
| 33 | New Mexico | 6,900 | 0.8% |
| 34 | Nebraska | 6,400 | 0.7% |
| 35 | Maine | 5,600 | 0.6% |
| 36 | New Hampshire | 5,000 | 0.6% |
| 37 | Montana | 4,000 | 0.5% |
| 38 | Alaska | 3,500 | 0.4% |
| 39 | Rhode Island | 3,400 | 0.4% |
| 40 | Delaware | 3,300 | 0.4% |
| 41 | South Dakota | 2,700 | 0.3% |
| 41 | Wyoming | 2,700 | 0.3% |
| 43 | Vermont | 2,300 | 0.3% |
| 44 | North Dakota | 1,800 | 0.2% |
| NA | California** | NA | NA |
| NA | Georgia** | NA | NA |
| NA | Hawaii** | NA | NA |
| NA | Indiana** | NA | NA |
| NA | Louisiana** | NA | NA |
| NA | Minnesota** | NA | NA |
| | District of Columbia | 1,800 | 0.2% |

Source: CQ Press using data from U.S. Department of Health and Human Services, National Center for Health Statistics
"National Vital Statistics System, Marriages and Divorces" (http://www.cdc.gov/nchs/mardiv.htm)
*Provisional estimates by state of occurrence. National total is only for reporting states.
**Not available.

# Divorce Rate in 2011

## Reporting States' Rate = 3.6 Divorces per 1,000 Population*

| ALPHA ORDER | | | RANK ORDER | | |
|---|---|---|---|---|---|
| RANK | STATE | RATE | RANK | STATE | RATE |
| 11 | Alabama | 4.3 | 1 | Nevada | 5.6 |
| 6 | Alaska | 4.8 | 2 | Arkansas | 5.3 |
| 17 | Arizona | 3.9 | 3 | Oklahoma | 5.2 |
| 2 | Arkansas | 5.3 | 3 | West Virginia | 5.2 |
| NA | California** | NA | 5 | Idaho | 4.9 |
| 9 | Colorado | 4.4 | 6 | Alaska | 4.8 |
| 35 | Connecticut | 3.1 | 6 | Wyoming | 4.8 |
| 25 | Delaware | 3.6 | 8 | Florida | 4.5 |
| 8 | Florida | 4.5 | 9 | Colorado | 4.4 |
| NA | Georgia** | NA | 9 | Kentucky | 4.4 |
| NA | Hawaii** | NA | 11 | Alabama | 4.3 |
| 5 | Idaho | 4.9 | 11 | Tennessee | 4.3 |
| 43 | Illinois | 2.6 | 13 | Maine | 4.2 |
| NA | Indiana** | NA | 14 | Washington | 4.1 |
| 44 | Iowa | 2.4 | 15 | Mississippi | 4.0 |
| 17 | Kansas | 3.9 | 15 | Montana | 4.0 |
| 9 | Kentucky | 4.4 | 17 | Arizona | 3.9 |
| NA | Louisiana** | NA | 17 | Kansas | 3.9 |
| 13 | Maine | 4.2 | 17 | Missouri | 3.9 |
| 36 | Maryland | 2.9 | 20 | New Hampshire | 3.8 |
| 41 | Massachusetts | 2.7 | 20 | Oregon | 3.8 |
| 28 | Michigan | 3.4 | 20 | Virginia | 3.8 |
| NA | Minnesota** | NA | 23 | North Carolina | 3.7 |
| 15 | Mississippi | 4.0 | 23 | Utah | 3.7 |
| 17 | Missouri | 3.9 | 25 | Delaware | 3.6 |
| 15 | Montana | 4.0 | 25 | Vermont | 3.6 |
| 27 | Nebraska | 3.5 | 27 | Nebraska | 3.5 |
| 1 | Nevada | 5.6 | 28 | Michigan | 3.4 |
| 20 | New Hampshire | 3.8 | 28 | Ohio | 3.4 |
| 36 | New Jersey | 2.9 | 30 | New Mexico | 3.3 |
| 30 | New Mexico | 3.3 | 30 | South Dakota | 3.3 |
| 36 | New York | 2.9 | 32 | Rhode Island | 3.2 |
| 23 | North Carolina | 3.7 | 32 | South Carolina | 3.2 |
| 41 | North Dakota | 2.7 | 32 | Texas | 3.2 |
| 28 | Ohio | 3.4 | 35 | Connecticut | 3.1 |
| 3 | Oklahoma | 5.2 | 36 | Maryland | 2.9 |
| 20 | Oregon | 3.8 | 36 | New Jersey | 2.9 |
| 40 | Pennsylvania | 2.8 | 36 | New York | 2.9 |
| 32 | Rhode Island | 3.2 | 36 | Wisconsin | 2.9 |
| 32 | South Carolina | 3.2 | 40 | Pennsylvania | 2.8 |
| 30 | South Dakota | 3.3 | 41 | Massachusetts | 2.7 |
| 11 | Tennessee | 4.3 | 41 | North Dakota | 2.7 |
| 32 | Texas | 3.2 | 43 | Illinois | 2.6 |
| 23 | Utah | 3.7 | 44 | Iowa | 2.4 |
| 25 | Vermont | 3.6 | NA | California** | NA |
| 20 | Virginia | 3.8 | NA | Georgia** | NA |
| 14 | Washington | 4.1 | NA | Hawaii** | NA |
| 3 | West Virginia | 5.2 | NA | Indiana** | NA |
| 36 | Wisconsin | 2.9 | NA | Louisiana** | NA |
| 6 | Wyoming | 4.8 | NA | Minnesota** | NA |
| | | | | District of Columbia | 2.9 |

Source: U.S. Department of Health and Human Services, National Center for Health Statistics
  "National Vital Statistics System, Marriages and Divorces" (http://www.cdc.gov/nchs/mardiv.htm)
*Provisional data by state of occurrence.  National rate is only for reporting states.
**Not available.

# Average Family Size in 2012

## National Average = 3.25 Persons per Family

ALPHA ORDER

| RANK | STATE | PERSONS |
|------|-------|---------|
| 19 | Alabama | 3.17 |
| 4 | Alaska | 3.44 |
| 10 | Arizona | 3.29 |
| 32 | Arkansas | 3.10 |
| 3 | California | 3.57 |
| 24 | Colorado | 3.14 |
| 23 | Connecticut | 3.15 |
| 18 | Delaware | 3.19 |
| 13 | Florida | 3.27 |
| 6 | Georgia | 3.34 |
| 2 | Hawaii | 3.61 |
| 17 | Idaho | 3.21 |
| 10 | Illinois | 3.29 |
| 24 | Indiana | 3.14 |
| 45 | Iowa | 2.98 |
| 30 | Kansas | 3.12 |
| 41 | Kentucky | 3.04 |
| 15 | Louisiana | 3.24 |
| 49 | Maine | 2.86 |
| 14 | Maryland | 3.26 |
| 21 | Massachusetts | 3.16 |
| 24 | Michigan | 3.14 |
| 39 | Minnesota | 3.05 |
| 15 | Mississippi | 3.24 |
| 34 | Missouri | 3.08 |
| 47 | Montana | 2.96 |
| 41 | Nebraska | 3.04 |
| 7 | Nevada | 3.32 |
| 45 | New Hampshire | 2.98 |
| 10 | New Jersey | 3.29 |
| 7 | New Mexico | 3.32 |
| 9 | New York | 3.31 |
| 30 | North Carolina | 3.12 |
| 48 | North Dakota | 2.95 |
| 34 | Ohio | 3.08 |
| 24 | Oklahoma | 3.14 |
| 37 | Oregon | 3.06 |
| 32 | Pennsylvania | 3.10 |
| 37 | Rhode Island | 3.06 |
| 28 | South Carolina | 3.13 |
| 34 | South Dakota | 3.08 |
| 28 | Tennessee | 3.13 |
| 4 | Texas | 3.44 |
| 1 | Utah | 3.64 |
| 50 | Vermont | 2.84 |
| 19 | Virginia | 3.17 |
| 21 | Washington | 3.16 |
| 39 | West Virginia | 3.05 |
| 44 | Wisconsin | 3.02 |
| 41 | Wyoming | 3.04 |

RANK ORDER

| RANK | STATE | PERSONS |
|------|-------|---------|
| 1 | Utah | 3.64 |
| 2 | Hawaii | 3.61 |
| 3 | California | 3.57 |
| 4 | Alaska | 3.44 |
| 4 | Texas | 3.44 |
| 6 | Georgia | 3.34 |
| 7 | Nevada | 3.32 |
| 7 | New Mexico | 3.32 |
| 9 | New York | 3.31 |
| 10 | Arizona | 3.29 |
| 10 | Illinois | 3.29 |
| 10 | New Jersey | 3.29 |
| 13 | Florida | 3.27 |
| 14 | Maryland | 3.26 |
| 15 | Louisiana | 3.24 |
| 15 | Mississippi | 3.24 |
| 17 | Idaho | 3.21 |
| 18 | Delaware | 3.19 |
| 19 | Alabama | 3.17 |
| 19 | Virginia | 3.17 |
| 21 | Massachusetts | 3.16 |
| 21 | Washington | 3.16 |
| 23 | Connecticut | 3.15 |
| 24 | Colorado | 3.14 |
| 24 | Indiana | 3.14 |
| 24 | Michigan | 3.14 |
| 24 | Oklahoma | 3.14 |
| 28 | South Carolina | 3.13 |
| 28 | Tennessee | 3.13 |
| 30 | Kansas | 3.12 |
| 30 | North Carolina | 3.12 |
| 32 | Arkansas | 3.10 |
| 32 | Pennsylvania | 3.10 |
| 34 | Missouri | 3.08 |
| 34 | Ohio | 3.08 |
| 34 | South Dakota | 3.08 |
| 37 | Oregon | 3.06 |
| 37 | Rhode Island | 3.06 |
| 39 | Minnesota | 3.05 |
| 39 | West Virginia | 3.05 |
| 41 | Kentucky | 3.04 |
| 41 | Nebraska | 3.04 |
| 41 | Wyoming | 3.04 |
| 44 | Wisconsin | 3.02 |
| 45 | Iowa | 2.98 |
| 45 | New Hampshire | 2.98 |
| 47 | Montana | 2.96 |
| 48 | North Dakota | 2.95 |
| 49 | Maine | 2.86 |
| 50 | Vermont | 2.84 |
| | District of Columbia | 3.25 |

Source: U.S. Bureau of the Census
"2012 American Community Survey-Table DP02" (http://www.census.gov/acs/www/index.html)

# Seats in the U.S. House of Representatives in 2014

## National Total = 435 Seats*

ALPHA ORDER

| RANK | STATE | SEATS | % of USA |
|---|---|---|---|
| 22 | Alabama | 7 | 1.6% |
| 44 | Alaska | 1 | 0.2% |
| 14 | Arizona | 9 | 2.1% |
| 30 | Arkansas | 4 | 0.9% |
| 1 | California | 53 | 12.2% |
| 22 | Colorado | 7 | 1.6% |
| 27 | Connecticut | 5 | 1.1% |
| 44 | Delaware | 1 | 0.2% |
| 3 | Florida | 27 | 6.2% |
| 8 | Georgia | 14 | 3.2% |
| 39 | Hawaii | 2 | 0.5% |
| 39 | Idaho | 2 | 0.5% |
| 5 | Illinois | 18 | 4.1% |
| 14 | Indiana | 9 | 2.1% |
| 30 | Iowa | 4 | 0.9% |
| 30 | Kansas | 4 | 0.9% |
| 25 | Kentucky | 6 | 1.4% |
| 25 | Louisiana | 6 | 1.4% |
| 39 | Maine | 2 | 0.5% |
| 18 | Maryland | 8 | 1.8% |
| 14 | Massachusetts | 9 | 2.1% |
| 8 | Michigan | 14 | 3.2% |
| 18 | Minnesota | 8 | 1.8% |
| 30 | Mississippi | 4 | 0.9% |
| 18 | Missouri | 8 | 1.8% |
| 44 | Montana | 1 | 0.2% |
| 36 | Nebraska | 3 | 0.7% |
| 30 | Nevada | 4 | 0.9% |
| 39 | New Hampshire | 2 | 0.5% |
| 11 | New Jersey | 12 | 2.8% |
| 36 | New Mexico | 3 | 0.7% |
| 3 | New York | 27 | 6.2% |
| 10 | North Carolina | 13 | 3.0% |
| 44 | North Dakota | 1 | 0.2% |
| 7 | Ohio | 16 | 3.7% |
| 27 | Oklahoma | 5 | 1.1% |
| 27 | Oregon | 5 | 1.1% |
| 5 | Pennsylvania | 18 | 4.1% |
| 39 | Rhode Island | 2 | 0.5% |
| 22 | South Carolina | 7 | 1.6% |
| 44 | South Dakota | 1 | 0.2% |
| 14 | Tennessee | 9 | 2.1% |
| 2 | Texas | 36 | 8.3% |
| 30 | Utah | 4 | 0.9% |
| 44 | Vermont | 1 | 0.2% |
| 12 | Virginia | 11 | 2.5% |
| 13 | Washington | 10 | 2.3% |
| 36 | West Virginia | 3 | 0.7% |
| 18 | Wisconsin | 8 | 1.8% |
| 44 | Wyoming | 1 | 0.2% |

RANK ORDER

| RANK | STATE | SEATS | % of USA |
|---|---|---|---|
| 1 | California | 53 | 12.2% |
| 2 | Texas | 36 | 8.3% |
| 3 | Florida | 27 | 6.2% |
| 3 | New York | 27 | 6.2% |
| 5 | Illinois | 18 | 4.1% |
| 5 | Pennsylvania | 18 | 4.1% |
| 7 | Ohio | 16 | 3.7% |
| 8 | Georgia | 14 | 3.2% |
| 8 | Michigan | 14 | 3.2% |
| 10 | North Carolina | 13 | 3.0% |
| 11 | New Jersey | 12 | 2.8% |
| 12 | Virginia | 11 | 2.5% |
| 13 | Washington | 10 | 2.3% |
| 14 | Arizona | 9 | 2.1% |
| 14 | Indiana | 9 | 2.1% |
| 14 | Massachusetts | 9 | 2.1% |
| 14 | Tennessee | 9 | 2.1% |
| 18 | Maryland | 8 | 1.8% |
| 18 | Minnesota | 8 | 1.8% |
| 18 | Missouri | 8 | 1.8% |
| 18 | Wisconsin | 8 | 1.8% |
| 22 | Alabama | 7 | 1.6% |
| 22 | Colorado | 7 | 1.6% |
| 22 | South Carolina | 7 | 1.6% |
| 25 | Kentucky | 6 | 1.4% |
| 25 | Louisiana | 6 | 1.4% |
| 27 | Connecticut | 5 | 1.1% |
| 27 | Oklahoma | 5 | 1.1% |
| 27 | Oregon | 5 | 1.1% |
| 30 | Arkansas | 4 | 0.9% |
| 30 | Iowa | 4 | 0.9% |
| 30 | Kansas | 4 | 0.9% |
| 30 | Mississippi | 4 | 0.9% |
| 30 | Nevada | 4 | 0.9% |
| 30 | Utah | 4 | 0.9% |
| 36 | Nebraska | 3 | 0.7% |
| 36 | New Mexico | 3 | 0.7% |
| 36 | West Virginia | 3 | 0.7% |
| 39 | Hawaii | 2 | 0.5% |
| 39 | Idaho | 2 | 0.5% |
| 39 | Maine | 2 | 0.5% |
| 39 | New Hampshire | 2 | 0.5% |
| 39 | Rhode Island | 2 | 0.5% |
| 44 | Alaska | 1 | 0.2% |
| 44 | Delaware | 1 | 0.2% |
| 44 | Montana | 1 | 0.2% |
| 44 | North Dakota | 1 | 0.2% |
| 44 | South Dakota | 1 | 0.2% |
| 44 | Vermont | 1 | 0.2% |
| 44 | Wyoming | 1 | 0.2% |
| | District of Columbia | 0 | 0.0% |

Source: U.S. Bureau of the Census
"Congressional Apportionment" (http://www.census.gov/population/apportionment/)
*This table shows the number of seats after reapportionment of the 2010 Census. This apportionment became effective with the Congress elected in November 2012 and that took office in January 2013.
**The District of Columbia has one non-voting delegate. Each state has two members in the U.S. Senate.

# Estimated Population per U.S. House Seat in 2014

## National Rate = 725,247 Persons per House Member*

| ALPHA ORDER | | | RANK ORDER | | |
|---|---|---|---|---|---|
| RANK | STATE | RATE | RANK | STATE | RATE |
| 41 | Alabama | 690,532 | 1 | Montana | 1,015,165 |
| 19 | Alaska | 735,132 | 2 | Delaware | 925,749 |
| 18 | Arizona | 736,292 | 3 | South Dakota | 844,877 |
| 17 | Arkansas | 739,843 | 4 | Idaho | 806,068 |
| 28 | California | 723,255 | 5 | Oregon | 786,013 |
| 11 | Colorado | 752,624 | 6 | Iowa | 772,604 |
| 31 | Connecticut | 719,216 | 7 | Louisiana | 770,912 |
| 2 | Delaware | 925,749 | 8 | Oklahoma | 770,114 |
| 25 | Florida | 724,180 | 9 | North Carolina | 757,543 |
| 34 | Georgia | 713,726 | 10 | Missouri | 755,521 |
| 37 | Hawaii | 702,027 | 11 | Colorado | 752,624 |
| 4 | Idaho | 806,068 | 12 | Virginia | 750,946 |
| 33 | Illinois | 715,674 | 13 | Mississippi | 747,802 |
| 22 | Indiana | 730,100 | 14 | Massachusetts | 743,647 |
| 6 | Iowa | 772,604 | 15 | New Jersey | 741,612 |
| 26 | Kansas | 723,489 | 16 | Maryland | 741,102 |
| 21 | Kentucky | 732,549 | 17 | Arkansas | 739,843 |
| 7 | Louisiana | 770,912 | 18 | Arizona | 736,292 |
| 44 | Maine | 664,151 | 19 | Alaska | 735,132 |
| 16 | Maryland | 741,102 | 20 | Texas | 734,672 |
| 14 | Massachusetts | 743,647 | 21 | Kentucky | 732,549 |
| 36 | Michigan | 706,830 | 22 | Indiana | 730,100 |
| 43 | Minnesota | 677,548 | 23 | New York | 727,820 |
| 13 | Mississippi | 747,802 | 24 | Utah | 725,218 |
| 10 | Missouri | 755,521 | 25 | Florida | 724,180 |
| 1 | Montana | 1,015,165 | 26 | Kansas | 723,489 |
| 47 | Nebraska | 622,839 | 27 | North Dakota | 723,393 |
| 38 | Nevada | 697,534 | 28 | California | 723,255 |
| 45 | New Hampshire | 661,730 | 29 | Ohio | 723,176 |
| 15 | New Jersey | 741,612 | 30 | Tennessee | 721,775 |
| 40 | New Mexico | 695,096 | 31 | Connecticut | 719,216 |
| 23 | New York | 727,820 | 32 | Wisconsin | 717,839 |
| 9 | North Carolina | 757,543 | 33 | Illinois | 715,674 |
| 27 | North Dakota | 723,393 | 34 | Georgia | 713,726 |
| 29 | Ohio | 723,176 | 35 | Pennsylvania | 709,656 |
| 8 | Oklahoma | 770,114 | 36 | Michigan | 706,830 |
| 5 | Oregon | 786,013 | 37 | Hawaii | 702,027 |
| 35 | Pennsylvania | 709,656 | 38 | Nevada | 697,534 |
| 50 | Rhode Island | 525,756 | 39 | Washington | 697,141 |
| 42 | South Carolina | 682,120 | 40 | New Mexico | 695,096 |
| 3 | South Dakota | 844,877 | 41 | Alabama | 690,532 |
| 30 | Tennessee | 721,775 | 42 | South Carolina | 682,120 |
| 20 | Texas | 734,672 | 43 | Minnesota | 677,548 |
| 24 | Utah | 725,218 | 44 | Maine | 664,151 |
| 46 | Vermont | 626,630 | 45 | New Hampshire | 661,730 |
| 12 | Virginia | 750,946 | 46 | Vermont | 626,630 |
| 39 | Washington | 697,141 | 47 | Nebraska | 622,839 |
| 48 | West Virginia | 618,101 | 48 | West Virginia | 618,101 |
| 32 | Wisconsin | 717,839 | 49 | Wyoming | 582,658 |
| 49 | Wyoming | 582,658 | 50 | Rhode Island | 525,756 |
| | | | | District of Columbia** | NA |

Source: CQ Press using data from U.S. Bureau of the Census
   "Congressional Apportionment" (http://www.census.gov/population/apportionment/)
*Rates calculated using 2013 population estimates and do not include population of the District of Columbia. The
District has one non-voting delegate. Each state has two members in the U.S. Senate. This table is based only on U.S.
Representatives and not U.S. Senate members. This table reflects reapportionment resulting from the 2010 census and
taking effect after the 2012 election. **Not applicable.

# State Legislators in 2013

## National Total = 7,383 Legislators*

| RANK | STATE | LEGISLATORS | % of USA |
|---|---|---|---|
| 27 | Alabama | 140 | 1.9% |
| 49 | Alaska | 60 | 0.8% |
| 43 | Arizona | 90 | 1.2% |
| 30 | Arkansas | 135 | 1.8% |
| 35 | California | 120 | 1.6% |
| 42 | Colorado | 100 | 1.4% |
| 9 | Connecticut | 187 | 2.5% |
| 48 | Delaware | 62 | 0.8% |
| 18 | Florida | 160 | 2.2% |
| 3 | Georgia | 236 | 3.2% |
| 46 | Hawaii | 76 | 1.0% |
| 39 | Idaho | 105 | 1.4% |
| 13 | Illinois | 177 | 2.4% |
| 19 | Indiana | 150 | 2.0% |
| 19 | Iowa | 150 | 2.0% |
| 17 | Kansas | 165 | 2.2% |
| 29 | Kentucky | 138 | 1.9% |
| 25 | Louisiana | 144 | 2.0% |
| 10 | Maine | 186 | 2.5% |
| 8 | Maryland | 188 | 2.5% |
| 6 | Massachusetts | 200 | 2.7% |
| 23 | Michigan | 148 | 2.0% |
| 5 | Minnesota | 201 | 2.7% |
| 14 | Mississippi | 174 | 2.4% |
| 7 | Missouri | 197 | 2.7% |
| 19 | Montana | 150 | 2.0% |
| 50 | Nebraska | 49 | 0.7% |
| 47 | Nevada | 63 | 0.9% |
| 1 | New Hampshire | 424 | 5.7% |
| 35 | New Jersey | 120 | 1.6% |
| 38 | New Mexico | 112 | 1.5% |
| 4 | New York | 213 | 2.9% |
| 15 | North Carolina | 170 | 2.3% |
| 26 | North Dakota | 141 | 1.9% |
| 32 | Ohio | 132 | 1.8% |
| 22 | Oklahoma | 149 | 2.0% |
| 43 | Oregon | 90 | 1.2% |
| 2 | Pennsylvania | 253 | 3.4% |
| 37 | Rhode Island | 113 | 1.5% |
| 15 | South Carolina | 170 | 2.3% |
| 39 | South Dakota | 105 | 1.4% |
| 32 | Tennessee | 132 | 1.8% |
| 11 | Texas | 181 | 2.5% |
| 41 | Utah | 104 | 1.4% |
| 12 | Vermont | 180 | 2.4% |
| 27 | Virginia | 140 | 1.9% |
| 24 | Washington | 147 | 2.0% |
| 31 | West Virginia | 134 | 1.8% |
| 32 | Wisconsin | 132 | 1.8% |
| 43 | Wyoming | 90 | 1.2% |

| RANK | STATE | LEGISLATORS | % of USA |
|---|---|---|---|
| 1 | New Hampshire | 424 | 5.7% |
| 2 | Pennsylvania | 253 | 3.4% |
| 3 | Georgia | 236 | 3.2% |
| 4 | New York | 213 | 2.9% |
| 5 | Minnesota | 201 | 2.7% |
| 6 | Massachusetts | 200 | 2.7% |
| 7 | Missouri | 197 | 2.7% |
| 8 | Maryland | 188 | 2.5% |
| 9 | Connecticut | 187 | 2.5% |
| 10 | Maine | 186 | 2.5% |
| 11 | Texas | 181 | 2.5% |
| 12 | Vermont | 180 | 2.4% |
| 13 | Illinois | 177 | 2.4% |
| 14 | Mississippi | 174 | 2.4% |
| 15 | North Carolina | 170 | 2.3% |
| 15 | South Carolina | 170 | 2.3% |
| 17 | Kansas | 165 | 2.2% |
| 18 | Florida | 160 | 2.2% |
| 19 | Indiana | 150 | 2.0% |
| 19 | Iowa | 150 | 2.0% |
| 19 | Montana | 150 | 2.0% |
| 22 | Oklahoma | 149 | 2.0% |
| 23 | Michigan | 148 | 2.0% |
| 24 | Washington | 147 | 2.0% |
| 25 | Louisiana | 144 | 2.0% |
| 26 | North Dakota | 141 | 1.9% |
| 27 | Alabama | 140 | 1.9% |
| 27 | Virginia | 140 | 1.9% |
| 29 | Kentucky | 138 | 1.9% |
| 30 | Arkansas | 135 | 1.8% |
| 31 | West Virginia | 134 | 1.8% |
| 32 | Ohio | 132 | 1.8% |
| 32 | Tennessee | 132 | 1.8% |
| 32 | Wisconsin | 132 | 1.8% |
| 35 | California | 120 | 1.6% |
| 35 | New Jersey | 120 | 1.6% |
| 37 | Rhode Island | 113 | 1.5% |
| 38 | New Mexico | 112 | 1.5% |
| 39 | Idaho | 105 | 1.4% |
| 39 | South Dakota | 105 | 1.4% |
| 41 | Utah | 104 | 1.4% |
| 42 | Colorado | 100 | 1.4% |
| 43 | Arizona | 90 | 1.2% |
| 43 | Oregon | 90 | 1.2% |
| 43 | Wyoming | 90 | 1.2% |
| 46 | Hawaii | 76 | 1.0% |
| 47 | Nevada | 63 | 0.9% |
| 48 | Delaware | 62 | 0.8% |
| 49 | Alaska | 60 | 0.8% |
| 50 | Nebraska | 49 | 0.7% |
| | District of Columbia** | NA | NA |

Source: National Conference of State Legislatures (Denver, CO)
    "2013 Partisan Composition" (http://www.ncsl.org/research/about-state-legislatures/partisan-composition.aspx)
*There are 1,972 state senators (including Nebraska's 49 unicameral seats) and 5,411 state house members.
**Not applicable.

# Population per State Legislator in 2013

## National Rate = 42,731 Population per Legislator*

ALPHA ORDER

| RANK | STATE | RATE |
|------|-------|------|
| 22 | Alabama | 34,527 |
| 42 | Alaska | 12,252 |
| 7 | Arizona | 73,629 |
| 32 | Arkansas | 21,921 |
| 1 | California | 319,438 |
| 12 | Colorado | 52,684 |
| 34 | Connecticut | 19,230 |
| 40 | Delaware | 14,931 |
| 3 | Florida | 122,205 |
| 20 | Georgia | 42,340 |
| 36 | Hawaii | 18,474 |
| 39 | Idaho | 15,354 |
| 8 | Illinois | 72,780 |
| 17 | Indiana | 43,806 |
| 33 | Iowa | 20,603 |
| 37 | Kansas | 17,539 |
| 25 | Kentucky | 31,850 |
| 24 | Louisiana | 32,121 |
| 45 | Maine | 7,141 |
| 26 | Maryland | 31,536 |
| 23 | Massachusetts | 33,464 |
| 9 | Michigan | 66,862 |
| 30 | Minnesota | 26,967 |
| 38 | Mississippi | 17,191 |
| 27 | Missouri | 30,681 |
| 46 | Montana | 6,768 |
| 21 | Nebraska | 38,133 |
| 16 | Nevada | 44,288 |
| 50 | New Hampshire | 3,121 |
| 6 | New Jersey | 74,161 |
| 35 | New Mexico | 18,619 |
| 4 | New York | 92,259 |
| 11 | North Carolina | 57,930 |
| 48 | North Dakota | 5,130 |
| 5 | Ohio | 87,658 |
| 31 | Oklahoma | 25,843 |
| 18 | Oregon | 43,667 |
| 13 | Pennsylvania | 50,489 |
| 43 | Rhode Island | 9,305 |
| 28 | South Carolina | 28,087 |
| 44 | South Dakota | 8,046 |
| 14 | Tennessee | 49,212 |
| 2 | Texas | 146,123 |
| 29 | Utah | 27,893 |
| 49 | Vermont | 3,481 |
| 10 | Virginia | 59,003 |
| 15 | Washington | 47,425 |
| 41 | West Virginia | 13,838 |
| 19 | Wisconsin | 43,505 |
| 47 | Wyoming | 6,474 |

RANK ORDER

| RANK | STATE | RATE |
|------|-------|------|
| 1 | California | 319,438 |
| 2 | Texas | 146,123 |
| 3 | Florida | 122,205 |
| 4 | New York | 92,259 |
| 5 | Ohio | 87,658 |
| 6 | New Jersey | 74,161 |
| 7 | Arizona | 73,629 |
| 8 | Illinois | 72,780 |
| 9 | Michigan | 66,862 |
| 10 | Virginia | 59,003 |
| 11 | North Carolina | 57,930 |
| 12 | Colorado | 52,684 |
| 13 | Pennsylvania | 50,489 |
| 14 | Tennessee | 49,212 |
| 15 | Washington | 47,425 |
| 16 | Nevada | 44,288 |
| 17 | Indiana | 43,806 |
| 18 | Oregon | 43,667 |
| 19 | Wisconsin | 43,505 |
| 20 | Georgia | 42,340 |
| 21 | Nebraska | 38,133 |
| 22 | Alabama | 34,527 |
| 23 | Massachusetts | 33,464 |
| 24 | Louisiana | 32,121 |
| 25 | Kentucky | 31,850 |
| 26 | Maryland | 31,536 |
| 27 | Missouri | 30,681 |
| 28 | South Carolina | 28,087 |
| 29 | Utah | 27,893 |
| 30 | Minnesota | 26,967 |
| 31 | Oklahoma | 25,843 |
| 32 | Arkansas | 21,921 |
| 33 | Iowa | 20,603 |
| 34 | Connecticut | 19,230 |
| 35 | New Mexico | 18,619 |
| 36 | Hawaii | 18,474 |
| 37 | Kansas | 17,539 |
| 38 | Mississippi | 17,191 |
| 39 | Idaho | 15,354 |
| 40 | Delaware | 14,931 |
| 41 | West Virginia | 13,838 |
| 42 | Alaska | 12,252 |
| 43 | Rhode Island | 9,305 |
| 44 | South Dakota | 8,046 |
| 45 | Maine | 7,141 |
| 46 | Montana | 6,768 |
| 47 | Wyoming | 6,474 |
| 48 | North Dakota | 5,130 |
| 49 | Vermont | 3,481 |
| 50 | New Hampshire | 3,121 |
| | District of Columbia** | NA |

Source: CQ Press using data from National Conference of State Legislatures (Denver, CO)
   "2013 Partisan Composition" (http://www.ncsl.org/research/about-state-legislatures/partisan-composition.aspx)
*There are 1,972 state senators (including Nebraska's 49 unicameral seats) and 5,411 state house members. National rate does not include population for the District of Columbia. Calculated using 2013 population estimates.
**Not applicable.

# Registered Voters in 2012

## National Total = 153,157,000

| ALPHA ORDER | | | | | RANK ORDER | | | |
|---|---|---|---|---|---|---|---|---|
| RANK | STATE | REGISTERED | % of USA | | RANK | STATE | REGISTERED | % of USA |
| 23 | Alabama | 2,556,000 | 1.7% | | 1 | California | 15,356,000 | 10.0% |
| 48 | Alaska | 361,000 | 0.2% | | 2 | Texas | 10,749,000 | 7.0% |
| 21 | Arizona | 2,812,000 | 1.8% | | 3 | Florida | 9,102,000 | 5.9% |
| 33 | Arkansas | 1,376,000 | 0.9% | | 4 | New York | 8,887,000 | 5.8% |
| 1 | California | 15,356,000 | 10.0% | | 5 | Pennsylvania | 6,795,000 | 4.4% |
| 22 | Colorado | 2,635,000 | 1.7% | | 6 | Illinois | 6,425,000 | 4.2% |
| 30 | Connecticut | 1,760,000 | 1.1% | | 7 | Ohio | 6,076,000 | 4.0% |
| 45 | Delaware | 470,000 | 0.3% | | 8 | Michigan | 5,620,000 | 3.7% |
| 3 | Florida | 9,102,000 | 5.9% | | 9 | North Carolina | 5,295,000 | 3.5% |
| 10 | Georgia | 4,767,000 | 3.1% | | 10 | Georgia | 4,767,000 | 3.1% |
| 44 | Hawaii | 547,000 | 0.4% | | 11 | New Jersey | 4,326,000 | 2.8% |
| 41 | Idaho | 745,000 | 0.5% | | 12 | Virginia | 4,210,000 | 2.7% |
| 6 | Illinois | 6,425,000 | 4.2% | | 13 | Massachusetts | 3,759,000 | 2.5% |
| 17 | Indiana | 3,270,000 | 2.1% | | 14 | Washington | 3,533,000 | 2.3% |
| 31 | Iowa | 1,745,000 | 1.1% | | 15 | Missouri | 3,384,000 | 2.2% |
| 32 | Kansas | 1,467,000 | 1.0% | | 16 | Wisconsin | 3,318,000 | 2.2% |
| 26 | Kentucky | 2,303,000 | 1.5% | | 17 | Indiana | 3,270,000 | 2.1% |
| 24 | Louisiana | 2,498,000 | 1.6% | | 18 | Tennessee | 3,210,000 | 2.1% |
| 39 | Maine | 787,000 | 0.5% | | 19 | Minnesota | 3,085,000 | 2.0% |
| 20 | Maryland | 2,888,000 | 1.9% | | 20 | Maryland | 2,888,000 | 1.9% |
| 13 | Massachusetts | 3,759,000 | 2.5% | | 21 | Arizona | 2,812,000 | 1.8% |
| 8 | Michigan | 5,620,000 | 3.7% | | 22 | Colorado | 2,635,000 | 1.7% |
| 19 | Minnesota | 3,085,000 | 2.0% | | 23 | Alabama | 2,556,000 | 1.7% |
| 29 | Mississippi | 1,794,000 | 1.2% | | 24 | Louisiana | 2,498,000 | 1.6% |
| 15 | Missouri | 3,384,000 | 2.2% | | 25 | South Carolina | 2,479,000 | 1.6% |
| 42 | Montana | 553,000 | 0.4% | | 26 | Kentucky | 2,303,000 | 1.5% |
| 38 | Nebraska | 901,000 | 0.6% | | 27 | Oregon | 2,086,000 | 1.4% |
| 34 | Nevada | 1,176,000 | 0.8% | | 28 | Oklahoma | 1,806,000 | 1.2% |
| 40 | New Hampshire | 752,000 | 0.5% | | 29 | Mississippi | 1,794,000 | 1.2% |
| 11 | New Jersey | 4,326,000 | 2.8% | | 30 | Connecticut | 1,760,000 | 1.1% |
| 37 | New Mexico | 978,000 | 0.6% | | 31 | Iowa | 1,745,000 | 1.1% |
| 4 | New York | 8,887,000 | 5.8% | | 32 | Kansas | 1,467,000 | 1.0% |
| 9 | North Carolina | 5,295,000 | 3.5% | | 33 | Arkansas | 1,376,000 | 0.9% |
| 47 | North Dakota | 383,000 | 0.3% | | 34 | Nevada | 1,176,000 | 0.8% |
| 7 | Ohio | 6,076,000 | 4.0% | | 35 | Utah | 1,138,000 | 0.7% |
| 28 | Oklahoma | 1,806,000 | 1.2% | | 36 | West Virginia | 982,000 | 0.6% |
| 27 | Oregon | 2,086,000 | 1.4% | | 37 | New Mexico | 978,000 | 0.6% |
| 5 | Pennsylvania | 6,795,000 | 4.4% | | 38 | Nebraska | 901,000 | 0.6% |
| 43 | Rhode Island | 552,000 | 0.4% | | 39 | Maine | 787,000 | 0.5% |
| 25 | South Carolina | 2,479,000 | 1.6% | | 40 | New Hampshire | 752,000 | 0.5% |
| 46 | South Dakota | 454,000 | 0.3% | | 41 | Idaho | 745,000 | 0.5% |
| 18 | Tennessee | 3,210,000 | 2.1% | | 42 | Montana | 553,000 | 0.4% |
| 2 | Texas | 10,749,000 | 7.0% | | 43 | Rhode Island | 552,000 | 0.4% |
| 35 | Utah | 1,138,000 | 0.7% | | 44 | Hawaii | 547,000 | 0.4% |
| 49 | Vermont | 357,000 | 0.2% | | 45 | Delaware | 470,000 | 0.3% |
| 12 | Virginia | 4,210,000 | 2.7% | | 46 | South Dakota | 454,000 | 0.3% |
| 14 | Washington | 3,533,000 | 2.3% | | 47 | North Dakota | 383,000 | 0.3% |
| 36 | West Virginia | 982,000 | 0.6% | | 48 | Alaska | 361,000 | 0.2% |
| 16 | Wisconsin | 3,318,000 | 2.2% | | 49 | Vermont | 357,000 | 0.2% |
| 50 | Wyoming | 268,000 | 0.2% | | 50 | Wyoming | 268,000 | 0.2% |
| | | | | | | District of Columbia | 385,000 | 0.3% |

Source: U.S. Bureau of the Census
"Voting and Registration" (Table 4a, http://www.census.gov/hhes/www/socdemo/voting/index.html)

# Percent of Eligible Voters Reported Registered in 2012

## National Percent = 71.2%*

ALPHA ORDER

| RANK | STATE | PERCENT |
|---|---|---|
| 18 | Alabama | 73.5 |
| 26 | Alaska | 72.8 |
| 46 | Arizona | 65.2 |
| 45 | Arkansas | 65.3 |
| 44 | California | 65.6 |
| 15 | Colorado | 74.4 |
| 33 | Connecticut | 70.4 |
| 21 | Delaware | 73.3 |
| 39 | Florida | 68.3 |
| 32 | Georgia | 70.7 |
| 50 | Hawaii | 58.9 |
| 34 | Idaho | 70.0 |
| 27 | Illinois | 72.7 |
| 36 | Indiana | 69.2 |
| 5 | Iowa | 78.2 |
| 15 | Kansas | 74.4 |
| 28 | Kentucky | 72.1 |
| 8 | Louisiana | 77.1 |
| 8 | Maine | 77.1 |
| 28 | Maryland | 72.1 |
| 4 | Massachusetts | 78.7 |
| 7 | Michigan | 77.8 |
| 2 | Minnesota | 79.0 |
| 1 | Mississippi | 84.2 |
| 10 | Missouri | 76.7 |
| 21 | Montana | 73.3 |
| 35 | Nebraska | 69.5 |
| 47 | Nevada | 65.0 |
| 11 | New Hampshire | 75.9 |
| 25 | New Jersey | 73.0 |
| 37 | New Mexico | 68.6 |
| 41 | New York | 67.9 |
| 3 | North Carolina | 78.9 |
| 14 | North Dakota | 74.5 |
| 31 | Ohio | 71.1 |
| 43 | Oklahoma | 66.1 |
| 17 | Oregon | 74.3 |
| 30 | Pennsylvania | 71.9 |
| 18 | Rhode Island | 73.5 |
| 21 | South Carolina | 73.3 |
| 12 | South Dakota | 74.8 |
| 37 | Tennessee | 68.6 |
| 42 | Texas | 66.9 |
| 49 | Utah | 63.5 |
| 20 | Vermont | 73.4 |
| 13 | Virginia | 74.6 |
| 24 | Washington | 73.1 |
| 40 | West Virginia | 68.1 |
| 6 | Wisconsin | 78.1 |
| 48 | Wyoming | 63.9 |

RANK ORDER

| RANK | STATE | PERCENT |
|---|---|---|
| 1 | Mississippi | 84.2 |
| 2 | Minnesota | 79.0 |
| 3 | North Carolina | 78.9 |
| 4 | Massachusetts | 78.7 |
| 5 | Iowa | 78.2 |
| 6 | Wisconsin | 78.1 |
| 7 | Michigan | 77.8 |
| 8 | Louisiana | 77.1 |
| 8 | Maine | 77.1 |
| 10 | Missouri | 76.7 |
| 11 | New Hampshire | 75.9 |
| 12 | South Dakota | 74.8 |
| 13 | Virginia | 74.6 |
| 14 | North Dakota | 74.5 |
| 15 | Colorado | 74.4 |
| 15 | Kansas | 74.4 |
| 17 | Oregon | 74.3 |
| 18 | Alabama | 73.5 |
| 18 | Rhode Island | 73.5 |
| 20 | Vermont | 73.4 |
| 21 | Delaware | 73.3 |
| 21 | Montana | 73.3 |
| 21 | South Carolina | 73.3 |
| 24 | Washington | 73.1 |
| 25 | New Jersey | 73.0 |
| 26 | Alaska | 72.8 |
| 27 | Illinois | 72.7 |
| 28 | Kentucky | 72.1 |
| 28 | Maryland | 72.1 |
| 30 | Pennsylvania | 71.9 |
| 31 | Ohio | 71.1 |
| 32 | Georgia | 70.7 |
| 33 | Connecticut | 70.4 |
| 34 | Idaho | 70.0 |
| 35 | Nebraska | 69.5 |
| 36 | Indiana | 69.2 |
| 37 | New Mexico | 68.6 |
| 37 | Tennessee | 68.6 |
| 39 | Florida | 68.3 |
| 40 | West Virginia | 68.1 |
| 41 | New York | 67.9 |
| 42 | Texas | 66.9 |
| 43 | Oklahoma | 66.1 |
| 44 | California | 65.6 |
| 45 | Arkansas | 65.3 |
| 46 | Arizona | 65.2 |
| 47 | Nevada | 65.0 |
| 48 | Wyoming | 63.9 |
| 49 | Utah | 63.5 |
| 50 | Hawaii | 58.9 |
| | District of Columbia | 83.4 |

Source: U.S. Bureau of the Census
"Voting and Registration" (Table 4a, http://www.census.gov/hhes/www/socdemo/voting/index.html)
*As a percent of citizen population 18 and older.

# Persons Voting in 2012

## National Total = 132,948,000

ALPHA ORDER

| RANK | STATE | VOTERS | % of USA |
|---|---|---|---|
| 24 | Alabama | 2,154,000 | 1.6% |
| 49 | Alaska | 289,000 | 0.2% |
| 22 | Arizona | 2,412,000 | 1.8% |
| 33 | Arkansas | 1,124,000 | 0.8% |
| 1 | California | 13,462,000 | 10.1% |
| 21 | Colorado | 2,495,000 | 1.9% |
| 29 | Connecticut | 1,568,000 | 1.2% |
| 45 | Delaware | 431,000 | 0.3% |
| 3 | Florida | 8,107,000 | 6.1% |
| 10 | Georgia | 4,168,000 | 3.1% |
| 43 | Hawaii | 480,000 | 0.4% |
| 41 | Idaho | 679,000 | 0.5% |
| 6 | Illinois | 5,428,000 | 4.1% |
| 18 | Indiana | 2,801,000 | 2.1% |
| 30 | Iowa | 1,548,000 | 1.2% |
| 32 | Kansas | 1,249,000 | 0.9% |
| 27 | Kentucky | 1,895,000 | 1.4% |
| 25 | Louisiana | 2,148,000 | 1.6% |
| 38 | Maine | 700,000 | 0.5% |
| 19 | Maryland | 2,609,000 | 2.0% |
| 13 | Massachusetts | 3,382,000 | 2.5% |
| 8 | Michigan | 4,832,000 | 3.6% |
| 16 | Minnesota | 2,859,000 | 2.2% |
| 28 | Mississippi | 1,588,000 | 1.2% |
| 17 | Missouri | 2,818,000 | 2.1% |
| 42 | Montana | 495,000 | 0.4% |
| 37 | Nebraska | 798,000 | 0.6% |
| 34 | Nevada | 1,048,000 | 0.8% |
| 40 | New Hampshire | 688,000 | 0.5% |
| 12 | New Jersey | 3,670,000 | 2.8% |
| 36 | New Mexico | 878,000 | 0.7% |
| 4 | New York | 7,675,000 | 5.8% |
| 9 | North Carolina | 4,624,000 | 3.5% |
| 47 | North Dakota | 328,000 | 0.2% |
| 7 | Ohio | 5,395,000 | 4.1% |
| 31 | Oklahoma | 1,431,000 | 1.1% |
| 26 | Oregon | 1,897,000 | 1.4% |
| 5 | Pennsylvania | 5,824,000 | 4.4% |
| 44 | Rhode Island | 469,000 | 0.4% |
| 23 | South Carolina | 2,187,000 | 1.6% |
| 46 | South Dakota | 370,000 | 0.3% |
| 20 | Tennessee | 2,606,000 | 2.0% |
| 2 | Texas | 8,643,000 | 6.5% |
| 35 | Utah | 1,022,000 | 0.8% |
| 48 | Vermont | 308,000 | 0.2% |
| 11 | Virginia | 3,778,000 | 2.8% |
| 14 | Washington | 3,172,000 | 2.4% |
| 39 | West Virginia | 690,000 | 0.5% |
| 15 | Wisconsin | 3,127,000 | 2.4% |
| 50 | Wyoming | 247,000 | 0.2% |

RANK ORDER

| RANK | STATE | VOTERS | % of USA |
|---|---|---|---|
| 1 | California | 13,462,000 | 10.1% |
| 2 | Texas | 8,643,000 | 6.5% |
| 3 | Florida | 8,107,000 | 6.1% |
| 4 | New York | 7,675,000 | 5.8% |
| 5 | Pennsylvania | 5,824,000 | 4.4% |
| 6 | Illinois | 5,428,000 | 4.1% |
| 7 | Ohio | 5,395,000 | 4.1% |
| 8 | Michigan | 4,832,000 | 3.6% |
| 9 | North Carolina | 4,624,000 | 3.5% |
| 10 | Georgia | 4,168,000 | 3.1% |
| 11 | Virginia | 3,778,000 | 2.8% |
| 12 | New Jersey | 3,670,000 | 2.8% |
| 13 | Massachusetts | 3,382,000 | 2.5% |
| 14 | Washington | 3,172,000 | 2.4% |
| 15 | Wisconsin | 3,127,000 | 2.4% |
| 16 | Minnesota | 2,859,000 | 2.2% |
| 17 | Missouri | 2,818,000 | 2.1% |
| 18 | Indiana | 2,801,000 | 2.1% |
| 19 | Maryland | 2,609,000 | 2.0% |
| 20 | Tennessee | 2,606,000 | 2.0% |
| 21 | Colorado | 2,495,000 | 1.9% |
| 22 | Arizona | 2,412,000 | 1.8% |
| 23 | South Carolina | 2,187,000 | 1.6% |
| 24 | Alabama | 2,154,000 | 1.6% |
| 25 | Louisiana | 2,148,000 | 1.6% |
| 26 | Oregon | 1,897,000 | 1.4% |
| 27 | Kentucky | 1,895,000 | 1.4% |
| 28 | Mississippi | 1,588,000 | 1.2% |
| 29 | Connecticut | 1,568,000 | 1.2% |
| 30 | Iowa | 1,548,000 | 1.2% |
| 31 | Oklahoma | 1,431,000 | 1.1% |
| 32 | Kansas | 1,249,000 | 0.9% |
| 33 | Arkansas | 1,124,000 | 0.8% |
| 34 | Nevada | 1,048,000 | 0.8% |
| 35 | Utah | 1,022,000 | 0.8% |
| 36 | New Mexico | 878,000 | 0.7% |
| 37 | Nebraska | 798,000 | 0.6% |
| 38 | Maine | 700,000 | 0.5% |
| 39 | West Virginia | 690,000 | 0.5% |
| 40 | New Hampshire | 688,000 | 0.5% |
| 41 | Idaho | 679,000 | 0.5% |
| 42 | Montana | 495,000 | 0.4% |
| 43 | Hawaii | 480,000 | 0.4% |
| 44 | Rhode Island | 469,000 | 0.4% |
| 45 | Delaware | 431,000 | 0.3% |
| 46 | South Dakota | 370,000 | 0.3% |
| 47 | North Dakota | 328,000 | 0.2% |
| 48 | Vermont | 308,000 | 0.2% |
| 49 | Alaska | 289,000 | 0.2% |
| 50 | Wyoming | 247,000 | 0.2% |
| | District of Columbia | 350,000 | 0.3% |

Source: U.S. Bureau of the Census
"Voting and Registration" (Table 4a, http://www.census.gov/hhes/www/socdemo/voting/index.html)

# Percent of Eligible Population Reported Voting in 2012

## National Percent = 61.8%*

| ALPHA ORDER | | | RANK ORDER | | |
|---|---|---|---|---|---|
| RANK | STATE | PERCENT | RANK | STATE | PERCENT |
| 27 | Alabama | 61.9 | 1 | Mississippi | 74.5 |
| 40 | Alaska | 58.4 | 2 | Wisconsin | 73.6 |
| 44 | Arizona | 55.9 | 3 | Minnesota | 73.2 |
| 47 | Arkansas | 53.3 | 4 | Massachusetts | 70.8 |
| 42 | California | 57.5 | 5 | Colorado | 70.4 |
| 5 | Colorado | 70.4 | 6 | Iowa | 69.4 |
| 25 | Connecticut | 62.7 | 6 | New Hampshire | 69.4 |
| 11 | Delaware | 67.3 | 8 | North Carolina | 68.9 |
| 35 | Florida | 60.8 | 9 | Maine | 68.6 |
| 27 | Georgia | 61.9 | 10 | Oregon | 67.6 |
| 49 | Hawaii | 51.6 | 11 | Delaware | 67.3 |
| 19 | Idaho | 63.9 | 12 | Virginia | 66.9 |
| 33 | Illinois | 61.5 | 13 | Michigan | 66.8 |
| 36 | Indiana | 59.3 | 14 | Louisiana | 66.3 |
| 6 | Iowa | 69.4 | 15 | Montana | 65.7 |
| 22 | Kansas | 63.3 | 16 | Washington | 65.6 |
| 36 | Kentucky | 59.3 | 17 | Maryland | 65.1 |
| 14 | Louisiana | 66.3 | 18 | South Carolina | 64.7 |
| 9 | Maine | 68.6 | 19 | Idaho | 63.9 |
| 17 | Maryland | 65.1 | 19 | Missouri | 63.9 |
| 4 | Massachusetts | 70.8 | 19 | North Dakota | 63.9 |
| 13 | Michigan | 66.8 | 22 | Kansas | 63.3 |
| 3 | Minnesota | 73.2 | 22 | Vermont | 63.3 |
| 1 | Mississippi | 74.5 | 24 | Ohio | 63.1 |
| 19 | Missouri | 63.9 | 25 | Connecticut | 62.7 |
| 15 | Montana | 65.7 | 26 | Rhode Island | 62.5 |
| 30 | Nebraska | 61.6 | 27 | Alabama | 61.9 |
| 41 | Nevada | 57.9 | 27 | Georgia | 61.9 |
| 6 | New Hampshire | 69.4 | 27 | New Jersey | 61.9 |
| 27 | New Jersey | 61.9 | 30 | Nebraska | 61.6 |
| 30 | New Mexico | 61.6 | 30 | New Mexico | 61.6 |
| 39 | New York | 58.7 | 30 | Pennsylvania | 61.6 |
| 8 | North Carolina | 68.9 | 33 | Illinois | 61.5 |
| 19 | North Dakota | 63.9 | 34 | South Dakota | 61.0 |
| 24 | Ohio | 63.1 | 35 | Florida | 60.8 |
| 48 | Oklahoma | 52.4 | 36 | Indiana | 59.3 |
| 10 | Oregon | 67.6 | 36 | Kentucky | 59.3 |
| 30 | Pennsylvania | 61.6 | 38 | Wyoming | 58.9 |
| 26 | Rhode Island | 62.5 | 39 | New York | 58.7 |
| 18 | South Carolina | 64.7 | 40 | Alaska | 58.4 |
| 34 | South Dakota | 61.0 | 41 | Nevada | 57.9 |
| 45 | Tennessee | 55.7 | 42 | California | 57.5 |
| 46 | Texas | 53.8 | 43 | Utah | 57.0 |
| 43 | Utah | 57.0 | 44 | Arizona | 55.9 |
| 22 | Vermont | 63.3 | 45 | Tennessee | 55.7 |
| 12 | Virginia | 66.9 | 46 | Texas | 53.8 |
| 16 | Washington | 65.6 | 47 | Arkansas | 53.3 |
| 50 | West Virginia | 47.8 | 48 | Oklahoma | 52.4 |
| 2 | Wisconsin | 73.6 | 49 | Hawaii | 51.6 |
| 38 | Wyoming | 58.9 | 50 | West Virginia | 47.8 |
| | | | | District of Columbia | 75.9 |

Source: U.S. Bureau of the Census
   "Voting and Registration" (Table 4a, http://www.census.gov/hhes/www/socdemo/voting/index.html)
*As a percent of citizen population 18 and older.

# Percent of Registered Population Reported Voting in 2012

## National Percent = 86.8%*

ALPHA ORDER

RANK ORDER

| RANK | STATE | PERCENT | | RANK | STATE | PERCENT |
|------|-------|---------|---|------|-------|---------|
| 41 | Alabama | 84.3 | | 1 | Colorado | 94.7 |
| 48 | Alaska | 80.1 | | 2 | Wisconsin | 94.2 |
| 33 | Arizona | 85.8 | | 3 | Minnesota | 92.7 |
| 44 | Arkansas | 81.7 | | 4 | Wyoming | 92.2 |
| 26 | California | 87.7 | | 5 | Delaware | 91.7 |
| 1 | Colorado | 94.7 | | 6 | New Hampshire | 91.5 |
| 16 | Connecticut | 89.1 | | 7 | Idaho | 91.1 |
| 5 | Delaware | 91.7 | | 8 | Oregon | 90.9 |
| 16 | Florida | 89.1 | | 9 | Maryland | 90.3 |
| 27 | Georgia | 87.4 | | 10 | Massachusetts | 90.0 |
| 25 | Hawaii | 87.8 | | 11 | New Mexico | 89.8 |
| 7 | Idaho | 91.1 | | 11 | Utah | 89.8 |
| 40 | Illinois | 84.5 | | 11 | Washington | 89.8 |
| 34 | Indiana | 85.7 | | 14 | Virginia | 89.7 |
| 21 | Iowa | 88.7 | | 15 | Montana | 89.5 |
| 37 | Kansas | 85.1 | | 16 | Connecticut | 89.1 |
| 43 | Kentucky | 82.3 | | 16 | Florida | 89.1 |
| 31 | Louisiana | 86.0 | | 16 | Nevada | 89.1 |
| 19 | Maine | 88.9 | | 19 | Maine | 88.9 |
| 9 | Maryland | 90.3 | | 20 | Ohio | 88.8 |
| 10 | Massachusetts | 90.0 | | 21 | Iowa | 88.7 |
| 31 | Michigan | 86.0 | | 22 | Nebraska | 88.6 |
| 3 | Minnesota | 92.7 | | 23 | Mississippi | 88.5 |
| 23 | Mississippi | 88.5 | | 24 | South Carolina | 88.2 |
| 42 | Missouri | 83.3 | | 25 | Hawaii | 87.8 |
| 15 | Montana | 89.5 | | 26 | California | 87.7 |
| 22 | Nebraska | 88.6 | | 27 | Georgia | 87.4 |
| 16 | Nevada | 89.1 | | 28 | North Carolina | 87.3 |
| 6 | New Hampshire | 91.5 | | 29 | New York | 86.4 |
| 39 | New Jersey | 84.8 | | 30 | Vermont | 86.3 |
| 11 | New Mexico | 89.8 | | 31 | Louisiana | 86.0 |
| 29 | New York | 86.4 | | 31 | Michigan | 86.0 |
| 28 | North Carolina | 87.3 | | 33 | Arizona | 85.8 |
| 36 | North Dakota | 85.6 | | 34 | Indiana | 85.7 |
| 20 | Ohio | 88.8 | | 34 | Pennsylvania | 85.7 |
| 49 | Oklahoma | 79.2 | | 36 | North Dakota | 85.6 |
| 8 | Oregon | 90.9 | | 37 | Kansas | 85.1 |
| 34 | Pennsylvania | 85.7 | | 38 | Rhode Island | 85.0 |
| 38 | Rhode Island | 85.0 | | 39 | New Jersey | 84.8 |
| 24 | South Carolina | 88.2 | | 40 | Illinois | 84.5 |
| 45 | South Dakota | 81.5 | | 41 | Alabama | 84.3 |
| 46 | Tennessee | 81.2 | | 42 | Missouri | 83.3 |
| 47 | Texas | 80.4 | | 43 | Kentucky | 82.3 |
| 11 | Utah | 89.8 | | 44 | Arkansas | 81.7 |
| 30 | Vermont | 86.3 | | 45 | South Dakota | 81.5 |
| 14 | Virginia | 89.7 | | 46 | Tennessee | 81.2 |
| 11 | Washington | 89.8 | | 47 | Texas | 80.4 |
| 50 | West Virginia | 70.3 | | 48 | Alaska | 80.1 |
| 2 | Wisconsin | 94.2 | | 49 | Oklahoma | 79.2 |
| 4 | Wyoming | 92.2 | | 50 | West Virginia | 70.3 |
| | | | | | District of Columbia | 90.9 |

Source: CQ Press using data from U.S. Bureau of the Census
"Voting and Registration" (Table 4a, http://www.census.gov/hhes/www/socdemo/voting/index.html)
*As a percent of citizen population 18 and older registered to vote.

# XIV. Social Welfare

# Poverty Rate in 2012

## National Rate = 15.7% of Population in Poverty*

| ALPHA ORDER | | | | RANK ORDER | | |
|---|---|---|---|---|---|---|
| RANK | STATE | PERCENT | | RANK | STATE | PERCENT |
| 6 | Alabama | 19.0 | | 1 | Mississippi | 23.0 |
| 48 | Alaska | 10.2 | | 2 | New Mexico | 21.0 |
| 9 | Arizona | 18.3 | | 3 | Louisiana | 19.6 |
| 4 | Arkansas | 19.3 | | 4 | Arkansas | 19.3 |
| 18 | California | 16.4 | | 5 | Kentucky | 19.2 |
| 33 | Colorado | 13.5 | | 6 | Alabama | 19.0 |
| 46 | Connecticut | 10.5 | | 7 | Georgia | 18.7 |
| 40 | Delaware | 11.9 | | 8 | South Carolina | 18.5 |
| 16 | Florida | 16.8 | | 9 | Arizona | 18.3 |
| 7 | Georgia | 18.7 | | 10 | Texas | 18.1 |
| 44 | Hawaii | 11.5 | | 10 | West Virginia | 18.1 |
| 19 | Idaho | 16.1 | | 12 | Tennessee | 17.9 |
| 26 | Illinois | 14.5 | | 13 | North Carolina | 17.8 |
| 23 | Indiana | 15.6 | | 14 | Michigan | 17.3 |
| 37 | Iowa | 12.7 | | 15 | Oklahoma | 17.1 |
| 30 | Kansas | 13.8 | | 16 | Florida | 16.8 |
| 5 | Kentucky | 19.2 | | 16 | Oregon | 16.8 |
| 3 | Louisiana | 19.6 | | 18 | California | 16.4 |
| 28 | Maine | 14.0 | | 19 | Idaho | 16.1 |
| 49 | Maryland | 10.1 | | 19 | Ohio | 16.1 |
| 43 | Massachusetts | 11.6 | | 21 | Nevada | 15.8 |
| 14 | Michigan | 17.3 | | 22 | Missouri | 15.7 |
| 42 | Minnesota | 11.7 | | 23 | Indiana | 15.6 |
| 1 | Mississippi | 23.0 | | 23 | New York | 15.6 |
| 22 | Missouri | 15.7 | | 25 | Montana | 15.2 |
| 25 | Montana | 15.2 | | 26 | Illinois | 14.5 |
| 36 | Nebraska | 13.0 | | 27 | Rhode Island | 14.2 |
| 21 | Nevada | 15.8 | | 28 | Maine | 14.0 |
| 50 | New Hampshire | 8.9 | | 29 | South Dakota | 13.9 |
| 46 | New Jersey | 10.5 | | 30 | Kansas | 13.8 |
| 2 | New Mexico | 21.0 | | 31 | Washington | 13.7 |
| 23 | New York | 15.6 | | 32 | Pennsylvania | 13.6 |
| 13 | North Carolina | 17.8 | | 33 | Colorado | 13.5 |
| 38 | North Dakota | 12.2 | | 34 | Utah | 13.2 |
| 19 | Ohio | 16.1 | | 34 | Wisconsin | 13.2 |
| 15 | Oklahoma | 17.1 | | 36 | Nebraska | 13.0 |
| 16 | Oregon | 16.8 | | 37 | Iowa | 12.7 |
| 32 | Pennsylvania | 13.6 | | 38 | North Dakota | 12.2 |
| 27 | Rhode Island | 14.2 | | 39 | Vermont | 12.0 |
| 8 | South Carolina | 18.5 | | 40 | Delaware | 11.9 |
| 29 | South Dakota | 13.9 | | 40 | Wyoming | 11.9 |
| 12 | Tennessee | 17.9 | | 42 | Minnesota | 11.7 |
| 10 | Texas | 18.1 | | 43 | Massachusetts | 11.6 |
| 34 | Utah | 13.2 | | 44 | Hawaii | 11.5 |
| 39 | Vermont | 12.0 | | 44 | Virginia | 11.5 |
| 44 | Virginia | 11.5 | | 46 | Connecticut | 10.5 |
| 31 | Washington | 13.7 | | 46 | New Jersey | 10.5 |
| 10 | West Virginia | 18.1 | | 48 | Alaska | 10.2 |
| 34 | Wisconsin | 13.2 | | 49 | Maryland | 10.1 |
| 40 | Wyoming | 11.9 | | 50 | New Hampshire | 8.9 |
| | | | | | District of Columbia | 18.8 |

Source: U.S. Bureau of the Census

"2012 American Community Survey-Table GCT1701" (http://www.census.gov/acs/www/index.html)

*Three-year average: 2010-2012.  The poverty threshold for a family of four (two children) in 2012 was $23,283.

# Percent of Senior Citizens Living in Poverty in 2012

## National Percent = 9.5%*

ALPHA ORDER

| RANK | STATE | PERCENT |
|------|-------|---------|
| 8 | Alabama | 11.1 |
| 50 | Alaska | 4.4 |
| 25 | Arizona | 8.3 |
| 9 | Arkansas | 10.9 |
| 11 | California | 10.4 |
| 34 | Colorado | 7.8 |
| 44 | Connecticut | 6.9 |
| 41 | Delaware | 7.4 |
| 12 | Florida | 10.2 |
| 7 | Georgia | 11.2 |
| 44 | Hawaii | 6.9 |
| 18 | Idaho | 9.7 |
| 22 | Illinois | 8.8 |
| 43 | Indiana | 7.2 |
| 34 | Iowa | 7.8 |
| 47 | Kansas | 6.7 |
| 3 | Kentucky | 12.3 |
| 2 | Louisiana | 12.6 |
| 28 | Maine | 8.2 |
| 37 | Maryland | 7.6 |
| 20 | Massachusetts | 9.3 |
| 25 | Michigan | 8.3 |
| 31 | Minnesota | 7.9 |
| 1 | Mississippi | 15.1 |
| 21 | Missouri | 9.0 |
| 24 | Montana | 8.6 |
| 41 | Nebraska | 7.4 |
| 29 | Nevada | 8.1 |
| 48 | New Hampshire | 6.6 |
| 31 | New Jersey | 7.9 |
| 4 | New Mexico | 11.9 |
| 6 | New York | 11.4 |
| 14 | North Carolina | 10.0 |
| 10 | North Dakota | 10.6 |
| 30 | Ohio | 8.0 |
| 17 | Oklahoma | 9.9 |
| 38 | Oregon | 7.5 |
| 25 | Pennsylvania | 8.3 |
| 18 | Rhode Island | 9.7 |
| 13 | South Carolina | 10.1 |
| 14 | South Dakota | 10.0 |
| 14 | Tennessee | 10.0 |
| 5 | Texas | 11.6 |
| 46 | Utah | 6.8 |
| 38 | Vermont | 7.5 |
| 31 | Virginia | 7.9 |
| 34 | Washington | 7.8 |
| 22 | West Virginia | 8.8 |
| 38 | Wisconsin | 7.5 |
| 49 | Wyoming | 4.8 |

RANK ORDER

| RANK | STATE | PERCENT |
|------|-------|---------|
| 1 | Mississippi | 15.1 |
| 2 | Louisiana | 12.6 |
| 3 | Kentucky | 12.3 |
| 4 | New Mexico | 11.9 |
| 5 | Texas | 11.6 |
| 6 | New York | 11.4 |
| 7 | Georgia | 11.2 |
| 8 | Alabama | 11.1 |
| 9 | Arkansas | 10.9 |
| 10 | North Dakota | 10.6 |
| 11 | California | 10.4 |
| 12 | Florida | 10.2 |
| 13 | South Carolina | 10.1 |
| 14 | North Carolina | 10.0 |
| 14 | South Dakota | 10.0 |
| 14 | Tennessee | 10.0 |
| 17 | Oklahoma | 9.9 |
| 18 | Idaho | 9.7 |
| 18 | Rhode Island | 9.7 |
| 20 | Massachusetts | 9.3 |
| 21 | Missouri | 9.0 |
| 22 | Illinois | 8.8 |
| 22 | West Virginia | 8.8 |
| 24 | Montana | 8.6 |
| 25 | Arizona | 8.3 |
| 25 | Michigan | 8.3 |
| 25 | Pennsylvania | 8.3 |
| 28 | Maine | 8.2 |
| 29 | Nevada | 8.1 |
| 30 | Ohio | 8.0 |
| 31 | Minnesota | 7.9 |
| 31 | New Jersey | 7.9 |
| 31 | Virginia | 7.9 |
| 34 | Colorado | 7.8 |
| 34 | Iowa | 7.8 |
| 34 | Washington | 7.8 |
| 37 | Maryland | 7.6 |
| 38 | Oregon | 7.5 |
| 38 | Vermont | 7.5 |
| 38 | Wisconsin | 7.5 |
| 41 | Delaware | 7.4 |
| 41 | Nebraska | 7.4 |
| 43 | Indiana | 7.2 |
| 44 | Connecticut | 6.9 |
| 44 | Hawaii | 6.9 |
| 46 | Utah | 6.8 |
| 47 | Kansas | 6.7 |
| 48 | New Hampshire | 6.6 |
| 49 | Wyoming | 4.8 |
| 50 | Alaska | 4.4 |
| | District of Columbia | 11.9 |

Source: U.S. Bureau of the Census
"2012 American Community Survey-Table GCT1703" (http://www.census.gov/acs/www/index.html)
*People 65 years and older living with incomes below the poverty level.

# Percent of Children Living in Poverty in 2012

## National Percent = 22.3%*

ALPHA ORDER

| RANK | STATE | PERCENT |
|------|-------|---------|
| 5 | Alabama | 27.3 |
| 48 | Alaska | 13.5 |
| 8 | Arizona | 26.6 |
| 3 | Arkansas | 28.1 |
| 18 | California | 23.5 |
| 31 | Colorado | 18.1 |
| 46 | Connecticut | 14.6 |
| 35 | Delaware | 17.1 |
| 13 | Florida | 25.1 |
| 6 | Georgia | 27.0 |
| 37 | Hawaii | 16.6 |
| 24 | Idaho | 20.4 |
| 24 | Illinois | 20.4 |
| 23 | Indiana | 22.0 |
| 39 | Iowa | 15.6 |
| 30 | Kansas | 18.7 |
| 9 | Kentucky | 26.2 |
| 4 | Louisiana | 28.0 |
| 24 | Maine | 20.4 |
| 48 | Maryland | 13.5 |
| 42 | Massachusetts | 15.0 |
| 14 | Michigan | 24.5 |
| 47 | Minnesota | 14.2 |
| 1 | Mississippi | 34.6 |
| 22 | Missouri | 22.2 |
| 27 | Montana | 19.8 |
| 34 | Nebraska | 17.5 |
| 17 | Nevada | 23.6 |
| 41 | New Hampshire | 15.1 |
| 40 | New Jersey | 15.2 |
| 2 | New Mexico | 29.2 |
| 20 | New York | 22.6 |
| 10 | North Carolina | 25.7 |
| 50 | North Dakota | 12.9 |
| 19 | Ohio | 23.4 |
| 16 | Oklahoma | 23.8 |
| 20 | Oregon | 22.6 |
| 28 | Pennsylvania | 19.4 |
| 29 | Rhode Island | 19.0 |
| 7 | South Carolina | 26.7 |
| 36 | South Dakota | 17.0 |
| 11 | Tennessee | 25.5 |
| 11 | Texas | 25.5 |
| 45 | Utah | 14.8 |
| 44 | Vermont | 14.9 |
| 42 | Virginia | 15.0 |
| 31 | Washington | 18.1 |
| 15 | West Virginia | 24.2 |
| 33 | Wisconsin | 17.9 |
| 37 | Wyoming | 16.6 |

RANK ORDER

| RANK | STATE | PERCENT |
|------|-------|---------|
| 1 | Mississippi | 34.6 |
| 2 | New Mexico | 29.2 |
| 3 | Arkansas | 28.1 |
| 4 | Louisiana | 28.0 |
| 5 | Alabama | 27.3 |
| 6 | Georgia | 27.0 |
| 7 | South Carolina | 26.7 |
| 8 | Arizona | 26.6 |
| 9 | Kentucky | 26.2 |
| 10 | North Carolina | 25.7 |
| 11 | Tennessee | 25.5 |
| 11 | Texas | 25.5 |
| 13 | Florida | 25.1 |
| 14 | Michigan | 24.5 |
| 15 | West Virginia | 24.2 |
| 16 | Oklahoma | 23.8 |
| 17 | Nevada | 23.6 |
| 18 | California | 23.5 |
| 19 | Ohio | 23.4 |
| 20 | New York | 22.6 |
| 20 | Oregon | 22.6 |
| 22 | Missouri | 22.2 |
| 23 | Indiana | 22.0 |
| 24 | Idaho | 20.4 |
| 24 | Illinois | 20.4 |
| 24 | Maine | 20.4 |
| 27 | Montana | 19.8 |
| 28 | Pennsylvania | 19.4 |
| 29 | Rhode Island | 19.0 |
| 30 | Kansas | 18.7 |
| 31 | Colorado | 18.1 |
| 31 | Washington | 18.1 |
| 33 | Wisconsin | 17.9 |
| 34 | Nebraska | 17.5 |
| 35 | Delaware | 17.1 |
| 36 | South Dakota | 17.0 |
| 37 | Hawaii | 16.6 |
| 37 | Wyoming | 16.6 |
| 39 | Iowa | 15.6 |
| 40 | New Jersey | 15.2 |
| 41 | New Hampshire | 15.1 |
| 42 | Massachusetts | 15.0 |
| 42 | Virginia | 15.0 |
| 44 | Vermont | 14.9 |
| 45 | Utah | 14.8 |
| 46 | Connecticut | 14.6 |
| 47 | Minnesota | 14.2 |
| 48 | Alaska | 13.5 |
| 48 | Maryland | 13.5 |
| 50 | North Dakota | 12.9 |
| | District of Columbia | 26.4 |

Source: U.S. Bureau of the Census
 "2012 American Community Survey-Table GCT1702" (http://www.census.gov/acs/www/index.html)
*Children 17 and under living in families with incomes below the poverty level.

# Percent of Families Living in Poverty in 2012

## National Percent = 11.6%*

ALPHA ORDER

| RANK | STATE | PERCENT |
|------|-------|---------|
| 4 | Alabama | 14.8 |
| 48 | Alaska | 7.2 |
| 11 | Arizona | 13.4 |
| 6 | Arkansas | 14.5 |
| 16 | California | 12.3 |
| 33 | Colorado | 9.2 |
| 44 | Connecticut | 7.7 |
| 41 | Delaware | 8.0 |
| 16 | Florida | 12.3 |
| 7 | Georgia | 14.4 |
| 40 | Hawaii | 8.1 |
| 21 | Idaho | 11.7 |
| 25 | Illinois | 10.6 |
| 23 | Indiana | 11.2 |
| 37 | Iowa | 8.4 |
| 30 | Kansas | 9.4 |
| 5 | Kentucky | 14.6 |
| 3 | Louisiana | 15.3 |
| 31 | Maine | 9.3 |
| 49 | Maryland | 7.0 |
| 38 | Massachusetts | 8.3 |
| 15 | Michigan | 12.4 |
| 45 | Minnesota | 7.6 |
| 1 | Mississippi | 18.2 |
| 23 | Missouri | 11.2 |
| 26 | Montana | 10.0 |
| 36 | Nebraska | 8.9 |
| 19 | Nevada | 11.9 |
| 50 | New Hampshire | 5.9 |
| 43 | New Jersey | 7.9 |
| 2 | New Mexico | 16.4 |
| 18 | New York | 12.0 |
| 12 | North Carolina | 13.3 |
| 45 | North Dakota | 7.6 |
| 20 | Ohio | 11.8 |
| 14 | Oklahoma | 12.8 |
| 21 | Oregon | 11.7 |
| 29 | Pennsylvania | 9.5 |
| 28 | Rhode Island | 9.7 |
| 8 | South Carolina | 14.1 |
| 34 | South Dakota | 9.1 |
| 10 | Tennessee | 13.6 |
| 8 | Texas | 14.1 |
| 27 | Utah | 9.9 |
| 45 | Vermont | 7.6 |
| 39 | Virginia | 8.2 |
| 31 | Washington | 9.3 |
| 13 | West Virginia | 13.1 |
| 35 | Wisconsin | 9.0 |
| 41 | Wyoming | 8.0 |

RANK ORDER

| RANK | STATE | PERCENT |
|------|-------|---------|
| 1 | Mississippi | 18.2 |
| 2 | New Mexico | 16.4 |
| 3 | Louisiana | 15.3 |
| 4 | Alabama | 14.8 |
| 5 | Kentucky | 14.6 |
| 6 | Arkansas | 14.5 |
| 7 | Georgia | 14.4 |
| 8 | South Carolina | 14.1 |
| 8 | Texas | 14.1 |
| 10 | Tennessee | 13.6 |
| 11 | Arizona | 13.4 |
| 12 | North Carolina | 13.3 |
| 13 | West Virginia | 13.1 |
| 14 | Oklahoma | 12.8 |
| 15 | Michigan | 12.4 |
| 16 | California | 12.3 |
| 16 | Florida | 12.3 |
| 18 | New York | 12.0 |
| 19 | Nevada | 11.9 |
| 20 | Ohio | 11.8 |
| 21 | Idaho | 11.7 |
| 21 | Oregon | 11.7 |
| 23 | Indiana | 11.2 |
| 23 | Missouri | 11.2 |
| 25 | Illinois | 10.6 |
| 26 | Montana | 10.0 |
| 27 | Utah | 9.9 |
| 28 | Rhode Island | 9.7 |
| 29 | Pennsylvania | 9.5 |
| 30 | Kansas | 9.4 |
| 31 | Maine | 9.3 |
| 31 | Washington | 9.3 |
| 33 | Colorado | 9.2 |
| 34 | South Dakota | 9.1 |
| 35 | Wisconsin | 9.0 |
| 36 | Nebraska | 8.9 |
| 37 | Iowa | 8.4 |
| 38 | Massachusetts | 8.3 |
| 39 | Virginia | 8.2 |
| 40 | Hawaii | 8.1 |
| 41 | Delaware | 8.0 |
| 41 | Wyoming | 8.0 |
| 43 | New Jersey | 7.9 |
| 44 | Connecticut | 7.7 |
| 45 | Minnesota | 7.6 |
| 45 | North Dakota | 7.6 |
| 45 | Vermont | 7.6 |
| 48 | Alaska | 7.2 |
| 49 | Maryland | 7.0 |
| 50 | New Hampshire | 5.9 |
| | District of Columbia | 14.6 |

Source: U.S. Bureau of the Census
   "2012 American Community Survey-Table DP03" (http://www.census.gov/acs/www/index.html)
*Families living with incomes below the poverty level.

# Percent of Female-Headed Families with Children Living in Poverty in 2012

## National Percent = 40.6%*

<u>ALPHA ORDER</u>

| RANK | STATE | PERCENT |
|------|-------|---------|
| 2 | Alabama | 49.8 |
| 49 | Alaska | 27.3 |
| 24 | Arizona | 40.1 |
| 5 | Arkansas | 48.4 |
| 34 | California | 37.4 |
| 40 | Colorado | 35.8 |
| 47 | Connecticut | 31.7 |
| 48 | Delaware | 30.7 |
| 32 | Florida | 38.4 |
| 15 | Georgia | 43.9 |
| 46 | Hawaii | 31.8 |
| 13 | Idaho | 44.6 |
| 22 | Illinois | 40.3 |
| 17 | Indiana | 43.0 |
| 29 | Iowa | 39.3 |
| 24 | Kansas | 40.1 |
| 4 | Kentucky | 49.7 |
| 5 | Louisiana | 48.4 |
| 27 | Maine | 39.5 |
| 50 | Maryland | 26.5 |
| 41 | Massachusetts | 35.7 |
| 8 | Michigan | 45.9 |
| 39 | Minnesota | 36.4 |
| 1 | Mississippi | 52.4 |
| 19 | Missouri | 41.9 |
| 19 | Montana | 41.9 |
| 30 | Nebraska | 38.8 |
| 42 | Nevada | 34.4 |
| 45 | New Hampshire | 32.1 |
| 44 | New Jersey | 33.2 |
| 10 | New Mexico | 45.4 |
| 33 | New York | 38.3 |
| 13 | North Carolina | 44.6 |
| 21 | North Dakota | 40.9 |
| 9 | Ohio | 45.7 |
| 12 | Oklahoma | 44.7 |
| 16 | Oregon | 43.7 |
| 23 | Pennsylvania | 40.2 |
| 36 | Rhode Island | 37.0 |
| 7 | South Carolina | 46.3 |
| 31 | South Dakota | 38.5 |
| 10 | Tennessee | 45.4 |
| 18 | Texas | 42.3 |
| 35 | Utah | 37.2 |
| 37 | Vermont | 36.9 |
| 43 | Virginia | 34.0 |
| 37 | Washington | 36.9 |
| 2 | West Virginia | 49.8 |
| 26 | Wisconsin | 39.7 |
| 28 | Wyoming | 39.4 |

<u>RANK ORDER</u>

| RANK | STATE | PERCENT |
|------|-------|---------|
| 1 | Mississippi | 52.4 |
| 2 | Alabama | 49.8 |
| 2 | West Virginia | 49.8 |
| 4 | Kentucky | 49.7 |
| 5 | Arkansas | 48.4 |
| 5 | Louisiana | 48.4 |
| 7 | South Carolina | 46.3 |
| 8 | Michigan | 45.9 |
| 9 | Ohio | 45.7 |
| 10 | New Mexico | 45.4 |
| 10 | Tennessee | 45.4 |
| 12 | Oklahoma | 44.7 |
| 13 | Idaho | 44.6 |
| 13 | North Carolina | 44.6 |
| 15 | Georgia | 43.9 |
| 16 | Oregon | 43.7 |
| 17 | Indiana | 43.0 |
| 18 | Texas | 42.3 |
| 19 | Missouri | 41.9 |
| 19 | Montana | 41.9 |
| 21 | North Dakota | 40.9 |
| 22 | Illinois | 40.3 |
| 23 | Pennsylvania | 40.2 |
| 24 | Arizona | 40.1 |
| 24 | Kansas | 40.1 |
| 26 | Wisconsin | 39.7 |
| 27 | Maine | 39.5 |
| 28 | Wyoming | 39.4 |
| 29 | Iowa | 39.3 |
| 30 | Nebraska | 38.8 |
| 31 | South Dakota | 38.5 |
| 32 | Florida | 38.4 |
| 33 | New York | 38.3 |
| 34 | California | 37.4 |
| 35 | Utah | 37.2 |
| 36 | Rhode Island | 37.0 |
| 37 | Vermont | 36.9 |
| 37 | Washington | 36.9 |
| 39 | Minnesota | 36.4 |
| 40 | Colorado | 35.8 |
| 41 | Massachusetts | 35.7 |
| 42 | Nevada | 34.4 |
| 43 | Virginia | 34.0 |
| 44 | New Jersey | 33.2 |
| 45 | New Hampshire | 32.1 |
| 46 | Hawaii | 31.8 |
| 47 | Connecticut | 31.7 |
| 48 | Delaware | 30.7 |
| 49 | Alaska | 27.3 |
| 50 | Maryland | 26.5 |
| | District of Columbia | 38.6 |

Source: U.S. Bureau of the Census
   "2012 American Community Survey-Table DP03" (http://www.census.gov/acs/www/index.html)
*Households headed by females with own children under 18 years living with them with incomes below the poverty level as a percent of all such female-headed households.

# State and Local Government Expenditures for Public Welfare Programs in 2011

## National Total = $492,007,114,000*

| ALPHA ORDER | | | | | RANK ORDER | | | |
|---|---|---|---|---|---|---|---|---|
| RANK | STATE | EXPENDITURES | % of USA | | RANK | STATE | EXPENDITURES | % of USA |
| 26 | Alabama | $5,940,027,000 | 1.2% | | 1 | California | $67,669,710,000 | 13.8% |
| 44 | Alaska | 1,857,227,000 | 0.4% | | 2 | New York | 50,390,083,000 | 10.2% |
| 18 | Arizona | 9,205,490,000 | 1.9% | | 3 | Texas | 30,825,703,000 | 6.3% |
| 32 | Arkansas | 4,501,060,000 | 0.9% | | 4 | Pennsylvania | 25,676,334,000 | 5.2% |
| 1 | California | 67,669,710,000 | 13.8% | | 5 | Florida | 23,542,869,000 | 4.8% |
| 30 | Colorado | 4,944,789,000 | 1.0% | | 6 | Ohio | 20,287,667,000 | 4.1% |
| 25 | Connecticut | 6,157,405,000 | 1.3% | | 7 | Illinois | 18,488,172,000 | 3.8% |
| 45 | Delaware | 1,755,102,000 | 0.4% | | 8 | Massachusetts | 14,508,196,000 | 2.9% |
| 5 | Florida | 23,542,869,000 | 4.8% | | 9 | New Jersey | 14,372,123,000 | 2.9% |
| 14 | Georgia | 10,119,428,000 | 2.1% | | 10 | Michigan | 13,293,251,000 | 2.7% |
| 42 | Hawaii | 2,147,032,000 | 0.4% | | 11 | Minnesota | 11,889,794,000 | 2.4% |
| 40 | Idaho | 2,210,201,000 | 0.4% | | 12 | North Carolina | 11,388,371,000 | 2.3% |
| 7 | Illinois | 18,488,172,000 | 3.8% | | 13 | Virginia | 10,188,489,000 | 2.1% |
| 20 | Indiana | 8,495,515,000 | 1.7% | | 14 | Georgia | 10,119,428,000 | 2.1% |
| 31 | Iowa | 4,830,388,000 | 1.0% | | 15 | Tennessee | 10,059,567,000 | 2.0% |
| 34 | Kansas | 3,566,432,000 | 0.7% | | 16 | Wisconsin | 10,035,317,000 | 2.0% |
| 22 | Kentucky | 7,235,398,000 | 1.5% | | 17 | Maryland | 9,502,330,000 | 1.9% |
| 24 | Louisiana | 6,417,506,000 | 1.3% | | 18 | Arizona | 9,205,490,000 | 1.9% |
| 36 | Maine | 2,926,188,000 | 0.6% | | 19 | Washington | 8,851,696,000 | 1.8% |
| 17 | Maryland | 9,502,330,000 | 1.9% | | 20 | Indiana | 8,495,515,000 | 1.7% |
| 8 | Massachusetts | 14,508,196,000 | 2.9% | | 21 | Missouri | 7,740,656,000 | 1.6% |
| 10 | Michigan | 13,293,251,000 | 2.7% | | 22 | Kentucky | 7,235,398,000 | 1.5% |
| 11 | Minnesota | 11,889,794,000 | 2.4% | | 23 | South Carolina | 6,812,062,000 | 1.4% |
| 29 | Mississippi | 5,180,726,000 | 1.1% | | 24 | Louisiana | 6,417,506,000 | 1.3% |
| 21 | Missouri | 7,740,656,000 | 1.6% | | 25 | Connecticut | 6,157,405,000 | 1.3% |
| 47 | Montana | 1,411,016,000 | 0.3% | | 26 | Alabama | 5,940,027,000 | 1.2% |
| 41 | Nebraska | 2,178,328,000 | 0.4% | | 27 | Oregon | 5,672,523,000 | 1.2% |
| 38 | Nevada | 2,346,121,000 | 0.5% | | 28 | Oklahoma | 5,433,864,000 | 1.1% |
| 43 | New Hampshire | 2,092,820,000 | 0.4% | | 29 | Mississippi | 5,180,726,000 | 1.1% |
| 9 | New Jersey | 14,372,123,000 | 2.9% | | 30 | Colorado | 4,944,789,000 | 1.0% |
| 33 | New Mexico | 4,429,189,000 | 0.9% | | 31 | Iowa | 4,830,388,000 | 1.0% |
| 2 | New York | 50,390,083,000 | 10.2% | | 32 | Arkansas | 4,501,060,000 | 0.9% |
| 12 | North Carolina | 11,388,371,000 | 2.3% | | 33 | New Mexico | 4,429,189,000 | 0.9% |
| 49 | North Dakota | 961,866,000 | 0.2% | | 34 | Kansas | 3,566,432,000 | 0.7% |
| 6 | Ohio | 20,287,667,000 | 4.1% | | 35 | West Virginia | 3,237,674,000 | 0.7% |
| 28 | Oklahoma | 5,433,864,000 | 1.1% | | 36 | Maine | 2,926,188,000 | 0.6% |
| 27 | Oregon | 5,672,523,000 | 1.2% | | 37 | Utah | 2,863,288,000 | 0.6% |
| 4 | Pennsylvania | 25,676,334,000 | 5.2% | | 38 | Nevada | 2,346,121,000 | 0.5% |
| 39 | Rhode Island | 2,332,616,000 | 0.5% | | 39 | Rhode Island | 2,332,616,000 | 0.5% |
| 23 | South Carolina | 6,812,062,000 | 1.4% | | 40 | Idaho | 2,210,201,000 | 0.4% |
| 48 | South Dakota | 973,120,000 | 0.2% | | 41 | Nebraska | 2,178,328,000 | 0.4% |
| 15 | Tennessee | 10,059,567,000 | 2.0% | | 42 | Hawaii | 2,147,032,000 | 0.4% |
| 3 | Texas | 30,825,703,000 | 6.3% | | 43 | New Hampshire | 2,092,820,000 | 0.4% |
| 37 | Utah | 2,863,288,000 | 0.6% | | 44 | Alaska | 1,857,227,000 | 0.4% |
| 46 | Vermont | 1,464,380,000 | 0.3% | | 45 | Delaware | 1,755,102,000 | 0.4% |
| 13 | Virginia | 10,188,489,000 | 2.1% | | 46 | Vermont | 1,464,380,000 | 0.3% |
| 19 | Washington | 8,851,696,000 | 1.8% | | 47 | Montana | 1,411,016,000 | 0.3% |
| 35 | West Virginia | 3,237,674,000 | 0.7% | | 48 | South Dakota | 973,120,000 | 0.2% |
| 16 | Wisconsin | 10,035,317,000 | 2.0% | | 49 | North Dakota | 961,866,000 | 0.2% |
| 50 | Wyoming | 764,252,000 | 0.2% | | 50 | Wyoming | 764,252,000 | 0.2% |
| | | | | | | District of Columbia | 2,833,753,000 | 0.6% |

Source: U.S. Bureau of the Census, Governments Division
    "2011 State and Local Government Finances" (http://www.census.gov/govs/local/)
*Direct general expenditures. Includes funds for cash assistance programs, medical and other vendor payments, welfare institutions, and other public welfare programs.

# Per Capita State and Local Government Expenditures
## for Public Welfare Programs in 2011
## National Per Capita = $1,579*

ALPHA ORDER

| RANK | STATE | PER CAPITA |
|------|-------|-----------|
| 41 | Alabama | $1,237 |
| 2 | Alaska | 2,566 |
| 29 | Arizona | 1,423 |
| 24 | Arkansas | 1,532 |
| 11 | California | 1,796 |
| 49 | Colorado | 966 |
| 16 | Connecticut | 1,717 |
| 10 | Delaware | 1,933 |
| 42 | Florida | 1,234 |
| 47 | Georgia | 1,031 |
| 23 | Hawaii | 1,558 |
| 33 | Idaho | 1,396 |
| 27 | Illinois | 1,438 |
| 36 | Indiana | 1,304 |
| 21 | Iowa | 1,576 |
| 40 | Kansas | 1,242 |
| 17 | Kentucky | 1,657 |
| 32 | Louisiana | 1,403 |
| 6 | Maine | 2,203 |
| 18 | Maryland | 1,627 |
| 7 | Massachusetts | 2,196 |
| 35 | Michigan | 1,346 |
| 4 | Minnesota | 2,224 |
| 15 | Mississippi | 1,740 |
| 38 | Missouri | 1,288 |
| 30 | Montana | 1,414 |
| 44 | Nebraska | 1,182 |
| 50 | Nevada | 863 |
| 20 | New Hampshire | 1,588 |
| 18 | New Jersey | 1,627 |
| 8 | New Mexico | 2,131 |
| 1 | New York | 2,584 |
| 46 | North Carolina | 1,180 |
| 31 | North Dakota | 1,405 |
| 12 | Ohio | 1,758 |
| 28 | Oklahoma | 1,436 |
| 25 | Oregon | 1,466 |
| 9 | Pennsylvania | 2,015 |
| 5 | Rhode Island | 2,220 |
| 26 | South Carolina | 1,458 |
| 44 | South Dakota | 1,182 |
| 22 | Tennessee | 1,572 |
| 43 | Texas | 1,203 |
| 48 | Utah | 1,017 |
| 3 | Vermont | 2,337 |
| 39 | Virginia | 1,257 |
| 37 | Washington | 1,297 |
| 14 | West Virginia | 1,745 |
| 12 | Wisconsin | 1,758 |
| 34 | Wyoming | 1,347 |

RANK ORDER

| RANK | STATE | PER CAPITA |
|------|-------|-----------|
| 1 | New York | $2,584 |
| 2 | Alaska | 2,566 |
| 3 | Vermont | 2,337 |
| 4 | Minnesota | 2,224 |
| 5 | Rhode Island | 2,220 |
| 6 | Maine | 2,203 |
| 7 | Massachusetts | 2,196 |
| 8 | New Mexico | 2,131 |
| 9 | Pennsylvania | 2,015 |
| 10 | Delaware | 1,933 |
| 11 | California | 1,796 |
| 12 | Ohio | 1,758 |
| 12 | Wisconsin | 1,758 |
| 14 | West Virginia | 1,745 |
| 15 | Mississippi | 1,740 |
| 16 | Connecticut | 1,717 |
| 17 | Kentucky | 1,657 |
| 18 | Maryland | 1,627 |
| 18 | New Jersey | 1,627 |
| 20 | New Hampshire | 1,588 |
| 21 | Iowa | 1,576 |
| 22 | Tennessee | 1,572 |
| 23 | Hawaii | 1,558 |
| 24 | Arkansas | 1,532 |
| 25 | Oregon | 1,466 |
| 26 | South Carolina | 1,458 |
| 27 | Illinois | 1,438 |
| 28 | Oklahoma | 1,436 |
| 29 | Arizona | 1,423 |
| 30 | Montana | 1,414 |
| 31 | North Dakota | 1,405 |
| 32 | Louisiana | 1,403 |
| 33 | Idaho | 1,396 |
| 34 | Wyoming | 1,347 |
| 35 | Michigan | 1,346 |
| 36 | Indiana | 1,304 |
| 37 | Washington | 1,297 |
| 38 | Missouri | 1,288 |
| 39 | Virginia | 1,257 |
| 40 | Kansas | 1,242 |
| 41 | Alabama | 1,237 |
| 42 | Florida | 1,234 |
| 43 | Texas | 1,203 |
| 44 | Nebraska | 1,182 |
| 44 | South Dakota | 1,182 |
| 46 | North Carolina | 1,180 |
| 47 | Georgia | 1,031 |
| 48 | Utah | 1,017 |
| 49 | Colorado | 966 |
| 50 | Nevada | 863 |

District of Columbia — 4,578

Source: CQ Press using data from U.S. Bureau of the Census, Governments Division

"2011 State and Local Government Finances" (http://www.census.gov/govs/local/)

*Direct general expenditures. Includes funds for cash assistance programs, medical and other vendor payments, welfare institutions, and other public welfare programs.

# State and Local Government Spending for Public Welfare Programs as a Percent of All State and Local Government Expenditures in 2011
## National Percent = 19.0%*

ALPHA ORDER

| RANK | STATE | PERCENT |
|------|-------|---------|
| 36 | Alabama | 16.8 |
| 46 | Alaska | 14.5 |
| 13 | Arizona | 21.6 |
| 11 | Arkansas | 21.7 |
| 21 | California | 19.1 |
| 49 | Colorado | 12.0 |
| 25 | Connecticut | 18.5 |
| 19 | Delaware | 20.4 |
| 34 | Florida | 17.1 |
| 39 | Georgia | 15.8 |
| 31 | Hawaii | 17.6 |
| 16 | Idaho | 21.1 |
| 30 | Illinois | 17.7 |
| 25 | Indiana | 18.5 |
| 27 | Iowa | 18.3 |
| 41 | Kansas | 15.5 |
| 9 | Kentucky | 22.4 |
| 43 | Louisiana | 15.0 |
| 1 | Maine | 25.8 |
| 21 | Maryland | 19.1 |
| 6 | Massachusetts | 23.6 |
| 28 | Michigan | 18.0 |
| 3 | Minnesota | 25.2 |
| 11 | Mississippi | 21.7 |
| 24 | Missouri | 18.7 |
| 33 | Montana | 17.4 |
| 43 | Nebraska | 15.0 |
| 48 | Nevada | 12.5 |
| 19 | New Hampshire | 20.4 |
| 31 | New Jersey | 17.6 |
| 8 | New Mexico | 22.8 |
| 15 | New York | 21.4 |
| 35 | North Carolina | 16.9 |
| 43 | North Dakota | 15.0 |
| 14 | Ohio | 21.5 |
| 16 | Oklahoma | 21.1 |
| 29 | Oregon | 17.8 |
| 6 | Pennsylvania | 23.6 |
| 2 | Rhode Island | 25.3 |
| 21 | South Carolina | 19.1 |
| 39 | South Dakota | 15.8 |
| 4 | Tennessee | 23.9 |
| 38 | Texas | 16.6 |
| 47 | Utah | 14.1 |
| 5 | Vermont | 23.7 |
| 37 | Virginia | 16.7 |
| 42 | Washington | 15.3 |
| 9 | West Virginia | 22.4 |
| 18 | Wisconsin | 21.0 |
| 50 | Wyoming | 10.1 |

RANK ORDER

| RANK | STATE | PERCENT |
|------|-------|---------|
| 1 | Maine | 25.8 |
| 2 | Rhode Island | 25.3 |
| 3 | Minnesota | 25.2 |
| 4 | Tennessee | 23.9 |
| 5 | Vermont | 23.7 |
| 6 | Massachusetts | 23.6 |
| 6 | Pennsylvania | 23.6 |
| 8 | New Mexico | 22.8 |
| 9 | Kentucky | 22.4 |
| 9 | West Virginia | 22.4 |
| 11 | Arkansas | 21.7 |
| 11 | Mississippi | 21.7 |
| 13 | Arizona | 21.6 |
| 14 | Ohio | 21.5 |
| 15 | New York | 21.4 |
| 16 | Idaho | 21.1 |
| 16 | Oklahoma | 21.1 |
| 18 | Wisconsin | 21.0 |
| 19 | Delaware | 20.4 |
| 19 | New Hampshire | 20.4 |
| 21 | California | 19.1 |
| 21 | Maryland | 19.1 |
| 21 | South Carolina | 19.1 |
| 24 | Missouri | 18.7 |
| 25 | Connecticut | 18.5 |
| 25 | Indiana | 18.5 |
| 27 | Iowa | 18.3 |
| 28 | Michigan | 18.0 |
| 29 | Oregon | 17.8 |
| 30 | Illinois | 17.7 |
| 31 | Hawaii | 17.6 |
| 31 | New Jersey | 17.6 |
| 33 | Montana | 17.4 |
| 34 | Florida | 17.1 |
| 35 | North Carolina | 16.9 |
| 36 | Alabama | 16.8 |
| 37 | Virginia | 16.7 |
| 38 | Texas | 16.6 |
| 39 | Georgia | 15.8 |
| 39 | South Dakota | 15.8 |
| 41 | Kansas | 15.5 |
| 42 | Washington | 15.3 |
| 43 | Louisiana | 15.0 |
| 43 | Nebraska | 15.0 |
| 43 | North Dakota | 15.0 |
| 46 | Alaska | 14.5 |
| 47 | Utah | 14.1 |
| 48 | Nevada | 12.5 |
| 49 | Colorado | 12.0 |
| 50 | Wyoming | 10.1 |
| | District of Columbia | 27.3 |

Source: CQ Press using data from U.S. Bureau of the Census, Governments Division
   "2011 State and Local Government Finances" (http://www.census.gov/govs/local/)
*As a percent of direct general expenditures. Includes funds for cash assistance programs, medical and other vendor payments, welfare institutions, and other public welfare programs.

# Social Security (OASDI) Payments in 2011

## National Total = $724,943,000,000*

| RANK | STATE | PAYMENTS | % of USA |
|------|-------|----------|----------|
| 20 | Alabama | $13,156,000,000 | 1.8% |
| 50 | Alaska | 1,010,000,000 | 0.1% |
| 18 | Arizona | 14,744,000,000 | 2.0% |
| 30 | Arkansas | 7,964,000,000 | 1.1% |
| 1 | California | 66,661,000,000 | 9.2% |
| 27 | Colorado | 9,382,000,000 | 1.3% |
| 29 | Connecticut | 9,111,000,000 | 1.3% |
| 45 | Delaware | 2,482,000,000 | 0.3% |
| 2 | Florida | 50,986,000,000 | 7.0% |
| 11 | Georgia | 19,578,000,000 | 2.7% |
| 42 | Hawaii | 3,056,000,000 | 0.4% |
| 41 | Idaho | 3,549,000,000 | 0.5% |
| 8 | Illinois | 28,189,000,000 | 3.9% |
| 13 | Indiana | 16,709,000,000 | 2.3% |
| 31 | Iowa | 7,840,000,000 | 1.1% |
| 33 | Kansas | 6,705,000,000 | 0.9% |
| 24 | Kentucky | 11,379,000,000 | 1.6% |
| 25 | Louisiana | 9,941,000,000 | 1.4% |
| 39 | Maine | 3,740,000,000 | 0.5% |
| 23 | Maryland | 11,879,000,000 | 1.6% |
| 15 | Massachusetts | 15,439,000,000 | 2.1% |
| 7 | Michigan | 28,270,000,000 | 3.9% |
| 22 | Minnesota | 12,123,000,000 | 1.7% |
| 32 | Mississippi | 7,415,000,000 | 1.0% |
| 16 | Missouri | 15,416,000,000 | 2.1% |
| 44 | Montana | 2,485,000,000 | 0.3% |
| 38 | Nebraska | 4,093,000,000 | 0.6% |
| 35 | Nevada | 5,607,000,000 | 0.8% |
| 40 | New Hampshire | 3,554,000,000 | 0.5% |
| 10 | New Jersey | 21,865,000,000 | 3.0% |
| 36 | New Mexico | 4,524,000,000 | 0.6% |
| 3 | New York | 45,819,000,000 | 6.3% |
| 9 | North Carolina | 23,505,000,000 | 3.2% |
| 48 | North Dakota | 1,519,000,000 | 0.2% |
| 6 | Ohio | 28,618,000,000 | 3.9% |
| 28 | Oklahoma | 9,136,000,000 | 1.3% |
| 26 | Oregon | 9,743,000,000 | 1.3% |
| 5 | Pennsylvania | 35,656,000,000 | 4.9% |
| 43 | Rhode Island | 2,739,000,000 | 0.4% |
| 21 | South Carolina | 12,453,000,000 | 1.7% |
| 46 | South Dakota | 1,934,000,000 | 0.3% |
| 14 | Tennessee | 16,512,000,000 | 2.3% |
| 4 | Texas | 44,966,000,000 | 6.2% |
| 37 | Utah | 4,385,000,000 | 0.6% |
| 47 | Vermont | 1,710,000,000 | 0.2% |
| 12 | Virginia | 17,400,000,000 | 2.4% |
| 17 | Washington | 15,317,000,000 | 2.1% |
| 34 | West Virginia | 5,867,000,000 | 0.8% |
| 19 | Wisconsin | 14,657,000,000 | 2.0% |
| 49 | Wyoming | 1,240,000,000 | 0.2% |

| RANK | STATE | PAYMENTS | % of USA |
|------|-------|----------|----------|
| 1 | California | $66,661,000,000 | 9.2% |
| 2 | Florida | 50,986,000,000 | 7.0% |
| 3 | New York | 45,819,000,000 | 6.3% |
| 4 | Texas | 44,966,000,000 | 6.2% |
| 5 | Pennsylvania | 35,656,000,000 | 4.9% |
| 6 | Ohio | 28,618,000,000 | 3.9% |
| 7 | Michigan | 28,270,000,000 | 3.9% |
| 8 | Illinois | 28,189,000,000 | 3.9% |
| 9 | North Carolina | 23,505,000,000 | 3.2% |
| 10 | New Jersey | 21,865,000,000 | 3.0% |
| 11 | Georgia | 19,578,000,000 | 2.7% |
| 12 | Virginia | 17,400,000,000 | 2.4% |
| 13 | Indiana | 16,709,000,000 | 2.3% |
| 14 | Tennessee | 16,512,000,000 | 2.3% |
| 15 | Massachusetts | 15,439,000,000 | 2.1% |
| 16 | Missouri | 15,416,000,000 | 2.1% |
| 17 | Washington | 15,317,000,000 | 2.1% |
| 18 | Arizona | 14,744,000,000 | 2.0% |
| 19 | Wisconsin | 14,657,000,000 | 2.0% |
| 20 | Alabama | 13,156,000,000 | 1.8% |
| 21 | South Carolina | 12,453,000,000 | 1.7% |
| 22 | Minnesota | 12,123,000,000 | 1.7% |
| 23 | Maryland | 11,879,000,000 | 1.6% |
| 24 | Kentucky | 11,379,000,000 | 1.6% |
| 25 | Louisiana | 9,941,000,000 | 1.4% |
| 26 | Oregon | 9,743,000,000 | 1.3% |
| 27 | Colorado | 9,382,000,000 | 1.3% |
| 28 | Oklahoma | 9,136,000,000 | 1.3% |
| 29 | Connecticut | 9,111,000,000 | 1.3% |
| 30 | Arkansas | 7,964,000,000 | 1.1% |
| 31 | Iowa | 7,840,000,000 | 1.1% |
| 32 | Mississippi | 7,415,000,000 | 1.0% |
| 33 | Kansas | 6,705,000,000 | 0.9% |
| 34 | West Virginia | 5,867,000,000 | 0.8% |
| 35 | Nevada | 5,607,000,000 | 0.8% |
| 36 | New Mexico | 4,524,000,000 | 0.6% |
| 37 | Utah | 4,385,000,000 | 0.6% |
| 38 | Nebraska | 4,093,000,000 | 0.6% |
| 39 | Maine | 3,740,000,000 | 0.5% |
| 40 | New Hampshire | 3,554,000,000 | 0.5% |
| 41 | Idaho | 3,549,000,000 | 0.5% |
| 42 | Hawaii | 3,056,000,000 | 0.4% |
| 43 | Rhode Island | 2,739,000,000 | 0.4% |
| 44 | Montana | 2,485,000,000 | 0.3% |
| 45 | Delaware | 2,482,000,000 | 0.3% |
| 46 | South Dakota | 1,934,000,000 | 0.3% |
| 47 | Vermont | 1,710,000,000 | 0.2% |
| 48 | North Dakota | 1,519,000,000 | 0.2% |
| 49 | Wyoming | 1,240,000,000 | 0.2% |
| 50 | Alaska | 1,010,000,000 | 0.1% |
|  | District of Columbia | 904,000,000 | 0.1% |

Source: Social Security Administration
   "Social Security Bulletin, Annual Statistical Supplement 2012" (http://www.ssa.gov/policy/docs/statcomps/supplement/2012/)
*"OASDI" is Old Age, Survivors and Disability Insurance.  National total includes $12,016,000,000 in payments to recipients in
U.S. territories and foreign countries.

# Per Capita Social Security (OASDI) Payments in 2011

## National Per Capita = $2,288*

| RANK | STATE | PER CAPITA |
|------|-------|-----------|
| 5 | Alabama | $2,740 |
| 50 | Alaska | 1,396 |
| 31 | Arizona | 2,279 |
| 8 | Arkansas | 2,710 |
| 47 | California | 1,770 |
| 46 | Colorado | 1,833 |
| 19 | Connecticut | 2,539 |
| 6 | Delaware | 2,734 |
| 10 | Florida | 2,672 |
| 45 | Georgia | 1,996 |
| 36 | Hawaii | 2,219 |
| 34 | Idaho | 2,241 |
| 38 | Illinois | 2,193 |
| 17 | Indiana | 2,564 |
| 18 | Iowa | 2,559 |
| 29 | Kansas | 2,337 |
| 13 | Kentucky | 2,606 |
| 41 | Louisiana | 2,173 |
| 3 | Maine | 2,817 |
| 44 | Maryland | 2,034 |
| 29 | Massachusetts | 2,337 |
| 2 | Michigan | 2,863 |
| 32 | Minnesota | 2,267 |
| 22 | Mississippi | 2,490 |
| 16 | Missouri | 2,565 |
| 21 | Montana | 2,491 |
| 35 | Nebraska | 2,222 |
| 43 | Nevada | 2,063 |
| 9 | New Hampshire | 2,696 |
| 24 | New Jersey | 2,474 |
| 40 | New Mexico | 2,177 |
| 27 | New York | 2,349 |
| 25 | North Carolina | 2,435 |
| 37 | North Dakota | 2,218 |
| 23 | Ohio | 2,478 |
| 26 | Oklahoma | 2,413 |
| 20 | Oregon | 2,519 |
| 4 | Pennsylvania | 2,798 |
| 12 | Rhode Island | 2,608 |
| 11 | South Carolina | 2,665 |
| 28 | South Dakota | 2,348 |
| 14 | Tennessee | 2,581 |
| 48 | Texas | 1,754 |
| 49 | Utah | 1,558 |
| 7 | Vermont | 2,730 |
| 42 | Virginia | 2,147 |
| 33 | Washington | 2,245 |
| 1 | West Virginia | 3,162 |
| 15 | Wisconsin | 2,567 |
| 39 | Wyoming | 2,186 |

| RANK | STATE | PER CAPITA |
|------|-------|-----------|
| 1 | West Virginia | $3,162 |
| 2 | Michigan | 2,863 |
| 3 | Maine | 2,817 |
| 4 | Pennsylvania | 2,798 |
| 5 | Alabama | 2,740 |
| 6 | Delaware | 2,734 |
| 7 | Vermont | 2,730 |
| 8 | Arkansas | 2,710 |
| 9 | New Hampshire | 2,696 |
| 10 | Florida | 2,672 |
| 11 | South Carolina | 2,665 |
| 12 | Rhode Island | 2,608 |
| 13 | Kentucky | 2,606 |
| 14 | Tennessee | 2,581 |
| 15 | Wisconsin | 2,567 |
| 16 | Missouri | 2,565 |
| 17 | Indiana | 2,564 |
| 18 | Iowa | 2,559 |
| 19 | Connecticut | 2,539 |
| 20 | Oregon | 2,519 |
| 21 | Montana | 2,491 |
| 22 | Mississippi | 2,490 |
| 23 | Ohio | 2,478 |
| 24 | New Jersey | 2,474 |
| 25 | North Carolina | 2,435 |
| 26 | Oklahoma | 2,413 |
| 27 | New York | 2,349 |
| 28 | South Dakota | 2,348 |
| 29 | Kansas | 2,337 |
| 29 | Massachusetts | 2,337 |
| 31 | Arizona | 2,279 |
| 32 | Minnesota | 2,267 |
| 33 | Washington | 2,245 |
| 34 | Idaho | 2,241 |
| 35 | Nebraska | 2,222 |
| 36 | Hawaii | 2,219 |
| 37 | North Dakota | 2,218 |
| 38 | Illinois | 2,193 |
| 39 | Wyoming | 2,186 |
| 40 | New Mexico | 2,177 |
| 41 | Louisiana | 2,173 |
| 42 | Virginia | 2,147 |
| 43 | Nevada | 2,063 |
| 44 | Maryland | 2,034 |
| 45 | Georgia | 1,996 |
| 46 | Colorado | 1,833 |
| 47 | California | 1,770 |
| 48 | Texas | 1,754 |
| 49 | Utah | 1,558 |
| 50 | Alaska | 1,396 |
| | District of Columbia | 1,459 |

Source: CQ Press using data from Social Security Administration
"Social Security Bulletin, Annual Statistical Supplement 2012" (http://www.ssa.gov/policy/docs/statcomps/supplement/2012/)
*"OASDI" is Old Age, Survivors and Disability Insurance. National per capita does not include payments or population in U.S. territories and foreign countries.

# Social Security (OASDI) Monthly Payments in 2011

## National Total = $62,213,382,000*

| ALPHA ORDER | | | | | RANK ORDER | | | |
|---|---|---|---|---|---|---|---|---|
| RANK | STATE | PAYMENTS | % of USA | | RANK | STATE | PAYMENTS | % of USA |
| 20 | Alabama | $1,111,578,000 | 1.8% | | 1 | California | $5,760,530,000 | 9.3% |
| 50 | Alaska | 87,416,000 | 0.1% | | 2 | Florida | 4,429,118,000 | 7.1% |
| 18 | Arizona | 1,282,882,000 | 2.1% | | 3 | New York | 3,934,524,000 | 6.3% |
| 30 | Arkansas | 673,482,000 | 1.1% | | 4 | Texas | 3,838,870,000 | 6.2% |
| 1 | California | 5,760,530,000 | 9.3% | | 5 | Pennsylvania | 3,044,365,000 | 4.9% |
| 27 | Colorado | 815,841,000 | 1.3% | | 6 | Ohio | 2,425,438,000 | 3.9% |
| 28 | Connecticut | 787,707,000 | 1.3% | | 7 | Michigan | 2,419,079,000 | 3.9% |
| 44 | Delaware | 214,792,000 | 0.3% | | 8 | Illinois | 2,407,184,000 | 3.9% |
| 2 | Florida | 4,429,118,000 | 7.1% | | 9 | North Carolina | 2,028,201,000 | 3.3% |
| 11 | Georgia | 1,684,659,000 | 2.7% | | 10 | New Jersey | 1,889,187,000 | 3.0% |
| 42 | Hawaii | 267,756,000 | 0.4% | | 11 | Georgia | 1,684,659,000 | 2.7% |
| 41 | Idaho | 307,240,000 | 0.5% | | 12 | Virginia | 1,498,922,000 | 2.4% |
| 8 | Illinois | 2,407,184,000 | 3.9% | | 13 | Indiana | 1,428,630,000 | 2.3% |
| 13 | Indiana | 1,428,630,000 | 2.3% | | 14 | Tennessee | 1,411,408,000 | 2.3% |
| 31 | Iowa | 671,839,000 | 1.1% | | 15 | Washington | 1,330,257,000 | 2.1% |
| 33 | Kansas | 575,137,000 | 0.9% | | 16 | Massachusetts | 1,324,894,000 | 2.1% |
| 24 | Kentucky | 954,128,000 | 1.5% | | 17 | Missouri | 1,313,771,000 | 2.1% |
| 26 | Louisiana | 826,634,000 | 1.3% | | 18 | Arizona | 1,282,882,000 | 2.1% |
| 39 | Maine | 319,869,000 | 0.5% | | 19 | Wisconsin | 1,265,027,000 | 2.0% |
| 23 | Maryland | 1,026,641,000 | 1.7% | | 20 | Alabama | 1,111,578,000 | 1.8% |
| 16 | Massachusetts | 1,324,894,000 | 2.1% | | 21 | South Carolina | 1,073,608,000 | 1.7% |
| 7 | Michigan | 2,419,079,000 | 3.9% | | 22 | Minnesota | 1,051,199,000 | 1.7% |
| 22 | Minnesota | 1,051,199,000 | 1.7% | | 23 | Maryland | 1,026,641,000 | 1.7% |
| 32 | Mississippi | 624,863,000 | 1.0% | | 24 | Kentucky | 954,128,000 | 1.5% |
| 17 | Missouri | 1,313,771,000 | 2.1% | | 25 | Oregon | 845,343,000 | 1.4% |
| 45 | Montana | 214,245,000 | 0.3% | | 26 | Louisiana | 826,634,000 | 1.3% |
| 38 | Nebraska | 350,845,000 | 0.6% | | 27 | Colorado | 815,841,000 | 1.3% |
| 34 | Nevada | 489,418,000 | 0.8% | | 28 | Connecticut | 787,707,000 | 1.3% |
| 40 | New Hampshire | 308,497,000 | 0.5% | | 29 | Oklahoma | 774,739,000 | 1.2% |
| 10 | New Jersey | 1,889,187,000 | 3.0% | | 30 | Arkansas | 673,482,000 | 1.1% |
| 36 | New Mexico | 388,287,000 | 0.6% | | 31 | Iowa | 671,839,000 | 1.1% |
| 3 | New York | 3,934,524,000 | 6.3% | | 32 | Mississippi | 624,863,000 | 1.0% |
| 9 | North Carolina | 2,028,201,000 | 3.3% | | 33 | Kansas | 575,137,000 | 0.9% |
| 48 | North Dakota | 128,944,000 | 0.2% | | 34 | Nevada | 489,418,000 | 0.8% |
| 6 | Ohio | 2,425,438,000 | 3.9% | | 35 | West Virginia | 487,983,000 | 0.8% |
| 29 | Oklahoma | 774,739,000 | 1.2% | | 36 | New Mexico | 388,287,000 | 0.6% |
| 25 | Oregon | 845,343,000 | 1.4% | | 37 | Utah | 379,672,000 | 0.6% |
| 5 | Pennsylvania | 3,044,365,000 | 4.9% | | 38 | Nebraska | 350,845,000 | 0.6% |
| 43 | Rhode Island | 235,870,000 | 0.4% | | 39 | Maine | 319,869,000 | 0.5% |
| 21 | South Carolina | 1,073,608,000 | 1.7% | | 40 | New Hampshire | 308,497,000 | 0.5% |
| 46 | South Dakota | 166,328,000 | 0.3% | | 41 | Idaho | 307,240,000 | 0.5% |
| 14 | Tennessee | 1,411,408,000 | 2.3% | | 42 | Hawaii | 267,756,000 | 0.4% |
| 4 | Texas | 3,838,870,000 | 6.2% | | 43 | Rhode Island | 235,870,000 | 0.4% |
| 37 | Utah | 379,672,000 | 0.6% | | 44 | Delaware | 214,792,000 | 0.3% |
| 47 | Vermont | 147,883,000 | 0.2% | | 45 | Montana | 214,245,000 | 0.3% |
| 12 | Virginia | 1,498,922,000 | 2.4% | | 46 | South Dakota | 166,328,000 | 0.3% |
| 15 | Washington | 1,330,257,000 | 2.1% | | 47 | Vermont | 147,883,000 | 0.2% |
| 35 | West Virginia | 487,983,000 | 0.8% | | 48 | North Dakota | 128,944,000 | 0.2% |
| 19 | Wisconsin | 1,265,027,000 | 2.0% | | 49 | Wyoming | 107,270,000 | 0.2% |
| 49 | Wyoming | 107,270,000 | 0.2% | | 50 | Alaska | 87,416,000 | 0.1% |
| | | | | | | District of Columbia | 77,584,000 | 0.1% |

Source: Social Security Administration
"Social Security Bulletin, Annual Statistical Supplement 2012" (http://www.ssa.gov/policy/docs/statcomps/supplement/2012/)
*For December 2011. "OASDI" is Old Age, Survivors and Disability Insurance. National total includes $1,003,799,000 in payments to recipients in U.S. territories and foreign countries.

# Social Security (OASDI) Beneficiaries in 2011

## National Total = 55,404,480*

ALPHA ORDER

| RANK | STATE | BENEFICIARIES | % of USA |
|---|---|---|---|
| 20 | Alabama | 1,037,438 | 1.9% |
| 50 | Alaska | 82,109 | 0.1% |
| 18 | Arizona | 1,104,545 | 2.0% |
| 29 | Arkansas | 647,077 | 1.2% |
| 1 | California | 5,129,529 | 9.3% |
| 27 | Colorado | 721,274 | 1.3% |
| 30 | Connecticut | 630,447 | 1.1% |
| 45 | Delaware | 176,885 | 0.3% |
| 2 | Florida | 3,894,179 | 7.0% |
| 10 | Georgia | 1,524,263 | 2.8% |
| 42 | Hawaii | 234,314 | 0.4% |
| 40 | Idaho | 278,563 | 0.5% |
| 7 | Illinois | 2,065,432 | 3.7% |
| 14 | Indiana | 1,219,879 | 2.2% |
| 32 | Iowa | 592,000 | 1.1% |
| 33 | Kansas | 498,707 | 0.9% |
| 22 | Kentucky | 913,548 | 1.6% |
| 25 | Louisiana | 809,450 | 1.5% |
| 39 | Maine | 306,600 | 0.6% |
| 24 | Maryland | 872,919 | 1.6% |
| 16 | Massachusetts | 1,161,122 | 2.1% |
| 8 | Michigan | 2,016,684 | 3.6% |
| 23 | Minnesota | 904,803 | 1.6% |
| 31 | Mississippi | 609,651 | 1.1% |
| 15 | Missouri | 1,188,437 | 2.1% |
| 44 | Montana | 198,230 | 0.4% |
| 38 | Nebraska | 313,087 | 0.6% |
| 35 | Nevada | 424,836 | 0.8% |
| 41 | New Hampshire | 262,952 | 0.5% |
| 11 | New Jersey | 1,500,403 | 2.7% |
| 36 | New Mexico | 370,911 | 0.7% |
| 4 | New York | 3,337,276 | 6.0% |
| 9 | North Carolina | 1,808,331 | 3.3% |
| 48 | North Dakota | 121,335 | 0.2% |
| 6 | Ohio | 2,166,271 | 3.9% |
| 28 | Oklahoma | 717,398 | 1.3% |
| 26 | Oregon | 734,841 | 1.3% |
| 5 | Pennsylvania | 2,617,879 | 4.7% |
| 43 | Rhode Island | 207,122 | 0.4% |
| 21 | South Carolina | 956,097 | 1.7% |
| 46 | South Dakota | 156,102 | 0.3% |
| 13 | Tennessee | 1,287,683 | 2.3% |
| 3 | Texas | 3,551,961 | 6.4% |
| 37 | Utah | 335,444 | 0.6% |
| 47 | Vermont | 132,268 | 0.2% |
| 12 | Virginia | 1,318,580 | 2.4% |
| 17 | Washington | 1,127,126 | 2.0% |
| 34 | West Virginia | 451,039 | 0.8% |
| 19 | Wisconsin | 1,085,632 | 2.0% |
| 49 | Wyoming | 93,748 | 0.2% |

RANK ORDER

| RANK | STATE | BENEFICIARIES | % of USA |
|---|---|---|---|
| 1 | California | 5,129,529 | 9.3% |
| 2 | Florida | 3,894,179 | 7.0% |
| 3 | Texas | 3,551,961 | 6.4% |
| 4 | New York | 3,337,276 | 6.0% |
| 5 | Pennsylvania | 2,617,879 | 4.7% |
| 6 | Ohio | 2,166,271 | 3.9% |
| 7 | Illinois | 2,065,432 | 3.7% |
| 8 | Michigan | 2,016,684 | 3.6% |
| 9 | North Carolina | 1,808,331 | 3.3% |
| 10 | Georgia | 1,524,263 | 2.8% |
| 11 | New Jersey | 1,500,403 | 2.7% |
| 12 | Virginia | 1,318,580 | 2.4% |
| 13 | Tennessee | 1,287,683 | 2.3% |
| 14 | Indiana | 1,219,879 | 2.2% |
| 15 | Missouri | 1,188,437 | 2.1% |
| 16 | Massachusetts | 1,161,122 | 2.1% |
| 17 | Washington | 1,127,126 | 2.0% |
| 18 | Arizona | 1,104,545 | 2.0% |
| 19 | Wisconsin | 1,085,632 | 2.0% |
| 20 | Alabama | 1,037,438 | 1.9% |
| 21 | South Carolina | 956,097 | 1.7% |
| 22 | Kentucky | 913,548 | 1.6% |
| 23 | Minnesota | 904,803 | 1.6% |
| 24 | Maryland | 872,919 | 1.6% |
| 25 | Louisiana | 809,450 | 1.5% |
| 26 | Oregon | 734,841 | 1.3% |
| 27 | Colorado | 721,274 | 1.3% |
| 28 | Oklahoma | 717,398 | 1.3% |
| 29 | Arkansas | 647,077 | 1.2% |
| 30 | Connecticut | 630,447 | 1.1% |
| 31 | Mississippi | 609,651 | 1.1% |
| 32 | Iowa | 592,000 | 1.1% |
| 33 | Kansas | 498,707 | 0.9% |
| 34 | West Virginia | 451,039 | 0.8% |
| 35 | Nevada | 424,836 | 0.8% |
| 36 | New Mexico | 370,911 | 0.7% |
| 37 | Utah | 335,444 | 0.6% |
| 38 | Nebraska | 313,087 | 0.6% |
| 39 | Maine | 306,600 | 0.6% |
| 40 | Idaho | 278,563 | 0.5% |
| 41 | New Hampshire | 262,952 | 0.5% |
| 42 | Hawaii | 234,314 | 0.4% |
| 43 | Rhode Island | 207,122 | 0.4% |
| 44 | Montana | 198,230 | 0.4% |
| 45 | Delaware | 176,885 | 0.3% |
| 46 | South Dakota | 156,102 | 0.3% |
| 47 | Vermont | 132,268 | 0.2% |
| 48 | North Dakota | 121,335 | 0.2% |
| 49 | Wyoming | 93,748 | 0.2% |
| 50 | Alaska | 82,109 | 0.1% |
| | District of Columbia | 75,755 | 0.1% |

Source: Social Security Administration
    "Social Security Bulletin, Annual Statistical Supplement 2012" (http://www.ssa.gov/policy/docs/statcomps/supplement/2012/)
*For December 2011. "OASDI" is Old Age, Survivors and Disability Insurance. National total includes 1,432,318 beneficiaries in U.S. territories and foreign countries.

# Average Monthly Social Security (OASDI) Payment in 2011

## National Average = $1,134 Each Month per Beneficiary*

ALPHA ORDER

| RANK | STATE | PER BENEFICIARY |
|---|---|---|
| 41 | Alabama | $1,071 |
| 43 | Alaska | 1,065 |
| 14 | Arizona | 1,161 |
| 48 | Arkansas | 1,041 |
| 27 | California | 1,123 |
| 26 | Colorado | 1,131 |
| 2 | Connecticut | 1,249 |
| 3 | Delaware | 1,214 |
| 22 | Florida | 1,137 |
| 33 | Georgia | 1,105 |
| 19 | Hawaii | 1,143 |
| 35 | Idaho | 1,103 |
| 10 | Illinois | 1,165 |
| 9 | Indiana | 1,171 |
| 24 | Iowa | 1,135 |
| 15 | Kansas | 1,153 |
| 46 | Kentucky | 1,044 |
| 50 | Louisiana | 1,021 |
| 47 | Maine | 1,043 |
| 7 | Maryland | 1,176 |
| 20 | Massachusetts | 1,141 |
| 4 | Michigan | 1,200 |
| 13 | Minnesota | 1,162 |
| 49 | Mississippi | 1,025 |
| 33 | Missouri | 1,105 |
| 38 | Montana | 1,081 |
| 30 | Nebraska | 1,121 |
| 16 | Nevada | 1,152 |
| 8 | New Hampshire | 1,173 |
| 1 | New Jersey | 1,259 |
| 45 | New Mexico | 1,047 |
| 6 | New York | 1,179 |
| 29 | North Carolina | 1,122 |
| 44 | North Dakota | 1,063 |
| 31 | Ohio | 1,120 |
| 40 | Oklahoma | 1,080 |
| 17 | Oregon | 1,150 |
| 12 | Pennsylvania | 1,163 |
| 21 | Rhode Island | 1,139 |
| 27 | South Carolina | 1,123 |
| 42 | South Dakota | 1,066 |
| 36 | Tennessee | 1,096 |
| 38 | Texas | 1,081 |
| 25 | Utah | 1,132 |
| 32 | Vermont | 1,118 |
| 22 | Virginia | 1,137 |
| 5 | Washington | 1,180 |
| 37 | West Virginia | 1,082 |
| 10 | Wisconsin | 1,165 |
| 18 | Wyoming | 1,144 |

RANK ORDER

| RANK | STATE | PER BENEFICIARY |
|---|---|---|
| 1 | New Jersey | $1,259 |
| 2 | Connecticut | 1,249 |
| 3 | Delaware | 1,214 |
| 4 | Michigan | 1,200 |
| 5 | Washington | 1,180 |
| 6 | New York | 1,179 |
| 7 | Maryland | 1,176 |
| 8 | New Hampshire | 1,173 |
| 9 | Indiana | 1,171 |
| 10 | Illinois | 1,165 |
| 10 | Wisconsin | 1,165 |
| 12 | Pennsylvania | 1,163 |
| 13 | Minnesota | 1,162 |
| 14 | Arizona | 1,161 |
| 15 | Kansas | 1,153 |
| 16 | Nevada | 1,152 |
| 17 | Oregon | 1,150 |
| 18 | Wyoming | 1,144 |
| 19 | Hawaii | 1,143 |
| 20 | Massachusetts | 1,141 |
| 21 | Rhode Island | 1,139 |
| 22 | Florida | 1,137 |
| 22 | Virginia | 1,137 |
| 24 | Iowa | 1,135 |
| 25 | Utah | 1,132 |
| 26 | Colorado | 1,131 |
| 27 | California | 1,123 |
| 27 | South Carolina | 1,123 |
| 29 | North Carolina | 1,122 |
| 30 | Nebraska | 1,121 |
| 31 | Ohio | 1,120 |
| 32 | Vermont | 1,118 |
| 33 | Georgia | 1,105 |
| 33 | Missouri | 1,105 |
| 35 | Idaho | 1,103 |
| 36 | Tennessee | 1,096 |
| 37 | West Virginia | 1,082 |
| 38 | Montana | 1,081 |
| 38 | Texas | 1,081 |
| 40 | Oklahoma | 1,080 |
| 41 | Alabama | 1,071 |
| 42 | South Dakota | 1,066 |
| 43 | Alaska | 1,065 |
| 44 | North Dakota | 1,063 |
| 45 | New Mexico | 1,047 |
| 46 | Kentucky | 1,044 |
| 47 | Maine | 1,043 |
| 48 | Arkansas | 1,041 |
| 49 | Mississippi | 1,025 |
| 50 | Louisiana | 1,021 |

District of Columbia     1,024

Source: CQ Press using data from Social Security Administration
   "Social Security Bulletin, Annual Statistical Supplement 2012" (http://www.ssa.gov/policy/docs/statcomps/supplement/2012/)
*As of December 2011. "OASDI" is Old Age, Survivors and Disability Insurance. National average does not include
beneficiaries or payments in U.S. territories or foreign countries.

# Social Security Supplemental Security Income Beneficiaries in 2011

## National Total = 8,112,773 Beneficiaries*

ALPHA ORDER

| RANK | STATE | BENEFICIARIES | % of USA |
|---|---|---|---|
| 15 | Alabama | 174,917 | 2.2% |
| 48 | Alaska | 12,675 | 0.2% |
| 23 | Arizona | 112,757 | 1.4% |
| 26 | Arkansas | 109,881 | 1.4% |
| 1 | California | 1,286,271 | 15.9% |
| 31 | Colorado | 68,725 | 0.8% |
| 33 | Connecticut | 59,731 | 0.7% |
| 45 | Delaware | 16,155 | 0.2% |
| 4 | Florida | 505,807 | 6.2% |
| 9 | Georgia | 238,751 | 2.9% |
| 42 | Hawaii | 25,330 | 0.3% |
| 40 | Idaho | 28,202 | 0.3% |
| 7 | Illinois | 276,332 | 3.4% |
| 21 | Indiana | 122,084 | 1.5% |
| 34 | Iowa | 48,903 | 0.6% |
| 35 | Kansas | 47,372 | 0.6% |
| 12 | Kentucky | 193,023 | 2.4% |
| 14 | Louisiana | 178,727 | 2.2% |
| 37 | Maine | 36,316 | 0.4% |
| 24 | Maryland | 111,275 | 1.4% |
| 11 | Massachusetts | 197,503 | 2.4% |
| 8 | Michigan | 264,699 | 3.3% |
| 28 | Minnesota | 88,731 | 1.1% |
| 20 | Mississippi | 126,307 | 1.6% |
| 19 | Missouri | 137,169 | 1.7% |
| 44 | Montana | 18,167 | 0.2% |
| 41 | Nebraska | 26,530 | 0.3% |
| 36 | Nevada | 43,713 | 0.5% |
| 43 | New Hampshire | 18,693 | 0.2% |
| 16 | New Jersey | 173,143 | 2.1% |
| 32 | New Mexico | 61,838 | 0.8% |
| 2 | New York | 690,258 | 8.5% |
| 10 | North Carolina | 224,780 | 2.8% |
| 49 | North Dakota | 8,361 | 0.1% |
| 6 | Ohio | 294,920 | 3.6% |
| 27 | Oklahoma | 95,510 | 1.2% |
| 30 | Oregon | 77,980 | 1.0% |
| 5 | Pennsylvania | 367,274 | 4.5% |
| 38 | Rhode Island | 32,114 | 0.4% |
| 22 | South Carolina | 114,819 | 1.4% |
| 47 | South Dakota | 14,154 | 0.2% |
| 13 | Tennessee | 179,350 | 2.2% |
| 3 | Texas | 639,869 | 7.9% |
| 39 | Utah | 29,412 | 0.4% |
| 46 | Vermont | 15,684 | 0.2% |
| 17 | Virginia | 150,804 | 1.9% |
| 18 | Washington | 142,848 | 1.8% |
| 29 | West Virginia | 80,734 | 1.0% |
| 25 | Wisconsin | 110,881 | 1.4% |
| 50 | Wyoming | 6,534 | 0.1% |

RANK ORDER

| RANK | STATE | BENEFICIARIES | % of USA |
|---|---|---|---|
| 1 | California | 1,286,271 | 15.9% |
| 2 | New York | 690,258 | 8.5% |
| 3 | Texas | 639,869 | 7.9% |
| 4 | Florida | 505,807 | 6.2% |
| 5 | Pennsylvania | 367,274 | 4.5% |
| 6 | Ohio | 294,920 | 3.6% |
| 7 | Illinois | 276,332 | 3.4% |
| 8 | Michigan | 264,699 | 3.3% |
| 9 | Georgia | 238,751 | 2.9% |
| 10 | North Carolina | 224,780 | 2.8% |
| 11 | Massachusetts | 197,503 | 2.4% |
| 12 | Kentucky | 193,023 | 2.4% |
| 13 | Tennessee | 179,350 | 2.2% |
| 14 | Louisiana | 178,727 | 2.2% |
| 15 | Alabama | 174,917 | 2.2% |
| 16 | New Jersey | 173,143 | 2.1% |
| 17 | Virginia | 150,804 | 1.9% |
| 18 | Washington | 142,848 | 1.8% |
| 19 | Missouri | 137,169 | 1.7% |
| 20 | Mississippi | 126,307 | 1.6% |
| 21 | Indiana | 122,084 | 1.5% |
| 22 | South Carolina | 114,819 | 1.4% |
| 23 | Arizona | 112,757 | 1.4% |
| 24 | Maryland | 111,275 | 1.4% |
| 25 | Wisconsin | 110,881 | 1.4% |
| 26 | Arkansas | 109,881 | 1.4% |
| 27 | Oklahoma | 95,510 | 1.2% |
| 28 | Minnesota | 88,731 | 1.1% |
| 29 | West Virginia | 80,734 | 1.0% |
| 30 | Oregon | 77,980 | 1.0% |
| 31 | Colorado | 68,725 | 0.8% |
| 32 | New Mexico | 61,838 | 0.8% |
| 33 | Connecticut | 59,731 | 0.7% |
| 34 | Iowa | 48,903 | 0.6% |
| 35 | Kansas | 47,372 | 0.6% |
| 36 | Nevada | 43,713 | 0.5% |
| 37 | Maine | 36,316 | 0.4% |
| 38 | Rhode Island | 32,114 | 0.4% |
| 39 | Utah | 29,412 | 0.4% |
| 40 | Idaho | 28,202 | 0.3% |
| 41 | Nebraska | 26,530 | 0.3% |
| 42 | Hawaii | 25,330 | 0.3% |
| 43 | New Hampshire | 18,693 | 0.2% |
| 44 | Montana | 18,167 | 0.2% |
| 45 | Delaware | 16,155 | 0.2% |
| 46 | Vermont | 15,684 | 0.2% |
| 47 | South Dakota | 14,154 | 0.2% |
| 48 | Alaska | 12,675 | 0.2% |
| 49 | North Dakota | 8,361 | 0.1% |
| 50 | Wyoming | 6,534 | 0.1% |
| | District of Columbia | 25,748 | 0.3% |

Source: Social Security Administration

"Social Security Bulletin, Annual Statistical Supplement 2012" (http://www.ssa.gov/policy/docs/statcomps/supplement/2012/)

*For December 2011. National total includes1,012 beneficiaries in U.S. territories or otherwise not distributed by state. The SSI program provides income support to persons age 65 and older and blind or disabled adults and children.

# Average Monthly Social Security
## Supplemental Security Income Payment in 2011
### National Average = $481.31 Each Month per Beneficiary*

ALPHA ORDER

| RANK | STATE | AVERAGE BENEFIT |
|---|---|---|
| 34 | Alabama | $466.61 |
| 37 | Alaska | 464.25 |
| 8 | Arizona | 492.17 |
| 28 | Arkansas | 472.96 |
| 22 | California | 479.76 |
| 30 | Colorado | 471.78 |
| 12 | Connecticut | 486.07 |
| 19 | Delaware | 482.70 |
| 21 | Florida | 480.15 |
| 31 | Georgia | 469.97 |
| 11 | Hawaii | 487.08 |
| 29 | Idaho | 472.14 |
| 4 | Illinois | 504.95 |
| 10 | Indiana | 490.90 |
| 43 | Iowa | 457.67 |
| 26 | Kansas | 473.15 |
| 23 | Kentucky | 478.10 |
| 15 | Louisiana | 483.88 |
| 47 | Maine | 451.97 |
| 6 | Maryland | 499.95 |
| 20 | Massachusetts | 481.48 |
| 3 | Michigan | 505.66 |
| 9 | Minnesota | 491.30 |
| 41 | Mississippi | 460.41 |
| 27 | Missouri | 473.08 |
| 42 | Montana | 458.21 |
| 44 | Nebraska | 457.61 |
| 14 | Nevada | 484.05 |
| 36 | New Hampshire | 464.94 |
| 33 | New Jersey | 467.36 |
| 40 | New Mexico | 461.06 |
| 7 | New York | 494.00 |
| 45 | North Carolina | 456.40 |
| 50 | North Dakota | 430.55 |
| 5 | Ohio | 501.33 |
| 24 | Oklahoma | 477.78 |
| 18 | Oregon | 482.85 |
| 1 | Pennsylvania | 507.50 |
| 13 | Rhode Island | 484.35 |
| 38 | South Carolina | 462.93 |
| 49 | South Dakota | 447.16 |
| 35 | Tennessee | 466.57 |
| 39 | Texas | 461.75 |
| 25 | Utah | 475.97 |
| 46 | Vermont | 452.13 |
| 32 | Virginia | 468.93 |
| 2 | Washington | 507.04 |
| 16 | West Virginia | 483.45 |
| 17 | Wisconsin | 483.21 |
| 48 | Wyoming | 449.87 |

RANK ORDER

| RANK | STATE | AVERAGE BENEFIT |
|---|---|---|
| 1 | Pennsylvania | $507.50 |
| 2 | Washington | 507.04 |
| 3 | Michigan | 505.66 |
| 4 | Illinois | 504.95 |
| 5 | Ohio | 501.33 |
| 6 | Maryland | 499.95 |
| 7 | New York | 494.00 |
| 8 | Arizona | 492.17 |
| 9 | Minnesota | 491.30 |
| 10 | Indiana | 490.90 |
| 11 | Hawaii | 487.08 |
| 12 | Connecticut | 486.07 |
| 13 | Rhode Island | 484.35 |
| 14 | Nevada | 484.05 |
| 15 | Louisiana | 483.88 |
| 16 | West Virginia | 483.45 |
| 17 | Wisconsin | 483.21 |
| 18 | Oregon | 482.85 |
| 19 | Delaware | 482.70 |
| 20 | Massachusetts | 481.48 |
| 21 | Florida | 480.15 |
| 22 | California | 479.76 |
| 23 | Kentucky | 478.10 |
| 24 | Oklahoma | 477.78 |
| 25 | Utah | 475.97 |
| 26 | Kansas | 473.15 |
| 27 | Missouri | 473.08 |
| 28 | Arkansas | 472.96 |
| 29 | Idaho | 472.14 |
| 30 | Colorado | 471.78 |
| 31 | Georgia | 469.97 |
| 32 | Virginia | 468.93 |
| 33 | New Jersey | 467.36 |
| 34 | Alabama | 466.61 |
| 35 | Tennessee | 466.57 |
| 36 | New Hampshire | 464.94 |
| 37 | Alaska | 464.25 |
| 38 | South Carolina | 462.93 |
| 39 | Texas | 461.75 |
| 40 | New Mexico | 461.06 |
| 41 | Mississippi | 460.41 |
| 42 | Montana | 458.21 |
| 43 | Iowa | 457.67 |
| 44 | Nebraska | 457.61 |
| 45 | North Carolina | 456.40 |
| 46 | Vermont | 452.13 |
| 47 | Maine | 451.97 |
| 48 | Wyoming | 449.87 |
| 49 | South Dakota | 447.16 |
| 50 | North Dakota | 430.55 |

| | District of Columbia | 521.39 |
|---|---|---|

Source: Social Security Administration
  "Social Security Bulletin, Annual Statistical Supplement 2012" (http://www.ssa.gov/policy/docs/statcomps/supplement/2012/)
*As of December 2011. National average includes payments to beneficiaries in U.S. territories and foreign countries. The SSI program provides income support to persons age 65 and older and blind or disabled adults and children.

# Medicare Enrollees in 2012

## National Total = 49,682,146 Enrollees*

ALPHA ORDER

| RANK | STATE | ENROLLEES | % of USA |
|------|-------|-----------|----------|
| 20 | Alabama | 896,274 | 1.8% |
| 50 | Alaska | 72,898 | 0.1% |
| 18 | Arizona | 1,009,292 | 2.0% |
| 30 | Arkansas | 558,620 | 1.1% |
| 1 | California | 5,111,208 | 10.3% |
| 26 | Colorado | 688,283 | 1.4% |
| 29 | Connecticut | 595,294 | 1.2% |
| 45 | Delaware | 161,422 | 0.3% |
| 2 | Florida | 3,621,057 | 7.3% |
| 11 | Georgia | 1,350,944 | 2.7% |
| 42 | Hawaii | 221,514 | 0.4% |
| 40 | Idaho | 249,626 | 0.5% |
| 7 | Illinois | 1,934,703 | 3.9% |
| 15 | Indiana | 1,064,511 | 2.1% |
| 31 | Iowa | 537,430 | 1.1% |
| 33 | Kansas | 453,927 | 0.9% |
| 24 | Kentucky | 804,245 | 1.6% |
| 25 | Louisiana | 729,271 | 1.5% |
| 39 | Maine | 281,968 | 0.6% |
| 21 | Maryland | 844,862 | 1.7% |
| 14 | Massachusetts | 1,125,661 | 2.3% |
| 8 | Michigan | 1,754,367 | 3.5% |
| 23 | Minnesota | 836,205 | 1.7% |
| 32 | Mississippi | 523,625 | 1.1% |
| 16 | Missouri | 1,058,418 | 2.1% |
| 44 | Montana | 181,710 | 0.4% |
| 38 | Nebraska | 291,333 | 0.6% |
| 35 | Nevada | 394,066 | 0.8% |
| 41 | New Hampshire | 240,551 | 0.5% |
| 10 | New Jersey | 1,397,532 | 2.8% |
| 36 | New Mexico | 336,413 | 0.7% |
| 4 | New York | 3,138,042 | 6.3% |
| 9 | North Carolina | 1,604,085 | 3.2% |
| 48 | North Dakota | 112,330 | 0.2% |
| 6 | Ohio | 2,003,455 | 4.0% |
| 28 | Oklahoma | 635,525 | 1.3% |
| 27 | Oregon | 671,822 | 1.4% |
| 5 | Pennsylvania | 2,385,084 | 4.8% |
| 43 | Rhode Island | 191,420 | 0.4% |
| 22 | South Carolina | 839,989 | 1.7% |
| 46 | South Dakota | 143,014 | 0.3% |
| 13 | Tennessee | 1,132,942 | 2.3% |
| 3 | Texas | 3,256,477 | 6.6% |
| 37 | Utah | 307,361 | 0.6% |
| 47 | Vermont | 119,759 | 0.2% |
| 12 | Virginia | 1,226,577 | 2.5% |
| 17 | Washington | 1,055,977 | 2.1% |
| 34 | West Virginia | 396,705 | 0.8% |
| 19 | Wisconsin | 966,151 | 1.9% |
| 49 | Wyoming | 85,708 | 0.2% |

RANK ORDER

| RANK | STATE | ENROLLEES | % of USA |
|------|-------|-----------|----------|
| 1 | California | 5,111,208 | 10.3% |
| 2 | Florida | 3,621,057 | 7.3% |
| 3 | Texas | 3,256,477 | 6.6% |
| 4 | New York | 3,138,042 | 6.3% |
| 5 | Pennsylvania | 2,385,084 | 4.8% |
| 6 | Ohio | 2,003,455 | 4.0% |
| 7 | Illinois | 1,934,703 | 3.9% |
| 8 | Michigan | 1,754,367 | 3.5% |
| 9 | North Carolina | 1,604,085 | 3.2% |
| 10 | New Jersey | 1,397,532 | 2.8% |
| 11 | Georgia | 1,350,944 | 2.7% |
| 12 | Virginia | 1,226,577 | 2.5% |
| 13 | Tennessee | 1,132,942 | 2.3% |
| 14 | Massachusetts | 1,125,661 | 2.3% |
| 15 | Indiana | 1,064,511 | 2.1% |
| 16 | Missouri | 1,058,418 | 2.1% |
| 17 | Washington | 1,055,977 | 2.1% |
| 18 | Arizona | 1,009,292 | 2.0% |
| 19 | Wisconsin | 966,151 | 1.9% |
| 20 | Alabama | 896,274 | 1.8% |
| 21 | Maryland | 844,862 | 1.7% |
| 22 | South Carolina | 839,989 | 1.7% |
| 23 | Minnesota | 836,205 | 1.7% |
| 24 | Kentucky | 804,245 | 1.6% |
| 25 | Louisiana | 729,271 | 1.5% |
| 26 | Colorado | 688,283 | 1.4% |
| 27 | Oregon | 671,822 | 1.4% |
| 28 | Oklahoma | 635,525 | 1.3% |
| 29 | Connecticut | 595,294 | 1.2% |
| 30 | Arkansas | 558,620 | 1.1% |
| 31 | Iowa | 537,430 | 1.1% |
| 32 | Mississippi | 523,625 | 1.1% |
| 33 | Kansas | 453,927 | 0.9% |
| 34 | West Virginia | 396,705 | 0.8% |
| 35 | Nevada | 394,066 | 0.8% |
| 36 | New Mexico | 336,413 | 0.7% |
| 37 | Utah | 307,361 | 0.6% |
| 38 | Nebraska | 291,333 | 0.6% |
| 39 | Maine | 281,968 | 0.6% |
| 40 | Idaho | 249,626 | 0.5% |
| 41 | New Hampshire | 240,551 | 0.5% |
| 42 | Hawaii | 221,514 | 0.4% |
| 43 | Rhode Island | 191,420 | 0.4% |
| 44 | Montana | 181,710 | 0.4% |
| 45 | Delaware | 161,422 | 0.3% |
| 46 | South Dakota | 143,014 | 0.3% |
| 47 | Vermont | 119,759 | 0.2% |
| 48 | North Dakota | 112,330 | 0.2% |
| 49 | Wyoming | 85,708 | 0.2% |
| 50 | Alaska | 72,898 | 0.1% |
| | District of Columbia | 82,493 | 0.2% |

Source: U.S. Department of Health and Human Services, Centers for Medicare and Medicaid Services
   "2013 Medicare and Medicaid Statistical Supplement" (Table 2.8)
      (www.cms.gov/Research-Statistics-Data-and-Systems/Statistics-Trends-and-Reports/MedicareMedicaidStatSupp/index.html)
*Includes aged and disabled enrollees. Total does not include enrollees in Puerto Rico and other outlying areas, foreign countries, or whose address is unknown.

# Percent of Population Enrolled in Medicare in 2012

## National Percent = 15.8% of Population*

| ALPHA ORDER | | | RANK ORDER | | |
|---|---|---|---|---|---|
| RANK | STATE | PERCENT | RANK | STATE | PERCENT |
| 7 | Alabama | 18.6 | 1 | West Virginia | 21.4 |
| 50 | Alaska | 10.0 | 2 | Maine | 21.2 |
| 38 | Arizona | 15.4 | 3 | Vermont | 19.1 |
| 4 | Arkansas | 18.9 | 4 | Arkansas | 18.9 |
| 46 | California | 13.4 | 5 | Florida | 18.7 |
| 47 | Colorado | 13.3 | 5 | Pennsylvania | 18.7 |
| 25 | Connecticut | 16.6 | 7 | Alabama | 18.6 |
| 14 | Delaware | 17.6 | 8 | Kentucky | 18.4 |
| 5 | Florida | 18.7 | 9 | New Hampshire | 18.2 |
| 45 | Georgia | 13.6 | 9 | Rhode Island | 18.2 |
| 31 | Hawaii | 15.9 | 11 | Montana | 18.1 |
| 36 | Idaho | 15.6 | 12 | Michigan | 17.8 |
| 40 | Illinois | 15.0 | 12 | South Carolina | 17.8 |
| 27 | Indiana | 16.3 | 14 | Delaware | 17.6 |
| 16 | Iowa | 17.5 | 14 | Missouri | 17.6 |
| 34 | Kansas | 15.7 | 16 | Iowa | 17.5 |
| 8 | Kentucky | 18.4 | 16 | Mississippi | 17.5 |
| 32 | Louisiana | 15.8 | 16 | Tennessee | 17.5 |
| 2 | Maine | 21.2 | 19 | Ohio | 17.4 |
| 43 | Maryland | 14.4 | 20 | Oregon | 17.2 |
| 22 | Massachusetts | 16.9 | 20 | South Dakota | 17.2 |
| 12 | Michigan | 17.8 | 22 | Massachusetts | 16.9 |
| 37 | Minnesota | 15.5 | 22 | Wisconsin | 16.9 |
| 16 | Mississippi | 17.5 | 24 | Oklahoma | 16.7 |
| 14 | Missouri | 17.6 | 25 | Connecticut | 16.6 |
| 11 | Montana | 18.1 | 26 | North Carolina | 16.4 |
| 34 | Nebraska | 15.7 | 27 | Indiana | 16.3 |
| 44 | Nevada | 14.3 | 28 | New Mexico | 16.1 |
| 9 | New Hampshire | 18.2 | 28 | North Dakota | 16.1 |
| 32 | New Jersey | 15.8 | 30 | New York | 16.0 |
| 28 | New Mexico | 16.1 | 31 | Hawaii | 15.9 |
| 30 | New York | 16.0 | 32 | Louisiana | 15.8 |
| 26 | North Carolina | 16.4 | 32 | New Jersey | 15.8 |
| 28 | North Dakota | 16.1 | 34 | Kansas | 15.7 |
| 19 | Ohio | 17.4 | 34 | Nebraska | 15.7 |
| 24 | Oklahoma | 16.7 | 36 | Idaho | 15.6 |
| 20 | Oregon | 17.2 | 37 | Minnesota | 15.5 |
| 5 | Pennsylvania | 18.7 | 38 | Arizona | 15.4 |
| 9 | Rhode Island | 18.2 | 39 | Washington | 15.3 |
| 12 | South Carolina | 17.8 | 40 | Illinois | 15.0 |
| 20 | South Dakota | 17.2 | 40 | Virginia | 15.0 |
| 16 | Tennessee | 17.5 | 42 | Wyoming | 14.9 |
| 48 | Texas | 12.5 | 43 | Maryland | 14.4 |
| 49 | Utah | 10.8 | 44 | Nevada | 14.3 |
| 3 | Vermont | 19.1 | 45 | Georgia | 13.6 |
| 40 | Virginia | 15.0 | 46 | California | 13.4 |
| 39 | Washington | 15.3 | 47 | Colorado | 13.3 |
| 1 | West Virginia | 21.4 | 48 | Texas | 12.5 |
| 22 | Wisconsin | 16.9 | 49 | Utah | 10.8 |
| 42 | Wyoming | 14.9 | 50 | Alaska | 10.0 |
| | | | | District of Columbia | 13.0 |

Source: U.S. Department of Health and Human Services, Centers for Medicare and Medicaid Services
 "2013 Medicare and Medicaid Statistical Supplement" (Table 2.8)
  (www.cms.gov/Research-Statistics-Data-and-Systems/Statistics-Trends-and-Reports/MedicareMedicaidStatSupp/index.html)
*Includes aged and disabled enrollees. National rate includes only residents of the 50 states and the District of Columbia.

# Medicare Program Payments in 2011

## National Total = $339,587,000,000*

ALPHA ORDER

| RANK | STATE | PAYMENTS | % of USA |
|---|---|---|---|
| 18 | Alabama | $5,949,000,000 | 1.8% |
| 50 | Alaska | 525,000,000 | 0.2% |
| 24 | Arizona | 5,277,000,000 | 1.6% |
| 30 | Arkansas | 3,580,000,000 | 1.1% |
| 1 | California | 31,038,000,000 | 9.1% |
| 31 | Colorado | 3,456,000,000 | 1.0% |
| 25 | Connecticut | 4,882,000,000 | 1.4% |
| 41 | Delaware | 1,400,000,000 | 0.4% |
| 3 | Florida | 25,495,000,000 | 7.5% |
| 12 | Georgia | 8,856,000,000 | 2.6% |
| 47 | Hawaii | 780,000,000 | 0.2% |
| 42 | Idaho | 1,287,000,000 | 0.4% |
| 5 | Illinois | 16,702,000,000 | 4.9% |
| 15 | Indiana | 7,556,000,000 | 2.2% |
| 29 | Iowa | 3,599,000,000 | 1.1% |
| 32 | Kansas | 3,226,000,000 | 0.9% |
| 20 | Kentucky | 5,783,000,000 | 1.7% |
| 21 | Louisiana | 5,739,000,000 | 1.7% |
| 37 | Maine | 1,768,000,000 | 0.5% |
| 14 | Maryland | 8,111,000,000 | 2.4% |
| 11 | Massachusetts | 9,222,000,000 | 2.7% |
| 7 | Michigan | 13,243,000,000 | 3.9% |
| 27 | Minnesota | 4,479,000,000 | 1.3% |
| 28 | Mississippi | 4,444,000,000 | 1.3% |
| 17 | Missouri | 7,011,000,000 | 2.1% |
| 44 | Montana | 1,014,000,000 | 0.3% |
| 36 | Nebraska | 2,162,000,000 | 0.6% |
| 35 | Nevada | 2,474,000,000 | 0.7% |
| 38 | New Hampshire | 1,736,000,000 | 0.5% |
| 9 | New Jersey | 12,473,000,000 | 3.7% |
| 39 | New Mexico | 1,712,000,000 | 0.5% |
| 4 | New York | 21,568,000,000 | 6.4% |
| 10 | North Carolina | 10,949,000,000 | 3.2% |
| 48 | North Dakota | 765,000,000 | 0.2% |
| 8 | Ohio | 12,760,000,000 | 3.8% |
| 26 | Oklahoma | 4,693,000,000 | 1.4% |
| 33 | Oregon | 2,732,000,000 | 0.8% |
| 6 | Pennsylvania | 14,091,000,000 | 4.1% |
| 43 | Rhode Island | 1,090,000,000 | 0.3% |
| 19 | South Carolina | 5,935,000,000 | 1.7% |
| 45 | South Dakota | 985,000,000 | 0.3% |
| 16 | Tennessee | 7,227,000,000 | 2.1% |
| 2 | Texas | 26,255,000,000 | 7.7% |
| 40 | Utah | 1,534,000,000 | 0.5% |
| 46 | Vermont | 852,000,000 | 0.3% |
| 13 | Virginia | 8,127,000,000 | 2.4% |
| 22 | Washington | 5,598,000,000 | 1.6% |
| 34 | West Virginia | 2,644,000,000 | 0.8% |
| 23 | Wisconsin | 5,406,000,000 | 1.6% |
| 49 | Wyoming | 617,000,000 | 0.2% |

RANK ORDER

| RANK | STATE | PAYMENTS | % of USA |
|---|---|---|---|
| 1 | California | $31,038,000,000 | 9.1% |
| 2 | Texas | 26,255,000,000 | 7.7% |
| 3 | Florida | 25,495,000,000 | 7.5% |
| 4 | New York | 21,568,000,000 | 6.4% |
| 5 | Illinois | 16,702,000,000 | 4.9% |
| 6 | Pennsylvania | 14,091,000,000 | 4.1% |
| 7 | Michigan | 13,243,000,000 | 3.9% |
| 8 | Ohio | 12,760,000,000 | 3.8% |
| 9 | New Jersey | 12,473,000,000 | 3.7% |
| 10 | North Carolina | 10,949,000,000 | 3.2% |
| 11 | Massachusetts | 9,222,000,000 | 2.7% |
| 12 | Georgia | 8,856,000,000 | 2.6% |
| 13 | Virginia | 8,127,000,000 | 2.4% |
| 14 | Maryland | 8,111,000,000 | 2.4% |
| 15 | Indiana | 7,556,000,000 | 2.2% |
| 16 | Tennessee | 7,227,000,000 | 2.1% |
| 17 | Missouri | 7,011,000,000 | 2.1% |
| 18 | Alabama | 5,949,000,000 | 1.8% |
| 19 | South Carolina | 5,935,000,000 | 1.7% |
| 20 | Kentucky | 5,783,000,000 | 1.7% |
| 21 | Louisiana | 5,739,000,000 | 1.7% |
| 22 | Washington | 5,598,000,000 | 1.6% |
| 23 | Wisconsin | 5,406,000,000 | 1.6% |
| 24 | Arizona | 5,277,000,000 | 1.6% |
| 25 | Connecticut | 4,882,000,000 | 1.4% |
| 26 | Oklahoma | 4,693,000,000 | 1.4% |
| 27 | Minnesota | 4,479,000,000 | 1.3% |
| 28 | Mississippi | 4,444,000,000 | 1.3% |
| 29 | Iowa | 3,599,000,000 | 1.1% |
| 30 | Arkansas | 3,580,000,000 | 1.1% |
| 31 | Colorado | 3,456,000,000 | 1.0% |
| 32 | Kansas | 3,226,000,000 | 0.9% |
| 33 | Oregon | 2,732,000,000 | 0.8% |
| 34 | West Virginia | 2,644,000,000 | 0.8% |
| 35 | Nevada | 2,474,000,000 | 0.7% |
| 36 | Nebraska | 2,162,000,000 | 0.6% |
| 37 | Maine | 1,768,000,000 | 0.5% |
| 38 | New Hampshire | 1,736,000,000 | 0.5% |
| 39 | New Mexico | 1,712,000,000 | 0.5% |
| 40 | Utah | 1,534,000,000 | 0.5% |
| 41 | Delaware | 1,400,000,000 | 0.4% |
| 42 | Idaho | 1,287,000,000 | 0.4% |
| 43 | Rhode Island | 1,090,000,000 | 0.3% |
| 44 | Montana | 1,014,000,000 | 0.3% |
| 45 | South Dakota | 985,000,000 | 0.3% |
| 46 | Vermont | 852,000,000 | 0.3% |
| 47 | Hawaii | 780,000,000 | 0.2% |
| 48 | North Dakota | 765,000,000 | 0.2% |
| 49 | Wyoming | 617,000,000 | 0.2% |
| 50 | Alaska | 525,000,000 | 0.2% |
| | District of Columbia | 783,000,000 | 0.2% |

Source: U.S. Department of Health and Human Services, Centers for Medicare and Medicaid Services
"2012 Medicare and Medicaid Statistical Supplement" (Table 3.5)
(www.cms.gov/Research-Statistics-Data-and-Systems/Statistics-Trends-and-Reports/MedicareMedicaidStatSupp/index.html)
*Figures for calendar year 2011.  Includes payments to aged and disabled enrollees.  Total does not include payments to beneficiaries in Puerto Rico and other outlying areas.

# Medicare Program Payments per Enrollee in 2011

## National Rate = $9,468*

| ALPHA ORDER | | | | RANK ORDER | | |
|---|---|---|---|---|---|---|
| RANK | STATE | PER ENROLLEE | | RANK | STATE | PER ENROLLEE |
| 29 | Alabama | $8,623 | | 1 | Maryland | $10,852 |
| 42 | Alaska | 7,740 | | 2 | Florida | 10,823 |
| 28 | Arizona | 8,663 | | 3 | Louisiana | 10,778 |
| 37 | Arkansas | 7,911 | | 4 | Texas | 10,596 |
| 11 | California | 9,903 | | 5 | New Jersey | 10,553 |
| 36 | Colorado | 7,939 | | 6 | Connecticut | 10,406 |
| 6 | Connecticut | 10,406 | | 7 | Michigan | 10,320 |
| 17 | Delaware | 9,369 | | 8 | Massachusetts | 10,264 |
| 2 | Florida | 10,823 | | 9 | New York | 10,255 |
| 24 | Georgia | 8,836 | | 10 | Minnesota | 10,000 |
| 50 | Hawaii | 6,368 | | 11 | California | 9,903 |
| 45 | Idaho | 7,531 | | 12 | Ohio | 9,882 |
| 15 | Illinois | 9,758 | | 13 | Pennsylvania | 9,769 |
| 20 | Indiana | 8,957 | | 14 | Mississippi | 9,767 |
| 39 | Iowa | 7,869 | | 15 | Illinois | 9,758 |
| 32 | Kansas | 8,336 | | 16 | Nevada | 9,539 |
| 21 | Kentucky | 8,936 | | 17 | Delaware | 9,369 |
| 3 | Louisiana | 10,778 | | 18 | Rhode Island | 9,046 |
| 44 | Maine | 7,538 | | 19 | Oklahoma | 8,987 |
| 1 | Maryland | 10,852 | | 20 | Indiana | 8,957 |
| 8 | Massachusetts | 10,264 | | 21 | Kentucky | 8,936 |
| 7 | Michigan | 10,320 | | 22 | South Carolina | 8,900 |
| 10 | Minnesota | 10,000 | | 23 | Tennessee | 8,859 |
| 14 | Mississippi | 9,767 | | 24 | Georgia | 8,836 |
| 27 | Missouri | 8,679 | | 25 | North Carolina | 8,725 |
| 49 | Montana | 6,759 | | 26 | West Virginia | 8,720 |
| 30 | Nebraska | 8,466 | | 27 | Missouri | 8,679 |
| 16 | Nevada | 9,539 | | 28 | Arizona | 8,663 |
| 33 | New Hampshire | 8,193 | | 29 | Alabama | 8,623 |
| 5 | New Jersey | 10,553 | | 30 | Nebraska | 8,466 |
| 47 | New Mexico | 7,266 | | 31 | Wisconsin | 8,352 |
| 9 | New York | 10,255 | | 32 | Kansas | 8,336 |
| 25 | North Carolina | 8,725 | | 33 | New Hampshire | 8,193 |
| 43 | North Dakota | 7,570 | | 34 | Virginia | 8,061 |
| 12 | Ohio | 9,882 | | 35 | Utah | 8,057 |
| 19 | Oklahoma | 8,987 | | 36 | Colorado | 7,939 |
| 48 | Oregon | 7,087 | | 37 | Arkansas | 7,911 |
| 13 | Pennsylvania | 9,769 | | 38 | South Dakota | 7,889 |
| 18 | Rhode Island | 9,046 | | 39 | Iowa | 7,869 |
| 22 | South Carolina | 8,900 | | 40 | Vermont | 7,812 |
| 38 | South Dakota | 7,889 | | 41 | Wyoming | 7,795 |
| 23 | Tennessee | 8,859 | | 42 | Alaska | 7,740 |
| 4 | Texas | 10,596 | | 43 | North Dakota | 7,570 |
| 35 | Utah | 8,057 | | 44 | Maine | 7,538 |
| 40 | Vermont | 7,812 | | 45 | Idaho | 7,531 |
| 34 | Virginia | 8,061 | | 46 | Washington | 7,510 |
| 46 | Washington | 7,510 | | 47 | New Mexico | 7,266 |
| 26 | West Virginia | 8,720 | | 48 | Oregon | 7,087 |
| 31 | Wisconsin | 8,352 | | 49 | Montana | 6,759 |
| 41 | Wyoming | 7,795 | | 50 | Hawaii | 6,368 |
| | | | | | District of Columbia | 10,953 |

Source: U.S. Department of Health and Human Services, Centers for Medicare and Medicaid Services
  "2012 Medicare and Medicaid Statistical Supplement" (Table 3.5)
    (www.cms.gov/Research-Statistics-Data-and-Systems/Statistics-Trends-and-Reports/MedicareMedicaidStatSupp/index.html)
*Figures for calendar year 2011.  Includes payments to aged and disabled enrollees.  National figure does not include enrollees in managed care plans in the denominator used to calculate average payments.  National rate also does not include payments or enrollees in Puerto Rico and other outlying areas.

# Medicaid Enrollment in 2011

## National Total = 57,106,941 Enrollees*

ALPHA ORDER

| RANK | STATE | ENROLLEES | % of USA |
|------|-------|-----------|----------|
| 20 | Alabama | 930,736 | 1.6% |
| 46 | Alaska | 120,611 | 0.2% |
| 12 | Arizona | 1,351,988 | 2.4% |
| 29 | Arkansas | 608,332 | 1.1% |
| 1 | California | 7,580,978 | 13.3% |
| 30 | Colorado | 583,618 | 1.0% |
| 31 | Connecticut | 578,620 | 1.0% |
| 42 | Delaware | 200,810 | 0.4% |
| 4 | Florida | 3,069,456 | 5.4% |
| 10 | Georgia | 1,548,090 | 2.7% |
| 38 | Hawaii | 272,218 | 0.5% |
| 41 | Idaho | 230,725 | 0.4% |
| 5 | Illinois | 2,787,200 | 4.9% |
| 18 | Indiana | 1,055,779 | 1.8% |
| 33 | Iowa | 440,993 | 0.8% |
| 35 | Kansas | 354,664 | 0.6% |
| 25 | Kentucky | 823,133 | 1.4% |
| 14 | Louisiana | 1,208,859 | 2.1% |
| 34 | Maine | 357,706 | 0.6% |
| 19 | Maryland | 986,304 | 1.7% |
| 9 | Massachusetts | 1,566,222 | 2.7% |
| 8 | Michigan | 1,818,312 | 3.2% |
| 24 | Minnesota | 847,638 | 1.5% |
| 28 | Mississippi | 621,607 | 1.1% |
| 22 | Missouri | 895,998 | 1.6% |
| 48 | Montana | 106,493 | 0.2% |
| 40 | Nebraska | 237,484 | 0.4% |
| 37 | Nevada | 297,640 | 0.5% |
| 45 | New Hampshire | 135,092 | 0.2% |
| 17 | New Jersey | 1,098,608 | 1.9% |
| 32 | New Mexico | 551,017 | 1.0% |
| 2 | New York | 4,925,236 | 8.6% |
| 11 | North Carolina | 1,488,263 | 2.6% |
| 50 | North Dakota | 66,698 | 0.1% |
| 7 | Ohio | 2,129,706 | 3.7% |
| 26 | Oklahoma | 684,387 | 1.2% |
| 27 | Oregon | 652,846 | 1.1% |
| 6 | Pennsylvania | 2,134,956 | 3.7% |
| 43 | Rhode Island | 197,248 | 0.3% |
| 23 | South Carolina | 862,145 | 1.5% |
| 47 | South Dakota | 120,474 | 0.2% |
| 13 | Tennessee | 1,218,676 | 2.1% |
| 3 | Texas | 3,943,189 | 6.9% |
| 39 | Utah | 269,643 | 0.5% |
| 44 | Vermont | 177,108 | 0.3% |
| 21 | Virginia | 915,038 | 1.6% |
| 15 | Washington | 1,182,587 | 2.1% |
| 36 | West Virginia | 326,749 | 0.6% |
| 16 | Wisconsin | 1,173,355 | 2.1% |
| 49 | Wyoming | 69,947 | 0.1% |

RANK ORDER

| RANK | STATE | ENROLLEES | % of USA |
|------|-------|-----------|----------|
| 1 | California | 7,580,978 | 13.3% |
| 2 | New York | 4,925,236 | 8.6% |
| 3 | Texas | 3,943,189 | 6.9% |
| 4 | Florida | 3,069,456 | 5.4% |
| 5 | Illinois | 2,787,200 | 4.9% |
| 6 | Pennsylvania | 2,134,956 | 3.7% |
| 7 | Ohio | 2,129,706 | 3.7% |
| 8 | Michigan | 1,818,312 | 3.2% |
| 9 | Massachusetts | 1,566,222 | 2.7% |
| 10 | Georgia | 1,548,090 | 2.7% |
| 11 | North Carolina | 1,488,263 | 2.6% |
| 12 | Arizona | 1,351,988 | 2.4% |
| 13 | Tennessee | 1,218,676 | 2.1% |
| 14 | Louisiana | 1,208,859 | 2.1% |
| 15 | Washington | 1,182,587 | 2.1% |
| 16 | Wisconsin | 1,173,355 | 2.1% |
| 17 | New Jersey | 1,098,608 | 1.9% |
| 18 | Indiana | 1,055,779 | 1.8% |
| 19 | Maryland | 986,304 | 1.7% |
| 20 | Alabama | 930,736 | 1.6% |
| 21 | Virginia | 915,038 | 1.6% |
| 22 | Missouri | 895,998 | 1.6% |
| 23 | South Carolina | 862,145 | 1.5% |
| 24 | Minnesota | 847,638 | 1.5% |
| 25 | Kentucky | 823,133 | 1.4% |
| 26 | Oklahoma | 684,387 | 1.2% |
| 27 | Oregon | 652,846 | 1.1% |
| 28 | Mississippi | 621,607 | 1.1% |
| 29 | Arkansas | 608,332 | 1.1% |
| 30 | Colorado | 583,618 | 1.0% |
| 31 | Connecticut | 578,620 | 1.0% |
| 32 | New Mexico | 551,017 | 1.0% |
| 33 | Iowa | 440,993 | 0.8% |
| 34 | Maine | 357,706 | 0.6% |
| 35 | Kansas | 354,664 | 0.6% |
| 36 | West Virginia | 326,749 | 0.6% |
| 37 | Nevada | 297,640 | 0.5% |
| 38 | Hawaii | 272,218 | 0.5% |
| 39 | Utah | 269,643 | 0.5% |
| 40 | Nebraska | 237,484 | 0.4% |
| 41 | Idaho | 230,725 | 0.4% |
| 42 | Delaware | 200,810 | 0.4% |
| 43 | Rhode Island | 197,248 | 0.3% |
| 44 | Vermont | 177,108 | 0.3% |
| 45 | New Hampshire | 135,092 | 0.2% |
| 46 | Alaska | 120,611 | 0.2% |
| 47 | South Dakota | 120,474 | 0.2% |
| 48 | Montana | 106,493 | 0.2% |
| 49 | Wyoming | 69,947 | 0.1% |
| 50 | North Dakota | 66,698 | 0.1% |
| | District of Columbia | 201,777 | 0.4% |

Source: U.S. Department of Health and Human Services, Centers for Medicare and Medicaid Services
"2011 Medicaid Managed Care Enrollment Report" (http://www.cms.gov/MedicaidDataSourcesGenInfo/)
*Unduplicated enrollment as of December 31, 2011. National total includes 1,099,982 Medicaid enrollees in Puerto Rico and the Virgin Islands.

# Percent of Population Enrolled in Medicaid in 2011

## National Percent = 18.0% of Population*

| ALPHA ORDER | | | RANK ORDER | | |
|---|---|---|---|---|---|
| **RANK** | **STATE** | **PERCENT** | **RANK** | **STATE** | **PERCENT** |
| 15 | Alabama | 19.4 | 1 | Vermont | 28.3 |
| 28 | Alaska | 16.7 | 2 | Maine | 26.9 |
| 9 | Arizona | 20.9 | 3 | New Mexico | 26.5 |
| 11 | Arkansas | 20.7 | 4 | Louisiana | 26.4 |
| 13 | California | 20.1 | 5 | New York | 25.3 |
| 44 | Colorado | 11.4 | 6 | Massachusetts | 23.7 |
| 30 | Connecticut | 16.1 | 7 | Delaware | 22.1 |
| 7 | Delaware | 22.1 | 8 | Illinois | 21.7 |
| 30 | Florida | 16.1 | 9 | Arizona | 20.9 |
| 33 | Georgia | 15.8 | 9 | Mississippi | 20.9 |
| 14 | Hawaii | 19.8 | 11 | Arkansas | 20.7 |
| 37 | Idaho | 14.6 | 12 | Wisconsin | 20.6 |
| 8 | Illinois | 21.7 | 13 | California | 20.1 |
| 29 | Indiana | 16.2 | 14 | Hawaii | 19.8 |
| 39 | Iowa | 14.4 | 15 | Alabama | 19.4 |
| 41 | Kansas | 12.4 | 16 | Tennessee | 19.0 |
| 17 | Kentucky | 18.8 | 17 | Kentucky | 18.8 |
| 4 | Louisiana | 26.4 | 17 | Rhode Island | 18.8 |
| 2 | Maine | 26.9 | 19 | Michigan | 18.4 |
| 25 | Maryland | 16.9 | 19 | Ohio | 18.4 |
| 6 | Massachusetts | 23.7 | 19 | South Carolina | 18.4 |
| 19 | Michigan | 18.4 | 22 | Oklahoma | 18.1 |
| 32 | Minnesota | 15.9 | 23 | West Virginia | 17.6 |
| 9 | Mississippi | 20.9 | 24 | Washington | 17.3 |
| 36 | Missouri | 14.9 | 25 | Maryland | 16.9 |
| 47 | Montana | 10.7 | 25 | Oregon | 16.9 |
| 40 | Nebraska | 12.9 | 27 | Pennsylvania | 16.8 |
| 46 | Nevada | 11.0 | 28 | Alaska | 16.7 |
| 48 | New Hampshire | 10.2 | 29 | Indiana | 16.2 |
| 41 | New Jersey | 12.4 | 30 | Connecticut | 16.1 |
| 3 | New Mexico | 26.5 | 30 | Florida | 16.1 |
| 5 | New York | 25.3 | 32 | Minnesota | 15.9 |
| 34 | North Carolina | 15.4 | 33 | Georgia | 15.8 |
| 49 | North Dakota | 9.7 | 34 | North Carolina | 15.4 |
| 19 | Ohio | 18.4 | 34 | Texas | 15.4 |
| 22 | Oklahoma | 18.1 | 36 | Missouri | 14.9 |
| 25 | Oregon | 16.9 | 37 | Idaho | 14.6 |
| 27 | Pennsylvania | 16.8 | 37 | South Dakota | 14.6 |
| 17 | Rhode Island | 18.8 | 39 | Iowa | 14.4 |
| 19 | South Carolina | 18.4 | 40 | Nebraska | 12.9 |
| 37 | South Dakota | 14.6 | 41 | Kansas | 12.4 |
| 16 | Tennessee | 19.0 | 41 | New Jersey | 12.4 |
| 34 | Texas | 15.4 | 43 | Wyoming | 12.3 |
| 50 | Utah | 9.6 | 44 | Colorado | 11.4 |
| 1 | Vermont | 28.3 | 45 | Virginia | 11.3 |
| 45 | Virginia | 11.3 | 46 | Nevada | 11.0 |
| 24 | Washington | 17.3 | 47 | Montana | 10.7 |
| 23 | West Virginia | 17.6 | 48 | New Hampshire | 10.2 |
| 12 | Wisconsin | 20.6 | 49 | North Dakota | 9.7 |
| 43 | Wyoming | 12.3 | 50 | Utah | 9.6 |
| | | | | District of Columbia | 32.6 |

Source: CQ Press using data from U.S. Department of Health and Human Services, Centers for Medicare and Medicaid Services
"2011 Medicaid Managed Care Enrollment Report" (http://www.cms.gov/MedicaidDataSourcesGenInfo/)
*Unduplicated enrollment as of December 31, 2011. National percent does not include recipients or population in U.S. territories.

# Estimated Medicaid Expenditures in 2013

## National Total = $419,337,000,000*

| ALPHA ORDER | | | | RANK ORDER | | | |
|---|---|---|---|---|---|---|---|
| RANK | STATE | EXPENDITURES | % of USA | RANK | STATE | EXPENDITURES | % of USA |
| 24 | Alabama | $5,835,000,000 | 1.4% | 1 | California | $55,885,000,000 | 13.3% |
| 42 | Alaska | 1,646,000,000 | 0.4% | 2 | New York | 38,792,000,000 | 9.3% |
| 12 | Arizona | 9,333,000,000 | 2.2% | 3 | Texas | 28,707,000,000 | 6.8% |
| 30 | Arkansas | 4,617,000,000 | 1.1% | 4 | Pennsylvania | 23,102,000,000 | 5.5% |
| 1 | California | 55,885,000,000 | 13.3% | 5 | Florida | 21,176,000,000 | 5.0% |
| 22 | Colorado | 6,377,000,000 | 1.5% | 6 | Illinois | 16,784,000,000 | 4.0% |
| 23 | Connecticut | 6,202,000,000 | 1.5% | 7 | Ohio | 14,419,000,000 | 3.4% |
| 44 | Delaware | 1,577,000,000 | 0.4% | 8 | Massachusetts | 12,830,000,000 | 3.1% |
| 5 | Florida | 21,176,000,000 | 5.0% | 9 | Michigan | 12,728,000,000 | 3.0% |
| 15 | Georgia | 8,289,000,000 | 2.0% | 10 | North Carolina | 12,137,000,000 | 2.9% |
| 43 | Hawaii | 1,627,000,000 | 0.4% | 11 | New Jersey | 10,442,000,000 | 2.5% |
| 40 | Idaho | 1,916,000,000 | 0.5% | 12 | Arizona | 9,333,000,000 | 2.2% |
| 6 | Illinois | 16,784,000,000 | 4.0% | 13 | Tennessee | 9,274,000,000 | 2.2% |
| 14 | Indiana | 8,789,000,000 | 2.1% | 14 | Indiana | 8,789,000,000 | 2.1% |
| 32 | Iowa | 3,665,000,000 | 0.9% | 15 | Georgia | 8,289,000,000 | 2.0% |
| 35 | Kansas | 2,823,000,000 | 0.7% | 16 | Missouri | 8,210,000,000 | 2.0% |
| 25 | Kentucky | 5,626,000,000 | 1.3% | 17 | Minnesota | 8,201,000,000 | 2.0% |
| 20 | Louisiana | 7,373,000,000 | 1.8% | 18 | Maryland | 7,718,000,000 | 1.8% |
| 36 | Maine | 2,509,000,000 | 0.6% | 19 | Virginia | 7,634,000,000 | 1.8% |
| 18 | Maryland | 7,718,000,000 | 1.8% | 20 | Louisiana | 7,373,000,000 | 1.8% |
| 8 | Massachusetts | 12,830,000,000 | 3.1% | 21 | Wisconsin | 7,341,000,000 | 1.8% |
| 9 | Michigan | 12,728,000,000 | 3.0% | 22 | Colorado | 6,377,000,000 | 1.5% |
| 17 | Minnesota | 8,201,000,000 | 2.0% | 23 | Connecticut | 6,202,000,000 | 1.5% |
| 28 | Mississippi | 5,050,000,000 | 1.2% | 24 | Alabama | 5,835,000,000 | 1.4% |
| 16 | Missouri | 8,210,000,000 | 2.0% | 25 | Kentucky | 5,626,000,000 | 1.3% |
| 47 | Montana | 1,081,000,000 | 0.3% | 26 | Oregon | 5,499,000,000 | 1.3% |
| 41 | Nebraska | 1,822,000,000 | 0.4% | 27 | Oklahoma | 5,225,000,000 | 1.2% |
| 38 | Nevada | 1,994,000,000 | 0.5% | 28 | Mississippi | 5,050,000,000 | 1.2% |
| 46 | New Hampshire | 1,285,000,000 | 0.3% | 29 | South Carolina | 4,890,000,000 | 1.2% |
| 11 | New Jersey | 10,442,000,000 | 2.5% | 30 | Arkansas | 4,617,000,000 | 1.1% |
| 33 | New Mexico | 3,599,000,000 | 0.9% | 31 | Washington | 4,524,000,000 | 1.1% |
| 2 | New York | 38,792,000,000 | 9.3% | 32 | Iowa | 3,665,000,000 | 0.9% |
| 10 | North Carolina | 12,137,000,000 | 2.9% | 33 | New Mexico | 3,599,000,000 | 0.9% |
| 49 | North Dakota | 774,000,000 | 0.2% | 34 | West Virginia | 3,093,000,000 | 0.7% |
| 7 | Ohio | 14,419,000,000 | 3.4% | 35 | Kansas | 2,823,000,000 | 0.7% |
| 27 | Oklahoma | 5,225,000,000 | 1.2% | 36 | Maine | 2,509,000,000 | 0.6% |
| 26 | Oregon | 5,499,000,000 | 1.3% | 37 | Utah | 2,124,000,000 | 0.5% |
| 4 | Pennsylvania | 23,102,000,000 | 5.5% | 38 | Nevada | 1,994,000,000 | 0.5% |
| 39 | Rhode Island | 1,986,000,000 | 0.5% | 39 | Rhode Island | 1,986,000,000 | 0.5% |
| 29 | South Carolina | 4,890,000,000 | 1.2% | 40 | Idaho | 1,916,000,000 | 0.5% |
| 48 | South Dakota | 816,000,000 | 0.2% | 41 | Nebraska | 1,822,000,000 | 0.4% |
| 13 | Tennessee | 9,274,000,000 | 2.2% | 42 | Alaska | 1,646,000,000 | 0.4% |
| 3 | Texas | 28,707,000,000 | 6.8% | 43 | Hawaii | 1,627,000,000 | 0.4% |
| 37 | Utah | 2,124,000,000 | 0.5% | 44 | Delaware | 1,577,000,000 | 0.4% |
| 45 | Vermont | 1,387,000,000 | 0.3% | 45 | Vermont | 1,387,000,000 | 0.3% |
| 19 | Virginia | 7,634,000,000 | 1.8% | 46 | New Hampshire | 1,285,000,000 | 0.3% |
| 31 | Washington | 4,524,000,000 | 1.1% | 47 | Montana | 1,081,000,000 | 0.3% |
| 34 | West Virginia | 3,093,000,000 | 0.7% | 48 | South Dakota | 816,000,000 | 0.2% |
| 21 | Wisconsin | 7,341,000,000 | 1.8% | 49 | North Dakota | 774,000,000 | 0.2% |
| 50 | Wyoming | 604,000,000 | 0.1% | 50 | Wyoming | 604,000,000 | 0.1% |
| | | | | | District of Columbia** | NA | NA |

Source: National Association of State Budget Officers
   "State Expenditure Report" (http://www.nasbo.org)
*Estimates for fiscal year 2013.
**Not available.

# Percent Change in Medicaid Expenditures: 2012 to 2013

## National Percent Change = 7.6% Increase*

ALPHA ORDER

| RANK | STATE | PERCENT CHANGE |
|---|---|---|
| 31 | Alabama | 3.7 |
| 4 | Alaska | 20.2 |
| 38 | Arizona | 2.2 |
| 28 | Arkansas | 4.4 |
| 1 | California | 29.8 |
| 20 | Colorado | 6.8 |
| 23 | Connecticut | 5.4 |
| 10 | Delaware | 11.0 |
| 12 | Florida | 9.9 |
| 44 | Georgia | (0.6) |
| 6 | Hawaii | 15.1 |
| 7 | Idaho | 12.4 |
| 2 | Illinois | 29.6 |
| 3 | Indiana | 22.4 |
| 47 | Iowa | (1.1) |
| 26 | Kansas | 5.2 |
| 49 | Kentucky | (2.7) |
| 41 | Louisiana | 2.0 |
| 18 | Maine | 7.5 |
| 32 | Maryland | 3.1 |
| 27 | Massachusetts | 4.7 |
| 33 | Michigan | 3.0 |
| 50 | Minnesota | (5.0) |
| 5 | Mississippi | 17.3 |
| 43 | Missouri | 0.3 |
| 14 | Montana | 8.5 |
| 11 | Nebraska | 10.5 |
| 33 | Nevada | 3.0 |
| 16 | New Hampshire | 8.3 |
| 46 | New Jersey | (0.7) |
| 33 | New Mexico | 3.0 |
| 48 | New York | (1.2) |
| 23 | North Carolina | 5.4 |
| 21 | North Dakota | 6.0 |
| 40 | Ohio | 2.1 |
| 28 | Oklahoma | 4.4 |
| 8 | Oregon | 12.0 |
| 30 | Pennsylvania | 3.9 |
| 42 | Rhode Island | 0.5 |
| 38 | South Carolina | 2.2 |
| 23 | South Dakota | 5.4 |
| 44 | Tennessee | (0.6) |
| 37 | Texas | 2.8 |
| 36 | Utah | 2.9 |
| 13 | Vermont | 9.5 |
| 14 | Virginia | 8.5 |
| 19 | Washington | 7.1 |
| 9 | West Virginia | 11.9 |
| 17 | Wisconsin | 7.6 |
| 22 | Wyoming | 5.6 |

RANK ORDER

| RANK | STATE | PERCENT CHANGE |
|---|---|---|
| 1 | California | 29.8 |
| 2 | Illinois | 29.6 |
| 3 | Indiana | 22.4 |
| 4 | Alaska | 20.2 |
| 5 | Mississippi | 17.3 |
| 6 | Hawaii | 15.1 |
| 7 | Idaho | 12.4 |
| 8 | Oregon | 12.0 |
| 9 | West Virginia | 11.9 |
| 10 | Delaware | 11.0 |
| 11 | Nebraska | 10.5 |
| 12 | Florida | 9.9 |
| 13 | Vermont | 9.5 |
| 14 | Montana | 8.5 |
| 14 | Virginia | 8.5 |
| 16 | New Hampshire | 8.3 |
| 17 | Wisconsin | 7.6 |
| 18 | Maine | 7.5 |
| 19 | Washington | 7.1 |
| 20 | Colorado | 6.8 |
| 21 | North Dakota | 6.0 |
| 22 | Wyoming | 5.6 |
| 23 | Connecticut | 5.4 |
| 23 | North Carolina | 5.4 |
| 23 | South Dakota | 5.4 |
| 26 | Kansas | 5.2 |
| 27 | Massachusetts | 4.7 |
| 28 | Arkansas | 4.4 |
| 28 | Oklahoma | 4.4 |
| 30 | Pennsylvania | 3.9 |
| 31 | Alabama | 3.7 |
| 32 | Maryland | 3.1 |
| 33 | Michigan | 3.0 |
| 33 | Nevada | 3.0 |
| 33 | New Mexico | 3.0 |
| 36 | Utah | 2.9 |
| 37 | Texas | 2.8 |
| 38 | Arizona | 2.2 |
| 38 | South Carolina | 2.2 |
| 40 | Ohio | 2.1 |
| 41 | Louisiana | 2.0 |
| 42 | Rhode Island | 0.5 |
| 43 | Missouri | 0.3 |
| 44 | Georgia | (0.6) |
| 44 | Tennessee | (0.6) |
| 46 | New Jersey | (0.7) |
| 47 | Iowa | (1.1) |
| 48 | New York | (1.2) |
| 49 | Kentucky | (2.7) |
| 50 | Minnesota | (5.0) |
| | District of Columbia** | NA |

Source: National Association of State Budget Officers
    "State Expenditure Report" (http://www.nasbo.org)
*Estimates for fiscal year 2013.
**Not available.

# Percent of Population Receiving Public Aid in 2011

## National Percent = 4.0% of Population*

ALPHA ORDER

| RANK | STATE | PERCENT |
|------|-------|---------|
| 8 | Alabama | 4.8 |
| 24 | Alaska | 3.2 |
| 43 | Arizona | 2.3 |
| 13 | Arkansas | 4.4 |
| 1 | California | 7.2 |
| 46 | Colorado | 2.0 |
| 41 | Connecticut | 2.5 |
| 21 | Delaware | 3.5 |
| 25 | Florida | 3.1 |
| 33 | Georgia | 2.8 |
| 17 | Hawaii | 3.9 |
| 46 | Idaho | 2.0 |
| 30 | Illinois | 2.9 |
| 41 | Indiana | 2.5 |
| 28 | Iowa | 3.0 |
| 33 | Kansas | 2.8 |
| 2 | Kentucky | 5.9 |
| 13 | Louisiana | 4.4 |
| 9 | Maine | 4.6 |
| 28 | Maryland | 3.0 |
| 11 | Massachusetts | 4.5 |
| 17 | Michigan | 3.9 |
| 38 | Minnesota | 2.6 |
| 5 | Mississippi | 5.1 |
| 20 | Missouri | 3.7 |
| 36 | Montana | 2.7 |
| 44 | Nebraska | 2.2 |
| 38 | Nevada | 2.6 |
| 44 | New Hampshire | 2.2 |
| 30 | New Jersey | 2.9 |
| 4 | New Mexico | 5.4 |
| 7 | New York | 5.0 |
| 33 | North Carolina | 2.8 |
| 48 | North Dakota | 1.9 |
| 15 | Ohio | 4.2 |
| 25 | Oklahoma | 3.1 |
| 17 | Oregon | 3.9 |
| 11 | Pennsylvania | 4.5 |
| 9 | Rhode Island | 4.6 |
| 23 | South Carolina | 3.3 |
| 38 | South Dakota | 2.6 |
| 5 | Tennessee | 5.1 |
| 30 | Texas | 2.9 |
| 49 | Utah | 1.5 |
| 21 | Vermont | 3.5 |
| 36 | Virginia | 2.7 |
| 16 | Washington | 4.0 |
| 3 | West Virginia | 5.5 |
| 25 | Wisconsin | 3.1 |
| 50 | Wyoming | 1.3 |

RANK ORDER

| RANK | STATE | PERCENT |
|------|-------|---------|
| 1 | California | 7.2 |
| 2 | Kentucky | 5.9 |
| 3 | West Virginia | 5.5 |
| 4 | New Mexico | 5.4 |
| 5 | Mississippi | 5.1 |
| 5 | Tennessee | 5.1 |
| 7 | New York | 5.0 |
| 8 | Alabama | 4.8 |
| 9 | Maine | 4.6 |
| 9 | Rhode Island | 4.6 |
| 11 | Massachusetts | 4.5 |
| 11 | Pennsylvania | 4.5 |
| 13 | Arkansas | 4.4 |
| 13 | Louisiana | 4.4 |
| 15 | Ohio | 4.2 |
| 16 | Washington | 4.0 |
| 17 | Hawaii | 3.9 |
| 17 | Michigan | 3.9 |
| 17 | Oregon | 3.9 |
| 20 | Missouri | 3.7 |
| 21 | Delaware | 3.5 |
| 21 | Vermont | 3.5 |
| 23 | South Carolina | 3.3 |
| 24 | Alaska | 3.2 |
| 25 | Florida | 3.1 |
| 25 | Oklahoma | 3.1 |
| 25 | Wisconsin | 3.1 |
| 28 | Iowa | 3.0 |
| 28 | Maryland | 3.0 |
| 30 | Illinois | 2.9 |
| 30 | New Jersey | 2.9 |
| 30 | Texas | 2.9 |
| 33 | Georgia | 2.8 |
| 33 | Kansas | 2.8 |
| 33 | North Carolina | 2.8 |
| 36 | Montana | 2.7 |
| 36 | Virginia | 2.7 |
| 38 | Minnesota | 2.6 |
| 38 | Nevada | 2.6 |
| 38 | South Dakota | 2.6 |
| 41 | Connecticut | 2.5 |
| 41 | Indiana | 2.5 |
| 43 | Arizona | 2.3 |
| 44 | Nebraska | 2.2 |
| 44 | New Hampshire | 2.2 |
| 46 | Colorado | 2.0 |
| 46 | Idaho | 2.0 |
| 48 | North Dakota | 1.9 |
| 49 | Utah | 1.5 |
| 50 | Wyoming | 1.3 |
| | District of Columbia | 7.3 |

Source: CQ Press using data from U.S. Social Security Administration and
U.S. Department of Health and Human Services

*As of December 2011. Includes recipients of Temporary Assistance to Needy Families (TANF) and/or Supplemental Security Income payments.

# Recipients of Temporary Assistance to Needy Families (TANF) Payments in 2013
## National Total = 3,683,855 Monthly Recipients*

ALPHA ORDER

| RANK | STATE | RECIPIENTS | % of USA |
|---|---|---|---|
| 19 | Alabama | 44,933 | 1.2% |
| 43 | Alaska | 9,436 | 0.3% |
| 24 | Arizona | 35,211 | 1.0% |
| 36 | Arkansas | 15,135 | 0.4% |
| 1 | California | 1,337,981 | 36.3% |
| 21 | Colorado | 38,973 | 1.1% |
| 27 | Connecticut | 28,849 | 0.8% |
| 40 | Delaware | 13,864 | 0.4% |
| 7 | Florida | 92,547 | 2.5% |
| 26 | Georgia | 33,569 | 0.9% |
| 30 | Hawaii | 25,765 | 0.7% |
| 49 | Idaho | 2,790 | 0.1% |
| 20 | Illinois | 43,892 | 1.2% |
| 31 | Indiana | 23,657 | 0.6% |
| 23 | Iowa | 36,188 | 1.0% |
| 34 | Kansas | 18,560 | 0.5% |
| 15 | Kentucky | 60,958 | 1.7% |
| 37 | Louisiana | 15,032 | 0.4% |
| 38 | Maine | 14,022 | 0.4% |
| 17 | Maryland | 51,563 | 1.4% |
| 8 | Massachusetts | 89,355 | 2.4% |
| 10 | Michigan | 76,014 | 2.1% |
| 18 | Minnesota | 46,568 | 1.3% |
| 32 | Mississippi | 19,780 | 0.5% |
| 12 | Missouri | 74,029 | 2.0% |
| 45 | Montana | 7,080 | 0.2% |
| 41 | Nebraska | 12,364 | 0.3% |
| 29 | Nevada | 26,238 | 0.7% |
| 44 | New Hampshire | 7,330 | 0.2% |
| 11 | New Jersey | 75,902 | 2.1% |
| 25 | New Mexico | 34,828 | 0.9% |
| 2 | New York | 274,228 | 7.4% |
| 22 | North Carolina | 36,712 | 1.0% |
| 48 | North Dakota | 3,546 | 0.1% |
| 4 | Ohio | 131,340 | 3.6% |
| 35 | Oklahoma | 16,117 | 0.4% |
| 16 | Oregon | 59,319 | 1.6% |
| 3 | Pennsylvania | 174,695 | 4.7% |
| 39 | Rhode Island | 13,931 | 0.4% |
| 28 | South Carolina | 27,745 | 0.8% |
| 47 | South Dakota | 6,199 | 0.2% |
| 5 | Tennessee | 118,084 | 3.2% |
| 9 | Texas | 86,148 | 2.3% |
| 42 | Utah | 9,761 | 0.3% |
| 46 | Vermont | 6,706 | 0.2% |
| 14 | Virginia | 61,908 | 1.7% |
| 6 | Washington | 104,720 | 2.8% |
| 33 | West Virginia | 19,094 | 0.5% |
| 13 | Wisconsin | 64,289 | 1.7% |
| 50 | Wyoming | 1,216 | 0.0% |

RANK ORDER

| RANK | STATE | RECIPIENTS | % of USA |
|---|---|---|---|
| 1 | California | 1,337,981 | 36.3% |
| 2 | New York | 274,228 | 7.4% |
| 3 | Pennsylvania | 174,695 | 4.7% |
| 4 | Ohio | 131,340 | 3.6% |
| 5 | Tennessee | 118,084 | 3.2% |
| 6 | Washington | 104,720 | 2.8% |
| 7 | Florida | 92,547 | 2.5% |
| 8 | Massachusetts | 89,355 | 2.4% |
| 9 | Texas | 86,148 | 2.3% |
| 10 | Michigan | 76,014 | 2.1% |
| 11 | New Jersey | 75,902 | 2.1% |
| 12 | Missouri | 74,029 | 2.0% |
| 13 | Wisconsin | 64,289 | 1.7% |
| 14 | Virginia | 61,908 | 1.7% |
| 15 | Kentucky | 60,958 | 1.7% |
| 16 | Oregon | 59,319 | 1.6% |
| 17 | Maryland | 51,563 | 1.4% |
| 18 | Minnesota | 46,568 | 1.3% |
| 19 | Alabama | 44,933 | 1.2% |
| 20 | Illinois | 43,892 | 1.2% |
| 21 | Colorado | 38,973 | 1.1% |
| 22 | North Carolina | 36,712 | 1.0% |
| 23 | Iowa | 36,188 | 1.0% |
| 24 | Arizona | 35,211 | 1.0% |
| 25 | New Mexico | 34,828 | 0.9% |
| 26 | Georgia | 33,569 | 0.9% |
| 27 | Connecticut | 28,849 | 0.8% |
| 28 | South Carolina | 27,745 | 0.8% |
| 29 | Nevada | 26,238 | 0.7% |
| 30 | Hawaii | 25,765 | 0.7% |
| 31 | Indiana | 23,657 | 0.6% |
| 32 | Mississippi | 19,780 | 0.5% |
| 33 | West Virginia | 19,094 | 0.5% |
| 34 | Kansas | 18,560 | 0.5% |
| 35 | Oklahoma | 16,117 | 0.4% |
| 36 | Arkansas | 15,135 | 0.4% |
| 37 | Louisiana | 15,032 | 0.4% |
| 38 | Maine | 14,022 | 0.4% |
| 39 | Rhode Island | 13,931 | 0.4% |
| 40 | Delaware | 13,864 | 0.4% |
| 41 | Nebraska | 12,364 | 0.3% |
| 42 | Utah | 9,761 | 0.3% |
| 43 | Alaska | 9,436 | 0.3% |
| 44 | New Hampshire | 7,330 | 0.2% |
| 45 | Montana | 7,080 | 0.2% |
| 46 | Vermont | 6,706 | 0.2% |
| 47 | South Dakota | 6,199 | 0.2% |
| 48 | North Dakota | 3,546 | 0.1% |
| 49 | Idaho | 2,790 | 0.1% |
| 50 | Wyoming | 1,216 | 0.0% |
| | District of Columbia | 15,664 | 0.4% |

Source: U.S. Department of Health and Human Services, Administration for Children and Families
"TANF Caseload Data" (http://www.acf.hhs.gov/programs/ofa/programs/tanf/data-reports)
*As of June 2013. National total includes 40,020 recipients in U.S. territories (35,585 in Puerto Rico).

# Percent Change in TANF Recipients: 2012 to 2013

## National Percent Change = 8.0% Decrease*

| ALPHA ORDER | | | | RANK ORDER | | |
|---|---|---|---|---|---|---|
| RANK | STATE | PERCENT CHANGE | | RANK | STATE | PERCENT CHANGE |
| 28 | Alabama | (9.5) | | 1 | Wyoming | 110.4 |
| 23 | Alaska | (8.4) | | 2 | Wisconsin | 7.4 |
| 35 | Arizona | (12.2) | | 3 | Colorado | 5.9 |
| 21 | Arkansas | (7.2) | | 4 | Kentucky | 1.2 |
| 10 | California | (2.9) | | 5 | Florida | 1.0 |
| 3 | Colorado | 5.9 | | 6 | Vermont | 0.5 |
| 9 | Connecticut | (1.9) | | 7 | New York | (0.1) |
| 16 | Delaware | (5.8) | | 8 | Nevada | (0.9) |
| 5 | Florida | 1.0 | | 9 | Connecticut | (1.9) |
| 15 | Georgia | (5.1) | | 10 | California | (2.9) |
| 20 | Hawaii | (6.9) | | 11 | Idaho | (3.2) |
| 11 | Idaho | (3.2) | | 12 | Minnesota | (4.2) |
| 50 | Illinois | (56.1) | | 13 | Nebraska | (4.4) |
| 46 | Indiana | (22.7) | | 14 | New Hampshire | (4.8) |
| 30 | Iowa | (10.0) | | 15 | Georgia | (5.1) |
| 48 | Kansas | (25.3) | | 16 | Delaware | (5.8) |
| 4 | Kentucky | 1.2 | | 17 | West Virginia | (6.0) |
| 45 | Louisiana | (22.4) | | 18 | South Dakota | (6.7) |
| 47 | Maine | (22.8) | | 19 | New Jersey | (6.8) |
| 32 | Maryland | (10.7) | | 20 | Hawaii | (6.9) |
| 23 | Massachusetts | (8.4) | | 21 | Arkansas | (7.2) |
| 49 | Michigan | (25.5) | | 22 | Virginia | (7.3) |
| 12 | Minnesota | (4.2) | | 23 | Alaska | (8.4) |
| 36 | Mississippi | (12.4) | | 23 | Massachusetts | (8.4) |
| 27 | Missouri | (9.2) | | 25 | North Carolina | (8.6) |
| 30 | Montana | (10.0) | | 26 | Pennsylvania | (9.1) |
| 13 | Nebraska | (4.4) | | 27 | Missouri | (9.2) |
| 8 | Nevada | (0.9) | | 28 | Alabama | (9.5) |
| 14 | New Hampshire | (4.8) | | 29 | South Carolina | (9.7) |
| 19 | New Jersey | (6.8) | | 30 | Iowa | (10.0) |
| 44 | New Mexico | (18.6) | | 30 | Montana | (10.0) |
| 7 | New York | (0.1) | | 32 | Maryland | (10.7) |
| 25 | North Carolina | (8.6) | | 33 | Rhode Island | (11.0) |
| 34 | North Dakota | (11.4) | | 34 | North Dakota | (11.4) |
| 43 | Ohio | (17.0) | | 35 | Arizona | (12.2) |
| 37 | Oklahoma | (12.6) | | 36 | Mississippi | (12.4) |
| 42 | Oregon | (13.8) | | 37 | Oklahoma | (12.6) |
| 26 | Pennsylvania | (9.1) | | 37 | Texas | (12.6) |
| 33 | Rhode Island | (11.0) | | 39 | Tennessee | (12.8) |
| 29 | South Carolina | (9.7) | | 39 | Utah | (12.8) |
| 18 | South Dakota | (6.7) | | 41 | Washington | (13.2) |
| 39 | Tennessee | (12.8) | | 42 | Oregon | (13.8) |
| 37 | Texas | (12.6) | | 43 | Ohio | (17.0) |
| 39 | Utah | (12.8) | | 44 | New Mexico | (18.6) |
| 6 | Vermont | 0.5 | | 45 | Louisiana | (22.4) |
| 22 | Virginia | (7.3) | | 46 | Indiana | (22.7) |
| 41 | Washington | (13.2) | | 47 | Maine | (22.8) |
| 17 | West Virginia | (6.0) | | 48 | Kansas | (25.3) |
| 2 | Wisconsin | 7.4 | | 49 | Michigan | (25.5) |
| 1 | Wyoming | 110.4 | | 50 | Illinois | (56.1) |
| | | | | District of Columbia | | 13.5 |

Source: CQ Press using data from U.S. Department of Health and Human Services, Administration for Children and Families
  "TANF Caseload Data" (http://www.acf.hhs.gov/programs/ofa/programs/tanf/data-reports)
*June 2012 to June 2013.  National percent includes recipients in U.S. territories.

# TANF Work Participation Rates in 2011

## National Rate = 43.6%*

| ALPHA ORDER | | | | RANK ORDER | | |
|---|---|---|---|---|---|---|
| RANK | STATE | PERCENT | | RANK | STATE | PERCENT |
| 24 | Alabama | 47.5 | | 1 | Idaho | 91.6 |
| 30 | Alaska | 44.2 | | 2 | Nebraska | 76.7 |
| 38 | Arizona | 41.1 | | 3 | Wisconsin | 73.4 |
| 29 | Arkansas | 44.5 | | 4 | Wyoming | 64.4 |
| 27 | California | 46.6 | | 5 | South Dakota | 62.9 |
| 28 | Colorado | 44.9 | | 6 | Mississippi | 61.9 |
| 11 | Connecticut | 58.3 | | 7 | North Carolina | 61.7 |
| 42 | Delaware | 37.3 | | 8 | Montana | 61.1 |
| 18 | Florida | 50.8 | | 9 | Georgia | 60.3 |
| 9 | Georgia | 60.3 | | 10 | Iowa | 58.4 |
| 19 | Hawaii | 50.0 | | 11 | Connecticut | 58.3 |
| 1 | Idaho | 91.6 | | 12 | Oklahoma | 56.4 |
| 14 | Illinois | 53.9 | | 13 | Minnesota | 55.1 |
| 45 | Indiana | 32.2 | | 14 | Illinois | 53.9 |
| 10 | Iowa | 58.4 | | 15 | North Dakota | 52.6 |
| 30 | Kansas | 44.2 | | 16 | Pennsylvania | 52.2 |
| 17 | Kentucky | 51.8 | | 17 | Kentucky | 51.8 |
| 35 | Louisiana | 42.0 | | 18 | Florida | 50.8 |
| 44 | Maine | 32.7 | | 19 | Hawaii | 50.0 |
| 25 | Maryland | 46.9 | | 19 | New Hampshire | 50.0 |
| 49 | Massachusetts | 15.6 | | 21 | Nevada | 48.6 |
| 33 | Michigan | 43.6 | | 22 | Texas | 48.2 |
| 13 | Minnesota | 55.1 | | 23 | West Virginia | 47.6 |
| 6 | Mississippi | 61.9 | | 24 | Alabama | 47.5 |
| 50 | Missouri | 13.5 | | 25 | Maryland | 46.9 |
| 8 | Montana | 61.1 | | 25 | Tennessee | 46.9 |
| 2 | Nebraska | 76.7 | | 27 | California | 46.6 |
| 21 | Nevada | 48.6 | | 28 | Colorado | 44.9 |
| 19 | New Hampshire | 50.0 | | 29 | Arkansas | 44.5 |
| 46 | New Jersey | 30.7 | | 30 | Alaska | 44.2 |
| 37 | New Mexico | 41.5 | | 30 | Kansas | 44.2 |
| 32 | New York | 44.0 | | 32 | New York | 44.0 |
| 7 | North Carolina | 61.7 | | 33 | Michigan | 43.6 |
| 15 | North Dakota | 52.6 | | 34 | Utah | 43.1 |
| 39 | Ohio | 40.1 | | 35 | Louisiana | 42.0 |
| 12 | Oklahoma | 56.4 | | 36 | South Carolina | 41.9 |
| 40 | Oregon | 39.8 | | 37 | New Mexico | 41.5 |
| 16 | Pennsylvania | 52.2 | | 38 | Arizona | 41.1 |
| 48 | Rhode Island | 28.1 | | 39 | Ohio | 40.1 |
| 36 | South Carolina | 41.9 | | 40 | Oregon | 39.8 |
| 5 | South Dakota | 62.9 | | 41 | Virginia | 37.6 |
| 25 | Tennessee | 46.9 | | 42 | Delaware | 37.3 |
| 22 | Texas | 48.2 | | 43 | Washington | 36.6 |
| 34 | Utah | 43.1 | | 44 | Maine | 32.7 |
| 47 | Vermont | 30.4 | | 45 | Indiana | 32.2 |
| 41 | Virginia | 37.6 | | 46 | New Jersey | 30.7 |
| 43 | Washington | 36.6 | | 47 | Vermont | 30.4 |
| 23 | West Virginia | 47.6 | | 48 | Rhode Island | 28.1 |
| 3 | Wisconsin | 73.4 | | 49 | Massachusetts | 15.6 |
| 4 | Wyoming | 64.4 | | 50 | Missouri | 13.5 |
| | | | | | District of Columbia | 22.7 |

Source: U.S. Department of Health and Human Services, Administration for Children and Families
"Characteristics and Financial Circumstances of TANF Recipients, Fiscal Year 2011 " (Table 28)
(http://www.acf.hhs.gov/programs/ofa/resource/characteristics-financial-circumstances-appendix-fy2011)
*For fiscal year 2011.  Percent of parents in TANF families who work for at least 30 hours per week, or 20 hours per week if they have children under age six.  National average includes recipients in U.S. territories.

# Average Monthly TANF Assistance per Family in 2011

## National Average = $386.90*

| ALPHA ORDER | | | | RANK ORDER | | |
|---|---|---|---|---|---|---|
| RANK | STATE | PER FAMILY | | RANK | STATE | PER FAMILY |
| 46 | Alabama | $195.70 | | 1 | Alaska | $598.40 |
| 1 | Alaska | 598.40 | | 2 | Hawaii | 555.20 |
| 41 | Arizona | 219.40 | | 3 | New York | 538.50 |
| 49 | Arkansas | 155.00 | | 4 | Utah | 511.30 |
| 5 | California | 499.50 | | 5 | California | 499.50 |
| 19 | Colorado | 366.70 | | 6 | New Hampshire | 487.90 |
| 10 | Connecticut | 441.90 | | 7 | Massachusetts | 472.80 |
| 36 | Delaware | 255.60 | | 8 | Vermont | 465.30 |
| 38 | Florida | 235.40 | | 9 | Maryland | 455.20 |
| 44 | Georgia | 211.20 | | 10 | Connecticut | 441.90 |
| 2 | Hawaii | 555.20 | | 11 | Wisconsin | 441.20 |
| 30 | Idaho | 299.30 | | 12 | Oregon | 436.10 |
| 35 | Illinois | 255.90 | | 13 | Rhode Island | 423.50 |
| 42 | Indiana | 216.10 | | 14 | Montana | 420.30 |
| 24 | Iowa | 318.00 | | 15 | Washington | 396.40 |
| 32 | Kansas | 284.80 | | 16 | Maine | 391.60 |
| 34 | Kentucky | 279.10 | | 17 | Michigan | 387.40 |
| 27 | Louisiana | 304.90 | | 18 | South Dakota | 385.90 |
| 16 | Maine | 391.60 | | 19 | Colorado | 366.70 |
| 9 | Maryland | 455.20 | | 20 | Wyoming | 362.10 |
| 7 | Massachusetts | 472.80 | | 21 | Ohio | 356.10 |
| 17 | Michigan | 387.40 | | 22 | Minnesota | 343.20 |
| 22 | Minnesota | 343.20 | | 23 | Nevada | 342.80 |
| 50 | Mississippi | 148.40 | | 24 | Iowa | 318.00 |
| 39 | Missouri | 230.20 | | 25 | New Jersey | 315.50 |
| 14 | Montana | 420.30 | | 26 | North Dakota | 313.80 |
| 31 | Nebraska | 291.60 | | 27 | Louisiana | 304.90 |
| 23 | Nevada | 342.80 | | 28 | New Mexico | 304.80 |
| 6 | New Hampshire | 487.90 | | 29 | Pennsylvania | 300.20 |
| 25 | New Jersey | 315.50 | | 30 | Idaho | 299.30 |
| 28 | New Mexico | 304.80 | | 31 | Nebraska | 291.60 |
| 3 | New York | 538.50 | | 32 | Kansas | 284.80 |
| 43 | North Carolina | 211.60 | | 33 | West Virginia | 284.20 |
| 26 | North Dakota | 313.80 | | 34 | Kentucky | 279.10 |
| 21 | Ohio | 356.10 | | 35 | Illinois | 255.90 |
| 45 | Oklahoma | 196.40 | | 36 | Delaware | 255.60 |
| 12 | Oregon | 436.10 | | 37 | Virginia | 254.50 |
| 29 | Pennsylvania | 300.20 | | 38 | Florida | 235.40 |
| 13 | Rhode Island | 423.50 | | 39 | Missouri | 230.20 |
| 47 | South Carolina | 178.90 | | 40 | Texas | 219.80 |
| 18 | South Dakota | 385.90 | | 41 | Arizona | 219.40 |
| 48 | Tennessee | 164.90 | | 42 | Indiana | 216.10 |
| 40 | Texas | 219.80 | | 43 | North Carolina | 211.60 |
| 4 | Utah | 511.30 | | 44 | Georgia | 211.20 |
| 8 | Vermont | 465.30 | | 45 | Oklahoma | 196.40 |
| 37 | Virginia | 254.50 | | 46 | Alabama | 195.70 |
| 15 | Washington | 396.40 | | 47 | South Carolina | 178.90 |
| 33 | West Virginia | 284.20 | | 48 | Tennessee | 164.90 |
| 11 | Wisconsin | 441.20 | | 49 | Arkansas | 155.00 |
| 20 | Wyoming | 362.10 | | 50 | Mississippi | 148.40 |
| | | | | | District of Columbia | 378.80 |

Source: U.S. Department of Health and Human Services, Administration for Children and Families
"Characteristics and Financial Circumstances of TANF Recipients, Fiscal Year 2011 " (Table 41)
(http://www.acf.hhs.gov/programs/ofa/resource/characteristics-financial-circumstances-appendix-fy2011)
*For fiscal year 2011. National average includes families in U.S. territories.

# Percent of Households with Food Insecurity in 2012

## National Percent = 14.7% of Households*

ALPHA ORDER

| RANK | STATE | PERCENT |
|------|-------|---------|
| 4 | Alabama | 17.9 |
| 42 | Alaska | 12.1 |
| 18 | Arizona | 14.9 |
| 2 | Arkansas | 19.7 |
| 12 | California | 15.6 |
| 26 | Colorado | 14.1 |
| 32 | Connecticut | 13.4 |
| 44 | Delaware | 11.6 |
| 20 | Florida | 14.8 |
| 6 | Georgia | 16.9 |
| 28 | Hawaii | 14.0 |
| 24 | Idaho | 14.3 |
| 36 | Illinois | 13.0 |
| 31 | Indiana | 13.5 |
| 40 | Iowa | 12.6 |
| 23 | Kansas | 14.4 |
| 12 | Kentucky | 15.6 |
| 11 | Louisiana | 15.7 |
| 18 | Maine | 14.9 |
| 36 | Maryland | 13.0 |
| 45 | Massachusetts | 11.4 |
| 32 | Michigan | 13.4 |
| 47 | Minnesota | 10.6 |
| 1 | Mississippi | 20.9 |
| 7 | Missouri | 16.7 |
| 26 | Montana | 14.1 |
| 32 | Nebraska | 13.4 |
| 8 | Nevada | 16.6 |
| 48 | New Hampshire | 9.9 |
| 42 | New Jersey | 12.1 |
| 17 | New Mexico | 15.2 |
| 35 | New York | 13.2 |
| 5 | North Carolina | 17.0 |
| 50 | North Dakota | 8.7 |
| 10 | Ohio | 16.1 |
| 16 | Oklahoma | 15.3 |
| 30 | Oregon | 13.6 |
| 41 | Pennsylvania | 12.3 |
| 14 | Rhode Island | 15.4 |
| 14 | South Carolina | 15.4 |
| 38 | South Dakota | 12.9 |
| 9 | Tennessee | 16.2 |
| 3 | Texas | 18.4 |
| 20 | Utah | 14.8 |
| 39 | Vermont | 12.7 |
| 49 | Virginia | 9.2 |
| 22 | Washington | 14.6 |
| 25 | West Virginia | 14.2 |
| 46 | Wisconsin | 11.2 |
| 29 | Wyoming | 13.8 |

RANK ORDER

| RANK | STATE | PERCENT |
|------|-------|---------|
| 1 | Mississippi | 20.9 |
| 2 | Arkansas | 19.7 |
| 3 | Texas | 18.4 |
| 4 | Alabama | 17.9 |
| 5 | North Carolina | 17.0 |
| 6 | Georgia | 16.9 |
| 7 | Missouri | 16.7 |
| 8 | Nevada | 16.6 |
| 9 | Tennessee | 16.2 |
| 10 | Ohio | 16.1 |
| 11 | Louisiana | 15.7 |
| 12 | California | 15.6 |
| 12 | Kentucky | 15.6 |
| 14 | Rhode Island | 15.4 |
| 14 | South Carolina | 15.4 |
| 16 | Oklahoma | 15.3 |
| 17 | New Mexico | 15.2 |
| 18 | Arizona | 14.9 |
| 18 | Maine | 14.9 |
| 20 | Florida | 14.8 |
| 20 | Utah | 14.8 |
| 22 | Washington | 14.6 |
| 23 | Kansas | 14.4 |
| 24 | Idaho | 14.3 |
| 25 | West Virginia | 14.2 |
| 26 | Colorado | 14.1 |
| 26 | Montana | 14.1 |
| 28 | Hawaii | 14.0 |
| 29 | Wyoming | 13.8 |
| 30 | Oregon | 13.6 |
| 31 | Indiana | 13.5 |
| 32 | Connecticut | 13.4 |
| 32 | Michigan | 13.4 |
| 32 | Nebraska | 13.4 |
| 35 | New York | 13.2 |
| 36 | Illinois | 13.0 |
| 36 | Maryland | 13.0 |
| 38 | South Dakota | 12.9 |
| 39 | Vermont | 12.7 |
| 40 | Iowa | 12.6 |
| 41 | Pennsylvania | 12.3 |
| 42 | Alaska | 12.1 |
| 42 | New Jersey | 12.1 |
| 44 | Delaware | 11.6 |
| 45 | Massachusetts | 11.4 |
| 46 | Wisconsin | 11.2 |
| 47 | Minnesota | 10.6 |
| 48 | New Hampshire | 9.9 |
| 49 | Virginia | 9.2 |
| 50 | North Dakota | 8.7 |
| | District of Columbia | 12.0 |

Source: U.S. Department of Agriculture, Economic Research Service
   "Household Food Security in the United States, 2012" (www.ers.usda.gov/publications/err-economic-research-report/err155.aspx)
*Three-year average for 2010-2012. Refers to households for which access to enough food is limited by a lack of money and other resources. About one-third of food-insecure households have very low food security, meaning that at times the food intake of some household members is reduced and their normal eating patterns are disrupted.

# Supplemental Nutrition Assistance Program Benefits in 2013

## National Total = $76,067,237,586*

ALPHA ORDER

| RANK | STATE | BENEFITS | % of USA |
|---|---|---|---|
| 19 | Alabama | $1,414,951,864 | 1.9% |
| 45 | Alaska | 189,565,646 | 0.2% |
| 13 | Arizona | 1,648,236,258 | 2.2% |
| 30 | Arkansas | 731,845,896 | 1.0% |
| 1 | California | 7,558,333,190 | 9.9% |
| 28 | Colorado | 823,529,608 | 1.1% |
| 31 | Connecticut | 707,654,612 | 0.9% |
| 43 | Delaware | 235,028,481 | 0.3% |
| 3 | Florida | 5,906,158,957 | 7.8% |
| 6 | Georgia | 3,188,743,586 | 4.2% |
| 36 | Hawaii | 494,182,027 | 0.6% |
| 40 | Idaho | 346,782,947 | 0.5% |
| 5 | Illinois | 3,378,095,657 | 4.4% |
| 15 | Indiana | 1,461,136,176 | 1.9% |
| 33 | Iowa | 586,542,123 | 0.8% |
| 37 | Kansas | 474,255,829 | 0.6% |
| 22 | Kentucky | 1,332,998,664 | 1.8% |
| 14 | Louisiana | 1,479,828,133 | 1.9% |
| 39 | Maine | 367,069,888 | 0.5% |
| 25 | Maryland | 1,178,661,930 | 1.5% |
| 20 | Massachusetts | 1,394,535,579 | 1.8% |
| 8 | Michigan | 2,911,624,110 | 3.8% |
| 29 | Minnesota | 771,699,773 | 1.0% |
| 26 | Mississippi | 993,077,956 | 1.3% |
| 17 | Missouri | 1,428,882,352 | 1.9% |
| 44 | Montana | 192,259,685 | 0.3% |
| 42 | Nebraska | 264,636,314 | 0.3% |
| 34 | Nevada | 535,230,693 | 0.7% |
| 47 | New Hampshire | 162,970,800 | 0.2% |
| 18 | New Jersey | 1,419,226,622 | 1.9% |
| 32 | New Mexico | 679,481,811 | 0.9% |
| 4 | New York | 5,621,405,246 | 7.4% |
| 10 | North Carolina | 2,491,197,794 | 3.3% |
| 49 | North Dakota | 85,530,266 | 0.1% |
| 7 | Ohio | 2,923,160,707 | 3.8% |
| 27 | Oklahoma | 958,684,325 | 1.3% |
| 23 | Oregon | 1,250,684,645 | 1.6% |
| 9 | Pennsylvania | 2,748,346,529 | 3.6% |
| 41 | Rhode Island | 302,979,333 | 0.4% |
| 21 | South Carolina | 1,381,782,118 | 1.8% |
| 46 | South Dakota | 165,040,184 | 0.2% |
| 11 | Tennessee | 2,127,681,953 | 2.8% |
| 2 | Texas | 5,934,441,831 | 7.8% |
| 38 | Utah | 377,903,214 | 0.5% |
| 48 | Vermont | 150,054,164 | 0.2% |
| 16 | Virginia | 1,442,442,319 | 1.9% |
| 12 | Washington | 1,678,737,077 | 2.2% |
| 35 | West Virginia | 504,485,785 | 0.7% |
| 24 | Wisconsin | 1,198,302,422 | 1.6% |
| 50 | Wyoming | 56,980,056 | 0.1% |

RANK ORDER

| RANK | STATE | BENEFITS | % of USA |
|---|---|---|---|
| 1 | California | $7,558,333,190 | 9.9% |
| 2 | Texas | 5,934,441,831 | 7.8% |
| 3 | Florida | 5,906,158,957 | 7.8% |
| 4 | New York | 5,621,405,246 | 7.4% |
| 5 | Illinois | 3,378,095,657 | 4.4% |
| 6 | Georgia | 3,188,743,586 | 4.2% |
| 7 | Ohio | 2,923,160,707 | 3.8% |
| 8 | Michigan | 2,911,624,110 | 3.8% |
| 9 | Pennsylvania | 2,748,346,529 | 3.6% |
| 10 | North Carolina | 2,491,197,794 | 3.3% |
| 11 | Tennessee | 2,127,681,953 | 2.8% |
| 12 | Washington | 1,678,737,077 | 2.2% |
| 13 | Arizona | 1,648,236,258 | 2.2% |
| 14 | Louisiana | 1,479,828,133 | 1.9% |
| 15 | Indiana | 1,461,136,176 | 1.9% |
| 16 | Virginia | 1,442,442,319 | 1.9% |
| 17 | Missouri | 1,428,882,352 | 1.9% |
| 18 | New Jersey | 1,419,226,622 | 1.9% |
| 19 | Alabama | 1,414,951,864 | 1.9% |
| 20 | Massachusetts | 1,394,535,579 | 1.8% |
| 21 | South Carolina | 1,381,782,118 | 1.8% |
| 22 | Kentucky | 1,332,998,664 | 1.8% |
| 23 | Oregon | 1,250,684,645 | 1.6% |
| 24 | Wisconsin | 1,198,302,422 | 1.6% |
| 25 | Maryland | 1,178,661,930 | 1.5% |
| 26 | Mississippi | 993,077,956 | 1.3% |
| 27 | Oklahoma | 958,684,325 | 1.3% |
| 28 | Colorado | 823,529,608 | 1.1% |
| 29 | Minnesota | 771,699,773 | 1.0% |
| 30 | Arkansas | 731,845,896 | 1.0% |
| 31 | Connecticut | 707,654,612 | 0.9% |
| 32 | New Mexico | 679,481,811 | 0.9% |
| 33 | Iowa | 586,542,123 | 0.8% |
| 34 | Nevada | 535,230,693 | 0.7% |
| 35 | West Virginia | 504,485,785 | 0.7% |
| 36 | Hawaii | 494,182,027 | 0.6% |
| 37 | Kansas | 474,255,829 | 0.6% |
| 38 | Utah | 377,903,214 | 0.5% |
| 39 | Maine | 367,069,888 | 0.5% |
| 40 | Idaho | 346,782,947 | 0.5% |
| 41 | Rhode Island | 302,979,333 | 0.4% |
| 42 | Nebraska | 264,636,314 | 0.3% |
| 43 | Delaware | 235,028,481 | 0.3% |
| 44 | Montana | 192,259,685 | 0.3% |
| 45 | Alaska | 189,565,646 | 0.2% |
| 46 | South Dakota | 165,040,184 | 0.2% |
| 47 | New Hampshire | 162,970,800 | 0.2% |
| 48 | Vermont | 150,054,164 | 0.2% |
| 49 | North Dakota | 85,530,266 | 0.1% |
| 50 | Wyoming | 56,980,056 | 0.1% |
| | District of Columbia | 235,020,570 | 0.3% |

Source: U.S. Department of Agriculture, Food, Nutrition and Consumer Services
   "Supplemental Nutrition Assistance Program" (http://www.fns.usda.gov/pd/snapmain.htm)
*Preliminary data for fiscal year 2013. National total includes $175,149,881 to U.S. territories. Costs are for benefits only and exclude administrative expenditures. Program formerly called the Food Stamp Program.

# Monthly Supplemental Nutrition Assistance Program Recipients in 2013

## National Total = 47,636,084 Recipients*

ALPHA ORDER

| RANK | STATE | RECIPIENTS | % of USA |
|------|-------|-----------:|---------:|
| 18 | Alabama | 915,322 | 1.9% |
| 48 | Alaska | 91,364 | 0.2% |
| 13 | Arizona | 1,111,105 | 2.3% |
| 30 | Arkansas | 504,621 | 1.1% |
| 1 | California | 4,159,031 | 8.7% |
| 29 | Colorado | 507,934 | 1.1% |
| 32 | Connecticut | 425,320 | 0.9% |
| 43 | Delaware | 153,137 | 0.3% |
| 3 | Florida | 3,556,473 | 7.5% |
| 6 | Georgia | 1,948,189 | 4.1% |
| 40 | Hawaii | 189,350 | 0.4% |
| 39 | Idaho | 227,006 | 0.5% |
| 5 | Illinois | 2,040,053 | 4.3% |
| 17 | Indiana | 926,011 | 1.9% |
| 33 | Iowa | 420,344 | 0.9% |
| 36 | Kansas | 316,983 | 0.7% |
| 22 | Kentucky | 872,439 | 1.8% |
| 15 | Louisiana | 940,100 | 2.0% |
| 38 | Maine | 249,119 | 0.5% |
| 25 | Maryland | 771,021 | 1.6% |
| 19 | Massachusetts | 887,619 | 1.9% |
| 9 | Michigan | 1,775,646 | 3.7% |
| 28 | Minnesota | 552,928 | 1.2% |
| 26 | Mississippi | 668,624 | 1.4% |
| 16 | Missouri | 929,943 | 2.0% |
| 44 | Montana | 128,531 | 0.3% |
| 42 | Nebraska | 179,711 | 0.4% |
| 34 | Nevada | 360,953 | 0.8% |
| 45 | New Hampshire | 117,315 | 0.2% |
| 20 | New Jersey | 876,266 | 1.8% |
| 31 | New Mexico | 440,362 | 0.9% |
| 4 | New York | 3,170,465 | 6.7% |
| 10 | North Carolina | 1,703,700 | 3.6% |
| 49 | North Dakota | 56,523 | 0.1% |
| 7 | Ohio | 1,824,675 | 3.8% |
| 27 | Oklahoma | 621,831 | 1.3% |
| 24 | Oregon | 817,575 | 1.7% |
| 8 | Pennsylvania | 1,784,790 | 3.7% |
| 41 | Rhode Island | 179,925 | 0.4% |
| 21 | South Carolina | 875,866 | 1.8% |
| 46 | South Dakota | 104,052 | 0.2% |
| 11 | Tennessee | 1,342,089 | 2.8% |
| 2 | Texas | 4,041,891 | 8.5% |
| 37 | Utah | 251,626 | 0.5% |
| 47 | Vermont | 100,536 | 0.2% |
| 14 | Virginia | 940,932 | 2.0% |
| 12 | Washington | 1,113,441 | 2.3% |
| 35 | West Virginia | 350,695 | 0.7% |
| 23 | Wisconsin | 856,730 | 1.8% |
| 50 | Wyoming | 38,046 | 0.1% |

RANK ORDER

| RANK | STATE | RECIPIENTS | % of USA |
|------|-------|-----------:|---------:|
| 1 | California | 4,159,031 | 8.7% |
| 2 | Texas | 4,041,891 | 8.5% |
| 3 | Florida | 3,556,473 | 7.5% |
| 4 | New York | 3,170,465 | 6.7% |
| 5 | Illinois | 2,040,053 | 4.3% |
| 6 | Georgia | 1,948,189 | 4.1% |
| 7 | Ohio | 1,824,675 | 3.8% |
| 8 | Pennsylvania | 1,784,790 | 3.7% |
| 9 | Michigan | 1,775,646 | 3.7% |
| 10 | North Carolina | 1,703,700 | 3.6% |
| 11 | Tennessee | 1,342,089 | 2.8% |
| 12 | Washington | 1,113,441 | 2.3% |
| 13 | Arizona | 1,111,105 | 2.3% |
| 14 | Virginia | 940,932 | 2.0% |
| 15 | Louisiana | 940,100 | 2.0% |
| 16 | Missouri | 929,943 | 2.0% |
| 17 | Indiana | 926,011 | 1.9% |
| 18 | Alabama | 915,322 | 1.9% |
| 19 | Massachusetts | 887,619 | 1.9% |
| 20 | New Jersey | 876,266 | 1.8% |
| 21 | South Carolina | 875,866 | 1.8% |
| 22 | Kentucky | 872,439 | 1.8% |
| 23 | Wisconsin | 856,730 | 1.8% |
| 24 | Oregon | 817,575 | 1.7% |
| 25 | Maryland | 771,021 | 1.6% |
| 26 | Mississippi | 668,624 | 1.4% |
| 27 | Oklahoma | 621,831 | 1.3% |
| 28 | Minnesota | 552,928 | 1.2% |
| 29 | Colorado | 507,934 | 1.1% |
| 30 | Arkansas | 504,621 | 1.1% |
| 31 | New Mexico | 440,362 | 0.9% |
| 32 | Connecticut | 425,320 | 0.9% |
| 33 | Iowa | 420,344 | 0.9% |
| 34 | Nevada | 360,953 | 0.8% |
| 35 | West Virginia | 350,695 | 0.7% |
| 36 | Kansas | 316,983 | 0.7% |
| 37 | Utah | 251,626 | 0.5% |
| 38 | Maine | 249,119 | 0.5% |
| 39 | Idaho | 227,006 | 0.5% |
| 40 | Hawaii | 189,350 | 0.4% |
| 41 | Rhode Island | 179,925 | 0.4% |
| 42 | Nebraska | 179,711 | 0.4% |
| 43 | Delaware | 153,137 | 0.3% |
| 44 | Montana | 128,531 | 0.3% |
| 45 | New Hampshire | 117,315 | 0.2% |
| 46 | South Dakota | 104,052 | 0.2% |
| 47 | Vermont | 100,536 | 0.2% |
| 48 | Alaska | 91,364 | 0.2% |
| 49 | North Dakota | 56,523 | 0.1% |
| 50 | Wyoming | 38,046 | 0.1% |
| | District of Columbia | 144,889 | 0.3% |

Source: U.S. Department of Agriculture, Food, Nutrition and Consumer Services
   "Supplemental Nutrition Assistance Program" (http://www.fns.usda.gov/pd/snapmain.htm)
*Preliminary for fiscal year 2013. National total includes 72,990 recipients in U.S. territories. Program was formerly called the Food Stamp Program.

# Average Monthly Supplemental Nutrition Assistance Program Benefit per Recipient in 2013
## National Average = $133.07 per Recipient*

| ALPHA ORDER | | | | | RANK ORDER | | |
|---|---|---|---|---|---|---|---|
| RANK | STATE | PER RECIPIENT | | | RANK | STATE | PER RECIPIENT |
| 20 | Alabama | $128.82 | | | 1 | Hawaii | $217.49 |
| 2 | Alaska | 172.90 | | | 2 | Alaska | 172.90 |
| 39 | Arizona | 123.62 | | | 3 | California | 151.44 |
| 45 | Arkansas | 120.86 | | | 4 | New York | 147.75 |
| 3 | California | 151.44 | | | 5 | Rhode Island | 140.33 |
| 11 | Colorado | 135.11 | | | 6 | Connecticut | 138.65 |
| 6 | Connecticut | 138.65 | | | 7 | Florida | 138.39 |
| 25 | Delaware | 127.90 | | | 8 | Illinois | 137.99 |
| 7 | Florida | 138.39 | | | 9 | Michigan | 136.65 |
| 10 | Georgia | 136.40 | | | 10 | Georgia | 136.40 |
| 1 | Hawaii | 217.49 | | | 11 | Colorado | 135.11 |
| 30 | Idaho | 127.30 | | | 12 | New Jersey | 134.97 |
| 8 | Illinois | 137.99 | | | 13 | Ohio | 133.50 |
| 16 | Indiana | 131.49 | | | 14 | South Dakota | 132.18 |
| 49 | Iowa | 116.28 | | | 15 | Tennessee | 132.11 |
| 35 | Kansas | 124.68 | | | 16 | Indiana | 131.49 |
| 29 | Kentucky | 127.33 | | | 17 | South Carolina | 131.47 |
| 18 | Louisiana | 131.18 | | | 18 | Louisiana | 131.18 |
| 41 | Maine | 122.79 | | | 19 | Massachusetts | 130.92 |
| 28 | Maryland | 127.39 | | | 20 | Alabama | 128.82 |
| 19 | Massachusetts | 130.92 | | | 21 | New Mexico | 128.58 |
| 9 | Michigan | 136.65 | | | 22 | Oklahoma | 128.48 |
| 48 | Minnesota | 116.31 | | | 23 | Pennsylvania | 128.32 |
| 38 | Mississippi | 123.77 | | | 24 | Missouri | 128.04 |
| 24 | Missouri | 128.04 | | | 25 | Delaware | 127.90 |
| 36 | Montana | 124.65 | | | 26 | Virginia | 127.75 |
| 42 | Nebraska | 122.71 | | | 27 | Oregon | 127.48 |
| 40 | Nevada | 123.57 | | | 28 | Maryland | 127.39 |
| 50 | New Hampshire | 115.76 | | | 29 | Kentucky | 127.33 |
| 12 | New Jersey | 134.97 | | | 30 | Idaho | 127.30 |
| 21 | New Mexico | 128.58 | | | 31 | North Dakota | 126.10 |
| 4 | New York | 147.75 | | | 32 | Washington | 125.64 |
| 44 | North Carolina | 121.85 | | | 33 | Utah | 125.15 |
| 31 | North Dakota | 126.10 | | | 34 | Wyoming | 124.80 |
| 13 | Ohio | 133.50 | | | 35 | Kansas | 124.68 |
| 22 | Oklahoma | 128.48 | | | 36 | Montana | 124.65 |
| 27 | Oregon | 127.48 | | | 37 | Vermont | 124.38 |
| 23 | Pennsylvania | 128.32 | | | 38 | Mississippi | 123.77 |
| 5 | Rhode Island | 140.33 | | | 39 | Arizona | 123.62 |
| 17 | South Carolina | 131.47 | | | 40 | Nevada | 123.57 |
| 14 | South Dakota | 132.18 | | | 41 | Maine | 122.79 |
| 15 | Tennessee | 132.11 | | | 42 | Nebraska | 122.71 |
| 43 | Texas | 122.35 | | | 43 | Texas | 122.35 |
| 33 | Utah | 125.15 | | | 44 | North Carolina | 121.85 |
| 37 | Vermont | 124.38 | | | 45 | Arkansas | 120.86 |
| 26 | Virginia | 127.75 | | | 46 | West Virginia | 119.88 |
| 32 | Washington | 125.64 | | | 47 | Wisconsin | 116.56 |
| 46 | West Virginia | 119.88 | | | 48 | Minnesota | 116.31 |
| 47 | Wisconsin | 116.56 | | | 49 | Iowa | 116.28 |
| 34 | Wyoming | 124.80 | | | 50 | New Hampshire | 115.76 |
| | | | | | | District of Columbia | 135.17 |

Source: U.S. Department of Agriculture, Food, Nutrition and Consumer Services
   "Supplemental Nutrition Assistance Program" (http://www.fns.usda.gov/pd/snapmain.htm)
*Preliminary for fiscal year 2013. National average includes recipients in U.S. territories. Program formerly called the Food Stamp Program.

# Percent of Population Receiving
## Supplemental Nutrition Assistance Program Benefits in 2013
### National Percent = 15.0%*

ALPHA ORDER

| RANK | STATE | PERCENT |
|------|-------|---------|
| 8 | Alabama | 18.9 |
| 37 | Alaska | 12.4 |
| 17 | Arizona | 16.8 |
| 15 | Arkansas | 17.1 |
| 42 | California | 10.8 |
| 45 | Colorado | 9.6 |
| 39 | Connecticut | 11.8 |
| 18 | Delaware | 16.5 |
| 12 | Florida | 18.2 |
| 7 | Georgia | 19.5 |
| 32 | Hawaii | 13.5 |
| 28 | Idaho | 14.1 |
| 23 | Illinois | 15.8 |
| 28 | Indiana | 14.1 |
| 31 | Iowa | 13.6 |
| 41 | Kansas | 11.0 |
| 6 | Kentucky | 19.8 |
| 5 | Louisiana | 20.3 |
| 10 | Maine | 18.8 |
| 34 | Maryland | 13.0 |
| 33 | Massachusetts | 13.3 |
| 13 | Michigan | 17.9 |
| 43 | Minnesota | 10.2 |
| 1 | Mississippi | 22.4 |
| 25 | Missouri | 15.4 |
| 36 | Montana | 12.7 |
| 45 | Nebraska | 9.6 |
| 35 | Nevada | 12.9 |
| 47 | New Hampshire | 8.9 |
| 44 | New Jersey | 9.8 |
| 2 | New Mexico | 21.1 |
| 19 | New York | 16.1 |
| 14 | North Carolina | 17.3 |
| 49 | North Dakota | 7.8 |
| 23 | Ohio | 15.8 |
| 19 | Oklahoma | 16.1 |
| 3 | Oregon | 20.8 |
| 30 | Pennsylvania | 14.0 |
| 15 | Rhode Island | 17.1 |
| 11 | South Carolina | 18.3 |
| 38 | South Dakota | 12.3 |
| 4 | Tennessee | 20.7 |
| 26 | Texas | 15.3 |
| 48 | Utah | 8.7 |
| 21 | Vermont | 16.0 |
| 40 | Virginia | 11.4 |
| 21 | Washington | 16.0 |
| 8 | West Virginia | 18.9 |
| 27 | Wisconsin | 14.9 |
| 50 | Wyoming | 6.5 |

RANK ORDER

| RANK | STATE | PERCENT |
|------|-------|---------|
| 1 | Mississippi | 22.4 |
| 2 | New Mexico | 21.1 |
| 3 | Oregon | 20.8 |
| 4 | Tennessee | 20.7 |
| 5 | Louisiana | 20.3 |
| 6 | Kentucky | 19.8 |
| 7 | Georgia | 19.5 |
| 8 | Alabama | 18.9 |
| 8 | West Virginia | 18.9 |
| 10 | Maine | 18.8 |
| 11 | South Carolina | 18.3 |
| 12 | Florida | 18.2 |
| 13 | Michigan | 17.9 |
| 14 | North Carolina | 17.3 |
| 15 | Arkansas | 17.1 |
| 15 | Rhode Island | 17.1 |
| 17 | Arizona | 16.8 |
| 18 | Delaware | 16.5 |
| 19 | New York | 16.1 |
| 19 | Oklahoma | 16.1 |
| 21 | Vermont | 16.0 |
| 21 | Washington | 16.0 |
| 23 | Illinois | 15.8 |
| 23 | Ohio | 15.8 |
| 25 | Missouri | 15.4 |
| 26 | Texas | 15.3 |
| 27 | Wisconsin | 14.9 |
| 28 | Idaho | 14.1 |
| 28 | Indiana | 14.1 |
| 30 | Pennsylvania | 14.0 |
| 31 | Iowa | 13.6 |
| 32 | Hawaii | 13.5 |
| 33 | Massachusetts | 13.3 |
| 34 | Maryland | 13.0 |
| 35 | Nevada | 12.9 |
| 36 | Montana | 12.7 |
| 37 | Alaska | 12.4 |
| 38 | South Dakota | 12.3 |
| 39 | Connecticut | 11.8 |
| 40 | Virginia | 11.4 |
| 41 | Kansas | 11.0 |
| 42 | California | 10.8 |
| 43 | Minnesota | 10.2 |
| 44 | New Jersey | 9.8 |
| 45 | Colorado | 9.6 |
| 45 | Nebraska | 9.6 |
| 47 | New Hampshire | 8.9 |
| 48 | Utah | 8.7 |
| 49 | North Dakota | 7.8 |
| 50 | Wyoming | 6.5 |
| | District of Columbia | 22.4 |

Source: CQ Press using data from U.S. Department of Agriculture, Food, Nutrition and Consumer Services "Supplemental Nutrition Assistance Program" (http://www.fns.usda.gov/pd/snapmain.htm)

*Preliminary data for fiscal year 2013. National rate does not include recipients in U.S. territories. Program formerly called the Food Stamp Program.

# Percent of Households Receiving
## Supplemental Nutrition Assistance Program Benefits in 2013
## National Percent = 19.9% of Households*

ALPHA ORDER

| RANK | STATE | PERCENT |
|------|-------|---------|
| 14 | Alabama | 22.8 |
| 37 | Alaska | 15.2 |
| 22 | Arizona | 19.9 |
| 25 | Arkansas | 19.6 |
| 37 | California | 15.2 |
| 45 | Colorado | 11.6 |
| 33 | Connecticut | 17.2 |
| 19 | Delaware | 21.2 |
| 3 | Florida | 27.0 |
| 6 | Georgia | 25.7 |
| 17 | Hawaii | 21.4 |
| 34 | Idaho | 16.8 |
| 18 | Illinois | 21.3 |
| 34 | Indiana | 16.8 |
| 36 | Iowa | 16.2 |
| 43 | Kansas | 13.4 |
| 8 | Kentucky | 24.6 |
| 7 | Louisiana | 24.8 |
| 12 | Maine | 23.5 |
| 29 | Maryland | 18.2 |
| 24 | Massachusetts | 19.8 |
| 10 | Michigan | 23.8 |
| 44 | Minnesota | 13.0 |
| 2 | Mississippi | 28.0 |
| 28 | Missouri | 18.5 |
| 40 | Montana | 14.5 |
| 47 | Nebraska | 10.8 |
| 32 | Nevada | 17.3 |
| 47 | New Hampshire | 10.8 |
| 42 | New Jersey | 13.5 |
| 5 | New Mexico | 25.8 |
| 11 | New York | 23.6 |
| 20 | North Carolina | 21.1 |
| 49 | North Dakota | 9.0 |
| 26 | Ohio | 19.5 |
| 22 | Oklahoma | 19.9 |
| 1 | Oregon | 29.8 |
| 31 | Pennsylvania | 17.5 |
| 9 | Rhode Island | 24.3 |
| 13 | South Carolina | 23.3 |
| 41 | South Dakota | 14.0 |
| 4 | Tennessee | 26.7 |
| 27 | Texas | 18.7 |
| 46 | Utah | 11.3 |
| 21 | Vermont | 20.2 |
| 39 | Virginia | 15.0 |
| 16 | Washington | 22.4 |
| 15 | West Virginia | 22.5 |
| 29 | Wisconsin | 18.2 |
| 50 | Wyoming | 7.3 |

RANK ORDER

| RANK | STATE | PERCENT |
|------|-------|---------|
| 1 | Oregon | 29.8 |
| 2 | Mississippi | 28.0 |
| 3 | Florida | 27.0 |
| 4 | Tennessee | 26.7 |
| 5 | New Mexico | 25.8 |
| 6 | Georgia | 25.7 |
| 7 | Louisiana | 24.8 |
| 8 | Kentucky | 24.6 |
| 9 | Rhode Island | 24.3 |
| 10 | Michigan | 23.8 |
| 11 | New York | 23.6 |
| 12 | Maine | 23.5 |
| 13 | South Carolina | 23.3 |
| 14 | Alabama | 22.8 |
| 15 | West Virginia | 22.5 |
| 16 | Washington | 22.4 |
| 17 | Hawaii | 21.4 |
| 18 | Illinois | 21.3 |
| 19 | Delaware | 21.2 |
| 20 | North Carolina | 21.1 |
| 21 | Vermont | 20.2 |
| 22 | Arizona | 19.9 |
| 22 | Oklahoma | 19.9 |
| 24 | Massachusetts | 19.8 |
| 25 | Arkansas | 19.6 |
| 26 | Ohio | 19.5 |
| 27 | Texas | 18.7 |
| 28 | Missouri | 18.5 |
| 29 | Maryland | 18.2 |
| 29 | Wisconsin | 18.2 |
| 31 | Pennsylvania | 17.5 |
| 32 | Nevada | 17.3 |
| 33 | Connecticut | 17.2 |
| 34 | Idaho | 16.8 |
| 34 | Indiana | 16.8 |
| 36 | Iowa | 16.2 |
| 37 | Alaska | 15.2 |
| 37 | California | 15.2 |
| 39 | Virginia | 15.0 |
| 40 | Montana | 14.5 |
| 41 | South Dakota | 14.0 |
| 42 | New Jersey | 13.5 |
| 43 | Kansas | 13.4 |
| 44 | Minnesota | 13.0 |
| 45 | Colorado | 11.6 |
| 46 | Utah | 11.3 |
| 47 | Nebraska | 10.8 |
| 47 | New Hampshire | 10.8 |
| 49 | North Dakota | 9.0 |
| 50 | Wyoming | 7.3 |
| | District of Columbia | 30.7 |

Source: CQ Press using data from U.S. Department of Agriculture, Food, Nutrition and Consumer Services
"Supplemental Nutrition Assistance Program" (http://www.fns.usda.gov/pd/snapmain.htm)
*Preliminary data for fiscal year 2013. Percent calculated using 2012 estimated total households. National percent excludes households in U.S. territories. Program formerly called the Food Stamp Program.

# Average Monthly Participants in Women, Infants, and Children (WIC) Special Nutrition Program in 2013
## National Total = 8,662,538 Participants*

ALPHA ORDER

| RANK | STATE | PARTICIPANTS | % of USA |
|---|---|---|---|
| 20 | Alabama | 139,001 | 1.6% |
| 43 | Alaska | 23,253 | 0.3% |
| 12 | Arizona | 182,501 | 2.1% |
| 30 | Arkansas | 89,777 | 1.0% |
| 1 | California | 1,431,778 | 16.5% |
| 28 | Colorado | 96,874 | 1.1% |
| 36 | Connecticut | 54,250 | 0.6% |
| 44 | Delaware | 20,787 | 0.2% |
| 4 | Florida | 483,566 | 5.6% |
| 5 | Georgia | 289,512 | 3.3% |
| 40 | Hawaii | 36,370 | 0.4% |
| 38 | Idaho | 43,292 | 0.5% |
| 6 | Illinois | 280,463 | 3.2% |
| 14 | Indiana | 159,525 | 1.8% |
| 34 | Iowa | 65,876 | 0.8% |
| 32 | Kansas | 70,615 | 0.8% |
| 21 | Kentucky | 129,710 | 1.5% |
| 19 | Louisiana | 139,856 | 1.6% |
| 41 | Maine | 24,369 | 0.3% |
| 17 | Maryland | 144,628 | 1.7% |
| 24 | Massachusetts | 119,954 | 1.4% |
| 9 | Michigan | 254,126 | 2.9% |
| 22 | Minnesota | 124,744 | 1.4% |
| 29 | Mississippi | 91,652 | 1.1% |
| 18 | Missouri | 140,821 | 1.6% |
| 46 | Montana | 19,848 | 0.2% |
| 39 | Nebraska | 40,151 | 0.5% |
| 31 | Nevada | 75,011 | 0.9% |
| 47 | New Hampshire | 15,679 | 0.2% |
| 13 | New Jersey | 167,872 | 1.9% |
| 35 | New Mexico | 61,405 | 0.7% |
| 3 | New York | 513,299 | 5.9% |
| 7 | North Carolina | 264,750 | 3.1% |
| 49 | North Dakota | 13,273 | 0.2% |
| 8 | Ohio | 263,570 | 3.0% |
| 25 | Oklahoma | 118,552 | 1.4% |
| 27 | Oregon | 107,859 | 1.2% |
| 10 | Pennsylvania | 253,258 | 2.9% |
| 42 | Rhode Island | 23,416 | 0.3% |
| 23 | South Carolina | 124,287 | 1.4% |
| 45 | South Dakota | 20,430 | 0.2% |
| 15 | Tennessee | 159,426 | 1.8% |
| 2 | Texas | 955,072 | 11.0% |
| 33 | Utah | 66,726 | 0.8% |
| 48 | Vermont | 14,836 | 0.2% |
| 16 | Virginia | 155,935 | 1.8% |
| 11 | Washington | 191,753 | 2.2% |
| 37 | West Virginia | 46,402 | 0.5% |
| 26 | Wisconsin | 113,763 | 1.3% |
| 50 | Wyoming | 11,980 | 0.1% |

RANK ORDER

| RANK | STATE | PARTICIPANTS | % of USA |
|---|---|---|---|
| 1 | California | 1,431,778 | 16.5% |
| 2 | Texas | 955,072 | 11.0% |
| 3 | New York | 513,299 | 5.9% |
| 4 | Florida | 483,566 | 5.6% |
| 5 | Georgia | 289,512 | 3.3% |
| 6 | Illinois | 280,463 | 3.2% |
| 7 | North Carolina | 264,750 | 3.1% |
| 8 | Ohio | 263,570 | 3.0% |
| 9 | Michigan | 254,126 | 2.9% |
| 10 | Pennsylvania | 253,258 | 2.9% |
| 11 | Washington | 191,753 | 2.2% |
| 12 | Arizona | 182,501 | 2.1% |
| 13 | New Jersey | 167,872 | 1.9% |
| 14 | Indiana | 159,525 | 1.8% |
| 15 | Tennessee | 159,426 | 1.8% |
| 16 | Virginia | 155,935 | 1.8% |
| 17 | Maryland | 144,628 | 1.7% |
| 18 | Missouri | 140,821 | 1.6% |
| 19 | Louisiana | 139,856 | 1.6% |
| 20 | Alabama | 139,001 | 1.6% |
| 21 | Kentucky | 129,710 | 1.5% |
| 22 | Minnesota | 124,744 | 1.4% |
| 23 | South Carolina | 124,287 | 1.4% |
| 24 | Massachusetts | 119,954 | 1.4% |
| 25 | Oklahoma | 118,552 | 1.4% |
| 26 | Wisconsin | 113,763 | 1.3% |
| 27 | Oregon | 107,859 | 1.2% |
| 28 | Colorado | 96,874 | 1.1% |
| 29 | Mississippi | 91,652 | 1.1% |
| 30 | Arkansas | 89,777 | 1.0% |
| 31 | Nevada | 75,011 | 0.9% |
| 32 | Kansas | 70,615 | 0.8% |
| 33 | Utah | 66,726 | 0.8% |
| 34 | Iowa | 65,876 | 0.8% |
| 35 | New Mexico | 61,405 | 0.7% |
| 36 | Connecticut | 54,250 | 0.6% |
| 37 | West Virginia | 46,402 | 0.5% |
| 38 | Idaho | 43,292 | 0.5% |
| 39 | Nebraska | 40,151 | 0.5% |
| 40 | Hawaii | 36,370 | 0.4% |
| 41 | Maine | 24,369 | 0.3% |
| 42 | Rhode Island | 23,416 | 0.3% |
| 43 | Alaska | 23,253 | 0.3% |
| 44 | Delaware | 20,787 | 0.2% |
| 45 | South Dakota | 20,430 | 0.2% |
| 46 | Montana | 19,848 | 0.2% |
| 47 | New Hampshire | 15,679 | 0.2% |
| 48 | Vermont | 14,836 | 0.2% |
| 49 | North Dakota | 13,273 | 0.2% |
| 50 | Wyoming | 11,980 | 0.1% |
| | District of Columbia | 15,674 | 0.2% |

Source: U.S. Department of Agriculture, Food, Nutrition and Consumer Services
"WIC Program (http://www.fns.usda.gov/pd/wicmain.htm)
*Preliminary data for fiscal year 2013. National total includes 211,014 participants in outlying areas not shown separately (Puerto Rico has 187,850 participants).

# Average Monthly Benefit per Participant in Women, Infants, and Children (WIC) Special Nutrition Program in 2013
## National Average = $43.46*

ALPHA ORDER

| RANK | STATE | AVERAGE BENEFIT |
|------|-------|-----------------|
| 11 | Alabama | $46.58 |
| 5 | Alaska | 50.43 |
| 25 | Arizona | 42.88 |
| 13 | Arkansas | 46.47 |
| 15 | California | 46.05 |
| 32 | Colorado | 40.61 |
| 28 | Connecticut | 41.80 |
| 29 | Delaware | 41.77 |
| 20 | Florida | 44.39 |
| 17 | Georgia | 45.50 |
| 4 | Hawaii | 51.97 |
| 43 | Idaho | 36.90 |
| 9 | Illinois | 48.13 |
| 41 | Indiana | 37.26 |
| 47 | Iowa | 33.03 |
| 38 | Kansas | 37.78 |
| 36 | Kentucky | 40.02 |
| 6 | Louisiana | 50.20 |
| 31 | Maine | 41.02 |
| 23 | Maryland | 43.10 |
| 36 | Massachusetts | 40.02 |
| 33 | Michigan | 40.46 |
| 18 | Minnesota | 45.37 |
| 2 | Mississippi | 53.88 |
| 40 | Missouri | 37.60 |
| 26 | Montana | 42.79 |
| 19 | Nebraska | 44.79 |
| 39 | Nevada | 37.62 |
| 48 | New Hampshire | 32.95 |
| 3 | New Jersey | 53.50 |
| 42 | New Mexico | 36.98 |
| 1 | New York | 56.89 |
| 24 | North Carolina | 42.93 |
| 8 | North Dakota | 49.67 |
| 45 | Ohio | 35.39 |
| 34 | Oklahoma | 40.38 |
| 35 | Oregon | 40.12 |
| 16 | Pennsylvania | 45.55 |
| 12 | Rhode Island | 46.51 |
| 14 | South Carolina | 46.38 |
| 10 | South Dakota | 47.47 |
| 27 | Tennessee | 41.98 |
| 50 | Texas | 26.47 |
| 44 | Utah | 36.10 |
| 7 | Vermont | 49.87 |
| 46 | Virginia | 33.28 |
| 30 | Washington | 41.16 |
| 21 | West Virginia | 43.94 |
| 22 | Wisconsin | 43.33 |
| 49 | Wyoming | 31.67 |

RANK ORDER

| RANK | STATE | AVERAGE BENEFIT |
|------|-------|-----------------|
| 1 | New York | $56.89 |
| 2 | Mississippi | 53.88 |
| 3 | New Jersey | 53.50 |
| 4 | Hawaii | 51.97 |
| 5 | Alaska | 50.43 |
| 6 | Louisiana | 50.20 |
| 7 | Vermont | 49.87 |
| 8 | North Dakota | 49.67 |
| 9 | Illinois | 48.13 |
| 10 | South Dakota | 47.47 |
| 11 | Alabama | 46.58 |
| 12 | Rhode Island | 46.51 |
| 13 | Arkansas | 46.47 |
| 14 | South Carolina | 46.38 |
| 15 | California | 46.05 |
| 16 | Pennsylvania | 45.55 |
| 17 | Georgia | 45.50 |
| 18 | Minnesota | 45.37 |
| 19 | Nebraska | 44.79 |
| 20 | Florida | 44.39 |
| 21 | West Virginia | 43.94 |
| 22 | Wisconsin | 43.33 |
| 23 | Maryland | 43.10 |
| 24 | North Carolina | 42.93 |
| 25 | Arizona | 42.88 |
| 26 | Montana | 42.79 |
| 27 | Tennessee | 41.98 |
| 28 | Connecticut | 41.80 |
| 29 | Delaware | 41.77 |
| 30 | Washington | 41.16 |
| 31 | Maine | 41.02 |
| 32 | Colorado | 40.61 |
| 33 | Michigan | 40.46 |
| 34 | Oklahoma | 40.38 |
| 35 | Oregon | 40.12 |
| 36 | Kentucky | 40.02 |
| 36 | Massachusetts | 40.02 |
| 38 | Kansas | 37.78 |
| 39 | Nevada | 37.62 |
| 40 | Missouri | 37.60 |
| 41 | Indiana | 37.26 |
| 42 | New Mexico | 36.98 |
| 43 | Idaho | 36.90 |
| 44 | Utah | 36.10 |
| 45 | Ohio | 35.39 |
| 46 | Virginia | 33.28 |
| 47 | Iowa | 33.03 |
| 48 | New Hampshire | 32.95 |
| 49 | Wyoming | 31.67 |
| 50 | Texas | 26.47 |
| | District of Columbia | 43.58 |

Source: U.S. Department of Agriculture, Food, Nutrition and Consumer Services
"WIC Program (http://www.fns.usda.gov/pd/wicmain.htm)
*Preliminary data for fiscal year 2013. National average includes outlying areas and Indian reservations not shown separately.

# Percent of Public Elementary and Secondary School Students Eligible for Free or Reduced-Price Meals in 2011
## National Percent = 47.9%*

ALPHA ORDER

| RANK | STATE | PERCENT |
|------|-------|---------|
| 10 | Alabama | 54.9 |
| 39 | Alaska | 38.4 |
| 24 | Arizona | 45.1 |
| 4 | Arkansas | 60.5 |
| 12 | California | 53.7 |
| 35 | Colorado | 39.9 |
| 47 | Connecticut | 34.0 |
| 19 | Delaware | 47.7 |
| 8 | Florida | 56.0 |
| 6 | Georgia | 57.4 |
| 21 | Hawaii | 46.8 |
| 25 | Idaho | 45.0 |
| 26 | Illinois | 44.3 |
| 22 | Indiana | 46.6 |
| 37 | Iowa | 38.9 |
| 19 | Kansas | 47.7 |
| 7 | Kentucky | 56.6 |
| 3 | Louisiana | 66.2 |
| 28 | Maine | 43.0 |
| 33 | Maryland | 40.1 |
| 46 | Massachusetts | 34.2 |
| 23 | Michigan | 46.3 |
| 45 | Minnesota | 36.5 |
| 1 | Mississippi | 70.6 |
| 26 | Missouri | 44.3 |
| 32 | Montana | 40.8 |
| 30 | Nebraska | 42.6 |
| 15 | Nevada | 50.3 |
| 50 | New Hampshire | 25.2 |
| 48 | New Jersey | 32.8 |
| 2 | New Mexico | 67.6 |
| 18 | New York | 48.1 |
| 15 | North Carolina | 50.3 |
| 49 | North Dakota | 31.7 |
| 30 | Ohio | 42.6 |
| 4 | Oklahoma | 60.5 |
| 14 | Oregon | 50.6 |
| 37 | Pennsylvania | 38.9 |
| 29 | Rhode Island | 42.9 |
| 11 | South Carolina | 54.5 |
| 41 | South Dakota | 37.1 |
| 9 | Tennessee | 55.0 |
| 17 | Texas | 50.1 |
| 40 | Utah | 38.2 |
| 43 | Vermont | 36.8 |
| 44 | Virginia | 36.7 |
| 33 | Washington | 40.1 |
| 13 | West Virginia | 51.5 |
| 36 | Wisconsin | 39.3 |
| 41 | Wyoming | 37.1 |

RANK ORDER

| RANK | STATE | PERCENT |
|------|-------|---------|
| 1 | Mississippi | 70.6 |
| 2 | New Mexico | 67.6 |
| 3 | Louisiana | 66.2 |
| 4 | Arkansas | 60.5 |
| 4 | Oklahoma | 60.5 |
| 6 | Georgia | 57.4 |
| 7 | Kentucky | 56.6 |
| 8 | Florida | 56.0 |
| 9 | Tennessee | 55.0 |
| 10 | Alabama | 54.9 |
| 11 | South Carolina | 54.5 |
| 12 | California | 53.7 |
| 13 | West Virginia | 51.5 |
| 14 | Oregon | 50.6 |
| 15 | Nevada | 50.3 |
| 15 | North Carolina | 50.3 |
| 17 | Texas | 50.1 |
| 18 | New York | 48.1 |
| 19 | Delaware | 47.7 |
| 19 | Kansas | 47.7 |
| 21 | Hawaii | 46.8 |
| 22 | Indiana | 46.6 |
| 23 | Michigan | 46.3 |
| 24 | Arizona | 45.1 |
| 25 | Idaho | 45.0 |
| 26 | Illinois | 44.3 |
| 26 | Missouri | 44.3 |
| 28 | Maine | 43.0 |
| 29 | Rhode Island | 42.9 |
| 30 | Nebraska | 42.6 |
| 30 | Ohio | 42.6 |
| 32 | Montana | 40.8 |
| 33 | Maryland | 40.1 |
| 33 | Washington | 40.1 |
| 35 | Colorado | 39.9 |
| 36 | Wisconsin | 39.3 |
| 37 | Iowa | 38.9 |
| 37 | Pennsylvania | 38.9 |
| 39 | Alaska | 38.4 |
| 40 | Utah | 38.2 |
| 41 | South Dakota | 37.1 |
| 41 | Wyoming | 37.1 |
| 43 | Vermont | 36.8 |
| 44 | Virginia | 36.7 |
| 45 | Minnesota | 36.5 |
| 46 | Massachusetts | 34.2 |
| 47 | Connecticut | 34.0 |
| 48 | New Jersey | 32.8 |
| 49 | North Dakota | 31.7 |
| 50 | New Hampshire | 25.2 |
| | District of Columbia | 73.0 |

Source: CQ Press using data from U.S. Department of Education, National Center for Education Statistics
   "Common Core of Data (CCD) Database" (http://nces.ed.gov/ccd/)
*For school year 2010-2011.

# Child Support Collections in 2012

## National Total = $27,360,483,997*

ALPHA ORDER

ALPHA ORDER

| RANK | STATE | COLLECTIONS | % of USA |
|---|---|---|---|
| 29 | Alabama | $290,572,812 | 1.1% |
| 41 | Alaska | 99,583,102 | 0.4% |
| 24 | Arizona | 323,093,647 | 1.2% |
| 32 | Arkansas | 219,645,476 | 0.8% |
| 2 | California | 2,208,751,449 | 8.1% |
| 28 | Colorado | 293,245,061 | 1.1% |
| 31 | Connecticut | 245,369,851 | 0.9% |
| 46 | Delaware | 74,451,056 | 0.3% |
| 5 | Florida | 1,466,273,345 | 5.4% |
| 11 | Georgia | 647,282,139 | 2.4% |
| 42 | Hawaii | 96,191,283 | 0.4% |
| 38 | Idaho | 151,981,715 | 0.6% |
| 9 | Illinois | 802,971,010 | 2.9% |
| 17 | Indiana | 580,545,272 | 2.1% |
| 26 | Iowa | 313,319,066 | 1.1% |
| 36 | Kansas | 189,363,684 | 0.7% |
| 21 | Kentucky | 389,349,338 | 1.4% |
| 22 | Louisiana | 380,063,605 | 1.4% |
| 40 | Maine | 99,657,835 | 0.4% |
| 20 | Maryland | 514,934,157 | 1.9% |
| 15 | Massachusetts | 604,380,725 | 2.2% |
| 6 | Michigan | 1,320,275,023 | 4.8% |
| 16 | Minnesota | 582,324,840 | 2.1% |
| 27 | Mississippi | 299,798,756 | 1.1% |
| 18 | Missouri | 573,548,550 | 2.1% |
| 49 | Montana | 59,935,863 | 0.2% |
| 33 | Nebraska | 200,318,373 | 0.7% |
| 37 | Nevada | 171,931,117 | 0.6% |
| 45 | New Hampshire | 83,176,973 | 0.3% |
| 8 | New Jersey | 1,131,352,192 | 4.1% |
| 39 | New Mexico | 112,170,094 | 0.4% |
| 3 | New York | 1,703,265,881 | 6.2% |
| 10 | North Carolina | 662,096,486 | 2.4% |
| 43 | North Dakota | 89,592,169 | 0.3% |
| 4 | Ohio | 1,697,143,384 | 6.2% |
| 25 | Oklahoma | 315,117,057 | 1.2% |
| 23 | Oregon | 349,474,272 | 1.3% |
| 7 | Pennsylvania | 1,320,237,119 | 4.8% |
| 47 | Rhode Island | 66,339,200 | 0.2% |
| 30 | South Carolina | 255,318,273 | 0.9% |
| 44 | South Dakota | 86,280,610 | 0.3% |
| 19 | Tennessee | 555,988,101 | 2.0% |
| 1 | Texas | 3,320,420,591 | 12.1% |
| 35 | Utah | 194,717,309 | 0.7% |
| 50 | Vermont | 45,987,161 | 0.2% |
| 14 | Virginia | 606,627,426 | 2.2% |
| 12 | Washington | 644,113,060 | 2.4% |
| 34 | West Virginia | 195,410,794 | 0.7% |
| 13 | Wisconsin | 611,876,491 | 2.2% |
| 48 | Wyoming | 64,255,732 | 0.2% |

RANK ORDER

| RANK | STATE | COLLECTIONS | % of USA |
|---|---|---|---|
| 1 | Texas | $3,320,420,591 | 12.1% |
| 2 | California | 2,208,751,449 | 8.1% |
| 3 | New York | 1,703,265,881 | 6.2% |
| 4 | Ohio | 1,697,143,384 | 6.2% |
| 5 | Florida | 1,466,273,345 | 5.4% |
| 6 | Michigan | 1,320,275,023 | 4.8% |
| 7 | Pennsylvania | 1,320,237,119 | 4.8% |
| 8 | New Jersey | 1,131,352,192 | 4.1% |
| 9 | Illinois | 802,971,010 | 2.9% |
| 10 | North Carolina | 662,096,486 | 2.4% |
| 11 | Georgia | 647,282,139 | 2.4% |
| 12 | Washington | 644,113,060 | 2.4% |
| 13 | Wisconsin | 611,876,491 | 2.2% |
| 14 | Virginia | 606,627,426 | 2.2% |
| 15 | Massachusetts | 604,380,725 | 2.2% |
| 16 | Minnesota | 582,324,840 | 2.1% |
| 17 | Indiana | 580,545,272 | 2.1% |
| 18 | Missouri | 573,548,550 | 2.1% |
| 19 | Tennessee | 555,988,101 | 2.0% |
| 20 | Maryland | 514,934,157 | 1.9% |
| 21 | Kentucky | 389,349,338 | 1.4% |
| 22 | Louisiana | 380,063,605 | 1.4% |
| 23 | Oregon | 349,474,272 | 1.3% |
| 24 | Arizona | 323,093,647 | 1.2% |
| 25 | Oklahoma | 315,117,057 | 1.2% |
| 26 | Iowa | 313,319,066 | 1.1% |
| 27 | Mississippi | 299,798,756 | 1.1% |
| 28 | Colorado | 293,245,061 | 1.1% |
| 29 | Alabama | 290,572,812 | 1.1% |
| 30 | South Carolina | 255,318,273 | 0.9% |
| 31 | Connecticut | 245,369,851 | 0.9% |
| 32 | Arkansas | 219,645,476 | 0.8% |
| 33 | Nebraska | 200,318,373 | 0.7% |
| 34 | West Virginia | 195,410,794 | 0.7% |
| 35 | Utah | 194,717,309 | 0.7% |
| 36 | Kansas | 189,363,684 | 0.7% |
| 37 | Nevada | 171,931,117 | 0.6% |
| 38 | Idaho | 151,981,715 | 0.6% |
| 39 | New Mexico | 112,170,094 | 0.4% |
| 40 | Maine | 99,657,835 | 0.4% |
| 41 | Alaska | 99,583,102 | 0.4% |
| 42 | Hawaii | 96,191,283 | 0.4% |
| 43 | North Dakota | 89,592,169 | 0.3% |
| 44 | South Dakota | 86,280,610 | 0.3% |
| 45 | New Hampshire | 83,176,973 | 0.3% |
| 46 | Delaware | 74,451,056 | 0.3% |
| 47 | Rhode Island | 66,339,200 | 0.2% |
| 48 | Wyoming | 64,255,732 | 0.2% |
| 49 | Montana | 59,935,863 | 0.2% |
| 50 | Vermont | 45,987,161 | 0.2% |
| | District of Columbia | 50,365,472 | 0.2% |

Source: U.S. Department of Health and Human Services, Office of Child Support Enforcement
   "Child Support Enforcement Preliminary Data Report" (www.acf.hhs.gov/programs/css/resource/fy2012-preliminary-report)
*Fiscal year 2012. Total does not include $358,561,790 collected in U.S. territories.

# XV. Transportation

# Federal Highway Funding in 2011

## National Total = $40,248,003,000*

| RANK | STATE | FUNDS | % of USA | | RANK | STATE | FUNDS | % of USA |
|------|-------|-------|----------|---|------|-------|-------|----------|
| 16 | Alabama | $787,303,000 | 2.0% | | 1 | California | $3,808,734,000 | 9.5% |
| 30 | Alaska | 520,331,000 | 1.3% | | 2 | Texas | 3,274,769,000 | 8.1% |
| 18 | Arizona | 759,261,000 | 1.9% | | 3 | Florida | 1,966,140,000 | 4.9% |
| 28 | Arkansas | 537,275,000 | 1.3% | | 4 | New York | 1,741,861,000 | 4.3% |
| 1 | California | 3,808,734,000 | 9.5% | | 5 | Pennsylvania | 1,702,633,000 | 4.2% |
| 27 | Colorado | 554,906,000 | 1.4% | | 6 | Illinois | 1,475,374,000 | 3.7% |
| 29 | Connecticut | 521,208,000 | 1.3% | | 7 | Ohio | 1,390,981,000 | 3.5% |
| 48 | Delaware | 175,540,000 | 0.4% | | 8 | Georgia | 1,339,911,000 | 3.3% |
| 3 | Florida | 1,966,140,000 | 4.9% | | 9 | Michigan | 1,092,590,000 | 2.7% |
| 8 | Georgia | 1,339,911,000 | 3.3% | | 10 | North Carolina | 1,080,286,000 | 2.7% |
| 49 | Hawaii | 175,514,000 | 0.4% | | 11 | Virginia | 1,056,004,000 | 2.6% |
| 41 | Idaho | 296,811,000 | 0.7% | | 12 | New Jersey | 1,036,117,000 | 2.6% |
| 6 | Illinois | 1,475,374,000 | 3.7% | | 13 | Indiana | 988,795,000 | 2.5% |
| 13 | Indiana | 988,795,000 | 2.5% | | 14 | Missouri | 982,398,000 | 2.4% |
| 33 | Iowa | 499,338,000 | 1.2% | | 15 | Tennessee | 876,909,000 | 2.2% |
| 36 | Kansas | 392,153,000 | 1.0% | | 16 | Alabama | 787,303,000 | 2.0% |
| 21 | Kentucky | 689,494,000 | 1.7% | | 17 | Wisconsin | 780,813,000 | 1.9% |
| 19 | Louisiana | 728,330,000 | 1.8% | | 18 | Arizona | 759,261,000 | 1.9% |
| 47 | Maine | 191,557,000 | 0.5% | | 19 | Louisiana | 728,330,000 | 1.8% |
| 26 | Maryland | 621,866,000 | 1.5% | | 20 | Washington | 703,485,000 | 1.7% |
| 25 | Massachusetts | 630,252,000 | 1.6% | | 21 | Kentucky | 689,494,000 | 1.7% |
| 9 | Michigan | 1,092,590,000 | 2.7% | | 22 | Minnesota | 676,679,000 | 1.7% |
| 22 | Minnesota | 676,679,000 | 1.7% | | 23 | Oklahoma | 658,138,000 | 1.6% |
| 32 | Mississippi | 501,891,000 | 1.2% | | 24 | South Carolina | 651,506,000 | 1.6% |
| 14 | Missouri | 982,398,000 | 2.4% | | 25 | Massachusetts | 630,252,000 | 1.6% |
| 35 | Montana | 425,773,000 | 1.1% | | 26 | Maryland | 621,866,000 | 1.5% |
| 40 | Nebraska | 299,946,000 | 0.7% | | 27 | Colorado | 554,906,000 | 1.4% |
| 38 | Nevada | 376,815,000 | 0.9% | | 28 | Arkansas | 537,275,000 | 1.3% |
| 50 | New Hampshire | 171,456,000 | 0.4% | | 29 | Connecticut | 521,208,000 | 1.3% |
| 12 | New Jersey | 1,036,117,000 | 2.6% | | 30 | Alaska | 520,331,000 | 1.3% |
| 37 | New Mexico | 381,081,000 | 0.9% | | 31 | Oregon | 518,684,000 | 1.3% |
| 4 | New York | 1,741,861,000 | 4.3% | | 32 | Mississippi | 501,891,000 | 1.2% |
| 10 | North Carolina | 1,080,286,000 | 2.7% | | 33 | Iowa | 499,338,000 | 1.2% |
| 44 | North Dakota | 257,633,000 | 0.6% | | 34 | West Virginia | 453,501,000 | 1.1% |
| 7 | Ohio | 1,390,981,000 | 3.5% | | 35 | Montana | 425,773,000 | 1.1% |
| 23 | Oklahoma | 658,138,000 | 1.6% | | 36 | Kansas | 392,153,000 | 1.0% |
| 31 | Oregon | 518,684,000 | 1.3% | | 37 | New Mexico | 381,081,000 | 0.9% |
| 5 | Pennsylvania | 1,702,633,000 | 4.2% | | 38 | Nevada | 376,815,000 | 0.9% |
| 45 | Rhode Island | 226,948,000 | 0.6% | | 39 | Utah | 334,327,000 | 0.8% |
| 24 | South Carolina | 651,506,000 | 1.6% | | 40 | Nebraska | 299,946,000 | 0.7% |
| 42 | South Dakota | 292,650,000 | 0.7% | | 41 | Idaho | 296,811,000 | 0.7% |
| 15 | Tennessee | 876,909,000 | 2.2% | | 42 | South Dakota | 292,650,000 | 0.7% |
| 2 | Texas | 3,274,769,000 | 8.1% | | 43 | Wyoming | 265,848,000 | 0.7% |
| 39 | Utah | 334,327,000 | 0.8% | | 44 | North Dakota | 257,633,000 | 0.6% |
| 46 | Vermont | 210,610,000 | 0.5% | | 45 | Rhode Island | 226,948,000 | 0.6% |
| 11 | Virginia | 1,056,004,000 | 2.6% | | 46 | Vermont | 210,610,000 | 0.5% |
| 20 | Washington | 703,485,000 | 1.7% | | 47 | Maine | 191,557,000 | 0.5% |
| 34 | West Virginia | 453,501,000 | 1.1% | | 48 | Delaware | 175,540,000 | 0.4% |
| 17 | Wisconsin | 780,813,000 | 1.9% | | 49 | Hawaii | 175,514,000 | 0.4% |
| 43 | Wyoming | 265,848,000 | 0.7% | | 50 | New Hampshire | 171,456,000 | 0.4% |
| | | | | | | District of Columbia | 165,578,000 | 0.4% |

ALPHA ORDER (left) — RANK ORDER (right)

Source: U.S. Department of Transportation, Federal Highway Administration
  "Federal-aid Highway Fund Apportionments" (http://www.fhwa.dot.gov/policyinformation/statistics/2011/)
*Fiscal Year 2011. National total does not include $185,153,000 in federal funds for U.S. territories.

# Per Capita Federal Highway Funding in 2011

## National Per Capita = $129*

ALPHA ORDER

| RANK | STATE | PER CAPITA |
|---|---|---|
| 15 | Alabama | $164 |
| 1 | Alaska | 719 |
| 39 | Arizona | 117 |
| 11 | Arkansas | 183 |
| 48 | California | 101 |
| 44 | Colorado | 108 |
| 22 | Connecticut | 145 |
| 9 | Delaware | 193 |
| 46 | Florida | 103 |
| 26 | Georgia | 137 |
| 35 | Hawaii | 127 |
| 10 | Idaho | 187 |
| 41 | Illinois | 115 |
| 21 | Indiana | 152 |
| 16 | Iowa | 163 |
| 26 | Kansas | 137 |
| 20 | Kentucky | 158 |
| 19 | Louisiana | 159 |
| 23 | Maine | 144 |
| 45 | Maryland | 106 |
| 49 | Massachusetts | 95 |
| 43 | Michigan | 111 |
| 35 | Minnesota | 127 |
| 14 | Mississippi | 169 |
| 16 | Missouri | 163 |
| 3 | Montana | 427 |
| 16 | Nebraska | 163 |
| 24 | Nevada | 139 |
| 32 | New Hampshire | 130 |
| 39 | New Jersey | 117 |
| 11 | New Mexico | 183 |
| 50 | New York | 89 |
| 42 | North Carolina | 112 |
| 4 | North Dakota | 376 |
| 37 | Ohio | 120 |
| 13 | Oklahoma | 174 |
| 30 | Oregon | 134 |
| 30 | Pennsylvania | 134 |
| 8 | Rhode Island | 216 |
| 24 | South Carolina | 139 |
| 5 | South Dakota | 355 |
| 26 | Tennessee | 137 |
| 34 | Texas | 128 |
| 38 | Utah | 119 |
| 6 | Vermont | 336 |
| 32 | Virginia | 130 |
| 46 | Washington | 103 |
| 7 | West Virginia | 244 |
| 26 | Wisconsin | 137 |
| 2 | Wyoming | 469 |

RANK ORDER

| RANK | STATE | PER CAPITA |
|---|---|---|
| 1 | Alaska | $719 |
| 2 | Wyoming | 469 |
| 3 | Montana | 427 |
| 4 | North Dakota | 376 |
| 5 | South Dakota | 355 |
| 6 | Vermont | 336 |
| 7 | West Virginia | 244 |
| 8 | Rhode Island | 216 |
| 9 | Delaware | 193 |
| 10 | Idaho | 187 |
| 11 | Arkansas | 183 |
| 11 | New Mexico | 183 |
| 13 | Oklahoma | 174 |
| 14 | Mississippi | 169 |
| 15 | Alabama | 164 |
| 16 | Iowa | 163 |
| 16 | Missouri | 163 |
| 16 | Nebraska | 163 |
| 19 | Louisiana | 159 |
| 20 | Kentucky | 158 |
| 21 | Indiana | 152 |
| 22 | Connecticut | 145 |
| 23 | Maine | 144 |
| 24 | Nevada | 139 |
| 24 | South Carolina | 139 |
| 26 | Georgia | 137 |
| 26 | Kansas | 137 |
| 26 | Tennessee | 137 |
| 26 | Wisconsin | 137 |
| 30 | Oregon | 134 |
| 30 | Pennsylvania | 134 |
| 32 | New Hampshire | 130 |
| 32 | Virginia | 130 |
| 34 | Texas | 128 |
| 35 | Hawaii | 127 |
| 35 | Minnesota | 127 |
| 37 | Ohio | 120 |
| 38 | Utah | 119 |
| 39 | Arizona | 117 |
| 39 | New Jersey | 117 |
| 41 | Illinois | 115 |
| 42 | North Carolina | 112 |
| 43 | Michigan | 111 |
| 44 | Colorado | 108 |
| 45 | Maryland | 106 |
| 46 | Florida | 103 |
| 46 | Washington | 103 |
| 48 | California | 101 |
| 49 | Massachusetts | 95 |
| 50 | New York | 89 |

District of Columbia     267

Source: CQ Press using data from U.S. Department of Transportation, Federal Highway Administration
"Federal-aid Highway Fund Apportionments" (http://www.fhwa.dot.gov/policyinformation/statistics/2011/)
*Fiscal Year 2011. National per capita does not include population or federal funds for U.S. territories.

# Public Road and Street Mileage in 2011

## National Total = 4,077,756 Miles*

### ALPHA ORDER

| RANK | STATE | MILES | % of USA |
|---|---|---|---|
| 17 | Alabama | 101,668 | 2.5% |
| 45 | Alaska | 16,675 | 0.4% |
| 32 | Arizona | 65,092 | 1.6% |
| 18 | Arkansas | 100,082 | 2.5% |
| 2 | California | 172,202 | 4.2% |
| 22 | Colorado | 88,415 | 2.2% |
| 44 | Connecticut | 21,445 | 0.5% |
| 49 | Delaware | 6,358 | 0.2% |
| 10 | Florida | 121,759 | 3.0% |
| 7 | Georgia | 123,546 | 3.0% |
| 50 | Hawaii | 4,405 | 0.1% |
| 35 | Idaho | 48,553 | 1.2% |
| 4 | Illinois | 139,498 | 3.4% |
| 19 | Indiana | 97,066 | 2.4% |
| 14 | Iowa | 114,387 | 2.8% |
| 3 | Kansas | 140,513 | 3.4% |
| 26 | Kentucky | 79,220 | 1.9% |
| 33 | Louisiana | 61,635 | 1.5% |
| 43 | Maine | 22,874 | 0.6% |
| 41 | Maryland | 32,321 | 0.8% |
| 40 | Massachusetts | 36,303 | 0.9% |
| 9 | Michigan | 122,086 | 3.0% |
| 5 | Minnesota | 138,702 | 3.4% |
| 27 | Mississippi | 75,119 | 1.8% |
| 6 | Missouri | 131,667 | 3.2% |
| 28 | Montana | 74,880 | 1.8% |
| 21 | Nebraska | 93,600 | 2.3% |
| 39 | Nevada | 36,839 | 0.9% |
| 46 | New Hampshire | 16,076 | 0.4% |
| 37 | New Jersey | 39,213 | 1.0% |
| 30 | New Mexico | 68,384 | 1.7% |
| 13 | New York | 114,592 | 2.8% |
| 16 | North Carolina | 105,869 | 2.6% |
| 23 | North Dakota | 86,851 | 2.1% |
| 8 | Ohio | 123,247 | 3.0% |
| 15 | Oklahoma | 112,808 | 2.8% |
| 34 | Oregon | 59,148 | 1.5% |
| 11 | Pennsylvania | 119,771 | 2.9% |
| 48 | Rhode Island | 6,485 | 0.2% |
| 31 | South Carolina | 65,997 | 1.6% |
| 25 | South Dakota | 82,459 | 2.0% |
| 20 | Tennessee | 95,492 | 2.3% |
| 1 | Texas | 312,911 | 7.7% |
| 36 | Utah | 45,635 | 1.1% |
| 47 | Vermont | 14,290 | 0.4% |
| 29 | Virginia | 74,461 | 1.8% |
| 24 | Washington | 83,743 | 2.1% |
| 38 | West Virginia | 38,646 | 0.9% |
| 12 | Wisconsin | 115,018 | 2.8% |
| 42 | Wyoming | 28,253 | 0.7% |

### RANK ORDER

| RANK | STATE | MILES | % of USA |
|---|---|---|---|
| 1 | Texas | 312,911 | 7.7% |
| 2 | California | 172,202 | 4.2% |
| 3 | Kansas | 140,513 | 3.4% |
| 4 | Illinois | 139,498 | 3.4% |
| 5 | Minnesota | 138,702 | 3.4% |
| 6 | Missouri | 131,667 | 3.2% |
| 7 | Georgia | 123,546 | 3.0% |
| 8 | Ohio | 123,247 | 3.0% |
| 9 | Michigan | 122,086 | 3.0% |
| 10 | Florida | 121,759 | 3.0% |
| 11 | Pennsylvania | 119,771 | 2.9% |
| 12 | Wisconsin | 115,018 | 2.8% |
| 13 | New York | 114,592 | 2.8% |
| 14 | Iowa | 114,387 | 2.8% |
| 15 | Oklahoma | 112,808 | 2.8% |
| 16 | North Carolina | 105,869 | 2.6% |
| 17 | Alabama | 101,668 | 2.5% |
| 18 | Arkansas | 100,082 | 2.5% |
| 19 | Indiana | 97,066 | 2.4% |
| 20 | Tennessee | 95,492 | 2.3% |
| 21 | Nebraska | 93,600 | 2.3% |
| 22 | Colorado | 88,415 | 2.2% |
| 23 | North Dakota | 86,851 | 2.1% |
| 24 | Washington | 83,743 | 2.1% |
| 25 | South Dakota | 82,459 | 2.0% |
| 26 | Kentucky | 79,220 | 1.9% |
| 27 | Mississippi | 75,119 | 1.8% |
| 28 | Montana | 74,880 | 1.8% |
| 29 | Virginia | 74,461 | 1.8% |
| 30 | New Mexico | 68,384 | 1.7% |
| 31 | South Carolina | 65,997 | 1.6% |
| 32 | Arizona | 65,092 | 1.6% |
| 33 | Louisiana | 61,635 | 1.5% |
| 34 | Oregon | 59,148 | 1.5% |
| 35 | Idaho | 48,553 | 1.2% |
| 36 | Utah | 45,635 | 1.1% |
| 37 | New Jersey | 39,213 | 1.0% |
| 38 | West Virginia | 38,646 | 0.9% |
| 39 | Nevada | 36,839 | 0.9% |
| 40 | Massachusetts | 36,303 | 0.9% |
| 41 | Maryland | 32,321 | 0.8% |
| 42 | Wyoming | 28,253 | 0.7% |
| 43 | Maine | 22,874 | 0.6% |
| 44 | Connecticut | 21,445 | 0.5% |
| 45 | Alaska | 16,675 | 0.4% |
| 46 | New Hampshire | 16,076 | 0.4% |
| 47 | Vermont | 14,290 | 0.4% |
| 48 | Rhode Island | 6,485 | 0.2% |
| 49 | Delaware | 6,358 | 0.2% |
| 50 | Hawaii | 4,405 | 0.1% |
| | District of Columbia | 1,501 | 0.0% |

Source: U.S. Department of Transportation, Federal Highway Administration
"Highway Statistics 2011" (Table HM-20, http://www.fhwa.dot.gov/policyinformation/statistics/2011/)
*Does not include 16,691 miles of roads and streets in Puerto Rico.

# Percent of Public Road and Street Mileage Federally Funded in 2011

## National Percent = 24.5% of Public Road and Street Mileage*

ALPHA ORDER

| RANK | STATE | PERCENT |
|------|-------|---------|
| 20 | Alabama | 25.4 |
| 10 | Alaska | 28.3 |
| 43 | Arizona | 20.4 |
| 37 | Arkansas | 21.9 |
| 2 | California | 32.3 |
| 44 | Colorado | 19.8 |
| 8 | Connecticut | 28.7 |
| 25 | Delaware | 24.2 |
| 39 | Florida | 21.6 |
| 21 | Georgia | 25.2 |
| 1 | Hawaii | 35.5 |
| 33 | Idaho | 23.4 |
| 19 | Illinois | 25.5 |
| 26 | Indiana | 24.0 |
| 35 | Iowa | 22.7 |
| 22 | Kansas | 24.9 |
| 49 | Kentucky | 17.7 |
| 38 | Louisiana | 21.7 |
| 12 | Maine | 27.6 |
| 24 | Maryland | 24.4 |
| 5 | Massachusetts | 30.6 |
| 6 | Michigan | 29.8 |
| 29 | Minnesota | 23.8 |
| 8 | Mississippi | 28.7 |
| 34 | Missouri | 23.3 |
| 46 | Montana | 19.5 |
| 36 | Nebraska | 22.0 |
| 47 | Nevada | 19.4 |
| 40 | New Hampshire | 21.2 |
| 18 | New Jersey | 26.3 |
| 50 | New Mexico | 16.9 |
| 26 | New York | 24.0 |
| 42 | North Carolina | 20.8 |
| 40 | North Dakota | 21.2 |
| 31 | Ohio | 23.6 |
| 11 | Oklahoma | 28.1 |
| 4 | Oregon | 30.7 |
| 31 | Pennsylvania | 23.6 |
| 14 | Rhode Island | 27.0 |
| 3 | South Carolina | 31.8 |
| 26 | South Dakota | 24.0 |
| 48 | Tennessee | 18.7 |
| 17 | Texas | 26.8 |
| 45 | Utah | 19.7 |
| 14 | Vermont | 27.0 |
| 7 | Virginia | 29.3 |
| 29 | Washington | 23.8 |
| 14 | West Virginia | 27.0 |
| 23 | Wisconsin | 24.6 |
| 12 | Wyoming | 27.6 |

RANK ORDER

| RANK | STATE | PERCENT |
|------|-------|---------|
| 1 | Hawaii | 35.5 |
| 2 | California | 32.3 |
| 3 | South Carolina | 31.8 |
| 4 | Oregon | 30.7 |
| 5 | Massachusetts | 30.6 |
| 6 | Michigan | 29.8 |
| 7 | Virginia | 29.3 |
| 8 | Connecticut | 28.7 |
| 8 | Mississippi | 28.7 |
| 10 | Alaska | 28.3 |
| 11 | Oklahoma | 28.1 |
| 12 | Maine | 27.6 |
| 12 | Wyoming | 27.6 |
| 14 | Rhode Island | 27.0 |
| 14 | Vermont | 27.0 |
| 14 | West Virginia | 27.0 |
| 17 | Texas | 26.8 |
| 18 | New Jersey | 26.3 |
| 19 | Illinois | 25.5 |
| 20 | Alabama | 25.4 |
| 21 | Georgia | 25.2 |
| 22 | Kansas | 24.9 |
| 23 | Wisconsin | 24.6 |
| 24 | Maryland | 24.4 |
| 25 | Delaware | 24.2 |
| 26 | Indiana | 24.0 |
| 26 | New York | 24.0 |
| 26 | South Dakota | 24.0 |
| 29 | Minnesota | 23.8 |
| 29 | Washington | 23.8 |
| 31 | Ohio | 23.6 |
| 31 | Pennsylvania | 23.6 |
| 33 | Idaho | 23.4 |
| 34 | Missouri | 23.3 |
| 35 | Iowa | 22.7 |
| 36 | Nebraska | 22.0 |
| 37 | Arkansas | 21.9 |
| 38 | Louisiana | 21.7 |
| 39 | Florida | 21.6 |
| 40 | New Hampshire | 21.2 |
| 40 | North Dakota | 21.2 |
| 42 | North Carolina | 20.8 |
| 43 | Arizona | 20.4 |
| 44 | Colorado | 19.8 |
| 45 | Utah | 19.7 |
| 46 | Montana | 19.5 |
| 47 | Nevada | 19.4 |
| 48 | Tennessee | 18.7 |
| 49 | Kentucky | 17.7 |
| 50 | New Mexico | 16.9 |

| | District of Columbia | 30.2 |

Source: CQ Press using data from U.S. Department of Transportation, Federal Highway Administration
"Highway Statistics 2011" (Table HM-15, http://www.fhwa.dot.gov/policyinformation/statistics/2011/)
*National percent does not include federally-funded highway miles in Puerto Rico.

# Interstate Highway Mileage in 2011

## National Total = 46,960 Miles*

ALPHA ORDER

| RANK | STATE | MILES | % of USA |
|---|---|---|---|
| 24 | Alabama | 906 | 1.9% |
| 17 | Alaska | 1,084 | 2.3% |
| 14 | Arizona | 1,168 | 2.5% |
| 35 | Arkansas | 656 | 1.4% |
| 2 | California | 2,453 | 5.2% |
| 19 | Colorado | 953 | 2.0% |
| 45 | Connecticut | 346 | 0.7% |
| 50 | Delaware | 41 | 0.1% |
| 7 | Florida | 1,495 | 3.2% |
| 8 | Georgia | 1,248 | 2.7% |
| 49 | Hawaii | 55 | 0.1% |
| 36 | Idaho | 612 | 1.3% |
| 3 | Illinois | 2,182 | 4.6% |
| 13 | Indiana | 1,172 | 2.5% |
| 29 | Iowa | 782 | 1.7% |
| 26 | Kansas | 874 | 1.9% |
| 28 | Kentucky | 801 | 1.7% |
| 25 | Louisiana | 898 | 1.9% |
| 44 | Maine | 369 | 0.8% |
| 42 | Maryland | 481 | 1.0% |
| 37 | Massachusetts | 574 | 1.2% |
| 9 | Michigan | 1,244 | 2.6% |
| 22 | Minnesota | 914 | 1.9% |
| 33 | Mississippi | 702 | 1.5% |
| 10 | Missouri | 1,206 | 2.6% |
| 11 | Montana | 1,192 | 2.5% |
| 41 | Nebraska | 482 | 1.0% |
| 38 | Nevada | 571 | 1.2% |
| 47 | New Hampshire | 225 | 0.5% |
| 43 | New Jersey | 431 | 0.9% |
| 18 | New Mexico | 1,000 | 2.1% |
| 5 | New York | 1,704 | 3.6% |
| 12 | North Carolina | 1,174 | 2.5% |
| 38 | North Dakota | 571 | 1.2% |
| 6 | Ohio | 1,574 | 3.4% |
| 21 | Oklahoma | 933 | 2.0% |
| 32 | Oregon | 730 | 1.6% |
| 4 | Pennsylvania | 1,855 | 4.0% |
| 48 | Rhode Island | 71 | 0.2% |
| 27 | South Carolina | 851 | 1.8% |
| 34 | South Dakota | 679 | 1.4% |
| 16 | Tennessee | 1,104 | 2.4% |
| 1 | Texas | 3,237 | 6.9% |
| 20 | Utah | 937 | 2.0% |
| 46 | Vermont | 320 | 0.7% |
| 15 | Virginia | 1,119 | 2.4% |
| 30 | Washington | 764 | 1.6% |
| 40 | West Virginia | 555 | 1.2% |
| 31 | Wisconsin | 742 | 1.6% |
| 22 | Wyoming | 914 | 1.9% |

RANK ORDER

| RANK | STATE | MILES | % of USA |
|---|---|---|---|
| 1 | Texas | 3,237 | 6.9% |
| 2 | California | 2,453 | 5.2% |
| 3 | Illinois | 2,182 | 4.6% |
| 4 | Pennsylvania | 1,855 | 4.0% |
| 5 | New York | 1,704 | 3.6% |
| 6 | Ohio | 1,574 | 3.4% |
| 7 | Florida | 1,495 | 3.2% |
| 8 | Georgia | 1,248 | 2.7% |
| 9 | Michigan | 1,244 | 2.6% |
| 10 | Missouri | 1,206 | 2.6% |
| 11 | Montana | 1,192 | 2.5% |
| 12 | North Carolina | 1,174 | 2.5% |
| 13 | Indiana | 1,172 | 2.5% |
| 14 | Arizona | 1,168 | 2.5% |
| 15 | Virginia | 1,119 | 2.4% |
| 16 | Tennessee | 1,104 | 2.4% |
| 17 | Alaska | 1,084 | 2.3% |
| 18 | New Mexico | 1,000 | 2.1% |
| 19 | Colorado | 953 | 2.0% |
| 20 | Utah | 937 | 2.0% |
| 21 | Oklahoma | 933 | 2.0% |
| 22 | Minnesota | 914 | 1.9% |
| 22 | Wyoming | 914 | 1.9% |
| 24 | Alabama | 906 | 1.9% |
| 25 | Louisiana | 898 | 1.9% |
| 26 | Kansas | 874 | 1.9% |
| 27 | South Carolina | 851 | 1.8% |
| 28 | Kentucky | 801 | 1.7% |
| 29 | Iowa | 782 | 1.7% |
| 30 | Washington | 764 | 1.6% |
| 31 | Wisconsin | 742 | 1.6% |
| 32 | Oregon | 730 | 1.6% |
| 33 | Mississippi | 702 | 1.5% |
| 34 | South Dakota | 679 | 1.4% |
| 35 | Arkansas | 656 | 1.4% |
| 36 | Idaho | 612 | 1.3% |
| 37 | Massachusetts | 574 | 1.2% |
| 38 | Nevada | 571 | 1.2% |
| 38 | North Dakota | 571 | 1.2% |
| 40 | West Virginia | 555 | 1.2% |
| 41 | Nebraska | 482 | 1.0% |
| 42 | Maryland | 481 | 1.0% |
| 43 | New Jersey | 431 | 0.9% |
| 44 | Maine | 369 | 0.8% |
| 45 | Connecticut | 346 | 0.7% |
| 46 | Vermont | 320 | 0.7% |
| 47 | New Hampshire | 225 | 0.5% |
| 48 | Rhode Island | 71 | 0.2% |
| 49 | Hawaii | 55 | 0.1% |
| 50 | Delaware | 41 | 0.1% |
| | District of Columbia | 13 | 0.0% |

Source: CQ Press using data from U.S. Department of Transportation, Federal Highway Administration
"Highway Statistics 2011" (Table HM-15, http://www.fhwa.dot.gov/policyinformation/statistics/2011/)
*Does not include 282 miles of highway in Puerto Rico that are part of the interstate system.

# Toll Road Mileage in 2010

## National Total = 4,841 Miles

ALPHA ORDER

| RANK | STATE | MILES | % of USA |
|------|-------|-------|----------|
| 27 | Alabama | 3 | 0.1% |
| 27 | Alaska | 3 | 0.1% |
| 21 | Arizona | 20 | 0.4% |
| 33 | Arkansas | 0 | 0.0% |
| 11 | California | 135 | 2.8% |
| 33 | Colorado | 0 | 0.0% |
| 33 | Connecticut | 0 | 0.0% |
| 17 | Delaware | 51 | 1.1% |
| 1 | Florida | 741 | 15.3% |
| 25 | Georgia | 6 | 0.1% |
| 33 | Hawaii | 0 | 0.0% |
| 33 | Idaho | 0 | 0.0% |
| 7 | Illinois | 288 | 5.9% |
| 9 | Indiana | 157 | 3.2% |
| 33 | Iowa | 0 | 0.0% |
| 8 | Kansas | 236 | 4.9% |
| 33 | Kentucky | 0 | 0.0% |
| 18 | Louisiana | 28 | 0.6% |
| 13 | Maine | 106 | 2.2% |
| 16 | Maryland | 64 | 1.3% |
| 10 | Massachusetts | 142 | 2.9% |
| 23 | Michigan | 9 | 0.2% |
| 19 | Minnesota | 27 | 0.6% |
| 33 | Mississippi | 0 | 0.0% |
| 33 | Missouri | 0 | 0.0% |
| 33 | Montana | 0 | 0.0% |
| 31 | Nebraska | 1 | 0.0% |
| 25 | Nevada | 6 | 0.1% |
| 12 | New Hampshire | 131 | 2.7% |
| 5 | New Jersey | 387 | 8.0% |
| 33 | New Mexico | 0 | 0.0% |
| 4 | New York | 549 | 11.3% |
| 23 | North Carolina | 9 | 0.2% |
| 33 | North Dakota | 0 | 0.0% |
| 33 | Ohio | 0 | 0.0% |
| 2 | Oklahoma | 596 | 12.3% |
| 29 | Oregon | 2 | 0.0% |
| 3 | Pennsylvania | 574 | 11.9% |
| 29 | Rhode Island | 2 | 0.0% |
| 20 | South Carolina | 24 | 0.5% |
| 33 | South Dakota | 0 | 0.0% |
| 33 | Tennessee | 0 | 0.0% |
| 6 | Texas | 362 | 7.5% |
| 31 | Utah | 1 | 0.0% |
| 33 | Vermont | 0 | 0.0% |
| 15 | Virginia | 78 | 1.6% |
| 22 | Washington | 15 | 0.3% |
| 14 | West Virginia | 88 | 1.8% |
| 33 | Wisconsin | 0 | 0.0% |
| 33 | Wyoming | 0 | 0.0% |

RANK ORDER

| RANK | STATE | MILES | % of USA |
|------|-------|-------|----------|
| 1 | Florida | 741 | 15.3% |
| 2 | Oklahoma | 596 | 12.3% |
| 3 | Pennsylvania | 574 | 11.9% |
| 4 | New York | 549 | 11.3% |
| 5 | New Jersey | 387 | 8.0% |
| 6 | Texas | 362 | 7.5% |
| 7 | Illinois | 288 | 5.9% |
| 8 | Kansas | 236 | 4.9% |
| 9 | Indiana | 157 | 3.2% |
| 10 | Massachusetts | 142 | 2.9% |
| 11 | California | 135 | 2.8% |
| 12 | New Hampshire | 131 | 2.7% |
| 13 | Maine | 106 | 2.2% |
| 14 | West Virginia | 88 | 1.8% |
| 15 | Virginia | 78 | 1.6% |
| 16 | Maryland | 64 | 1.3% |
| 17 | Delaware | 51 | 1.1% |
| 18 | Louisiana | 28 | 0.6% |
| 19 | Minnesota | 27 | 0.6% |
| 20 | South Carolina | 24 | 0.5% |
| 21 | Arizona | 20 | 0.4% |
| 22 | Washington | 15 | 0.3% |
| 23 | Michigan | 9 | 0.2% |
| 23 | North Carolina | 9 | 0.2% |
| 25 | Georgia | 6 | 0.1% |
| 25 | Nevada | 6 | 0.1% |
| 27 | Alabama | 3 | 0.1% |
| 27 | Alaska | 3 | 0.1% |
| 29 | Oregon | 2 | 0.0% |
| 29 | Rhode Island | 2 | 0.0% |
| 31 | Nebraska | 1 | 0.0% |
| 31 | Utah | 1 | 0.0% |
| 33 | Arkansas | 0 | 0.0% |
| 33 | Colorado | 0 | 0.0% |
| 33 | Connecticut | 0 | 0.0% |
| 33 | Hawaii | 0 | 0.0% |
| 33 | Idaho | 0 | 0.0% |
| 33 | Iowa | 0 | 0.0% |
| 33 | Kentucky | 0 | 0.0% |
| 33 | Mississippi | 0 | 0.0% |
| 33 | Missouri | 0 | 0.0% |
| 33 | Montana | 0 | 0.0% |
| 33 | New Mexico | 0 | 0.0% |
| 33 | North Dakota | 0 | 0.0% |
| 33 | Ohio | 0 | 0.0% |
| 33 | South Dakota | 0 | 0.0% |
| 33 | Tennessee | 0 | 0.0% |
| 33 | Vermont | 0 | 0.0% |
| 33 | Wisconsin | 0 | 0.0% |
| 33 | Wyoming | 0 | 0.0% |
| | District of Columbia | 0 | 0.0% |

Source: U.S. Department of Transportation, Federal Highway Administration
"Highway Statistics 2010" (Table HM-25, http://www.fhwa.dot.gov/policyinformation/statistics/2010/index.cfm)

# Rural Road and Street Mileage in 2011

## National Total = 2,982,383 Rural Miles*

| ALPHA ORDER | | | | | RANK ORDER | | | |
|---|---|---|---|---|---|---|---|---|
| RANK | STATE | MILES | % of USA | | RANK | STATE | MILES | % of USA |
| 17 | Alabama | 76,416 | 2.6% | | 1 | Texas | 213,725 | 7.2% |
| 42 | Alaska | 13,987 | 0.5% | | 2 | Kansas | 127,532 | 4.3% |
| 34 | Arizona | 41,594 | 1.4% | | 3 | Minnesota | 117,885 | 4.0% |
| 10 | Arkansas | 87,069 | 2.9% | | 4 | Missouri | 107,827 | 3.6% |
| 14 | California | 81,877 | 2.7% | | 5 | Iowa | 102,986 | 3.5% |
| 23 | Colorado | 68,883 | 2.3% | | 6 | Illinois | 98,226 | 3.3% |
| 47 | Connecticut | 6,252 | 0.2% | | 7 | Oklahoma | 96,673 | 3.2% |
| 48 | Delaware | 3,361 | 0.1% | | 8 | Wisconsin | 92,537 | 3.1% |
| 35 | Florida | 40,288 | 1.4% | | 9 | Nebraska | 87,170 | 2.9% |
| 13 | Georgia | 83,548 | 2.8% | | 10 | Arkansas | 87,069 | 2.9% |
| 49 | Hawaii | 2,050 | 0.1% | | 11 | Michigan | 86,596 | 2.9% |
| 33 | Idaho | 43,000 | 1.4% | | 12 | North Dakota | 84,932 | 2.8% |
| 6 | Illinois | 98,226 | 3.3% | | 13 | Georgia | 83,548 | 2.8% |
| 21 | Indiana | 70,171 | 2.4% | | 14 | California | 81,877 | 2.7% |
| 5 | Iowa | 102,986 | 3.5% | | 15 | South Dakota | 79,492 | 2.7% |
| 2 | Kansas | 127,532 | 4.3% | | 16 | Ohio | 78,209 | 2.6% |
| 24 | Kentucky | 66,588 | 2.2% | | 17 | Alabama | 76,416 | 2.6% |
| 32 | Louisiana | 44,466 | 1.5% | | 18 | Pennsylvania | 73,620 | 2.5% |
| 40 | Maine | 19,867 | 0.7% | | 19 | Montana | 71,698 | 2.4% |
| 41 | Maryland | 14,323 | 0.5% | | 20 | North Carolina | 70,197 | 2.4% |
| 45 | Massachusetts | 7,988 | 0.3% | | 21 | Indiana | 70,171 | 2.4% |
| 11 | Michigan | 86,596 | 2.9% | | 22 | Tennessee | 69,975 | 2.3% |
| 3 | Minnesota | 117,885 | 4.0% | | 23 | Colorado | 68,883 | 2.3% |
| 26 | Mississippi | 64,107 | 2.1% | | 24 | Kentucky | 66,588 | 2.2% |
| 4 | Missouri | 107,827 | 3.6% | | 25 | New York | 66,157 | 2.2% |
| 19 | Montana | 71,698 | 2.4% | | 26 | Mississippi | 64,107 | 2.1% |
| 9 | Nebraska | 87,170 | 2.9% | | 27 | New Mexico | 60,480 | 2.0% |
| 38 | Nevada | 28,622 | 1.0% | | 28 | Washington | 60,059 | 2.0% |
| 44 | New Hampshire | 11,147 | 0.4% | | 29 | Virginia | 50,391 | 1.7% |
| 46 | New Jersey | 7,296 | 0.2% | | 30 | South Carolina | 49,623 | 1.7% |
| 27 | New Mexico | 60,480 | 2.0% | | 31 | Oregon | 46,237 | 1.6% |
| 25 | New York | 66,157 | 2.2% | | 32 | Louisiana | 44,466 | 1.5% |
| 20 | North Carolina | 70,197 | 2.4% | | 33 | Idaho | 43,000 | 1.4% |
| 12 | North Dakota | 84,932 | 2.8% | | 34 | Arizona | 41,594 | 1.4% |
| 16 | Ohio | 78,209 | 2.6% | | 35 | Florida | 40,288 | 1.4% |
| 7 | Oklahoma | 96,673 | 3.2% | | 36 | Utah | 34,463 | 1.2% |
| 31 | Oregon | 46,237 | 1.6% | | 37 | West Virginia | 33,275 | 1.1% |
| 18 | Pennsylvania | 73,620 | 2.5% | | 38 | Nevada | 28,622 | 1.0% |
| 50 | Rhode Island | 1,225 | 0.0% | | 39 | Wyoming | 25,468 | 0.9% |
| 30 | South Carolina | 49,623 | 1.7% | | 40 | Maine | 19,867 | 0.7% |
| 15 | South Dakota | 79,492 | 2.7% | | 41 | Maryland | 14,323 | 0.5% |
| 22 | Tennessee | 69,975 | 2.3% | | 42 | Alaska | 13,987 | 0.5% |
| 1 | Texas | 213,725 | 7.2% | | 43 | Vermont | 12,824 | 0.4% |
| 36 | Utah | 34,463 | 1.2% | | 44 | New Hampshire | 11,147 | 0.4% |
| 43 | Vermont | 12,824 | 0.4% | | 45 | Massachusetts | 7,988 | 0.3% |
| 29 | Virginia | 50,391 | 1.7% | | 46 | New Jersey | 7,296 | 0.2% |
| 28 | Washington | 60,059 | 2.0% | | 47 | Connecticut | 6,252 | 0.2% |
| 37 | West Virginia | 33,275 | 1.1% | | 48 | Delaware | 3,361 | 0.1% |
| 8 | Wisconsin | 92,537 | 3.1% | | 49 | Hawaii | 2,050 | 0.1% |
| 39 | Wyoming | 25,468 | 0.9% | | 50 | Rhode Island | 1,225 | 0.0% |
| | | | | | | District of Columbia | 0 | 0.0% |

Source: U.S. Department of Transportation, Federal Highway Administration
"Highway Statistics 2011" (Table HM-20, http://www.fhwa.dot.gov/policyinformation/statistics/2011/)
*Does not include 3,104 miles of rural roads and streets in Puerto Rico.

# Urban Road and Street Mileage in 2011

## National Total = 1,095,373 Urban Miles*

| ALPHA ORDER | | | | | RANK ORDER | | | |
|---|---|---|---|---|---|---|---|---|
| RANK | STATE | MILES | % of USA | | RANK | STATE | MILES | % of USA |
| 15 | Alabama | 25,252 | 2.3% | | 1 | Texas | 99,185 | 9.1% |
| 47 | Alaska | 2,688 | 0.2% | | 2 | California | 90,324 | 8.2% |
| 19 | Arizona | 23,498 | 2.1% | | 3 | Florida | 81,471 | 7.4% |
| 28 | Arkansas | 13,013 | 1.2% | | 4 | New York | 48,435 | 4.4% |
| 2 | California | 90,324 | 8.2% | | 5 | Pennsylvania | 46,151 | 4.2% |
| 22 | Colorado | 19,531 | 1.8% | | 6 | Ohio | 45,038 | 4.1% |
| 27 | Connecticut | 15,193 | 1.4% | | 7 | Illinois | 41,273 | 3.8% |
| 44 | Delaware | 2,997 | 0.3% | | 8 | Georgia | 39,998 | 3.7% |
| 3 | Florida | 81,471 | 7.4% | | 9 | North Carolina | 35,673 | 3.3% |
| 8 | Georgia | 39,998 | 3.7% | | 10 | Michigan | 35,490 | 3.2% |
| 48 | Hawaii | 2,355 | 0.2% | | 11 | New Jersey | 31,917 | 2.9% |
| 38 | Idaho | 5,553 | 0.5% | | 12 | Massachusetts | 28,315 | 2.6% |
| 7 | Illinois | 41,273 | 3.8% | | 13 | Indiana | 26,895 | 2.5% |
| 13 | Indiana | 26,895 | 2.5% | | 14 | Tennessee | 25,517 | 2.3% |
| 32 | Iowa | 11,401 | 1.0% | | 15 | Alabama | 25,252 | 2.3% |
| 29 | Kansas | 12,980 | 1.2% | | 16 | Virginia | 24,070 | 2.2% |
| 31 | Kentucky | 12,632 | 1.2% | | 17 | Missouri | 23,839 | 2.2% |
| 24 | Louisiana | 17,169 | 1.6% | | 18 | Washington | 23,683 | 2.2% |
| 43 | Maine | 3,007 | 0.3% | | 19 | Arizona | 23,498 | 2.1% |
| 23 | Maryland | 17,998 | 1.6% | | 20 | Wisconsin | 22,481 | 2.1% |
| 12 | Massachusetts | 28,315 | 2.6% | | 21 | Minnesota | 20,817 | 1.9% |
| 10 | Michigan | 35,490 | 3.2% | | 22 | Colorado | 19,531 | 1.8% |
| 21 | Minnesota | 20,817 | 1.9% | | 23 | Maryland | 17,998 | 1.6% |
| 34 | Mississippi | 11,011 | 1.0% | | 24 | Louisiana | 17,169 | 1.6% |
| 17 | Missouri | 23,839 | 2.2% | | 25 | South Carolina | 16,374 | 1.5% |
| 42 | Montana | 3,182 | 0.3% | | 26 | Oklahoma | 16,135 | 1.5% |
| 37 | Nebraska | 6,430 | 0.6% | | 27 | Connecticut | 15,193 | 1.4% |
| 35 | Nevada | 8,217 | 0.8% | | 28 | Arkansas | 13,013 | 1.2% |
| 41 | New Hampshire | 4,929 | 0.4% | | 29 | Kansas | 12,980 | 1.2% |
| 11 | New Jersey | 31,917 | 2.9% | | 30 | Oregon | 12,911 | 1.2% |
| 36 | New Mexico | 7,904 | 0.7% | | 31 | Kentucky | 12,632 | 1.2% |
| 4 | New York | 48,435 | 4.4% | | 32 | Iowa | 11,401 | 1.0% |
| 9 | North Carolina | 35,673 | 3.3% | | 33 | Utah | 11,172 | 1.0% |
| 49 | North Dakota | 1,919 | 0.2% | | 34 | Mississippi | 11,011 | 1.0% |
| 6 | Ohio | 45,038 | 4.1% | | 35 | Nevada | 8,217 | 0.8% |
| 26 | Oklahoma | 16,135 | 1.5% | | 36 | New Mexico | 7,904 | 0.7% |
| 30 | Oregon | 12,911 | 1.2% | | 37 | Nebraska | 6,430 | 0.6% |
| 5 | Pennsylvania | 46,151 | 4.2% | | 38 | Idaho | 5,553 | 0.5% |
| 40 | Rhode Island | 5,260 | 0.5% | | 39 | West Virginia | 5,371 | 0.5% |
| 25 | South Carolina | 16,374 | 1.5% | | 40 | Rhode Island | 5,260 | 0.5% |
| 45 | South Dakota | 2,968 | 0.3% | | 41 | New Hampshire | 4,929 | 0.4% |
| 14 | Tennessee | 25,517 | 2.3% | | 42 | Montana | 3,182 | 0.3% |
| 1 | Texas | 99,185 | 9.1% | | 43 | Maine | 3,007 | 0.3% |
| 33 | Utah | 11,172 | 1.0% | | 44 | Delaware | 2,997 | 0.3% |
| 50 | Vermont | 1,465 | 0.1% | | 45 | South Dakota | 2,968 | 0.3% |
| 16 | Virginia | 24,070 | 2.2% | | 46 | Wyoming | 2,785 | 0.3% |
| 18 | Washington | 23,683 | 2.2% | | 47 | Alaska | 2,688 | 0.2% |
| 39 | West Virginia | 5,371 | 0.5% | | 48 | Hawaii | 2,355 | 0.2% |
| 20 | Wisconsin | 22,481 | 2.1% | | 49 | North Dakota | 1,919 | 0.2% |
| 46 | Wyoming | 2,785 | 0.3% | | 50 | Vermont | 1,465 | 0.1% |
| | | | | | | District of Columbia | 1,501 | 0.1% |

Source: U.S. Department of Transportation, Federal Highway Administration
   "Highway Statistics 2011" (Table HM-20, http://www.fhwa.dot.gov/policyinformation/statistics/2011/)
*Does not include 13,587 miles of urban roads and streets in Puerto Rico.

# Percent of Roadways in Mediocre or Poor Condition in 2011

## National Percent = 21.5%*

| ALPHA ORDER | | | RANK ORDER | | |
|---|---|---|---|---|---|
| RANK | STATE | PERCENT | RANK | STATE | PERCENT |
| 41 | Alabama | 8.5 | 1 | Kansas | 52.1 |
| 18 | Alaska | 24.0 | 2 | Connecticut | 47.9 |
| 32 | Arizona | 14.1 | 3 | New Jersey | 44.6 |
| 10 | Arkansas | 30.8 | 4 | Hawaii | 38.8 |
| 5 | California | 36.6 | 5 | California | 36.6 |
| 28 | Colorado | 19.3 | 6 | Oklahoma | 36.0 |
| 2 | Connecticut | 47.9 | 7 | West Virginia | 33.3 |
| 26 | Delaware | 20.2 | 8 | Rhode Island | 32.6 |
| 37 | Florida | 11.0 | 9 | Michigan | 31.5 |
| 42 | Georgia | 8.3 | 10 | Arkansas | 30.8 |
| 4 | Hawaii | 38.8 | 11 | Maine | 30.0 |
| 30 | Idaho | 17.7 | 12 | Mississippi | 29.9 |
| 21 | Illinois | 22.6 | 13 | Washington | 27.1 |
| 22 | Indiana | 22.5 | 14 | Pennsylvania | 26.8 |
| 19 | Iowa | 23.5 | 15 | New York | 26.0 |
| 1 | Kansas | 52.1 | 16 | New Mexico | 25.3 |
| 43 | Kentucky | 7.9 | 17 | New Hampshire | 25.0 |
| 25 | Louisiana | 21.2 | 18 | Alaska | 24.0 |
| 11 | Maine | 30.0 | 19 | Iowa | 23.5 |
| 24 | Maryland | 22.1 | 20 | Vermont | 23.3 |
| 34 | Massachusetts | 13.4 | 21 | Illinois | 22.6 |
| 9 | Michigan | 31.5 | 22 | Indiana | 22.5 |
| 31 | Minnesota | 15.3 | 23 | Wisconsin | 22.3 |
| 12 | Mississippi | 29.9 | 24 | Maryland | 22.1 |
| 48 | Missouri | 6.3 | 25 | Louisiana | 21.2 |
| 45 | Montana | 7.1 | 26 | Delaware | 20.2 |
| 38 | Nebraska | 10.6 | 27 | Ohio | 19.9 |
| 47 | Nevada | 6.4 | 28 | Colorado | 19.3 |
| 17 | New Hampshire | 25.0 | 29 | Virginia | 17.9 |
| 3 | New Jersey | 44.6 | 30 | Idaho | 17.7 |
| 16 | New Mexico | 25.3 | 31 | Minnesota | 15.3 |
| 15 | New York | 26.0 | 32 | Arizona | 14.1 |
| 40 | North Carolina | 10.1 | 33 | South Dakota | 14.0 |
| 50 | North Dakota | 5.9 | 34 | Massachusetts | 13.4 |
| 27 | Ohio | 19.9 | 35 | Texas | 12.1 |
| 6 | Oklahoma | 36.0 | 36 | Utah | 11.4 |
| 46 | Oregon | 6.8 | 37 | Florida | 11.0 |
| 14 | Pennsylvania | 26.8 | 38 | Nebraska | 10.6 |
| 8 | Rhode Island | 32.6 | 39 | South Carolina | 10.4 |
| 39 | South Carolina | 10.4 | 40 | North Carolina | 10.1 |
| 33 | South Dakota | 14.0 | 41 | Alabama | 8.5 |
| 44 | Tennessee | 7.7 | 42 | Georgia | 8.3 |
| 35 | Texas | 12.1 | 43 | Kentucky | 7.9 |
| 36 | Utah | 11.4 | 44 | Tennessee | 7.7 |
| 20 | Vermont | 23.3 | 45 | Montana | 7.1 |
| 29 | Virginia | 17.9 | 46 | Oregon | 6.8 |
| 13 | Washington | 27.1 | 47 | Nevada | 6.4 |
| 7 | West Virginia | 33.3 | 48 | Missouri | 6.3 |
| 23 | Wisconsin | 22.3 | 49 | Wyoming | 6.1 |
| 49 | Wyoming | 6.1 | 50 | North Dakota | 5.9 |

| District of Columbia | 96.8 |
|---|---|

Source: CQ Press using data from U.S. Department of Transportation, Bureau of Transportation Statistics
   "State Transportation Statistics 2012" (http://www.bts.gov/publications/state_transportation_statistics/)
*Does not include 24,875 miles for which the condition is not reported.   Road condition ratings are derived from the International Roughness Index (IRI) and the Present Serviceability Rating (PSR).  States are required to report to the Federal Highway Administration (FHWA) IRI data for the Interstate system, other principal arterials, rural minor arterials, and the National Highway System regardless of functional system.

# Bridges in 2012

## National Total = 605,132 Bridges*

| ALPHA ORDER | | | | RANK ORDER | | | |
|---|---|---|---|---|---|---|---|
| RANK | STATE | BRIDGES | % of USA | RANK | STATE | BRIDGES | % of USA |
| 15 | Alabama | 16,070 | 2.7% | 1 | Texas | 52,260 | 8.6% |
| 47 | Alaska | 1,173 | 0.2% | 2 | Ohio | 27,045 | 4.5% |
| 29 | Arizona | 7,835 | 1.3% | 3 | Illinois | 26,514 | 4.4% |
| 23 | Arkansas | 12,696 | 2.1% | 4 | Kansas | 25,176 | 4.2% |
| 5 | California | 24,812 | 4.1% | 5 | California | 24,812 | 4.1% |
| 27 | Colorado | 8,591 | 1.4% | 6 | Iowa | 24,496 | 4.0% |
| 39 | Connecticut | 4,208 | 0.7% | 7 | Missouri | 24,334 | 4.0% |
| 49 | Delaware | 862 | 0.1% | 8 | Oklahoma | 23,781 | 3.9% |
| 24 | Florida | 11,982 | 2.0% | 9 | Pennsylvania | 22,669 | 3.7% |
| 17 | Georgia | 14,739 | 2.4% | 10 | Tennessee | 19,985 | 3.3% |
| 48 | Hawaii | 1,131 | 0.2% | 11 | Indiana | 18,789 | 3.1% |
| 38 | Idaho | 4,214 | 0.7% | 12 | North Carolina | 18,165 | 3.0% |
| 3 | Illinois | 26,514 | 4.4% | 13 | New York | 17,420 | 2.9% |
| 11 | Indiana | 18,789 | 3.1% | 14 | Mississippi | 17,061 | 2.8% |
| 6 | Iowa | 24,496 | 4.0% | 15 | Alabama | 16,070 | 2.7% |
| 4 | Kansas | 25,176 | 4.2% | 16 | Nebraska | 15,393 | 2.5% |
| 19 | Kentucky | 14,031 | 2.3% | 17 | Georgia | 14,739 | 2.4% |
| 21 | Louisiana | 13,175 | 2.2% | 18 | Wisconsin | 14,057 | 2.3% |
| 45 | Maine | 2,408 | 0.4% | 19 | Kentucky | 14,031 | 2.3% |
| 34 | Maryland | 5,294 | 0.9% | 20 | Virginia | 13,769 | 2.3% |
| 35 | Massachusetts | 5,120 | 0.8% | 21 | Louisiana | 13,175 | 2.2% |
| 25 | Michigan | 11,000 | 1.8% | 22 | Minnesota | 13,121 | 2.2% |
| 22 | Minnesota | 13,121 | 2.2% | 23 | Arkansas | 12,696 | 2.1% |
| 14 | Mississippi | 17,061 | 2.8% | 24 | Florida | 11,982 | 2.0% |
| 7 | Missouri | 24,334 | 4.0% | 25 | Michigan | 11,000 | 1.8% |
| 35 | Montana | 5,120 | 0.8% | 26 | South Carolina | 9,271 | 1.5% |
| 16 | Nebraska | 15,393 | 2.5% | 27 | Colorado | 8,591 | 1.4% |
| 46 | Nevada | 1,798 | 0.3% | 28 | Washington | 7,840 | 1.3% |
| 44 | New Hampshire | 2,429 | 0.4% | 29 | Arizona | 7,835 | 1.3% |
| 32 | New Jersey | 6,554 | 1.1% | 30 | Oregon | 7,633 | 1.3% |
| 40 | New Mexico | 3,924 | 0.6% | 31 | West Virginia | 7,093 | 1.2% |
| 13 | New York | 17,420 | 2.9% | 32 | New Jersey | 6,554 | 1.1% |
| 12 | North Carolina | 18,165 | 3.0% | 33 | South Dakota | 5,870 | 1.0% |
| 37 | North Dakota | 4,453 | 0.7% | 34 | Maryland | 5,294 | 0.9% |
| 2 | Ohio | 27,045 | 4.5% | 35 | Massachusetts | 5,120 | 0.8% |
| 8 | Oklahoma | 23,781 | 3.9% | 35 | Montana | 5,120 | 0.8% |
| 30 | Oregon | 7,633 | 1.3% | 37 | North Dakota | 4,453 | 0.7% |
| 9 | Pennsylvania | 22,669 | 3.7% | 38 | Idaho | 4,214 | 0.7% |
| 50 | Rhode Island | 757 | 0.1% | 39 | Connecticut | 4,208 | 0.7% |
| 26 | South Carolina | 9,271 | 1.5% | 40 | New Mexico | 3,924 | 0.6% |
| 33 | South Dakota | 5,870 | 1.0% | 41 | Wyoming | 3,101 | 0.5% |
| 10 | Tennessee | 19,985 | 3.3% | 42 | Utah | 2,947 | 0.5% |
| 1 | Texas | 52,260 | 8.6% | 43 | Vermont | 2,727 | 0.5% |
| 42 | Utah | 2,947 | 0.5% | 44 | New Hampshire | 2,429 | 0.4% |
| 43 | Vermont | 2,727 | 0.5% | 45 | Maine | 2,408 | 0.4% |
| 20 | Virginia | 13,769 | 2.3% | 46 | Nevada | 1,798 | 0.3% |
| 28 | Washington | 7,840 | 1.3% | 47 | Alaska | 1,173 | 0.2% |
| 31 | West Virginia | 7,093 | 1.2% | 48 | Hawaii | 1,131 | 0.2% |
| 18 | Wisconsin | 14,057 | 2.3% | 49 | Delaware | 862 | 0.1% |
| 41 | Wyoming | 3,101 | 0.5% | 50 | Rhode Island | 757 | 0.1% |
| | | | | | District of Columbia | 239 | 0.0% |

Source: U.S. Department of Transportation, Federal Highway Administration
    "Deficient Bridges by State and Highway System, 2012" (http://www.fhwa.dot.gov/bridge/deficient.htm)
*As of December 2012. Includes federal-aid and nonfederal-aid system bridges. National total does not include 2,248 bridges in Puerto Rico.

# Deficient Bridges in 2012

## National Total = 150,283 Deficient Bridges*

ALPHA ORDER

| RANK | STATE | BRIDGES | % of USA |
|------|-------|---------|----------|
| 19 | Alabama | 3,653 | 2.4% |
| 48 | Alaska | 275 | 0.2% |
| 37 | Arizona | 968 | 0.6% |
| 21 | Arkansas | 2,929 | 1.9% |
| 3 | California | 7,156 | 4.8% |
| 33 | Colorado | 1,473 | 1.0% |
| 32 | Connecticut | 1,476 | 1.0% |
| 50 | Delaware | 175 | 0.1% |
| 27 | Florida | 2,026 | 1.3% |
| 22 | Georgia | 2,749 | 1.8% |
| 45 | Hawaii | 505 | 0.3% |
| 40 | Idaho | 837 | 0.6% |
| 12 | Illinois | 4,287 | 2.9% |
| 13 | Indiana | 4,224 | 2.8% |
| 8 | Iowa | 6,475 | 4.3% |
| 10 | Kansas | 4,617 | 3.1% |
| 11 | Kentucky | 4,463 | 3.0% |
| 16 | Louisiana | 3,815 | 2.5% |
| 42 | Maine | 792 | 0.5% |
| 34 | Maryland | 1,467 | 1.0% |
| 23 | Massachusetts | 2,707 | 1.8% |
| 20 | Michigan | 3,026 | 2.0% |
| 31 | Minnesota | 1,613 | 1.1% |
| 17 | Mississippi | 3,774 | 2.5% |
| 5 | Missouri | 6,893 | 4.6% |
| 39 | Montana | 908 | 0.6% |
| 15 | Nebraska | 3,837 | 2.6% |
| 49 | Nevada | 256 | 0.2% |
| 41 | New Hampshire | 807 | 0.5% |
| 25 | New Jersey | 2,368 | 1.6% |
| 44 | New Mexico | 657 | 0.4% |
| 6 | New York | 6,887 | 4.6% |
| 9 | North Carolina | 5,488 | 3.7% |
| 36 | North Dakota | 993 | 0.7% |
| 7 | Ohio | 6,773 | 4.5% |
| 4 | Oklahoma | 6,986 | 4.6% |
| 30 | Oregon | 1,774 | 1.2% |
| 2 | Pennsylvania | 9,910 | 6.6% |
| 47 | Rhode Island | 411 | 0.3% |
| 28 | South Carolina | 1,981 | 1.3% |
| 35 | South Dakota | 1,445 | 1.0% |
| 14 | Tennessee | 3,864 | 2.6% |
| 1 | Texas | 10,052 | 6.7% |
| 46 | Utah | 469 | 0.3% |
| 38 | Vermont | 931 | 0.6% |
| 18 | Virginia | 3,671 | 2.4% |
| 26 | Washington | 2,059 | 1.4% |
| 24 | West Virginia | 2,547 | 1.7% |
| 29 | Wisconsin | 1,936 | 1.3% |
| 43 | Wyoming | 713 | 0.5% |

RANK ORDER

| RANK | STATE | BRIDGES | % of USA |
|------|-------|---------|----------|
| 1 | Texas | 10,052 | 6.7% |
| 2 | Pennsylvania | 9,910 | 6.6% |
| 3 | California | 7,156 | 4.8% |
| 4 | Oklahoma | 6,986 | 4.6% |
| 5 | Missouri | 6,893 | 4.6% |
| 6 | New York | 6,887 | 4.6% |
| 7 | Ohio | 6,773 | 4.5% |
| 8 | Iowa | 6,475 | 4.3% |
| 9 | North Carolina | 5,488 | 3.7% |
| 10 | Kansas | 4,617 | 3.1% |
| 11 | Kentucky | 4,463 | 3.0% |
| 12 | Illinois | 4,287 | 2.9% |
| 13 | Indiana | 4,224 | 2.8% |
| 14 | Tennessee | 3,864 | 2.6% |
| 15 | Nebraska | 3,837 | 2.6% |
| 16 | Louisiana | 3,815 | 2.5% |
| 17 | Mississippi | 3,774 | 2.5% |
| 18 | Virginia | 3,671 | 2.4% |
| 19 | Alabama | 3,653 | 2.4% |
| 20 | Michigan | 3,026 | 2.0% |
| 21 | Arkansas | 2,929 | 1.9% |
| 22 | Georgia | 2,749 | 1.8% |
| 23 | Massachusetts | 2,707 | 1.8% |
| 24 | West Virginia | 2,547 | 1.7% |
| 25 | New Jersey | 2,368 | 1.6% |
| 26 | Washington | 2,059 | 1.4% |
| 27 | Florida | 2,026 | 1.3% |
| 28 | South Carolina | 1,981 | 1.3% |
| 29 | Wisconsin | 1,936 | 1.3% |
| 30 | Oregon | 1,774 | 1.2% |
| 31 | Minnesota | 1,613 | 1.1% |
| 32 | Connecticut | 1,476 | 1.0% |
| 33 | Colorado | 1,473 | 1.0% |
| 34 | Maryland | 1,467 | 1.0% |
| 35 | South Dakota | 1,445 | 1.0% |
| 36 | North Dakota | 993 | 0.7% |
| 37 | Arizona | 968 | 0.6% |
| 38 | Vermont | 931 | 0.6% |
| 39 | Montana | 908 | 0.6% |
| 40 | Idaho | 837 | 0.6% |
| 41 | New Hampshire | 807 | 0.5% |
| 42 | Maine | 792 | 0.5% |
| 43 | Wyoming | 713 | 0.5% |
| 44 | New Mexico | 657 | 0.4% |
| 45 | Hawaii | 505 | 0.3% |
| 46 | Utah | 469 | 0.3% |
| 47 | Rhode Island | 411 | 0.3% |
| 48 | Alaska | 275 | 0.2% |
| 49 | Nevada | 256 | 0.2% |
| 50 | Delaware | 175 | 0.1% |
| | District of Columbia | 185 | 0.1% |

Source: U.S. Department of Transportation, Federal Highway Administration
   "Deficient Bridges by State and Highway System, 2012" (http://www.fhwa.dot.gov/bridge/deficient.htm)
*As of December 2012. Includes federal-aid and nonfederal-aid system bridges. National total does not include 1,214 deficient bridges in Puerto Rico. Bridges classified as deficient are either functionally obsolete or structurally deficient and are not necessarily unsafe.

# Deficient Bridges as a Percent of Total Bridges in 2012

## National Percent = 24.8% of Bridges are Deficient*

| ALPHA ORDER | | | | RANK ORDER | | |
|---|---|---|---|---|---|---|
| RANK | STATE | PERCENT | | RANK | STATE | PERCENT |
| 30 | Alabama | 22.7 | | 1 | Rhode Island | 54.3 |
| 26 | Alaska | 23.4 | | 2 | Massachusetts | 52.9 |
| 49 | Arizona | 12.4 | | 3 | Hawaii | 44.7 |
| 28 | Arkansas | 23.1 | | 4 | Pennsylvania | 43.7 |
| 16 | California | 28.8 | | 5 | New York | 39.5 |
| 42 | Colorado | 17.1 | | 6 | New Jersey | 36.1 |
| 8 | Connecticut | 35.1 | | 7 | West Virginia | 35.9 |
| 35 | Delaware | 20.3 | | 8 | Connecticut | 35.1 |
| 43 | Florida | 16.9 | | 9 | Vermont | 34.1 |
| 39 | Georgia | 18.7 | | 10 | New Hampshire | 33.2 |
| 3 | Hawaii | 44.7 | | 11 | Maine | 32.9 |
| 36 | Idaho | 19.9 | | 12 | Kentucky | 31.8 |
| 45 | Illinois | 16.2 | | 13 | North Carolina | 30.2 |
| 31 | Indiana | 22.5 | | 14 | Oklahoma | 29.4 |
| 21 | Iowa | 26.4 | | 15 | Louisiana | 29.0 |
| 40 | Kansas | 18.3 | | 16 | California | 28.8 |
| 12 | Kentucky | 31.8 | | 17 | Missouri | 28.3 |
| 15 | Louisiana | 29.0 | | 18 | Maryland | 27.7 |
| 11 | Maine | 32.9 | | 19 | Michigan | 27.5 |
| 18 | Maryland | 27.7 | | 20 | Virginia | 26.7 |
| 2 | Massachusetts | 52.9 | | 21 | Iowa | 26.4 |
| 19 | Michigan | 27.5 | | 22 | Washington | 26.3 |
| 50 | Minnesota | 12.3 | | 23 | Ohio | 25.0 |
| 33 | Mississippi | 22.1 | | 24 | Nebraska | 24.9 |
| 17 | Missouri | 28.3 | | 25 | South Dakota | 24.6 |
| 41 | Montana | 17.7 | | 26 | Alaska | 23.4 |
| 24 | Nebraska | 24.9 | | 27 | Oregon | 23.2 |
| 47 | Nevada | 14.2 | | 28 | Arkansas | 23.1 |
| 10 | New Hampshire | 33.2 | | 29 | Wyoming | 23.0 |
| 6 | New Jersey | 36.1 | | 30 | Alabama | 22.7 |
| 44 | New Mexico | 16.7 | | 31 | Indiana | 22.5 |
| 5 | New York | 39.5 | | 32 | North Dakota | 22.3 |
| 13 | North Carolina | 30.2 | | 33 | Mississippi | 22.1 |
| 32 | North Dakota | 22.3 | | 34 | South Carolina | 21.4 |
| 23 | Ohio | 25.0 | | 35 | Delaware | 20.3 |
| 14 | Oklahoma | 29.4 | | 36 | Idaho | 19.9 |
| 27 | Oregon | 23.2 | | 37 | Tennessee | 19.3 |
| 4 | Pennsylvania | 43.7 | | 38 | Texas | 19.2 |
| 1 | Rhode Island | 54.3 | | 39 | Georgia | 18.7 |
| 34 | South Carolina | 21.4 | | 40 | Kansas | 18.3 |
| 25 | South Dakota | 24.6 | | 41 | Montana | 17.7 |
| 37 | Tennessee | 19.3 | | 42 | Colorado | 17.1 |
| 38 | Texas | 19.2 | | 43 | Florida | 16.9 |
| 46 | Utah | 15.9 | | 44 | New Mexico | 16.7 |
| 9 | Vermont | 34.1 | | 45 | Illinois | 16.2 |
| 20 | Virginia | 26.7 | | 46 | Utah | 15.9 |
| 22 | Washington | 26.3 | | 47 | Nevada | 14.2 |
| 7 | West Virginia | 35.9 | | 48 | Wisconsin | 13.8 |
| 48 | Wisconsin | 13.8 | | 49 | Arizona | 12.4 |
| 29 | Wyoming | 23.0 | | 50 | Minnesota | 12.3 |
| | | | | | District of Columbia | 77.4 |

Source: CQ Press using data from U.S. Department of Transportation, Federal Highway Administration
   "Deficient Bridges by State and Highway System, 2012" (http://www.fhwa.dot.gov/bridge/deficient.htm)
*As of December 2012. Includes federal-aid and nonfederal-aid system bridges. National percent does not include bridges in Puerto Rico. Bridges classified as deficient are either functionally obsolete or structurally deficient and are not necessarily unsafe.

# Vehicle-Miles of Travel in 2011

## National Total = 2,946,131,000,000 Miles

<table>
<tr><td colspan="4">ALPHA ORDER</td><td colspan="4">RANK ORDER</td></tr>
<tr><td>RANK</td><td>STATE</td><td>MILES</td><td>% of USA</td><td>RANK</td><td>STATE</td><td>MILES</td><td>% of USA</td></tr>
<tr><td>16</td><td>Alabama</td><td>64,914,000,000</td><td>2.2%</td><td>1</td><td>California</td><td>320,784,000,000</td><td>10.9%</td></tr>
<tr><td>50</td><td>Alaska</td><td>4,593,000,000</td><td>0.2%</td><td>2</td><td>Texas</td><td>237,440,000,000</td><td>8.1%</td></tr>
<tr><td>17</td><td>Arizona</td><td>59,574,000,000</td><td>2.0%</td><td>3</td><td>Florida</td><td>191,855,000,000</td><td>6.5%</td></tr>
<tr><td>30</td><td>Arkansas</td><td>32,953,000,000</td><td>1.1%</td><td>4</td><td>New York</td><td>127,726,000,000</td><td>4.3%</td></tr>
<tr><td>1</td><td>California</td><td>320,784,000,000</td><td>10.9%</td><td>5</td><td>Ohio</td><td>111,990,000,000</td><td>3.8%</td></tr>
<tr><td>26</td><td>Colorado</td><td>46,606,000,000</td><td>1.6%</td><td>6</td><td>Georgia</td><td>108,454,000,000</td><td>3.7%</td></tr>
<tr><td>32</td><td>Connecticut</td><td>31,197,000,000</td><td>1.1%</td><td>7</td><td>North Carolina</td><td>103,772,000,000</td><td>3.5%</td></tr>
<tr><td>46</td><td>Delaware</td><td>9,028,000,000</td><td>0.3%</td><td>8</td><td>Illinois</td><td>103,234,000,000</td><td>3.5%</td></tr>
<tr><td>3</td><td>Florida</td><td>191,855,000,000</td><td>6.5%</td><td>9</td><td>Pennsylvania</td><td>99,204,000,000</td><td>3.4%</td></tr>
<tr><td>6</td><td>Georgia</td><td>108,454,000,000</td><td>3.7%</td><td>10</td><td>Michigan</td><td>94,754,000,000</td><td>3.2%</td></tr>
<tr><td>43</td><td>Hawaii</td><td>10,066,000,000</td><td>0.3%</td><td>11</td><td>Virginia</td><td>80,974,000,000</td><td>2.7%</td></tr>
<tr><td>39</td><td>Idaho</td><td>15,937,000,000</td><td>0.5%</td><td>12</td><td>Indiana</td><td>76,485,000,000</td><td>2.6%</td></tr>
<tr><td>8</td><td>Illinois</td><td>103,234,000,000</td><td>3.5%</td><td>13</td><td>New Jersey</td><td>73,094,000,000</td><td>2.5%</td></tr>
<tr><td>12</td><td>Indiana</td><td>76,485,000,000</td><td>2.6%</td><td>14</td><td>Tennessee</td><td>70,751,000,000</td><td>2.4%</td></tr>
<tr><td>31</td><td>Iowa</td><td>31,274,000,000</td><td>1.1%</td><td>15</td><td>Missouri</td><td>68,789,000,000</td><td>2.3%</td></tr>
<tr><td>33</td><td>Kansas</td><td>30,021,000,000</td><td>1.0%</td><td>16</td><td>Alabama</td><td>64,914,000,000</td><td>2.2%</td></tr>
<tr><td>24</td><td>Kentucky</td><td>48,061,000,000</td><td>1.6%</td><td>17</td><td>Arizona</td><td>59,574,000,000</td><td>2.0%</td></tr>
<tr><td>27</td><td>Louisiana</td><td>46,513,000,000</td><td>1.6%</td><td>18</td><td>Washington</td><td>56,955,000,000</td><td>1.9%</td></tr>
<tr><td>40</td><td>Maine</td><td>14,248,000,000</td><td>0.5%</td><td>19</td><td>Minnesota</td><td>56,685,000,000</td><td>1.9%</td></tr>
<tr><td>20</td><td>Maryland</td><td>56,221,000,000</td><td>1.9%</td><td>20</td><td>Maryland</td><td>56,221,000,000</td><td>1.9%</td></tr>
<tr><td>21</td><td>Massachusetts</td><td>54,792,000,000</td><td>1.9%</td><td>21</td><td>Massachusetts</td><td>54,792,000,000</td><td>1.9%</td></tr>
<tr><td>10</td><td>Michigan</td><td>94,754,000,000</td><td>3.2%</td><td>22</td><td>Wisconsin</td><td>54,402,000,000</td><td>1.8%</td></tr>
<tr><td>19</td><td>Minnesota</td><td>56,685,000,000</td><td>1.9%</td><td>23</td><td>South Carolina</td><td>48,730,000,000</td><td>1.7%</td></tr>
<tr><td>28</td><td>Mississippi</td><td>38,851,000,000</td><td>1.3%</td><td>24</td><td>Kentucky</td><td>48,061,000,000</td><td>1.6%</td></tr>
<tr><td>15</td><td>Missouri</td><td>68,789,000,000</td><td>2.3%</td><td>25</td><td>Oklahoma</td><td>47,464,000,000</td><td>1.6%</td></tr>
<tr><td>42</td><td>Montana</td><td>11,660,000,000</td><td>0.4%</td><td>26</td><td>Colorado</td><td>46,606,000,000</td><td>1.6%</td></tr>
<tr><td>37</td><td>Nebraska</td><td>19,093,000,000</td><td>0.6%</td><td>27</td><td>Louisiana</td><td>46,513,000,000</td><td>1.6%</td></tr>
<tr><td>36</td><td>Nevada</td><td>24,189,000,000</td><td>0.8%</td><td>28</td><td>Mississippi</td><td>38,851,000,000</td><td>1.3%</td></tr>
<tr><td>41</td><td>New Hampshire</td><td>12,720,000,000</td><td>0.4%</td><td>29</td><td>Oregon</td><td>33,373,000,000</td><td>1.1%</td></tr>
<tr><td>13</td><td>New Jersey</td><td>73,094,000,000</td><td>2.5%</td><td>30</td><td>Arkansas</td><td>32,953,000,000</td><td>1.1%</td></tr>
<tr><td>35</td><td>New Mexico</td><td>25,533,000,000</td><td>0.9%</td><td>31</td><td>Iowa</td><td>31,274,000,000</td><td>1.1%</td></tr>
<tr><td>4</td><td>New York</td><td>127,726,000,000</td><td>4.3%</td><td>32</td><td>Connecticut</td><td>31,197,000,000</td><td>1.1%</td></tr>
<tr><td>7</td><td>North Carolina</td><td>103,772,000,000</td><td>3.5%</td><td>33</td><td>Kansas</td><td>30,021,000,000</td><td>1.0%</td></tr>
<tr><td>45</td><td>North Dakota</td><td>9,131,000,000</td><td>0.3%</td><td>34</td><td>Utah</td><td>26,222,000,000</td><td>0.9%</td></tr>
<tr><td>5</td><td>Ohio</td><td>111,990,000,000</td><td>3.8%</td><td>35</td><td>New Mexico</td><td>25,533,000,000</td><td>0.9%</td></tr>
<tr><td>25</td><td>Oklahoma</td><td>47,464,000,000</td><td>1.6%</td><td>36</td><td>Nevada</td><td>24,189,000,000</td><td>0.8%</td></tr>
<tr><td>29</td><td>Oregon</td><td>33,373,000,000</td><td>1.1%</td><td>37</td><td>Nebraska</td><td>19,093,000,000</td><td>0.6%</td></tr>
<tr><td>9</td><td>Pennsylvania</td><td>99,204,000,000</td><td>3.4%</td><td>38</td><td>West Virginia</td><td>18,963,000,000</td><td>0.6%</td></tr>
<tr><td>48</td><td>Rhode Island</td><td>7,901,000,000</td><td>0.3%</td><td>39</td><td>Idaho</td><td>15,937,000,000</td><td>0.5%</td></tr>
<tr><td>23</td><td>South Carolina</td><td>48,730,000,000</td><td>1.7%</td><td>40</td><td>Maine</td><td>14,248,000,000</td><td>0.5%</td></tr>
<tr><td>47</td><td>South Dakota</td><td>9,002,000,000</td><td>0.3%</td><td>41</td><td>New Hampshire</td><td>12,720,000,000</td><td>0.4%</td></tr>
<tr><td>14</td><td>Tennessee</td><td>70,751,000,000</td><td>2.4%</td><td>42</td><td>Montana</td><td>11,660,000,000</td><td>0.4%</td></tr>
<tr><td>2</td><td>Texas</td><td>237,440,000,000</td><td>8.1%</td><td>43</td><td>Hawaii</td><td>10,066,000,000</td><td>0.3%</td></tr>
<tr><td>34</td><td>Utah</td><td>26,222,000,000</td><td>0.9%</td><td>44</td><td>Wyoming</td><td>9,245,000,000</td><td>0.3%</td></tr>
<tr><td>49</td><td>Vermont</td><td>7,141,000,000</td><td>0.2%</td><td>45</td><td>North Dakota</td><td>9,131,000,000</td><td>0.3%</td></tr>
<tr><td>11</td><td>Virginia</td><td>80,974,000,000</td><td>2.7%</td><td>46</td><td>Delaware</td><td>9,028,000,000</td><td>0.3%</td></tr>
<tr><td>18</td><td>Washington</td><td>56,955,000,000</td><td>1.9%</td><td>47</td><td>South Dakota</td><td>9,002,000,000</td><td>0.3%</td></tr>
<tr><td>38</td><td>West Virginia</td><td>18,963,000,000</td><td>0.6%</td><td>48</td><td>Rhode Island</td><td>7,901,000,000</td><td>0.3%</td></tr>
<tr><td>22</td><td>Wisconsin</td><td>54,402,000,000</td><td>1.8%</td><td>49</td><td>Vermont</td><td>7,141,000,000</td><td>0.2%</td></tr>
<tr><td>44</td><td>Wyoming</td><td>9,245,000,000</td><td>0.3%</td><td>50</td><td>Alaska</td><td>4,593,000,000</td><td>0.2%</td></tr>
<tr><td></td><td></td><td></td><td></td><td></td><td>District of Columbia</td><td>3,568,000,000</td><td>0.1%</td></tr>
</table>

Source: U.S. Department of Transportation, Federal Highway Administration
"Highway Statistics 2011" (Table VM-2, http://www.fhwa.dot.gov/policyinformation/statistics/2011/)

# Highway Fatalities in 2011

## National Total = 32,367 Fatalities

ALPHA ORDER

| RANK | STATE | FATALITIES | % of USA |
|---|---|---|---|
| 11 | Alabama | 894 | 2.8% |
| 48 | Alaska | 72 | 0.2% |
| 14 | Arizona | 825 | 2.5% |
| 24 | Arkansas | 549 | 1.7% |
| 2 | California | 2,791 | 8.6% |
| 27 | Colorado | 447 | 1.4% |
| 37 | Connecticut | 220 | 0.7% |
| 46 | Delaware | 99 | 0.3% |
| 3 | Florida | 2,398 | 7.4% |
| 6 | Georgia | 1,223 | 3.8% |
| 45 | Hawaii | 100 | 0.3% |
| 40 | Idaho | 167 | 0.5% |
| 10 | Illinois | 918 | 2.8% |
| 17 | Indiana | 750 | 2.3% |
| 30 | Iowa | 360 | 1.1% |
| 28 | Kansas | 386 | 1.2% |
| 18 | Kentucky | 721 | 2.2% |
| 20 | Louisiana | 675 | 2.1% |
| 42 | Maine | 136 | 0.4% |
| 25 | Maryland | 485 | 1.5% |
| 32 | Massachusetts | 337 | 1.0% |
| 12 | Michigan | 889 | 2.7% |
| 29 | Minnesota | 368 | 1.1% |
| 21 | Mississippi | 630 | 1.9% |
| 15 | Missouri | 784 | 2.4% |
| 38 | Montana | 209 | 0.6% |
| 39 | Nebraska | 181 | 0.6% |
| 35 | Nevada | 246 | 0.8% |
| 47 | New Hampshire | 90 | 0.3% |
| 22 | New Jersey | 627 | 1.9% |
| 31 | New Mexico | 353 | 1.1% |
| 7 | New York | 1,169 | 3.6% |
| 5 | North Carolina | 1,227 | 3.8% |
| 41 | North Dakota | 148 | 0.5% |
| 8 | Ohio | 1,016 | 3.1% |
| 19 | Oklahoma | 696 | 2.2% |
| 34 | Oregon | 331 | 1.0% |
| 4 | Pennsylvania | 1,286 | 4.0% |
| 49 | Rhode Island | 66 | 0.2% |
| 13 | South Carolina | 828 | 2.6% |
| 44 | South Dakota | 111 | 0.3% |
| 9 | Tennessee | 946 | 2.9% |
| 1 | Texas | 3,016 | 9.3% |
| 36 | Utah | 240 | 0.7% |
| 50 | Vermont | 55 | 0.2% |
| 16 | Virginia | 764 | 2.4% |
| 26 | Washington | 457 | 1.4% |
| 32 | West Virginia | 337 | 1.0% |
| 23 | Wisconsin | 582 | 1.8% |
| 43 | Wyoming | 135 | 0.4% |

RANK ORDER

| RANK | STATE | FATALITIES | % of USA |
|---|---|---|---|
| 1 | Texas | 3,016 | 9.3% |
| 2 | California | 2,791 | 8.6% |
| 3 | Florida | 2,398 | 7.4% |
| 4 | Pennsylvania | 1,286 | 4.0% |
| 5 | North Carolina | 1,227 | 3.8% |
| 6 | Georgia | 1,223 | 3.8% |
| 7 | New York | 1,169 | 3.6% |
| 8 | Ohio | 1,016 | 3.1% |
| 9 | Tennessee | 946 | 2.9% |
| 10 | Illinois | 918 | 2.8% |
| 11 | Alabama | 894 | 2.8% |
| 12 | Michigan | 889 | 2.7% |
| 13 | South Carolina | 828 | 2.6% |
| 14 | Arizona | 825 | 2.5% |
| 15 | Missouri | 784 | 2.4% |
| 16 | Virginia | 764 | 2.4% |
| 17 | Indiana | 750 | 2.3% |
| 18 | Kentucky | 721 | 2.2% |
| 19 | Oklahoma | 696 | 2.2% |
| 20 | Louisiana | 675 | 2.1% |
| 21 | Mississippi | 630 | 1.9% |
| 22 | New Jersey | 627 | 1.9% |
| 23 | Wisconsin | 582 | 1.8% |
| 24 | Arkansas | 549 | 1.7% |
| 25 | Maryland | 485 | 1.5% |
| 26 | Washington | 457 | 1.4% |
| 27 | Colorado | 447 | 1.4% |
| 28 | Kansas | 386 | 1.2% |
| 29 | Minnesota | 368 | 1.1% |
| 30 | Iowa | 360 | 1.1% |
| 31 | New Mexico | 353 | 1.1% |
| 32 | Massachusetts | 337 | 1.0% |
| 32 | West Virginia | 337 | 1.0% |
| 34 | Oregon | 331 | 1.0% |
| 35 | Nevada | 246 | 0.8% |
| 36 | Utah | 240 | 0.7% |
| 37 | Connecticut | 220 | 0.7% |
| 38 | Montana | 209 | 0.6% |
| 39 | Nebraska | 181 | 0.6% |
| 40 | Idaho | 167 | 0.5% |
| 41 | North Dakota | 148 | 0.5% |
| 42 | Maine | 136 | 0.4% |
| 43 | Wyoming | 135 | 0.4% |
| 44 | South Dakota | 111 | 0.3% |
| 45 | Hawaii | 100 | 0.3% |
| 46 | Delaware | 99 | 0.3% |
| 47 | New Hampshire | 90 | 0.3% |
| 48 | Alaska | 72 | 0.2% |
| 49 | Rhode Island | 66 | 0.2% |
| 50 | Vermont | 55 | 0.2% |
| | District of Columbia | 27 | 0.1% |

Source: U.S. Department of Transportation, National Highway Traffic Safety Administration
"Traffic Safety Facts 2011" (http://www-nrd.nhtsa.dot.gov/cats/index.aspx)

# Highway Fatality Rate in 2011

## National Rate = 1.10 Fatalities per 100 Million Vehicle-Miles of Travel

ALPHA ORDER

| RANK | STATE | RATE |
|---|---|---|
| 12 | Alabama | 1.38 |
| 7 | Alaska | 1.57 |
| 12 | Arizona | 1.38 |
| 4 | Arkansas | 1.67 |
| 41 | California | 0.87 |
| 32 | Colorado | 0.96 |
| 47 | Connecticut | 0.71 |
| 25 | Delaware | 1.10 |
| 19 | Florida | 1.25 |
| 24 | Georgia | 1.13 |
| 29 | Hawaii | 0.99 |
| 27 | Idaho | 1.05 |
| 40 | Illinois | 0.89 |
| 31 | Indiana | 0.98 |
| 22 | Iowa | 1.15 |
| 17 | Kansas | 1.29 |
| 8 | Kentucky | 1.50 |
| 11 | Louisiana | 1.45 |
| 33 | Maine | 0.95 |
| 42 | Maryland | 0.86 |
| 50 | Massachusetts | 0.62 |
| 35 | Michigan | 0.94 |
| 49 | Minnesota | 0.65 |
| 5 | Mississippi | 1.62 |
| 23 | Missouri | 1.14 |
| 1 | Montana | 1.79 |
| 33 | Nebraska | 0.95 |
| 28 | Nevada | 1.02 |
| 47 | New Hampshire | 0.71 |
| 42 | New Jersey | 0.86 |
| 12 | New Mexico | 1.38 |
| 37 | New York | 0.92 |
| 21 | North Carolina | 1.18 |
| 5 | North Dakota | 1.62 |
| 39 | Ohio | 0.91 |
| 9 | Oklahoma | 1.47 |
| 29 | Oregon | 0.99 |
| 16 | Pennsylvania | 1.30 |
| 44 | Rhode Island | 0.84 |
| 3 | South Carolina | 1.70 |
| 20 | South Dakota | 1.23 |
| 15 | Tennessee | 1.34 |
| 18 | Texas | 1.27 |
| 37 | Utah | 0.92 |
| 46 | Vermont | 0.77 |
| 35 | Virginia | 0.94 |
| 45 | Washington | 0.80 |
| 2 | West Virginia | 1.78 |
| 26 | Wisconsin | 1.07 |
| 10 | Wyoming | 1.46 |

RANK ORDER

| RANK | STATE | RATE |
|---|---|---|
| 1 | Montana | 1.79 |
| 2 | West Virginia | 1.78 |
| 3 | South Carolina | 1.70 |
| 4 | Arkansas | 1.67 |
| 5 | Mississippi | 1.62 |
| 5 | North Dakota | 1.62 |
| 7 | Alaska | 1.57 |
| 8 | Kentucky | 1.50 |
| 9 | Oklahoma | 1.47 |
| 10 | Wyoming | 1.46 |
| 11 | Louisiana | 1.45 |
| 12 | Alabama | 1.38 |
| 12 | Arizona | 1.38 |
| 12 | New Mexico | 1.38 |
| 15 | Tennessee | 1.34 |
| 16 | Pennsylvania | 1.30 |
| 17 | Kansas | 1.29 |
| 18 | Texas | 1.27 |
| 19 | Florida | 1.25 |
| 20 | South Dakota | 1.23 |
| 21 | North Carolina | 1.18 |
| 22 | Iowa | 1.15 |
| 23 | Missouri | 1.14 |
| 24 | Georgia | 1.13 |
| 25 | Delaware | 1.10 |
| 26 | Wisconsin | 1.07 |
| 27 | Idaho | 1.05 |
| 28 | Nevada | 1.02 |
| 29 | Hawaii | 0.99 |
| 29 | Oregon | 0.99 |
| 31 | Indiana | 0.98 |
| 32 | Colorado | 0.96 |
| 33 | Maine | 0.95 |
| 33 | Nebraska | 0.95 |
| 35 | Michigan | 0.94 |
| 35 | Virginia | 0.94 |
| 37 | New York | 0.92 |
| 37 | Utah | 0.92 |
| 39 | Ohio | 0.91 |
| 40 | Illinois | 0.89 |
| 41 | California | 0.87 |
| 42 | Maryland | 0.86 |
| 42 | New Jersey | 0.86 |
| 44 | Rhode Island | 0.84 |
| 45 | Washington | 0.80 |
| 46 | Vermont | 0.77 |
| 47 | Connecticut | 0.71 |
| 47 | New Hampshire | 0.71 |
| 49 | Minnesota | 0.65 |
| 50 | Massachusetts | 0.62 |

| | | |
|---|---|---|
| | District of Columbia | 0.76 |

Source: U.S. Department of Transportation, National Highway Traffic Safety Administration
"Traffic Safety Facts 2011" (http://www-nrd.nhtsa.dot.gov/cats/index.aspx)

# Percent of Traffic Fatalities That Were Speeding-Related in 2011

## National Percent = 30.7%*

ALPHA ORDER

| RANK | STATE | PERCENT |
|---|---|---|
| 23 | Alabama | 33.3 |
| 16 | Alaska | 36.1 |
| 18 | Arizona | 35.6 |
| 49 | Arkansas | 15.7 |
| 27 | California | 31.9 |
| 7 | Colorado | 40.9 |
| 26 | Connecticut | 33.2 |
| 20 | Delaware | 34.3 |
| 50 | Florida | 12.3 |
| 46 | Georgia | 18.0 |
| 4 | Hawaii | 45.0 |
| 39 | Idaho | 26.9 |
| 2 | Illinois | 47.8 |
| 43 | Indiana | 20.4 |
| 47 | Iowa | 17.8 |
| 37 | Kansas | 28.2 |
| 44 | Kentucky | 19.6 |
| 28 | Louisiana | 31.7 |
| 1 | Maine | 50.7 |
| 34 | Maryland | 29.3 |
| 31 | Massachusetts | 30.6 |
| 40 | Michigan | 26.8 |
| 41 | Minnesota | 23.4 |
| 48 | Mississippi | 16.5 |
| 8 | Missouri | 39.5 |
| 14 | Montana | 36.4 |
| 45 | Nebraska | 18.2 |
| 30 | Nevada | 30.9 |
| 5 | New Hampshire | 43.3 |
| 38 | New Jersey | 27.8 |
| 6 | New Mexico | 41.6 |
| 35 | New York | 28.9 |
| 9 | North Carolina | 38.6 |
| 19 | North Dakota | 34.5 |
| 33 | Ohio | 29.4 |
| 31 | Oklahoma | 30.6 |
| 29 | Oregon | 31.1 |
| 2 | Pennsylvania | 47.8 |
| 36 | Rhode Island | 28.8 |
| 23 | South Carolina | 33.3 |
| 23 | South Dakota | 33.3 |
| 42 | Tennessee | 22.7 |
| 9 | Texas | 38.6 |
| 13 | Utah | 37.5 |
| 14 | Vermont | 36.4 |
| 12 | Virginia | 37.6 |
| 16 | Washington | 36.1 |
| 21 | West Virginia | 33.8 |
| 22 | Wisconsin | 33.5 |
| 11 | Wyoming | 37.8 |

RANK ORDER

| RANK | STATE | PERCENT |
|---|---|---|
| 1 | Maine | 50.7 |
| 2 | Illinois | 47.8 |
| 2 | Pennsylvania | 47.8 |
| 4 | Hawaii | 45.0 |
| 5 | New Hampshire | 43.3 |
| 6 | New Mexico | 41.6 |
| 7 | Colorado | 40.9 |
| 8 | Missouri | 39.5 |
| 9 | North Carolina | 38.6 |
| 9 | Texas | 38.6 |
| 11 | Wyoming | 37.8 |
| 12 | Virginia | 37.6 |
| 13 | Utah | 37.5 |
| 14 | Montana | 36.4 |
| 14 | Vermont | 36.4 |
| 16 | Alaska | 36.1 |
| 16 | Washington | 36.1 |
| 18 | Arizona | 35.6 |
| 19 | North Dakota | 34.5 |
| 20 | Delaware | 34.3 |
| 21 | West Virginia | 33.8 |
| 22 | Wisconsin | 33.5 |
| 23 | Alabama | 33.3 |
| 23 | South Carolina | 33.3 |
| 23 | South Dakota | 33.3 |
| 26 | Connecticut | 33.2 |
| 27 | California | 31.9 |
| 28 | Louisiana | 31.7 |
| 29 | Oregon | 31.1 |
| 30 | Nevada | 30.9 |
| 31 | Massachusetts | 30.6 |
| 31 | Oklahoma | 30.6 |
| 33 | Ohio | 29.4 |
| 34 | Maryland | 29.3 |
| 35 | New York | 28.9 |
| 36 | Rhode Island | 28.8 |
| 37 | Kansas | 28.2 |
| 38 | New Jersey | 27.8 |
| 39 | Idaho | 26.9 |
| 40 | Michigan | 26.8 |
| 41 | Minnesota | 23.4 |
| 42 | Tennessee | 22.7 |
| 43 | Indiana | 20.4 |
| 44 | Kentucky | 19.6 |
| 45 | Nebraska | 18.2 |
| 46 | Georgia | 18.0 |
| 47 | Iowa | 17.8 |
| 48 | Mississippi | 16.5 |
| 49 | Arkansas | 15.7 |
| 50 | Florida | 12.3 |

| | District of Columbia | 37.0 |
|---|---|---|

Source: CQ Press using data from U.S. Department of Transportation, National Highway Traffic Safety Administration
"Traffic Safety Facts 2011" (http://www-nrd.nhtsa.dot.gov/cats/index.aspx)
*A speeding-related crash is if the driver was charged with a speeding-related offense or if an officer indicated that racing, driving too fast for conditions, or exceeding the posted speed limit was a contributing factor in the crash.

# Percent of Vehicles Involved in Fatal Crashes That Were Large Trucks in 2011

## National Percent = 8.2%*

ALPHA ORDER

| RANK | STATE | PERCENT |
|---|---|---|
| 26 | Alabama | 7.8 |
| 50 | Alaska | 0.0 |
| 43 | Arizona | 5.8 |
| 3 | Arkansas | 13.7 |
| 35 | California | 7.0 |
| 26 | Colorado | 7.8 |
| 47 | Connecticut | 4.8 |
| 33 | Delaware | 7.1 |
| 41 | Florida | 6.1 |
| 13 | Georgia | 9.9 |
| 48 | Hawaii | 2.1 |
| 24 | Idaho | 8.3 |
| 16 | Illinois | 9.6 |
| 4 | Indiana | 12.5 |
| 10 | Iowa | 10.4 |
| 9 | Kansas | 10.8 |
| 21 | Kentucky | 8.8 |
| 22 | Louisiana | 8.7 |
| 12 | Maine | 10.1 |
| 44 | Maryland | 5.5 |
| 41 | Massachusetts | 6.1 |
| 46 | Michigan | 4.9 |
| 10 | Minnesota | 10.4 |
| 28 | Mississippi | 7.7 |
| 17 | Missouri | 9.5 |
| 17 | Montana | 9.5 |
| 5 | Nebraska | 11.3 |
| 23 | Nevada | 8.5 |
| 39 | New Hampshire | 6.7 |
| 40 | New Jersey | 6.5 |
| 7 | New Mexico | 11.0 |
| 30 | New York | 7.3 |
| 35 | North Carolina | 7.0 |
| 1 | North Dakota | 17.0 |
| 25 | Ohio | 7.9 |
| 6 | Oklahoma | 11.1 |
| 7 | Oregon | 11.0 |
| 19 | Pennsylvania | 9.1 |
| 49 | Rhode Island | 1.2 |
| 32 | South Carolina | 7.2 |
| 29 | South Dakota | 7.4 |
| 38 | Tennessee | 6.8 |
| 14 | Texas | 9.8 |
| 33 | Utah | 7.1 |
| 20 | Vermont | 9.0 |
| 30 | Virginia | 7.3 |
| 44 | Washington | 5.5 |
| 37 | West Virginia | 6.9 |
| 15 | Wisconsin | 9.7 |
| 2 | Wyoming | 16.6 |

RANK ORDER

| RANK | STATE | PERCENT |
|---|---|---|
| 1 | North Dakota | 17.0 |
| 2 | Wyoming | 16.6 |
| 3 | Arkansas | 13.7 |
| 4 | Indiana | 12.5 |
| 5 | Nebraska | 11.3 |
| 6 | Oklahoma | 11.1 |
| 7 | New Mexico | 11.0 |
| 7 | Oregon | 11.0 |
| 9 | Kansas | 10.8 |
| 10 | Iowa | 10.4 |
| 10 | Minnesota | 10.4 |
| 12 | Maine | 10.1 |
| 13 | Georgia | 9.9 |
| 14 | Texas | 9.8 |
| 15 | Wisconsin | 9.7 |
| 16 | Illinois | 9.6 |
| 17 | Missouri | 9.5 |
| 17 | Montana | 9.5 |
| 19 | Pennsylvania | 9.1 |
| 20 | Vermont | 9.0 |
| 21 | Kentucky | 8.8 |
| 22 | Louisiana | 8.7 |
| 23 | Nevada | 8.5 |
| 24 | Idaho | 8.3 |
| 25 | Ohio | 7.9 |
| 26 | Alabama | 7.8 |
| 26 | Colorado | 7.8 |
| 28 | Mississippi | 7.7 |
| 29 | South Dakota | 7.4 |
| 30 | New York | 7.3 |
| 30 | Virginia | 7.3 |
| 32 | South Carolina | 7.2 |
| 33 | Delaware | 7.1 |
| 33 | Utah | 7.1 |
| 35 | California | 7.0 |
| 35 | North Carolina | 7.0 |
| 37 | West Virginia | 6.9 |
| 38 | Tennessee | 6.8 |
| 39 | New Hampshire | 6.7 |
| 40 | New Jersey | 6.5 |
| 41 | Florida | 6.1 |
| 41 | Massachusetts | 6.1 |
| 43 | Arizona | 5.8 |
| 44 | Maryland | 5.5 |
| 44 | Washington | 5.5 |
| 46 | Michigan | 4.9 |
| 47 | Connecticut | 4.8 |
| 48 | Hawaii | 2.1 |
| 49 | Rhode Island | 1.2 |
| 50 | Alaska | 0.0 |

District of Columbia    6.9

Source: U.S. Department of Transportation, National Highway Traffic Safety Administration
"Traffic Safety Facts: Large Trucks" (http://www-nrd.nhtsa.dot.gov/cats/Index.aspx)
*Large trucks are those with gross vehicle weight greater than 10,000 pounds. In 2011, 3,608 large trucks were involved in fatal crashes.

# Lives Saved by Child Restraints, Seat Belts,
## Air Bags, and Motorcycle Helmets in 2011
## National Total = 16,033 Lives

ALPHA ORDER

| RANK | STATE | LIVES | % of USA |
|---|---|---|---|
| 10 | Alabama | 454 | 2.8% |
| 47 | Alaska | 32 | 0.2% |
| 20 | Arizona | 320 | 2.0% |
| 25 | Arkansas | 266 | 1.7% |
| 2 | California | 1,506 | 9.4% |
| 30 | Colorado | 192 | 1.2% |
| 37 | Connecticut | 105 | 0.7% |
| 44 | Delaware | 39 | 0.2% |
| 3 | Florida | 939 | 5.9% |
| 5 | Georgia | 678 | 4.2% |
| 47 | Hawaii | 32 | 0.2% |
| 40 | Idaho | 69 | 0.4% |
| 12 | Illinois | 422 | 2.6% |
| 13 | Indiana | 415 | 2.6% |
| 32 | Iowa | 187 | 1.2% |
| 29 | Kansas | 200 | 1.2% |
| 16 | Kentucky | 364 | 2.3% |
| 19 | Louisiana | 322 | 2.0% |
| 41 | Maine | 66 | 0.4% |
| 26 | Maryland | 227 | 1.4% |
| 34 | Massachusetts | 148 | 0.9% |
| 7 | Michigan | 541 | 3.4% |
| 28 | Minnesota | 207 | 1.3% |
| 18 | Mississippi | 326 | 2.0% |
| 17 | Missouri | 338 | 2.1% |
| 39 | Montana | 86 | 0.5% |
| 38 | Nebraska | 87 | 0.5% |
| 36 | Nevada | 111 | 0.7% |
| 49 | New Hampshire | 23 | 0.1% |
| 22 | New Jersey | 317 | 2.0% |
| 31 | New Mexico | 190 | 1.2% |
| 6 | New York | 603 | 3.8% |
| 4 | North Carolina | 692 | 4.3% |
| 42 | North Dakota | 59 | 0.4% |
| 11 | Ohio | 447 | 2.8% |
| 21 | Oklahoma | 318 | 2.0% |
| 27 | Oregon | 209 | 1.3% |
| 8 | Pennsylvania | 505 | 3.1% |
| 49 | Rhode Island | 23 | 0.1% |
| 15 | South Carolina | 390 | 2.4% |
| 46 | South Dakota | 38 | 0.2% |
| 9 | Tennessee | 489 | 3.0% |
| 1 | Texas | 1,690 | 10.5% |
| 35 | Utah | 125 | 0.8% |
| 44 | Vermont | 39 | 0.2% |
| 14 | Virginia | 403 | 2.5% |
| 23 | Washington | 279 | 1.7% |
| 33 | West Virginia | 166 | 1.0% |
| 24 | Wisconsin | 275 | 1.7% |
| 43 | Wyoming | 57 | 0.4% |

RANK ORDER

| RANK | STATE | LIVES | % of USA |
|---|---|---|---|
| 1 | Texas | 1,690 | 10.5% |
| 2 | California | 1,506 | 9.4% |
| 3 | Florida | 939 | 5.9% |
| 4 | North Carolina | 692 | 4.3% |
| 5 | Georgia | 678 | 4.2% |
| 6 | New York | 603 | 3.8% |
| 7 | Michigan | 541 | 3.4% |
| 8 | Pennsylvania | 505 | 3.1% |
| 9 | Tennessee | 489 | 3.0% |
| 10 | Alabama | 454 | 2.8% |
| 11 | Ohio | 447 | 2.8% |
| 12 | Illinois | 422 | 2.6% |
| 13 | Indiana | 415 | 2.6% |
| 14 | Virginia | 403 | 2.5% |
| 15 | South Carolina | 390 | 2.4% |
| 16 | Kentucky | 364 | 2.3% |
| 17 | Missouri | 338 | 2.1% |
| 18 | Mississippi | 326 | 2.0% |
| 19 | Louisiana | 322 | 2.0% |
| 20 | Arizona | 320 | 2.0% |
| 21 | Oklahoma | 318 | 2.0% |
| 22 | New Jersey | 317 | 2.0% |
| 23 | Washington | 279 | 1.7% |
| 24 | Wisconsin | 275 | 1.7% |
| 25 | Arkansas | 266 | 1.7% |
| 26 | Maryland | 227 | 1.4% |
| 27 | Oregon | 209 | 1.3% |
| 28 | Minnesota | 207 | 1.3% |
| 29 | Kansas | 200 | 1.2% |
| 30 | Colorado | 192 | 1.2% |
| 31 | New Mexico | 190 | 1.2% |
| 32 | Iowa | 187 | 1.2% |
| 33 | West Virginia | 166 | 1.0% |
| 34 | Massachusetts | 148 | 0.9% |
| 35 | Utah | 125 | 0.8% |
| 36 | Nevada | 111 | 0.7% |
| 37 | Connecticut | 105 | 0.7% |
| 38 | Nebraska | 87 | 0.5% |
| 39 | Montana | 86 | 0.5% |
| 40 | Idaho | 69 | 0.4% |
| 41 | Maine | 66 | 0.4% |
| 42 | North Dakota | 59 | 0.4% |
| 43 | Wyoming | 57 | 0.4% |
| 44 | Delaware | 39 | 0.2% |
| 44 | Vermont | 39 | 0.2% |
| 46 | South Dakota | 38 | 0.2% |
| 47 | Alaska | 32 | 0.2% |
| 47 | Hawaii | 32 | 0.2% |
| 49 | New Hampshire | 23 | 0.1% |
| 49 | Rhode Island | 23 | 0.1% |
| | District of Columbia | 8 | 0.0% |

Source: CQ Press using data from U.S. Department of Transportation, National Highway Traffic Safety Administration
"Traffic Safety Facts: Lives Saved in 2011" (http://www-nrd.nhtsa.dot.gov/cats/Index.aspx)

# Safety Belt Usage Rate in 2012

## National Rate = 86.0% Use Safety Belts

ALPHA ORDER

| RANK | STATE | PERCENT |
|---|---|---|
| 17 | Alabama | 89.5 |
| 19 | Alaska | 88.1 |
| 32 | Arizona | 82.2 |
| 48 | Arkansas | 71.9 |
| 3 | California | 95.5 |
| 36 | Colorado | 80.7 |
| 23 | Connecticut | 86.8 |
| 20 | Delaware | 87.9 |
| 22 | Florida | 87.4 |
| 11 | Georgia | 92.0 |
| 9 | Hawaii | 93.4 |
| 41 | Idaho | 79.0 |
| 5 | Illinois | 93.6 |
| 5 | Indiana | 93.6 |
| 10 | Iowa | 92.4 |
| 38 | Kansas | 79.5 |
| 28 | Kentucky | 83.7 |
| 40 | Louisiana | 79.3 |
| 24 | Maine | 84.4 |
| 13 | Maryland | 91.1 |
| 47 | Massachusetts | 72.7 |
| 5 | Michigan | 93.6 |
| 5 | Minnesota | 93.6 |
| 31 | Mississippi | 83.2 |
| 39 | Missouri | 79.4 |
| 46 | Montana | 76.3 |
| 42 | Nebraska | 78.6 |
| 14 | Nevada | 90.5 |
| 49 | New Hampshire | 68.6 |
| 18 | New Jersey | 88.3 |
| 12 | New Mexico | 91.4 |
| 16 | New York | 90.4 |
| 21 | North Carolina | 87.5 |
| 35 | North Dakota | 80.9 |
| 33 | Ohio | 82.0 |
| 27 | Oklahoma | 83.8 |
| 2 | Oregon | 96.8 |
| 30 | Pennsylvania | 83.5 |
| 44 | Rhode Island | 77.5 |
| 14 | South Carolina | 90.5 |
| 50 | South Dakota | 66.5 |
| 28 | Tennessee | 83.7 |
| 4 | Texas | 94.0 |
| 34 | Utah | 81.9 |
| 25 | Vermont | 84.2 |
| 43 | Virginia | 78.4 |
| 1 | Washington | 96.9 |
| 26 | West Virginia | 84.0 |
| 37 | Wisconsin | 79.9 |
| 45 | Wyoming | 77.0 |

RANK ORDER

| RANK | STATE | PERCENT |
|---|---|---|
| 1 | Washington | 96.9 |
| 2 | Oregon | 96.8 |
| 3 | California | 95.5 |
| 4 | Texas | 94.0 |
| 5 | Illinois | 93.6 |
| 5 | Indiana | 93.6 |
| 5 | Michigan | 93.6 |
| 5 | Minnesota | 93.6 |
| 9 | Hawaii | 93.4 |
| 10 | Iowa | 92.4 |
| 11 | Georgia | 92.0 |
| 12 | New Mexico | 91.4 |
| 13 | Maryland | 91.1 |
| 14 | Nevada | 90.5 |
| 14 | South Carolina | 90.5 |
| 16 | New York | 90.4 |
| 17 | Alabama | 89.5 |
| 18 | New Jersey | 88.3 |
| 19 | Alaska | 88.1 |
| 20 | Delaware | 87.9 |
| 21 | North Carolina | 87.5 |
| 22 | Florida | 87.4 |
| 23 | Connecticut | 86.8 |
| 24 | Maine | 84.4 |
| 25 | Vermont | 84.2 |
| 26 | West Virginia | 84.0 |
| 27 | Oklahoma | 83.8 |
| 28 | Kentucky | 83.7 |
| 28 | Tennessee | 83.7 |
| 30 | Pennsylvania | 83.5 |
| 31 | Mississippi | 83.2 |
| 32 | Arizona | 82.2 |
| 33 | Ohio | 82.0 |
| 34 | Utah | 81.9 |
| 35 | North Dakota | 80.9 |
| 36 | Colorado | 80.7 |
| 37 | Wisconsin | 79.9 |
| 38 | Kansas | 79.5 |
| 39 | Missouri | 79.4 |
| 40 | Louisiana | 79.3 |
| 41 | Idaho | 79.0 |
| 42 | Nebraska | 78.6 |
| 43 | Virginia | 78.4 |
| 44 | Rhode Island | 77.5 |
| 45 | Wyoming | 77.0 |
| 46 | Montana | 76.3 |
| 47 | Massachusetts | 72.7 |
| 48 | Arkansas | 71.9 |
| 49 | New Hampshire | 68.6 |
| 50 | South Dakota | 66.5 |

|  |  |  |
|---|---|---|
| | District of Columbia | 92.4 |

Source: U.S. Department of Transportation, National Highway Traffic Safety Administration
"Traffic Safety Facts: Seat Belt Use in 2012" (http://www-nrd.nhtsa.dot.gov/cats/Index.aspx)

# Percent of Passenger Car Occupant Fatalities
## Where Victim Used a Seat Belt in 2011
## National Percent = 44% of Passenger Car Occupant Fatalities*

ALPHA ORDER

| RANK | STATE | PERCENT |
|---|---|---|
| 28 | Alabama | 39 |
| 44 | Alaska | 30 |
| 28 | Arizona | 39 |
| 35 | Arkansas | 37 |
| 1 | California | 60 |
| 35 | Colorado | 37 |
| 26 | Connecticut | 40 |
| 19 | Delaware | 44 |
| 14 | Florida | 46 |
| 19 | Georgia | 44 |
| 33 | Hawaii | 38 |
| 35 | Idaho | 37 |
| 14 | Illinois | 46 |
| 10 | Indiana | 49 |
| 22 | Iowa | 43 |
| 25 | Kansas | 41 |
| 22 | Kentucky | 43 |
| 38 | Louisiana | 36 |
| 14 | Maine | 46 |
| 13 | Maryland | 47 |
| 42 | Massachusetts | 31 |
| 6 | Michigan | 55 |
| 12 | Minnesota | 48 |
| 33 | Mississippi | 38 |
| 44 | Missouri | 30 |
| 42 | Montana | 31 |
| 44 | Nebraska | 30 |
| 28 | Nevada | 39 |
| 50 | New Hampshire | 20 |
| 5 | New Jersey | 56 |
| 7 | New Mexico | 54 |
| 3 | New York | 57 |
| 9 | North Carolina | 50 |
| 48 | North Dakota | 26 |
| 28 | Ohio | 39 |
| 28 | Oklahoma | 39 |
| 2 | Oregon | 59 |
| 44 | Pennsylvania | 30 |
| 39 | Rhode Island | 35 |
| 17 | South Carolina | 45 |
| 49 | South Dakota | 25 |
| 26 | Tennessee | 40 |
| 10 | Texas | 49 |
| 19 | Utah | 44 |
| 3 | Vermont | 57 |
| 17 | Virginia | 45 |
| 7 | Washington | 54 |
| 41 | West Virginia | 32 |
| 22 | Wisconsin | 43 |
| 39 | Wyoming | 35 |

RANK ORDER

| RANK | STATE | PERCENT |
|---|---|---|
| 1 | California | 60 |
| 2 | Oregon | 59 |
| 3 | New York | 57 |
| 3 | Vermont | 57 |
| 5 | New Jersey | 56 |
| 6 | Michigan | 55 |
| 7 | New Mexico | 54 |
| 7 | Washington | 54 |
| 9 | North Carolina | 50 |
| 10 | Indiana | 49 |
| 10 | Texas | 49 |
| 12 | Minnesota | 48 |
| 13 | Maryland | 47 |
| 14 | Florida | 46 |
| 14 | Illinois | 46 |
| 14 | Maine | 46 |
| 17 | South Carolina | 45 |
| 17 | Virginia | 45 |
| 19 | Delaware | 44 |
| 19 | Georgia | 44 |
| 19 | Utah | 44 |
| 22 | Iowa | 43 |
| 22 | Kentucky | 43 |
| 22 | Wisconsin | 43 |
| 25 | Kansas | 41 |
| 26 | Connecticut | 40 |
| 26 | Tennessee | 40 |
| 28 | Alabama | 39 |
| 28 | Arizona | 39 |
| 28 | Nevada | 39 |
| 28 | Ohio | 39 |
| 28 | Oklahoma | 39 |
| 33 | Hawaii | 38 |
| 33 | Mississippi | 38 |
| 35 | Arkansas | 37 |
| 35 | Colorado | 37 |
| 35 | Idaho | 37 |
| 38 | Louisiana | 36 |
| 39 | Rhode Island | 35 |
| 39 | Wyoming | 35 |
| 41 | West Virginia | 32 |
| 42 | Massachusetts | 31 |
| 42 | Montana | 31 |
| 44 | Alaska | 30 |
| 44 | Missouri | 30 |
| 44 | Nebraska | 30 |
| 44 | Pennsylvania | 30 |
| 48 | North Dakota | 26 |
| 49 | South Dakota | 25 |
| 50 | New Hampshire | 20 |
| | District of Columbia | 31 |

Source: U.S. Department of Transportation, National Highway Traffic Safety Administration
   "Traffic Safety Facts: Occupant Protection" (http://www-nrd.nhtsa.dot.gov/cats/Index.aspx)
*Only those fatalities where seat belts are known to have been used are counted.

# Fatalities in Alcohol-Related Crashes in 2011

## National Total = 11,510 Fatalities*

ALPHA ORDER

| RANK | STATE | FATALITIES | % of USA |
|---|---|---|---|
| 11 | Alabama | 309 | 2.7% |
| 49 | Alaska | 24 | 0.2% |
| 16 | Arizona | 263 | 2.3% |
| 23 | Arkansas | 194 | 1.7% |
| 2 | California | 886 | 7.7% |
| 26 | Colorado | 173 | 1.5% |
| 34 | Connecticut | 99 | 0.9% |
| 43 | Delaware | 43 | 0.4% |
| 3 | Florida | 854 | 7.4% |
| 9 | Georgia | 323 | 2.8% |
| 42 | Hawaii | 50 | 0.4% |
| 40 | Idaho | 55 | 0.5% |
| 9 | Illinois | 323 | 2.8% |
| 19 | Indiana | 243 | 2.1% |
| 35 | Iowa | 96 | 0.8% |
| 28 | Kansas | 131 | 1.1% |
| 22 | Kentucky | 201 | 1.7% |
| 17 | Louisiana | 255 | 2.2% |
| 45 | Maine | 39 | 0.3% |
| 24 | Maryland | 192 | 1.7% |
| 30 | Massachusetts | 130 | 1.1% |
| 14 | Michigan | 294 | 2.6% |
| 28 | Minnesota | 131 | 1.1% |
| 27 | Mississippi | 163 | 1.4% |
| 13 | Missouri | 299 | 2.6% |
| 37 | Montana | 88 | 0.8% |
| 41 | Nebraska | 54 | 0.5% |
| 36 | Nevada | 91 | 0.8% |
| 47 | New Hampshire | 29 | 0.3% |
| 20 | New Jersey | 227 | 2.0% |
| 31 | New Mexico | 119 | 1.0% |
| 6 | New York | 387 | 3.4% |
| 5 | North Carolina | 417 | 3.6% |
| 38 | North Dakota | 67 | 0.6% |
| 8 | Ohio | 358 | 3.1% |
| 18 | Oklahoma | 249 | 2.2% |
| 32 | Oregon | 116 | 1.0% |
| 4 | Pennsylvania | 464 | 4.0% |
| 48 | Rhode Island | 27 | 0.2% |
| 7 | South Carolina | 379 | 3.3% |
| 46 | South Dakota | 37 | 0.3% |
| 12 | Tennessee | 307 | 2.7% |
| 1 | Texas | 1,397 | 12.1% |
| 39 | Utah | 63 | 0.5% |
| 50 | Vermont | 23 | 0.2% |
| 15 | Virginia | 274 | 2.4% |
| 25 | Washington | 182 | 1.6% |
| 33 | West Virginia | 106 | 0.9% |
| 20 | Wisconsin | 227 | 2.0% |
| 44 | Wyoming | 41 | 0.4% |

RANK ORDER

| RANK | STATE | FATALITIES | % of USA |
|---|---|---|---|
| 1 | Texas | 1,397 | 12.1% |
| 2 | California | 886 | 7.7% |
| 3 | Florida | 854 | 7.4% |
| 4 | Pennsylvania | 464 | 4.0% |
| 5 | North Carolina | 417 | 3.6% |
| 6 | New York | 387 | 3.4% |
| 7 | South Carolina | 379 | 3.3% |
| 8 | Ohio | 358 | 3.1% |
| 9 | Georgia | 323 | 2.8% |
| 9 | Illinois | 323 | 2.8% |
| 11 | Alabama | 309 | 2.7% |
| 12 | Tennessee | 307 | 2.7% |
| 13 | Missouri | 299 | 2.6% |
| 14 | Michigan | 294 | 2.6% |
| 15 | Virginia | 274 | 2.4% |
| 16 | Arizona | 263 | 2.3% |
| 17 | Louisiana | 255 | 2.2% |
| 18 | Oklahoma | 249 | 2.2% |
| 19 | Indiana | 243 | 2.1% |
| 20 | New Jersey | 227 | 2.0% |
| 20 | Wisconsin | 227 | 2.0% |
| 22 | Kentucky | 201 | 1.7% |
| 23 | Arkansas | 194 | 1.7% |
| 24 | Maryland | 192 | 1.7% |
| 25 | Washington | 182 | 1.6% |
| 26 | Colorado | 173 | 1.5% |
| 27 | Mississippi | 163 | 1.4% |
| 28 | Kansas | 131 | 1.1% |
| 28 | Minnesota | 131 | 1.1% |
| 30 | Massachusetts | 130 | 1.1% |
| 31 | New Mexico | 119 | 1.0% |
| 32 | Oregon | 116 | 1.0% |
| 33 | West Virginia | 106 | 0.9% |
| 34 | Connecticut | 99 | 0.9% |
| 35 | Iowa | 96 | 0.8% |
| 36 | Nevada | 91 | 0.8% |
| 37 | Montana | 88 | 0.8% |
| 38 | North Dakota | 67 | 0.6% |
| 39 | Utah | 63 | 0.5% |
| 40 | Idaho | 55 | 0.5% |
| 41 | Nebraska | 54 | 0.5% |
| 42 | Hawaii | 50 | 0.4% |
| 43 | Delaware | 43 | 0.4% |
| 44 | Wyoming | 41 | 0.4% |
| 45 | Maine | 39 | 0.3% |
| 46 | South Dakota | 37 | 0.3% |
| 47 | New Hampshire | 29 | 0.3% |
| 48 | Rhode Island | 27 | 0.2% |
| 49 | Alaska | 24 | 0.2% |
| 50 | Vermont | 23 | 0.2% |
| | District of Columbia | 13 | 0.1% |

Source: U.S. Department of Transportation, National Highway Traffic Safety Administration
"Traffic Safety Facts: Alcohol-Impaired Driving" (http://www-nrd.nhtsa.dot.gov/cats/Index.aspx)
*Drivers with Blood Alcohol Content (BAC) of .01 or more. "Legally Drunk" BAC differs from state to state but is often .08 or higher.

# Fatalities in Alcohol-Related Crashes
## as a Percent of All Highway Fatalities in 2011
## National Percent = 36% of Highway Fatalities*

| ALPHA ORDER | | | | RANK ORDER | | |
|---|---|---|---|---|---|---|
| RANK | STATE | PERCENT | | RANK | STATE | PERCENT |
| 24 | Alabama | 35 | | 1 | Hawaii | 50 |
| 33 | Alaska | 33 | | 2 | South Carolina | 46 |
| 37 | Arizona | 32 | | 2 | Texas | 46 |
| 24 | Arkansas | 35 | | 4 | Connecticut | 45 |
| 37 | California | 32 | | 4 | North Dakota | 45 |
| 12 | Colorado | 39 | | 6 | Delaware | 44 |
| 4 | Connecticut | 45 | | 7 | Montana | 42 |
| 6 | Delaware | 44 | | 7 | Vermont | 42 |
| 18 | Florida | 36 | | 9 | Rhode Island | 41 |
| 48 | Georgia | 26 | | 10 | Maryland | 40 |
| 1 | Hawaii | 50 | | 10 | Washington | 40 |
| 33 | Idaho | 33 | | 12 | Colorado | 39 |
| 24 | Illinois | 35 | | 12 | Massachusetts | 39 |
| 37 | Indiana | 32 | | 12 | Wisconsin | 39 |
| 47 | Iowa | 27 | | 15 | Louisiana | 38 |
| 29 | Kansas | 34 | | 15 | Missouri | 38 |
| 46 | Kentucky | 28 | | 17 | Nevada | 37 |
| 15 | Louisiana | 38 | | 18 | Florida | 36 |
| 45 | Maine | 29 | | 18 | Minnesota | 36 |
| 10 | Maryland | 40 | | 18 | New Jersey | 36 |
| 12 | Massachusetts | 39 | | 18 | Oklahoma | 36 |
| 33 | Michigan | 33 | | 18 | Pennsylvania | 36 |
| 18 | Minnesota | 36 | | 18 | Virginia | 36 |
| 48 | Mississippi | 26 | | 24 | Alabama | 35 |
| 15 | Missouri | 38 | | 24 | Arkansas | 35 |
| 7 | Montana | 42 | | 24 | Illinois | 35 |
| 44 | Nebraska | 30 | | 24 | Ohio | 35 |
| 17 | Nevada | 37 | | 24 | Oregon | 35 |
| 37 | New Hampshire | 32 | | 29 | Kansas | 34 |
| 18 | New Jersey | 36 | | 29 | New Mexico | 34 |
| 29 | New Mexico | 34 | | 29 | North Carolina | 34 |
| 33 | New York | 33 | | 29 | South Dakota | 34 |
| 29 | North Carolina | 34 | | 33 | Alaska | 33 |
| 4 | North Dakota | 45 | | 33 | Idaho | 33 |
| 24 | Ohio | 35 | | 33 | Michigan | 33 |
| 18 | Oklahoma | 36 | | 33 | New York | 33 |
| 24 | Oregon | 35 | | 37 | Arizona | 32 |
| 18 | Pennsylvania | 36 | | 37 | California | 32 |
| 9 | Rhode Island | 41 | | 37 | Indiana | 32 |
| 2 | South Carolina | 46 | | 37 | New Hampshire | 32 |
| 29 | South Dakota | 34 | | 37 | Tennessee | 32 |
| 37 | Tennessee | 32 | | 37 | West Virginia | 32 |
| 2 | Texas | 46 | | 43 | Wyoming | 31 |
| 48 | Utah | 26 | | 44 | Nebraska | 30 |
| 7 | Vermont | 42 | | 45 | Maine | 29 |
| 18 | Virginia | 36 | | 46 | Kentucky | 28 |
| 10 | Washington | 40 | | 47 | Iowa | 27 |
| 37 | West Virginia | 32 | | 48 | Georgia | 26 |
| 12 | Wisconsin | 39 | | 48 | Mississippi | 26 |
| 43 | Wyoming | 31 | | 48 | Utah | 26 |
| | | | | | District of Columbia | 50 |

Source: U.S. Department of Transportation, National Highway Traffic Safety Administration
   "Traffic Safety Facts: Alcohol-Impaired Driving" (http://www-nrd.nhtsa.dot.gov/cats/Index.aspx)
*Drivers with Blood Alcohol Content (BAC) of .01 or more. "Legally Drunk" BAC differs from state to state but is often .08 or higher.

# Percent of Fatal Traffic Accidents Involving Older Drivers in 2011

## National Percent = 12.5%*

ALPHA ORDER

| RANK | STATE | PERCENT |
|---|---|---|
| 37 | Alabama | 11.7 |
| 46 | Alaska | 9.9 |
| 25 | Arizona | 13.5 |
| 35 | Arkansas | 11.9 |
| 44 | California | 10.3 |
| 45 | Colorado | 10.1 |
| 31 | Connecticut | 13.1 |
| 9 | Delaware | 14.9 |
| 27 | Florida | 13.4 |
| 10 | Georgia | 14.7 |
| 40 | Hawaii | 11.4 |
| 13 | Idaho | 14.5 |
| 34 | Illinois | 12.2 |
| 21 | Indiana | 13.7 |
| 1 | Iowa | 19.0 |
| 16 | Kansas | 14.0 |
| 39 | Kentucky | 11.6 |
| 49 | Louisiana | 8.8 |
| 7 | Maine | 15.4 |
| 37 | Maryland | 11.7 |
| 27 | Massachusetts | 13.4 |
| 15 | Michigan | 14.3 |
| 4 | Minnesota | 17.3 |
| 47 | Mississippi | 9.8 |
| 35 | Missouri | 11.9 |
| 21 | Montana | 13.7 |
| 30 | Nebraska | 13.2 |
| 16 | Nevada | 14.0 |
| 2 | New Hampshire | 18.3 |
| 14 | New Jersey | 14.4 |
| 43 | New Mexico | 10.7 |
| 32 | New York | 12.9 |
| 33 | North Carolina | 12.5 |
| 18 | North Dakota | 13.9 |
| 23 | Ohio | 13.6 |
| 20 | Oklahoma | 13.8 |
| 5 | Oregon | 17.1 |
| 23 | Pennsylvania | 13.6 |
| 5 | Rhode Island | 17.1 |
| 42 | South Carolina | 11.2 |
| 10 | South Dakota | 14.7 |
| 25 | Tennessee | 13.5 |
| 48 | Texas | 9.3 |
| 41 | Utah | 11.3 |
| 3 | Vermont | 18.2 |
| 27 | Virginia | 13.4 |
| 18 | Washington | 13.9 |
| 10 | West Virginia | 14.7 |
| 8 | Wisconsin | 15.0 |
| 50 | Wyoming | 8.6 |

RANK ORDER

| RANK | STATE | PERCENT |
|---|---|---|
| 1 | Iowa | 19.0 |
| 2 | New Hampshire | 18.3 |
| 3 | Vermont | 18.2 |
| 4 | Minnesota | 17.3 |
| 5 | Oregon | 17.1 |
| 5 | Rhode Island | 17.1 |
| 7 | Maine | 15.4 |
| 8 | Wisconsin | 15.0 |
| 9 | Delaware | 14.9 |
| 10 | Georgia | 14.7 |
| 10 | South Dakota | 14.7 |
| 10 | West Virginia | 14.7 |
| 13 | Idaho | 14.5 |
| 14 | New Jersey | 14.4 |
| 15 | Michigan | 14.3 |
| 16 | Kansas | 14.0 |
| 16 | Nevada | 14.0 |
| 18 | North Dakota | 13.9 |
| 18 | Washington | 13.9 |
| 20 | Oklahoma | 13.8 |
| 21 | Indiana | 13.7 |
| 21 | Montana | 13.7 |
| 23 | Ohio | 13.6 |
| 23 | Pennsylvania | 13.6 |
| 25 | Arizona | 13.5 |
| 25 | Tennessee | 13.5 |
| 27 | Florida | 13.4 |
| 27 | Massachusetts | 13.4 |
| 27 | Virginia | 13.4 |
| 30 | Nebraska | 13.2 |
| 31 | Connecticut | 13.1 |
| 32 | New York | 12.9 |
| 33 | North Carolina | 12.5 |
| 34 | Illinois | 12.2 |
| 35 | Arkansas | 11.9 |
| 35 | Missouri | 11.9 |
| 37 | Alabama | 11.7 |
| 37 | Maryland | 11.7 |
| 39 | Kentucky | 11.6 |
| 40 | Hawaii | 11.4 |
| 41 | Utah | 11.3 |
| 42 | South Carolina | 11.2 |
| 43 | New Mexico | 10.7 |
| 44 | California | 10.3 |
| 45 | Colorado | 10.1 |
| 46 | Alaska | 9.9 |
| 47 | Mississippi | 9.8 |
| 48 | Texas | 9.3 |
| 49 | Louisiana | 8.8 |
| 50 | Wyoming | 8.6 |

District of Columbia          3.4

Source: U.S. Department of Transportation, National Highway Traffic Safety Administration
"Traffic Safety Facts: Older Population" (http://www-nrd.nhtsa.dot.gov/cats/Index.aspx)
*Drivers 65 years old and older.  People 65 or older make up 13 percent of the total U.S. population.

# Percent of Highway Fatalities Who Were Young Drivers in 2011

## National Percent = 6.1% of Fatalities*

ALPHA ORDER

| RANK | STATE | PERCENT |
|------|-------|---------|
| 13 | Alabama | 7.2 |
| 47 | Alaska | 4.2 |
| 39 | Arizona | 5.0 |
| 32 | Arkansas | 5.8 |
| 46 | California | 4.3 |
| 23 | Colorado | 6.7 |
| 34 | Connecticut | 5.5 |
| 38 | Delaware | 5.1 |
| 42 | Florida | 4.9 |
| 34 | Georgia | 5.5 |
| 39 | Hawaii | 5.0 |
| 1 | Idaho | 13.2 |
| 30 | Illinois | 6.1 |
| 13 | Indiana | 7.2 |
| 6 | Iowa | 8.3 |
| 8 | Kansas | 8.0 |
| 37 | Kentucky | 5.4 |
| 9 | Louisiana | 7.6 |
| 3 | Maine | 10.3 |
| 18 | Maryland | 7.0 |
| 20 | Massachusetts | 6.8 |
| 17 | Michigan | 7.1 |
| 12 | Minnesota | 7.3 |
| 23 | Mississippi | 6.7 |
| 5 | Missouri | 8.8 |
| 13 | Montana | 7.2 |
| 6 | Nebraska | 8.3 |
| 50 | Nevada | 2.8 |
| 23 | New Hampshire | 6.7 |
| 43 | New Jersey | 4.8 |
| 45 | New Mexico | 4.5 |
| 48 | New York | 3.4 |
| 26 | North Carolina | 6.5 |
| 20 | North Dakota | 6.8 |
| 13 | Ohio | 7.2 |
| 31 | Oklahoma | 6.0 |
| 43 | Oregon | 4.8 |
| 9 | Pennsylvania | 7.6 |
| 49 | Rhode Island | 3.0 |
| 20 | South Carolina | 6.8 |
| 27 | South Dakota | 6.3 |
| 18 | Tennessee | 7.0 |
| 27 | Texas | 6.3 |
| 39 | Utah | 5.0 |
| 2 | Vermont | 10.9 |
| 29 | Virginia | 6.2 |
| 34 | Washington | 5.5 |
| 4 | West Virginia | 9.5 |
| 33 | Wisconsin | 5.7 |
| 11 | Wyoming | 7.4 |

RANK ORDER

| RANK | STATE | PERCENT |
|------|-------|---------|
| 1 | Idaho | 13.2 |
| 2 | Vermont | 10.9 |
| 3 | Maine | 10.3 |
| 4 | West Virginia | 9.5 |
| 5 | Missouri | 8.8 |
| 6 | Iowa | 8.3 |
| 6 | Nebraska | 8.3 |
| 8 | Kansas | 8.0 |
| 9 | Louisiana | 7.6 |
| 9 | Pennsylvania | 7.6 |
| 11 | Wyoming | 7.4 |
| 12 | Minnesota | 7.3 |
| 13 | Alabama | 7.2 |
| 13 | Indiana | 7.2 |
| 13 | Montana | 7.2 |
| 13 | Ohio | 7.2 |
| 17 | Michigan | 7.1 |
| 18 | Maryland | 7.0 |
| 18 | Tennessee | 7.0 |
| 20 | Massachusetts | 6.8 |
| 20 | North Dakota | 6.8 |
| 20 | South Carolina | 6.8 |
| 23 | Colorado | 6.7 |
| 23 | Mississippi | 6.7 |
| 23 | New Hampshire | 6.7 |
| 26 | North Carolina | 6.5 |
| 27 | South Dakota | 6.3 |
| 27 | Texas | 6.3 |
| 29 | Virginia | 6.2 |
| 30 | Illinois | 6.1 |
| 31 | Oklahoma | 6.0 |
| 32 | Arkansas | 5.8 |
| 33 | Wisconsin | 5.7 |
| 34 | Connecticut | 5.5 |
| 34 | Georgia | 5.5 |
| 34 | Washington | 5.5 |
| 37 | Kentucky | 5.4 |
| 38 | Delaware | 5.1 |
| 39 | Arizona | 5.0 |
| 39 | Hawaii | 5.0 |
| 39 | Utah | 5.0 |
| 42 | Florida | 4.9 |
| 43 | New Jersey | 4.8 |
| 43 | Oregon | 4.8 |
| 45 | New Mexico | 4.5 |
| 46 | California | 4.3 |
| 47 | Alaska | 4.2 |
| 48 | New York | 3.4 |
| 49 | Rhode Island | 3.0 |
| 50 | Nevada | 2.8 |

| | District of Columbia | 7.4 |

Source: CQ Press using data from U.S. Department of Transportation, National Highway Traffic Safety Administration
"Traffic Safety Facts: Young Drivers" (http://www-nrd.nhtsa.dot.gov/cats/Index.aspx)
*Drivers 15 to 20 years old. Based on 1,987 fatalities of young drivers. An additional 2,780 passengers and nonoccupants were killed in crashes involving young drivers. Young drivers accounted for 6.4 percent of all drivers.

# Licensed Drivers in 2011

## National Total = 211,874,649 Licensed Drivers

| ALPHA ORDER | | | | | RANK ORDER | | | |
|---|---|---|---|---|---|---|---|---|
| RANK | STATE | DRIVERS | % of USA | | RANK | STATE | DRIVERS | % of USA |
| 21 | Alabama | 3,798,552 | 1.8% | | 1 | California | 23,856,600 | 11.3% |
| 48 | Alaska | 521,280 | 0.2% | | 2 | Texas | 15,122,518 | 7.1% |
| 16 | Arizona | 4,592,398 | 2.2% | | 3 | Florida | 13,882,423 | 6.6% |
| 32 | Arkansas | 1,956,091 | 0.9% | | 4 | New York | 11,210,783 | 5.3% |
| 1 | California | 23,856,600 | 11.3% | | 5 | Pennsylvania | 8,796,774 | 4.2% |
| 22 | Colorado | 3,669,816 | 1.7% | | 6 | Illinois | 8,373,969 | 4.0% |
| 26 | Connecticut | 2,986,267 | 1.4% | | 7 | Ohio | 7,982,149 | 3.8% |
| 45 | Delaware | 716,109 | 0.3% | | 8 | Michigan | 7,059,509 | 3.3% |
| 3 | Florida | 13,882,423 | 6.6% | | 9 | Indiana | 6,569,665 | 3.1% |
| 11 | Georgia | 6,505,690 | 3.1% | | 10 | North Carolina | 6,569,341 | 3.1% |
| 42 | Hawaii | 911,660 | 0.4% | | 11 | Georgia | 6,505,690 | 3.1% |
| 39 | Idaho | 1,083,992 | 0.5% | | 12 | New Jersey | 5,977,458 | 2.8% |
| 6 | Illinois | 8,373,969 | 4.0% | | 13 | Virginia | 5,467,045 | 2.6% |
| 9 | Indiana | 6,569,665 | 3.1% | | 14 | Washington | 5,178,789 | 2.4% |
| 30 | Iowa | 2,191,715 | 1.0% | | 15 | Massachusetts | 4,683,323 | 2.2% |
| 31 | Kansas | 2,025,581 | 1.0% | | 16 | Arizona | 4,592,398 | 2.2% |
| 27 | Kentucky | 2,959,881 | 1.4% | | 17 | Tennessee | 4,543,759 | 2.1% |
| 25 | Louisiana | 3,186,227 | 1.5% | | 18 | Missouri | 4,277,037 | 2.0% |
| 41 | Maine | 1,014,826 | 0.5% | | 19 | Wisconsin | 4,147,470 | 2.0% |
| 20 | Maryland | 3,856,604 | 1.8% | | 20 | Maryland | 3,856,604 | 1.8% |
| 15 | Massachusetts | 4,683,323 | 2.2% | | 21 | Alabama | 3,798,552 | 1.8% |
| 8 | Michigan | 7,059,509 | 3.3% | | 22 | Colorado | 3,669,816 | 1.7% |
| 24 | Minnesota | 3,306,139 | 1.6% | | 23 | South Carolina | 3,408,318 | 1.6% |
| 33 | Mississippi | 1,926,603 | 0.9% | | 24 | Minnesota | 3,306,139 | 1.6% |
| 18 | Missouri | 4,277,037 | 2.0% | | 25 | Louisiana | 3,186,227 | 1.5% |
| 43 | Montana | 752,483 | 0.4% | | 26 | Connecticut | 2,986,267 | 1.4% |
| 37 | Nebraska | 1,356,377 | 0.6% | | 27 | Kentucky | 2,959,881 | 1.4% |
| 35 | Nevada | 1,700,829 | 0.8% | | 28 | Oregon | 2,773,956 | 1.3% |
| 40 | New Hampshire | 1,056,889 | 0.5% | | 29 | Oklahoma | 2,370,643 | 1.1% |
| 12 | New Jersey | 5,977,458 | 2.8% | | 30 | Iowa | 2,191,715 | 1.0% |
| 36 | New Mexico | 1,418,641 | 0.7% | | 31 | Kansas | 2,025,581 | 1.0% |
| 4 | New York | 11,210,783 | 5.3% | | 32 | Arkansas | 1,956,091 | 0.9% |
| 10 | North Carolina | 6,569,341 | 3.1% | | 33 | Mississippi | 1,926,603 | 0.9% |
| 49 | North Dakota | 490,146 | 0.2% | | 34 | Utah | 1,747,487 | 0.8% |
| 7 | Ohio | 7,982,149 | 3.8% | | 35 | Nevada | 1,700,829 | 0.8% |
| 29 | Oklahoma | 2,370,643 | 1.1% | | 36 | New Mexico | 1,418,641 | 0.7% |
| 28 | Oregon | 2,773,956 | 1.3% | | 37 | Nebraska | 1,356,377 | 0.6% |
| 5 | Pennsylvania | 8,796,774 | 4.2% | | 38 | West Virginia | 1,198,837 | 0.6% |
| 44 | Rhode Island | 749,706 | 0.4% | | 39 | Idaho | 1,083,992 | 0.5% |
| 23 | South Carolina | 3,408,318 | 1.6% | | 40 | New Hampshire | 1,056,889 | 0.5% |
| 46 | South Dakota | 603,258 | 0.3% | | 41 | Maine | 1,014,826 | 0.5% |
| 17 | Tennessee | 4,543,759 | 2.1% | | 42 | Hawaii | 911,660 | 0.4% |
| 2 | Texas | 15,122,518 | 7.1% | | 43 | Montana | 752,483 | 0.4% |
| 34 | Utah | 1,747,487 | 0.8% | | 44 | Rhode Island | 749,706 | 0.4% |
| 47 | Vermont | 521,666 | 0.2% | | 45 | Delaware | 716,109 | 0.3% |
| 13 | Virginia | 5,467,045 | 2.6% | | 46 | South Dakota | 603,258 | 0.3% |
| 14 | Washington | 5,178,789 | 2.4% | | 47 | Vermont | 521,666 | 0.2% |
| 38 | West Virginia | 1,198,837 | 0.6% | | 48 | Alaska | 521,280 | 0.2% |
| 19 | Wisconsin | 4,147,470 | 2.0% | | 49 | North Dakota | 490,146 | 0.2% |
| 50 | Wyoming | 421,928 | 0.2% | | 50 | Wyoming | 421,928 | 0.2% |
| | | | | | | District of Columbia | 395,442 | 0.2% |

Source: U.S. Department of Transportation, Federal Highway Administration
"Highway Statistics 2011" (Table DL-22, http://www.fhwa.dot.gov/policyinformation/statistics/2011/)

# Licensed Drivers per 1,000 Driving Age Population in 2011

## National Ratio = 860 Licensed Drivers

ALPHA ORDER

| RANK | STATE | RATIO |
|---|---|---|
| 4 | Alabama | 997 |
| 10 | Alaska | 939 |
| 17 | Arizona | 911 |
| 38 | Arkansas | 848 |
| 44 | California | 808 |
| 15 | Colorado | 913 |
| 2 | Connecticut | 1,038 |
| 5 | Delaware | 986 |
| 24 | Florida | 893 |
| 34 | Georgia | 856 |
| 42 | Hawaii | 826 |
| 20 | Idaho | 901 |
| 42 | Illinois | 826 |
| 1 | Indiana | 1,287 |
| 19 | Iowa | 906 |
| 18 | Kansas | 910 |
| 35 | Kentucky | 854 |
| 27 | Louisiana | 890 |
| 13 | Maine | 928 |
| 41 | Maryland | 831 |
| 28 | Massachusetts | 875 |
| 21 | Michigan | 898 |
| 48 | Minnesota | 785 |
| 40 | Mississippi | 833 |
| 21 | Missouri | 898 |
| 11 | Montana | 938 |
| 8 | Nebraska | 947 |
| 46 | Nevada | 797 |
| 6 | New Hampshire | 984 |
| 37 | New Jersey | 851 |
| 28 | New Mexico | 875 |
| 50 | New York | 714 |
| 33 | North Carolina | 862 |
| 26 | North Dakota | 892 |
| 31 | Ohio | 870 |
| 45 | Oklahoma | 802 |
| 24 | Oregon | 893 |
| 36 | Pennsylvania | 852 |
| 30 | Rhode Island | 872 |
| 14 | South Carolina | 916 |
| 11 | South Dakota | 938 |
| 23 | Tennessee | 894 |
| 49 | Texas | 777 |
| 32 | Utah | 863 |
| 3 | Vermont | 1,009 |
| 39 | Virginia | 847 |
| 7 | Washington | 954 |
| 47 | West Virginia | 791 |
| 15 | Wisconsin | 913 |
| 9 | Wyoming | 942 |

RANK ORDER

| RANK | STATE | RATIO |
|---|---|---|
| 1 | Indiana | 1,287 |
| 2 | Connecticut | 1,038 |
| 3 | Vermont | 1,009 |
| 4 | Alabama | 997 |
| 5 | Delaware | 986 |
| 6 | New Hampshire | 984 |
| 7 | Washington | 954 |
| 8 | Nebraska | 947 |
| 9 | Wyoming | 942 |
| 10 | Alaska | 939 |
| 11 | Montana | 938 |
| 11 | South Dakota | 938 |
| 13 | Maine | 928 |
| 14 | South Carolina | 916 |
| 15 | Colorado | 913 |
| 15 | Wisconsin | 913 |
| 17 | Arizona | 911 |
| 18 | Kansas | 910 |
| 19 | Iowa | 906 |
| 20 | Idaho | 901 |
| 21 | Michigan | 898 |
| 21 | Missouri | 898 |
| 23 | Tennessee | 894 |
| 24 | Florida | 893 |
| 24 | Oregon | 893 |
| 26 | North Dakota | 892 |
| 27 | Louisiana | 890 |
| 28 | Massachusetts | 875 |
| 28 | New Mexico | 875 |
| 30 | Rhode Island | 872 |
| 31 | Ohio | 870 |
| 32 | Utah | 863 |
| 33 | North Carolina | 862 |
| 34 | Georgia | 856 |
| 35 | Kentucky | 854 |
| 36 | Pennsylvania | 852 |
| 37 | New Jersey | 851 |
| 38 | Arkansas | 848 |
| 39 | Virginia | 847 |
| 40 | Mississippi | 833 |
| 41 | Maryland | 831 |
| 42 | Hawaii | 826 |
| 42 | Illinois | 826 |
| 44 | California | 808 |
| 45 | Oklahoma | 802 |
| 46 | Nevada | 797 |
| 47 | West Virginia | 791 |
| 48 | Minnesota | 785 |
| 49 | Texas | 777 |
| 50 | New York | 714 |
|  | District of Columbia | 755 |

Source: U.S. Department of Transportation, Federal Highway Administration
"Highway Statistics 2011" (Table DL-1C, http://www.fhwa.dot.gov/policyinformation/statistics/2011/)

# Motor Vehicle Registrations in 2011

## National Total = 253,215,681 Motor Vehicles*

ALPHA ORDER

| RANK | STATE | VEHICLES | % of USA |
|---|---|---|---|
| 21 | Alabama | 4,811,943 | 1.9% |
| 49 | Alaska | 757,954 | 0.3% |
| 19 | Arizona | 5,109,254 | 2.0% |
| 31 | Arkansas | 2,448,310 | 1.0% |
| 1 | California | 29,176,697 | 11.5% |
| 22 | Colorado | 4,332,251 | 1.7% |
| 30 | Connecticut | 2,828,794 | 1.1% |
| 45 | Delaware | 929,415 | 0.4% |
| 3 | Florida | 15,469,189 | 6.1% |
| 10 | Georgia | 7,533,735 | 3.0% |
| 43 | Hawaii | 1,148,041 | 0.5% |
| 38 | Idaho | 1,625,204 | 0.6% |
| 4 | Illinois | 10,445,208 | 4.1% |
| 13 | Indiana | 6,132,772 | 2.4% |
| 27 | Iowa | 3,496,576 | 1.4% |
| 32 | Kansas | 2,445,966 | 1.0% |
| 26 | Kentucky | 3,763,027 | 1.5% |
| 23 | Louisiana | 4,052,596 | 1.6% |
| 42 | Maine | 1,171,280 | 0.5% |
| 24 | Maryland | 3,905,629 | 1.5% |
| 15 | Massachusetts | 5,695,327 | 2.2% |
| 8 | Michigan | 9,182,847 | 3.6% |
| 20 | Minnesota | 4,909,634 | 1.9% |
| 34 | Mississippi | 2,036,524 | 0.8% |
| 18 | Missouri | 5,169,994 | 2.0% |
| 41 | Montana | 1,219,158 | 0.5% |
| 35 | Nebraska | 1,886,956 | 0.7% |
| 33 | Nevada | 2,152,407 | 0.9% |
| 40 | New Hampshire | 1,278,484 | 0.5% |
| 9 | New Jersey | 7,939,956 | 3.1% |
| 37 | New Mexico | 1,772,040 | 0.7% |
| 5 | New York | 10,430,559 | 4.1% |
| 12 | North Carolina | 6,249,592 | 2.5% |
| 48 | North Dakota | 785,866 | 0.3% |
| 7 | Ohio | 10,217,277 | 4.0% |
| 28 | Oklahoma | 3,428,689 | 1.4% |
| 29 | Oregon | 3,128,120 | 1.2% |
| 6 | Pennsylvania | 10,302,980 | 4.1% |
| 46 | Rhode Island | 918,823 | 0.4% |
| 25 | South Carolina | 3,827,208 | 1.5% |
| 44 | South Dakota | 995,423 | 0.4% |
| 16 | Tennessee | 5,302,335 | 2.1% |
| 2 | Texas | 19,617,055 | 7.7% |
| 36 | Utah | 1,883,410 | 0.7% |
| 50 | Vermont | 605,054 | 0.2% |
| 11 | Virginia | 6,998,385 | 2.8% |
| 14 | Washington | 5,880,793 | 2.3% |
| 39 | West Virginia | 1,458,222 | 0.6% |
| 17 | Wisconsin | 5,244,195 | 2.1% |
| 47 | Wyoming | 798,296 | 0.3% |

RANK ORDER

| RANK | STATE | VEHICLES | % of USA |
|---|---|---|---|
| 1 | California | 29,176,697 | 11.5% |
| 2 | Texas | 19,617,055 | 7.7% |
| 3 | Florida | 15,469,189 | 6.1% |
| 4 | Illinois | 10,445,208 | 4.1% |
| 5 | New York | 10,430,559 | 4.1% |
| 6 | Pennsylvania | 10,302,980 | 4.1% |
| 7 | Ohio | 10,217,277 | 4.0% |
| 8 | Michigan | 9,182,847 | 3.6% |
| 9 | New Jersey | 7,939,956 | 3.1% |
| 10 | Georgia | 7,533,735 | 3.0% |
| 11 | Virginia | 6,998,385 | 2.8% |
| 12 | North Carolina | 6,249,592 | 2.5% |
| 13 | Indiana | 6,132,772 | 2.4% |
| 14 | Washington | 5,880,793 | 2.3% |
| 15 | Massachusetts | 5,695,327 | 2.2% |
| 16 | Tennessee | 5,302,335 | 2.1% |
| 17 | Wisconsin | 5,244,195 | 2.1% |
| 18 | Missouri | 5,169,994 | 2.0% |
| 19 | Arizona | 5,109,254 | 2.0% |
| 20 | Minnesota | 4,909,634 | 1.9% |
| 21 | Alabama | 4,811,943 | 1.9% |
| 22 | Colorado | 4,332,251 | 1.7% |
| 23 | Louisiana | 4,052,596 | 1.6% |
| 24 | Maryland | 3,905,629 | 1.5% |
| 25 | South Carolina | 3,827,208 | 1.5% |
| 26 | Kentucky | 3,763,027 | 1.5% |
| 27 | Iowa | 3,496,576 | 1.4% |
| 28 | Oklahoma | 3,428,689 | 1.4% |
| 29 | Oregon | 3,128,120 | 1.2% |
| 30 | Connecticut | 2,828,794 | 1.1% |
| 31 | Arkansas | 2,448,310 | 1.0% |
| 32 | Kansas | 2,445,966 | 1.0% |
| 33 | Nevada | 2,152,407 | 0.9% |
| 34 | Mississippi | 2,036,524 | 0.8% |
| 35 | Nebraska | 1,886,956 | 0.7% |
| 36 | Utah | 1,883,410 | 0.7% |
| 37 | New Mexico | 1,772,040 | 0.7% |
| 38 | Idaho | 1,625,204 | 0.6% |
| 39 | West Virginia | 1,458,222 | 0.6% |
| 40 | New Hampshire | 1,278,484 | 0.5% |
| 41 | Montana | 1,219,158 | 0.5% |
| 42 | Maine | 1,171,280 | 0.5% |
| 43 | Hawaii | 1,148,041 | 0.5% |
| 44 | South Dakota | 995,423 | 0.4% |
| 45 | Delaware | 929,415 | 0.4% |
| 46 | Rhode Island | 918,823 | 0.4% |
| 47 | Wyoming | 798,296 | 0.3% |
| 48 | North Dakota | 785,866 | 0.3% |
| 49 | Alaska | 757,954 | 0.3% |
| 50 | Vermont | 605,054 | 0.2% |
|  | District of Columbia | 316,231 | 0.1% |

Source: U.S. Department of Transportation, Federal Highway Administration
   "Highway Statistics 2011" (Table MV-1, http://www.fhwa.dot.gov/policyinformation/statistics/2011/)
*Includes automobiles, trucks and buses.  Does not include motorcycles.

# Motor Vehicles per Driving Age Population in 2011

## National Rate = 1.03 Motor Vehicles*

ALPHA ORDER

ALPHA ORDER

RANK ORDER

| RANK | STATE | RATE | RANK | STATE | RATE |
|------|-------|------|------|-------|------|
| 10 | Alabama | 1.26 | 1 | Wyoming | 1.78 |
| 6 | Alaska | 1.36 | 2 | South Dakota | 1.55 |
| 36 | Arizona | 1.01 | 3 | Montana | 1.52 |
| 30 | Arkansas | 1.06 | 4 | Iowa | 1.44 |
| 42 | California | 0.99 | 5 | North Dakota | 1.43 |
| 25 | Colorado | 1.08 | 6 | Alaska | 1.36 |
| 44 | Connecticut | 0.98 | 7 | Idaho | 1.35 |
| 9 | Delaware | 1.28 | 8 | Nebraska | 1.32 |
| 40 | Florida | 1.00 | 9 | Delaware | 1.28 |
| 42 | Georgia | 0.99 | 10 | Alabama | 1.26 |
| 32 | Hawaii | 1.04 | 11 | Indiana | 1.20 |
| 7 | Idaho | 1.35 | 12 | New Hampshire | 1.19 |
| 34 | Illinois | 1.03 | 13 | Michigan | 1.17 |
| 11 | Indiana | 1.20 | 13 | Minnesota | 1.17 |
| 4 | Iowa | 1.44 | 13 | Vermont | 1.17 |
| 21 | Kansas | 1.10 | 16 | Oklahoma | 1.16 |
| 22 | Kentucky | 1.09 | 17 | Wisconsin | 1.15 |
| 18 | Louisiana | 1.13 | 18 | Louisiana | 1.13 |
| 28 | Maine | 1.07 | 18 | New Jersey | 1.13 |
| 48 | Maryland | 0.84 | 20 | Ohio | 1.11 |
| 30 | Massachusetts | 1.06 | 21 | Kansas | 1.10 |
| 13 | Michigan | 1.17 | 22 | Kentucky | 1.09 |
| 13 | Minnesota | 1.17 | 22 | Missouri | 1.09 |
| 47 | Mississippi | 0.88 | 22 | New Mexico | 1.09 |
| 22 | Missouri | 1.09 | 25 | Colorado | 1.08 |
| 3 | Montana | 1.52 | 25 | Virginia | 1.08 |
| 8 | Nebraska | 1.32 | 25 | Washington | 1.08 |
| 36 | Nevada | 1.01 | 28 | Maine | 1.07 |
| 12 | New Hampshire | 1.19 | 28 | Rhode Island | 1.07 |
| 18 | New Jersey | 1.13 | 30 | Arkansas | 1.06 |
| 22 | New Mexico | 1.09 | 30 | Massachusetts | 1.06 |
| 50 | New York | 0.66 | 32 | Hawaii | 1.04 |
| 49 | North Carolina | 0.82 | 32 | Tennessee | 1.04 |
| 5 | North Dakota | 1.43 | 34 | Illinois | 1.03 |
| 20 | Ohio | 1.11 | 34 | South Carolina | 1.03 |
| 16 | Oklahoma | 1.16 | 36 | Arizona | 1.01 |
| 36 | Oregon | 1.01 | 36 | Nevada | 1.01 |
| 40 | Pennsylvania | 1.00 | 36 | Oregon | 1.01 |
| 28 | Rhode Island | 1.07 | 36 | Texas | 1.01 |
| 34 | South Carolina | 1.03 | 40 | Florida | 1.00 |
| 2 | South Dakota | 1.55 | 40 | Pennsylvania | 1.00 |
| 32 | Tennessee | 1.04 | 42 | California | 0.99 |
| 36 | Texas | 1.01 | 42 | Georgia | 0.99 |
| 46 | Utah | 0.93 | 44 | Connecticut | 0.98 |
| 13 | Vermont | 1.17 | 45 | West Virginia | 0.96 |
| 25 | Virginia | 1.08 | 46 | Utah | 0.93 |
| 25 | Washington | 1.08 | 47 | Mississippi | 0.88 |
| 45 | West Virginia | 0.96 | 48 | Maryland | 0.84 |
| 17 | Wisconsin | 1.15 | 49 | North Carolina | 0.82 |
| 1 | Wyoming | 1.78 | 50 | New York | 0.66 |
| | | | | District of Columbia | 0.60 |

Source: CQ Press using data from U.S. Department of Transportation, Federal Highway Administration
"Highway Statistics 2011" (Table MV-1, http://www.fhwa.dot.gov/policyinformation/statistics/2011/)
*Persons age 16 and older.  Motor Vehicles include automobiles, trucks and buses.  Motorcycles are not included.

# Average Travel Time to Work in 2012

## National Average = 25.7 Minutes*

| ALPHA ORDER | | | | RANK ORDER | | |
|---|---|---|---|---|---|---|
| RANK | STATE | MINUTES | | RANK | STATE | MINUTES |
| 20 | Alabama | 24.5 | | 1 | Maryland | 31.9 |
| 43 | Alaska | 19.6 | | 2 | New York | 31.8 |
| 19 | Arizona | 24.6 | | 3 | New Jersey | 30.7 |
| 39 | Arkansas | 21.4 | | 4 | Massachusetts | 28.3 |
| 7 | California | 27.5 | | 5 | Illinois | 28.0 |
| 20 | Colorado | 24.5 | | 6 | Virginia | 27.9 |
| 18 | Connecticut | 24.8 | | 7 | California | 27.5 |
| 14 | Delaware | 25.8 | | 8 | Georgia | 26.9 |
| 10 | Florida | 26.2 | | 9 | New Hampshire | 26.3 |
| 8 | Georgia | 26.9 | | 10 | Florida | 26.2 |
| 12 | Hawaii | 26.0 | | 11 | Pennsylvania | 26.1 |
| 42 | Idaho | 20.2 | | 12 | Hawaii | 26.0 |
| 5 | Illinois | 28.0 | | 12 | Washington | 26.0 |
| 28 | Indiana | 23.5 | | 14 | Delaware | 25.8 |
| 45 | Iowa | 18.8 | | 15 | Texas | 25.3 |
| 44 | Kansas | 19.0 | | 16 | Louisiana | 25.2 |
| 34 | Kentucky | 22.9 | | 16 | West Virginia | 25.2 |
| 16 | Louisiana | 25.2 | | 18 | Connecticut | 24.8 |
| 28 | Maine | 23.5 | | 19 | Arizona | 24.6 |
| 1 | Maryland | 31.9 | | 20 | Alabama | 24.5 |
| 4 | Massachusetts | 28.3 | | 20 | Colorado | 24.5 |
| 24 | Michigan | 24.0 | | 22 | Rhode Island | 24.4 |
| 34 | Minnesota | 22.9 | | 22 | Tennessee | 24.4 |
| 24 | Mississippi | 24.0 | | 24 | Michigan | 24.0 |
| 32 | Missouri | 23.1 | | 24 | Mississippi | 24.0 |
| 46 | Montana | 18.4 | | 24 | Nevada | 24.0 |
| 47 | Nebraska | 18.2 | | 27 | North Carolina | 23.7 |
| 24 | Nevada | 24.0 | | 28 | Indiana | 23.5 |
| 9 | New Hampshire | 26.3 | | 28 | Maine | 23.5 |
| 3 | New Jersey | 30.7 | | 28 | South Carolina | 23.5 |
| 39 | New Mexico | 21.4 | | 31 | Ohio | 23.2 |
| 2 | New York | 31.8 | | 32 | Missouri | 23.1 |
| 27 | North Carolina | 23.7 | | 32 | Vermont | 23.1 |
| 49 | North Dakota | 17.4 | | 34 | Kentucky | 22.9 |
| 31 | Ohio | 23.2 | | 34 | Minnesota | 22.9 |
| 41 | Oklahoma | 21.1 | | 36 | Oregon | 22.7 |
| 36 | Oregon | 22.7 | | 37 | Utah | 22.0 |
| 11 | Pennsylvania | 26.1 | | 38 | Wisconsin | 21.8 |
| 22 | Rhode Island | 24.4 | | 39 | Arkansas | 21.4 |
| 28 | South Carolina | 23.5 | | 39 | New Mexico | 21.4 |
| 50 | South Dakota | 16.7 | | 41 | Oklahoma | 21.1 |
| 22 | Tennessee | 24.4 | | 42 | Idaho | 20.2 |
| 15 | Texas | 25.3 | | 43 | Alaska | 19.6 |
| 37 | Utah | 22.0 | | 44 | Kansas | 19.0 |
| 32 | Vermont | 23.1 | | 45 | Iowa | 18.8 |
| 6 | Virginia | 27.9 | | 46 | Montana | 18.4 |
| 12 | Washington | 26.0 | | 47 | Nebraska | 18.2 |
| 16 | West Virginia | 25.2 | | 48 | Wyoming | 18.1 |
| 38 | Wisconsin | 21.8 | | 49 | North Dakota | 17.4 |
| 48 | Wyoming | 18.1 | | 50 | South Dakota | 16.7 |
| | | | | | District of Columbia | 29.9 |

Source: U.S. Bureau of the Census
   "2012 American Community Survey-Table R0801" (http://www.census.gov/acs/www/index.html)
*Workers 16 and older not working at home.

# Percent of Commuters Who Drive to Work Alone in 2012

## National Percent = 76.3%*

| ALPHA ORDER | | | | RANK ORDER | | |
|---|---|---|---|---|---|---|
| RANK | STATE | PERCENT | | RANK | STATE | PERCENT |
| 1 | Alabama | 85.3 | | 1 | Alabama | 85.3 |
| 48 | Alaska | 66.2 | | 2 | Tennessee | 83.6 |
| 34 | Arizona | 76.7 | | 3 | Mississippi | 83.5 |
| 11 | Arkansas | 82.2 | | 4 | Ohio | 83.3 |
| 42 | California | 73.4 | | 5 | South Carolina | 82.9 |
| 38 | Colorado | 74.4 | | 6 | Kentucky | 82.7 |
| 28 | Connecticut | 78.6 | | 7 | Louisiana | 82.5 |
| 15 | Delaware | 81.5 | | 7 | Michigan | 82.5 |
| 24 | Florida | 79.3 | | 9 | Indiana | 82.4 |
| 22 | Georgia | 79.6 | | 10 | Oklahoma | 82.3 |
| 49 | Hawaii | 65.2 | | 11 | Arkansas | 82.2 |
| 31 | Idaho | 77.8 | | 11 | Kansas | 82.2 |
| 40 | Illinois | 73.6 | | 13 | New Hampshire | 81.9 |
| 9 | Indiana | 82.4 | | 14 | West Virginia | 81.7 |
| 21 | Iowa | 79.9 | | 15 | Delaware | 81.5 |
| 11 | Kansas | 82.2 | | 16 | Missouri | 81.3 |
| 6 | Kentucky | 82.7 | | 17 | North Carolina | 80.6 |
| 7 | Louisiana | 82.5 | | 18 | Nebraska | 80.2 |
| 33 | Maine | 76.9 | | 18 | Wisconsin | 80.2 |
| 42 | Maryland | 73.4 | | 20 | Texas | 80.1 |
| 46 | Massachusetts | 71.9 | | 21 | Iowa | 79.9 |
| 7 | Michigan | 82.5 | | 22 | Georgia | 79.6 |
| 29 | Minnesota | 78.0 | | 23 | North Dakota | 79.5 |
| 3 | Mississippi | 83.5 | | 24 | Florida | 79.3 |
| 16 | Missouri | 81.3 | | 25 | New Mexico | 78.9 |
| 38 | Montana | 74.4 | | 26 | Rhode Island | 78.8 |
| 18 | Nebraska | 80.2 | | 27 | South Dakota | 78.7 |
| 29 | Nevada | 78.0 | | 28 | Connecticut | 78.6 |
| 13 | New Hampshire | 81.9 | | 29 | Minnesota | 78.0 |
| 45 | New Jersey | 72.0 | | 29 | Nevada | 78.0 |
| 25 | New Mexico | 78.9 | | 31 | Idaho | 77.8 |
| 50 | New York | 53.7 | | 32 | Virginia | 77.3 |
| 17 | North Carolina | 80.6 | | 33 | Maine | 76.9 |
| 23 | North Dakota | 79.5 | | 34 | Arizona | 76.7 |
| 4 | Ohio | 83.3 | | 35 | Pennsylvania | 76.5 |
| 10 | Oklahoma | 82.3 | | 36 | Utah | 75.7 |
| 47 | Oregon | 71.2 | | 36 | Wyoming | 75.7 |
| 35 | Pennsylvania | 76.5 | | 38 | Colorado | 74.4 |
| 26 | Rhode Island | 78.8 | | 38 | Montana | 74.4 |
| 5 | South Carolina | 82.9 | | 40 | Illinois | 73.6 |
| 27 | South Dakota | 78.7 | | 41 | Vermont | 73.5 |
| 2 | Tennessee | 83.6 | | 42 | California | 73.4 |
| 20 | Texas | 80.1 | | 42 | Maryland | 73.4 |
| 36 | Utah | 75.7 | | 44 | Washington | 72.2 |
| 41 | Vermont | 73.5 | | 45 | New Jersey | 72.0 |
| 32 | Virginia | 77.3 | | 46 | Massachusetts | 71.9 |
| 44 | Washington | 72.2 | | 47 | Oregon | 71.2 |
| 14 | West Virginia | 81.7 | | 48 | Alaska | 66.2 |
| 18 | Wisconsin | 80.2 | | 49 | Hawaii | 65.2 |
| 36 | Wyoming | 75.7 | | 50 | New York | 53.7 |
| | | | | | District of Columbia | 34.1 |

Source: U.S. Bureau of the Census
"2012 American Community Survey-Table R0802" (http://www.census.gov/acs/www/index.html)
*Workers 16 and older who traveled to work by car, truck or van.

# Percent of Commuters Who Drive to Work in Carpools in 2012

## National Percent = 9.7%*

ALPHA ORDER

| RANK | STATE | PERCENT |
|---|---|---|
| 32 | Alabama | 9.5 |
| 2 | Alaska | 13.3 |
| 8 | Arizona | 11.0 |
| 6 | Arkansas | 11.2 |
| 7 | California | 11.1 |
| 27 | Colorado | 9.7 |
| 45 | Connecticut | 8.2 |
| 46 | Delaware | 8.1 |
| 27 | Florida | 9.7 |
| 17 | Georgia | 10.4 |
| 1 | Hawaii | 15.3 |
| 21 | Idaho | 10.1 |
| 39 | Illinois | 8.9 |
| 33 | Indiana | 9.4 |
| 37 | Iowa | 9.0 |
| 27 | Kansas | 9.7 |
| 25 | Kentucky | 9.8 |
| 23 | Louisiana | 9.9 |
| 8 | Maine | 11.0 |
| 25 | Maryland | 9.8 |
| 48 | Massachusetts | 7.8 |
| 37 | Michigan | 9.0 |
| 39 | Minnesota | 8.9 |
| 12 | Mississippi | 10.7 |
| 27 | Missouri | 9.7 |
| 12 | Montana | 10.7 |
| 22 | Nebraska | 10.0 |
| 11 | Nevada | 10.9 |
| 49 | New Hampshire | 7.2 |
| 44 | New Jersey | 8.3 |
| 5 | New Mexico | 11.3 |
| 50 | New York | 6.9 |
| 16 | North Carolina | 10.5 |
| 27 | North Dakota | 9.7 |
| 46 | Ohio | 8.1 |
| 17 | Oklahoma | 10.4 |
| 17 | Oregon | 10.4 |
| 39 | Pennsylvania | 8.9 |
| 39 | Rhode Island | 8.9 |
| 35 | South Carolina | 9.3 |
| 36 | South Dakota | 9.1 |
| 33 | Tennessee | 9.4 |
| 8 | Texas | 11.0 |
| 3 | Utah | 12.2 |
| 20 | Vermont | 10.2 |
| 23 | Virginia | 9.9 |
| 12 | Washington | 10.7 |
| 15 | West Virginia | 10.6 |
| 39 | Wisconsin | 8.9 |
| 4 | Wyoming | 11.6 |

RANK ORDER

| RANK | STATE | PERCENT |
|---|---|---|
| 1 | Hawaii | 15.3 |
| 2 | Alaska | 13.3 |
| 3 | Utah | 12.2 |
| 4 | Wyoming | 11.6 |
| 5 | New Mexico | 11.3 |
| 6 | Arkansas | 11.2 |
| 7 | California | 11.1 |
| 8 | Arizona | 11.0 |
| 8 | Maine | 11.0 |
| 8 | Texas | 11.0 |
| 11 | Nevada | 10.9 |
| 12 | Mississippi | 10.7 |
| 12 | Montana | 10.7 |
| 12 | Washington | 10.7 |
| 15 | West Virginia | 10.6 |
| 16 | North Carolina | 10.5 |
| 17 | Georgia | 10.4 |
| 17 | Oklahoma | 10.4 |
| 17 | Oregon | 10.4 |
| 20 | Vermont | 10.2 |
| 21 | Idaho | 10.1 |
| 22 | Nebraska | 10.0 |
| 23 | Louisiana | 9.9 |
| 23 | Virginia | 9.9 |
| 25 | Kentucky | 9.8 |
| 25 | Maryland | 9.8 |
| 27 | Colorado | 9.7 |
| 27 | Florida | 9.7 |
| 27 | Kansas | 9.7 |
| 27 | Missouri | 9.7 |
| 27 | North Dakota | 9.7 |
| 32 | Alabama | 9.5 |
| 33 | Indiana | 9.4 |
| 33 | Tennessee | 9.4 |
| 35 | South Carolina | 9.3 |
| 36 | South Dakota | 9.1 |
| 37 | Iowa | 9.0 |
| 37 | Michigan | 9.0 |
| 39 | Illinois | 8.9 |
| 39 | Minnesota | 8.9 |
| 39 | Pennsylvania | 8.9 |
| 39 | Rhode Island | 8.9 |
| 39 | Wisconsin | 8.9 |
| 44 | New Jersey | 8.3 |
| 45 | Connecticut | 8.2 |
| 46 | Delaware | 8.1 |
| 46 | Ohio | 8.1 |
| 48 | Massachusetts | 7.8 |
| 49 | New Hampshire | 7.2 |
| 50 | New York | 6.9 |
| | District of Columbia | 5.6 |

Source: U.S. Bureau of the Census
  "2012 American Community Survey-Table R0803" (http://www.census.gov/acs/www/index.html)
*Workers 16 and older who traveled to work by car, truck or van.

# Percent of Commuters Who Travel to Work by Public Transportation in 2012

## National Percent = 5.0%*

ALPHA ORDER

| RANK | STATE | PERCENT |
|------|-------|---------|
| 47 | Alabama | 0.4 |
| 23 | Alaska | 1.6 |
| 20 | Arizona | 2.0 |
| 44 | Arkansas | 0.5 |
| 9 | California | 5.2 |
| 15 | Colorado | 3.2 |
| 10 | Connecticut | 4.8 |
| 17 | Delaware | 2.5 |
| 19 | Florida | 2.2 |
| 20 | Georgia | 2.0 |
| 6 | Hawaii | 6.7 |
| 37 | Idaho | 0.8 |
| 5 | Illinois | 8.5 |
| 31 | Indiana | 1.1 |
| 31 | Iowa | 1.1 |
| 41 | Kansas | 0.6 |
| 35 | Kentucky | 1.0 |
| 29 | Louisiana | 1.2 |
| 41 | Maine | 0.6 |
| 4 | Maryland | 8.9 |
| 3 | Massachusetts | 9.4 |
| 27 | Michigan | 1.3 |
| 14 | Minnesota | 3.3 |
| 47 | Mississippi | 0.4 |
| 27 | Missouri | 1.3 |
| 35 | Montana | 1.0 |
| 41 | Nebraska | 0.6 |
| 13 | Nevada | 3.6 |
| 39 | New Hampshire | 0.7 |
| 2 | New Jersey | 10.6 |
| 31 | New Mexico | 1.1 |
| 1 | New York | 27.3 |
| 31 | North Carolina | 1.1 |
| 47 | North Dakota | 0.4 |
| 23 | Ohio | 1.6 |
| 47 | Oklahoma | 0.4 |
| 12 | Oregon | 4.1 |
| 8 | Pennsylvania | 5.4 |
| 16 | Rhode Island | 3.1 |
| 44 | South Carolina | 0.5 |
| 44 | South Dakota | 0.5 |
| 37 | Tennessee | 0.8 |
| 23 | Texas | 1.6 |
| 17 | Utah | 2.5 |
| 29 | Vermont | 1.2 |
| 11 | Virginia | 4.4 |
| 7 | Washington | 5.8 |
| 39 | West Virginia | 0.7 |
| 22 | Wisconsin | 1.8 |
| 26 | Wyoming | 1.5 |

RANK ORDER

| RANK | STATE | PERCENT |
|------|-------|---------|
| 1 | New York | 27.3 |
| 2 | New Jersey | 10.6 |
| 3 | Massachusetts | 9.4 |
| 4 | Maryland | 8.9 |
| 5 | Illinois | 8.5 |
| 6 | Hawaii | 6.7 |
| 7 | Washington | 5.8 |
| 8 | Pennsylvania | 5.4 |
| 9 | California | 5.2 |
| 10 | Connecticut | 4.8 |
| 11 | Virginia | 4.4 |
| 12 | Oregon | 4.1 |
| 13 | Nevada | 3.6 |
| 14 | Minnesota | 3.3 |
| 15 | Colorado | 3.2 |
| 16 | Rhode Island | 3.1 |
| 17 | Delaware | 2.5 |
| 17 | Utah | 2.5 |
| 19 | Florida | 2.2 |
| 20 | Arizona | 2.0 |
| 20 | Georgia | 2.0 |
| 22 | Wisconsin | 1.8 |
| 23 | Alaska | 1.6 |
| 23 | Ohio | 1.6 |
| 23 | Texas | 1.6 |
| 26 | Wyoming | 1.5 |
| 27 | Michigan | 1.3 |
| 27 | Missouri | 1.3 |
| 29 | Louisiana | 1.2 |
| 29 | Vermont | 1.2 |
| 31 | Indiana | 1.1 |
| 31 | Iowa | 1.1 |
| 31 | New Mexico | 1.1 |
| 31 | North Carolina | 1.1 |
| 35 | Kentucky | 1.0 |
| 35 | Montana | 1.0 |
| 37 | Idaho | 0.8 |
| 37 | Tennessee | 0.8 |
| 39 | New Hampshire | 0.7 |
| 39 | West Virginia | 0.7 |
| 41 | Kansas | 0.6 |
| 41 | Maine | 0.6 |
| 41 | Nebraska | 0.6 |
| 44 | Arkansas | 0.5 |
| 44 | South Carolina | 0.5 |
| 44 | South Dakota | 0.5 |
| 47 | Alabama | 0.4 |
| 47 | Mississippi | 0.4 |
| 47 | North Dakota | 0.4 |
| 47 | Oklahoma | 0.4 |

District of Columbia    38.6

Source: U.S. Bureau of the Census
   "2012 American Community Survey-Table R0804" (http://www.census.gov/acs/www/index.html)
*Workers 16 and older.

# Annual Miles per Vehicle in 2011

## National Annual Average = 11,635 Miles*

ALPHA ORDER

| RANK | STATE | MILES |
|------|-------|-------|
| 8 | Alabama | 13,490 |
| 50 | Alaska | 6,060 |
| 22 | Arizona | 11,660 |
| 9 | Arkansas | 13,459 |
| 30 | California | 10,995 |
| 32 | Colorado | 10,758 |
| 29 | Connecticut | 11,028 |
| 40 | Delaware | 9,714 |
| 16 | Florida | 12,402 |
| 4 | Georgia | 14,396 |
| 48 | Hawaii | 8,768 |
| 39 | Idaho | 9,806 |
| 38 | Illinois | 9,883 |
| 15 | Indiana | 12,472 |
| 47 | Iowa | 8,944 |
| 17 | Kansas | 12,274 |
| 13 | Kentucky | 12,772 |
| 27 | Louisiana | 11,477 |
| 19 | Maine | 12,164 |
| 5 | Maryland | 14,395 |
| 43 | Massachusetts | 9,621 |
| 35 | Michigan | 10,319 |
| 26 | Minnesota | 11,546 |
| 1 | Mississippi | 19,077 |
| 11 | Missouri | 13,305 |
| 44 | Montana | 9,564 |
| 36 | Nebraska | 10,118 |
| 28 | Nevada | 11,238 |
| 37 | New Hampshire | 9,949 |
| 45 | New Jersey | 9,206 |
| 3 | New Mexico | 14,409 |
| 18 | New York | 12,245 |
| 2 | North Carolina | 16,605 |
| 23 | North Dakota | 11,619 |
| 31 | Ohio | 10,961 |
| 7 | Oklahoma | 13,843 |
| 33 | Oregon | 10,669 |
| 42 | Pennsylvania | 9,629 |
| 49 | Rhode Island | 8,599 |
| 14 | South Carolina | 12,733 |
| 46 | South Dakota | 9,043 |
| 10 | Tennessee | 13,343 |
| 20 | Texas | 12,104 |
| 6 | Utah | 13,923 |
| 21 | Vermont | 11,802 |
| 25 | Virginia | 11,570 |
| 41 | Washington | 9,685 |
| 12 | West Virginia | 13,004 |
| 34 | Wisconsin | 10,374 |
| 24 | Wyoming | 11,581 |

RANK ORDER

| RANK | STATE | MILES |
|------|-------|-------|
| 1 | Mississippi | 19,077 |
| 2 | North Carolina | 16,605 |
| 3 | New Mexico | 14,409 |
| 4 | Georgia | 14,396 |
| 5 | Maryland | 14,395 |
| 6 | Utah | 13,923 |
| 7 | Oklahoma | 13,843 |
| 8 | Alabama | 13,490 |
| 9 | Arkansas | 13,459 |
| 10 | Tennessee | 13,343 |
| 11 | Missouri | 13,305 |
| 12 | West Virginia | 13,004 |
| 13 | Kentucky | 12,772 |
| 14 | South Carolina | 12,733 |
| 15 | Indiana | 12,472 |
| 16 | Florida | 12,402 |
| 17 | Kansas | 12,274 |
| 18 | New York | 12,245 |
| 19 | Maine | 12,164 |
| 20 | Texas | 12,104 |
| 21 | Vermont | 11,802 |
| 22 | Arizona | 11,660 |
| 23 | North Dakota | 11,619 |
| 24 | Wyoming | 11,581 |
| 25 | Virginia | 11,570 |
| 26 | Minnesota | 11,546 |
| 27 | Louisiana | 11,477 |
| 28 | Nevada | 11,238 |
| 29 | Connecticut | 11,028 |
| 30 | California | 10,995 |
| 31 | Ohio | 10,961 |
| 32 | Colorado | 10,758 |
| 33 | Oregon | 10,669 |
| 34 | Wisconsin | 10,374 |
| 35 | Michigan | 10,319 |
| 36 | Nebraska | 10,118 |
| 37 | New Hampshire | 9,949 |
| 38 | Illinois | 9,883 |
| 39 | Idaho | 9,806 |
| 40 | Delaware | 9,714 |
| 41 | Washington | 9,685 |
| 42 | Pennsylvania | 9,629 |
| 43 | Massachusetts | 9,621 |
| 44 | Montana | 9,564 |
| 45 | New Jersey | 9,206 |
| 46 | South Dakota | 9,043 |
| 47 | Iowa | 8,944 |
| 48 | Hawaii | 8,768 |
| 49 | Rhode Island | 8,599 |
| 50 | Alaska | 6,060 |

District of Columbia      11,283

Source: CQ Press using data from U.S. Department of Transportation, Federal Highway Administration
"Highway Statistics 2011" (Tables MV-1 and VM-2, http://www.fhwa.dot.gov/policyinformation/statistics/2011/)
*Includes automobiles, trucks, buses and motorcycles.

# Average Miles per Gallon in 2011

## National Average = 17.5 Miles per Gallon*

| RANK | STATE | MILES PER GALLON |
|---|---|---|
| 3 | Alabama | 19.7 |
| 50 | Alaska | 11.4 |
| 18 | Arizona | 17.8 |
| 36 | Arkansas | 16.7 |
| 8 | California | 18.8 |
| 18 | Colorado | 17.8 |
| 14 | Connecticut | 18.3 |
| 5 | Delaware | 19.2 |
| 1 | Florida | 20.9 |
| 10 | Georgia | 18.6 |
| 3 | Hawaii | 19.7 |
| 21 | Idaho | 17.7 |
| 33 | Illinois | 17.0 |
| 14 | Indiana | 18.3 |
| 47 | Iowa | 14.1 |
| 29 | Kansas | 17.3 |
| 37 | Kentucky | 16.6 |
| 40 | Louisiana | 15.6 |
| 35 | Maine | 16.9 |
| 17 | Maryland | 18.1 |
| 26 | Massachusetts | 17.5 |
| 14 | Michigan | 18.3 |
| 8 | Minnesota | 18.8 |
| 13 | Mississippi | 18.4 |
| 31 | Missouri | 17.1 |
| 39 | Montana | 15.9 |
| 40 | Nebraska | 15.6 |
| 18 | Nevada | 17.8 |
| 38 | New Hampshire | 16.3 |
| 43 | New Jersey | 15.0 |
| 21 | New Mexico | 17.7 |
| 7 | New York | 19.0 |
| 2 | North Carolina | 19.8 |
| 49 | North Dakota | 12.8 |
| 21 | Ohio | 17.7 |
| 10 | Oklahoma | 18.6 |
| 31 | Oregon | 17.1 |
| 42 | Pennsylvania | 15.2 |
| 12 | Rhode Island | 18.5 |
| 43 | South Carolina | 15.0 |
| 47 | South Dakota | 14.1 |
| 25 | Tennessee | 17.6 |
| 45 | Texas | 14.7 |
| 33 | Utah | 17.0 |
| 5 | Vermont | 19.2 |
| 29 | Virginia | 17.3 |
| 21 | Washington | 17.7 |
| 27 | West Virginia | 17.4 |
| 27 | Wisconsin | 17.4 |
| 46 | Wyoming | 14.5 |

| RANK | STATE | MILES PER GALLON |
|---|---|---|
| 1 | Florida | 20.9 |
| 2 | North Carolina | 19.8 |
| 3 | Alabama | 19.7 |
| 3 | Hawaii | 19.7 |
| 5 | Delaware | 19.2 |
| 5 | Vermont | 19.2 |
| 7 | New York | 19.0 |
| 8 | California | 18.8 |
| 8 | Minnesota | 18.8 |
| 10 | Georgia | 18.6 |
| 10 | Oklahoma | 18.6 |
| 12 | Rhode Island | 18.5 |
| 13 | Mississippi | 18.4 |
| 14 | Connecticut | 18.3 |
| 14 | Indiana | 18.3 |
| 14 | Michigan | 18.3 |
| 17 | Maryland | 18.1 |
| 18 | Arizona | 17.8 |
| 18 | Colorado | 17.8 |
| 18 | Nevada | 17.8 |
| 21 | Idaho | 17.7 |
| 21 | New Mexico | 17.7 |
| 21 | Ohio | 17.7 |
| 21 | Washington | 17.7 |
| 25 | Tennessee | 17.6 |
| 26 | Massachusetts | 17.5 |
| 27 | West Virginia | 17.4 |
| 27 | Wisconsin | 17.4 |
| 29 | Kansas | 17.3 |
| 29 | Virginia | 17.3 |
| 31 | Missouri | 17.1 |
| 31 | Oregon | 17.1 |
| 33 | Illinois | 17.0 |
| 33 | Utah | 17.0 |
| 35 | Maine | 16.9 |
| 36 | Arkansas | 16.7 |
| 37 | Kentucky | 16.6 |
| 38 | New Hampshire | 16.3 |
| 39 | Montana | 15.9 |
| 40 | Louisiana | 15.6 |
| 40 | Nebraska | 15.6 |
| 42 | Pennsylvania | 15.2 |
| 43 | New Jersey | 15.0 |
| 43 | South Carolina | 15.0 |
| 45 | Texas | 14.7 |
| 46 | Wyoming | 14.5 |
| 47 | Iowa | 14.1 |
| 47 | South Dakota | 14.1 |
| 49 | North Dakota | 12.8 |
| 50 | Alaska | 11.4 |

| | District of Columbia | 29.0 |

Source: CQ Press using data from U.S. Department of Transportation, Federal Highway Administration
"Highway Statistics 2011" (Table VM-2, http://www.fhwa.dot.gov/policyinformation/statistics/2011/)
*Total vehicle-miles for 2011 divided by total highway motor-fuel use.  Includes gasoline, gasohol, diesel, and other "special fuels."

# Airports in 2011

## National Total = 13,205 Airports*

| RANK | STATE | AIRPORTS | % of USA |
|------|-------|----------|----------|
| 32 | Alabama | 182 | 1.4% |
| 2 | Alaska | 549 | 4.2% |
| 30 | Arizona | 188 | 1.4% |
| 26 | Arkansas | 213 | 1.6% |
| 3 | California | 522 | 4.0% |
| 22 | Colorado | 259 | 2.0% |
| 47 | Connecticut | 51 | 0.4% |
| 49 | Delaware | 30 | 0.2% |
| 4 | Florida | 497 | 3.8% |
| 14 | Georgia | 335 | 2.5% |
| 48 | Hawaii | 32 | 0.2% |
| 24 | Idaho | 224 | 1.7% |
| 6 | Illinois | 479 | 3.6% |
| 9 | Indiana | 404 | 3.1% |
| 29 | Iowa | 196 | 1.5% |
| 16 | Kansas | 329 | 2.5% |
| 34 | Kentucky | 153 | 1.2% |
| 25 | Louisiana | 223 | 1.7% |
| 38 | Maine | 114 | 0.9% |
| 35 | Maryland | 148 | 1.1% |
| 43 | Massachusetts | 77 | 0.6% |
| 12 | Michigan | 362 | 2.7% |
| 16 | Minnesota | 329 | 2.5% |
| 31 | Mississippi | 186 | 1.4% |
| 13 | Missouri | 359 | 2.7% |
| 23 | Montana | 232 | 1.8% |
| 28 | Nebraska | 207 | 1.6% |
| 40 | Nevada | 98 | 0.7% |
| 46 | New Hampshire | 52 | 0.4% |
| 39 | New Jersey | 101 | 0.8% |
| 37 | New Mexico | 143 | 1.1% |
| 10 | New York | 395 | 3.0% |
| 14 | North Carolina | 335 | 2.5% |
| 21 | North Dakota | 265 | 2.0% |
| 5 | Ohio | 490 | 3.7% |
| 19 | Oklahoma | 302 | 2.3% |
| 18 | Oregon | 322 | 2.4% |
| 8 | Pennsylvania | 433 | 3.3% |
| 50 | Rhode Island | 9 | 0.1% |
| 33 | South Carolina | 158 | 1.2% |
| 36 | South Dakota | 144 | 1.1% |
| 27 | Tennessee | 209 | 1.6% |
| 1 | Texas | 1,450 | 11.0% |
| 42 | Utah | 90 | 0.7% |
| 45 | Vermont | 62 | 0.5% |
| 20 | Virginia | 290 | 2.2% |
| 11 | Washington | 366 | 2.8% |
| 44 | West Virginia | 76 | 0.6% |
| 7 | Wisconsin | 439 | 3.3% |
| 41 | Wyoming | 93 | 0.7% |

| RANK | STATE | AIRPORTS | % of USA |
|------|-------|----------|----------|
| 1 | Texas | 1,450 | 11.0% |
| 2 | Alaska | 549 | 4.2% |
| 3 | California | 522 | 4.0% |
| 4 | Florida | 497 | 3.8% |
| 5 | Ohio | 490 | 3.7% |
| 6 | Illinois | 479 | 3.6% |
| 7 | Wisconsin | 439 | 3.3% |
| 8 | Pennsylvania | 433 | 3.3% |
| 9 | Indiana | 404 | 3.1% |
| 10 | New York | 395 | 3.0% |
| 11 | Washington | 366 | 2.8% |
| 12 | Michigan | 362 | 2.7% |
| 13 | Missouri | 359 | 2.7% |
| 14 | Georgia | 335 | 2.5% |
| 14 | North Carolina | 335 | 2.5% |
| 16 | Kansas | 329 | 2.5% |
| 16 | Minnesota | 329 | 2.5% |
| 18 | Oregon | 322 | 2.4% |
| 19 | Oklahoma | 302 | 2.3% |
| 20 | Virginia | 290 | 2.2% |
| 21 | North Dakota | 265 | 2.0% |
| 22 | Colorado | 259 | 2.0% |
| 23 | Montana | 232 | 1.8% |
| 24 | Idaho | 224 | 1.7% |
| 25 | Louisiana | 223 | 1.7% |
| 26 | Arkansas | 213 | 1.6% |
| 27 | Tennessee | 209 | 1.6% |
| 28 | Nebraska | 207 | 1.6% |
| 29 | Iowa | 196 | 1.5% |
| 30 | Arizona | 188 | 1.4% |
| 31 | Mississippi | 186 | 1.4% |
| 32 | Alabama | 182 | 1.4% |
| 33 | South Carolina | 158 | 1.2% |
| 34 | Kentucky | 153 | 1.2% |
| 35 | Maryland | 148 | 1.1% |
| 36 | South Dakota | 144 | 1.1% |
| 37 | New Mexico | 143 | 1.1% |
| 38 | Maine | 114 | 0.9% |
| 39 | New Jersey | 101 | 0.8% |
| 40 | Nevada | 98 | 0.7% |
| 41 | Wyoming | 93 | 0.7% |
| 42 | Utah | 90 | 0.7% |
| 43 | Massachusetts | 77 | 0.6% |
| 44 | West Virginia | 76 | 0.6% |
| 45 | Vermont | 62 | 0.5% |
| 46 | New Hampshire | 52 | 0.4% |
| 47 | Connecticut | 51 | 0.4% |
| 48 | Hawaii | 32 | 0.2% |
| 49 | Delaware | 30 | 0.2% |
| 50 | Rhode Island | 9 | 0.1% |
| | District of Columbia | 3 | 0.0% |

Source: U.S. Department of Transportation, Bureau of Transportation Statistics
"State Transportation Statistics 2012" (http://www.bts.gov/publications/state_transportation_statistics/)
*This table comprises all U.S. public use and private use airports. Public use facilities are open to the public with no prior authorization or permission required. Private use facilities are not open to the general public and include medical, law enforcement, corporate, and other such facilities.

# Inland Waterway Mileage in 2011

## National Total = 29,620 Miles*

ALPHA ORDER

| RANK | STATE | MILES | % of USA |
|---|---|---|---|
| 6 | Alabama | 1,270 | 4.3% |
| 1 | Alaska | 5,500 | 18.6% |
| 40 | Arizona | 0 | 0.0% |
| 3 | Arkansas | 1,860 | 6.3% |
| 26 | California | 290 | 1.0% |
| 40 | Colorado | 0 | 0.0% |
| 31 | Connecticut | 120 | 0.4% |
| 34 | Delaware | 100 | 0.3% |
| 5 | Florida | 1,540 | 5.2% |
| 14 | Georgia | 720 | 2.4% |
| 40 | Hawaii | 0 | 0.0% |
| 33 | Idaho | 110 | 0.4% |
| 8 | Illinois | 1,100 | 3.7% |
| 24 | Indiana | 350 | 1.2% |
| 19 | Iowa | 490 | 1.7% |
| 31 | Kansas | 120 | 0.4% |
| 4 | Kentucky | 1,590 | 5.4% |
| 2 | Louisiana | 2,820 | 9.5% |
| 37 | Maine | 70 | 0.2% |
| 18 | Maryland | 530 | 1.8% |
| 35 | Massachusetts | 90 | 0.3% |
| 40 | Michigan | 0 | 0.0% |
| 27 | Minnesota | 260 | 0.9% |
| 12 | Mississippi | 870 | 2.9% |
| 10 | Missouri | 1,030 | 3.5% |
| 40 | Montana | 0 | 0.0% |
| 25 | Nebraska | 320 | 1.1% |
| 40 | Nevada | 0 | 0.0% |
| 39 | New Hampshire | 10 | 0.0% |
| 23 | New Jersey | 360 | 1.2% |
| 40 | New Mexico | 0 | 0.0% |
| 22 | New York | 390 | 1.3% |
| 7 | North Carolina | 1,150 | 3.9% |
| 40 | North Dakota | 0 | 0.0% |
| 21 | Ohio | 440 | 1.5% |
| 30 | Oklahoma | 150 | 0.5% |
| 15 | Oregon | 680 | 2.3% |
| 27 | Pennsylvania | 260 | 0.9% |
| 38 | Rhode Island | 40 | 0.1% |
| 20 | South Carolina | 480 | 1.6% |
| 36 | South Dakota | 80 | 0.3% |
| 11 | Tennessee | 950 | 3.2% |
| 13 | Texas | 830 | 2.8% |
| 40 | Utah | 0 | 0.0% |
| 40 | Vermont | 0 | 0.0% |
| 17 | Virginia | 670 | 2.3% |
| 9 | Washington | 1,060 | 3.6% |
| 15 | West Virginia | 680 | 2.3% |
| 29 | Wisconsin | 230 | 0.8% |
| 40 | Wyoming | 0 | 0.0% |

RANK ORDER

| RANK | STATE | MILES | % of USA |
|---|---|---|---|
| 1 | Alaska | 5,500 | 18.6% |
| 2 | Louisiana | 2,820 | 9.5% |
| 3 | Arkansas | 1,860 | 6.3% |
| 4 | Kentucky | 1,590 | 5.4% |
| 5 | Florida | 1,540 | 5.2% |
| 6 | Alabama | 1,270 | 4.3% |
| 7 | North Carolina | 1,150 | 3.9% |
| 8 | Illinois | 1,100 | 3.7% |
| 9 | Washington | 1,060 | 3.6% |
| 10 | Missouri | 1,030 | 3.5% |
| 11 | Tennessee | 950 | 3.2% |
| 12 | Mississippi | 870 | 2.9% |
| 13 | Texas | 830 | 2.8% |
| 14 | Georgia | 720 | 2.4% |
| 15 | Oregon | 680 | 2.3% |
| 15 | West Virginia | 680 | 2.3% |
| 17 | Virginia | 670 | 2.3% |
| 18 | Maryland | 530 | 1.8% |
| 19 | Iowa | 490 | 1.7% |
| 20 | South Carolina | 480 | 1.6% |
| 21 | Ohio | 440 | 1.5% |
| 22 | New York | 390 | 1.3% |
| 23 | New Jersey | 360 | 1.2% |
| 24 | Indiana | 350 | 1.2% |
| 25 | Nebraska | 320 | 1.1% |
| 26 | California | 290 | 1.0% |
| 27 | Minnesota | 260 | 0.9% |
| 27 | Pennsylvania | 260 | 0.9% |
| 29 | Wisconsin | 230 | 0.8% |
| 30 | Oklahoma | 150 | 0.5% |
| 31 | Connecticut | 120 | 0.4% |
| 31 | Kansas | 120 | 0.4% |
| 33 | Idaho | 110 | 0.4% |
| 34 | Delaware | 100 | 0.3% |
| 35 | Massachusetts | 90 | 0.3% |
| 36 | South Dakota | 80 | 0.3% |
| 37 | Maine | 70 | 0.2% |
| 38 | Rhode Island | 40 | 0.1% |
| 39 | New Hampshire | 10 | 0.0% |
| 40 | Arizona | 0 | 0.0% |
| 40 | Colorado | 0 | 0.0% |
| 40 | Hawaii | 0 | 0.0% |
| 40 | Michigan | 0 | 0.0% |
| 40 | Montana | 0 | 0.0% |
| 40 | Nevada | 0 | 0.0% |
| 40 | New Mexico | 0 | 0.0% |
| 40 | North Dakota | 0 | 0.0% |
| 40 | Utah | 0 | 0.0% |
| 40 | Vermont | 0 | 0.0% |
| 40 | Wyoming | 0 | 0.0% |
| | District of Columbia | 10 | 0.0% |

Source: U.S. Department of Transportation, Bureau of Transportation Statistics
  "State Transportation Statistics 2012" (http://www.bts.gov/publications/state_transportation_statistics/)
*Waterway mileage was determined by including the length of channels 1) with a controlling draft of nine feet or greater, 2) with commercial cargo traffic reported for 1998 and 1999, but 3) were not offshore.  Channels within major bays are included (e.g., Chesapeake Bay, San Francisco Bay, Puget Sound, Long Island Sound, and major sounds and straits in southeastern Alaska). Channels in the Great Lakes are not included.  Approximately 4,300 miles are counted twice as several are state boundaries.

# Percent of Recreational Boating Accidents Involving Alcohol in 2012

## National Percent = 8.2% of Accidents*

<table>
<tr><td colspan="3">ALPHA ORDER</td><td colspan="3">RANK ORDER</td></tr>
<tr><td>RANK</td><td>STATE</td><td>PERCENT</td><td>RANK</td><td>STATE</td><td>PERCENT</td></tr>
<tr><td>6</td><td>Alabama</td><td>15.5</td><td>1</td><td>Wyoming</td><td>22.2</td></tr>
<tr><td>25</td><td>Alaska</td><td>8.7</td><td>2</td><td>Colorado</td><td>21.7</td></tr>
<tr><td>34</td><td>Arizona</td><td>7.1</td><td>3</td><td>Iowa</td><td>21.2</td></tr>
<tr><td>19</td><td>Arkansas</td><td>11.8</td><td>4</td><td>North Dakota</td><td>20.0</td></tr>
<tr><td>43</td><td>California</td><td>3.8</td><td>5</td><td>New Mexico</td><td>16.7</td></tr>
<tr><td>2</td><td>Colorado</td><td>21.7</td><td>6</td><td>Alabama</td><td>15.5</td></tr>
<tr><td>18</td><td>Connecticut</td><td>12.2</td><td>7</td><td>Delaware</td><td>15.4</td></tr>
<tr><td>7</td><td>Delaware</td><td>15.4</td><td>8</td><td>Pennsylvania</td><td>15.3</td></tr>
<tr><td>41</td><td>Florida</td><td>4.5</td><td>9</td><td>Idaho</td><td>15.2</td></tr>
<tr><td>33</td><td>Georgia</td><td>7.2</td><td>10</td><td>Massachusetts</td><td>14.7</td></tr>
<tr><td>48</td><td>Hawaii</td><td>0.0</td><td>11</td><td>Louisiana</td><td>13.8</td></tr>
<tr><td>9</td><td>Idaho</td><td>15.2</td><td>12</td><td>Washington</td><td>13.3</td></tr>
<tr><td>15</td><td>Illinois</td><td>12.9</td><td>13</td><td>South Carolina</td><td>13.0</td></tr>
<tr><td>23</td><td>Indiana</td><td>9.3</td><td>13</td><td>Texas</td><td>13.0</td></tr>
<tr><td>3</td><td>Iowa</td><td>21.2</td><td>15</td><td>Illinois</td><td>12.9</td></tr>
<tr><td>21</td><td>Kansas</td><td>11.1</td><td>16</td><td>Kentucky</td><td>12.8</td></tr>
<tr><td>16</td><td>Kentucky</td><td>12.8</td><td>17</td><td>Wisconsin</td><td>12.7</td></tr>
<tr><td>11</td><td>Louisiana</td><td>13.8</td><td>18</td><td>Connecticut</td><td>12.2</td></tr>
<tr><td>36</td><td>Maine</td><td>6.3</td><td>19</td><td>Arkansas</td><td>11.8</td></tr>
<tr><td>29</td><td>Maryland</td><td>7.6</td><td>20</td><td>Oklahoma</td><td>11.3</td></tr>
<tr><td>10</td><td>Massachusetts</td><td>14.7</td><td>21</td><td>Kansas</td><td>11.1</td></tr>
<tr><td>28</td><td>Michigan</td><td>7.8</td><td>22</td><td>Minnesota</td><td>10.7</td></tr>
<tr><td>22</td><td>Minnesota</td><td>10.7</td><td>23</td><td>Indiana</td><td>9.3</td></tr>
<tr><td>35</td><td>Mississippi</td><td>7.0</td><td>24</td><td>Nebraska</td><td>8.9</td></tr>
<tr><td>26</td><td>Missouri</td><td>8.5</td><td>25</td><td>Alaska</td><td>8.7</td></tr>
<tr><td>48</td><td>Montana</td><td>0.0</td><td>26</td><td>Missouri</td><td>8.5</td></tr>
<tr><td>24</td><td>Nebraska</td><td>8.9</td><td>27</td><td>New York</td><td>8.1</td></tr>
<tr><td>38</td><td>Nevada</td><td>5.3</td><td>28</td><td>Michigan</td><td>7.8</td></tr>
<tr><td>31</td><td>New Hampshire</td><td>7.5</td><td>29</td><td>Maryland</td><td>7.6</td></tr>
<tr><td>40</td><td>New Jersey</td><td>5.2</td><td>29</td><td>North Carolina</td><td>7.6</td></tr>
<tr><td>5</td><td>New Mexico</td><td>16.7</td><td>31</td><td>New Hampshire</td><td>7.5</td></tr>
<tr><td>27</td><td>New York</td><td>8.1</td><td>32</td><td>Ohio</td><td>7.4</td></tr>
<tr><td>29</td><td>North Carolina</td><td>7.6</td><td>33</td><td>Georgia</td><td>7.2</td></tr>
<tr><td>4</td><td>North Dakota</td><td>20.0</td><td>34</td><td>Arizona</td><td>7.1</td></tr>
<tr><td>32</td><td>Ohio</td><td>7.4</td><td>35</td><td>Mississippi</td><td>7.0</td></tr>
<tr><td>20</td><td>Oklahoma</td><td>11.3</td><td>36</td><td>Maine</td><td>6.3</td></tr>
<tr><td>46</td><td>Oregon</td><td>1.4</td><td>37</td><td>South Dakota</td><td>5.6</td></tr>
<tr><td>8</td><td>Pennsylvania</td><td>15.3</td><td>38</td><td>Nevada</td><td>5.3</td></tr>
<tr><td>45</td><td>Rhode Island</td><td>3.2</td><td>38</td><td>West Virginia</td><td>5.3</td></tr>
<tr><td>13</td><td>South Carolina</td><td>13.0</td><td>40</td><td>New Jersey</td><td>5.2</td></tr>
<tr><td>37</td><td>South Dakota</td><td>5.6</td><td>41</td><td>Florida</td><td>4.5</td></tr>
<tr><td>42</td><td>Tennessee</td><td>4.1</td><td>42</td><td>Tennessee</td><td>4.1</td></tr>
<tr><td>13</td><td>Texas</td><td>13.0</td><td>43</td><td>California</td><td>3.8</td></tr>
<tr><td>47</td><td>Utah</td><td>1.0</td><td>44</td><td>Virginia</td><td>3.4</td></tr>
<tr><td>48</td><td>Vermont</td><td>0.0</td><td>45</td><td>Rhode Island</td><td>3.2</td></tr>
<tr><td>44</td><td>Virginia</td><td>3.4</td><td>46</td><td>Oregon</td><td>1.4</td></tr>
<tr><td>12</td><td>Washington</td><td>13.3</td><td>47</td><td>Utah</td><td>1.0</td></tr>
<tr><td>38</td><td>West Virginia</td><td>5.3</td><td>48</td><td>Hawaii</td><td>0.0</td></tr>
<tr><td>17</td><td>Wisconsin</td><td>12.7</td><td>48</td><td>Montana</td><td>0.0</td></tr>
<tr><td>1</td><td>Wyoming</td><td>22.2</td><td>48</td><td>Vermont</td><td>0.0</td></tr>
<tr><td></td><td></td><td></td><td></td><td>District of Columbia</td><td>0.0</td></tr>
</table>

Source: CQ Press using data from United States Coast Guard
"Boating Statistics 2012" (http://www.uscgboating.org/statistics/accident_statistics.aspx)
*Alcohol involvement in a boating accident includes any accident in which alcoholic beverages are consumed in the boat and the investigating official has determined that the operator was impaired or affected while operating the boat.

# Railroad Accidents and Incidents in 2012

## National Total = 10,926*

ALPHA ORDER

RANK ORDER

| RANK | STATE | ACCIDENTS | % of USA | | RANK | STATE | ACCIDENTS | % of USA |
|------|-------|-----------|----------|---|------|-------|-----------|----------|
| 14 | Alabama | 200 | 1.8% | | 1 | New York | 1,178 | 10.8% |
| 39 | Alaska | 74 | 0.7% | | 2 | Illinois | 867 | 7.9% |
| 37 | Arizona | 94 | 0.9% | | 3 | California | 817 | 7.5% |
| 20 | Arkansas | 169 | 1.5% | | 4 | Texas | 799 | 7.3% |
| 3 | California | 817 | 7.5% | | 5 | New Jersey | 672 | 6.2% |
| 26 | Colorado | 141 | 1.3% | | 6 | Pennsylvania | 623 | 5.7% |
| 33 | Connecticut | 115 | 1.1% | | 7 | Indiana | 289 | 2.6% |
| 40 | Delaware | 60 | 0.5% | | 8 | Ohio | 273 | 2.5% |
| 9 | Florida | 259 | 2.4% | | 9 | Florida | 259 | 2.4% |
| 11 | Georgia | 254 | 2.3% | | 10 | Louisiana | 256 | 2.3% |
| 50 | Hawaii | 0 | 0.0% | | 11 | Georgia | 254 | 2.3% |
| 43 | Idaho | 49 | 0.4% | | 12 | Nebraska | 224 | 2.1% |
| 2 | Illinois | 867 | 7.9% | | 13 | Minnesota | 210 | 1.9% |
| 7 | Indiana | 289 | 2.6% | | 14 | Alabama | 200 | 1.8% |
| 21 | Iowa | 166 | 1.5% | | 14 | Missouri | 200 | 1.8% |
| 17 | Kansas | 196 | 1.8% | | 16 | Massachusetts | 198 | 1.8% |
| 25 | Kentucky | 150 | 1.4% | | 17 | Kansas | 196 | 1.8% |
| 10 | Louisiana | 256 | 2.3% | | 18 | Washington | 194 | 1.8% |
| 48 | Maine | 16 | 0.1% | | 19 | Virginia | 184 | 1.7% |
| 27 | Maryland | 134 | 1.2% | | 20 | Arkansas | 169 | 1.5% |
| 16 | Massachusetts | 198 | 1.8% | | 21 | Iowa | 166 | 1.5% |
| 27 | Michigan | 134 | 1.2% | | 21 | Tennessee | 166 | 1.5% |
| 13 | Minnesota | 210 | 1.9% | | 23 | North Carolina | 164 | 1.5% |
| 34 | Mississippi | 111 | 1.0% | | 24 | Oklahoma | 162 | 1.5% |
| 14 | Missouri | 200 | 1.8% | | 25 | Kentucky | 150 | 1.4% |
| 35 | Montana | 106 | 1.0% | | 26 | Colorado | 141 | 1.3% |
| 12 | Nebraska | 224 | 2.1% | | 27 | Maryland | 134 | 1.2% |
| 44 | Nevada | 37 | 0.3% | | 27 | Michigan | 134 | 1.2% |
| 49 | New Hampshire | 3 | 0.0% | | 29 | North Dakota | 131 | 1.2% |
| 5 | New Jersey | 672 | 6.2% | | 29 | Wisconsin | 131 | 1.2% |
| 38 | New Mexico | 78 | 0.7% | | 31 | Oregon | 121 | 1.1% |
| 1 | New York | 1,178 | 10.8% | | 31 | South Carolina | 121 | 1.1% |
| 23 | North Carolina | 164 | 1.5% | | 33 | Connecticut | 115 | 1.1% |
| 29 | North Dakota | 131 | 1.2% | | 34 | Mississippi | 111 | 1.0% |
| 8 | Ohio | 273 | 2.5% | | 35 | Montana | 106 | 1.0% |
| 24 | Oklahoma | 162 | 1.5% | | 35 | West Virginia | 106 | 1.0% |
| 31 | Oregon | 121 | 1.1% | | 37 | Arizona | 94 | 0.9% |
| 6 | Pennsylvania | 623 | 5.7% | | 38 | New Mexico | 78 | 0.7% |
| 46 | Rhode Island | 21 | 0.2% | | 39 | Alaska | 74 | 0.7% |
| 31 | South Carolina | 121 | 1.1% | | 40 | Delaware | 60 | 0.5% |
| 45 | South Dakota | 32 | 0.3% | | 41 | Wyoming | 58 | 0.5% |
| 21 | Tennessee | 166 | 1.5% | | 42 | Utah | 54 | 0.5% |
| 4 | Texas | 799 | 7.3% | | 43 | Idaho | 49 | 0.4% |
| 42 | Utah | 54 | 0.5% | | 44 | Nevada | 37 | 0.3% |
| 47 | Vermont | 20 | 0.2% | | 45 | South Dakota | 32 | 0.3% |
| 19 | Virginia | 184 | 1.7% | | 46 | Rhode Island | 21 | 0.2% |
| 18 | Washington | 194 | 1.8% | | 47 | Vermont | 20 | 0.2% |
| 35 | West Virginia | 106 | 1.0% | | 48 | Maine | 16 | 0.1% |
| 29 | Wisconsin | 131 | 1.2% | | 49 | New Hampshire | 3 | 0.0% |
| 41 | Wyoming | 58 | 0.5% | | 50 | Hawaii | 0 | 0.0% |
| | | | | | | District of Columbia | 109 | 1.0% |

Source: U.S. Department of Transportation, Federal Railroad Administration, Office of Safety Analysis

"Railroad Accidents and Incidents" (http://safetydata.fra.dot.gov/OfficeofSafety/publicsite/Query/stateoverview.aspx)

*Accidents or incidents include all events reportable to the U.S. Department of Transportation. These include train accidents causing damage above an established threshold; highway-rail grade crossing incidents involving impact between railroad equipment and highway users at crossings; and all other reportable incidents that cause a fatality or injury to any person or an occupational illness to a railroad employee. There were 694 fatalities involving railroads.

# Railroad Mileage Operated in 2011

## National Total = 138,565 Miles of Railroad*

ALPHA ORDER

| RANK | STATE | MILES | % of USA |
|---|---|---|---|
| 17 | Alabama | 3,255 | 2.3% |
| 45 | Alaska | 506 | 0.4% |
| 36 | Arizona | 1,645 | 1.2% |
| 25 | Arkansas | 2,698 | 1.9% |
| 4 | California | 5,327 | 3.8% |
| 26 | Colorado | 2,667 | 1.9% |
| 46 | Connecticut | 364 | 0.3% |
| 48 | Delaware | 250 | 0.2% |
| 24 | Florida | 2,902 | 2.1% |
| 7 | Georgia | 4,666 | 3.4% |
| 50 | Hawaii | 0 | 0.0% |
| 37 | Idaho | 1,622 | 1.2% |
| 2 | Illinois | 7,027 | 5.1% |
| 9 | Indiana | 4,273 | 3.1% |
| 11 | Iowa | 3,855 | 2.8% |
| 6 | Kansas | 4,855 | 3.5% |
| 28 | Kentucky | 2,562 | 1.8% |
| 23 | Louisiana | 2,912 | 2.1% |
| 40 | Maine | 1,116 | 0.8% |
| 43 | Maryland | 762 | 0.5% |
| 42 | Massachusetts | 892 | 0.6% |
| 12 | Michigan | 3,632 | 2.6% |
| 8 | Minnesota | 4,449 | 3.2% |
| 29 | Mississippi | 2,432 | 1.8% |
| 10 | Missouri | 3,958 | 2.9% |
| 21 | Montana | 3,172 | 2.3% |
| 18 | Nebraska | 3,247 | 2.3% |
| 39 | Nevada | 1,192 | 0.9% |
| 47 | New Hampshire | 344 | 0.2% |
| 41 | New Jersey | 983 | 0.7% |
| 34 | New Mexico | 1,835 | 1.3% |
| 13 | New York | 3,532 | 2.5% |
| 19 | North Carolina | 3,245 | 2.3% |
| 15 | North Dakota | 3,328 | 2.4% |
| 3 | Ohio | 5,338 | 3.9% |
| 16 | Oklahoma | 3,273 | 2.4% |
| 30 | Oregon | 2,396 | 1.7% |
| 5 | Pennsylvania | 5,127 | 3.7% |
| 49 | Rhode Island | 19 | 0.0% |
| 31 | South Carolina | 2,292 | 1.7% |
| 35 | South Dakota | 1,754 | 1.3% |
| 27 | Tennessee | 2,651 | 1.9% |
| 1 | Texas | 10,425 | 7.5% |
| 38 | Utah | 1,343 | 1.0% |
| 44 | Vermont | 590 | 0.4% |
| 20 | Virginia | 3,214 | 2.3% |
| 22 | Washington | 3,157 | 2.3% |
| 32 | West Virginia | 2,213 | 1.6% |
| 14 | Wisconsin | 3,385 | 2.4% |
| 33 | Wyoming | 1,860 | 1.3% |

RANK ORDER

| RANK | STATE | MILES | % of USA |
|---|---|---|---|
| 1 | Texas | 10,425 | 7.5% |
| 2 | Illinois | 7,027 | 5.1% |
| 3 | Ohio | 5,338 | 3.9% |
| 4 | California | 5,327 | 3.8% |
| 5 | Pennsylvania | 5,127 | 3.7% |
| 6 | Kansas | 4,855 | 3.5% |
| 7 | Georgia | 4,666 | 3.4% |
| 8 | Minnesota | 4,449 | 3.2% |
| 9 | Indiana | 4,273 | 3.1% |
| 10 | Missouri | 3,958 | 2.9% |
| 11 | Iowa | 3,855 | 2.8% |
| 12 | Michigan | 3,632 | 2.6% |
| 13 | New York | 3,532 | 2.5% |
| 14 | Wisconsin | 3,385 | 2.4% |
| 15 | North Dakota | 3,328 | 2.4% |
| 16 | Oklahoma | 3,273 | 2.4% |
| 17 | Alabama | 3,255 | 2.3% |
| 18 | Nebraska | 3,247 | 2.3% |
| 19 | North Carolina | 3,245 | 2.3% |
| 20 | Virginia | 3,214 | 2.3% |
| 21 | Montana | 3,172 | 2.3% |
| 22 | Washington | 3,157 | 2.3% |
| 23 | Louisiana | 2,912 | 2.1% |
| 24 | Florida | 2,902 | 2.1% |
| 25 | Arkansas | 2,698 | 1.9% |
| 26 | Colorado | 2,667 | 1.9% |
| 27 | Tennessee | 2,651 | 1.9% |
| 28 | Kentucky | 2,562 | 1.8% |
| 29 | Mississippi | 2,432 | 1.8% |
| 30 | Oregon | 2,396 | 1.7% |
| 31 | South Carolina | 2,292 | 1.7% |
| 32 | West Virginia | 2,213 | 1.6% |
| 33 | Wyoming | 1,860 | 1.3% |
| 34 | New Mexico | 1,835 | 1.3% |
| 35 | South Dakota | 1,754 | 1.3% |
| 36 | Arizona | 1,645 | 1.2% |
| 37 | Idaho | 1,622 | 1.2% |
| 38 | Utah | 1,343 | 1.0% |
| 39 | Nevada | 1,192 | 0.9% |
| 40 | Maine | 1,116 | 0.8% |
| 41 | New Jersey | 983 | 0.7% |
| 42 | Massachusetts | 892 | 0.6% |
| 43 | Maryland | 762 | 0.5% |
| 44 | Vermont | 590 | 0.4% |
| 45 | Alaska | 506 | 0.4% |
| 46 | Connecticut | 364 | 0.3% |
| 47 | New Hampshire | 344 | 0.2% |
| 48 | Delaware | 250 | 0.2% |
| 49 | Rhode Island | 19 | 0.0% |
| 50 | Hawaii | 0 | 0.0% |
| | District of Columbia | 23 | 0.0% |

Source: Association of American Railroads
"Railroads and States" (http://www.aar.org/KeyIssues/Railroads-States.aspx)
*Includes Class I and non-Class I miles. Excludes trackage rights. Synonymous with route-miles, so that a mile of single track
is counted the same as a mile of double track.

# Sources

**ACT, Inc.**
500 ACT Drive, P.O. Box 168
Iowa City, IA 52243-0168
319-337-1000
www.act.org

**Administration for Children and Families**
U.S. Department of Health and Human Services
370 L'Enfant Promenade, SW
Washington, DC 20447
202-401-9215
www.acf.hhs.gov

**American Cancer Society, Inc.**
250 Williams Street, NW
Atlanta, GA 30303
800-227-2345
www.cancer.org

**American Dental Association**
211 E. Chicago Avenue
Chicago, IL 60611-2678
800-621-8335
www.ada.org

**American Hospital Association**
155 N. Wacker Drive
Chicago, IL 60611-5885
312-422-3000
www.aha.org

**American Medical Association**
330 N. Wabash Avenue
Chicago, IL 60654
800-621-8335
www.ama-assn.org

**Association of American Railroads**
425 Third Street, SW. Suite 1000
Washington, DC 20024
202-639-2100
www.aar.org

**Bureau of the Census**
4600 Silver Hill Road
Washington, DC 20233-0001
800-923-8282
www.census.gov

**Bureau of Economic Analysis**
U.S. Department of Commerce
1441 L Street, NW
Washington, DC 20230
202-606-9900
www.bea.gov

**Bureau of Justice Statistics**
U.S. Department of Justice
810 Seventh Street, NW
Washington, DC 20531
202-307-0765
www.bjs.gov

**Bureau of Labor Statistics**
U.S. Department of Labor
2 Massachusetts Avenue, NE
Washington, DC 20212-0001
202-691-5200
www.bls.gov

**Bureau of Transportation Statistics**
US Department of Transportation
1200 New Jersey Avenue, SE
Washington, DC 20590
800-853-1351
www.bts.gov

**Centers for Disease Control and Prevention**
1600 Clifton Road
Atlanta, GA 30333
800-232-4636
www.cdc.gov

**Centers for Medicare and Medicaid Services**
7500 Security Boulevard
Baltimore, MD 21244-1850
877-267-2323
www.cms.hhs.gov

**College Board**
45 Columbus Avenue
New York, NY 10023-6992
212-713-8000
www.collegeboard.com

**Economic Research Service**
U.S. Department of Agriculture
1400 Independence Avenue, SW
Mail Stop 1800
Washington, DC 20250-0002
202-694-5050
www.ers.usda.gov

**Energy Information Administration**
US Department of Energy
1000 Independence Avenue, SW
Washington, DC 20585
202-586-8800
www.eia.doe.gov

**Environmental Protection Agency**
Ariel Rios Building
1200 Pennsylvania Avenue, NW
Washington, DC 20460
202-272-0167
www.epa.gov

**Federal Bureau of Investigation**
J Edgar Hoover Building
935 Pennsylvania Avenue, NW
Washington, DC 20535-0001
202-324-3000
www.fbi.gov

**Federal Highway Administration**
US Department of Transportation
1200 New Jersey Avenue, SE
Washington, DC 20590
202-366-4000
www.fhwa.dot.gov

**Federation of Tax Administrators**
444 North Capitol Street, NW. Suite 348
Washington, DC 20001
202-624-5890
www.taxadmin.org

**Food and Nutrition Service**
U.S. Department of Agriculture
3101 Park Center Drive
Alexandria, VA 22302
703-305-2062
www.fns.usda.gov/fns

**General Services Administration**
One Constitution Square
1800 F Street NW
Washington, DC 20540
800-488-3111
www.gsa.gov

**Health Resources and Services Administration**
Division of Practitioner Data Banks
5600 Fishers Lane
Rockville, MD 20857
800-275-4772
www.hrsa.gov

**Institute of Museum and Library Services**
1800 M Street, NW, 9th Floor
Washington, DC 20036-5802
202-653-4657
www.imls.gov

**Internal Revenue Service**
U.S. Department of the Treasury
10th Street and Pennsylvania Avenue, NW
Washington, DC 20004
800-829-1040
www.irs.gov

**Medical Expenditure Panel Survey**
Agency for Healthcare Research and Quality
540 Gaither Road
Rockville, MD 20850
301-427-1364
www.meps.ahrq.gov

**National Agricultural Statistics Service**
1400 Independence Avenue, SW
Washington, DC 20250
800-727-9540
www.nass.usda.gov

**National Assembly of State Arts Agencies**
1029 Vermont Avenue, NW. 2nd Floor
Washington, DC 20005
202-347-6352
www.nasaa-arts.org

**National Association of Realtors**
430 N. Michigan Avenue
Chicago, IL 60611
800-874-6500
www.realtor.org

**National Association of State Park Directors**
8829 Woodyhill Road
Raleigh, NC 27613
919-676-8365
www.naspd1.org

**National Center for Education Statistics**
U.S. Department of Education
1990 K Street, NW
Washington, DC 20006
202-502-7300
www.nces.ed.gov

**National Center for Health Statistics**
U.S. Department of Health and Human Services
3311 Toledo Road
Hyattsville, MD 20782
800-232-4636
www.cdc.gov/nchs

**National Conference of State Legislatures**
7700 E. First Place
Denver, CO 80230
303-364-7700
www.ncsl.org

**National Education Association**
1201 16th Street, NW
Washington, DC 20036-3290
202-833-4000
www.nea.org

**National Highway Traffic Safety Administration**
1200 New Jersey Avenue, SE
Washington, DC 20590
888-327-4236
www.nhtsa.dot.gov

**National Institute on Alcohol Abuse and Alcoholism**
5635 Fishers Lane, MSC 9304
Bethesda, MD 20892-9304
301-443-3860
www.niaaa.nih.gov

**National Oceanic & Atmospheric Administration**
**U.S. Department of Commerce**
1401 Constitution Avenue, NW. Room 5128
Washington, DC 20230
202-482-6090
www.noaa.gov

**Office of Management and Budget**
USAspending.gov
725 17th Street, NW
Washington, DC 20503
202-395-3080
www.USAspending.gov

**Social Security Administration**
Windsor Park Building
6401 Security Boulevard
Baltimore, MD 21235
800-772-1213 (information)
www.ssa.gov

**Storm Prediction Center**
National Weather Service
120 David Boren Boulevard
Norman, OK 73072
405-579-0771
www.spc.noaa.gov

**Tax Foundation**
529 14th Street, NW. Suite 420
Washington, DC 20045-1000
202-464-6200
www.taxfoundation.org

**U.S. Department of Defense**
Directorate for Public Inquiry and Analysis
Room 2E565 The Pentagon
1400 Defense Pentagon
Washington, DC 20301-1400
703-571-3343
www.defense.gov

**U.S. Department of Veterans Affairs**
810 Vermont Avenue, NW
Washington, DC 20420
202-273-5400
www.va.gov

**U.S. Geological Survey**
12201 Sunrise Valley Drive
Reston, VA 20192
703-648-5953
www.usgs.gov

# Index